Photography

Today

Photography Today

Mark Durden

Contents

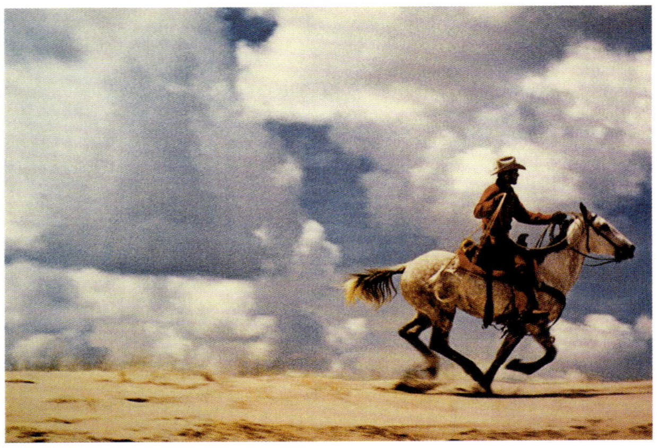

Richard Prince
Untitled (Cowboy), 1989

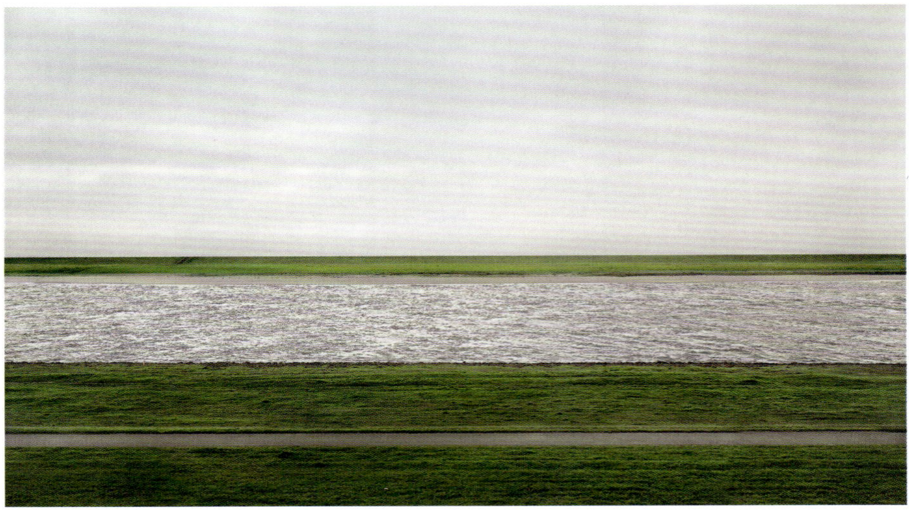

Andreas Gursky
Rhein II, 1999

Preface

Photography is now unequivocally a dominant contemporary art form. Prices for art photography continue to escalate: the first photograph to break the million dollar mark at public auction was the American artist Richard Prince's 1989 *Untitled (Cowboy)*, sold for $1,248,000 at a sale of contemporary art at Christie's in New York in November 2005. Six years later, in November 2011, at the same venue, Andreas Gursky's *Rhein II*, from 1999, the first in an edition of six copies of a large (385 cm x 207 cm) colour photograph offering a spare and minimal portrayal of Germany's river as a horizontal band running the width of the picture, set a world record for a photograph at auction at $4,338,500.

Photography's identity as art has not always been so certain. As a reproducible medium, photography upsets traditional assumptions about artistic value. A photograph is not a unique cultural form like a painting. That said, when it comes to the auction house the fact that photographs are in editions can actually bolster their value. The success of Gursky's *Rhein II* was no doubt aided by the fact that other copies were held in major museum collections around the world, including the Museum of Modern Art, New York, and Tate Modern, London.

This book begins in the 1960s, at a time when photography was not unimportant to art but when the relationship was complex and fraught with contradiction. Chapter One, *The Copy: Authorship and Reproduction*, shows how photography became important to Conceptual artists and others who wanted to strip art of its traditional romantic and expressive characteristics. Photography appealed precisely because of its perceived ease and limited aesthetic value. It also became integral to dismantling assumptions about art's separation from ordinary life.

Parallel to but distinct from these developments, photography was being championed for its own aesthetic characteristics by the director of the Department of Photography at New York's Museum of Modern Art, John Szarkowski. Taking up this position in 1962, Szarkowski had a tremendous impact on our understanding of photography as art and was instrumental in establishing the

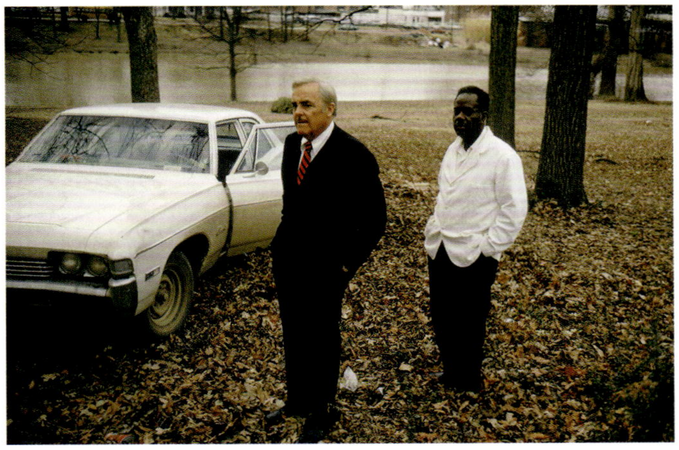

William Eggleston
Untitled (Sumner, Mississippi, Cassidy Bayou in Background), 1971

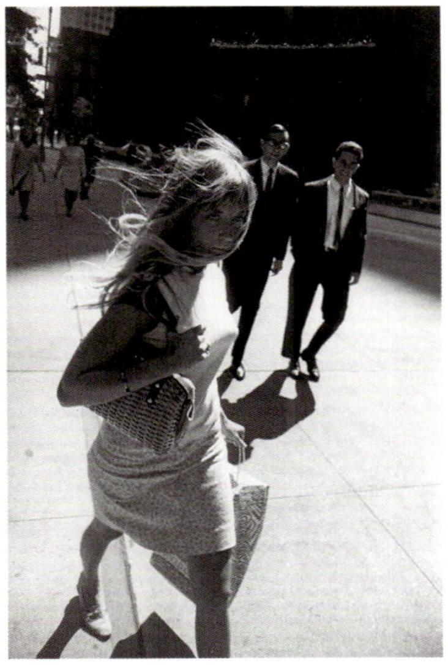

Garry Winogrand
New York, 1965

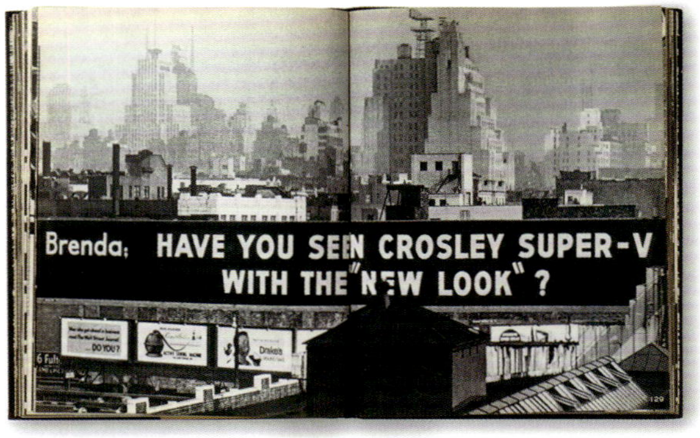

William Klein
Life is Good and Good For You in New York: Trance Witness Revels, 1956

reputations of major twentieth-century photographers, notably Diane Arbus, William Eggleston, Lee Friedlander and Garry Winogrand. Their influence is arguably even stronger today than ever, and all will feature significantly in this book.

In the late 1970s and early 1980s a number of photographers, responding to developments in colour-print technology, started making photographs at a large scale. This has had a transformative effect on the relationship of photography to the museum, and some grand claims have been made about the transition. For the art historian Michael Fried, it was only when photographs were made for the museum wall – 'to be looked at like paintings' – that they began to matter as contemporary art.[1]

Until this time, although photographs were admittedly matted, framed and exhibited on the gallery wall, there was something rather arbitrary about such a mode of display. Such photography was too small for the museum wall and only really worked in books and catalogues. Photography lends itself to print media and, in many senses, and despite Fried's claims about the importance of this shift in image size, the book remains its ideal context. Discussion of photobooks will thus play an important part in this book, from two groundbreaking publications by William Klein and Daido Moriyama to Joachim Schmid's recent encyclopedic publications of images appropriated and edited from the billions stored on the photo sharing site Flickr.com. With digital technology facilitating greater ease of publication, more photographs are being published in books than ever before.

With its many photographic reproductions, this publication, too, benefits from the close affinity between photography and the book. The images form an important part of my arguments. All the photographs included for reproduction have been carefully selected and arranged in terms of both the dynamic they set up with each other and their links with the text. As much as some of my selections and arrangements of pictures might please and confirm expectations, I am also deliberately shaking up the expected and familiar order and pattern of photographic history. This book is written in full

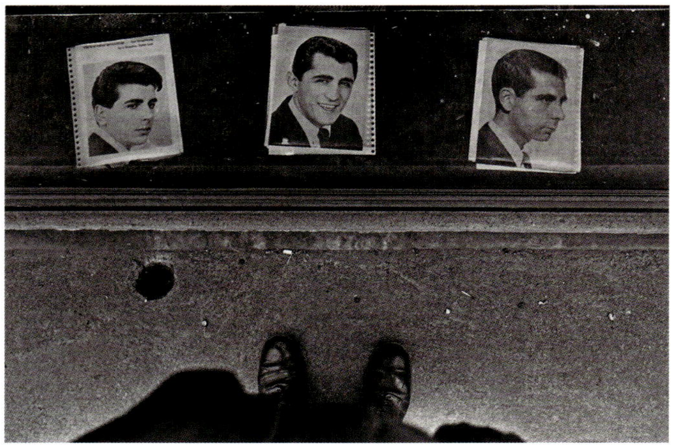

Lee Friedlander
Albany, New York, 1967

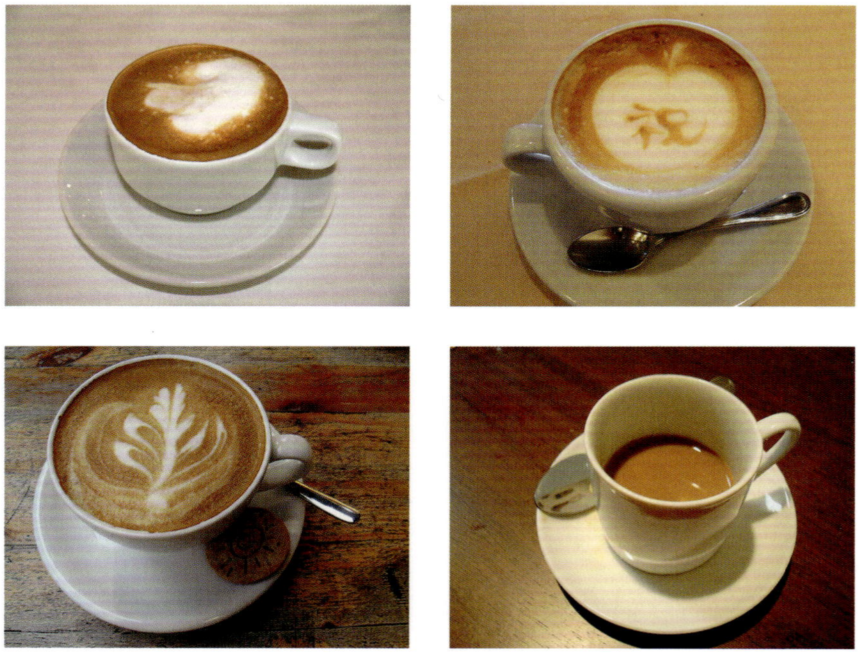

Joachim Schmid
Coffee (detail) From 'Other People's Photographs', 2008–11

awareness of the dangers of simply reiterating an established canon – though, of course, I have not completely ignored it; as you will see, my respect for the orginality and vision of John Szarkowski as a writer and curator throughout this book bears this out.

Szarkowski held a somewhat critical relation to documentary. This was important in his definition of what was distinctive in the approach of photographers like Winogrand, Arbus and Friedlander, whose art was more personal and open than traditional documentary forms, motivated by causes and issues. Nevertheless an important element of this book concerns what are essentially documentary uses of photography. In the most generous application of the term, all photographs of the phenomenal world, all photographs taken from life, could be described as documentary. My discussion of documentary in Chapter Eight will, however, largely be concerned with work that is engaged with or implies some kind of political agenda, showing us inequities and injustices, social ills and problems. From its continuity in the 1960s and 1970s from earlier reformist documentary traditions during the Great Depression, documentary photography has become an important form of contemporary art. Very often, however, this involves a knowing disruption of the tradition's codes and expectations, and in some cases a deliberate disregard for its core values. Documentary photography has also fed our appetite for sensational and shocking images.

If one were to distinguish between two primary characteristics of photography in the last fifty years, one would tend to divide them in terms of those photographers who still use and explore – and on occasion also exploit – the realist qualities of the medium for directly taking photographs from the world, and those practitioners who occupy a more self-conscious and distanced – and on occasion critical – engagement with photography as a realist form. For those who appropriate other photographs or those who construct images to photograph, photography to a certain extent becomes their subject. Their art tends to reflect upon other pictures or speak about photography. Digital technology has not really altered this situation, lending itself just as effectively to both realist and non-realist uses of photography. What has been transformed in

Alfredo Jaar
Lament of the Images, 2002

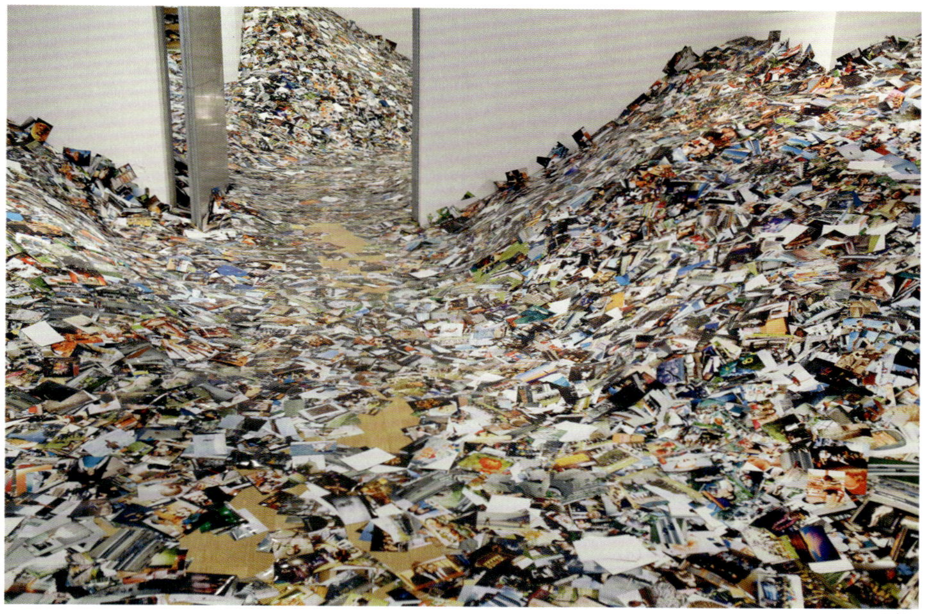

Erik Kessels
24 Hrs In Photos, 2012

our digital age, however, is the photographic landscape, as more people take photographs than ever before. While some artists are beginning to respond directly to this ubiquity of photography, the full impact such a proliferation of images will have on art photography is, one feels, yet to be seen.

Mapping a way through over fifty years of photography's history has determined certain selections. Even a book as big as this cannot be fully comprehensive. I have tried to select and consider work that I think will last, which is sometimes easy when looking back but more difficult when the work is very recent and contemporary. A characteristic of photography's recent history has been that photography has become more global; the current worldwide dimension and breadth of photography marks a significant shift from the relatively parochial First World concentration of photography in the 1960s.

Each chapter of this book follows a loose chronology, beginning in the 1960s and often concluding with work made in the last few years. Photography can be hard to classify, and I am very much aware that the definitions and names we often use to identify and understand photographs are not always adequate. I have therefore mainly used themes or genres simply as a means to try and hold on and stabilize the dizzying array of different approaches to photography that characterizes the last half a century of its history.

A closing chapter discusses the work of artists that might be seen to point the way towards a photography tomorrow. My examples include what I refer to as an extreme photography – beginning and closing with two memorable but distinct installations, the absence of photographs in Alfredo Jaar's 2002 *Lament of the Images* and Erik Kessel's 2011 exhibition of hundreds of thousands of images that were uploaded to Flickr over twenty-four hours. While the breadth and range of such artists' approaches to photography might be seen to map out some of the recurring and salient concerns of photography now and in the future, tomorrow's photography could just as well lie in the lesser-known works of exciting younger artists that are discussed throughout this book.

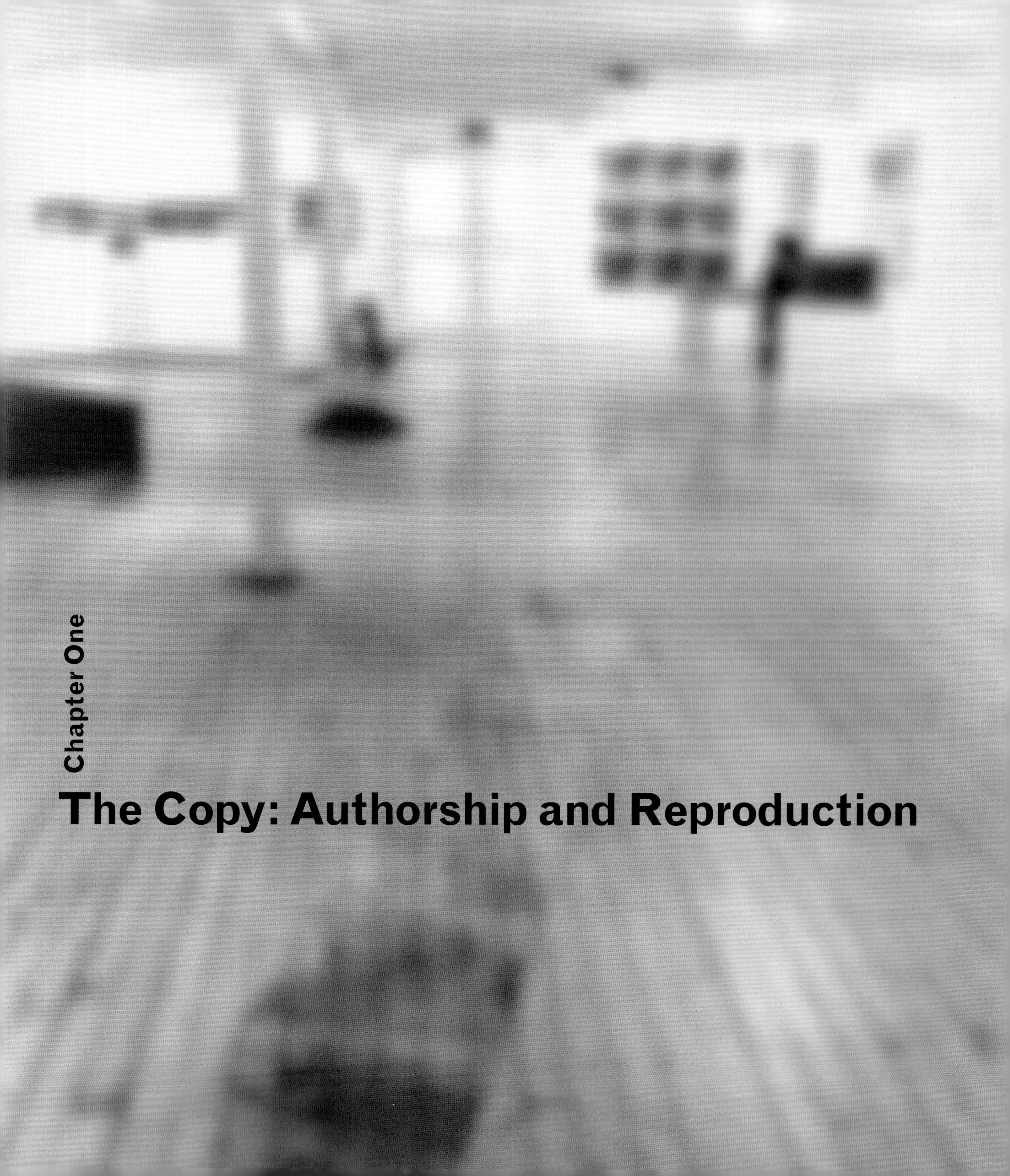

Chapter One

The Copy: Authorship and Reproduction

Copying and reproduction raise various considerations in terms of photography's identity and status as art. Photography played a key role in the transformation of American painting in relation to Pop art in the 1960s, and also had a central role to play in the experiments of Conceptual art in the 1960s and 1970s, when it provided artists with a medium to fulfil their desire to break with the objecthood, materiality and expressivity of art. Such relationships are particularly telling about how photographs are valued and used beyond the narrower confines of an exclusively photographic history. Indeed, it was in relationship to both Conceptual art and Pop art that photography became accepted as an avant-garde art form.

Conceptualism led to appropriation art, a practice involving re-photographing photographs. This practice, which has often been identified as postmodern, had repercussions beyond its defining moment in the 1980s. Meanwhile, the school of photography that emerged in Düsseldorf was valued for objectivity and neutrality, but remained predicated on the value of photography as art: authored, distinctive and big in scale.

A relationship between photography and painting recurs throughout this first chapter. It becomes important to the work of Sherrie Levine when she photographs reproductions of nineteenth-century paintings and continues in both Andreas Gursky's and Thomas Struth's photographs of art on display in museums, which involves them deliberately positioning their own photographs alongside and in relationship to a tradition of great painting.

Robert Rauschenberg

Robert Rauschenberg began adding photographs and found reproductions to the surfaces of his paintings as early as 1951, and in 1954 he coined the term 'combine paintings', or simply 'combines', to describe his paintings and assemblages. He used mostly found images or reproductions cut from newspapers, but sometimes also used old family photographs or his own photographs. Collaged onto the picture surface along with objects – including brooms, pillows, clothing – the photographs realized the artist's expressed desire to work in the gap between art and life.

Photographic reproduction also enabled Rauschenberg to demonstrate the inimitable nature of the gestural painted mark in his repeat combines *Factum I* and *Factum II* (1957) in which non-identical drips of paint were played off against the ability of mechanically reproduced photographs and prints to appear identical in each painting. Rauschenberg worked on the canvases together and was, he said, interested in how different two paintings would be that looked that much alike. In a subtle reiteration of the perceptual games going on between the two paintings, the reproduced images used for each painting themselves contain pictorial repetitions and doublings. The repeated photographs depicting twin trees, show similar but not identical natural forms, and the double-frame *Daily News* images at the bottom of each canvas represent the same burning buildings, but from different distances and moments. Differences also emerge with the two Eisenhower portraits at the top right of each canvas, differences in terms of how they are cut from newspapers and the variations in paint markings on the images' surfaces. Photography is introduced as a medium for repetition and duplication, but at the same time this identity and role begins to stutter and waver.

Having discovered the technique on a visit to Andy Warhol's studio in 1962, Rauschenberg introduced the photo silkscreen into his work, enabling him to vary the size of his reproductions. Appropriating images from magazines and newspapers, the silkscreen paintings collided specific media images of historical and political events with more banal subjects derived from photographs taken by Rauschenberg himself. Gestural painted marks variously enhanced, denied or played against the illusory and insubstantial photo-silkscreen images. The silkscreen itself was used expressively. The images were not screened uniformly: Rauschenberg varied the amount of ink, so some images would be dense and others ghostlike.

Rauschenberg later remarked about this work that he was 'bombarded with TV sets and magazines, by the refuse, by the excess of the world.'[1] Critic Brian O'Doherty related the work to a distinctly urban effect, allying the impact of Rauschenberg's layered and discordant imagery with the indiscriminate, wandering attention we have in the street. Rauschenberg's silkscreen paintings replaced the 'art audience's stare' with what O'Doherty calls the 'vernacular glance.'[2]

Rauschenberg used photography to disrupt painting; smears and drips might break the photographs' illusionism, reducing them to surfaces, but photography's overriding significance was to bring into his paintings something from life and the everyday, similar to the objects he incorporates into his work. Photography transformed painting as a result, moving it away from ritual and aura, but in terms of the relationship between painting and photography, Rauschenberg never vanquished pictorial and painterly elements. It was only with Andy Warhol that art fully gave itself over to the serial reproductive capacity of photography. Warhol took the effect of photography on painting to an extreme as he abandoned collage aesthetics for isolated, centralized representations, displayed as single or multi units.

Robert Rauschenberg
Factum I, 1957
Oil, ink, pencil, crayon, paper, fabric, newspaper, printed reproductions and printed paper on canvas
156.2 × 90.8 cm / 61½ × 35¾ in

Factum II, 1957
Oil, ink, pencil, crayon, paper, fabric, newspaper, printed reproductions and printed paper on canvas
155.9 × 90.2 cm / 61⅜ × 35½ in

Estate, 1963
Oil and silkscreened ink on canvas
243.2 × 177.2 cm / 95¾ × 69¾ in

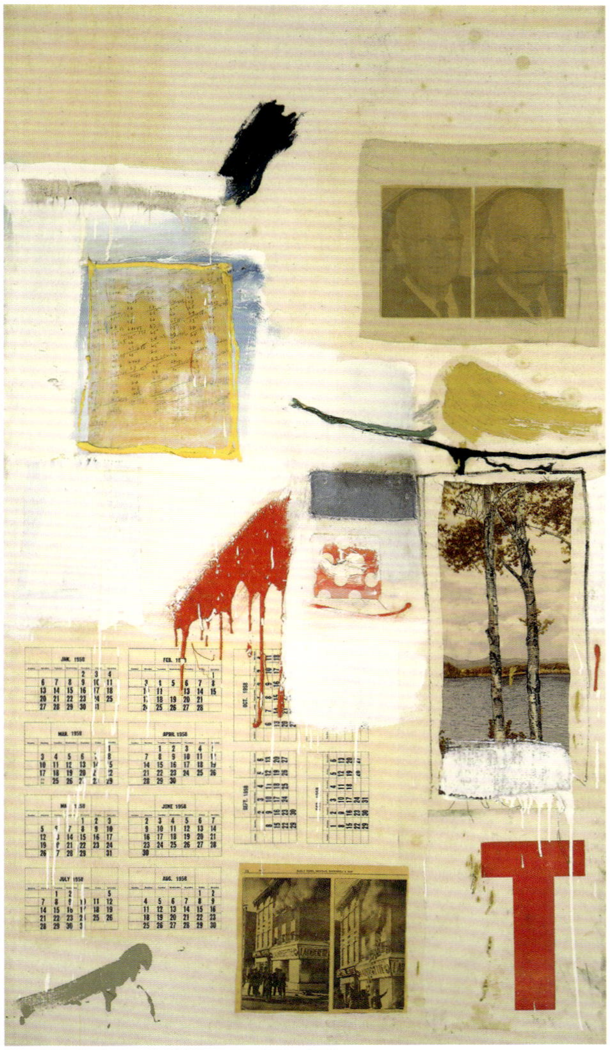

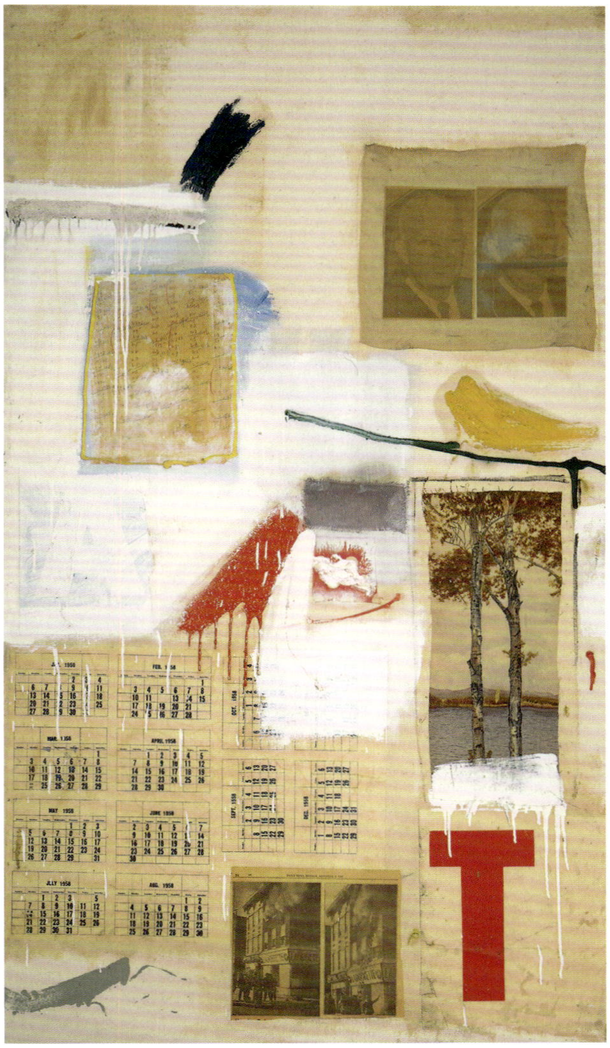

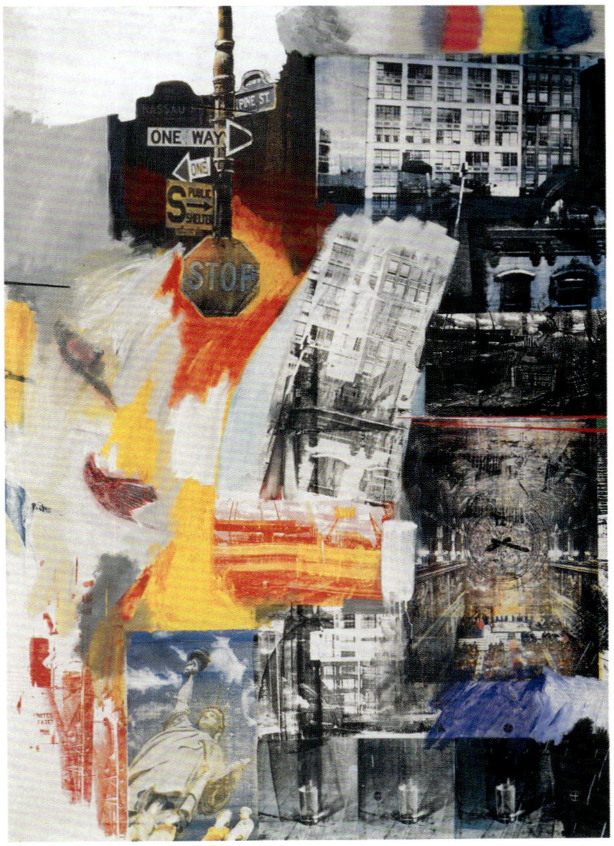
NASSAU
PINE ST
ONE WAY
STOP

William Klein

William Klein's *Life is Good & Good For You in New York: Trance Witness Revels* began as a commission for a feature on New York City for American *Vogue*, but the pictures he took during an intensive period of six months were rejected as too crude and anti-American. Klein failed to find a publisher in the United States and the pictures were only published as a book in France by Éditions du Seuil in 1956, and then only because of the influence of the filmmaker Chris Marker, who threatened to resign as editor of the publishing house if they did not publish Klein's book.

A New Yorker, Klein had returned to his home city from a position of exile, having spent eight years in Paris, where he had studied painting under the French artist Fernand Léger. His pictures of his home city were intended to convey what he referred to as 'the kinetic quality of New York – the kids, dirt, madness'.[3] He felt the city needed 'a kick in the balls'. The title of the book, a bit like a jingle from an advertisment, was of course deeply ironic. The more engimatic subtitle, 'Trance Witness Revels', as well as being a possible word play on a tabloid headline, 'Chance Witness Reveals', might also suggest the street photographer's spellbound absorption as he revels in the city. Printed in rotorgravure with a high contrast range and with a dynamic and varied layout that Klein was able to develop using the state-of-the-art Photostat machine in *Vogue*'s offices, the book is in many senses a savage and brutal portrayal of a city choking with signs and bereft of humanity.

Klein's response to the city frequently played upon a collision of different kinds of pictures and messages, through a constantly varying arrangement of photographs across the book's pages and a recurrent fascination with spectacle and display: there are pictures of advertisements, window displays, neon lights, movie houses, movie posters, graffiti, homemade signs, parades, crowds and protests. Klein exploits the difference between the book as a form from the picture on the museum wall. There is a kinetic quality to the photography in the book: the reader does not just scan the surface but moves back and forth between pictures. In this respect the book could be seen to extend the kind of looking associated with the street that Brian O'Doherty raises in relationship to Robert Rauschenberg's silkscreens, the sense of a roving and mobile gaze. The book's glut of signs is played out against a predominantly bleak and fractured portrayal of humanity, cued by an opening image that shows us a tight close-up of four heads from a crowd, four very different individuals, all looking away from each other. People often show or parade themselves to camera, are very much on display. Some, like the zombiefied, bespectacled man pictured delicately holding the end of a banner's pole are just not with it; they are detached, not part of the passion and excitement of the public event. Klein's pictures of women can be harsh, like the puffy-faced saleswoman at a Woolworth's store counter selling a new spot-removing product, whose gesture and look provide a sad echo of the youthful beauty on the product's promotional image. Klein makes a lot of comparisons and juxtapositions: women shoppers with their trolleys at the check-out in a Broadway supermarket and elderly folk dressed up for an Easter parade set against a following double-spread of fashion shots of cover girls, or the laughing young women in their party frocks, uncannily alike, cruelly paired against a close-up showing saucy cartoons of women decorating men's fancy ties.

The book format allows Klein to deploy words and signs effectively. In one remarkable double-page spread a cryptic message taken from an advertising hoarding – *Brenda; HAVE YOU SEEN CROSLEY SUPER-V WITH THE "NEW LOOK"?* – runs as a horizontal strip across the full width of the open pages, cutting up Klein's view of New York City. In the caption booklet attached by a string to the original book (with dynamic graphics and cut-out news stories, headlines and ads), Klein comically explains how: 'Brenda is for snob appeal. The Super-V is probably uranium-plated. Anyway, there is something terrifying about this phrase written on the face of the city. Who asks this question that echoed through the sky?' Klein has said he saw the book like 'a monster big-city *Daily Bugle* with its scandals and scoops that you'd find blowing the streets at three in the morning'. He photographed a fan-like spread of tabloid newspapers on display in a newsstand. Presented as a half-page image, with the facing page left blank, it offers a relatively rare caesura in the book; denoting a shift in subject matter, the section is given the simple heading 'Gun' in the book's table of contents. The close-up of newspapers plays with the repetitive details of the headline 'GUNMAN', a word which, like the front-page picture of cops and a corpse, is broken up and replayed over and over. The photograph plays out a numb and repetitive fascination with a sensational violent culture. It also introduces the play of toy-gun-toting children in two following spreads, beginning with the aggressive and confrontational dynamic of one kid thrusting his gun straight at the camera.

The repeated, broken details of tabloid newspapers Klein photographed might in some senses be seen as a precursor to Andy Warhol's fascination with repeated disaster images of car crashes and suicides culled from press photographs.

William Klein
Life is Good & Good For You in New York: Trance Witness Revels, Editions du Seuil, Album Petit Planete, Paris, 1956
27.5 × 22 cm / 10 × 8½ in, 194pp with 16pp caption booklet, hardcover with full black cloth and jacket, 188 black and white photographs, design by William Klein

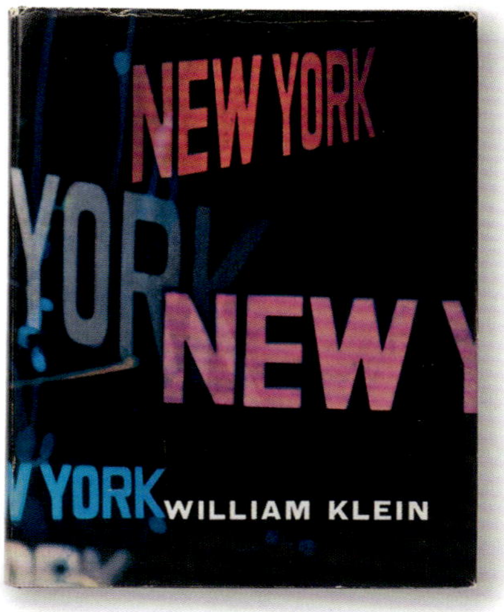
NEW YORK
WILLIAM KLEIN

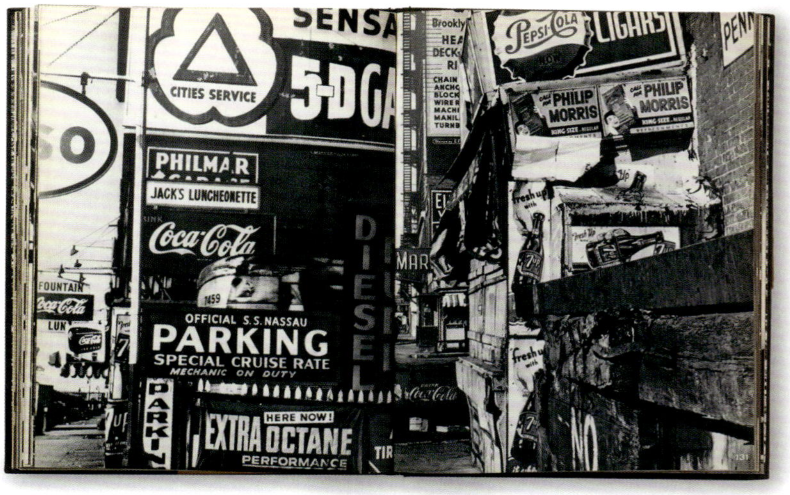
CITIES SERVICE
PHILMAR
JACK'S LUNCHEONETTE
Coca-Cola
OFFICIAL S.S.NASSAU
PARKING
SPECIAL CRUISE RATE
MECHANIC ON DUTY
DIESEL
HERE NOW!
EXTRA OCTANE
PERFORMANCE
Pepsi-Cola
CIGARS
PHILIP MORRIS

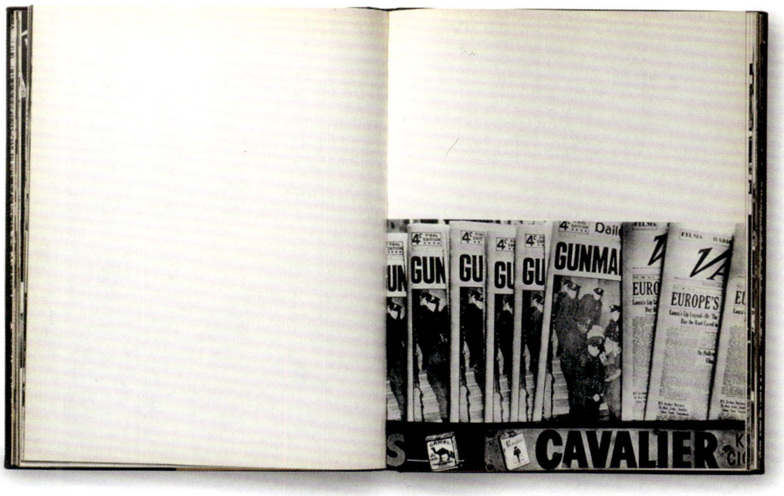
GUNMA
EUROPE'S
CAVALIER

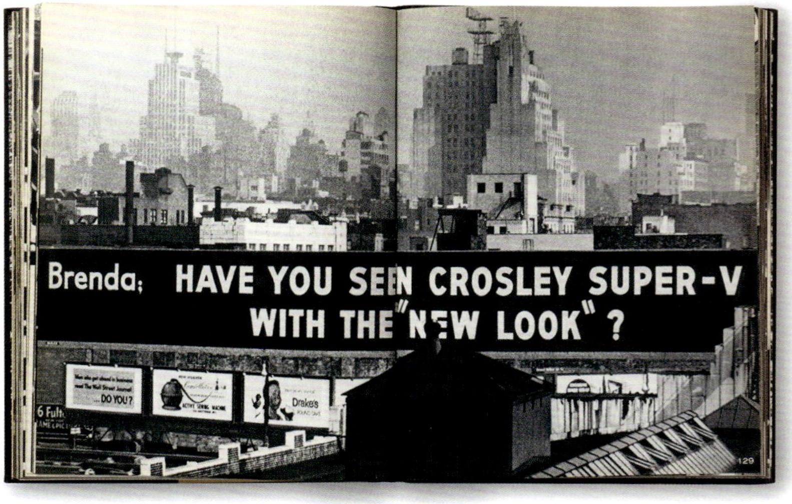
Brenda: HAVE YOU SEEN CROSLEY SUPER-V
WITH THE "NEW LOOK" ?

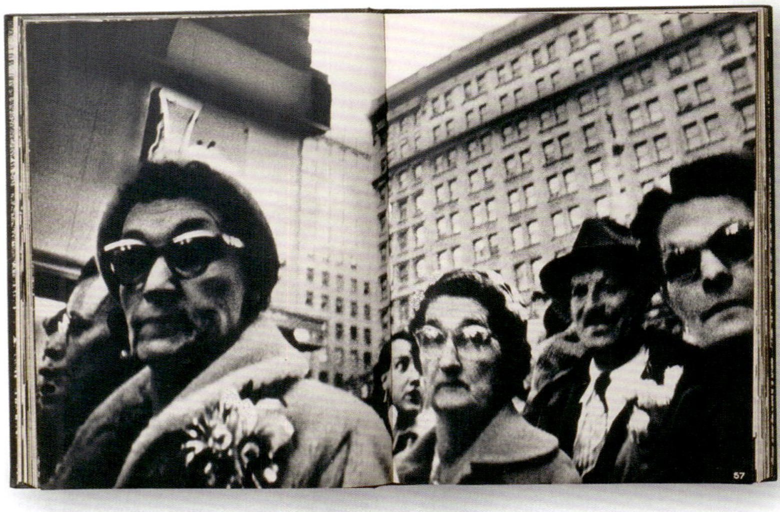

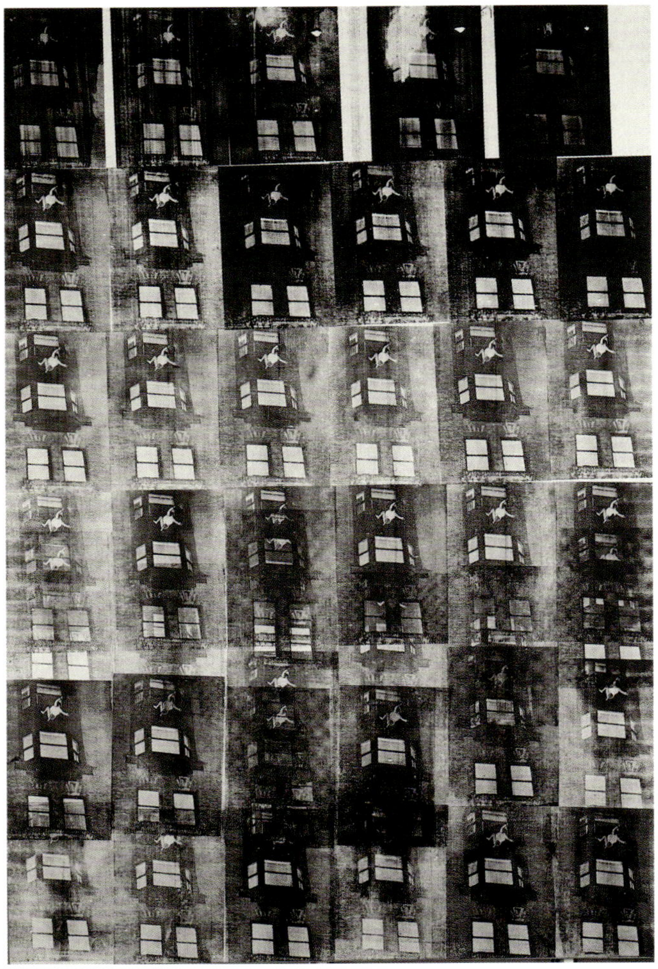

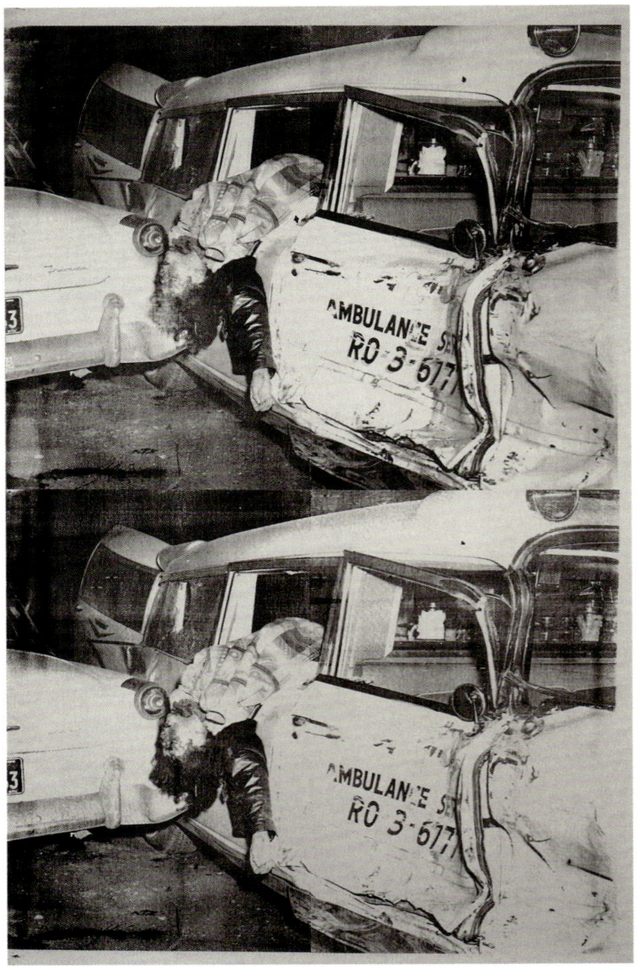
AMBULANCE
AMBULANCE

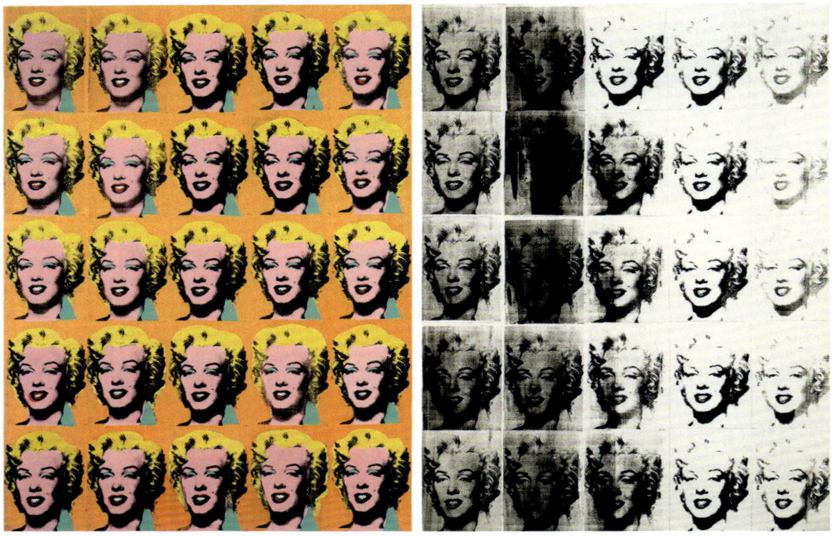

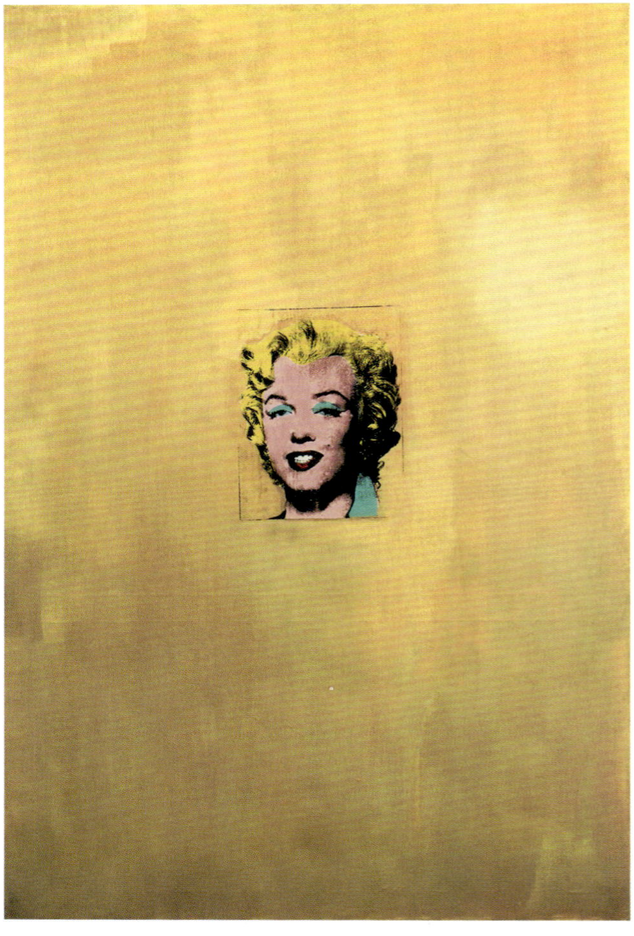

Mass Culture

Andy Warhol

In the 1950s, Andy Warhol was among one of New York's most successful commercial artists. Moving into the sphere of high art from the field of advertising design, his work radically overhauled traditional cultural and aesthetic distinctions. His art alerts us to the way in which the images and objects of consumer culture have taken over public experience. Sex-goddesses of the cinema screen provided new ersatz icons: in one famous version of his Marilyn Monroe pictures, *Gold Marilyn Monroe* (1962), the star's face adorns a gilded tondo formerly associated with sacred paintings of the Madonna and Child.

Warhol has been seen as reaching the threshold of painting's abolition. He takes art uncomfortably close to both the vulgarities and the glamour of mass culture. As a result, his relationship to mass culture remains ambiguous. Are we to see his art as one of detachment and disengagement, a depthless blank mirroring of aspects of the culture industry? Or are we to read a critical commentary in the way his art collides the aura of stars and celebrities with the macabre voyeuristic horror show of car accidents and suicides? In one tragic sense the anonymous deaths replayed over and over in the 'Disaster' series also parallel Warhol's portraits of stars, with the artist highlighting, as one writer has put it, 'the flash of fame that these little-known victims achieve in death, as their pictures are repeated in thousands of copies of newspapers'.[4]

Death also marks Warhol's celebrity portraits. He began producing his silkscreen portraits of Marilyn Monroe shortly after her suicide in 1962. The art historian Thomas Crow has suggested that *Marilyn Diptych* (1962) sets out a tension between presence and absence, life and death, initially signalled by the stripping of colour from one panel to the next. But if we then see the unevenly registered blocks of monchrome portraits evoking the material of film, with Marilyn's memory being 'most vividly carried in the flickering passage of film exposures', this transition from life to death could also be seen to reverse itself, as she is seen to be more alive in the monochrome filmic portraits.[5] As portraiture, Warhol's *Marilyn* paintings radically undermine the genre. There is no sense of somebody outside the portrait, just the bland hollow mask of the star's eternally smiling face.

Andy Warhol
A Woman's Suicide, 1963
Silkscreen ink and pencil on linen
313.1 × 212.7 cm / 123¼ × 83¾ in

Ambulance Disaster, 1963–4
Silkscreen ink on linen
316.2 × 202.9 cm / 124½ × 79⅞ in

Marilyn Diptych, 1962
Acrylic paint on canvas support each
205.7 × 144.8 cm / 81 × 57 in

Gold Marilyn Monroe, 1962
Silkscreen ink on synthetic polymer paint on canvas, 211.5 × 144.8 cm / 83¼ × 57 in

Daido Moriyama

Influenced by both William Klein and Andy Warhol, Daido Moriyama exploits photography's identity as a reproducible medium, pushing it to the limits of all coherence, sense and meaning in his book *Sashin yo Sayonara* (Bye Bye Photography) (1972), one of the most inventive, daring and experimental photography books ever published. For Moriyama 'My photographs are made complete on the printed page', and publication was more important than the display of pictures on the museum wall.[6] What is striking about *Sashin yo Sayonara* is its formlessness, and the dominance of the processes of reproduction. Everything collapses into an intense and overwhelming succession of seemingly undifferentiated representations, where appropriated images readily blur and confuse with those snatched – for the sense here is of photography done quickly – from life.

The book takes us to a limit point of photography, giving us pictures of nothingness, black and blank white frames, and scratched and grainy fields of static. The photographer Nobuyoshi Araki went so far to say that the book 'suggests the total negation of all former styles of photography'.[7] There is a sense that the viewer is not sure what he or she is seeing; there are so many images they begin to merge into each other. The book consists of 137 double-page spreads, the majority of which feature full-bleed single images although on occasions two or more images are spread out across the pages. In terms of sequencing, Moriyama has said that the 'layout was one continuous sequence'. He handed his prints to two editors and 'let them do what they wanted'.

When he was making the prints he did 'a lot of trimming, using one part of a negative or those of other people ... using whatever negatives had fallen on the darkroom floor'.[8] The aesthetic here is very much to do with the materiality of analogue photography and the meshes, dots and grain of mechanical reproduction. It is very hard to get a sense of what is pictured. Often a murky darkness and greyness obscures the images, we are too close up to faces, or there are shots of the floor or feet and the backs of people. Prints run into whiteness as light leaks onto the negative and we get partial images of a naked human form. A woman's lower back and bottom emerge from the sheets only to be lost in the whiteness of a negative as it is flooded by light, the very process here signalling that flesh and beauty are mortal. A preceding double-page photograph has introduced death through an image showing the white-draped corpse of a road accident victim.

The impact of the book is memorable and unforgettable. One double spread looks like the grainy black-and-white enlargement at the core of Michelangelo Antonioni's 1966 film, *Blow-Up*. Centred on interferences and breakdowns in communication and understanding, it is a film that is close to Moriyama's art. The pictures in *Sashin yo Sayonara* are like a radio transmission drifting in and out of tune. A similar quality has been identified as characterizing Robert Rauschenberg's silkscreens; the critic Leo Steinberg, for example, referred to their 'optical noise'[9].

It is hard to get a sense of a subject or vision in Moriyama's book, a seemingly unedited photography, grabbing from anywhere. Much as there is a loss of faith in form and coherence, viewed over thirty years later the book does now have a particular beauty, caught up with a certain nostalgia for the processes of chemical-based photography, of pictures with dust motes, hairs, chemical stains, scratches and grain. A few spreads carry particular affinities to Warhol: displays of commodities, stacks of Jolly Green Giant cans and washing detergent, products that have become unappetizing in their grainy and smudgy rendition. There is also the close-up of a commercial smile that has turned sour through its degraded copy in a blow-up of halftone newsprint. The vacuity at the heart of a commodity-driven culture, discernible in Klein's portrait of the heart of capitalism, is also evident in such pictures.

Klein and Moriyama remain photographers, and their chief concerns are to do with the implications of photography as a reproducible medium. They are fascinated with the play of pictures within pictures, how photographs circulate within culture, on movie posters, advertisements and so on. Like Warhol viewed in relationship to Rauschenberg, Moriyama can be seen as going further than Klein in pushing representation as a form: his pictures are more degraded and hollow. With Warhol's repeat silkscreen car crashes, the interferences and flaws in the silkscreen process can be as wounding as the carnage they show. Critical as it is, Klein still preserves a faith in the expressivity of portraiture, whereas people are not present in Moriyama's book: landscapes of litter, the empty sea or spaces of abandonment recur, as well as the crackle and buzz of broken images on TV channels, giving us diffused images of wrestlers, of Nixon or of helicopters from Vietnam.

Daido Moriyama
Sashin yo Sayonara (Bye Bye Photography), Shashin Hyoron-sha, Tokyo, 1972
23 × 18.2 cm / 9 × 7¼ in, 308pp, paperback with jacket, 137 black and white double page photographs

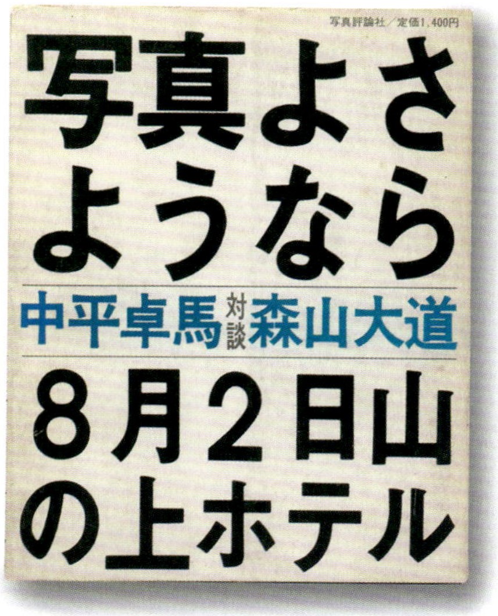
写真評論社 定価1,400円
写真よさようなら
中平卓馬 対談 森山大道
8月2日山の上ホテル

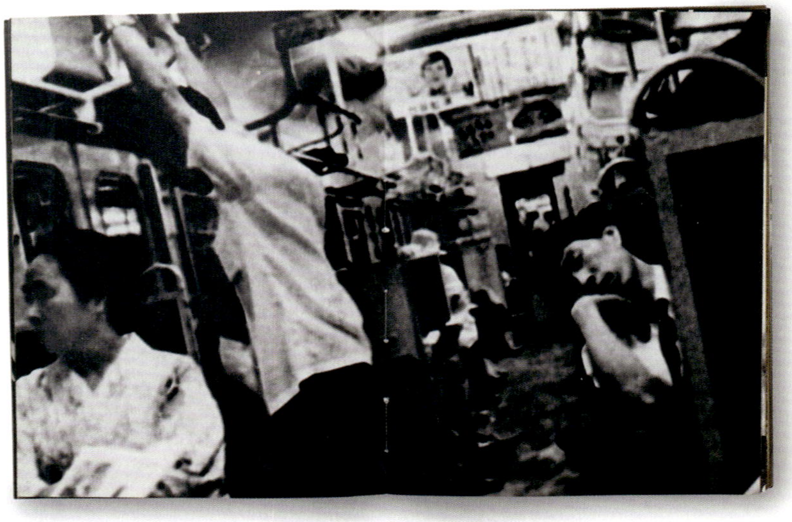

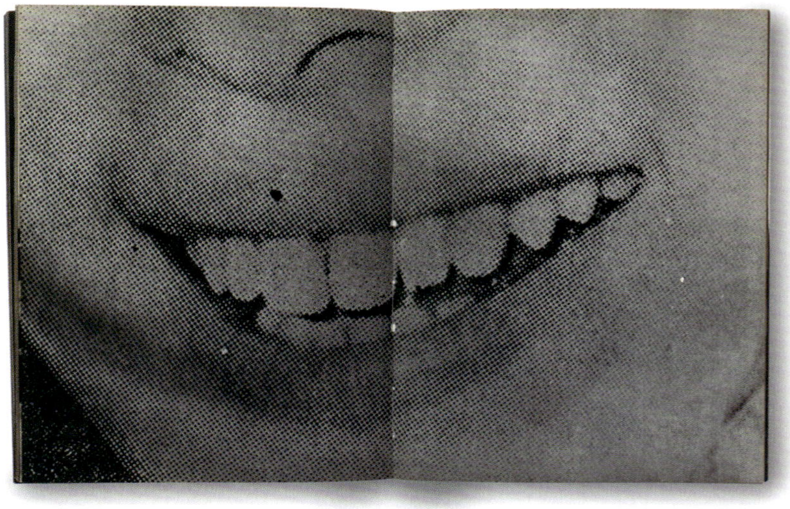

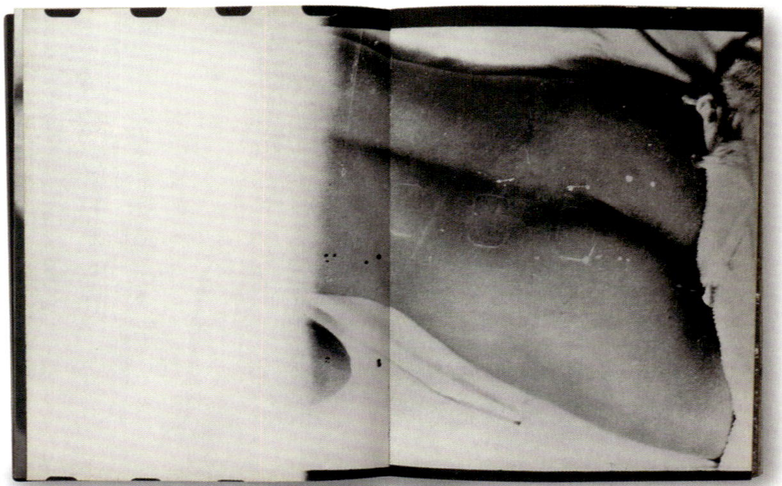

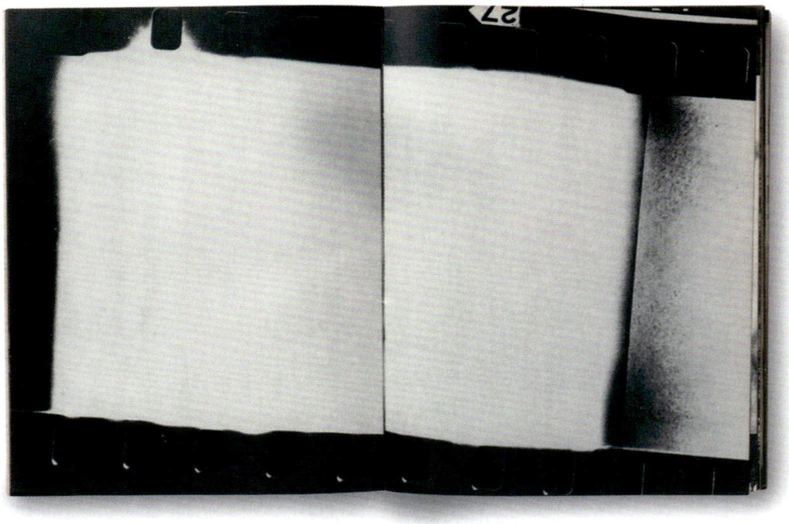

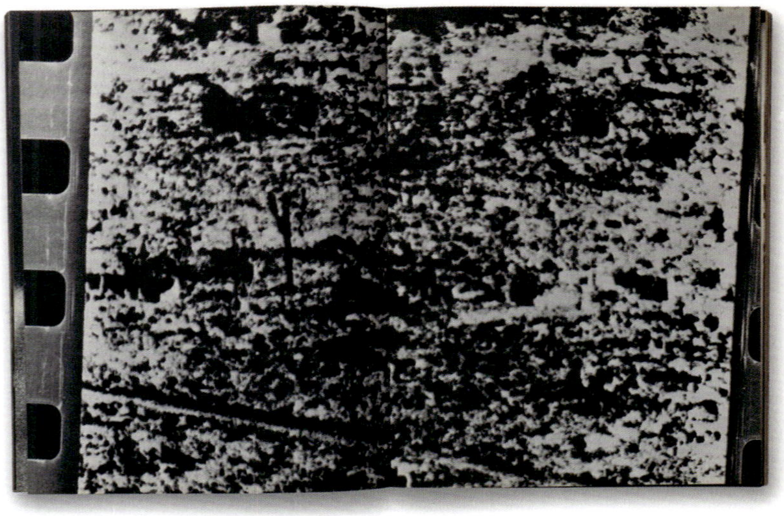

The dematerialization of the art object within Conceptual art was represented in various photographic forms as photography was deployed as a medium to document art's ephemeral events or performances. In an argument about photography becoming an art akin to modernist painting and sculpture, both of which had moved away from representation, the Canadian artist-photographer Jeff Wall spoke of the need for photography to break with and interrogate its twin traditions of depiction: reportage and the fine-art pictorialist photograph.[10] In this approach, bad photography, amateurism and deskilling was seen as one of the ways to make photography important as an avant-garde medium.

Among the key examples of this process, Wall cites the photobooks of Ed Ruscha. While Ruscha took most of the pictures himself, they are generally considered to be taken with a disregard for the craft of the medium. This casual mode of documenting began with his book *Twentysix Gasoline Stations* (prepared in 1962 and published in 1963), the first in a series of books that included *Some Los Angeles Apartments* (1965), *Every Building on the Sunset Strip* (1966), *Thirtyfour Parking Lots* (1967), *Nine Swimming Pools and a Broken Glass* (1968) and *Real Estate Opportunities* (1970). Ruscha had initially worked as a graphic artist, designing first ads and then magazines, including *Artforum* from 1965 to 1967. Ruscha's anti-pictorial and seemingly anti-aesthetic use of the medium offered a kind of degree-zero photography. *Twentysix Gasoline Stations*, he said, 'is not a book to house a collection of art photographs – they are technical data like industrial photography. To me, they are nothing more than snapshots.'[11] The photographs recorded service stations passed on journeys between Los Angeles and his Oklahoma family home along the legendary Route 66. The structure of Ruscha's books, the fixation on a certain number and the recourse to matter-of-fact documents – *Twentysix Gasoline Stations*, no more and no less – corresponded with the seriality and neutrality found in Warhol's art, whose paintings of 32 varieties of Campbell's soup cans were shown at LA's Ferus gallery in the summer of 1962.

Ruscha's photobooks were commercially produced and were deliberately intended to counter the elitism and the whole concept of the crafted artist's book. Ruscha once said he wanted to be the Henry Ford of book-making. The books' mass production allowed for the distribution of an artwork outside the rarefied space of the art gallery and also set up considerable uncertainties as to their identity. Ruscha said he did not see himself as a photographer, he just used the camera 'to shoot the pictures I have to shoot' in the same way he would pick up 'an axe when I've got to chop down a tree.' He mimed the jobbing work of an estate agent photographer with the dry factuality of the presentation of properties in *Some Los Angeles Apartments* and with the depictions of vacant lots and scrubby bits of land dominated by For Sale signs in *Real Estate Opportunities*. The pictures for *Every Building on the Sunset Strip* were taken with a motorized camera while standing in the back of a slow-moving pickup truck. Nothing is edited out in this total document of all the street fronts and intersections Ruscha passed on his journey up and down the strip. The photographs were pasted together to form one long page: in an accordion fold it ran to 27 feet (8.2 metres), with pictures of each side of the Strip forming horizontal bands top and bottom of the page and the blank band between indicating the road. The form of the book very much corresponds with Ruscha's description of Los Angeles as a succession of surfaces with nothing behind: the city is 'like a series of store fronts and planes that are all vertical from the street, and there's almost like nothing behind the facades.'

For *Nine Swimming Pools and a Broken Glass* Ruscha used expensive colour reproduction. Colour, which was associated at the time with commercial photography for fashion and advertising, makes the book look like a brochure or catalogue. He said the book was about 'the lifestyle, the particular issues about how a swimming pool would look – the waterness, the ripples, a particular kind of indulgence…'. Taken in cheap motels, however, the pools look somewhat shabby and unkempt. They are also all depicted without people. As in Ruscha's other books, the overriding note is one of emptiness and hollowness, a quality further accented by the inclusion of a large amount of blank pages, nearly five times the number of colour plates. The jarring closing picture of a broken glass upsets both the sense and the order of the book: a small but significant moment of drama that suggests an incident and event, contrasting with the stasis and eventlessness of his otherwise neutral photographs of unoccupied pools (wet footprints around a diving board in one picture are the only suggestion of use).

Ed Ruscha
Twentysix Gasoline Stations, Ed Ruscha, Los Angeles, California, 1963
17.9 × 14 / 7 1/16 × 5 1/2 in, 48pp
Paperback with glassine jacket
26 black and white photographs

Nine Swimming Pools and a Broken Glass, Ed Ruscha, Los Angeles, California, 1968–1997
17.8 × 14 cm / 7 × 5 1/2 in, 64pp
Paperback with glassine jacket
10 colour photographs

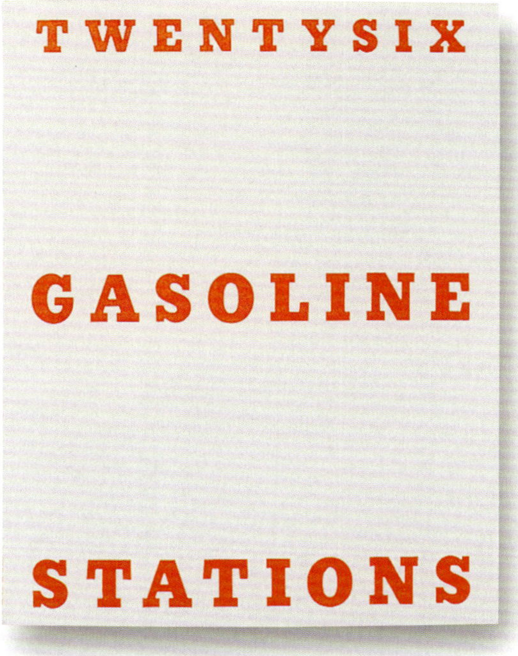
TWENTYSIX
GASOLINE
STATIONS

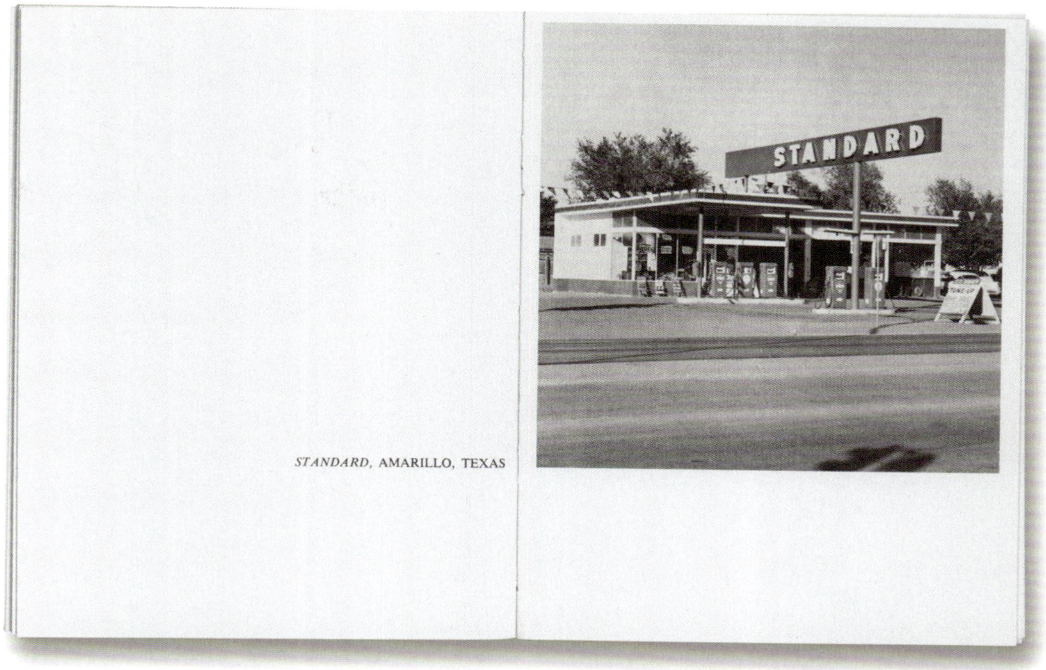
STANDARD
STANDARD, AMARILLO, TEXAS

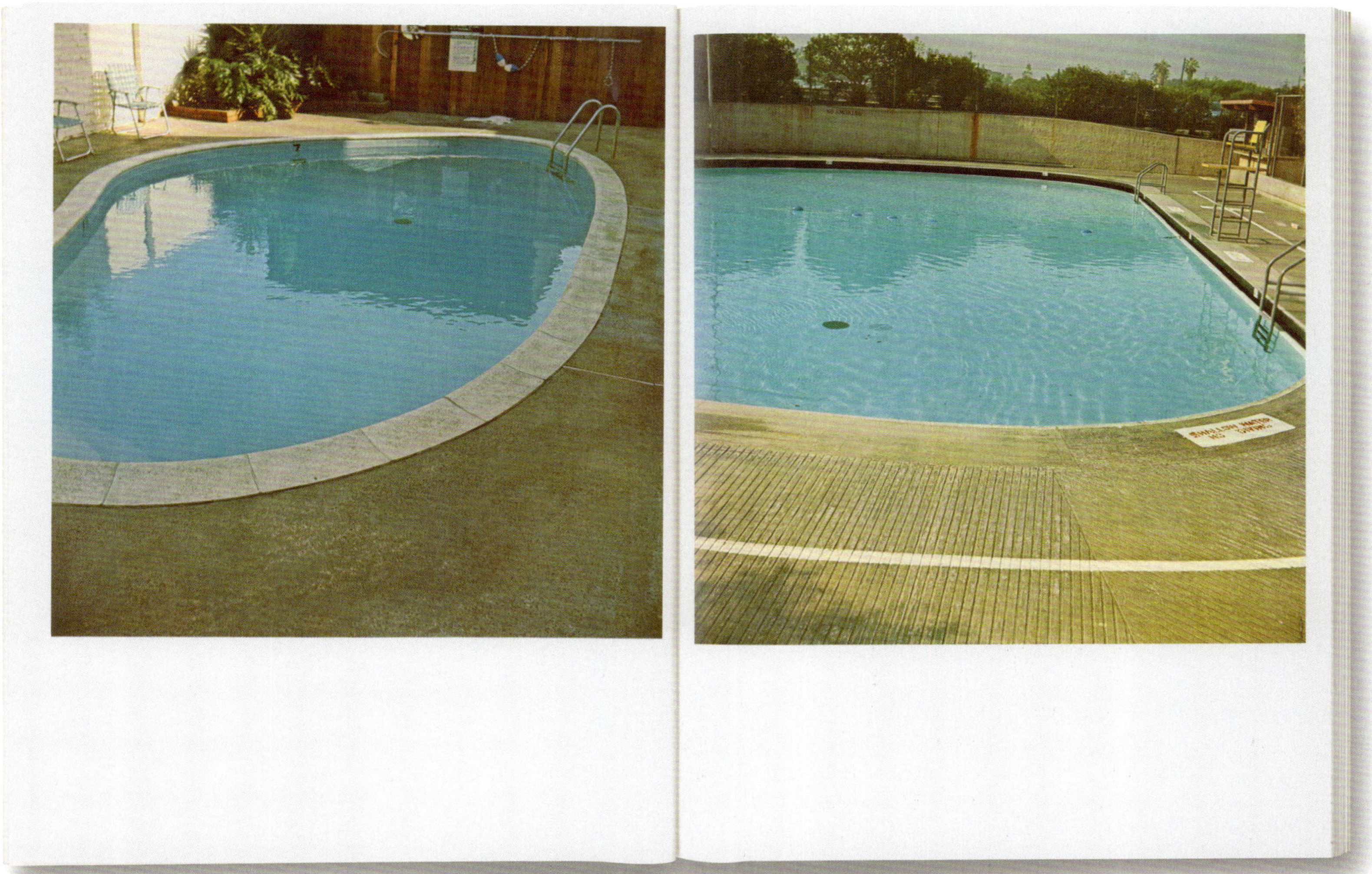

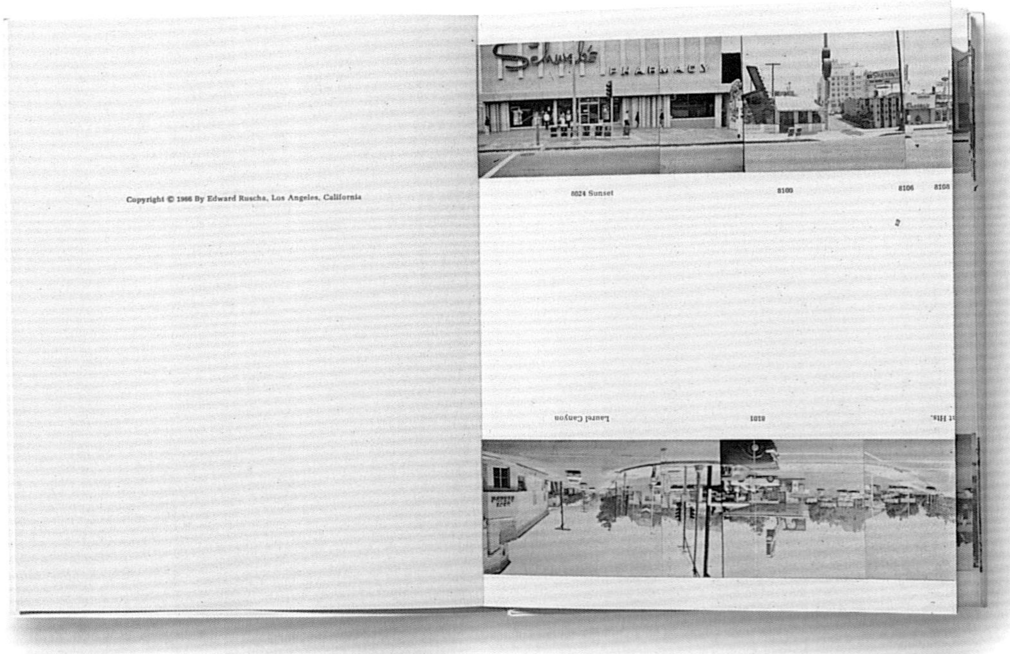

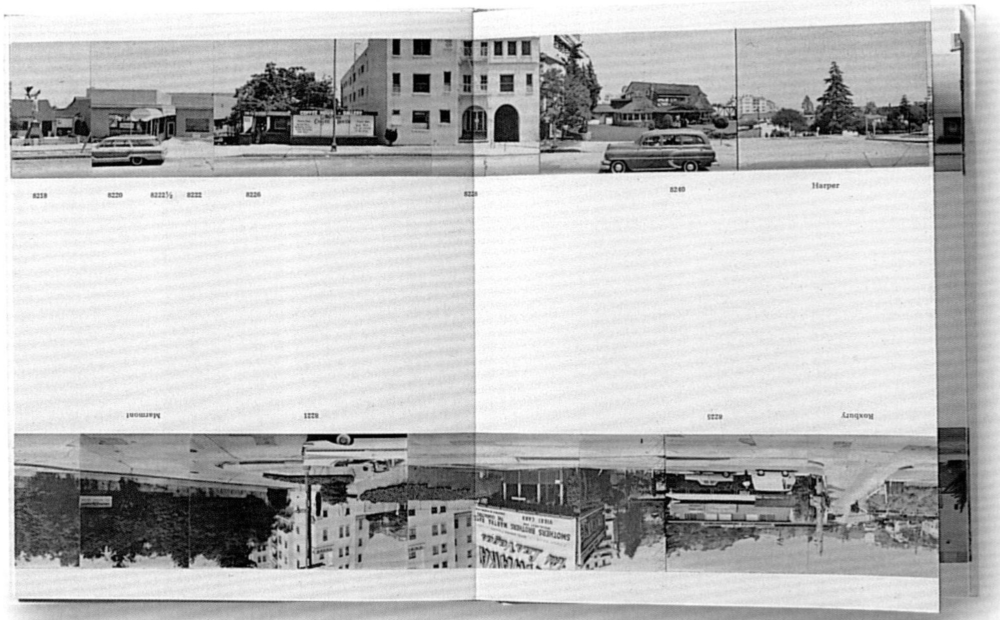

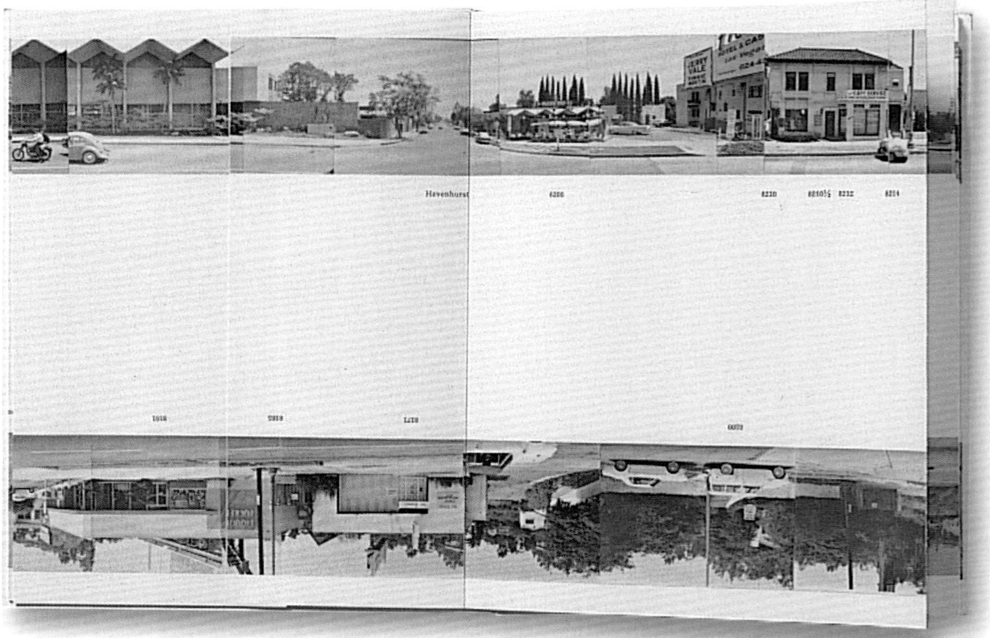

Ed Ruscha
Every Building on the Sunset Strip,
Ed Ruscha, Los Angeles, California, 1966
18 × 14.6 / 7 × 5½ in, 54pp
Paperback with an accordian fold-out page attached to card cover in white card slipcase and white paper bellyband (not shown), numerous black and white photographs

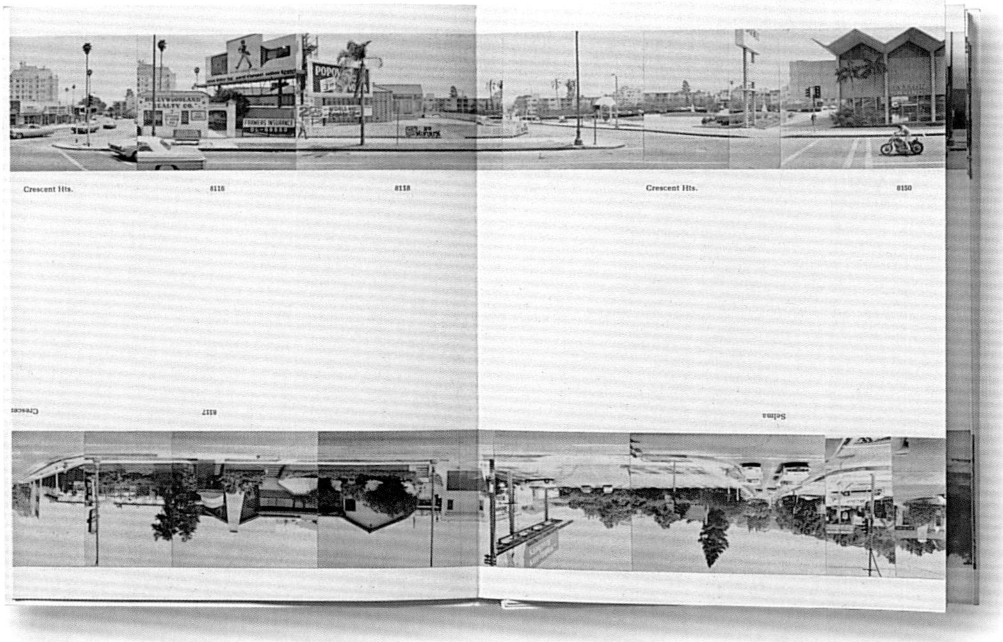

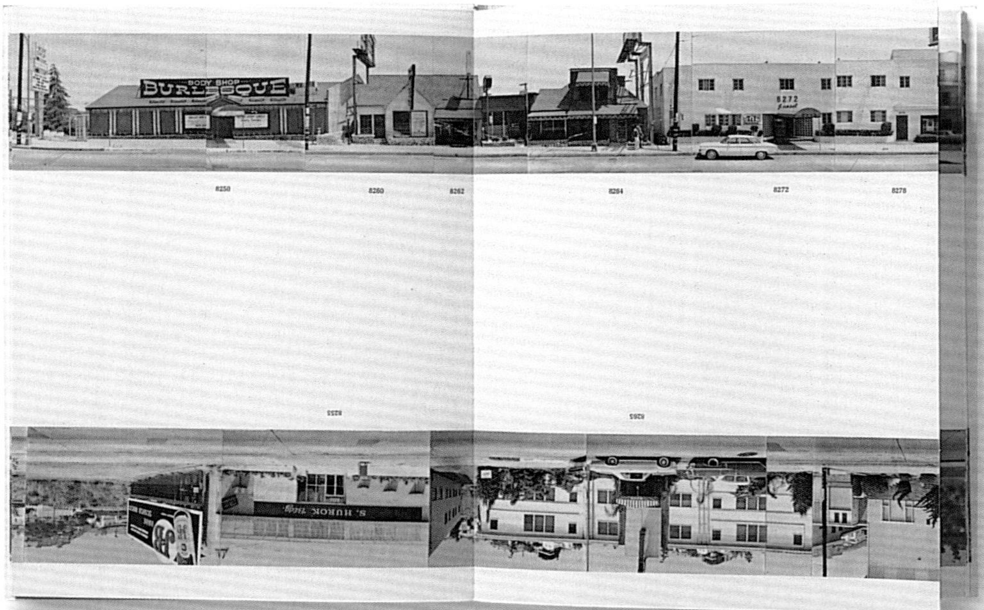

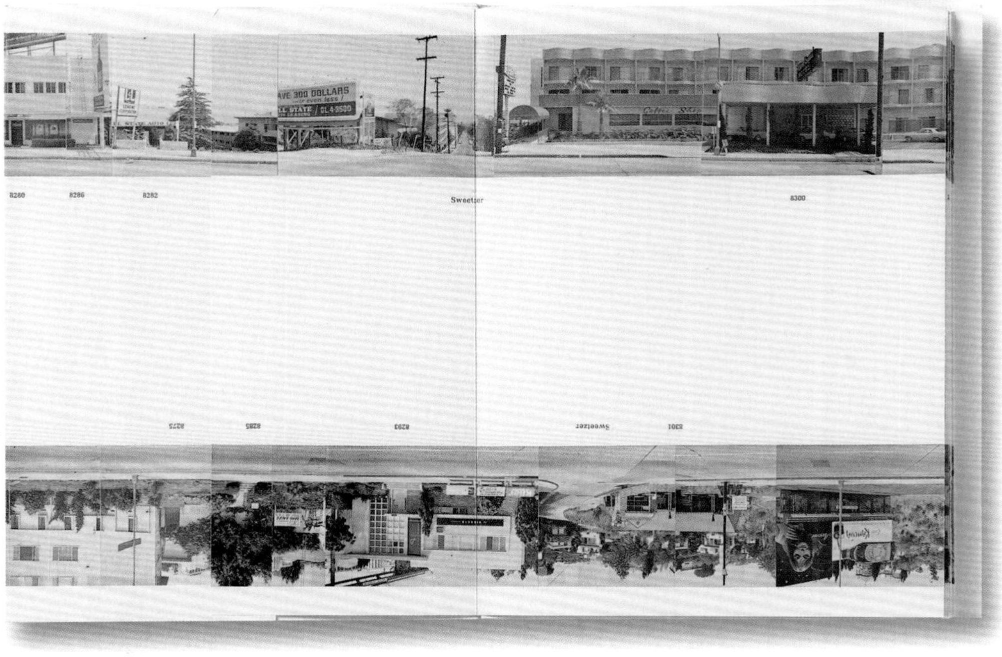

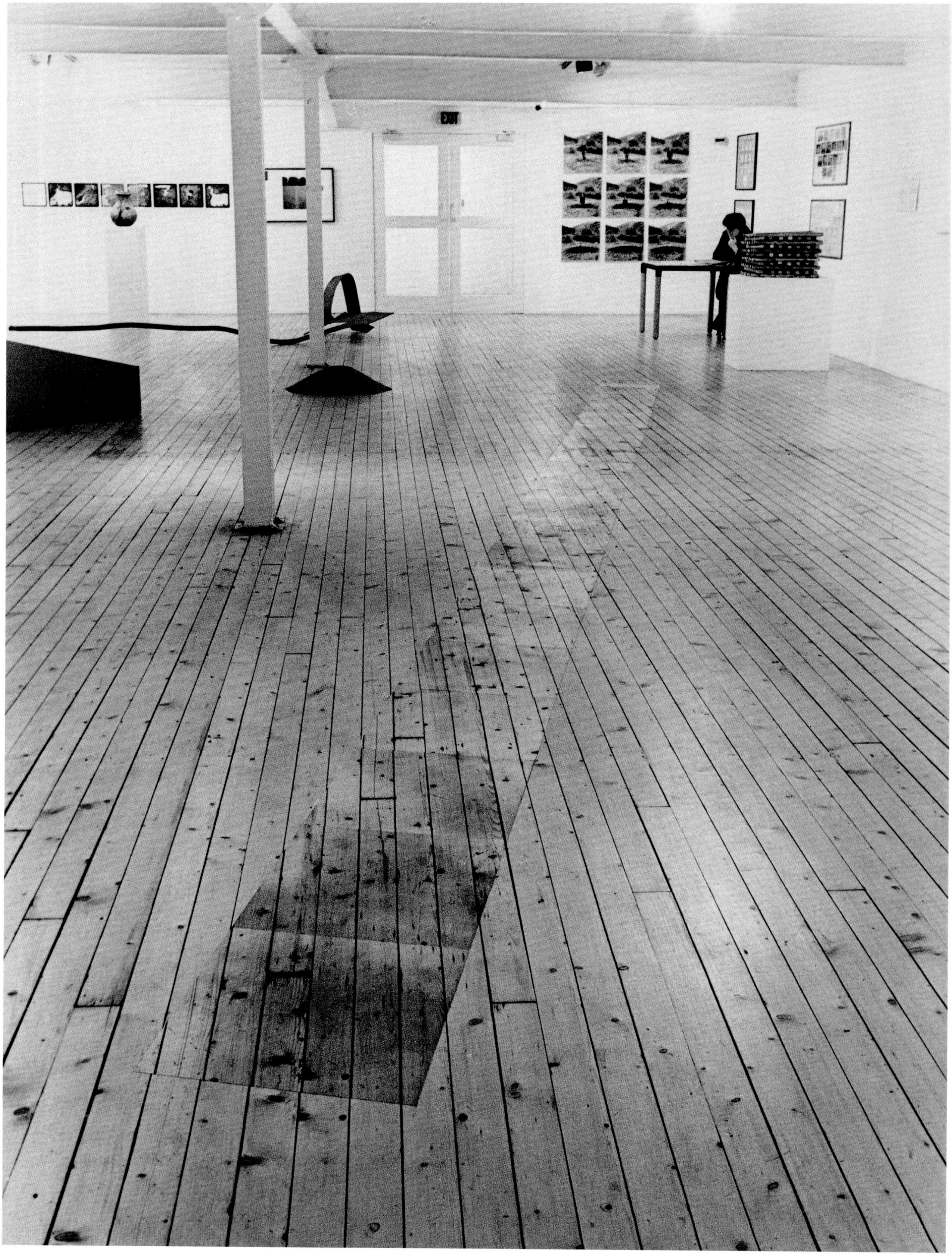

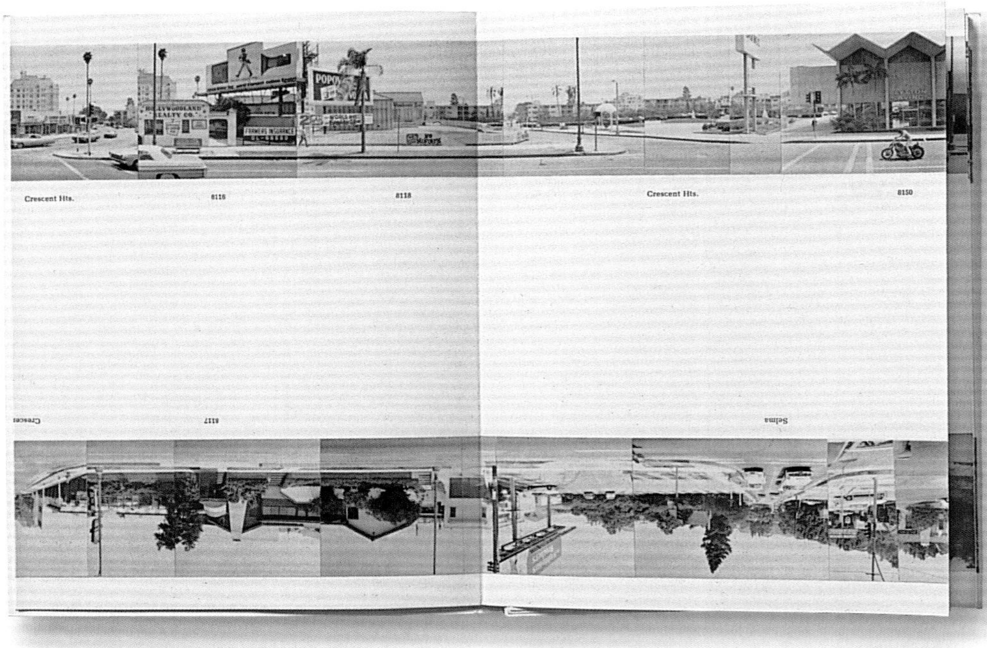
Crescent Hts.
Crescent Hts.

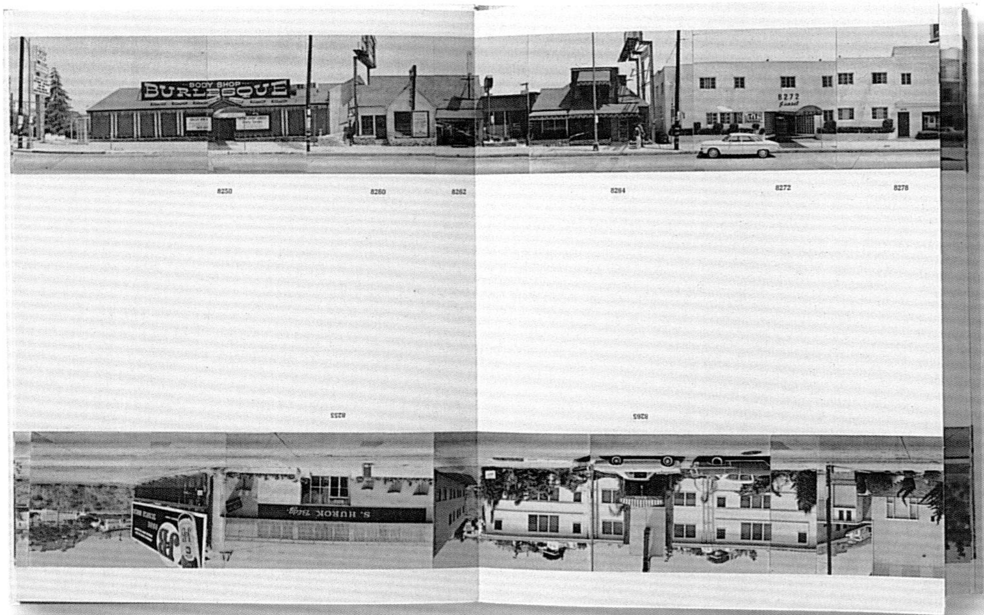

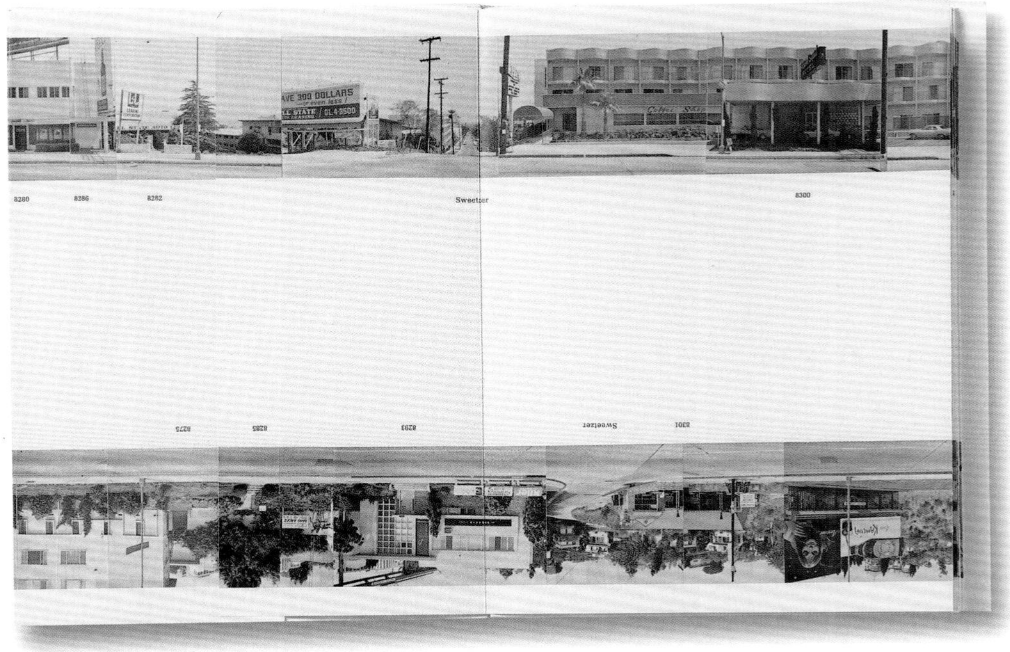
Sweetzer

John Baldessari

John Baldessari produced a series of phototext canvases in the late 1960s that, like Ed Ruscha's books, deliberately flouted aesthetic conventions. He said that he 'wanted to be less artful than Robert Rauschenberg and Andy Warhol.'[12] Experimenting with light-sensitive emulsion allowed him to print his photographs on canvas and raise them to the status of art. But being presented in this way only exacerbated the deliberately banal and dumb characteristic of his photographic images. Baldessari described how he took some of them: 'I drove with one hand and pointed the camera out the window with the other, not looking where I was shooting pictures. Then I would stop the car and just write down the location … I wanted things the way they were, with ugly wires and telephone poles, without beautification and with the quality of newspaper photo-reportage.' Beneath each image, the names of the places appear in plain and functional lettering made by a sign painter Baldessari had hired.

In the photo-emulsion painting *Wrong* (1966–8), Baldessari appears as the subject. The single word of the title is combined with a portrait of the photographer standing in front of his home in National City, a working-class industrial suburb of San Diego. What is wrong with the picture is comically clear: Baldessari stands in front of a palm tree that looks as though it is growing out of his head. Amateur photography guides are the most obvious point of reference here. There is much humour and pleasure in this blatant show of doing something wrong. The work also rebounds on bigger questions about the hierarchies and distinctions integral to judgements about aesthetic worth and value, of what is proper and correct in terms of composition. The error also, of course, plays upon something integral to photographic representation: its ability to collapse space.

Photography becomes important to Baldessari because its identity as art is less clear-cut. Its shortcomings in relationship to art become the subject of one photo-emulsion canvas in particular, showing a messy, nondescript view, through trees, plants and bushes, of cars in a parking lot. The picture is accompanied by the text: 'An artist is not merely the slavish announcer of a series of facts, which in this case the camera has had to accept and mechanically record.' Photography's 'slavish' documentary description is insufficient as art and this quality is compounded by the evident lack of pictorial interest of Baldessari's photography, and its insistence on his prosaic and ordinary surroundings.

In *The Pencil Story* (1972–3) Baldessari uses photography and text to raise questions about the nature of art. The text reveals that he had an old pencil on the dashboard of his car; every time he saw it, he 'felt uncomfortable since its point was so dull and dirty.' He always intended to sharpen it, and when he did he thought it might have 'something to do with art.' Two colour photographs show us the pencil: in one its stub is blunt and in the other it is sharpened to a point. The shift is a nice way of presenting a thought about art in relation to a common object. The blunt, 'dull and dirty' point also becomes an apposite symbol of the grubby world of daily realities and human inadequacies out of which Baldessari makes his art.

John Baldessari
An Artist is Not Merely the Slavish Announcer, 1966–8
Acrylic and photo-emulsion on canvas
150.1 × 114.6 cm / 59 × 45⅛ in

Wrong, 1966–8
Photo-emulsion and acrylic on canvas
55.9 × 69.2 cm / 22 × 27¼ in

The Pencil Story, 1972–3
2 colour photographs mounted on board
55.9 × 69.2 cm / 22 × 27¼ in

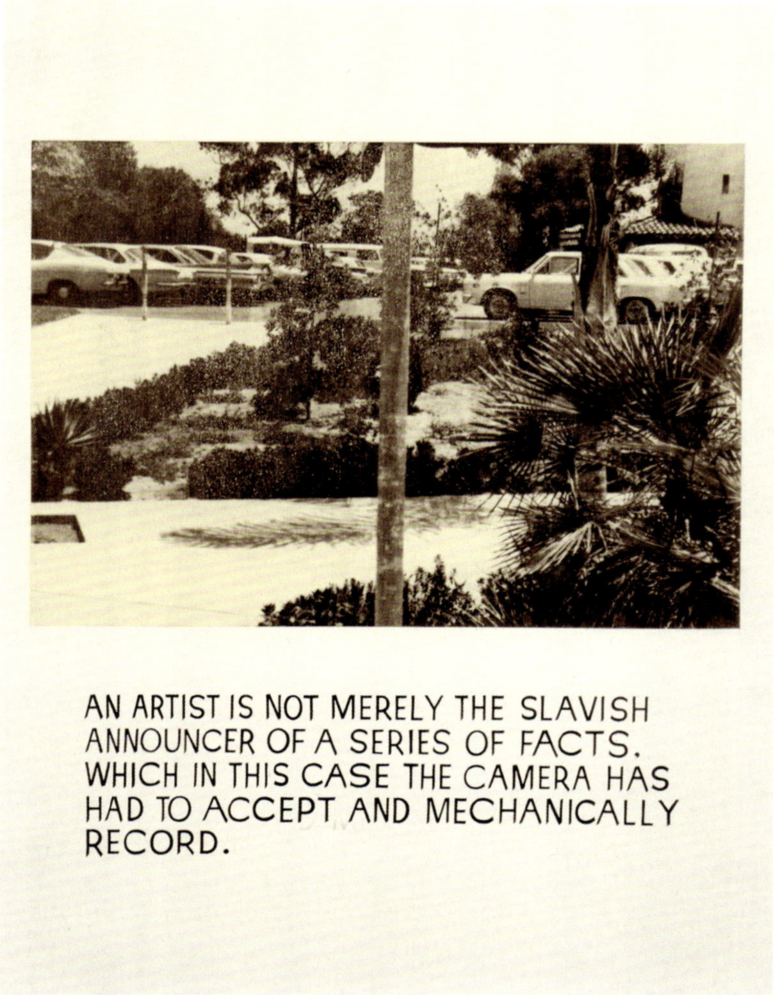
AN ARTIST IS NOT MERELY THE SLAVISH ANNOUNCER OF A SERIES OF FACTS. WHICH IN THIS CASE THE CAMERA HAS HAD TO ACCEPT AND MECHANICALLY RECORD.

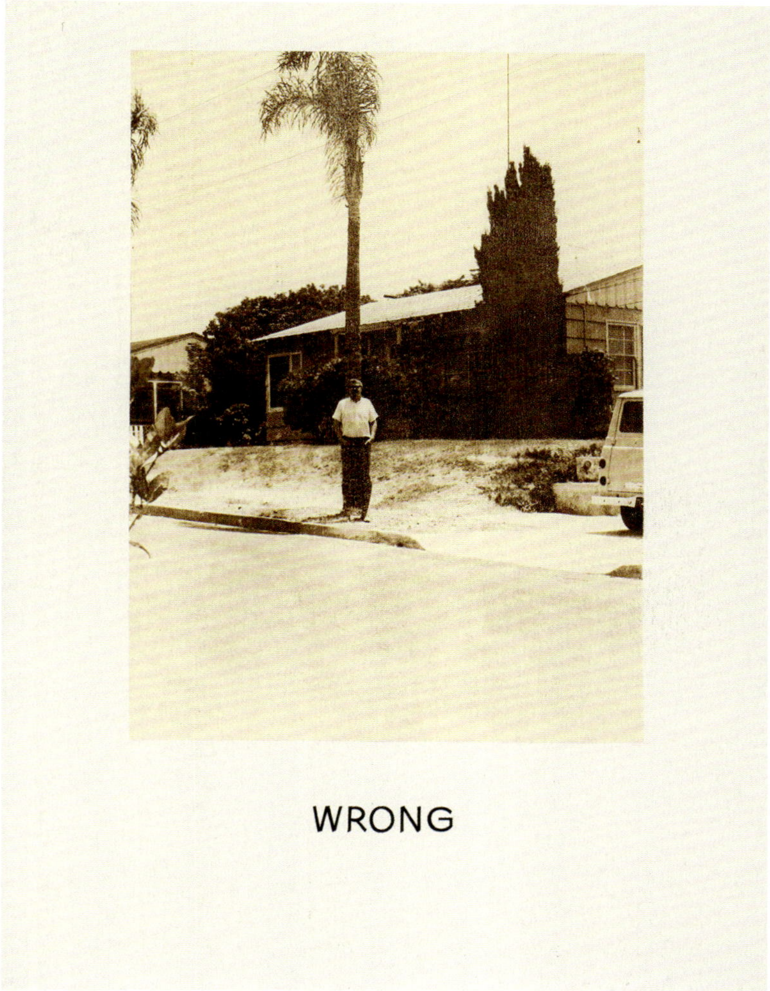
WRONG

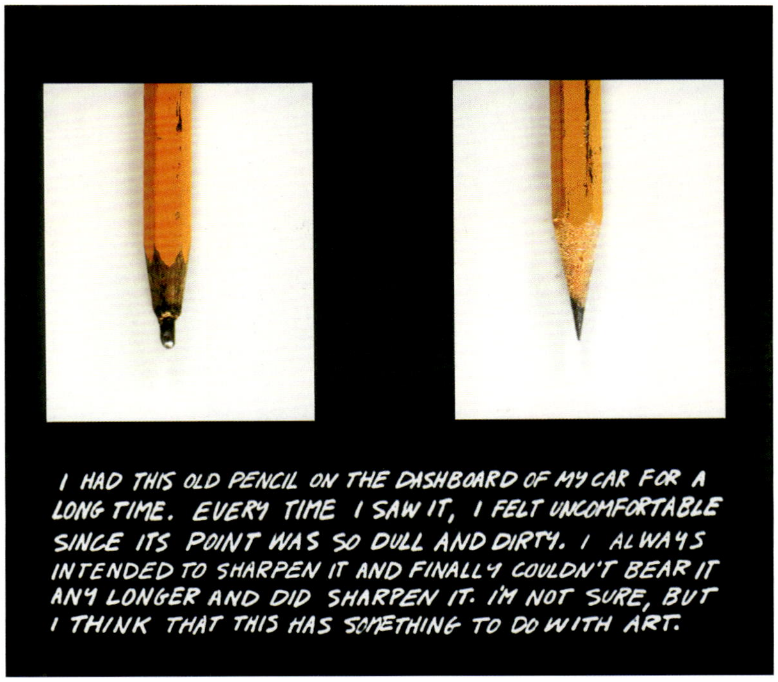
I HAD THIS OLD PENCIL ON THE DASHBOARD OF MY CAR FOR A LONG TIME. EVERY TIME I SAW IT, I FELT UNCOMFORTABLE SINCE ITS POINT WAS SO DULL AND DIRTY. I ALWAYS INTENDED TO SHARPEN IT AND FINALLY COULDN'T BEAR IT ANY LONGER AND DID SHARPEN IT. I'M NOT SURE, BUT I THINK THAT THIS HAS SOMETHING TO DO WITH ART.

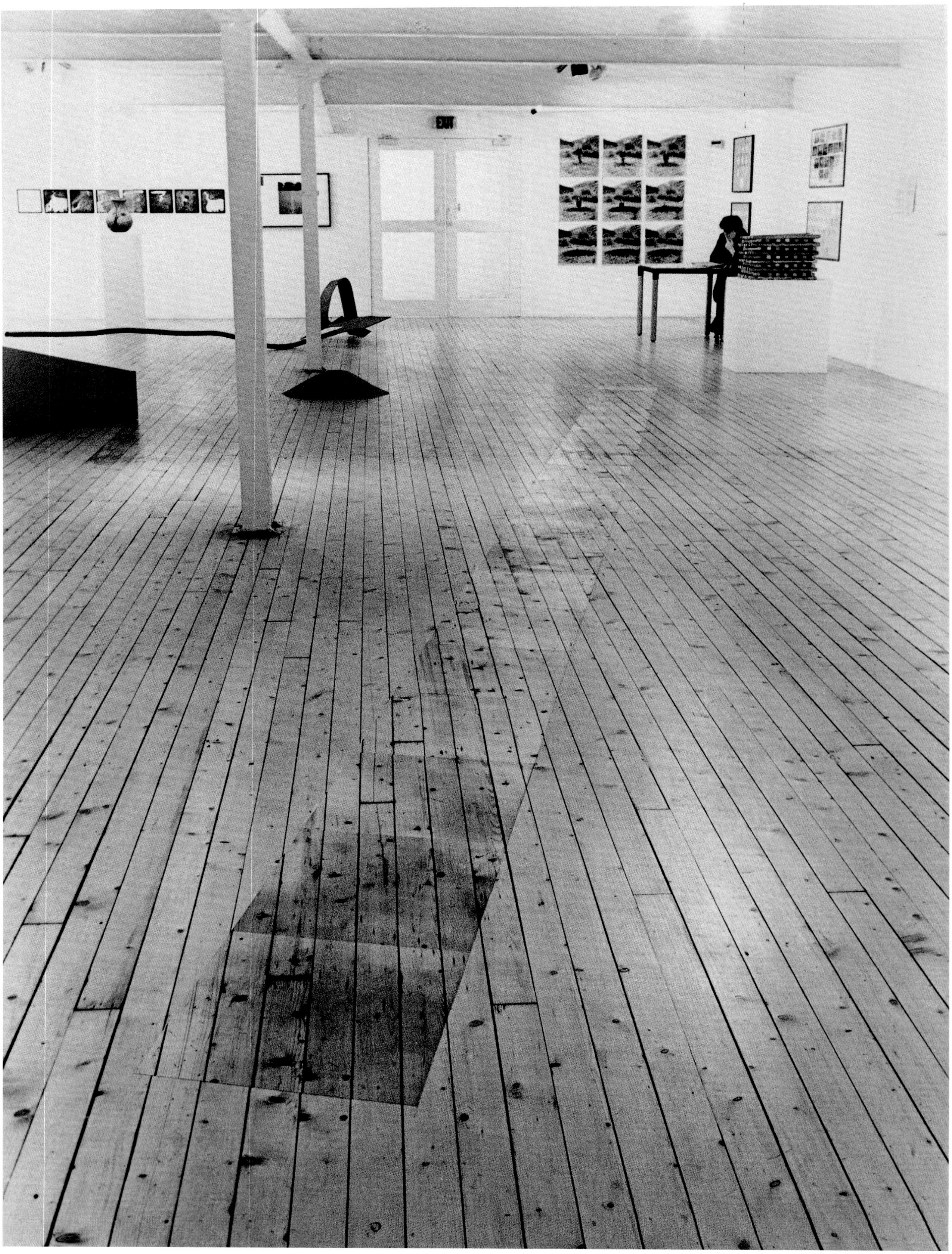
EXIT

Victor Burgin

The British artist Victor Burgin pursued an interesting dialogue with both minimalist sculpture and Conceptual art through his site-specific installation *Photopath*, exhibited at the London venue of 'Live in Your Head: When Attitudes Become Form' in 1969. This is a literal use of the photograph as a copying medium. The work questions the adequacy of photography as a document by using photographs to cover areas of the gallery floor they represent. Divesting photography of seeming aesthetic value and worth, all we have is a black and white document of a blank area of the floor. Yet, if we follow the logic of Jeff Wall's argument, this can also be seen to mark photography's emergence as an avant-garde art form. Such conceptual (and sculptural) uses of photography paralleled the autonomy and reflexivity of minimalist sculpture, such as Carl Andre's plates of differing metals laid edge to edge to form flat extended squares that rest directly on the floor.

Burgin was a student in the Graduate School of Art and Architecture at Yale in the mid 1960s, at the height of minimalism, when the teachers there included Robert Morris and Donald Judd. Burgin's investigations into photography's status and adequacy as a realist form has a clear relationship to Joseph Kosuth's earlier formal-philosophical interrogations into photography's identity in such works as *One and Three Chairs* (1965–7), where the photograph functioned as a document of a quotidian object, alongside that physical object and a dictionary definition of the name of that object. The point of comparison seemed to be to show the limits and insufficiencies of photography as a representation of an object.

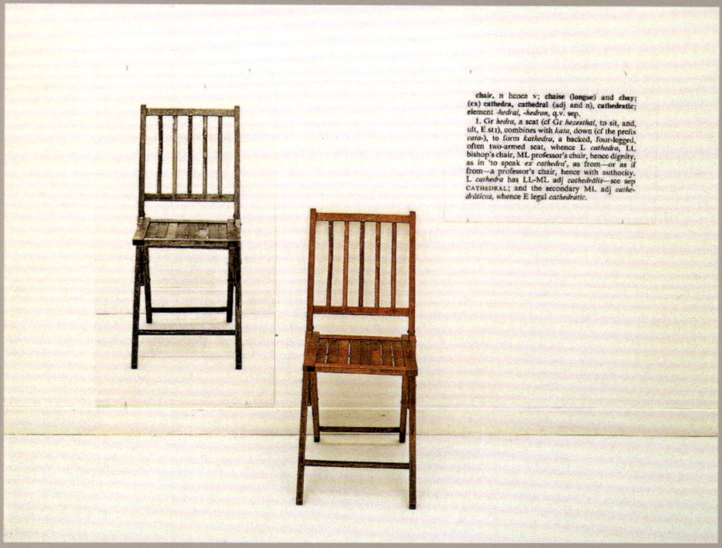

Joseph Kosuth
One and Three Chairs, 1965–7
Photograph of chair to scale, wooden folding chair, photographic enlargement of dictionary definition, dimensions variable

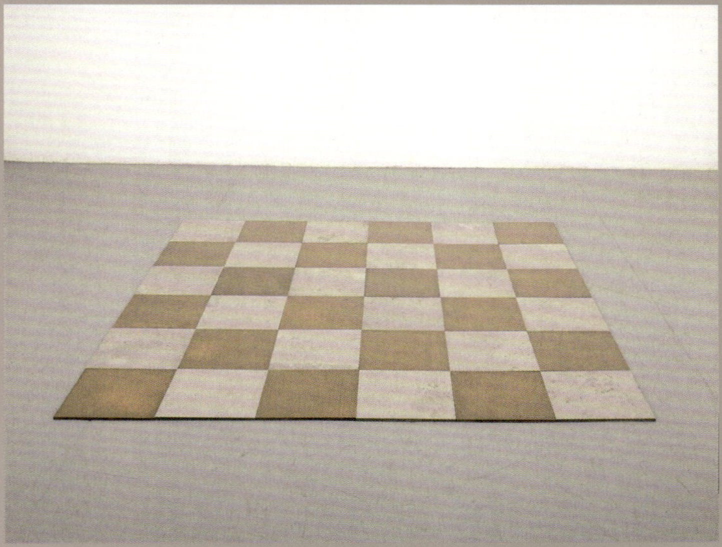

Carl Andre
Copper - Magnesium Plain, New York, 1969
Copper and magnesium, 36-unit square, on floor, each metal alternating
95 × 182.9 × 182.9 cm / ⅜ × 72 × 72 in

Victor Burgin
Photopath, 1967
Photographic print, dimensions variable

Sherrie Levine

Sherrie Levine's infamous gesture was to photograph other photographers' work. Levine is one of a group of artists who have come to be referred to as the Pictures Generation, a title stemming from the groundbreaking 1977 New York show 'Pictures', curated by Douglas Crimp, which highlighted art involving various forms of image appropriation. Crimp described such work as postmodern in the way it dismantled the core values identified with the artwork: authorship, orginality and expressivity. Levine adapted Marcel Duchamp's premise of the readymade to photography. Duchamp invented the term to describe a series of common objects designated as artworks simply because he had chosen them and displayed them in the gallery. He famously proposed an upturned factory-made urinal to New York's Armory Show in 1917.

Levine exhibited copies of photographic reproductions by such photographers as Edward Weston and Walker Evans, matted, framed and behind glass, just as the original works would have been displayed. The shock and difficulty of such work was that there was nothing new to look at. A number of writers read a feminist agenda into the fact that Levine was appropriating the work of canonical male artists. Her work was also produced in the wake of a photography boom that saw prices skyrocket and the re-evaluation of all kinds of photographs as individual, authored works. Levine's appropriations can also be set against the revival of expressionism in painting, announced by such exhibitions as London's Royal Academy of Art's 'A New Spirit in Painting' in 1981, the year her selection of twenty-one photographs after Walker Evans were shown in her one-person exhibition at Metro Pictures in New York. Raising questions about authorship rebounded on what Evans was doing in representing the poor tenant families of Alabama, and of the rights and legimitacy he had in making art from prying into the lives of others. In 1995–6 Levine made copies of Claude Monet's *Rouen Cathedral* paintings from colour reproductions. She produced both black and white 10×8 inch gelatin silver prints from the paintings and a computerized averaging of Monet's colour in the form of Iris prints. Like her silver prints after Degas and Cézanne, the Monet photographs have, as Howard Singerman has argued, a certain autonomy as photographs: their size was that of a classic photograph rather than that of the 'original' reproductions in books.

Levine's use of photography is subtle and intelligent, reflecting upon art history and the copy at a time when the reception of photography within the art market was changing. Her photographs after paintings from the 1990s onwards attest to a shift away from the initial postmodern framework and possess their own distinctive aesthetic as photographs. Levine was also producing drawings, paintings and sculpture. For example, in *Fountain* (1991), her series of six urinals after Marcel Duchamp's most famous readymade were transformed into distinctly aesthetic objects, cast in highly polished bronze and replete with allusions to the modernist sculpture of Brancusi and Jean Arp.

Sherrie Levine
After Cézanne: 1–9, 1993
(detail), gelatin silver prints
Each 20.3 × 25.4 cm / 8 × 10 in

Cathedral 5, 1996
Gelatin silver print
25.4 × 20.3 cm / 10 × 8 in

Installation view of *After Walker Evans: 1–22*, 1981
Whitney Museum of American Art, New York
21 gelatin silver prints, each
25.4 × 20.3 cm / 10 × 8 in

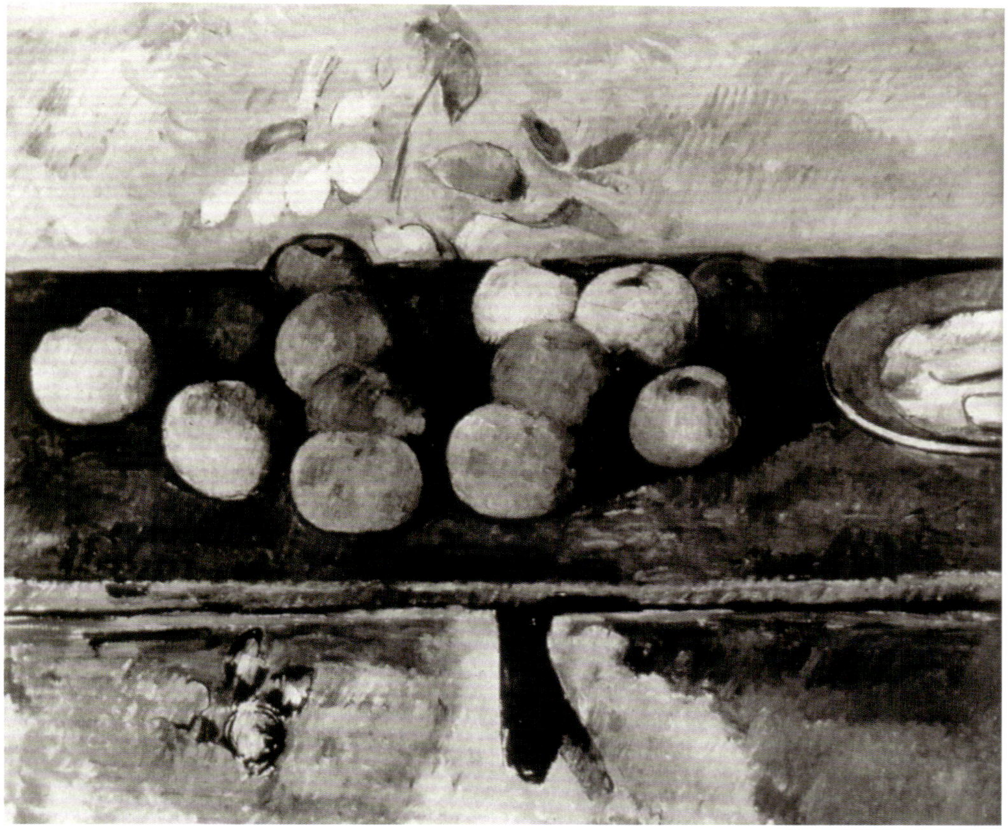

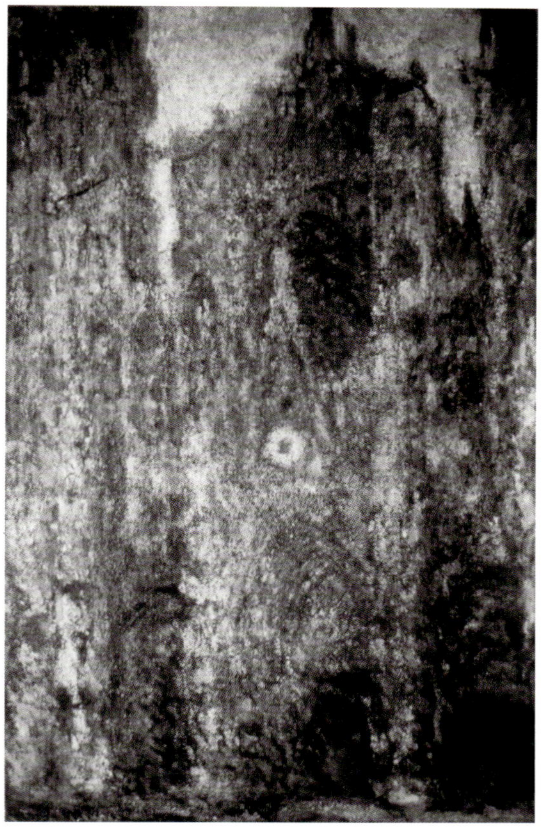

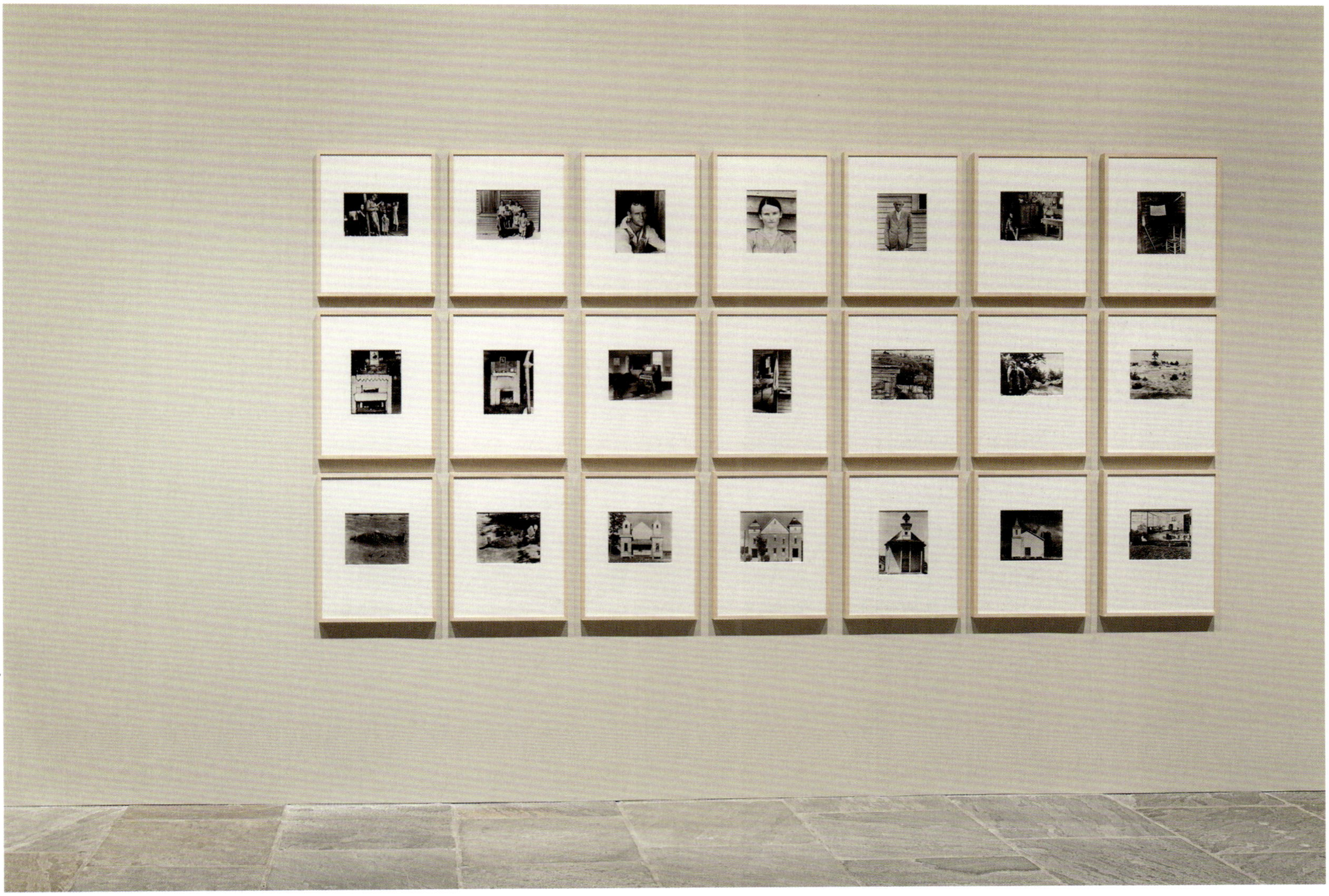

Larry Sultan and Mike Mandel

In California in 1977, the same year as the 'Pictures' exhibition in New York, Larry Sultan and Mike Mandel published a book of photographs entitled *Evidence.* While not associated with the Pictures Generation, Sultan and Mandel also appropriate images. *Evidence* was the culmination of a three-year search through the files and archives of over one hundred U.S. government agencies, educational institutions and corporations. Sifting through some two million images, the artists assembled a careful sequence of fifty-nine pictures for the book.

Printing full frame from the original 5×4 inch negatives, Sultan and Mandel are fascinated with the contingent information outside the images' original illustrational role. They give us a bigger, more inclusive picture as a result, but in doing so only create greater ambiguity and mystery.

Sultan and Mandel considered the pictures they used as found objects, fully within the tradition of Marcel Duchamp's readymades. Pictures are taken out of context and become meaningful in terms of new associations, affected both by the political context of the 1970s and by their similarities to performance-based and installation art. Mandel acknowledged the influence of the performance artist Chris Burden, in which the body was subjected to such violent acts as in *Shoot* (1971), for which the artist was shot in his upper left arm. The pictures begin with forensic details: footprints across a patio floor, the cast of a human hand with a small identification portrait, a snapshot on a plastic chair that has survived a fire. One photograph shows a gloved hand holding a rope in the form of a noose. When figures are included they appear very often as scientific functionaries. Suited or hard-hatted, they are shown experimenting, measuring, investigating and testing. One picture shows a deep grave-shaped hole above which a man holds a long tape in order to measure its depth. Science and technology is set in relationship to an increasing sense of uncertainty and not-knowing. Two pictures of human figures, towards the end of the book, bear this out. One shows a lone figure in tie, shirt and galoshes looking back from the black void of a tunnel filled with a tar-like substance, while the other is an aerial view looking down at a human figure in a concrete subway holding a large case; the figure is shown moving up a pile of rubble and away from the ladder that offers an exit from the hole he is in.

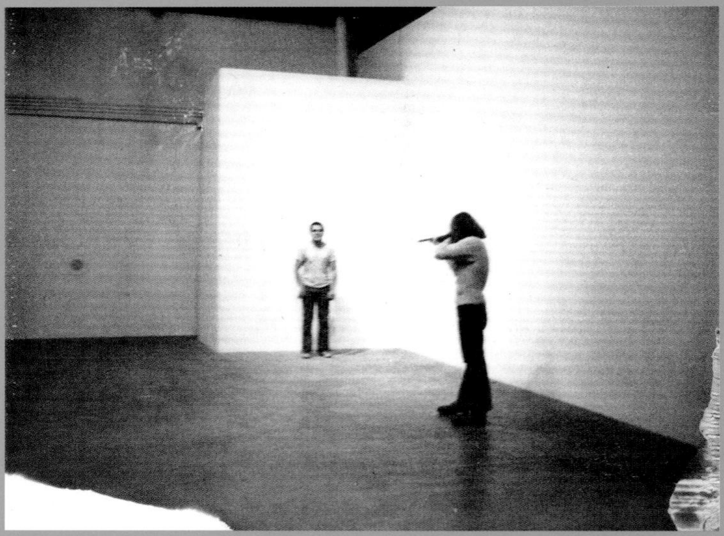

Chris Burden
Shoot, 1971
F Space, Santa Ana, California
Still from video

Larry Sultan and Mike Mandel
Evidence, Clatworthy Colorvues, Greenbrae, Santa Cruz, California, 1977
(2003 edition illustrated)
23 × 24.7 cm / 9 × 9¾ in, 72pp
Hardback, 59 black and white photographs

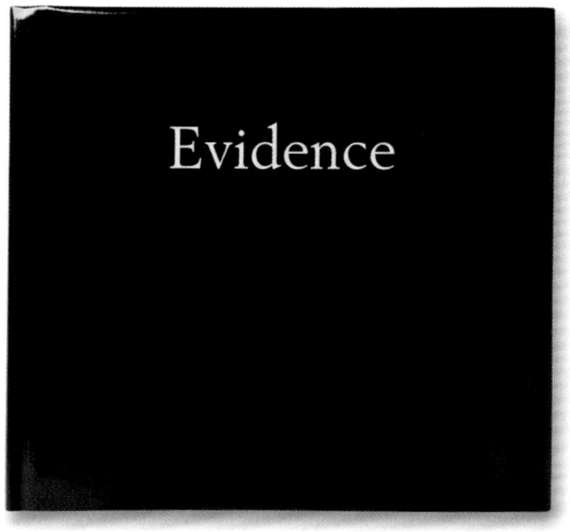
Evidence

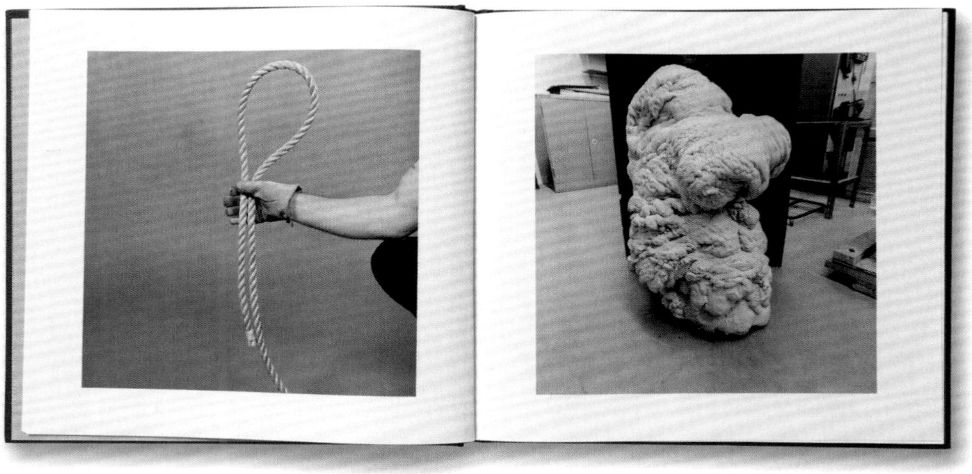

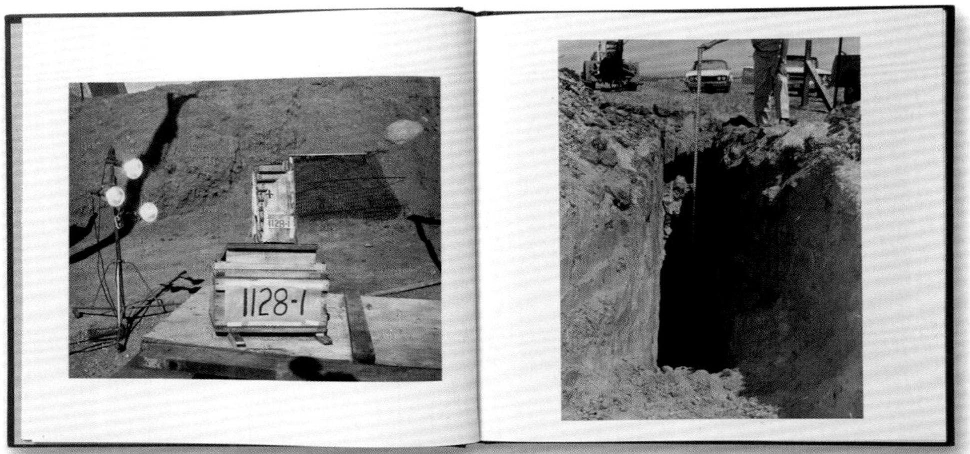
1128-1

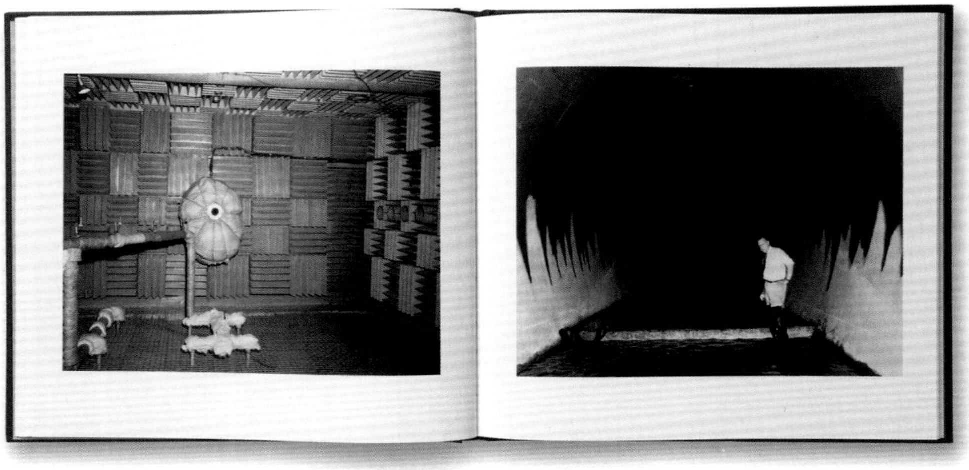

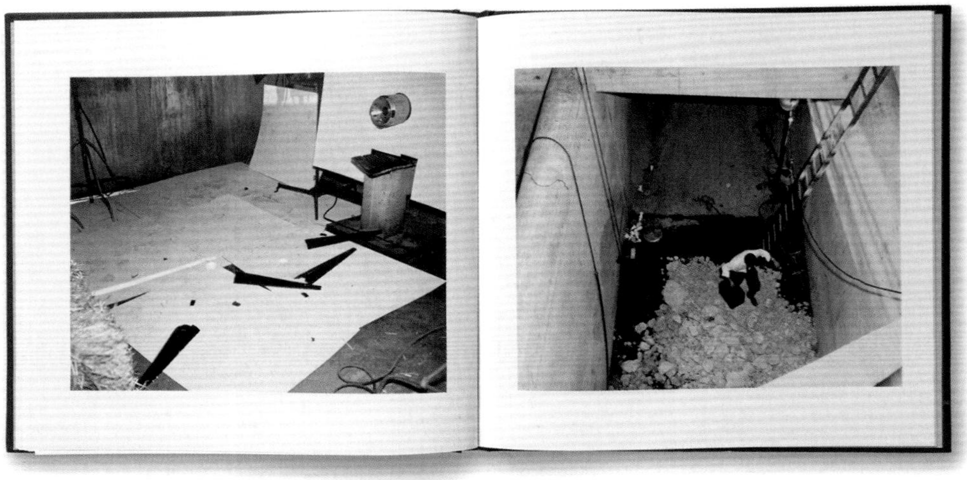

Richard Prince

Richard Prince appropriates images from consumer and popular culture. Working for *Time-Life*, he was clipping editorials from different magazines for staff writers when in 1977 he began photographing adverts, with all ad copy excised. He likens commercial advertisements in magazines to freeze frames from a movie. As Prince crops and manipulates pictures that have already been retouched and manipulated, he is magnifying and distorting the fakeries and artifices of commercial photography. Caught up with the desires and fantasies that circulate around commodities, his art also serves to block them, as his process of rephotography begins to debase and de-idealize the source images, accenting their awkward plasticity. One could argue that there is a sense in Prince's rephotography of adverts of an over-embellishment, the aesthetic enhancement having gone too far. They are too slicked up and we sense the plastic artifice. The face colours of his models do not look like flesh, and the models are rendered like mannequins or automata, as in his *Untitled (Couple)* (1977). His most famous images appropriated from the Marlboro Man cowboy cigarette adverts – begun when the marketing company stopped using the imagery – replay imagery that taps into a powerful nostalgic mythology of the Wild West, symbolic of American democracy and independence.

Prince's most scandalous and infamous rephotography was that of Gary Gross's 1975 photograph of a naked and clearly eroticized ten-year-old Brooke Shields. Gross had got consent to take this picture from Shields's mother, who had been managing her daughter's career as a model since she was a baby (she first appeared in an advert at eleven months). Prince first displayed the picture on its own in a cheap gold frame beneath a picture light in a storefront gallery he opened in a run-down part of Lower Manhattan. Both the picture and the gallery were called 'Spiritual America.' The title was lifted from an Alfred Stieglitz 1923 photograph of the rear quarters of a castrated and trussed-up horse, a photograph Prince had seen in New York's Metropolitan Museum and a picture that is generally seen as an ironic commentary on America's lack of spiritual life, of a culture bereft of passion and sexuality.

Sexuality is the very source of anxiety in Prince's 'Spiritual America,' a work that introduces a sordid affair about images and exploitation. By the time of Prince's installation of the picture, Brooke Shields had gained star status and notoriety through her roles and nude appearances as a child prostitute in Louis Malle's 1978 film *Pretty Baby* and as a teenage lover in the 1980 film *Blue Lagoon*. She had also appeared in the controversial 'What Comes Between Me and My Calvins?' campaign for Calvin Klein jeans. In 1981 Brooke Shields had convinced the Supreme Court of New York to issue an injunction against Gross to prevent further sales of his 1975 picture of her. Eight months before Prince opened his 'Spiritual America,' exhibition, the injunction had been overturned because a child cannot break a contract signed by a parent or guardian. So Prince's appropriation reflects upon the ownership, commodification and exploitation of a child. The picture was contested before he appropriated it for his art, indeed its very pre-history is integral to its meaning – a pre-history that taps into anxieties about sexualized images of children, as well as opening copyright issues to broader questions about ownership and possession in what is in effect the unnatural commercial exchange of a daughter's body and image by her mother. In this respect, Prince's work marks a decisive shift in appropriation art, raising important questions about how images are used and valued, and how they circulate outside the rarefied space of the art museum.

Richard Prince
Untitled (Couple), 1977
Ektacolor photograph
51 × 61 cm / 20 × 24 in

Untitled (Cowboy), 1993
Ektacolor photograph
121.9 × 182.9 cm / 48 × 72 in

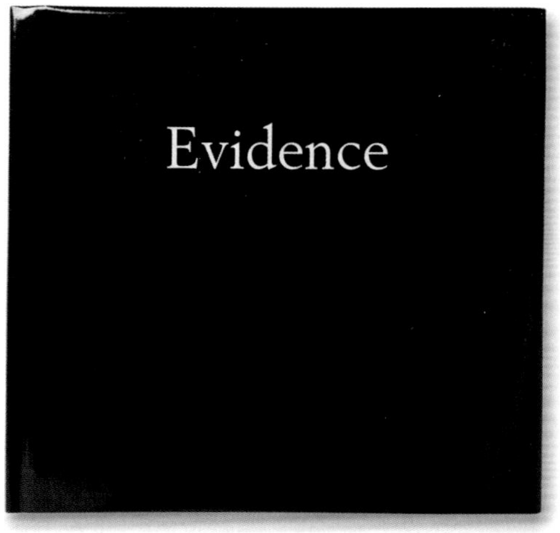
Evidence

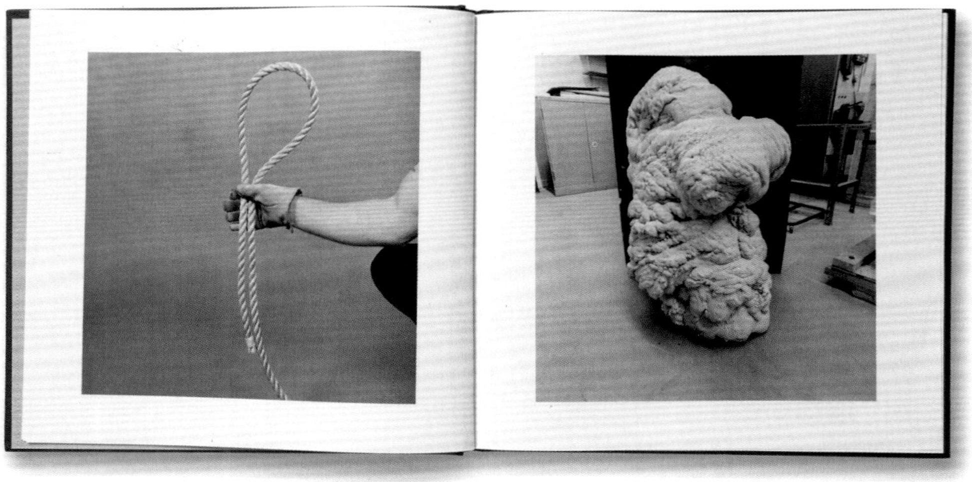

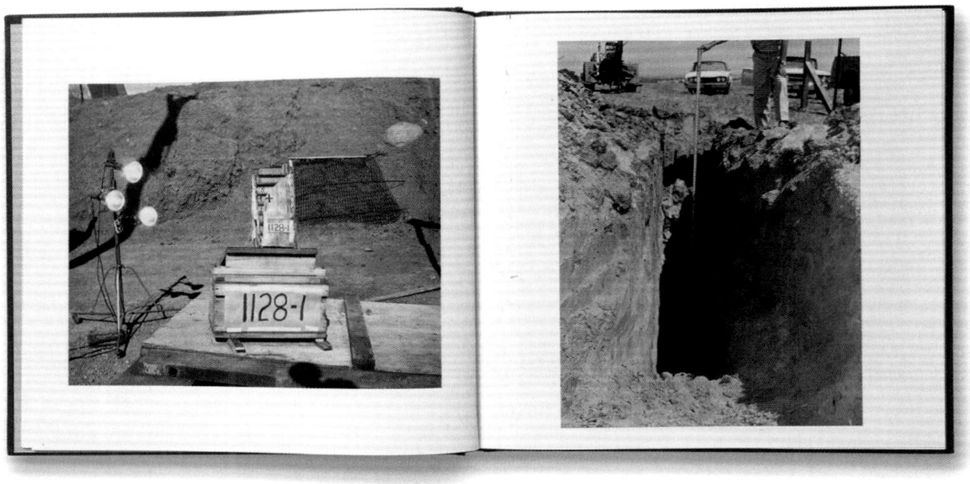
1128-1

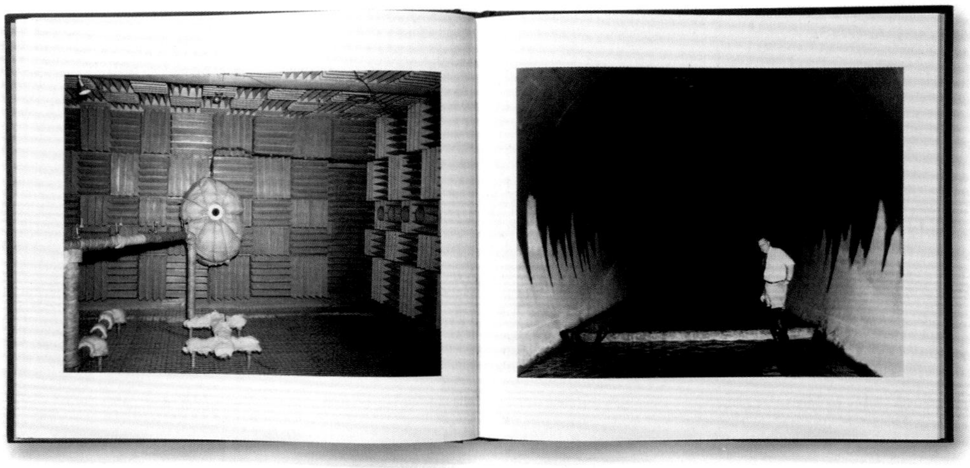

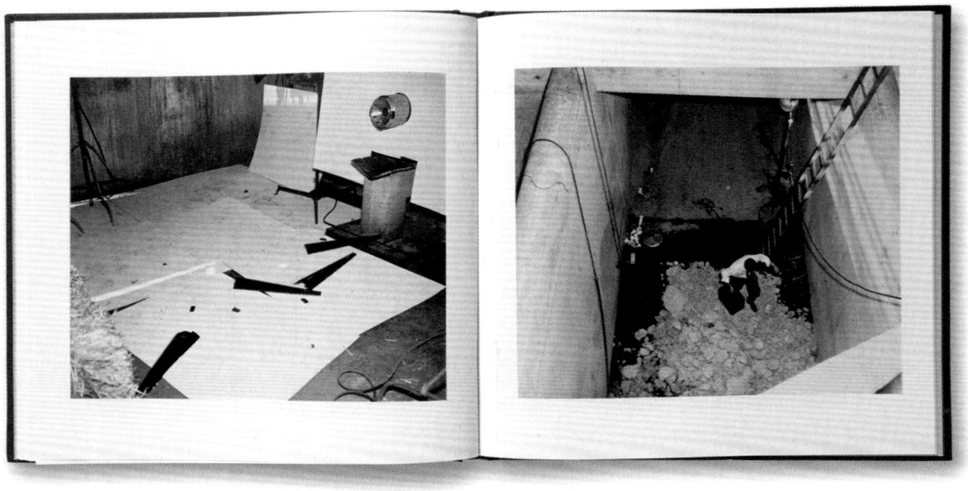

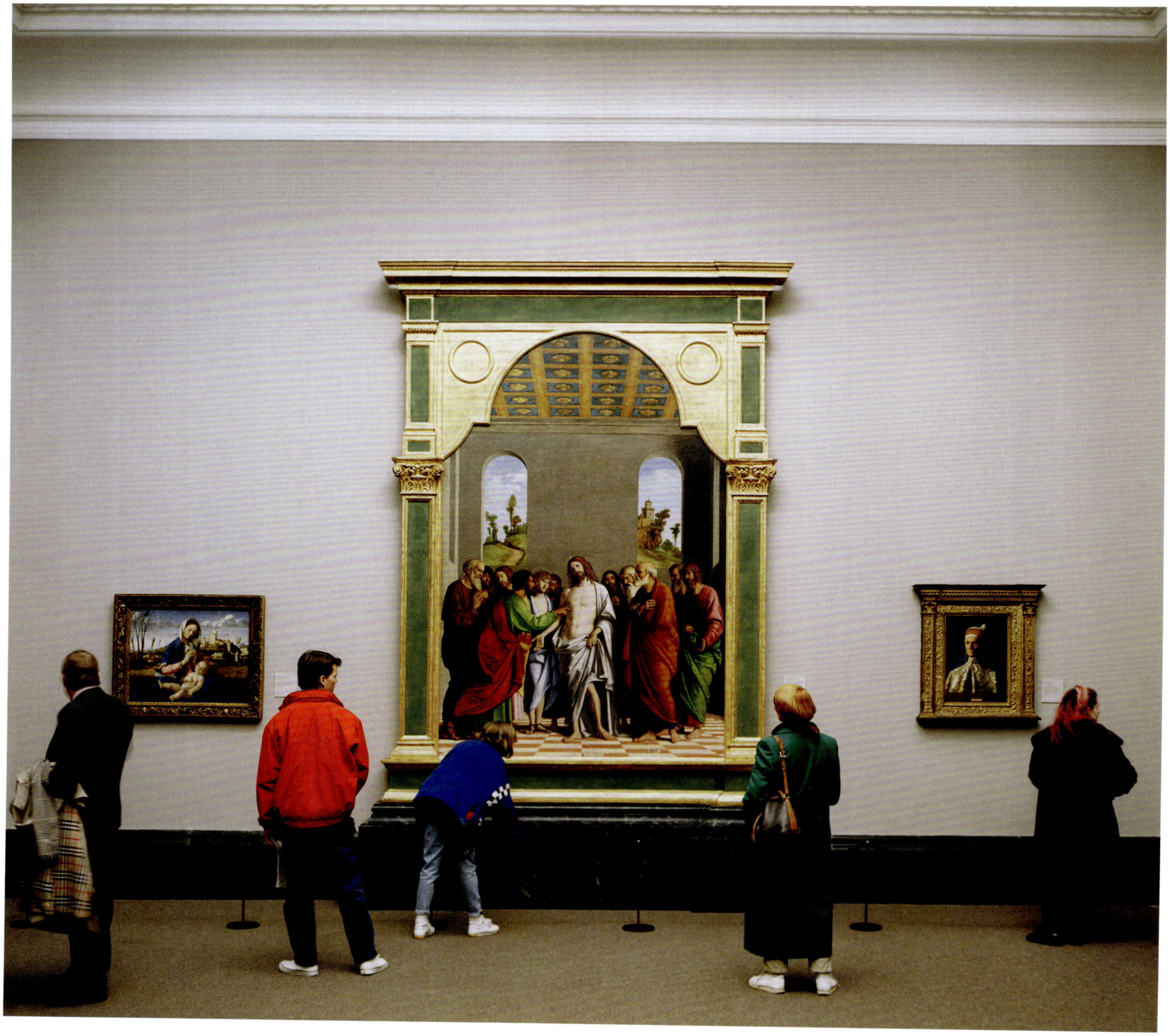

Thomas Struth
National Gallery 1 London, 1989
C-print
134 × 152 cm / 52¾ × 59⅞ in

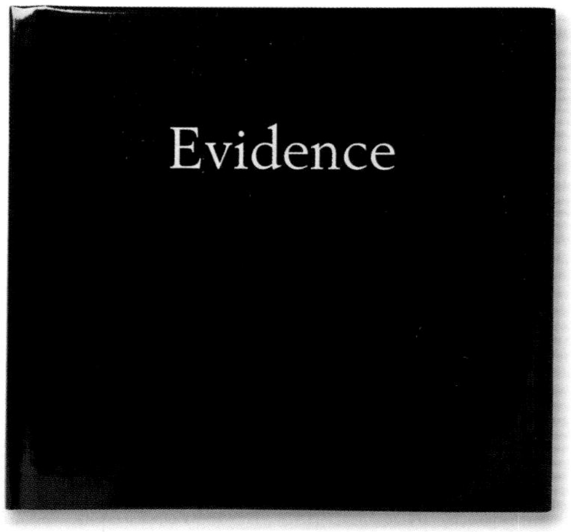
Evidence

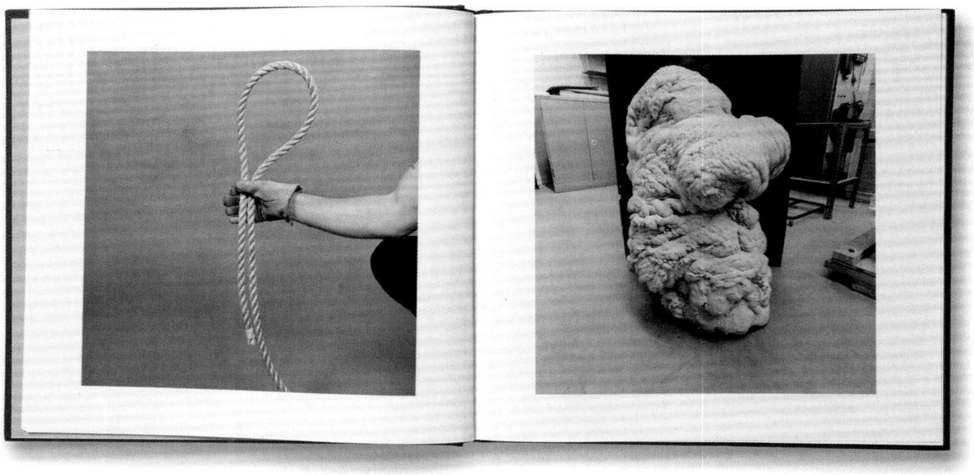

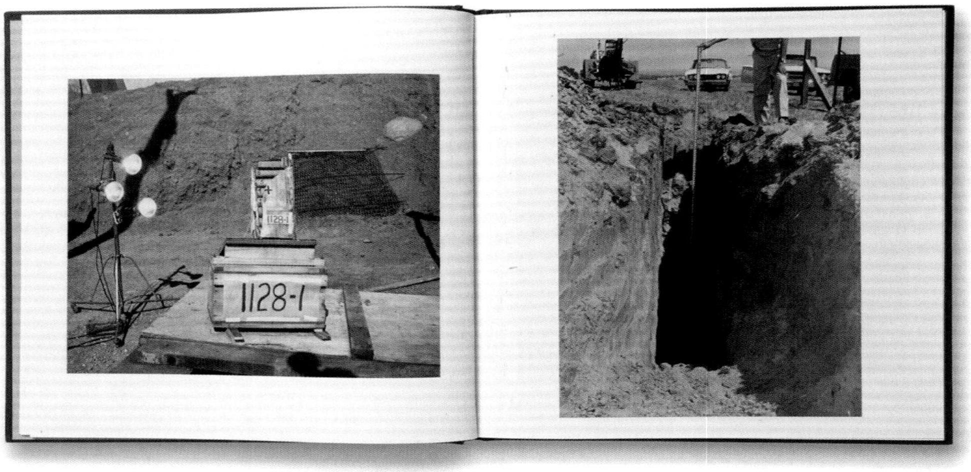
1128-1

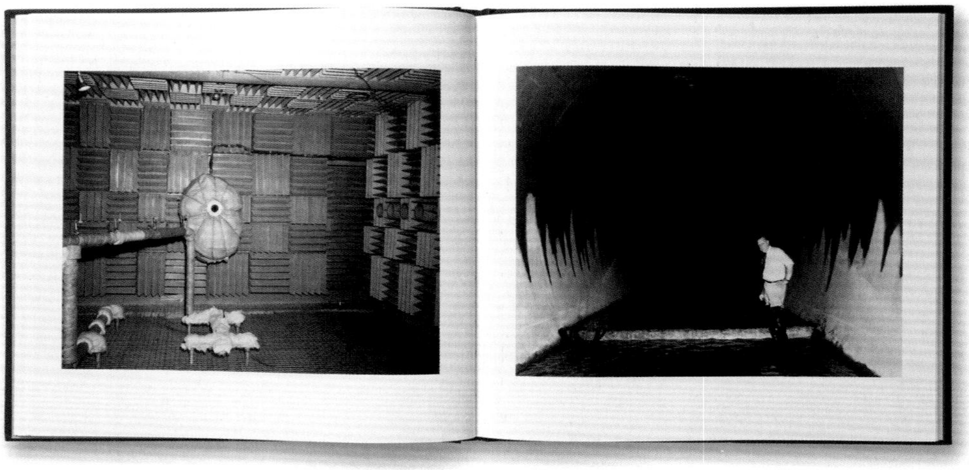

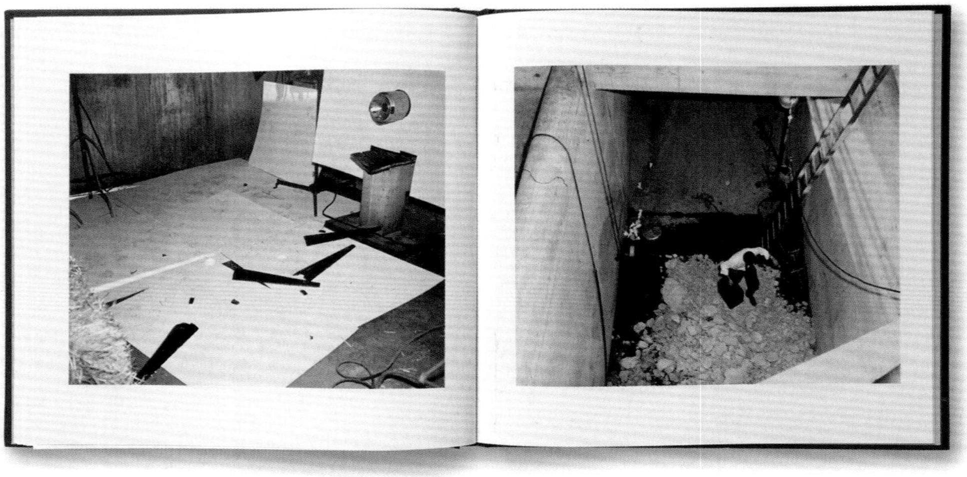

Louise Lawler

While not included in the 1977 'Pictures' show, Louise Lawler is often associated with the Pictures Generation. Her art pictures the work of other artists in its various contexts of display to give a documentary revelation of how art circulates as a commodity in private rooms, museums, galleries, auction houses and corporate spaces. She is concerned with the physical and material contexts of art's exhibition, from the functional and mundane stands on which pictures hang in auction houses to the collisions and rhymes set up between artworks and the interior décor and objects against which they are set in collectors' homes: in *Pollock and Tureen* (1984), for example, a Jackson Pollock drip painting is interplayed with the floral patterning of an upmarket soup tureen placed on a sideboard.

Much as Lawler's work plays with the status of the artwork and reflects on art's literal dispersal in the world, the gesture is still reflexive and ultimately aesthetic. Her use of composition is never neutral. Her dramatic cropping and reframing of artworks draws attention to the pictorial conventions she deploys, exaggerating her own aesthetic impositions and interventions. Her framing of a Frank Stella 'protractor' painting accents its aura as it is pictured glowing in the polished floor of its museum space.

The picture's focus on reflection is linked to the implications of the miniature repackaging of her own photographs in the form of glass paperweights, presented in vitrines and on pedestals. These miniatures of her own work mean that the displayed art she photographs is now further refracted and condensed in the little glass domes, which, functioning as kitsch objects, could be seen to point to art's inevitable dispersal into spectacle.

Louise Lawler
Does Marilyn Monroe Make You Cry?, 1988
Cibachrome print, plexiglass wall label
69.2 × 99.1 cm / 27¼ × 39 in

Pollock and Tureen, 1984
Cibachrome print, 71.1 × 99.1 cm / 28 × 39 in

How Many Pictures, 1989
Cibachrome print
122.1 cm × 157.2 cm / 48 1/16 × 61⅞ in

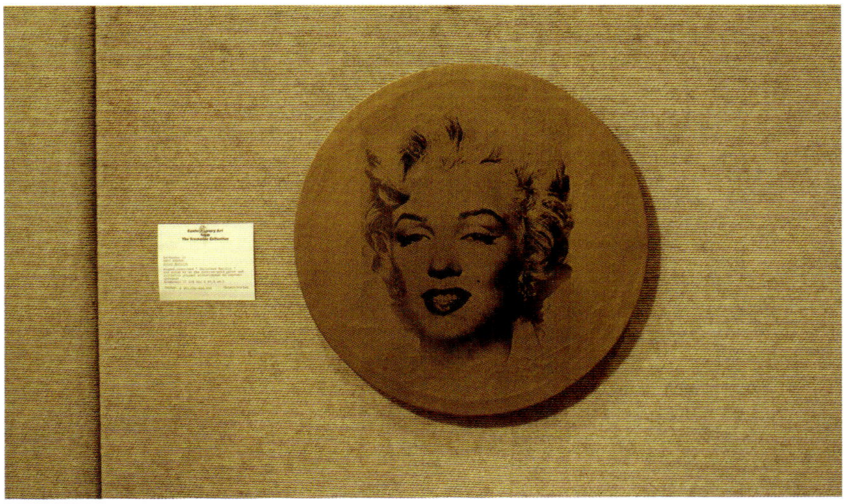

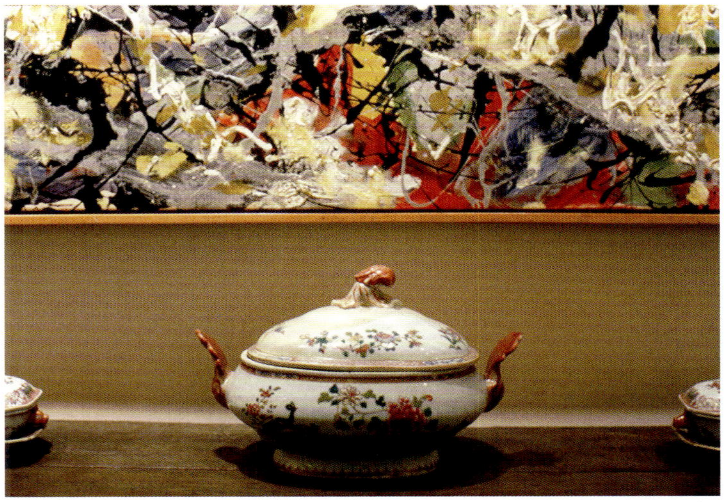

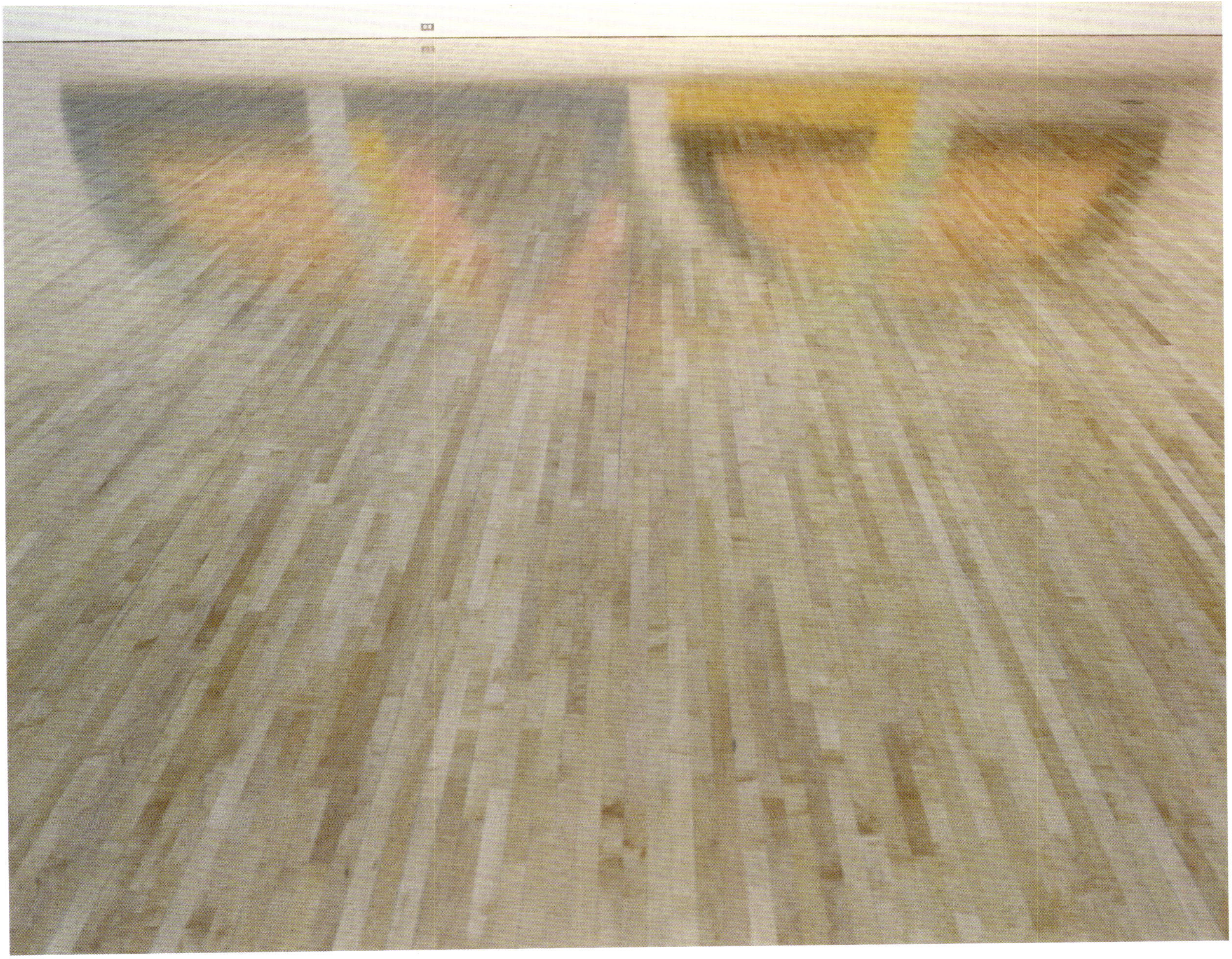

Richard Prince

Richard Prince appropriates images from consumer and popular culture. Working for *Time-Life*, he was clipping editorials from different magazines for staff writers when in 1977 he began photographing adverts, with all ad copy excised. He likens commercial advertisements in magazines to freeze frames from a movie. As Prince crops and manipulates pictures that have already been retouched and manipulated, he is magnifying and distorting the fakeries and artifices of commercial photography. Caught up with the desires and fantasies that circulate around commodities, his art also serves to block them, as his process of rephotography begins to debase and de-idealize the source images, accenting their awkward plasticity. One could argue that there is a sense in Prince's rephotography of adverts of an over-embellishment, the aesthetic enhancement having gone too far. They are too slicked up and we sense the plastic artifice. The face colours of his models do not look like flesh, and the models are rendered like mannequins or automata, as in his *Untitled (Couple)* (1977). His most famous images appropriated from the Marlboro Man cowboy cigarette adverts – begun when the marketing company stopped using the imagery – replay imagery that taps into a powerful nostalgic mythology of the Wild West, symbolic of American democracy and independence.

Prince's most scandalous and infamous rephotography was that of Gary Gross's 1975 photograph of a naked and clearly eroticized ten-year-old Brooke Shields. Gross had got consent to take this picture from Shields's mother, who had been managing her daughter's career as a model since she was a baby (she first appeared in an advert at eleven months). Prince first displayed the picture on its own in a cheap gold frame beneath a picture light in a storefront gallery he opened in a run-down part of Lower Manhattan. Both the picture and the gallery were called 'Spiritual America.' The title was lifted from an Alfred Stieglitz 1923 photograph of the rear quarters of a castrated and trussed-up horse, a photograph Prince had seen in New York's Metropolitan Museum and a picture that is generally seen as an ironic commentary on America's lack of spiritual life, of a culture bereft of passion and sexuality.

Sexuality is the very source of anxiety in Prince's 'Spiritual America,' a work that introduces a sordid affair about images and exploitation. By the time of Prince's installation of the picture, Brooke Shields had gained star status and notoriety through her roles and nude appearances as a child prostitute in Louis Malle's 1978 film *Pretty Baby* and as a teenage lover in the 1980 film *Blue Lagoon*. She had also appeared in the controversial 'What Comes Between Me and My Calvins?' campaign for Calvin Klein jeans. In 1981 Brooke Shields had convinced the Supreme Court of New York to issue an injunction against Gross to prevent further sales of his 1975 picture of her. Eight months before Prince opened his 'Spiritual America,' exhibition, the injunction had been overturned because a child cannot break a contract signed by a parent or guardian. So Prince's appropriation reflects upon the ownership, commodification and exploitation of a child. The picture was contested before he appropriated it for his art, indeed its very pre-history is integral to its meaning – a pre-history that taps into anxieties about sexualized images of children, as well as opening copyright issues to broader questions about ownership and possession in what is in effect the unnatural commercial exchange of a daughter's body and image by her mother. In this respect, Prince's work marks a decisive shift in appropriation art, raising important questions about how images are used and valued, and how they circulate outside the rarefied space of the art museum.

Richard Prince
Untitled (Couple), 1977
Ektacolor photograph
51 × 61 cm / 20 × 24 in

Untitled (Cowboy), 1993
Ektacolor photograph
121.9 × 182.9 cm / 48 × 72 in

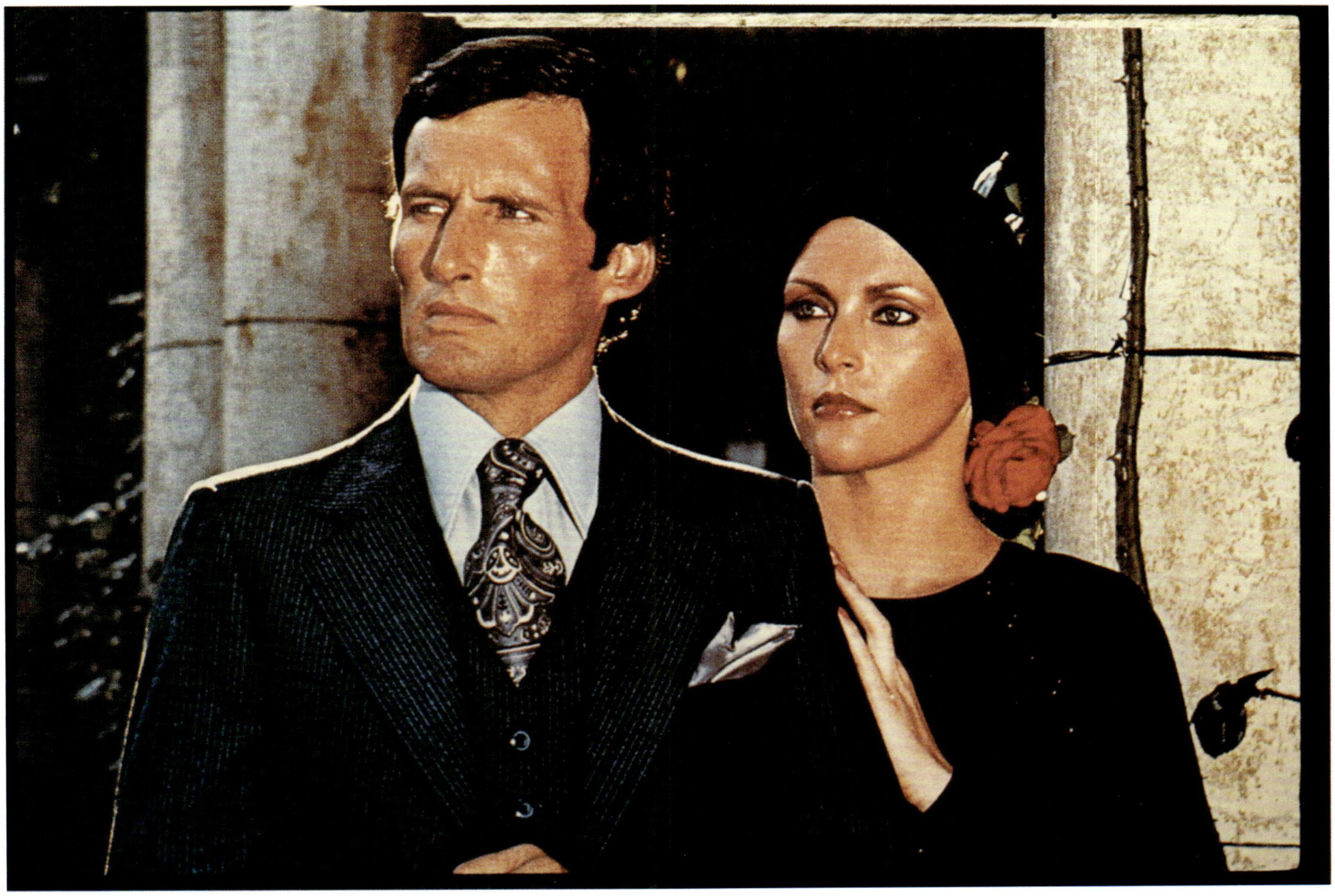

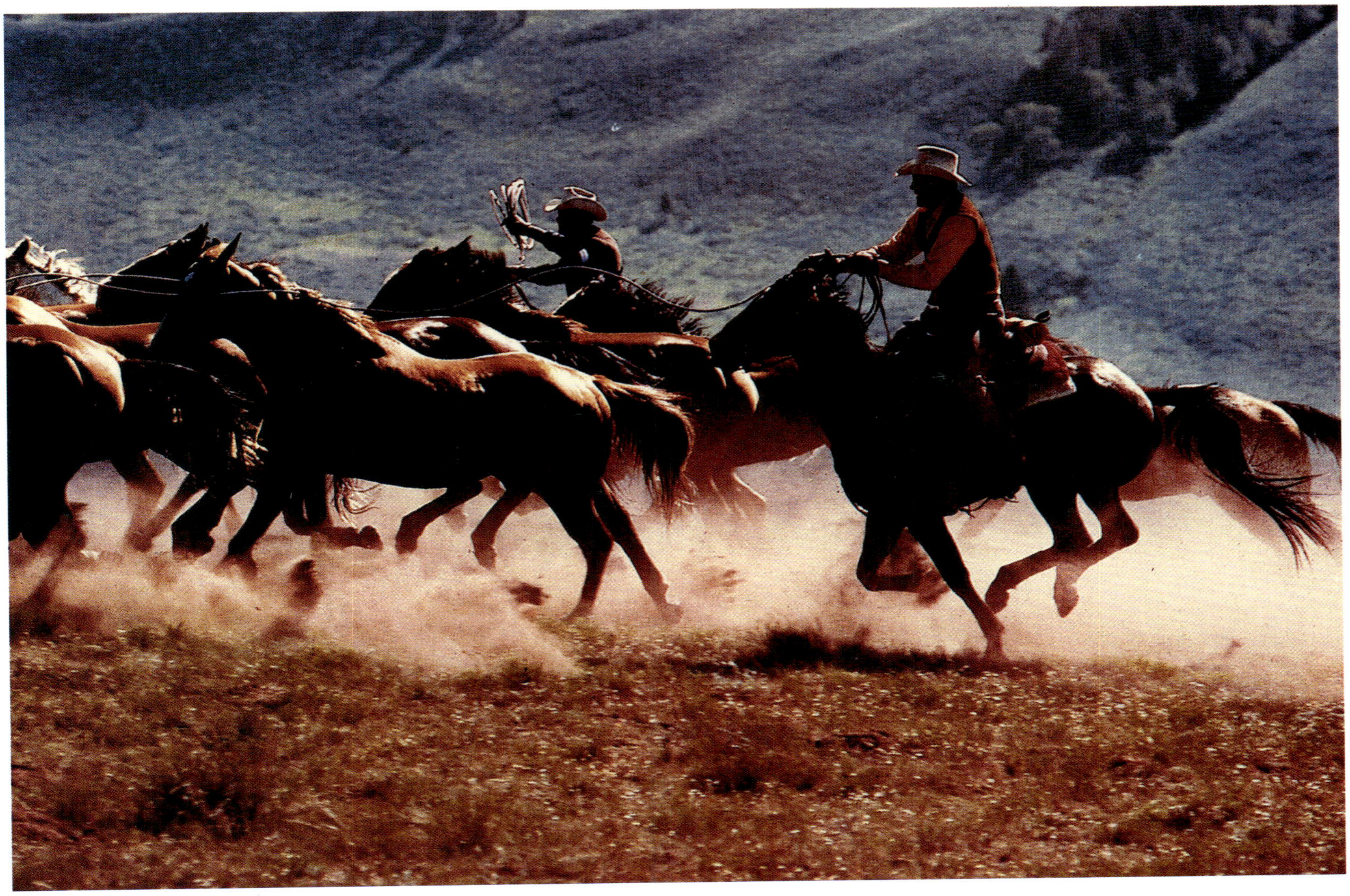

Eugenio Dittborn

Appropriation

Chilean artist Eugenio Dittborn's 'Airmail Paintings', begun in 1984, serve as powerful and haunting reminders of the specific political contexts of his homeland, far from the art metropolises to and from which his paintings journey. Dittborn uses the international postal system to send his art to the global art centres around the world. He exhibits the works – on brown paper or sheets of synthetic white fabric and cotton, replete with a variety of markings that are sewn, drawn, painted or photo-mechanical – alongside the envelopes in which they are mailed. Their trans-global circulation and display is integral to these paintings' meaning, raising questions about geographical margins, borders and centres, and is linked with the imagery and texts of these works, which is often associated with the brutal history of his homeland. 'Power in our country constructs a social, political and cultural space which is characterized by a monstrous capacity to empty and exclude any possibility of memory. My artistic work puts itself forward, in its travels, as a little model of a possible memory.'[13] As Guy Brett has put it: 'The survival of people, either in bodily form through preservation in the water, the sand, the snow etc., or in mediated forms through images, inscriptions, drawings and other memorials – set against their destruction and disappearance – is a persistent theme in Dittborn's work.' *Liquid Ashes, Airmail Painting No. 96* (1992), for example, contains the photosilkscreened images of two mummified bodies: Lindow Man, a Celtic sacrifice to the gods whose body was preserved in a bog for two thousand years and discovered in 1984, and a young Chilean man, abducted and murdered by the Pinochet dictatorship in the 1970s, whose body, preserved in the sand of the Tarapacá desert, was found in 1990.

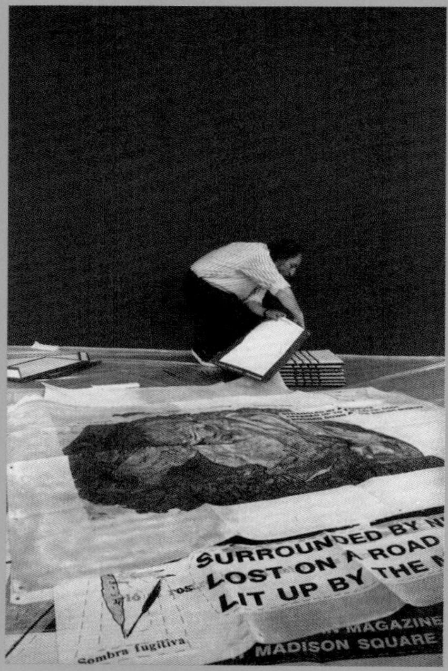

Eugenio Dittborn
The artist at Documenta IX, June 1992
Envelopes of *Airmail Painting No. 96* being opened before installation

Gerhard Richter

Photography in Painting

In the midst of the hyped-up artworld of the 1980s, the German artist Gerhard Richter used photography to affirm painting and emotion. His *October 18, 1977* (1988) consists of fifteen grey paintings drawn from photographs taken from the press, the police and the underground showing the capture, deaths and burial of members of the Red Army Faction (RAF), also known as the Baader-Meinhof Group, an organization that had terrorized West Germany in the 1970s. The title of the cycle commemorates the day the bodies of Andreas Baader and Gudrun Ensslin – along with the dying Jan-Carl Raspe and the wounded Irmgard Möller – were discovered in their cells in a high-security prison in Stammheim. Almost three years earlier, Holger Meins had died from starvation during a hunger strike protesting prison conditions. Ulrike Meinhof had been found hanging in her cell in May 1976, shortly before she and the others were sentenced to life. While her death was ruled a suicide, as were those of Baader, Ensslin and Raspe, there was suspicion that all of them had been murdered by the state.

What did it mean for a well-respected and established painter to trawl up such an explosive moment in his country's history? In some senses the cycle of paintings can be seen as using evidential and documentary photographs to revive history painting, albeit in a somewhat skewed way: Richter's is a history painting that does not glorify the state but that instead is fixated with the deaths of its enemies. The artist has referred to the series as a 'leave-taking', both in the sense that it deals with the deaths of specific persons and 'ideologically, a leave-taking from a specific doctrine of salvation and beyond that from the illusion that unacceptable circumstances of life can be changed by this conventional expedient of violent struggle (this kind of revolutionary thought and action is futile and passé).'[14]

The cycle of paintings begins with a sentimental studio shot of Ulrike Meinhof, *Youth Portrait*, while the rest fix upon images connected with the deaths of these young people in their prison cells. In blunt contrast to the studio portrait of Ulrike, three small pictures offer different painted permutations drawn from the same forensic photograph showing the head of Meinhof after her purported suicide, including the ligature marks left around her neck when she was cut down. Documentary photographic source images are blurred, diffused and smeared as they are translated into paintings. This effect is created by dragging brushes or squeegees across the surface of the canvas, a process at odds with the hyper-verisimilitude of Photorealism. Much as this veils and diffuses, it also gives a certain duration and animation to the paintings in contrast to the cold clinical gaze of photography. Haunted by the tragically flawed idealism of these young people, Richter creates a powerfully affective series of paintings, imbued with sadness and pain.

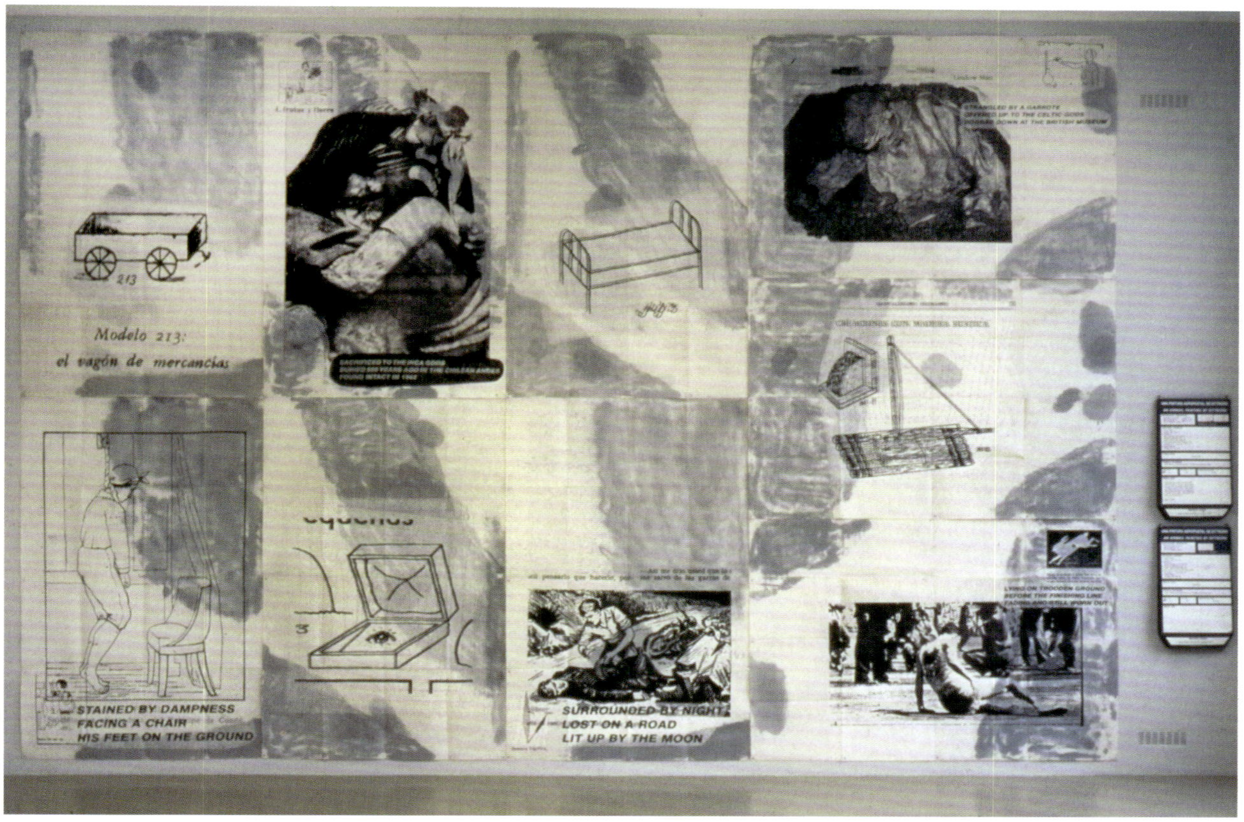

Eugenio Dittborn
Liquid Ashes, Airmail Painting No. 96, 1992
Paint, stitching and photosilkscreen on 11 sections of non-woven fabric
420 × 980 cm / 165 × 385 in

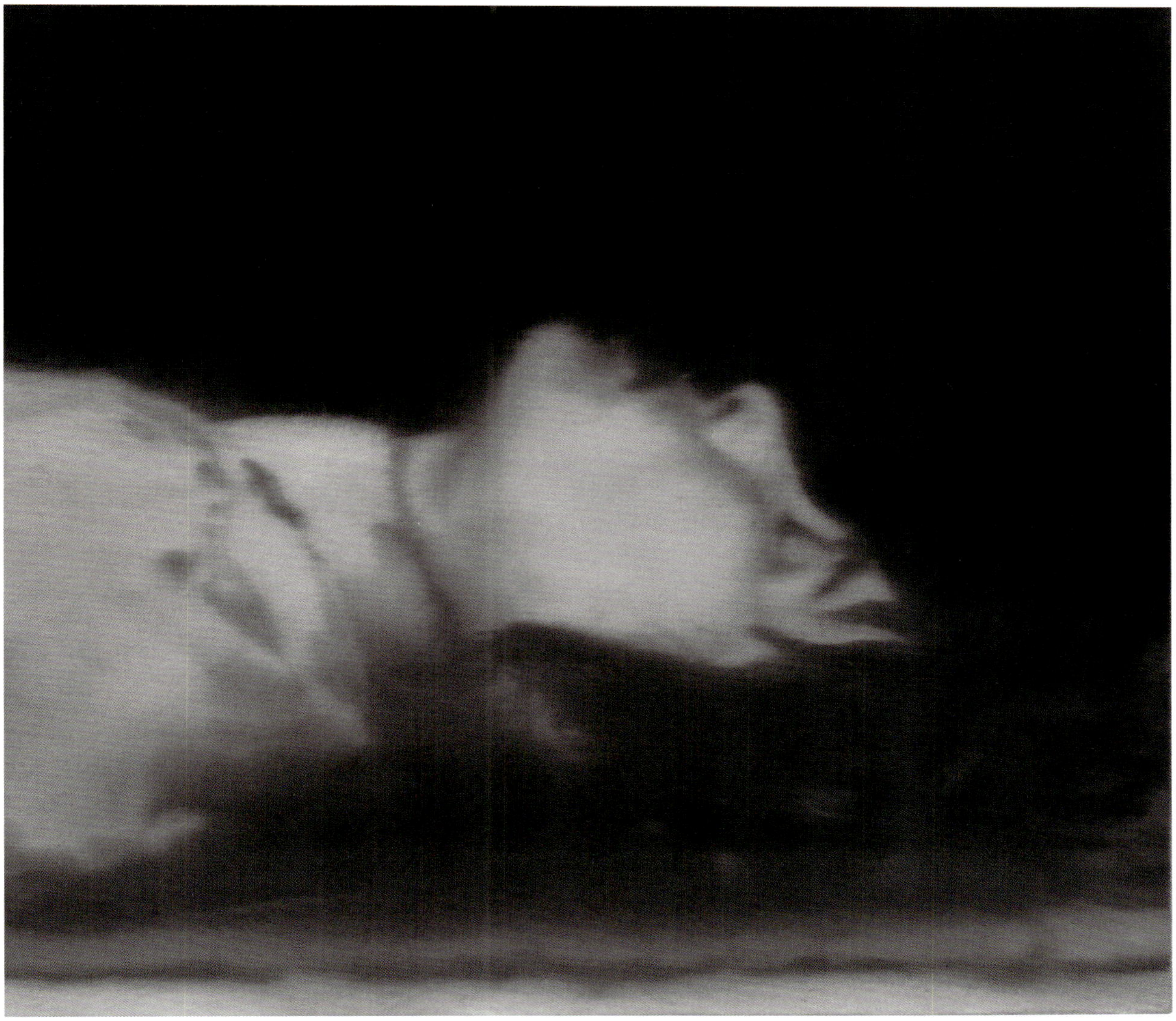

Gerhard Richter
Dead, from the series 'October 18', 1988
Oil on canvas, 62 × 67 cm / 24⅜ × 26⅜ in

Thomas Struth

Thomas Struth's large-scale series of photographs of art museums (1989–2005) are clearly indebted to Louise Lawler, but they are less concerned with art as commodity. Instead they return us to a sense of the enduring aesthetic value of both art and photography. Gerhard Richter used photography to rehabilitate painting while Struth used painting to rehabilitate photography.

The museum photographs draw attention to formal correspondences between viewers and the artwork they have come to see. People in the gallery – single figures, small groups and crowds – are photographed before famous art collections. One might see this as a commentary on the invasion of cultural institutions by mass tourism, but the interplay Struth sets up between viewers and artworks starts to speak about something else. The point is that many of the ordinary people Struth photographs in the museum are given a certain aesthetic elevation, as the colours of their clothing, their gestures and poses echo those of the figures in the paintings they are viewing. Struth's work is in part a statement about the value of photography in relation to the great figurative painting tradition. In many senses he is making a claim about his own artistic heritage. The art in the museum is never lowered or devalued by being photographed; instead the art bestows beauty on the everyday world within which it is framed.

In Struth's later work made in museums, the gallery crowd replaces the artwork. His series 'Audience' (2004), for example, concentrates solely on the art tourists gathered to view Michelangelo's Renaissance masterpiece *David*, with the sculpture remaining outside the picture. What we are presented with is a kind of street photography within the museum. Like Andreas Gursky, Struth's relationship to art history made him aware of the question and problem of photography as a medium of spectacle: in a picture of New York City's Times Square he turns his large format photography upon the spectacle of commodity culture, and within his *National Museum of Art, Toyko* (1999), the theatrical public display of a Eugène Delacroix painting in Japan gives it something of the look of a cinema projection.

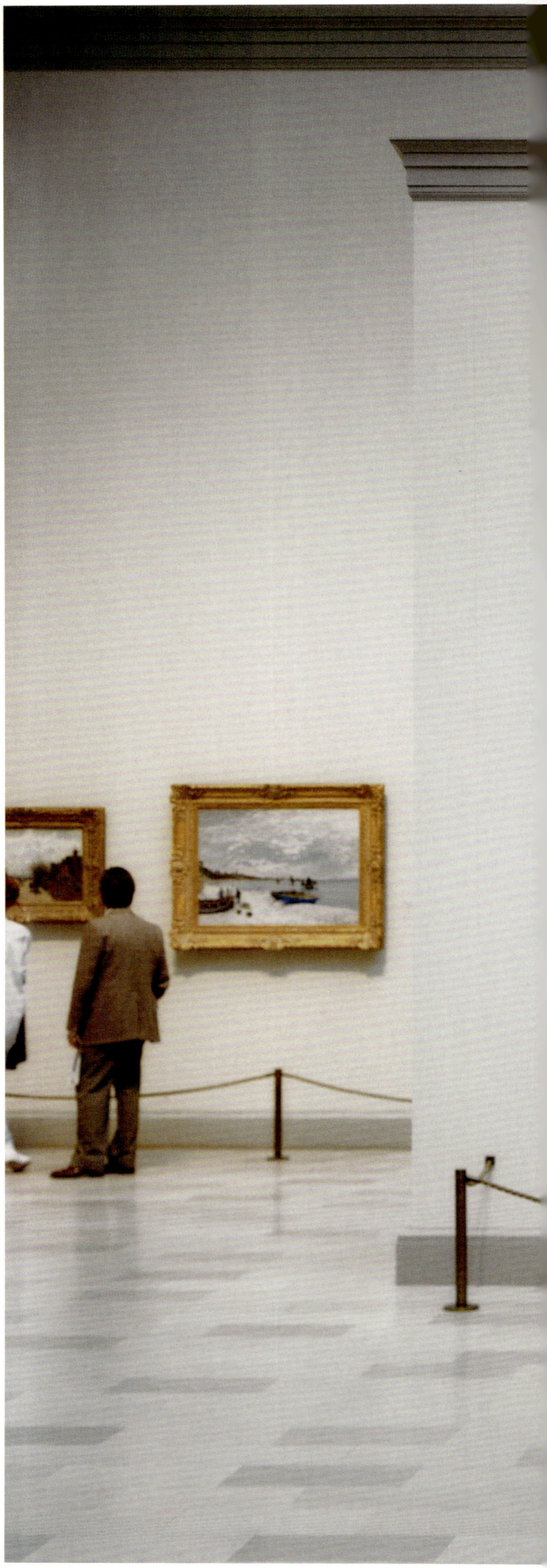

Thomas Struth
Art Institute of Chicago 2
Chicago, 1990
C-print
137.5 × 174.5 cm / 54⅛ × 68¾ in

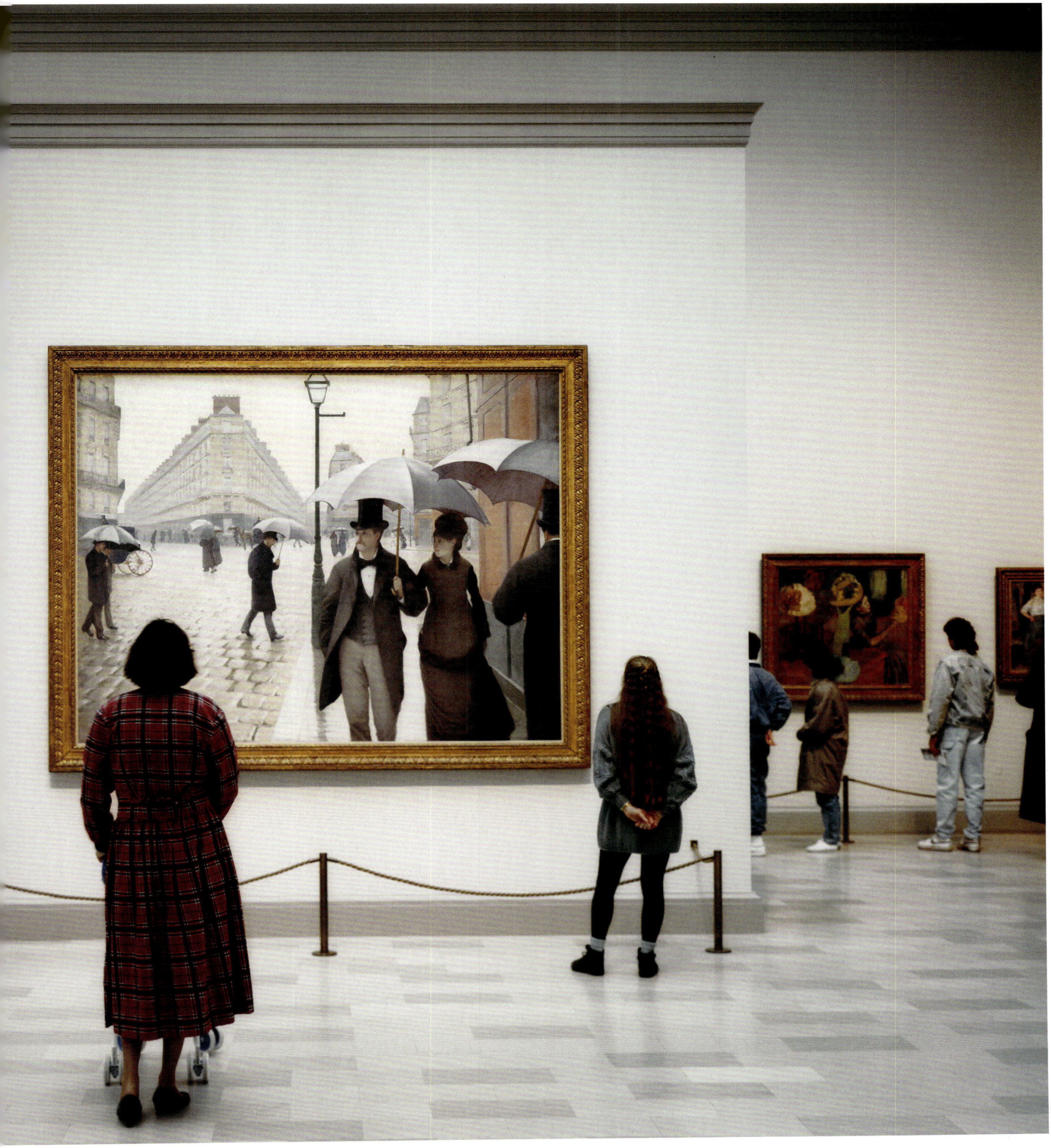

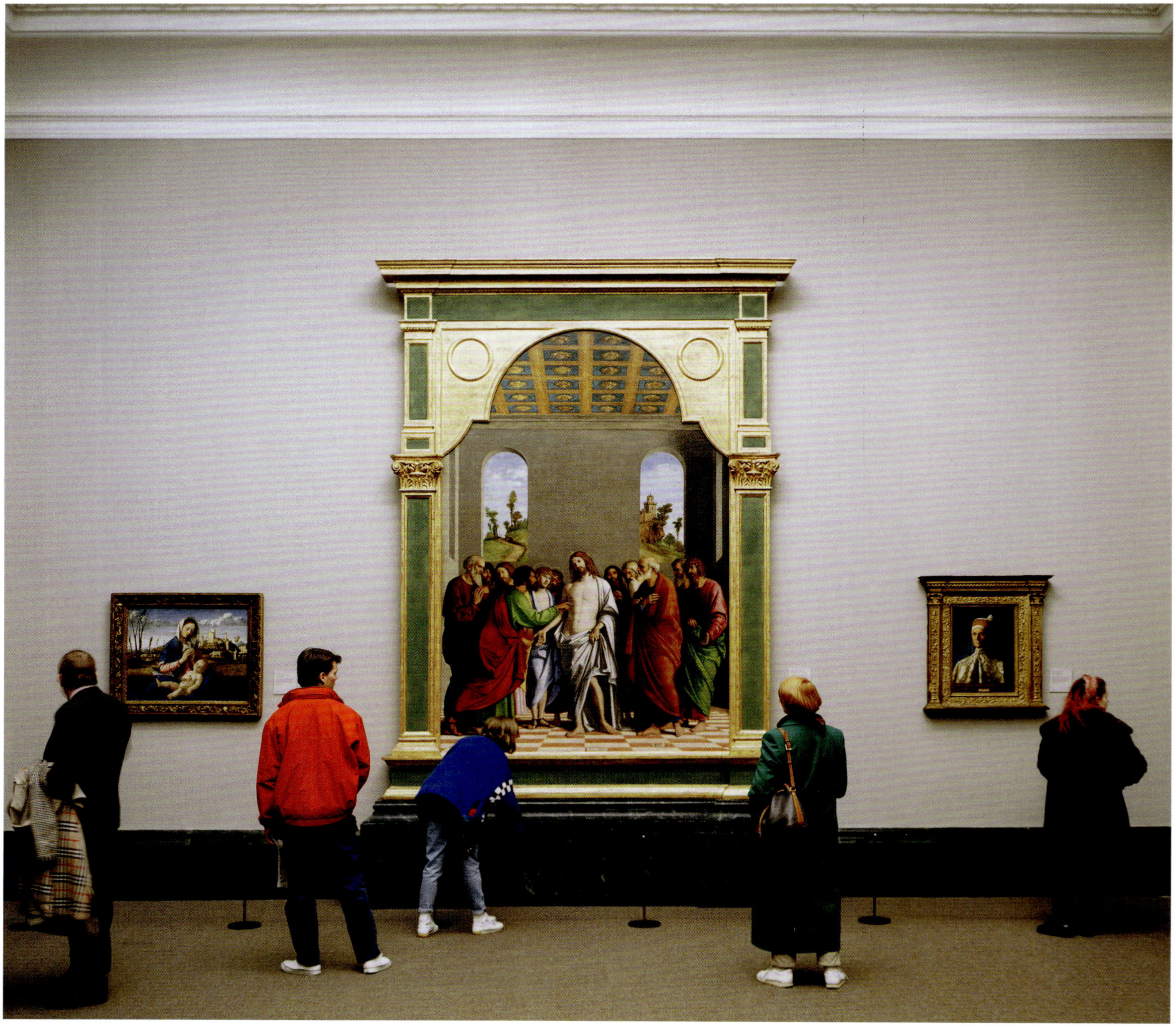

Thomas Struth
National Gallery 1 London, 1989
C-print
134 × 152 cm / 52¾ × 59⅞ in

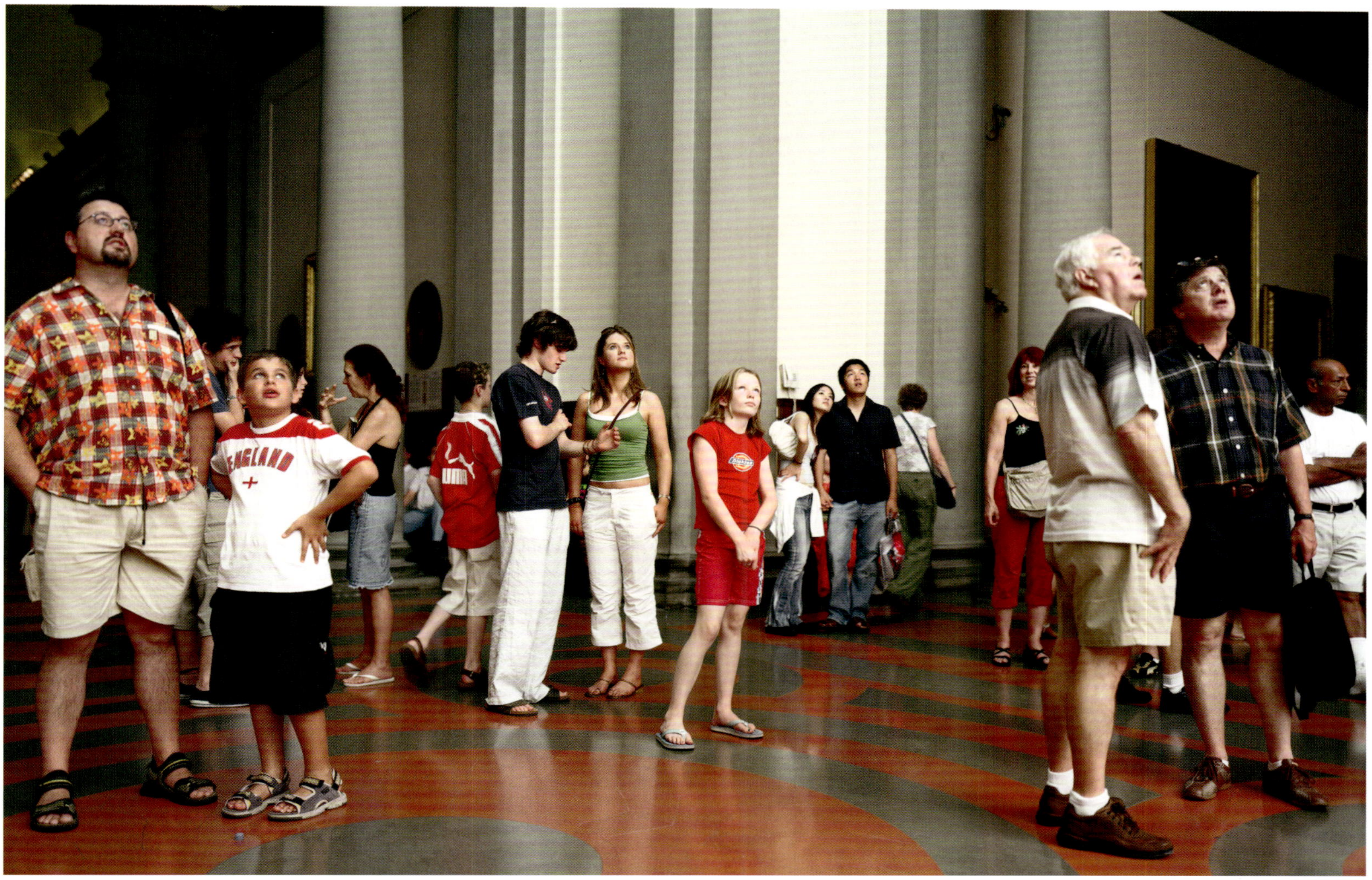

Thomas Struth
Audience 1 Florence, 2004
C-print
178 × 286.5 cm / 70 1/8 × 113 in

Bernd and Hilla Becher

Thomas Struth studied under both Gerhard Richter and the photographers Bernd and Hilla Becher at the now famous Künstakademie in Düsseldorf. Bernd Becher was employed to teach photography there in 1976, and Struth, one of the Bechers' first students, graduated in 1980. The Bechers' influential photography department looked back to the German tradition of 1920s' *Neue Sachlichkeit* (New Objectivity). A leading exponent of *Neue Sachlichkeit*, Albert Renger-Patzsch, who is famous for his book *The World is Beautiful* (1928), championed the distinctive and modern nature of a precise photographic aesthetic vision as distinct from painting.

Working with large-format cameras at Düsseldorf, the Bechers' students came to establish and define a school that entailed a restorative use of the precision of the medium, producing formal and detailed photographic renditions of the phenomenal world. Such emphasis on skilled, high technical accomplishment and crafted pictures was in contrast to both Conceptual art's anti-aesthetic and de-skilling photographic strategies and postmodern image appropriations. The school came to dominate the agendas of contemporary art: many of its photographers are lead players in Michael Fried's 2008 book, *Why Photography Matters as Contemporary Art*, and the Bechers' student, Andreas Gursky, has recently been commanding high prices in the auction house.

The Bechers' art embraced the anonymity of record photography through their meticulous and longstanding detailing of such industrial structures as water towers, grain elevators, winding towers, gas tanks and cooling towers. They started picturing the industrial structures in 1957, when Bernd was an art student and Hilla a professional photographer: 'Since these structures were disappearing more and more, we could imagine that conserving these things photographically would someday be of general interest.'[15] These were first appreciated in the context of Conceptual and minimal art. The minimalist sculptor Carl Andre wrote an essay on the Bechers in 1972, but they claimed: 'Our idea of showing the material has much more to do with the nineteenth century, with the encyclopedic approach used on botany or zoology, where plants of the same variety, or animals of the same species are compared with one another in individual pages of the lexicon.' Their photography pays homage to the work of the anonymous engineers and architects who built the structures, celebrating their beauty through the precision and clarity of their exhaustive and encyclopedic photographic depictions. Their pictures elevated and celebrated these industrial constructions as sculpture; their first monograph was entitled, *Anonyme Skulpturen* (*Anonymous Sculptures*) (1970) and they were awarded the Golden Lion for sculpture in the 1991 Venice Biennale.

Bernd and Hilla Becher
Winding Towers, 1997
12 gelatin silver prints
173.3 × 191.1 cm / 68¼ × 75¼ in

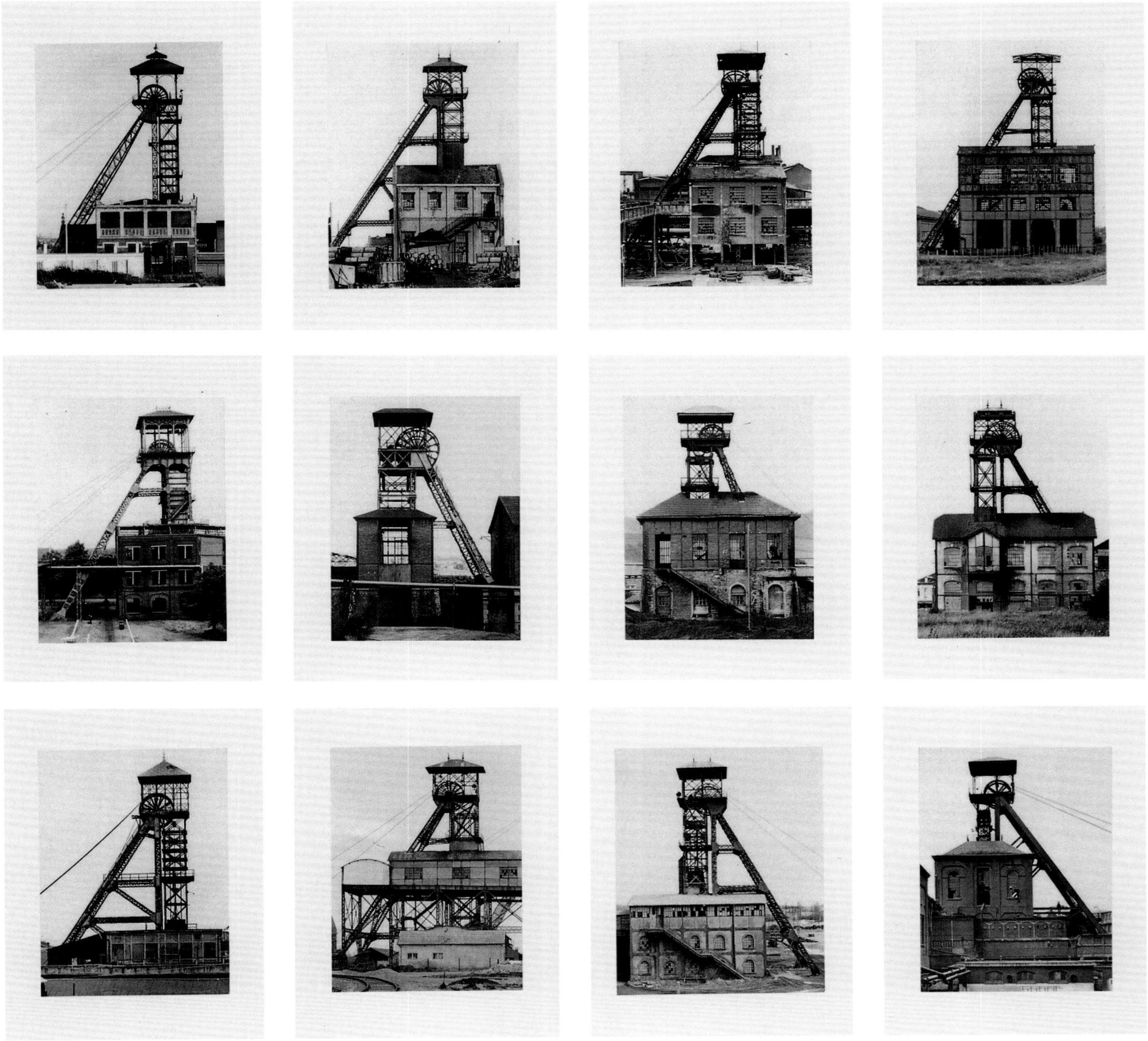

Thomas Ruff

Thomas Ruff is the most experimental of the artists to emerge from the Düsseldorf School. His relationship to the medium of photography, both analogue and digital, is adventurous and testing. His photographs of stars, 'Sterne' (1989–92), for example, were made by cropping and printing from negatives he bought in the archive of the European Southern Observatory. Ruff's appropriation here makes an aesthetic and pictorial elevation of astronomical records. Such beautiful pictures, much as they reflect upon the heavens, the ultimate sublime, also prompt thoughts about photography's very being as a medium of light-writing. Ordinarily the analogue photograph as a trace of its subject in light fixes one temporal moment from the past, but before these photographs, as Ruff says, 'the stars are different distances away from us, which means that they have different lengths of time and paths behind them. That is to say we are looking at different levels of the past at the same time.'[16]

Ruff's 'nudes' (1999–), culled from pornography on the internet, distances us from the originary illicit use of such images by the way in which they have been processed. Enlarged and digitally filtered, the images are given a pictorial beauty and grace, an aesthetic that rubs against the extremity of what many of the images still appear to disclose, albeit erotically veiled through pixellation and blurring. Entitling them 'nudes' underscores the fact that the process of image manipulation idealizes. Referring to this work, Ruff joked that he was also interested in returning the blur that had been stolen from photography by Gerhard Richter back from painting to photography.

Andreas Gursky

Painting and art is a key point of reference for Andreas Gursky. He even made a clear reference to Gerhard Richter's grey abstract painting in his photograph of an expanse of grey carpet, *Untitled 1* (1993), a joke that is also about the assertion of the ceaseless beauty and fascination photography can uncover within the humdrum and everyday. Gursky, like Thomas Struth, has also pictured paintings, only his interest is with modernist rather than figurative works: three late semi-abstract Turners on display at the Clore Gallery, London, and Jackson Pollock's all-over abstraction, *One: Number 31* (1950), in New York's Museum of Modern Art. Here Gursky's homage is to a kind of representation that is the very antithesis of photography, of pictures without perspective and illusion. Both Turner's dissolution of the landscape to atmospheric aerial paintings about light, energy and motion and Pollock's magnificent 17-foot all-over drip painting, one of the defining works of twentieth-century art, can be seen in relationship to Gursky's own monumental photographs of our contemporary global landscapes, with their predilection for god's-eye aerial views that sublimely put us back into perspective by showing how small and insignificant we all really are. There is also another dimension to Gursky's pictures of paintings. His photographs of art on display in museums must also be seen in relation to his pictures of the serial display of commodities, shelves of Nike trainers, for example, or the empty minimalist displays at Prada. Art, such photographs remind us, is never that far away from the spectacle of commodities.

Thomas Ruff
nudes pe11, 2011
from the series 'nudes'
C-print
156 × 110 cm / 61$\frac{3}{8}$ × 43$\frac{3}{8}$ in

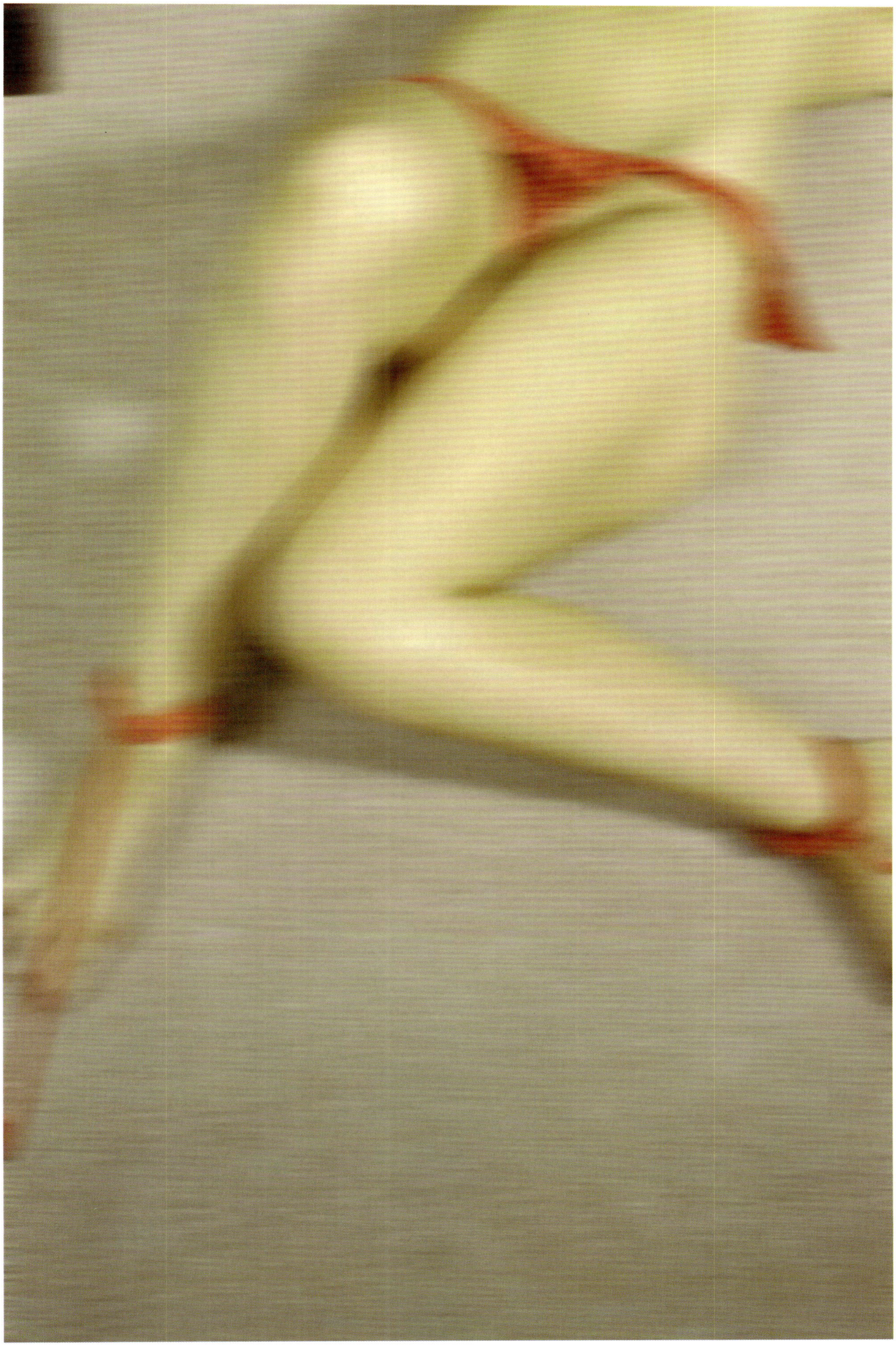

Thomas Ruff
19h 10m/-30°, 1992
from the series 'Sterne'
(Stars), C-print
260 × 188 cm / 102 × 74 in

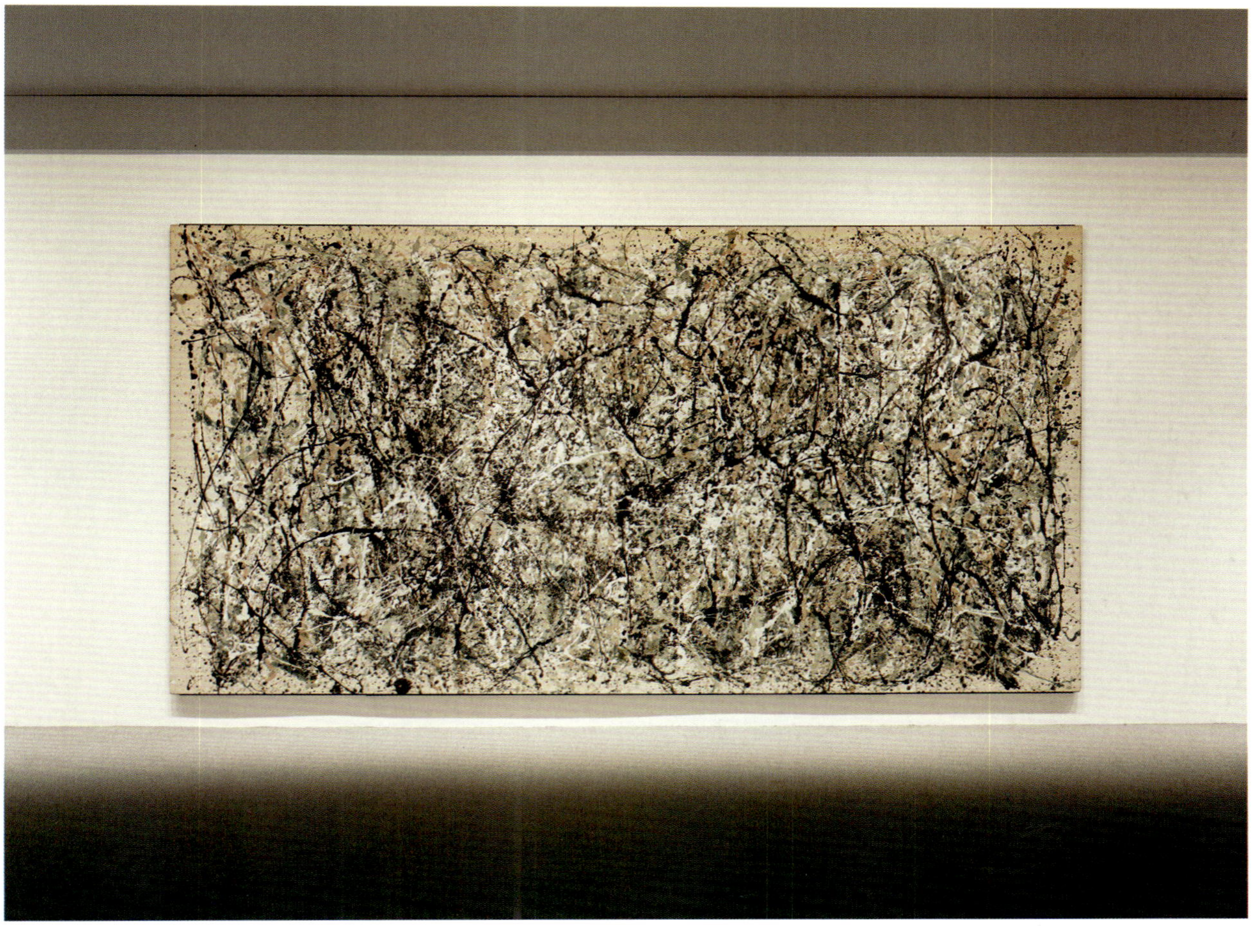

Andreas Gursky
Untitled I, 1993
Inkjet-print
220 × 276 × 6.2 cm /
86⅝ × 108⅝ × 2⅜ in

Untitled VI, 1997
C-print
236.1 × 315.2 × 6.2 cm /
93 × 124 × 2⅜ in

Art in Photography

Hiroshi Sugimoto

The Japanese artist Hiroshi Sugimoto, who trained in Los Angeles, uses the medium of photography to counter spectacle. His black-and-white photographs, such as 'Theatres' (1975–2001), are produced by exposing the photographic negative for the full duration of a movie's projection. The result are pictures with, as he says, 'a very brilliant white rectangle coming from the screen, shining through the whole theatre.'[17] One could see such photography as being directed against the movies. Using still photography to absorb and photograph a complete showing of a motion film, Sugimoto produces a subtle and mesmerizing Zen-like aesthetic, a world away from the more transient thrills and sensations of the entertainment industry.

Sugimoto uses photography to establish an aesthetic of a high order. His 'Seascapes' (1980–), for example, concentrate us on uniformally composed and structured photographs depicting the world's oceans and seas, each view bisected (when visible) by the marine horizon. We are invited to observe and compare the variations in water surface and light from one picture to the next. Bereft of any distracting human or cultural details that might invite narrative associations, such photography approaches the condition of abstract art.

Appropriation Now

Idris Khan

Idris Khan's digital composites give the appearance of speeding up the slow process of other photographers' artistic work. His art revisits and replays well-known pictures from the history of photography, collapsing and condensing a succession of source images into large-scale beautiful and distinctive single pictures, which often have the appearance and quality of drawings, as in *Every... Bernd and Hilla Becher Spherical Type Gasholders* (2004) or *Every... photograph of Nicholas Nixon's Brown Sisters* (2004). The use of digital technology to appropriate old photographic forms might invite a reading which sees Khan's work in terms of a dynamic between the two modes: the digital picking over and reprocessing the corpse of photography.

With Khan the final single pictures we view are to be set against the slow production process of the photographers' work appropriated: the Bechers had been photographing industrial structures for over forty years; his composite of Nicholas Nixon's portraits of his wife and her three sisters spanned twenty-five years. With his composites of the Bechers' photographs, the effect is to energize and animate their degree-zero deadpan photography and give it an unexpected expressive force. Nixon's portraits testify to the inevitable mortality of the flesh. Their pathos rests upon the tension between those portrayed and the cruel facticity of the photographic medium, which meticulously and indifferently logs the women's physical ageing. In Khan's composite, the sitters appear to turn to stone. They have become monumental, sepulchral and eternally petrified.

Hiroshi Sugimoto
Cabot Street Cinema, Massachusetts, 1978
Gelatin silver print
119.4 × 149.2 cm / 48 × 58¾ in

Baltic Sea, Rugen, 1996
Gelatin silver print
50.8 × 61 cm / 20 × 24 in

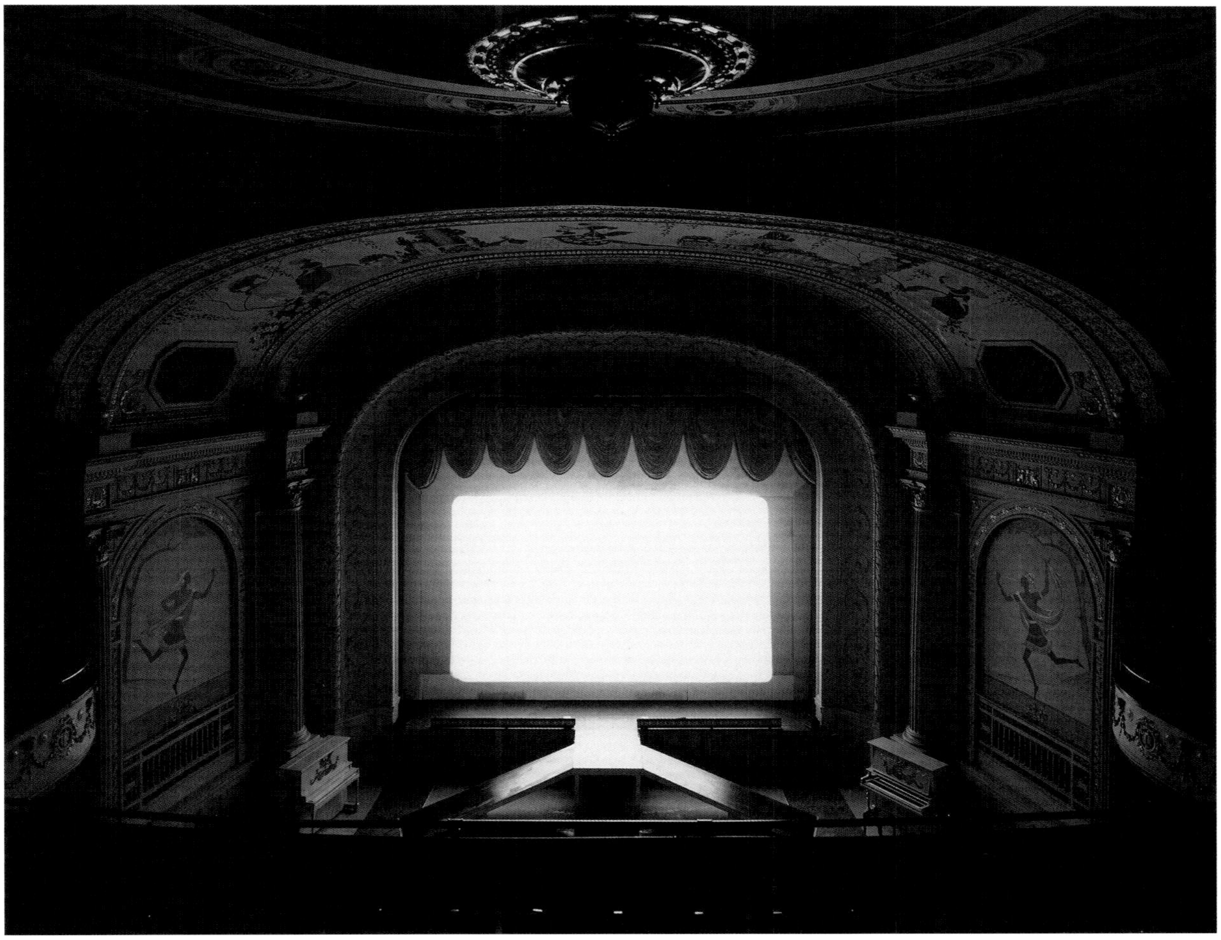

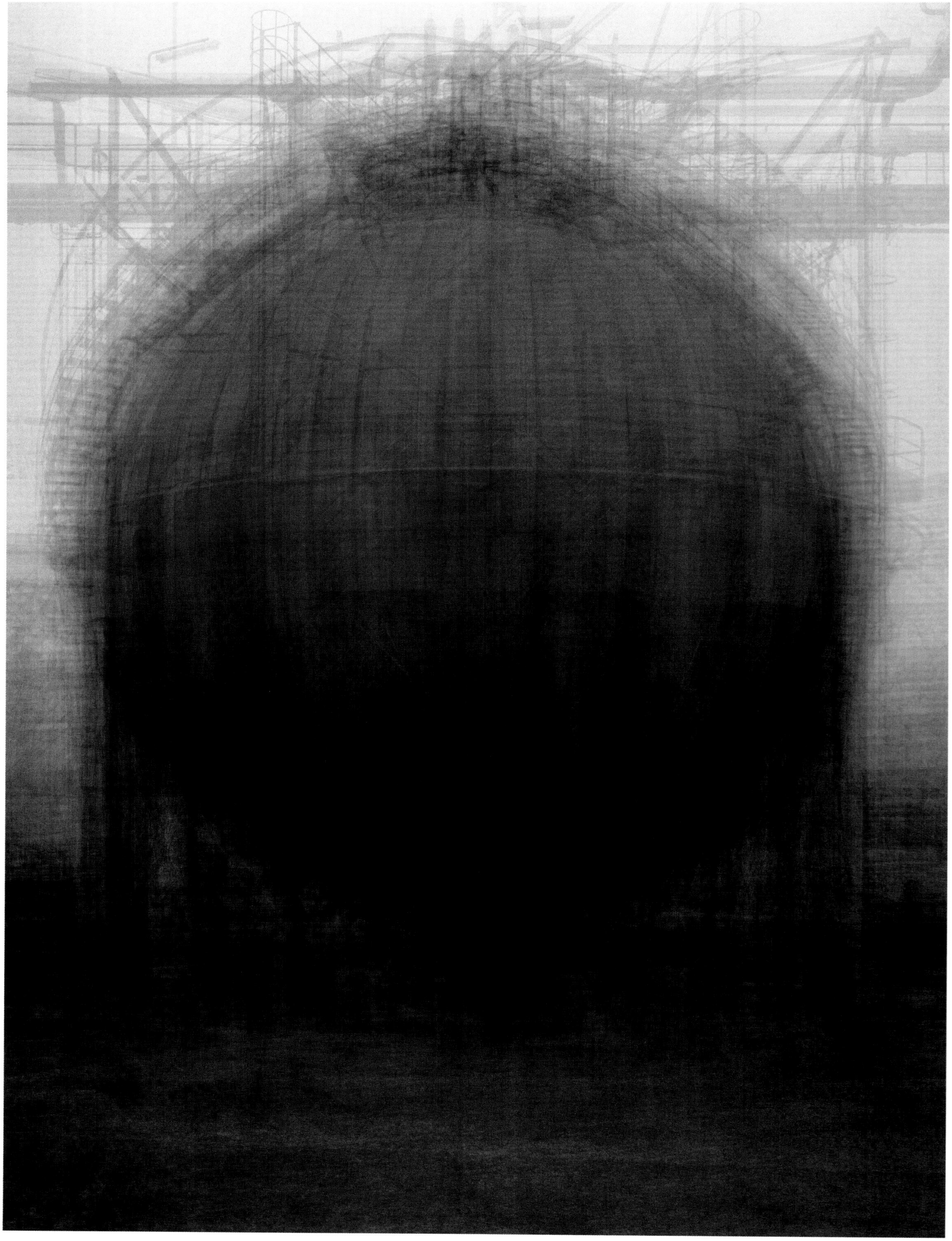

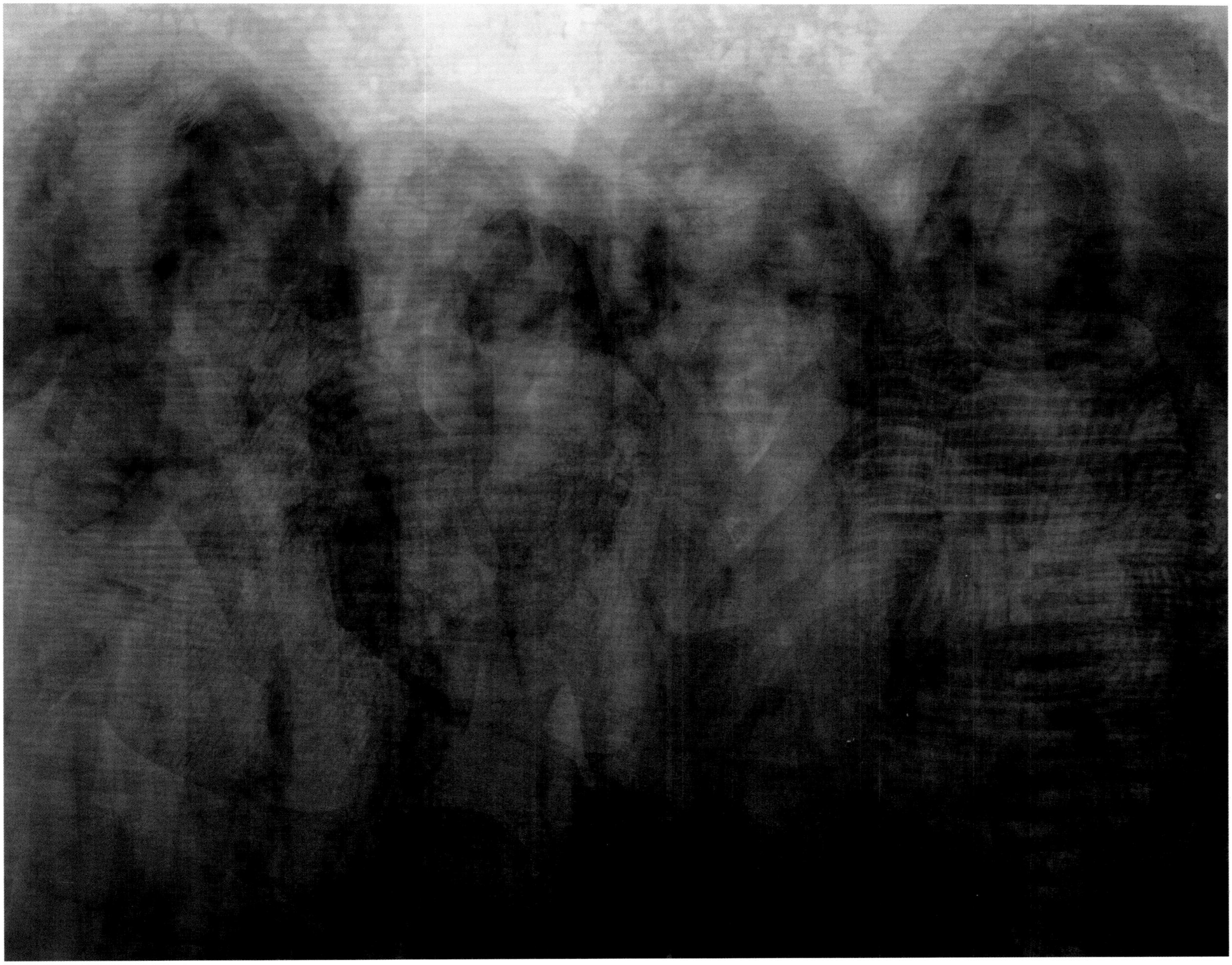

Idris Kahn
Every...Bernd and Hilla Becher Spherical Type Gasholders, 2004
Photographic print
119.4 × 149.2 cm / 47 × 58¾ in

Every...photograph of Nicholas Nixon's Brown Sisters, 2004
Digital C-print mounted on aluminium
113 × 135 cm / 44½ × 53⅛ in

Bohnchang Koo

For his series 'Vessels' (2004–7), Bohnchang Koo adopts the role of a museum copy photographer to take his beautiful and meticulous pictures of delicate white Korean porcelain vessels from the Joseon dynasty (1392–1910), used for tombs and tableware. Koo travelled 42,000 miles in order to photograph these objects, housed in museum collections all over the world. His careful record of the treasures can be seen as an act of restoration and tribute to the artistic achievements of Korea: his sensuous photography highlights and valorizes the craft underlying the delicate porcelain forms. Photography also shows the stains, cracks and wear of everyday use on these vessels, and concentrates our attention upon their human and material aspects. Koo's slow and minimal still lifes counter contemporary Korea's fast-paced culture. Photography allows him to erase the context of the museum, symbolically returning home treasures integral to his country's enduring and spiritual traditional culture, rebuilding a collection dispersed and broken up by the legacies of imperialism.

Bohnchang Koo
Vessel (HA 11), 2005
C-print, dimensions variable
Location of pottery: Leeum, Samsung Museum, Seoul

Anne Collier

Like Idris Khan, Anne Collier offers another fascinating contemporary response to appropriation. Using a large-format camera she makes meticulous and sensuous copies of an array of products, including self-help books and tapes, record sleeves, posters, jigsaw puzzles, the covers of art and photography magazines and film stills. Often photographed flat against black or white backgrounds, or propped up against a plain studio wall, such cheap and tawdry popular and vernacular cultural forms are given a particular import and value. Collier is fascinated by the dated but still alluring styles of LP covers, arranging and selecting them in terms of their imagery: an arty solitary Smiths record sleeve bearing a still from Jean Cocteau's *Orphée*, for example, or two Marilyn Monroe covers placed side by side, with a clear nod to Warhol.

Postmodern photographers such as Sherrie Levine and Richard Prince were interested in pictures that had already been seen. Collier is, too. But she plays up this quality through the fact that her items have been well used. The timeworn record sleeves and creased posters are suggestive of the strong personal meanings and fantasies we invest in commercial media. The photographs of self-help books and cassette tapes introduce a slightly different element, drawing attention to the ways in which our fears, desires and hopes can be managed and controlled. Collier's still-life photography relies on the tension between the psychological content of her items and their ordered and clinical mode of presentation. *Developing Tray, #2* (2009) presents us with a black-and-white close-up photographic print of her open eye afloat in a shallow chemical tray, an animate and visceral self-portrait that challenges the viewer's gaze. The picture links with and counters a series of photographs in which vision and looking is the subject, from the use of eyes as illustrations in technical photographic books to the unusual erotica that used to adorn the covers of popular camera magazines, such as a 1979 issue of *Zoom* with a camera-headed naked female.

Puzzle (Jackson Pollock, Convergence) (2009) offers a neat counterpoint to Andreas Gursky's more reverential homage to the great painter. There is the immediate joke of the photographed object itself, a box full of the unassembled pieces of a very difficult jigsaw puzzle based upon the formless image of one of Jackson Pollock's abstract drip paintings. One also starts musing on the hobbyist activity of the person doing the puzzle, and the particular engagement they would have to this version of a sublime artwork as they struggle to make the picture from the scrambled fragments. As with much of her work, Collier is fascinated with relationships and attachments to pictures and things that don't quite fit expected modes of viewing or thinking about art.

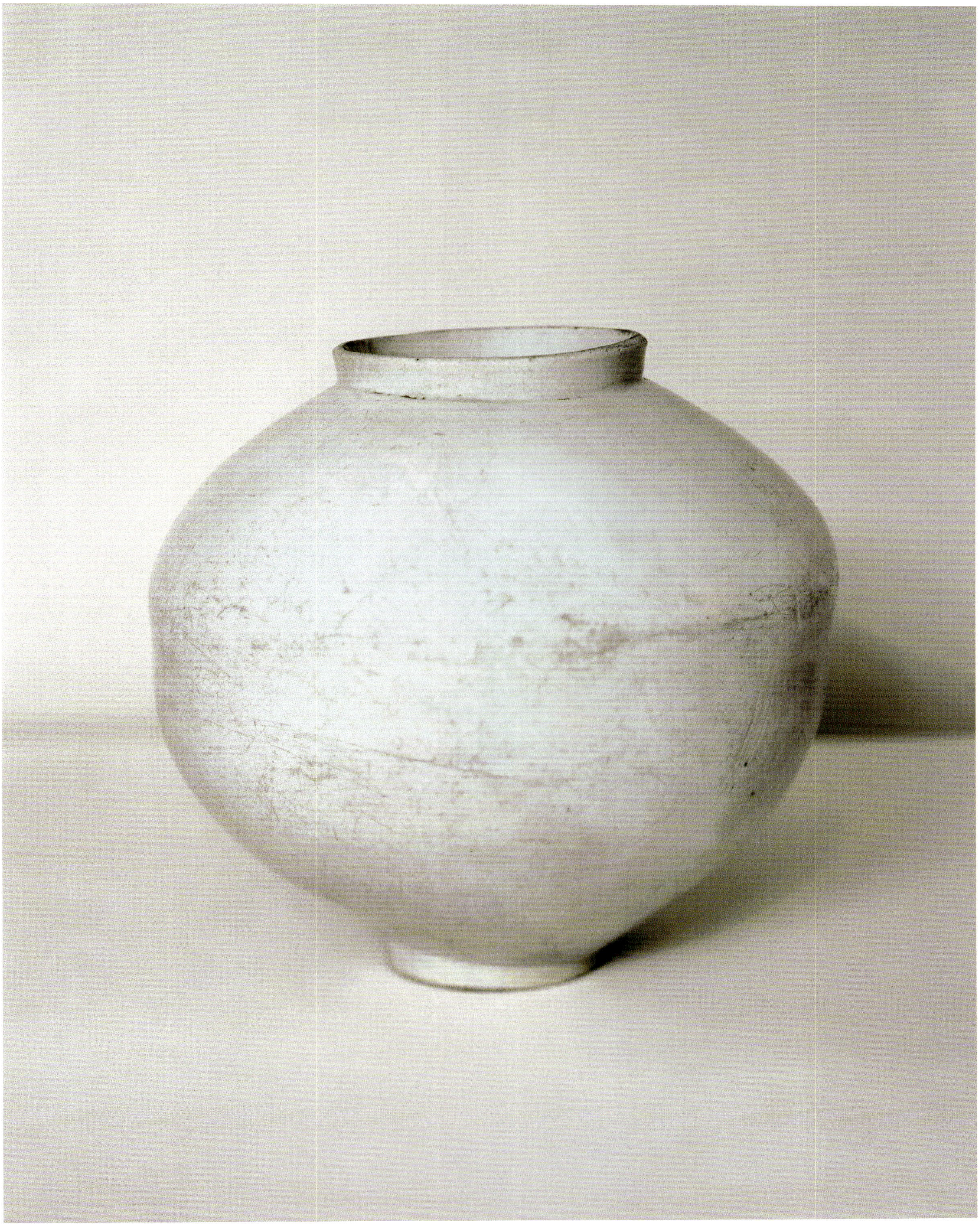

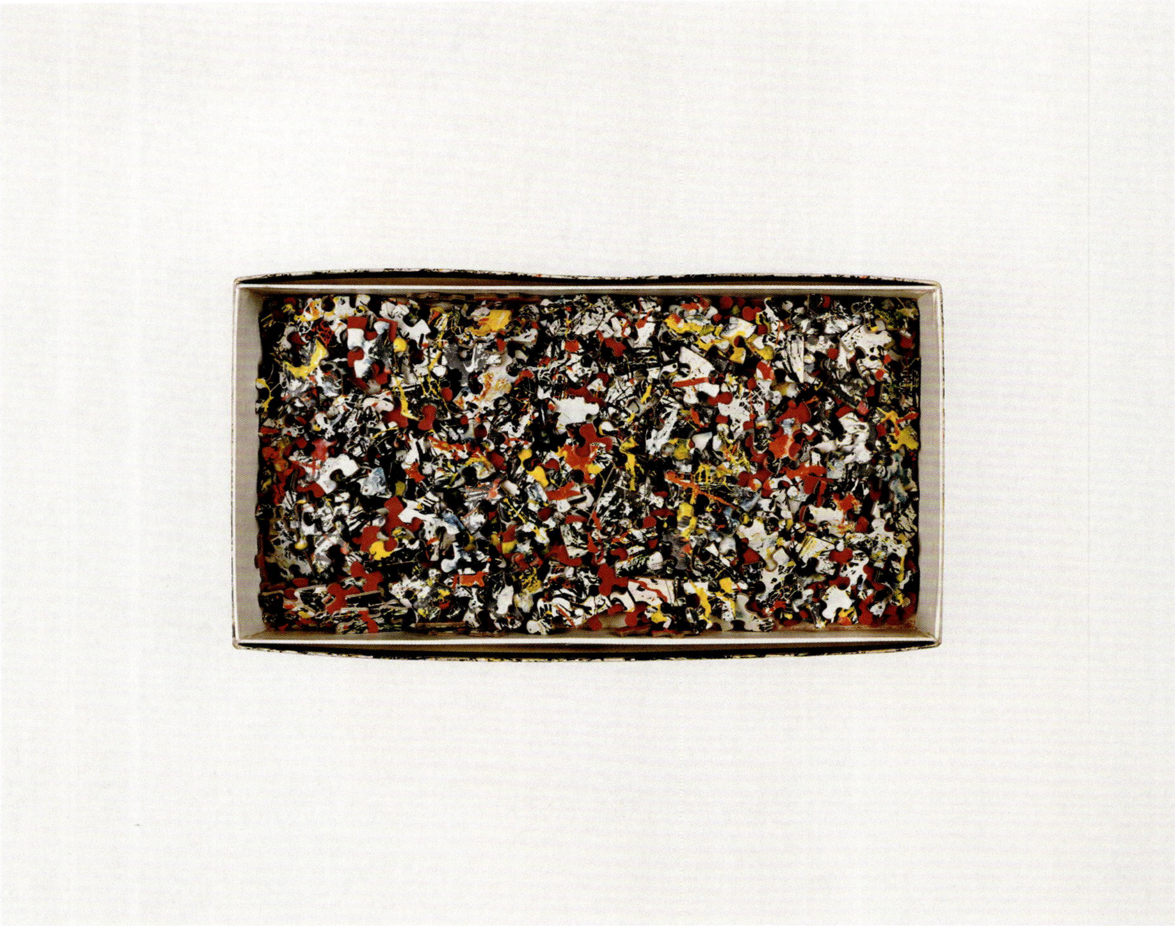

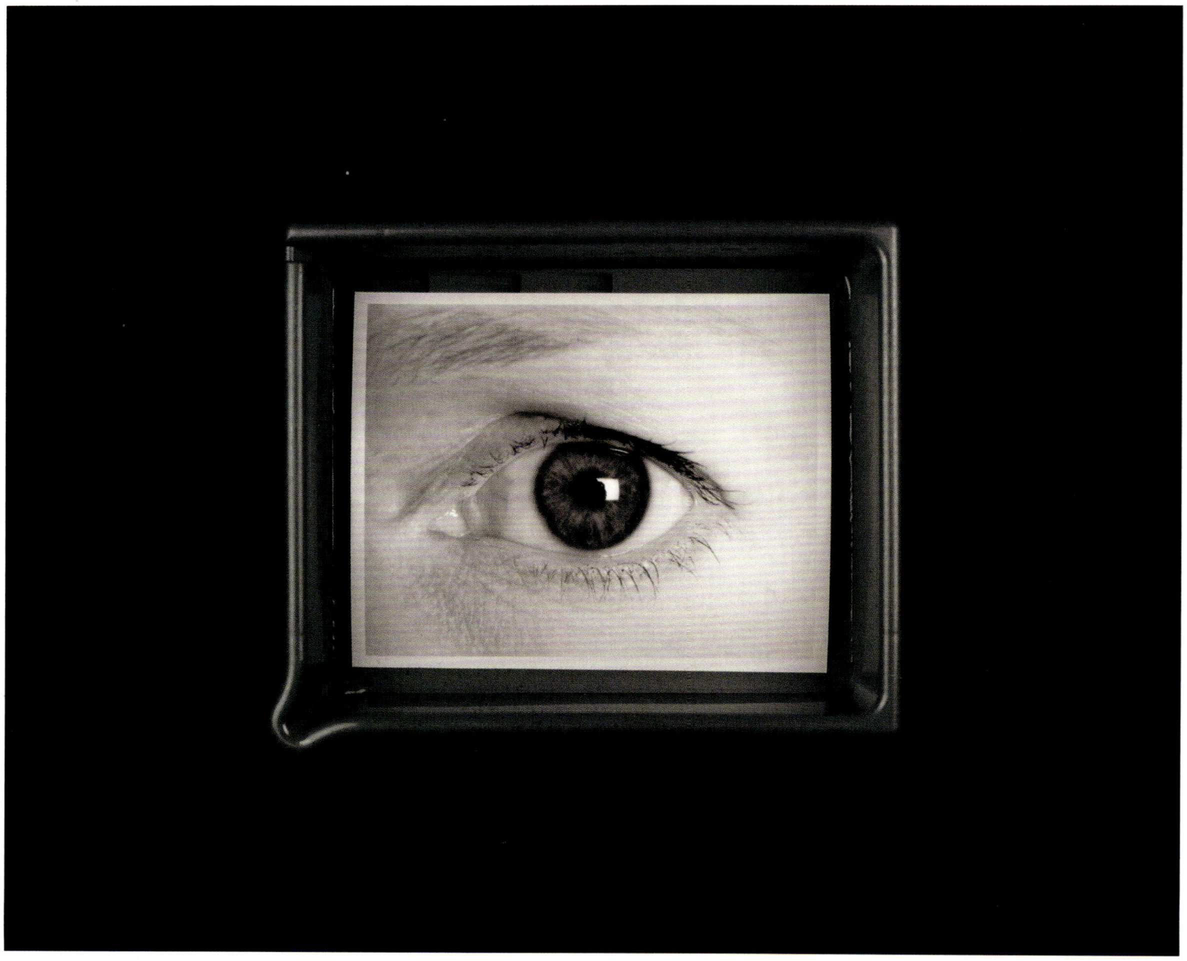

Anne Collier
Puzzle (Jackson Pollock, Convergence), 2009
C-print
113.8 × 142.2 / 44 13/16 × 56 in

Developing Tray #2 (Grey), 2009
C-print
109.2 × 133.3 cm / 43 × 52½ in

Double Marilyn, 2007
C-print
123.2 × 161.3 cm / 48½ × 63½ in

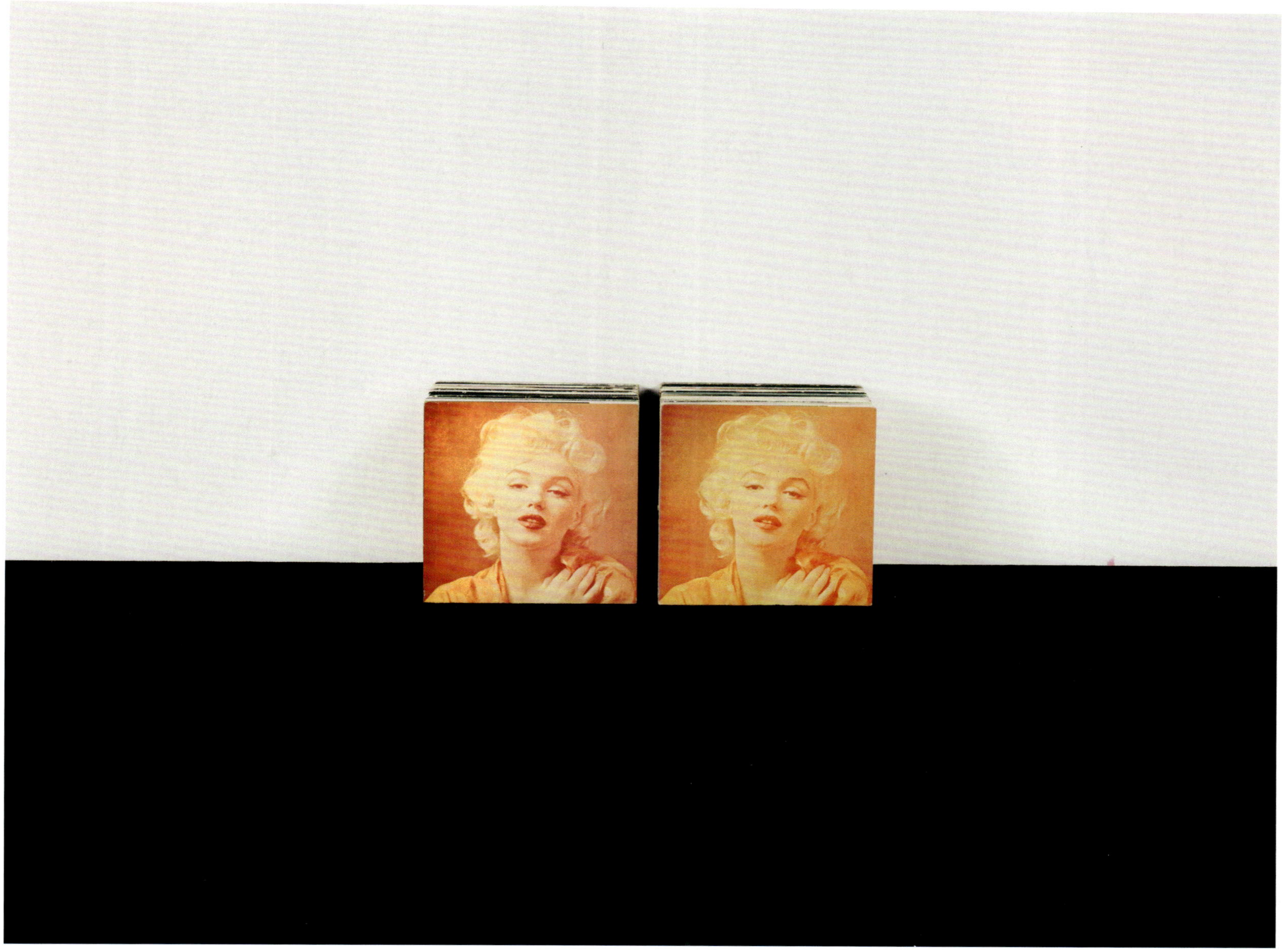

Joachim Schmid

The German artist Joachim Schmid challenges the order and value system integral to the museum through his use of found photographs. While more recent work has involved the production of books with images readily appropriated from such photo-sharing internet sites as Flickr, his work began with photographs picked up from the street or bought from flea markets. For example, 'Bilder von der Straße' (Pictures from the street), begun in 1982 and finished in 2012, consists of a thousand photos, often degraded and fragmentary, which the artist picked up from cities around the world. Integral to 'Bilder...' is a ritualized and superstitious relationship to the photograph. It is an extraordinary tribute to the power and value of the photographic medium as well as increasingly now a testament to the obsolescence of a certain kind of material and physical relationship to the photograph. Many of these found photos, with their ripped edges, abrasions and missing parts, are testimony to something that has gone wrong and are often suggestive of some social discord. Some even start to invite us to look for signs of future unhappiness. For example, in the curious Polaroid showing a couple reflected in the bathroom mirror – *No. 75, Berlin May 1990* – we start to think something already might have gone awry in their relationship because of the woman's sad expression. As well as signs of a breakdown in human relations, of hatred and anger, many probably result from the unfortunate case of a treasured portrait being lost or stolen. Others have ended up on the pavement because of a photographic mistake, a picture that hasn't worked or has fallen short of someone's desires for a good portrait or good photograph. The anonymity of such pictures – identified only by their location and time when found – is mirrored in their archival display, presented neutrally one after the other, in chronological order, as actual artefacts in a gallery or isolated against blank pages in book form. The work is nevertheless subjectively charged and part of the attraction to the material is, as Schmid says, a result of what he refers to as their 'destructive energy'.[18]

Preoccupied with the low and banal elements of common cultural practices, Schmid draws attention to the social uses and psychological functions of photography. His display of photographic litter and waste visual material might also be seen as an anti-capitalist and anti-art market gesture. Schmid, relishing uncertainties and insecurities about the fundamental creative value and status of photography, constructs his own counter-history, a deliberate and conscious celebration of the everyday and amateur.

Schmid's practice has a bearing on the work of the group of artists and people behind the European magazine *Useful Photography*: Hans Aaarsman, Claudie de Cleen, Julian Germain, Erik Kessels and Hans van der Meer. As they declare in the magazine, their intention is 'to give a platform to imagery that is part of our everyday lives but which is rarely studied or appreciated'. *Issue #003*, 2004, was made up of photographs supplied by the National Missing Persons Helpline – studio portraits, snapshots, photocopies, passport photos, digital prints – used to search for people who have gone missing. Each picture has a caption of the person's details and when and where they were last seen. This issue of the magazine shifts the purpose of appropriation from a familiar artistic and aesthetic gesture to one that acknowledges the multiple uses of photography and the social and communicative value of reproduced images. This is a canny move that taps into a recurring obsession with portrait photography's pathos-imbued identity as a trace in light of its subject. Only in this case the severance from the moment recorded is not a cue to romantic musings but is anchored in painful social realities and real-life dramas. The project highlights the core ambivalence about the photograph as an artistic medium: much as it is used and pulled into the orbit of art, much as it is transformed as art, it is still very often a medium in which what is pictured dominates. The implications of this issue of *Useful Photography* also introduce concerns of the next chapter, as it explores the varied ways photography has been used as a medium for portraiture.

Joachim Schmid
No. 75, Berlin, May 1990
from the series 'Bilder von der Straße' (Pictures from the Street), 1982–2012
Photograph mounted on board
29.7 × 21 cm / 11¾ × 8¼ in

No. 140, Belo Horizonte, August 1992
from the series 'Bilder von der Straße' (Pictures from the Street), 1982–2012
Photograph mounted on board
29.7 × 21 cm / 11¾× 8¼ in

Useful Photography, Issue #003
Artimo, Amsterdam, 2003
21 × 29.7 cm / 21¼ × 11¾ in, 160pp
Paperback, 86 photographs
Photographs collected and edited by Hans Aarsman, Claudie De Cleen, Julian Germain, Erik Kessels and Hans Van der Meer

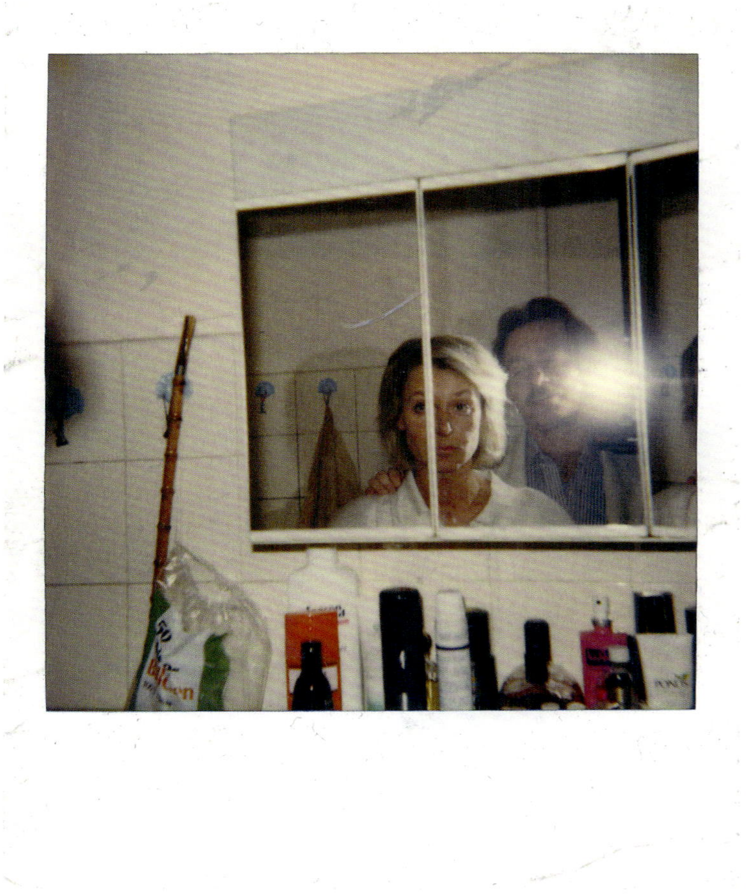

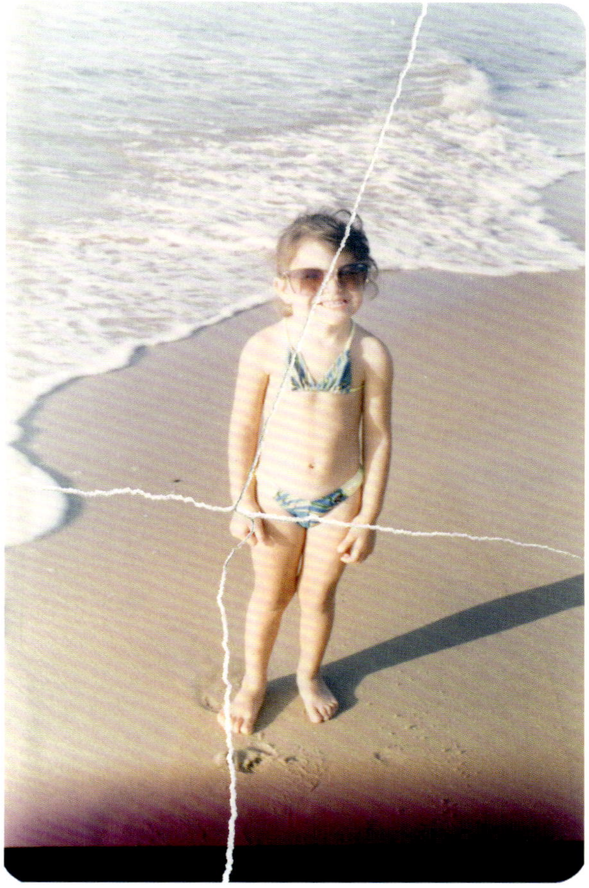

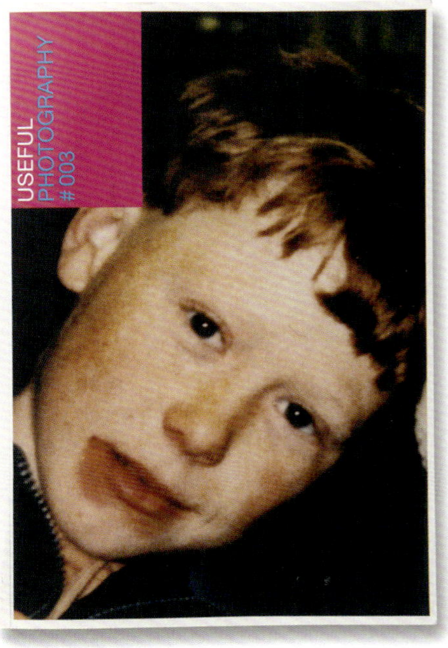
USEFUL
PHOTOGRAPHY
003

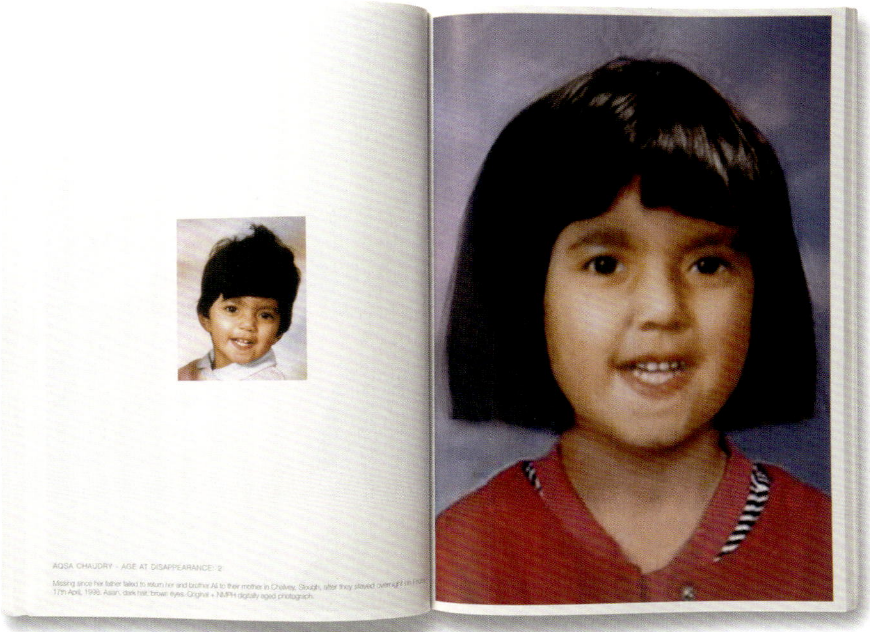
AQSA CHAUDRY - AGE AT DISAPPEARANCE: 2

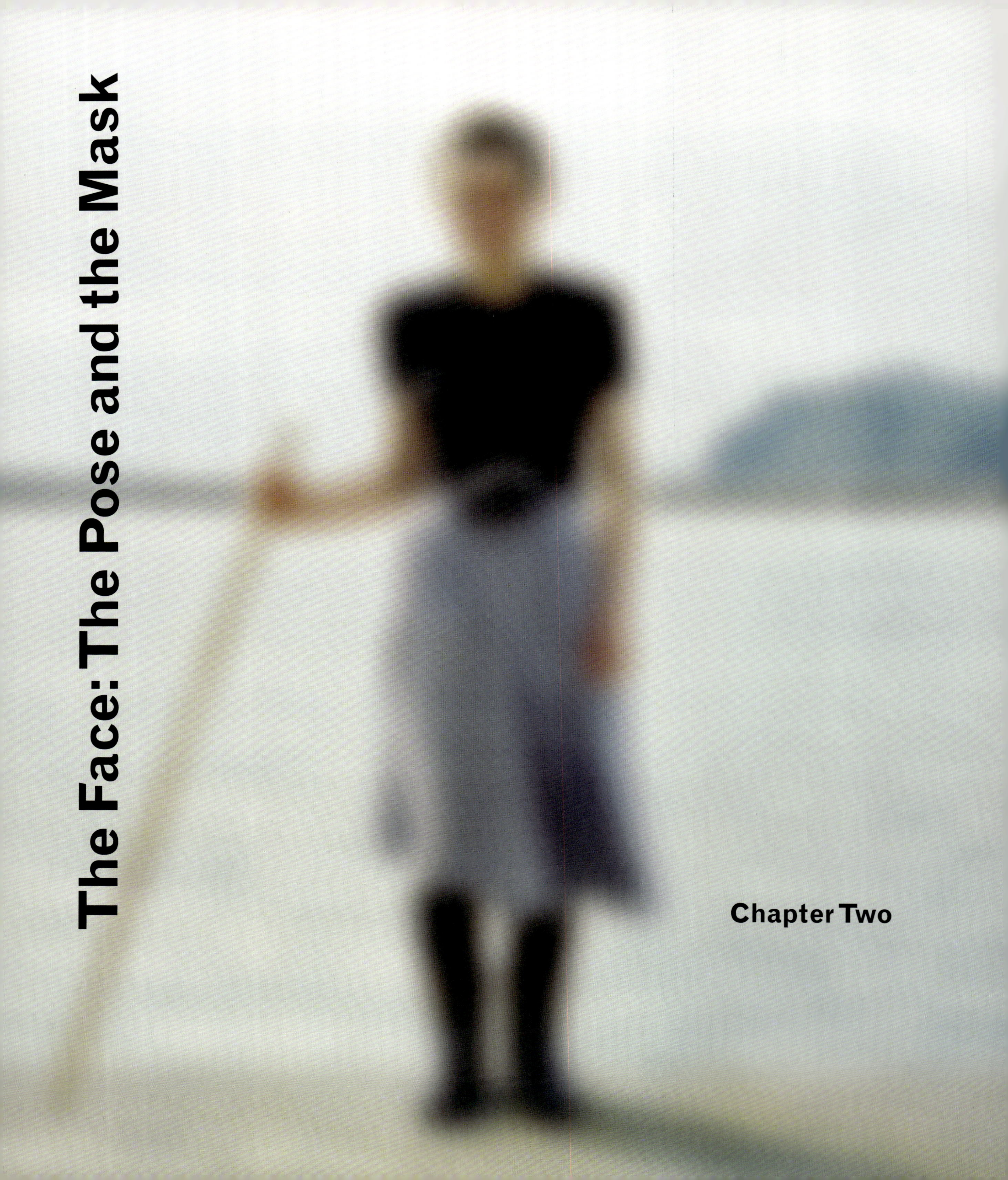

The Face: The Pose and the Mask

Chapter Two

Even though photography can of course distort and idealize, the interest of many photographers in portraiture stems from its evidential certitude, that is, the peculiar and enduring power that we are looking at someone who once existed. The French literary theorist Roland Barthes, in his 1980 book on photography, *Camera Lucida*, is clear about this characteristic. The whole book stems from a desire to explain the enduring 'amazement' of a mid-nineteenth century photographic portrait of Jerome Bonaparte, Napoleon's younger brother: 'I am looking at eyes that looked at the Emperor'.[1] Painting could never offer that same existential guarantee.

Traditionally, the portrait sets up the expectation that something of the sitter's identity will be revealed. While a number of artists use the genre of photographic portraiture to interrogate and undermine such an expectation, many continue to draw upon it. As this chapter will show, there are essentially two approaches to photographic portraiture: on one hand work that plays with the possibility of psychological disclosure or unmasking, and on the other hand work that erases this and simply acknowledges the ultimate inadequacy of the photographic portrait to portray character.

Cindy Sherman

Cindy Sherman radically challenged the conventions of portraiture with her 'Untitled Film Stills' (1977–80). Sherman's photographs have been much discussed and in many ways have come to exemplify postmodernism in the way they appear to remove the self and challenge expression. In tableaux staged for camera, Sherman performs an inventory of stereotypical female images drawn from films, both mainstream and art house. Viewed as portraits any quest for a secure identity is denied, all one gets is an endless mirroring of other representations. In an early important postmodern reading of Sherman, Craig Owens wrote about how 'Untitled Film Stills' refutes the masculine desire for a 'stable and stabilizing identity' from images of women; the fact that we can see the same model adopting a succession of different roles and poses means there is 'a trembling around the edges of that identity'.[2]

Sherman's work reflects upon the way images shape our perceptions of the world. While the movies provide a repertoire of poses she can adopt, some photographs interrogate the pose itself. *Untitled Film Still* 2 (1977), for example, presents a grainy image that gives us a predatory and voyeuristic view of an unguarded woman in a bathroom. She is shown striking a pose within the mirror, a reflected image that fulfils a certain ideal of femininity and a contrast, as Kaja Silverman has highlighted, with the less stylized depiction of her body as she stands in the bathroom, wrapped in a towel. The postmodern reading of Sherman's 'Untitled Film Stills' is that woman is nothing but image, that there is nothing beneath the masks. *Untitled Film Still* 2's fractured image hints at something else, showing us how aspirations fall short of an ideal self image.

ORLAN the French multimedia/performance artist takes the postmodern idea that there is nothing beyond the image to a disturbing extreme. Her face is physically altered in 'performances' in which she undergoes plastic surgery and relays the operations by live video and satellite links to art galleries across the world. This began in 1990, when she underwent the first of seven planned cosmetic surgery operations, each altering her face according to the features of Old Master paintings of idealized feminine beauty. Yet as the theorist Parveen Adams has argued, ORLAN's art is far from the 'narcissistic optimism of cosmetic surgery'.[3] Adams draws attention to the shocking moment in a facial operation when we see ORLAN's face begin to detach itself from her head, a graphically blunt display of the face as nothing but facade, as mask. There is nothing beneath.

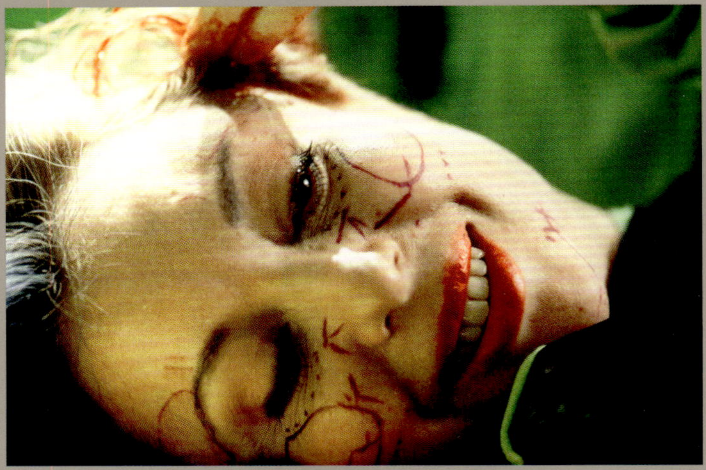

ORLAN
Close-up of laughter during the operation, from the seventh surgery-performance *Omnipresence*, New York, 21st Nov 1993
Cibachrome print in diasec mount, 165 × 110 cm / 65 × 43.3 in

Cindy Sherman
Untitled Film Still 2, 1977
Gelatin silver print
24.1 × 19.2 cm / 9½ × 7½ in

Untitled Film Still 54, 1980
Gelatin silver print
17.3 × 24 cm / 6¾ × 9½ in

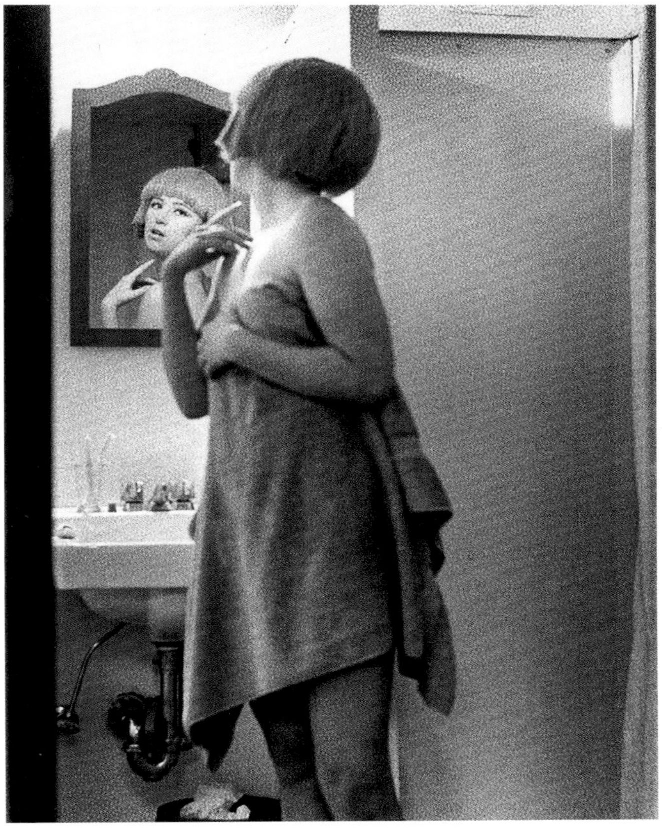

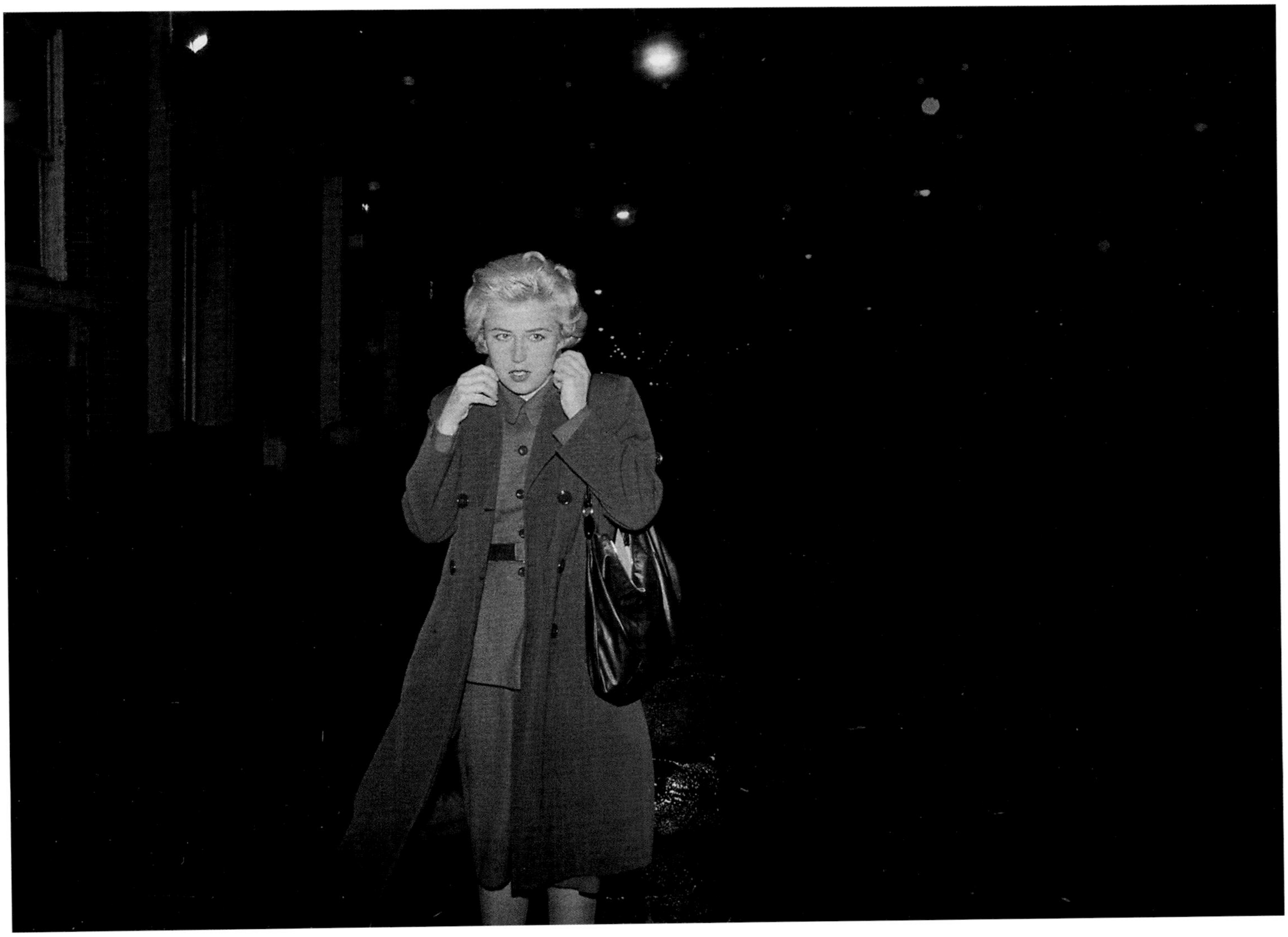

Diane Arbus

Diane Arbus's enduring and powerful series of portraits often rely upon the tension between a projected self-image, a subject's public 'front', and a sense of the person beneath this social mask. Her head-on portrayal of subjects, often drawn from those sidelined by traditional bourgeois portraiture – dwarfs, midgets, giants, homes for the mentally handicapped, transvestites, nudists, carnival performers and so on – at the same time borrows from the dignifying frontal photographic portrait tradition, stemming from and typified by the genteel and middle-class *cartes de visite* of the Victorian era. Only Arbus's subjects all tend to be rather loosely centred in the square format of her Rolleiflex camera: the form is more casual than clinical, an imprecision that accords with the specific awkwardness and imperfections in the world she pictures.

Arbus deliberately seems to upturn the conventions of the domestic and family grouping. The benign form of picturing typified by the family snapshot is literally turned on its head in such pictures as *Jewish Giant at Home with his Parents in the Bronx, N.Y. 1970*, which shows the stooped figure of the son towering over his mother and father, who appear more like his children. In another grouping, *A Young Brooklyn Family Going for a Sunday Outing, N.Y.C. 1966*, the adults' controlled and groomed self images – apparently modelled on fanzine culture, with the man trying to look like James Dean and the woman like Elizabeth Taylor – is disrupted by the facial gesture of their child, which suggests some emotional or mental disturbance. His facial expression undermines his parents' attempt at stylization and coherence, and introduces the loss of pose and composure that was to become integral to Arbus's pictures made of the residents in homes for the mentally handicapped, a series which, in terms of Arbus the legend, have been seen as symbolic of the photographer's own inner turmoil and suffering, and a presentiment of their maker's suicide. They are important, like the child of the Brooklyn family, because they are integral to the whole problem of the pose. The subjects' very innocence means they lack the pose and possess unselfconsciousness before the camera. The relation between photography and the pose is further complicated in this series by the way in which masks enter the work. It is there, too, albeit more subliminally, in the Brookyln couple's attempt to mimic the 'model' look of movie stars. In Arbus's last works, the fixed, stylized grimaces and grotesquery of the Halloween masks contrast with the wild, uncontrolled expressions and expressivity of her subjects, all lacking the capacity to control their self-image.

Brought up in an upper-middle-class Jewish environment, and having worked for many years in partnership with her husband in their fashion photography business, Arbus was fully aware of how an idealized vision could condone and feed the sensibilities of the middle and upper classes. In turning her camera on more outsider and 'freakish' subjects, despite all the talk of intimacy and dignity in relation to such pictures, the distance of her own privileged class is still very much present. But much as class is clearly factored into the differences set up by some of her subjects – it is cuttingly evident in the cruelty behind some of her portraits of the middle and upper classes, such as her up-close portrait of the veiled, puffy, made-up face of a late-middle-aged woman on Fifth Avenue – it is instead the physical manifestations of difference within the body that provide the central focus in Arbus's work. Her spectrum of portraits of more 'normal' couples and single figures on the street or in their homes, of differing ages and ethnicities, are made strange and 'other' in relation to the portraits of the marginal and outsider subjects. Even those well-known pictures which reveal a fascination with mirroring in nature – her portraits of twins and triplets, whose mirroring rebounds on the reproductive process of photography itself – are predicated upon difference. Dressed identically to amplify the oddity of their biological repetition, the subjects' facial expressions, gestures and composure nevertheless slip out of the cultural uniformity imposed upon them. Indeed, if one considers this further then one can come to appreciate the unsettling late portraits as ultimately signalling, not despair and inner turmoil, but playful freedom and innocent excess. The joy of play is clearly registered in these pictures.

Arbus's portraits focus upon what she has referred to as 'the gap between intention and effect'.[4] She was discussing the way in which what we intend to project to others never quite matches up with what is seen: 'Our whole guise is like giving a sign to the world to think of us in a certain way, but there's a point between what you want people to know about you and what you can't help people knowing about you.'

The discrepancy or slippage between projected self-image and what is actually seen is integral to Arbus's work. Many of her portraits give the sense of cutting through the 'self-images' projected by her subjects. The realm of 'intent' is shown up as artifice, associated with make-up, dress or masking, the cultural adornment of those pictured. And all this cultural garb, this 'front', never quite accords with the subjects. What lies behind is only the irreducible physicality of different bodies, imperfect, unidealized and all heightened somewhat hallucinogenically through the very surfeit of detail the 'harsh' and 'cold' camera can bring out. As Arbus said, 'If you scrutinize reality closely enough, if in some way you really, really get to it, it becomes fantastic.'

Diane Arbus
A Young Brooklyn Family Going for a Sunday Outing, N.Y.C., 1966
Gelatin silver print, dimensions variable

Identical twins, Roselle, N.J., 1967
Gelatin silver print, dimensions variable

Untitled (4), 1970–1
Gelatin silver print, dimensions variable

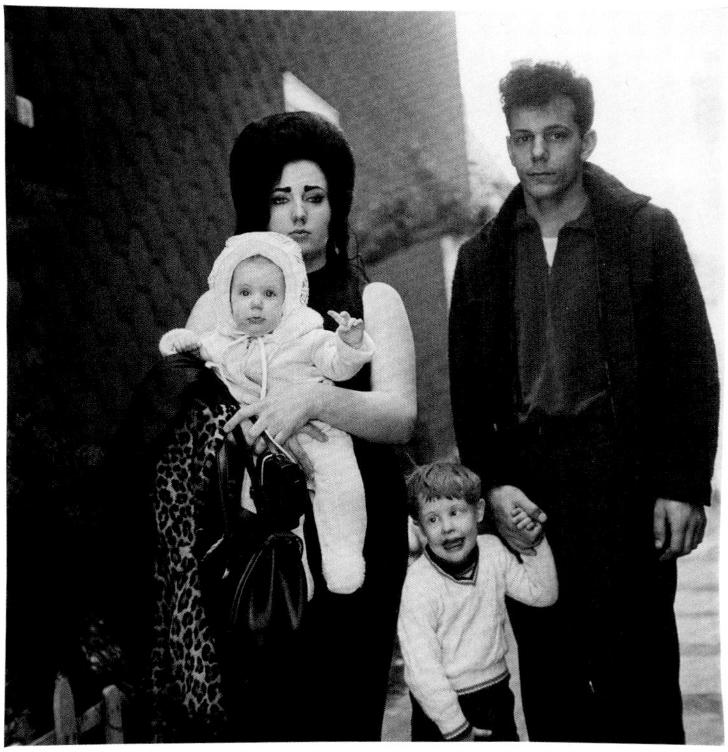

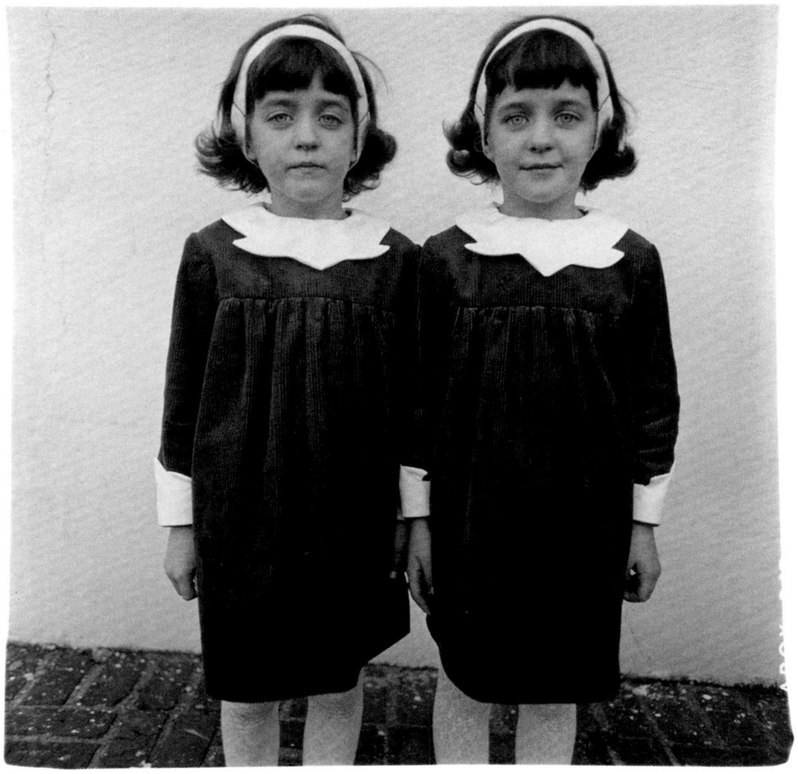

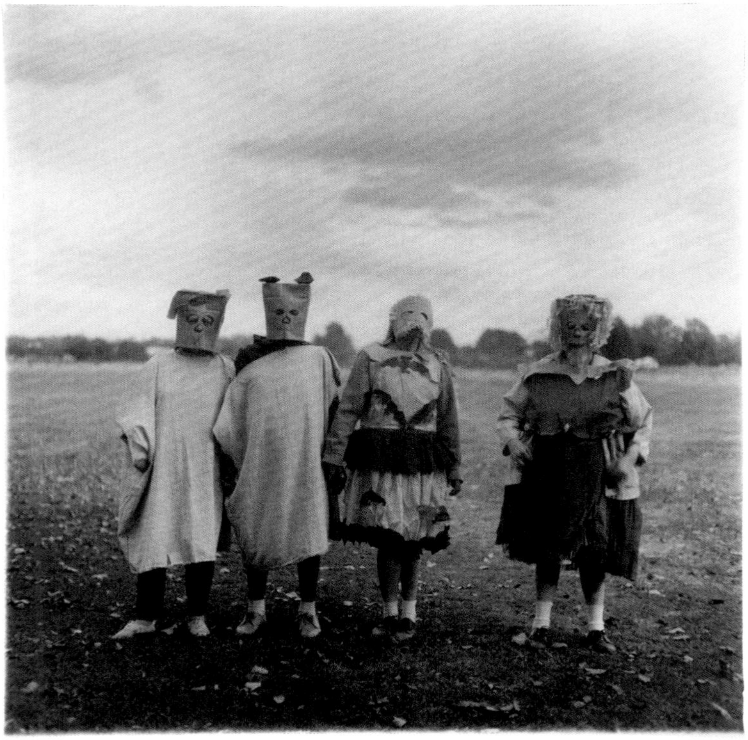

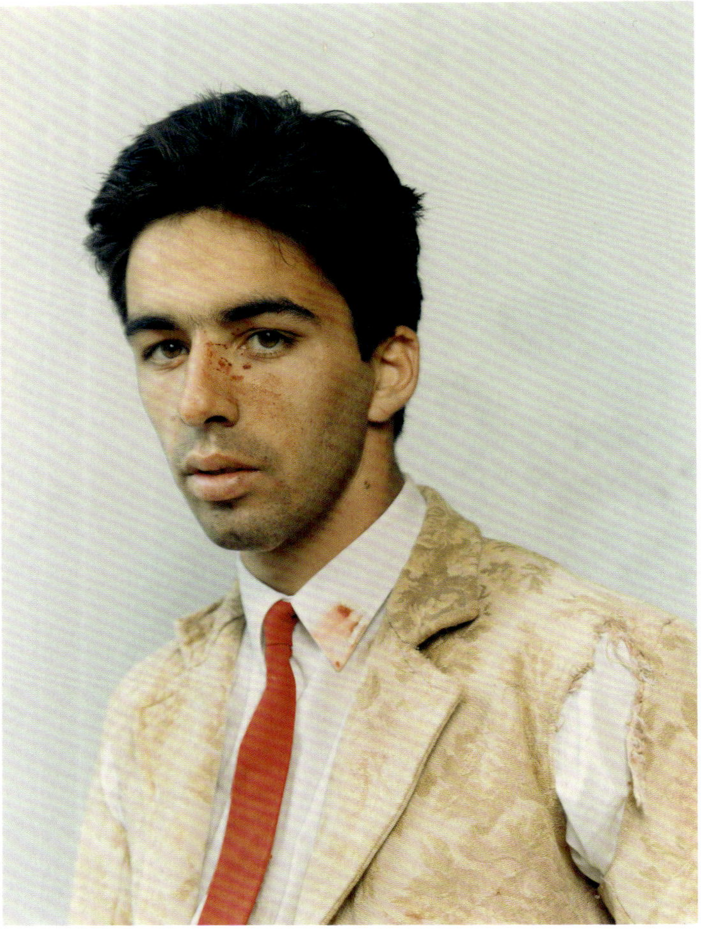

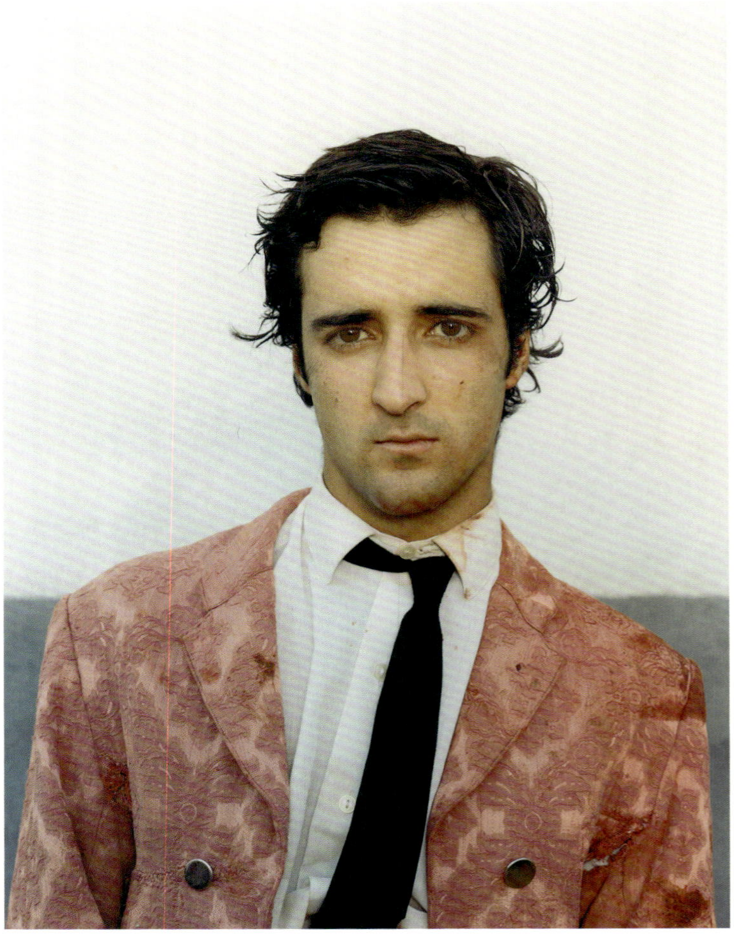

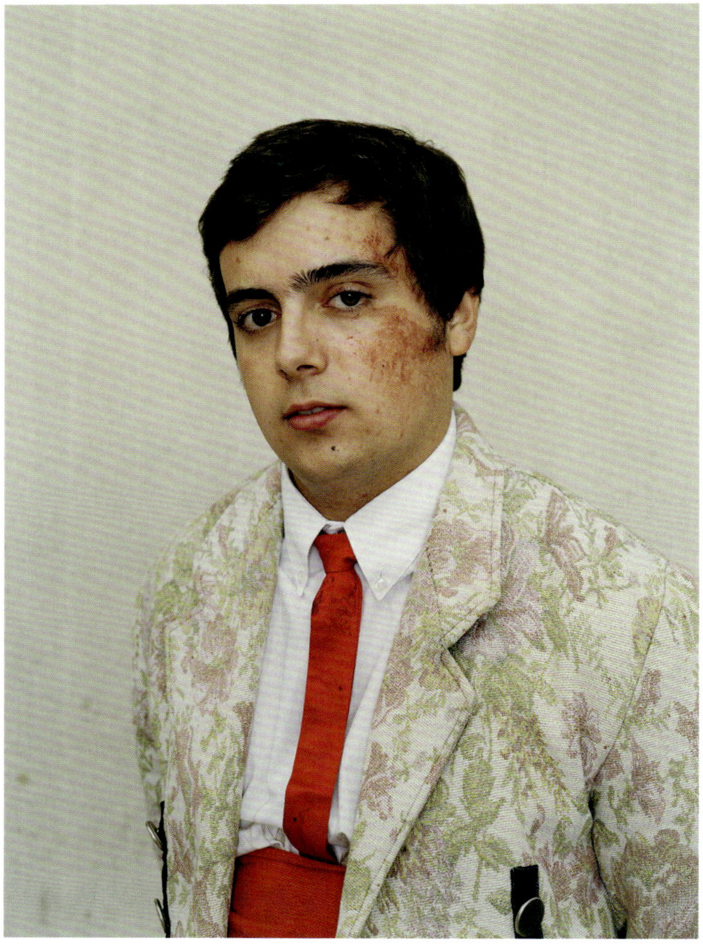

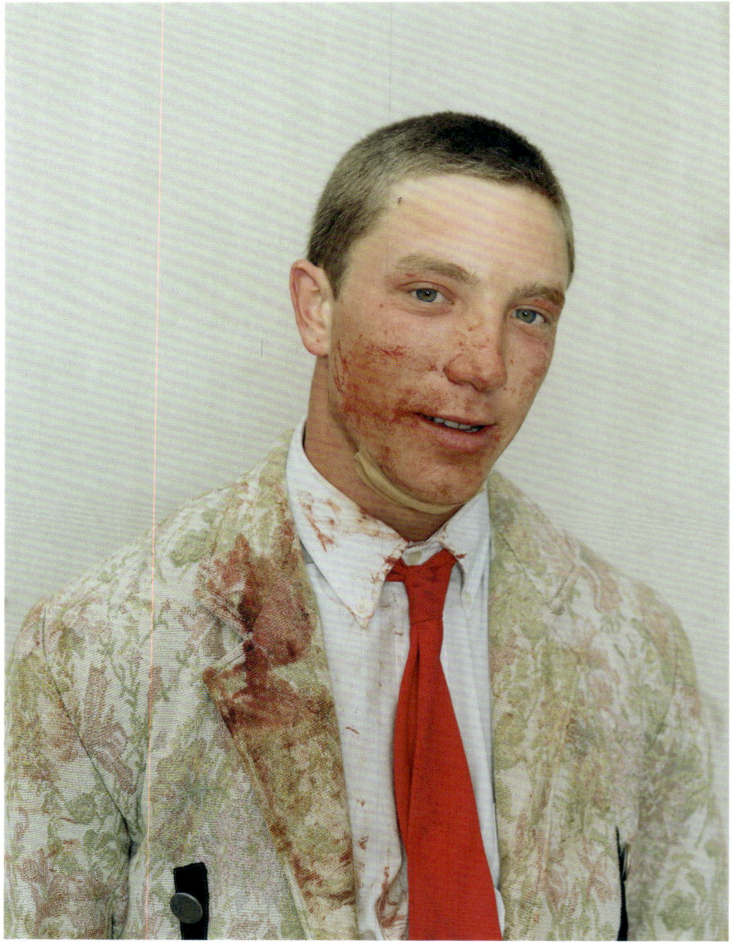

Rineke Dijkstra

In her approach to portraiture, Rineke Dijkstra acknowledges the influence of Diane Arbus and the importance of what she said about 'looking for the "gap between intention and effect."'[5] As Dijkstra puts it: 'People think that they present themselves one way, but they cannot help but show something else as well. It's impossible to have everything under control.'

Dijsktra's portraiture reveals a fascination with subjects, primarily youthful, who are not fully in control. Many portraits entail a slippage of the defensive nature of the pose and the sense of the vulnerable and exposed individual beneath. Dijkstra photographs her subjects at moments when the mask of the pose slips. In her series of extraordinary portraits of Portuguese bullfighters, she pictures young men who have just come out of the ring. The bravery, machismo and pomp associated with their performance is undercut by the biting realism of these portraits. The photographs are exposés in the sense in which their subjects' bloodied faces, soiled and torn clothes or crooked ties testify to their lack of composure: the men look somewhat dazed, not quite themselves. Played out against the spectacle and display of the bullfight, such counter-idealizing portraits upset the ceremonial display of self, giving us more a sense of vulnerability than one of vanity and pride.

She has also made portraits of young soldiers in Israel, in camouflage and together with their machine guns, after a first day's training exercise in the Golan Heights (1999/2000). As with the portraits of the toreros, the face is seen as a potential register of the dramatic situation and event that closely precedes the portrait's taking. Poses are disrupted or rather marked by this situation.

For her first important work, (1992–6) she made full-length portraits of teenagers on beaches before the sea – a celebration of the awkward beauty of the transitional state of adolescence. Beginning in the Netherlands, Dijkstra moved on to photograph in the United States, where she found teenagers who, as she said, 'take their examples from photos in glamour magazines they want to imitate.'[6] These were in contrast to the youths she then portrayed on beaches in Eastern Europe, in Poland, Ukraine and Croatia.

Video allows a longer look at her subjects. The dual screen video projection Buzz Club/Mysteryworld (1996–7) moves between portraits of young girls in a northern English night club and the harsher more male-dominated music scene of a Dutch techno club. Both groups of young clubbers are filmed against blank walls away from the dance floor, a context that abstracts and isolates the rituals of their performances to camera, gives the work an anthropological edge. In one long and rather cruel video portrait, the camera concentrates on the face of a youth from the Dutch nightclub, smoking and chewing gum he appears somewhat out of it, drifting back and forth between a consciousness of being filmed, as he looks straight to camera, and distraction, as he closes his eyes to us and the world. As with her photographic portraits, Dijkstra studies groups of people, only here we move between two distinctive subcultures, each with their particular looks and styles and types of music. In the video the intensity and emotional expression desired is not of one moment, instead we move between a lack of inhibition and a loss of self in the music and the atmosphere of the nightclubs and the awkward self-consciousness that comes from knowing they are performing to camera.

Rineke Dijkstra
Villa Franca, Portugal, May 8, 1994, 1994
Inkjet print, printed in large and small formats

Montemor, Portugal, May 1, 1994, 1994
Inkjet print, printed in large and small formats

Forte da Casa, Portugal, May 20, 2000, 2000
C-print, printed in large and small formats

Forte da Casa, Portugal, May 20, 2000, 2000
C-print, printed in large and small formats

Ralph Eugene Meatyard

Ralph Eugene Meatyard worked as an optician and took photographs at the weekends. His world is much more private and intimate than Diane Arbus's, but like her he was fascinated with the problem of the pose in portraiture. The mask was also an integral element to his work, only he used the literal mask to acknowledge the incapacity and inadequacy of the portrait convention as a means of psychological disclosure.

Meatyard's pictures offer an emotive mix of autobiography, comedy and tragedy in response to an intimate portrait tradition. He borrows from and subverts the tradition of the family snapshot portrait in his remarkable posthumous book, *The Family Album of Lucybelle Crater* (1974), the photographs for which he took and prepared for publication in the last two years of his life, when he had been diagnosed with terminal cancer. The book's photographs depict two masked figures in various middle-class suburban and domestic spaces, both outdoors and indoors, in Lexington, Kentucky. Meatyard's wife, Madelyn, is present in all the pictures wearing a grotesque mask with two protruding teeth and warts. She has the title role, Lucybelle Crater, and in each photograph she is accompanied by a different person, each wearing a transparent plastic mask of an old man, aging the subject grotesquely. Meatyard felt that the clear mask was a portrait of its wearer in forty years' time, a portrait of a future self. The real names of the masked people are revealed at the end of the book and represent a close circle: Meatyard himself, his wife, his sons, daughter, mother, neighbours, colleagues and friends. He gave few directions to his sitters and permitted them to pose in whatever clothes they were wearing after their locations had been chosen.

It is possible to see the mask as a metaphor for the way family snapshots tend to mask their subjects, highlighting snapshot photography's standardized artifice. Yet, much as these pictures might be seen to disrupt family album conventions, they nevertheless draw upon the emotive and affective potential of the genre. The point lies in the discrepancy between the masks and the poignant personal context of the project, which represents a dying photographer's final gathering of all those who are close and dear to him. In the first and last images, Meatyard pictures himself with his wife, both masked. In the first he is identified as Lucybelle's husband. In the last picture, taken on their twenty-fifth wedding anniversary and in a favourite spot of Madelyn's, the sitters have switched clothes and masks. This suggests their closeness and intimacy, and the ultimate privacy of this album.

As Marianne Hirsch has proposed, the book in this respect points to 'the limitation of family photography, that which it cannot record or tell.'[7] She also suggests that, by hiding their subjects, masks make the portraits generic, engaging viewers in a scene of recognition and connection, in as much as the interiors and locations of suburban culture in a small part of Kentucky in the 1970s can be a point of collective recognition.

The critic A.D. Coleman gives Meatyard's pictures an existential slant, claiming their 'theme is the essential otherness and shifting personae of people, even those to whom one is closest.'[8] But the context of Meatyard's illness and the social groupings suggest something else. There is an intimacy here, something close and private that is never disclosed and remains incommunicable. In this respect one might see the masked subjects as a reverse of the videos made by British artist Gillian Wearing in *Confess All On Video. Don't Worry You Will Be in Disguise. Intrigued? Call Gillian…* (1994), which show fixed head shots of variously disguised subjects who freely confess to the camera; incessant interior disclosures and monologues that feed our curiosity and fascination with the lives of others. For Wearing's subjects the mask is there to hide behind. For Meatyard's subjects the masks have the same function, but the use of the mask also suggests the incapacity to express an emotional situation. The repetition of the fixed grotesquery of the masks draws attention to the poses and gestures of the different subjects, which, although they follow the familiar poses of family-album photography, carry more emotional weight precisely because they are the only clues to character we are given.

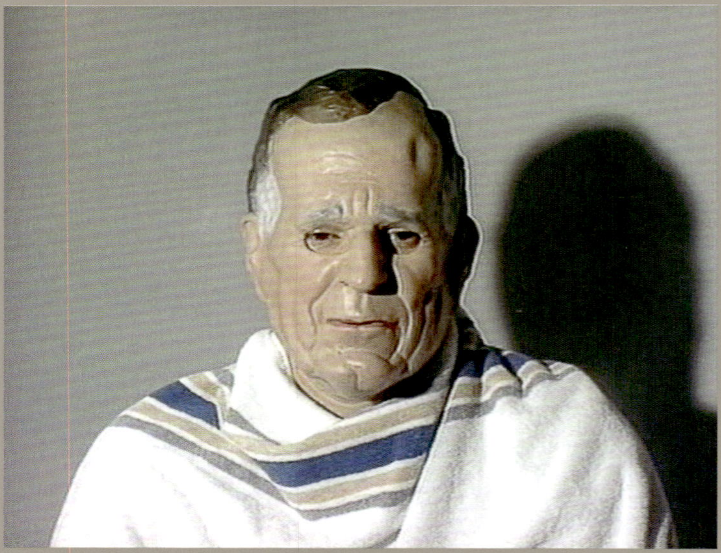

Gillian Wearing
Confess All On Video. Don't Worry, You Will Be In Disguise. Intrigued? Call Gillian…, 1994
Still from colour video for monitor with sound, 30 minutes

Ralph Eugene Meatyard
From the book *The Family Album of Lucybelle Crater*, 1970–2
Gelatin silver print
19.3 × 19.3 cm / 7½ × 7½ in

Lucybelle Crater and Gnomist Friend, from the book *The Family Album of Lucybelle Crater*, 1970–2
Gelatin silver print
19.3 × 19.3 cm / 7½ × 7½ in

Lucybelle Crater and close friend Lucybelle Crater in the grape arbor, from the book *The Family Album of Lucybelle Crater*, 1970–2
Gelatin silver print
19.3 × 19.3 cm / 7½ × 7½ in

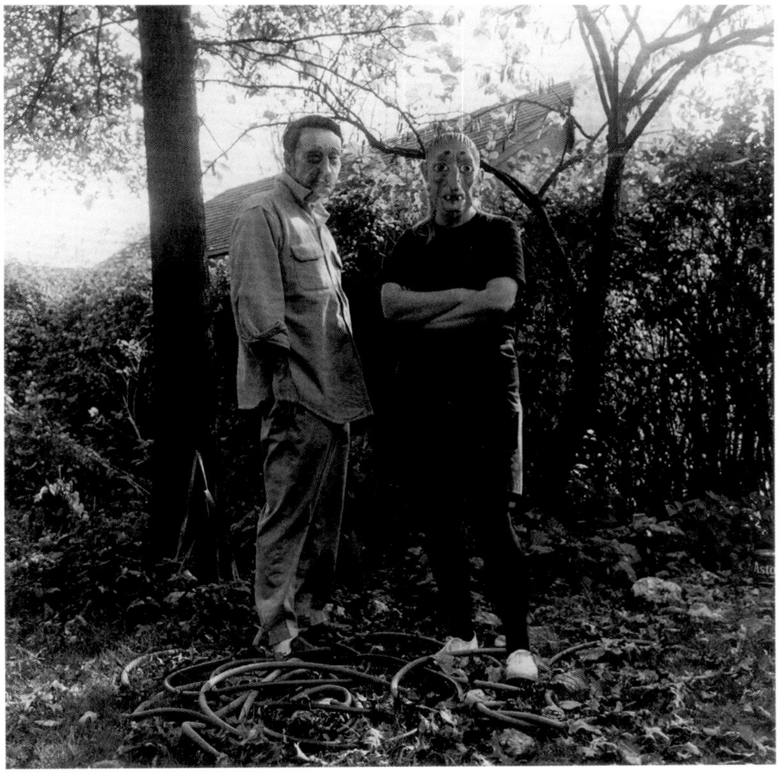

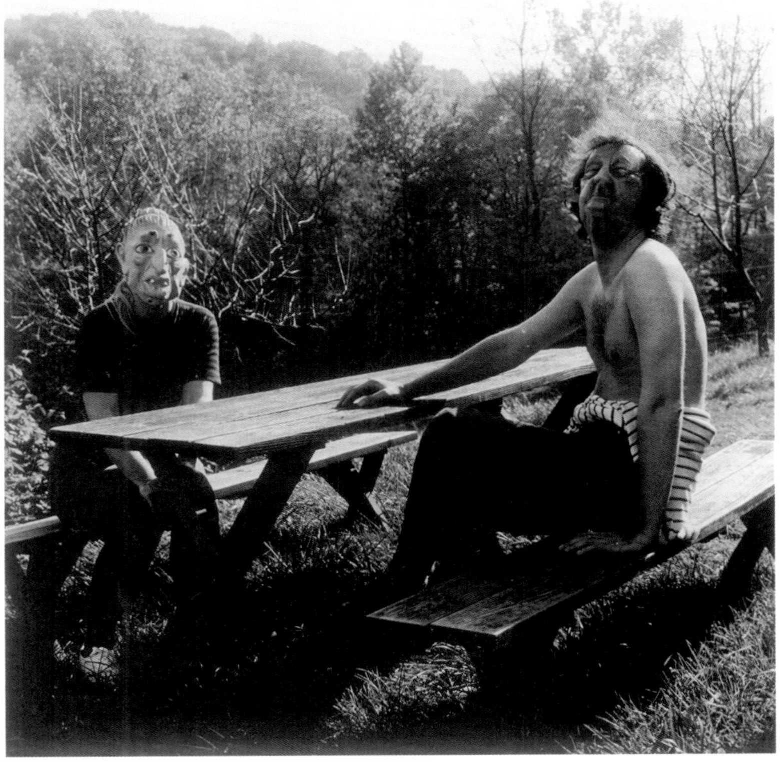

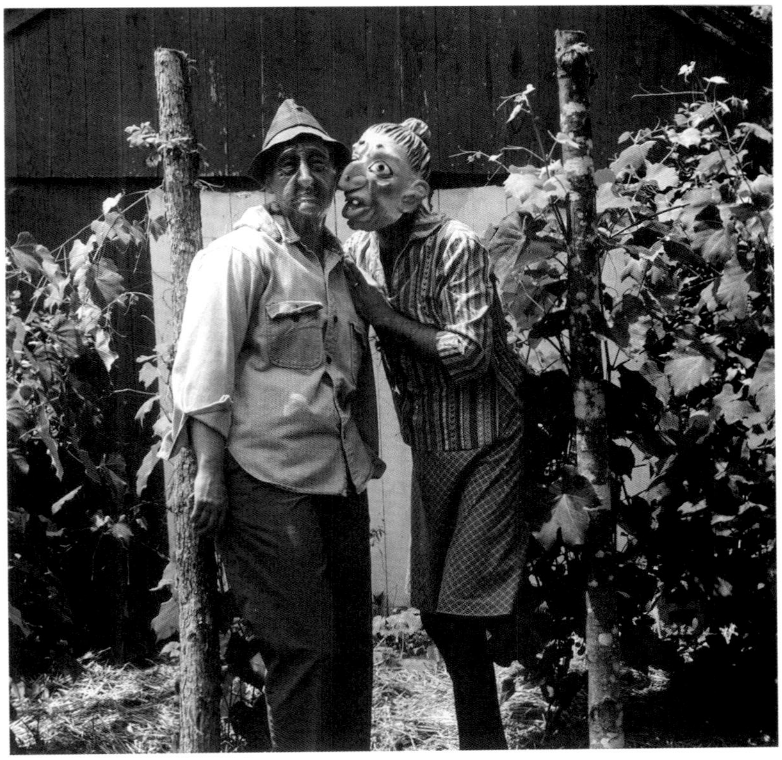

Seiichi Furuya

The Japanese-born but Austrian-based photographer Seiichi Furuya makes public his grief and love through books and exhibitions that present the mass of intimate portraits he took of his late wife, Christine Furuya-Gössler. He began taking photographs of her the day they met in 1978. In 1985, after several periods in hospital for depression, she committed suicide by jumping from the ninth floor of their apartment block in East Berlin. Furuya's portraits invite us into his personal tragedy to share his demand for some kind of disclosure and meaning from the photographic portrait. The pictures were, he says, 'compiled to record, in photographs, proof of the life Christine and I lived and at the same time they are filled with the wish that someday Komyo [their son] will read them. They were made with the idea that those things I cannot speak of, and those that Komyo does not want to know, must, unfailingly, be set down.'[9]

Furuya develops a metaphoric and poetic use of photography that engages powerfully with a sense of loss. It marks an unusually obsessive use of the photographic portrait, entangled in deep emotions. As writer Monika Faber has put it: 'Does the incomprehensible event lose something of its horror through the repeated attempt to come closer to it? Or must we fear the opposite: does the repeatedly encountered suffering become perpetuated rather than disappearing into the past, constantly revived instead of losing power?'[10]

The portraits continue after Christine's death with a photograph of her picture floating in the liquid of a developer tray. Like the beautiful and unusual close-up portrait of her in the bath, in which her face appears like a mask detached from the rest of her body which is submerged in the soapy water, this image points to a sense of fragility and impermanence, the tenuousness of our hold on others. Such portraits shift between a sense of Christine's presence and absence.

Furuya rarely photographed Christine in the last year of her life. The few photographs he has published are some of the most powerful and moving, providing a searing contrast with one of his first portraits of her in 1978, taken in his hometown of Nishi-Izu and redolent of joy, lightness and serenity. In one portrait of Christine from 1985, one gets a sense of intruding into something very private and intense. She looks straight into the camera and, from her watery eyes, it looks as if she has just been crying. The image is taken in red and ochre twilight in front of a copy of Jean-François's Millet's famous painting, *The Angelus*, its sunset scene adding to the charged atmosphere of Furuya's portrait. In another of the last images, Christine, her hair now shaved, is huddled up against an empty interior; beautifully lit, she is framed by a patch of natural daylight, her gaze uplifted, detached, elsewhere.

Seiichi Furuya
Izu, 1978
C-print, dimensions variable

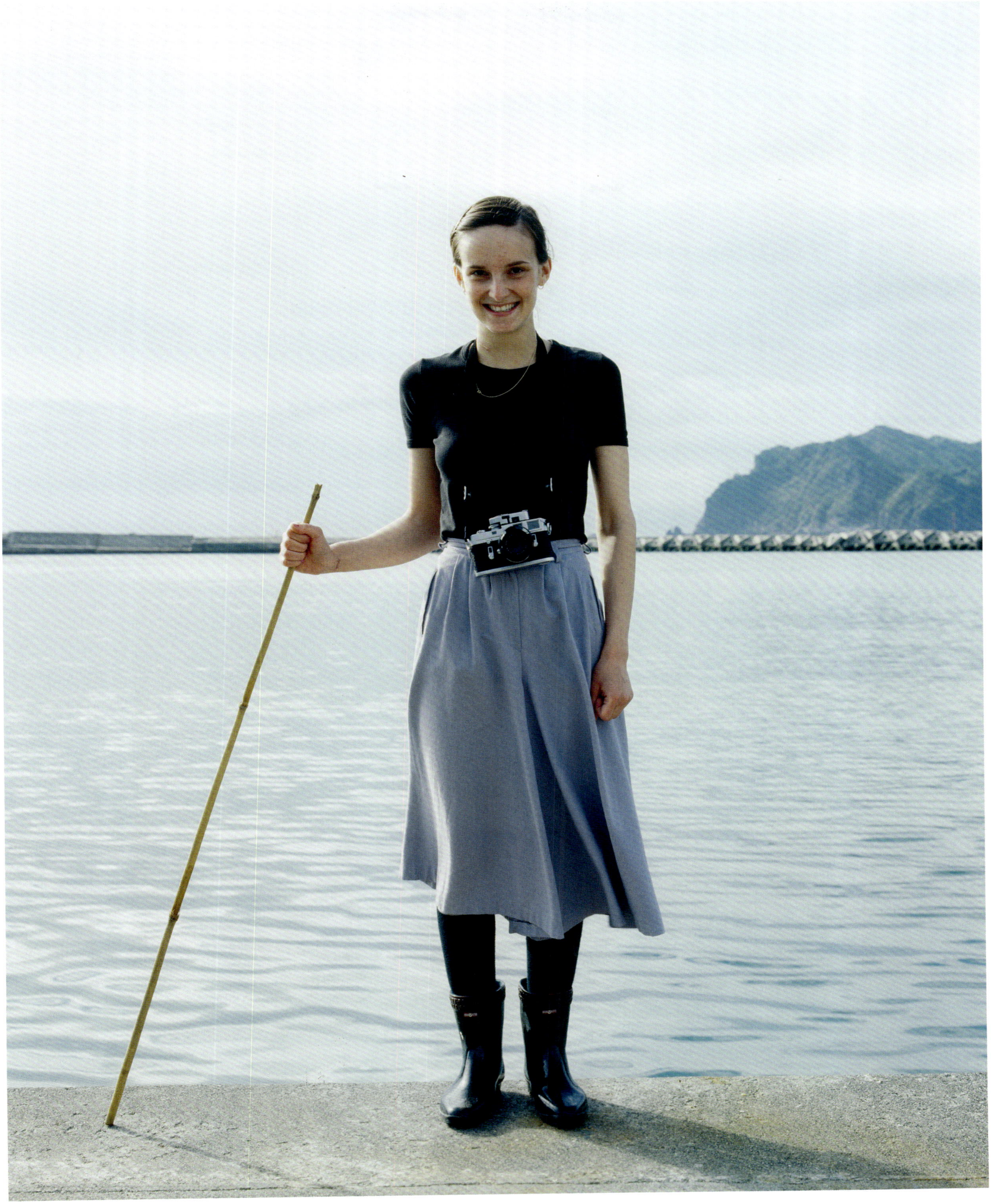

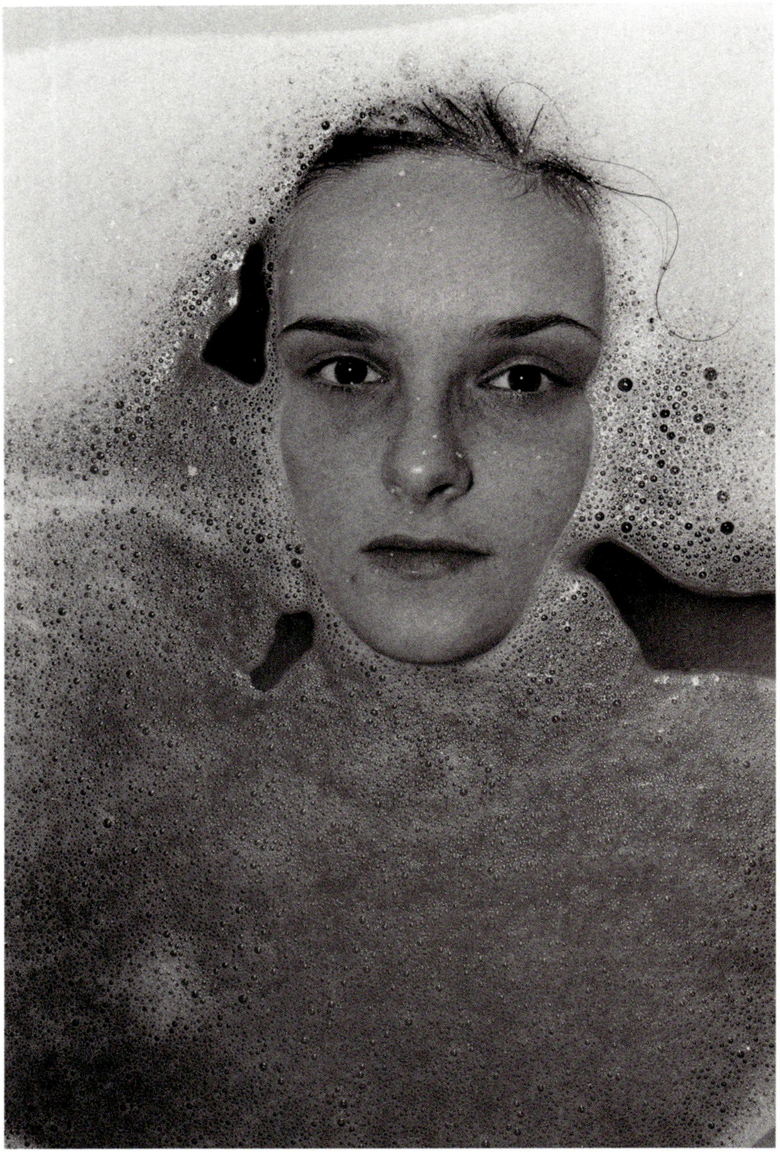

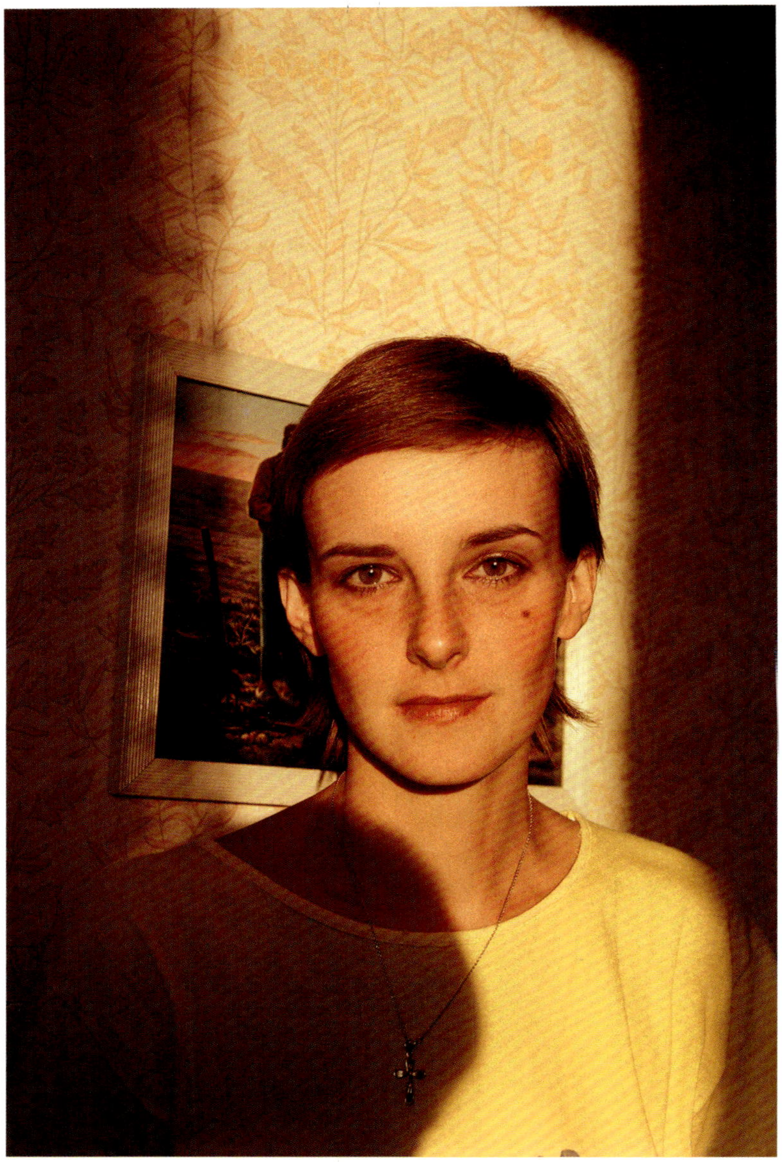

Seiichi Furuya
Graz, 1979
Gelatin silver print, dimensions variable

East Berlin, 1985
C-print, dimensions variable

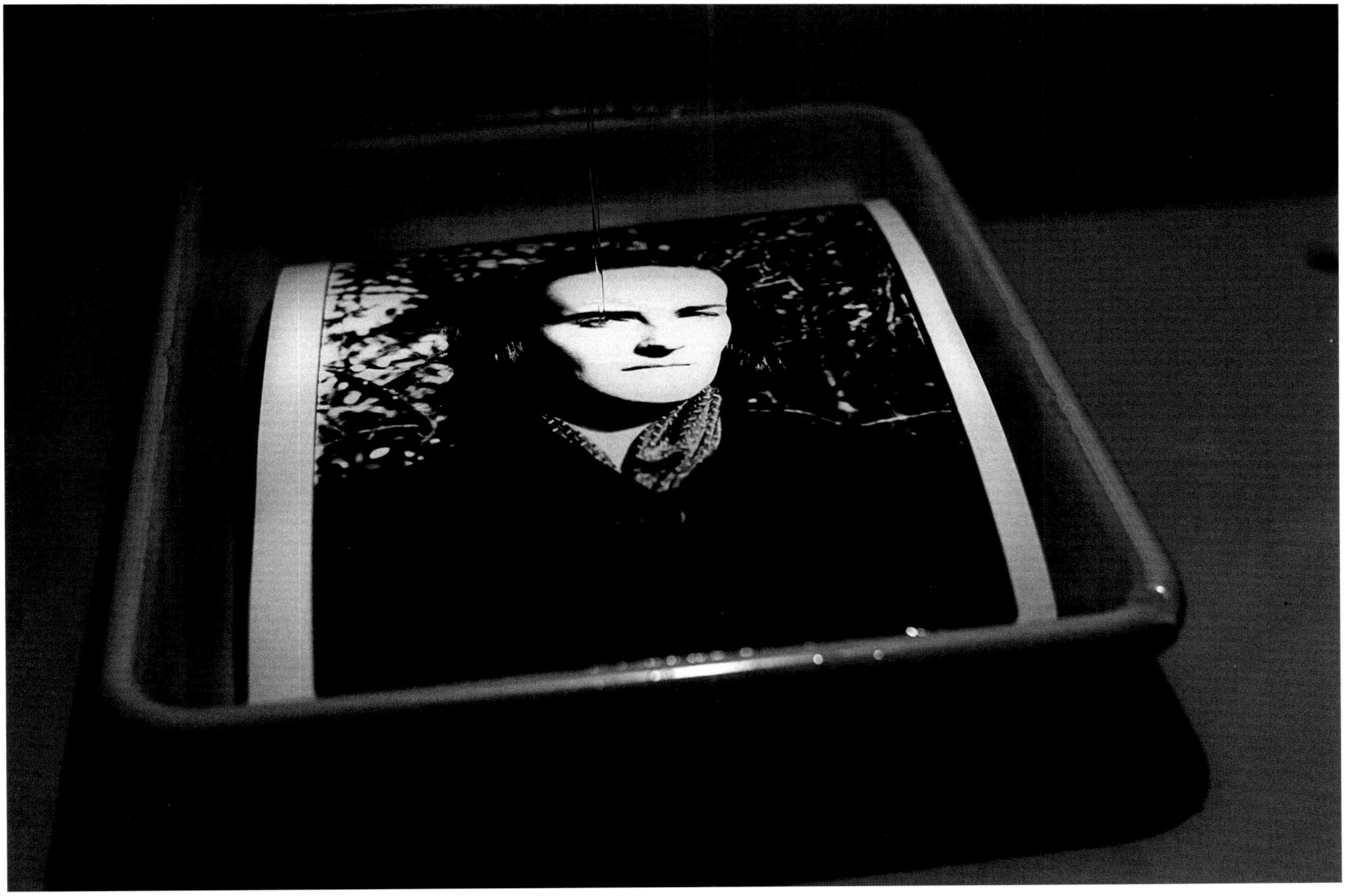

Graz, 1987
Gelatin silver print, dimensions variable

Nicholas Nixon

In terms of its intimacy and duration, Seiichi Furuya's project has revealing points of comparison with *The Brown Sisters* by the American photographer Nicholas Nixon who, every year since 1975, has taken a portrait of his wife and her three sisters. But Nixon's is a much less poetic and varied mode of portraiture than Furuya's. It is more analytic and systematic. The four women always pose in the same order. In their seriality the pictures echo the structure of minimalist art, and establish a tension between the discipline of their form and the subjective and intimate nature of their content. *The Brown Sisters* offers an interesting variant on family photography and at the same time highlights the pathos integral to the photographic medium, a pathos here made vivid through the women's ageing. It illustrates the characteristic of photography to highlight temporal melt as well as to show genealogical ties. Here technical precision – using a large-format 10x8 inch camera and contact printing from the negatives – allows for the revelation of details not always desired in portraiture and maintains a formal distinction between the camera's cold scrutinizing record and the familial intimacy that underlies the pictures' production. The photographs say little about the specific details of these women's lives, but instead turns them into abstract symbols for everyone's irrevocable mortality. Nixon's portraits of people dying of AIDS provide an awkward parallel to the project. He presents an extended series of portraits of individuals succumbing to the illness, detailing its harrowing progression right up until moments before death. While attempts at intimacy and closeness – Peter Galassi refers to the pictures' 'untimid tenderness' – countered much of the abusive media stereotyping of people with AIDS, Nixon's reduction of the subjects to pitiable 'victims' and the ready equation of people with AIDS with death invited much criticism.[11]

Nicholas Nixon
Tom Moran, Boston, January, 1988
Gelatin silver contact print
20.3 × 25.4 cm / 8 × 10 in

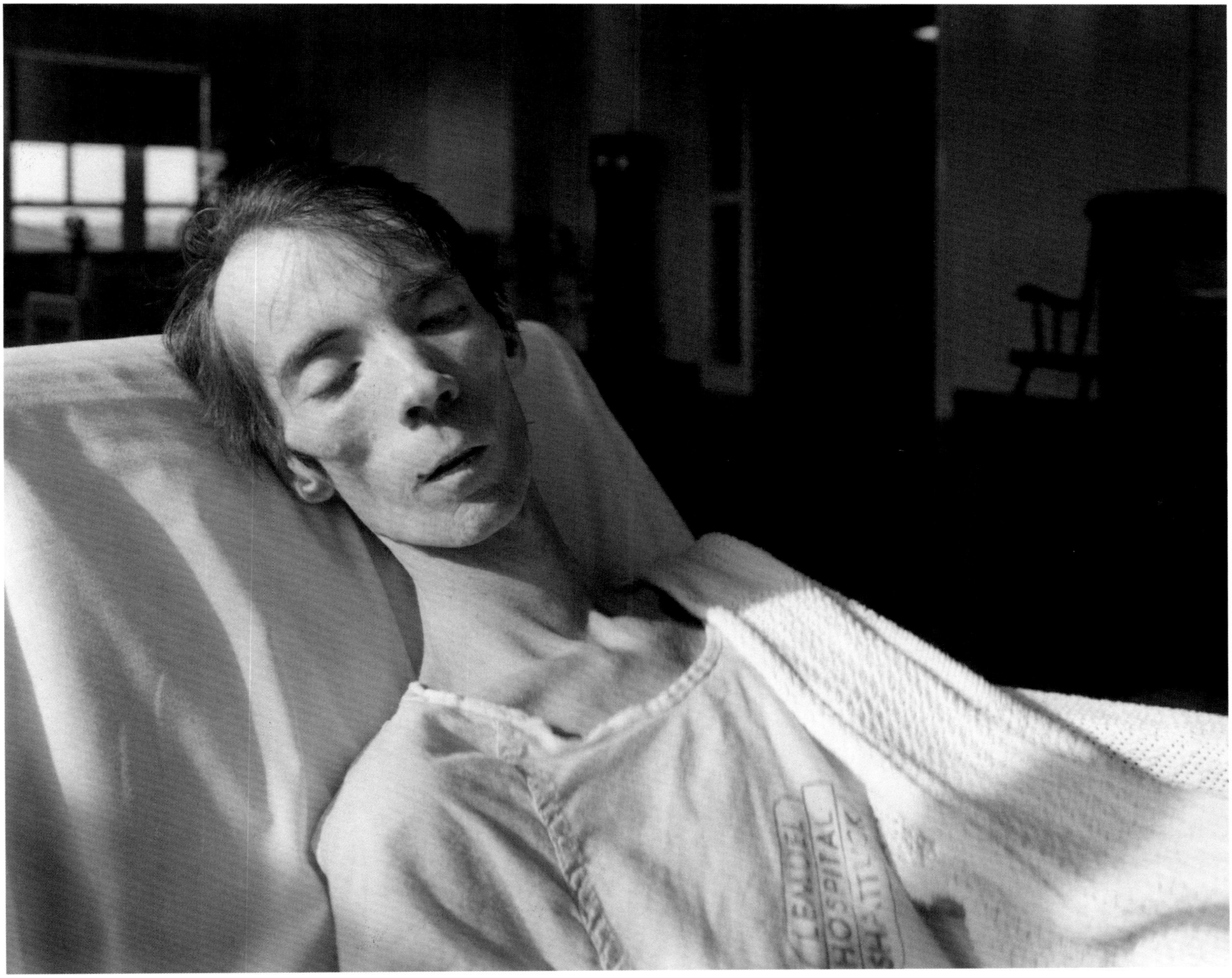
HOSPITAL

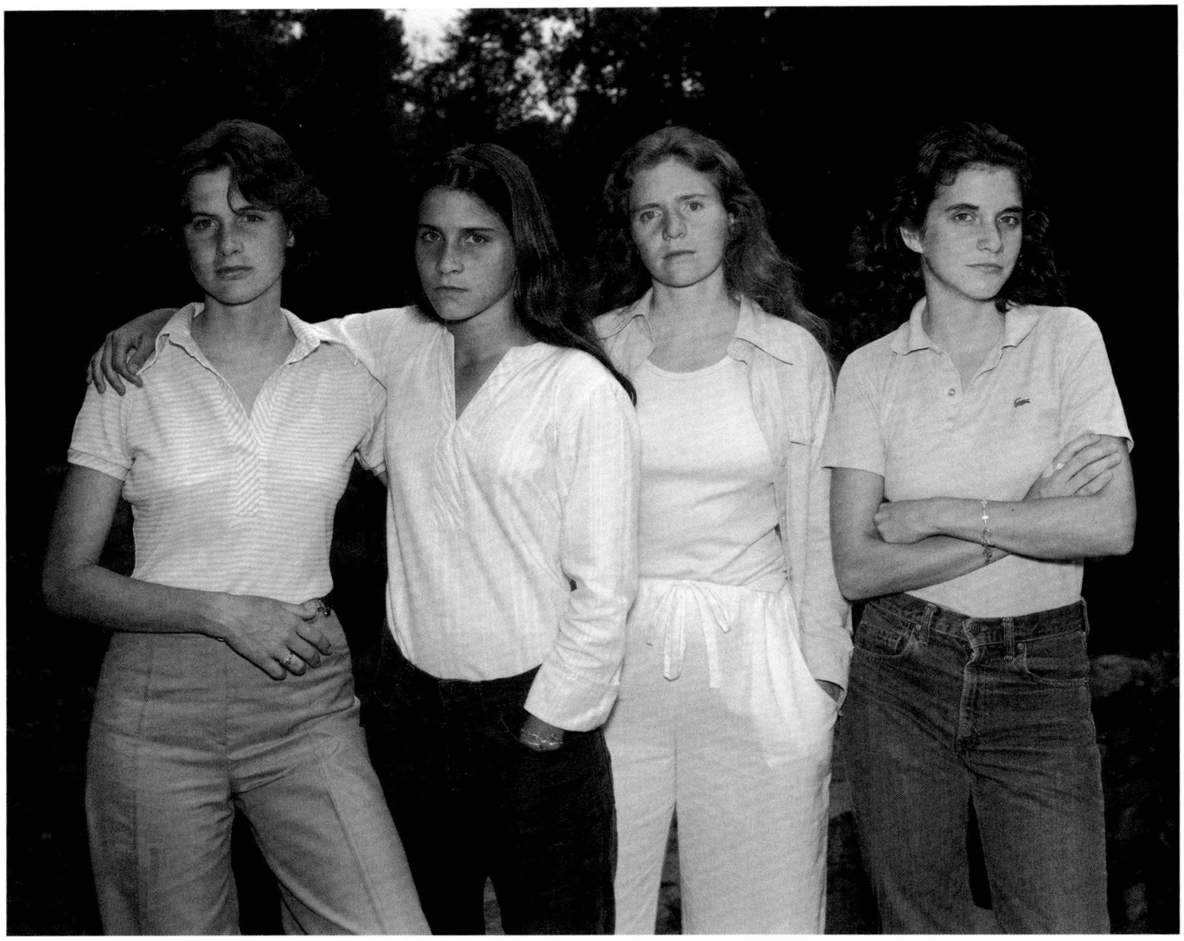

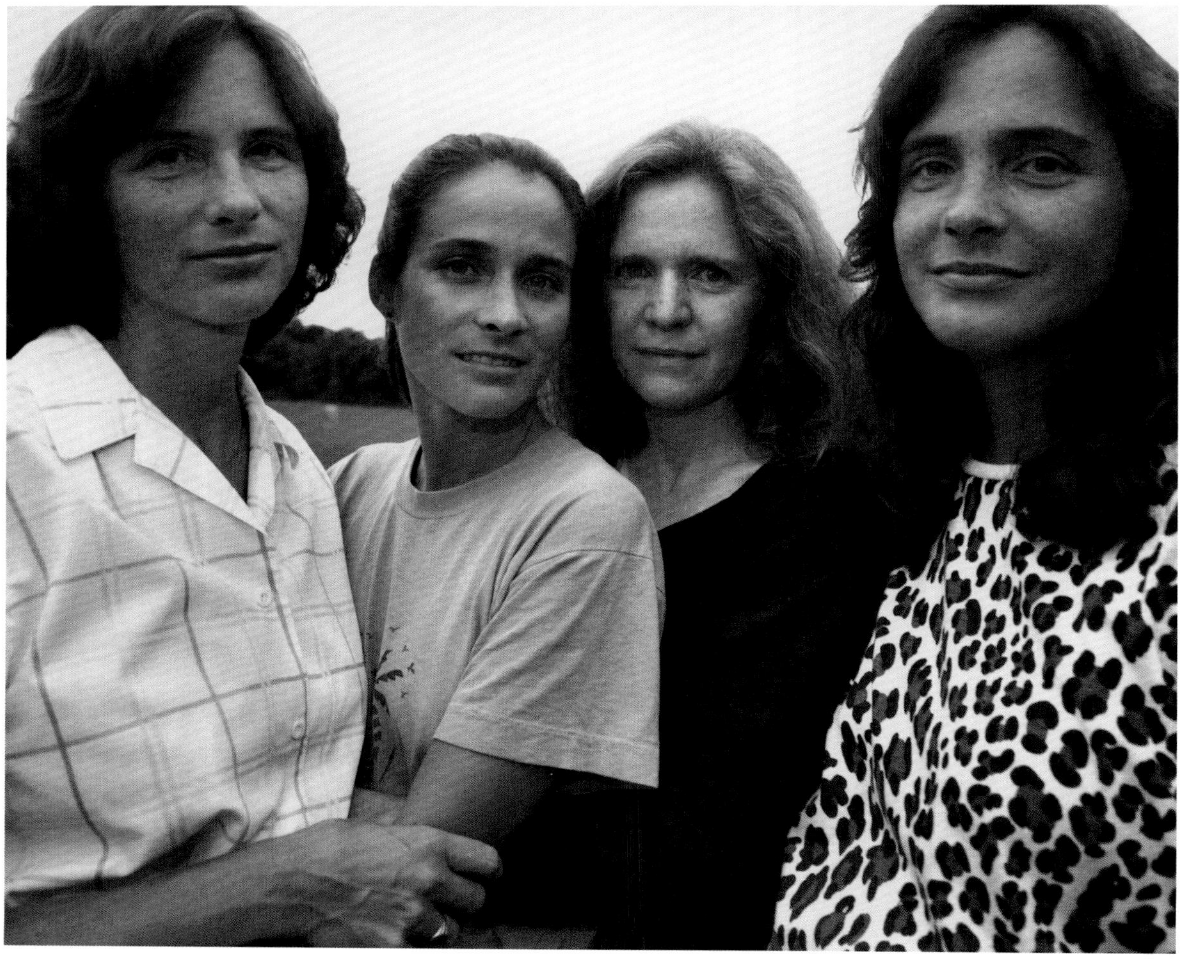

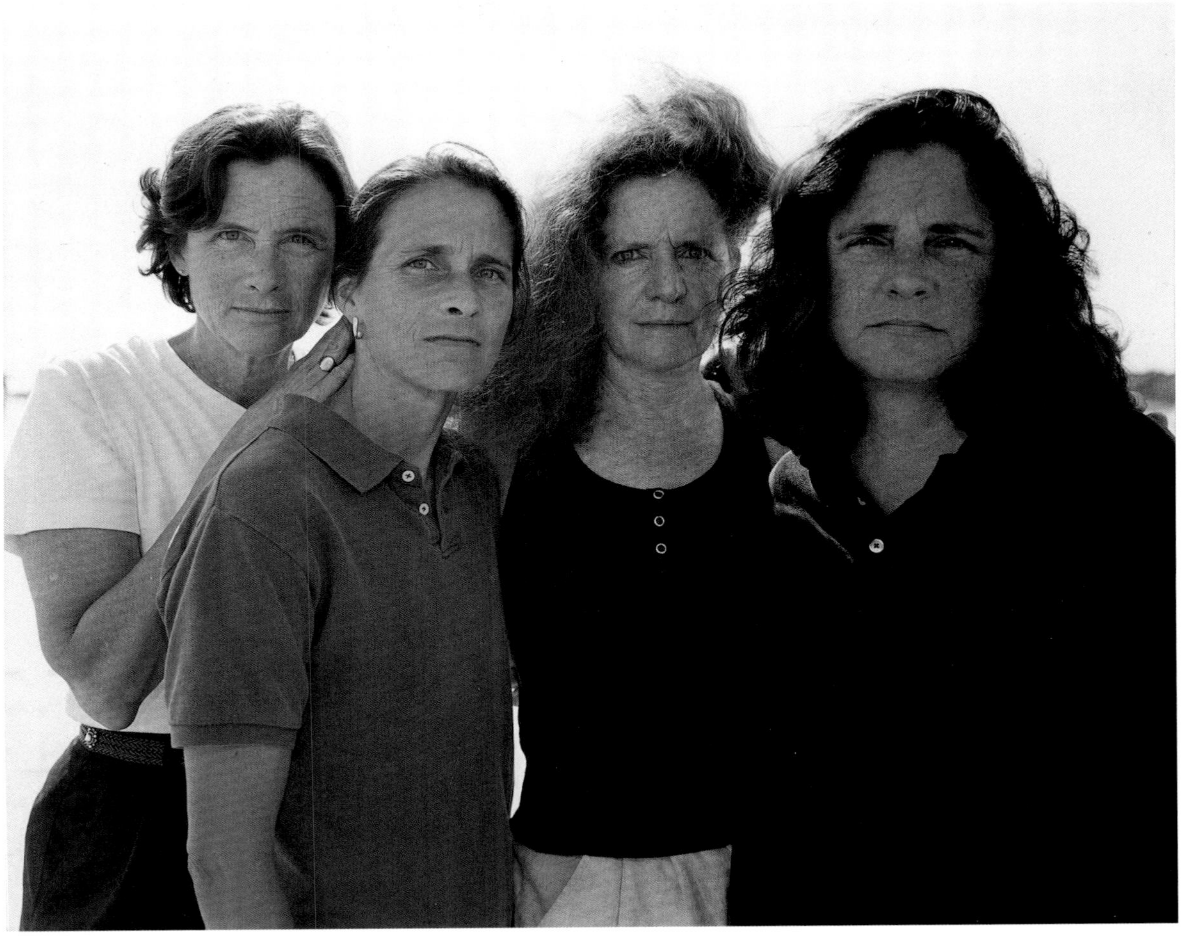

Nicholas Nixon
The Brown Sisters, New Canaan, Connecticut, 1975
Gelatin silver print
19.5 × 24.5 cm / 7¾ × 9¾ in

The Brown Sisters, Wellesley, Massachusetts, 1988
Gelatin silver print
19.5 × 24.5 cm / 7¾ × 9¾ in

The Brown Sisters, Ipswich Massachusetts, 2003
Gelatin silver print
19.5 × 24.5 cm / 7¾ × 9¾ in

Sarah Jones

Sarah Jones both makes explicit the psychological dimensions and demands of portrait photography and dismantles them in her 'Consulting Room' series, which began in 1995. While these images might seem to sit rather awkwardly in relation to the conventions of portrait photography, the insistence on something beyond photography, the energy and residue of the charged and emotive encounters which take place in these spaces, is integral to their meaning. One can also approach such work in reaction to the abstract use of psychoanalytical theory in photography and film discourses during the 1980s. Jones's photographs reflect a fixation with the literal working space of the psychiatrist. Décor and details become significant as a sense of trauma and neurosis tends to be associated with the disruptive expressive details of the creases on the couches or the dark expanses beneath them. There is a haunted and charged quality to the pictures that is also present in the unease and disquiet that disrupts the social and economic order in her portraits of teenage girls in upper middle-class homes, *Francis Place* and *Mulberry Lodge* (1997–9). The psychological intensity of such work is created through the tensions set up between the figures and their settings. The antique objects, furniture and decoration in many of the interiors serve as overbearing signs of an imperial and patriarchal order which, coupled with the rigorous formality of many of Jones's compositions, serves to oppress and constrain the young girls. The girls' gestures are not about play or cohesion but express a social distance, a disengagement from one another and from us. The girls remain aloof, introspective and moody. They might be reflected in the polished dining room tables, but the environment is ultimately oppressive and alien to them. Objects also begin to carry a potential dual function, serving not just as signs of bourgeois opulence and class privilege but also as symbols we start to link with the teenagers' emotional states: the lidded tureen that features in some of the images, for example, seems to hold a mystery, linking it with the secrets of the introspective girls posed around it.

Sarah Jones
Consulting Room (Couch) (X), 1997
C-print on aluminium
150 × 150 cm / 59 × 59 in

Dining Room (Francis Place) (II), 1997
C-print on aluminium
150 × 150 cm / 59 × 59 in

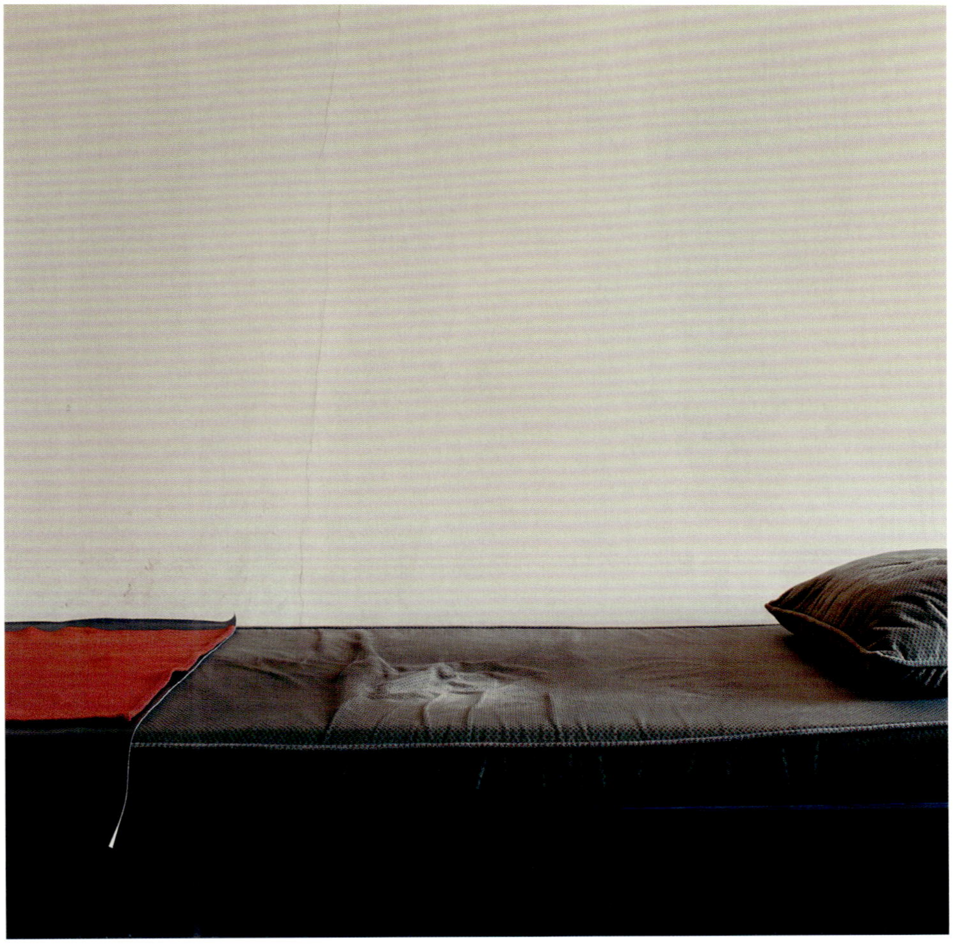

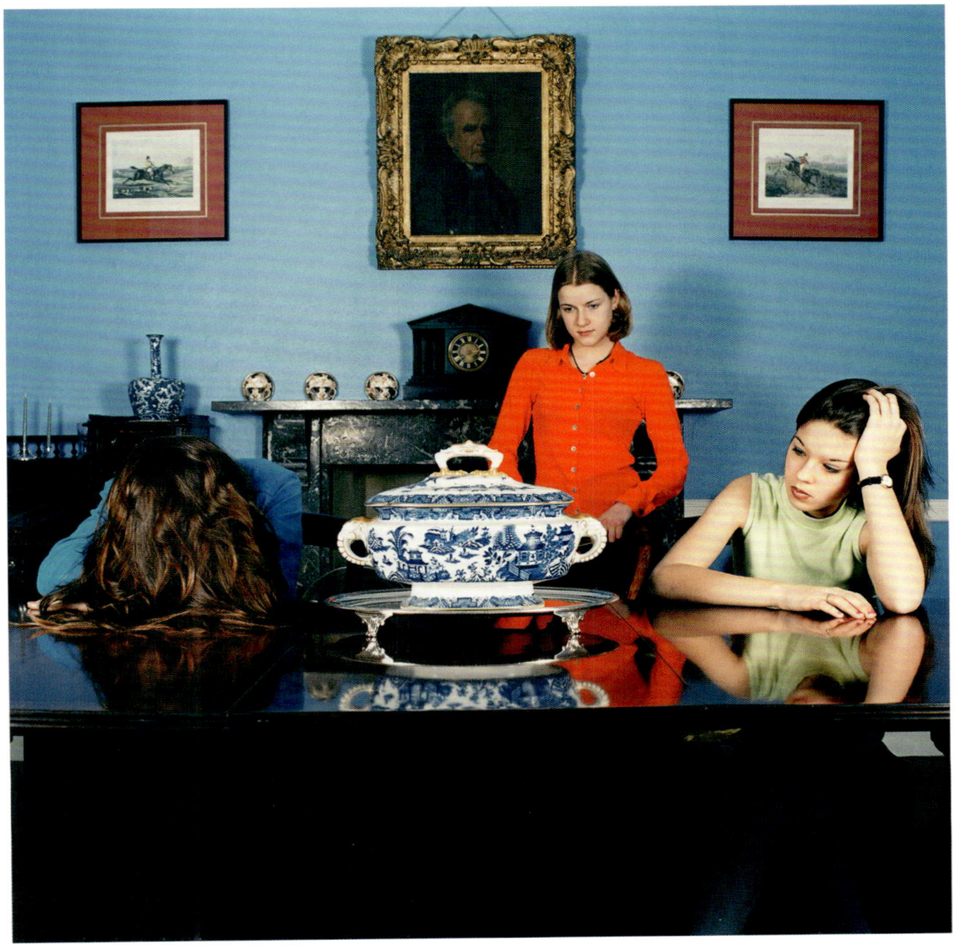

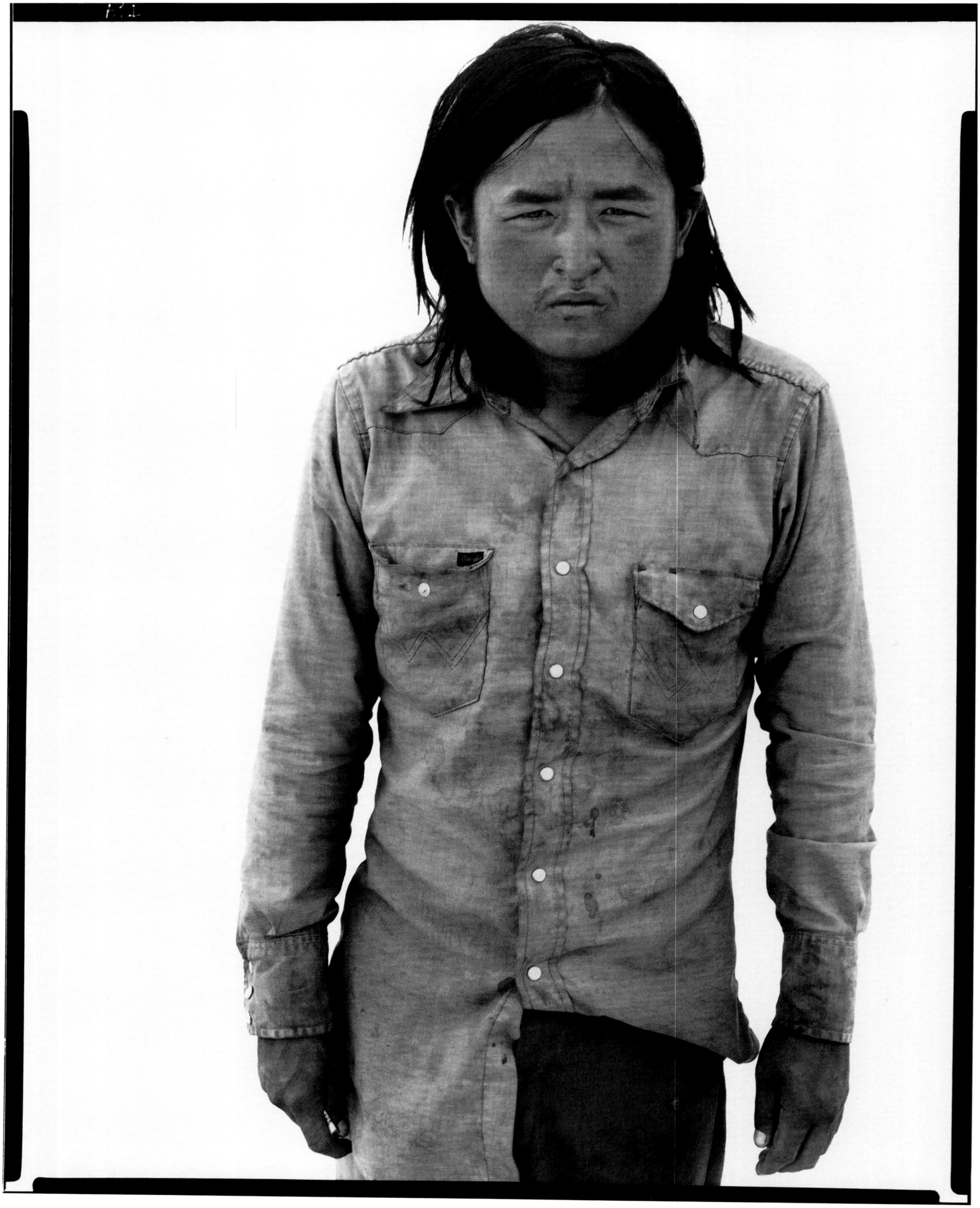

Monumental Portraits

Richard Avedon

Richard Avedon's monumental portraits 'In the American West' (1979–85) extend the qualities of harshness found in some of the photographs of Diane Arbus. In these pictures we have a rugged and romantic portrait of the labouring and unemployed classes of America: drifters, factory workers, meat packers, prisoners, ranch hands, waitresses, the mentally ill. Avedon said he chose 'men and women who work at hard, uncelebrated jobs.'[12] All of his subjects are set against a blank white backdrop, associated with studio photography, and photographed in the shade of natural sunlight. But it is hard to see the process as in any way dignifying or elevating those depicted. Instead, 'In the American West's' unglamorous parade of the socially disadvantaged and marginalized is very much the antithesis of Avedon's fashion work. The photographer not only isolates his subjects from their contexts, but also plays with asymmetrical compositions within the picture plane. His subjects are decentred or misaligned in the frame, and this serves further to highlight the awkwardness of many of their stances and gestures.

The subjects are made to seem as if they don't quite fit within the frame. And although they face the camera, many are shown squinting and seem uncertain or uneasy about being photographed. In this way the conventions of a dignifying portrait tradition are taken apart and we are invited to muse over these people as fascinating fields of texture, expensive and lavish blow-ups of an underclass that provide a collective portrait of a blighted and damaged American West. Studies of slaughtered sheep and steer underscore the visceral, physical accent of the portraits and the sense of a raw exposure of a harsh reality. In some of the most memorable pictures, the faces and limbs of slaughterhouse workers, miners or oil-field workers bear the gypsum, coal, blood, oil and grease of their labour. They are so wedded to the land and its resources that they carry traces of their environment into the studio-like setting of their portraits.

Avedon can be seen as representing an approach to portraiture that disfigures the genre's more dignifying and traditional conventions. Like much of the work discussed so far, Avedon's pictures mark a point of extremity, a hyperbolic, self-conscious use of the portrait convention.

Richard Avedon
Benson James, drifter, Route 66, Gallup, New Mexico, June 30, 1979, 1979
Gelatin silver print
127.3 × 99.7 cm / 50⅛ × 39¼ in

Thomas Struth

Thomas Struth's ongoing project of large-scale family portraits is unusual in its seeming revival of the possibility of a dignifying portrait tradition. The subjects are mostly friends and acquaintances of the artist, and his portraits often involve long relationships with the sitters. The portraits are formal, characterized by a controlled frontality in the sitters' bodies and faces. The photographs' intensity reflects the ritualized nature of their production: people are lifted out of their day-to-day existence for the formal ceremonial portrait. Picturing families of differing nationalities but from predominantly first-world economic positions – a family in Lima is the notable exception – Struth resurrects the ideal of a benign and civil bourgeois portraiture. The scale and detail of the large-format works allows us to see each sitter's face, a scrutiny uniquely facilitated by the medium. Because we are so habituated to the smiling faces of commercial photography, these faces might strike us as initially inexpressive or deadpan, but the series is full of energies connected with the various attachments and identifications that bind the different family groups. They possess a latent expressivity.

Thomas Ruff

Thomas Ruff has said how, 'Photography can only depict the surface of things.'[13] His 'Portraits' (1980–90) reduce and minimize the humanist and affective qualities of portraiture. Choosing sitters through similarity of age, Ruff has them all adopt a uniform frontal pose when facing the camera. Such formality and in-expressivity means that there is little psychological depth to these portraits. Blown-up to larger than life size, the clarity of details such as the textures and imperfections of the skin absorbs the viewer. As a result, the portraits lose specificity and the human dimension, and become instead blank icons. All Ruff's sitters are successful at masking themselves through the formal pose. That he photographs youthful fresh faces also means they are relatively bereft of the character of older subjects. Nevertheless Ruff sees the portraits as carrying a political meaning. He described how they were made 'in the years leading up to 1984, in the vague expectancy of the coming of Big Brother and the form it would take. We in Germany had had the R.A.F.[the militant Red Army Faction group] and all the hysteria and the control that went with it. So the portraits are like "vis-à-vis". He's looking at us, and we are trying to look back. And if we show no movement, no emotion, maybe he can ignore us.'[14] Such allusions were further highlighted in another series, 'Other Portraits' (1994–5), when Ruff used outdated techniques of police photography to make composite portraits. Such work is to be read in relation to a specific institutional portraiture. Exchanges of power within the photographic portrait, highlighted in the tradition of the criminalmugshot, shadows our viewing of Ruff's portraits.

Thomas Ruff
Porträt (O. Cieslik), 1990
from the series 'Portraits'
C-print
210 × 165 cm / 82¾ × 65 in

Thomas Struth
Untitled, (New York Family 1), New York
2001
C-print
115.3 × 146 cm / 45¾ × 57½ in

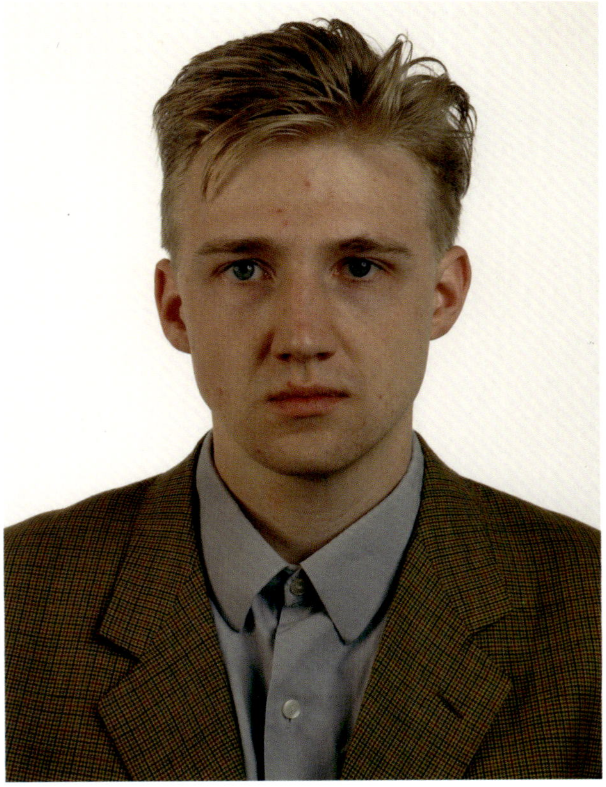

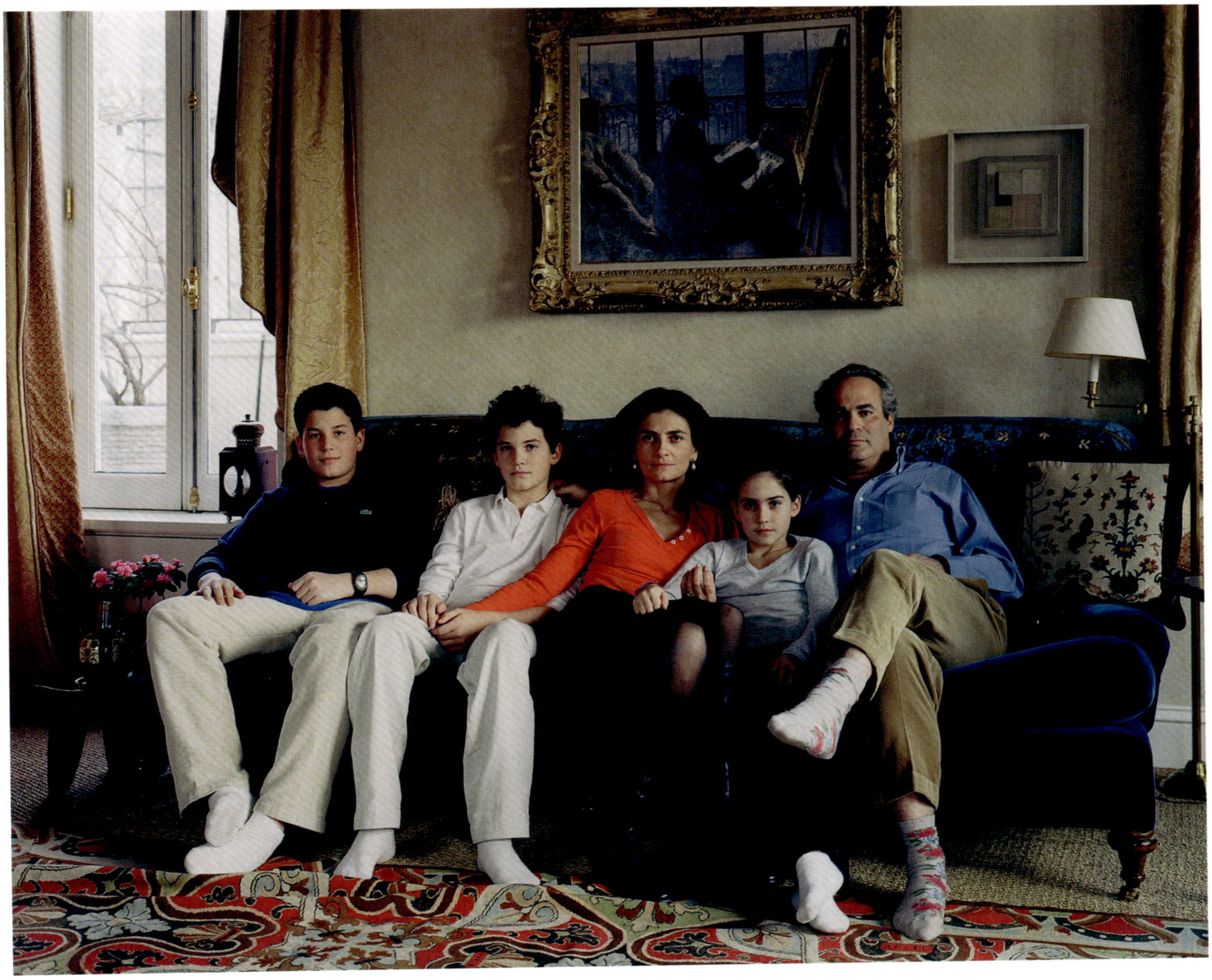

Anna Fox

For the British photographer Anna Fox, portraiture is a theatrical event. Her 'Zwarte Piet' portraits (1993–8) draw upon a Dutch Christmas tradition in which people have their faces blacked up, dress in clown costumes and give out sweets to children. In Fox's portraits, the dark backgrounds and white collars of the costumes recall Dutch portraiture of the seventeenth century. The cultural and traditional weight of such portraiture collides with the crude racism underpinning the more invidious *Zwarte Piet* tradition and all the issues and anxieties associated with its preservation in the present day. Some of the most interesting portraits make us aware of the tawdriness of this theatre: the make-up is poorly applied, the collars are torn, shabby and stained, and one begins to think about the person behind the racist mask.

Andres Serrano

Andres Serrano's portraits of members of the Ku Klux Klan, 'The Klan' (1990) deliberately confronts the racial and cultural divide between him and his subjects; he was born in New York to a Cuban-born mother and Honduran father. The pictures are disquieting in that they not only appear non-judgmental but actually seem to glamourize the subjects. The members of the group only agreed to be photographed if they were portrayed in a positive light. Hidden behind their hoods, they remain anonymous and faceless, representative of racial hatred and extreme prejudice. But if these images might initially be seen as 'recruitment posters for the Klan',[15] the way a number highlight the bad stitching of the homemade outfits pulls against the symbolism and grandeur. Such a marker of poverty also gives a class inflection to the portraits and makes one think about the vulnerability of the poorest members of society to extremist ideology.

Anna Fox
Zwarte Piet 14, 1999
Matt light jet print archival
73.6 × 73.6 cm / 29 × 29 in

Andres Serrano
Klan (Imperial Wizard III), 1990
Cibachrome, plexiglass mounted
127 × 152.4 cm / 50 × 60 in

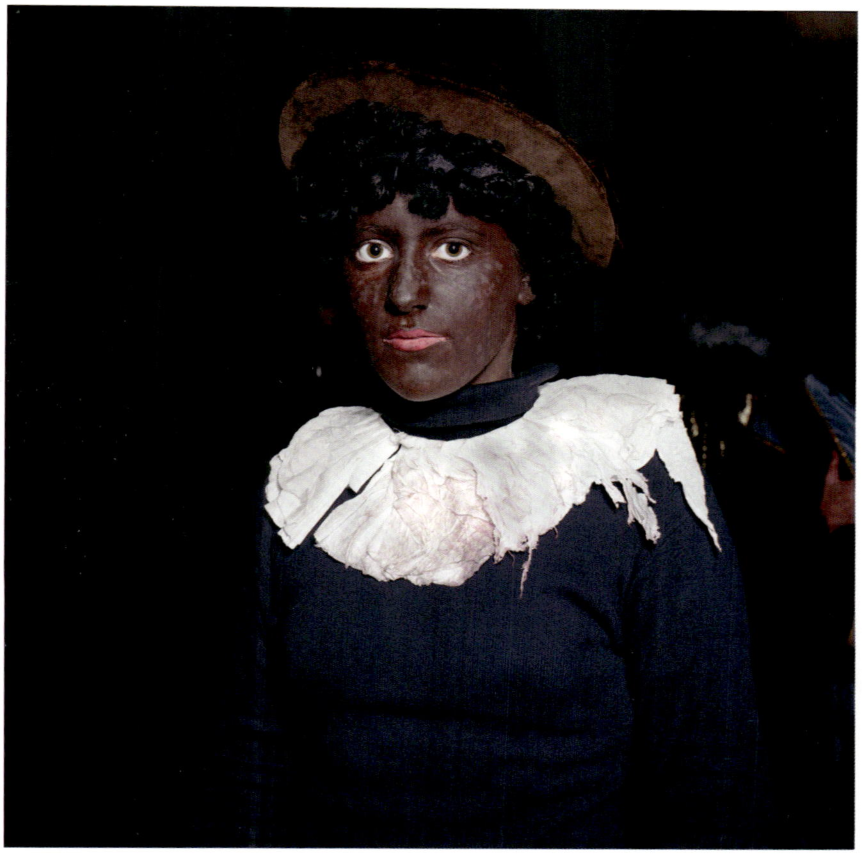

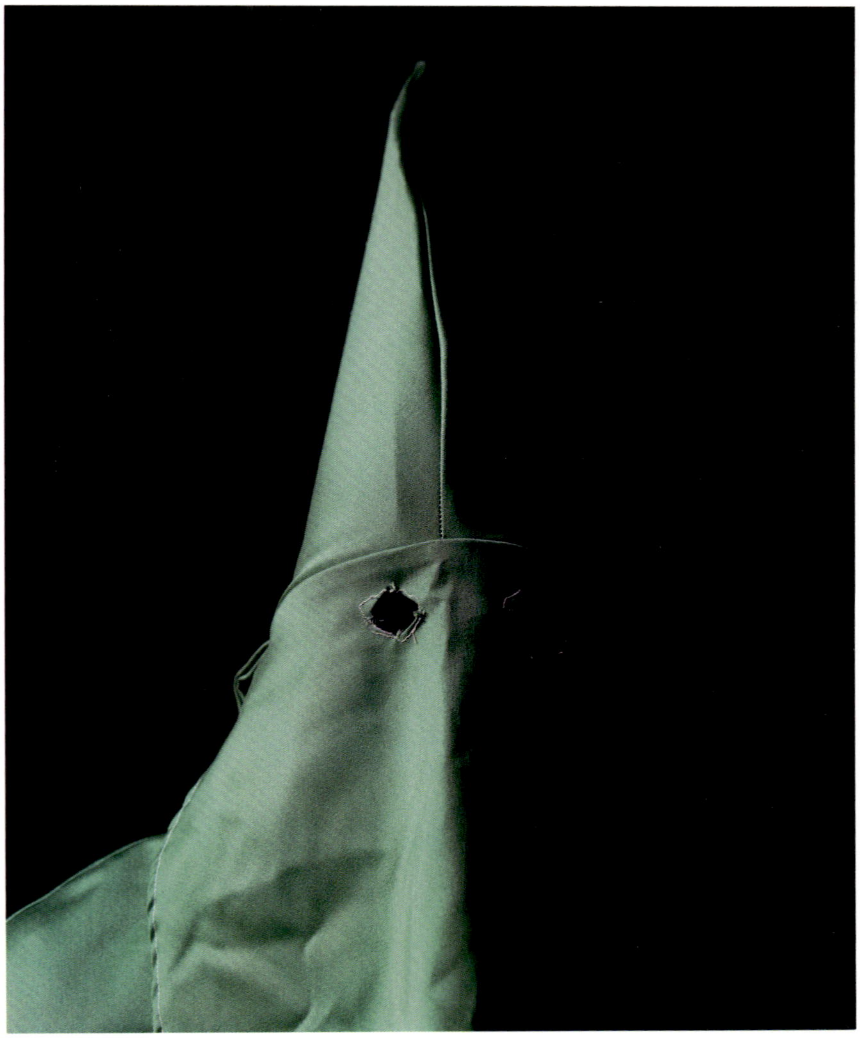

Ad van Denderen

In 2005 an issue of the European journal *Useful Photography #004* presented a disturbing series of photographs by the Dutch photojournalist, Ad van Denderen, taken in the West Bank. Turning away from the usual newsworthy scenes, Denderen photographs the posters made by Palestinian activists and glued onto buildings and walls. For the Palestinians such posters represent heroic memorial portraits of the martyred dead: suicide bombers, militants, intifada fighters and bystanders killed in the conflict with Israel. Cheaply produced and printed, they would last for several weeks until covered with new posters or were ripped down by young Palestinians with an Israeli gun in their back. The iconography is intriguing, on the one hand offering us a glimpse into a mode of portraiture that is not intended for the West, and which very much contradicts media representations of the terrorist, but on the other hand showing how the Arabic slogans and Islamic iconography are mixed up with Western imagery. Some images have the look of Hollywood movie posters, as the sitters' machismo, gun-toting poses mimic the appearance of such stars as Stallone or Schwarzenegger.
In contrast, the more weathered and bleached posters underscore their role as memorials in their resemblance of Roman funerary portraits. The overriding impact is a sense of the youthfulness and the humanness of these subjects, women as well as men, framed by the symbols and slogans of the ideology that fed their defiance, hatred and desire for martyrdom.

Fazal Sheikh

The American Fazal Sheikh's portraits use a formal and dignifying tradition to challenge the social inequities embedded in the anthropological and photojournalist representations of non-Western cultures and communities. Sheikh provides a compassionate portrayal of refugees driven from their homelands by civil wars, drought and famine. Sheikh was born in New York to a father who was born in Kenya; his grandfather was born in a part of India that is now Pakistan. Part of Sheikh's work explores his ancestral history, so he is not completely detached from the lands and people he photographs. He spends time living with the people he photographs and his portraits are often presented alongside texts that explain the political situation depicted and occasionally include testaments by the individuals he pictures. Sheikh's work functions to counter the brutal and sensational way suffering is represented in mainstream agency photographs. His *A Sense of Common Ground* (1996), for example, portrays the elders and residents of the refugee communities in north-eastern Kenya in a series of beautiful and elegant Polaroid formal portraits, group and individual, of displaced peoples from Sudan, Ethiopia, Somalia, Mozambique and Rwanda. In *The Victor Weeps* (1998) Sheikh returns to the land of his grandfather, making respectful and contemplative portraits of people displaced from their homeland on the border between northern Pakistan and Afghanistan. Sheikh also pictures hands holding tiny portraits of lost loved ones, offering the viewer a cherishing of pictures that is integral to his own tender portrayal of his subjects.

Ad van Denderen
From 'See you in Paradise', *Kayed Khalil, Nablus, West Bank*, 2002
C-print
120 × 170 cm / 47¼ × 67 in

From 'See you in Paradise', *Ramallah, West Bank*, 2002
C-print
120 × 170 cm / 47¼ × 67 in

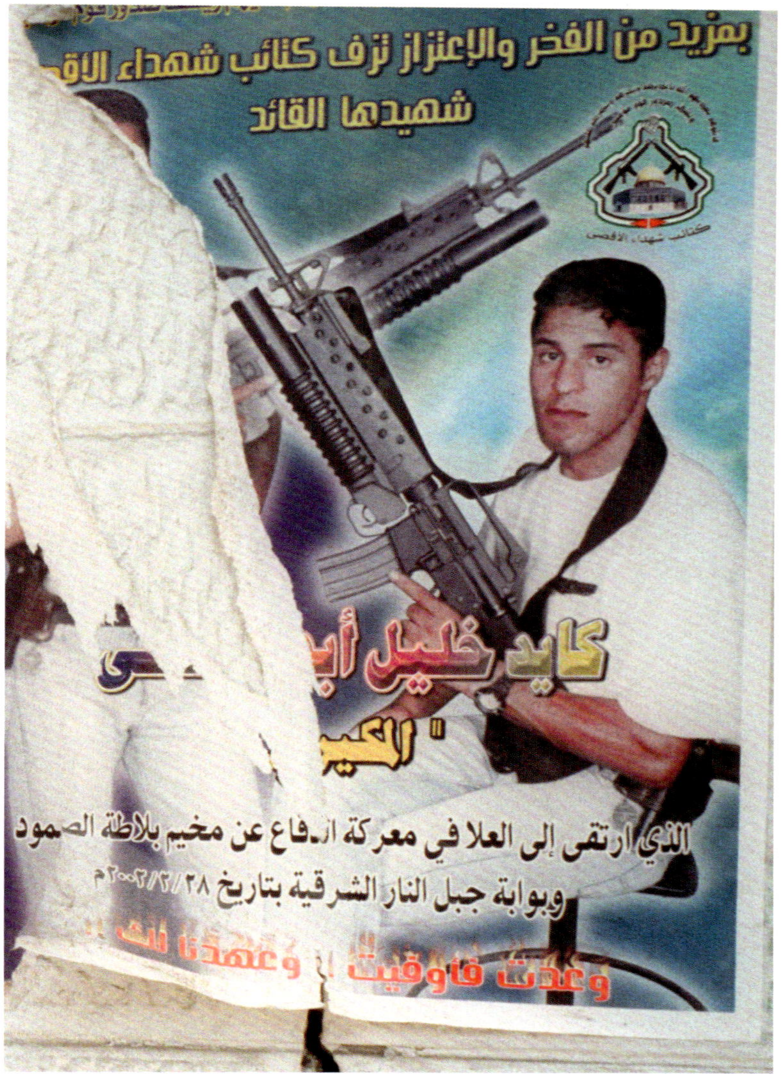
بمزيد من الفخر والإعتزاز تزف كتائب شهداء
شهيدها القائد
وبوابة جبل النار الشرقية بتاريخ ٢٨/٢/٢٠٠٢م

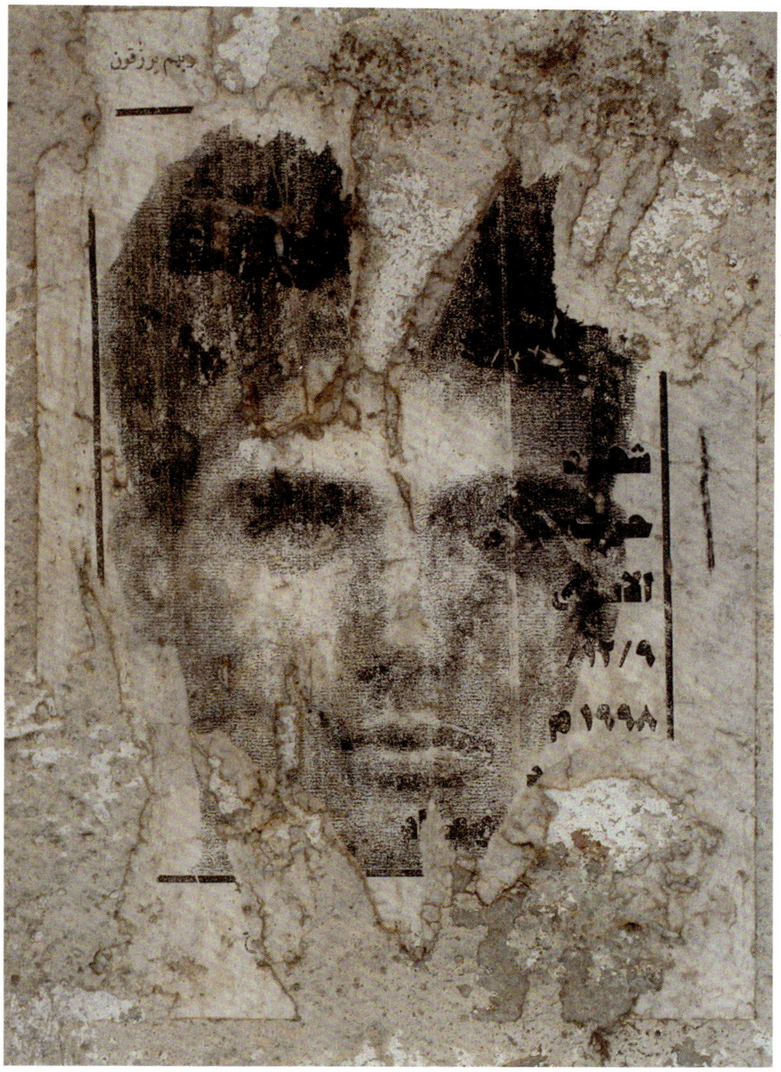
١٩٩٨م

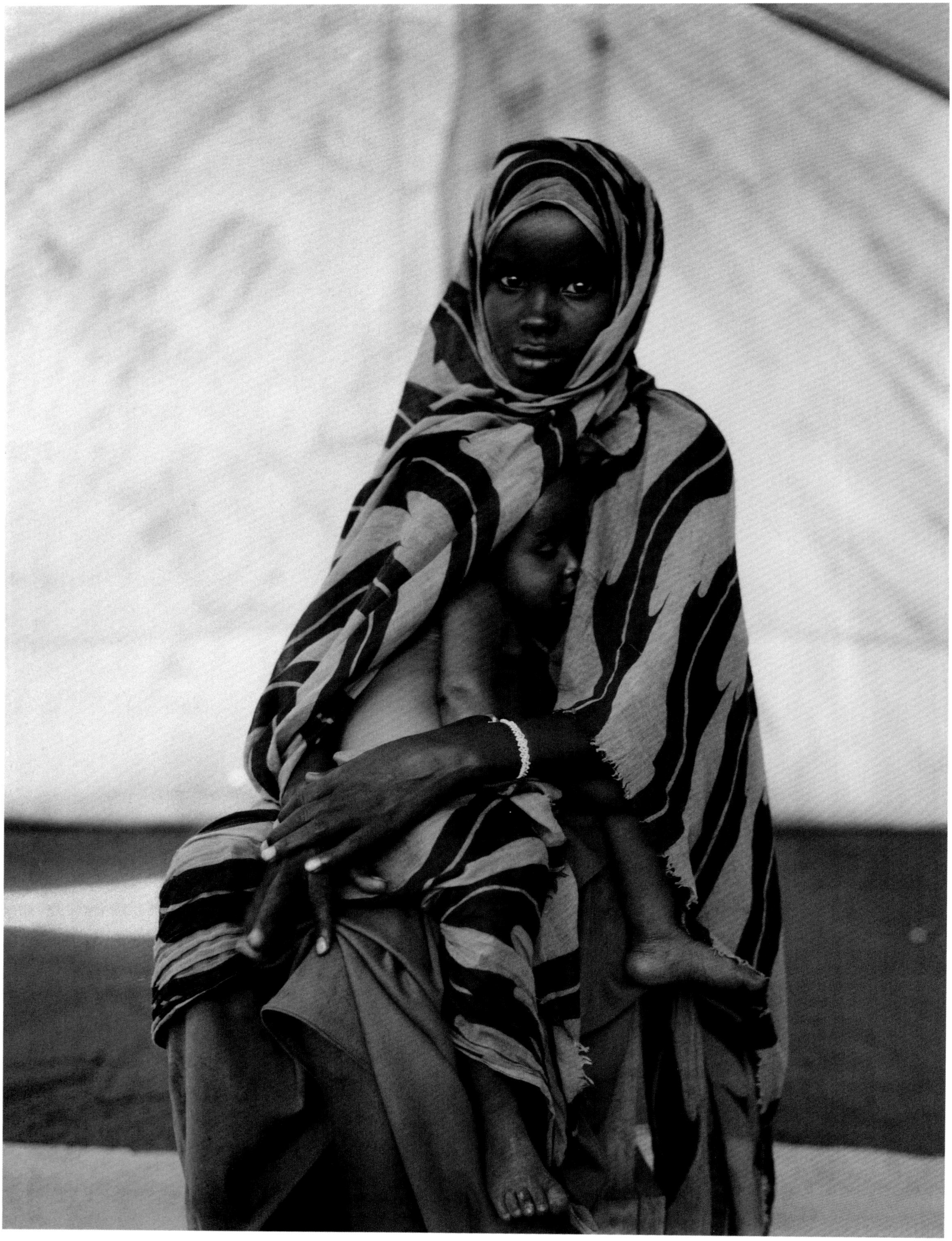

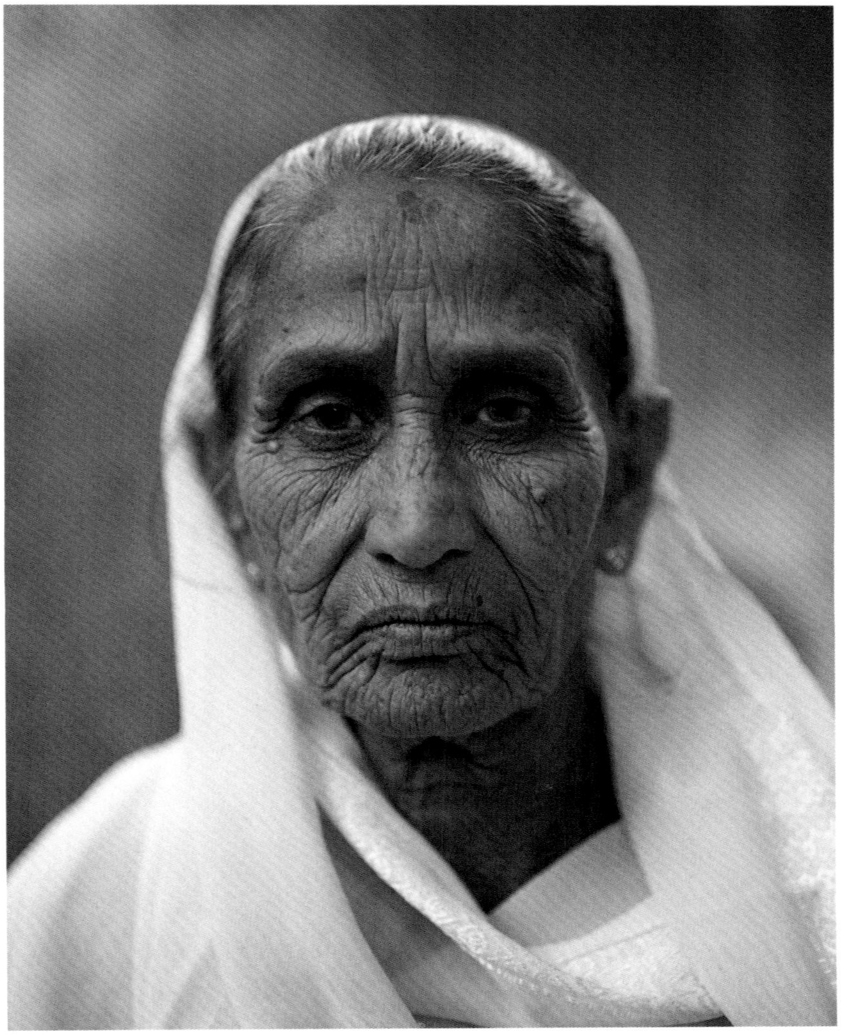

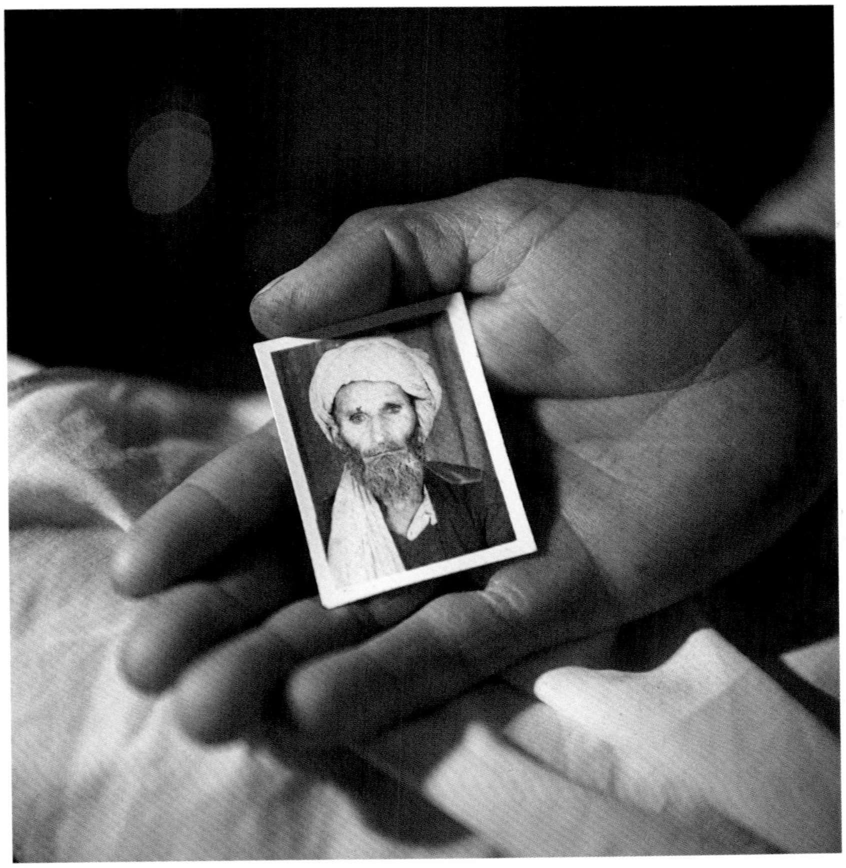

Fazal Sheikh
Jamaa Abdullai and Adan, Somali Refugee Camp, Mandera, Kenya, 1993
Gelatin silver print
43.5 × 36.5 cm / 17⅛ × 14⅜ in

Shahjahan Apa, Delhi, India, 2007
Carbon pigment print
57.1 × 46 cm / 22½ × 18⅛ in

Haji Abdul holding a photograph of his father, Haji Gholam Sadiq, Afghan refugee village, Miran Shah, Northwestern Frontier Province, Pakistan, 1997
Carbon pigment print
57.1 × 46 cm / 22½ × 18⅛ in

Seydou Keïta

The Malian Seydou Keïta's studio photo portraits also offer sensitive and humane portraits of a people who tend to be de-individualized by mass-media reportage. But there is a big difference. Keïta's photographs date from the late 1940s but only began to circulate within an artistic context in the 1990s as a result of three large-scale exhibitions of African photography at New York's Guggenheim, London's Barbican and Paris's House of European Photography.

As a studio photographer producing pictures for his urban clientele in Bamako, Mali, Keita did not intend his photos to be viewed as art objects. Self-trained, he opened his studio in 1948 and was a master of postcard-sized portraits until he became Mali's official photographer in 1962 and closed his business. The portraits were commissioned by and for Africans, to be printed on an intimate scale and circulated among family and friends. The people he photographed were from traditional middle-class Bamako families – businessmen and their wives, landlords and civil servants – and Keïta's role was to make them look as if they fitted well into the town's bourgeoisie and middle-class. The photographer often provided costumes and props to help construct his clients' desired look, and accessories such as fountain pens, radios and wristwatches frequently appear in the photographs. Whether adorned in finest tribal costumes or the (borrowed) attire of Western businessmen, many of Keïta's subjects are marked by self-possession and dignity.

Malick Sidibé

Malick Sidibé's portraits shows how the youth of 1960s' Mali adopted the consumer habits of an international youth culture. Like Seydou Keïta he did not consider himself an artist: 'Photographers in Bamako were no different than barbers or tailors: they all beautified their clients or provided them with styles for the visual pleasure of people in Bamako.'[16]

When independence arrived in 1960 and the colonial administration gave way, the socialist Malian government created a militia to ensure that people's behaviour conformed with socialist values. Curfews were set, and youths caught wearing mini-skirts, bell-bottom pants or Afro hairdos were sent to re-education camps. Young Malians turned to Pan-Africanism and the African disapora as powerful sources to express their defiant freedom, as Sidibé's pictures celebrated. He made his subjects look like the film and pop stars they wanted to be. The Bamako youth could more readily identify with James Brown or Mohammad Ali than with any other motif of independence at the time.

Both Keïta's and Sidibé's portraits highlight the enduring power of and fascination with more vernacular photographic traditions and conventions. But their aesthetic evaluation and celebration since the 1990s is fraught with contradiction. On the one hand they open up the history of African photography and break with the deadpan blankness that is often played out within the Western portrait tradition; but on the other hand they can be seen to have become trophies in a voracious art market: exotic spectacles of neocolonial appropriation and distortion.

Seydou Keïta
Untitled, 1956/7
Gelatin silver print
50 × 60 cm / 19 × 23 in

Untitled, 1952/55
Gelatin silver print
60 × 50 cm / 23 × 19 in

Malick Sidibé
Les Tres bon Amis dans la Meme Tenue, 1972/2008
Gelatin silver print
50.8 × 35.5 cm / 20¼ × 13⅞ in

Un Ye Ye en Position, 1963/2003
Gelatin silver print
94 × 95.9 cm / 37 × 37¾ in

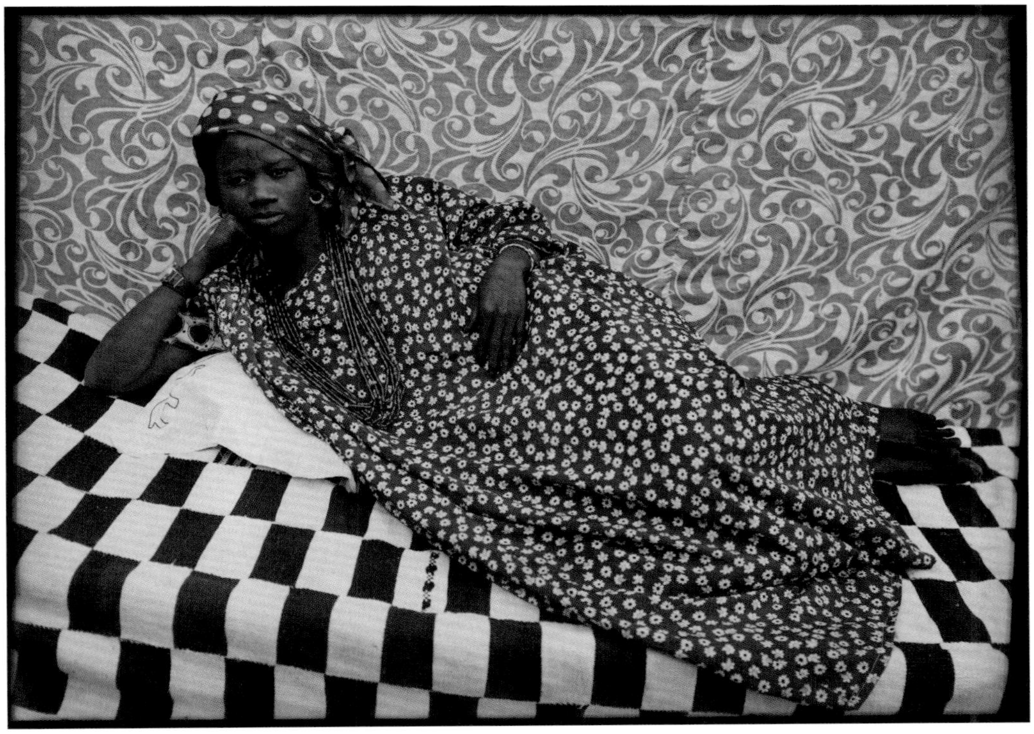

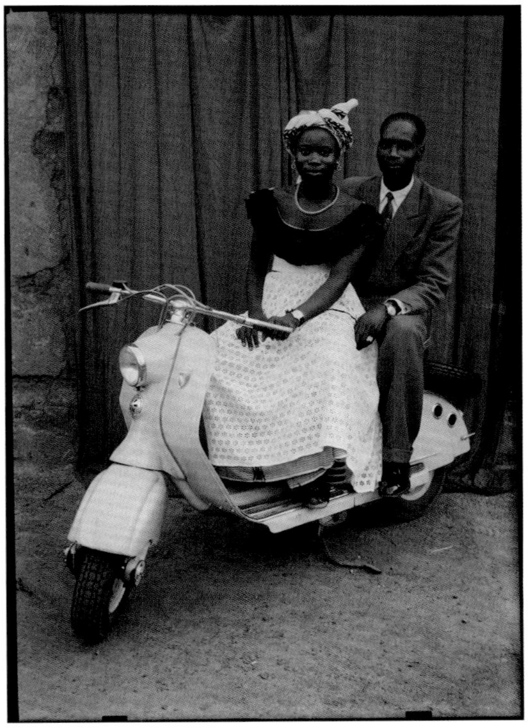

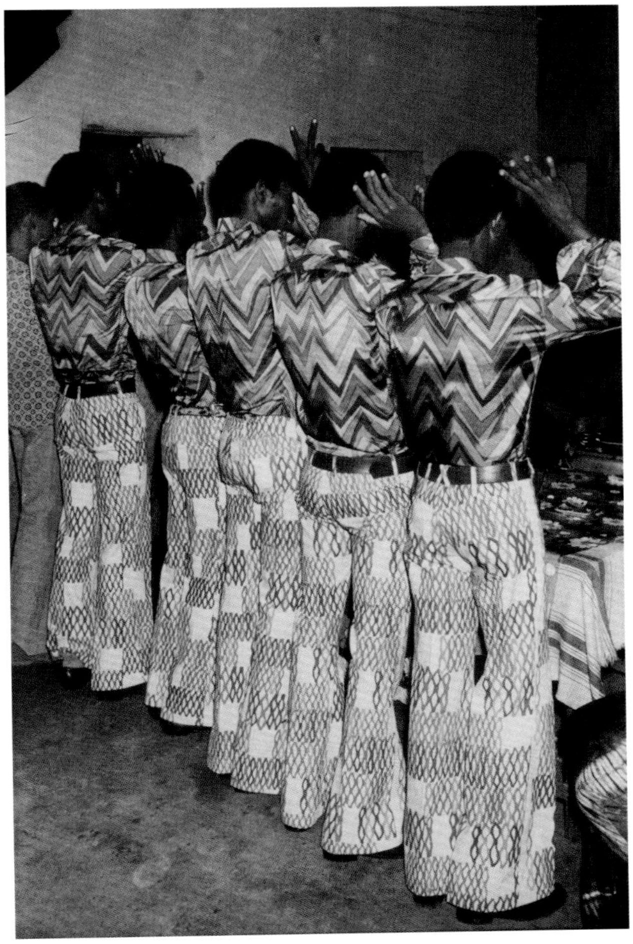

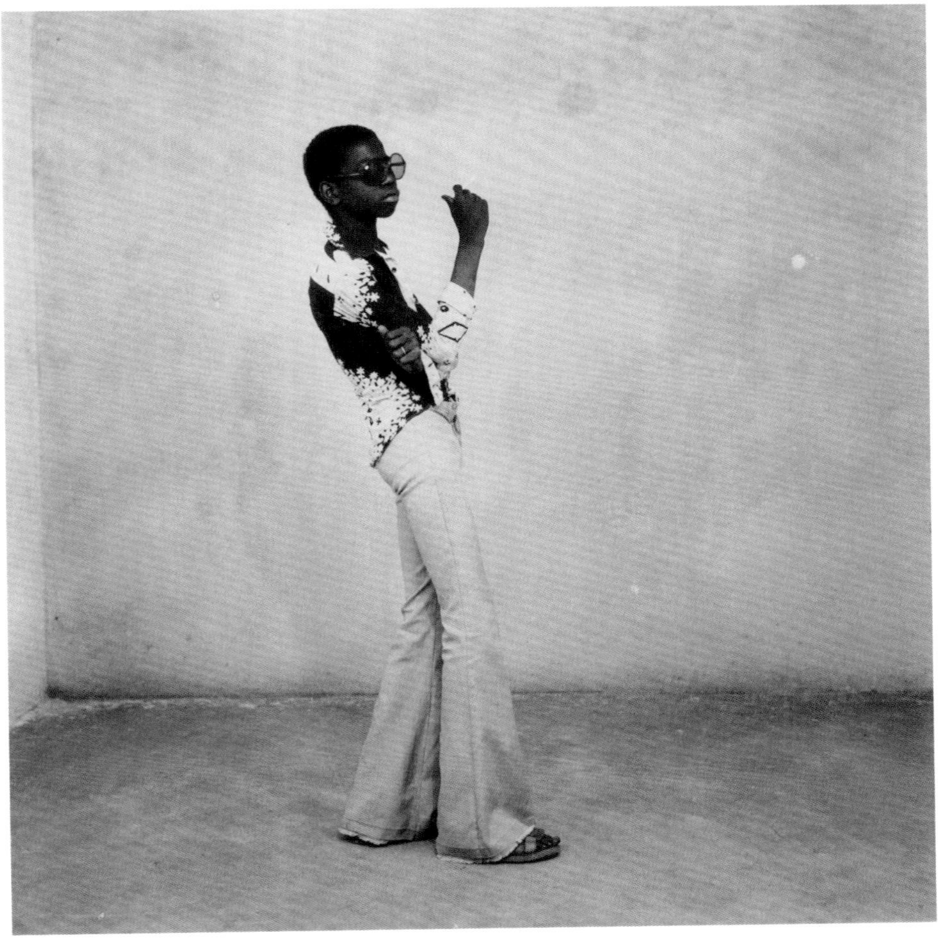

Sanggil Kim

The tension between the global expectation of a Western market and a specific cultural tradition is integral to Sanggil Kim's group portraits. Kim researched online to find various internet communities in South Korea and then made formal portraits of the groups when they met. He photographs people united through their consumer interests: a love of the luxury British clothing firm, Burberry, for example, or Harley Davidsons, Nike or the film *The Sound of Music*. Such portraiture is about conformity as well as about the global dominance of Western commodity culture. Kim's work takes us back to the question of the mask and identity, showing people united for a traditional group portrait that visibly marks their unity – they are all attired in Burberry, for example – while at the same time the portraiture is edged by the shallowness of consumerism. Viewing Kim's *off-line_burberry internet community* (2003), one is struck by the collision between their uniformity as a group of Korean young women, and one young man, and the Western product they are championing. In some senses such a picture comes close to product advertisements: it is a marker of Burberry's global success. Dressed up, the young people denote a wealthy and privileged group showing their status through the products they wear, but at the same time we are conscious of the de-individualizing effect of such consumerism.

Mintio

The Singapore artist Mintio offers another perspective on the relationships between individuals and mass culture in her recent series of extraordinary portraits, T.H.O.H.Y (*aka The Hall of Hyperdelic Youths*) (2010), which is a reaction to Singaporean teenagers' addiction to computer games. Through multiple exposures, she shows us both the faces of gamers lit by their computer screens and the virtual worlds in which they are absorbed, including on-screen icons, messages and commands. In these portraits, Mintio is, she says, extracting, 'imagery from both their psychological landscape and the landscapes of the games they play.'[17] In Sanggil Kim's picture, the Burberry fans all look back at us. Although the context for the gathering may be unusual, the formal pose and address to camera is typical of much portrait photography. Mintio, however, opens out portraiture to something quite different and unusual. Her multiple exposures mean her gamers appear locked into their game worlds, completely immersed and shut off from everything around them. Irradiated by the synthetic colours of the computer screen, her subjects become spectres in this melancholic testimony to mass culture's hold on the young. The glow of colour de-realizes these young gamers and serves to create the effect of fusing them into the virtual worlds that they are hooked into and hooked upon. Mintio's use of synthetic colour calls upon a particularly rich history in art photography, one in which artists have deliberately exploited the particular aesthetic effects and connotations of colour. This is the subject of the next chapter, *Colour: Surface and Depth*.

Sanggil Kim
off-line_burberry internet community, 2003
C-print
188 × 238 cm / 74 × 93¾ in

Mintio
~T.H.O.H.Y~ (aka The Hall of Hyperdelic Youths), from the series '~xLUV, Audition', 2010
Lambda print on metallic paper
58 × 73 cm / 22⅞ × 28¾ in

~T.H.O.H.Y~ (aka The Hall of Hyperdelic Youths), from the series '~xLUV, Audition', 2010
Lambda print on metallic paper
58 × 73 cm / 22⅞ × 28¾ in

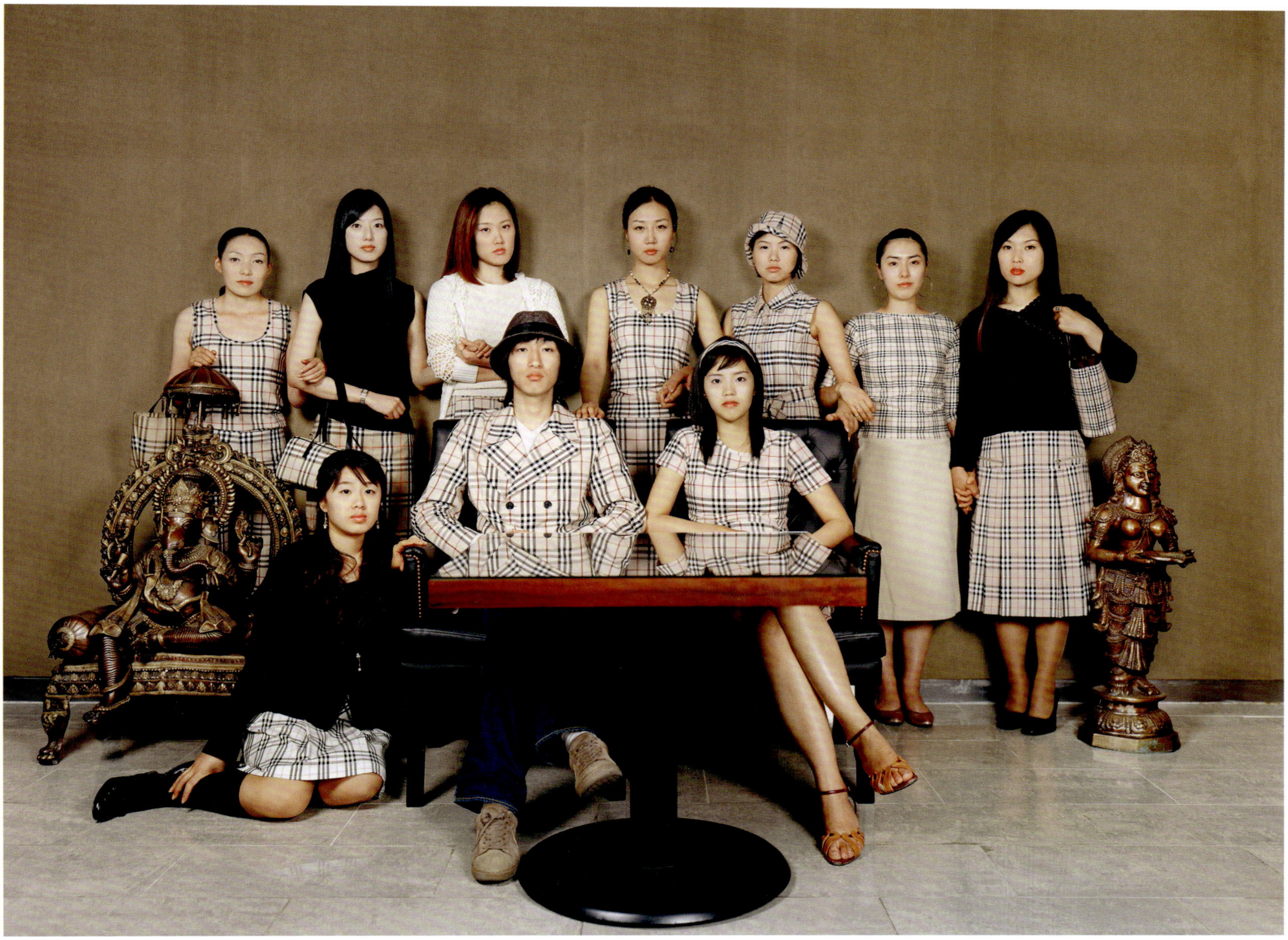

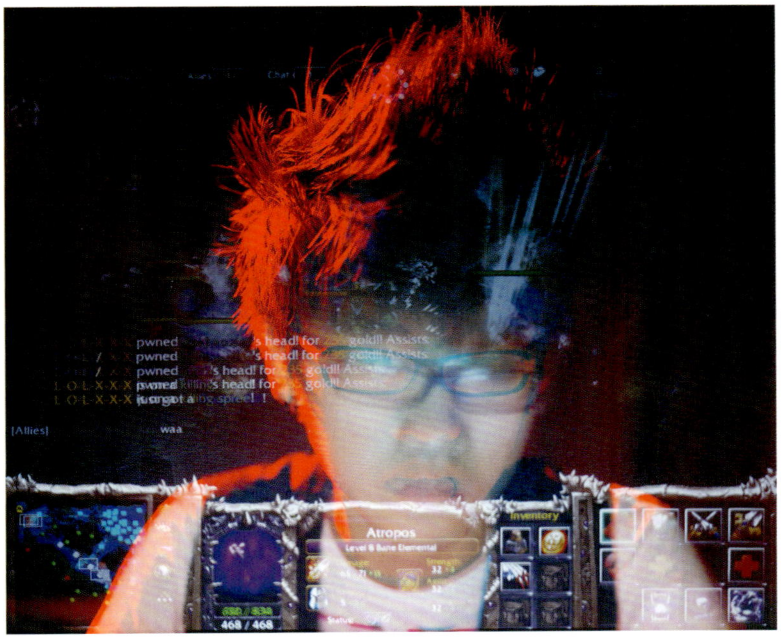
[Allies]
Atropos
Inventory

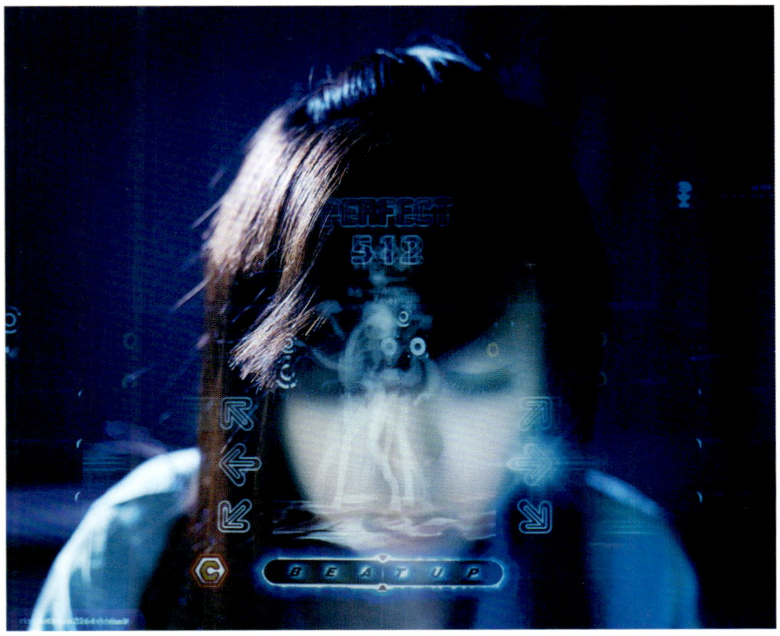
PERFECT
BEAT UP

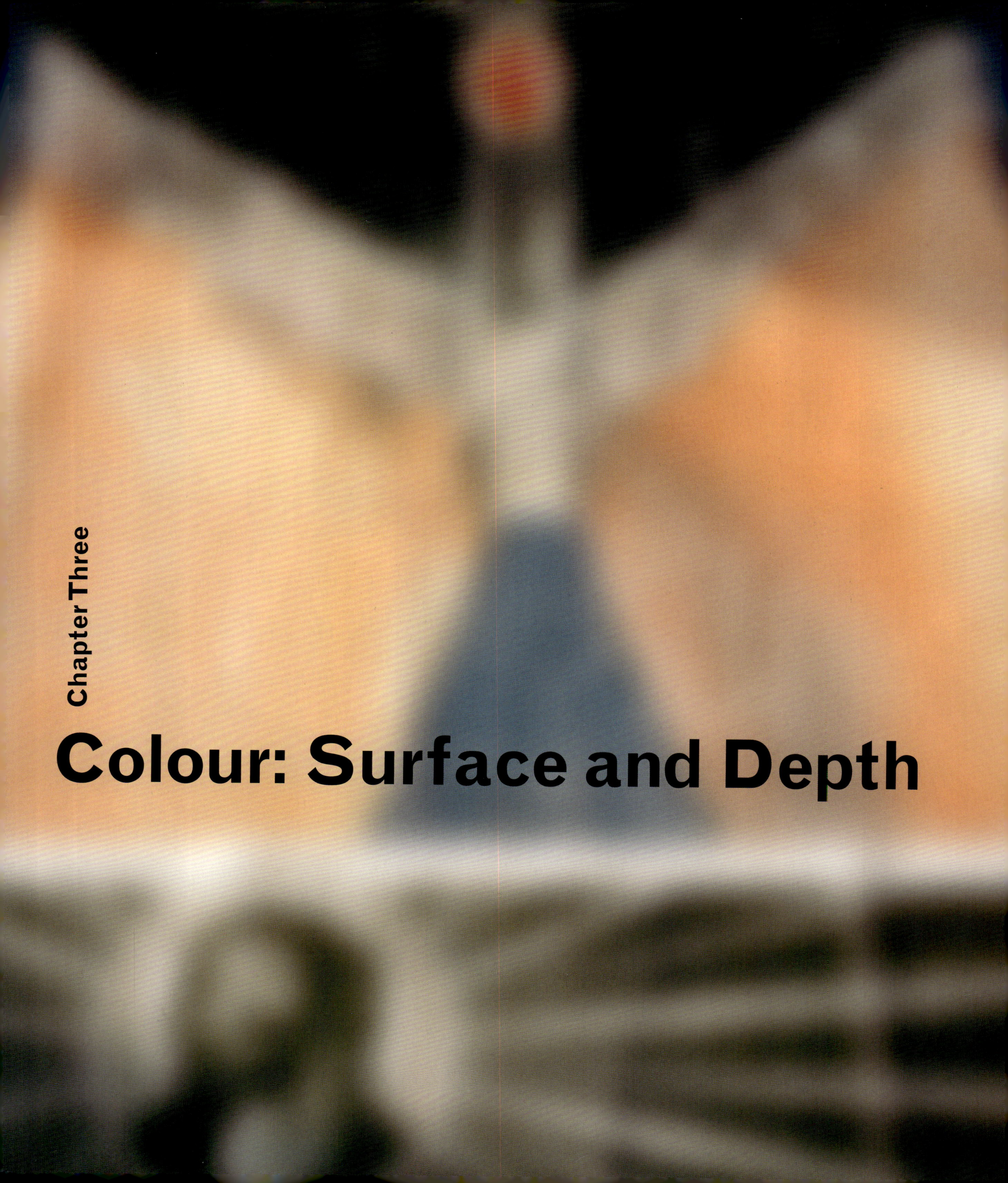

Chapter Three

Colour: Surface and Depth

During the 1930s in the United States, the first use of colour reproductions in such general-interest magazines as *Look* and *Life* energized consumer culture. Colour was used almost exclusively for advertising for thirty years. Costly and time-consuming, colour reproduction was only practical for advertisers, and eventually became synonymous with selling. As a result, serious art photography tended to disdain colour and decorative appeal, which it saw as being allied to the shallowness and superficiality of consumerism. In 1969 Walker Evans, for example, declared colour photography 'vulgar'; he saw it as valid for depicting only vulgar things and artificial colours.[1]

While colour can draw attention to what is vulgar, brash or kitsch, it is also integral to the affirmative qualities of photography. Colour underpins both William Eggleston's and Stephen Shore's discovery of a new beauty in the most ordinary and commonplace aspects of American culture. It was significant in Susan Meiselas's portrayal of people in Nicaragua and also fitted with the celebratory spirit of her record of revolution. Colour also had a key role to play in terms of documentary: Mary Ellen Mark's use of colour in the depiction of the women in Falkland Road avoided the potentially bleaker and harsher qualities of black-and-white documentary.

The Mundane World

William Eggleston
Stephen Shore

Illusionism and Abstraction

Luigi Ghirri
Andres Serrano

The Colour of War

Larry Burrows
Catherine Leroy
Susan Meiselas
Simon Norfolk
Alex Webb

Documentary Colour

Mary Ellen Mark
Raghubir Singh
Paul Graham
Richard Billingham
Daniela Rossell

Consumerism

Martin Parr

New Intensities

Peter Fraser
Gabriel Orozco
Saïdou Dicko

William Eggleston

A generally cited pivotal moment in the acceptance of colour as a non-commercial art is William Eggleston's solo show at the Museum of Modern Art in New York in 1976. (This was in fact not MoMA's first colour photography exhibition: colour photographs by Eliot Porter were exhibited as early as 1943, and John Szarkowski had shown Helen Levitt's colour slides at MoMA two years before Eggleston's show.)

There is an anecdote about Eggleston in the mid-1960s, watching in the middle of the night as hundreds of colour snapshots were churned out of developing machines at one of the first industrial photofinishing laboratories. Such an experience marked a turning point in his photography, influencing his use of colour to depict ordinary subject matter drawn from his own private milieu. But the mundane world was nevertheless transformed through Eggleston's distinctive use of super-saturated colour, the result of the expensive dye-transfer printing process, which had previously mainly been used for commercial photography and magazine publication. The process meant, as Eggleston has said, 'it doesn't look at all like the scene, which in some cases is what you want.'[2] In relation to his photograph, *Greenwood, Mississippi* (1973), showing a cross of white cables leading to the central lightbulb on a red ceiling in his friend's guestroom, he noted, 'When you look at the dye, it is like red blood that's wet on the wall.' The colour also gives a distinct erotic association to the interior space, which is echoed by the detail of a poster showing diagrams of differing sexual positions. The poster's depictions of interlocked bodies might even be seen as giving suggestive connotations to the cluster of little plugs drawing electricity from the cable that lights the bare bulb.

In his essay for *Eggleston's Guide*, the book accompanying the MoMA show and the first colour catalogue of photography the museum had published, John Szarkowski refers to how Eggleston's pictures, with their subjects drawn from the ordinary inhabitants and surroundings of suburban Memphis and Mississippi, are 'consistently local and private.'[3] The book is presented as a mock photo album with its leatherette cover and begins with a cheery sunny image of a front door decorated with a basket of flowers. Yet a number of pictures suggest darker undercurrents: there is a chilling emptiness to the photographs of the inside of a domestic gas oven and a green-tiled shower cubicle. And the pictures of people are often bereft of the intimacy we might expect from family portraits. A number of Eggleston's subjects are pictured on their own, such as the vulnerable and troubled, naked figure who seems to be scratching his head in uncertainty in a red room adorned with graffiti. One solitary male is shown tenderly touching a huge red U.S. Air Force missile. In one outdoors scene at the edge of woodland, a white male in a dark suit stands in front of a black male in white jacket and dark trousers. Hands in pockets, both adopt similar waiting-and-watching poses beside a car with its door open and its driver just discernible behind the windscreen. The event or occasion behind the picture remains unclear, but it seems formal and serious. (They are in fact attending a funeral.) Much as the picture highlights a correspondence of stance and pose, it also accents the separation between the two figures, a distance that here is also suggestive of the South's continued racial divide.

An inescapable influence on Eggleston was Walker Evans, whose photography, in the words of Mark Holborn, 'transformed the ordinary with a clarity that was extraordinary.'[4] But if there are certain continuities in terms of subject matter, Eggleston's pictures involved a radical break from Evans's photography in terms of their formal style: 'If there was anything about Walker Evans's work that I disliked, it was his determination always to use that same, square, frontal view. I never cared much for any photographs with such frontal fields.' Instead, Eggleston adopted unorthodox viewing positions, from the fly's-eye view of the red ceiling to the view from the ground of the child's bike that adorned the cover of *Eggleston's Guide*. 'Sometimes I like the idea of making a picture that does not look like a human picture. Humans make pictures which tend to be about five feet above the ground looking out horizontally. I like very fast flying insects moving all over and I wonder what their view is from moment to moment.'

Eggleston says it was in 1976 that he first abandoned using the viewfinder. As a result, he felt, 'You end up looking more intensely as you walk around.' He made an analogy between photographing without a viewfinder and firing a shotgun rather than a rifle: 'You don't look down the barrel and line things up.' Instead, 'With a shotgun it's done with feel.' Such analogies help explain the extraordinary liberational and open aspect of so many of Eggleston's pictures – their sense of perceptual freedom, a roaming, lyrical, unencumbered response to things in the world.

While colour was used by Eggleston primarily to depict the unspectacular world of middle-class life and the scenery of the American South, on one occasion he did use colour for vulgar subject matter when he turned his camera on the excessive décor of Elvis Presley's Graceland home in Memphis. Eggleston's photographs from the series were initially commissioned and published in a souvenir guidebook (in 1983) that was sold at the mansion, an unusual context in light of their general critical reflection upon the King's extravagant and indulgent taste. Photographed with flash, at night and with curtains drawn, the pictures convey a sense of a cloistered, hellish, fantasy world, irrevocably linked to the sensationalist stories of the star's tragic final years cooped up inside.

William Eggleston
William Eggleston's Guide, The Museum of Modern Art, New York, 1976
23.5 × 23.5 cm / 9¼ × 9¼ in, 112pp
Harback with full black leatherette and photograph mounted on, 48 colour photographs and 1 black and white photograph, essay by John Szarkowski

Untitled (Greenwood, Mississippi), 1970
Dye-transfer print
61 × 50.8 cm / 24 × 20 in

Untitled, (TV Room, Graceland), from 'The Graceland Portfolio', 1984
Dye-transfer print
61 × 50.8 cm / 24 × 20 in

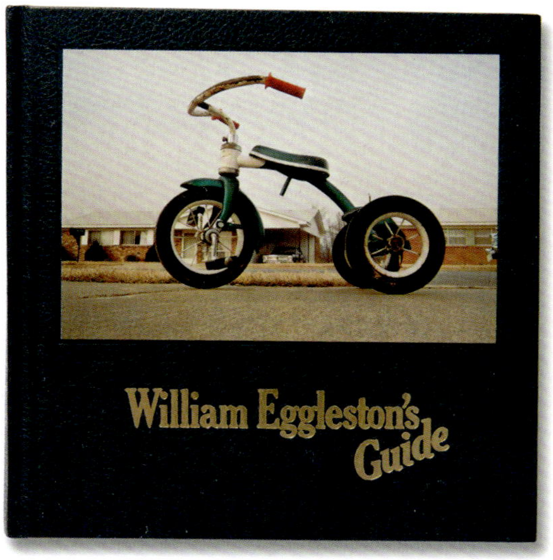
William Eggleston's
Guide

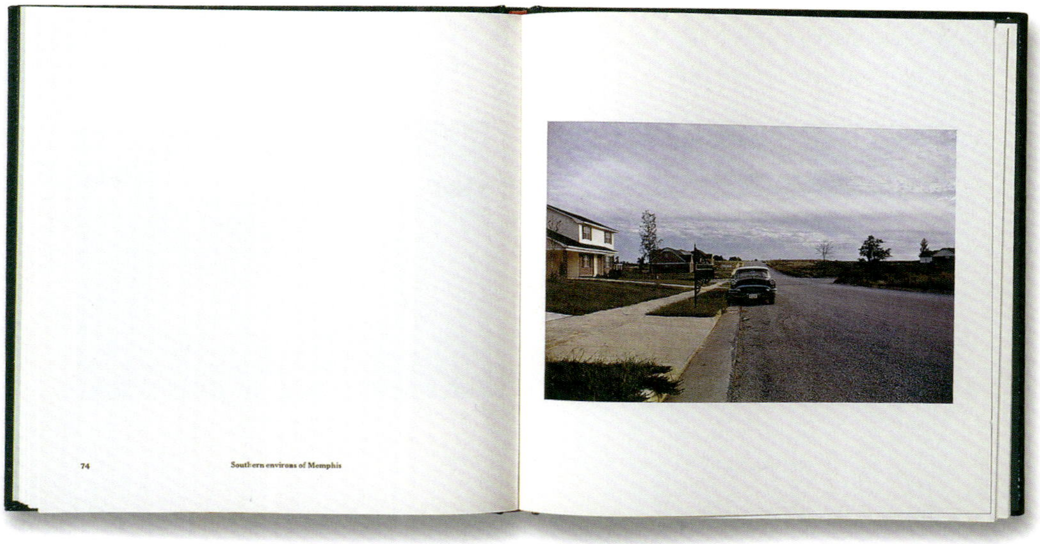
74
Southern environs of Memphis

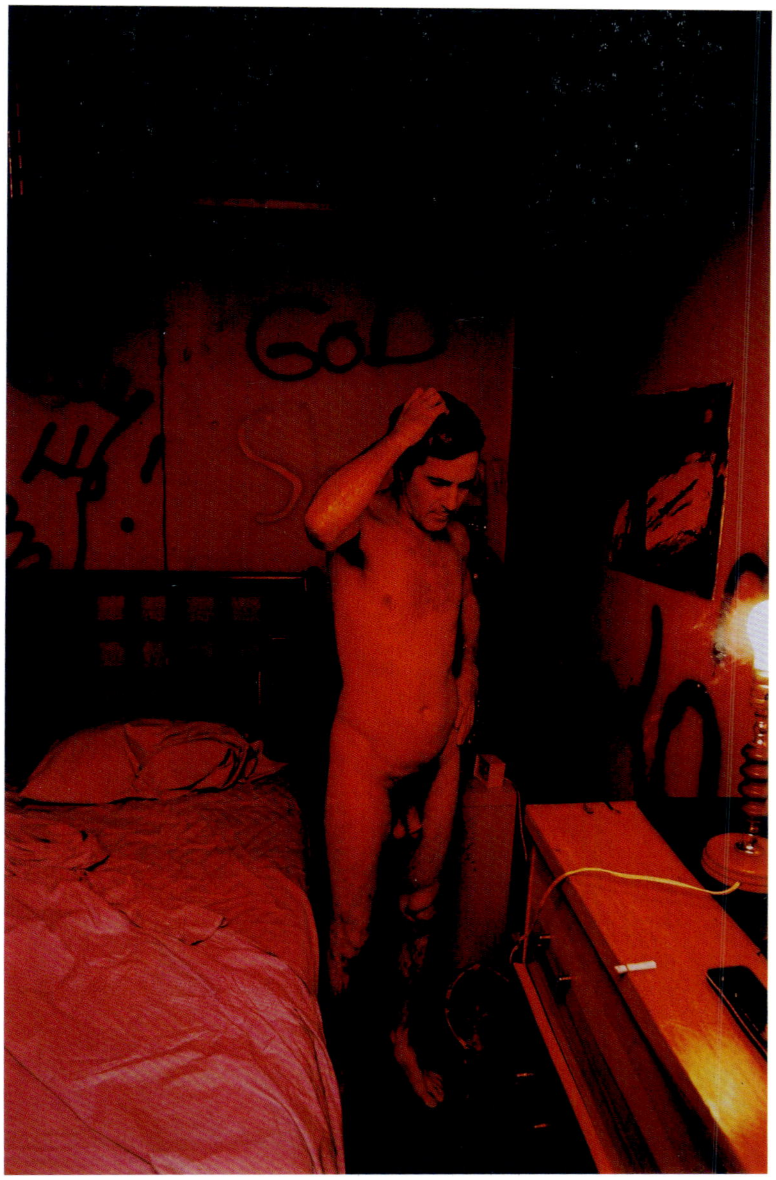

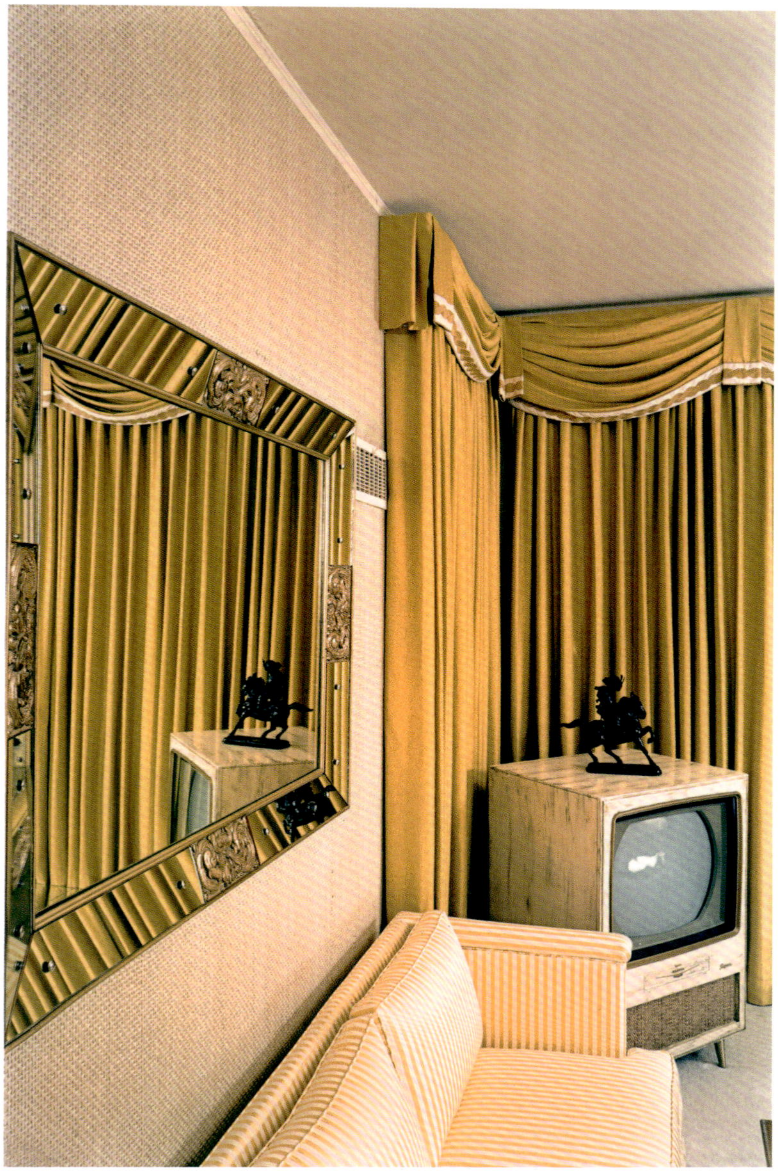

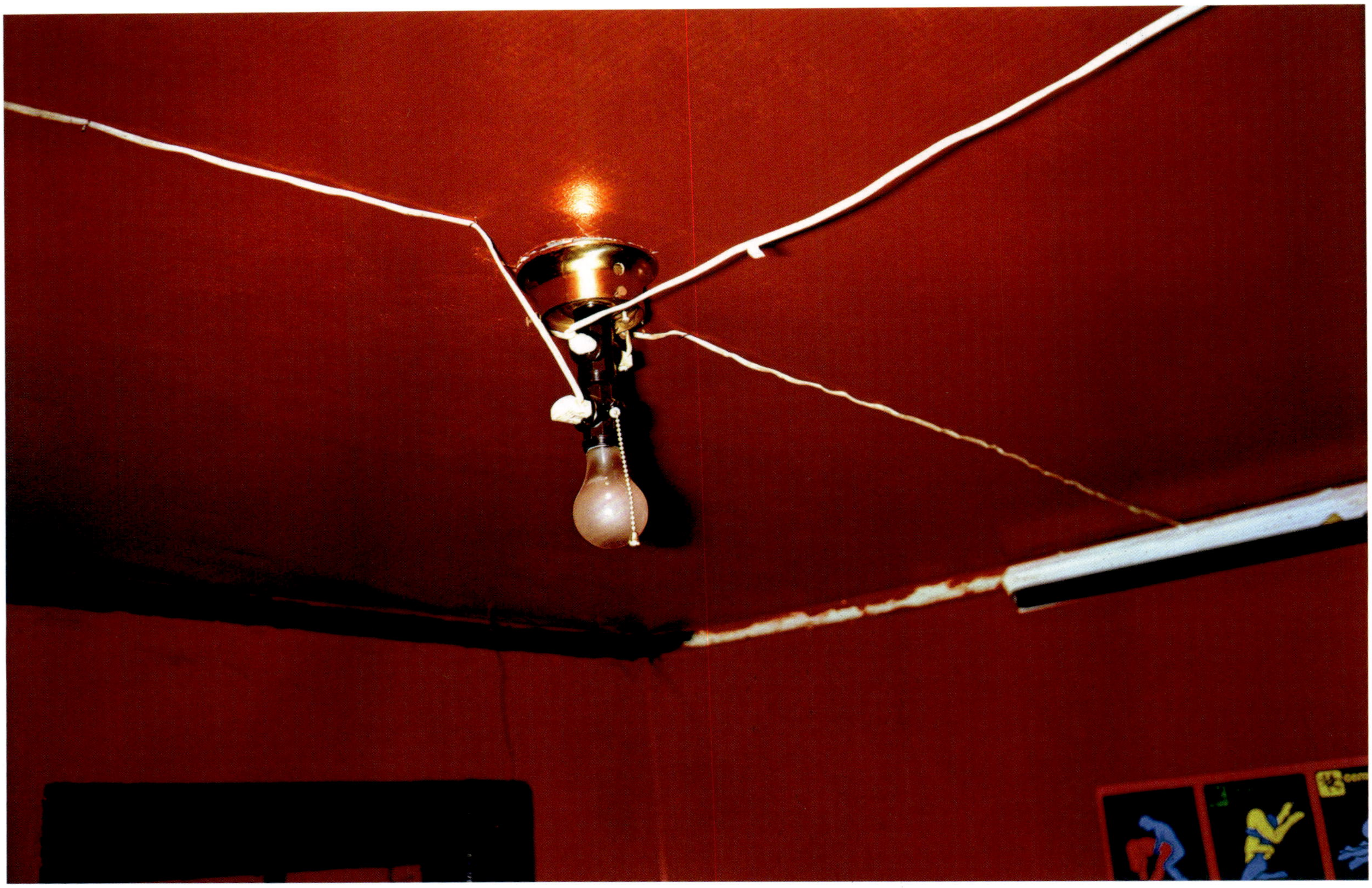

William Eggleston
Untitled (Greenwood, Mississippi), 1973
Dye-transfer print
40.6 × 50.8 cm / 16 × 20 in

Untitled (Sumner, Mississippi, Cassidy Bayou in Background), 1971
Dye-transfer print
50.8 × 61 cm / 20 × 24 in

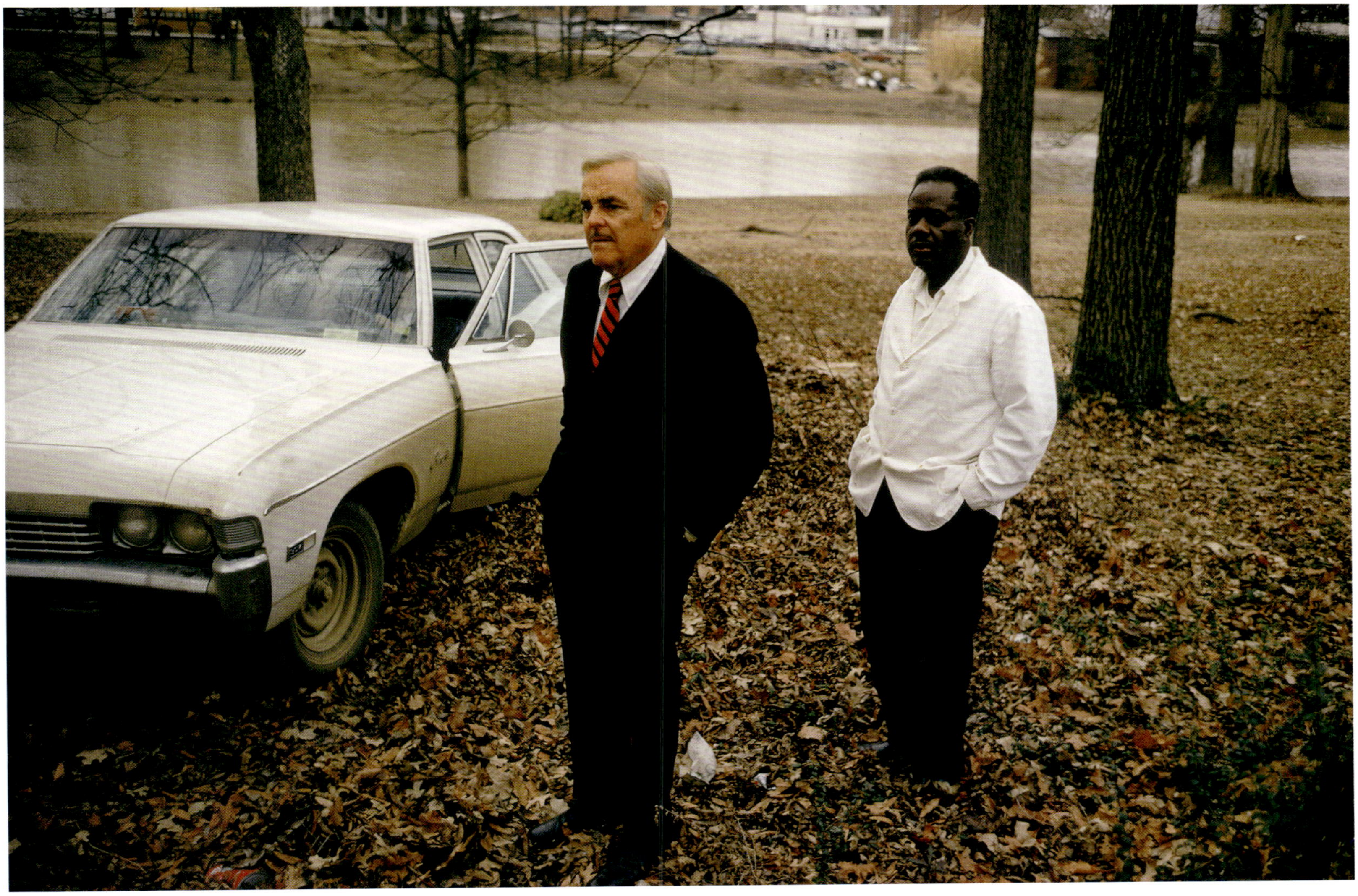

Stephen Shore

Stephen Shore, like William Eggleston, was closely engaged with the language of amateur photography. But while Eggleston's view of the everyday was presented through the expensive dye-transfer process more familiar from the world of advertising, Shore dropped his films off at local camera shops and displayed the resultant 3×5 inch glossy prints with white borders as they were, taping them directly onto the gallery wall. Such pictures were first shown in a small, back room of New York's The Light Gallery in 1972.

Shore, very much influenced by the experience of having photographed at Andy Warhol's Factory studio from 1965 to 1969, brought a certain Pop sensibility to his photography: a numb, detached perspective on the everyday world about him he referred to as Warhol's 'distanced delight in culture'.[5] Another important influence was the deadpan aesthetic that characterized Ed Ruscha's books. Fascinated by Ruscha's *Every Building on the Sunset Strip*, Shore apparently bought up all Ruscha's books. One can see the influence in Shore's seriality and his depiction of everyday, vernacular architecture, as well as an attention and concern with surfaces rather than depth. These pictures were very much, as the title of the collection made clear, 'American Surfaces'. Through the hundreds of snapshots that make up this work, Shore gives us a more extensive catalogue of his everyday world than Ruscha. He also includes people, so his pictures are not devoid of life, although people, whether serving him at a petrol pump, serving him his meals or snapped on the street, are treated with the same matter-of-factness and indifference as the objects he photographs: the hotel beds, toilets, the televisons in his motel rooms, the pictures on the walls and the food he eats. He said of the work, 'I was interested more in the ordinary, of things not happening in your life... I started photographing everyone I met, every meal, every toilet, every bed I slept in, the streets I walked on...'.[6]

Shore's is a Pop America, a world of tacky décor and fast food. Much as it is a road trip, it is one bereft of romanticism. Nothing much happens on his journeying. Instead, he is preoccupied with a primarily synthetic world in which the cheapness of the photographs' production and display is in accordance with the cheapness and tackiness of the mass products and consumer culture he often pictures.

Having pictured the United States with a snapshot camera, Shore, on the advice of John Szarkowski, returned to the iconography of the journey with a large-format camera. He has described the effects of working with a 10x8 inch camera as providing 'the photographic means of communicating what the world looks like in a state of heightened awareness'. The change in format means the pictures are less candid. Gone is the stark flashbulb lighting that characterized many of the photographs in 'American Surfaces', so one is much more aware of natural light in these pictures. There was a certain rawness to 'American Surfaces' connected with the immediacy, informality and directness of the handheld snapshot camera. Here there is more distance, as the preoccupation is with a formal translation of events: the colour of signage and the layering of space, the architecture at intersections, a gas station, a rainbow over a car park, the beautiful rendition of the plastic interior of a fast-food restaurant, a pancake and melon breakfast, an incomplete jigsaw puzzle. There is tension between the sensuousness and richness of the photographs and the ordinariness and commonality of the things and places depicted, but as time passes and products, commodities and fashions change, this ordinariness nevertheless gets more special and interesting. Photography allows a detachment and separation from the immediate world, making Shore and us see things differently. Intimacy and attachment are therefore not markers of these pictures. Figures are often static and stationary amidst the signage of the city. In the picture of a couple embracing on a sofa, the fascination is not with their attachment but with the richness of the photographic rendition of the scene, the texture and patterning of the sofa and carpet and the domestic clutter. The man looks back to camera and, as we are drawn to his gaze, we are struck by the reflective nature of his glasses, a mirroring in miniature of the precision of Shore's distanced and detailed pictorial representation.

Stephen Shore
Macon, Georgia, June, 1972, 1972
From the series 'American Surfaces'
C-print, 12.7 × 19 cm / 5 × 7½ in

Santa Rosa, New Mexico, June, 1972, 1972, from the series 'American Surfaces'
C-print, 12.7 × 19 cm / 5 × 7½ in

Albuquerque, New Mexico, June, 1972, 1972, from the series 'American Surfaces'
C-print 12.7 × 19 cm / 5 × 7½ in

Cerrillos, New Mexico, June, 1972, 1972,
From the series 'American Surfaces'
C-print, 12.7 × 19 cm / 5 × 7½ in

Sandusky, Ohio, July, 1972, 1972
From the series 'American Surfaces'
C-print, 12.7 × 19 cm / 5 × 7½ in

St. Louis Missouri, July 1972, 1972
From the series 'American Surfaces'
C-print, 12.7 × 19 cm / 5 × 7½ in

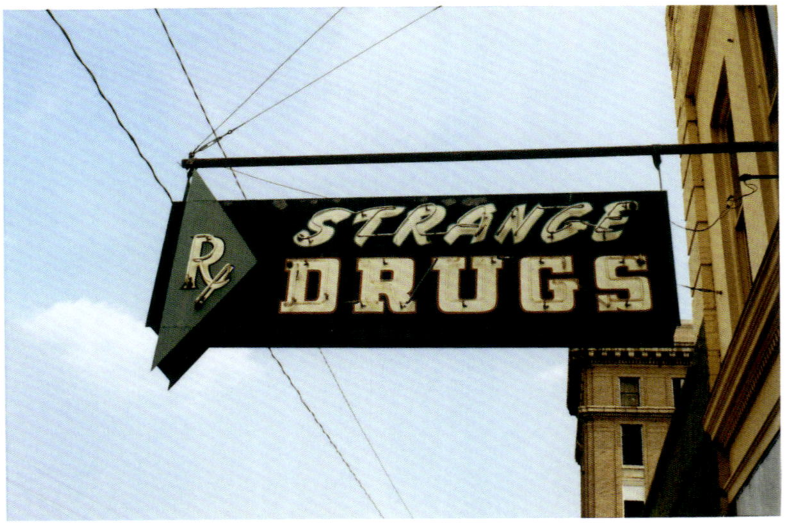
STRANGE
DRUGS

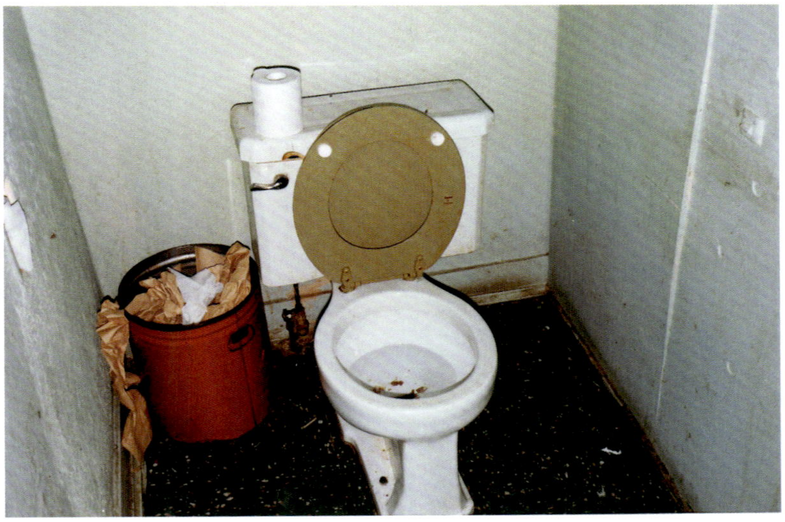

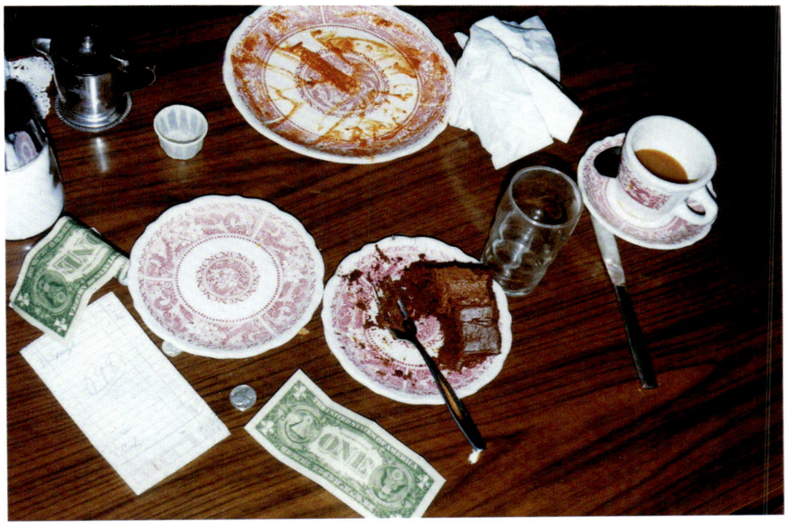
ONE

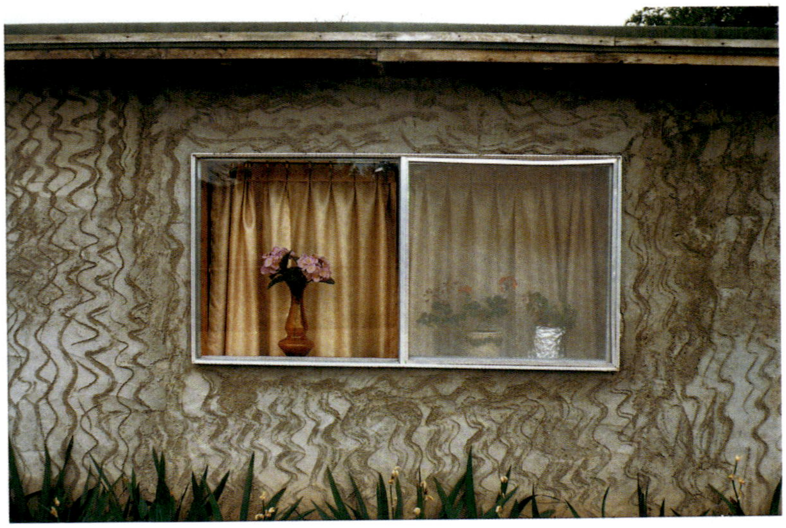

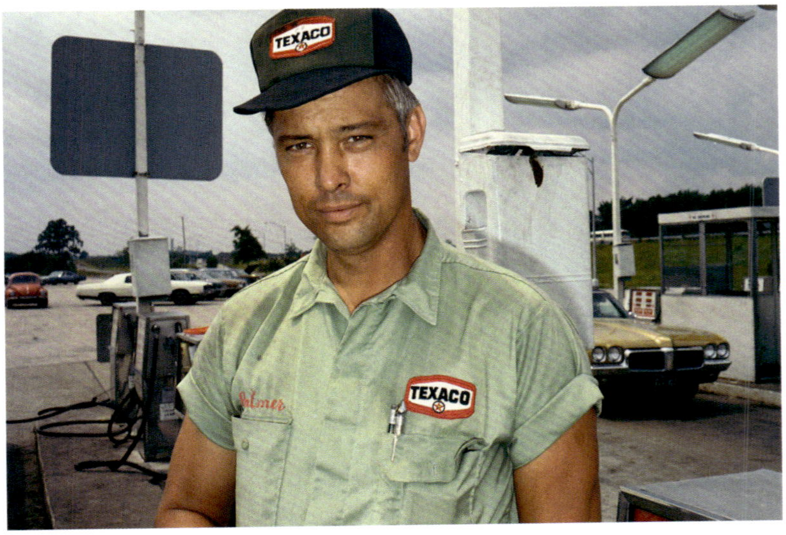
TEXACO
TEXACO

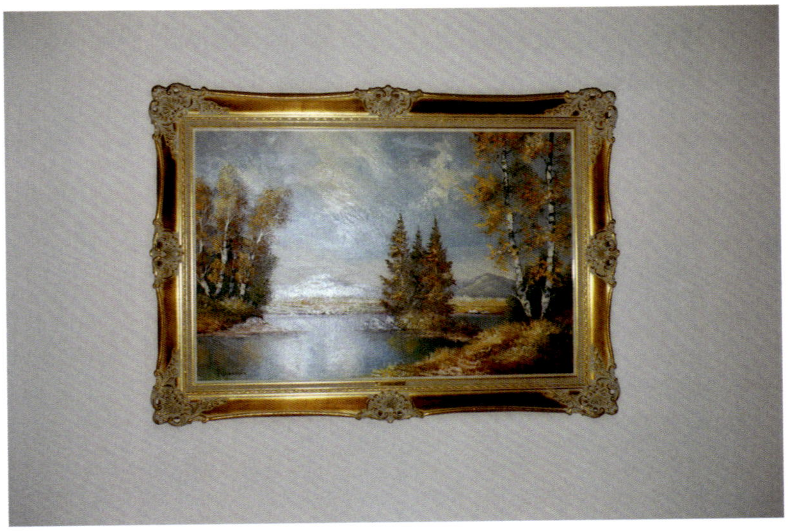

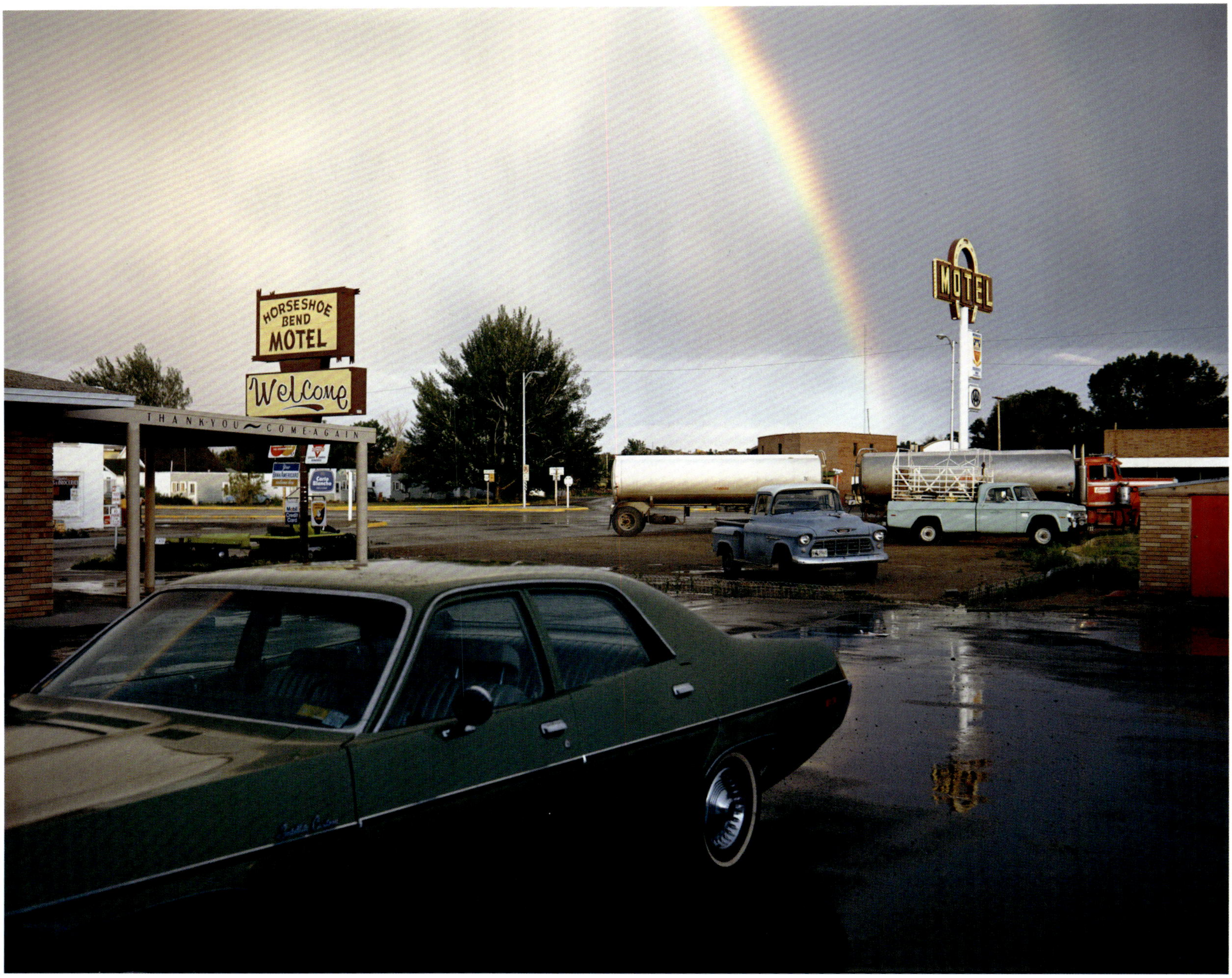

Stephen Shore
Horseshoe Bend Hotel, Lovell, Wyoming, July 16, 1973, 1973, from the series 'Uncommon Places'
C-print, 43.2 × 55.2 cm / 17 × 21¾ in

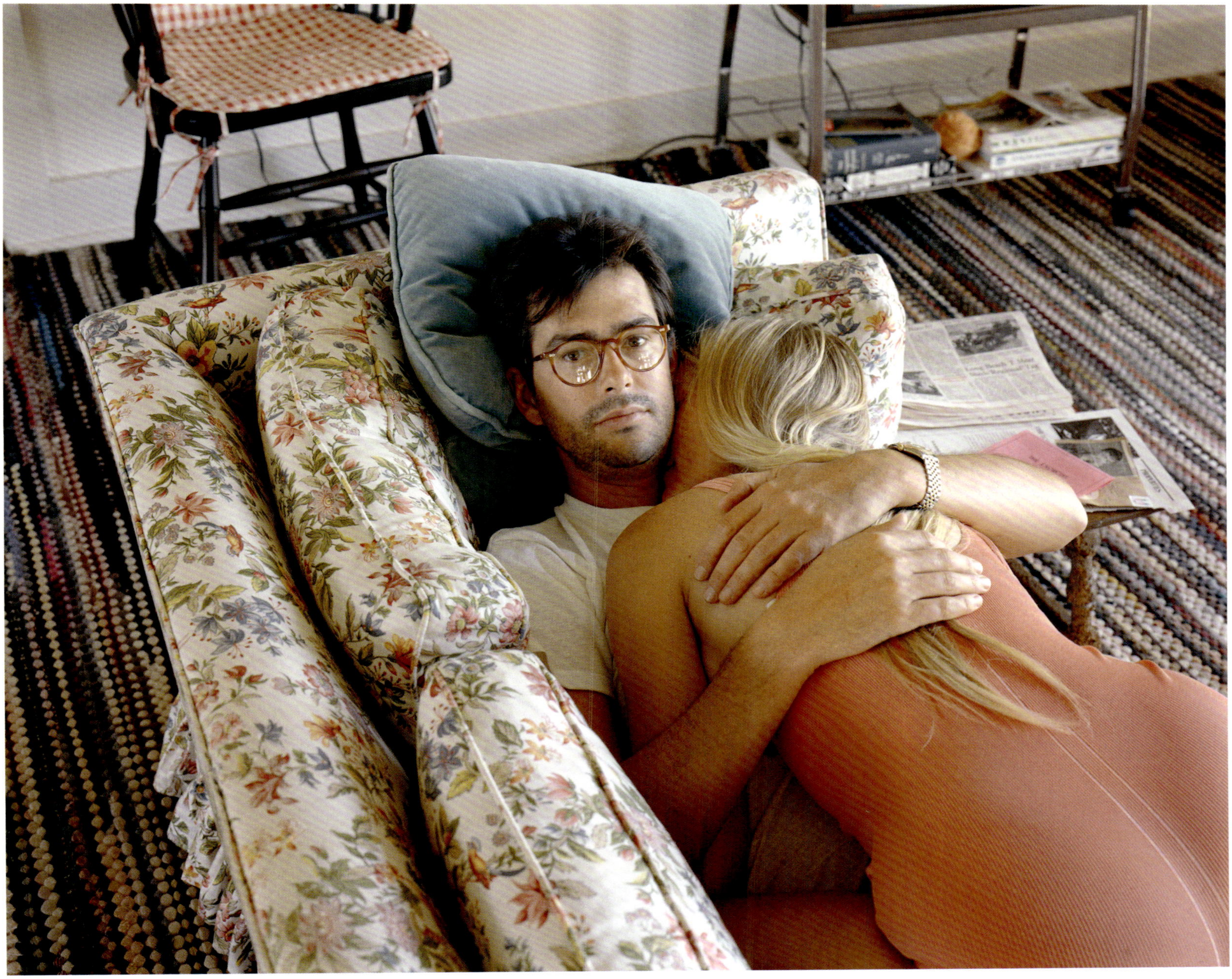

Michael and Sandy Marsh, Amarillo, Texas, 1974, 1974, from the series 'Uncommon Places'
C-print, 19.1 × 24.1 cm / 7½ × 9½ in

Luigi Ghirri

The Italian Luigi Ghirri was preoccupied with photography as an illusionistic medium and photography's place as an integral feature of the world. Ghirri's photography combines references to both an enduring classical tradition and the Pop commercial landscapes of Italy. His subject is representation in the age of spectacle. Advertising and street posters become especially fascinating, opening up a rich and playful iconic realm, replete with such comic cultural collisions as in his detail of a layering of poster images that puts Christ's head below the thighs and tinseled pants of a dancer, *Modena* (1973). With *Calvi* (1976), Ghirri pictures a rack of postcards showing sunsets and nightscapes of the tourist spot, a glut of kitsch that comments on the way landscape is processed and manufactured and the impossibility of viewing nature beyond cliché or free from such images. One central rack has no postcards and we see the wall beneath, an absence that serves as a reminder that photography itself is merely an alluring play of surfaces. Walls are the subject of the 1973 photograph *Egmond am Zee*, which sets a billboard's escapist picture of a view to the sky through a broken brick wall against an actual brick wall. Ghirri loves accenting the material surfaces of his photographed images; pictured in strong sunlight, a corner of the advertisement has peeled away and casts a distinctive shadow.

If many of his pictures are caught up in the imagery of advertising, posters and tourist postcards, Ghirri also shifted register and colour in a series of photographs taken in the studio of the painter Giorgio Morandi. Ghirri's photographs respond to the spare beauty of the painter's still lifes in 'Atelier Giorgio Morandi, Grizzana, Bologna' (1989–90). The colour and the natural light of Morandi's studio become a means of paying homage to the artist. One rather unusual picture from the series goes in close to the artist's easel and focuses on the thick layers of colourless paint that have accumulated within its tray, presumably as the artist scraped and wiped paint away from his pictures. The paint has also partly covered a large rag used by the artist. With the beautiful natural light of the studio, Ghirri has made his own still life out of the matter of paint. Photographed, the paint suggests the gathering of dust. Much as the image is a tribute to Morandi, it is also about photography's aesthetic as distinct from that of painting, which is to do with the ability to discover unexpected beauty and riches in almost nothing – from material that is literally left out of a painting.

Andres Serrano

Monochromes are common in the history of painting but much rarer in photography. Andres Serrano produced a series of colour monochromes in works that profoundly challenged assumptions about abstraction in art. What appeared as fields of pure colour, red, white and yellow were produced through fluids – blood, milk and urine – replete with particular associations. It is not the look of these pictures that is troubling but what is used to create their aesthetic quality. The pictures are not in this respect – and can never be – pure abstraction. In a key reading of such work, bell hooks drew attention to the symbolism and import of blood within the Christian church and the way in which Serrano knowingly recodes and revalues it. His celebratory and beautiful pictures of menstrual blood in his 'Red River' series countered the taboo attached to women's periods. As hooks points out, Christian patriarchal law only allows us to celebrate the blood of Christ, which is 'precious, sacred, a sign of compassion and forgiveness'; women's blood in contrast is deemed unclean and shameful.[7] hooks also sets Serrano's affirmative use of blood imagery against the media panic over AIDS and its images of 'dangerous blood'.

Luigi Ghirri
Egmond am Zee, 1973, from the series 'Kodachrome'
Vintage C-print
Dimensions variable

Modena, 1973, from the series 'Kodachrome'
Vintage C-print
Dimensions variable

Calvi, 1976, from the series 'Kodachrome'
Vintage C-print
Dimensions variable

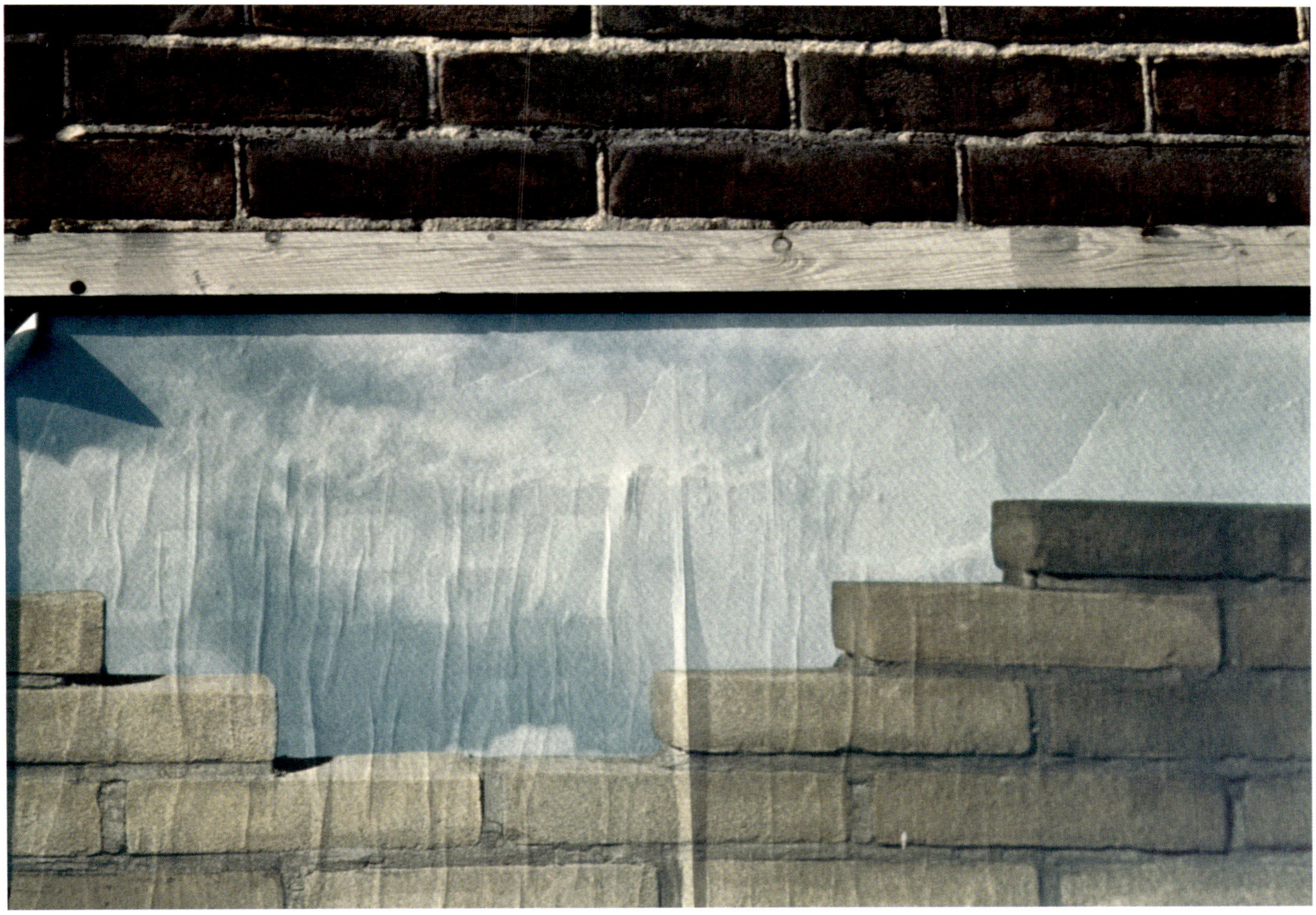

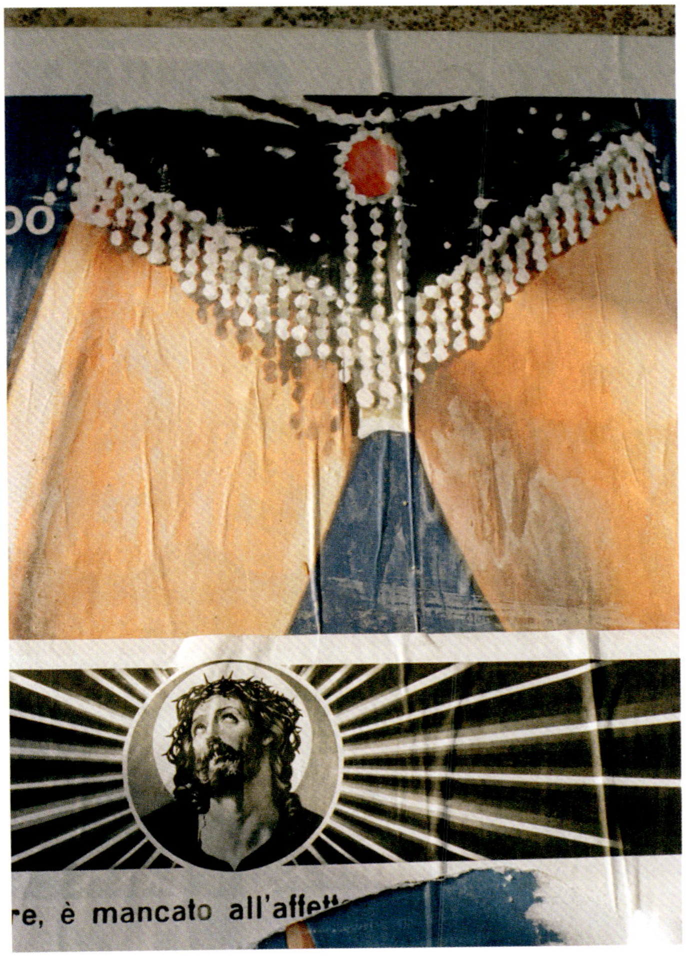
re, è mancato all'affett

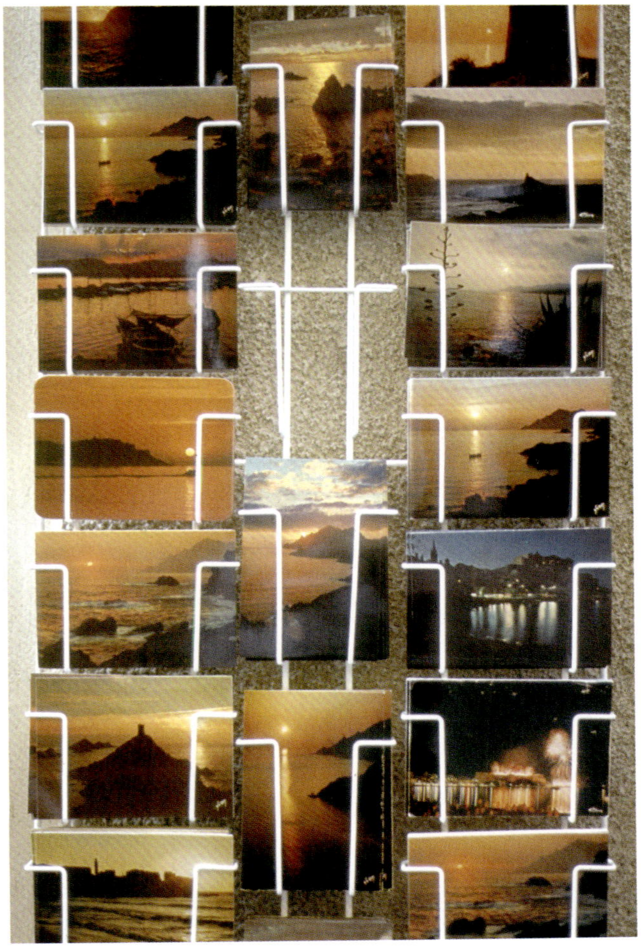

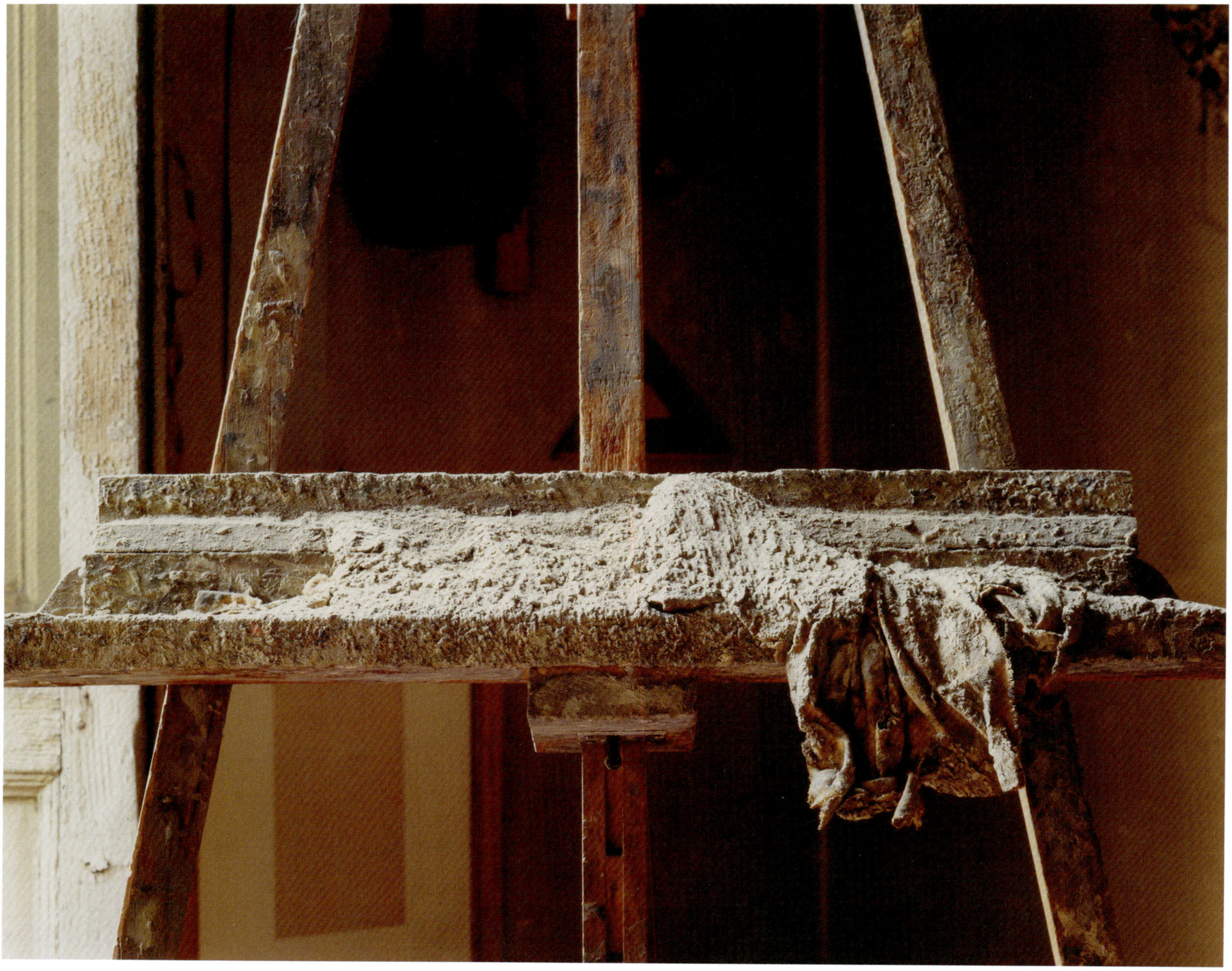

Luigi Ghirri
Atelier Giorgio Morandi,
Via Fondazza, Bologna, 1989–90
Vintage C-print, dimensions variable

Andres Serrano
Milk/Blood, 1986
Cibachrome, plexiglass mounted
101.6 × 152.4 cm / 40 × 60 in

Bloodscape, 1987
Cibachrome, plexiglass mounted
101.6 × 152.4 cm / 40 × 60 in

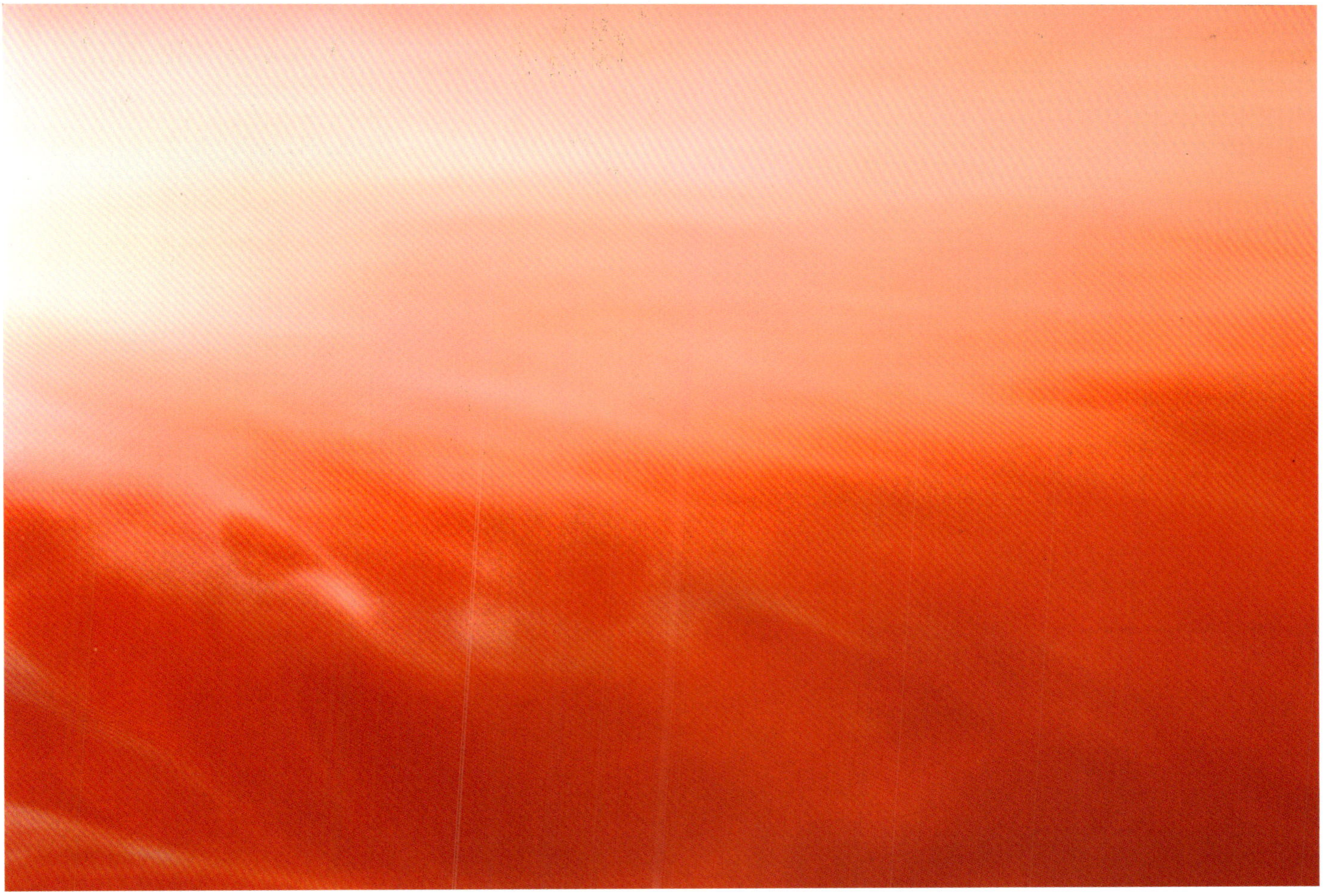

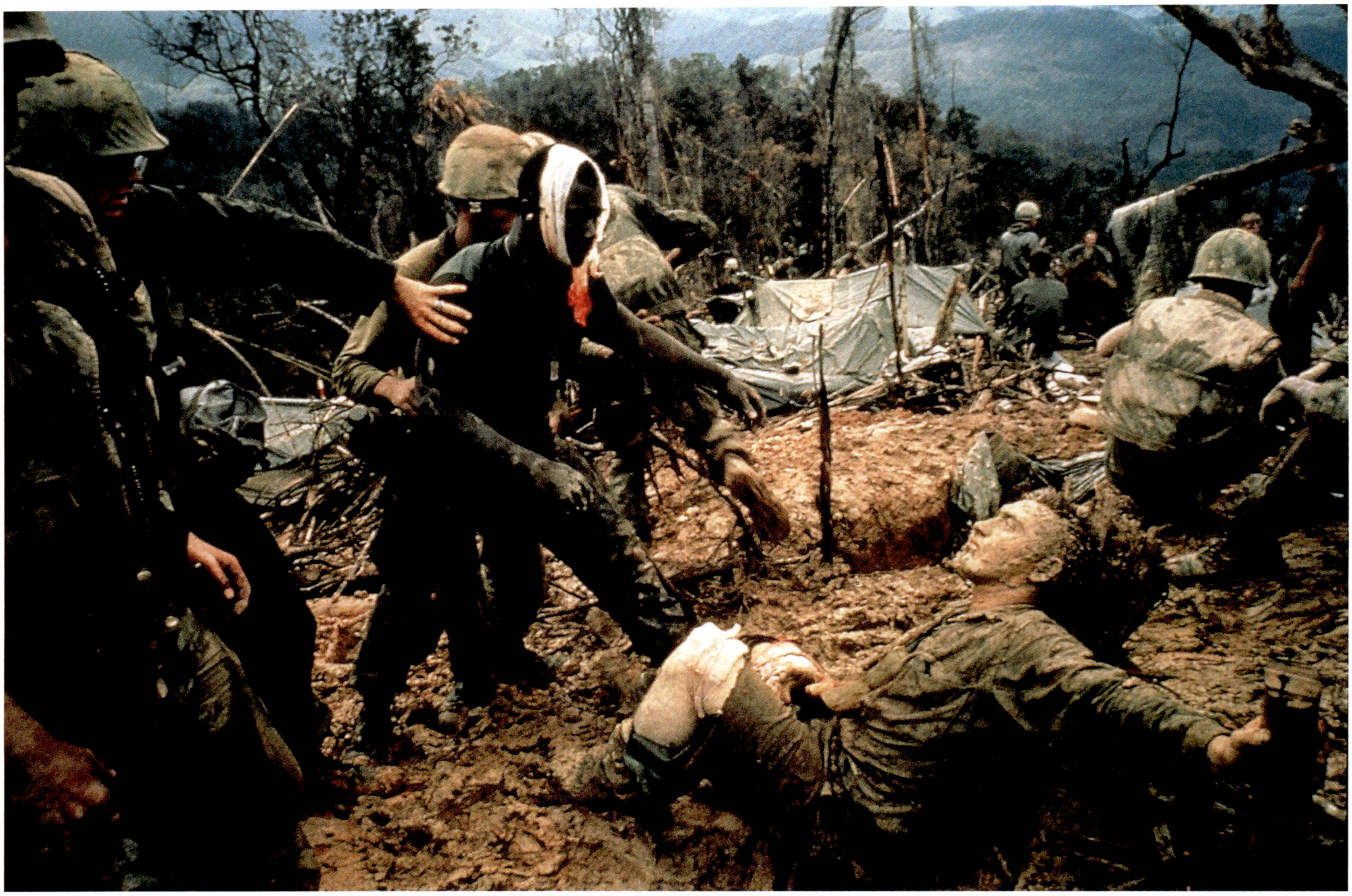

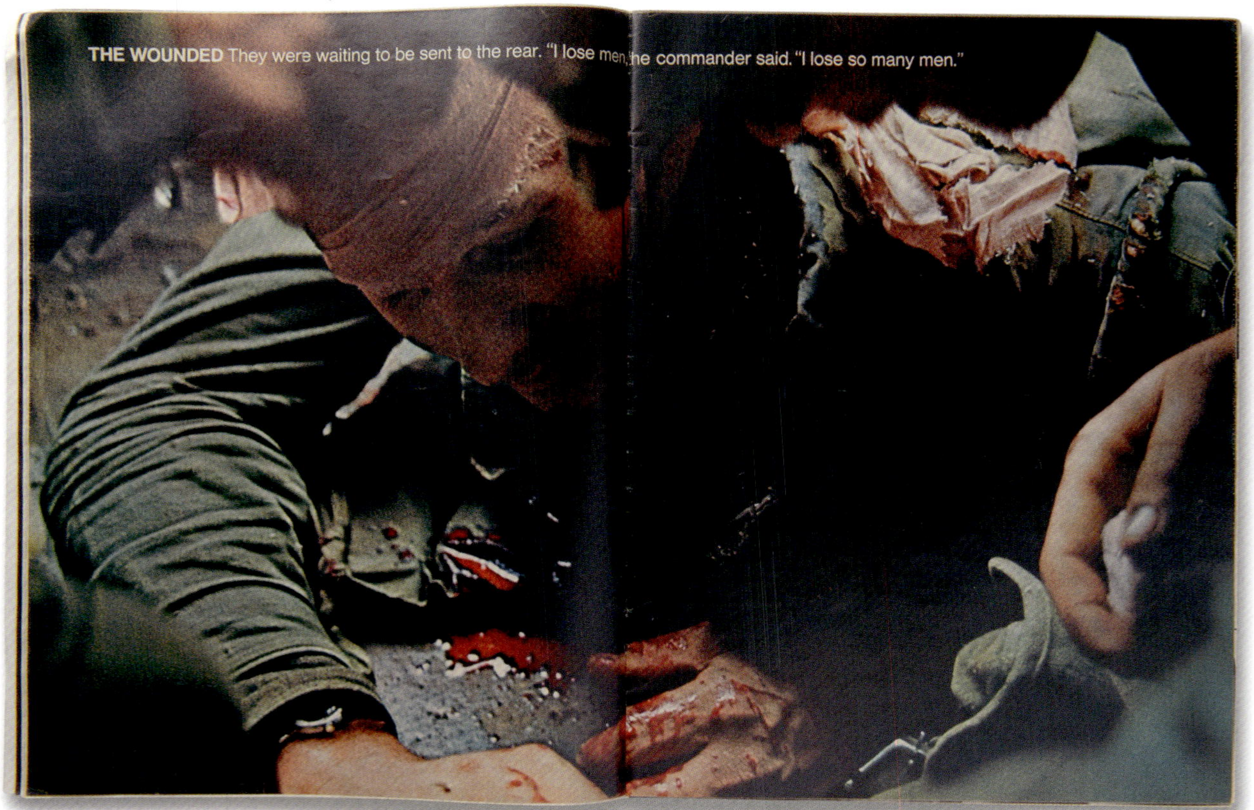
THE WOUNDED They were waiting to be sent to the rear. "I lose men," the commander said. "I lose so many men."

Larry Burrows

Colour's visceral association was central to both its importance to photojournalism and the problems it created. Colour had already become important in relation to both *Look* and *Life*'s coverage of the war in Vietnam. Such early and ubiquitous use of colour photography in news magazines served also to highlight a contrast to the television coverage, which cameramen shot primarily in black-and-white.

Colour met much resistance from some photojournalists. David Duncan, for example, upheld the value of black-and-white for the sonorous subjects of war photography, arguing that colour 'violates too many of the human decencies and the great privacy of the battlefield.'[8] It was seen as more 'voyeuristic' than black-and-white. In the words of the French photojournalist Gilles Peress, 'Black and white is more abstract, more conceptual, more ideological. Colour is sensual.'[9]

Larry Burrows, a photographer working for *Life Magazine*, covered the Vietnam War from 1962 until his death in 1971, when the helicopter he was riding in was shot down over Laos. Burrows worked in both black-and-white and colour, but believed colour gave 'far more realism to the beauty and harshness' of the war.[10] For Burrows the muted colours found in Ektachrome slide film were closer to the colours of Vietnam. One of his best-known pictures of Vietnam, taken in 1966 as part of a series that showed injured and wounded American soldiers during the battle for Nui Cay Tri Ridge, was not published until *Life* ran a memorial issue on Burrows on February 26, 1971, a month after his death. It was taken in a Marine first aid centre on a hillside awash with mud, with the hills of the jungle in the background. It captures the moment when a black soldier, with a blood-stained bandage wrapped round his head, strides towards a stricken white Marine who is propped against the stump of a tree and whose position, as many commentators have noted, is Christ-like, with his left hand stretched out towards us as it holds another stump towards the bottom right corner of the picture. It has been suggested that this photograph can be seen as an allegory of the way in which the United States itself was mired in the conflict in Vietnam.

Catherine Leroy

In contrast to Larry Burrows, who pictured a scene of war like a tableau or a painting, the images of the French photojournalist Catherine Leroy are marked by their rawness and immediacy. Leroy used the visceral impact of colour to shock in a series of full-bleed single- and double-page spreads that ran in *Look* on May 14, 1968. The photo historian Susan Moeller has described the pictures as 'the most visually striking of all the photo-essays of all the publications for all the war.'[11] The most dramatic of the photographs shows a close up of an American casualty. The browns, greens and black of the photograph are offset by the brilliant red of the blood oozing from the man's wounds onto the ground. Through such powerful pictures, as Moeller puts it, '*Look* tried to convince its readers to reassess American policy in Vietnam by transporting them to the war and rubbing their faces in its ubiquitous, anonymous horrors.'

Larry Burrows
South of the DMZ, South Vietnam,
1966
C-print, dimensions variable

Catherine LeRoy
Look magazine May 14, 1968
33 × 26.5 cm / 13 × 10½ in

Susan Meiselas

Susan Meiselas's book *Nicaragua* (1981) documents the thirteen-month, Sandinista-led popular uprising against Nicaragua's U.S.-backed Somoza government in 1978–9. Mesielas shot in both black-and-white and colour, but used colour because, she said, it caught 'the spirit of optimism about what was happening.'[12]

The photographs begin by presenting us with the social reality that preceded the Nicaraguan revolution: squalid muddy country crossroads, a woman washing clothes in a sewer in Managua. This accents the contrast with the picture showing the leisure and affluence of a country club in Managua and the white suits of Somoza and his men at the opening of a new session of the National Congress. Colour signals celebration and affirmation. The spirit and optimism of the revolution is shown especially well in the colourful dress of both the Muchachos (young rebels) and the people of Nicaragua, in contrast to the colourlessness of the grey armoured forces of Somoza.

Nicaragua is a layered and varied book. While some images accord with photojournalistic conventions and are taken close to the street fighting, showing scenes of destruction and the death of innocents, others are caught up with a reflection upon the nature of photography itself. A number of pictures running through the book show the public display and use of photographic portraits, from a poster of Somoza in front of which young recruits march to the black-and-white memorial portrait of a beautiful female revolutionary held up at a funeral and the picture showing a dead National Guardsman whose body goes up in flames, together with a portrait of his leader.

Martha Rosler has argued that Meiselas's reportorial work is marred by the book's appeal as an art book. The problem, for Rosler, was colour. At the time of *Nicaragua's* publication, colour was becoming the standard in *Time* and *Newsweek*. But because colour was still most widely used in advertising, signifying commodification and the exotic, the book's photography could not escape such associations. Meiselas was nevertheless aware how colour is keyed into a consciousness of the exotic and beautiful, setting up a jarring collision between the *National Geographic*-quality of the Nicaraguan landscape and the horrors committed there in what was for her the central image of the book, a picture showing a dismembered corpse on a hillside outside Managua known as 'Cuesta del Plomo', the site where executions were carried out by the National Guard. Meiselas had previously been unable to publish such a picture in the news media. Colour is integral to establishing the contradiction between the beautiful vista of fields, lake and mountains and the remains of the man's body in the foreground, which was left there as part of the terrorizing display of the brutal power of Somoza's regime.

Susan Meiselas
Ciudad Sandino, searching everyone traveling by car, truck, bus or foot, 1978–9
C-print, dimensions variable

Jinotepe, a funeral procession for assassinated student leaders. Demonstrators carry a photograph of Arlen Siu, an FSLN guerrilla fighter killed in the mountains three years earlier, 1978–9
C-print, dimensions variable

Managua, 'Cuesta del Plomo', a hillside outside Managua, a well known site of many assassinations carried out by the National Guard, 1978–9
C-print, dimensions variable

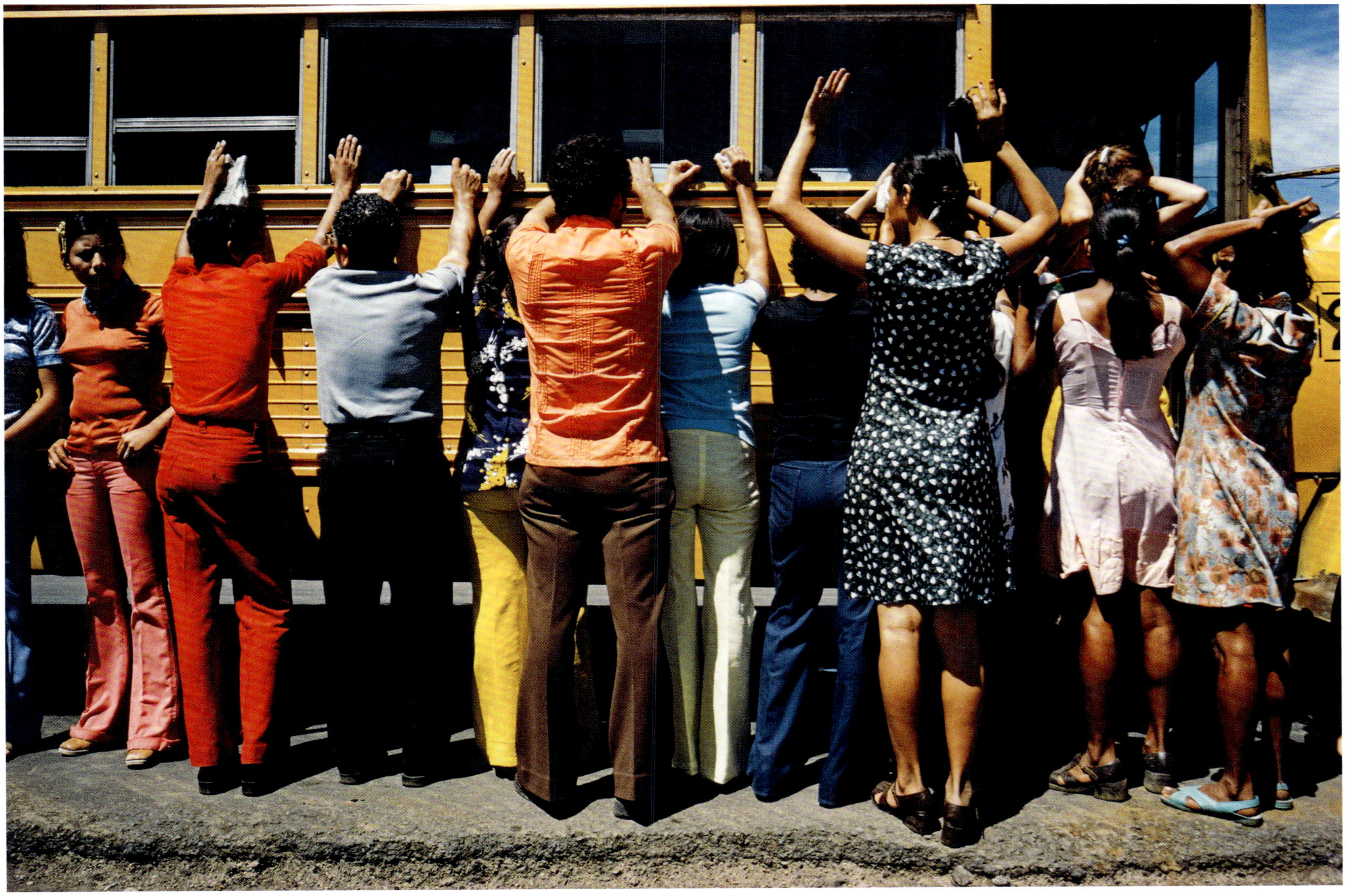

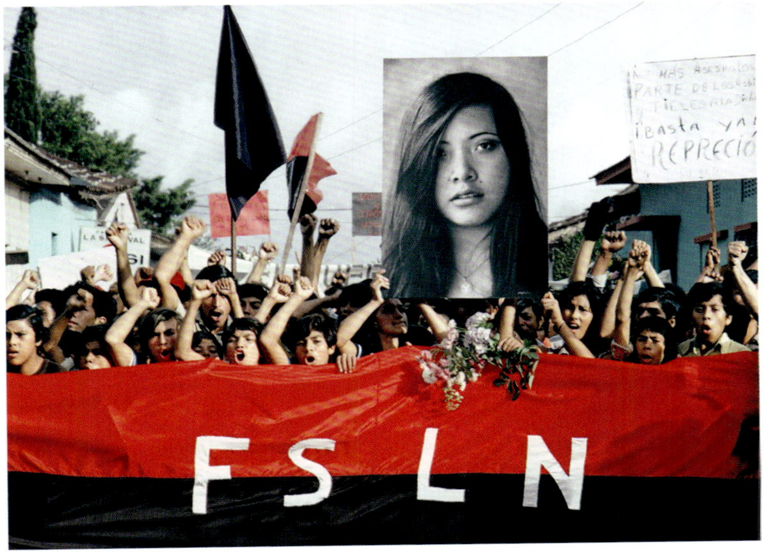
FSLN

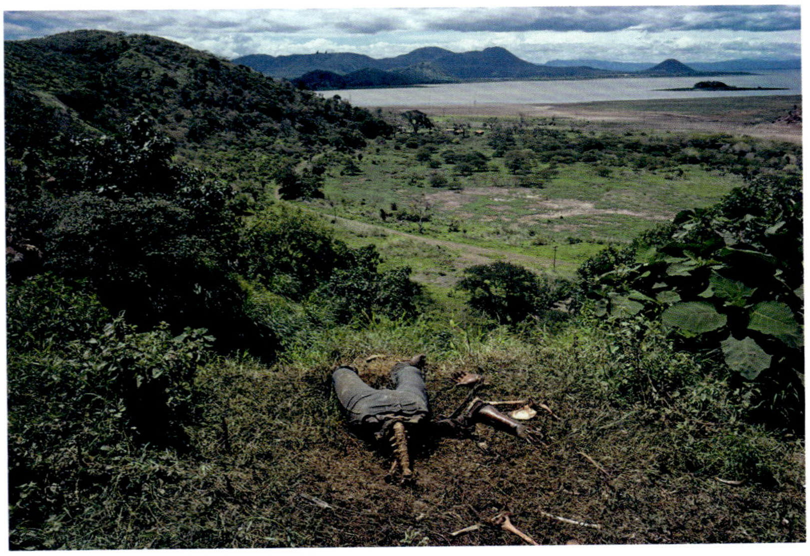

Simon Norfolk

Simon Norfolk is described as a 'landscape photographer' on the jacket of his book *Bleed*, (2005), which consists of a series of landscapes made at the sites of massacres in Bosnia. The beauty of the views collides with the knowledge of what took place on these sites during the Bosnian War of 1992–5, when more than 200,000 people died, most of them civilians. Norfolk's 'landscapes' are an allegorical response to the impact of war on the region, and Norfolk is absorbed with the pictorial allure and beauty of winter landscapes at the often remote sites of secondary mass graves to which the bodies of Bosnians had been moved by Serbian forces in order to hide evidence of their war crimes. Norfolk's pictures rely on captioning texts to supplement our view and identify the atrocities that occurred in these places. The traumatic history of these landscapes is often symbolically relayed through significant details: the red painted trees that define a still-active minefield alongside a path leading up to the mass-grave site at Crni Vrh or the blood-like stain on the frozen surface of an aluminium waste pond at Petkovici, into which the bodies of Bosnian men and boys are believed to have been thrown.

Alex Webb

Alex Webb's extraordinary book *Under a Grudging Sun* also used colour to exploit the tensions between aesthetics and atrocity. Unlike Susan Meiselas's portrayal of Nicaragua, the American photojournalist's photographs document only a momentary period of optimism and hope in Haiti Libéré, between 1986 and 1988. Like Susan Meiselas, Webb was aware of contradictions: 'Colours are out there. You go into a country like Haiti. It is poor. Shockingly poor. There's tremendous repression. Yet the walls are bright pink and bright green and it's incredibly beautiful. The complexity of that kind of response that one can have in colour interests me.'[13] His pictures attest to this complexity and push the boundaries of photojournalism to new extremes.

Webb's sequence of photographs show a transition from pre-election hope, during the brief period after the departure of the Haitian dictator, Jean-Claude Duvalier, to brutality and a return to suspicion. Webb had made several trips to Haiti before Duvalier left, but when he returned during Haiti Libéré he was struck by a new sense of freedom and openness among the people. Never before had he found Haitians on the streets feeling free enough to talk to him about what the future might hold. The first pictures show this climate and then the tone of the book changes as he chronicles repression and the massacres of the November 1987 elections, but it is not marked by a shift in colour. The colours of things remain just as beautiful despite the brutality; so much so that, in one picture of a man slumped in an alcove, killed by the army, the body is lost in the dominant colours of the painted walls. The dead becomes secondary to the colourful aesthetic of the composition. It is as if Webb is testing our habituation to horror, countering our expectation that the photograph can register a response. While Webb has spoken of 'the splash of colours that almost seem chosen to ward off the inevitable tragedy of Haitian life', such pictures show otherwise.[14] The exoticism of colour is never separated from the tragedy.

Simon Norfolk
Bleed, Petkovici, Bosnia, 2005
Digital C-print
101.6 × 127 cm / 40 × 50 in

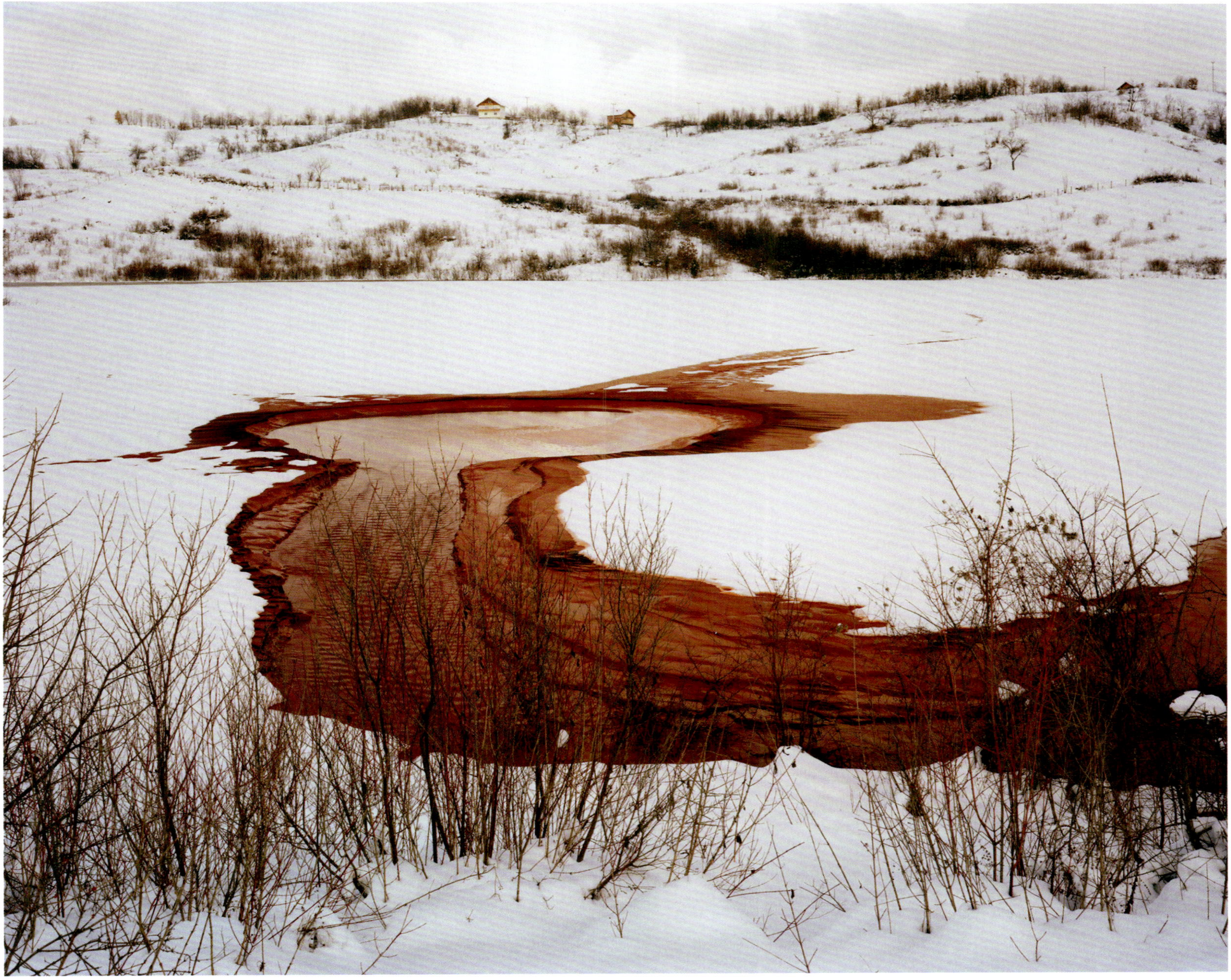

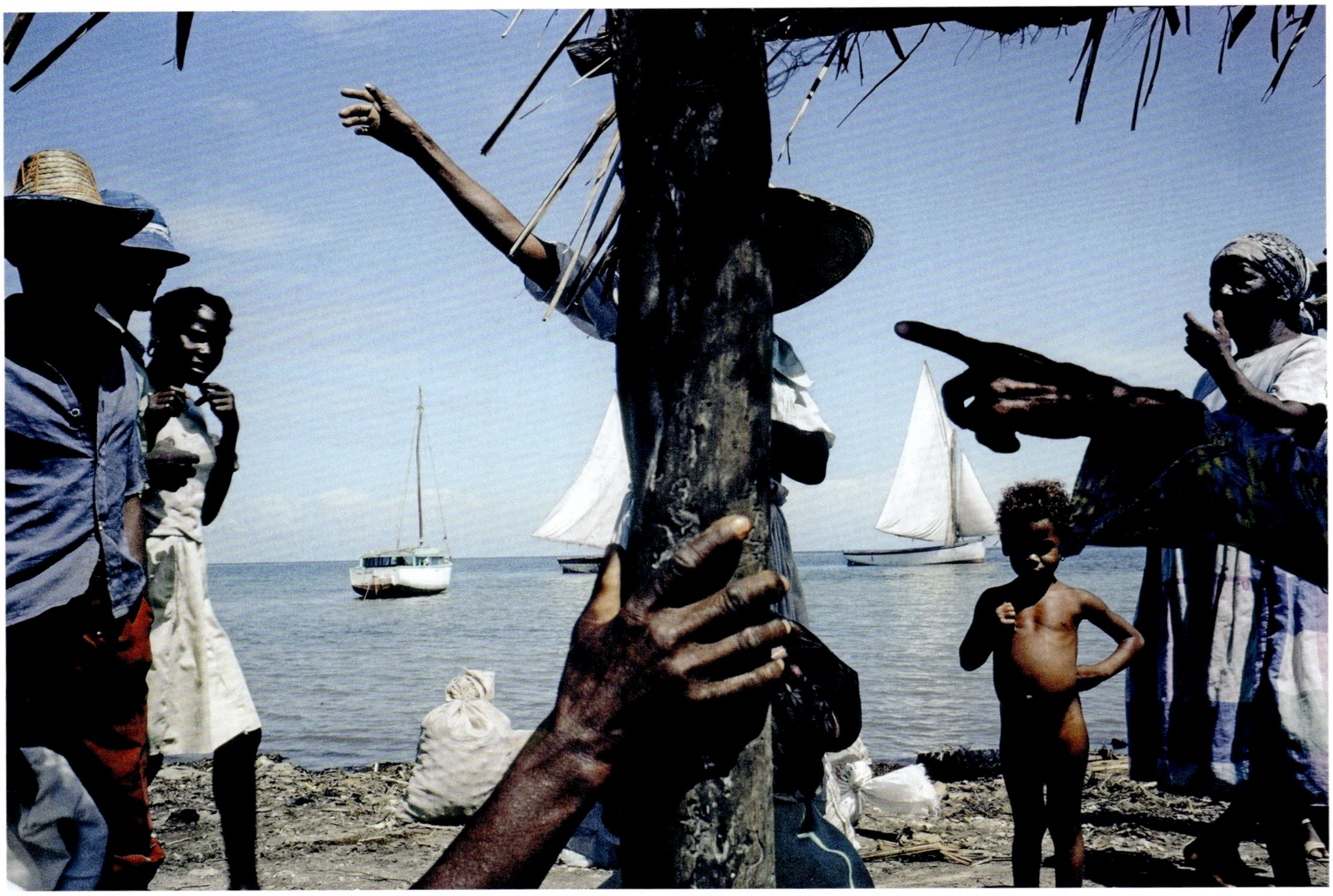

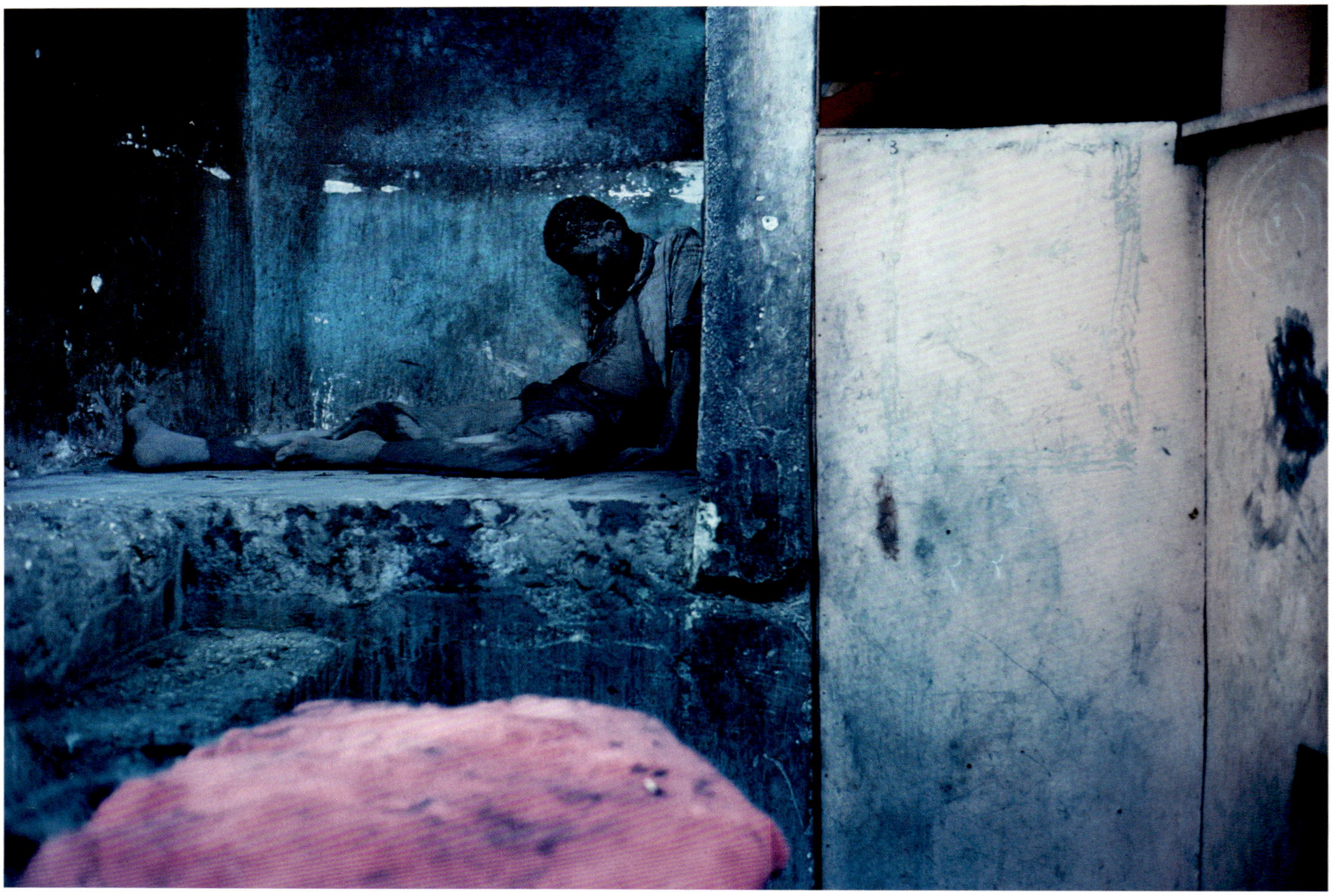

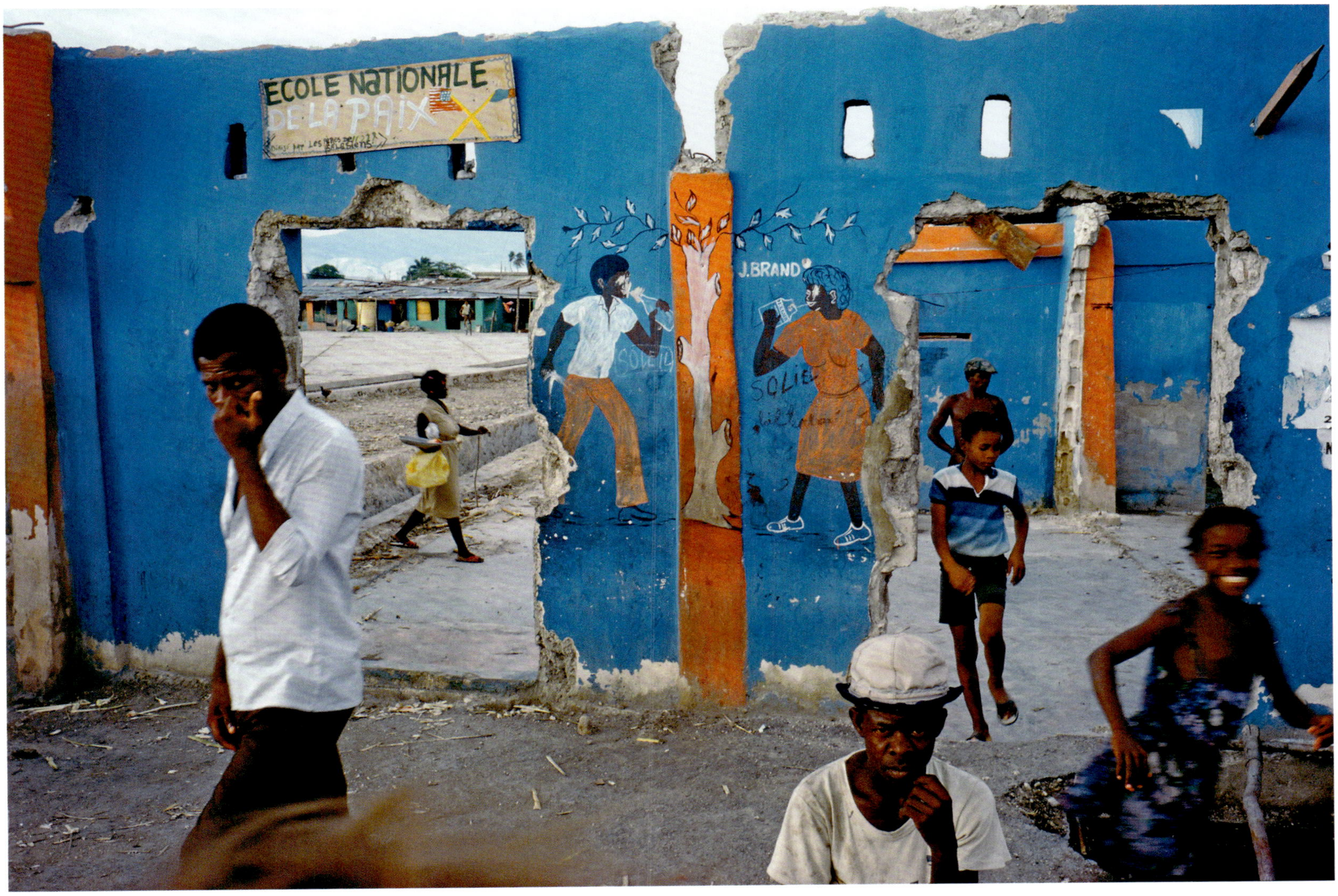

Alex Webb
Haiti, Etroits, La Gonave, 1986
C-print, dimensions variable

Haiti, Port-au-Prince, Killed by the Army, 1987
C-print, dimensions variable

Haiti. Cite Soleil, 1986
C-print, dimensions variable

Mary Ellen Mark

Colour's use within photojournalism was paralleled by its use within documentary, where it again prompted much anxiety as to its appropriateness. Colour could be seen as feeding exoticism, which becomes an issue in Mary Ellen Mark's Aperture book *Falkland Road* (1981). The book's title refers to a notorious street in Bombay, 'where the less expensive prostitutes live and work, an area famous for the cage-like houses in which some of the women live.'[15] The pictures were commissioned by *GEO* magazine's U.S. edition, but not eventually published because they were felt to be too explicit. Thirteen pictures were, however, published in Germany's *Stern* magazine in 1981.

The book names and is dedicated to the 'very special women' on Falkland Road that Mark got to know. Quotes from the girls also accompany some of the pictures, which are both intimate and voyeuristic studies. Colour helps give a sense of individual life and dignity to those portrayed, counteracting the sense of squalor that could very easily be associated with such a subject and helping give a more affirmative portrait of the women's lives. What is notable is the eloquence and formal sophistication of the pictures as colours suggest moods, from the melancholy of blues and greens to the more warm and exuberant celebratory moments, the play of patterns and colour, that offset the sense of alienating interiors. In celebrating these women's working lives, rooms are cramped but often brightly coloured and clean.

Raghubir Singh

For Raghubir Singh colour is integral to Indian life and culture. However much Indians might admire 'the black and white arts of the West,' he claims the 'Indian photographers cannot produce the angst and alienation rooted in Western photographers such as Brassaï, Bill Brandt, Robert Frank and Diane Arbus.'[16] He grew up in Nehru's post-colonial India, but spent most of his adult life in the West, living at various times in Hong Kong, Paris and London. His career began by covering news stories and assignments through the local press bureaux for *Life International* and *The New York Times*. He shifted to colour when he began working on an extended project to document the Ganges. In his pictures of Indian life on the street the pictorial field is always teeming and full as the competing different elements in the photographs set up a remarkably rich and complex visual interplay of colours, gestures and forms. Singh also especially loved the spatial uncertainties created by mirrored surfaces, as well as the ambiguities set up by the inclusion of other life-like pictures within the frame. While Singh was influenced by Henri Cartier-Bresson, his pictures of street life in many respects went further since his compositions were rarely centred on one decisive moment and they were in colour. This is beautifully brought out in his photograph showing the rhyming tea-pouring and tea-drinking figures in a bustling Mumbai market or the splendid correspondences set up between the gestures of a street barber and the flailing stone arms and hands of unpainted stone Kali figures, icons of faith and tradition interwoven with more humdrum and mundane daily activities.

Singh's pictures might become an exoticism to Western viewers, but the aesthetic and colour is integral to his philosophy and to Indian culture. Singh's photography confirms what he refers to as 'the Indian view of life,' one resonating 'with optimism, with sparkle, with illusion, with lively pictorialism and with the bonding spirit of community.'

Mary Ellen Mark
Putla, Falkland Road, Bombay, India, 1978
Cibachrome print
40.6 × 50.8 cm / 16 × 20 in

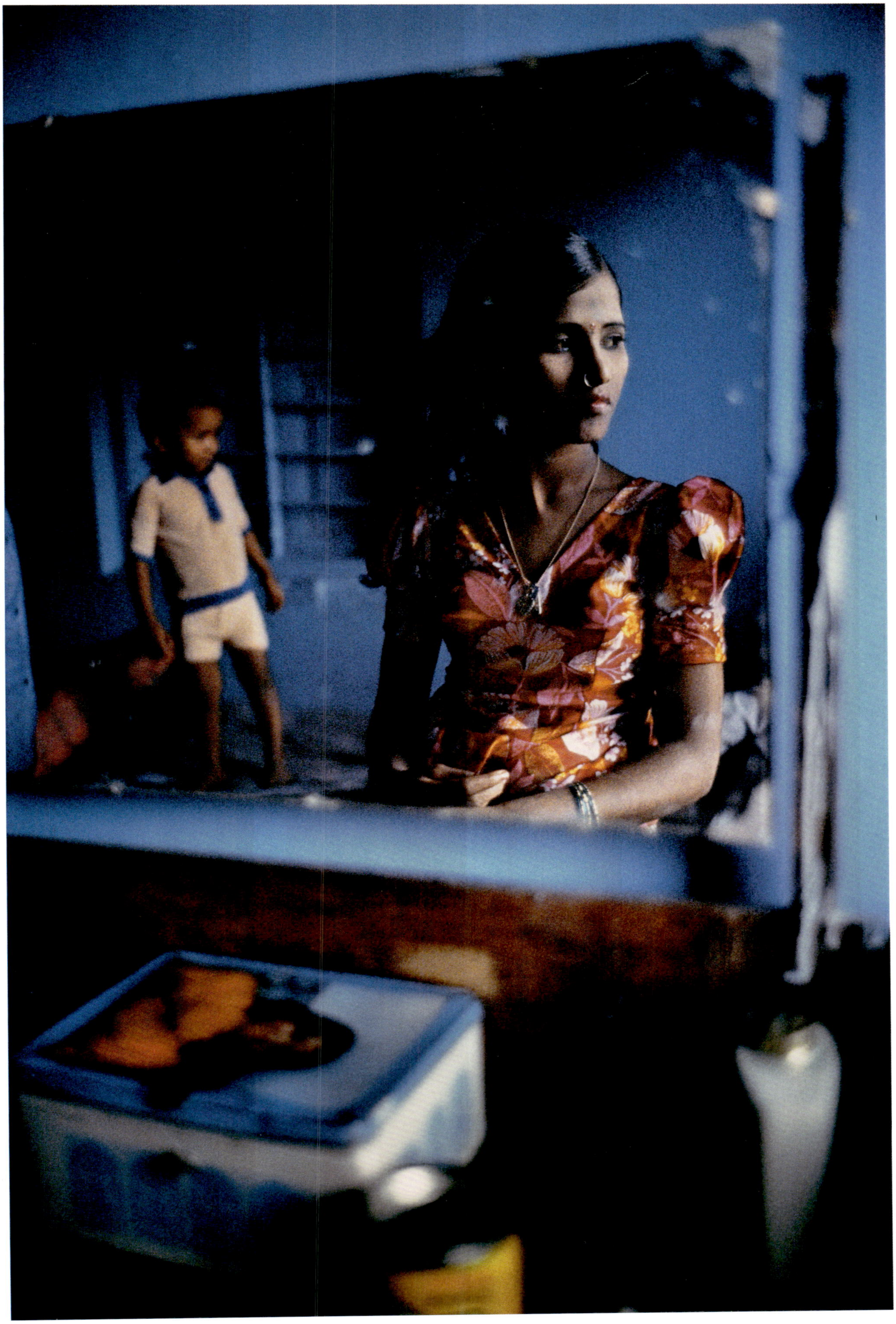

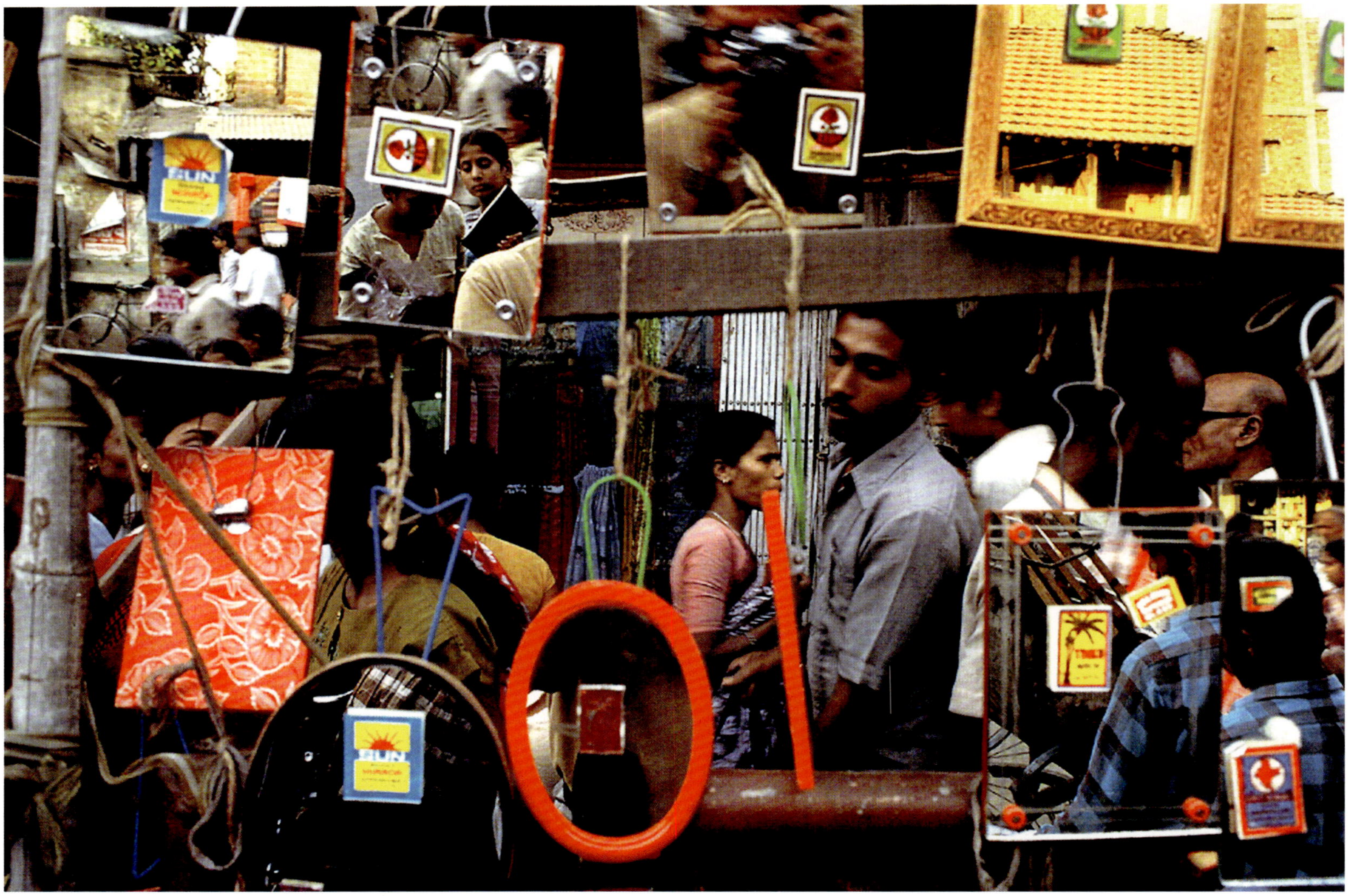

Raghubir Singh
Pavement Mirror Shop, Howrah, West Bengal, 1991
C-print, 40.6 × 59.6 cm / $23\frac{5}{8} \times 31\frac{1}{2}$ in

Barber and goddess Kali, Calcutta, West Bengal, 1987
C-print, 40.6 × 59.6 cm / $23\frac{5}{8} \times 31\frac{1}{2}$ in

Crawford Market, Mumbai, Maharashtra, 1993
C-print, 40.6 × 59.6 cm / $23\frac{5}{8} \times 31\frac{1}{2}$ in

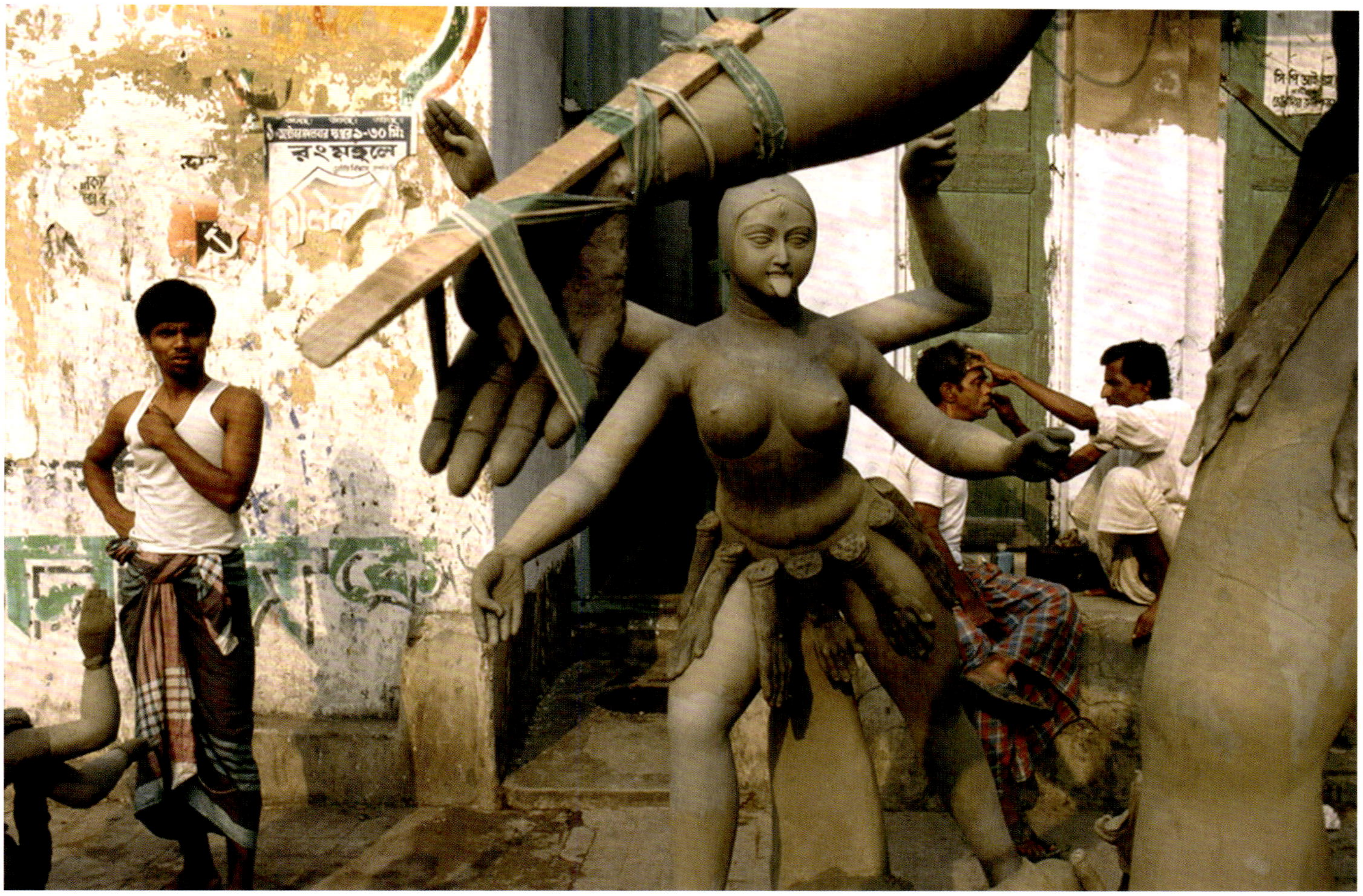

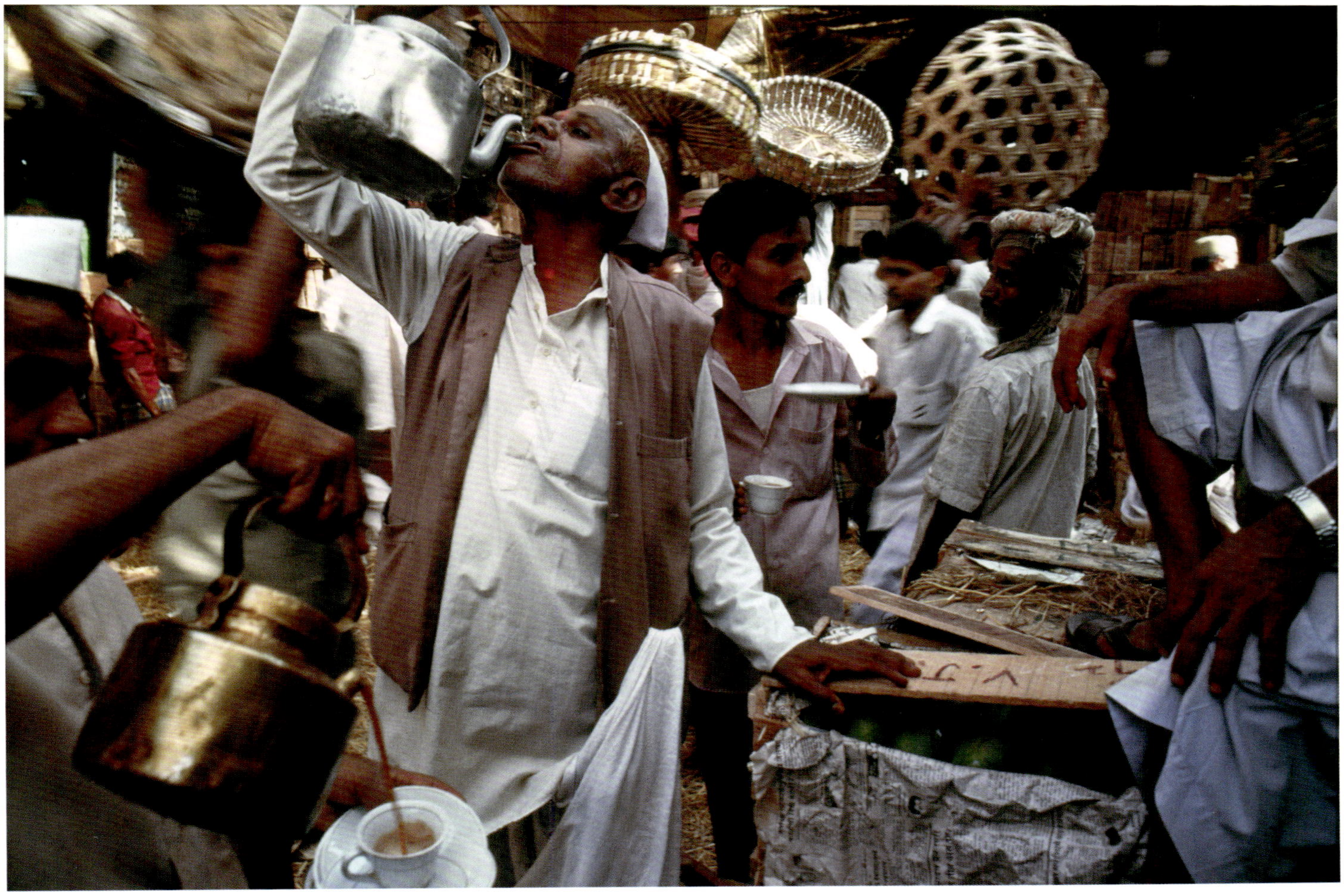

Paul Graham

Paul Graham's use of colour challenged the British social documentary photographic tradition. There was an assumption that colour's close association with advertising meant it was not possible to be critical of the effects of capitalism through a form so integral to consumer culture. Influenced by the new colour photography in the United States, Graham used colour to document the damaging effects of the destruction of an old industrial order and its replacement by an American-style market economy under Margaret Thatcher's Conservative government (1979–90).

Through a series of interior photographs of unemployment benefit offices up and down the United Kingdom, Graham's 'Beyond Caring' (1984–5) shows the decay of Britain's Welfare State under Margaret Thatcher and a sense of the government's neglect of a large section of the population (by 1982 more than three million people were out of work). Graham's pictures appear to be taken surreptitiously; some are off-kilter and taken with a low viewpoint, showing expanses of grimy and often littered floors. The fractured and awkward compositions seem to accord with the social disunity of the groups of people pictured in the spaces. The stasis and stillness of those shown waiting underscores a sense of the wasting of these people's lives. The alienation Graham shows speaks not about some existential condition, as in William Eggleston's portrayal of lone male figures, for example, but is instead determined by economic forces. Colour, as the critic David Chandler notes, is integral to these pictures. It conveys the discordant and stifling atmosphere of the rooms as well as showing us 'the false optimism of those orange benches and yellow walls, contrived to "brighten up" the experience.'[17]

Paul Graham
Mother and Baby, Highgate DHSS, North London, 1984
Colour photograph
68 × 87.5 cm / 26¾ × 34⅜ in

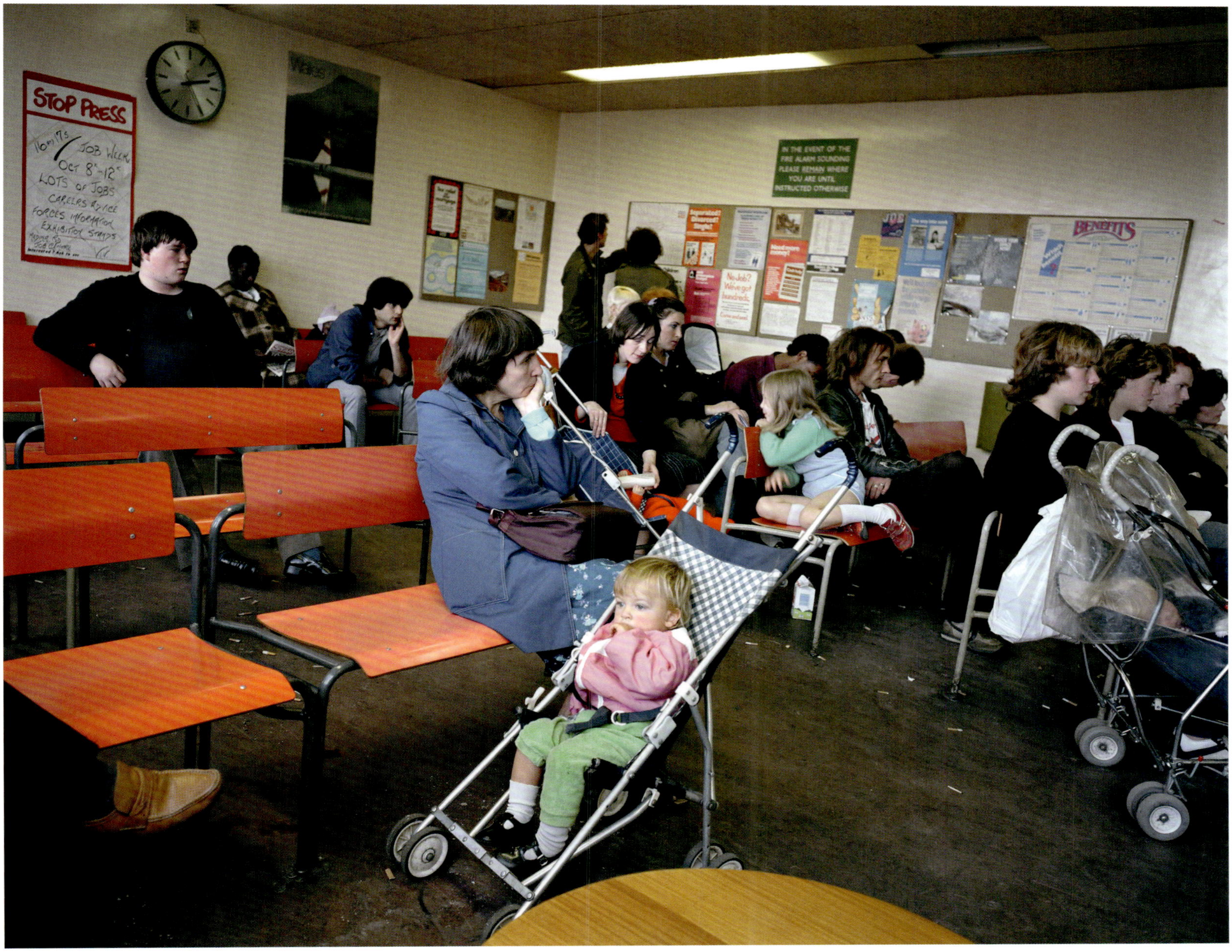
STOP PRESS
16 or 17s
JOB WEEK
OCT 8th–12th
LOTS OF JOBS
CAREERS ADVICE
FORCES INFORMATION
EXHIBITION STANDS
IN THE EVENT OF THE
FIRE ALARM SOUNDING
PLEASE REMAIN WHERE
YOU ARE UNTIL
INSTRUCTED OTHERWISE
Need more money?
BENEFITS

Richard Billingham

Colour was integral to Richard Billingham's groundbreaking 1996 book, *Ray's a Laugh*. Picturing his own family, he raises issues about judgements of taste and attitudes towards class. For all the flaws and imperfections of the snapshot and artless look – a look which aids a sense of realism and directness – the visual effect and style of these pictures is deliberate and knowing. Originally made as reference material for paintings while a student at Sunderland University, Billingham's photographs possess a distinctive visual richness and understanding of form. The pictures rely on the tensions and contradictions between an essentially abject and counter-idealizing vision and a pictorial richness. Much of their aesthetic effect is caught up in a class collision of taste, where the spectacle of kitsch ornamentation, legible to middle-class viewers as working-class 'bad taste', both maintains a cultural and class difference that keeps the subjects in their place, apart and separate, and yet gives the pictures an aesthetic distinction that raises them beyond mere documentary. One of Billingham's most visually rich images is a portrait of his mother doing a jigsaw puzzle which sets up collisions between its mosaic of colours, the blue box of Sky cigarettes on the half-formed jigsaw landscape on the table top, the box of jigsaw pieces and his mother's floral dress. In another picture, showing a potentially violent argument – with Billingham's mother looking as though she's about to thump her husband and his brother hovering awkwardly in the background and only just intruding into frame – the camera also catches a visual interplay of patterns, the floral tattoos all over his mother's arm, the pattern on her dress, the wallpaper and the ornaments on the cabinet shelves in the background. While such beauty could be seen as separating Billingham's photographs from a more despairing and degrading documentary, it was also integral to lifting them into the artistic mainstream and making them more easily commodifiable.

Richard Billingham
Untitled, 1995
C-print
120 × 80 cm / 47¼ × 31½ in

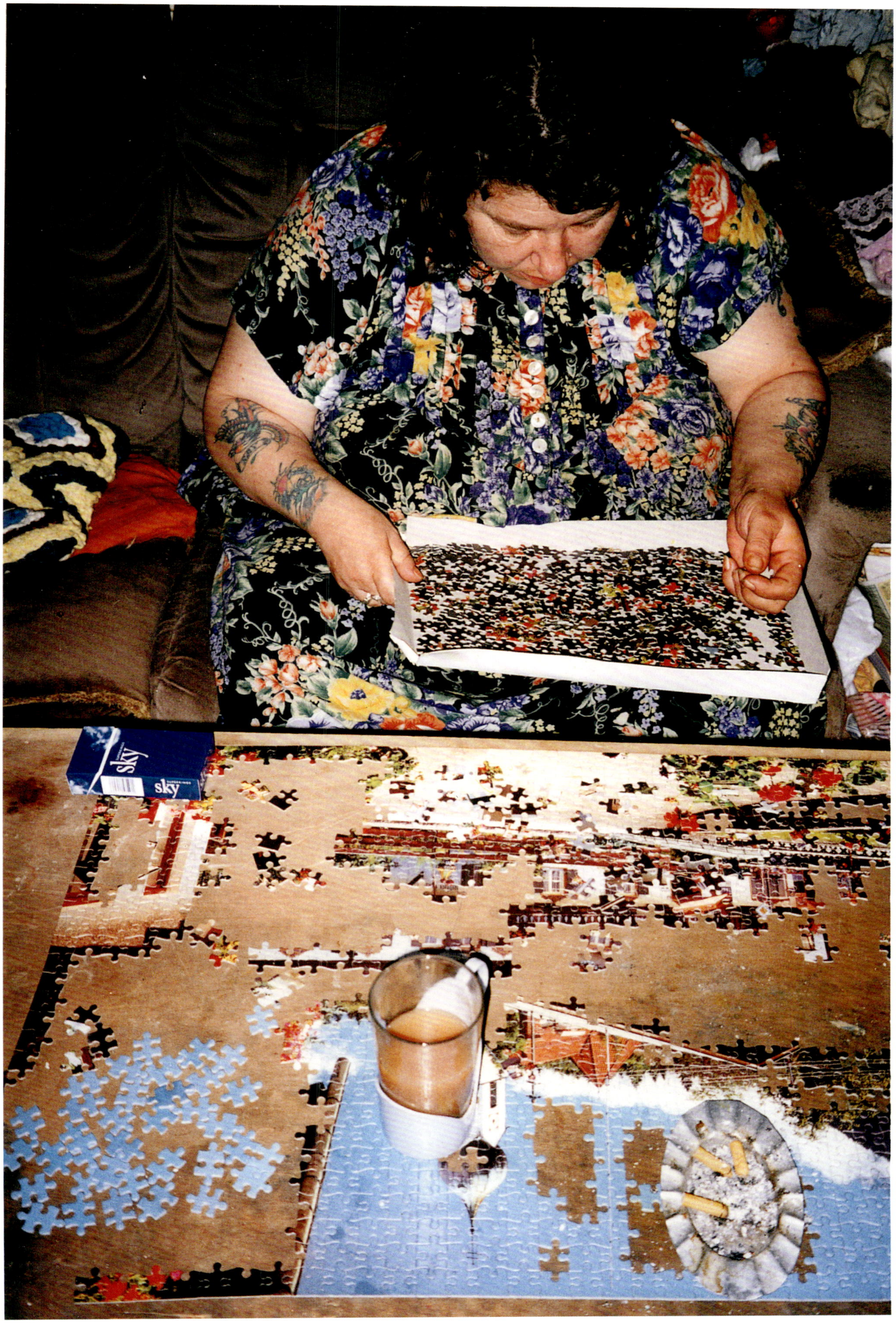
sky
sky

Daniela Rossell

Documentary Colour

The Mexican Daniela Rossell pictures her own class, and here colour is integral in bringing out the lavishness and excesses of their conspicuous consumption. Her 'Ricas y Famosas' images feature Mexico City's super-rich women, oligarchs' wives, in various poses, amidst ludicruous interiors where they have been able to play out their fantasies. The spaces are full of colonial décor, harem murals, stuffed tigers, giant Buddhas, kitsch painted portraits of themselves, religious icons and cuddly toys. Rossell came of age in this milieu. Turning twenty-one in 1994, she took the first images of 'Ricas y Famosas' in the lavish settings of her childhood home. She is complicit with her subjects. She does not censor their world, but shows it as it is. In the introduction to her book published in 2002, she declares, 'The images depict actual settings. The photographic subjects are representing themselves. Any resemblance [to] real world events is not coincidental.'[18] In one picture her subjects mimic the postures of the women in a harem mural behind them. Such colonial kitsch is made all the more powerful in contrast to typical Mexican photography, with its emphasis on ritual and poverty. When Rossell includes maids and servants to frame some of her depictions, they often look awkward as their female employers perform and parade themselves to camera. Material possessions emanate from the dolled-up subjects. The photographs are all the more excessive and obscene because of their contrast with the poverty in Mexico. One photograph includes representations of Mexican peasants in the form of kitsch, generic decorative pictures adorning the wall behind the figure of a young redheaded woman in an armchair.

These lavish spectacles are not seamless. The very collisions and contrasts set up within the photographs become important and meaningful. In some, an aerial viewpoint accords with a Baroque sensibility, as the photography creates a groundless sense of trompe l'oeil effects and mirrored surfaces. With Richard Billingham the ornamentation and decoration is class-marked. Kitsch speaks of working-class British taste. In Rossell's pictures kitsch is linked with the decadence of a ruling elite. The excess of decoration reflects an imperial and neocolonial pomposity that brings out the ludicrousness of the fantasies of her subjects and their naivety. Much of the imagery is steeped in colonial fantasies, which reflects the situation of these privileged white women in Mexico, but at the same time the very excess, the straining of credulity and the real, is suggestive of the ultimate hollowness and sadness of the lives of people cocooned in such luxurious isolation.

Martin Parr

Consumerism

The perceived vulgarity of colour means it still has a close relation to the commercial world. Colour is very much the garish form of commodity culture. The work of the British documentary photographer Martin Parr deliberately engages with issues of colour, consumerism and class.

Lurid colour is integral to Parr's critique of global consumerism in his 1999 book *Common Sense*. The book replays a theme earlier introduced in his series 'Last Resort', documentary photographs made between 1983 and 1986 in which holidaymakers wallowed in a sea of waste in the run-down northern British seaside town of New Brighton. The pictures in *Common Sense* were taken in every continent and the book's launch was celebrated by simultaneous exhibitions in more than 30 different cities worldwide that blanketed gallery walls with multiple images. The book flags up its worldwide theme with the cover detail of a rusty and battered moneybox globe. While some pictures clearly invite national stereotypes – from Germany's periscope-shaped salami to an abundance of signs for Englishness, such as a cup of tea, wasps in jam, a torso with a nationalist 'Made In England' tattoo – differences are subsumed by the overriding uniform, repetitive act of consumption. And it is in this respect one understands the full significance of the book's title: that the common sense is the sense we have in common, which Parr shows to be the affluent West's base sense of greedy overconsumption. The globe on the cover is a cue for the orgy of world consumption pictured within the book. But Parr's depiction of the excesses of consumption is coupled with a sense of waste and decay. Interrupting the pictures of people stuffing their faces are occasional abject details: a sticky lollipop dropped on the floor, a putrefying banana, a degraded bar code, a bruised apple.

The colour images offer details and close ups of half-eaten food, of hands stuffing mouths with sweets, ice creams, burgers, popcorn and meat. It is a world of excess and indulgence conveyed through a glut of over-the-top photographs. Parr mostly avoids identifiable pictures of people. He goes in so close to his subjects we only see the consumers through punchy fragmentary details: bits of faces, a freshly lipsticked smile, a $100 dollar bill hanging out of a woman's mouth. Instead of human faces and expressions, we have only the stunned, gaping or blank stares of mannequins and sex dolls. Parr's aesthetic is deliberately facile, cheap, low and gauche. His critique of consumerist excesses through mimicry indicates a dangerous endgame within consumerism, as colour's very vulgarity becomes integral to the savageness of this compelling but messy series.

Daniela Rossell
Harem Room, 2002, from the series 'Ricas y Famosas'
C-print
127 × 152.4 cm / 50 × 60 in

Janita Office, 1999, from the series 'Ricas y Famosas'
C-print
127 × 152.4 cm / 50 × 60 in

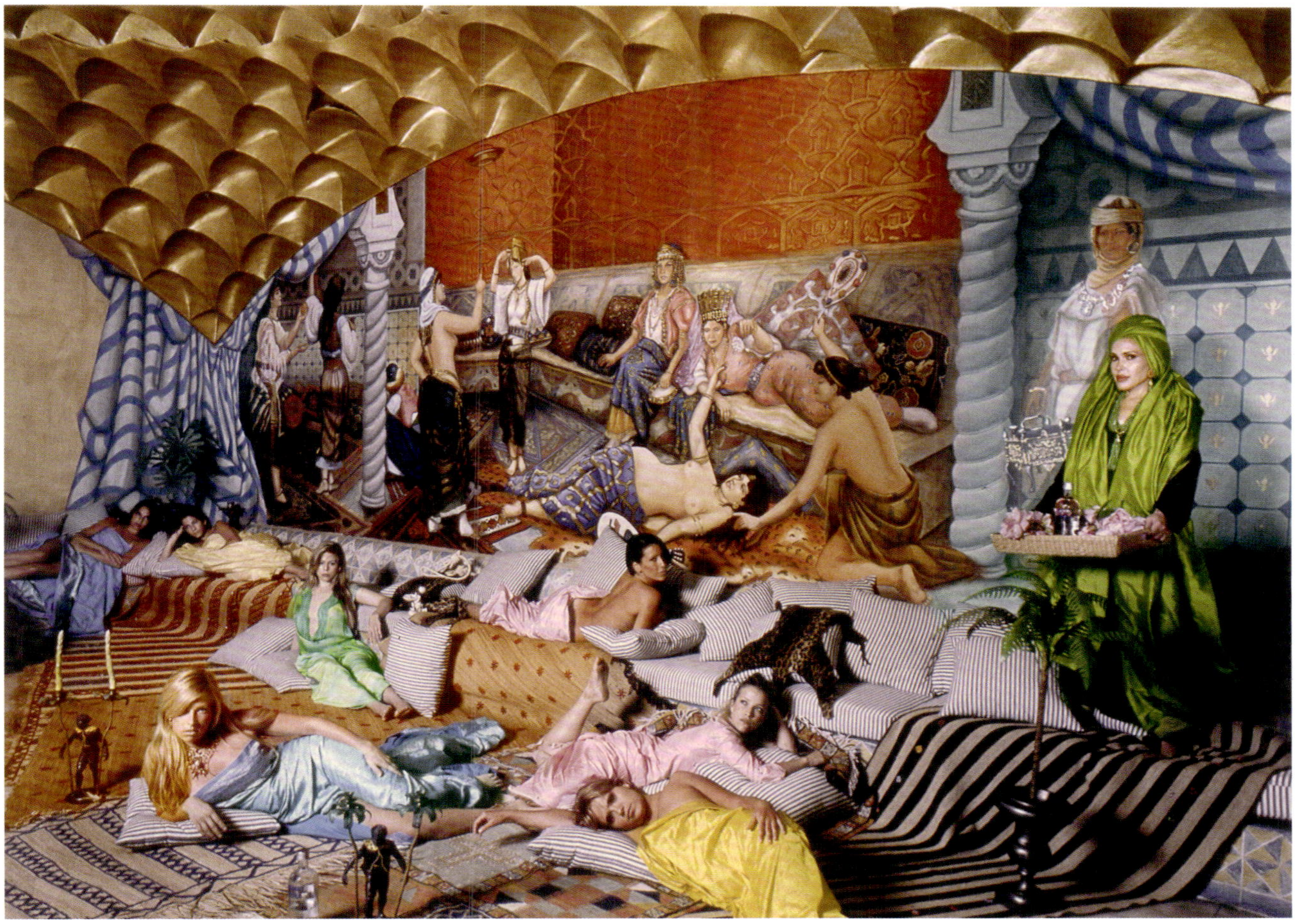

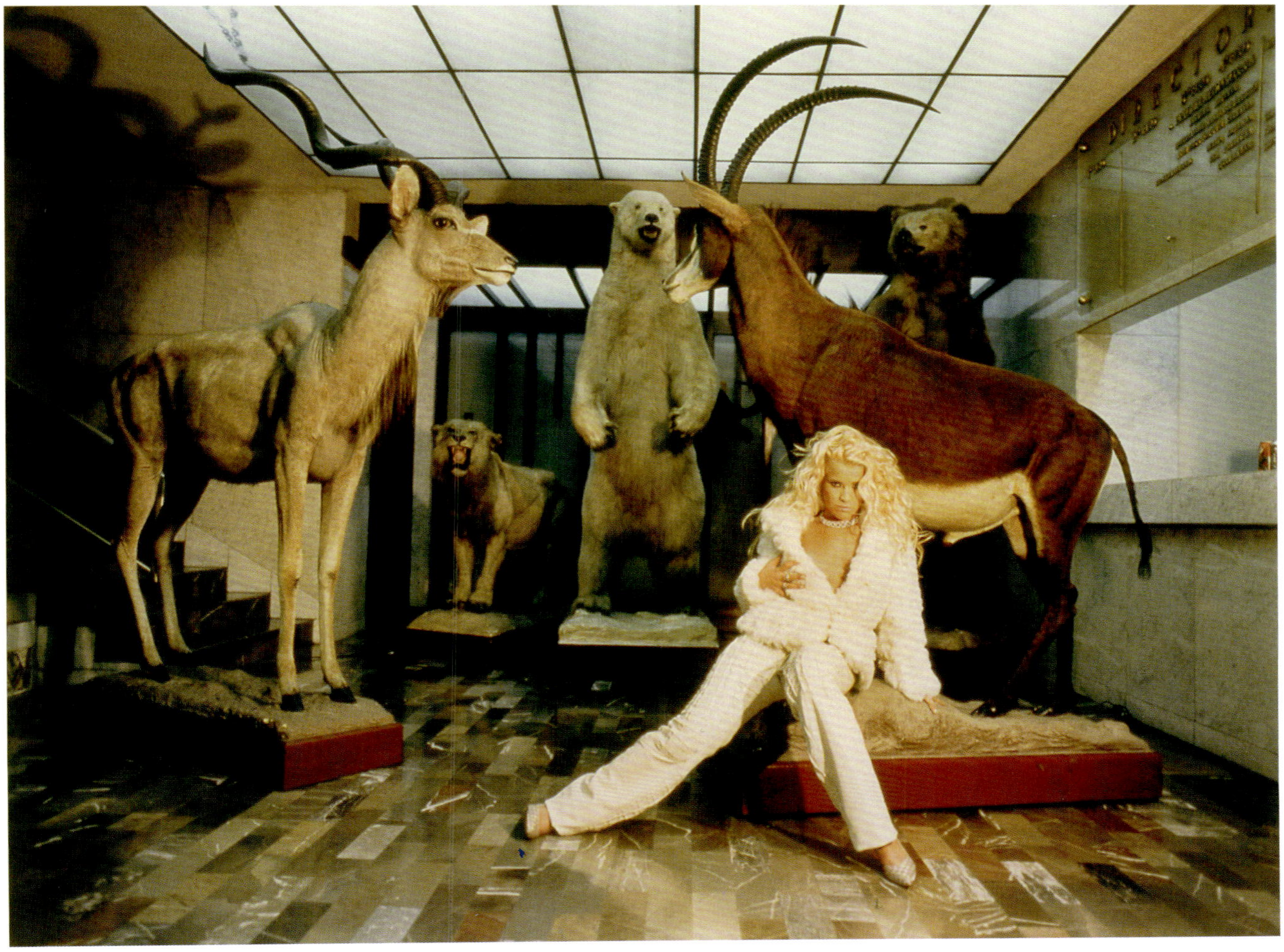

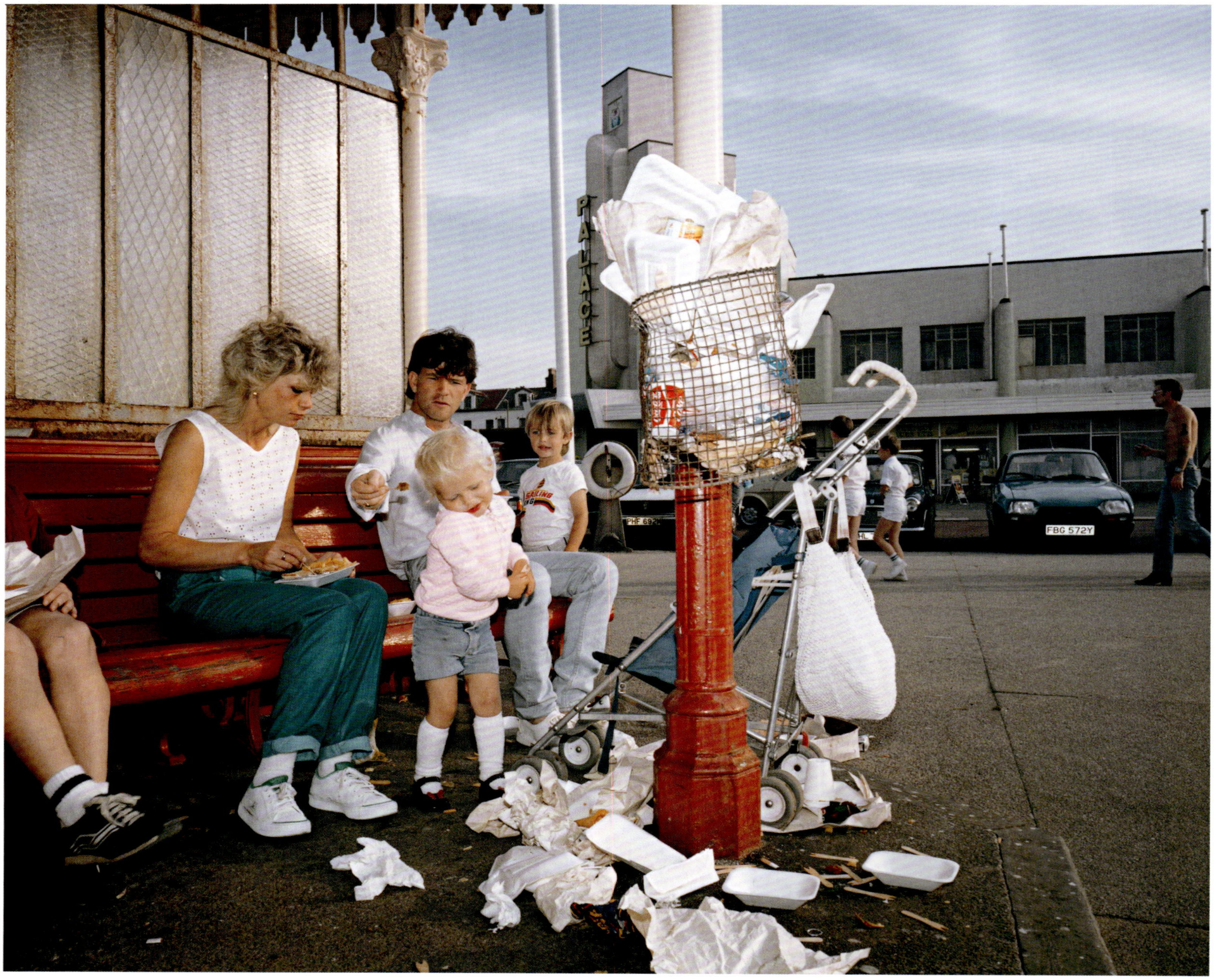

Martin Parr
New Brighton, Merseyside, from the series 'The Last Resort', 1983–6, C-print, dimensions variable

Sand Bay, England, GB, 1997, from the series 'Common Sense' C-print, dimensions variable

Sand Bay, England. GB, 1997, from the series 'Common Sense' and 'New British', C-print, dimensions variable

Las Vegas, USA, 1998, from the series 'Common Sense' C-print, dimensions variable

Zurich, Switzerland, 1997, from the series 'Common Sense' C-print, dimensions variable

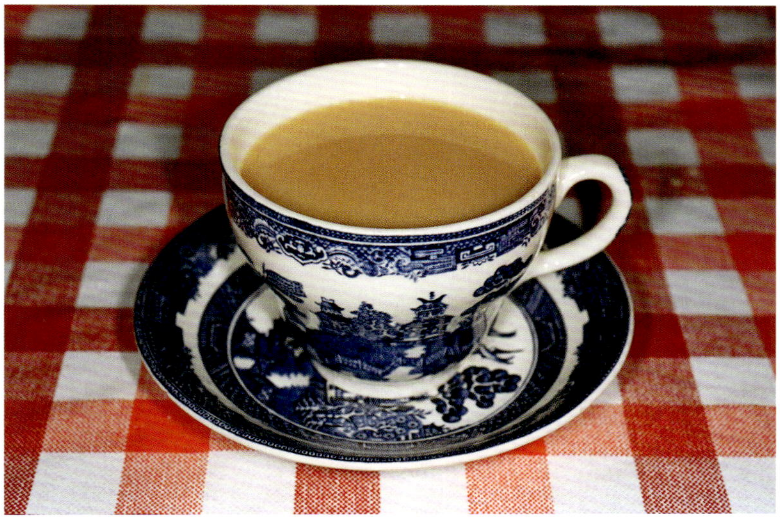

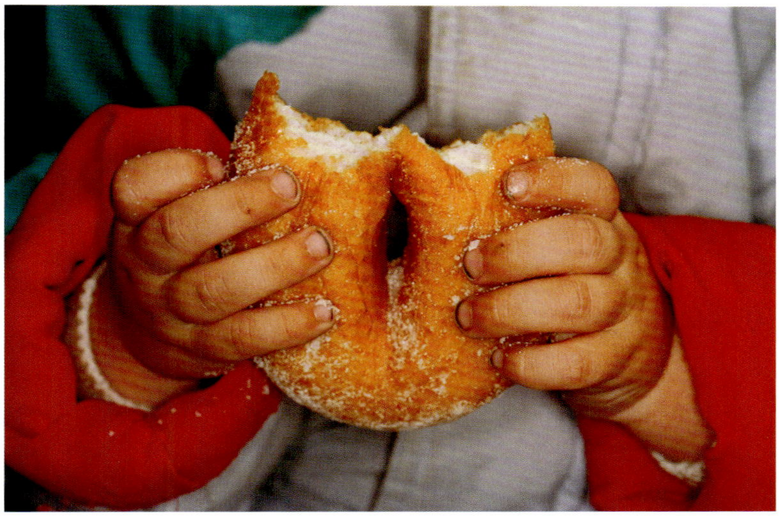

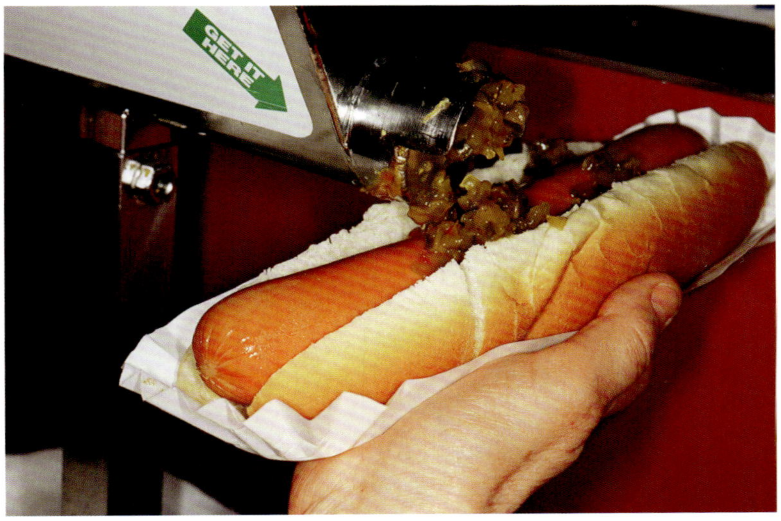
GET IT HERE

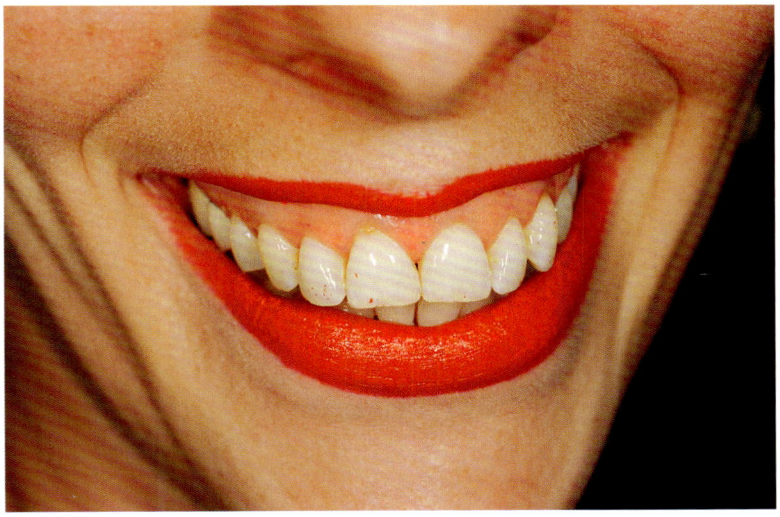

Peter Fraser

Peter Fraser's pictures involve subjective, deeply felt, instinctual responses to the look of things in the world. Chance is a recurrent element in Fraser's photography. There is the sense of a searching use of the camera and an openness to the potentially infinite pictorial possibilities of what is around him. Colour is integral to the ways in which his photography opens up new and unexpected ways of depicting aspects of the everyday and ordinary, such as the subtle tonal shift in blues between two plastic buckets.

Questions about aesthetic value and judgement often lie at the heart of Fraser's work. One of his early and most iconic photographs, taken in Wales in 1985, shows a corrugated green shed bearing the graffito 'I Hate Green' across its doors. When Fraser's picture adorned the cover of what was one of the first colour issues of the leading photography journal in Britain in the 1980s, *Creative Camera*, it served as a witty riposte to the detractors of colour photography. The picture was a celebration of the colour green, not only of the green of the painted shed, but also of the grass, vegetation and trees. Fraser's sentiments were clearly far from those of the anonymous graffitist, unlike those magazine readers at the time still clinging to the value and import of black-and-white photography.

An early important inspiration for Fraser was the 1968 film *Powers of Ten*, written and directed by Ray and Charles Eames, with its macro and micro views. The film starts with a view of a picnicking couple in a park by a lake in Michigan, but the human measure is soon lost, both in the vastness of space as we are given a succession of receding aerial views and in the unfathomable depths of the body's interior as a subsequent succession of magnified close-ups takes us through the skin of the man's hand to cells, coils of the DNA and down to the quarks in a proton of a carbon atom. The sublime disordering effect of scale, of losing a sense of measure and a grip on things in the world, is characteristic of many of Fraser's photographs.

Science is important to his photography. Not as something knowable, but for opening up an unfathomable beyond. It became the subject in 'Deep Blue' (1997), a title taken from the evocative name given to the computer that beat the world-renowned Grand Master Gary Kasparov at chess and a project that reveals a fascination with the appearance of advanced scientific machines at many different sites from around the world, from Cambridge University to CERN's vast underground particle-physics laboratory in Geneva. Fraser used a series of colourful backdrops in his depiction of the machines. Much as these precise, complex technological objects can be seen to represent a non-human world, the use of colour introduces a subjective aesthetic element linked to human tastes, feelings and values. It is a reminder of what still might differentiate us from such super-intelligent machines.

While making 'Deep Blue', Fraser became aware of how such research environments were highly controlled to keep them free from contamination. His following series, 'Material' (2002), concentrates upon the other abject realm to these technological spaces, a world of detritus, dirt and formless matter. Fraser began by taking forensic close-ups of technology to show the imperfections, disorder and chaos, and the brilliant colours, within its electronic circuitry and components. 'Material' also included pictures of industrial objects and substances, of rusted pipes, oily chains, dried-up cans of paint, swarf, foam and grease. One distinctive flash-lit picture, taken at night outside an empty factory, shows a tar- and grit-encrusted little cube of splintered wood. Photographed and enlarged so we lose a sense of scale, this rough-hewn geometric form becomes a strange totemic object. Set against an impenetrable blackness, it invites reflection on our desire to discern beauty, form and order among the chaos and emptiness.

Peter Fraser
Communications Satellite, from the series 'Deep Blue', 1997
Pigment print, 135 × 165 cm / 53⅛ × 65 in

Cheddar No 5, from the series 'Everyday Icons', 1985–6
Pigment print
50 × 60 cm / 19⅝ × 23⅝ in

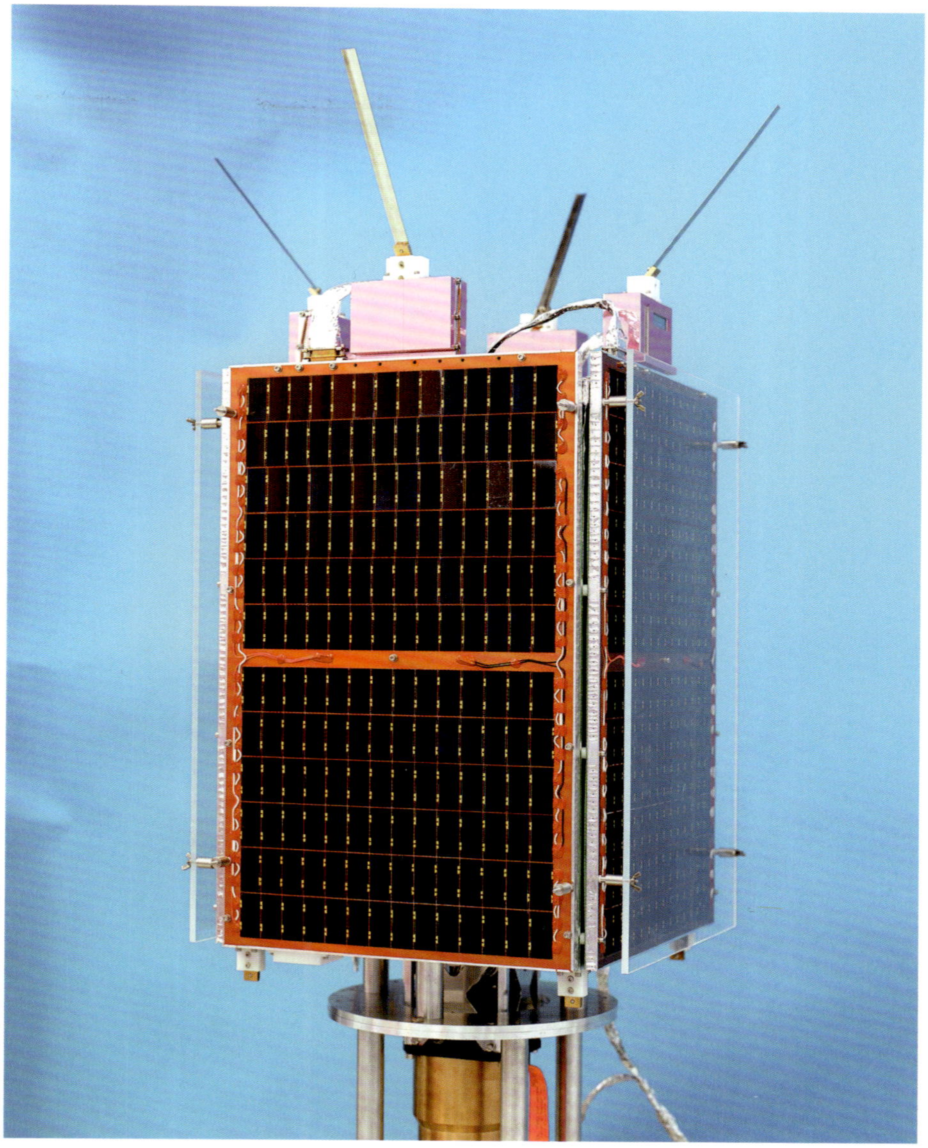

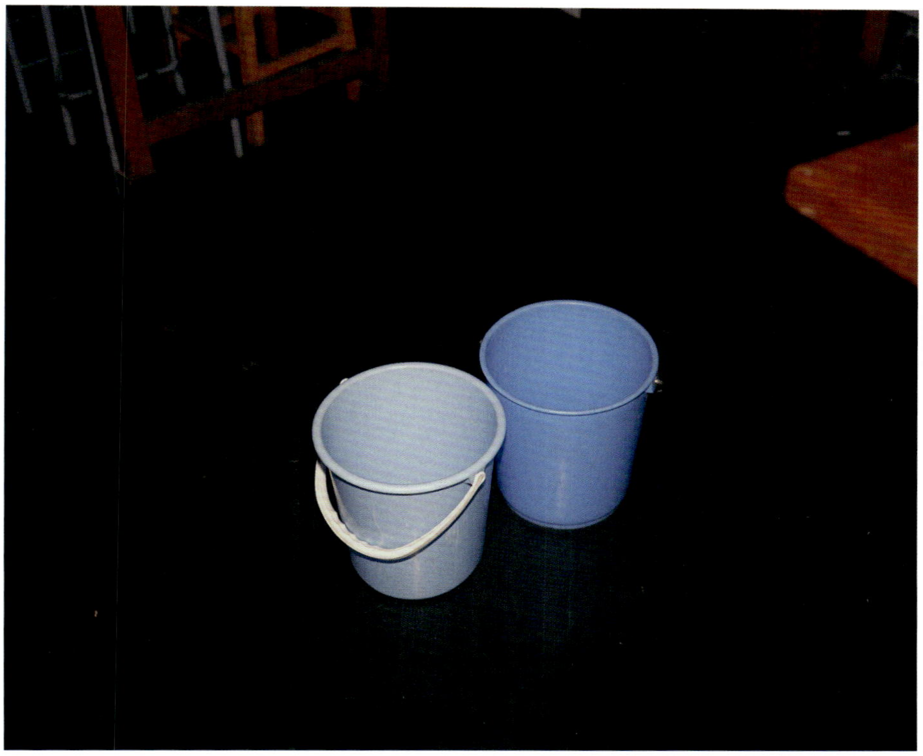

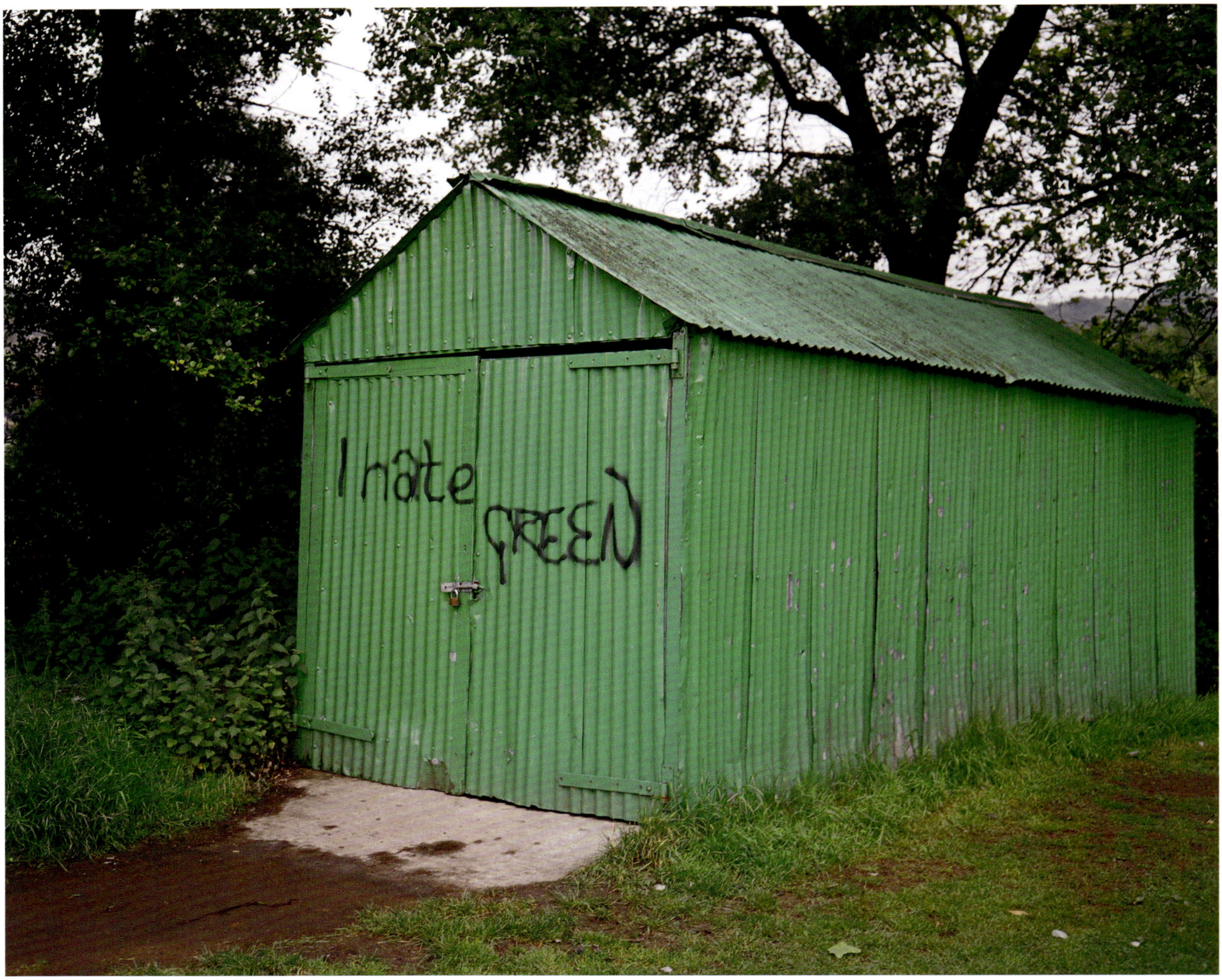

Peter Fraser
Pontypridd No 1, from the series 'Valleys Project', 1985
Pigment print, 50 × 60 cm / 19⅝ × 23⅝ in

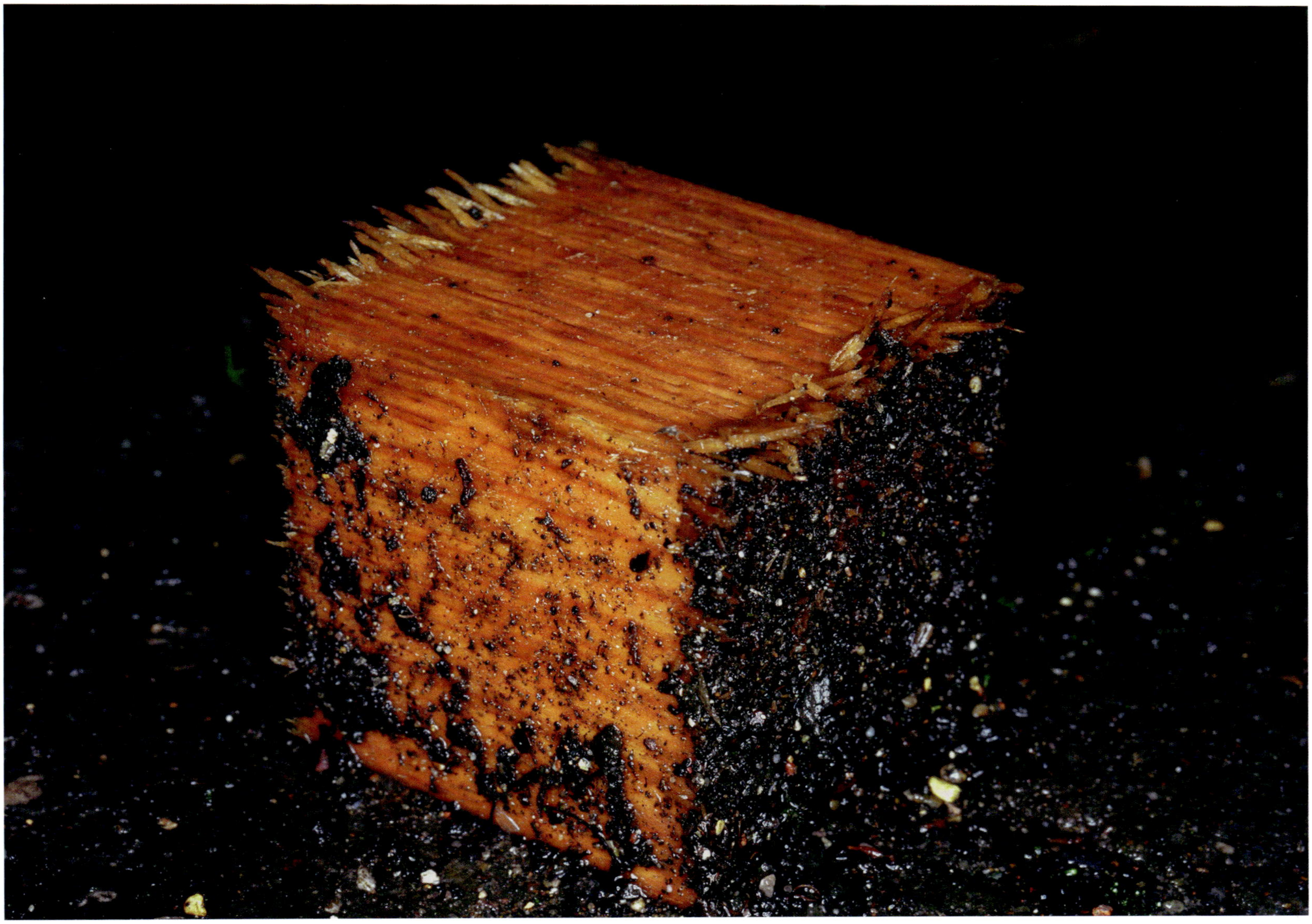

Peter Fraser
Untitled, from the series 'Material',
2002
Pigment print, 50 × 60 cm /
19⅝ × 23⅝ in

Gabriel Orozco

The photography of the Mexican artist Gabriel Orozco reveals the sensibility of a sculptor. His photography often involves interventions and manipulations. He alters things in the world and photographs the results: an arrangements of wooden scraps that he assembles to echo the New York skyline behind (*Island Within an Island*, 1993), oranges set out on wooden tables in a market after hours in Brazil (*Crazy Tourist*, 1991), circles left by the tyres of his bicycle as he rides through puddles (*Extension of Reflection*, 1992) or the trace of his breath on the closed lid of a piano (*Breath on Piano*, 1993). Sometimes he isolates other people's gestures, as with what one critic wittily called the 'greasy halos' above the empty Eames-inspired plastic chairs in a museum in Calcutta, formed by the imprints of the heads of all the people who once sat there (*Waiting Chairs*, 1998).[19]

Orozco calls the photograph 'a container I use to transport what I pick up in my interactions.'[20] And containers recur within his iconography, from the way a used and deflated ball has become a receptacle for a little puddle of water in *Pinched Ball* (1993) to the sensuous and intimate close up of the island-like and egg-like form of a pregnant belly, edged with the white froth of bubbles in a bath (*La Isla de Simon*, 2005).

The idea of the receptacle is also important in one of Orozco's favourite artworks, *Empty Shoe Box*. When it was first shown in the 1993 Venice Biennale its slightness and seeming insignificance served as an effective counterpoint to the spectacle of art on display at such festivals. It was presented on the floor, where it could (and did) get crushed, kicked or thrown away. The light touch of this nevertheless important intervention is echoed in the qualities of his photography. As *Empty Shoe Box* countered the excesses of the biennale jamboree, Orozco's photography is drawn from the everyday and resists the spectacular tendencies of the medium. Attentive to the imaginative potential of his encounters with things in the world, predominantly in places away from the centres of capital, Orozco's photography is integral to his playful and open approach to art-making and his way of bringing art closer to life.

Gabriel Orozco
Island within an Island, 1993
Silver dye bleach print
40.6 × 50.8 cm / 16 × 20 in

Crazy Tourist, 1991
C-print, 40.6 × 50.8 cm / 16 × 20 in

Waiting Chairs, 1998
Silver dye bleach print
40.6 × 50.8 cm / 16 × 20 in

Pinched Ball, 1993
Silver dye bleach print
40.6 × 50.8 cm / 16 × 20 in

La Isla de Simon, 2005
C-print, 40.6 × 50.8 cm / 16 × 20 in

Empty Shoe Box, 1993
Shoe box, 12.4 × 33 × 21.6 cm /
4⅞ × 13 × 8½ in

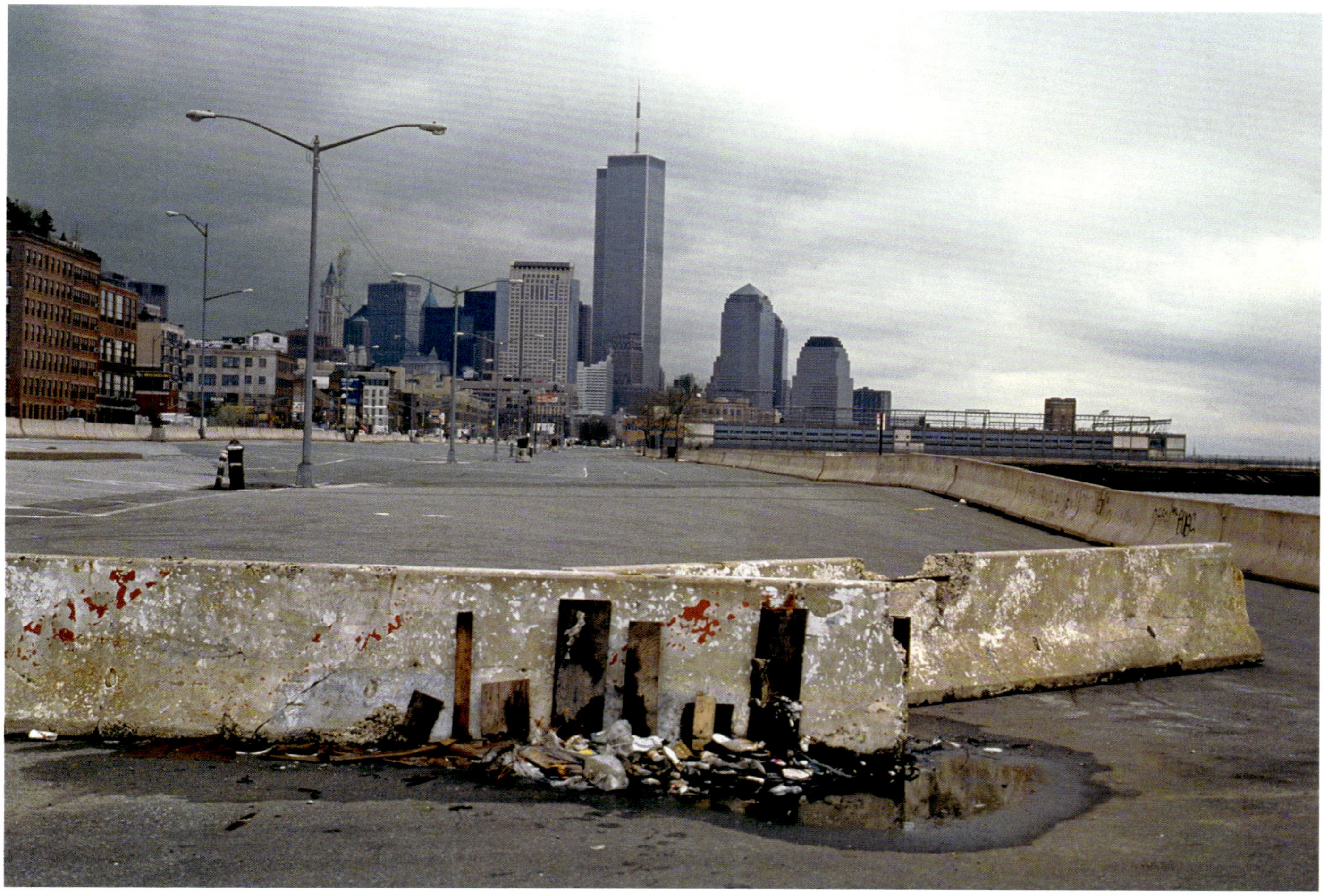

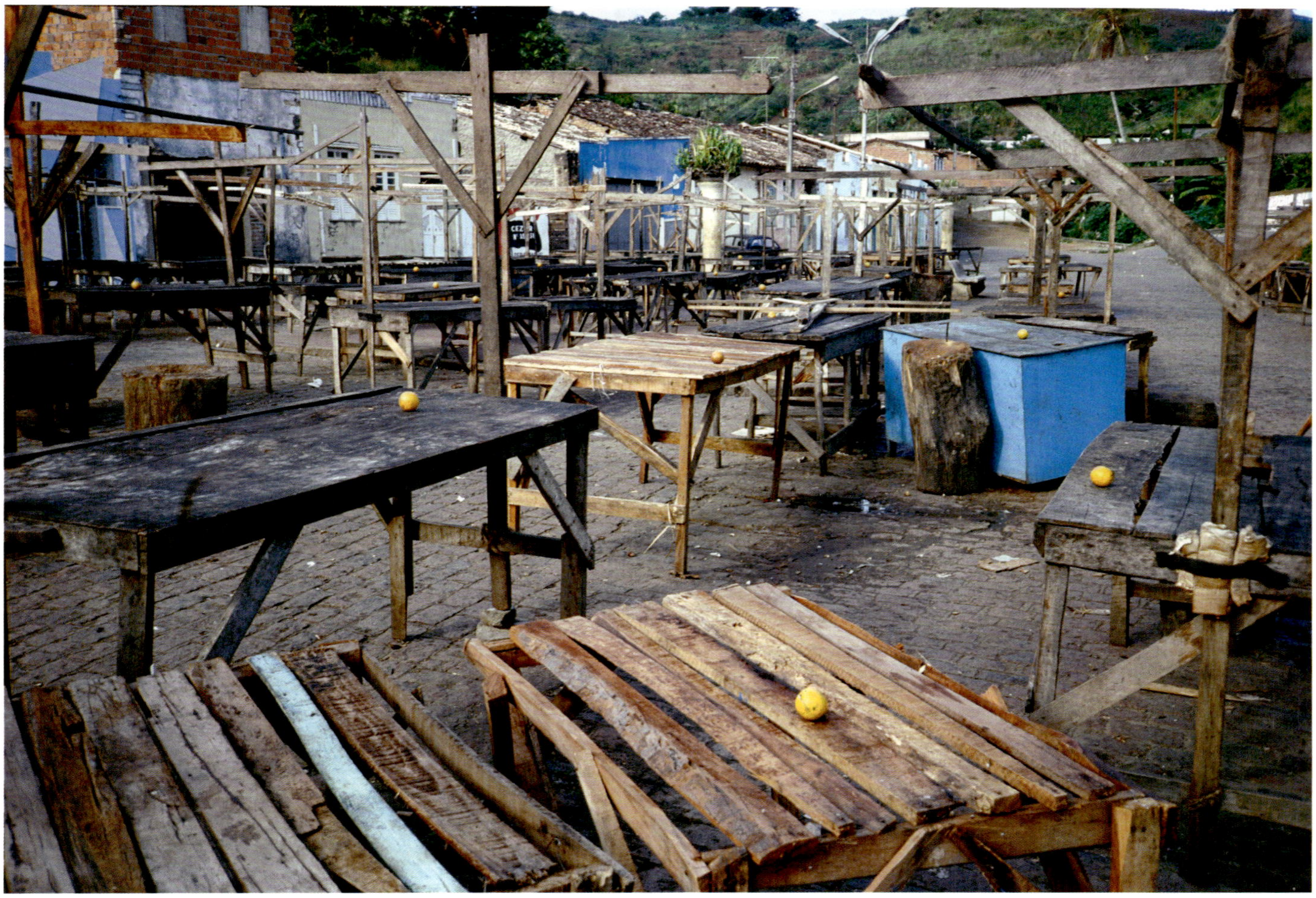

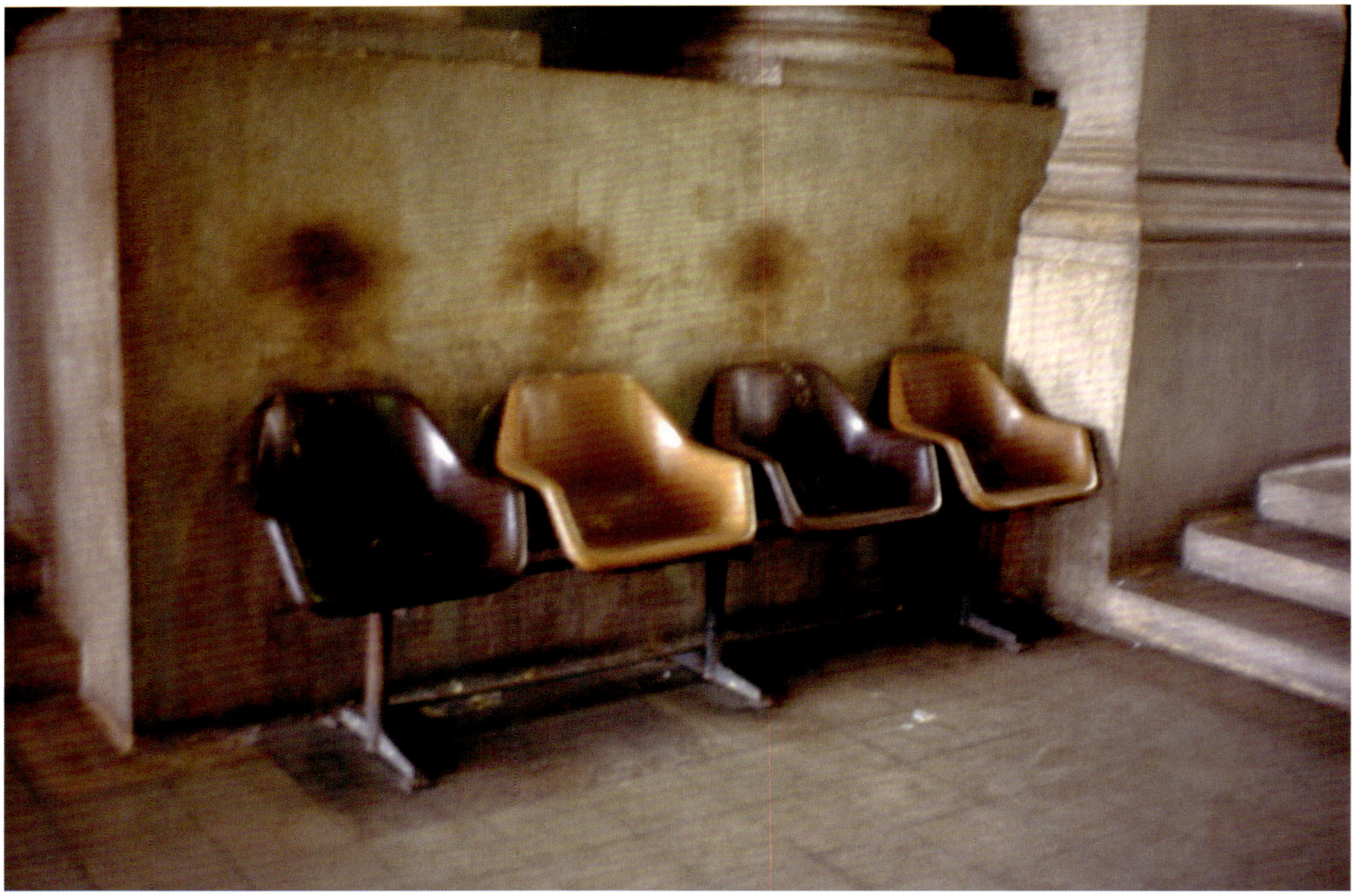

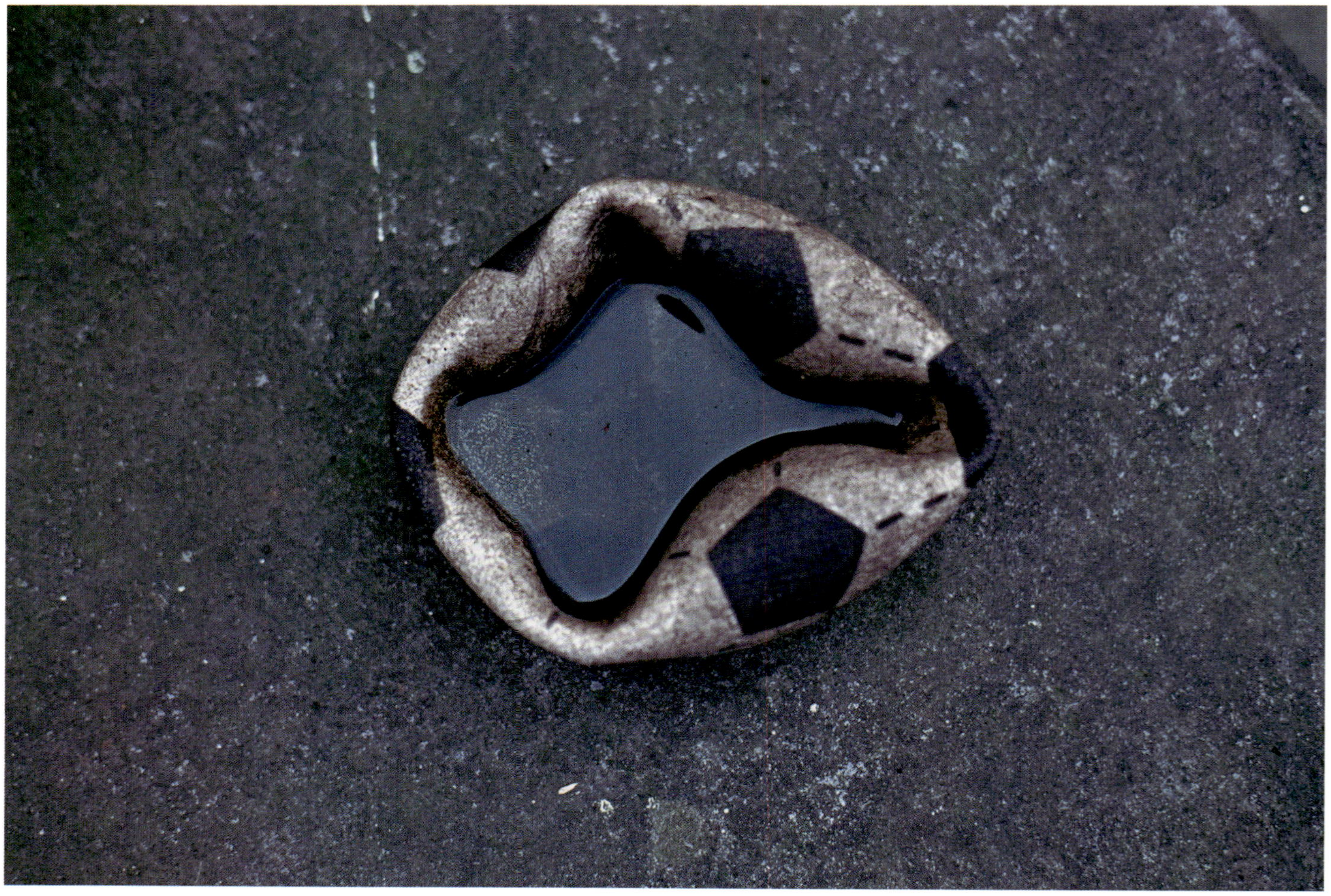

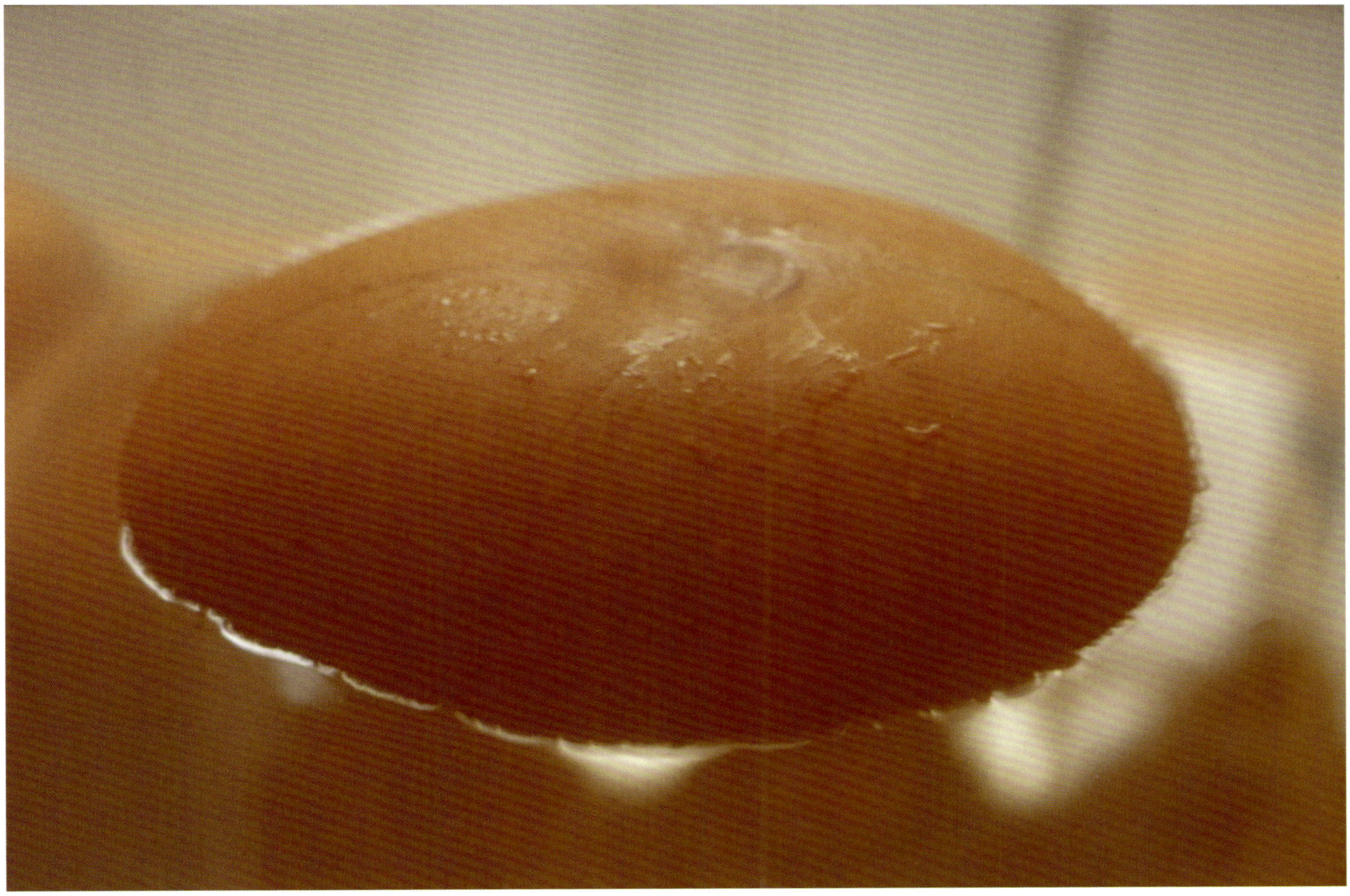

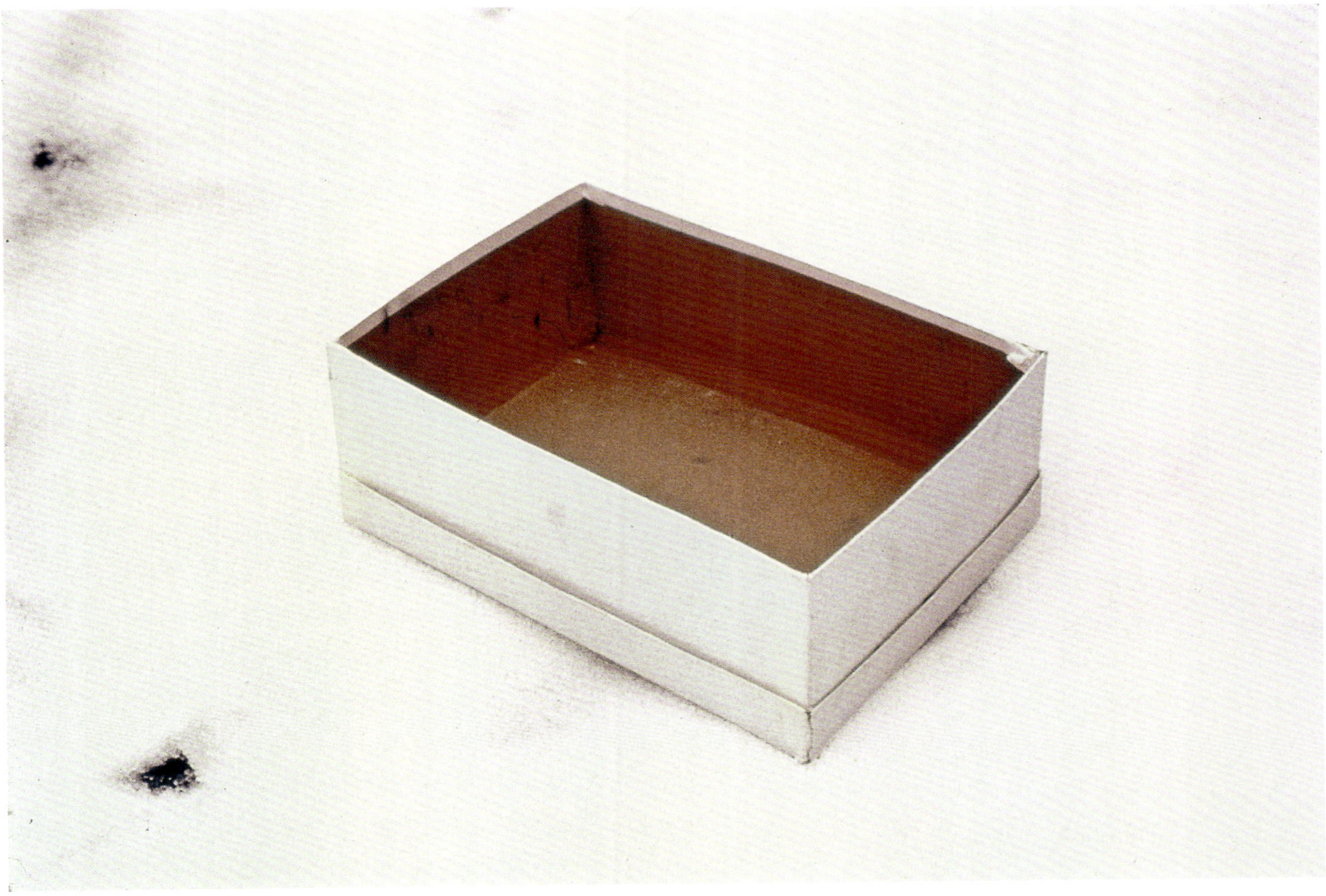

Saïdou Dicko

A remarkable series of colour photographs made in Africa by the artist Saïdou Dicko, who is also a painter, continue this affirmative and joyful use of colour. Born in Déou, Burkina Faso, where he worked as a herdsman between the ages of five and nine, Dicko now lives and works in Dakar, Senegal. His photographs show the shadows of people and animals. One can see his work as countering the colonial fascination with the African body, which was the basis of a history of anthropological looking that fixed and measured its subjects as specimens for scrutiny. Dicko's subjects remain mostly non-visible, and are given a different and new visibility and freedom in absentia by the way the camera fixes their shadows. We get a sense that this photography takes us inside the life of the subjects he pictures with such an intimacy and closeness. Light and vibrant colour are central to the sensousness of these images. While they reflect a painter's vision and celebratory joy in colour, at the same time the shadow motif is inextricably connected to photography. One of the earliest names for photography was skiagraphy, or 'shadow-writing,' and Dicko's skiagraphies are not about darkness or negativity but the exuberance of life. The shadows are always full of colour. In an unexpected sense, they are also embodied; they give us a sense of where they were taken from, and the artist's own shadow, on occasion, dances among the shadows of others. This is very much a visceral colour photography, accenting the colours and textures of a people's environment as the shadows are cast against brightly painted and tiled walls, oil drums, vehicles, bricks and the textures of the earth itself.

Dicko uses colour as an affirmation of both people and place. As with Peter Fraser and Gabriel Orozco, we are dealing here with a basic and primary use of photography. It is very much an open photography, which is responsive to a lifeworld of seemingly limitless possibilities, and colour is integral to its joy and apparent lightness of touch. Dicko's concentration on shadows shifts us away from things to suggest a world that is forever changing, with the accent on moments that capture gestures, the fun of games or dancing figures, or more tender portraits as shown in the profiles of mothers holding or carrying their children. Sometimes Dicko presents a simple action, such as the drinking of water, through a succession of pictures. With their fascination with the lyricism of gesture, Dicko's shadow photographs could well be seen in terms of street photography, a key and enduring artistic use of the medium which is explored in the following chapter.

Saïdou Dicko
Suka, 2005
Digital C-print, dimensions variable

Entre-Deux, 2005
Digital C-print, dimensions variable

L'eau, 2007
Digital C-print, dimensions variable

Marché Tilène, 2007
Digital C-print, dimensions variable

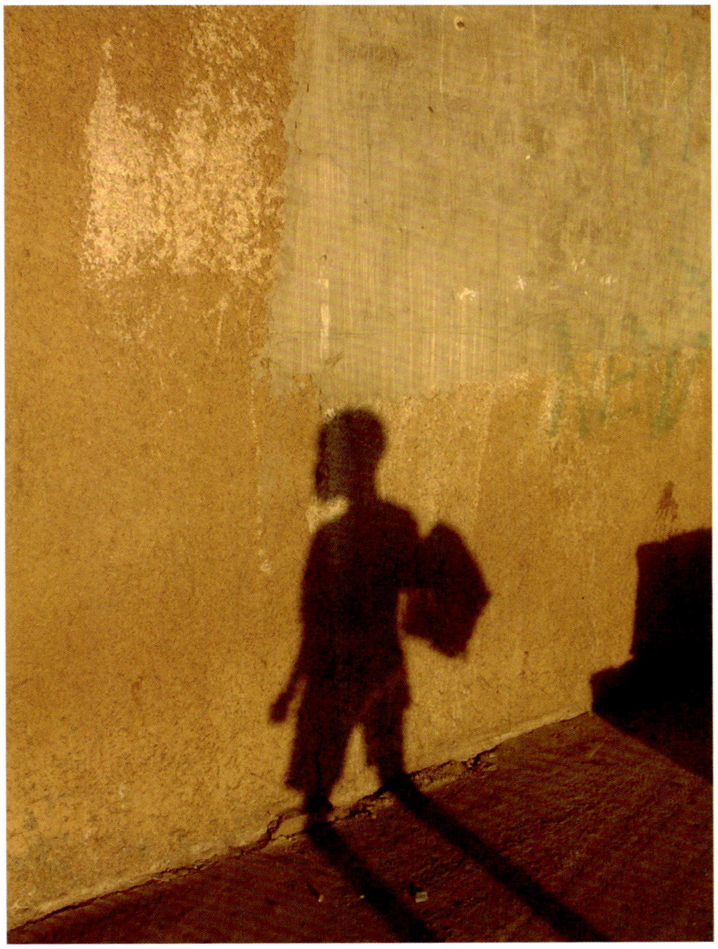
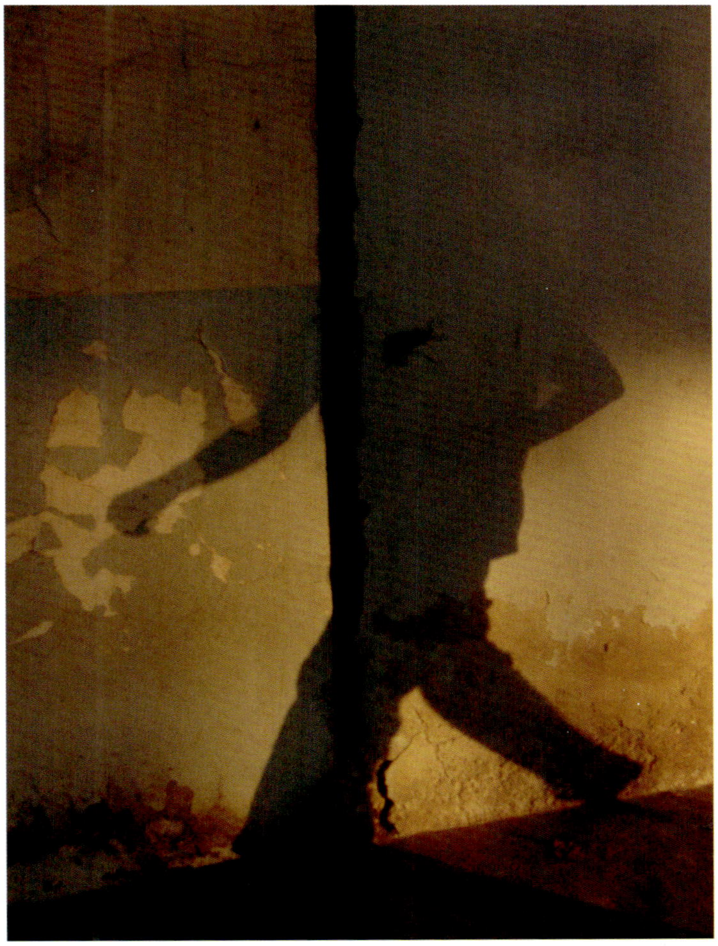
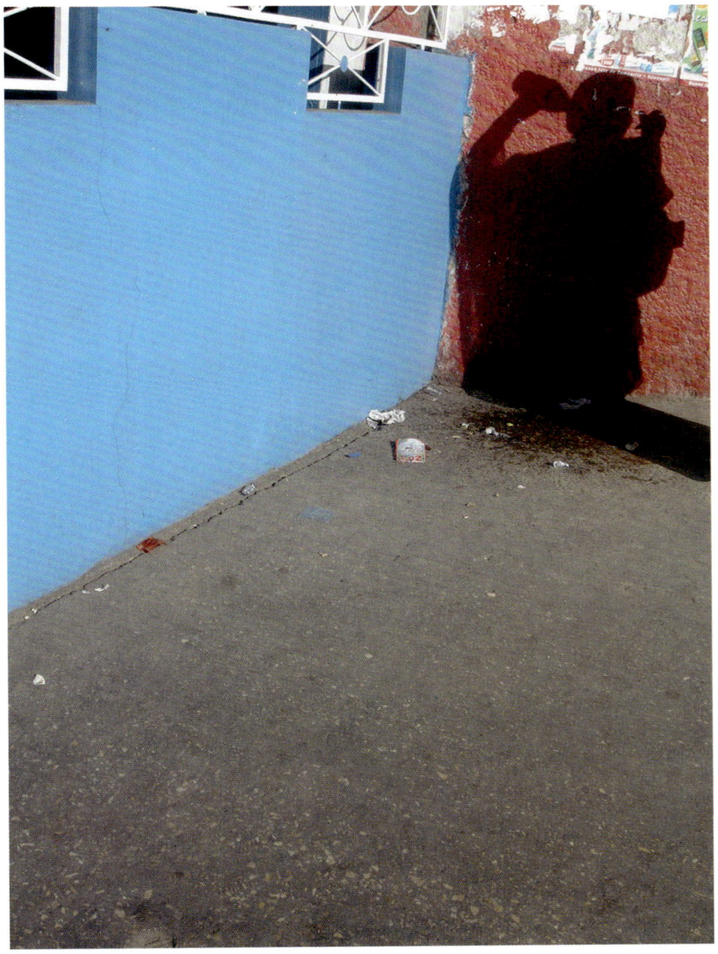
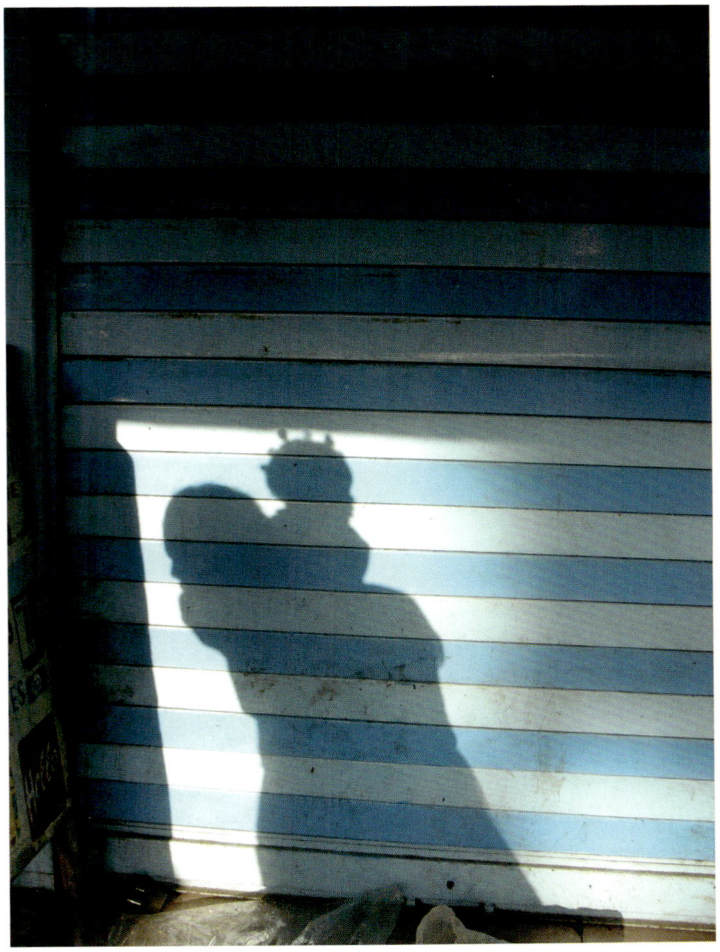

Chapter Four

The Street: Discord and Harmony

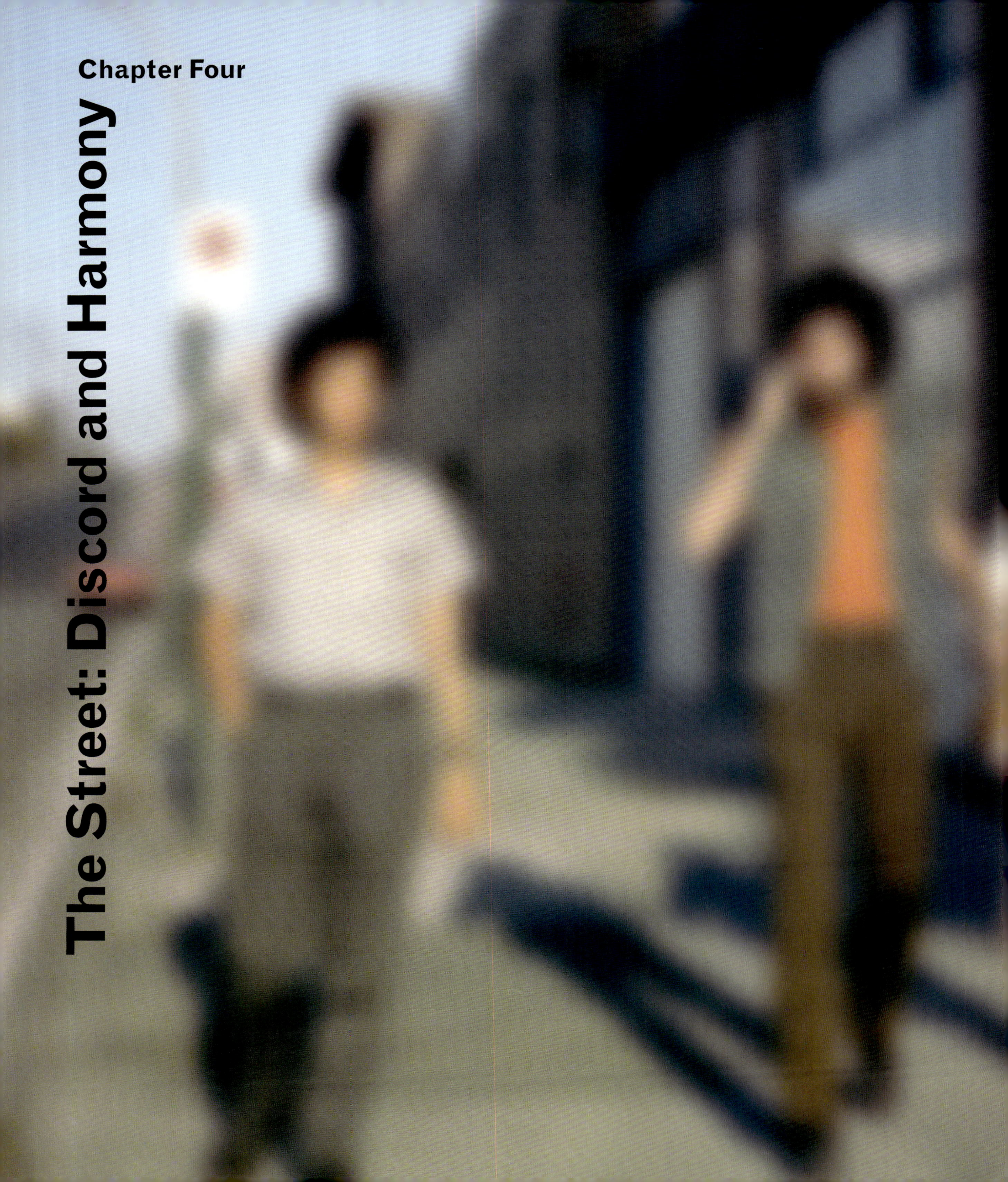

Everyday life on the street is characterized by constantly shifting configurations and micro events that often escape notice. Street photography is preoccupied with capturing such moments and, in doing so, explores properties that are particular to photography. According to Colin Westerbeck and Joel Meyerowitz, street photography explores and exploits the properties of instantaneity and multiplicity: taking multiple shots, the street photographer can either strive for the singular image, a perfect composition that condenses and trumps all other possibilities, or can present us with pictures that are more 'open-ended'; lacking autonomy, such pictures 'can't stand alone and need to be played off one another in groups or runs in books'.[1]

The choice can be presented as one between the 'decisive moment' of Henri Cartier-Bresson's photography or the happenstance of Robert Frank's formally less coherent pictures, which, one might argue, are closer to the flux of life. One can also see the distinction between the two approaches as being a distinction between affirmation and alienation. Cartier-Bresson's decisive moment was caught up with a lyrical and transcendent form: 'To me photography is the simultaneous recognition, in a fraction of a second, of the significance of an event as well as of a precise organization of forms which give that event its proper expression'.[2] In contrast to the affirmative note struck by Cartier-Bresson's photography, Robert Frank, an immigrant to the United States from Switzerland, created a darker, harsher vision of humanity. His 1959 book *The Americans* (first published in Paris by Robert Delpire a year earlier) used under-exposed, off-balance and on occasion even out-of-focus photographs to create a predominantly bleak portrait of a nation riven by division and characterized by malaise.

As this chapter shows much photography of everyday life in the street reflects assumptions about the urban experience in cities, which is generally portrayed in a bleak, dystopian light in which subjects are isolated. Themes of loss, alienation and despair govern perspectives on street photography. Pessimism and nihilism pervade photographers' visions of urban life, which are often seen as an exposure of the vacuity at the heart of a consumer-driven capitalist culture. There are important exceptions to this, but there is nevertheless a recurrence of depictions of urban everyday life and spaces as bereft of humanity and harmony.

Joel Meyerowitz

Joel Meyerowitz's colour street photography extends Henri Cartier-Bresson's lyrical form. Consider, for example, the remarkable coincidences of dress, colour and light in his 1975 New York City street picture of a couple, both wearing similar yellow camel coats and walking away from camera. A patch of sunlight and a white cloud of steam lift them out of the shadowy crowds. The beautiful epiphanic moment is made even more extraordinary because the picture also manages to capture the backs of two other people wearing similar coats, each bearing the clearly defined shadow of another person behind them, the two shadows appearing like a cut-out negative of the central couple.

At about the time he took that photograph, Meyerowitz explained how he was trying to make pictures on the street about what he refers to as the 'all of it' – pictures without a central subject, such as his kaleidoscopic street scene *New York City* (1976), teeming with signs and people competing for attention – where he 'wanted all the information, near and far to hold our interest equally' and, importantly, was 'trying to unlock photography from the aesthetic of the decisive moment'.[3] Stepping back allowed more depth of field and greater clarity in the picture as Meyerowitz tried to bring the photograph closer to the 'inchoate and unresolved' experience of being on the street. There is no central point of focus in this picture, despite its organization around classical perspectival recession. What appears to be a dodgy monetary transaction by two men in the lower centre of the picture maintains a fragile connection with the decisive moment, but it is a moment that is soon offset by other distractions in the picture, such as the static portrait of the cigar-smoking and sunglass-wearing, short, elderly male figure staring straight at the camera.

Joel Meyerowitz
New York City, 1975
C-print, dimensions variable

New York City, 1976
C-print, dimensions variable

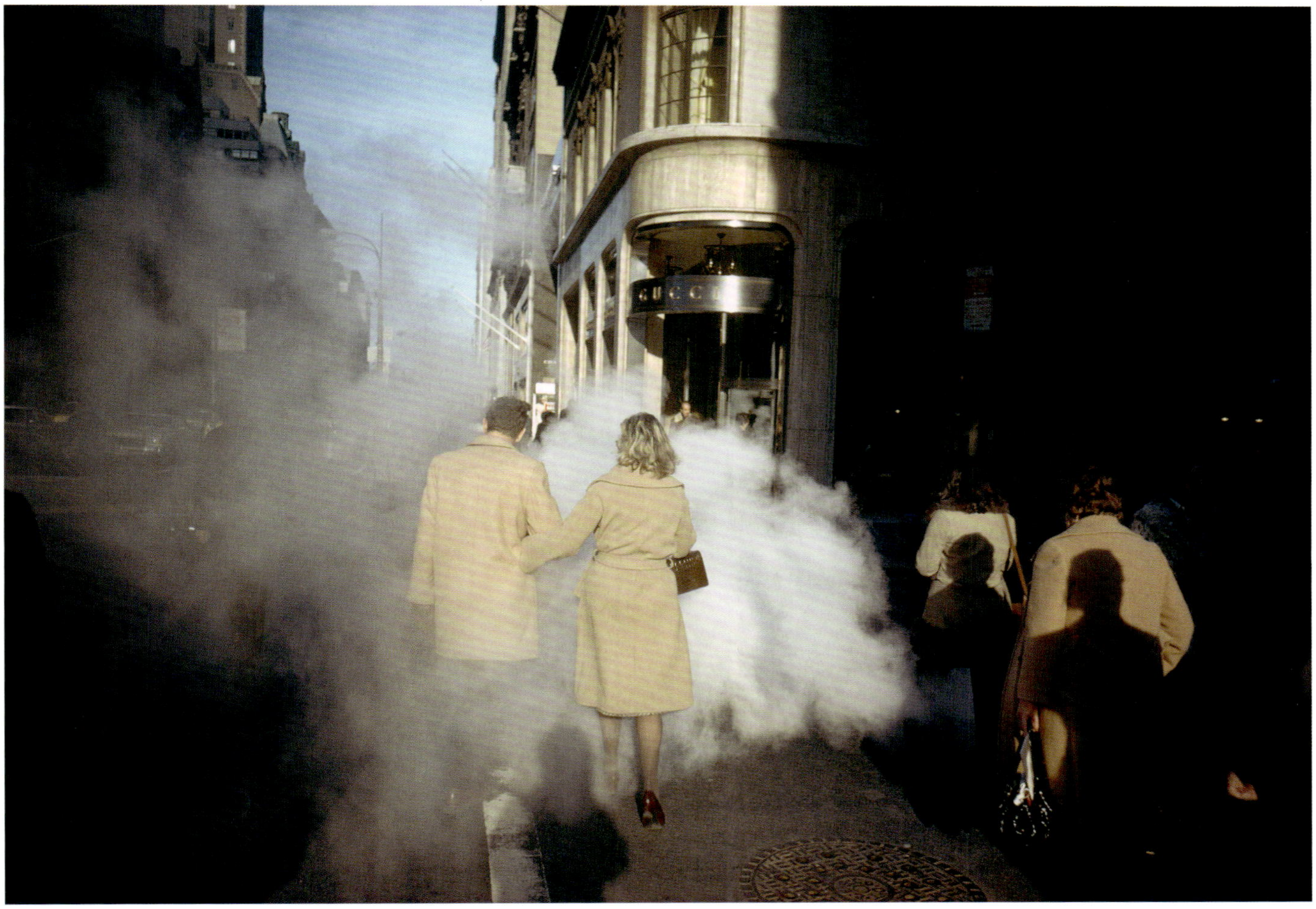

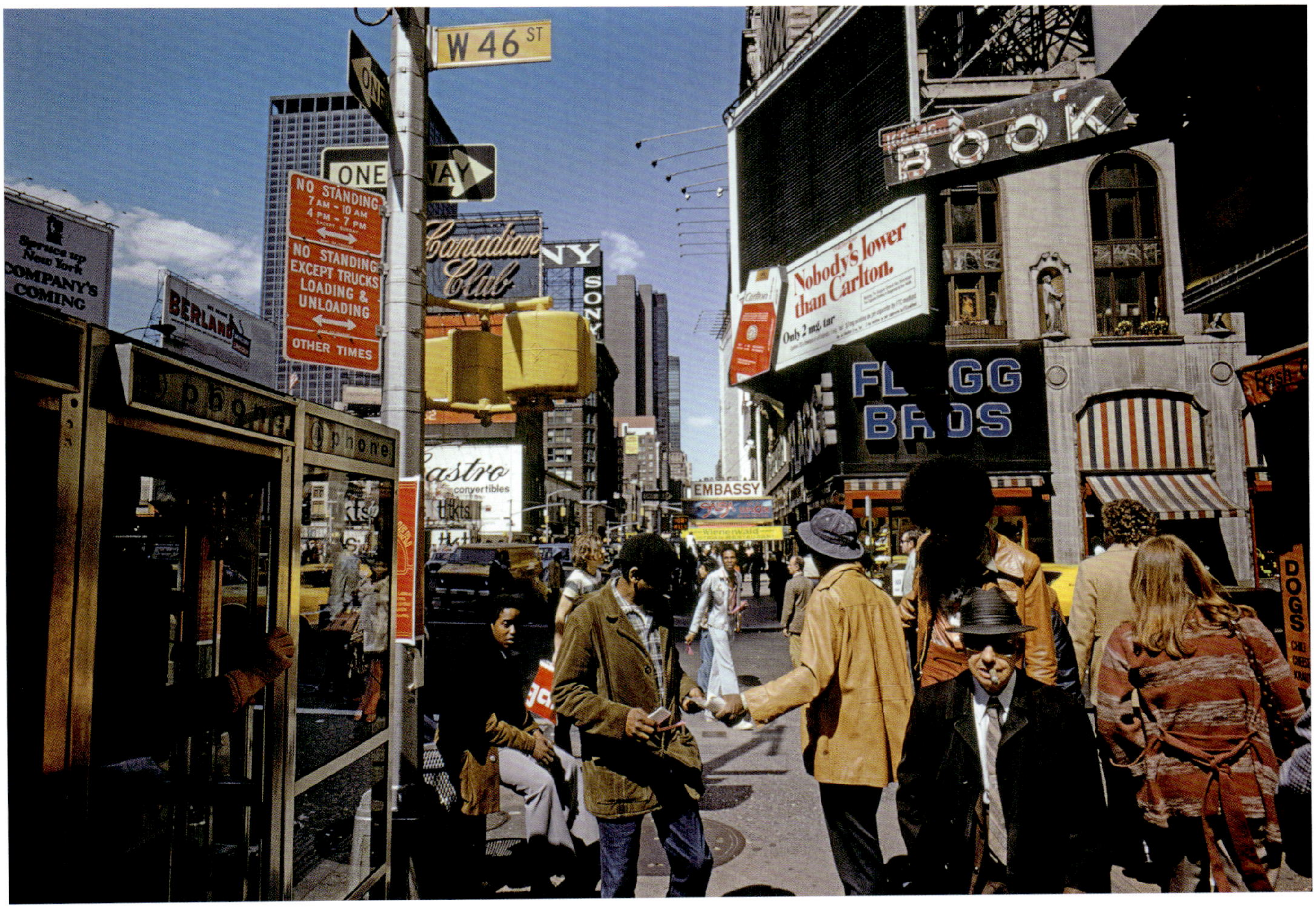
W 46 ST
ONE WAY
ONE WAY
NO STANDING
7 AM - 10 AM
4 PM - 7 PM
NO STANDING
EXCEPT TRUCKS
LOADING &
UNLOADING
OTHER TIMES
Canadian Club
SONY
COMPANY'S COMING
BERLAND
BOOK
Nobody's lower than Carlton.
Only 2 mg. tar
EMBASSY
phone
phone
DOGS

Garry Winogrand

Garry Winogrand's photographic background involved both photojournalism and advertising. He came to prominence as an art photographer through shows organized by John Szarkowksi at New York's Museum of Modern Art, including 'New Documents' in 1967, which also included Diane Arbus and Lee Freidlander. Winogrand was part of what Szarkowksi defined as a shift away from the social concern of documentary 'toward more personal ends'[4]

In his most extensive and informative interview, just a few years before his death from pancreatic cancer in 1984, Winogrand gave an especially clarifying account of his street photography. He distinguished photography from ideas of simple transparency by saying 'how the fact of putting four edges around a collection of information or facts transforms it.'[5] For him, the act of photographing changes things to such an extent that 'a new world is created.' Thus, while Winogrand's pictures can be seen as indexing events and particular moments in time, they are also highly concerned with the still photograph's alteration of those events. There is no such thing as a photograph that functions as a window on the world. What we see are things transformed, in Winogrand's case by the speed of the camera's record of life on the street, human gestures and situations caught on the fly. Winogrand's seemingly simple assertion, 'I photograph to find out what something will look like photographed,' is actually quite complex and precise in terms of his particular relation to and interest in the photographic as not only distinct from, but also transformative of, the event or thing in the world it represents.[6]

While harsh and often brutal in their depiction of humanity, Winogrand's pictures are not without a certain lyricism. They are expressive and gestural, through the tilting wide-angle view of figures on the street, epitomized by the desire-filled and celebratory pictures in his series published as *Women Are Beautiful* (1975), and the dynamic exchanges that are often set up between his subjects on the street, caught looking at or away from one another, or through uncanny chance similarities of dress, gesture, expressions and pose.

When Winogrand shows American legionnaires at a street corner, they ignore the legless man on the pavement and their looks go in every direction except toward the centre from which he confronts the viewer. Looking becomes the subject, as it does in so many of Winogrand's pictures. Here the viewer is invited to reflect on what it is to not look at such a person. Is it callousness or politeness? Photography's fixing of a moment charges the dynamic, so that they all seem to be looking away. One might sense a certain return to Cartier-Bresson here, but the formal effect of the picture is used to augment a sense of social dis-unity.

Winogrand has an ability to capture the awkwardness of social interactions by isolating moments that can seem cruel and unflattering. Moments of both adolescent ardour and frustration are caught in his sidewalk photograph showing one girl being kissed by a cadet in a doorway while her younger, plump female companion faces the camera, alone and unloved (*New York*, before 1976). The girl being embraced catches the photographer out of the corner of her eye with a look that seems less one of anger and more one of happiness that this moment might be being recorded, while the other girl is much less at ease, her quizzical stare speaking volumes about the uncertainty of her position.

The photographs of zoos that make up the 1969 book *The Animals* perhaps offer Winogrand's bleakest view of humanity. As Szarkowski has eloquently put it, he shows us 'a surreal Disneyland where unlikely human beings and jaded careerist animals stare at each through bars, exhibiting bad manners and a mutual failure to recognize their own ludicrous predicaments.'[7] The zoo becomes a dystopian world in miniature of often desperate and cruelly treated animals that have lost their nobility and magnificence in their confinement. Winogrand often highlights their sorry and sad state: an elephant straining to get titbits with his trunk, the gaping jaws of a caged hippo that disclose a discarded food packet, the orangutan holding a half-eaten lolly, the chimpanzee urinating into another's mouth or the lion, the king of the beasts, caught in the undignified moment as he struggles – 'half-heartedly and unsuccessfully,' Szarkowski suggests – to mount his mate. Even the title of the book gives a sense of Winogrand's view of humanity: *The Animals*, of course, can apply just as much to the visitors to the zoo as to the creatures they have come to see. The correspondence becomes comically clear when he photographs over the shoulder of a woman while she takes a picture of her smartly dressed companion posing in front of a caged zebra, or more menacing when a young man's look toward his female companion – his eye made to appear evil as it is caught in shadow – is linked to the wolf's predatory movement in the cage behind them (*New York*, ca. 1962).

From 1969 until 1976, Winogrand photographed what he referred to as 'the effects of the media on events.'[8] According to Szarkowski he used up 700 rolls of film at public and semi-public events and printed up 6,500 proof prints which were then edited for the book and exhibition, *Public Relations*, by Tod Papageorge. The photographs are about the way scheduled events are designed to be reported; after twenty years as a photojournalist, Winogrand knew that such events were not spontaneous, and decided to show their construction and theatre. At the same time, what so many of these pictures do so well is to show us moments that don't go to script, as in the over-self-satisfied grin of the seated mayor surrounded by press and adulators. The pictures are replete with an air of mystery and ambiguity. Winogrand does not judge when he depicts rallies and protestors. Amidst all the petitioning and emotion, he does not petition the viewer. He is there as a witness but is not part of the rallies and protests. This again distinguishes these pictures from the rhetoric of message-driven press reportage.

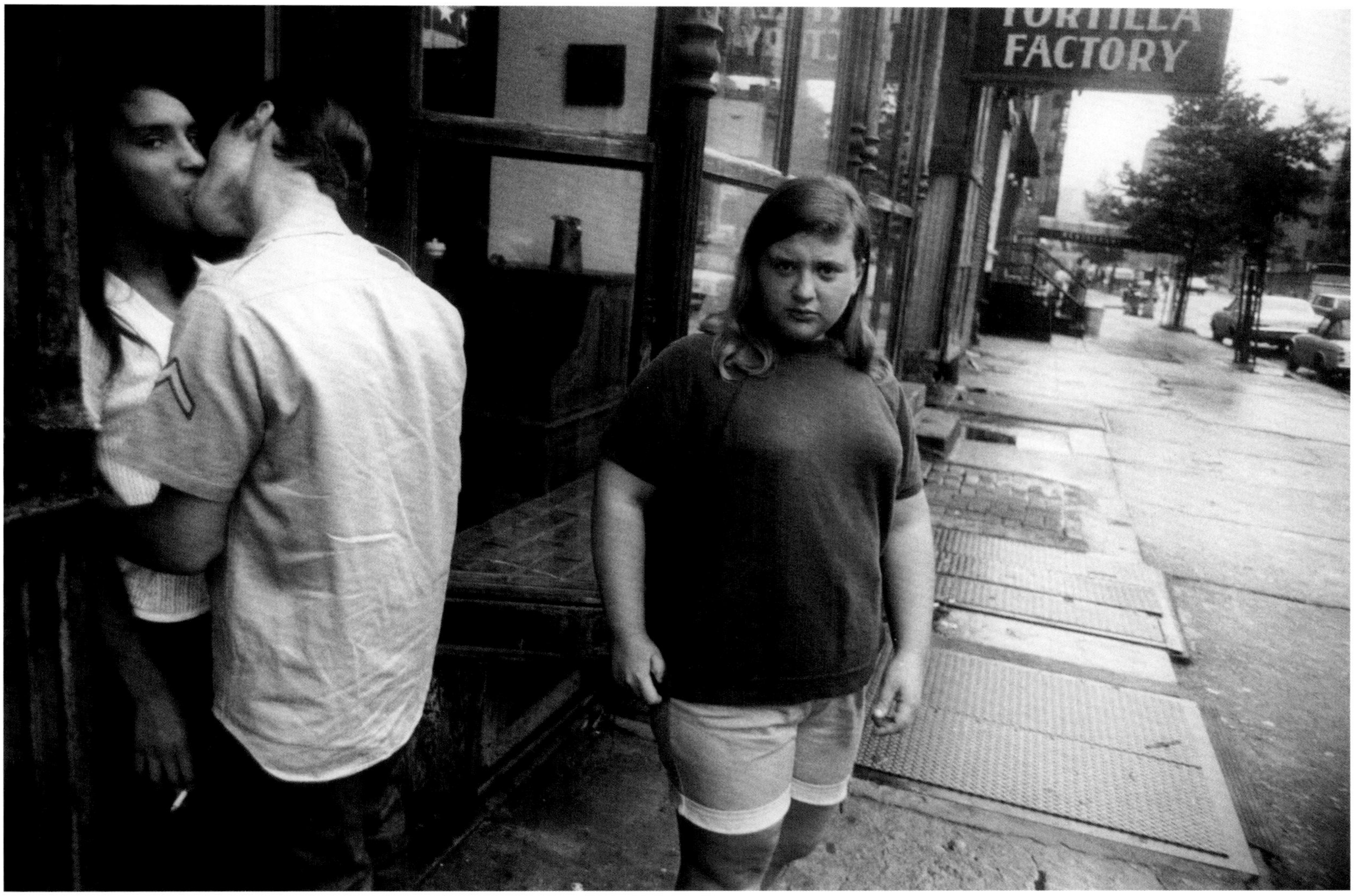

Garry Winogrand
New York, before 1976
Gelatin silver print
26 × 38.1 cm / 10¼ × 15½ in

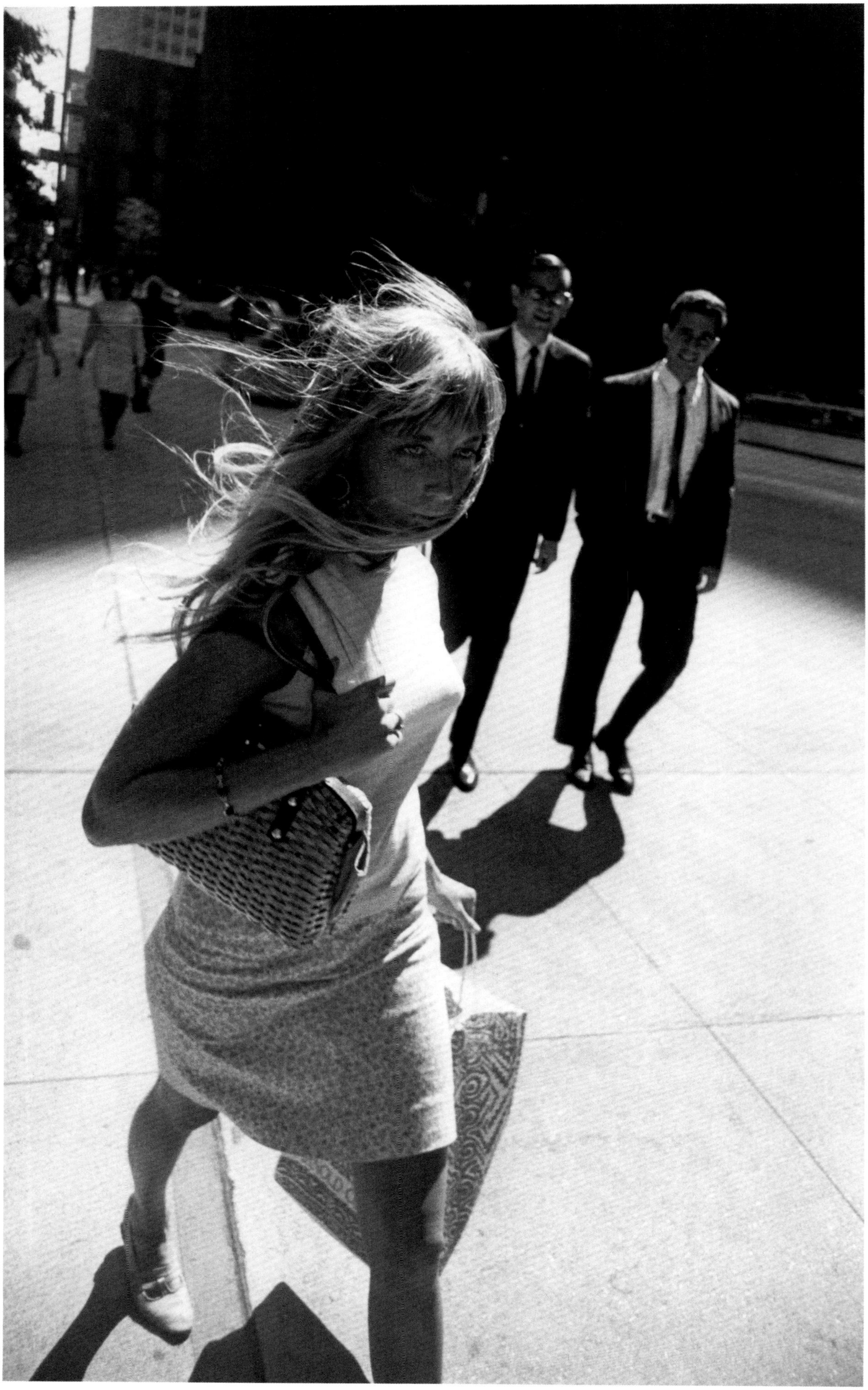

Garry Winogrand
New York, 1965
Gelatin silver print
35.5 × 27.9 cm / 14 × 11 in

New York, *c.*1962
Gelatin silver print
27.9 × 35.5 cm / 11 × 14 in

Mayor John Lindsay, Central Park, New York City, 1969
Gelatin silver print
35.5 × 43.1 cm / 11 × 14 in

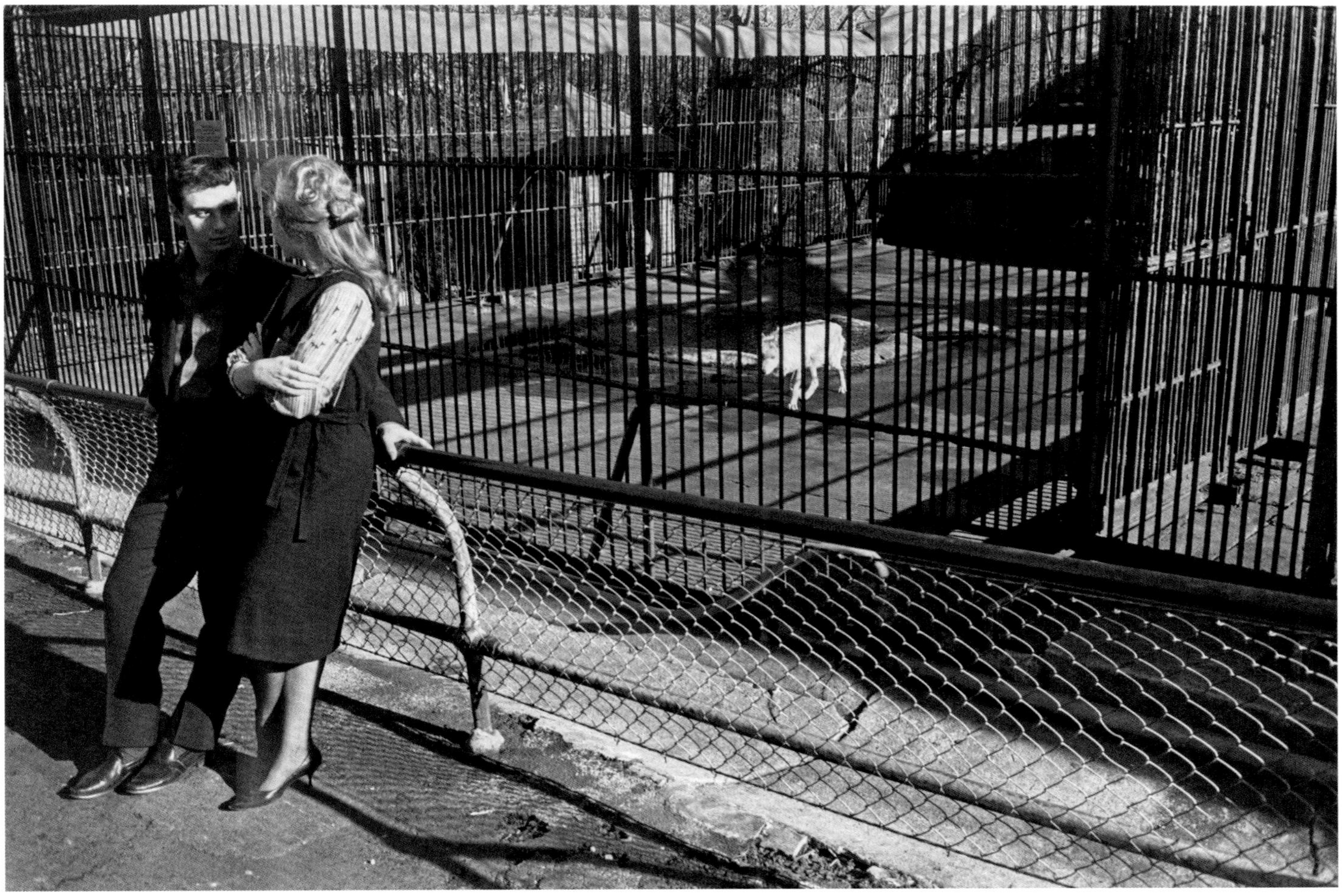

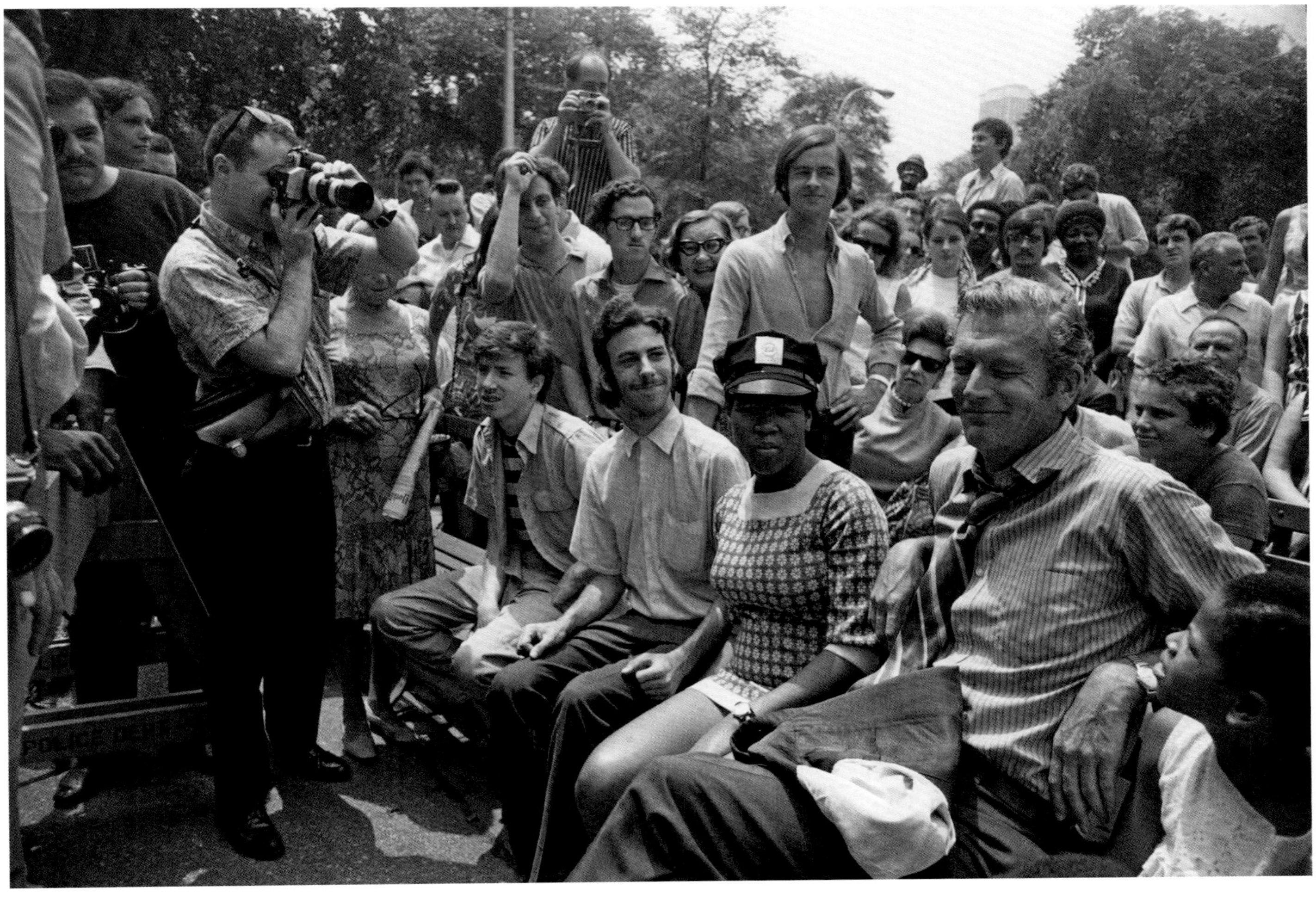

Tod Papageorge

Discord and Distraction

Tod Papageorge's brilliant introduction to *Public Relations* notes how, although Garry Winogrand would say his pictures had little to do with the Vietnam War, they nevertheless gave Americans 'a unilateral report of how we behaved under pressure during a time of costumes and causes, and of how extravagantly, outrageously, and continuously we displayed what we wanted.'[9] The statement also has a bearing on Papageorge's own work from the period. In 1970 he travelled the United States to record a series of major national sporting events at the height of the Vietnam War, picturing the crowds gathered in the arena to enjoy the spectacle in order to give us a collective portrait of the American people in pictures that are tumultuous, chaotic and teeming. These have only recently been published in book form as *American Sports 1970*, or *How We Spent the War in Vietnam* (2007). Papageorge sets his photographs of the mass of crowds against the mass of American troops who lost their lives during 1970. The total deaths are included at the book's close – 4,221 – paired with a photograph showing the bowed figure of a late middle-aged male passing before a war memorial in Indianapolis on a wet day. One sees the book as an indictment of American culture and behaviour at a time of national moment. The people absorbed and distracted by the spectacle of sports create a sense of misdirected energy, of a desperate escapism that wants to forget the political turmoil of the times. At the same time, we look to the gatherings of men, women and children – but predominantly men – as a register of the contemporary events taking place in Vietnam. While some of the young males' energy and behaviour seems displaced or inappropriate, others, such as the naval officers Papageorge depicts, suggest in their anxious looks that their thoughts might be with their absent fellows.

Tod Papageorge
Cotton Bowl (Notre Dame vs. Texas), Cotton Bowl Stadium, Dallas,
January 1, 1971
Gelatin silver print
30 × 43.1 cm / 11⅞ × 17⅞ in

Opening Day (Boston vs. New York), Yankee Stadium, New York
April 7, 1970
Gelatin silver print
30 × 43.1 cm / 11⅞ × 17⅞ in

Lee Friedlander

Readymade Montages

Lee Friedlander's street photography in many ways parallels the discordant and fragmentary collaged surfaces of Robert Rauschenberg's paintings. But Friedlander achieves this through straight photography. He found readymade montages in the environment of the street, through reflections and the continual framing and reframing of people, things and other pictures, especially other photographs – of John and Jackie Kennedy, of hairstyle models, of strippers and film stars. In a remarkable picture taken face-on to a storefront in Los Angeles against a reflected backdrop that includes the city's iconic palm trees, he depicts the smiling cut-out figures of a man and woman taped to the window, a cheap display suggestive of the broader depthlessness of such a culture.

Friedlander's photography, as Jonathan Green has argued, makes 'no distinction between the celebrity and the common man.'[10] He perceives the world coolly and without hierarchy: everything is equally anonymous and matter of fact. People are, as Peter Galassi puts it, simply part of 'the furniture of the street, as solid and immobile as the poles and hydrants and motionless doors that surround and enclose them.'[11] Friedlander turns what might be seen as pictorial errors or mistakes into an integral element of his pictures: awkward cropping, the interruption of views by passing pedestrians, the spatial and pictorial confusions set up by glass surfaces, especially shop fronts, or the deliberate inclusion of the photographer's shadow or reflection in pictures. The inclusion of himself in many of his street pictures led to Friedlander's first book, *Self-Portrait*, distinguished by his own impersonal attitude towards himself, which is far from the egocentric perspectives of Abstract Expressionism. In one comic picture, *Albany, New York* (1967), we see just his feet, set before photographs of a choice of three groomed masculine heads displayed in a barber's grubby window. In some photographs he becomes a stalker and voyeur, turning the camera on himself as he stands outside a peep show or lurks behind an unsuspecting female. In *Colorado* (1967), he links the reflection of his body to a portrait of John F. Kennedy on a display stand inside a rather neglected-looking community centre. The relation with the portrait is at the same time broken by the blank white surface of the back of a poster taped onto the glass from inside, an interruptive void that seems to echo the fact that the picture was taken four years after the president's assassination. Friedlander was unravelling the centrality of the author figure in his pictures in favour of an indifference and blankness associated with the camera itself. In this respect his work is far from the romantic idea of the prowling instinctual and expressive practice of street photography. It is as if Friedlander has incorporated the isolation and vacuity often associated with the street into his pictures' very form.

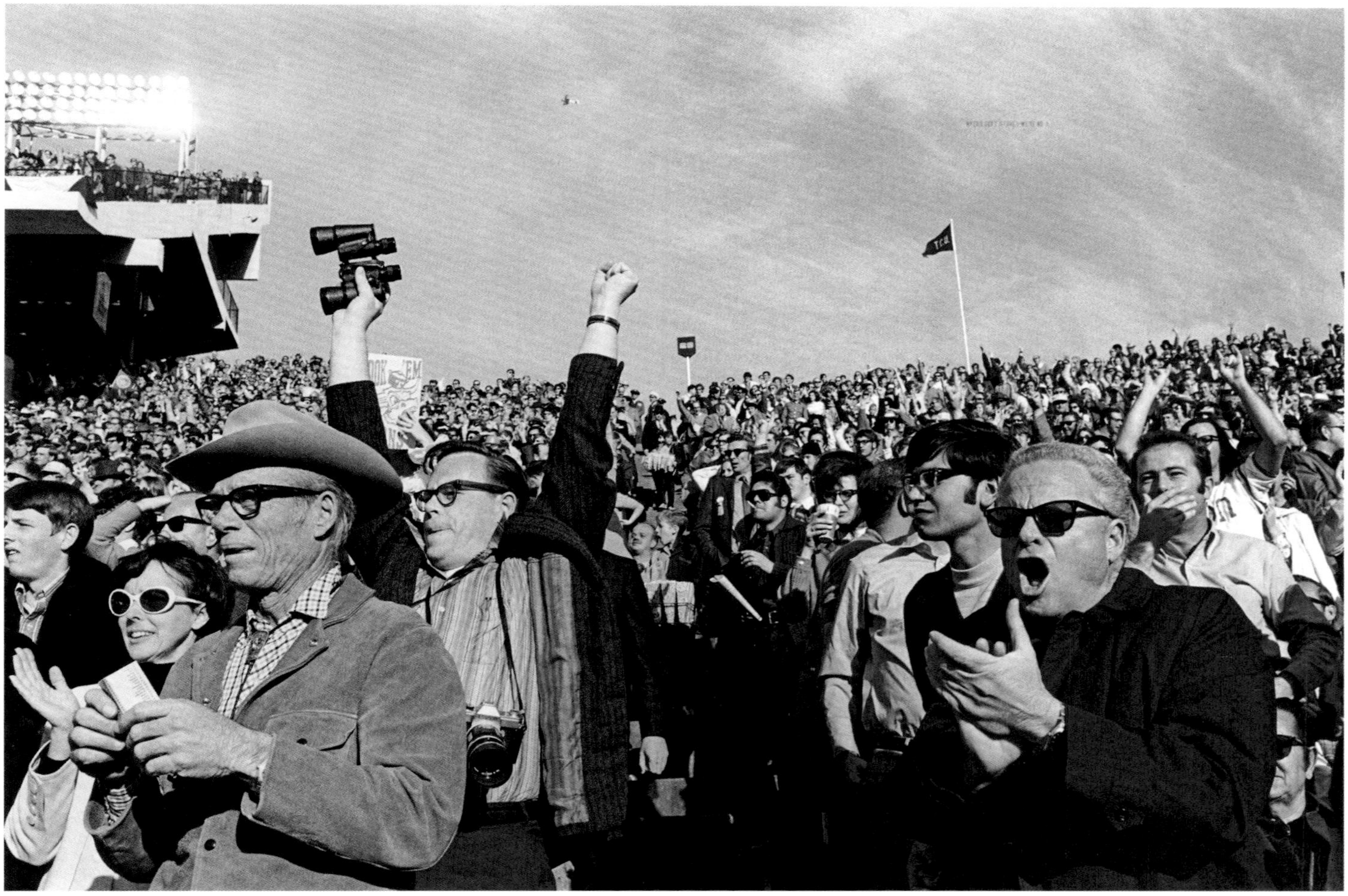

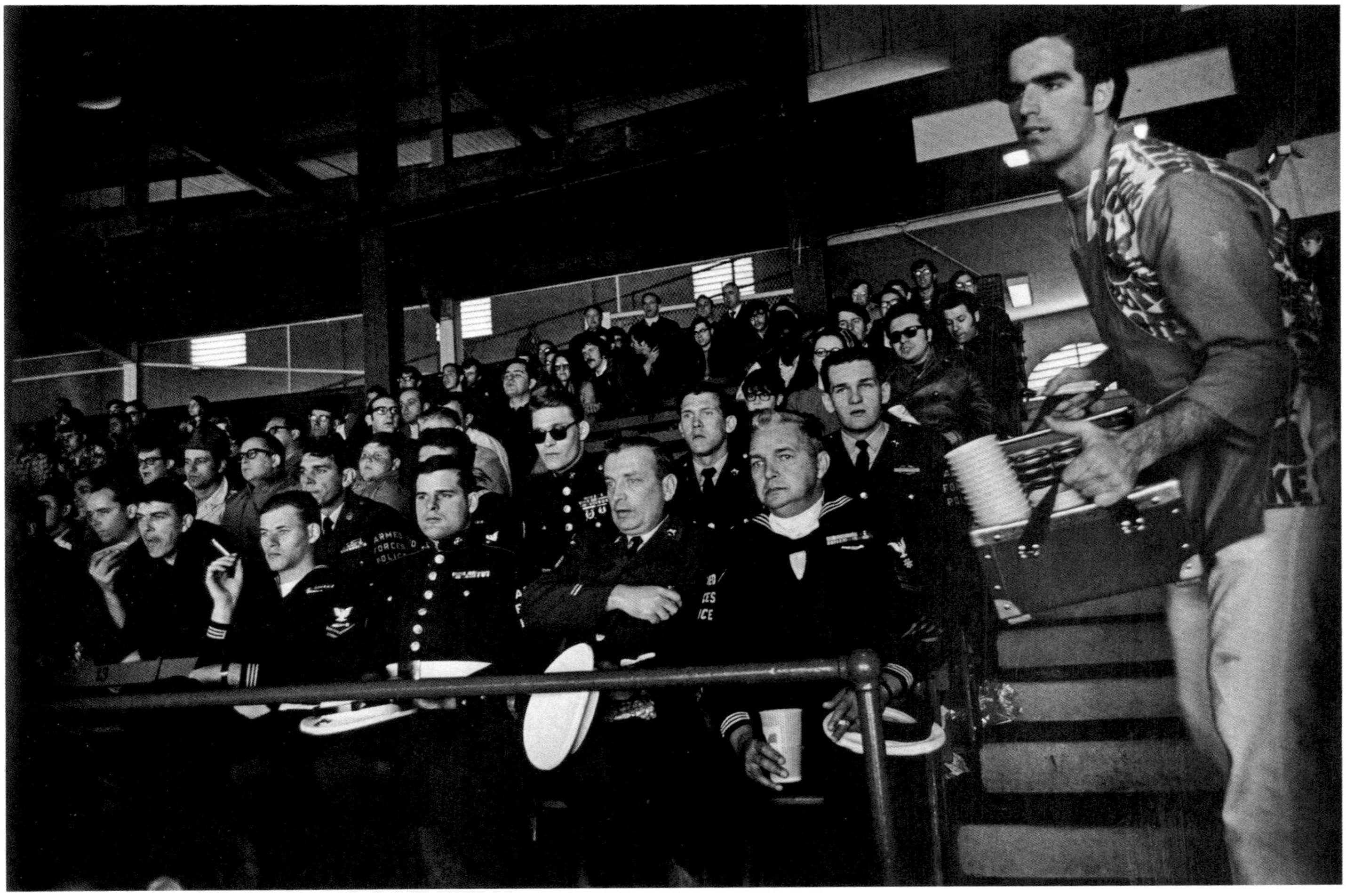

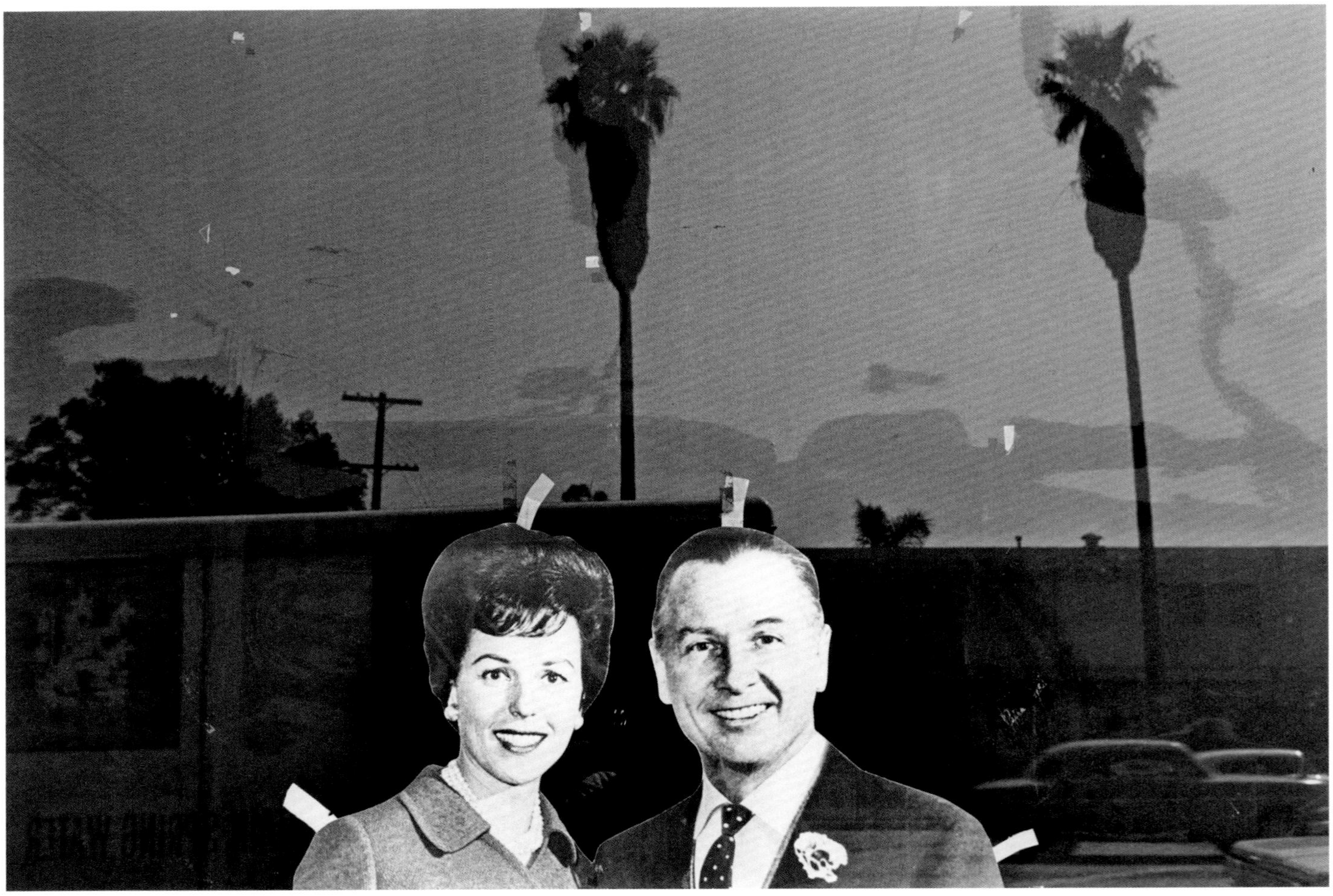

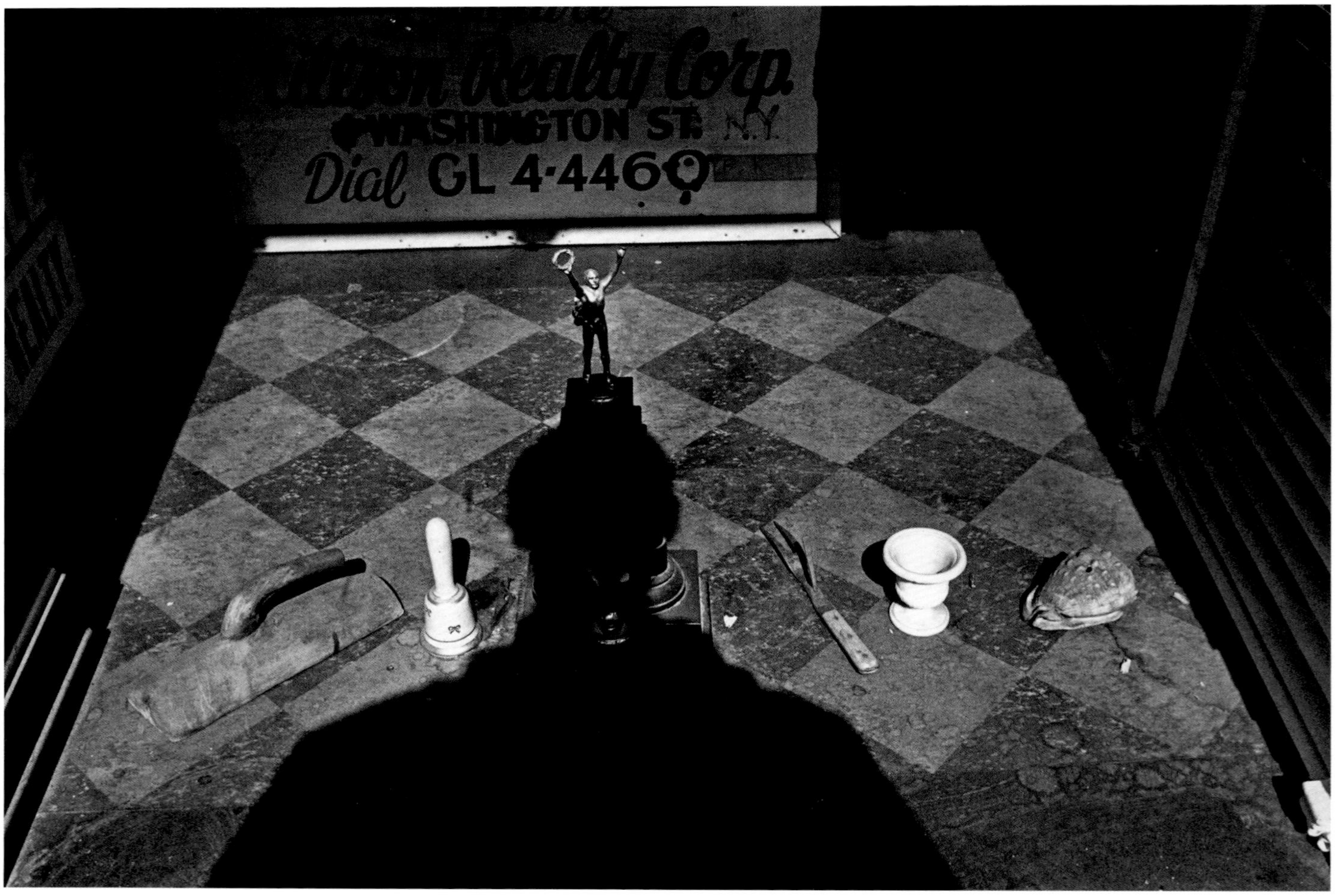

Lee Friedlander
Los Angeles, 1965
Gelatin silver print
27.9 × 35.6 cm /
11 × 14 in

Newburgh,
New York, 1966
Gelatin silver print
27.9 × 35.5 cm /
11 × 14 in

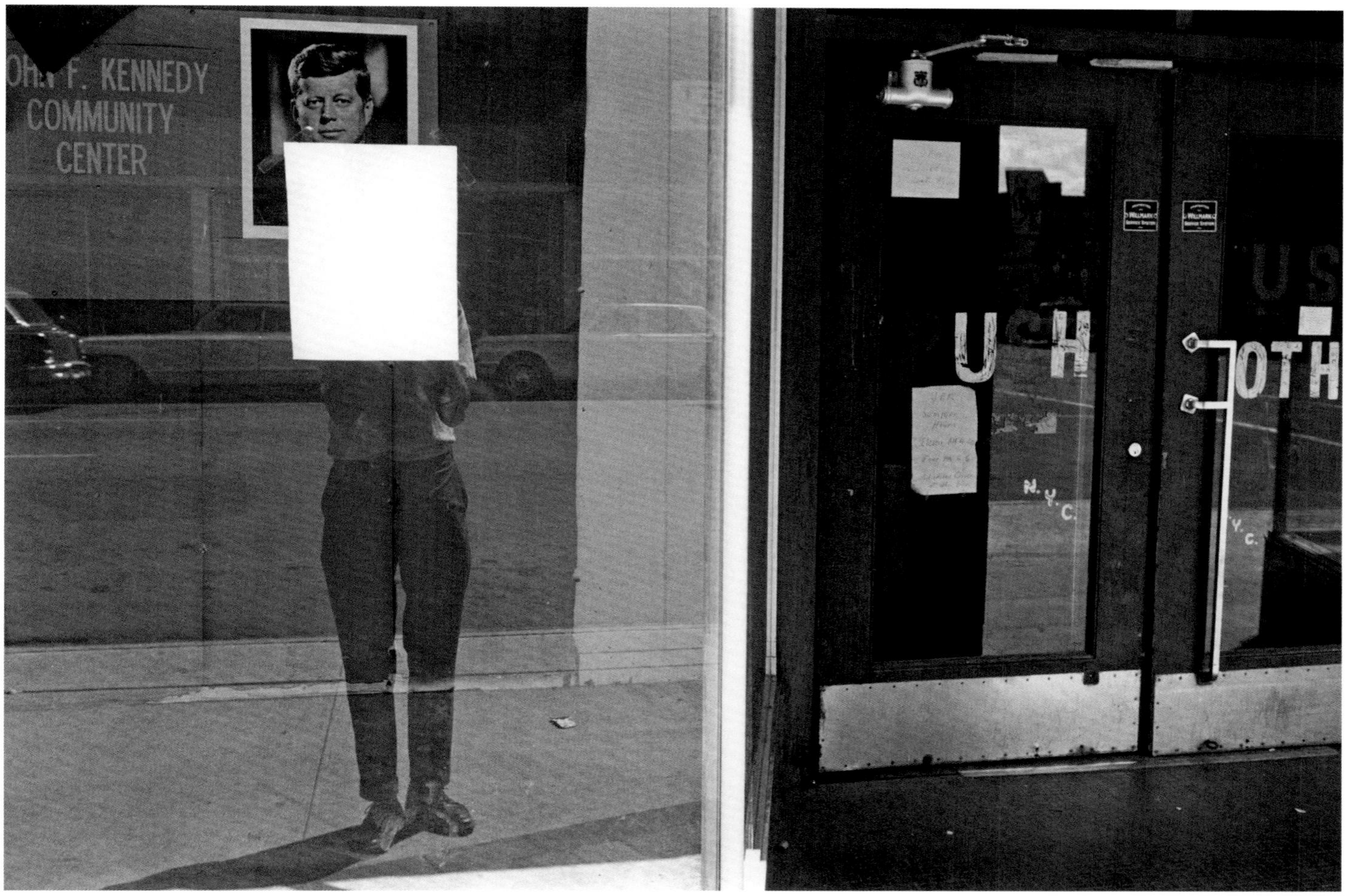

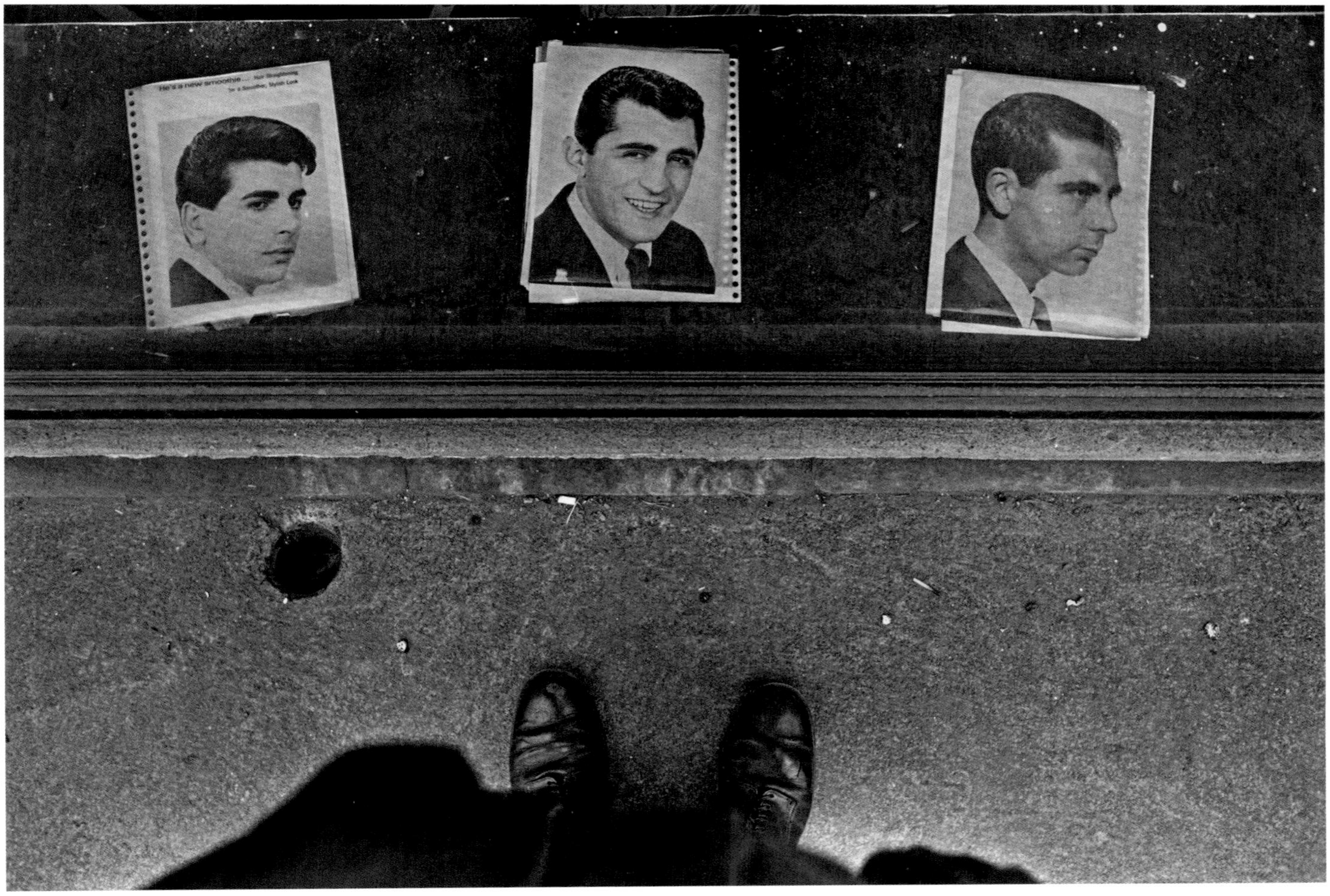

Colorado, 1967
Gelatin silver print
27.9 × 35.6 cm /
11 × 14 in

Albany, New York,
1967
Gelatin silver print
19 × 28.6 cm /
7½ × 11¼ in

Roy DeCarava

Roy DeCarava's photography also signals a significant shift in the tradition of street photography. Having trained as a painter and printmaker, DeCarava turned to photography in the 1940s and in 1952 became the first African American photographer to receive a Guggenheim fellowship. In his first extended personal photographic project, he aimed to achieve 'a creative expression' rather than a 'documentary or sociological statement.'[12] Born in Harlem, and having almost always lived and worked in New York, he spoke about this first project in terms of black identity and its strength: 'I want to photograph Harlem through the Negro people, morning, noon, night, at work, going to work, coming home from work, at play, in the streets... I want to show the strength, the wisdom, the dignity of the Negro people. Not the famous and the well-known, but the unknown and the unnamed.'

Often motivated by identification with the people he depicts, DeCarava's work is at its core humane and compassionate. Black-and-white photography is used in a particular way here. He is famous, as Peter Galassi notes, 'for his luxurious shadows, for the delicate interplay of tones in pictures that reside at the dark end of the photographic scale.'[13] The rich tonality of DeCarava's prints brings a particular sensuousness and beauty to his depiction of people that is integral to the feelings that often underly them.

DeCarava was present during the historic Civil Rights March on Washington of August 28, 1963. In *Mississippi Freedom Marcher, Washington D.C.* he goes in close to concentrate on the face of a resolute young woman. Isolating her from the other protestors, he uses the occasion to make an expressive and emotional portrait, and to elicit identification through a face-to-face encounter. Galassi has spoken about a 'patient contemplation' at the heart of DeCarava's photography, and it is beautifully realized in such a picture. DeCarava also went in close with his extraordinary *Five Men*, a photograph that gains meaning and significance when we understand its specific context: 'The motivation at that moment was my political understanding of the treatment of black people and their response to injustice. This moment occurred during a memorial service for the children killed in a church in Birmingham, Alabama, in 1964. The photograph shows men coming out of the service at a church in Harlem. I was aware of all this, and I wanted to make a picture, to commemorate that day.' Again the picture draws attention to an expressive interiority, of something often missing in the reportage photographs of such an event.

DeCarava's photography has a temporal difference from many of the pictures we have been discussing so far. The isolation of the faces of protestors and mourners appears to slow down time. Abstracted from the historical moment, the weight of the event is registered through individuals and their dignified and beautiful representation. DeCarava's is an emotional identification, conveying a sense of inner reserve and resilience, finding reflective pauses amidst the public spectacle the media makes of such events. The sensitivity shown towards their subjects in such images can be contrasted with the way in which personal power is displayed in the depiction of the white male passenger in *Cab 173* (1962). With his face completely lost in shadow, he is present only through the detail of his hand, with the telling detail of a brash, gold signet ring on his little finger.

In 1963 DeCarava photographed a demonstration organized by African-American residents of a Brooklyn neighbourhood to protest the razing of their homes to clear the ground for an addition to the Downstate Medical Center. Power is, as he shows us in this splendid decisive-moment picture, 'insidious' and non-monumental. DeCarava said that in *Force, Downstate*, which shows the removal of one of the residents, 'I wanted to express something that always seems to happen to people, black people in this particular case. They are removing this woman from a demonstration and it is a display of force. Force is short for force and violence... Force, violence isn't always spectacular and monumental and epic. Sometimes it is very quiet and insidious, almost imperceptible.'[14]

Roy DeCarava
Mississippi Freedom Marcher, Washington D.C., 1963
Gelatin silver print
27.9 × 36 cm / 11 × 14 in

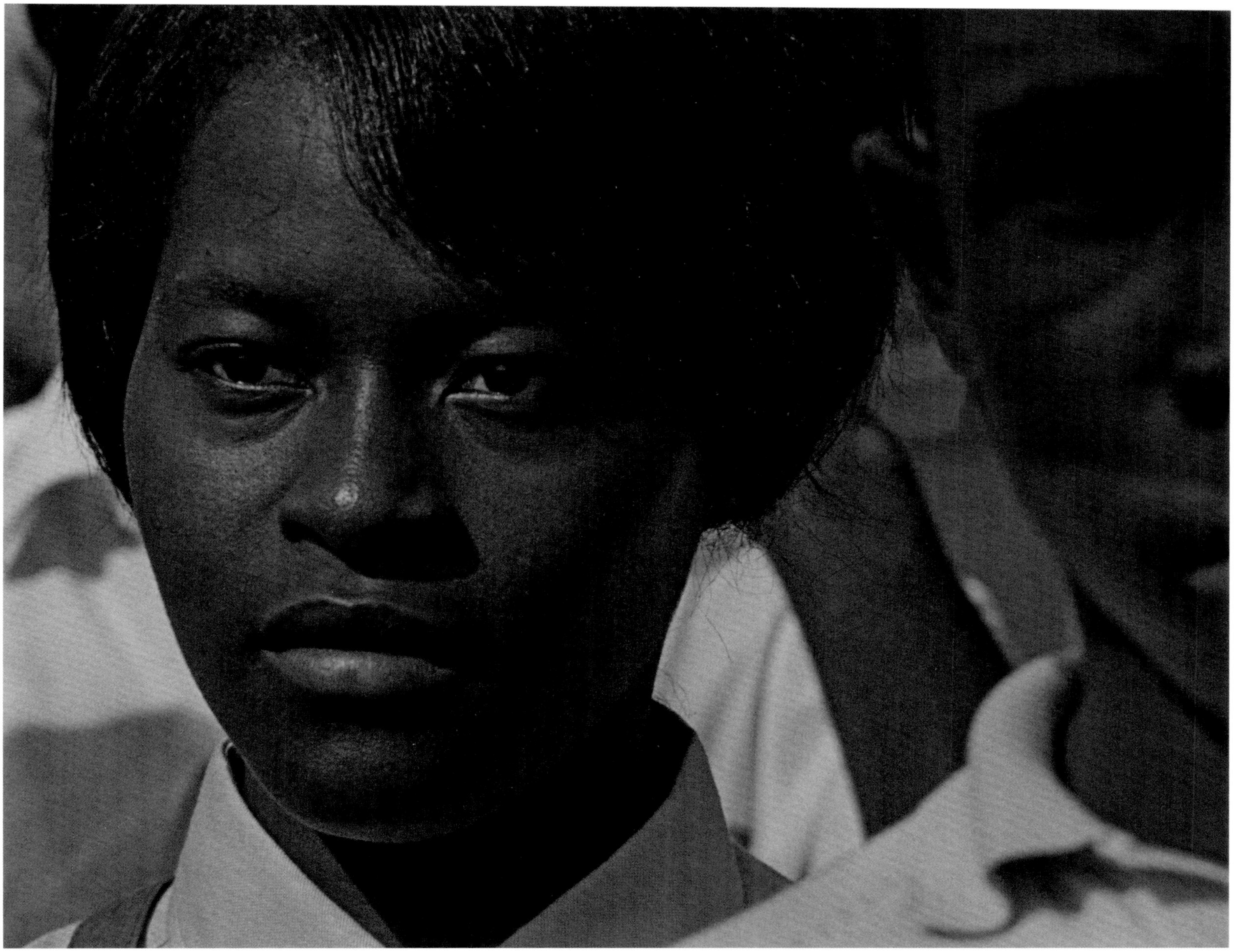

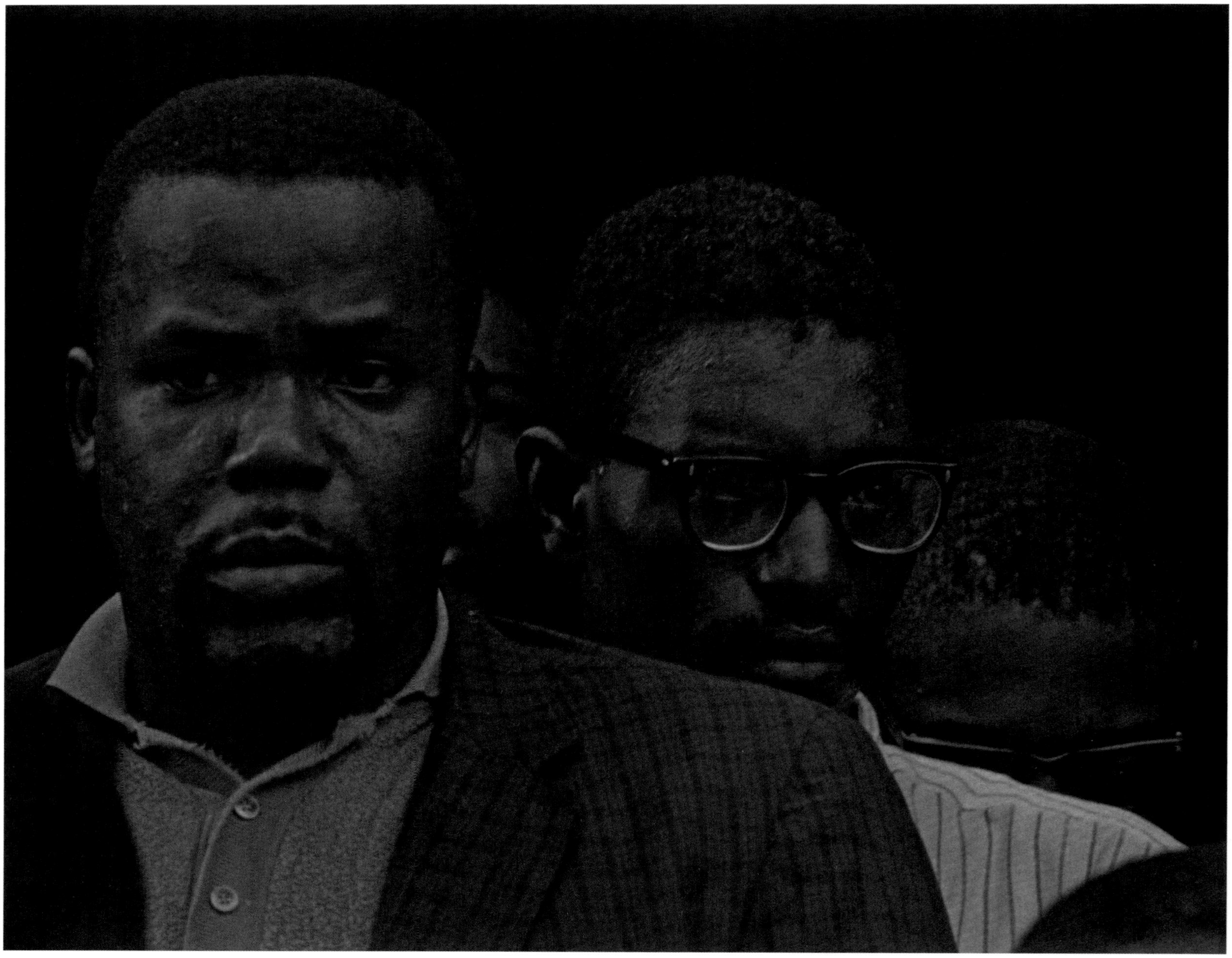

Roy DeCarava
Five Men, 1964
Gelatin silver print
27.9 × 36 cm / 11 × 14 in

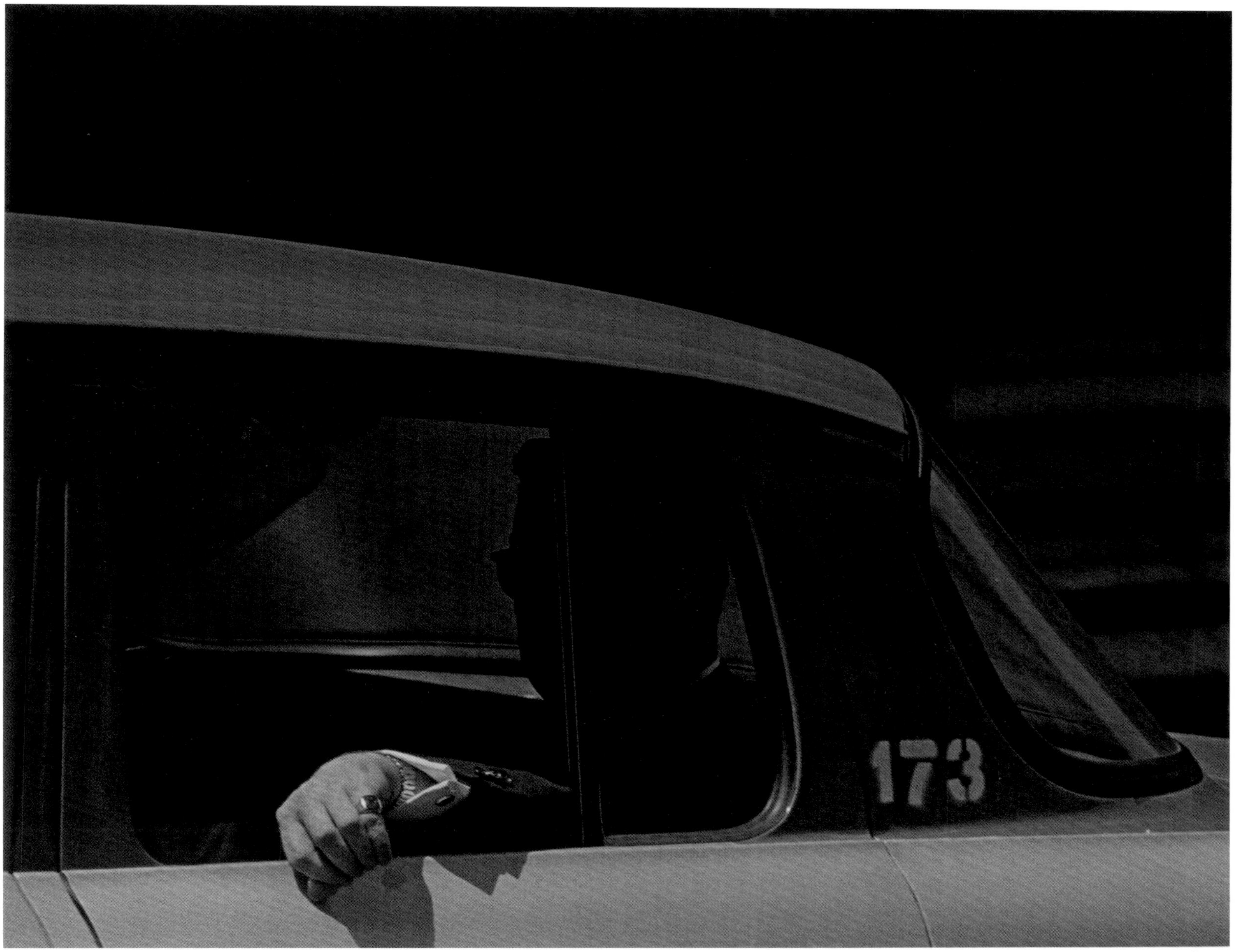

Cab 173, 1962
Gelatin silver print
27.9 × 36 cm / 11 × 14 in

Daido Moriyama

Like Lee Friedlander's photography, Daido Moriyama's art grabs from anywhere and everything. Details from the television screen and movie posters interrupt and compete with pictures taken from life. Any constancy in Friedlander's self-portraits comes from his portrayal as an anonymous figure walking the street, unromantic and unheroic. Moriyama's analogies are even more lowly – the Japanese photographer likens himself to a dog.

His *Memories of a Dog*, an autobiographical collection of essays, links the dog of the title to what has become an emblematic Moriyama image: a threatening picture of a stray dog photographed low down and close up, 'showing the whites of its eyes and snarling, on the streets outside a U.S. air base in the town of Misawa.'[15] 'That dog and I,' Moriyama says, 'came to be seen and talked about as if superimposed on each other… The figure I cast, roaming around town and on the back streets, carrying my camera, appeared in others' eyes very much like a stray dog.' Stray dogs on the street recur through his photography as an emblem of both his own roaming and also the wild and untamed sense of his mode of picturing. His photographs are nearly always taken on the fly, often out of focus, grainy, high contrast and off centre. There is no fixed or central point of view, but instead a constant sense of a shifting and restless looking.

For Moriyama, photography can only offer elusive and vague fragments of what is experienced. 'I hold my camera as a means of continually confirming the self and examining the question "what does my life mean?" in this grotesque, scandalous and utterly accidental world in which I live and participate.'[16] His pictures provide a fascinating mix of raw photos snatched from life with a recurrent fascination with mediation and the processes of image production. Moriyama sees no difference between a photographed photograph and photographed people. He has an interest in the brutality of images, borne out by his picture of a movie poster showing a violent death from the film *Bonnie and Clyde* or the series of photos *Smash-up* (1969), blown-up details of a traffic safety poster. Such pictures testify to the formal fascination of replaying a horrific event, and also to the numbing effect of such spectacles of violence. Pop is brutalized. Moriyama's is a violent, even nihilist vision, fuelled by his anger at the destruction and subsequent occupation of his homeland by the United States.

The concept of the predatory street photographer was parodied and critiqued by Friedlander, who knowingly played with the menacing associations of the lone male wandering the streets. Moriyama's picture of a barefooted female running away from the camera in a back alley is more blunt in its depiction of the threatening, aggressive activity of the male street photographer.

Daido Moriyama
Smash-up, from the series 'Accident', 1969
Gelatin silver print
16.8 × 24.2 cm / 6 ½ × 9 ½ in

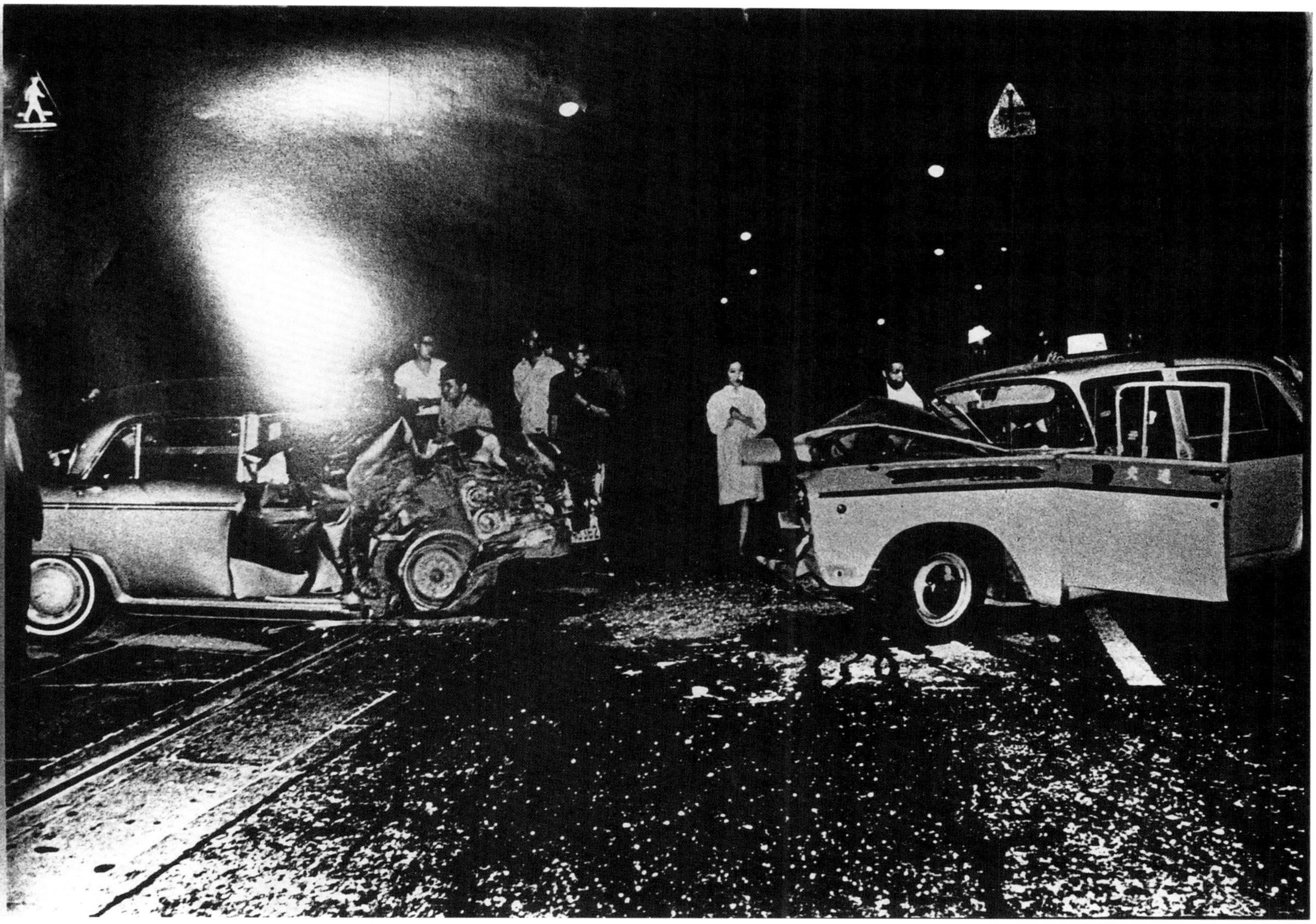

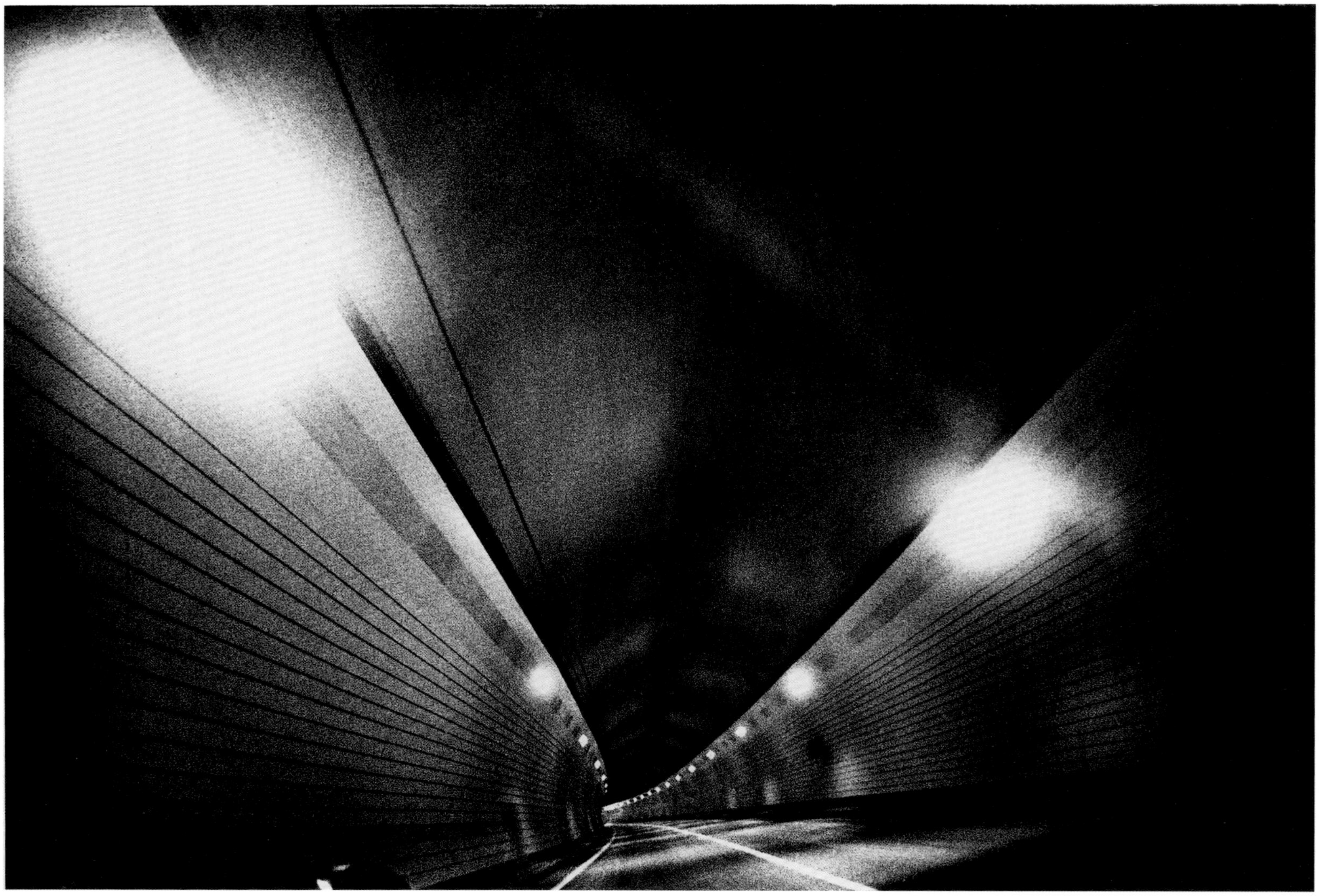

Daido Moriyama
Highway Shizuoka, Japan, 1969
Gelatin silver print
Dimensions variable

Yokosuka, from the series
'Another Country 18', 1970
Gelatin silver print
35 × 43 cm / 14 × 17 in

Boy, Miagi, Japan, 1973
Gelatin silver print
50.8 × 61 cm / 20 × 24 in

Stray Dog, Misawa,
Aomori, 1971
Gelatin silver print
48 × 71.2 cm / 18⅞ × 28 in

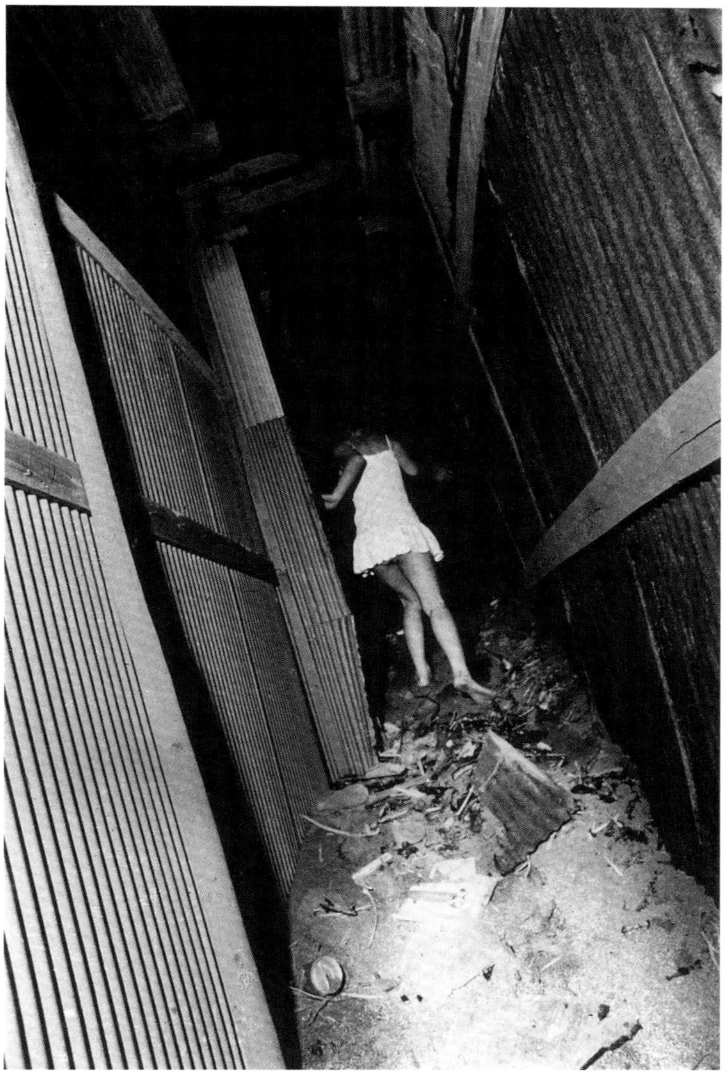

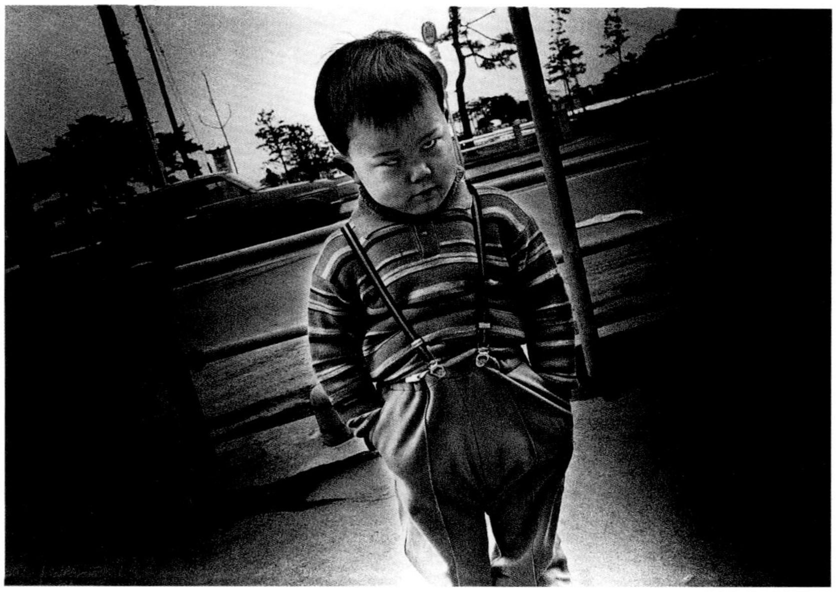

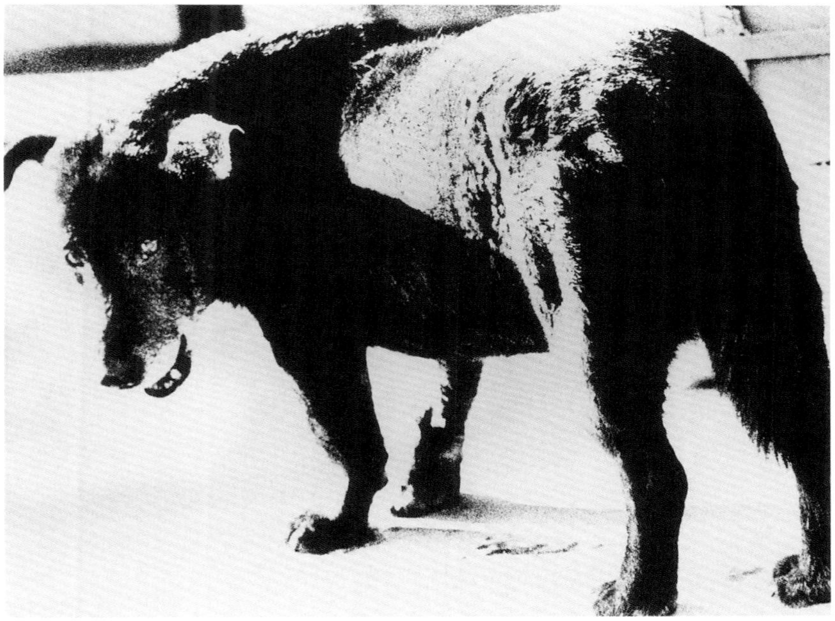

Laurie Anderson

In 1973, Laurie Anderson's photo-conceptual work 'Fully Automated Nikon (Object/Objection/Objectivity)' offered a feminist intervention into the tradition of street photography. The work was made in response to the female artist being harassed by men on the street. Armed with a camera, she took photographs of anyone who made insinuating comments to her as she walked down Huston Street in New York. The camera was a means of defence. The text accompanying these 'portraits' speaks of 'photography as a kind of mugging – a kind of assault'. Photography provides the means of retaliation. By the time Anderson takes their picture, the men are posing, flattered by the attention and smiling. Only their eyes are blanked out. This maintains their anonymity, but can also be seen to disempower them and to criminalize them by association. Anderson has the last word. In an earlier and convivial variant on this, the photographer, Ed van der Elsken, would sometimes call to the women he was photographing on the street, picturing their response as they wave back.

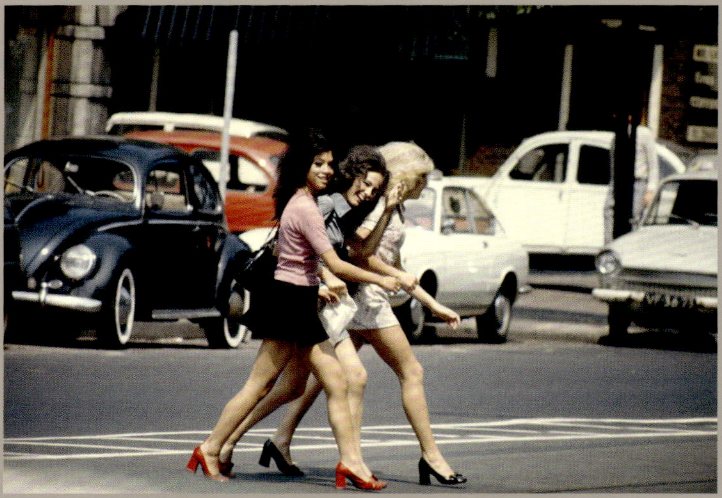

Ed van der Elsken
Beethovenstraat, 1967
Colour photograph
30 × 40 cm / 11¾ × 15¾ in

Victor Burgin

The British photographer Victor Burgin adapts the conventions of street photography in his series 'US77'. Texts overlaid on the pictures underscore his intention to use the photography to spell out the links between patriarchy, consumerism and capitalism. Burgin draws upon an academic language in his phototexts and the body of essays that further supplements this work. As with earlier street photographers, he often plays out a theme of alienation, but the texts explain the causes of such situations. There is an illustrational tendency to Burgin's image-text work that brings it closer to the advertisements that it often reframes and critiques. In *Framed*, for example, a particularly drab urban spot provides the setting for a Marlboro ad, its icon of masculinity the foil for a text that tells the story of a woman wanting her hairstyle to match that of a model in a magazine. Another picture from the series, *Omnipotence*, shows a man in a car adopting a Marlboro look, setting up a contrast to the line of suited men behind him. An accompanying text informs us how oppression in the workplace is mirrored in the home.

Laurie Anderson
From 'Fully Automated Nikon (Object/Objection/Objectivity)', 1973
Black and white photographs, text, dimensions variable

Fully Automated Nikon
1973

In a seafood restaurant in Chincoteague, Virginia, a woman approached me, convinced that I was a soap opera actress -
"the one on 'The Secret Storm' who's in love with the doctor who..."

"No, I'm not her," I said. "I guess I just look like her."
This seemed to delight and excite her.

"Of course you deny it!" she said. "You don't want to be recognized!" I smiled."See! You smile just like her!"

I denied it again but the more I denied it, the more convinced she was. The conversation was slowly turning into an argument and partly to assert myself, I asked if I could take her picture.

As I shot her, I realised that photography is a kind of mugging- a kind of assault.

When I got back to New York, I decided to take pictures of men who made comments as I passed them on the street. I had always resented this invasion of privacy. Now, suddenly I had the means of my revenge.
As I walked through the Lower East Side with my fully automated Nikon, I felt armed, ready.
The standard street technique was: the female passes and the male speaks at the last possible moment, forcing the woman to backtrack if she should dare to object.

My first shot was a man who muttered "Wanna fuck?" just after I passed by.
I wheeled around, furious.
"DID YOU SAY THAT?"
He looked around surprised, then defiant. I raised my Nikon, took aim. His eyes darted back and forth. Undercover cop? Huh? CLICK.
As it turned out, most of the men I shot that day had similar reactions. When I questioned them, they acted innocent -even offended- like some nasty invisible ventriloquist had tricked them into saying dirty words against their will.
By the time I started to shoot, they were posing. They seemed flattered, like taking their pictures was the least I could do.

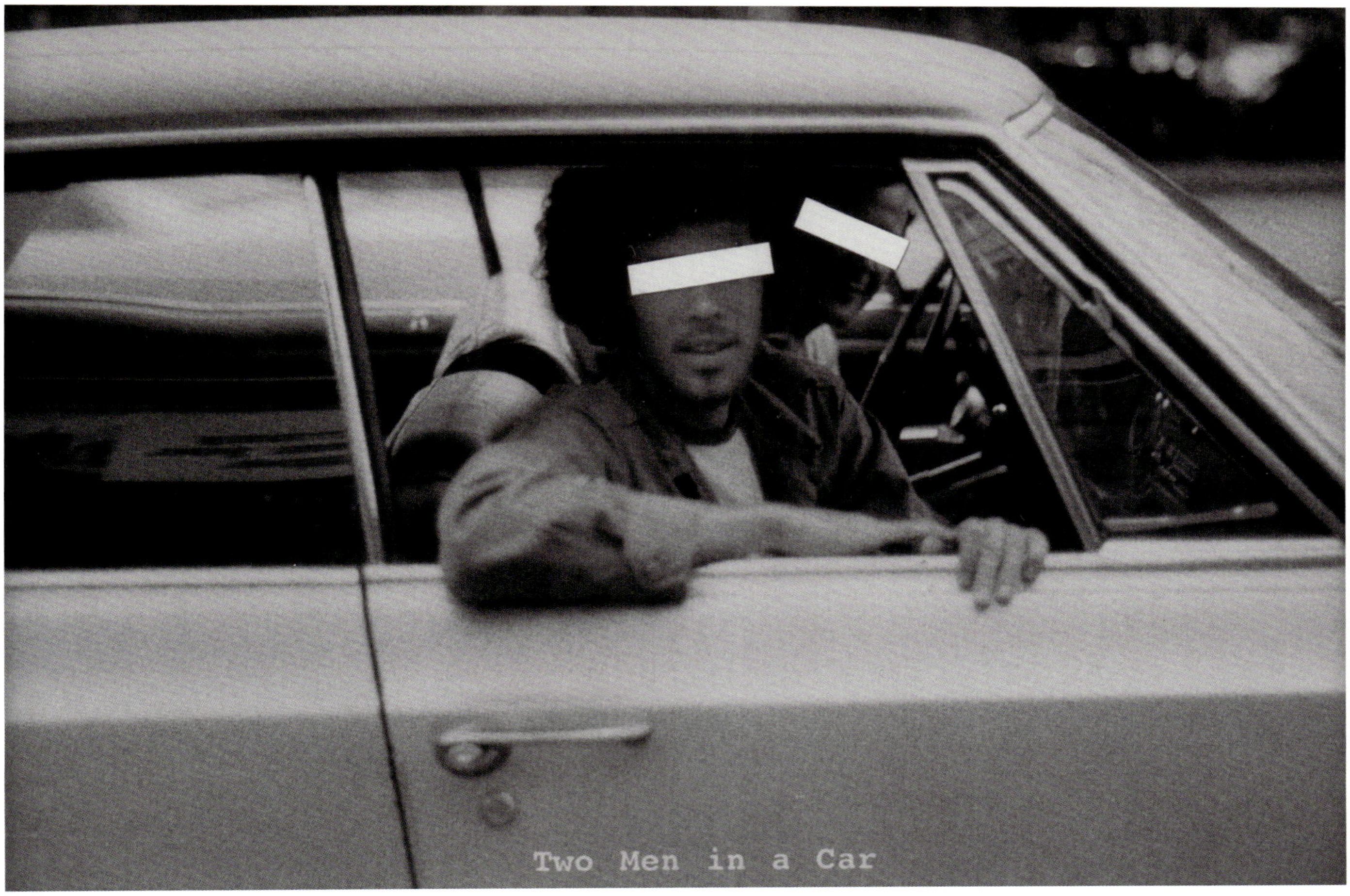

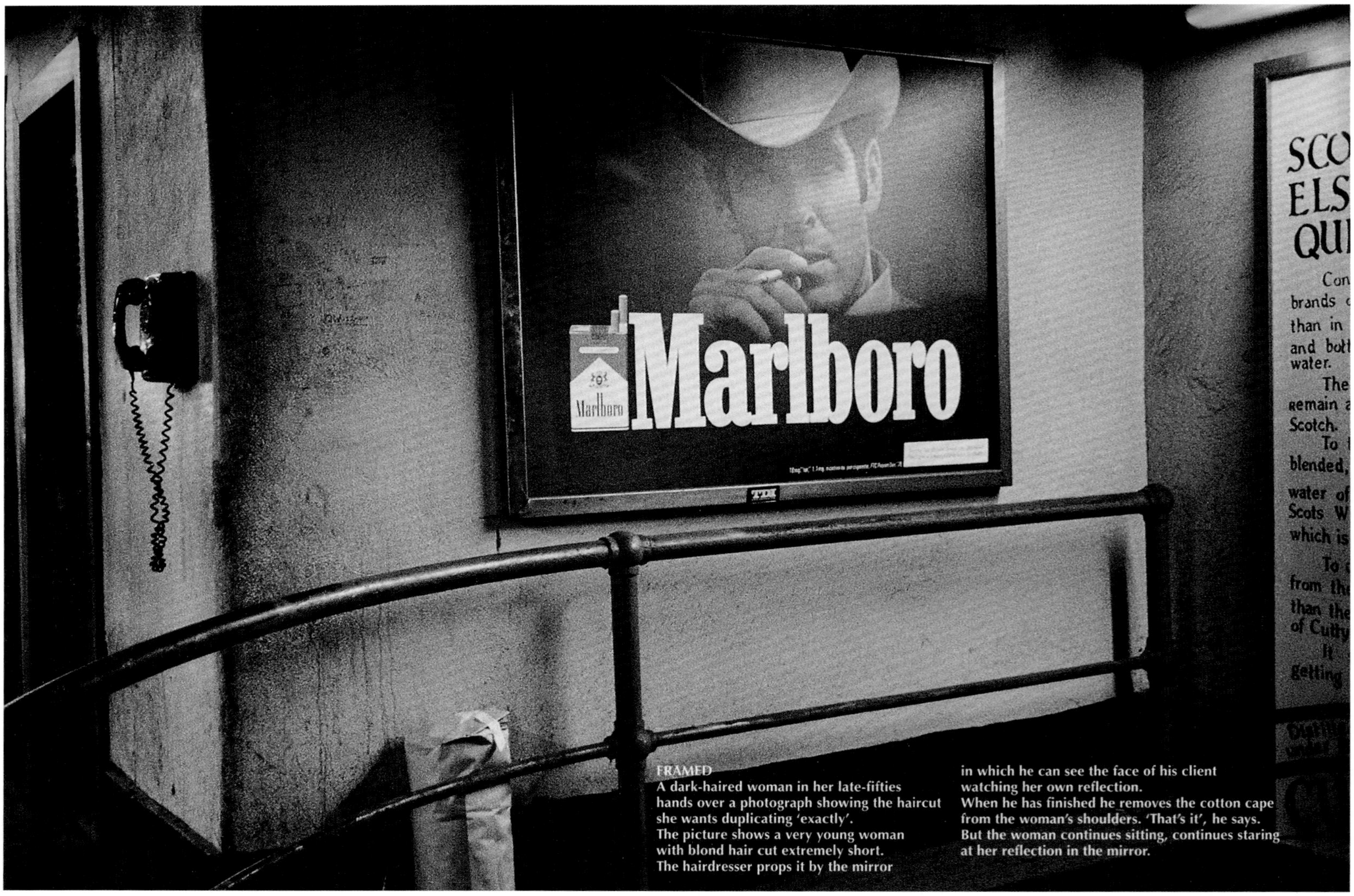

Victor Burgin
Framed, from the series 'US 77', 1977
Photographic prints and text
12 panels each 100 × 150 cm /
39⅜ × 59 in

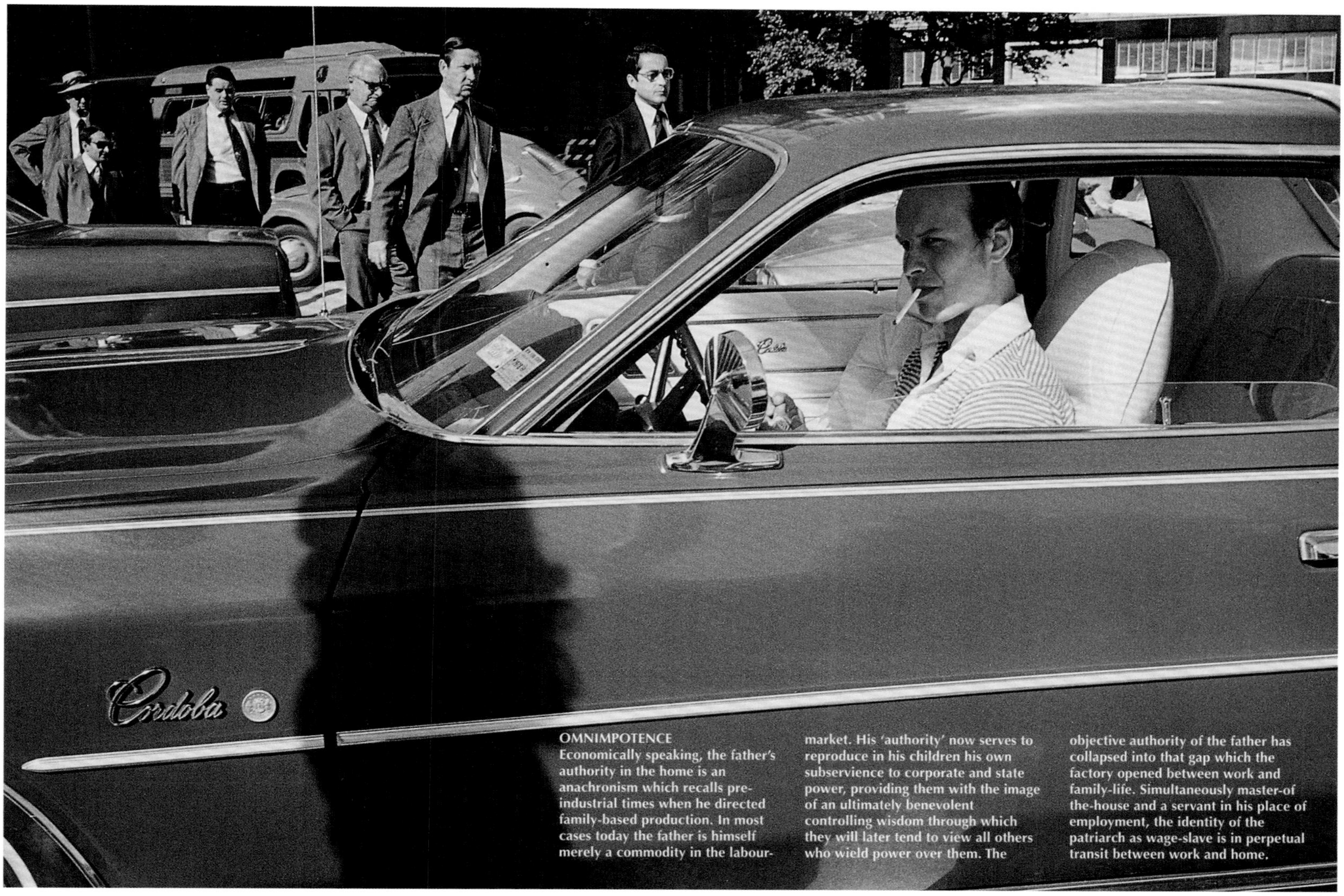

Victor Burgin
Omnimpotence, from the series 'US 77', 1977
Photographic prints and text
12 panels each 100 × 150 cm / 39⅜ × 59 in

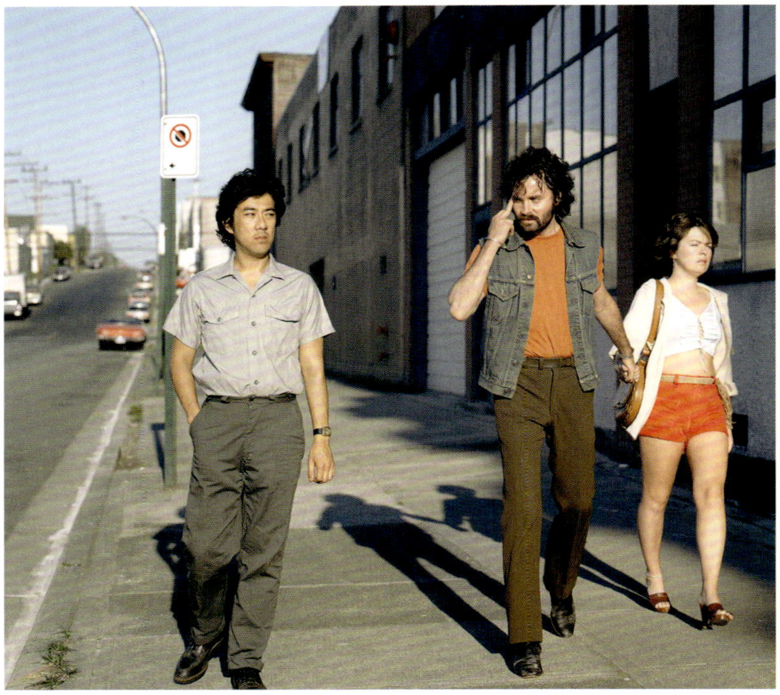

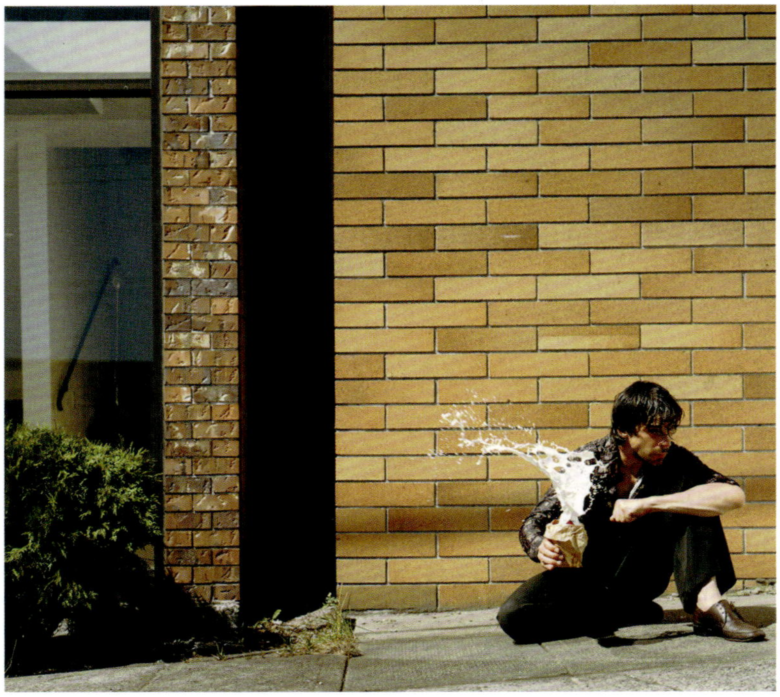

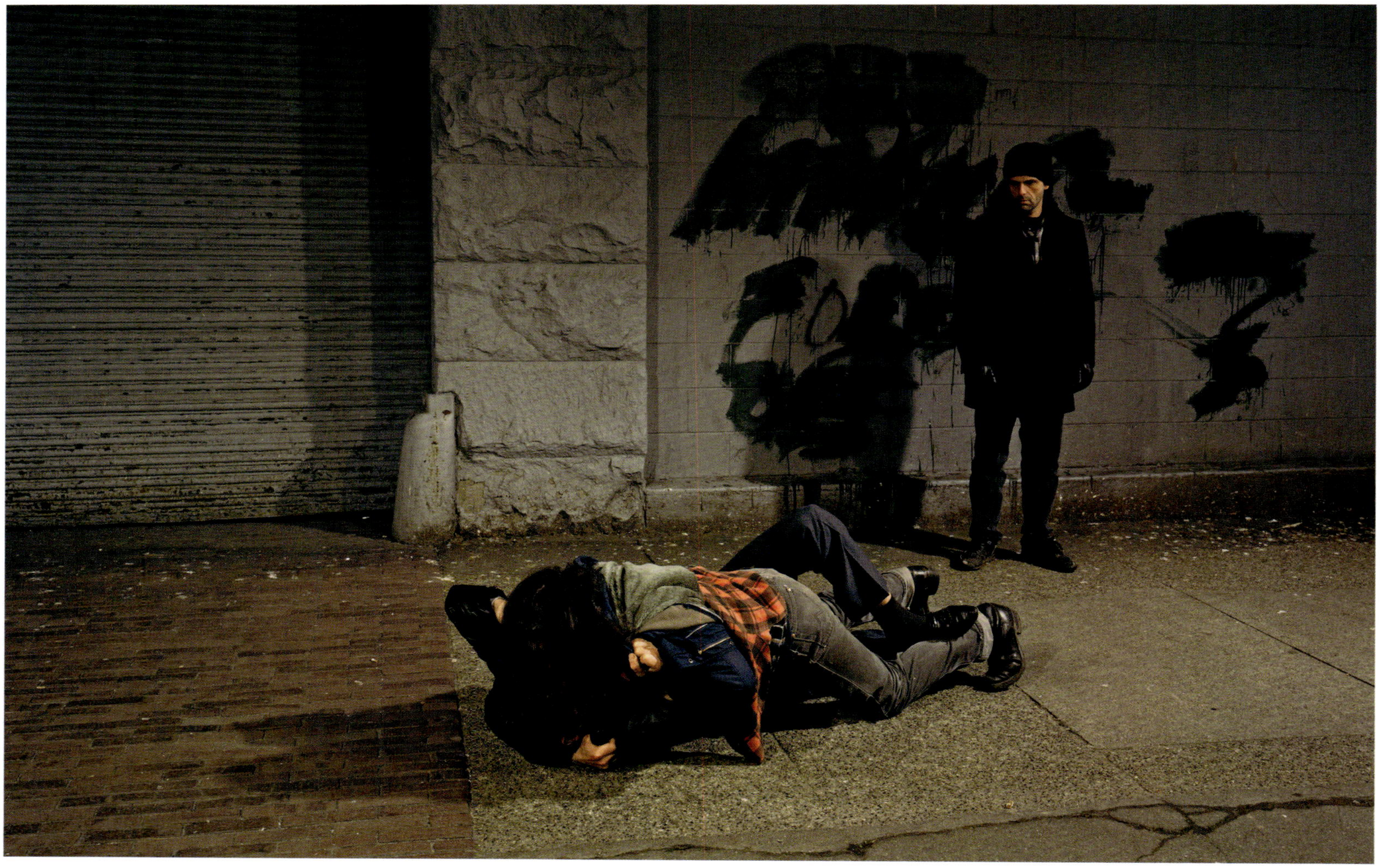

Jeff Wall

Jeff Wall draws upon the language of street photography in a number of his staged tableaux, a process that allows him to render street scenes with a large-format camera in such detail they can be enlarged to the scale of the human figures depicted within them. He has said of his images that 'They do not refer to a condition or moment that needs to have existed historically or socially.'[17] Most of the pictures involve artifice and stagecraft: they are meticulously controlled as scenes are set up and performers carefully posed. As a result they are indebted to the history of art as much as to street photography. Édouard Manet's aesthetics of estrangement is integral to the quality of many of Wall's tableaux. The use of the black-lit lightbox mirrors the form of late capitalist spectacle, a form of luminosity and display that is often contradicted by the scenes of social breakdown and disorder it carries. Wall's street scenes are hyperbolic, over the top: *Mimic* (1982), for example, freezes a racist slur as a scruffy bearded male pulling his girlfriend along the street – implying another level of subjugation and abuse – raises his finger to his eye as they pass an Asian male. *Milk* (1984) introduces a distracting and beautiful abstract form created as the milk explodes from a carton held by a dishevelled-looking man seated on the sidewalk. Wall is interested in what he calls the 'importance of complicated natural forms' frozen in an instant, an effect that alludes both to Harold Edgerton's scientific high speed photography stilling a splash of milk and to an expressive, gestural, painterly expression.[18]

Wall brings the formal in tension with the social implications of life on the street. The same opposition continues with *A Fight on the Sidewalk* (1994), which sets its act of violence in a shallow theatrical space and lends a degree of eroticism to the two figures fighting on the ground, who are so entwined with one another it is hard to tell them apart. A tension lies between the violent act and the calmness and order of the surrounding tableau. The man in a black coat, hat and gloves who stands impassively watching the fight adds to the picture's contradictory sense of quiet stillness. The figure's detachment echoes our position before the tableau. The energy lacking in the staged violence is evident in the expressionist gestures of the black painted marks that cover up the writing on the wall behind the standing figure, a pictorial element that echoes the explosive splash of milk and continues Wall's dual preoccupation with the pictorial and the real. Witnessed violence can attain a formal stillness and beauty, as highlighted by Roy DeCarava's *Force*, but it is often less coherent. Wall might set up formal oppositions and tensions, but there is an overriding clarity and legibility to his tableaux that can be seen as diminishing and reducing the very qualities of street photography. Street life is filtered and anaesthetized through the tableau form.

Jeff Wall
Mimic, 1982
Transparency in lightbox
198 × 228.5 cm / 78 × 90 in

Milk, 1984
Transparency in lightbox
187 × 229 cm / 73⅝ × 90⅛ in

A Fight on the Sidewalk, 1994
Transparency in lightbox
189 × 303.5 cm / 74⅜ × 119½ in

Ken Lum

Ken Lum, a Canadian artist of Chinese heritage, mixes Pop art, advertising and street photography in a series of diptychs about everyday life (1993–4) which pair large-scale colour photographs with bright-coloured enamel screens on which are printed texts like comic speech bubbles that appear to present the thoughts or voices of the subjects depicted. The text panels give duration to the still photographs and augment the experiences they show. They subjectivise the portraits, making up for the limitations of photography's ability to represent the social world.

Lum has said that he is 'interested in moments and what is real – resistences, drives, desires, wishes and so on.'[19] The photographs are staged, like Wall's street scenes, but are more naturalistic in appearance. The texts are repetitive and simple, like a mantra or chant. A photograph showing a distressed female wearing denim with white stilettos in conversation in a phone booth is paired with the text: 'You don't love me, You've never loved me! When have you ever loved me? When have you ever given a shit about me?!' Lum notes his relation to Pop art and the paintings of Roy Lichtenstein: 'No matter how flat and stiff his characters are, because they are derived from comic books, the problems they are articulating are problems real people can identify with. They are always about subjectivity. For example, the famous Brad… oh Brad type paintings are so great because the resonance of the text, or the emotional outbursts, contradicts so oppositionally the form of the picture, which is very cool and objective. It's about the problem of how to have feelings in a world which doesn't feel (which sounds like a cliché), but that's a problem of everyday life.'

In Lum's work, where the dynamic is between a comic strip text and a photograph, the elements are more discordant. The texts bring out a concern with emotional states in an attempt to supplement what he felt was missing from street photography. Garry Winogrand's work does not go far enough for Lum because it is 'directed to how sensuous the world is.' It is far from Lum's more prescriptive responses to everyday life. As he puts it, 'If you can't control it, the reading of the work is not going to be directed.' While a number of his pictures focus on typical situations of social breakdown or discord, Lum also deals with the idea of nothingness in his picture about someone taking time out, a photograph of an Asian teenager reclined on wooden steps, cigarette in hand, which is paired with a series of words – or rather sounds – intended to convey their chilled state, when little or anything is on their mind: 'Hum, hum hummm hum hummmm Hum hummmm…'.

Ken Lum
You don't love me, 1994
C-print, aluminium, enamel, sintra
183 × 243 cm / 72 × 95⅝ in

Hum, hum, hummm, 1994
C-print, lacquer and enamel on aluminium
183 × 243 cm / 72 × 95⅝ in

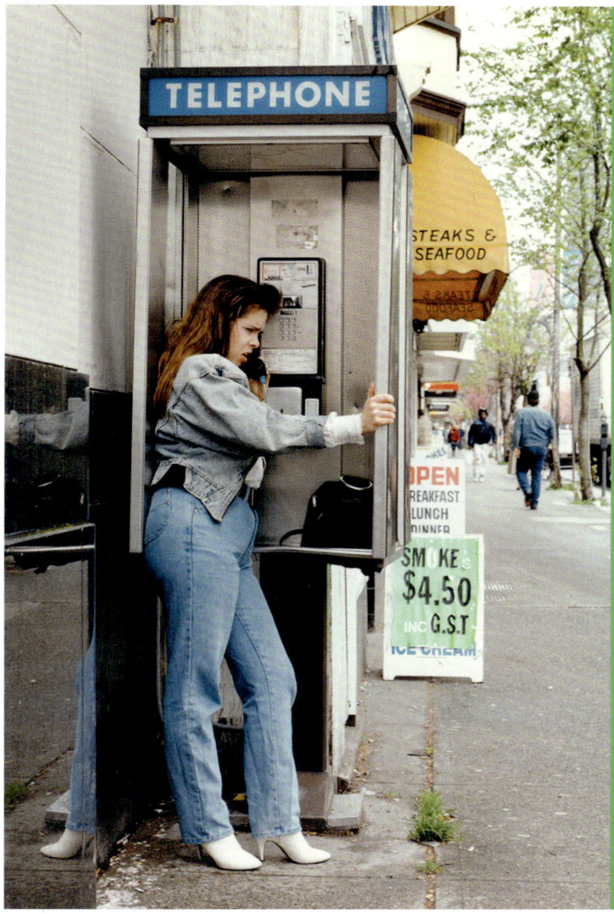

You don't love me
You've never
loved me!
When have you ever
loved me?
When have you ever
given a shit
about me?!

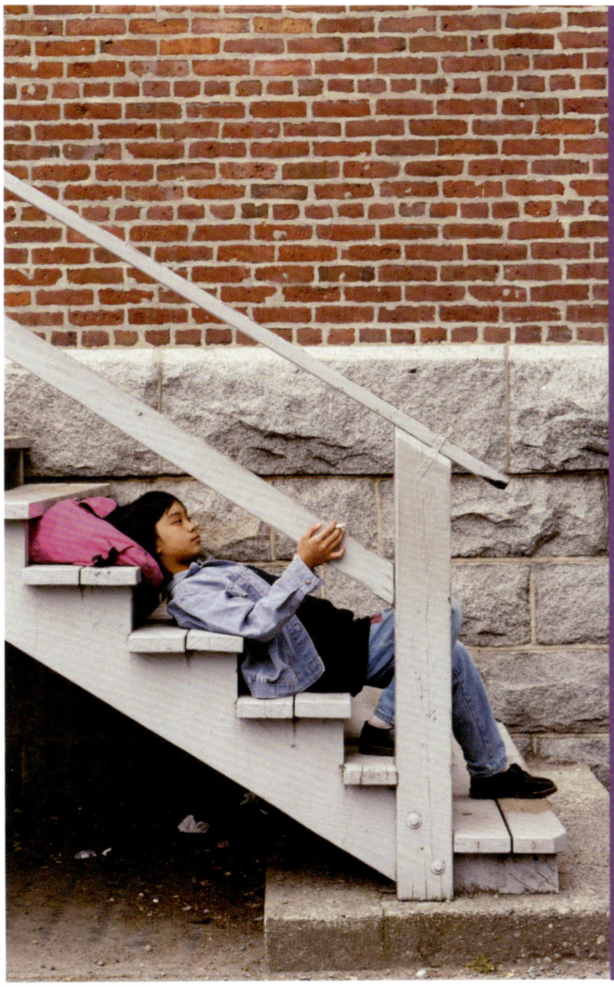

Hum hum hummm
hum hummmm
Hum hummmm
hum hum hummm
Hum hum hummm
hum hummmm
Hum hummmm
hum hum hummm

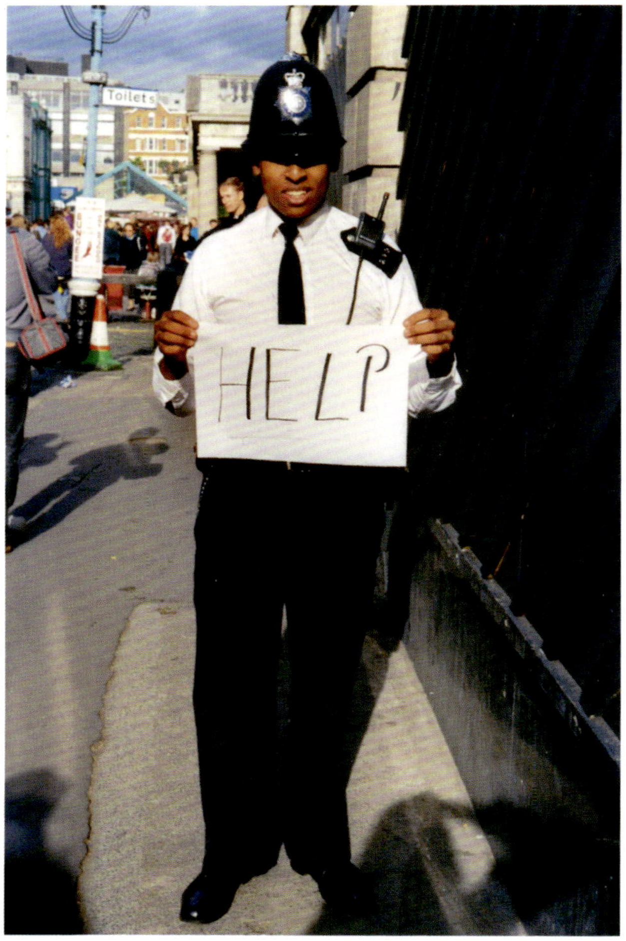
Toilets
HELP

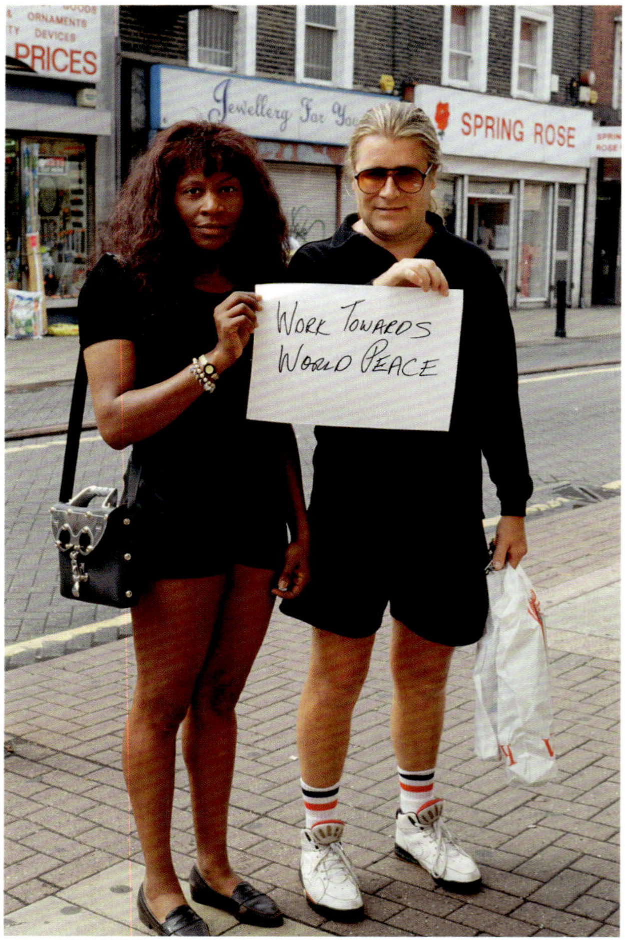
PRICES
Jewellery For You
SPRING ROSE
WORK TOWARDS
WORLD PEACE

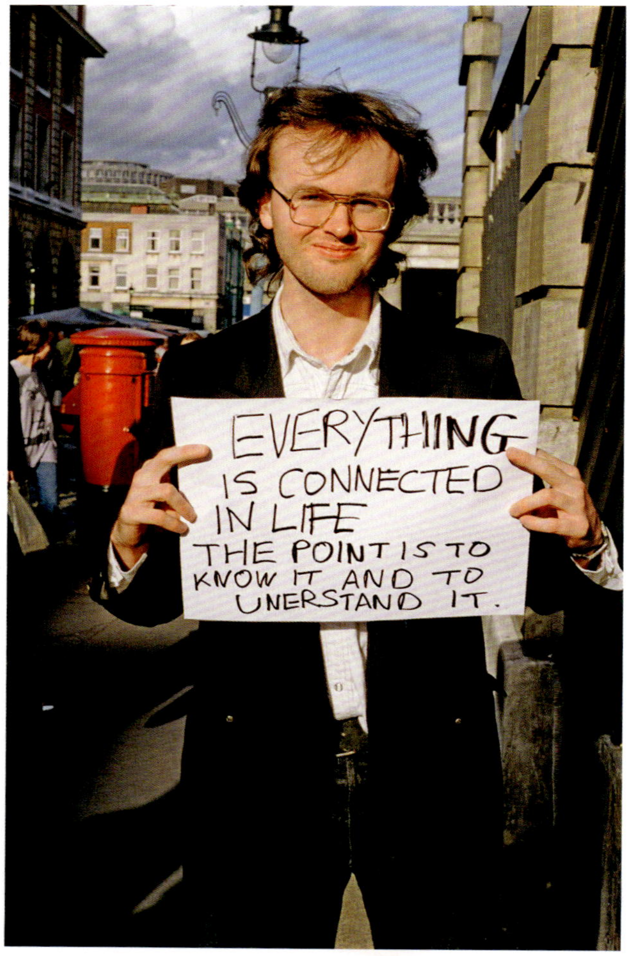
EVERYTHING
IS CONNECTED
IN LIFE
THE POINT IS TO
KNOW IT AND TO
UNERSTAND IT.

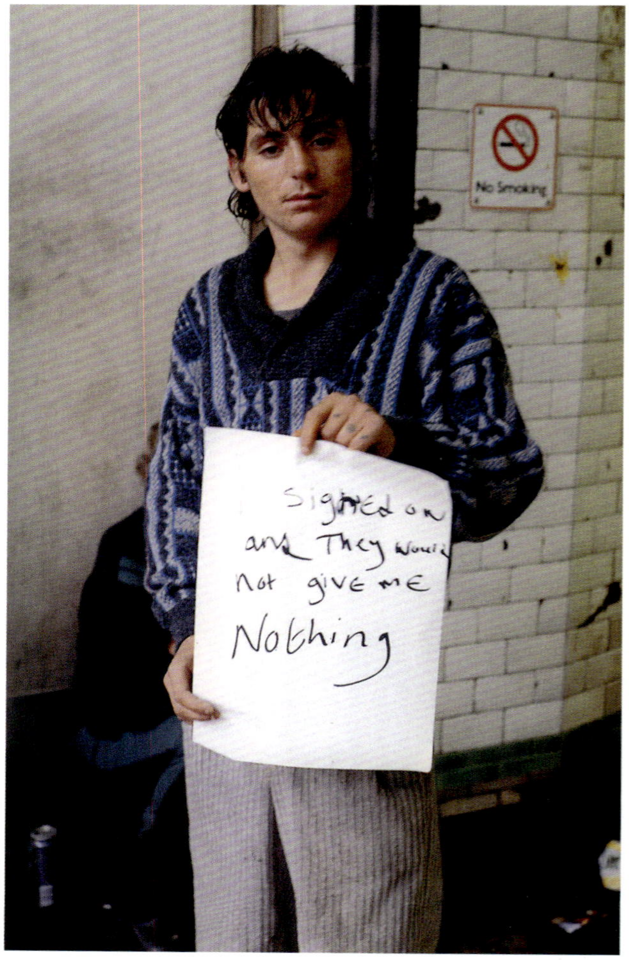
No Smoking
Signed on
and They would
not give me
Nothing

Gillian Wearing

The tradition of street photography is acknowledged in Gillian Wearing's series of photographs 'Signs that Say What You Want to Say and Not Signs that Say What Someone Else Wants You to Say' (1992–3). To make these pictures, Wearing stopped people in the street and got them to write down what they were thinking before photographing them. Her photographs are nothing special as photographs: an informal colour snapshot record of her subjects looking to camera as they each hold their statements, which are presented in the form of handwritten notes on white sheets of paper. With the display of self to camera supplemented by the personal disclosures made within the signs, there is an element of unmasking here. Picturing a range of people in terms of age, gender, class and ethnicity, this *vox populi* street portraiture both draws upon and unsettles stereotypes as we try and read the look of the person in relation to the slogans they make public. This visually forceful work rests upon our fascination and curiosity about what strangers are like on the street, with the varying revelations and disclosures made in their handwritten signs, either interrupting or confirming the expectations and assumptions made about her subjects in terms of their expressions, gestures and dress.

Gillian Wearing
Signs that Say What You Want Them To Say and Not Signs that Say What Someone Else Wants You To Say, HELP, 1992–3
C-print mounted on aluminium
44.5 × 29.7 cm / 17½ × 11¾ in

Signs that Say What You Want Them To Say and Not Signs that Say What Someone Else Wants You To Say, WORK TOWARDS WORLD PEACE, 1992–3
C-print mounted on aluminium
44.5 × 29.7 cm / 17½ × 11¾ in

Signs that Say What You Want Them To Say and Not Signs that Say What Someone Else Wants You To Say, EVERYTHING IS CONNECTED IN LIFE THE POINT IS TO KNOW IT AND TO UNDERSTAND IT, 1992–3
C-print mounted on aluminium
44.5 × 29.7 cm / 17½ × 11¾ in

Signs that Say What You Want Them To Say and Not Signs that Say What Someone Else Wants You To Say, SIGNED ON AND THEY WOULD NOT GIVE ME NOTHING, 1992–3
C-print mounted on aluminium
44.5 × 29.7 cm / 17½ × 11¾ in

Joel Sternfeld

A number of Joel Sternfeld's photographs from his series 'Passing Strangers' (1987–2000) rely on the tension set up by the formal demands of using a large-format camera on the street, which decisively breaks with the more random and snapshot qualities that have come to characterize the tradition of street photography. Getting strangers to interrupt their day-to-day activities and pose for a photograph, Sternfeld is concerned with the distinctive look and less expected qualities of his subjects. The sense of the posed portrait is far from the instantaneity of the handheld camera, and links these pictures with what the great American writer James Agee identified as monumental photography, which for him was the complete opposite of lyrical street photography. For Agee, monumental, static photography involved a different way of looking that was 'generally the richest in meditativeness, in mentality, in attentiveness to the wonder of materials and of objects'.[20] This is certainly the effect of Sternfeld's photographs.

The lonely business executive eating his evening meal on the street or the lawyer carrying his laundry fascinate us because they are caught at more informal moments, outside their familiar roles. But they nevertheless chime with the wider idea of these men's hurried existence, pressured by a work that seems to have taken over their lives. Details in the pictures serve as surprises that help break expectations about their subjects, giving the series a certain surreal air: the flamboyant tattoos on a runner's arm and leg; the pet rabbit carried in a transparent container by a woman out shopping, its pink lid matching her jacket; the red trainers worn by the bare-chested homeless man, photographed with his blankets over his shoulder. This is a non-judgemental and non-hierarchical portrait of American people. The recurrent look to camera is an invitation to identify with them, yet the scrutiny invited by Sternfeld's detailed depiction creates a separation that keeps us outside and apart from their worlds.

Joel Sternfeld
A Homeless Man with his Bedding, New York, New York, July 1994, 1994
C-print
118.1 × 96.5 cm / 46½ × 38 in

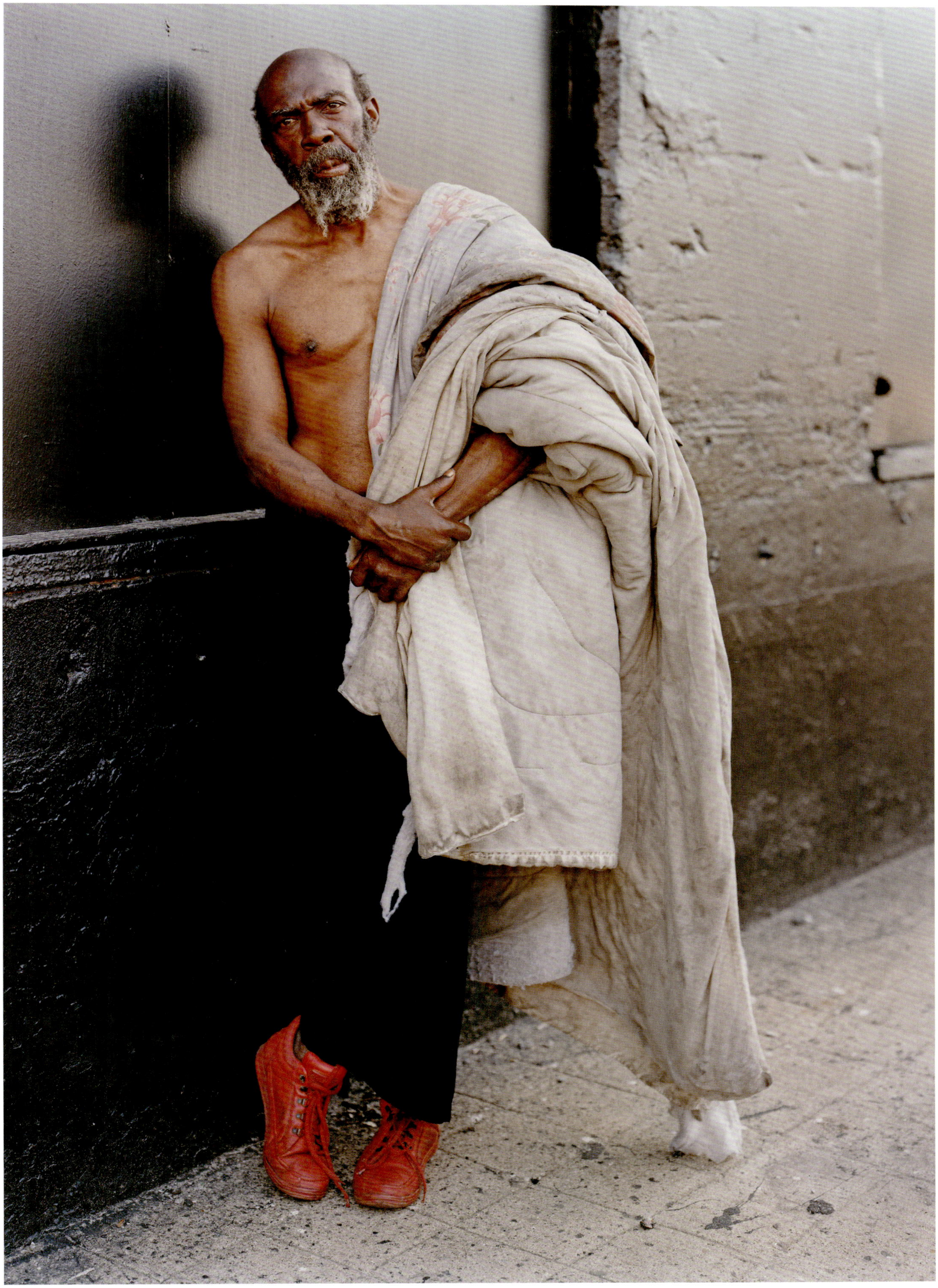

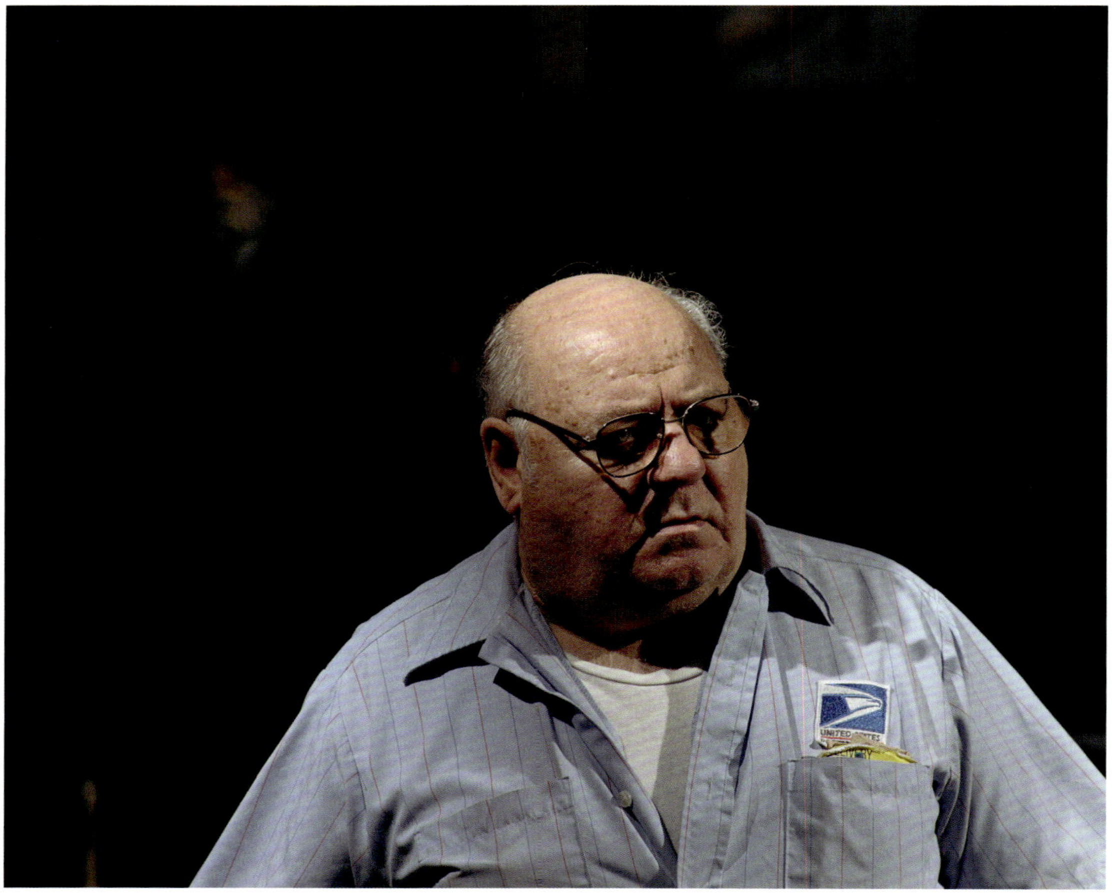

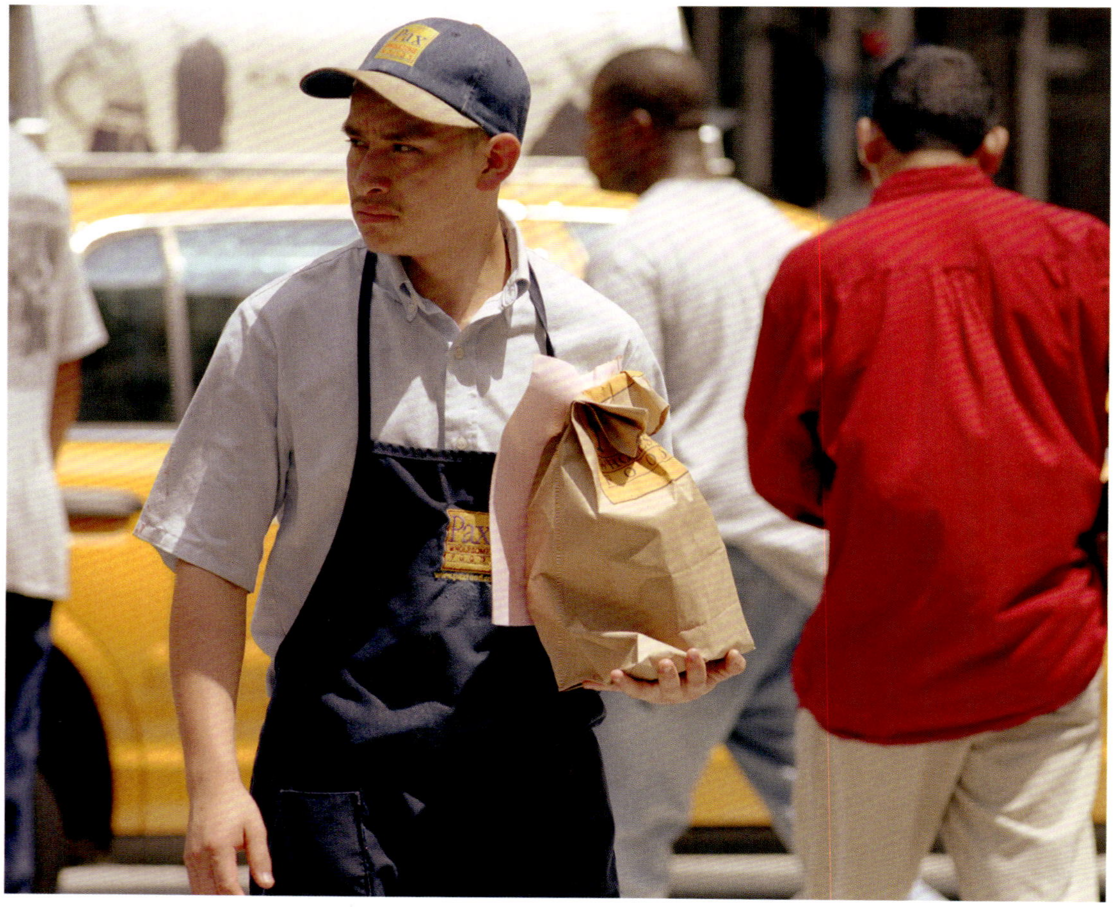
Pax

Philip-Lorca diCorcia

Both Gillian Wearing's and Joel Sternfeld's photography involves transactional street photography. The subjects who pose before the photographer are complicit in having their picture taken. The work of Philip-Lorca diCorcia and Beat Streuli returns us to the candid tradition of street photography and its fascination with people's unguarded, less self-conscious moments. Both photographers are attentive to faces in the crowd, focusing on individuals and difference but at the same time are concerned with a sense of collectivity and commonality.

DiCorcia's 'Heads', face-on portraits of unsuspecting passersby, all taken at the same spot in Times Square, can be seen as pointing to a soullessness beneath America's spectacle culture, placing them in street photography's long-standing tradition of representations of lone and lonely subjects in urban spaces. In order to take the photographs, diCorcia rigged up an overhead strobe on scaffolding in Times Square, which he triggered as his unsuspecting passersby walked over an × marked on the sidewalk. Spot-lit, his ordinary subjects are given a theatrical presence as a result. They appear to be elsewhere, distracted, absorbed in their own thoughts, cares and worries. For all the details of difference, we feel that somehow they are all the same, that we are witnessing a plurality of isolations.

Beat Streuli

In marked contrast, the Swiss artist Beat Streuli's close-up portraits of people from crowds, taken in various cities from all over the world, are predominantly upbeat. This is photography in the humanist tradition of the 1955 exhibition 'The Family of Man', the famous worldwide touring show that celebrated what Roland Barthes called the 'solid rock of a universal human nature' and removed history in the process.[21] Presented in the form of slide projections whose images slowly dissolve into one another or as large photographic prints, larger than life size, Streuli's photographs invite us to linger on the sensuousness and beauty of people's facial expressions or gestures. Streuli has said: 'I want to have installations that are big and beautiful just as the movies are, or great billboards, and without selling stupid products.'[22] Nevertheless his pictures vie with the spectacle of global advertising, especially when they are shown on streets as billboard posters. One cannot help but sense that Streuli's succession of youthful figures blend too readily into the mirroring facades of global advertising. They may not sell stupid products, but those photographed nevertheless become commodities in the process. The people he photographs are not models or stars but anonymous citizens, strangers in crowds, who take on a certain aura through his pictorial elevation of them. Streuli's street portraiture is not inclusive but quite selective. Avoiding the exotic, abject or bizarre, he photographs mostly young and rather good-looking people in sunlight, which inevitably has a bearing on how they look and how we view them. He takes his pictures in recreational areas or downtown in big cities, in places that, as he says, 'provide a few hours of paradise for everybody'.[23]

Philip-Lorca diCorcia
Head #9, 2001
Fujicolor Crystal Archive print
121.9 × 152.4 cm / 48 × 60 in

Beat Streuli
8th Avenue / 35th Street, 2002
C-print
150 × 200 cm / 59 × 78¾ in

Tom Wood

Tom Wood opened street photography to new formal possibilities through the series of remarkable photographs he made between 1978 and 1998 while journeying on buses in Merseyside in the north of England. The people, location and economic context remain very specific and local, yet the portrait of street life is varied and multi-layered. Travelling on the bus, Wood gives us mobile views, shifting portraits of people and their environment. The photographs begin in black-and-white then explode in colour in a shift that also entails a greater interplay with images from adverts. In this respect, his work is distinct from Beat Streuli's street photography. When Wood's photographs show how the hairstyles of models on advertisements are mirrored by those of his subjects, we nevertheless remain fully aware of what separates them. These passengers on public transport tend to define a particular economic group and class.

Reflections create a layering to some of Wood's photographs, a rich composite effect in which the worlds outside and inside come together, formally counterpointed by the juxtapositions set up between the bus interiors and the landscapes outside. The cut of montage is beautifully articulated by the configuration of cutting blades of a Silk Cut cigarette advert, cropped by the frame of the bus window. Below the knives stand a mother and daughter in the street, both dressed in white, framed by the jagged hazard-road markings, which themselves are played off against the repetitive bars of the seats in the bus interior.

The multiple pictures set up through reflections and montages make us think of more than one moment, of accumulated time. In addition, the idea of the bus travel in terms of a journey through life is evoked through pictures that pick out groups of people that show us differences in generations, of children, parents and the elderly. The buses follow the same routes over and over, but the pictures are not repetitive – there is breadth and variety here, and a sensitivity to a range of moods implied by the gestures and expressions of people as they go about their everyday lives, an everyday which Wood is both part of and separate from. The windows on the bus function like extensions of the camera, opening up views – landscapes as well as street scenes – framing individuals and crowds, blurring and diffusing what is outside or collapsing what is outside with what is inside through reflections. Wood's is an essentially celebratory and affirmative street photography. Henri Cartier-Bresson spoke about a desire to 'preserve life in the act of living' in his photographs, and this tautology describes very well what Tom Wood does.[24] And he does it in the face of the alienating and fragmentary experience of urban life and street photography's more characteristic bleaker history. He does not idealize. His pictures might seem to depart from the real in their play with reflective and mirrored images, but they remain firmly attached to the people, places and things we are shown.

Michael Wolf

Michael Wolf's pictures introduce a peculiarly rich but dark reflection on people and street photography. He gives us close-ups of commuters in Tokyo, where individuals are squashed up against the glass of train windows, creating a screen that allows him to photograph them up close while remaining safe and separate from them. These street portraits present an endless series of people – women and men, old and young – all huddled together. Some are aware of the camera and try to hide their faces or stare back aggressively at the photographer, while others are caught in their own worlds. Condensation on the glass can have the beautiful pictorial effect of blurring and diffusing faces, while other more disturbing photographs show us how the coldness of the glass makes the faces and hands that come into contact with it appear cadaverous.

Wolf's street portraits of commuters link up with his appropriated images from Google Street View – a street photography from the armchair, attentive to the surprises and unpredictability of events that Google's totalizing and exhaustive mapping process has documented. It is not surprising that Wolf should liken himself to the photographer-turned-detective in Michelangelo's Antonioni's 1966 film *Blow-Up*, who enlarges photographs he has taken in a park to seek evidence about the murder he has unintentionally documented. In Wolf's blow-ups, everything is filtered through the screen of the computer and the anonymous gaze of Google Street View's machinery. He sometimes even incorporates on-screen directional arrows and markings as an integral pictorial element of his photographs. It perhaps becomes inevitable that such an exhaustive and global project might find variants, albeit much more impoverished, of classic street photographs. While Wolf highlights those who target the camera with anger, giving it the finger, there is also much unexpected magic, beauty, comedy and calamity in his pictures. There is a distinctly postmodern aspect to such appropriations, but at the same time what is so absorbing and fascinating are the glimmers of the real that can be found within the surveillance images. Wolf's photography does not signal the death of traditional street photography. Viewing his pictures still brings us back to the pleasures and joys of the genre; indeed, they only really make sense in relationship to the traditions of a photography from the street.

Tom Wood
Stanley Road, Kirkdale (flower streets), 1989
From 'All Zones Off Peak'
C-print, dimensions variable

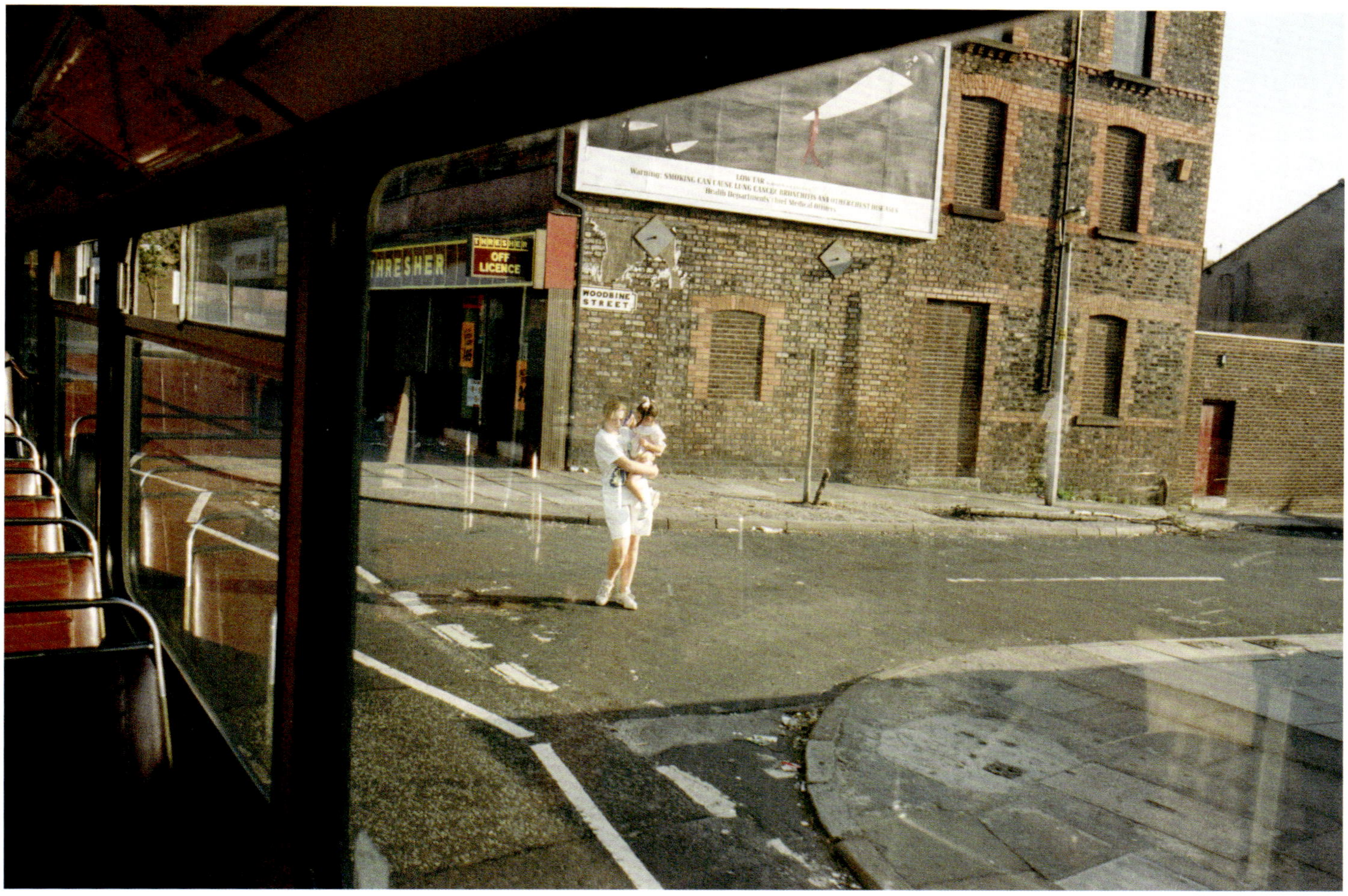
THRESHER
THRESHER OFF LICENCE
WOODBINE STREET
LOW TAR

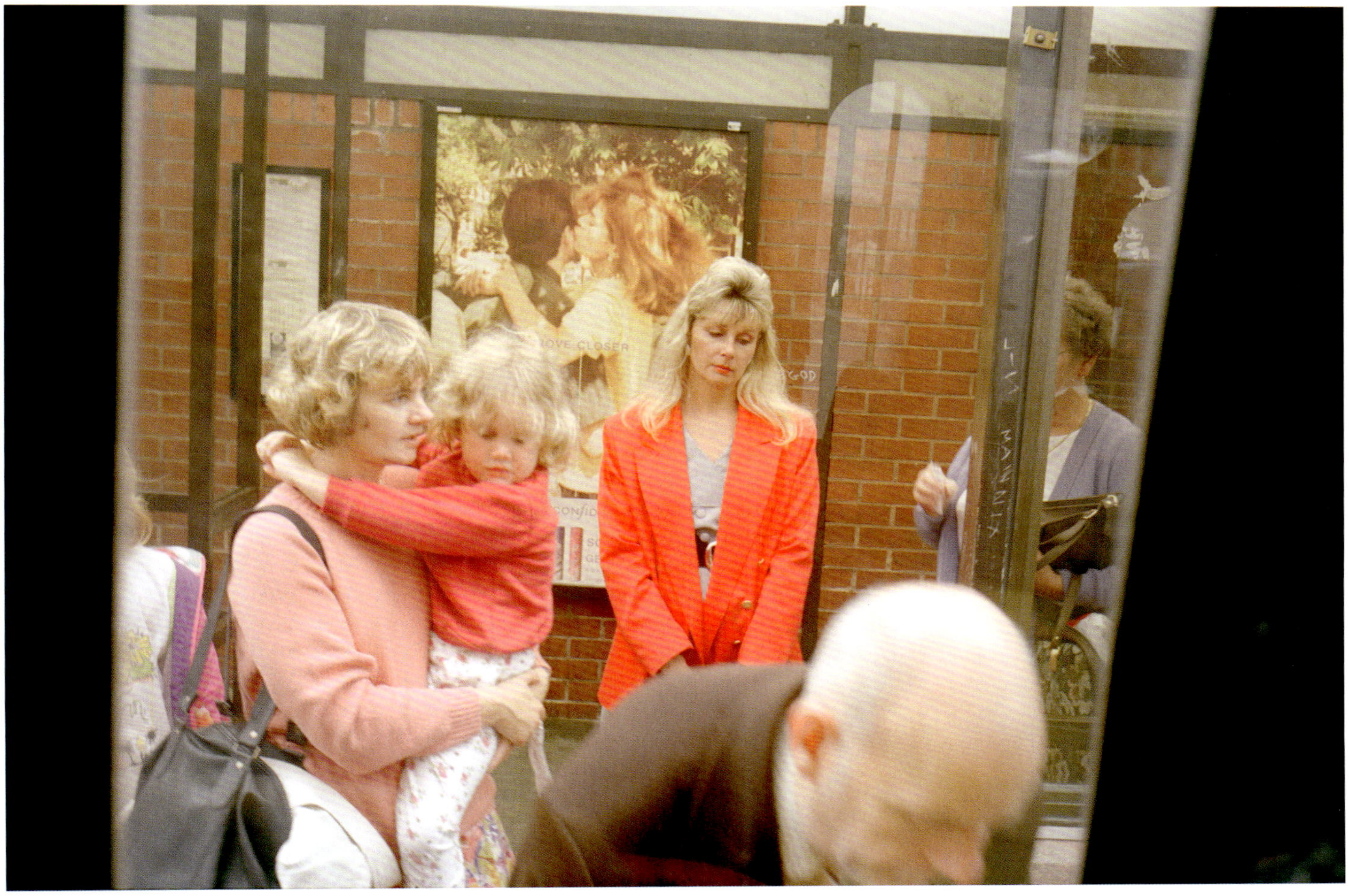

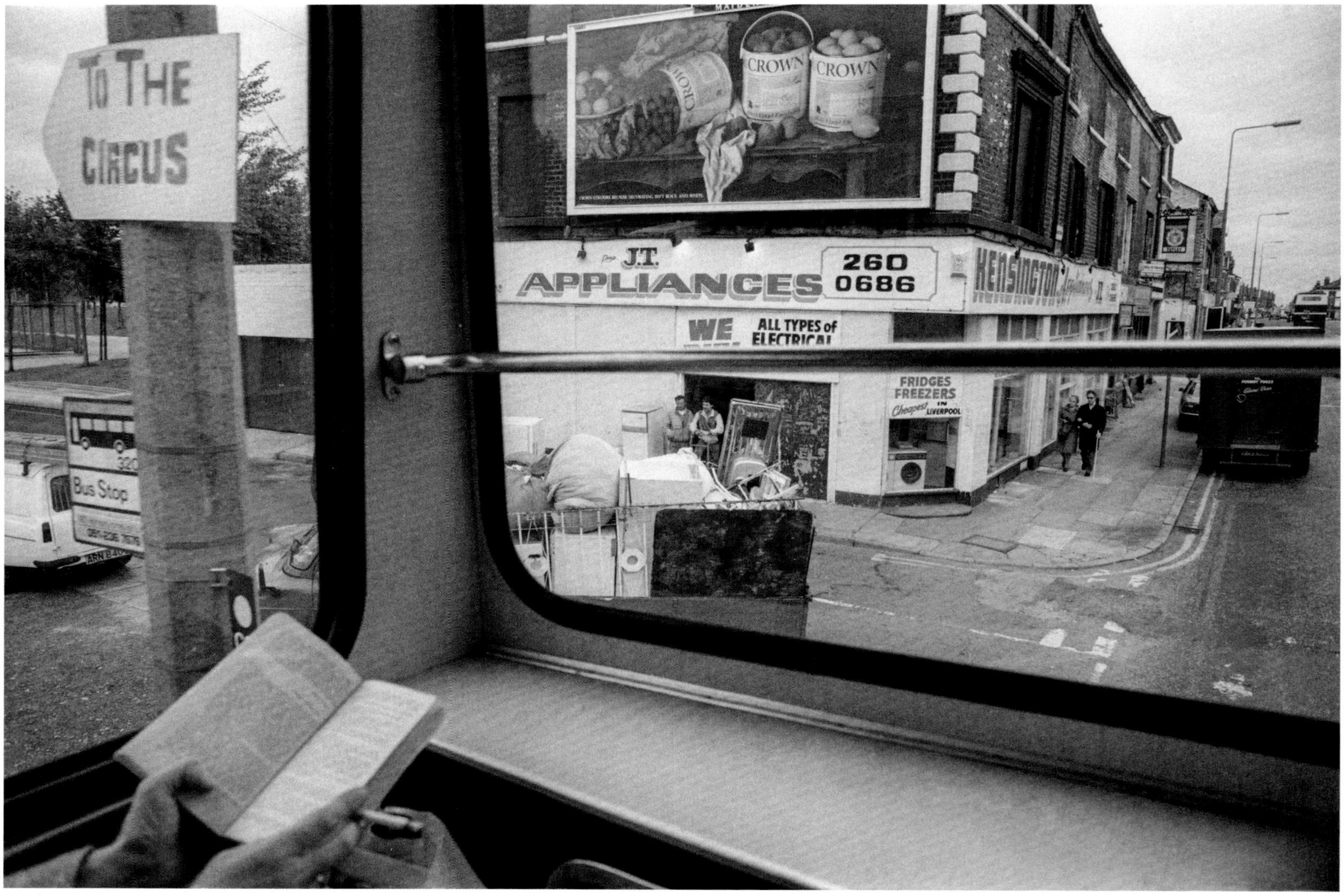

Tom Wood
Kensington, 1988, from the series
'All Zones Off Peak'
C-print, dimensions variable

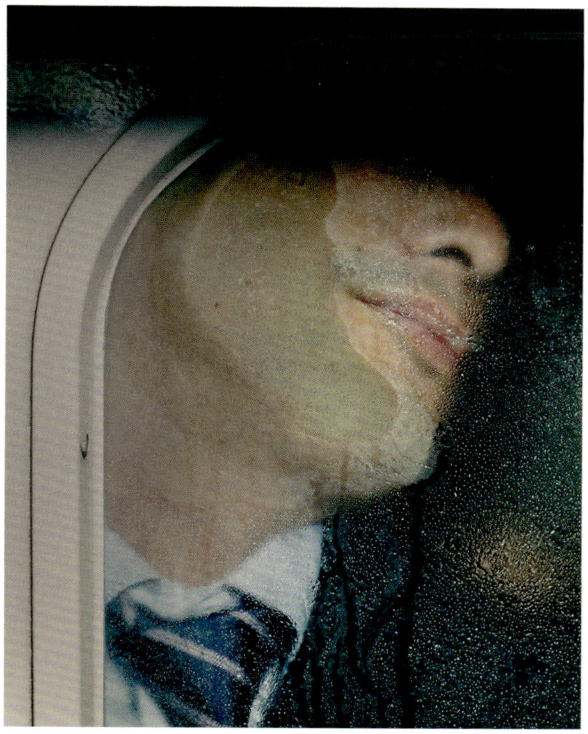

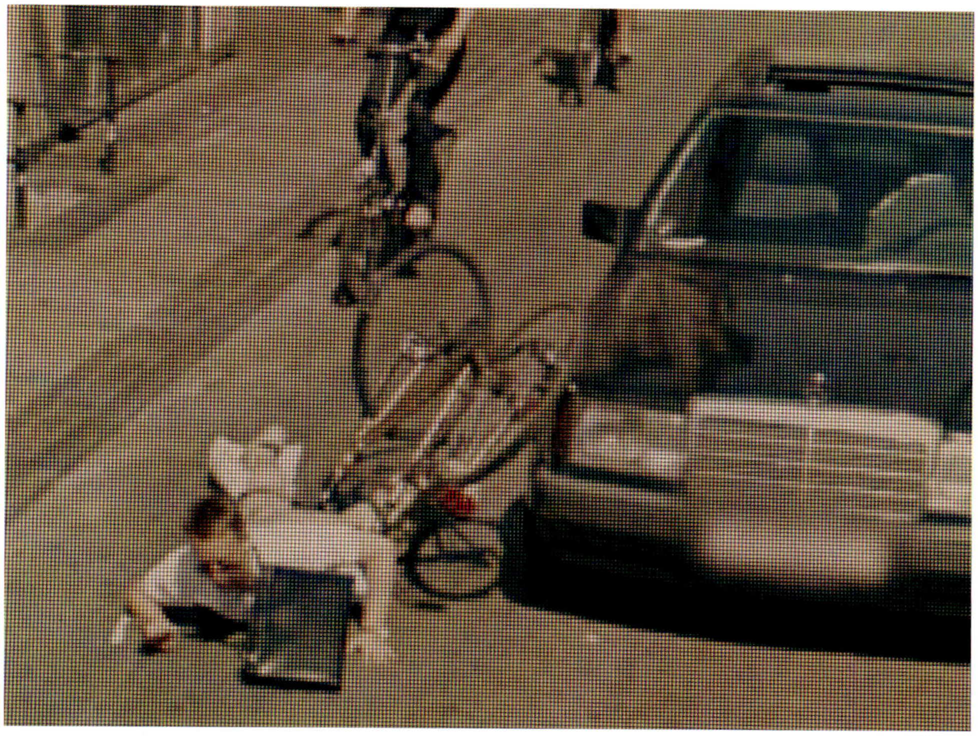

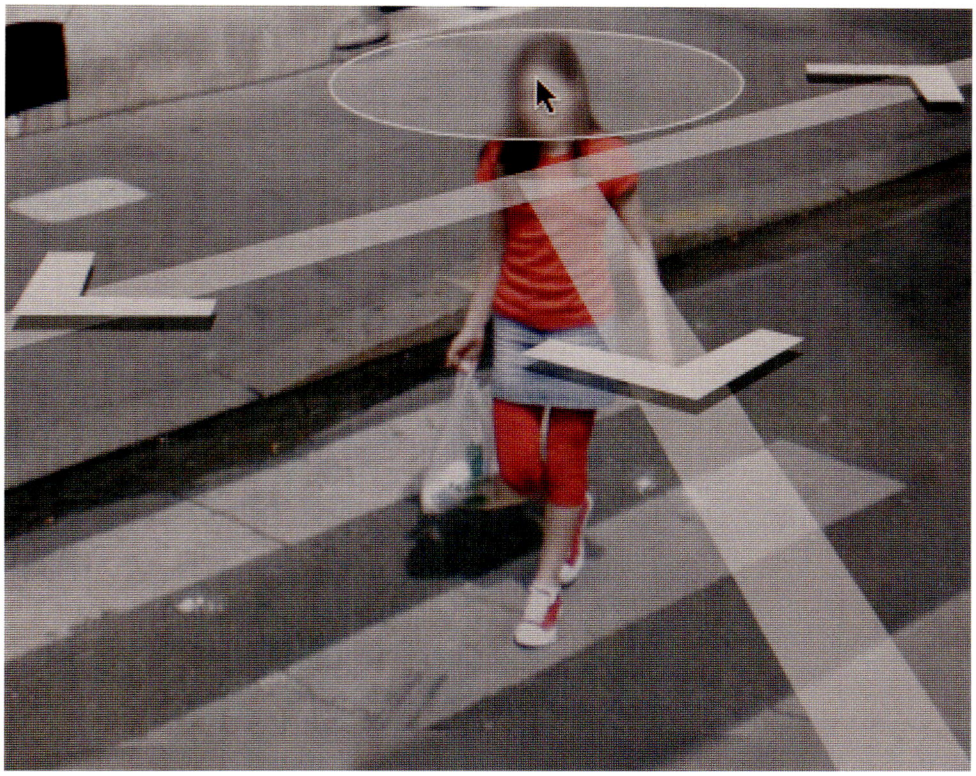

Michael Wolf
Tokyo Compression #5, 2010
Ink jet print, dimensions variable

A Series of Unfortunate Events #51, 2010
C-print, dimensions variable

Paris Street View #48, 2010
C-print, dimensions variable

Chapter Five

Landscapes: Nature, Culture and Power

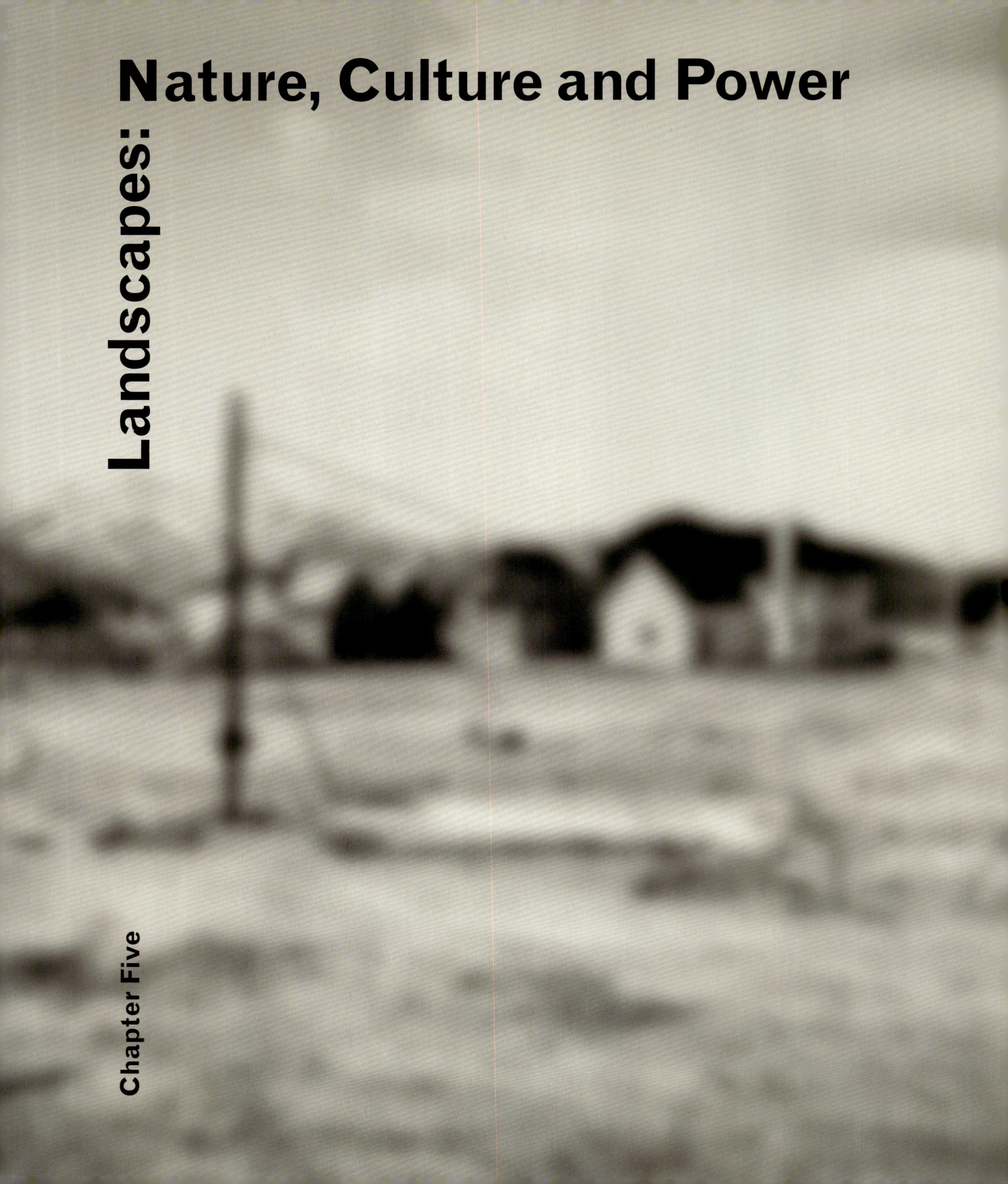

Since the 1960s, many artists concerned with landscape have marked a decisive shift away from the idealized notion of nature untouched by human presence typified by the work of the great American photographer Ansel Adams. Landscape now is rarely viewed innocent of the effects we have upon it.

This chapter begins with a discussion of a primarily aesthetic relationship to the landscape in the work of Thomas Struth and Andreas Gursky. Discussion of the 'New West' of urban sprawls, industrial parks and wastelands by Lewis Baltz and Robert Adams establishes an important and influential post-romantic approach to the landscape, which will continue in the work of a number of other artists discussed here. Industrial landscapes were used as a site of experimentation by the artist Robert Smithson with his photographs of photo markers and mirrors placed within specific sites. His work introduces a conceptual and experimental relationship to landscape which continues with the work of such artists as John Hilliard, Roger Palmer and Sophy Rickett. Both Richard Misrach and Edward Burtynsky make spectacular pictures from sites of ecological destruction. This political dimension will continue in the work of photographic artists who foreground the power relationships inherent in their depictions of place.

Sublime

Thomas Struth
Andreas Gursky

New Topography

Robert Adams
Lewis Baltz

Process and Experimentation

Robert Smithson
John Hilliard
Richard Long
Roger Palmer
Sophy Rickett

Romantic

Thomas Joshua Cooper
Roni Horn
Jem Southam

Documentary Landscapes

Joel Sternfeld
Richard Misrach
Edward Burtynsky

Viewing Positons

Wille Doherty
Jorma Puranen
Paul Seawright

Exclusion

Yto Barrada
George Georgiou
Vandy Rattana

Thomas Struth

The very concept of landscape itself implies a cultural view of nature. Viewing Thomas Struth's 1999 photograph of the sublime sunlit rock formation of El Capitan, the largest exposed granite face in the world, in California's Yosemite National Park, one cannot forget how Ansel Adams had already defined the very same landscape scenery. Struth is very much concerned with photography's identity and status as art, and his image is a response to Adams. Struth's picture is in colour, monumental in scale and framed by lines of cars and tourists who have also stopped to take in the breathtaking view. But while the picture might include tourists, it nevertheless represents something very special and distinct from a tourist view. The formal qualities of the picture raise it above tourism: like Adams, Struth makes art. Struth is primarily concerned with the value of photography in face of its reduction through popular and commercial photography. He takes seriously the sublime grandeur of the rocks and seeks to represent it through photography. This is not a post-romantic photograph, like much photography that will be considered in this chapter. Struth's art is about holding onto the value of the picture in the face of its reduction to spectacle and commerce. One should contrast Struth's picture with Martin Parr's comic reflections on global tourism in his 1995 book *Small World*, a photography more preoccupied with the spectacle of sightseers than the places they have come to see.

As John Szarkowski has noted, Ansel Adams was not alone when he took some of his best pictures in the High Sierra. Many were made 'during hours that could be spared from his duties as assistant trail boss of a great moveable picnic, composed of up to two hundred nature lovers'.[1] Adams's pictures construct the myth of romantic solitude, editing out the tourism of which he himself was fully aware.

Struth has also produced a series of remarkable pictures of wild nature, taken in the jungles of Australia, Japan and China, 'Paradise'. The all-over layers of dense vegetation create a formlessness that parallels abstract painting; as a reference point for these pictures, Struth cites Brice Marden's 'Cold Mountain' calligraphic paintings. The landscape pictorial tradition is disassembled, since these are no longer landscapes in the sense of landscape as a cultural convention of viewing nature. Nature is not framed as a tourist spectacle as it is in the picture of El Capitan. Before the dense screens of foliage in Struth's 'Paradise' pictures we have a loss of perspective and confront the fundamental otherness of nature. The work resists connotation and brings us up against a pure photographic seeing with minimum association, just the dense accumulation of details of natural phenomena, out of time and bereft of any social or historical information.

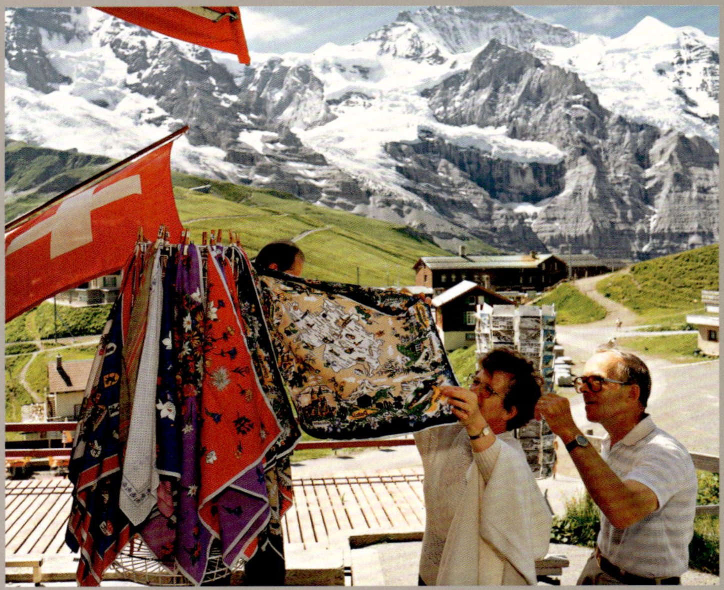

Martin Parr
Kleine Scheidegg, Switzerland, 1990, from the series 'Small World'
C-print, dimensions variable

Thomas Struth
El Capitan, Yosemite National Park, 1999
Cibachrome print, 169.5 × 216 cm / 66¾ × 85 in

Paradise 09, Xi Shuang Banna, China, 1999
C-print
267.9 × 337.9 cm / 105 × 133 in

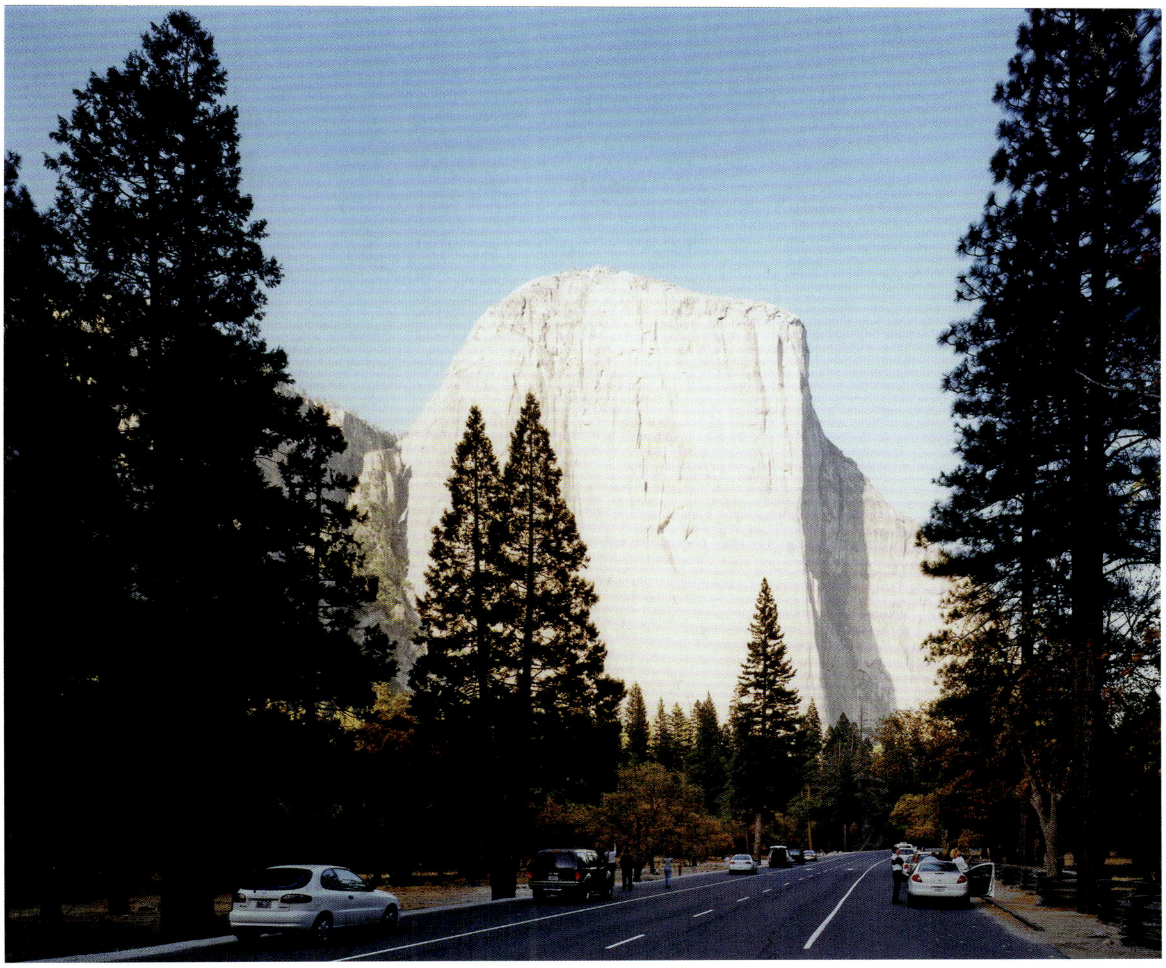

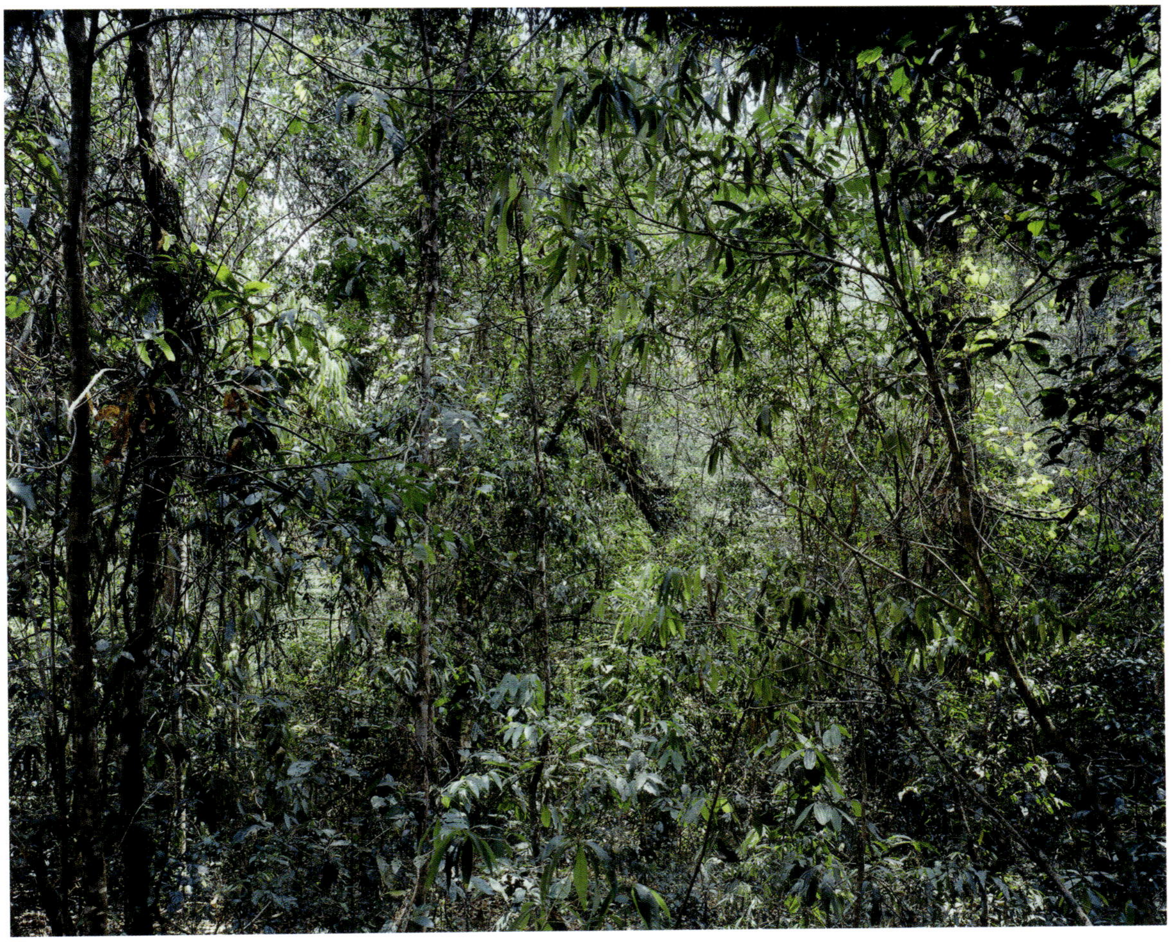

Andreas Gursky

Andreas Gursky's *Theben West* (1993), like Thomas Struth's *El Capitan* (1999), engages with tourism. Gursky is not among the tourists, but looks down upon them from an elevated vantage point high up on the pyramid. His picture allows us to see in both depth and time: from tourists, archaeological excavations and a strip of asphalt road against the desert sands, and further back to green fertile plains and the Nile itself on the horizon. Gursky's landscapes, global in their vision, show us spectacular manifestations of the contemporary landscape from such tourist sites to factories, airports, stock exchanges, pop concerts, sport events, shops and art museums. Both the scale of his pictures and his recurrent use of the aerial view combine to elicit awe. But the point is to show up the scale of things, and thus highlight our own insignificance.

Gursky's *Rhein II* (1996) parallels the formal concerns and preoccupations of Thomas Struth's 'Paradise' pictures. Only rather than an excess of detail, Gursky's photograph is spare and minimal. Here he moves away from the awe of the vista and instead presents us with a view in which the elements of the landscape are spread across the field of vision in the form of horizontal bands or stripes, parallel to the picture plane. For Gursky, such purity and abstraction looks back to the abstract paintings of Barnett Newman. But as the art historian Michael Fried has noted, formally the photograph is closer to Kenneth Noland's high modernist stripe or band pictures of the late 1960s and early 1970s[2]. *Rhein II* is part of a shift in Gursky's work, in which, as he has said, 'A visual structure appears to dominate the real events shown in my picture.'[3] Aided by digital manipulation, which in this case allowed him to erase a factory from the scene, *Rhein II* is drained of anecdotal and narrative detail. But much as it might allude to abstract painting and strive for a similar autonomy, the detailed and varied rendition of the river's shimmering surface still maintains a distinctive photographic element.

Andreas Gursky
Theben West, 1993
C-print
226.5 × 184.5 × 6.2 cm /
89¼ × 72⅝ × 2⅜ in

Rhein II, 1999
C-print
187 × 346 × 6.2 cm /
73⅝ × 136 × 2⅜ in

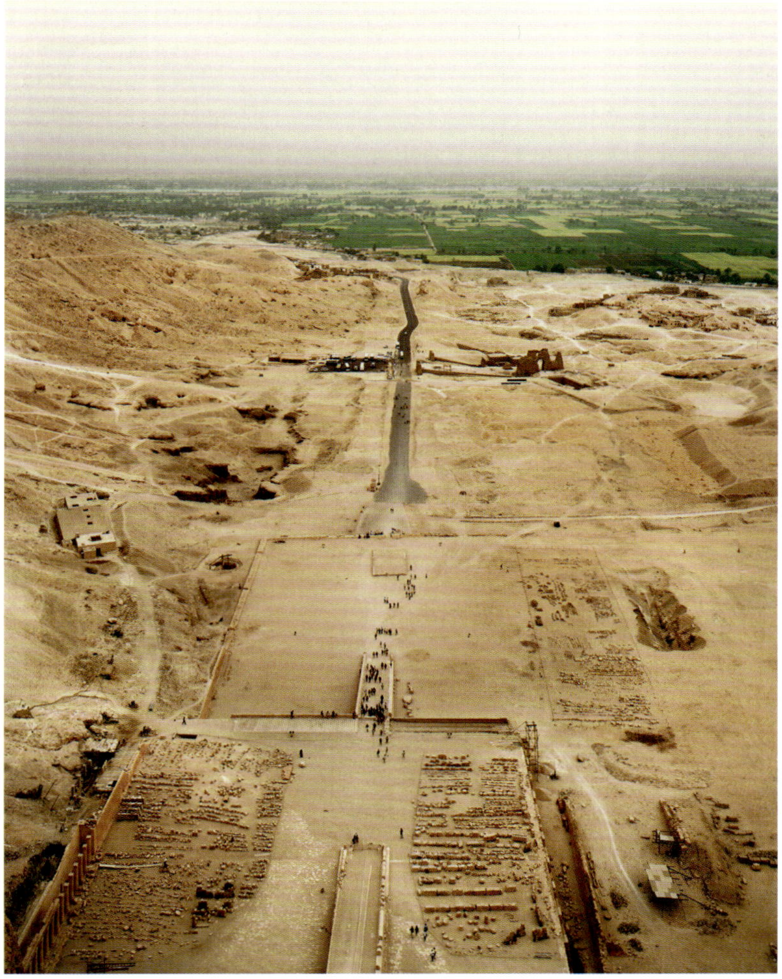

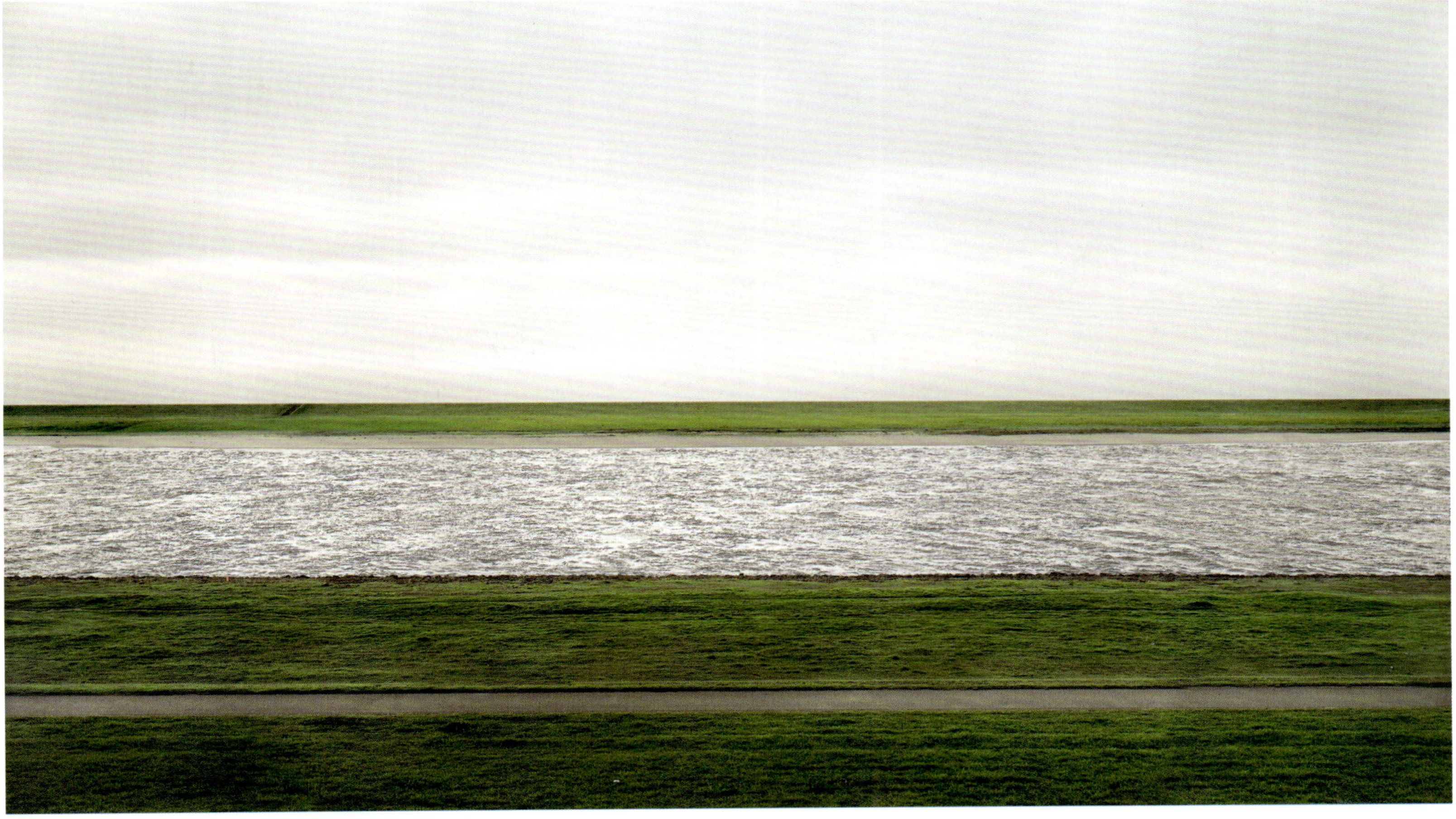

Robert Adams

Following World War II, rapid urbanization and commercialism transformed the American West. Pictures of the effects of this transformation marked a significant shift in the tradition of landscape photography in the United States. Photographers such as Robert Adams and Lewis Baltz – both identified with the New Topographic movement following an important exhibition named 'New Topographics: Photographs of a Man-Altered Landscape' at George Eastman House in 1975 – turned their cameras on this process of change, inaugurating what might be best described as a post-romantic photography, countering the grandeur of Ansel Adams's photography, with a less expressive, more evidential and documentary record of the New West of urban sprawls, wastegrounds, highways, industrial parks and tract housing.

In an interview published in 2006, Adams asserted that the American West has no future, 'just a history.' There are only 'tiny shards of the Mythic West that remain.'[4] Adams's pictures convey a sense of loss and melancholy in their acknowledgement of his country's reckless stewardship of the land. He began to photograph on the Colorado high plains in 1965, and his subjects have included the suburban landscape of Denver in the 1960s and 1970s, the disused orange estates of outer Los Angeles in the 1970s and 1980s and the ruined forests of coastal Oregon from the 1990s to the present. The use of black-and-white, as the critic Max Kozloff has put it, 'strikes a memorial note' that projects his photographs 'back into a nineteenth-century tradition.'[5] Adams was influenced by nineteenth-century explorer photographers of the American West, in particular Timothy O'Sullivan, a cache of whose prints he discovered in a Denver library in the 1960s.

Light was seen as redemptive in Adams's portrayal of shoddy and temporary building structures in the New West. Printed at the bright end of the grey scale his photographs, as Tod Papageorge has put it, 'distill the brilliant Colorado sunlight to a nearly nuclear intensity that, even as it glared down on the poor things it exposed, seemed to envelop, succor them.'[6] In his introduction to *The New West*, Adams refers to his subject as light, 'the source of all form' and how 'nothing permanently diminishes the affirmation of the sun.'[7]

Through his writings on photography and numerous books of photographs, Adams has consistently been concerned with questions about our use and abuse of the land. His work is austere and undramatic, but neither ironic nor neutral. Much as his pictures show us evidence of maltreatment of the land, he nevertheless refuses to turn away from what artists have traditionally celebrated in life: beauty – although this is very much a fragile beauty.

Lewis Baltz

Lewis Baltz was the first photographer to be shown, in 1971, at the prestigious Leo Castelli Gallery in New York, notable for showing artists such as Jasper Johns, Robert Rauschenberg and Donald Judd. In maintaining fine black-and-white prints, however, Baltz's photography was clearly positioned against the more casual and anti-aesthetic use of photography by Conceptual artists. Often displayed in minimalist grid-like structures, his frontal, deadpan, middle-distanced depictions of the featureless built environment of California present us with a sense of alienation and inertia, an elemental blankness that counters the spectacle of consumer culture within the United States. Photographing tract houses under construction, and new warehouses, offices and industrial structures, enabled him to make specific allusions to minimalist art. Baltz used photography to show how high modernist forms are mirrored in the banality and featurelessness of the new urban housing and industrial parks. He went on to photograph indeterminate waste grounds, implying construction as much as ruin – 'Park City' (1978–9), for example, documents the rapid growth of a ski resort and second-home development east of Salt Lake City. Subsequent series of photographs foresenically depicted junked objects in dumping grounds and trashed landscapes, a dystopian counterpoint to his earlier fixation with the minimalist facades of new industrial and urban buildings. 'Candlestick Point' (1987–9) concentrates on a landfill site going out into the sea on a spit of land between San Francisco and its airpor – pictures that while pristine in the clarity of their depiction are, as he himself has said, 'flat,' in that no one photograph is more important than another.[8]

Robert Adams
San Bernardino County, Santa Ana Wash, 1982
Gelatin silver print
22.9 × 28.7 cm / 9 × 11½ in

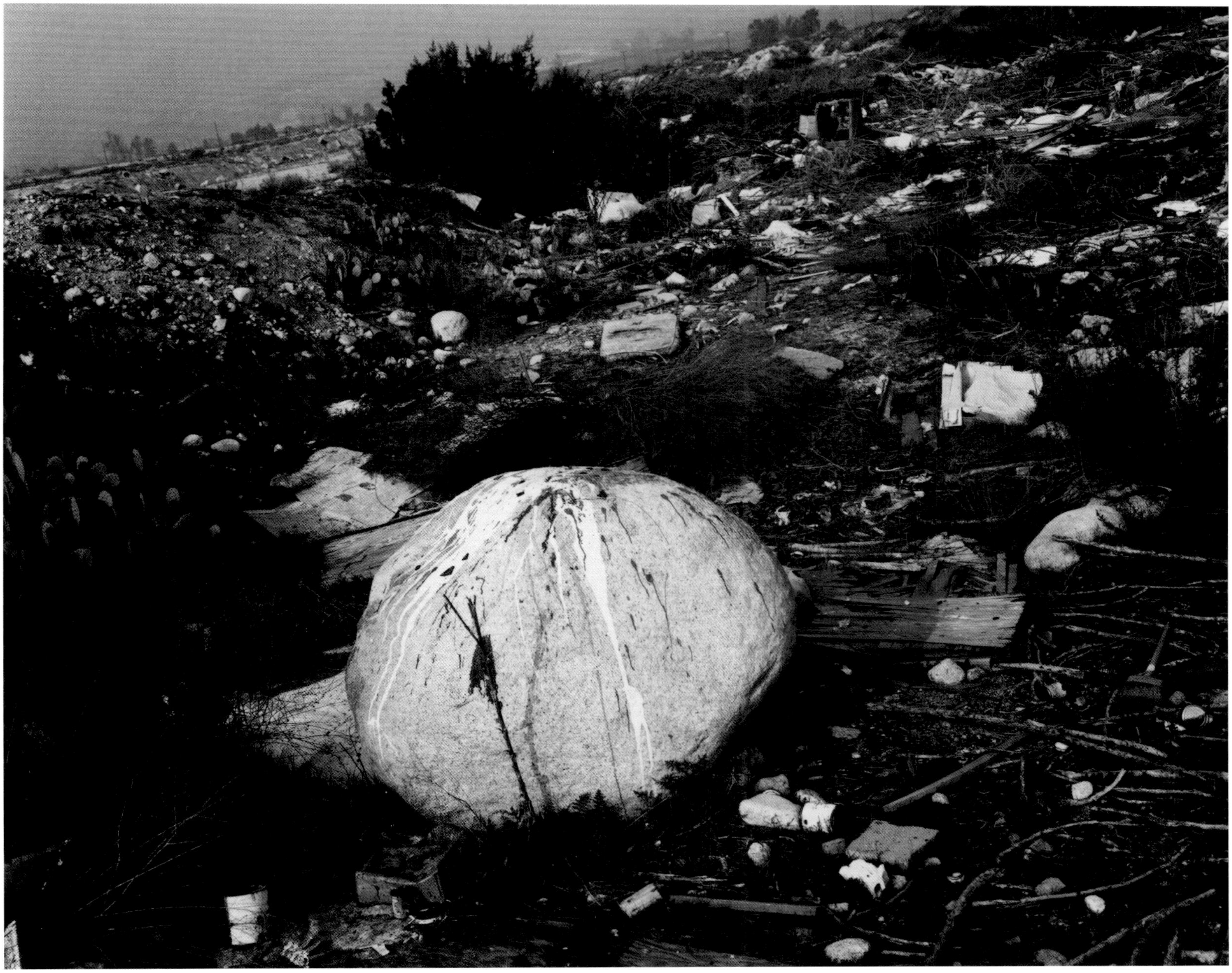

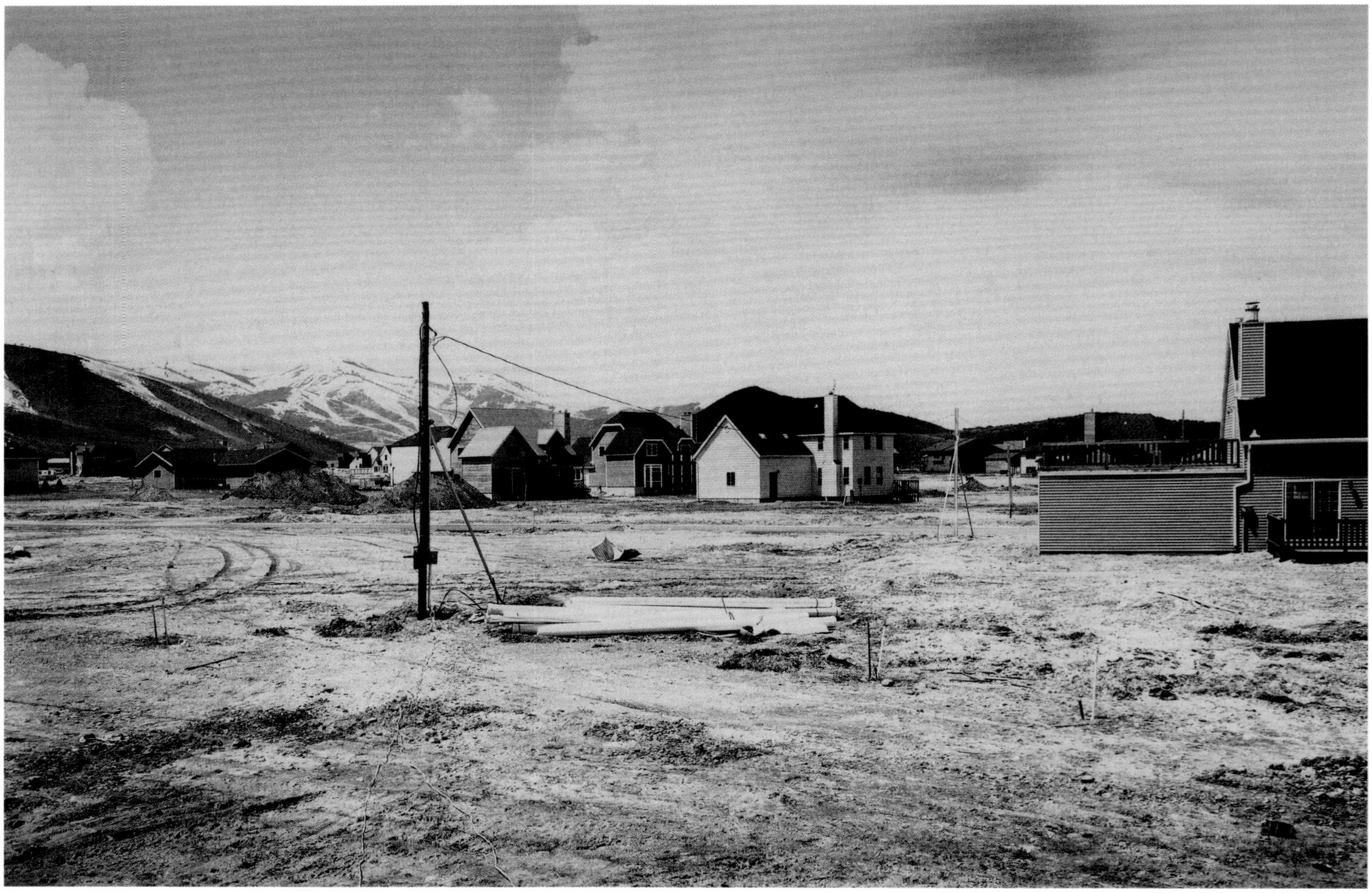

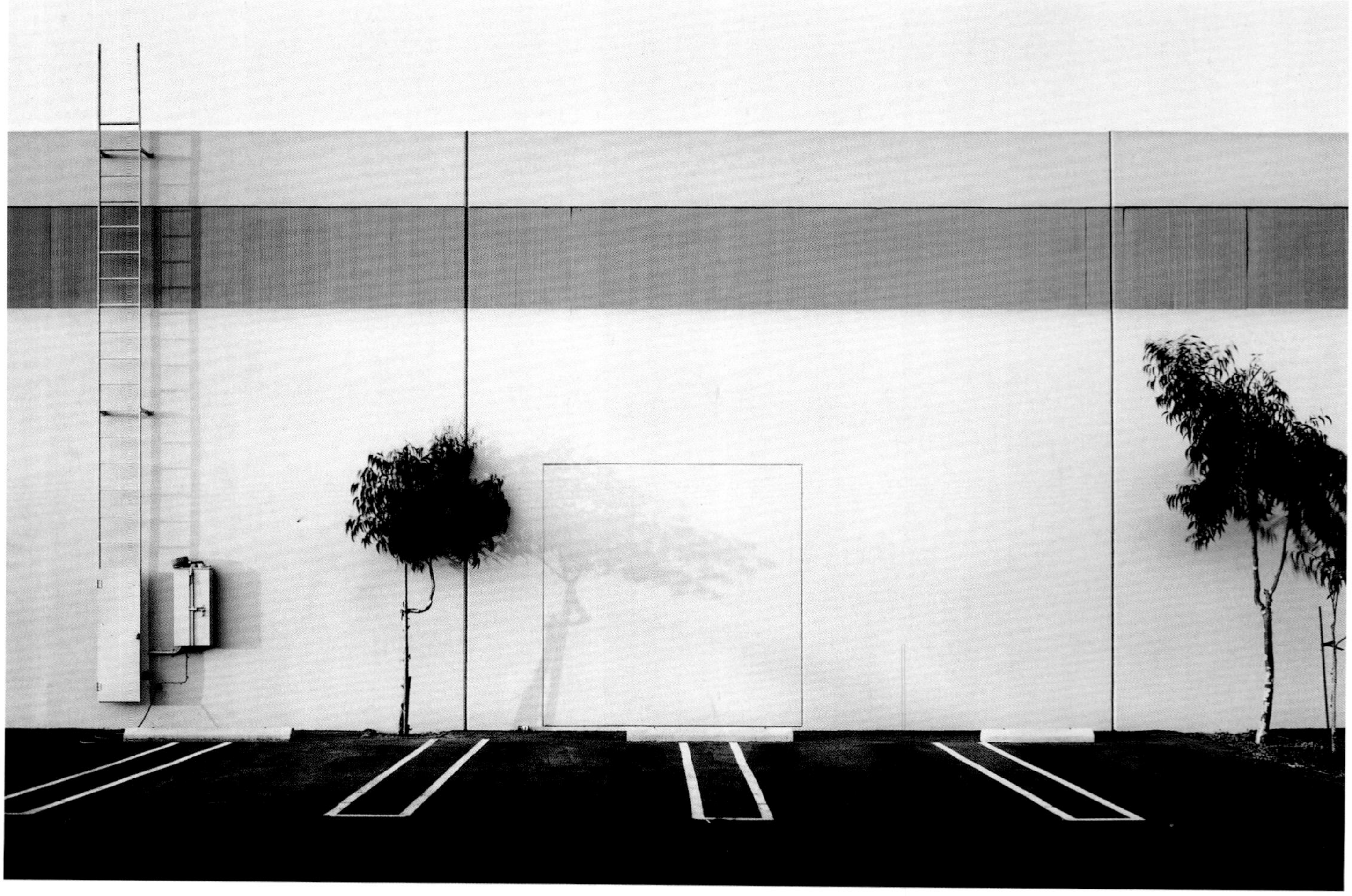

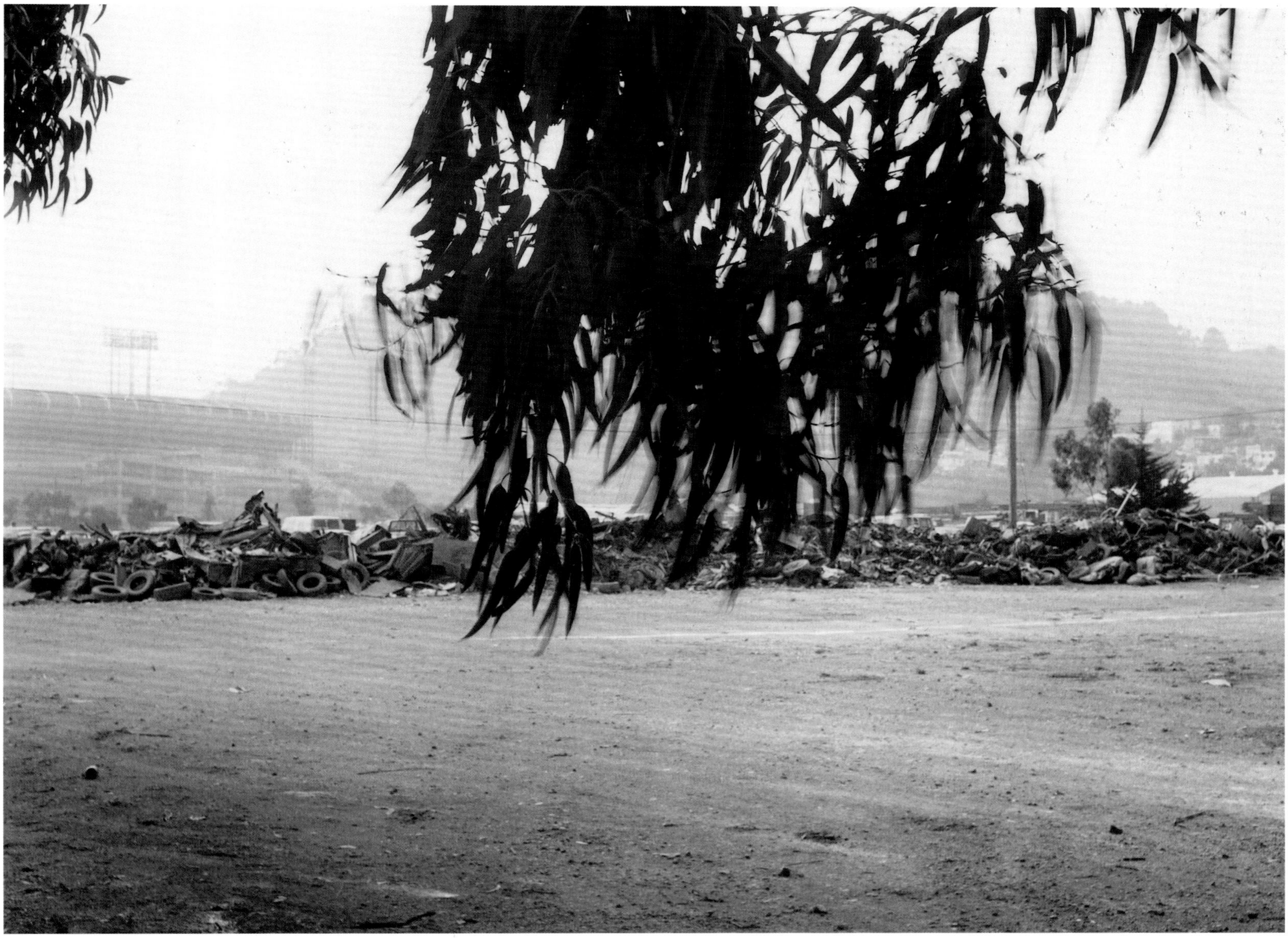

Lewis Baltz
Park City 25, 1979
Gelatin silver print
20 × 25 cm / 8 × 10 in

The New Industrial Parks Near Irvine, 1974
Gelatin silver print
20 × 25 cm / 8 × 10 in

From the series 'Candlestick Point', 1987–9
Gelatin silver print
27.9 × 35.5 cm / 11 × 14 in

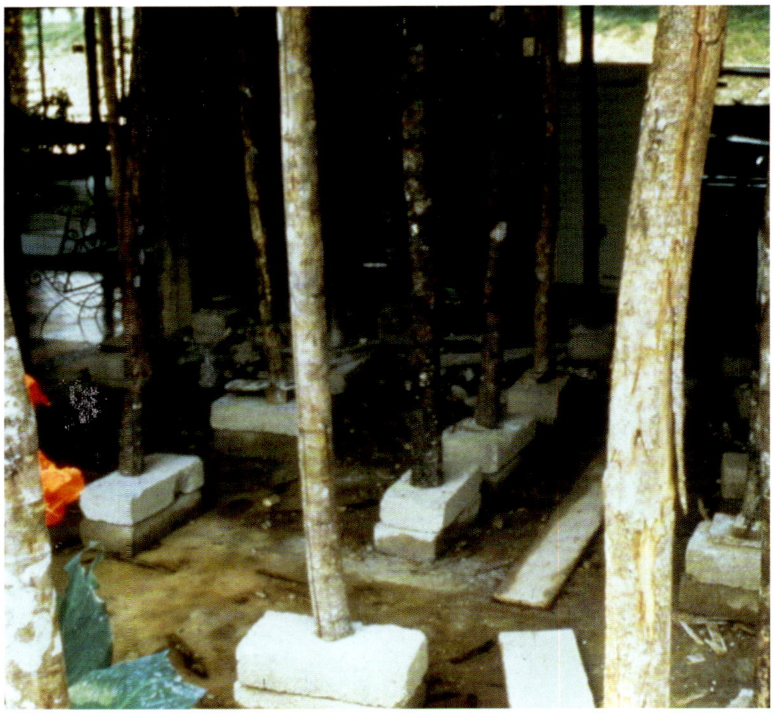
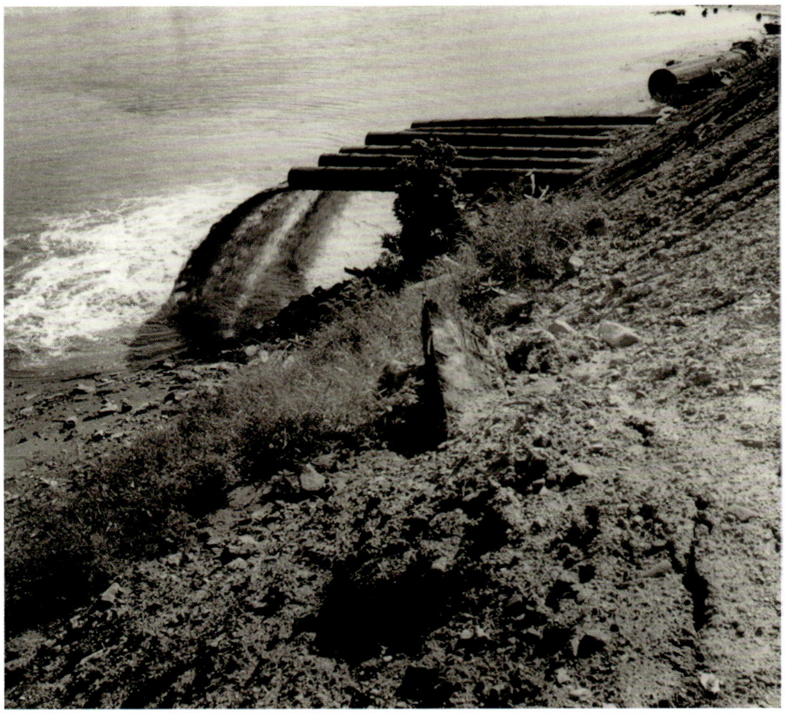
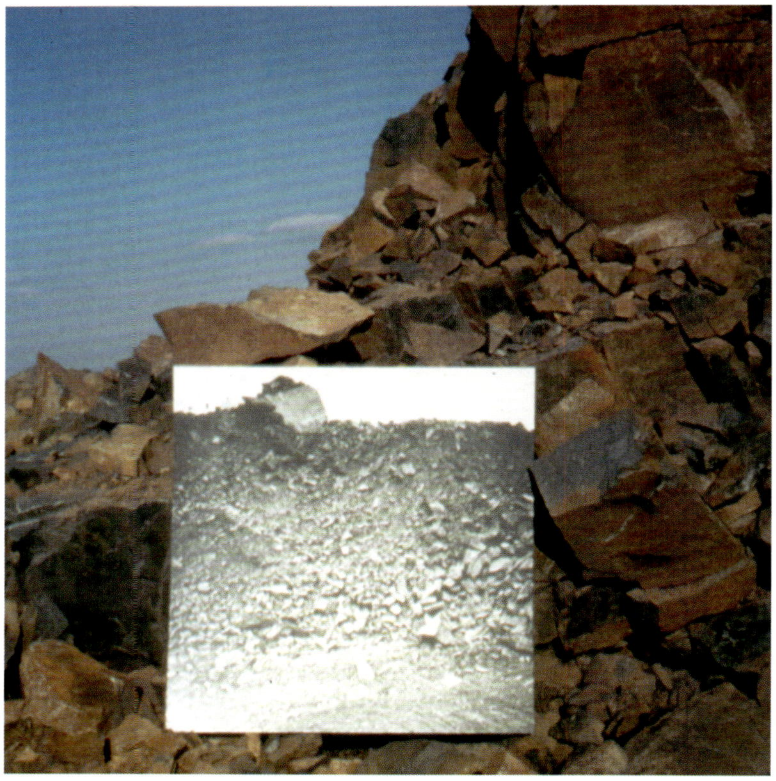
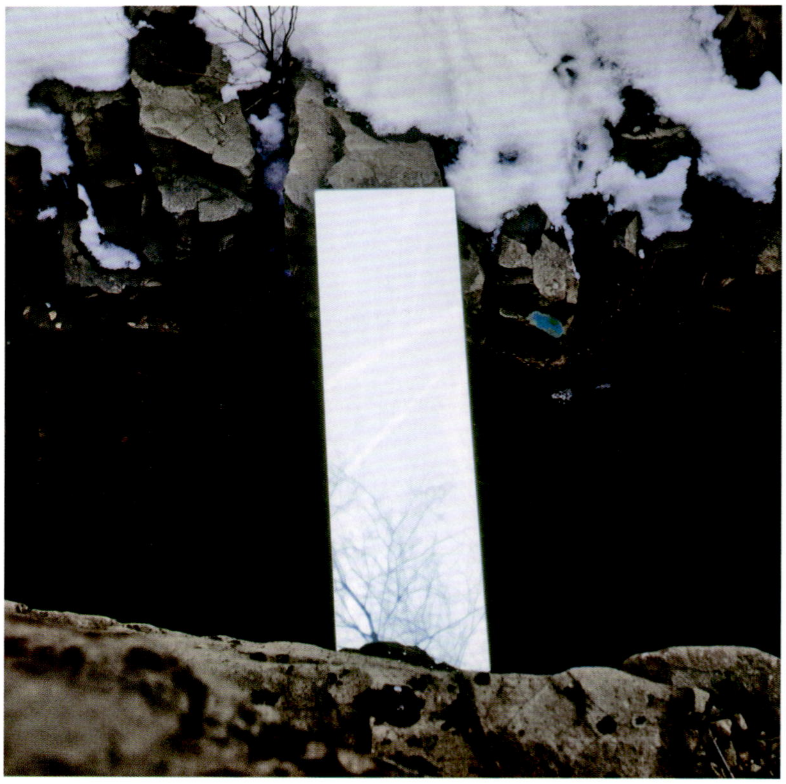

Robert Smithson

Smithson's photo-essay 'Monuments of Passaic' (1967) surveyed signs of industrial disintegration in his native New Jersey, a travelogue through a distressed landscape in which gas holders, waste pipes and derricks became evidence of energy rundown and entropy. Two years later Smithson visited Palenque in Mexico, famed for the Mayan temples nearby. But instead of depicting such historical attractions, he conducted a photographic study of what he referred to as the 'contemporary ruin' of the half-built Hotel Palenque, caught in an indeterminate state between construction and disintegration.

For Smithson the landscape was a place for experimentation and intervention. In his 'Photo-Markers' of 1968, Smithson took photographs of several nondescript sites in New Jersey and returned the photographs as large, physical black-and-white prints into the sites they represented. He then photographed the images in situ and in colour. Such pictures within pictures demonstrate photography's limitations as document: what it shows is insufficient and inadequate. The black-and-white photograph presented in this way makes us think about it as a fixed moment against the ongoing, irreversible changes taking place in the natural world. The theme was further explored in Smithson's colour photographs of arrangements of mirrors within the landscape, 'Mirror Displacements'. The reflective mirrors, introducing elements of a landscape outside the frame of the camera to the picture, served to fracture and disorder photography's static, monocular viewpoint. The sense of the mirror as a disruptive cut in the picture was especially well shown in *Mirror Span*, in which a rectangular mirror that opened up a spatial void in the picture was itself placed over the void of a deep crevice between rocks.

Robert Smithson
Hotel Palenque, Palenque, Mexico (detail), 1969
31 original 126 format chromogenic-development transparencies, with audio recording

The Fountain Monument, Side View, from the series 'Monuments of Passaic', New Jersey, 1967
6 photographs and one cut photostat map

Photo-Markers (6 Stops on a section), Laurel Hill, New Jersey, 1968
Reproduced from an original 126 format chromogenic-development transparency

Mirror Span, 1968 Montclair Quarry, New Jersey
Reproduced from an original 126 format chromogenic-development transparency

John Hilliard

John Hilliard has used the romantic associations of the landscape and played these off against the material limits of film itself. Hilliard moved to photography from sculpture. Initially his photographs systematically revealed the limits of photographic depiction through reflexive documents showing the camera's own mechanics, pictures of darkroom clocks registering the exposure and over exposure of the film recording the passage of time. When he turned to the landscape as subject matter, he used it to continue questioning the nature and limits of photographic representation. In a series of diptychs, *Over Mount Caburn* (1978) for example, Hilliard produced two different but formally rhyming pictures from the same landscape view, with each photograph exposed and printed alternatively for land and sky.

Hilliard confronted us with the idea of a photography of nothing in his *Black Depths, White Expanse, Grey Extent* (1974). Here the three tones which make up black-and-white photography, are shown as blank expanses squares of black, white and grey. Each blank square is associated with specific natural phenomena through captions and a second series of images, which explains the captions. *White Expanse*, for example, consists of four identical white squares. Each is given a caption, identifying different subjects, drawn from the four elements, air, earth, water and fire: the texts 'The expanse of the sky', 'The expanse of the sands', 'The expanse of the fjord', 'The expanse of autumn smoke', are explained by the second part of the work, which reveals, in four rectangular pictures, what was cropped out of the initial 'blank' images: an airplane, footprints, boats and fire. Such illustrationally simplistic work provides both a materialist exposé of the mechanics and ambiguities of photographic framing and plays with the romantic motif of an elemental void. Hilliard is using landscape as a motif to play with, to test the formal possibilities of the medium of film.

Jan Dibbets' 'Perspective Corrections' (1968–9) disrupt assumptions about the photograph as document. Dibbets made perceptual jokes by using photographs to depict trapezoid geometrical markings he had made in the landscape, which when photographed from a certain position gave the illusion of being a square shape perpendicular to the picture plane. The critic David Green has described the paradox of this work succinctly: 'the camera records a trapezoid that cannot be "seen" and a square that does not "exist"'.[9]

With Dibbets it is only through the photographic record that the visual joke can be made. The work is only realized in photographic form. Dibbets' photographs exploit the problem of illusion and parallel the philosophical reflections on representation evident in such photo-conceptual works as Victor Burgin's 1969 *Photopath*.

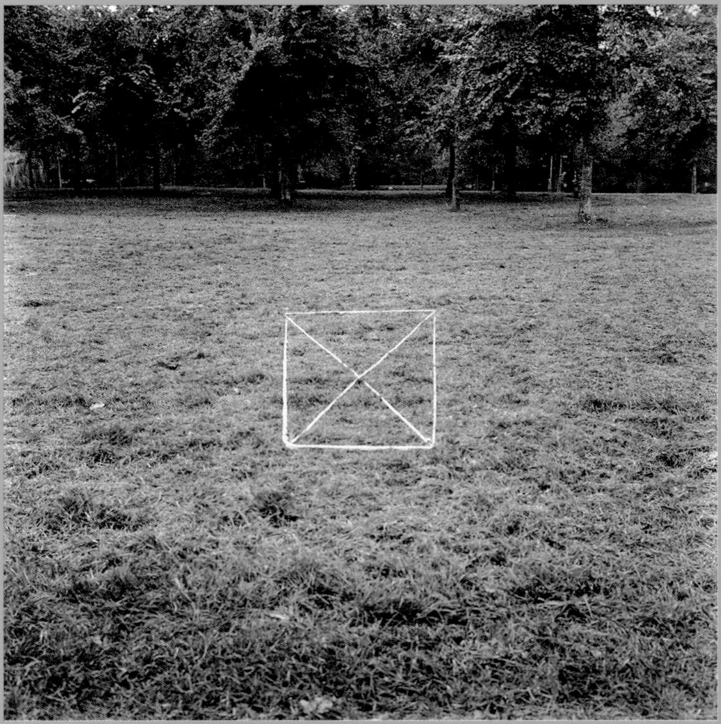

Jan Dibbets
Perspective Corrections (Square with Two Diagonals), 1968
Gelatin silver print on photographic canvas, 120 × 120 cm / 47¼ × 47¼ in

John Hilliard
Over Mount Caburn, 1978
Gelatin silver prints and Letraset on museum board
84 × 132 cm / 33 × 52 in

White Expanse, 1974
Gelatin silver prints and Letraset on museum board
Each 2 × 80 × 80 cm / ¾ × 31 × 31 in

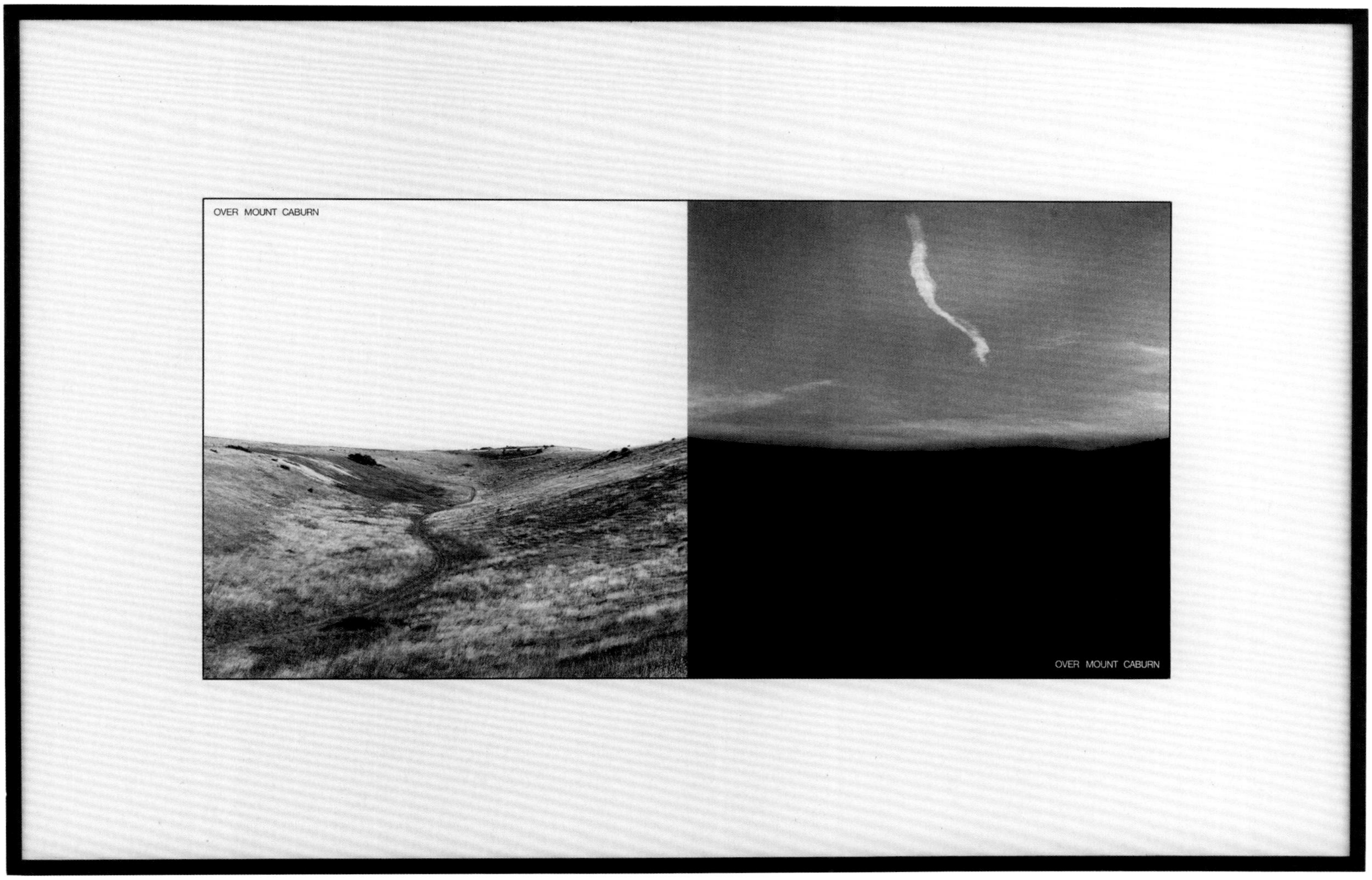
OVER MOUNT CABURN
OVER MOUNT CABURN

The expanse of the sky
The expanse of autumn smoke
The expanse of the fjord
The expanse of the sands

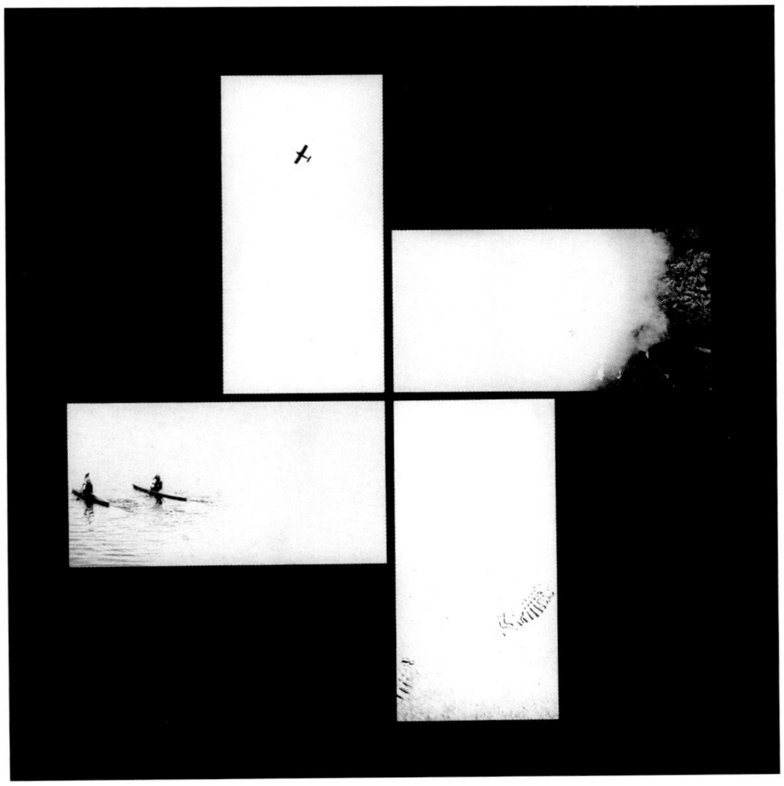

Richard Long

Richard Long produced his groundbreaking *A Line Made by Walking* while a twenty-two-year-old student at St. Martin's School of Art, London. Seeing himself as a sculptor rather than a performance artist, Long's art involved him walking repetitively in a straight line in a field for twenty minutes in the summer of 1967. The line of trampled grass was then photographed. In relation to the grandeur of the American tradition of Land Art, which as in the work of Walter De Maria and Robert Smithson involved heavy industrial equipment to move the earth, this is a modest and subtle intervention into the landscape.

Long's walking a line in the field is an action that leaves a trace. His non-personalised aesthetic, carrying affinities with the formal language of minimalist art, contrasts with the expressivity of the painter's action. For Jackson Pollock the canvas became an arena in which he could perform, accumulating the drips and traces in paint from the artist's body. Here a natural field provides the arena in which Long leaves his mark, a much less personalised and expressive trace, but one which nevertheless invites us to think of the process of its production.

Long did not like the description of his work in terms of performance art, which was for him seen as theatrical and too personalised. His action involved an ordinary, day-to-day activity. The photograph he made of the residue of this action looks down the line in the field towards the horizon and is pictured in such a way the trampled grass catches the light and is clearly defined. What we get in the photographic record is both the instant of the moment pictured, the landscape on that summer's day, and the accumulated time implied by the line made in the field. The imprints left in the grass might also be seen in photographic terms, with the field bearing the trace of the artist's movement across it akin to the way the negative registers imprints in light from its subject.

Roger Palmer

Roger Palmer's subtle and intelligent black-and-white photographs continue a conceptual approach to the landscape tradition. Palmer's earlier photographs explored the interrelationships between text and image in terms of pictorial landscape conventions – which in terms of those made in Britain concentrated on fairly empty and non-descript sites, marked in some cases by traces of an earlier history. Each was accompanied by a short text, as 'precisely dispassionate as the photographs.'[10] His '*The Village of Plashetts Submerged by Kielder Reservoir*', for example, pictured an uninviting and barren area: a track that led to the former mining village that now leads directly to the water, edged by a bit of wire fencing. While a jetty structure in the reservoir points to its new leisure uses, the overriding sense is one of neglect and abandonment. As a landscape this picture is to a certain extent without a view, reflecting on an absence, on a village that is no more.

Palmer's photography is now drawn from many places in the world and reveals a fascination with the landscape as a pictorial form. He often invites us to see the landscape view as a picture within a picture. Language – often in broken bits as words and letters – also enters many of these photographs as an opaque pictorial presence, obstructing, overlaying and competing with the photographic view. Sometimes the words prompt meanings and associations that resonate with the views we are given. In *White Cliffs* (2002), for example, Palmer frames part of a sign, CLIFFS, against a scree of broken rocks. The individual letters of the word, doubled by shadows, appear to be slipping down, breaking up like the fragments of stone they overlay. The fortuitous detail of a passing truck in the right corner of the picture, barely visible in the dust it has created – a glimpse into another landscape – seems to fit with the sense of break up, disintegration and entropy.

The idea of the landscape view as partial or fragmented often recurs in these photographs. In *Georgetown* (2001), a tear in the surface of a banner gives us a miniature landscape, a beautifully composed view in deep perspective in which the receding lines of road, grass verge and reflective watery ditch pull the viewer into its illusory depths. The depth of the landscape is set against the flatness of the slightly out-of-focus grey surface of the banner and the single lower-case letter 'a' upon it, which seems to have been given just the same weight and presence as the ragged-edged landscape. Palmer's are very much meta-landscapes, pictures about rather than of landscapes.

Richard Long
A Line Made by Walking, England, 1967
Gelatin silver print
37.5 × 32 cm / 15 × 12½ in

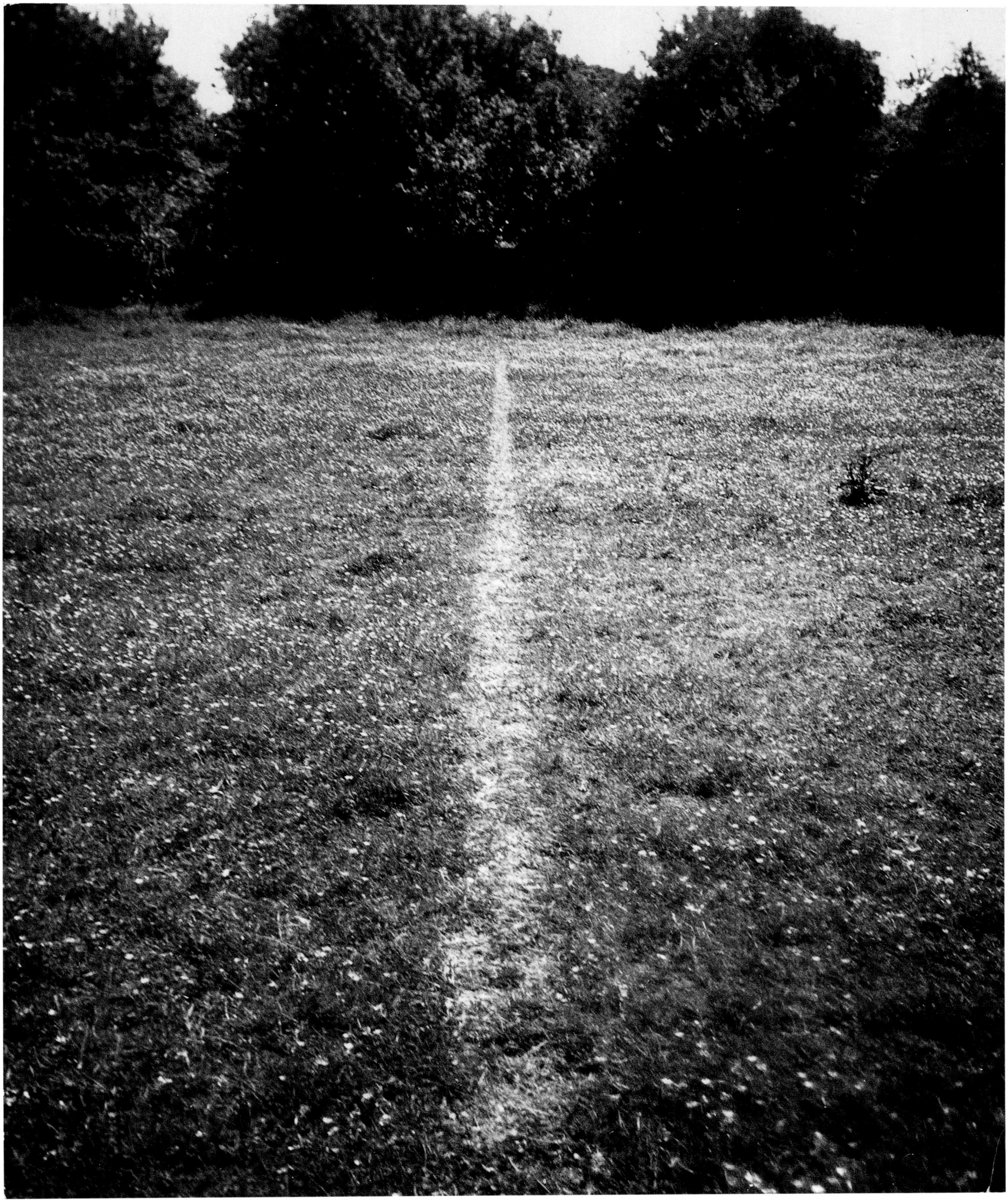

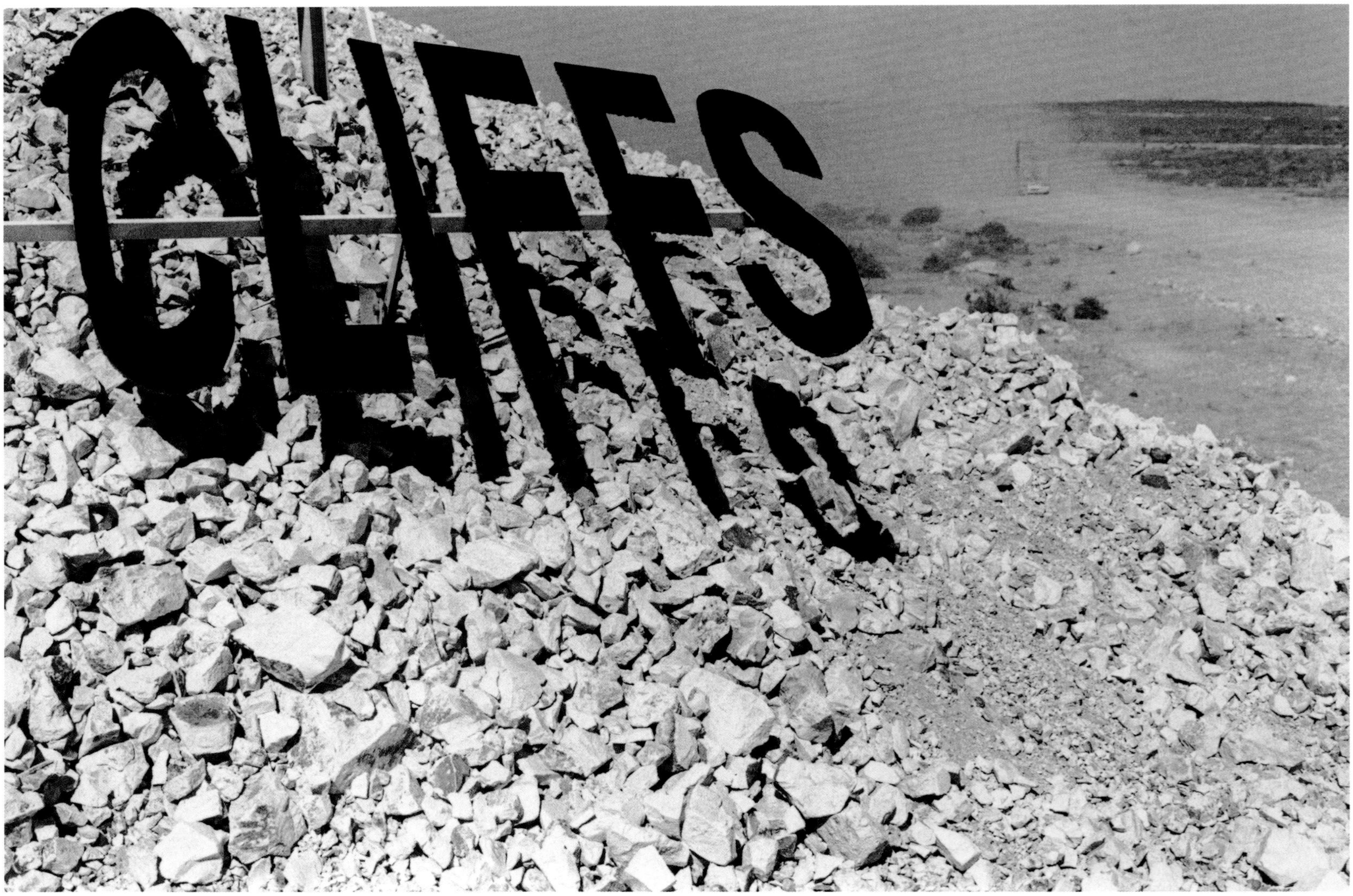

Roger Palmer
White Cliffs, 2002
Gelatin silver print
100 × 125 cm / 39⅜ × 49¼ in

Georgetown, 2001
Gelatin silver print
100 × 125 cm / 39⅜ × 49¼ in

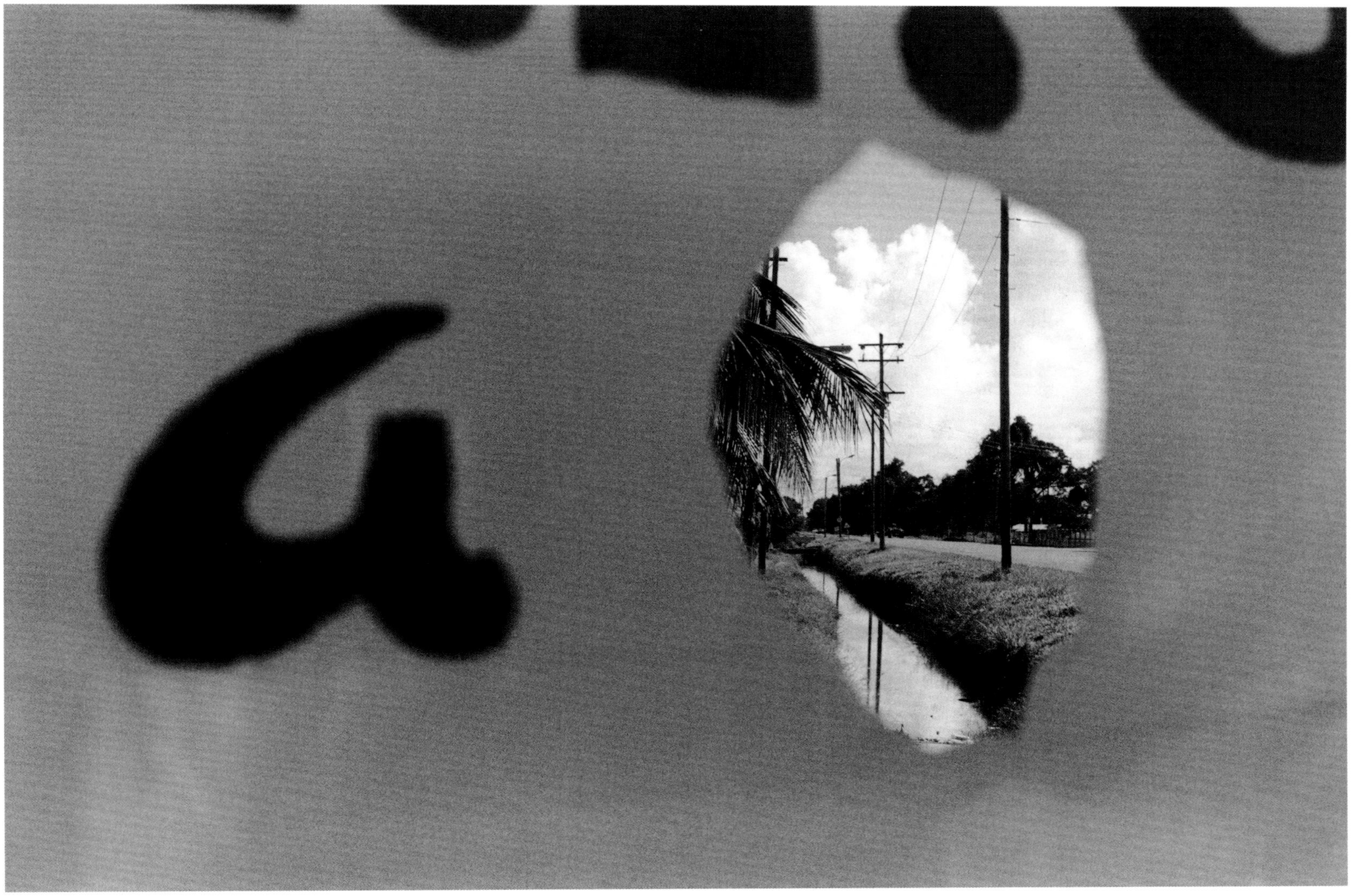

Sophy Rickett

Sophy Rickett uses the night to explore perceptual and formal issues intrinsic to photographic representation. Using the landscape as a motif, she strips down its elements. Introducing artificial light into the spaces she photographs, she makes her panoramic 'Untitled Landscapes' look like stages. They are also reflections upon the mechanics and limits of photographic seeing. As single projected beams, light appears in these pictures as lines or cuts in the image. One of Rickett's sparest and most minimal pictures, shows nothing more than a sliver of projected light as it illuminates the ground, cutting a horizontal line across the photograph. In other photographs from the series, figures are present to indicate scale and provide a measure against the blackness. Some images give a viewpoint looking up and from a distance at what appear to be the railings on a bridge, illuminated in such a way that they appear as a series of markings, as if calibrating or mapping the empty and ambiguous space. The source of light remains out of frame. Such photographs graphically literalize the mechanics of monocular perspective, but at the same time complicate such illustrational simplicity by un-grounding our viewing position. While showing the principles of perspectival seeing, they also bring out its limits and accent its fundamental partiality and incompleteness.

Rickett uses the landscape to experiment with representation: the use of artificial light within her night scenes allows her to manipulate and construct landscapes. Her more recent work, in the form of a multi-video and sound installation, has turned to the issue of spectatorship. In *To The River* (2011), we watch and listen to people who have come to see the natural phenomenon of the Severn Bore, a tidal surge of water that sweeps up the River Severn in western England. Rickett combines fragments of conversations with video portraits of those, young and old, who have come to see the Bore. We do not see it, but we hear it pass as a rush of water. In her focus on the crowds, Rickett draws attention to the everyday in relation to a sublime event. This ordinary frame or context is nevertheless lifted out from the day-to-day by being illuminated by floodlights, an embellishment that fits with the state of heightened expectancy of such an event. Accompanying the installation are a series of archival pictures and documents about the Severn Bore, including material to do with the making of the project itself. Rickett includes a letter from someone with whom the artist worked, saying how he was sorry he did not get to give her one last hug and say goodbye. The inclusion of the personal letter accords with the way in which Rickett's installation responds to a natural phenomenon through the emotions and feelings of others; it also fits with the overall melancholy tone of the work, and its sense that our expectancy and desire for something are often never fulfilled.

Sophy Rickett,
To The River (archive) 23 (left) and
To the River (archive) 54 (right),
2010/2012
Letter from and photograph of
Ian Bendall
21 × 19 cm / 9 × 7½ in

To The River, 2011
Still from 3-screen video projection
with 14 channels of sound

Untitled Landscape 2, 1998
Silver bromide print, mounted on
aluminium
1.3 × 0.4 m / 50 × 16½ in

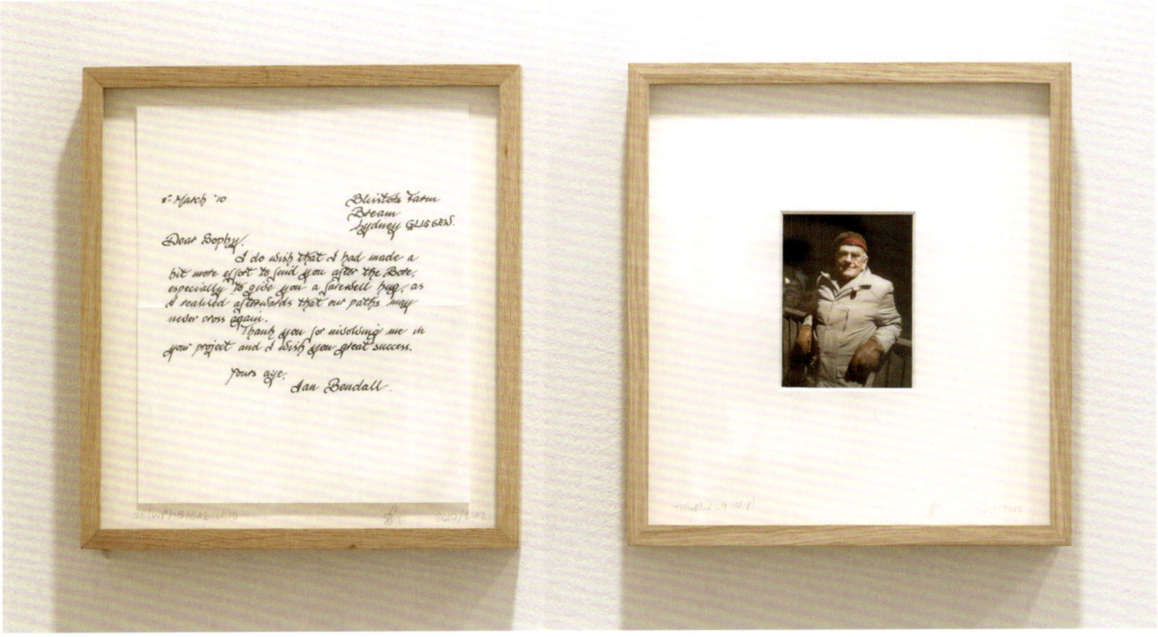
March '10
Blistors Farm
Bream
Lydney GL15 6EW.
Dear Sophy,
I do wish that I had made a bit more effort to find you after the Bote, especially to give you a farewell hug, as I realised afterwards that our paths may never cross again.
Thank you for involving me in your project and I wish you great success.
Yours aye,
Ian Bendall.

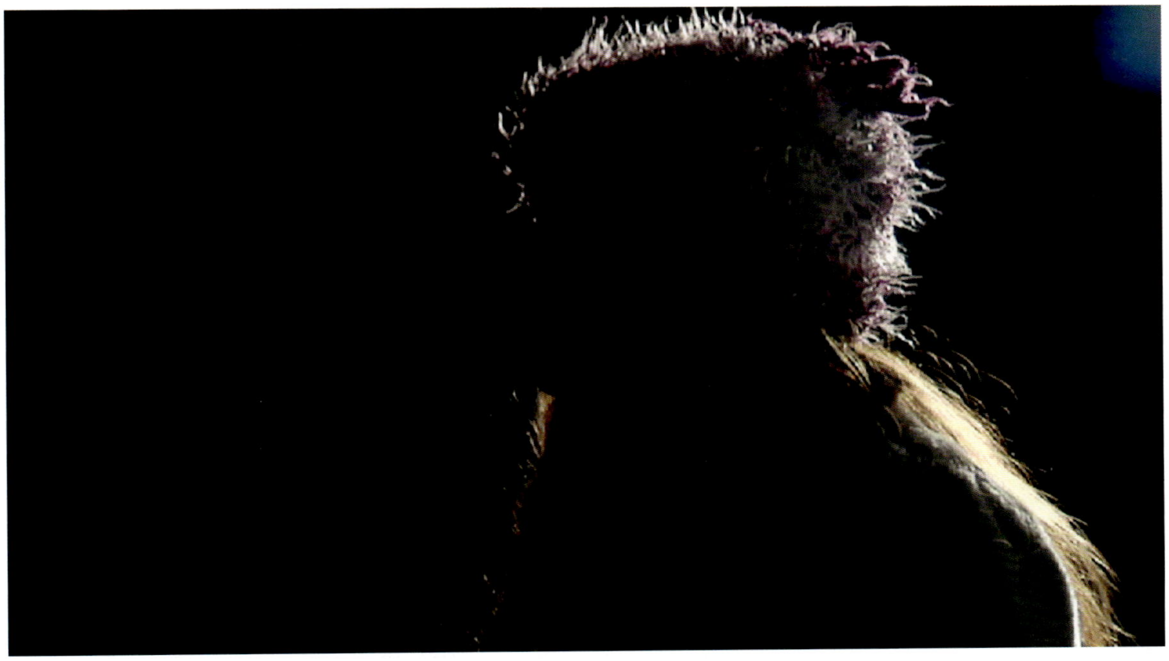

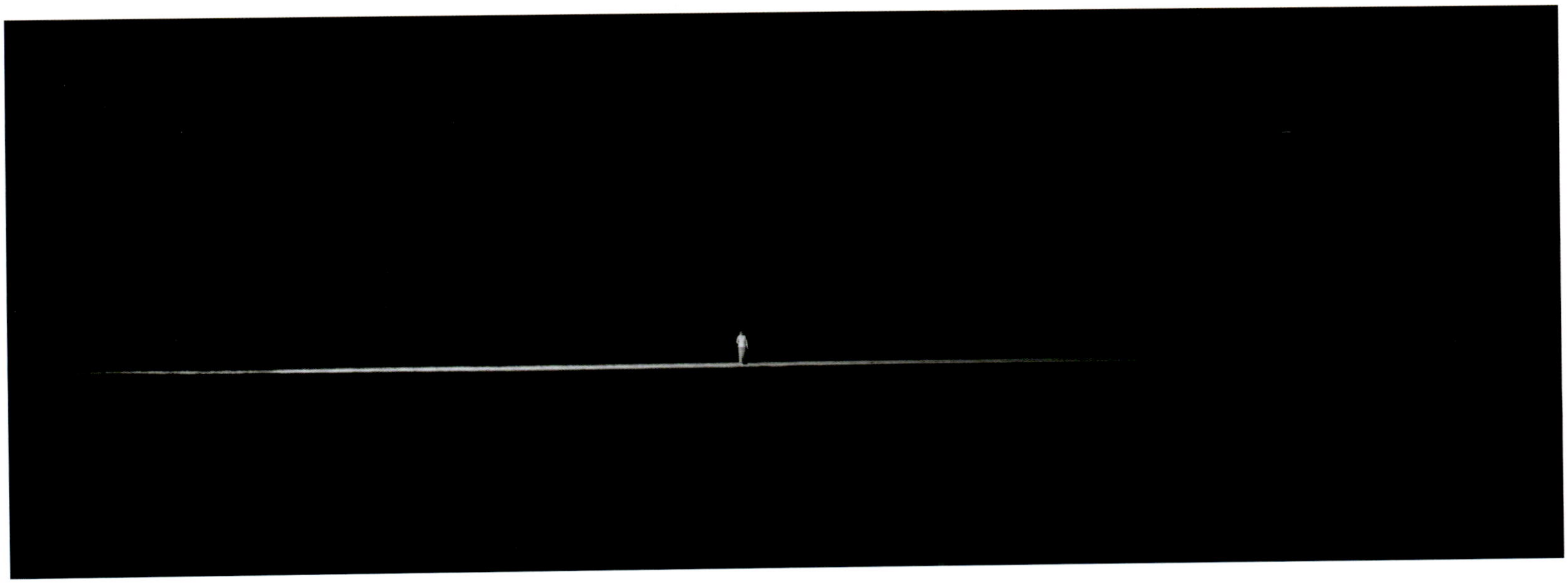

Thomas Joshua Cooper

Thomas Joshua Cooper's art involves a solitary engagement with natural phenomena. Indeed, Cooper's work is valuable in its singular refusal to engage with the contemporary world: he is out there on his own as a photographer, just as he is very often out there on his own on the remote and difficult promontories from which he makes his pictures. There is a distinct heroic element to Cooper's epic quest to take pictures from the extremities of the land and islands from the furthest point north to the furthest point south on both sides of the Atlantic Ocean. 'The World's Edge – The Atlantic Basin Project – An Atlas of Emptiness and Extremity' was begun in 1992 and is still ongoing. It was initiated by Cooper's reading of a book by an American historian, William Manchester, which argued that the greatest achievement of the Renaissance was Ferdinand Magellan's circumnavigation of the world. Cooper's use of a nineteenth-century camera, film and old processes – resulting in the creation of beautiful silver prints, often toned with layers of selenium and gold chloride – fits the retrospective nature of this whole remarkable project. The succession of vertiginous views from rocky edges onto expanses of often animate seas and oceans concentrate us upon primary and elemental expanses and voids, steeped in the aura and myths associated with the world's first exploration. This unequivocally romantic work, bereft of the damaging evidence and effects of globalization, nevertheless makes us muse upon its origins.

Thomas Joshua Cooper
Moonlight – West, Southwest – The Mid Atlantic Ocean, Cap Manuel, Dakar, The Cape Verde Peninsula, Senegal, 2004, the South-most point of the Cape Verde Peninsula
Selenium and gold chloride toned gelatin silver print
101.6 × 391.2 cm / 40 × 54 in

North, The Mediterranean Sea, "Little" Ras Angela, #2, Tunisia, 2004
Selenium and gold chloride toned gelatin silver print
71.1 × 91.4 cm / 28 × 36 in

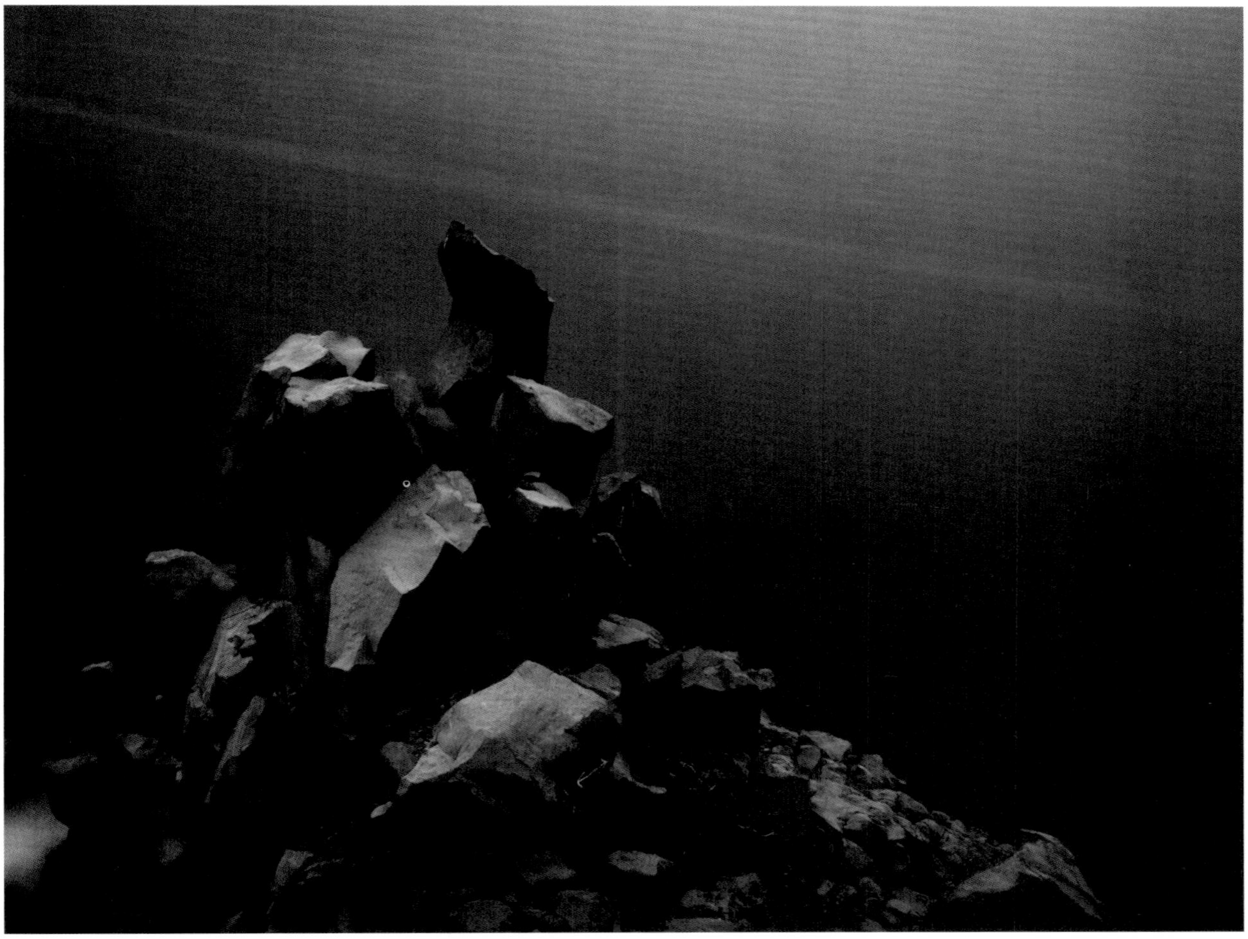

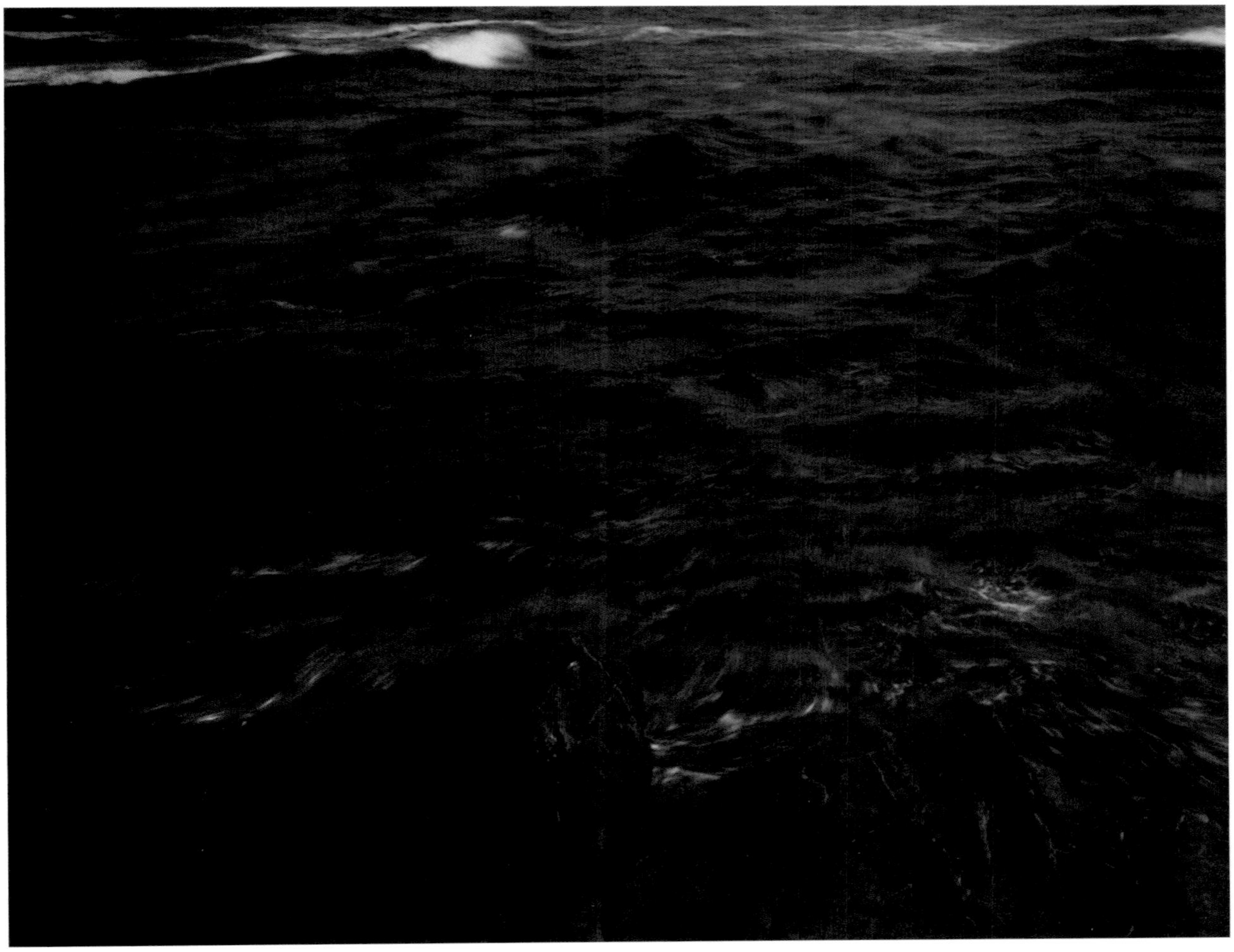

Roni Horn

Roni Horn's 'Another Water' (2000) explores the poetic associations of a dirty, polluted river through a series of closely cropped depictions of the mutable surface of the waters of London's River Thames, photographed at various times of the day in various weather conditions. Horn's work strips many of the picturesque and pictorial connotations of water, instead highlighting the river's fearful opacity and viscosity. In one version of the work, the surface of each photograph is overlaid with tiny white numbers that serve to indicate the footnotes beneath, consisting of a series of anecdotes and thoughts made in response to the river, a repetitive and garrulous stream of consciousness that is often fixated with the darker associations this river carries. Horn is especially fascinated with the high number of suicides in the Thames and details about them provide a recurrent element among the footnotes. In a book version of the series, she also interrupts pictures of the river with detailed matter-of-fact case histories based on police reports of deaths in the river, giving distinguishing details of corpses and lists of possessions found on the bodies.

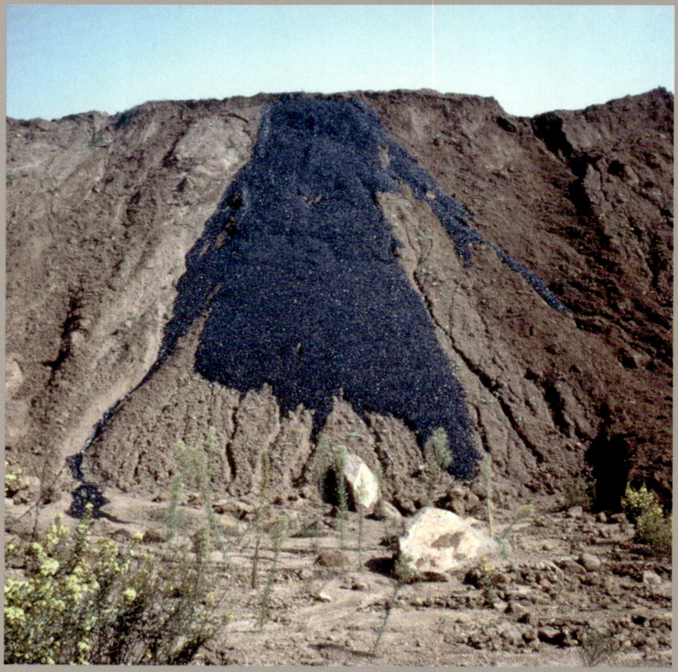

Robert Smithson
Asphalt Rundown, 1969, outside Rome, Italy
Reproduced from an original 126 format, chromogenic-development transparency

Jem Southam

Jem Southam's photographs meticulously record, with the precision of a 10x8 inch view camera, both sublime landscape phenomena on the British coast and more commonplace and mundane landscapes. His 'Rockfall' pictures, documenting evidence of coastal erosion, reflect upon remorseless change. They look back both to a Romantic British landscape painting tradition – James Ward's 1813 *Gordale Scar*, for example – and to the entropic events orchestrated by the artist Robert Smithson in the late 1960s: his 1969 *Asphalt Rundown*, for example, in which a dump truck poured fresh asphalt over a cliff near Rome.

Conveying both a sense of deep geological time and the inexorable impermanence and mutability of all things, Southam's photographs of coastal erosion become powerfully suggestive of uncertainty and insignificance. His series of photographs, 'The Pond at Upton Pyne,' concentrate upon a small, unprepossessing piece of land near Exeter, in Devon. The pictures, taken over time, show the various improvements of what was an eyesore and rubbish dump when Southam first photographed it in 1996. His photographs follow the formation and construction of a landscape, document local and modest acts of landscape gardening, peoples' vision of a small arcadia. This work links with the series of photographs 'Painter's Pool' (2002–3), in which Southam pays homage to a painter colleague, Mike Garton, who until his death had spent over two decades depicting the undergrowth and trees in an area of ancient woodland north of Exeter. Garton created a pond in the woods by damming a stream, but only painted it a year or so before he died. The painter's obsessive attempts to depict the complexity of this small part of nature are integral to Southam's detailed photographs of the woodland and pool. He pictures a landscape that both acknowledges and is determined by the vision of another artist. Southam's photographs serve as ambiguous memorials to Garton's realism. With the painter's presence just perceptible through a few sad details – an easel, bits of string, wooden poles – the photographs can also be read as showing the folly of the artist's realist quest, especially compared with the quality and precision of Southam's own mode of representation.

Roni Horn
Still Water (The River Thames, for Example) (detail), 1999
15 photographs with text, each
77.5 × 105 cm / 30½ × 41½ in

Still Water (The River Thames, for Example) (detail), 1999
15 photographs with text, each
77.5 × 105 cm / 30½ × 41½ in

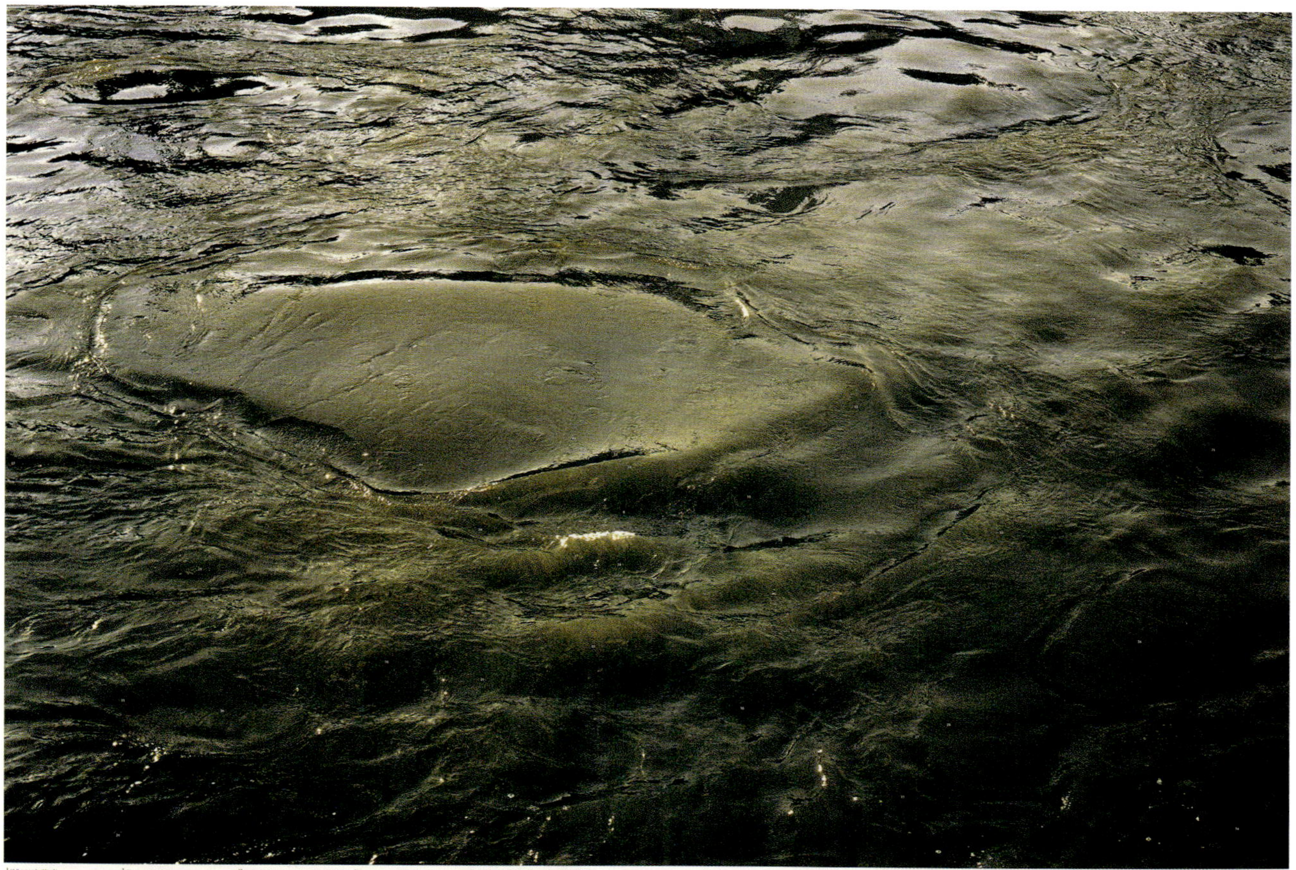

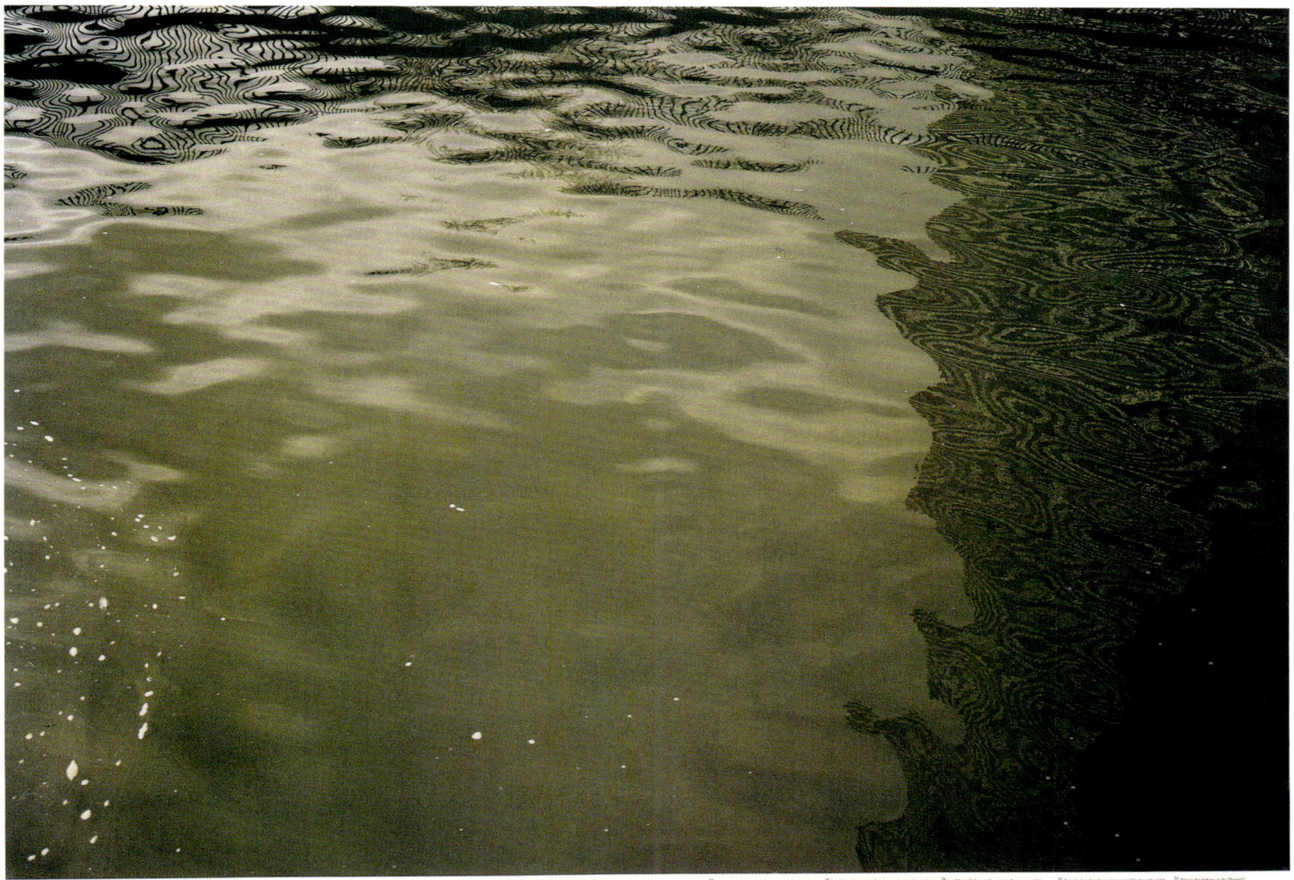

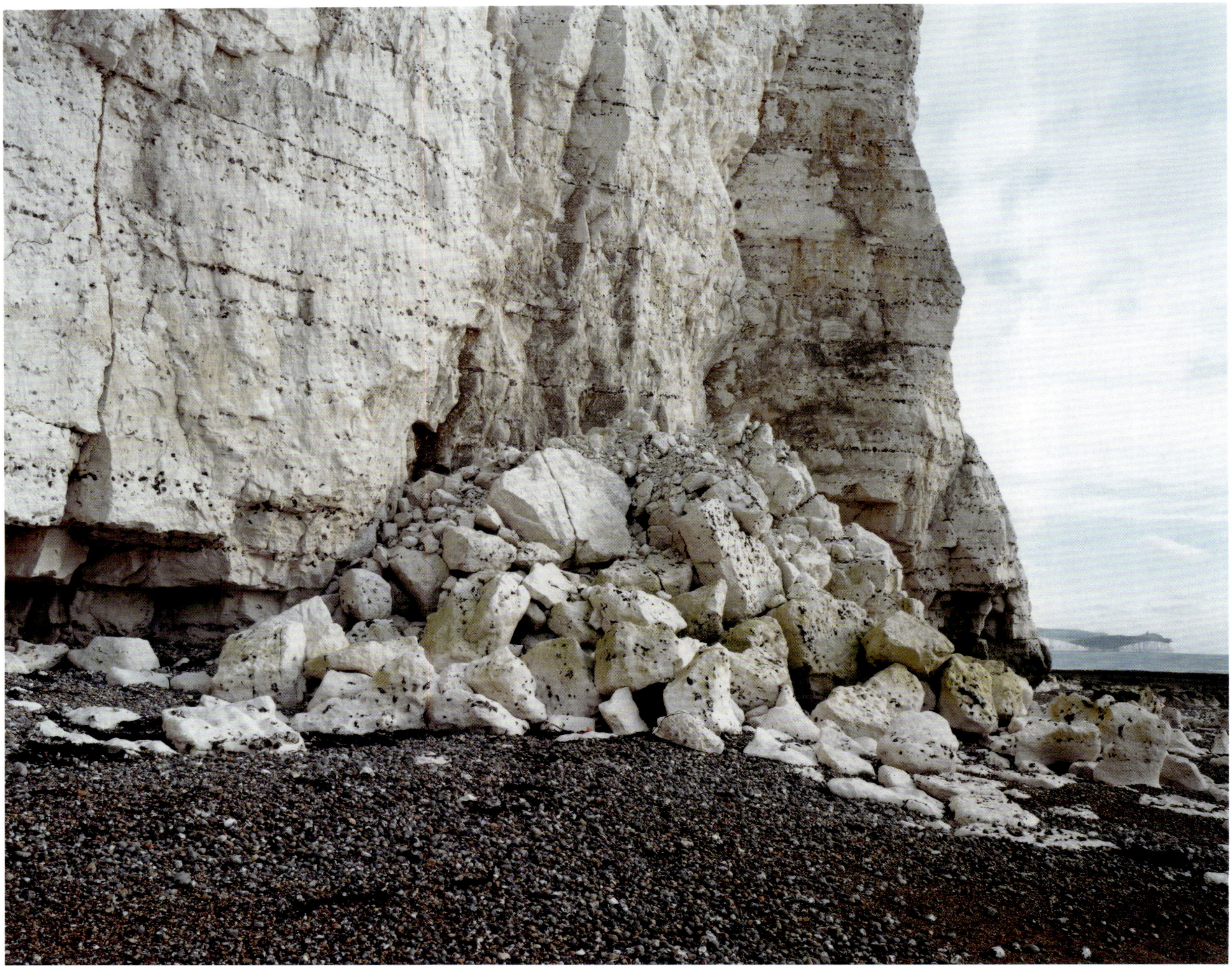

Jem Southam
Rockfall, Seaford Head, 2008, 2008
Chromogenic dye coupler print
91 × 114 cm / 35⅞ × 44⅞ in

The Painter's Pool, 03 February 2002 (Left), 2002
Chromogenic dye coupler print
91 × 114 cm / 35⅞ × 44⅞ in

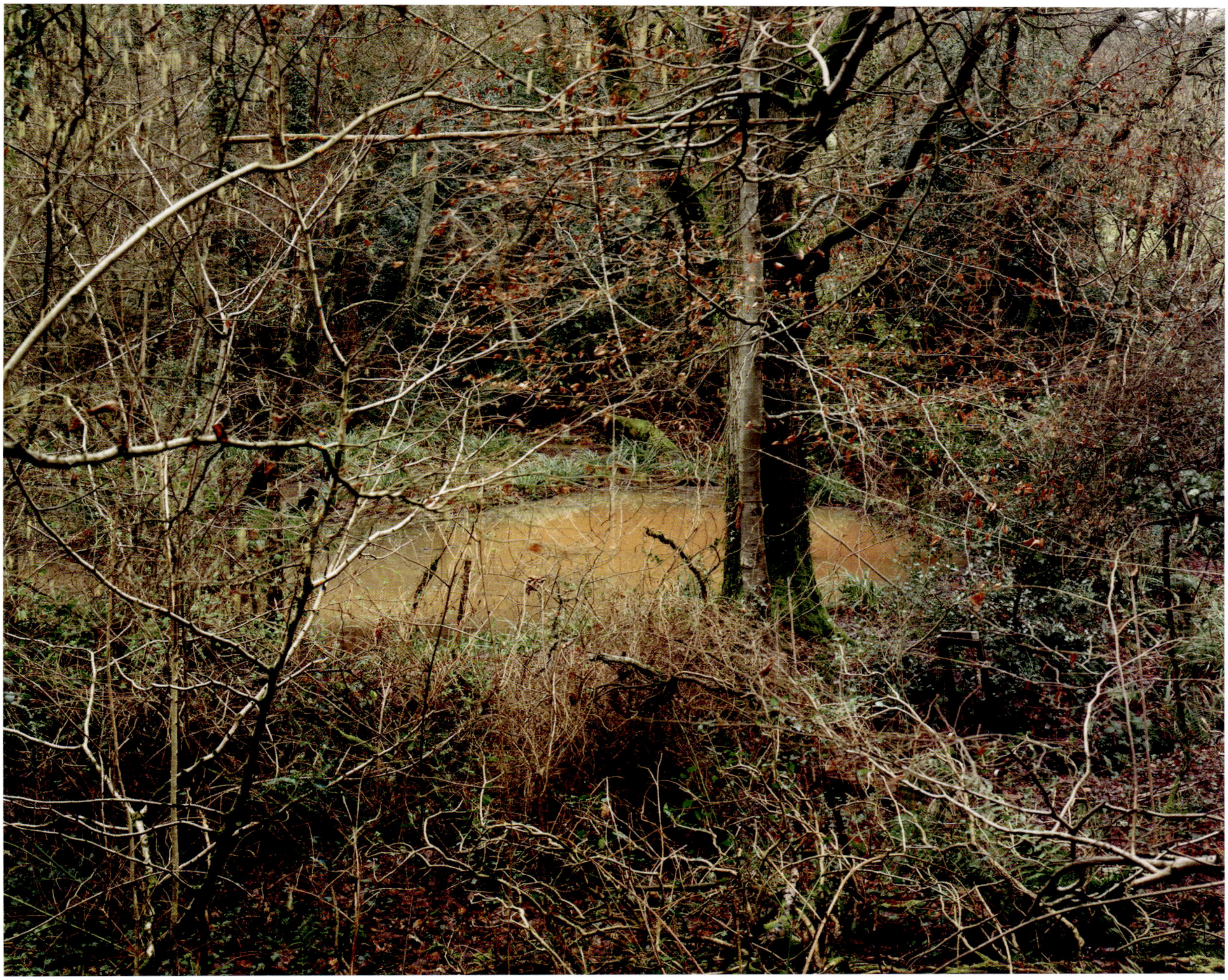

Joel Sternfeld

Joel Sternfeld's pictures from his series 'American Prospects' have a documentary inflection, offering wry commentaries on the state of the nation through depictions of its landscape. The title itself puns on the idea of the prospect as a view, as well as invoking the future. Judging from Sternfeld's pictures, the prospects are not good. Some pictures introduce to the landscape genre the drama and significance usually associated with reportage or photojournalism, as exemplified by one of his best-known photographs, *Exhausted Renegade Elephant* (1979). It is tempting to see in this picture of a large creature collapsed and drained of energy, a metaphor for America's exhaustion. Certainly, all is not well in the world Sternfeld pictures. Houses burn and a fireman buys pumpkins. Paradises are artificial, as splendidly shown in a photograph of a swimming pool in the desert with its solar-powered petals. Sternfeld also accents the temporariness and fragility of our inhabitation of the land with his depiction of a destroyed family home set against a sense of deep geological time, suddenly exposed by the indiscriminate wrath of nature in *After a Flash Flood, Rancho Mirage, California, July 1979*.

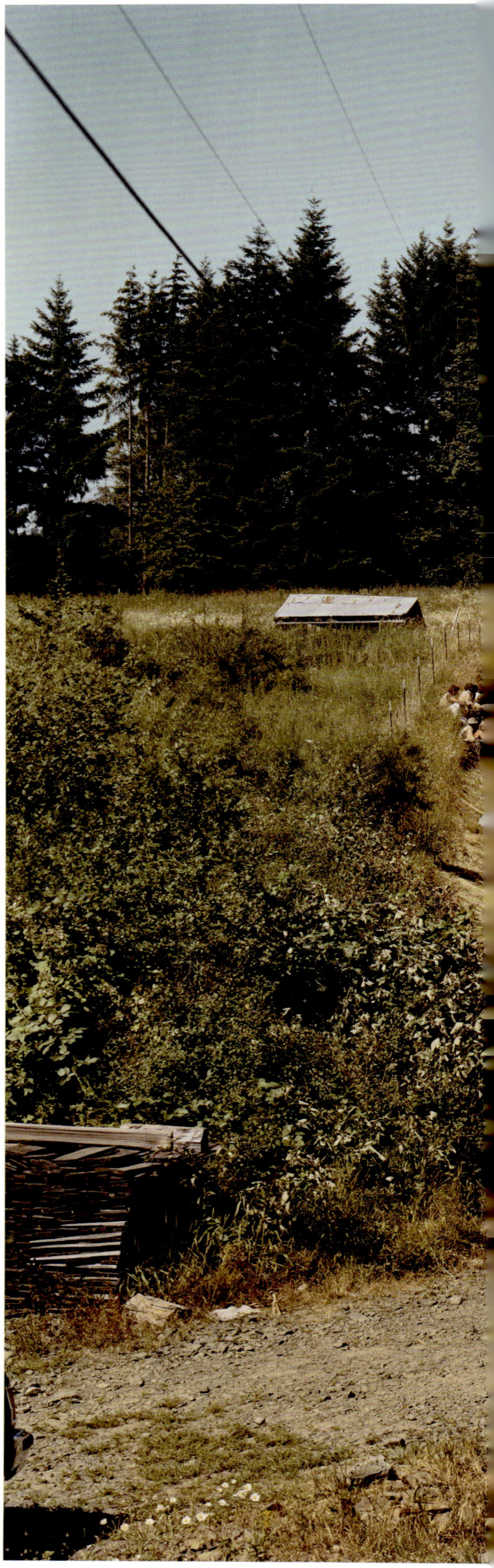

Joel Sternfeld
Exhausted Renegade Elephant, Woodland, Washington, June, 1979,
1979
Digital C-print
106.7 × 133.3 / 42 × 52½ in

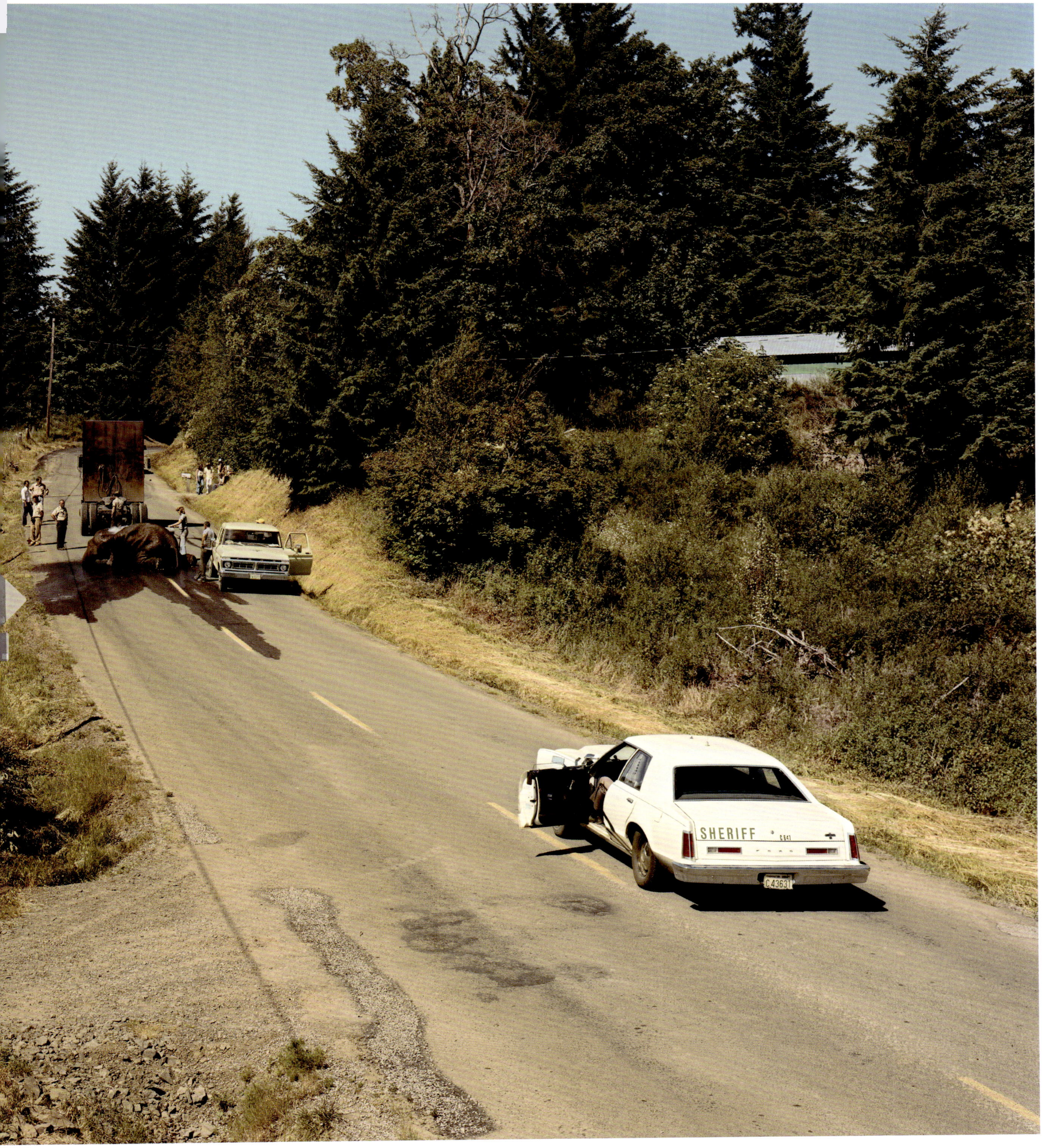
SHERIFF
C43631

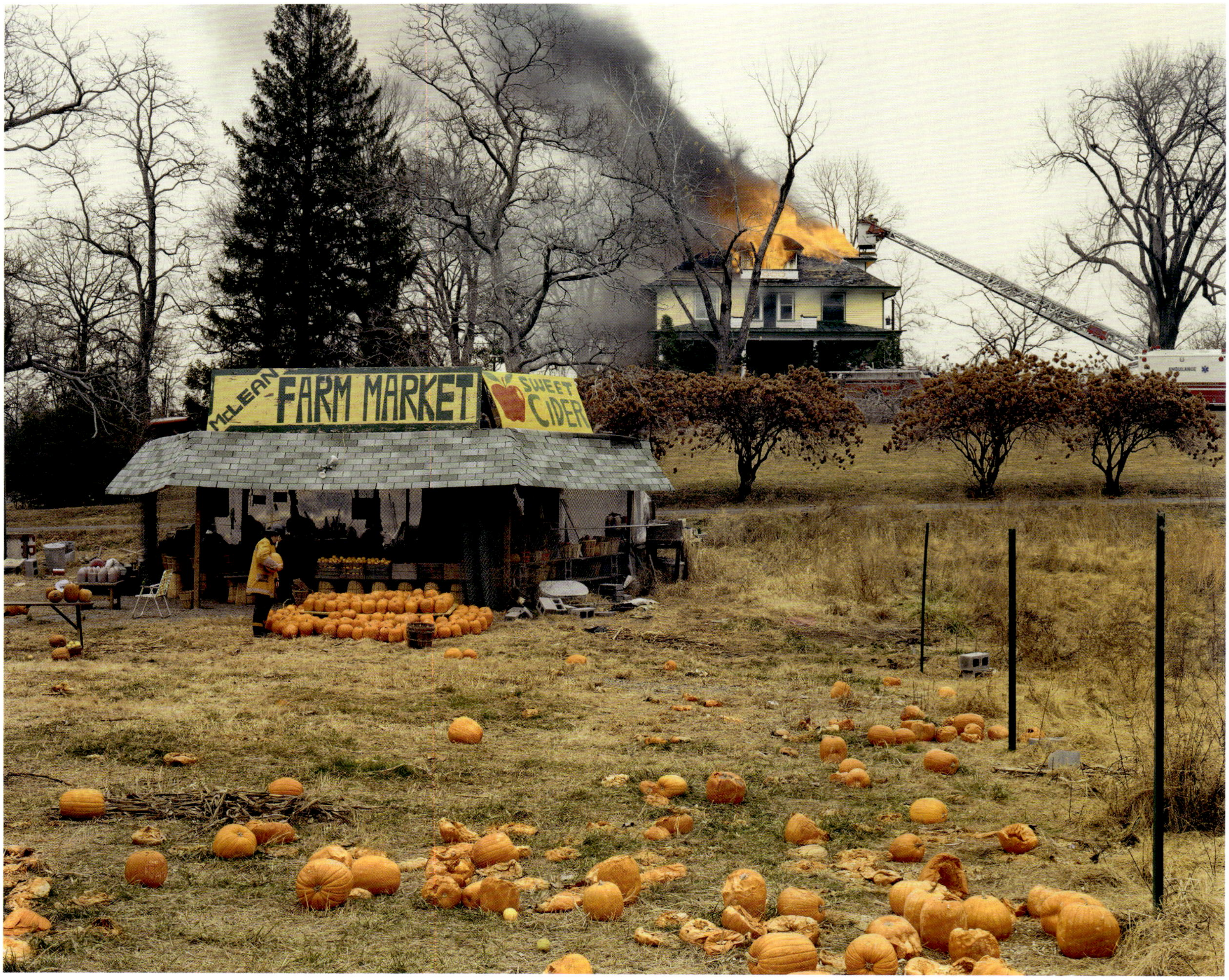

Joel Sternfeld
McLean, Virginia, December, 1978,
1978
Digital C-print
106.7 × 133.3 / 42 × 52½ in

After A Flash Flood, Rancho Mirage, California, *1979*, 1979
Digital C-print
106.7 × 133.3 / 42 × 52½ in

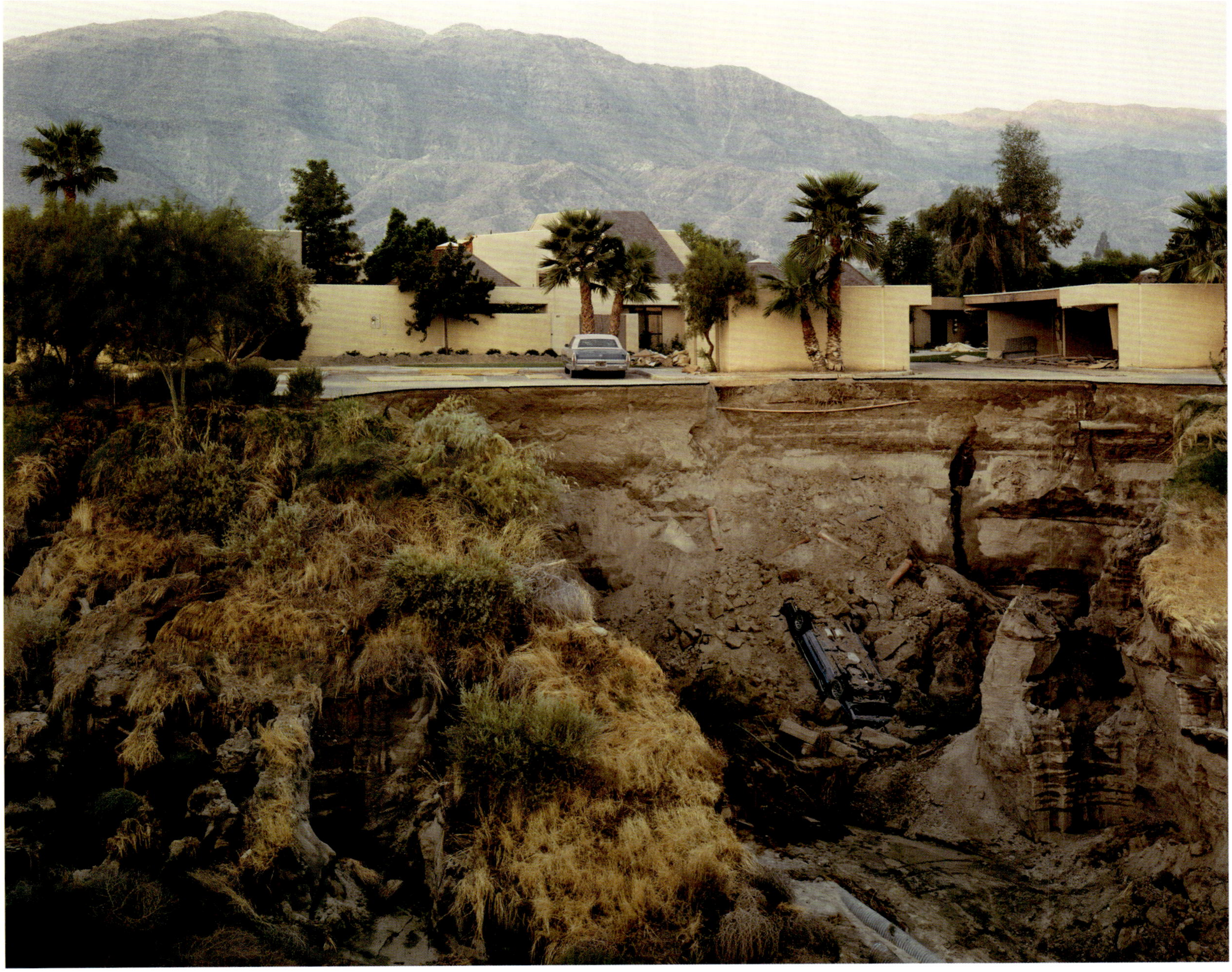

Richard Misrach

Photographing the military testing grounds within the Nevada desert, Richard Misrach gives us an apocalyptic view of the American West. The scale, lighting and colour of his pictures gives them something of the gloss and spectacle associated with the cinema and advertising – associations which jar with the devastation he pictures. The desert landscape, iconic of American identity, is shown scarred, pitted by bomb craters and littered with missiles; as he puts it, 'a more accurate myth of today's West would be Frankenstein.'[11] In this way he makes his own landscape Other. Such a process of estrangement is further underlined by Misrach's series of violent images symbolic of the destruction of American culture: the photographs show bullet-ridden pages of *Playboy* magazine that have been used as target practice. As critic Max Kozloff put it, 'Misrach has no trouble in revealing how a macho culture has literally vomited all over the very same environment that in yesteryear it had held up as the territory of its heroic aggression.'[12]

The symbolic destruction of culture through the 'Playboy' series contrasts with the more literal evidencing of death in what amount to Misrach's most apocalyptic and visceral pictures, 'The Pit.' Here he draws attention to livestock, cattle and horses that have died of unexplained or unexamined causes, although the suggestion is that their deaths are linked to the lethal pollutants created by military testing. The pictures of dead horses in the desert become especially meaningful. These landscapes invert the cowboy mythology of the Old West, from the westerns of John Ford to the Marlboro cigarette ads.

Misrach's *Destroy This Memory* (2010) is a powerful testimony to the devastating impact on people's lives of Hurricane Katrina. Taken with a 4 megapixel pocket digital camera between October and December 2005, the photographs register the impact upon the people and their response as they return to what is left of their homes and possessions. The images are published as a book with no other words than those of the people who went through the destruction and who were left to fend for themselves in the aftermath of the hurricane. Each document of wreckage includes the messages left in the landscape and upon the structures that remain: calls for help, warnings, threats, announcements, memorials, even jokes – ELVIS HAS LEFT THE HOUSE. Such words bring home the scenes of destruction by introducing human responses to the tragedy. Played out against the images of destruction, the cumulative effect of all these signs is to convey the psychological impact upon the people of what they have been through. Their messages convey their fears, faith, despair, anger, humour and resilience. Many want to forget. As the graffiti over the wrecked house on the book's cover says, 'Destroy This Memory.' Many of those who went through the tragedy want to banish it from their memory and start anew, but Misrach as documentarian does not want us to forget.

Richard Misrach
Dead Animals #001, 1987
C-print
101.6 × 127 cm / 40 × 50 in

Dead Animals #327, Nevada, 1987
C-print
46.4 × 59.1 cm / 18¼ × 23¼ in

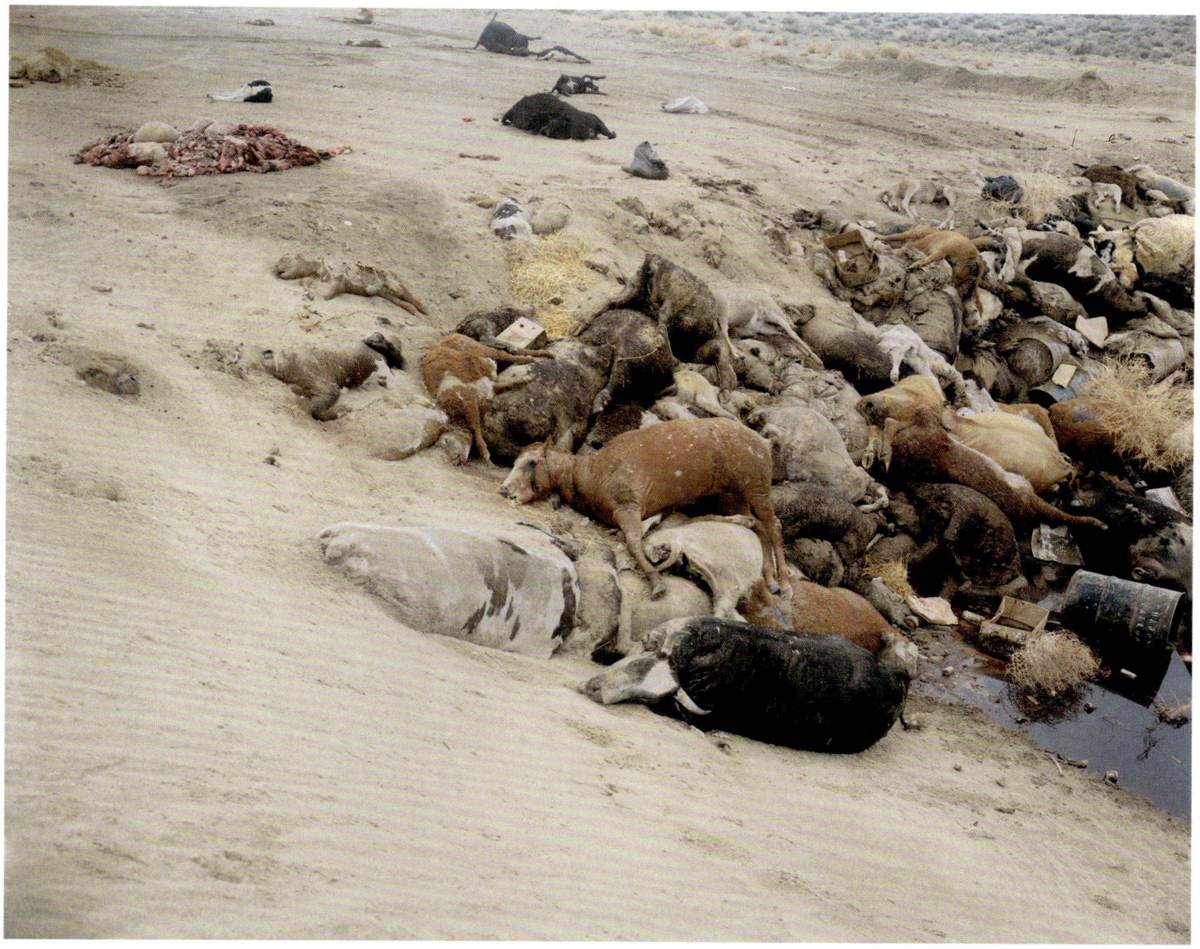

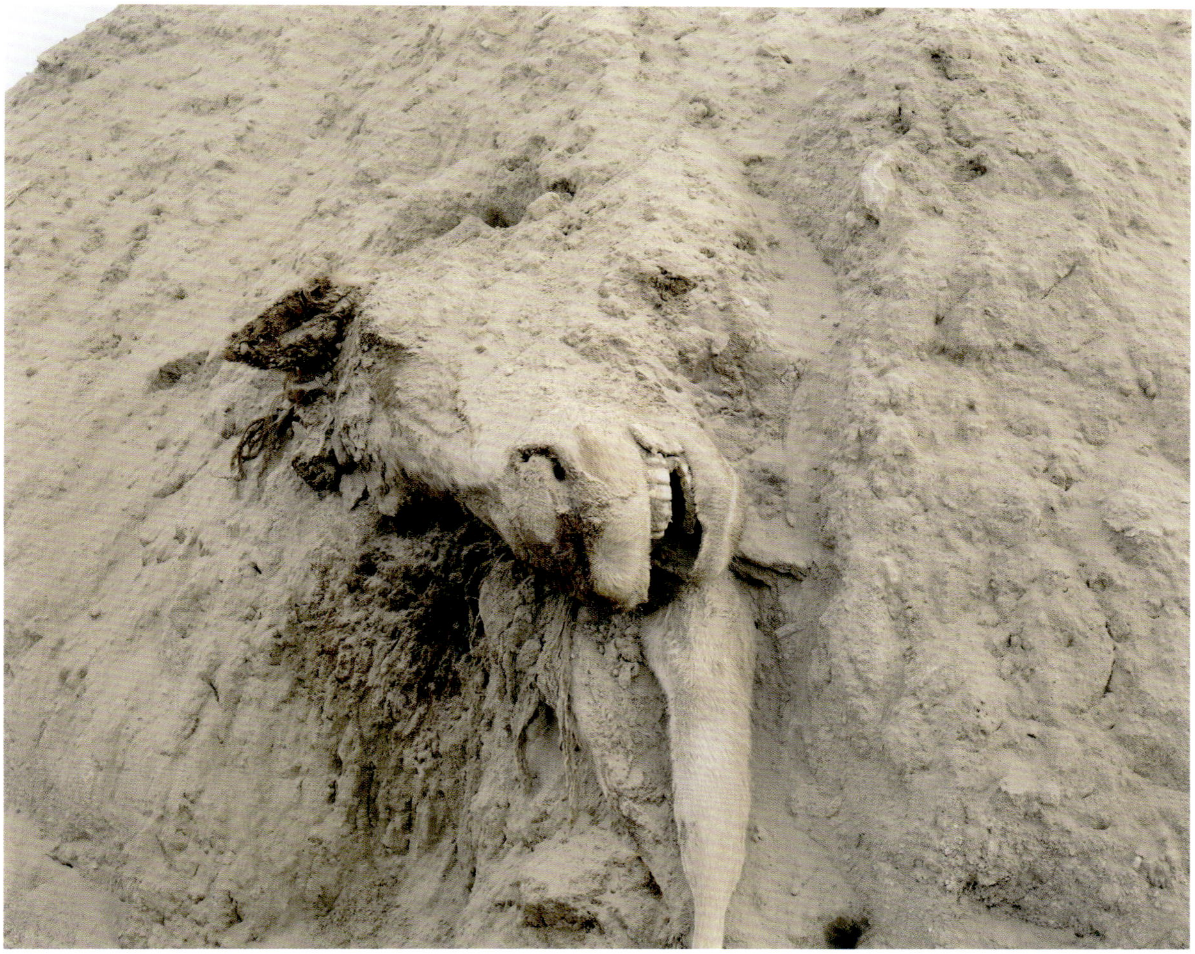

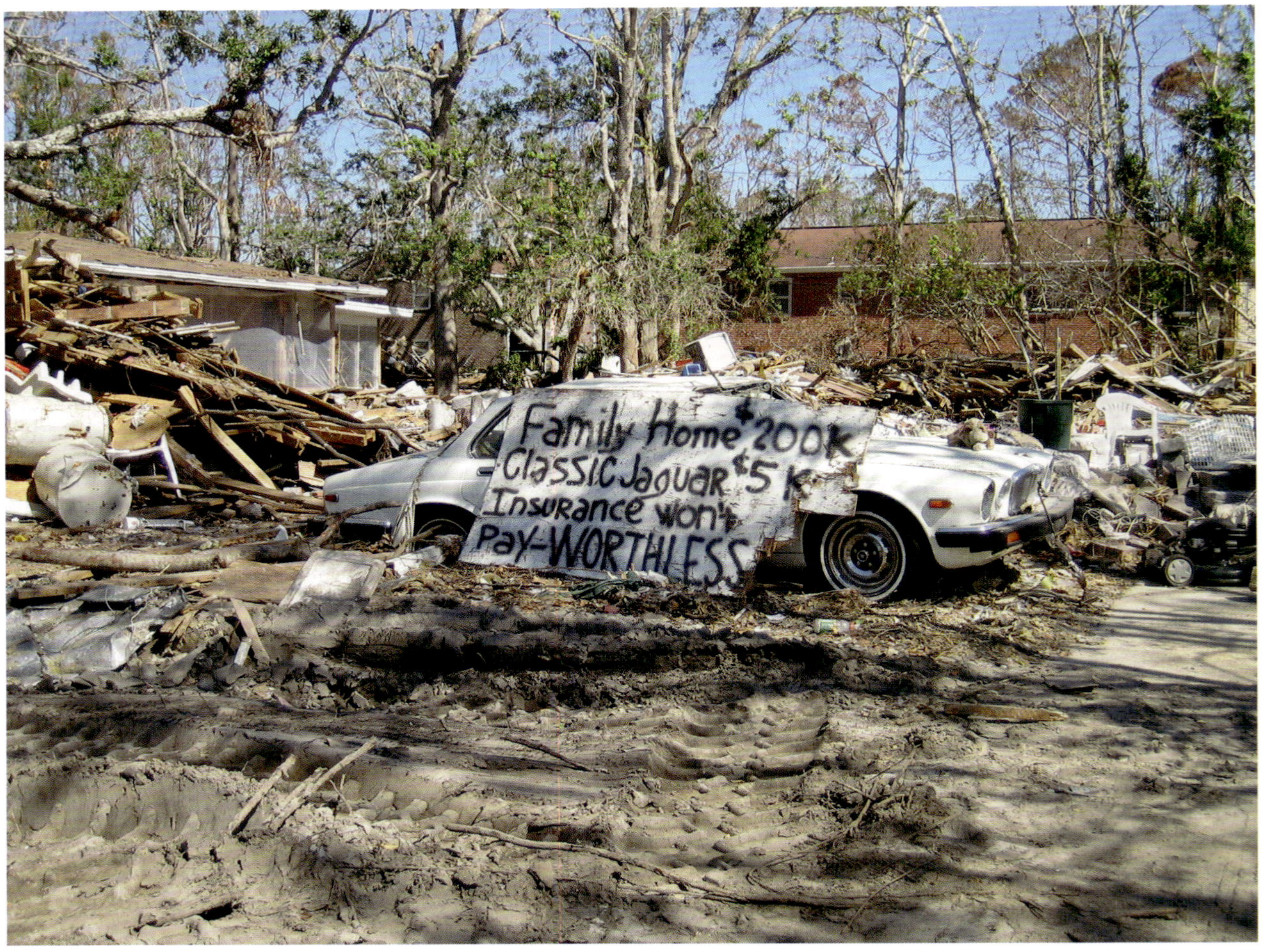

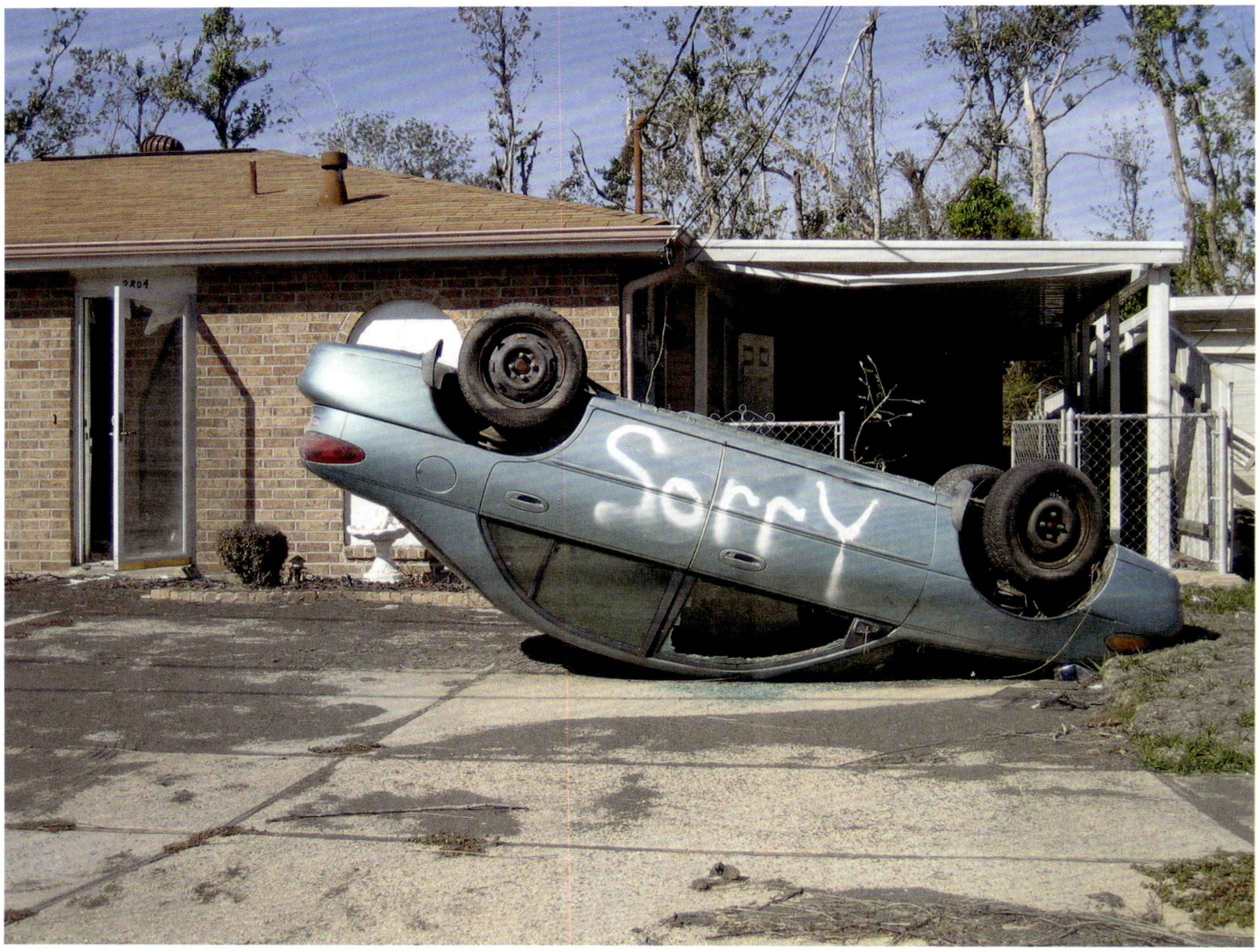

Richard Misrach
Untitled (New Orleans and the Gulf Coast), 2005, from the series 'Destroy This Memory'
Pigment print
27.9 × 36.8 cm /
$10\frac{7}{8} \times 14\frac{1}{2}$ in

Untitled (New Orleans and the Gulf Coast), 2005, from the series 'Destroy This Memory'
Pigment print
27.9 × 36.8 cm /
$10\frac{7}{8} \times 14\frac{1}{2}$ in

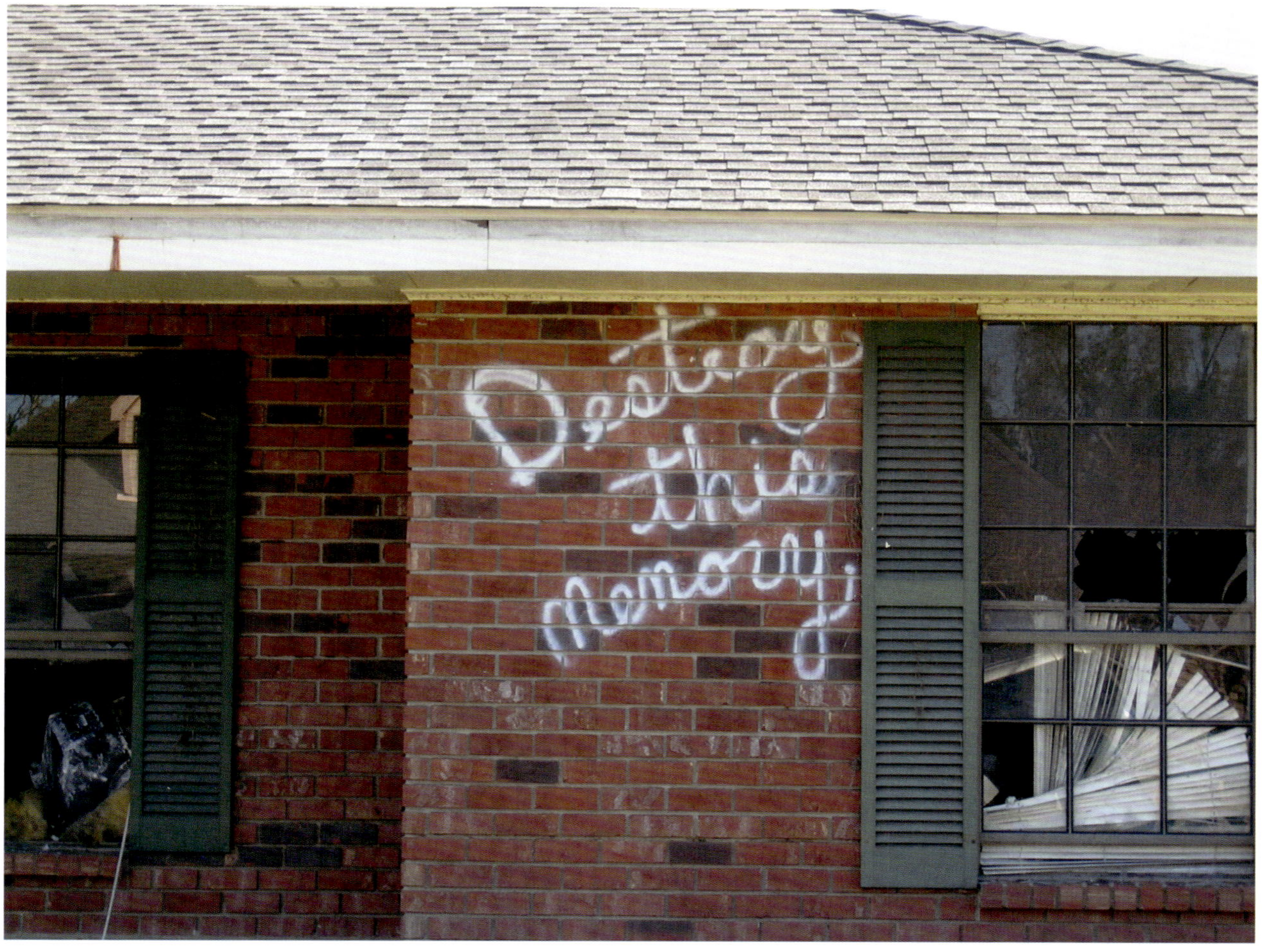

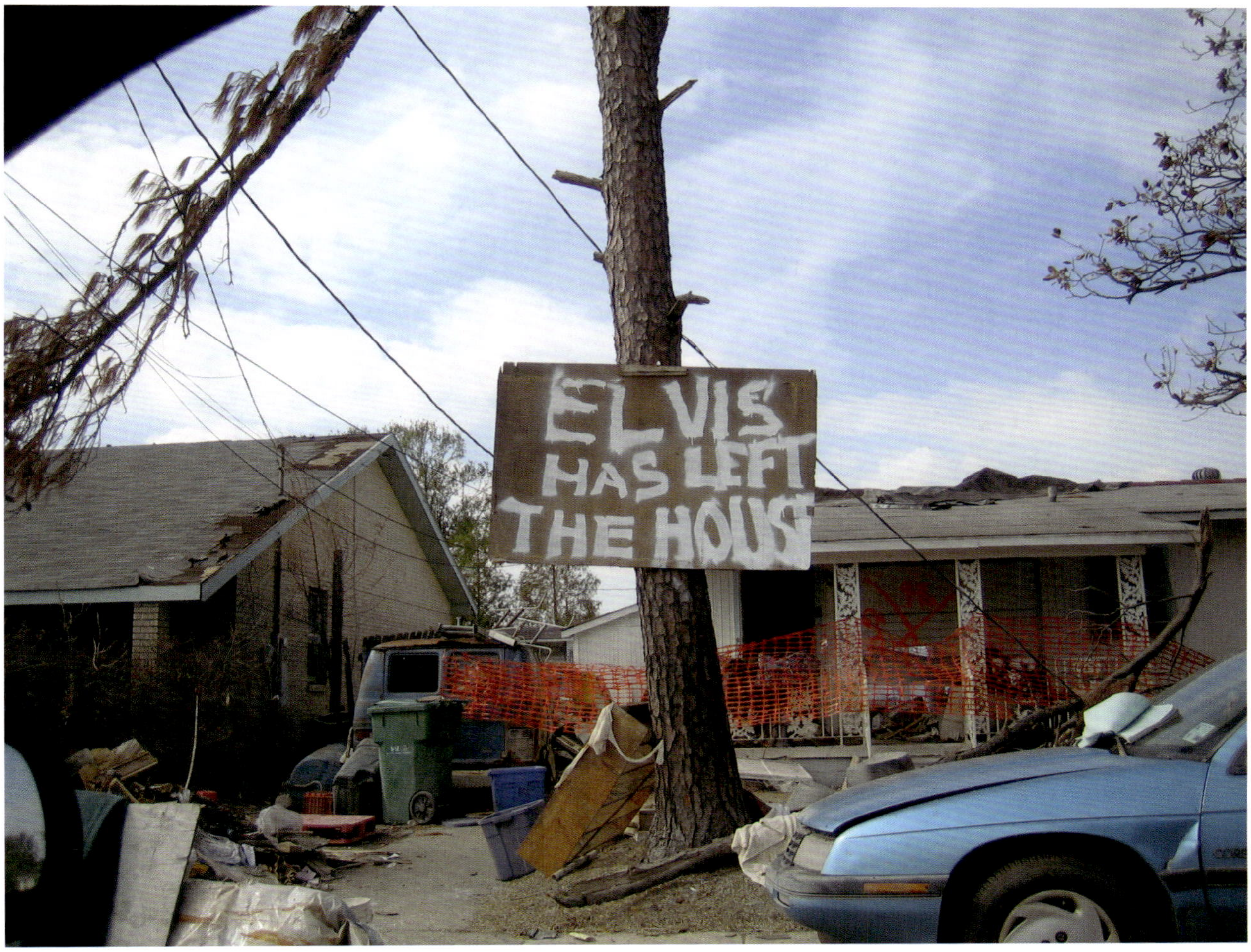

Untitled (New Orleans and the Gulf Coast), 2005, from the series 'Destroy This Memory'
Pigment print
27.9 × 36.8 cm /
11 × 14½ in

Untitled (New Orleans and the Gulf Coast), 2005, from the series 'Destroy This Memory'
Pigment print
27.9 × 36.8 cm /
11 × 14½ in

Edward Burtynsky

The Canadian Edward Burtynsky shows us the vastness and grandeur of the excavation of the world's diminishing global resources. His spectacular and beautiful epic landscapes play out a dystopian vision of our overworked and polluted planet. Burtynsky has spoken about how, 'We are surrounded by all kinds of consumer goods, and yet we are profoundly detached from the sources of those things. Our lifestyles are made possible by industries all around the world, but we take them for granted, as background to our existence.'[13] Beginning with photographs of mining and tailing in the mid-1980s, his photography has gone on to encompass an increasingly global vision of what he describes as 'nature transformed through industry', including the quarrying of marble around the world, ship-breaking on the shores of Bangladesh, the rapid industrial expansion and transformation of China, including the devasting consequences of the construction of the Three Gorges Dam, and a whole series about the extraction and refinery of oil, as well as aerial views of oil spills at sea.[14]

In showing us the material consequences of capitalism, Burtynsky's pictures still function as opulent, luxurious objects. There is an awkward collision between the aesthetic richness of his mode of picturing and the destruction and depletion his photographs evidence. Richard Misrach's *Destroy this Memory* allowed an important shift to the human dimension and perspective through the signs and messages people had left facing the wreckage, disrupting the viewer's comfort in simply looking at one spectacle of destruction after another. Burtynsky, on the other hand, rarely shifts his god-like perspective and viewpoint. In the pictures of shipbreaking in Bangladesh, the spectacle of the disassembled ships, somewhat suggestive of the heavy metal sculptures of Richard Serra, is interrupted by the presence of workers. There to signal scale, they also testify to exploitation, performing such dangerous work with no protective clothing. Burtynsky predominantly maintains a distanced view, however, and even here, we never get too close.

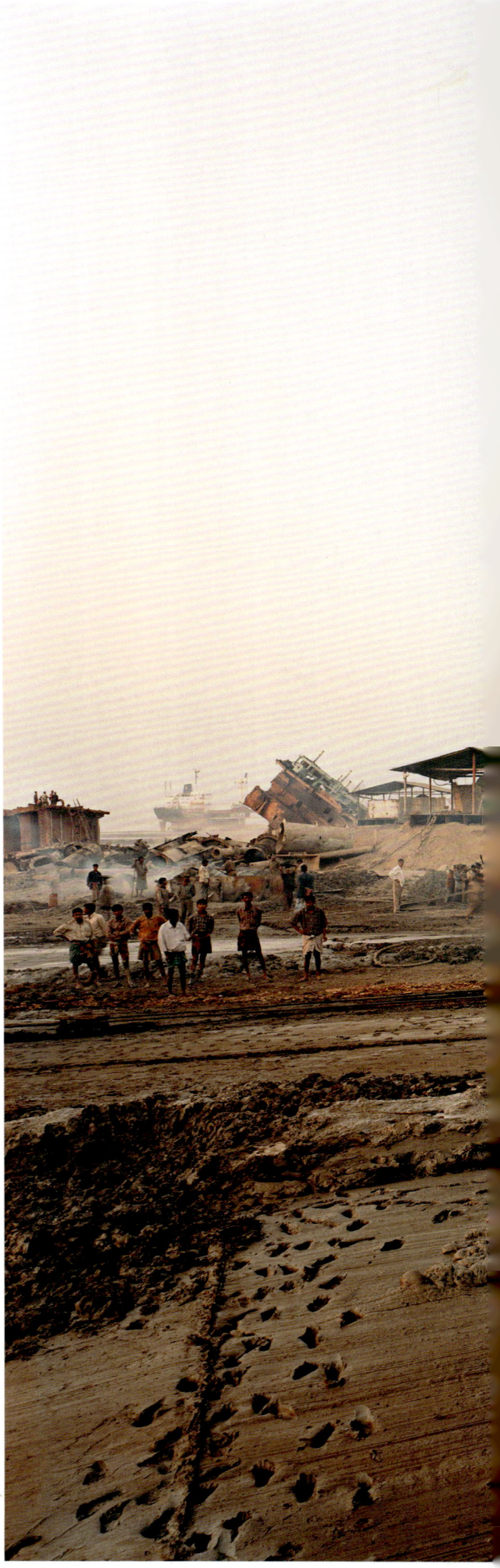

Edward Burtynsky
Shipbreaking #9B Chittagong, Bangladesh, 2000 (detail from original diptych)
C-print, dimensions variable

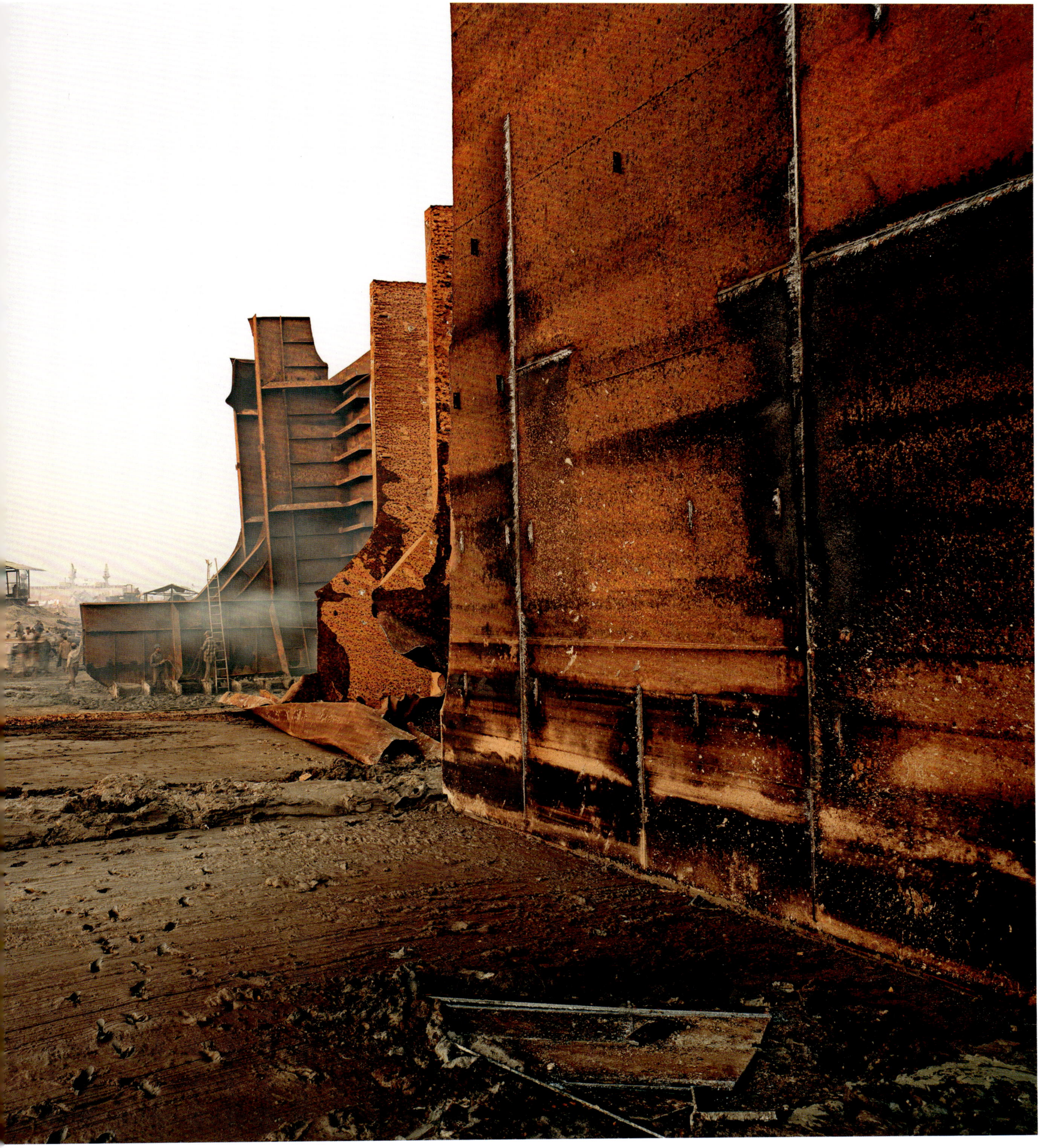

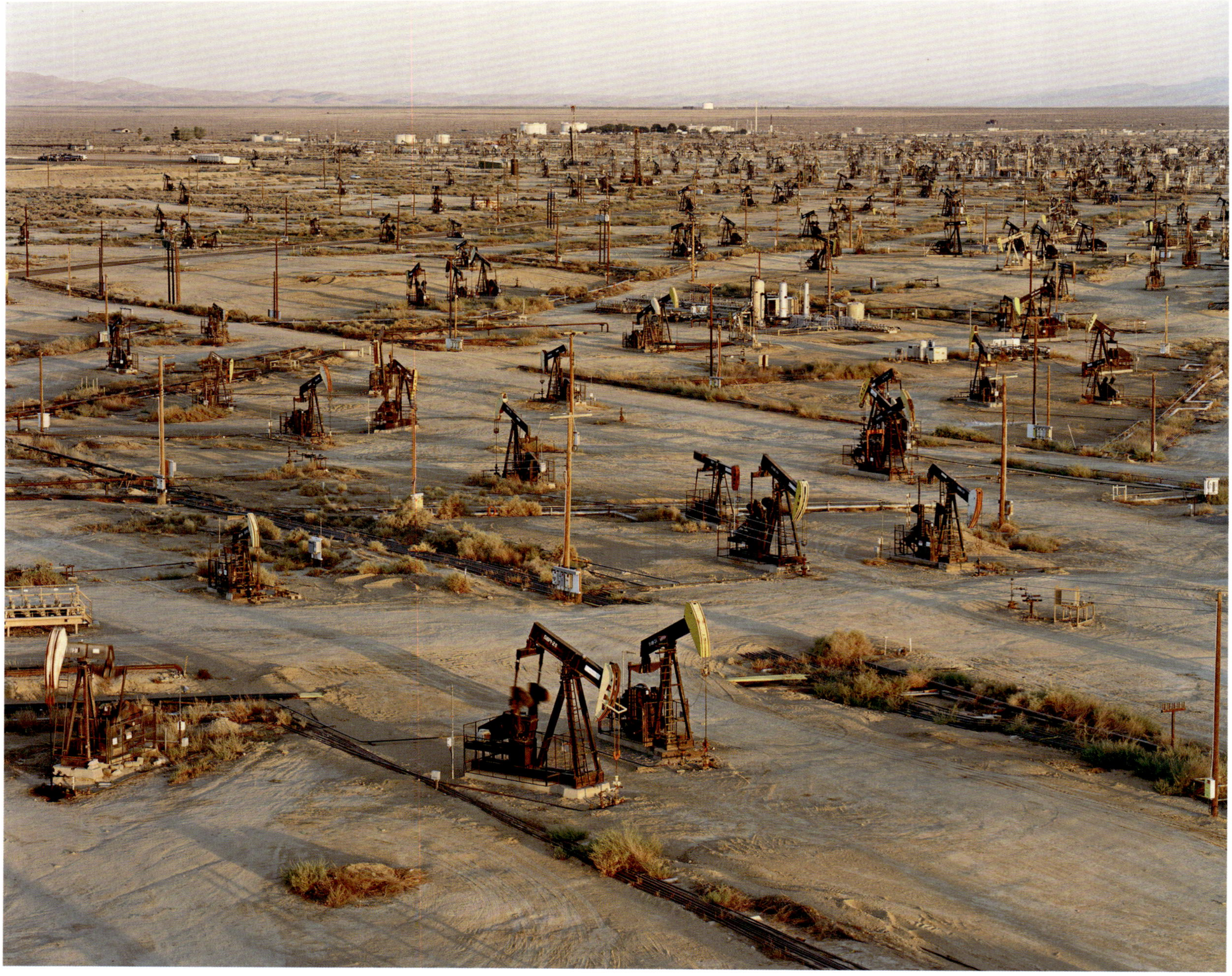

Edward Burtynsky,
Oil Fields #19A, Belridge California, USA, 2003
Medium C-print
Dimensions variable

Oil Fields #19B, Belridge California, USA, 2003
Medium C-print
Dimensions variable

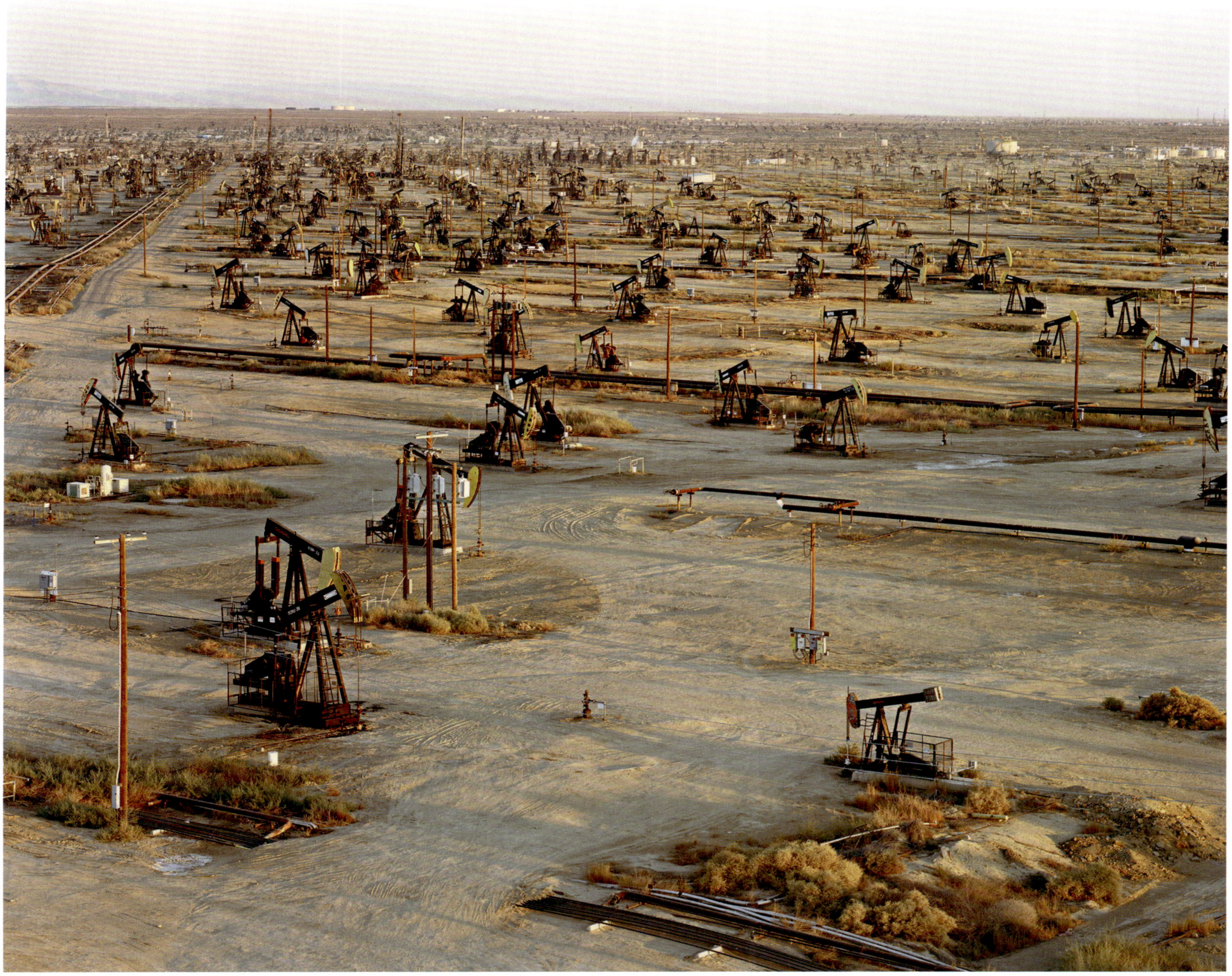

Willie Doherty

Willie Doherty's photography and video respond to both the beautiful Irish landscape and its urban wastegrounds. Beginning in the 1980s Doherty used the duality of photography and text to address political identification with land in Ireland in pictures that make the viewer very conscious about his or her own viewing position. His panorama of Derry, *The Walls* (1987), usurped the colonialist gaze of the British security forces by viewing the lower Catholic 'Bogside' from inside the city's walls. Doherty's politicized landscape representation also showed how romantic and pictorial views of the Irish landscape were never empty of ideology, being potentially caught up in either Republican or Loyalist sentiment. This was shown in such works as *Blue Skies of Ulster*, which set up an ironic collision between a Loyalist slogan and a panoramic view of a mist-laden River Foyle, which separates the predominantly Protestant East Bank and Catholic West Bank of Derry. This veiled, mist-filled view was inscribed with the words: WE SHALL NEVER FORSAKE THE BLUE SKIES OF ULSTER FOR THE GREY MISTS OF AN IRISH REPUBLIC.

Doherty's artistic response to the violent history of conflict in his homeland has been to work against the one-sided news management of these events. His work often mirrors the fractured social and political context of Ireland through its double mode of address in which two forms, two languages, representative of two world views and ideologies, are set against each other. Yet it would be wrong to infer from this that the artist occupied a unique and privileged position outside of any identification with any side. As he has said, 'My work refutes such a position and comes from my knowledge and experience of a nationalist background.'[15]

The iconography of many of Doherty's photographic and video works from the 1990s onwards has concerned the depiction of indeterminate spaces on the peripheries of urban areas: wastegrounds, abandoned architectural interiors, empty factories, forbidden and foreboding terrain. Doherty works to counter the colonizing and imperial vista through these scruffy and derelict sites.

Willie Doherty
We Shall Never Forsake the Blue Skies of Ulster for the Grey Mists of an Irish Republic, 1986
Black and white photograph with text, 152 × 46 cm / 5⅞ × 8¼ in

The Walls, 1987
Black and white photograph with text mounted on masonite
61 × 152.5 cm / 24 × 60 in

WE SHALL NEVER FORSAKE THE BLUE SKIES OF ULSTER
FOR THE GREY MISTS OF AN IRISH REPUBLIC

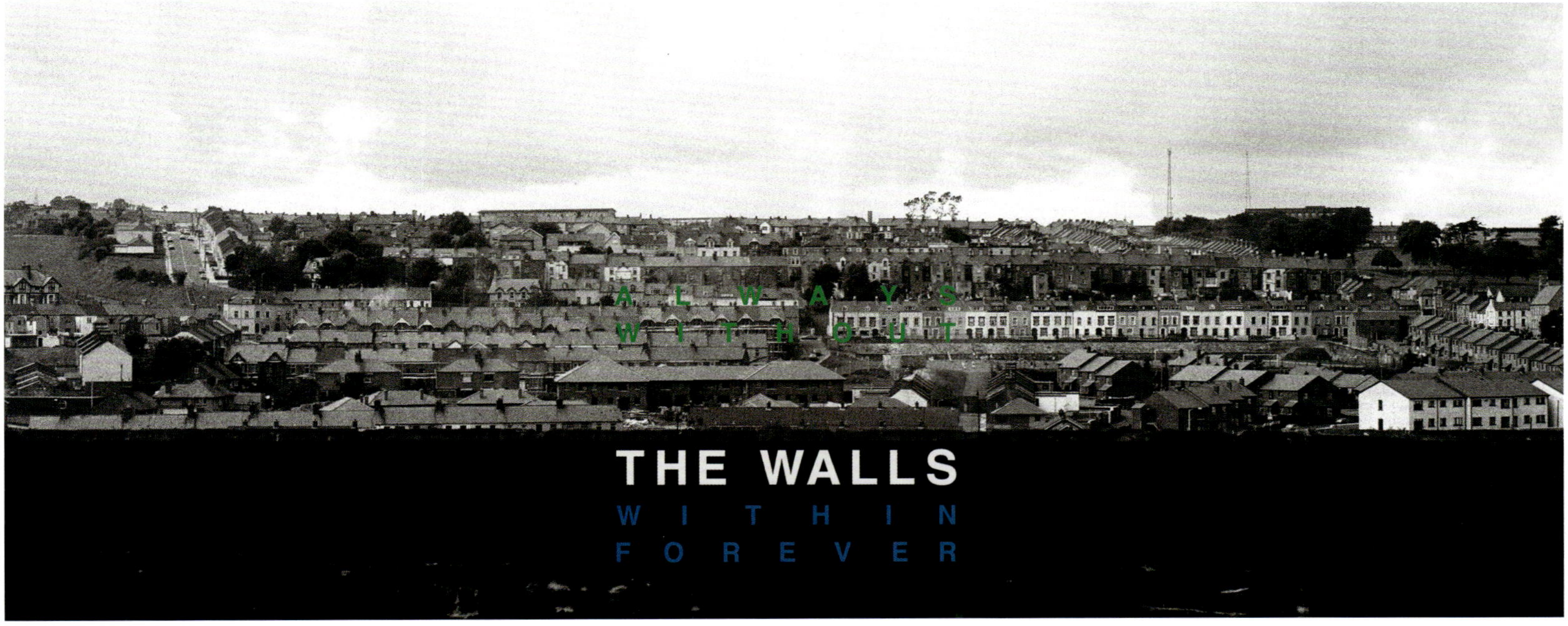
A L W A Y S
W I T H O U T
THE WALLS
W I T H I N
F O R E V E R

Jorma Puranen

In 'Imaginary Homecoming' (1991–7) the Finnish artist Jorma Puranen engages with historical images of the minority Sami people of northern Norway, Finland, Sweden and Russia, and sets up a symbolic act of colonial reparation by returning them to the landscape of northern Scandinavia. His starting point was a book showing archival potraits of Sami people from the Musée de l'Homme in Paris, which were taken under the supervision of Prince Bonaparte on a visit to northern Scandinavia in 1884. He rephotographed these and other historical anthropological portraits of the Sami testifying to colonial subjugation and control, then printed them on large plexiglass panels or as positives and negatives on polyester sheets. The images were then physically returned to the land of the Sami and inserted in the ground, wrapped around trees or hung in bushes. Re-photographed in their landscape settings, the portraits circulate as art, inviting a different kind of looking and engagement. No longer subjects of a colonial gaze, the portraits now serve to challenge and disrupt the view. As Puranen says, 'The historical portraits as it were block our path when we might be tempted simply to admire the beauty of the landscape.'[16]

Jorma Puranen
From the series 'Imaginary Homecoming', 1991
Gelatin silver print
90 × 120 cm / 35⅜ × 47¼ in

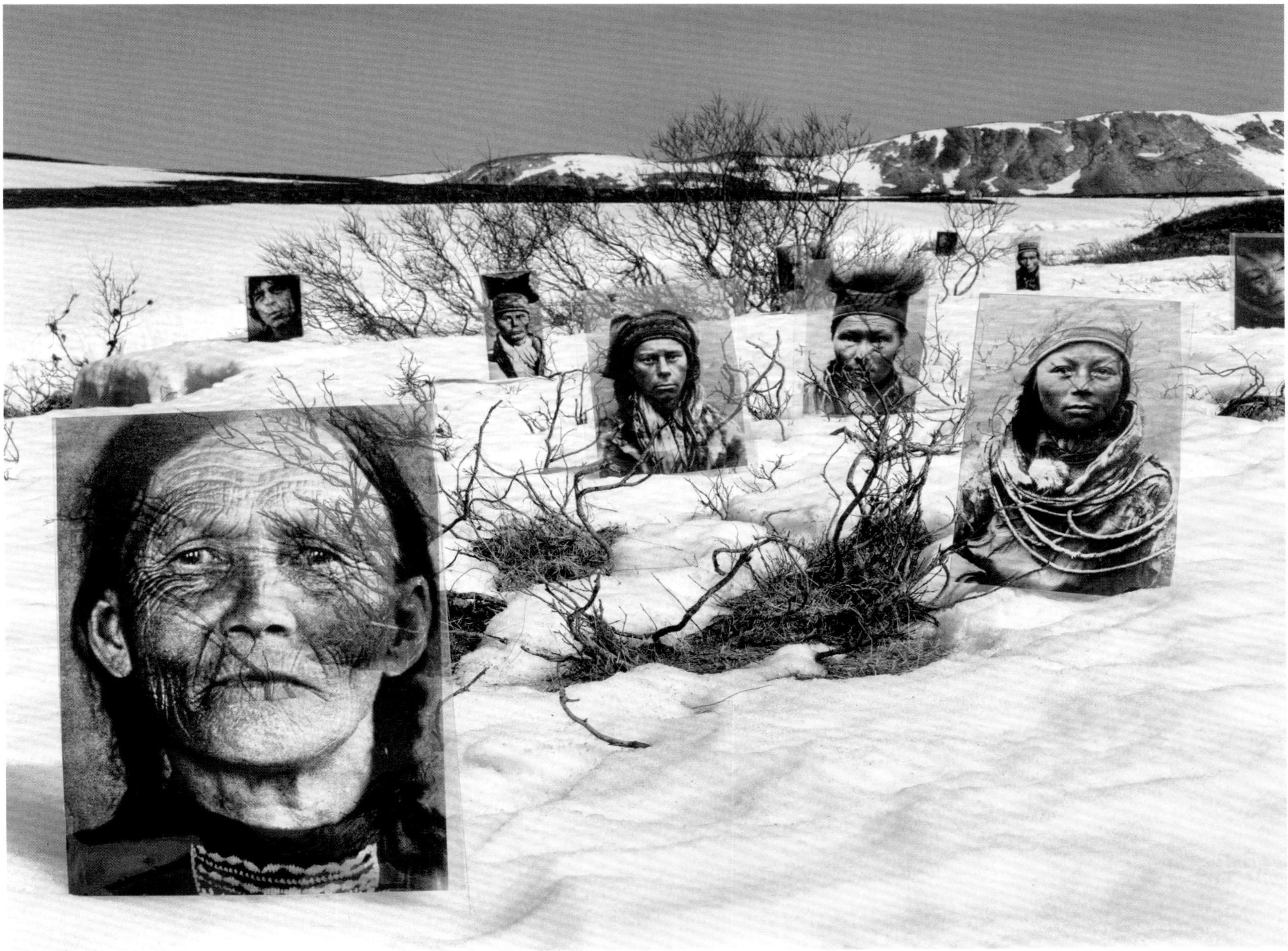

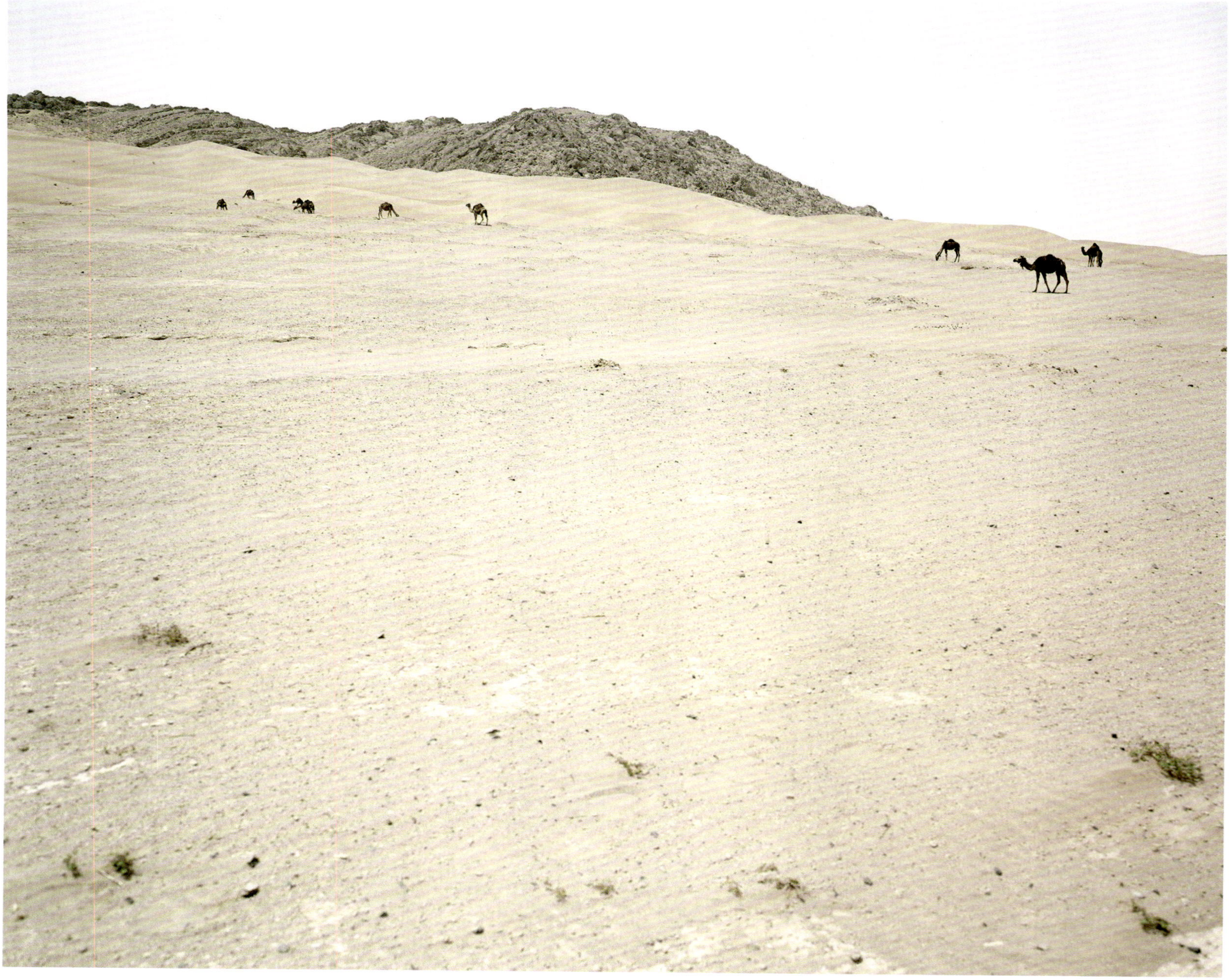

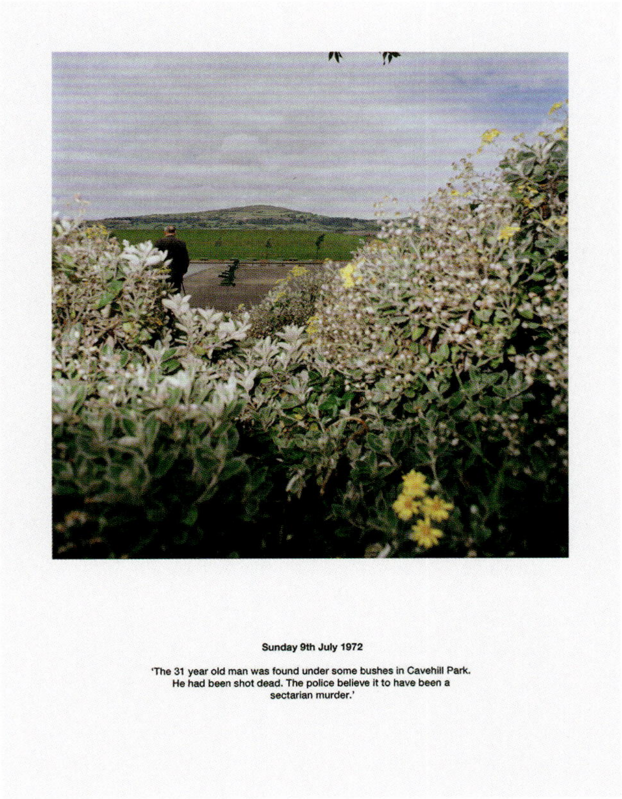

Paul Seawright

Paul Seawright's photography is characterized by a disavowal of the kind of photojournalist imagery that came to dominate the newspaper coverage of the conflict in his hometown, Belfast in Northern Ireland. His 'Sectarian Murder' (1988), for example, involved the artist revisiting and photographing the scenes of sectarian killings in Belfast in the 1970s a decade later. Many of the photographs from this series possess a pictorial innocence, a contradictory sense of calm and normalcy. One also finds an attempt to confront that which cannot be seen, the sense of an invisible threat and menace. It was a documentary made in response to events that had passed but that continued to determine and shape people's relationships to the city. As the writer Justin Carville has said, 'Sectarian Murder' 'challenge[s] the viewer to confront the ideological and psychological territorialism that sectarian murder engenders in the communities affected.'[17]

When he agreed to undertake an Imperial War Museum commission to go to Afghanistan as an artist in 2002, Seawright would be in the very colonial and 'outsider' position so much of the work made in his homeland had sought to challenge and undermine. As a result many of the pictures from this series, 'Hidden', explored the colonial associations of vistas of the desert landscapes of Afghanistan. Countering the media's portrayal of the war-torn country as a spectacle of ruins, as well as Simon Norfolk's contemporary colour-saturated pictures of Afghanistan showing layers of destruction and devastation, Seawright's spare, ashen photographs are preoccupied with the hidden malevolence of heavily-mined landscapes. The desert as minefield allows him to evoke Victorian travel photography, replete with its imperialist and colonialist connotations, and combine it with the invisible menace of the lethal weaponry of modern warfare. Seawright came to this war zone after much of the fighting was over, and used the idea of the unexploded mine as an effective means of stressing the continued violent destructiveness of conflict, long after wars are said to be over.

Paul Seawright
Minefield from the series 'Hidden', 2002
C-type Fuji Crystal Archive print
152 × 127 cm / 59⅞ × 50 in

Sunday 9th July 1972, from the series 'Sectarian Murder', 1988
C-type Fuji Crystal Archive print
66 × 51 cm / 26 × 20 in

Yto Barrada

Since 1991 Africans have been unable to cross the Strait of Gibraltar without visas, but the narrow sea-crossing has become one of the main gateways for illegal immigrants seeking to reach Europe. Yto Barrada's photographs from her series 'The Strait Project: A Life Full of Holes' (1998–2004) reflect, she says, 'on the condition of a country whose people are all leaving or trying to leave'.[18] Born in Paris to Moroccan parents, Barrada can travel freely between Europe and Africa, and is therefore able to record the sense of exclusion that the majority of the population of Tangier now experience.

Although Barrada does give us one photograph showing illegal immigrants crossing into the Spanish enclave of Ceuta, her pictures are generally not documentary in their response; instead they provide a metaphorical and poetic reflection upon the impact the division of the Strait has on Morocco, and especially Tangier: 'I try to expose the metonymic character of the Strait through a series of images that reveal the tension – which restlessly animates the streets of my home town – between its allegorical nature and immediate, harsh reality.' Barrada uses the divisions and wastegrounds of Tangier and its surrounding landscape to suggest the experience of a people caught in limbo. Borrowing the *Rückenfigur* from German Romantic landscape painting, in which we see the back of figures absorbed in the views before them, she presents figures facing walls in a landscape of blockage, with no clear exit, an allegory of the stasis and inertia of those trapped within Tangier. The borders and divisions are everywhere: the innocence of play is caught up with the political context as she shows us children leaving a football ground through a hole in a surrounding fence. Even a detail showing the trace of a football's imprint on a white wall is redolent of a sense of containment and restricted movement. In one street scene, the wide expanse of asphalt serves as a clear sign of the division created by the border of the Strait. Viewed from on high, there are people at the edges of the picture on either side the road: a group of women on one side are about to cross while, on the other side, a man carrying a model sailing ship looks towards them. The street's very name is a reminder of what many cannot have: *Avenue d'Espagne* (Strait – Spanish Avenue).

Europe figures only as a dream for many of Barrada's subjects, and this is shown through her picture of an Alpine landscape wallpaper, its false nature evident through its visible seam. While closed to Africans, the border is open to European tourists, as acknowledged through the picture of a swimming pool on a hoarding advertising a tourist development in Briech. One picture looking up to the blue sky through the rust holes in the top of a shipping container is suggestive of both the porosity of Tangier and the idea of the stowaway. In her series, 'Public Park' (2006), a sense of the immigrant experience is conveyed through figures pictured lying down or sleeping in public places, with their faces hidden by clothing. Many of the hopeful immigrants burn their papers, so that if they are caught the authorities will not know where to return them to. Such anonymous sleepers are powerful representations of the forced stateless condition of the immigrant, and a wider reminder, like all Barrada's work, that our view of landscape is never innocent.

Yto Barrada
Avenue d'Espagne, Tangier, 2003
C-print
60 × 60 cm / 48⅞ × 48⅞ in

Girl in red playing Jacks, Tangier, 1999
C-print
125 × 125 cm / 48⅞ × 48⅞ in

Dormeurs (The Sleepers), Fig.2, 2006
C-print
125 × 125 cm / 49¼ × 49¼ in

Dormeurs (The Sleepers), Fig.3, 2006
C-print
125 × 125 cm / 49¼ × 49¼ in

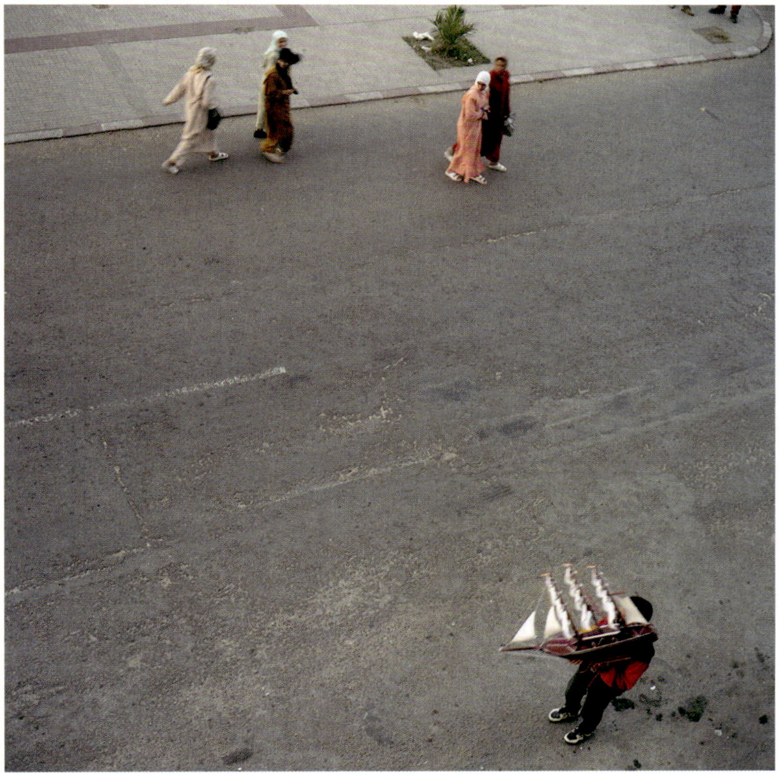

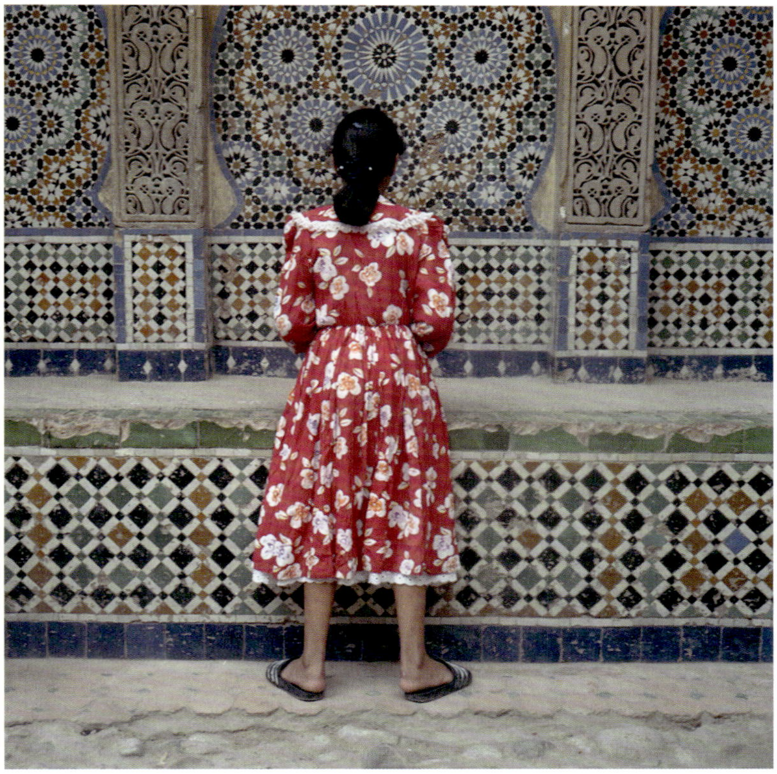

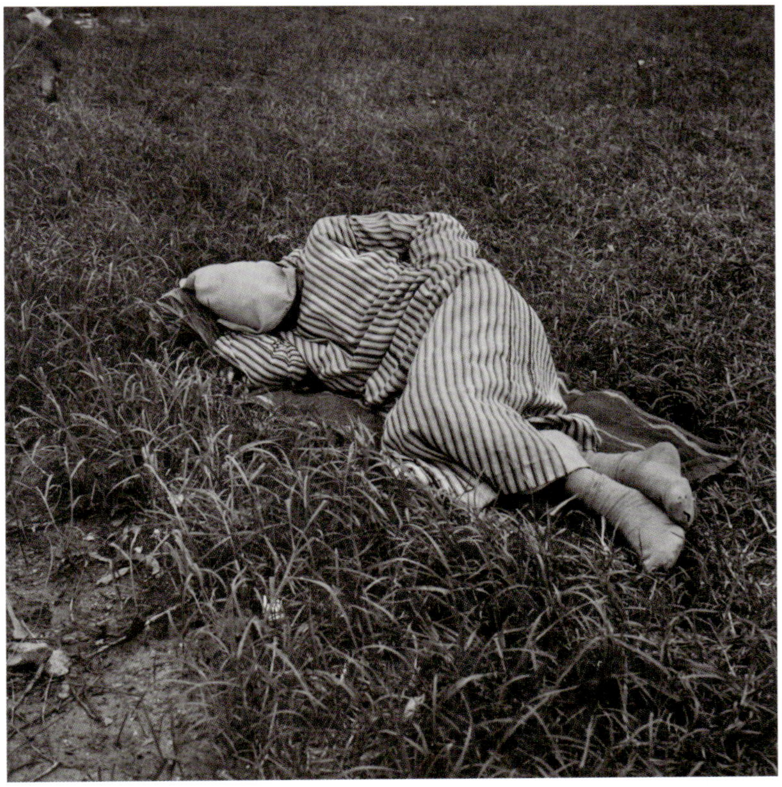

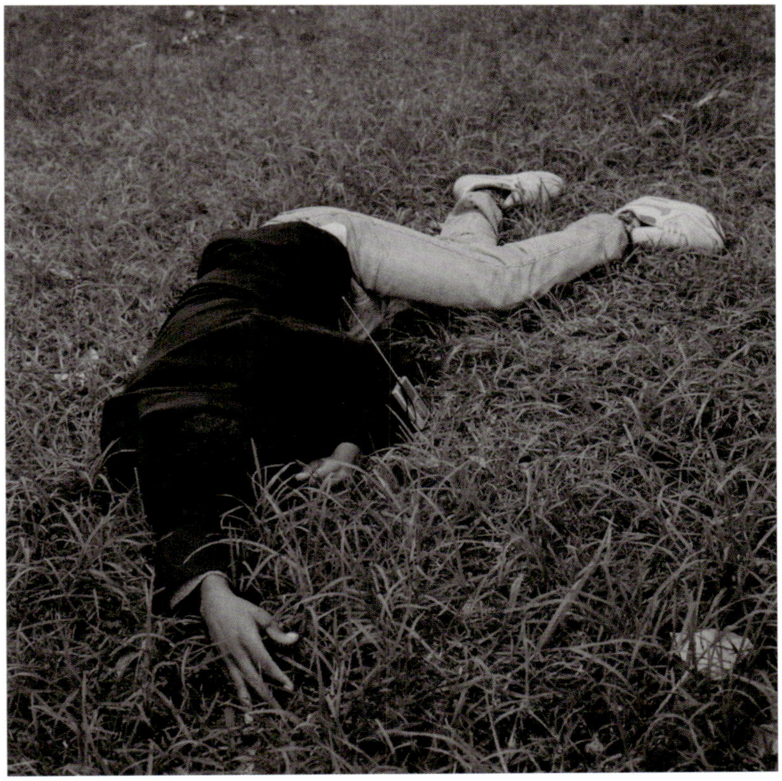

George Georgiou

'My work seeks to address and question the concept of East and West and the process of modernization, urbanization, and national identity that is happening against a rising tide of nationalism and religion. I have chosen to represent the changes by focusing on the quiet everyday life that most people in Turkey experience.'[19] This is how the British-born photographer George Georgiou introduces his work 'Fault Lines/Turkey/East/West', drawn from over a decade's worth of pictures taken in Eastern Europe and Turkey. Georgiou explores the landscapes of the Balkans and the collisions and tensions between the impact of modernity and the traditions of Turkish people. 'We are used to seeing Istanbul or the Mediterranean resorts', says Georgiou, 'but most of Turkey is on a huge plateau above 1000m. I wanted to get this non-romantic version of Turkey where the landscape represents the harshness of its geography and its topographical place in the East.'[20] His tableaux-like pictures often set individuals caught up in everyday activities against their environments: a solitary male in a highly built-up urban area hoses down a grey terrace, bereft of flowers and vegetation; a woman returns from shopping to new apartments, the produce in her bag a reminder of the village life and community that has been lost with the move to modern homes. Georgiou captures the modernization of Turkey and how it is reshaping landscapes, towns and cities, showing the onset of large apartment blocks and extensive road networks in a landscape that reflects the collisions and tensions between tradition and modernity, faith and secularism. This state of transformation is often set against the grandeur and beauty of the Turkish landscape, a backdrop that accents the sense of superficiality of the country's emergent new global consumer culture: fittingly in one of Georgiou's views, a brash red supermarket sign remains unfinished.

Georgiou's approach to landscape reflects the social concerns and interests that characterize and motivate the documentary photographic tradition. In this respect, like the work of a number of other artists discussed so far, landscape is always viewed in relation to history.

Vandy Rattana

Vandy Rattana's remarkable series of colour landscapes 'Takeo' (2009), picture the remains of America's secret bombing campaign in Cambodia during the Vietnam War. Between 1964 and 1975, the United States dropped 2,756,941 tons of bombs (230,516 sorties on 113,716 sites) on the officially neutral country. This figure went unacknowledged until 2000, when Bill Clinton travelled to Vietnam and released previously classified Air Force data on American bombings in former Indochina.

Rattana pictures the craters made by the bombings, known in the Khmer language as the 'bomb ponds'. To make these landscapes he went to the ten most severely bombed provinces in Cambodia and consulted with older villagers to find where craters existed. The pictures are quiet and contemplative, their tranquility belying the violence of their formation and the toxicity of their waters. A number of the photographs show the ponds' precise circular shapes, a sign that these are unnatural and manmade, but a precision that also further contributes to the beauty of these landscapes. As documents the pictures give evidence of a history kept silent. Born in the period of recovery after the official fall of the Khmer Rouge as part of Cambodia's so-called 'new generation', Rattana grew up with little knowledge of his country's recent war history. His photographs are about not forgetting the past. They are subtle memorials to Cambodia's violent history and also reminders of the continued acts of military destruction worldwide, often unseen and undocumented.

George Georgiou
Konya, Market, 2008, from the series 'Fault Lines/Turkey/East/West'
Digital C-print
100 × 70cm / 39⅜ × 27⅝ in

Hakkari, 2007, from the series 'Fault Lines/Turkey/East/West'
Digital C-print
100 × 70cm / 39⅜ × 27½ in

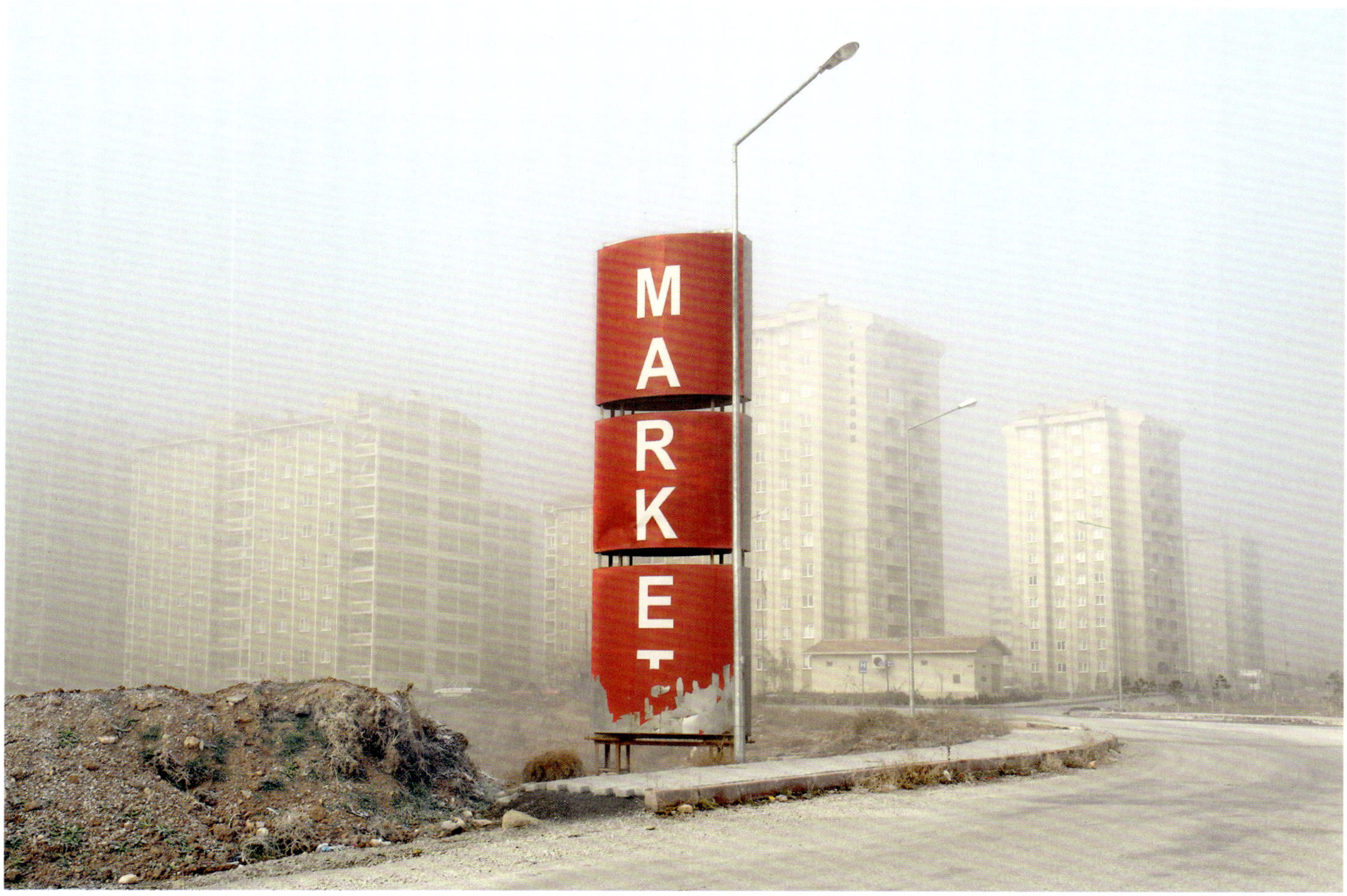
MARKE

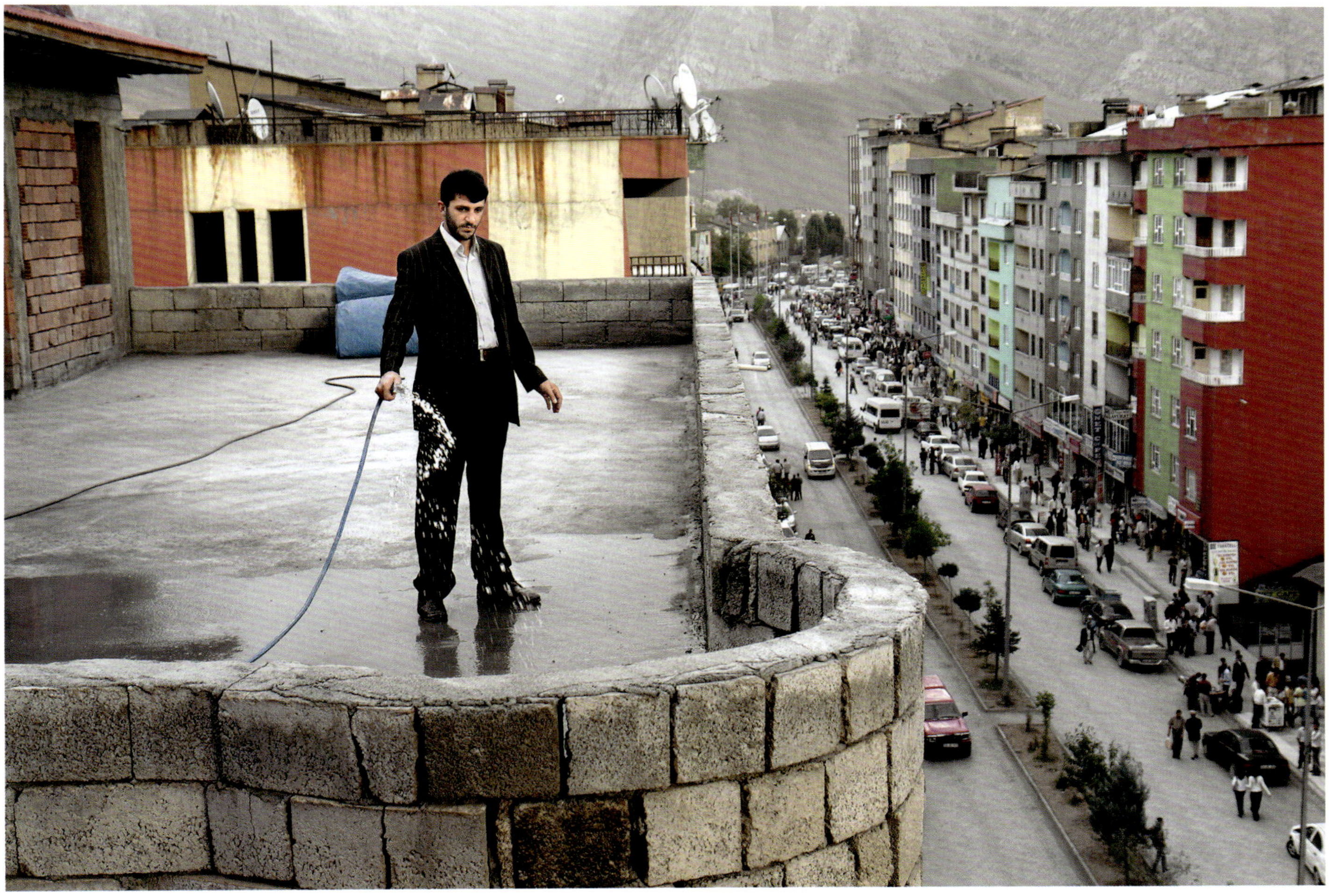

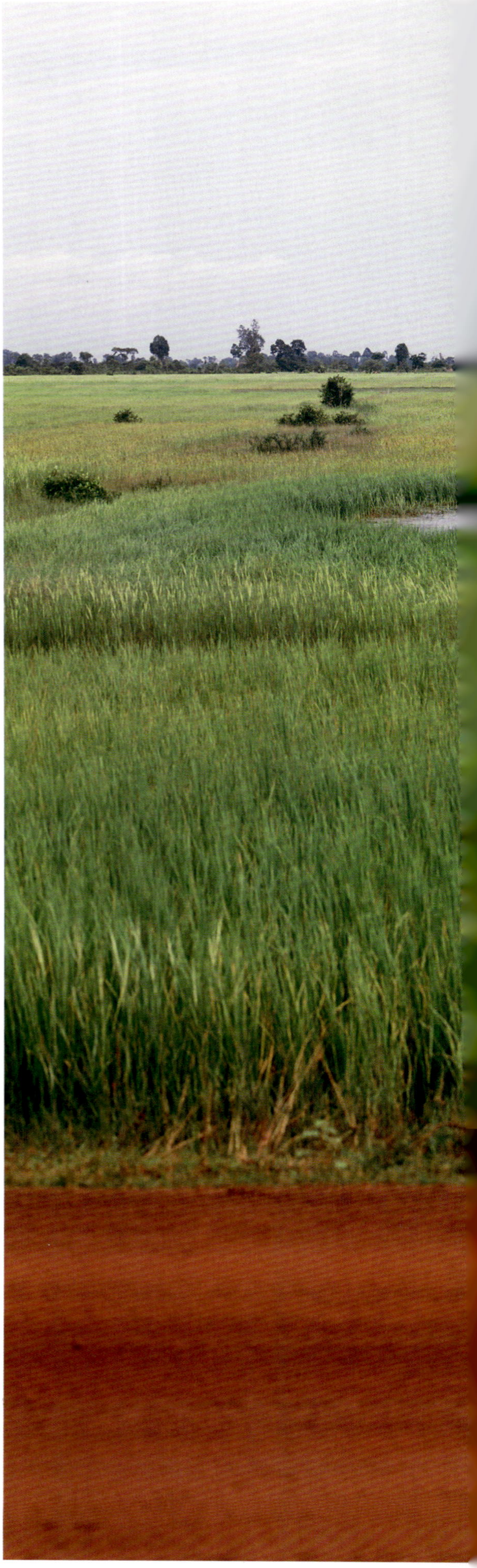

Vandy Rattana
Bomb Ponds, Kompong Thom,
2009
Digital C-print
96 × 111 cm / 37⅞ × 43¾ in

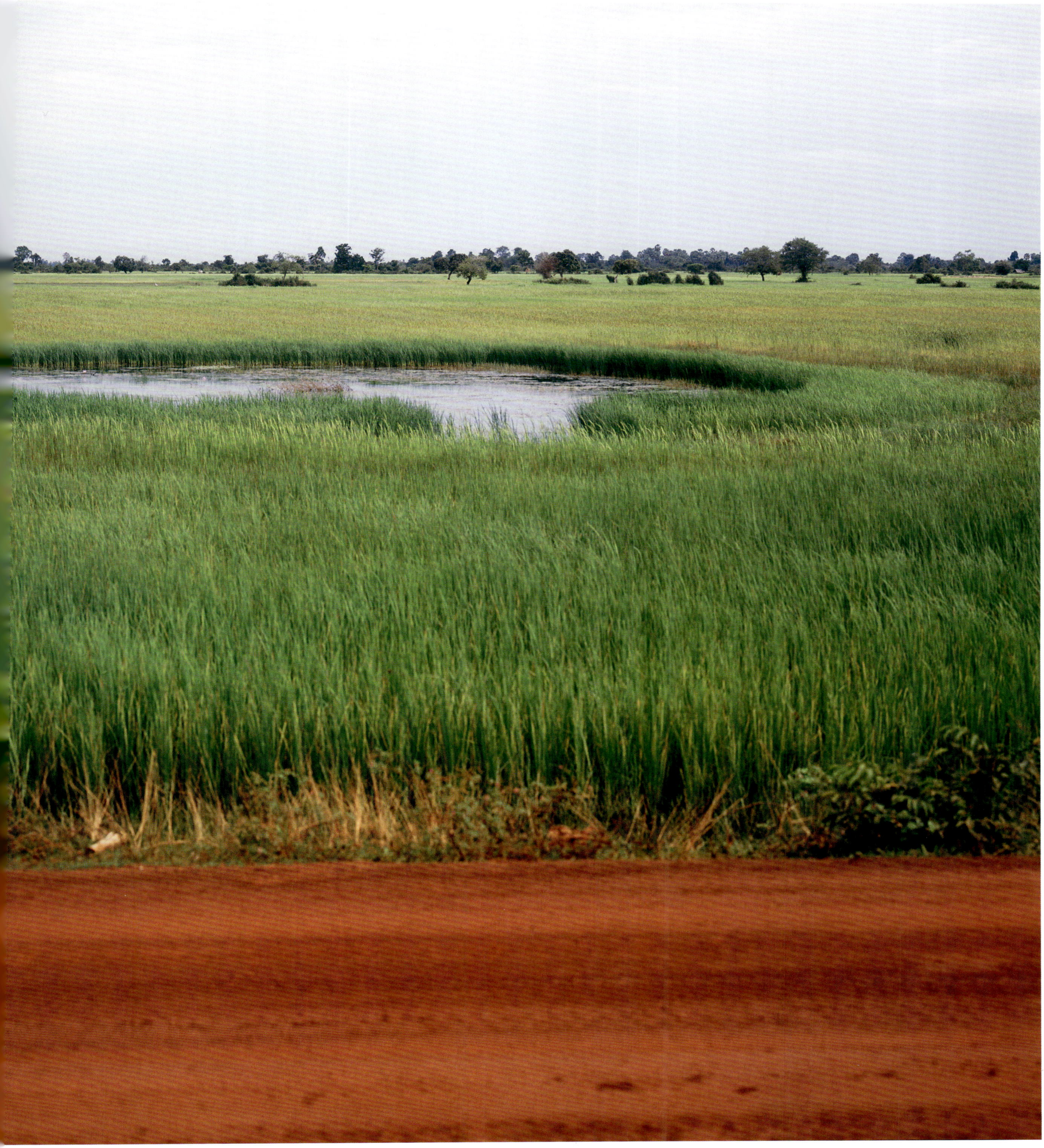

Chapter Six

History: Witnessing Atrocity

Photography has often been used in response to traumatic historical events, but how adequate is it for a role as witness and evidence provider? Artists and photographers use different strategies to try and respond to the atrocities they have seen, but the question of impact is central to them all: how does the photographer or artist best relay the pain, suffering and horror witnessed to an audience that is often distant and detached from what is being shown? Such a question applies to both photographs made within the context of art, positioned within the art gallery or the book, and photojournalism within the news media.

Writing in 1987 in *The New York Times*, Andy Grundberg suggested that photojournalism was reclaiming its 'former glamourous, legendary status', fifteen years after the demise of *Life Magazine* as a weekly publication.[1] Grundberg's point was that pictures taken on assignment for magazines and newspapers were now regularly appearing as framed pictures on the walls of museums and galleries. He identified this 'New Photojournalism' as reflecting the desire of the photojournalist to have credence as a creative photographer as books and galleries took the place of the declining number of news magazines willing to run photo essays. Taken off the page and folded into the museum, the 'New Photojournalism' became simply another genre in the realm of art, which Grundberg calls 'dysfunctional but beautiful'.

The tensions between art and documentary that underlie Grundberg's argument are particularly important in relation to photography that attempts to witness and evidence historical events and their aftermath. One way of seeing the use of the gallery and the book to display pictures ordinarily associated with the magazine and the newspaper is a greater self-consciousness on the part of photographers in relation to what they are doing. The aesthetic can too readily be a catch-all, dismissive term that does not acknowledge the complexity of our engagement with images, especially when those images are so visibly marked by the often traumatic events that have been witnessed.

James Nachtwey

James Nachtwey is one of the world's leading war photographers. With complete dedication and extreme risk to his own life, he has spent over thirty years acting on behalf of others. His mission is to represent those who suffer, are disadvantaged and distressed, living under and effected by oppressive regimes, or in the areas of our world ripped apart by war. The people he photographs have no access to the media. They have no voice. Nachtwey and his camera act as their witness and his brutally compassionate photographs bring their plight to our attention with the plea that we might act and, in turn, make a difference.

The photographs in his monumental book, *Inferno* (1999), take the pictorial and rhetorical possibilities of photojournalism to extremes. The outward sombreness of the book fits the subject – 'a record of crimes against humanity that occurred during the final decade of the 20th century'.[2] The 382 pictures form nine chapters, echoing Dante's nine circles of hell. The first circle shows the disease-wracked bodies of neglected children in orphanages in Romania after the fall of Nicolae Ceausescu's regime and the book ends with the violence that erupted in Kosovo between Serbian armed forces and Albanian Kosovars in 1999. Page after page of horror, cruelty and destruction committed by man on his fellow man. The unrelenting terror refuses to be silenced and forces the reader to engage and realise the depth and breadth of the atrocities inflicted in our lifetime. We can visit museums dedicated to the horrors of the past and feel somehow absolved that we will 'never forget', but Nachtwey reminds us that we need to look at ourselves, today. We may 'not forget' what happened in times past, but we haven't learnt. We have not changed. We continue to commit the same crimes and these pictures are a call to action.

The 5th circle of hell takes place in Bosnia where Muslims, Catholics and Orthodox Christians had once lived peacefully as neighbours. By the early 1990s the Muslim minority was subjected to kidnapping, rape, internment and mass execution by the warring Serb and Croat militia spurred on by their megalomaniac leaders. Nachtwey's most powerful picture of this bloody war of attrition is perhaps a photograph taken in Mostar. A bedroom, normally a refuge of rest and intimacy, has become a battlefield. The sheets are dirty and crumpled; a pillow sits, as if broken, against the headboard and the paper peels from the wall. The bedroom has become a place of terror and destruction. Its sole inhabitant, a lone Croat sniper, who has perhaps requisitioned this space and made it his own, carefully aims his AK47 at the enemy below, in what was once a normal residential street.

Guns are not the only tools used to eliminate 'undesirables'. Food, or lack of it, can also be manipulated into a weapon of mass destruction. By controlling the production and distribution of food in Somalia and Sudan leaders subjected hundreds of thousands to slow death by starvation and disease. In Rwanda the principal murder weapons were axes, clubs and machetes. One of Nachtwey's most memorable images is of a young Hutu man with horrendous facial scars. The photograph evokes the physical pain and mental torture suffered at the hand of his aggressors.

What is remarkable about Nachtwey is his ability to consistently create such impactful pictures. As Luc Sante points out in the book's introduction: '...Nachtwey's pictures are always compositions. Maybe we expect that the photographer...will be rendered incompetent by the sight, just as we would be incapable of finding the words to describe such a scene. Maybe it seems that the only moral option...would be to take haphazard, ill focussed snapshots. Maybe we are just projecting, wanting the camera to fall away just as we would. Nachtwey's photographs are always clear and striking compositions in part because he is probably physically incapable of taking a bad picture, but also and more importantly because he is honest and clear in his stance'.[3]

James Nachtwey
Inferno, Phaidon Press, London, 1999
38 × 27.5 cm / 15 × 10⅞ in, 480 pp
Hardback with full black cloth
382 tritone photographs
Introduction by Luc Sante; afterword by James Nachtwey; design by Stuart Smith

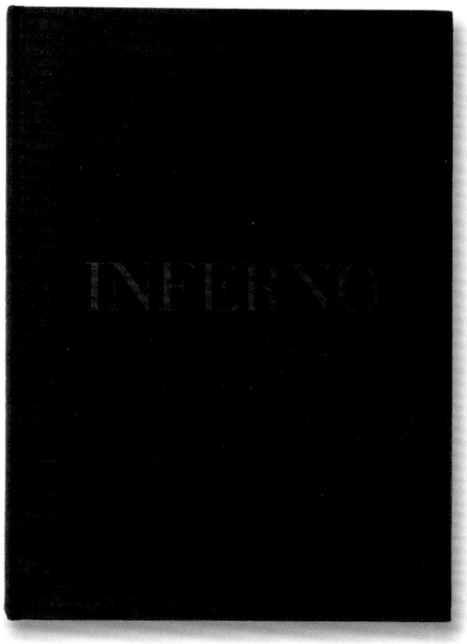
INFERNO

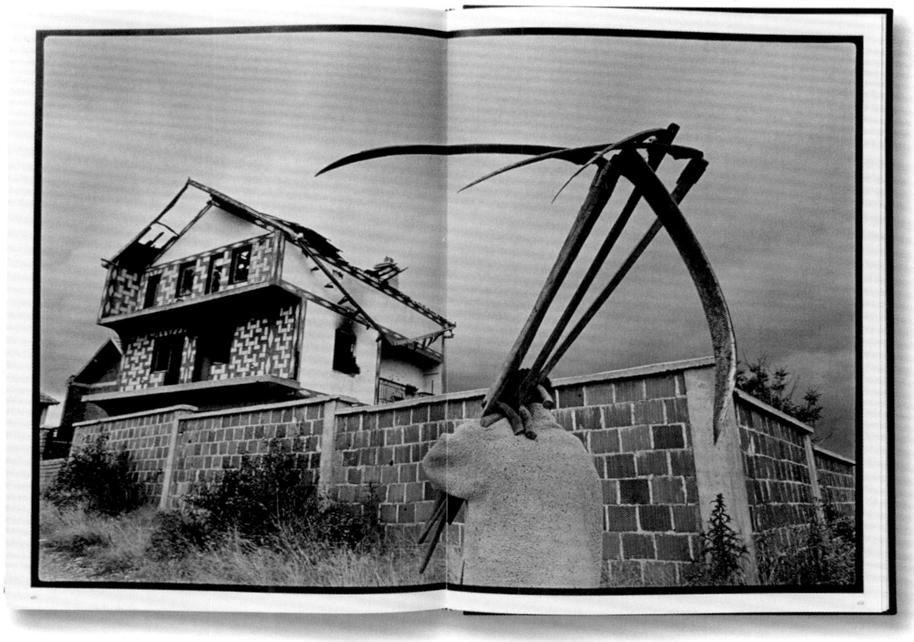

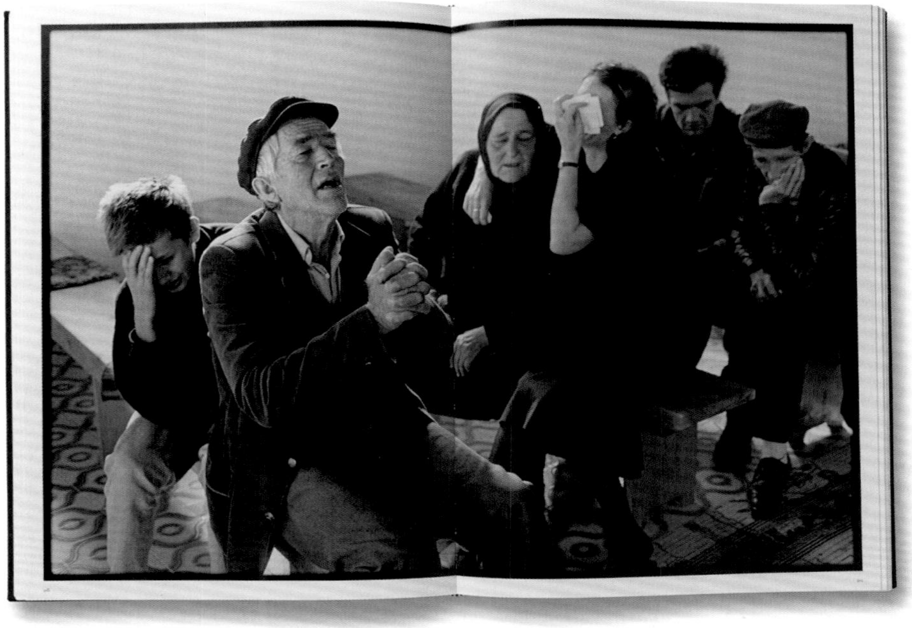

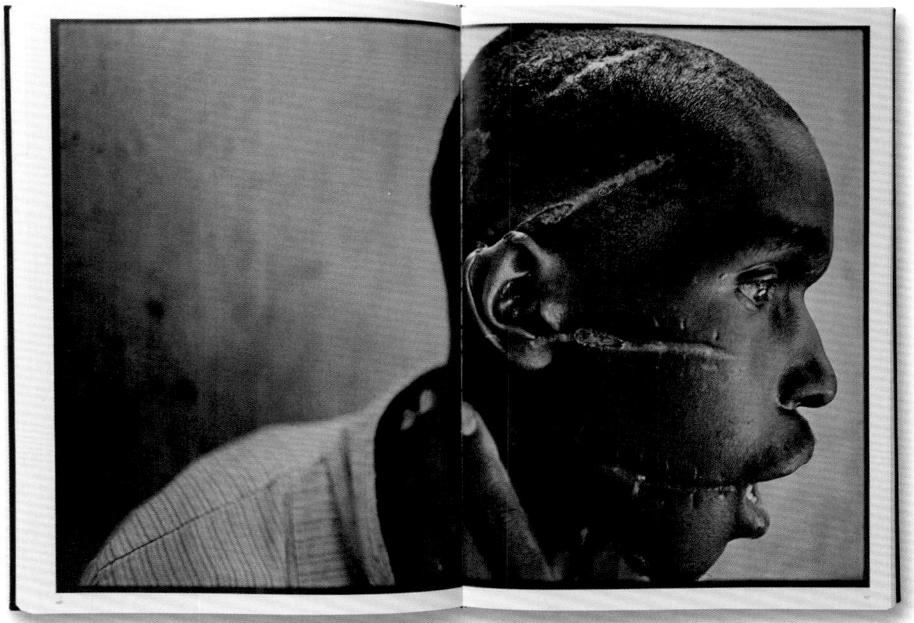

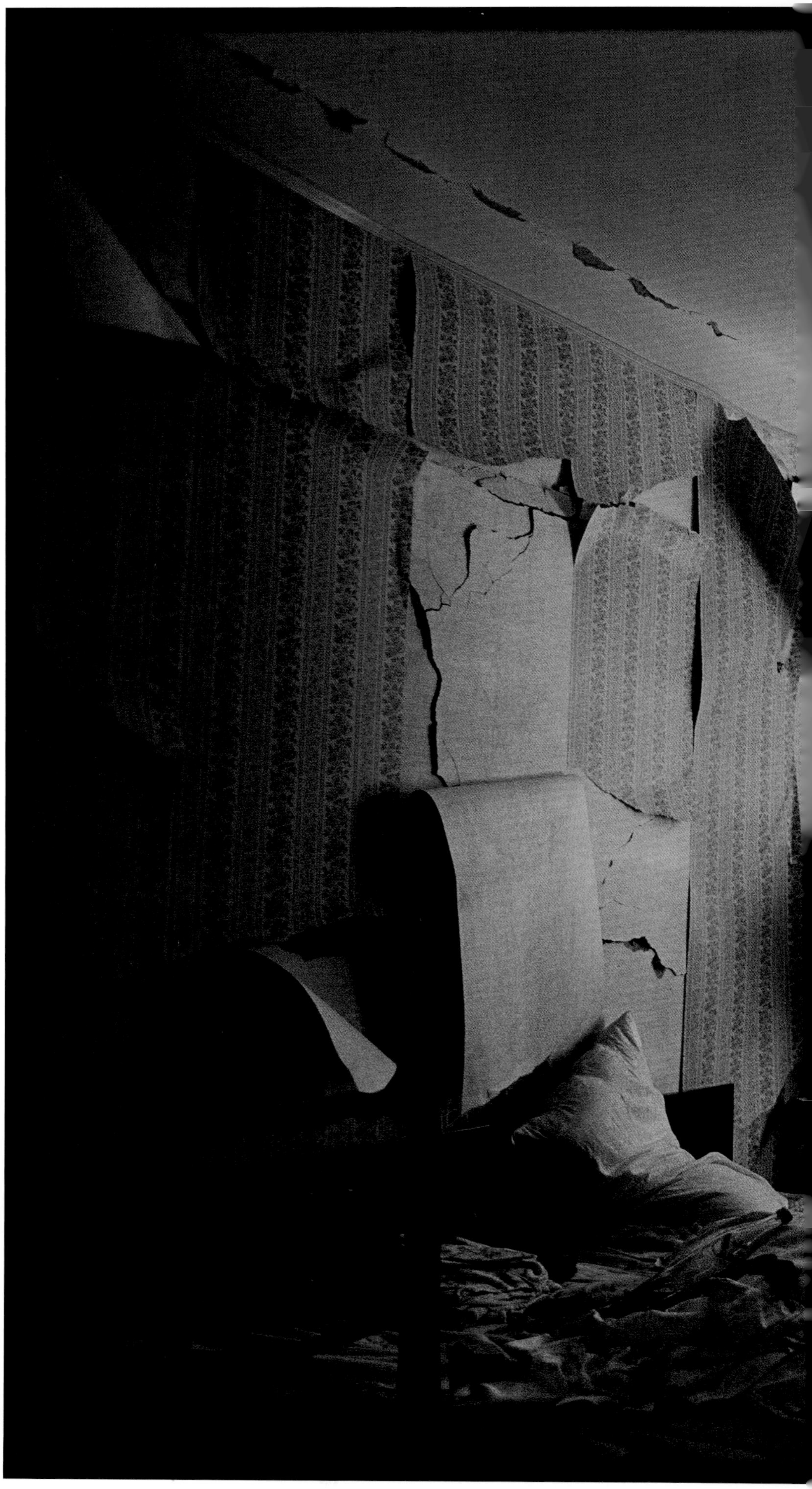

James Nachtwey
Bosnia, 1993
Ethnic cleansing in Mostar. Croat militiaman fires on his Moslem neighbours

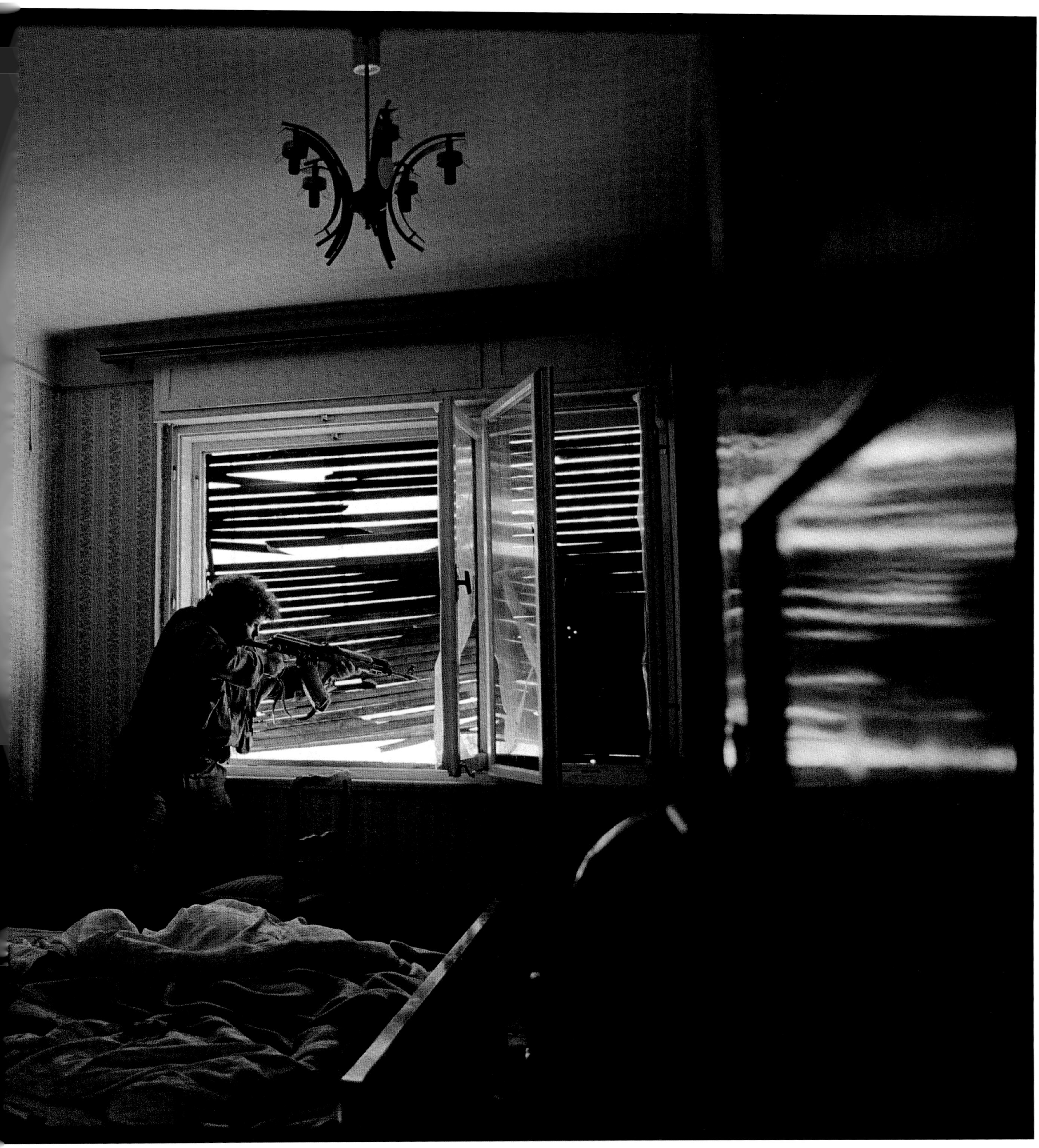

Sebastião Salgado

Beauty in photojournalism can be seen as integral to the value given those who are photographed. It is in this respect, too, that one understands why beauty is so integral to the work of Brazilian-born Sebastião Salgado. His black-and-white depiction of starvation in the Sahel desert, the Indian peoples of Latin America, and his monumental series 'Workers', a portrayal of conditions of labour around the world, have been criticised for their beauty, as if the political power of the image may be dissipated by its aesthetic look. But as art historian Julian Stallabrass has noted, Salgado's pictures 'show an expenditure of time and skill which may be taken as a homage, especially when compared with the speedy gathering of horrific images by the newspaper photographers'.[4] And for Salgado: 'I wanted to respect people as much as I could, to work to get the best composition and the most beautiful light... If you can show a situation this way – get the beauty and nobility along with the despair – then you can show someone in America or France that these people are not different. I wanted Americans to look at the pictures of these people and see themselves'.[5]

Between 1984 and 1985 Salgado spent fifteen months documenting the drought-striken Sahel region of Africa in the countries of Chad, Ethiopia, Mali and the Sudan, where approximately a million people died from malnutrition. They were notably distinct from the typical tendencies of disaster photojournalism, that made the African people, as Fred Ritchin put it, 'different from us in their victimization – bereft with swollen bellies, covered in flies, surrendering to their cirumstances'.[6] Published only as books in Europe at the time when they were taken, the pictures had to wait two decades before becoming a book in the USA.

Salagado has said that he never puts himself into the situation where he has a moral question about whether he has the right to photograph 'when the death is there in front of me'. This is because he has asked himself the more important questions – 'Do we have the right to the division of resources that we have in the world? Do I have the right to have the house that I have, to live where I live? Do I have the right to eat when others don't eat?'[7]

Sebastião Salgado
Draped in blankets to keep out the cold morning wind, refugees wait outside Korem camp, Ethiopia, 1984
Gelatin silver print, dimensions variable

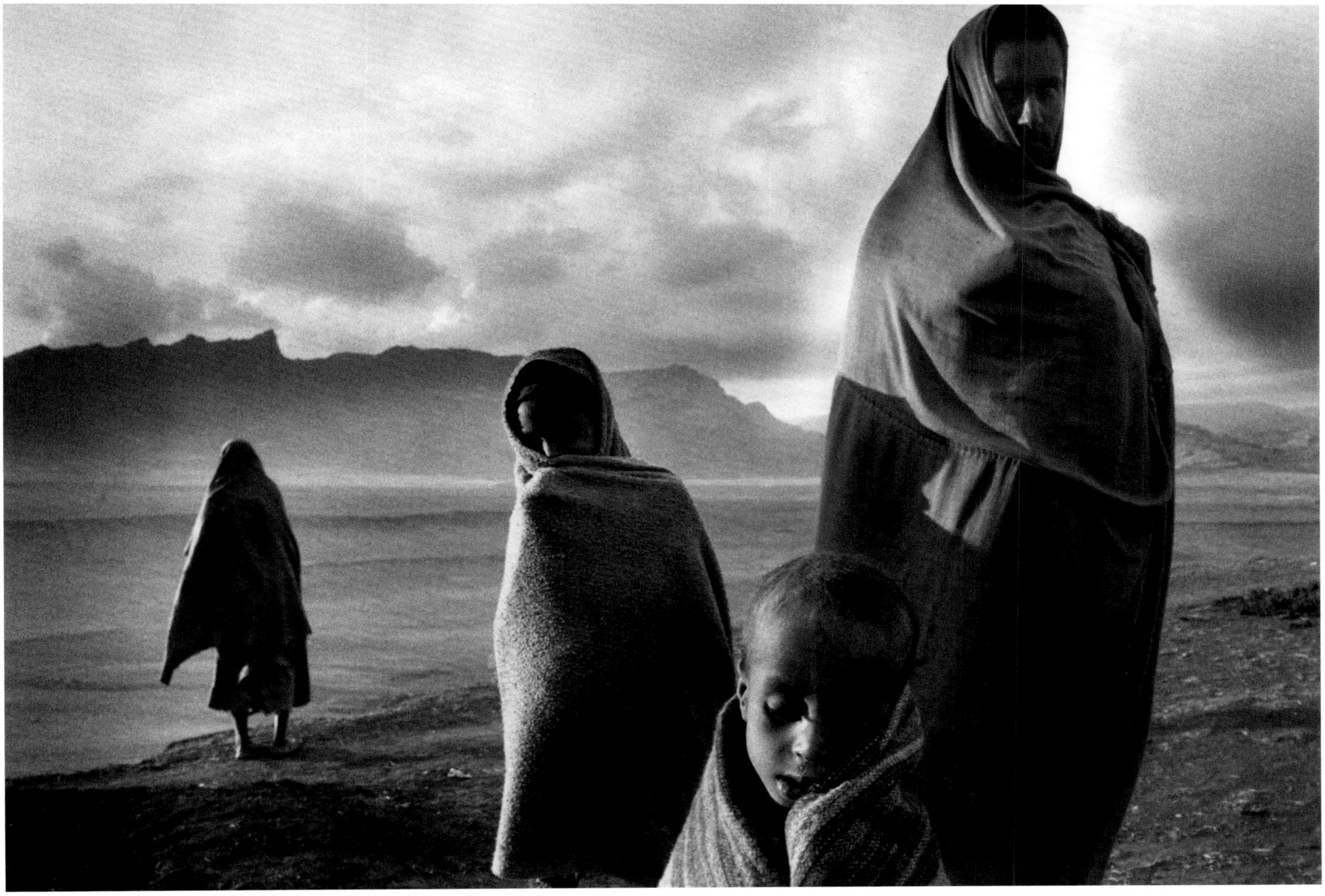

Vietnam

Larry Burrows

In looking at the strategies photographers have adopted in representing traumatic historical events, the question of aesthetics is integral. In some senses the New Photojournalism could be traced back earlier than Andy Grundberg suggested. In the coverage of war in Vietnam, much of what characterized the New Photojournalism was already evident in the work of such feature photographers as Don McCullin and Larry Burrows. As Susan Moeller has pointed out, the most iconic pictures of the war – Malcolm Browne's 1963 picture of a burning monk, Eddie Adams's 1968 photograph of the Tet execution, Huynh Cong (Nick) Ut's 1972 photograph of napalmed children – were those taken by the breaking-news photojournalists, working at such speed and immediacy they had to turn a story around in a couple of days.[8] As a feature photographer, Larry Burrows had the leisure to work on an article for a month to six weeks.

Burrows' 1965 *Life Magazine* picture story, 'One Ride with Yankee Papa 13', has as its subject a young lance-corporal, James Farley, crew chief of the helicopter Yankee Papa 13; the photographer saw him as being like the kid next door. The dramatic and emotional story that unfolds through the pictures shows the impact of war on one individual and narrates his loss of innocence. Burrows 'with a brave crew in a deadly fight' – as *Life's* front page headlines the story – shows Farley's attempted but failed rescue of the pilot of another helicopter that had been shot down. Burrows shows us how, having rescued the co-pilot and crewman, Farley is devastated as he is unable to stop the co-pilot dying from his injuries. The sequence ends with a portrait of Farley alone in a storeroom, sobbing. The picture is in stark contrast to the earlier full-length smiling portrait as he loads his machine guns, as well as a dramatic photograph taken from a camera mounted on a rig attached to his machine gun as Farley fires it from his helicopter.

This picture story is about being close to the action. At the same time, however, we are not just shown atrocity. Witnessing here is also indirect, as it is mediated through the central character. Through Farley's portrait we get a human response to the horror of war.

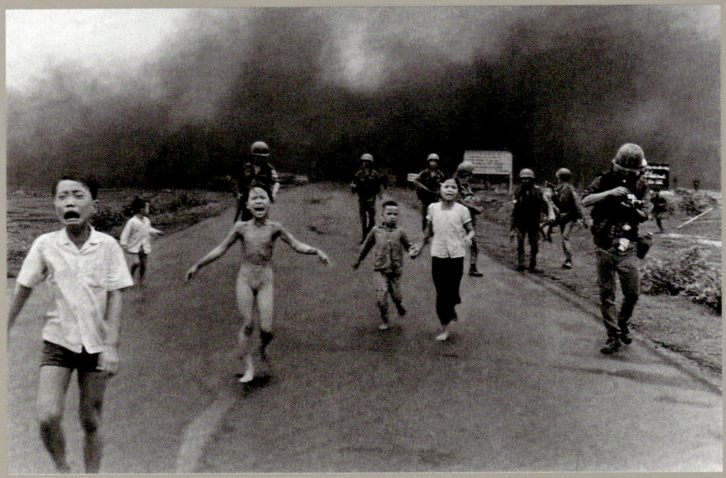

Nick Ut
Children Fleeing an American Napalm Strike, 1972
Gelatin silver print, dimensions variable

Larry Burrows
Life Magazine, April 16, 1965
34 × 26.2 cm / 13⅜ × 10⅜ in

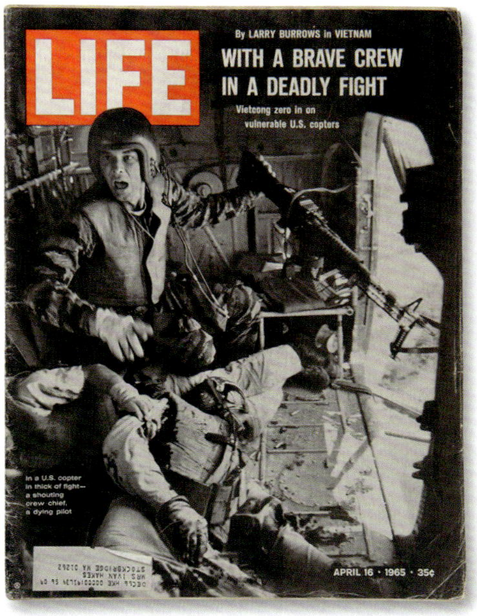

LIFE

By LARRY BURROWS in VIETNAM

WITH A BRAVE CREW IN A DEADLY FIGHT

Vietcong zero in on vulnerable U.S. copters

In a U.S. copter in thick of fight—a shouting crew chief, a dying pilot

APRIL 16 · 1965 · 35¢

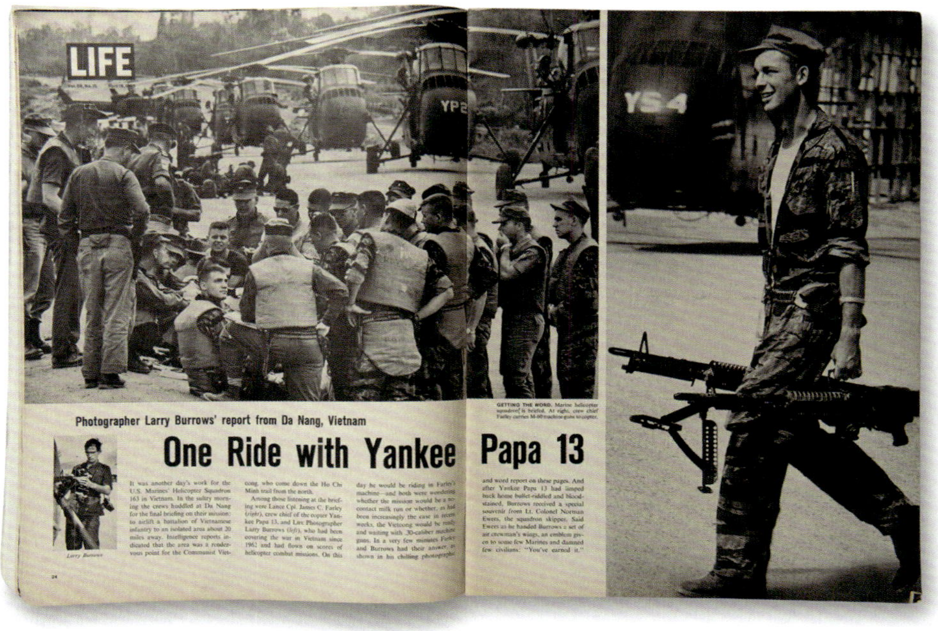

LIFE

Photographer Larry Burrows' report from Da Nang, Vietnam

One Ride with Yankee Papa 13

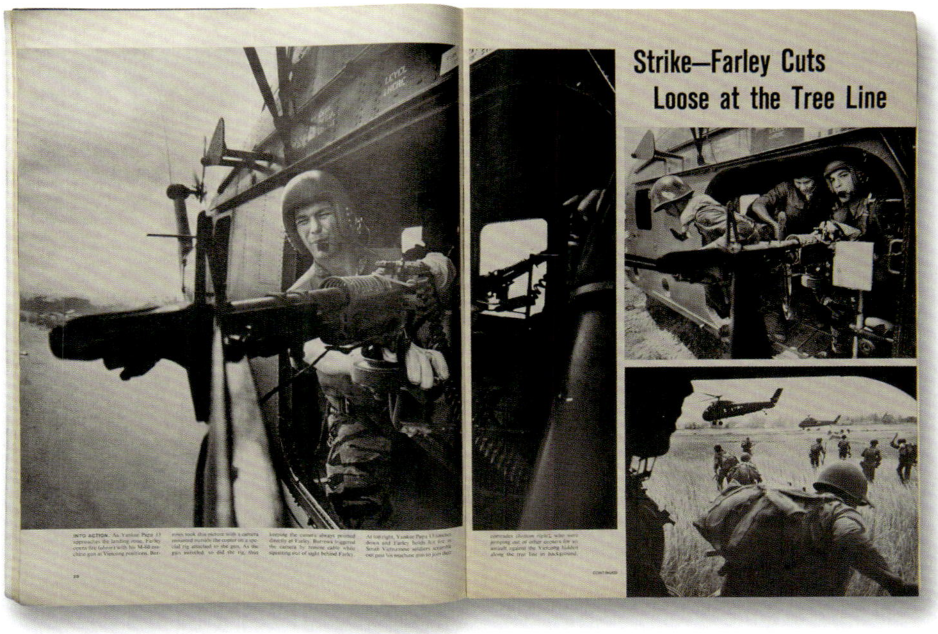

Strike—Farley Cuts Loose at the Tree Line

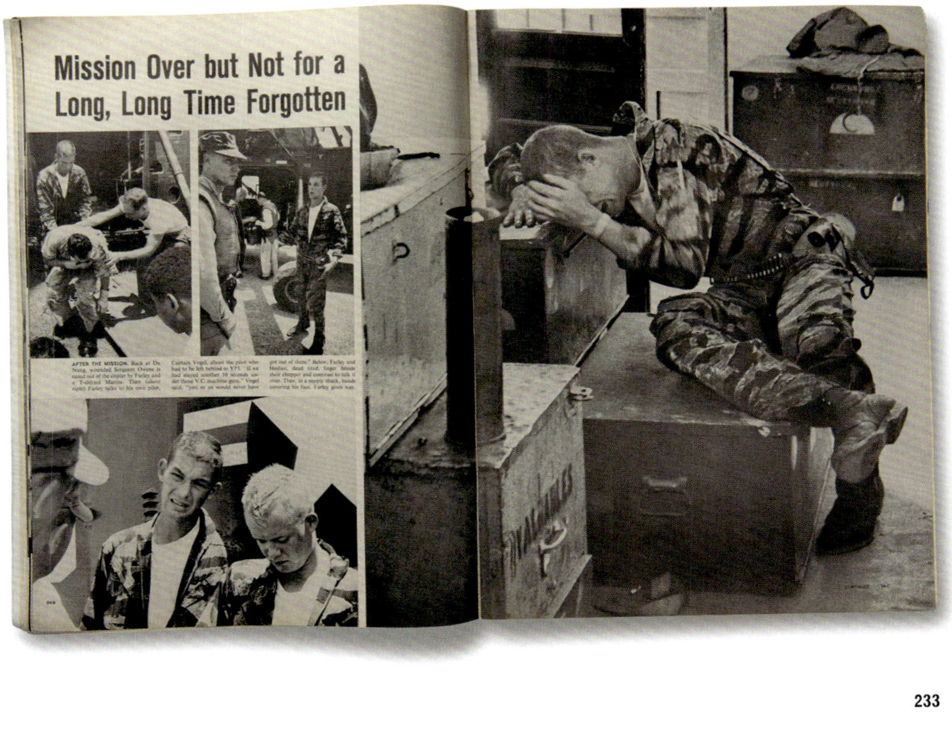

Mission Over but Not for a Long, Long Time Forgotten

Judith Joy Ross

Judith Joy Ross is not a war photographer, but she has made work that pays tribute to the psychological effect of war. The emphasis on the subjective and affective response to the conflict lies behind the series of photographs that she took at the Washington Vietnam Veterans Memorial. Ross makes portraits of those who have come to view the memorial, far from both the atrocities of war itself and from photojournalism. Ross's work offers a reflective space that parallels the introspective effect and purpose of the memorial itself but also acknowledges something felt and experienced through a variety of people. This sense of distraction and absorption makes demands of the viewer that are different from the engagement with the immediacy and impact of pictures in a newspaper or magazine. It is a photographic augmentation of the memorial itself and addresses us in a very different way from photojournalism, in which the message is often immediate and there is little space for reflection. There is also a temporal shift as we encounter the stillness of the portrait as opposed to the drama of photo-reportage.

Judith Joy Ross
Untitled, from the series 'Portraits at the Vietnam Veterans Memorial, Washington, D.C.', 1984
Gold-toned gelatin silver print
24.4 × 19.4 cm / 9½ × 7½ in

Untitled, from the series 'Portraits at the Vietnam Veterans Memorial, Washington, D.C.', 1984
Gold-toned gelatin silver print
24.4 × 19.4 cm / 9½ × 7½ in

Untitled, from the series 'Portraits at the Vietnam Veterans Memorial, Washington, D.C.', 1984
Gold-toned gelatin silver print
24.4 × 19.4 cm / 9½ × 7½ in

Untitled, from the series 'Portraits at the Vietnam Veterans Memorial, Washington, D.C.', 1984
Gold-toned gelatin silver print
24.4 × 19.4 cm / 9½ × 7½ in

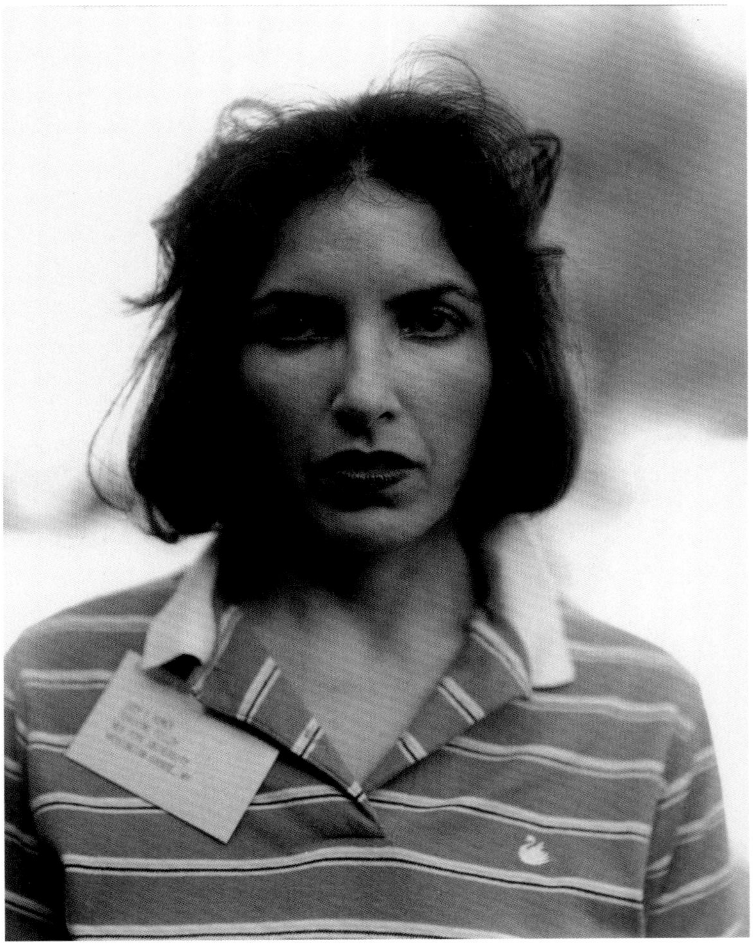

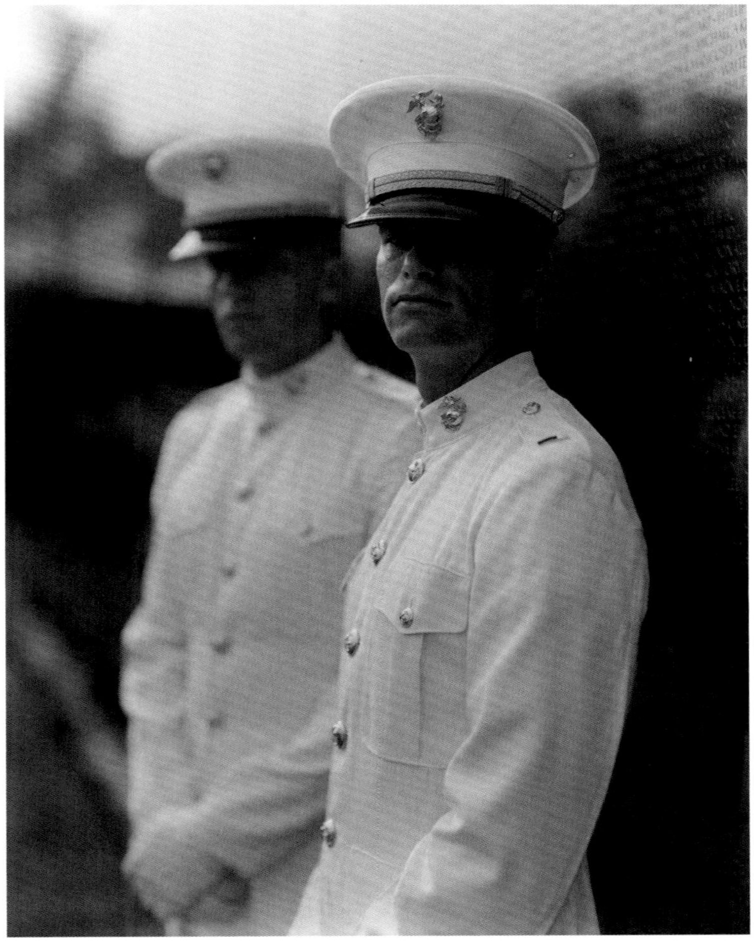

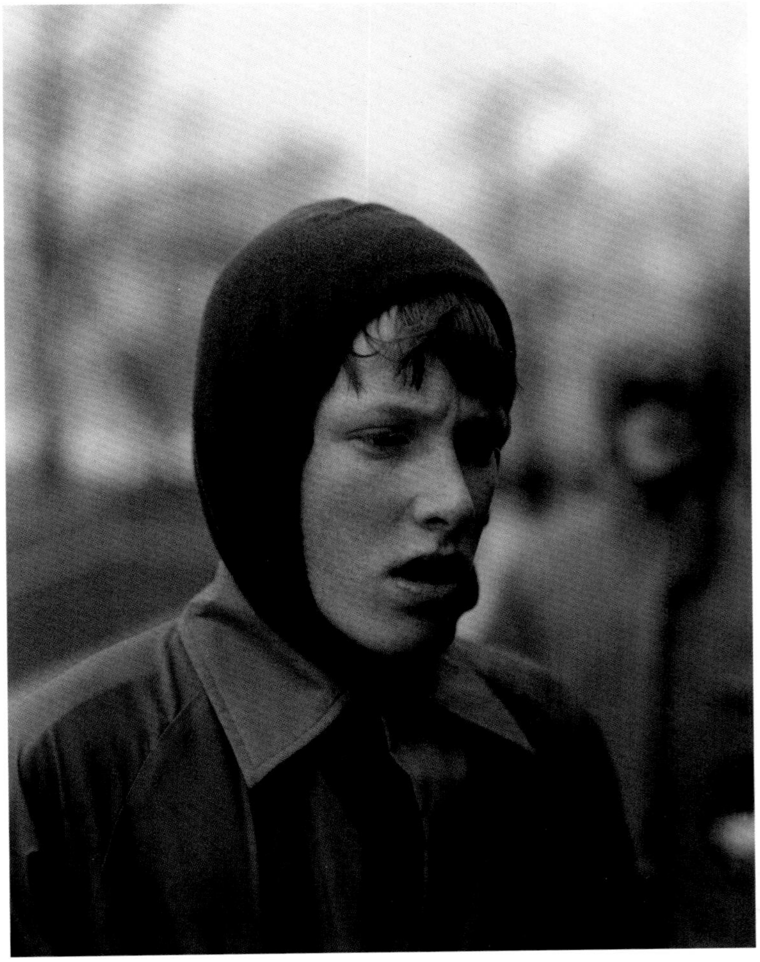

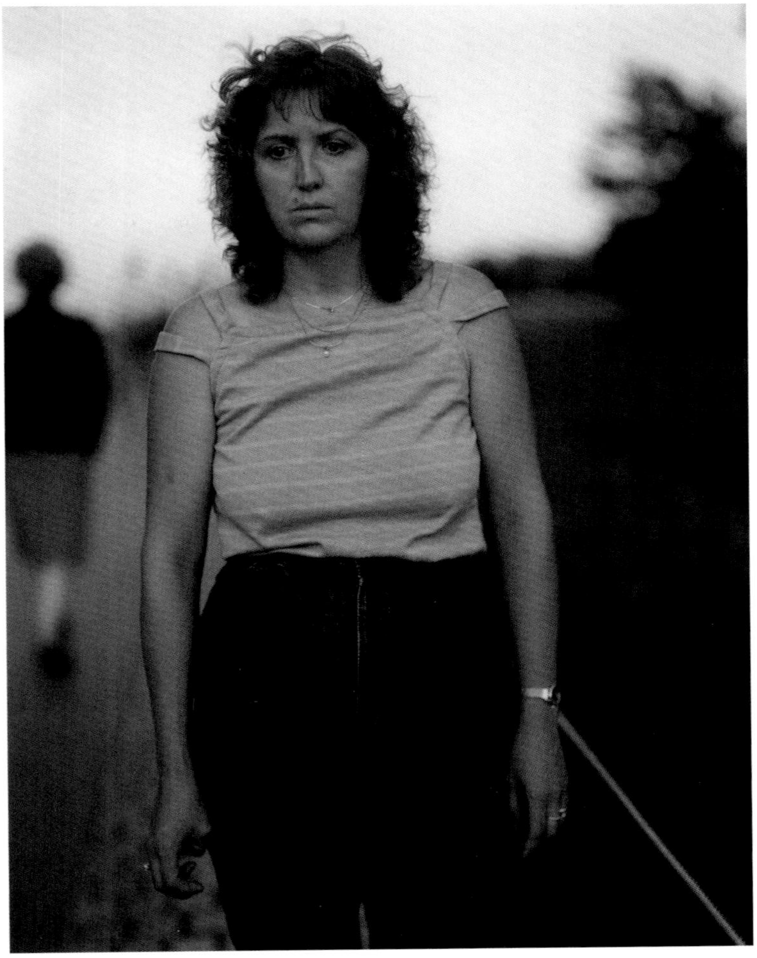

Paul Graham

In relation to media coverage of violent events in Northern Ireland, the British artist Paul Graham makes a powerful intervention with his *Man Watching TV News Broadcast of Lynching, Belfast* (1988). Here he shows us a man's response to the shocking news footage of the murder of two soldiers trapped in the middle of a Republican funeral. The TV is out of frame and instead Graham's photograph concentrates upon the man's expression: mouth agape, his stunned absorption in the broadcast registers an emotionalism in contrast to the dispassionate recording of the awful event by cameramen who dared not intervene.

Graham's use of ellipsis points to certain inadequacies and insufficiencies within direct photographic reporting. Like Judith Joy Ross's work, his picture is about mediation. But nevertheless, much as it sets up a contrast with media coverage, it also acknowledges the power of that reporting. The man is moved not by art, but by the power of an horrific news event as it is broadcast.

Paul Graham
Man Watching TV News Broadcast of Lynching, Belfast, 1988
Colour photograph
152 × 114 cm / 59⅞ × 44⅞ in

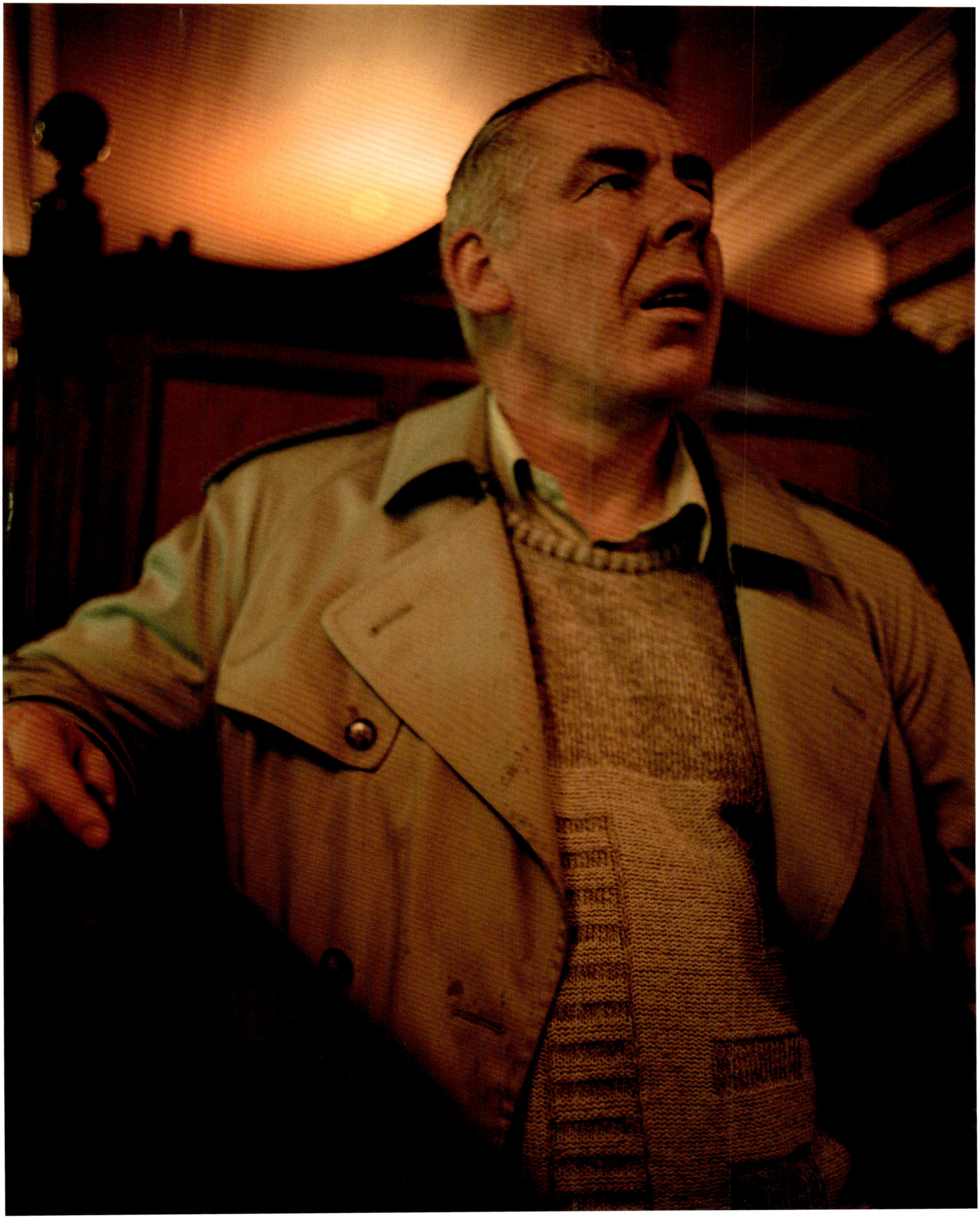

An-My Lê

An-My Lê uses the genre of landscape photography to explore how we remember, glorify and imagine war. Born in Saigon in 1960, she moved to the United States as a refugee in 1975. She went back to Vietnam several times, and her beautiful, meticulous black-and-white pictures of her home country represent her attempts to reconcile memories of her childhood home with the contemporary landscape. She created this series to explore, as she has put it, 'the Vietnam of the mind'.[9]

Her photography deals with how war is remembered and also, in the case of the war re-enactors, reconstructed. In her series 'Small Wars' she recorded the performances of Vietnam War re-enactment societies in Virginia in the United States. On one hand this is a postmodern gesture, about how conflict cannot be represented and how attempts to represent it are caught up in other images. But on the other it also deals with Lê's own relationship to history. Participating in the reconstructions, she had to enter into fantasy worlds and play the 'enemy' soldier. Such photographs tap into the peculiar imaginings and identifications associated with the Vietnam War, and the anomaly of using an American landscape as the setting is significant. Its distinction is evident in its contrast with the landscapes Lê made back in Vietnam, and her work also reflects how American war films have shaped her attempts to represent her native land.

An-My Lê
Untitled, Lao Bao il, 1998
Gelatin silver print
50.8 × 60.9 cm / 20 × 24 in

Le Sniper 1, 1999–2002
Gelatin silver print
67.3 × 96.5 cm / 26½ × 38 in

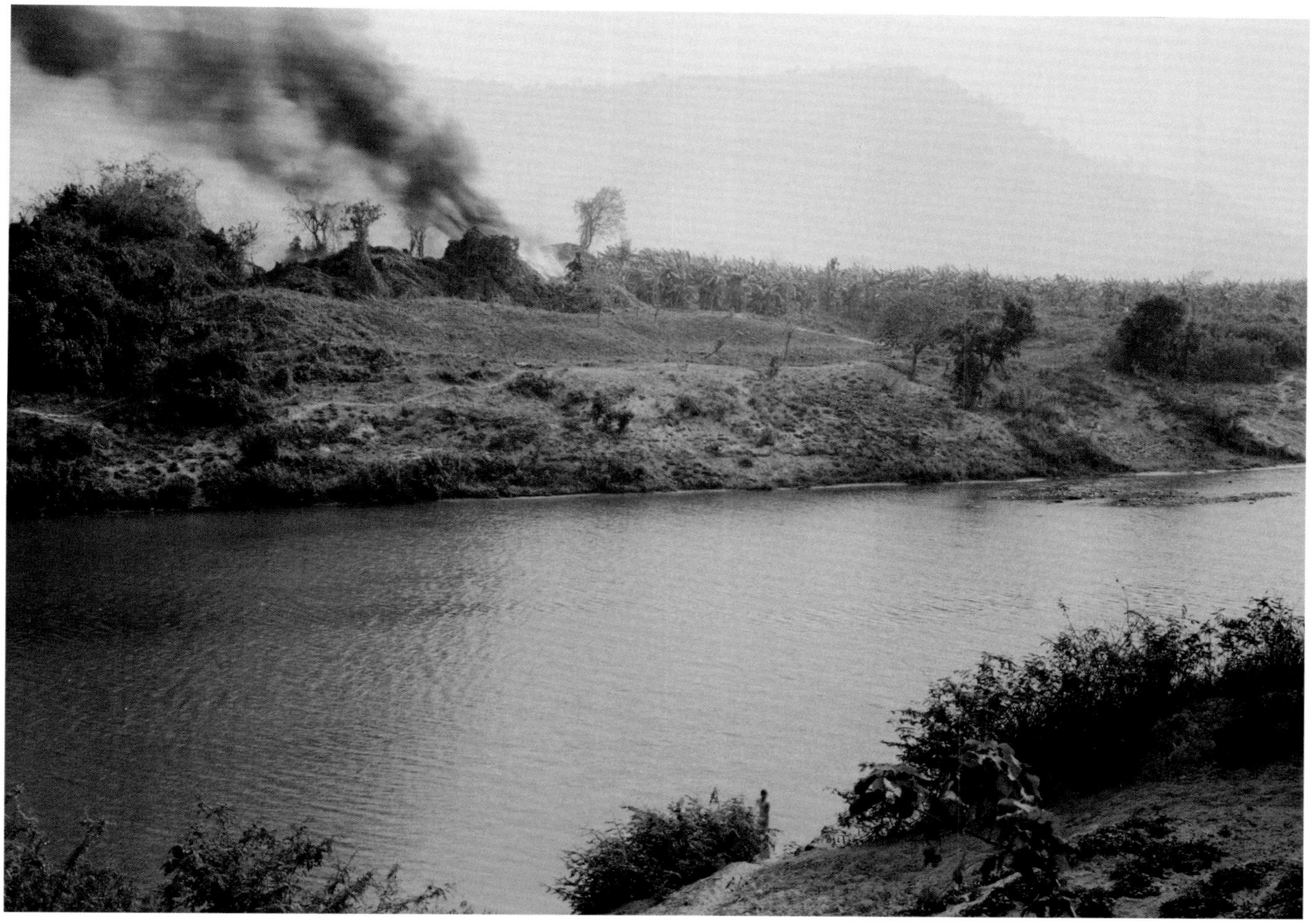

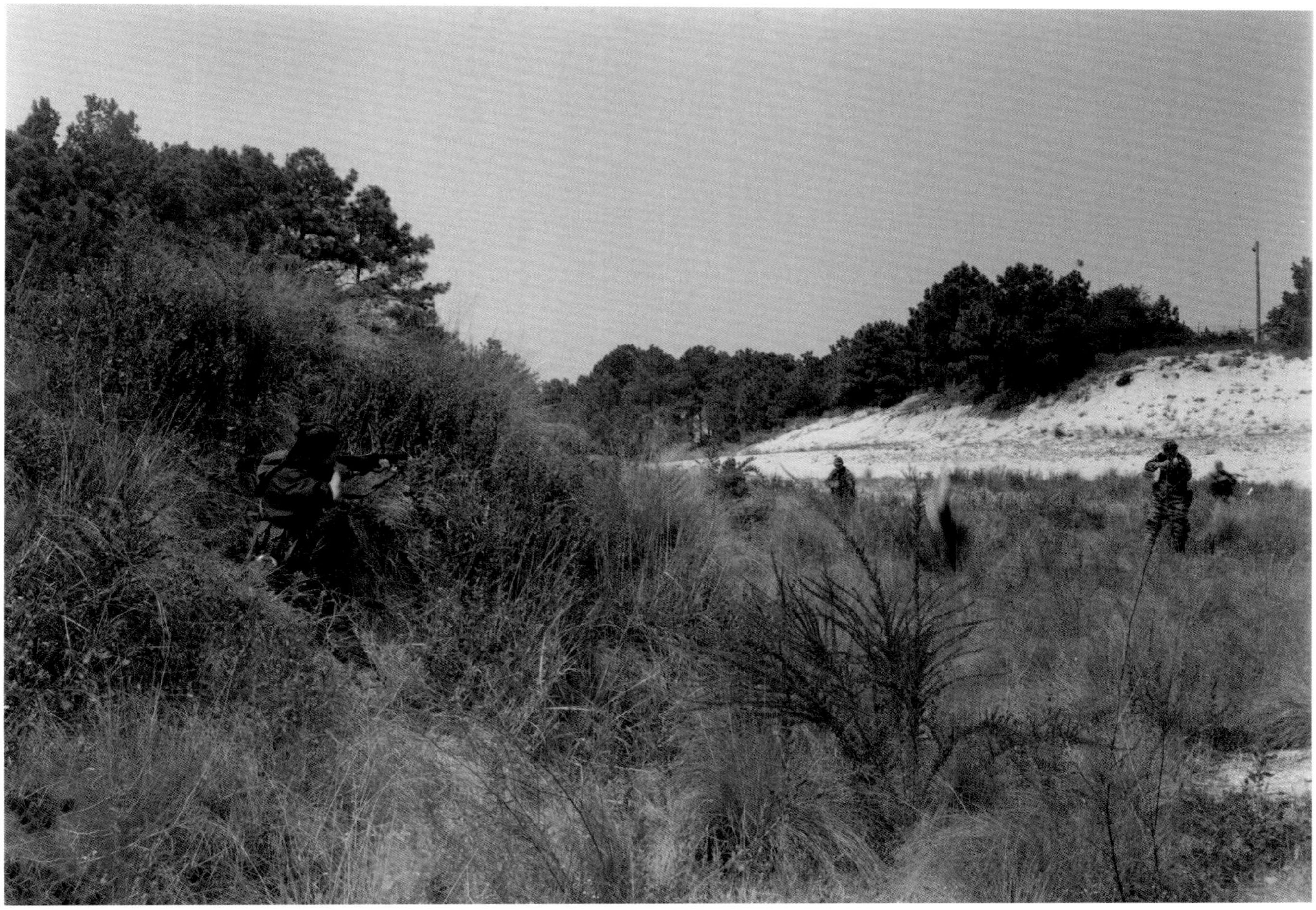

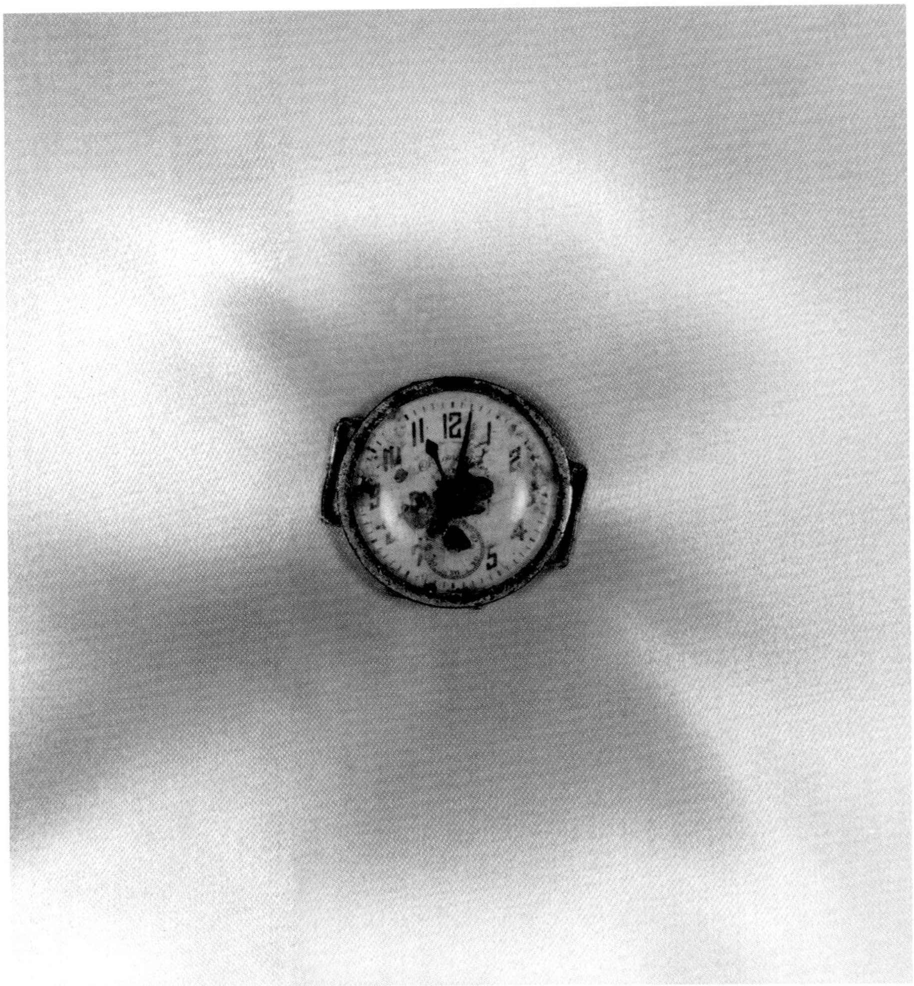

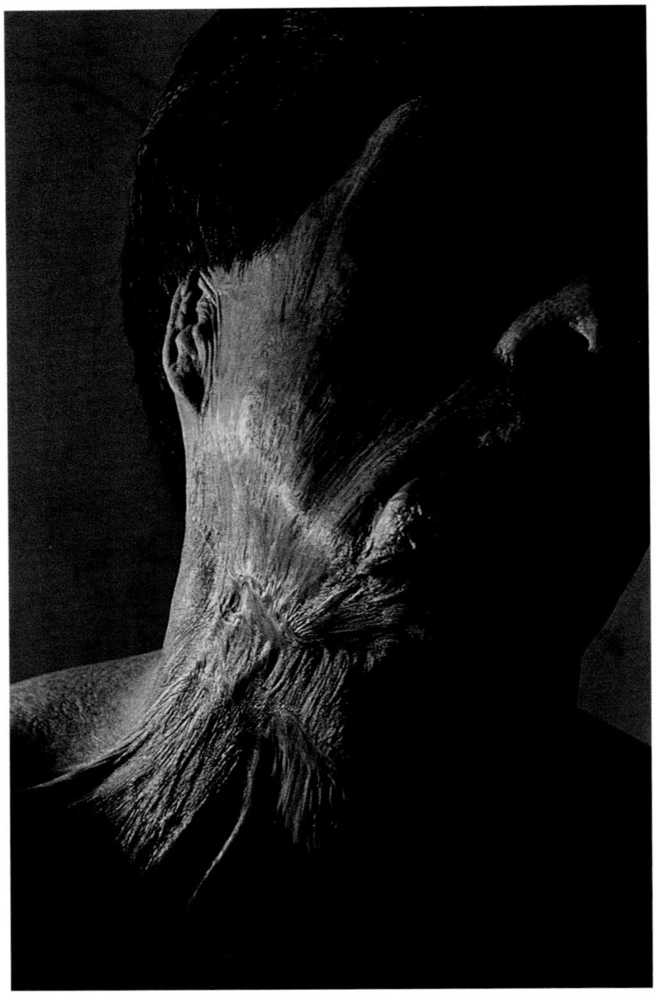

Shomei Tomatsu

Aftermath

When the Americans arrived in defeated Japan in 1945, they confiscated Japanese film footage of the effects of the atomic bombs and ordered all photographs to be handed over. The first feature photographs of Nagasaki and Hiroshima did not appear until 1952, four months after the US occupation ended. Shomei Tomatsu's photographs offer a poetic and elliptical response to the horrific devastation of the atomic bomb. He uses photography in an allegorical way, seeing in the medium's light writing an awful corollary of the effects of the atomic blast itself. Tomatsu was commissioned to photograph Nagasaki by the Japan Council Against Atomic and Hydrogen Bombs. They proposed a book to be published in English and Russian to represent the legacy of Hiroshima and Nagasaki, to remind of the horrors caused by nuclear weapons. Tomatsu was commissioned to photograph Nagasaki while Ken Domon photographed Hiroshima. Their joint collection was published in 1961, but Tomatsu did not publish all his pictures until 1966 in the book *11:02 Nagasaki*, its title taken from one of his most iconic pictures, of a watch stopped at the time the bomb detonated. Tomatsu's pictures were not polemical but subtle. In contrast, Domon photographed gruesome close-ups of reconstructive surgery. Pain in Tomatsu's pictures is registered using analogies with photography, from a stopped watch, the precise index of the time of the blast, and a familiar and touching everyday human detail, to the iconoclastic destruction unleashed by the bomb, seen in the faceless head of a statue of an angel in the Catholic cathedral at Urakami, located almost directly below where the bomb was dropped.

There was an inclination in Japan to ostracize the surviving victims of the atomic blast. Burns and chronic sickness were thought shameful and hidden away by families. Tomatsu made a series of powerful portraits of such survivors, their scarred bodies and faces evidence of the awful destruction of the atomic blast. In his portrait *Yamaguchi Senji, who was injured 1.2 kilometres from the epicentre of the blast, Nagasaki* (1962), the very lighting of the picture, as Ian Jeffrey has noted, restages the blinding of the explosion.[10] The man turns away from the camera, the light dramatically illuminating the terrible scarring. He seems to be re-enacting the event, turning away from the brightness as if protecting his eyes.

In memorializing and making a poetic tribute to an event that is beyond adequate representation, documentary becomes inappropriate. Tomatsu's photography is both evidentiary and poetic, shifting between a record of objects distorted and damaged by the blast and moving portraits in which scars are a raw, painful and graphic index of the blast. Tomatsu's pictures might be identified as aftermath photography: he comes after the event and makes pictures in response to the enduring effects of the horror.

Shomei Tomatsu
A wristwatch dug up approximately 0.7 km from the epicenter of the explosion. Nagasaki, 1961
Gelatin silver print
Dimensions variable

Yamaguchi Senji who was injured 1.2 km from the epicentre of the blast, Nagasaki, 1962
Gelatin silver print
Dimensions variable

Christian Boltanski

Christian Boltanski's mother was a French Catholic while his father was a Polish-Jewish Frenchman who survived World War II by hiding in the family home. In a 1992 interview Boltanski acknowleged that the Holocaust is important in his work, but clarified, '[The work] is perhaps after, around, but not about the Holocaust.'[11] In relation to documentary footage he has said: 'I have never used images from the camps, it would be impossible for me, it would be something too shameful to use, too sacred.'[12] Instead, Boltanski's installations from the 1980s rely on the potential pathos and affective charge of photography. Ellipsis is a strategy Boltanski uses in relation to the Holocaust, avoiding explicit documentary photographs.

Boltanski made a series of works involving reshooting portraits taken from grammar school group photographs and high-school yearbooks of Jewish children from the 1930s. In *Autel Lycée Chases*, the source was a 1931 graduating-class portrait from a Jewish high school that Boltanski found in a book on Jews of Vienna. From 1987 to 1990 he made numerous variations based on this photo and on a 1939 group portrait of Jewish children posing in costume for Purim, the holiday that celebrates the biblical escape of Persian Jews from mass extermination. He isolates each of the children's faces, blown up and rephotographed so they lose individual features. The blown-up faces are no longer subjects. The photographic portrait is emptied out and made cadaverous; as Boltanski says, they 'became a sort of skull.'[13] In some installations, rusty tin boxes provide support for the photographs, each portrait is lit with overhanging desk lamps that blind and obscure the faces, their cables running down over the pictures. The lamps suggest interrogation and with their light burning into the portraits, served to emphasize the vulnerability and fragility of both the photographs and the people depicted.

While he never used pictures of the death camps, Boltanski did rephotograph gruesome images of murders for the series 'El Caso', first shown at the Museo nacional centro de arte Reina Sofia in Madrid in May 1988. The title of the work borrows from a Spanish tabloid that is infamous for its sensational use of pictures of violent and brutal deaths. In the installation, snapshot portraits of the victims, with lamps above the faces, were each displayed above a tin box containing newspaper photos of the victim's corpse. In a commission made for the Swiss art journal *Parkett*, Boltanski made the hidden pictures visible in the form of a pocket-size book. The miniature size acknowledges our awkward relation to the atrocity images; the book is so small you could hide it in your hands when viewing.

Christian Boltanski
El Caso, 1989
Booklet with 17 photographs
5 × 8 × 0.6 cm / 2 × 3 × ¼ in

Autel Lycée Chases, 1988
Cans, lamps, black and white photographs
240 × 165 cm / 94½ × 65 in

Réserve des Suisses morts, 1990
1,168 boxes, photographs, lamps
Dimensions variable

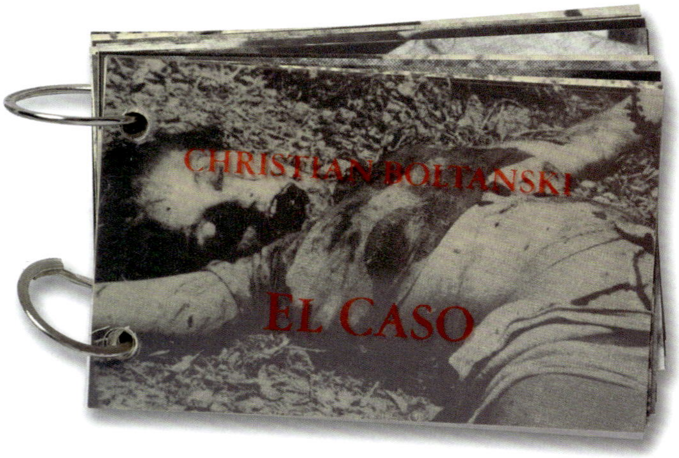
CHRISTIAN BOLTANSKI
EL CASO

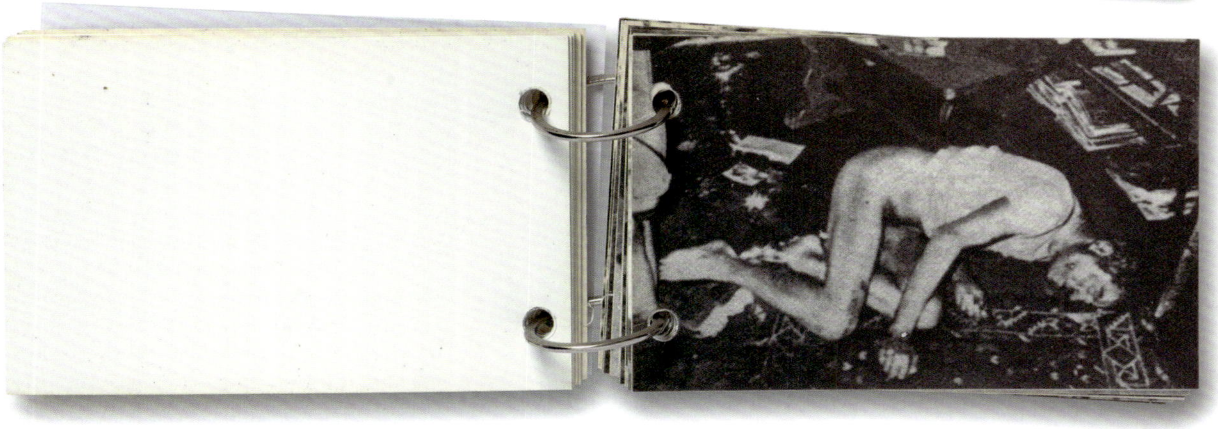

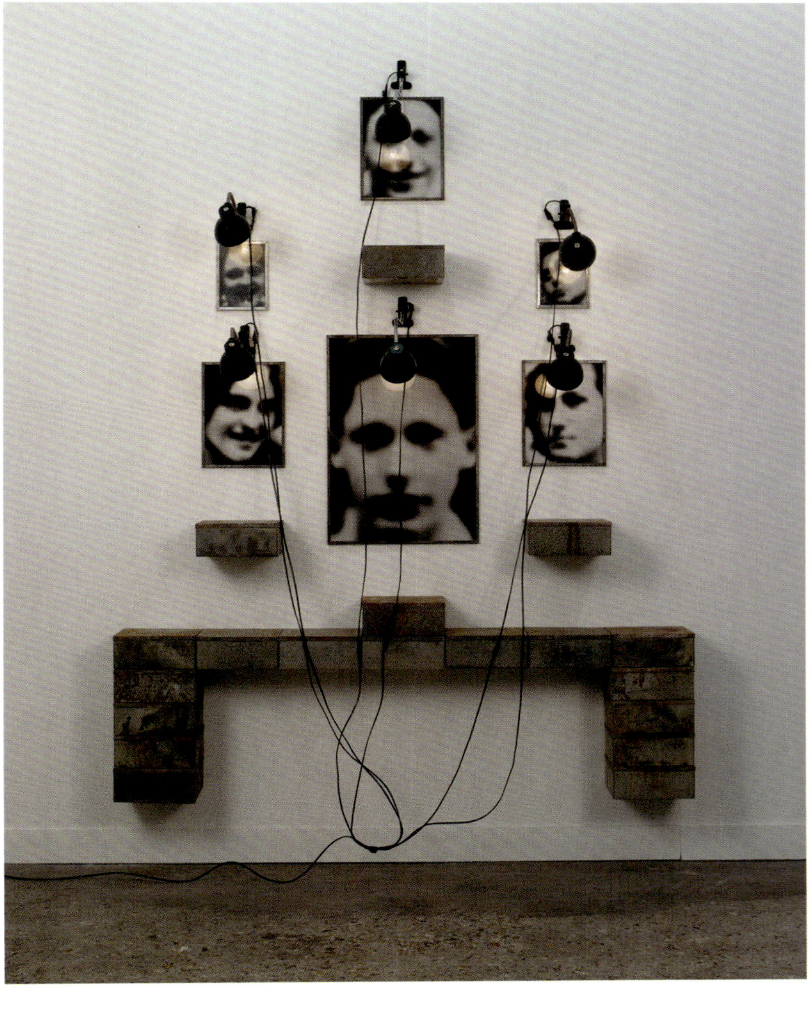

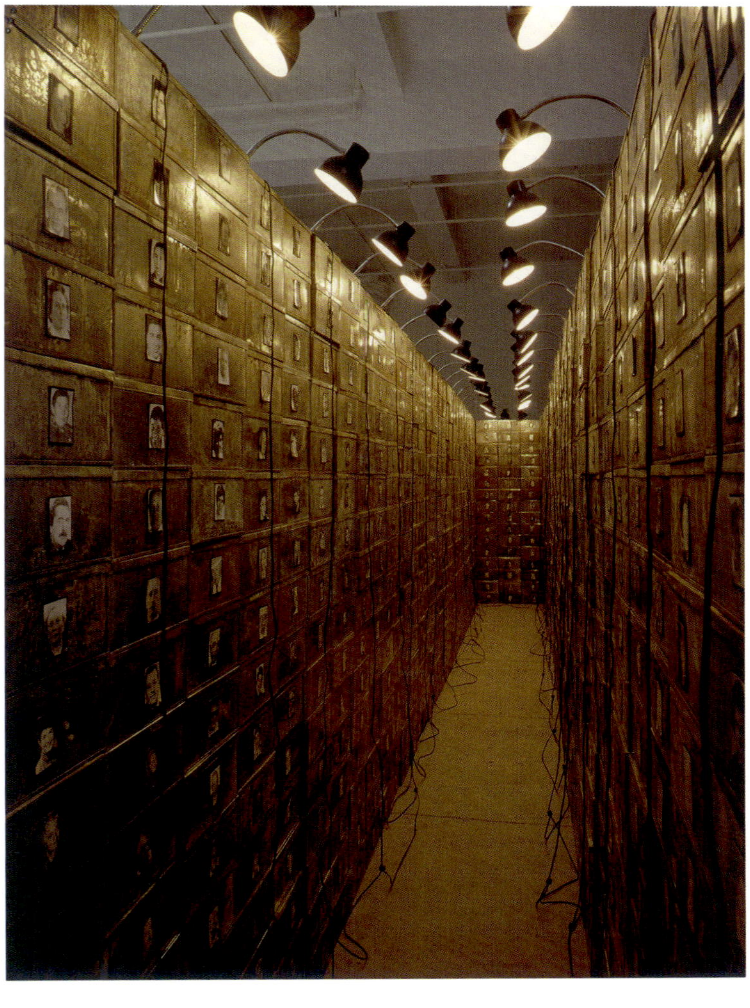

Daniel Blaufuks

The Portuguese artist Daniel Blaufuks fixes and dwells on the past in relation to the disappearance of beings, their brutal extinction and vanishing. Blaufuks slowed down and saturated red fragments of footage of a 1944 'Staged Nazi Film' (the words are stamped throughout the film in its top right corner) of Theresienstadt, a concentration camp that had been cleaned up and transformed in order to deceive a visiting Red Cross consortium. He also made photographic stills of people and faces from the film, again all stained red. One shows children and adults gathered around a table, the iconography redolent of the normalcy and familiarity of a family snapshot, an allusion intended to disguise the very abnormality, inhumanity and horrors of the camp.

Theresienstadt, now called Terezín, was a former military garrison used by the Nazis not as an extermination camp – although 30,000 people died there of starvation and disease – but as a holding station in which Jews were housed until they were sent to other camps to be murdered. Blaufuks went to Terezín, now a museum, as a result of an obsession with a photograph used in W.G. Sebald's book *Austerlitz*, showing what appears to be an office space, its walls filled from floor to ceiling with shelves bearing files. Blaufuks made his own photograph of the bureaucratic space, in colour. The office-like room was a *Geschaftszimmer*, a business room, located in the prison in the camp and used as a control room.

Blaufuks' photograph of the control room is in effect a picture of an archive. In this way it is integral to his characteristic use of photography, which involves the neutrality and dry formality of a forensic and classifying mode of depiction. But this simple gathering of evidence has a recurrent emphasis on absences, of things missing or not disclosed: the back of a photograph bearing only the stamped message, 'PORST KONIGSBILD August 1989'; a 35mm colour negative strip that maintains the privacy of its four snapshot images, locked in the negative like fossils in amber.

Two paired black-and-white photographs show a clock face at six o'clock and a quarter past six. The clock suggests a connection with administration and bureaucracy. The gap between the photographs and the times they show is important, and like much of Blaufuks' art puts emphasis on something that is absent or escapes representation. What happened in the fifteen minutes that elapsed? The two pictures of the clock are terrifying in many ways, a stark reminder that what happened happened, that the clock cannot be turned back, that nothing can change what took place. The clock is thus a brutal and ruthless counterpoint to the obsession with the faces of the Jews in the Theresienstadt film, the need to restore and prolong their presence, however ghostly, in the wake of their brutal erasure. We may well look at the appearance of a family seated around a dining table, but we see it fully aware that the Final Solution wiped out whole families, leaving no-one to remember them.

Daniel Blaufuks
Fifteen Minutes, from the series 'The Business of Living', 2010
Inkjet print, 30 × 40 × 2 cm / 11⅞ × 15¾ × ¾ in

Fifteen Minutes, from the series 'The Business of Living', 2010
Inkjet print, 30 × 40 × 2 cm / 11⅞ × 15¾ × ¾ in

Untitled, from the series 'Terezin', 2007
Inkjet print, 100 × 160 cm / 39⅜ × 63 in

Album Nr. 22, from the series 'The Archive', 2008
C-print, 100 × 80 cm / 39⅜ × 31½ in →

Untitled, from the series 'Terezin', 2007
Inkjet print, 100 × 160 cm / 39⅜ × 63 in →

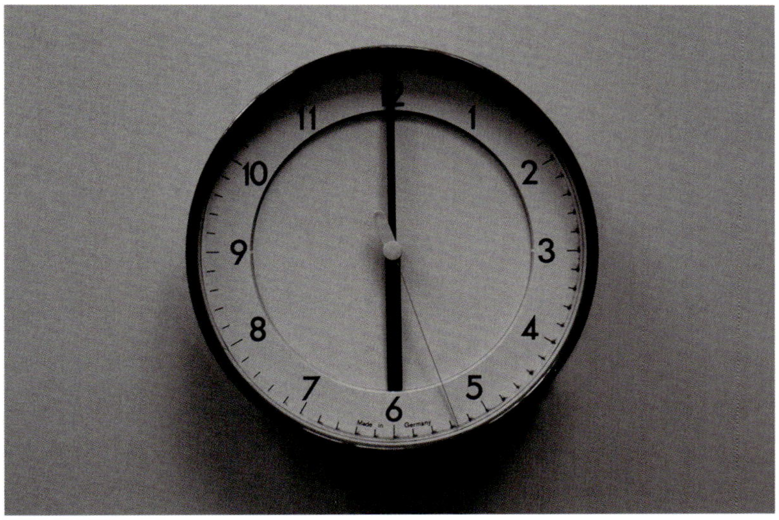

Made in Germany

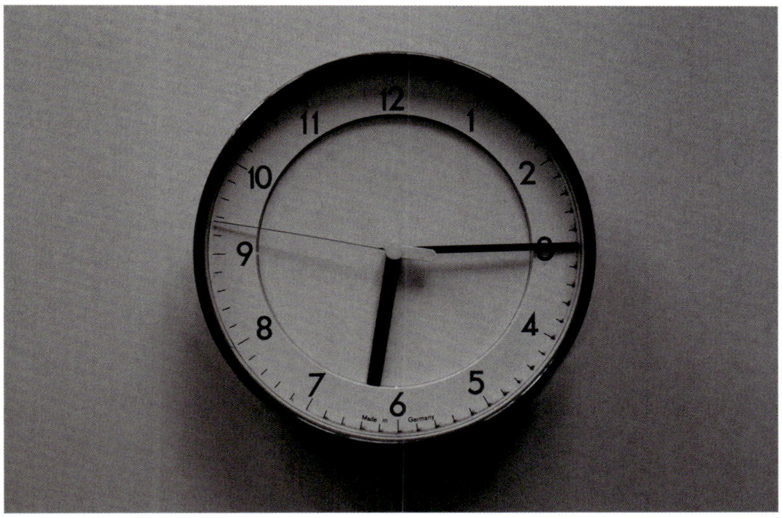

Made in Germany

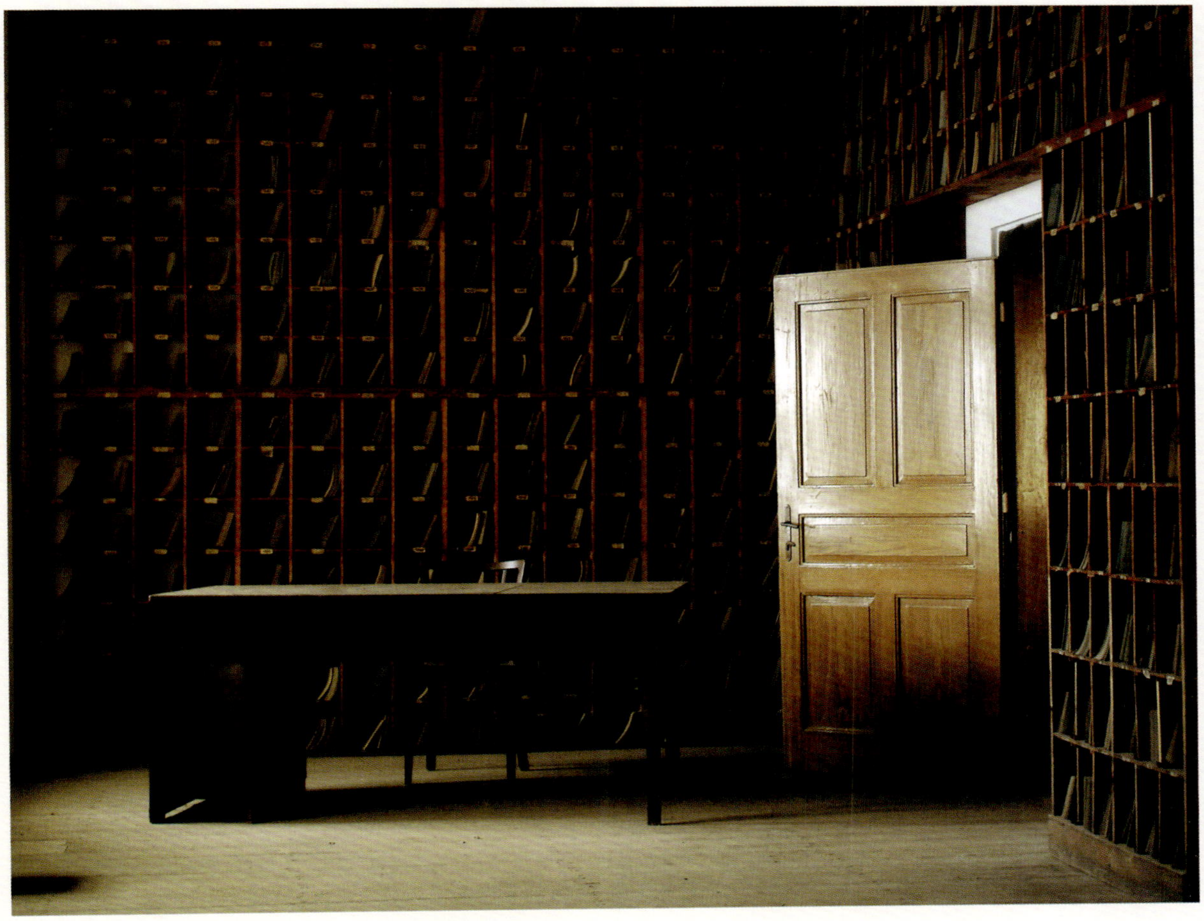

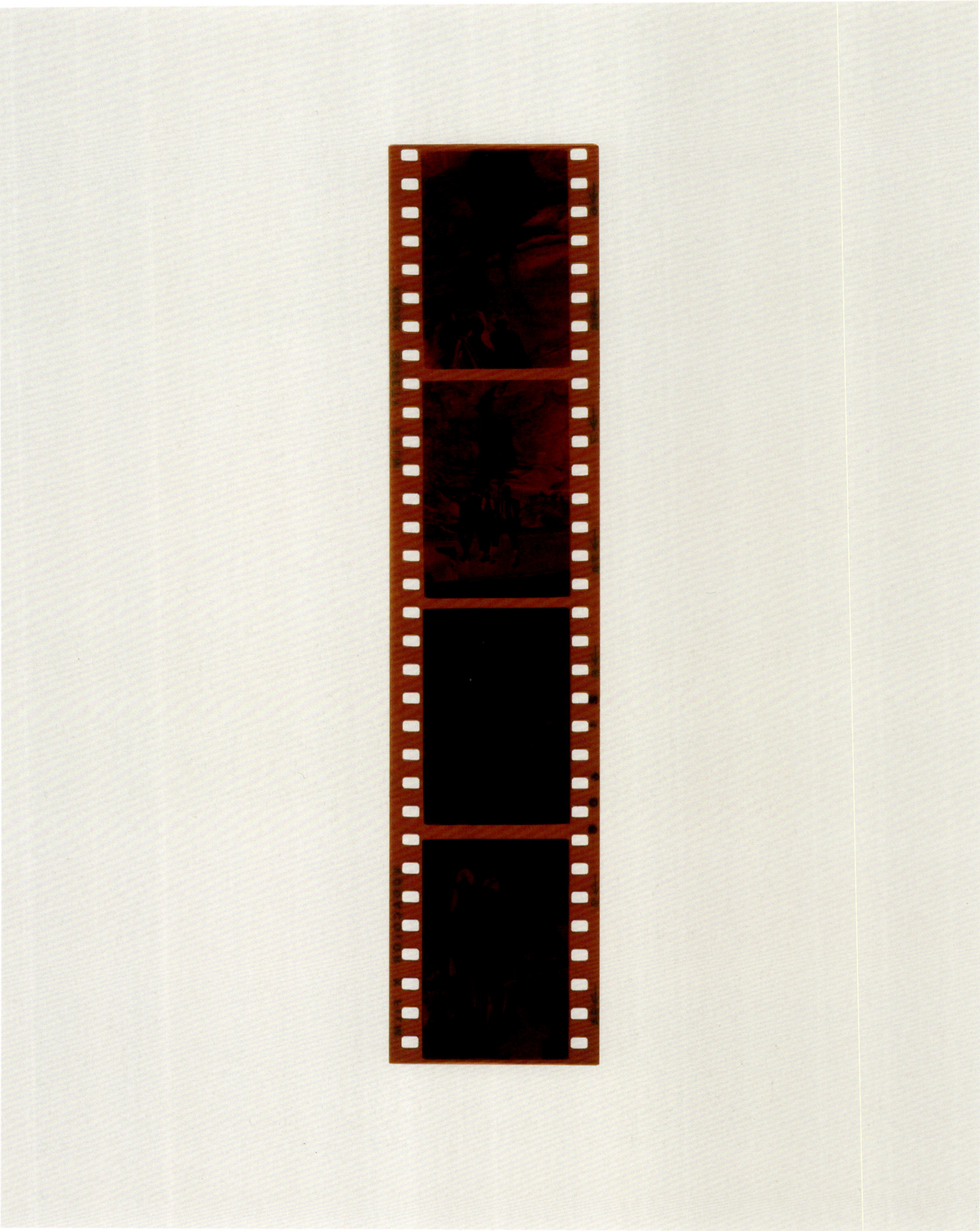

Alfredo Jaar

Critical of the media coverage of the genocide in Rwanda, Alfredo Jaar refused to show any of the photographs of the horror he took when he visited the African country shortly after the killings in 1994. One of his first works acknowledged this by hiding photographs in boxes covered with descriptions of what was pictured. The display of stacked black boxes, *Real Pictures* (1995), carried allusions to both minimalist sculpture and memorials.

When Jaar does use photographs, they are often elliptical. In his remarkable installation *The Eyes of Gutete Emerita* (1996) he shows only images of the eyes of a witness to atrocity. This is a powerful means of calling up horror in the face of public indifference, and avoids some of the problems of media coverage reliant on actual horror. Such eye-to-eye address directly brings home a geographically distant atrocity.

Jaar's installation relies on language not only to name and individualize the woman whose eyes we see but also to tell us of the tragedy she has witnessed. Thus, before we look into her eyes, we read a fifteen-foot long text – displayed in a single line and at eye level – which informs us, among other things, that her husband and two sons were 'killed with machetes before her eyes.' Following this, an adjoining room displays a million slides heaped up on a huge lightbox table. There are a million slides for the estimated million Tutsi and moderate Hutu murdered by Hutu in Rwanda. Each slide is identical and shows a close-up of the eyes of Gutete Emerita. Magnifiers installed along the edges of the table invite us to look closely, again and again, into her eyes. The display is meant to counter the ephemerality of our encounter with pictures in the print media.

The Eyes of Gutete Emerita draws upon a familiar strategy of photojournalism, the look of the innocent. Jaar's work is best seen as a slowing down of the exhortational and rhetorical techniques of photojournalism, and an acknowledgement of photography's inadequacies in the face of trauma. Jaar avoids graphic depictions of the horror of genocide, yet the work remains powerful through ellipsis. The act of looking into the face of a witness to horror can bring atrocity home, providing a human and subjective register of witnessed pain and injury. But empathy becomes nearly impossible when the events are so terrible that we cannot begin to comprehend the horror.

Alfredo Jaar
The Eyes of Gutete Emerita, 1996
Illuminated text, light table, slides
Dimensions variable

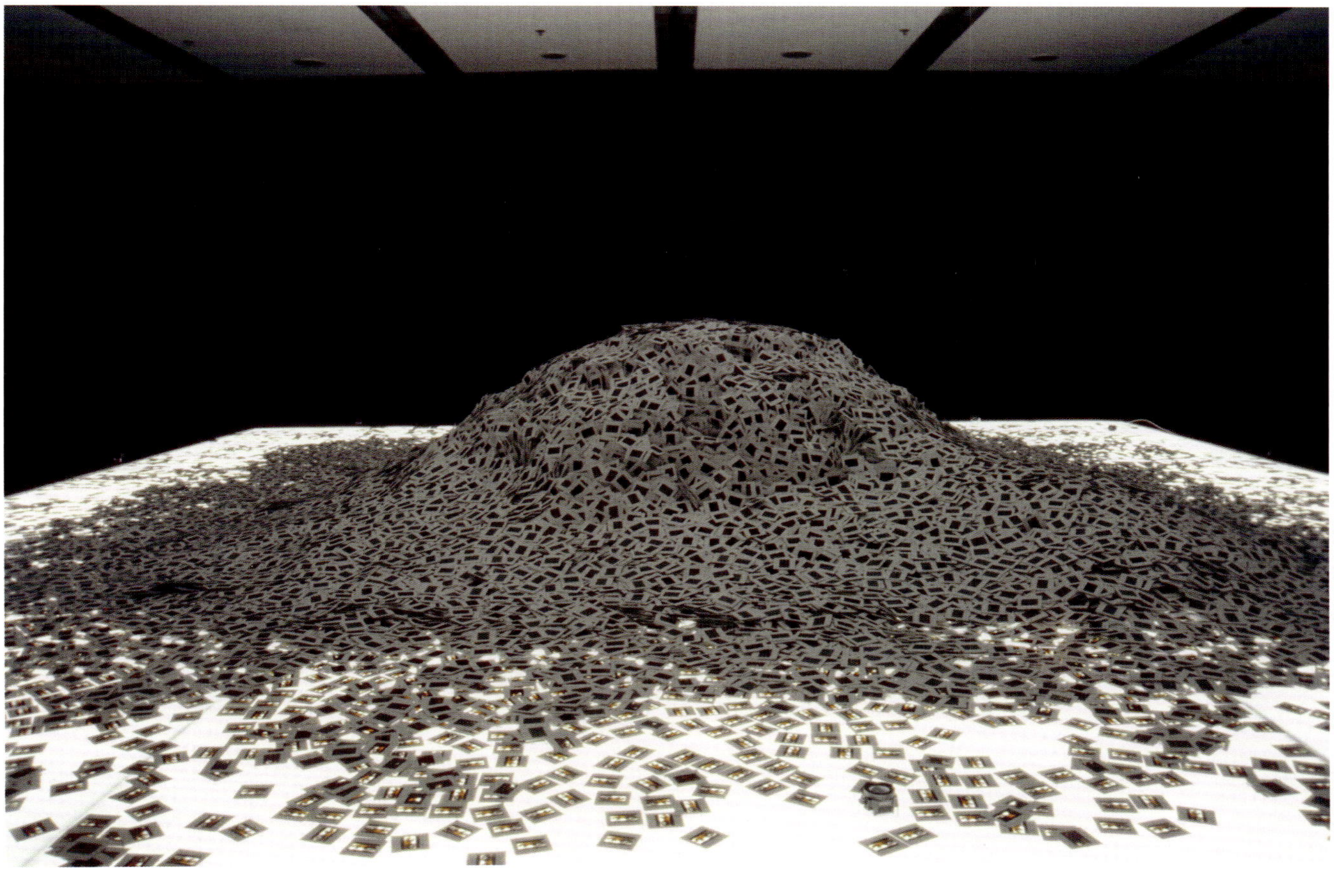

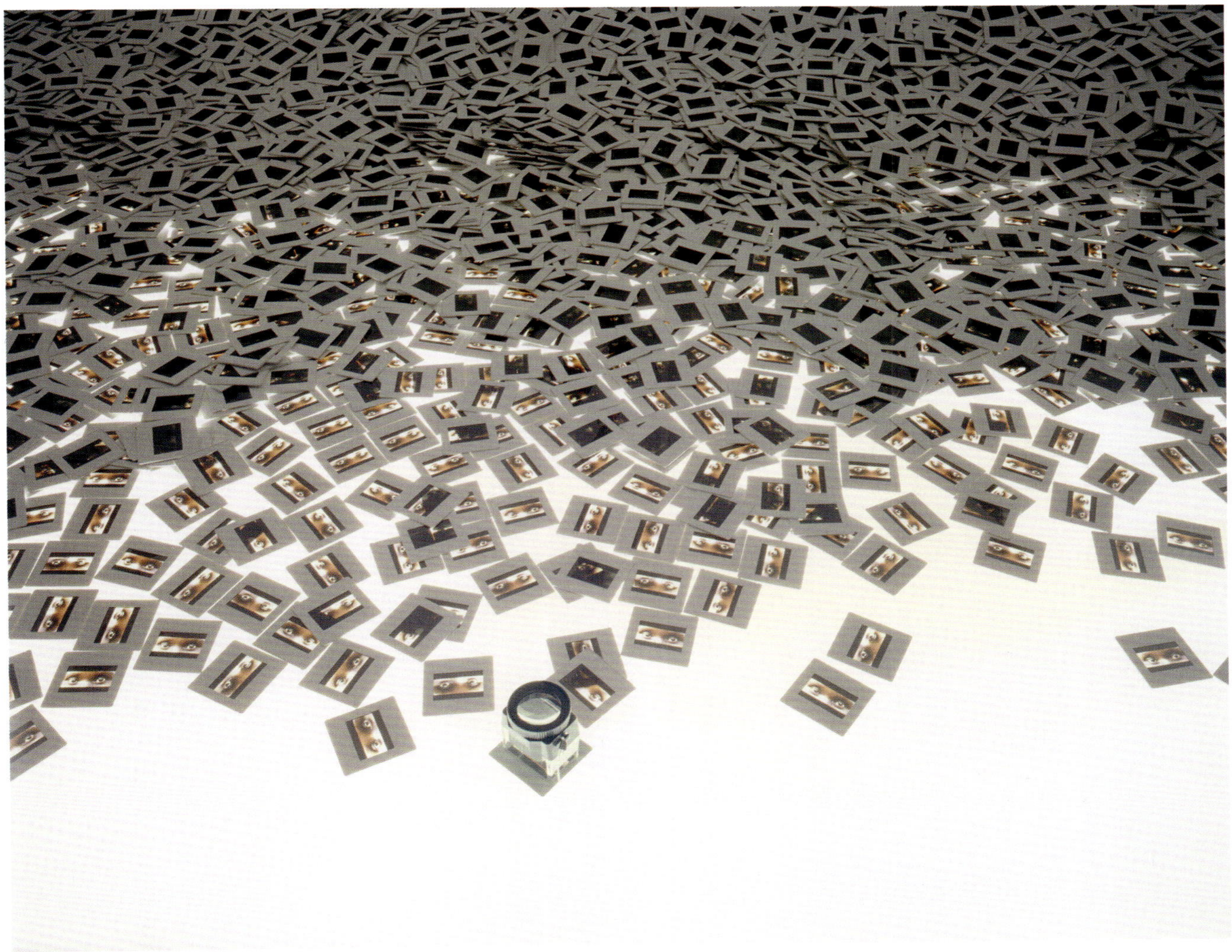

Gilles Peress

Gilles Peress's smallish book of black-and-white pictures in response to the genocide in Rwanda, *The Silence* (1995), relentlessly shows the brutal and wounding excesses of atrocity. Although they are not identical, his uncaptioned images become familiar and repetitive. Peress seeks to shock us out of habituation and indifference by the relentless nature of his representation. Yet these images raise problems in relation to atrocity images of 'foreign bodies', or the readiness with which barbaric violence is associated with non-Western cultures.

The first and last photographs in Peress's book are, however, different. Taken three minutes apart, they rest on an exchange of looks between the subject and the photographer. An opening caption identifies the person in the photograph as 'a prisoner, a killer'. In the first image he is self absorbed, reflecting, the caption leads us to assume, on the brutality of the crimes he has committed and witnessed. By the second image he has made eye contact with Peress; his look is antagonistic, non-reciprocal. After the horrors of the book, we return to this individual, almost as if the weight of the atrocious events Peress has documented rests on his shoulders. That it is the aggressive look of a killer rather than the face of the innocent means that the kind of empathic relation ordinarily invited by such eye-to-eye contact is disrupted. But if empathy is broken, the viewer is nevertheless led to think about precisely what kind of identification he or she might have with such a subject. Could not the Western viewer, through his or her very indifference to such atrocities in 'foreign' countries, share a certain culpability? Like the book as a whole, such a look serves as a challenge to the Western gaze, an indictment of indifference and complacency, 'our' compassion fatigue. Peress's hyperbolic use of portraiture indicts the very assumptions of difference and distance, and the very indifference that characterizes relations between the First World and the so called Third World – relations which, it could be said, allowed and continue to allow such atrocities as those which took place in Rwanda to happen.

In 1997 Peress said: 'I work very much like a forensic photographer in a certain way, collecting evidence. I've started to take more still lifes, like a police photographer, collecting evidence as a witness… The work is much more factual and much less about good photography. I don't care that much about good photography.'[14] The forensic and evidential functioning of Peress's photography is paralleled by the work of those pictured in his book (with Eric Stover) *The Graves*, which documents in unrelenting detail the grim labour of excavating human remains in order to provide evidence of mass murders and war crimes in Srebenica and Vukovar. The book also pays tribute to the labour of the people who do such work. *The Graves*, like *The Silence*, sets up counterpoints between atrocity and portraiture – only in *The Graves* it is conveyed through a series of portraits of the women whose husbands or sons are missing.

Gilles Peress
The Silence, Scalo, New York, 1995
22.9 × 17.1 cm / 9 × 6¾ in, 200pp
Paperback, 100 duotone photographs

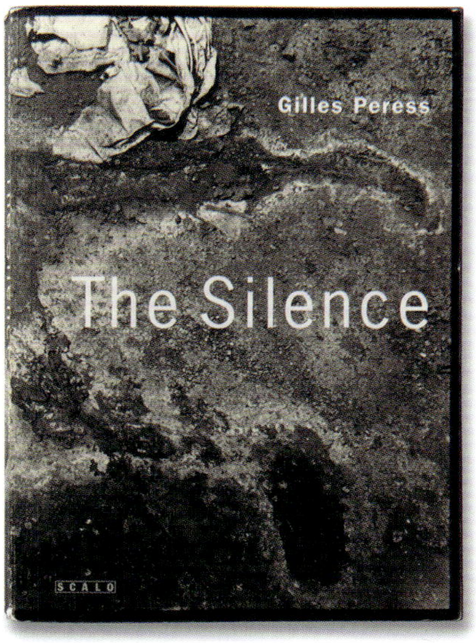
Gilles Peress
The Silence
SCALO

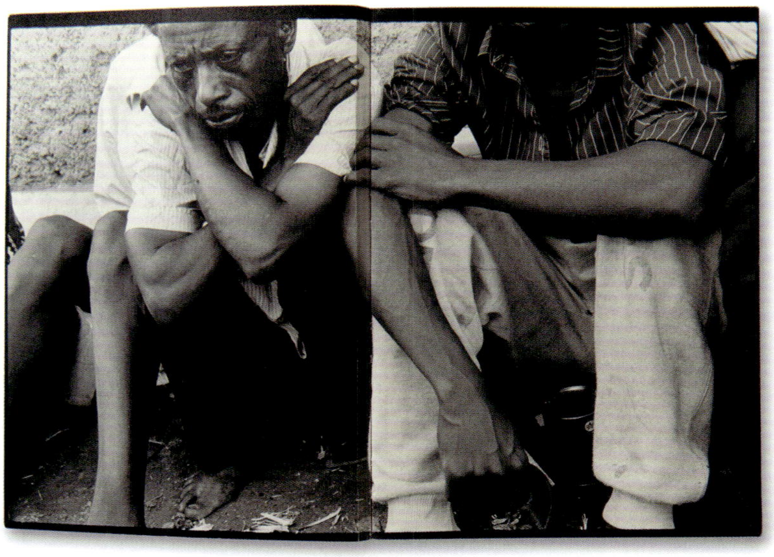

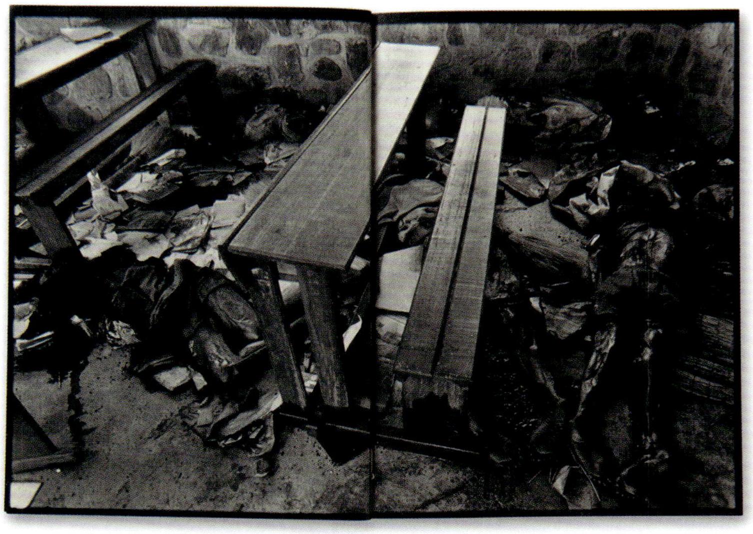

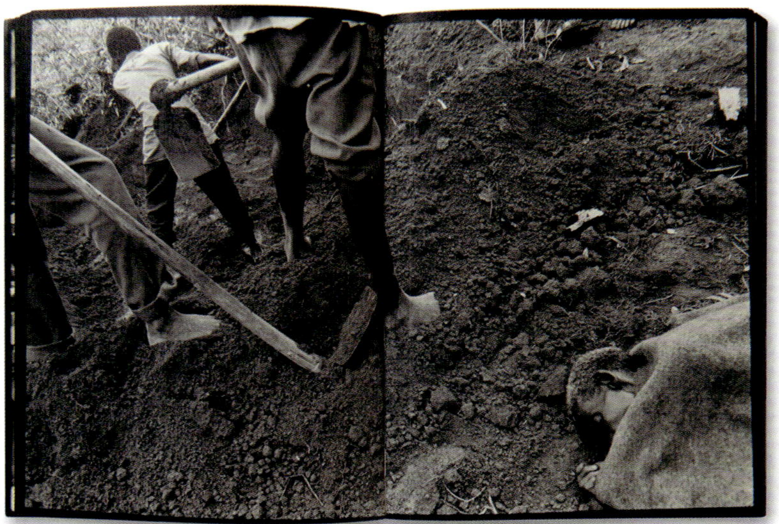

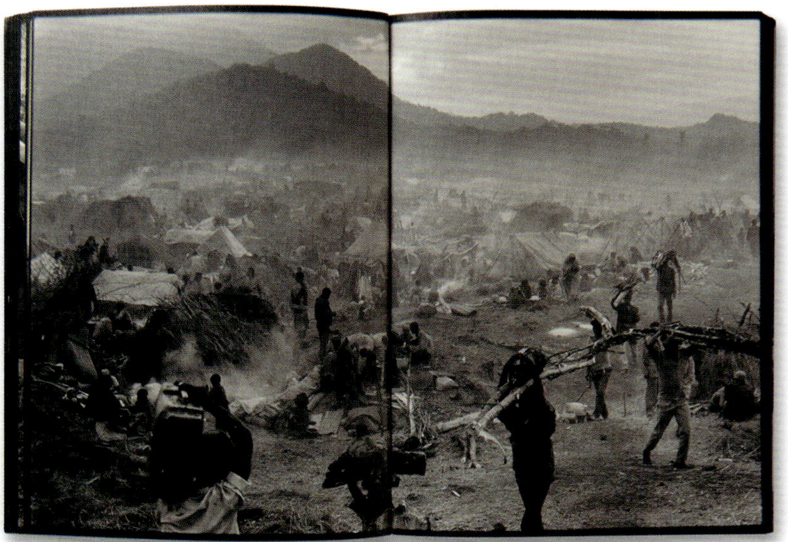

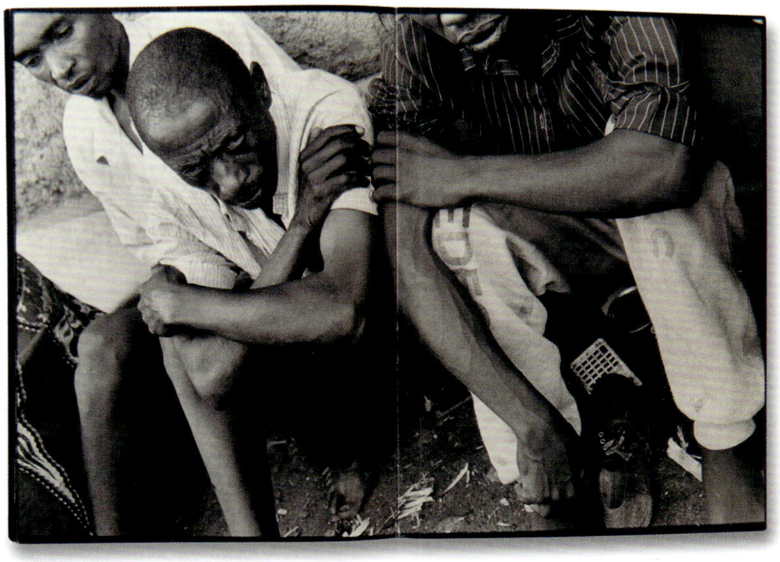

Thomas Hirschhorn

Responding to the absence of media images of the dead in the wars in the Middle East, Afghanistan and Iraq, the Swiss artist Thomas Hirschhorn confronts us with an uncensored and relentless display of what war does to human bodies in his *Incommensurable Banner* (2007). The eighteen-foot banner is covered with images culled from the internet, newspapers and magazines, showing bodies torn apart by contemporary munitions. By using the improvised and DIY form of display of the protestor, Hirschhorn positions the atrocity images in the context of the impassioned commitment, urgency and outrage of those protesting against such wars. A sense of the human is conveyed through the form of display, and is integral to how we are affected and moved by this work.

Hirschhorn did not go to places of conflict to make such work. His strategy is twofold: he not only appropriates images but also borrows the language of the war protestor to challenge the sanitized media images of current wars. Atrocity images are repositioned as a form of protest. Such work is far from the humanist tradition of photojournalism. Hirschhorn's work highlights the problem that the use of images of victims to trigger an affective response can be seen as a violation of those subjects: it fails to respect their dignity.

Luc Delahaye

Luc Delahaye, a French photographer, uses subject matter drawn from globally newsworthy events, but presented in the form of aesthetically beautiful, large-scale colour photographs that are exhibited as art. In some pictures, Delahaye gives us long-distance views of events and situations linked to international news, a totalizing, vivid representation which, while offering a sense of an overview – the bigger picture – nevertheless also highlights how limited and partial our view is. While many of Delahaye's photographs might offer a seeming order and visual control in relation to what must have often been chaotic, dangerous and violent situations, there is no sense of a mastering and omniscient gaze.

In opposition to the instantaneous image capture and global distribution associated with contemporary news media, Delahaye's pictures entail a slow record of newsworthy and historical moments. They rely on the power of photography's evidentiality, the role of witness, of being there, but at the same time they do not pretend to register a clear response to what is witnessed. Instead, Delahaye is absorbed in the artistry of making good pictures. Questions of form, beauty, composition and pictorial allusion are integral to our relationship to his photographs.

Figures of power are often dwarfed by their settings, like Pope John Paul II, tiny amidst the Renaissance splendour of the Vatican. Delahaye also shows the bustle of the media as it records news events, underscoring that he is standing outside this hubbub and frenzy. Occasionally, Delahaye reverses the scale and takes us closer: *Taliban* (2001), for example, not only brings us close in its documenting of an anonymous dead soldier from the war in Afghanistan but, deliberately or not, likens him to depictions of the dead Christ, a symbolic and cultural elevation which contradicts the dominant media view of the Taliban as the West's extreme evil Other.

In their exposé of the media circus and the collision between the organization and spectacles of the mechanics of Western power and the disastrous and devastating events on the ground, Delahaye's epic photographs articulate their critique subtly. His extensive documentation never amounts to a seamless vision; collectively his pictures show us the fractures and contradictions that underly the current global world order. The panoramic view accents the ruptures and splits between our privileged position and the situations he presents to us with a scale and detail that gives them a weight and density distinct from the fleeting encounter with the newspaper, TV or digital screen image.

Thomas Hirschhorn
The Incommensurable Banner, 2007
Fabric, spray paint, printed materials, plastic, adhesive tape
Approx. 4 × 18 m / 158 × 709 in

Luc Delahaye
Security Council, 2003
C-print
241 × 112 cm / 94⅞ × 44 in

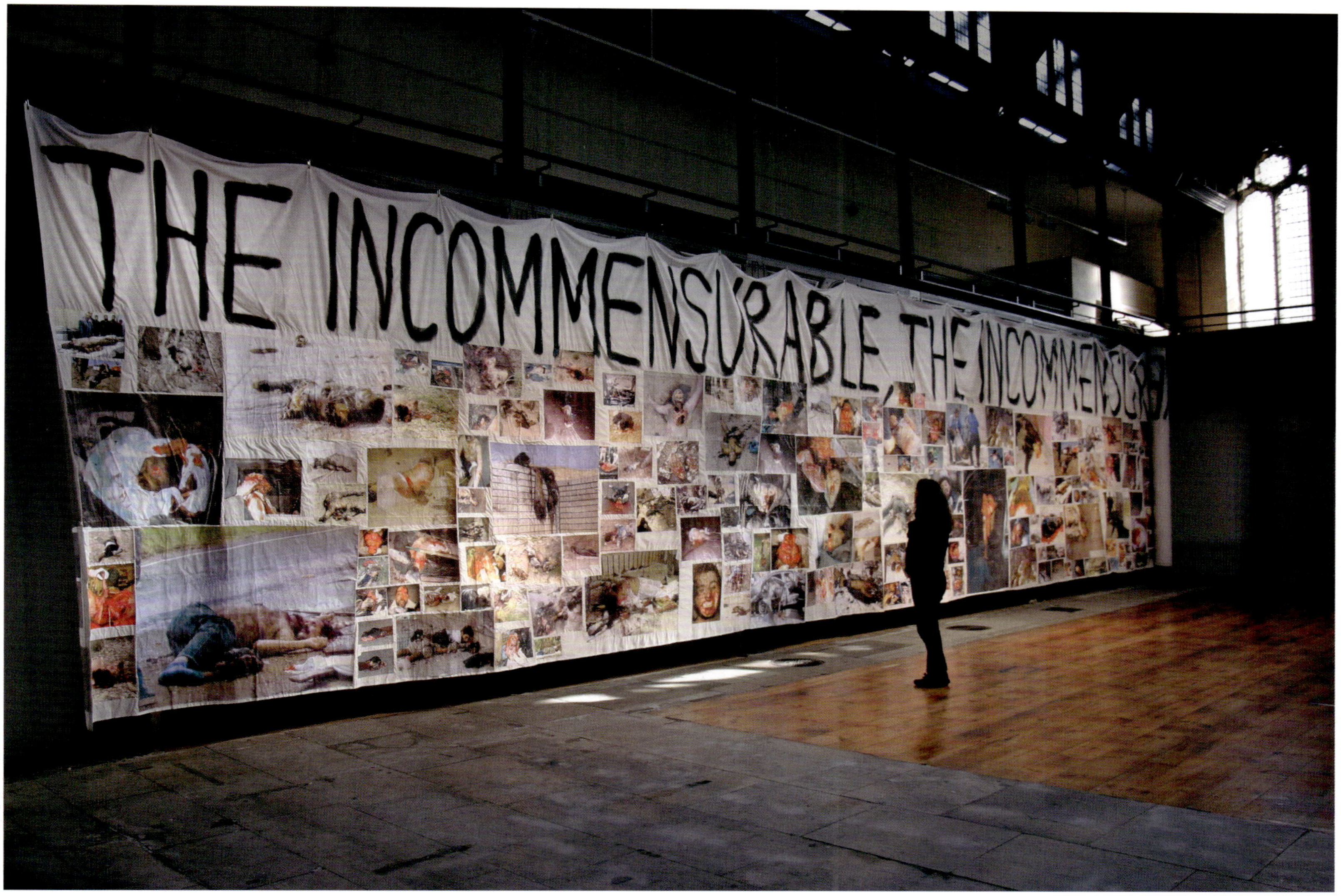
THE INCOMMENSURABLE, THE

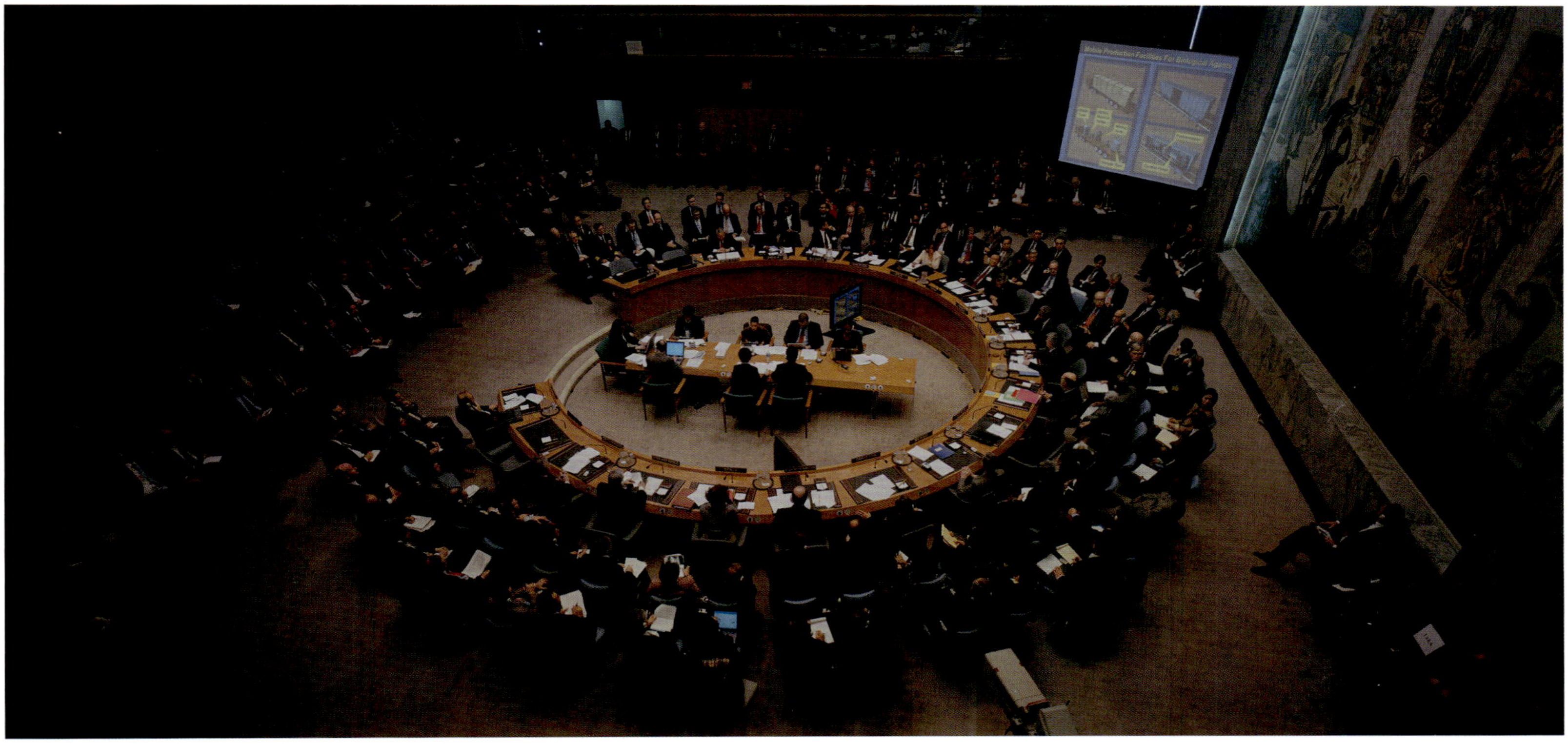

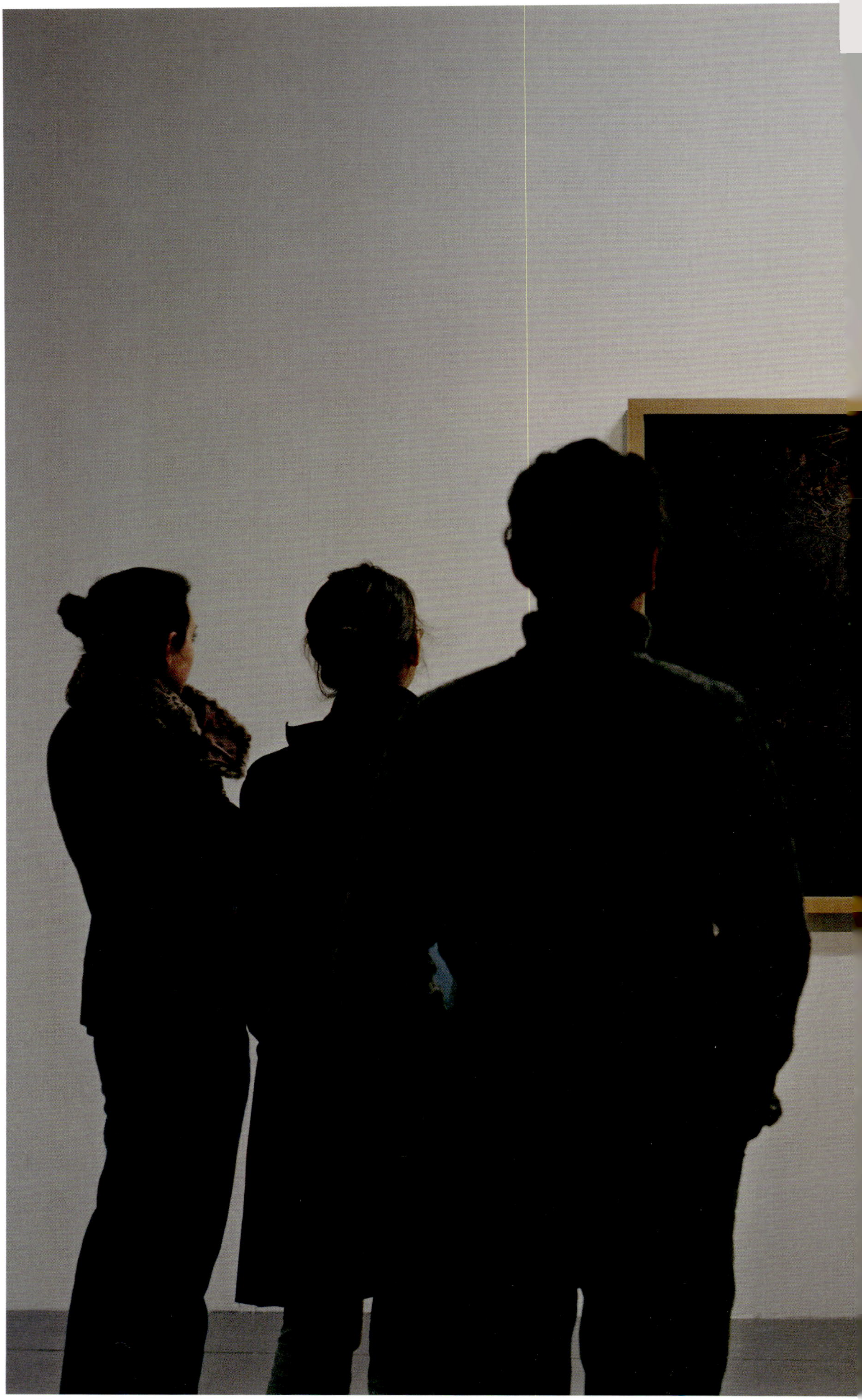

Luc Delahaye
Taliban, 2001
C-print
237 × 111 cm / 93⅜ × 43¾ in

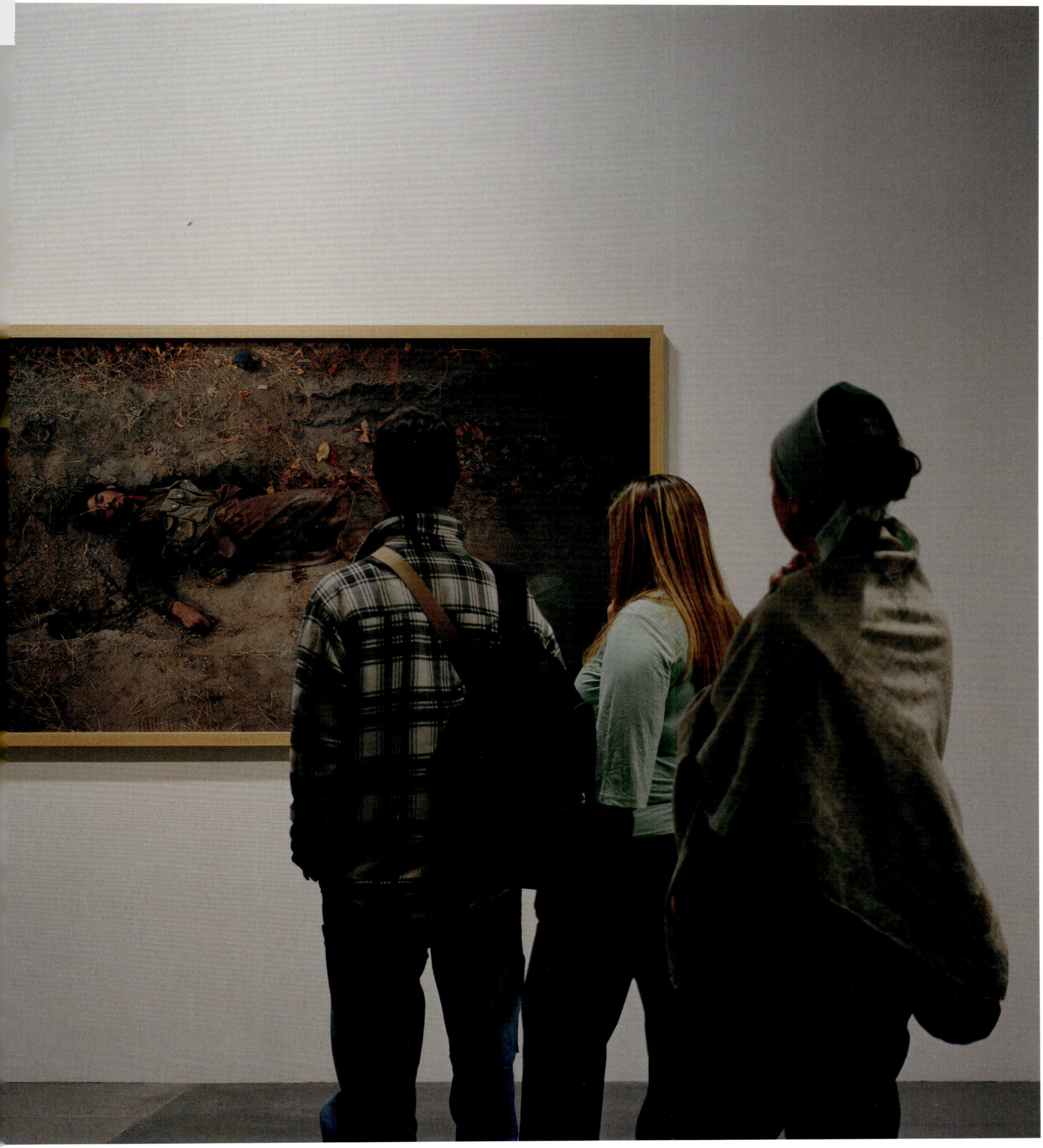

Craigie Horsfield

A powerful film and series of stills made in response to 9/11 by the British artist, Craigie Horsfield, achieves an enduring experience of trauma. In the large stills extracted from his four-to-five hour film, showing people on Broadway gathered on the site of the Twin Towers a short time after their destruction, human subjectivity becomes the focus amidst the incomprehensibility of this mass atrocity. Horsfield's art turns both inwards and outwards, voyeuristically closing in on the faces of people caught at private moments of reflection – grief, mourning, disbelief, shock and so on – as they survey the devastation caused by a world-changing event, a spectacle that remains off-screen and, in many senses for Horsfield, un-representable. Horsfield trades very heavily on the dramatic emotional context from which his picture is drawn. The faces fascinate as we look to these witnesses as carriers of something of the traumatic effect of 9/11. The human face serves as a more sensitive and powerful register of the event than any direct photographic witnessing. These people's collective responsiveness can be seen as opposing the photographic spectacles of the scene of devastation itself, where, as Horsfield puts it, the 'moment [is] fixed, frozen, without consequence.'[15] Restoration of human value is integral to the politics of the Broadway work, in opposition to the barbarism behind the felling of the towers.

Craigie Horsfield
Broadway, 15th Day, 38 minutes from dusk, New York, Sept 2001, 2005
Dry print, 102 × 128 cm /
40⅛ × 50⅜ in

Joel Meyerowitz
Ralph and Paul Guidel, New York City, 2001
C-print, dimensions variable

Joel Meyerowitz

Joel Meyerowitz made the only existing photographic record of Ground Zero after the attacks on the World Trade Center. Motivated by the necessity to document for history the impact of the destruction, he managed through sheer persistence to get access and photograph Ground Zero, which was otherwise fenced off, guarded and declared a crime scene, with no photography allowed: the site became known as 'the forbidden city.' Meyerowitz took over 8,000 large-format photographs in nine months, using a 10x8 wooden box-view camera. For him, working with such a camera was important because the exquisite detail of its record gave his pictures a physical impact: 'So those people in the future who looked at this work – not as a work of art but as history, as what happened here – could literally look at the photographs and feel what it was like to stand in front of the pile.'[15]

One form the photographs have taken is in an oversize book, *Aftermath* (2006). Its very size and weight means it is physically difficult to look at – a response to the scale of the destruction itself and a way of trying to recognize the exhaustive physical and emotive labour of all those people who undertook the task of recovery and clearance. The overwhelming effect of the destruction is conveyed through the sheer accumulation and variety of photographs, from pictures showing the 'awful beauty' of the site, of this 'spectacle with a cast of thousands,' to details that register the violent force of the towers' collapse – a tree severed by flying metal, a melted parking meter – and the memorials, the messages written on walls, or in the dust on windows and marble facades, as well as the portraits of people working on the site, the police officers, the firefighters, engineers, workers, the volunteers involved in the clean-up.[17] The pictures of *Aftermath* are driven by compassion and warmth. The human dimension is integral to Meyerowitz's portrayal of this site of destruction, brought out through the attention given to the people working on the site: the way a father helps his son climb up the last remaining column on the site, so he can put up a photograph of his missing brother, and the care with which workers rake and pick over the rubble for any traces of human remains.

The traumatic ruins of the World Trade Center served an important ideological role as a global reminder of a city wounded by terrorism. Patricia Harrison, Assistant Secretary of State for Educational and Cultural Affairs, was key in convincing State Department chiefs that a photography exhibition could be an effective weapon in countering misinformation about the United States, arguing that it was necessary to convey to foreign audiences the physical and human dimensions of the recovery effort. Harrison worked with Meyerowitz to construct a touring exhibition of some of his photographs of Ground Zero. Launched by US Secretary of State Colin Powell in Washington in February 2002, by 2012 the exhibition's 32 travelling shows had been seen by a total of around four million people in approximately sixty countries. Travelling the world, these apocalyptic scenes at the heart of its wealthiest nation were intended to shape and maintain a public memory of the 9/11 attacks and their aftermath.

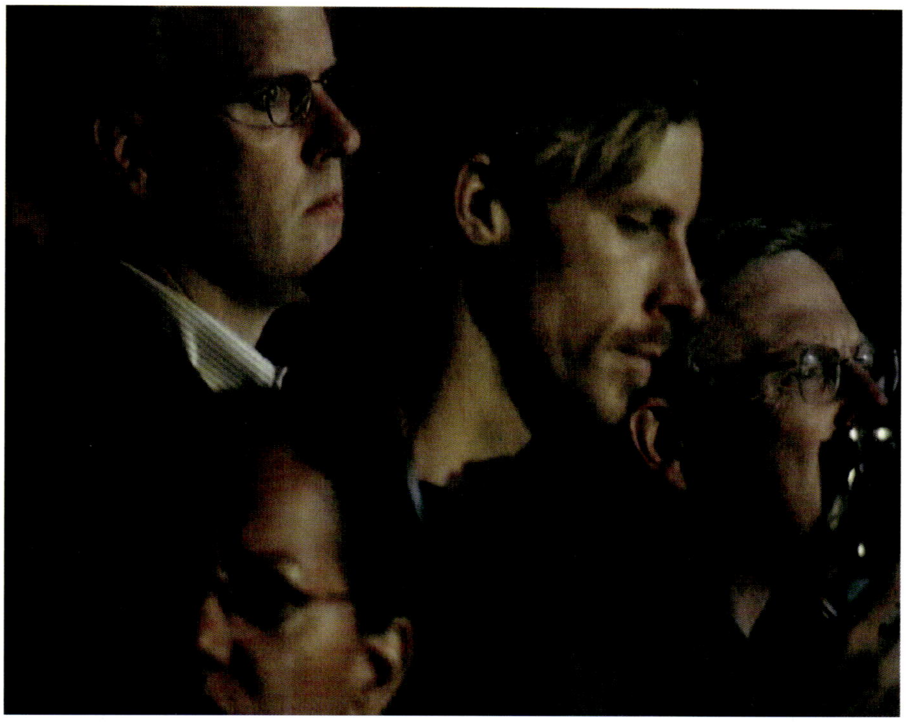

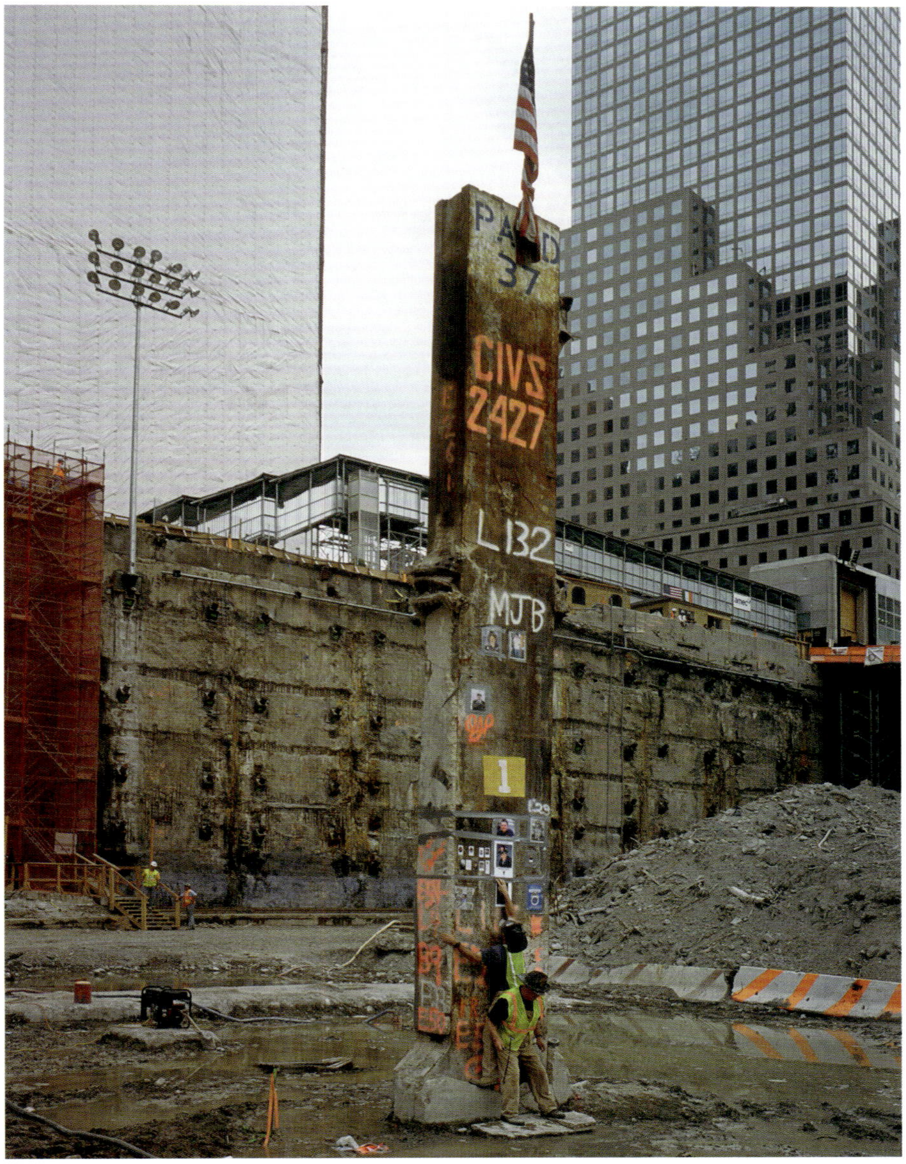
37
CIVS
2427
L132
MJB
1

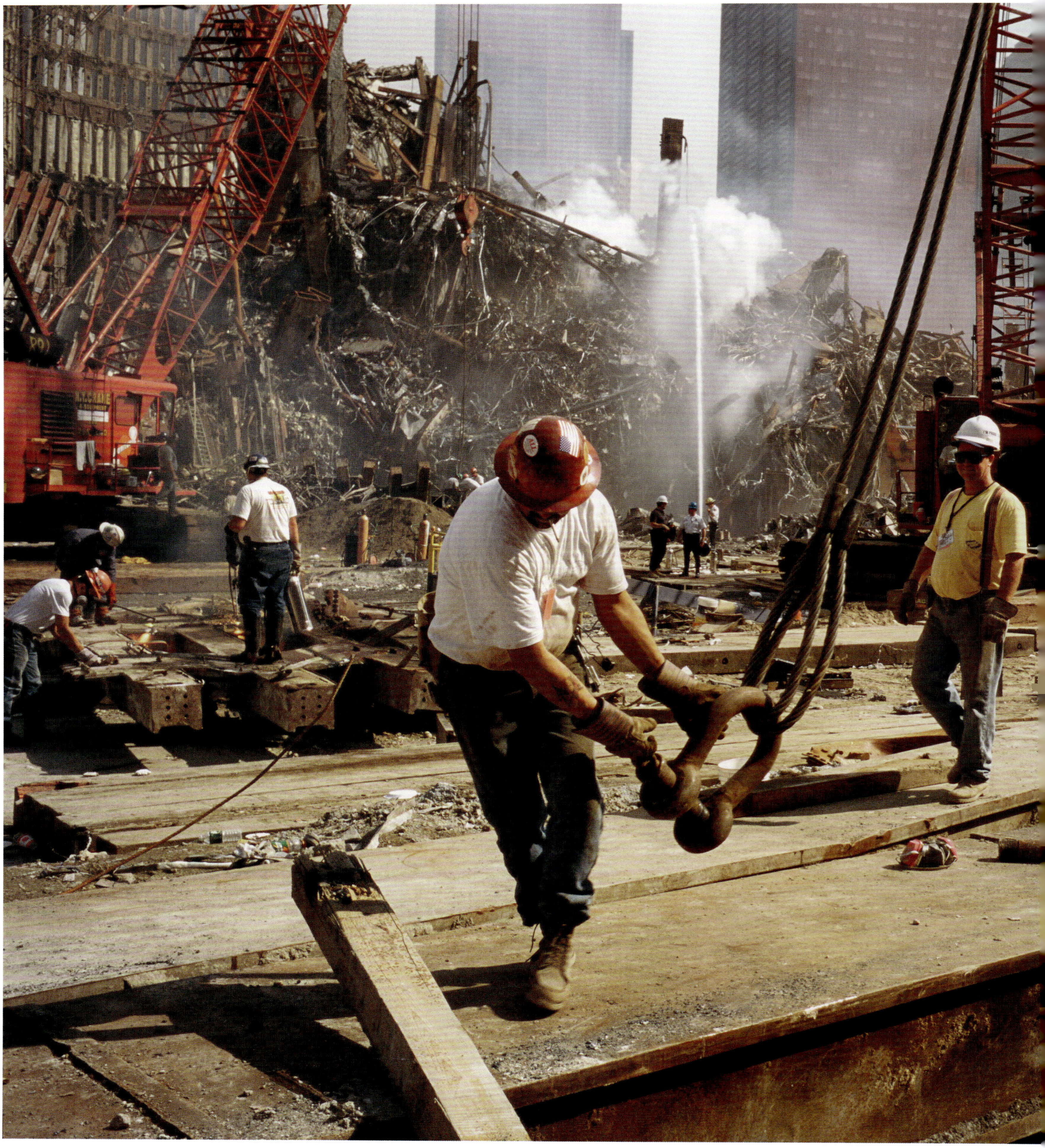

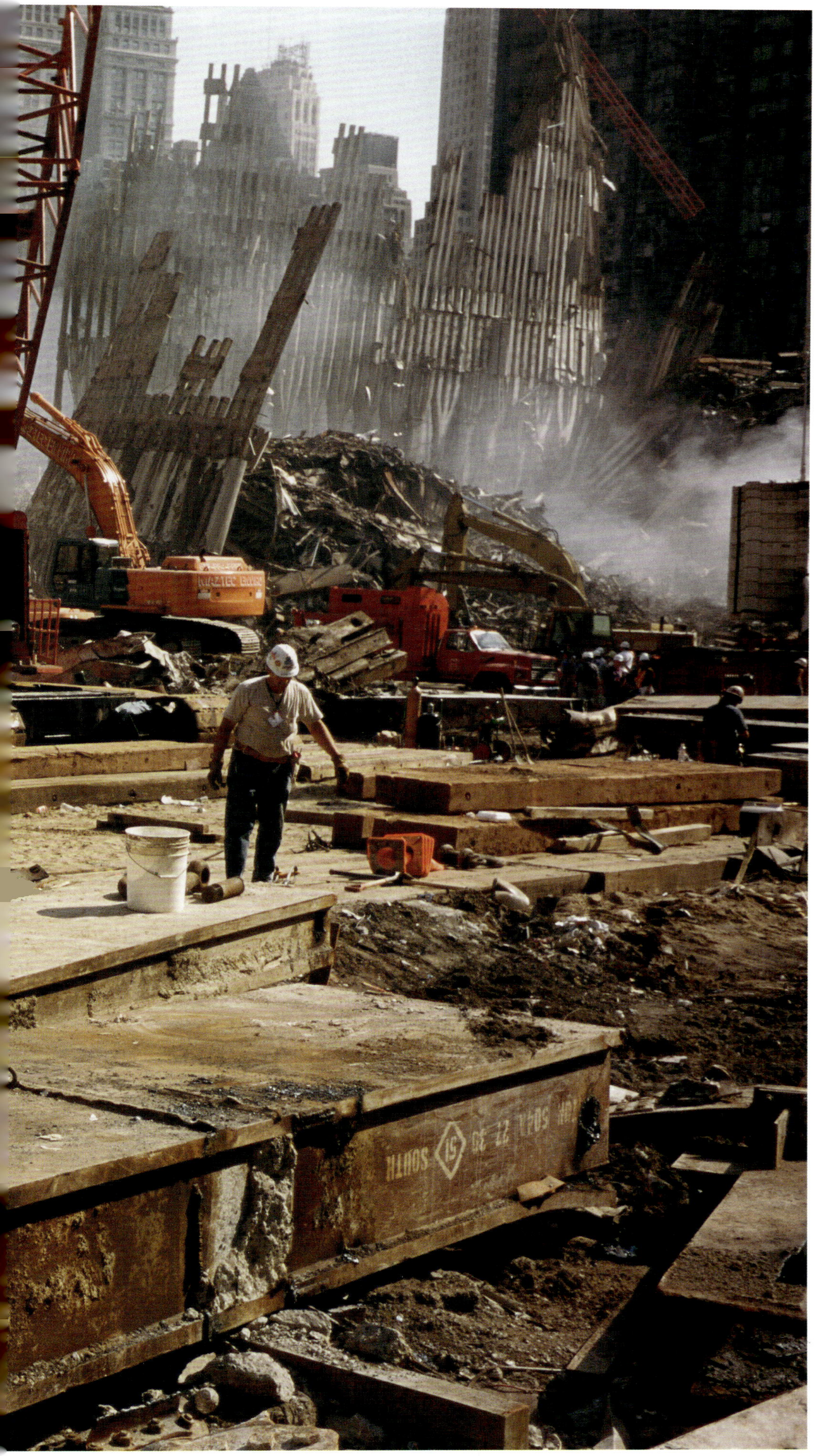

Joel Meyerowitz
Ironworkers, New York City, 2001
C-print, dimensions variable

Geert van Kesteren

Photojournalism is closely allied with the emotionalism of dramatic and expressive situations. It is very much about closeness: closeness to the witnessed event, of being there, and closeness in terms of empathic affiliation with the lives of those who are pictured. The Dutch photographer Geert van Kesteren's books, *Why Mister, Why?* (2004) and *Baghdad Calling* (2008), are both important in this respect. *Why Mister, Why?* mixes pictures taken while being un-embedded and embedded, depicting the brutal regime of Saddam Hussein and the richness of Iraqi culture as well as the brutality of US troops during the insurgency in Iraq: showing, close-up, their violent subjugation of civilians. Many are visceral and expressive pictures, often taken at dramatic moments. In *Baghdad Calling* van Kesteren takes us closer to the everyday world of the Iraqis, creating a view of their world from inside by publishing their mobile phone images of day-to-day life in Iraq: pictures not just of friends, family and home, but also of destruction, injury and death. Combined with accounts of Iraqis' experiences in their homeland, taken from interviews with refugees in Turkey, Syria and Jordan, the result is particularly powerful and emotive. It draws out the pathos and intimacy of photography of everyday moments, familiar family-album pictures, but the portraits of people dying and injured in hospitals, graves, wrecked cityscapes or plumes of smoke from nearby explosions also draw out the sense of a pervasive violence and death within which these ordinary moments are set. Van Kesteren takes us inside the war zone through its inhabitants' snapshots – low-grade camera-phone pictures that bring us close to the appalling reality of what is happening there through their everyday intimacy. The use of such images of war acknowledges the limits of traditional photojournalism in the face of the violence of contemporary conflict – van Kesteren is using other people's images because it is too dangerous to photograph in Iraq – but at the same time also works with something integral to it. As he has said, 'Too often politicians talk about "collateral damage" or the "death toll": they try to dehumanize war as much as possible. The less they talk about people the less responsibility they have to take for their actions. The truth is that they are talking about human beings, people who have a family, a home and desires, just like you, to grow up peacefully.' Because of this, he says, his showing of the family album is 'essential'.[18]

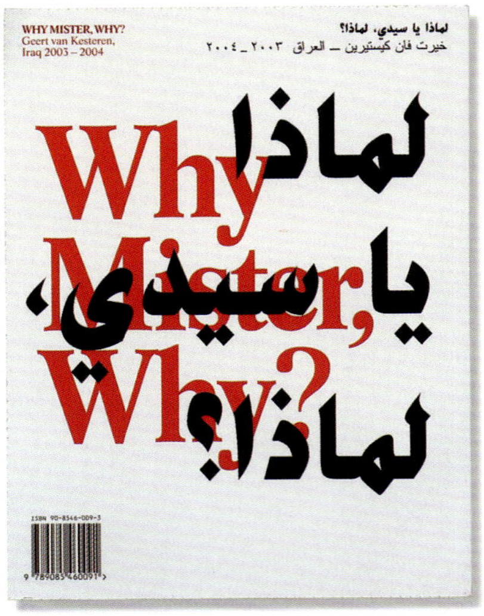

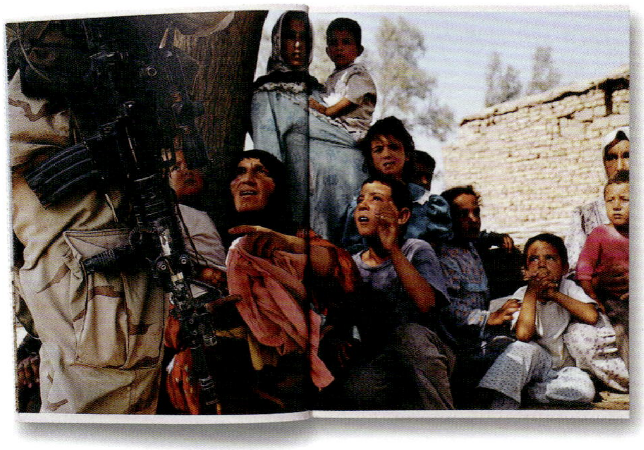

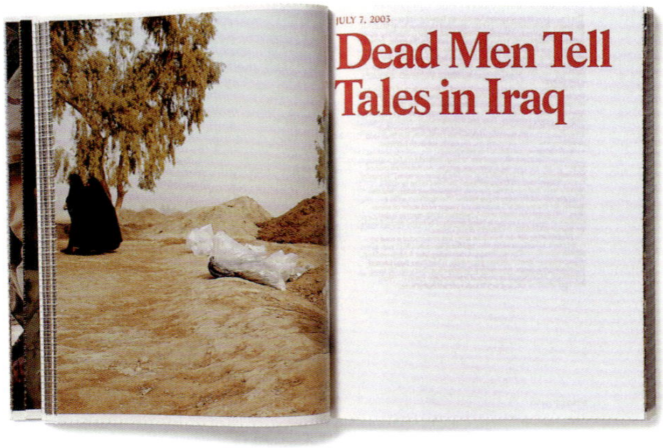

Geert van Kesteren
Why Mister, Why? Artimo, Amsterdam, 2004 (English-Arabic and Dutch-Arabic editions)
22 × 17 cm / 8½ × 6¾ in, 544 pp
Paperback with English and Arabic covers, 252 colour photographs
Foreword by Jan Guiters; introduction by Michael Hirsh; text and photo-edited by Geert van Kersteren; edited by Edie Peters; design by Mevis & Van Deursen with Marijke Cobbenhagen

Baghdad Calling: Reports from Turkey, Syria, Jordan and Iraq
Episode, Amsterdam, 2008
241 × 19 cm / 9.12 × 7.12 in, 388 pp
Paperback, Numerous colour photographs
Essays by Jan Gruiters and Brigitte Lardinois; edited by Geert van Kesteren; design by Mevis and Van Deursen

From the book *Baghdad Calling*, Iraq, 2005–7
Mobile phone images made by Iraqi citizens and sent to relatives or friends living as refugees abroad

'This is one of the best areas in Baghdad. Some pictures by which we can remember our great capital and how it is nowadays'.

'This is a wedding in 2006, they are Muslims and Christian people. They were so scared but happy at the same time.'

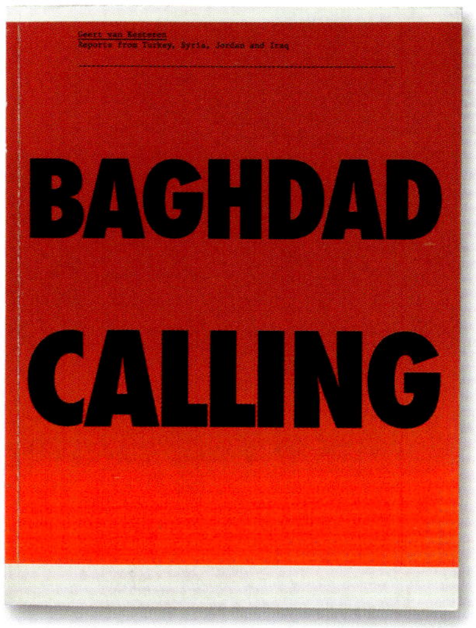

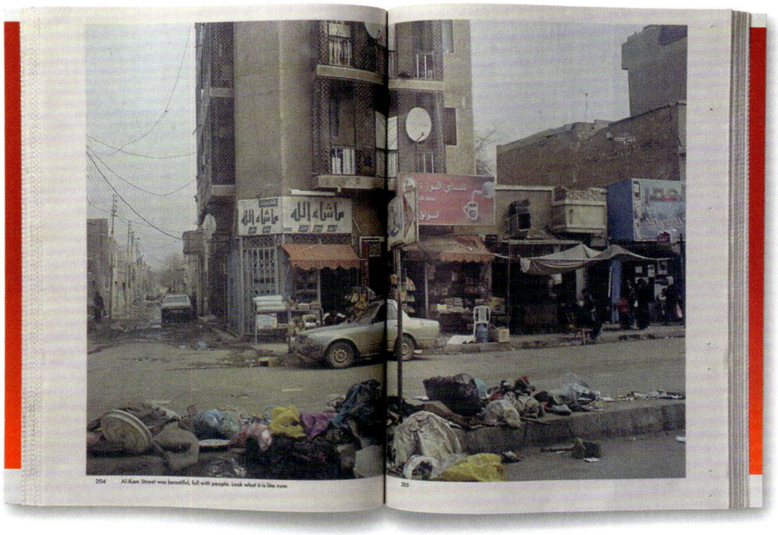

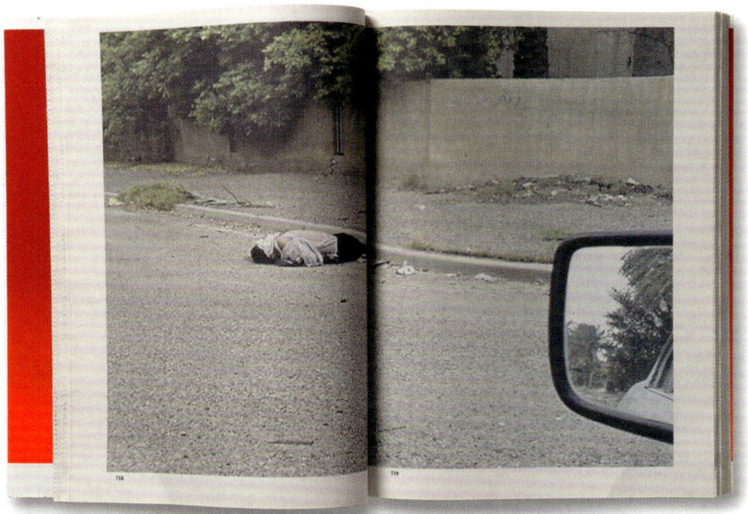

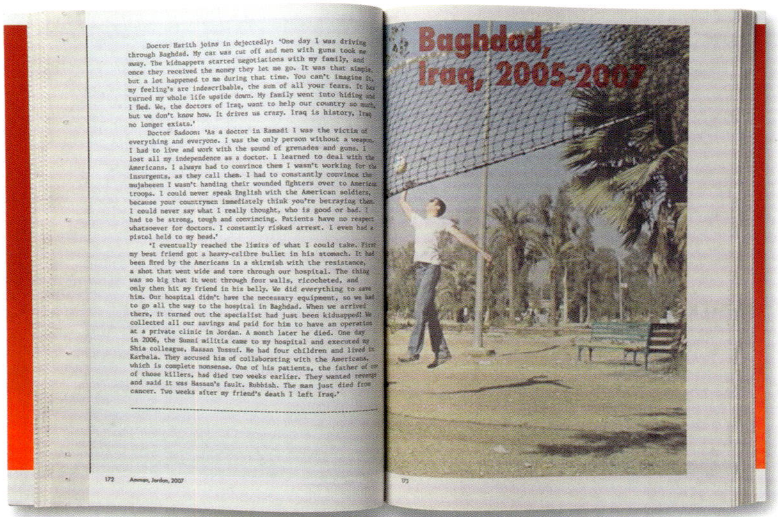
Doctor Harith joins in dejectedly: 'One day I was driving through Baghdad. My car was cut off and men with guns took me away. The kidnappers started negotiations with my family, and once they received the money they let me go. It was that simple, but a lot happened to me during that time. You can't imagine it, my feeling's are indescribable, the sum of all your fears. It has turned my whole life upside down. My family went into hiding and I fled. We, the doctors of Iraq, want to help our country so much, but we don't know how. It drives us crazy. Iraq is history, Iraq no longer exists.'

Doctor Sadoon: 'As a doctor in Ramadi I was the victim of everything and everyone. I was the only person without a weapon. I had to live and work with the sound of grenades and guns. I lost all my independence as a doctor. I learned to deal with the Americans. I always had to convince them I wasn't working for the insurgents, as they call them. I had to constantly convince the mujaheeen I wasn't handing their wounded fighters over to American troops. I could never speak English with the American soldiers, because your countrymen immediately think you're betraying them. I could never say what I really thought, who is good or bad. I had to be strong, tough and convincing. Patients have no respect whatsoever for doctors. I constantly risked arrest. I even had a pistol held to my head.'

'I eventually reached the limits of what I could take. First my best friend got a heavy-calibre bullet in his stomach. It had been fired by the Americans in a skirmish with the resistance, a shot that went wide and tore through our hospital. The thing was so big that it went through four walls, ricocheted, and only then hit my friend in his belly. We did everything to save him. Our hospital didn't have the necessary equipment, so we had to go all the way to the hospital in Baghdad. When we arrived there, it turned out the specialist had just been kidnapped! We collected all our savings and paid for him to have an operation at a private clinic in Jordan. A month later he died. One day in 2006, the Sunni militia came to my hospital and executed my Shia colleague, Hassan Yussuf. He had four children and lived in Karbala. They accused him of collaborating with the Americans, which is complete nonsense. One of his patients, the father of one of those killers, had died two weeks earlier. They wanted revenge and said it was Hassan's fault. Rubbish. The man just died from cancer. Two weeks after my friend's death I left Iraq.'

172 Amman, Jordan, 2007

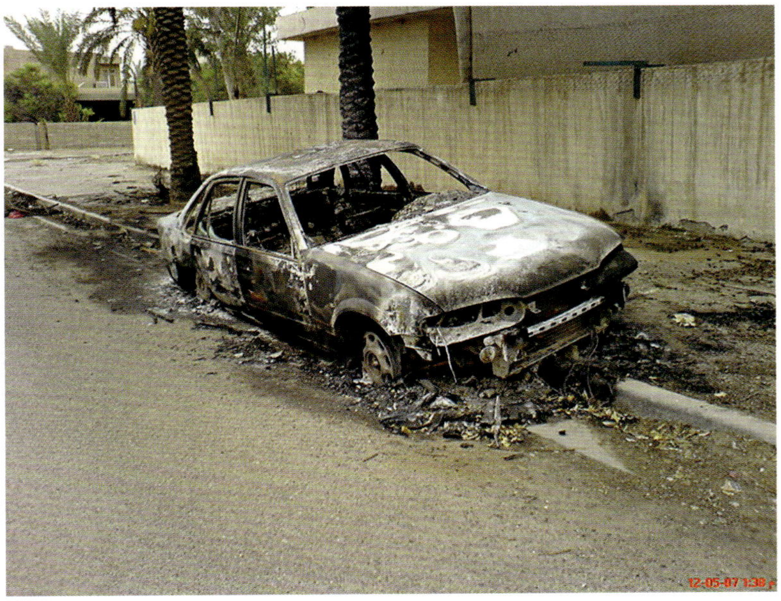

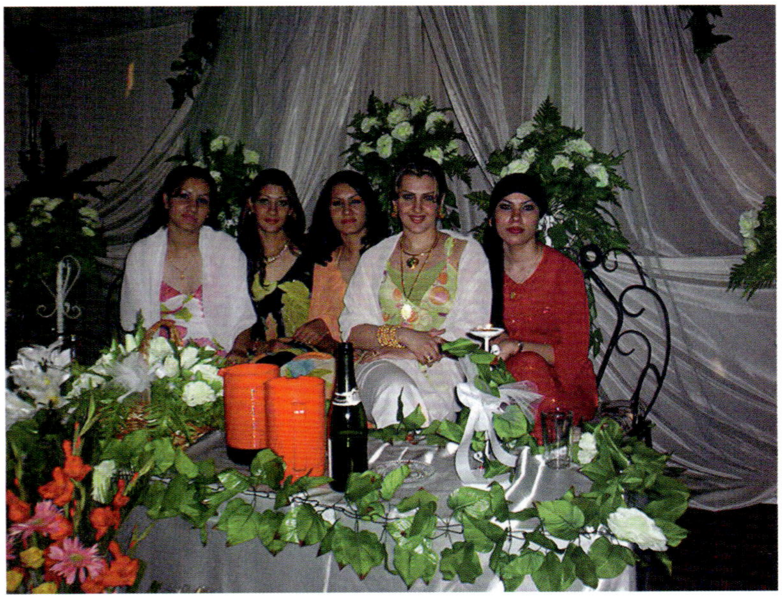

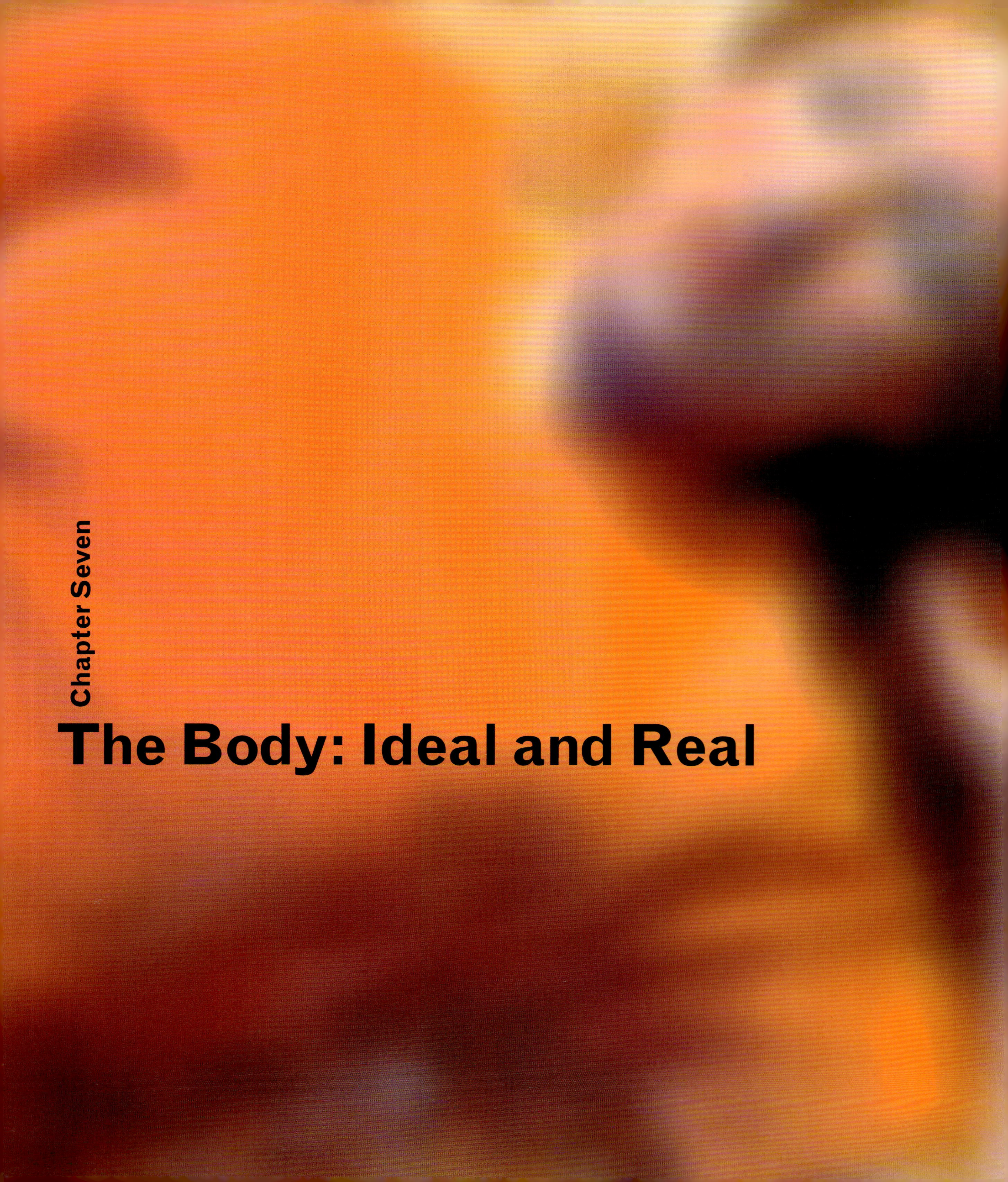

Chapter Seven

The Body: Ideal and Real

One of the key problems in photographing the human body is the objectification and abstraction that photography can involve as a result of the way in which the medium can fix, fetishize and idealize the body. A dominant artistic use of photography in its representation of the body has been to challenge this mode of depiction. It is the conflict between the body, or rather bodies, and the process of representation that will be explored here. Because this particular dynamic comes strongly to the fore when photography (and also film and video) is used to document the performing body, performance art and its documentation will also provide an important aspect of this chapter.

Representations of the human body are often used to suggest something universal and collective. The body suggests what we all have in common and can relate to; it signifies our humanness. But while it can be hard to get away from this way of thinking, much of the work discussed here uses photography to disrupt our expectations of how bodies should be depicted and shown, often concentrating on differences or showing how the body is affected by gender, sexuality, economics, health, race, age and physical ability or disability.

Bas Jan Ader

The Dutch artist Bas Jan Ader's series of filmic and photographic 'falls' of 1970–74, as he documented himself falling from the roof of his house in Los Angeles or riding a bike into a canal in Amsterdam, entail performances in which the artist gives up any dramatic control and agency. In many senses, these are un-heroic performances. As one critic put it, they rest upon 'an act of total surrender, as autonomy, will, strength, balance and all the other forces that we marshal at every moment just to remain animate are willingly renounced.'[1] The sequence of photos or films show the human subject becoming a passive object. In the few public statements he made, Ader said: 'I do not make body sculpture, body art or body works. When I fell off the roof of my house or into a canal, it was because gravity made itself master over me.'[2] The priority is upon the literal body and its subjugation to a force over which the artist has no control. The slapstick of the comic pratfall is given pathos and gravitas. In some respects these performances can be seen as symbolic of the physical decline of ageing, a rehearsal of the ultimate fall to death. Ader's life was cut tragically short when he was lost at sea in his attempt to sail single-handed across the Atlantic, for part of his art work, *In Search of the Miraculous* (1975–6).

Yves Klein

The French artist Yves Klein constructed an illusion, *Leap into the Void*, a 1960-montage in which he appears to be launching himself into the air from a roof ledge. In contrast to Bas Jan Ader's performances, the fall here is a symbolic moment of aggrandisement. It was intended to speak of the mystical powers of the artist, allowing as one critic put it, 'a fall to miraculously become an ascent.'[3] It is a fictionalized photographic document showing Klein making a superhuman leap onto the street below. Such a picture fed the mythic aspects of the artist's career. What was not visible in the doctored photograph were the dozen or so students from the nearby judo academy who held an outstretched tarpaulin to break the artist's fall.

Yves Klein
Leap into the Void, 1960
(photographed by Harry Shunk and Janos Kender)
Gelatin silver print
25.9 × 20 cm / 10 × 8 in

Bas Jan Ader
Fall II, 1970
Still from 16mm film

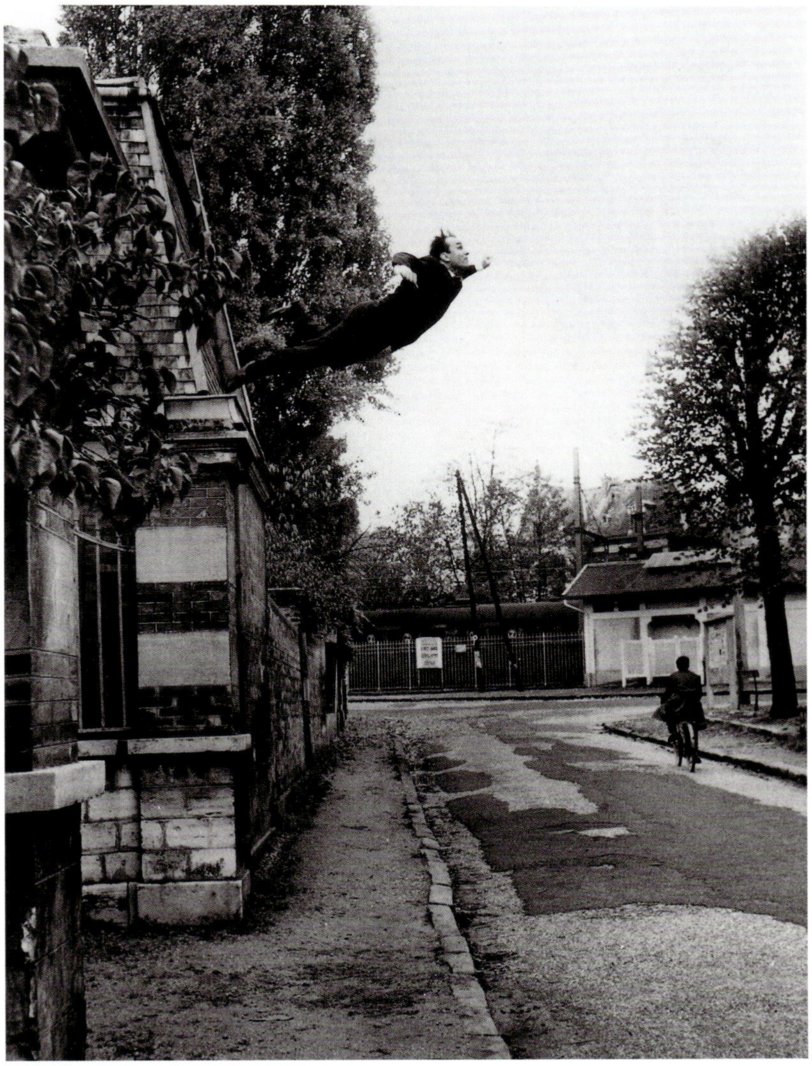

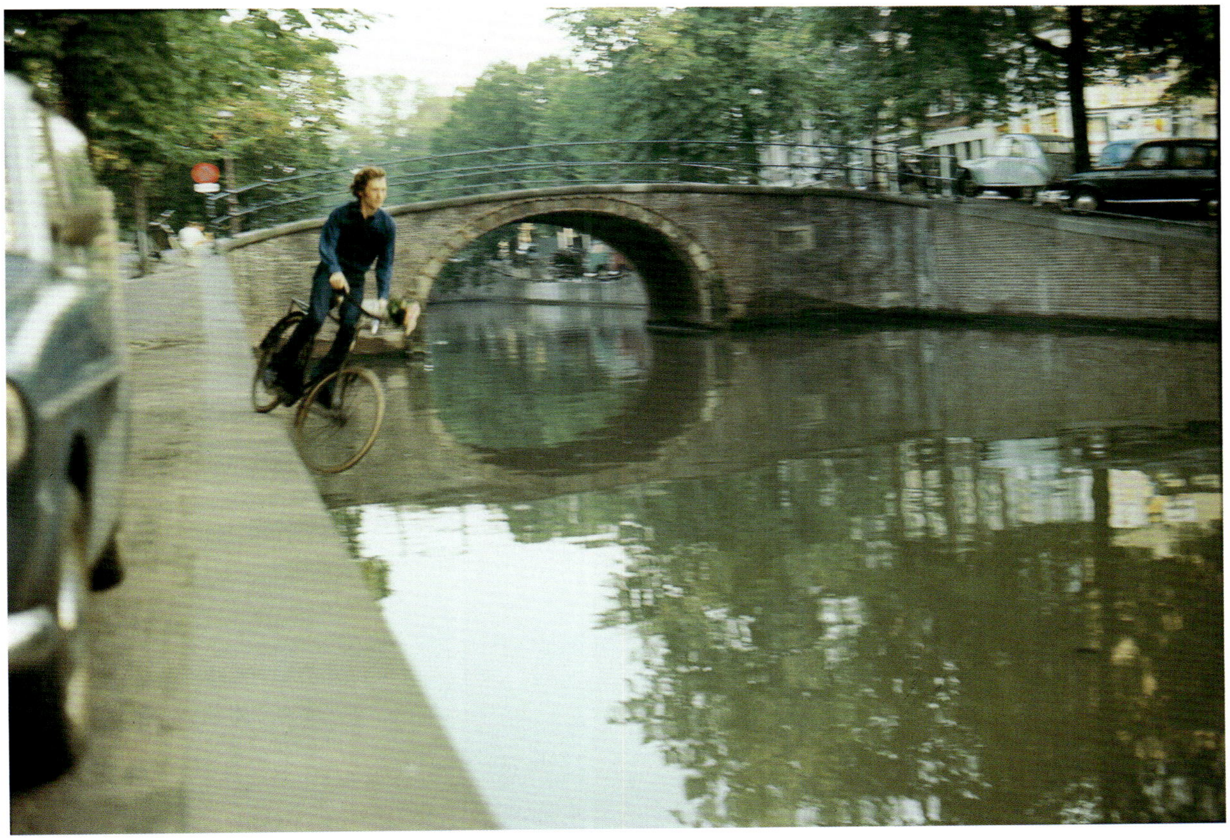

Erwin Wurm

Erwin Wurm uses ordinary bodies, his own and that of others, to expand the principles of sculpture. For his ongoing 'One Minute Sculptures' (1997–) the human body is placed into absurd, witty and often precarious relationships with everyday objects, such as pens, fruit, vegetables, chairs, balls or brooms. The work takes the form of drawn instructions, live performances, videos and photographs. As with Bas Jan Ader's work, it has a deliberate anti-heroic aspect. Funny, pathetic and ridiculous, his 'One Minute Sculptures' show the limits and awkwardness of the human body. For Ader the body becomes a mere object, subject to gravity. In many of Wurm's works the human body is treated as a sculptural form, adopting bizarre and unexpected positions as individuals attempt to perform the artist's instructions. Wurm's is an art for all, where anyone can make art. It is also about the misuse of familiar and ordinary things to enliven and animate the everyday world. Art is made out of the day to day, a DIY aesthetic involving acts of short-lived improvisation in which the relationships and familiar patterns of object use are radically disrupted – the face that becomes a receptacle to hold various stationary equipment, or a male (identified as 'The Museum Director') positioned upside down and head first in a dustbin, a subversive prank that also overturns for a moment his position of power.

Tehching Hsieh

The Taiwanese artist Tehching Hsieh stretches the act of performance to the limits of duration. In many senses his is one of the purest forms of performance art, in which the body is subjected to a self-imposed discipline. *One Year Performance* (1980–1) involved the ritual of punching a time card every hour on the hour for a year. The extensive documentation of this performance fills a whole gallery room. Each time he punches the clock Hsieh makes a portrait by exposing one frame from a 16mm movie camera. Thousands of individual prints from each film frame, printed in sequence as strips registering a day at a time, each with their time cards, fill the walls, and the documentation also includes the time clock, the projected film of the stills and a vitrine containing the uniform the artist wore and statements, descriptions and letters detailing and authenticating the performance. Bas Jan Ader and Erwin Wurm treated the body like sculpture, but in actions and events that were brief. Hsieh's work is in contrast about endurance and the measuring of time through a punishing ritual. Time is measured not only through the clock but also through the body: the artist shaves his hair at the outset, and we can see it grow in the filmic and photographic documentation of the year-long performance. The artwork is about an extraordinary discipline, but it is not faultless: there are times when Hsieh sleeps through and misses an hour, or does not hit the clock at the right time. The cumulative power of this record is a testament to how a body is totally given over to a system. The thousands of portraits that record the repeated punching of the time clock underline the punishing severity of the timetabling and disciplining of the body, as well as a sense of the sheer weight and presence of the passage of time. That Hsieh uses a time clock and wears a worker's uniform makes us think of the labouring body in relation to disciplinary and controlling systems.

Erwin Wurm
From the series 'One Minute Sculptures', 1997
C-print, 45 × 30 cm / 17¾ × 11⅞ in

The Museum Director (Appenzell), 1998
C-print, 120 × 80 cm / 47¼ × 31½ in

Tehching Hsieh
One Year Performance 1980–1
8,760 hours of images, April 11, 1980–April 11, 1982
16mm film, dimensions variable

Punching the Time Clock, 1981, from *One Year Performance, 1980–1*
Photograph by Michael Shen
April 11, 1980
C-print, 21.6 × 28.6 cm / 8.5 × 11.2 in

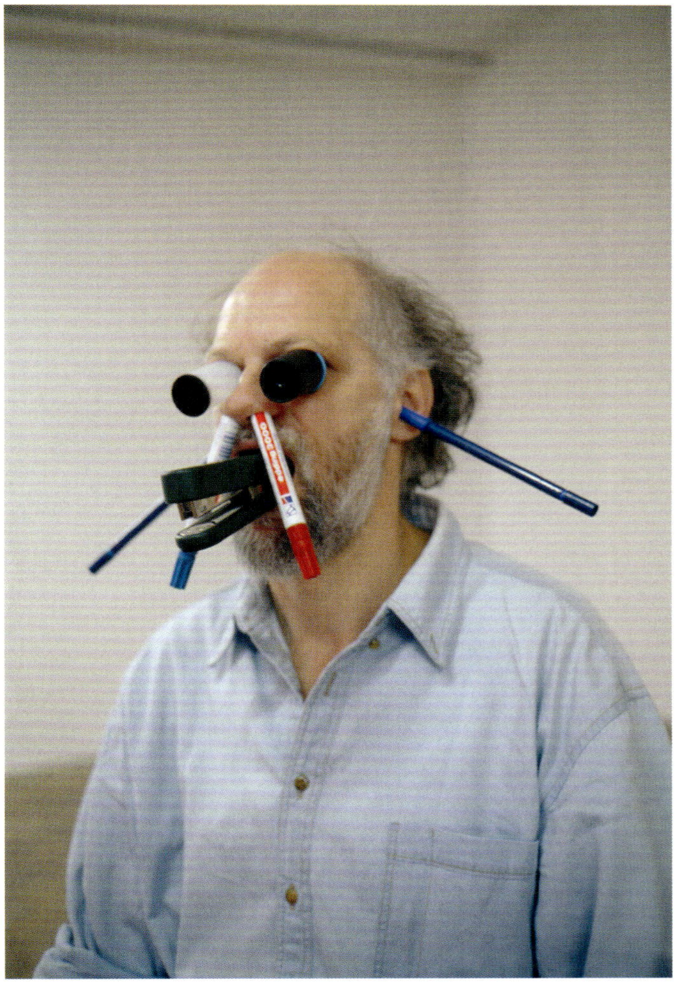

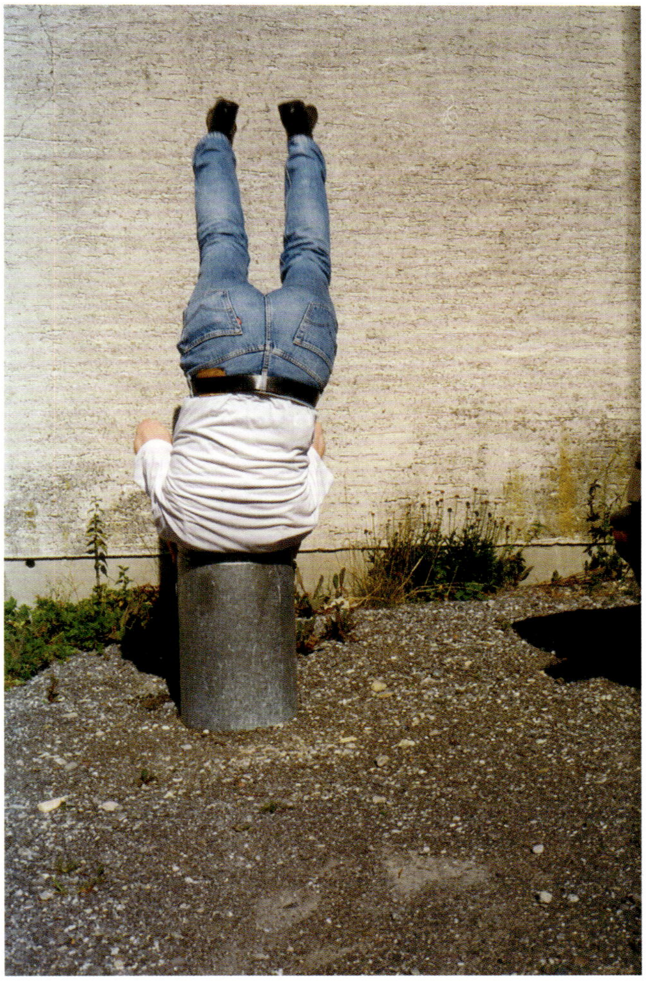

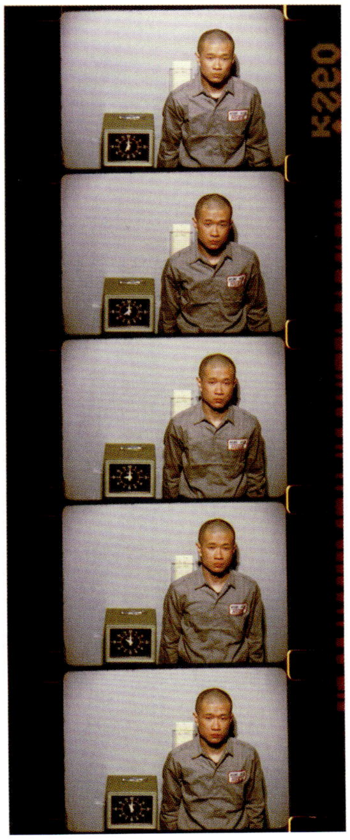

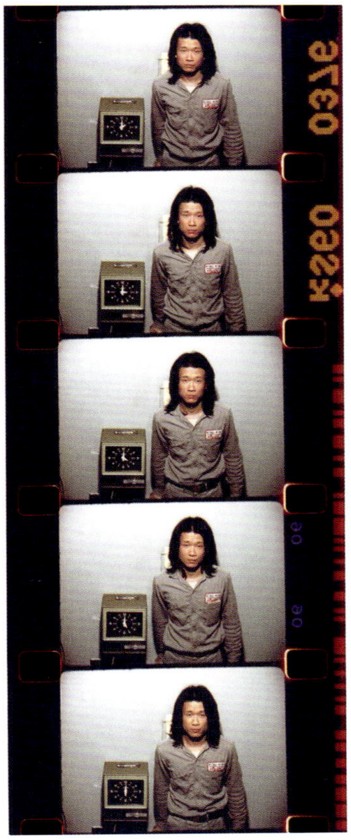

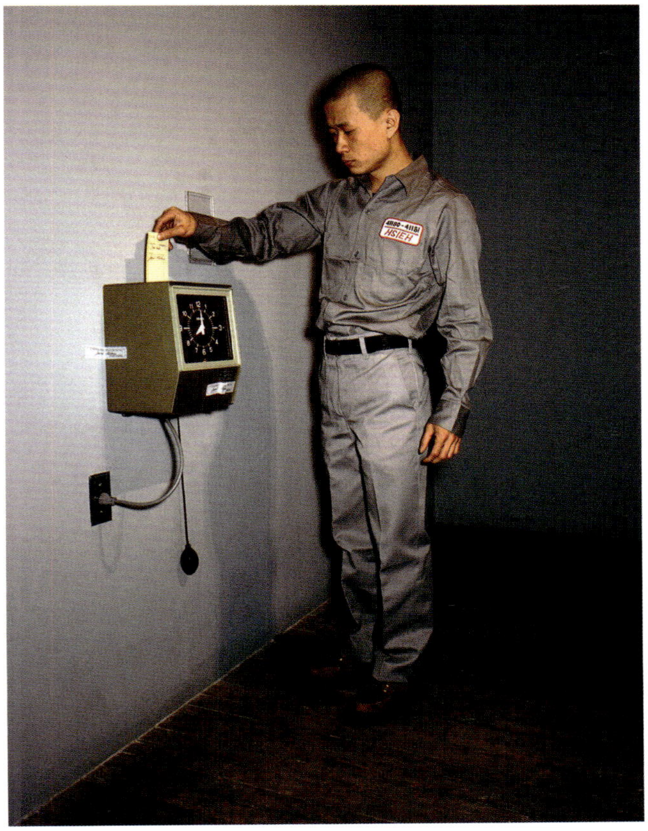

Carolee Schneemann

Photography plays a crucial role in the documentation of the explicit display of the female body in performance art. Carolee Schneemann's performance, *Interior Scroll* (1975), for example, involved her unravelling and reading a script from her vagina. Such a literal display of the artist's female body during a live performance event was seen as a challenge to the aesthetic containment of the female body countering the stabilizing and fetishizing process of voyeurism, as well as the framing of the female figure through the symbolic and conventional forms of art. Such work bluntly opposed the dominant and traditional pictorial conventions that portrayed the nude as a contained, idealized and abstract female form.

Ana Mendieta

Cuban-born Ana Mendieta made performance pieces in the 1970s that documented erasure. In contrast to Schneemann's physical display of her own body, in Mendieta's art disembodied traces replaced the presence of the artist. Her *Silueta* series (1973–7) consisted of female silhouettes based on the outline of the artist's own body, marked or drawn on the landscape in different ways: carved in stone, moulded from the earth or snow, shaped with rocks and traced in flowers, fire or blood. Emblems of death and rebirth, these images could be also seen as symbols of Mendieta's uprootedness. Raised in Havana by a prominent family, she was sent to a foster home in Iowa as part of Operation Pedro Pan, a US Catholic-sponsored programme responsible for the immigration of some 20,000 Cuban children in the early 1960s. Disembodiment might be seen as symbolic of Mendieta's own experience as an exile, but it also entails an attempt to maintain a sense of her cultural heritage. Her ritual fascination with primitive art and cultures stems from her childhood in Cuba.

Carolee Schneemann
Interior Scroll, 1975
East Hampton, Long Island
Performance

Ana Mendieta
Untitled, 1973, from the series
'Silueta Series, Mexico', 1973–7
12 colour photographs each
50.8 × 40.6 cm / 20 × 16 in

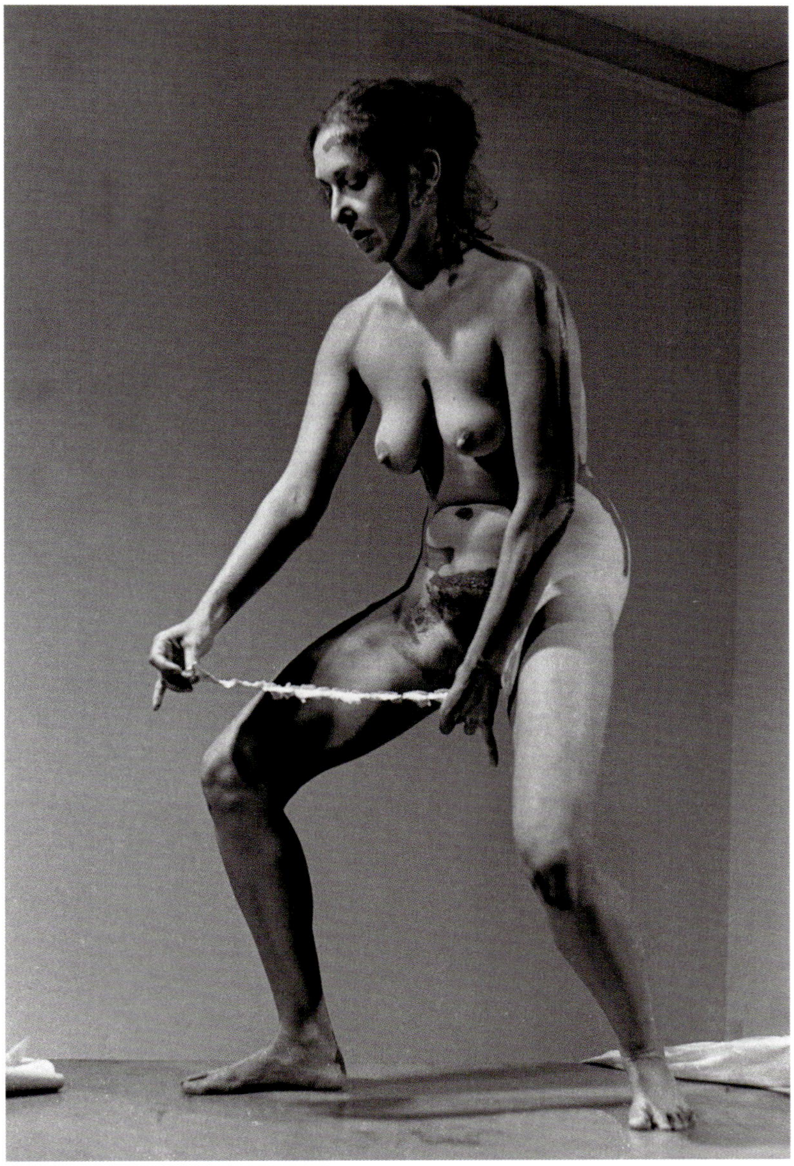 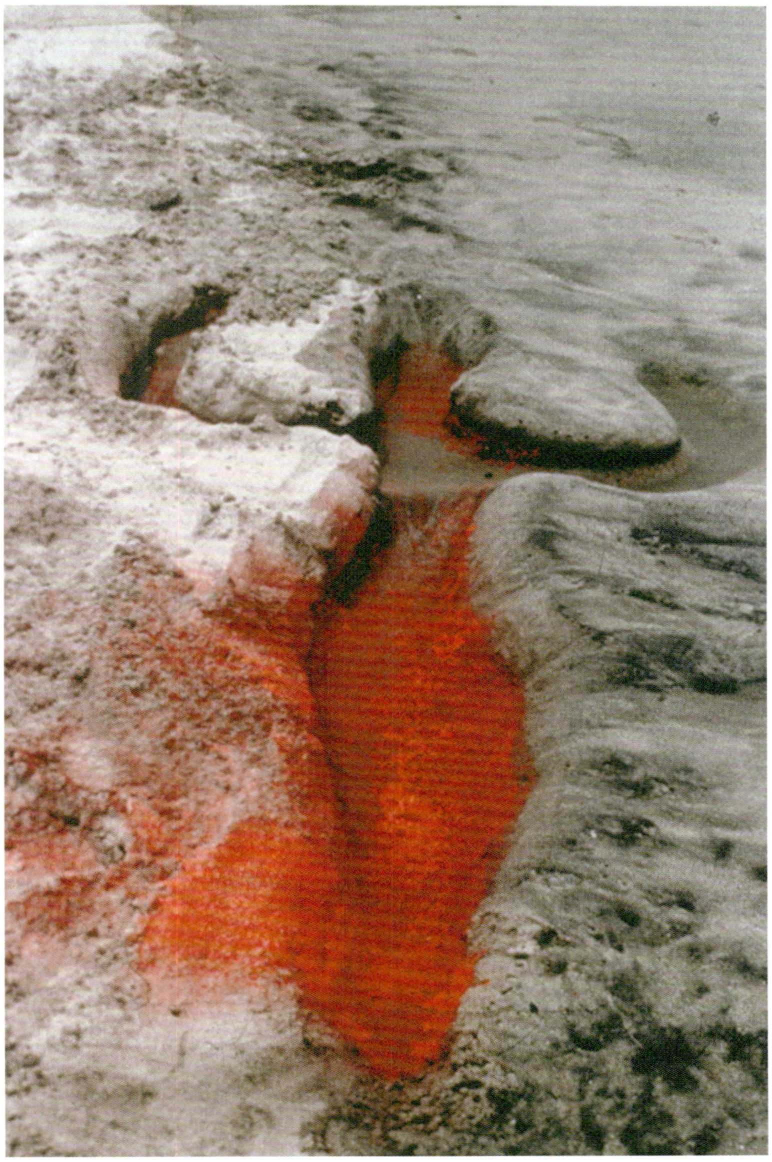

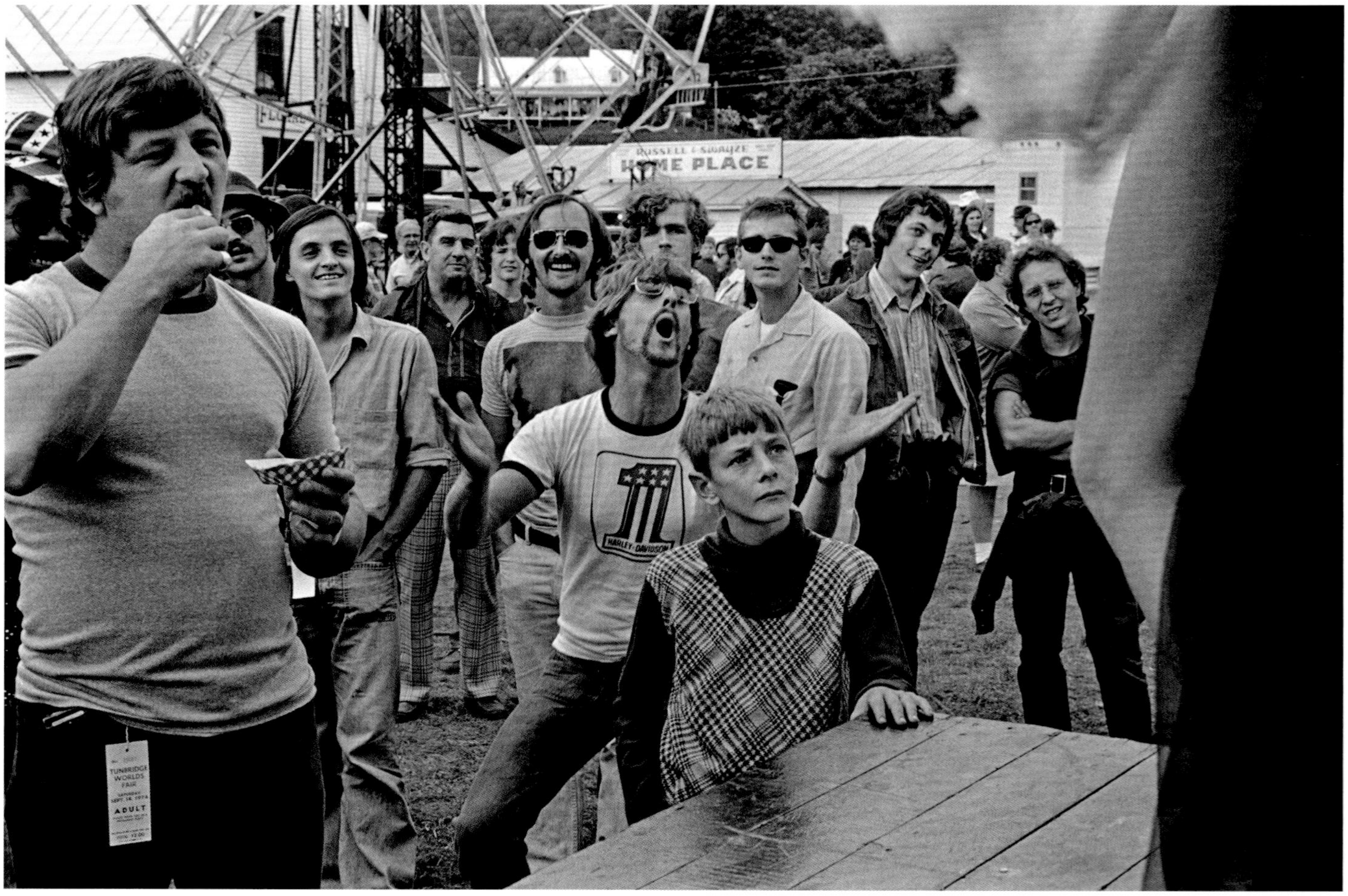
TUNBRIDGE
WORLDS
FAIR
ADULT

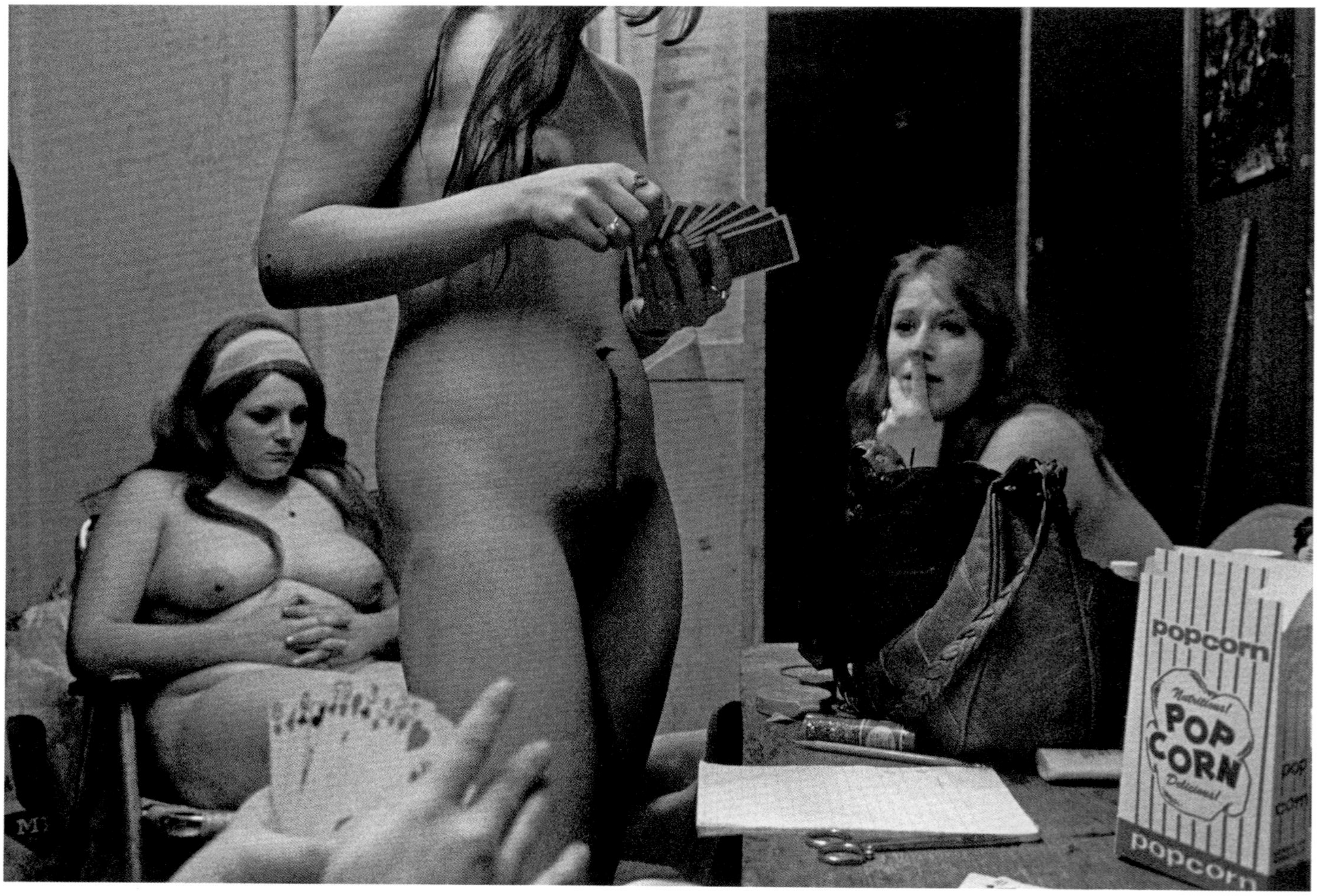
popcorn
POP
CORN
popcorn

Susan Meiselas

An important use of the photographic medium to show and expose the sex industry was made by Susan Meiselas in her book *Carnival Strippers* (1976). While Carolee Schneemann displayed the artist's body in defiance of the masculine framing of woman as symbol, Meiselas uses a documentary strategy to reveal the operations of carnival strip shows that formed part of travelling circuses and state fairs in the 1970s. She shows the women not simply as victims but as workers. They are photographed both on-stage and between performances. Such raw and gritty counter-idealizing representations offered a multi-faceted portrait of these sex workers. The photographs came out of a specific documentary tradition and practice: they are accompanied by extracts from 150 hours of taped interviews Meiselas recorded with the girls, managers, bouncers and audiences. As the lives of the women are vividly brought out, this work becomes about political affiliation and understanding. Much as *Carnival Strippers* is about showing the demeaning work of these women – Meiselas's pictures reveal that many of these acts allowed the male audience to touch and even lick the girls – it is also a homage to their strength and self-preservation, even dignity. They remain in control as much as they can. One of the girls who is interviewed goes so far as to say that: 'The Women look at it as revolutionary – for the first time in their lives to say, "I've got you eating out of the palm of my hand."' Sensitive to the class context that determines and necessitates this work – one writer calls it 'a social documentary about a workplace' – the pictures are also revealing in their display of male lust: greedy and animalistic.[4]

Susan Meiselas
From the series'Carnival Strippers'
Tunbridge, Vermont, USA
Afternoon tease, 1974
Gelatin silver print, dimensions variable

From the series'Carnival Strippers'
Fryeburg, Maine, USA
The dressing room, 1975
Gelatin silver print, dimensions variable

Helmut Newton

As Rosetta Brooks has claimed, no particular look dominated fashion photography in the 1970s and there was no equivalent of such recognizable models from the 1960s as Jean Shrimpton or Twiggy. Instead, fashion photography was characterized by a conspicuous repression of the model's distinctive individuality. Helmut Newton's photography epitomizes this shift, in which 'the model is presented with the cold distance of a fleshy automaton, an extension of the technology which manipulates her and converts her into an object'.[5] Newton adeptly both highlighted and parodied this relationship in his work.

In *Self-Portrait with Wife June and Models, Vogue Studio, Paris* (1981), Newton plays with the conventions and clichés of fashion photography, showing us what is in effect the staging of an erotic fantasy. We see both the back of a naked model as well her full frontal reflection in a mirror. By photographing into a mirror, Newton also puts himself into the picture and alongside the reflection of the body of his model. Adorned in high heels, she adopts a typical 'pin-up' pose for camera, while Newton wears a raincoat, which as Victor Burgin has noted, can be seen as a jokey acknowledgement of his role as both a voyeur and flasher. We do not see his face as he is looking down into the viewfinder of his camera to take his picture. The model turns her head and closes her eyes as she poses. The mirror also reflects the legs and high heels of another model in the studio. We can see nothing else of this woman in the frame of Newton's picture. Contained in the mirror, it is as if both the model and the disembodied pair of legs are part of an imaginary realm conjured up by Newton. The foreground's slightly blurred depiction of the back of the model appears less idealized than her reflected image. The inclusion of his wife in the picture, seated in a director's chair to the right of the mirror and looking towards her husband and the models, further complicates this photograph. A door behind her opens out onto the street, which has the effect of linking her with the outside world, a realm distinct from the magical and fantastical space of the studio, Newton's space, but one which she nevertheless is watching over.

Guy Bourdin

The French fashion photographer, Guy Bourdin, like Helmut Newton, knowingly played with the codes and conventions of fashion photography, often organizing his images around the divide of the double page, the centrefold. In the March 1978 issue of French *Vogue* a Charles Jourdan advertisement showed a model crouching in black swimwear on an urban walkway, the gutter of the page and the vanishing point of the picture falling at the point between her spread legs. Opening and closing the pages would also open and close the model's high-heeled bare legs. The conventional pornographic display was however obstructed by a black-and-white photograph of the model in a similar pose, which was held up to the viewer by the woman so it concealed the colour photographic depiction of her body from below her eyes to above her crotch. This picture within a picture unsettles the pattern of voyeurism and, as Rosetta Brooks has put it, showed how the model 'was the possessor of the image and of its falsity and shared the joke with the predominantly female readership of the magazine'.[6]

Bourdin cleverly plays with and blurs the distinctions between the mannequin and human model in his photograph published in the May 1975 issue of French *Vogue*. A series of dummies in a shop's interior have been styled and arranged so they take on an uncanny lifelikeness. So much so that their varied and animate gestures contrast with the standardised uniformity of the two female models striding down the street outside.

Helmut Newton
Self-Portrait with Wife June and Models, Vogue Studio, Paris, 1981
Gelatin silver print
Dimensions variable

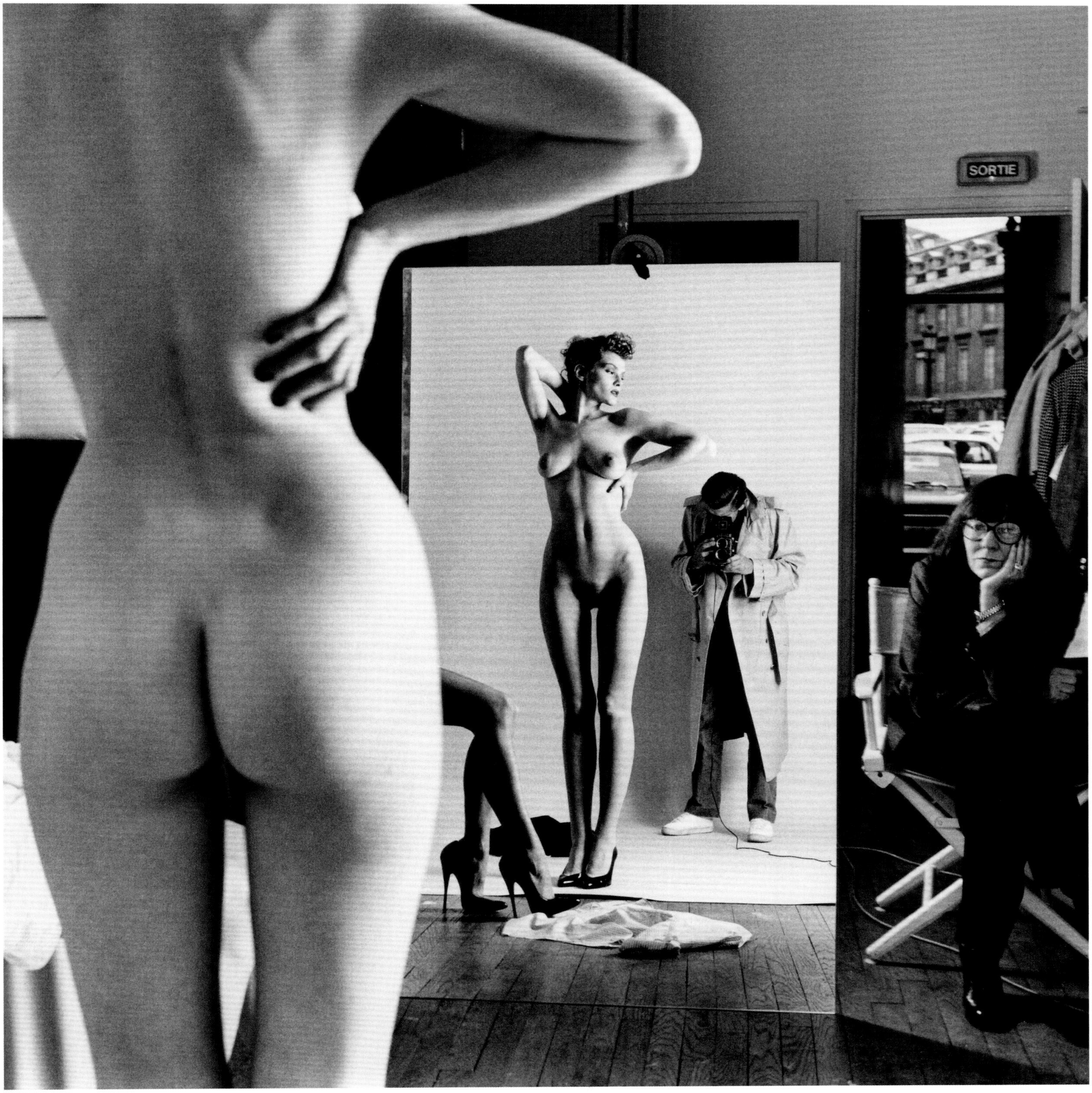
SORTIE

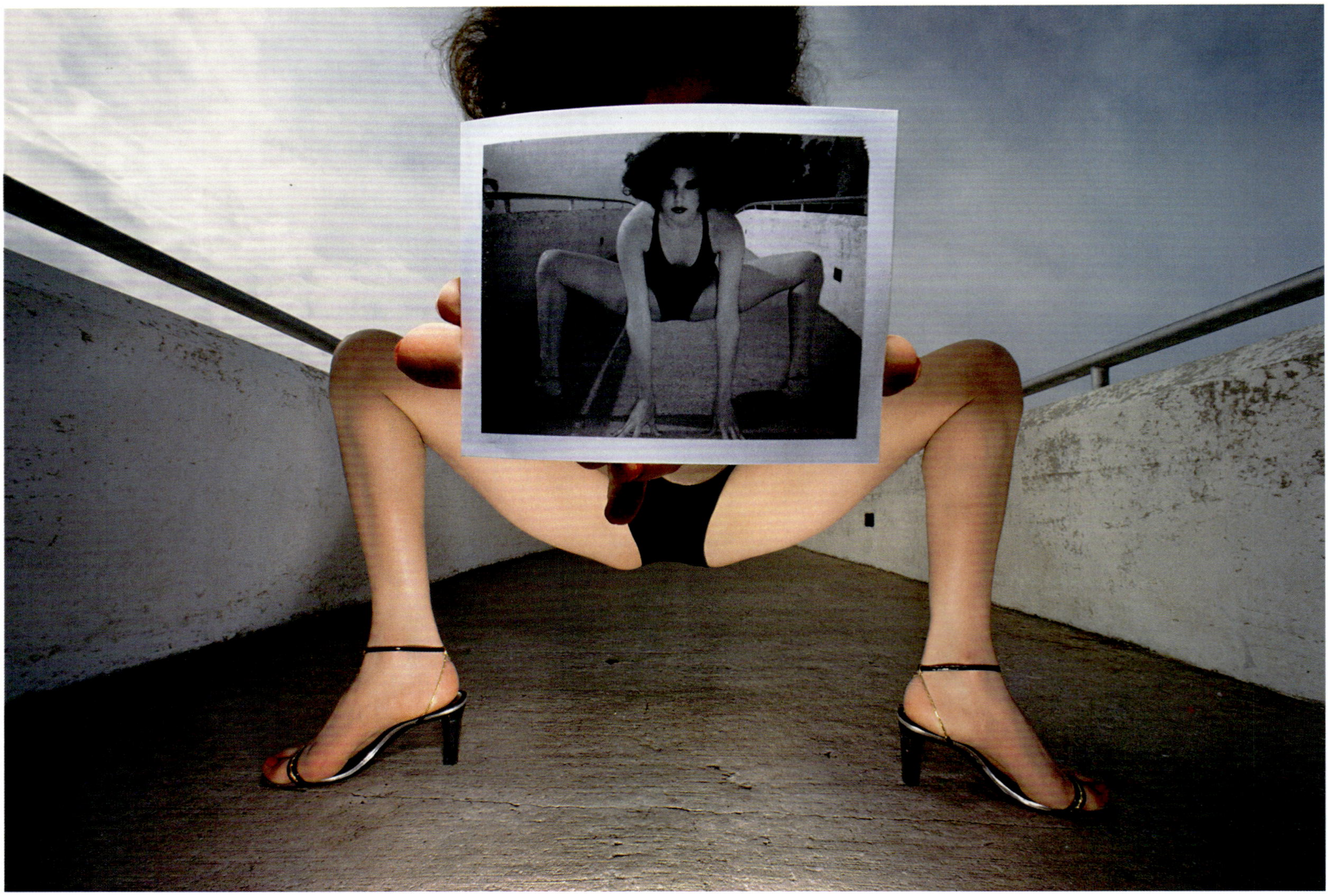

Guy Bourdin
Charles Jourdan, Spring 1978

Vogue Paris, May 1975

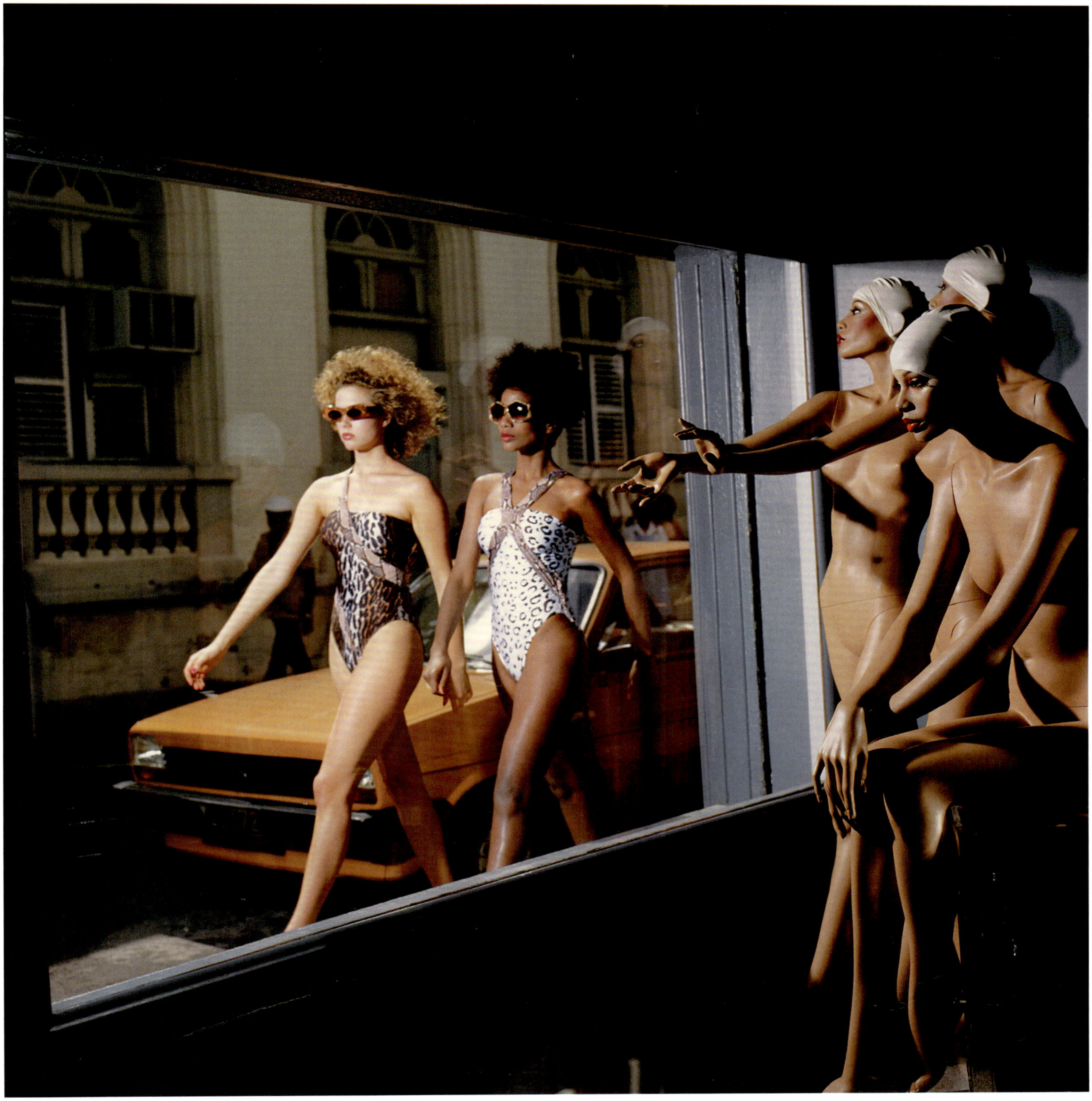

Robert Mapplethorpe

Helmut Newton's mannequin-like models find their parallel in the pumped-up masculinity on show in many of Robert Mapplethorpe's photographs of black male bodies. In his *Black Book* (1986), we look through a sequence of individual, named African-American men but, as the theorist Kobena Mercer has argued, their portrayal can be seen as maintaining racial and sexual fantasies about the black male body. There is nothing here about their lives, histories or experiences. Instead, the black body is reduced to a 'passive decorative *objet d'art*.'[7] In this respect, Mapplethorpe's sexualized and fetishizing representations of the black male body can be seen to echo Leni Riefensthal's ethnographic photographs of the Nuba, first published in Germany in 1973 and in the United States a year later. Susan Sontag's well-known attack on Riefensthal's pictures read them as carrying a continuity with the fascist aesthetic of her propagandistic film work for the Nazis, *Triumph of the Will* and *Olympia*. In this colonial context, the subjects are bereft of history and become exotic specimens for Riefensthal's delectation. Drawn to the male Nuba because of their healthy and physical bodies, Riefensthal makes pictures whose idealized view feeds an exoticizing colonial fantasy, 'one more lament for vanishing primitives,' as Sontag puts it.[8]

The conventional subject of the nude is the white female body and Mapplethorpe draws on the codes of this genre to frame his way of seeing black male bodies as abstract, beautiful 'things.' Additionally, a number of Mapplethorpe's depictions of black men make use of racial myths that exploit black virility. *Man In Polyester Suit* (1980) not only de-individualizes by cropping out the subject's head, but reduces the black male figure to his sex, which in accordance with colonial fears and fantasies is portrayed as something 'excessive/other.' The use of the suit further compounds such ideas, suggesting that the black male is unable to fully accede to civilizing culture because of his sex. That the suit is made of cheap polyester and its seams are coming undone adds a class connotation, alluding to the poverty and low social position of the black male subject.

Mapplethorpe's photographs brought a formal charge of obscenity, the first made against an art gallery in American history. In 1990 Dennis Barrie, the director of the Contemporary Arts Centre in Cincinnati, went on trial for showing seven works by Mapplethorpe accused of being obscene, two of children and five showing scenes of sado-masochistic homosexuality. The argument that Mapplethorpe was a master of classical form won Barrie and the museum an aquittal. Aesthetics excused the supposed obscene content of the pictures.

Crucial changes in context brought about by the moral panic in the United States around the homoerotic content of Mapplethorpe's work have affected readings of his pictures. His death in 1989 from AIDS, the subsequent obscenity trial and the political assault by the political Right on funding for the arts in the United States led to a re-appraisal of Mapplethorpe's photography. Kobena Mercer, for example, shifted his initial critical response to the photographer's work. He noted that 'Mapplethorpe was hardly representative of the hegemonic model of straight, white, bourgeois male identity traditionally privileged in Western art history as the centred subject and agent of representation.' Mercer began to see something both affirmative and subversive in Mapplethorpe's depiction of black bodies with the ideals of Classical Greek sculpture. Black men in the United States, 'disenfranchised, disadvantaged and disempowered as a distinct collective subject in the late-capitalist underclass,' are 'elevated onto the pedestal of the transcendental Western aesthetic ideal.' The critic Peggy Phelan, also attentive to the importance of the classicizing of the black male body in Mapplethorpe's work, went so far as to suggest that 'his photographs demonstrate that love and understanding of a body, while always involving objectification… do not have to violate or eliminate the private grace and power of the model.'[9]

Robert Mapplethorpe
Ken Moody, 1983
Gelatin silver print
38.4 × 38.7 cm / 15⅛ × 15¼ in

Ajitto, 1981
Gelatin silver print, 50.8 × 40.6 cm / 20 × 16 in

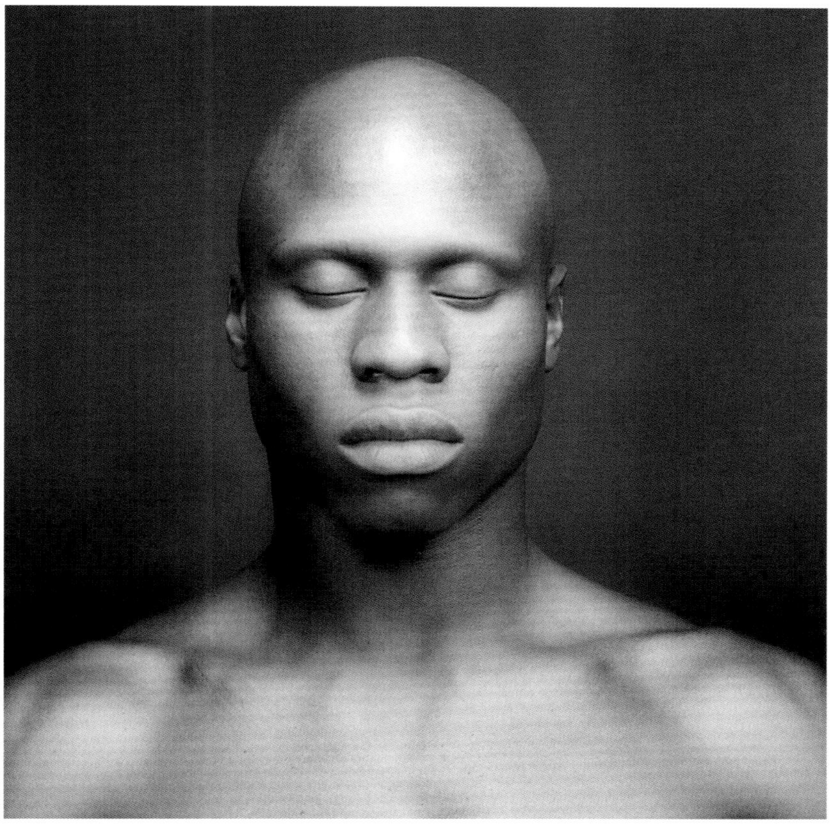

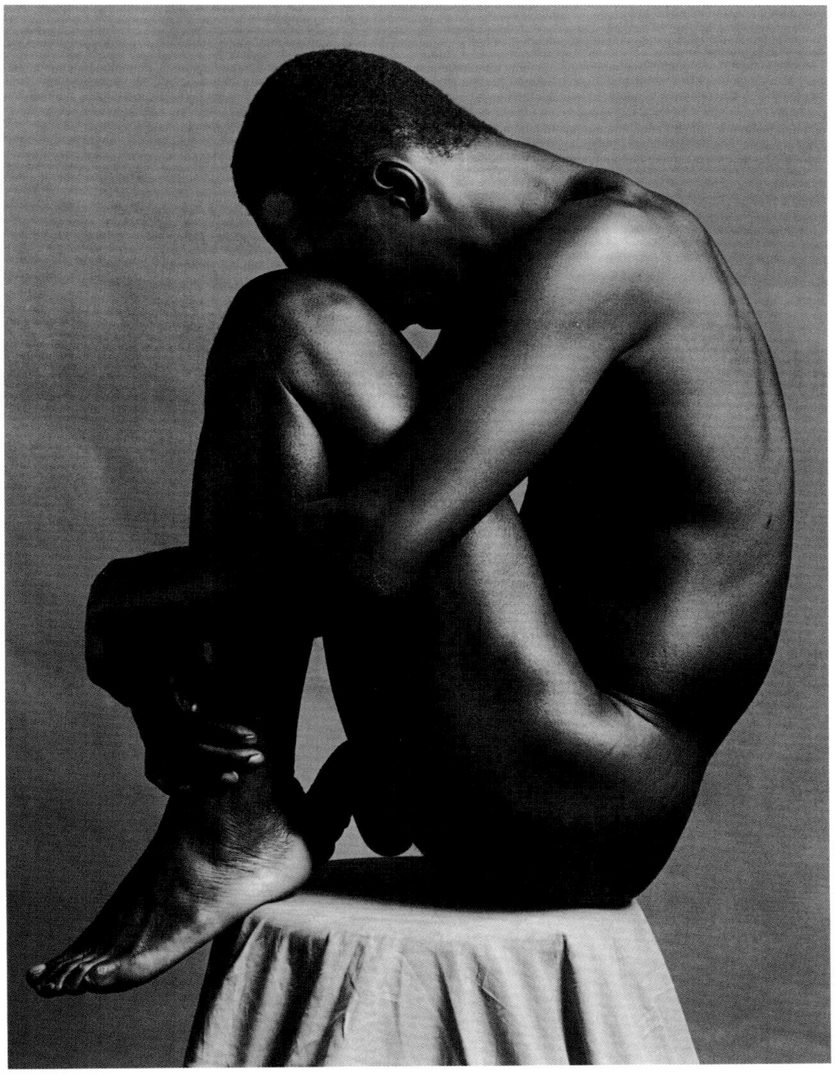

Sally Mann's pictures of her son and two daughters became embroiled in the panic over children and sexuality prompted by the furore over Robert Mapplethorpe's work. Mann's photographs in her books, *At Twelve: Portraits of Young Women* (1988) and *Immediate Family* (1992), explore anxieties over the representation of children. Many of the pictures of adolescent girls in *At Twelve* show innocence as either under threat or lost, and adults as no longer protective but threatening and dangerous. The book's cover shows a picture that sets the sexuality of one of the book's young women, 'Sherry', against an old photograph propped up on a chair, showing her grandmother at the age of twelve. The demure formal Victorian portrait is crumbling and mottled, suggesting that innocence is something irretrievably past, in distinct contrast to the bodily presence of the girl posing next to the photo, cropped at knees and chest. Mann has framed Sherry in such a way that everything centres upon her vulva, as revealed through the creases of her closely fitting shorts. Adults in Mann's pictures do not offer support but signal danger and threat. They are, as one picture reveals, a shadowy and oppressive dark force, out of place in the child's world, symbolized by the little playhouse the man dwarfs. Many of the girls' poses mime those of adults. A sullen-faced girl stretches out on the hood of a car, 'Showing me how her mother's boyfriend pretended to hang himself out in the back yard', according to Mann's accompanying caption. Unease and menace is signalled by the word DOOM, written in the dust on the bonnet, while the butterfly net is suggestive of entrapment and vulnerability. Captions, on occasion, expand upon what is implied in the pictures: in the most dramatic, the tension between the male adult and the child posing with him sensationally explodes in the accompanying narrative: 'The child was distinctly reluctant to stand closer to her mother's boyfriend... Several months later her mother shot him in the face with a .22. She testified that while she worked nights at a local truck stop he was "at home partying and harassing my daughter"'.

Immediate Family went on to explore the unease and uncertainties of childhood from the perspective of the mother. Mann pictured her three children – Emmett, Jessie and Virginia – over a period of seven years in the Arcadian setting of her Virginia home, a thirty-acre garden established by Mann's father in the foothills of the Blue Ridge Mountains. Taken with a Victorian large-format camera and printed in black and white, the pictures have a look of the past, recalling the allegorical photographs of the English photographer Julia Margaret Cameron. In many senses Mann's images extend and magnify the sensuality and eroticism of the earlier pictures.

The old process and look of these pictures, the beauty of the children and the idyllic setting evoke fantasies of an innocent, natural childhood. But innocence is always under threat, tainted and skewed. Many depictions play upon the fears of the mother. Children are shown bitten, with bloody noses, with cuts needing stitches, even dead-looking. In *The Wet Bed*, showing the youngest child asleep at the age of two, the state of angelic innocence is offset by the connotations of the pale stain that spreads on the mattress. This is extended in photographs that show children injured or soiled and caked in mud. Much as they appear knowing, active, in control, the children also can appear tentative and vulnerable. In *Hayhook* (1989), clothed adults are shown indifferent to a nude Jessie, hanging from a large chain and hook at the centre of the picture. Is Mann, as Marianne Hirsch has suggested, 'revealing the exposure and vulnerability of childhood in a world of uncaring and self-involved adults? Or is she revealing her own fears, projected onto Jessie's taut body, fears of her own exposure as her image hangs like her daughter from hooks amid uninvolved spectators'?[10]

In Mann's recent 'Proud Flesh' (2003–9)series the use of the messy Victorian wet-collodion process in which the negatives are coated with chemicals and exposed when wet, gives an expressive and sensual dimension to her still photographs of the naked body of her husband. Bathed in daylight the flesh of her lover can appear akin to classical statuary while in others there is a more literal, blunt and even medical detailing of his ageing and wasted body. Her husband is suffering from muscular dystrophy and her pictures are in part a reflection upon and response to his physical debilitation. Imperfections in the printing process, the way the various stains, scratches, mottling and spattering appear to mark and lacerate the surfaces of skin can also be suggestive of the pain and loss of her lover's physical well-being, as well as the sense of the mortality of all flesh.

Sally Mann
Theresa and the Tattooed Man, 1983–5
Gelatin silver print
20.3 × 25.4 cm / 8 × 10 in

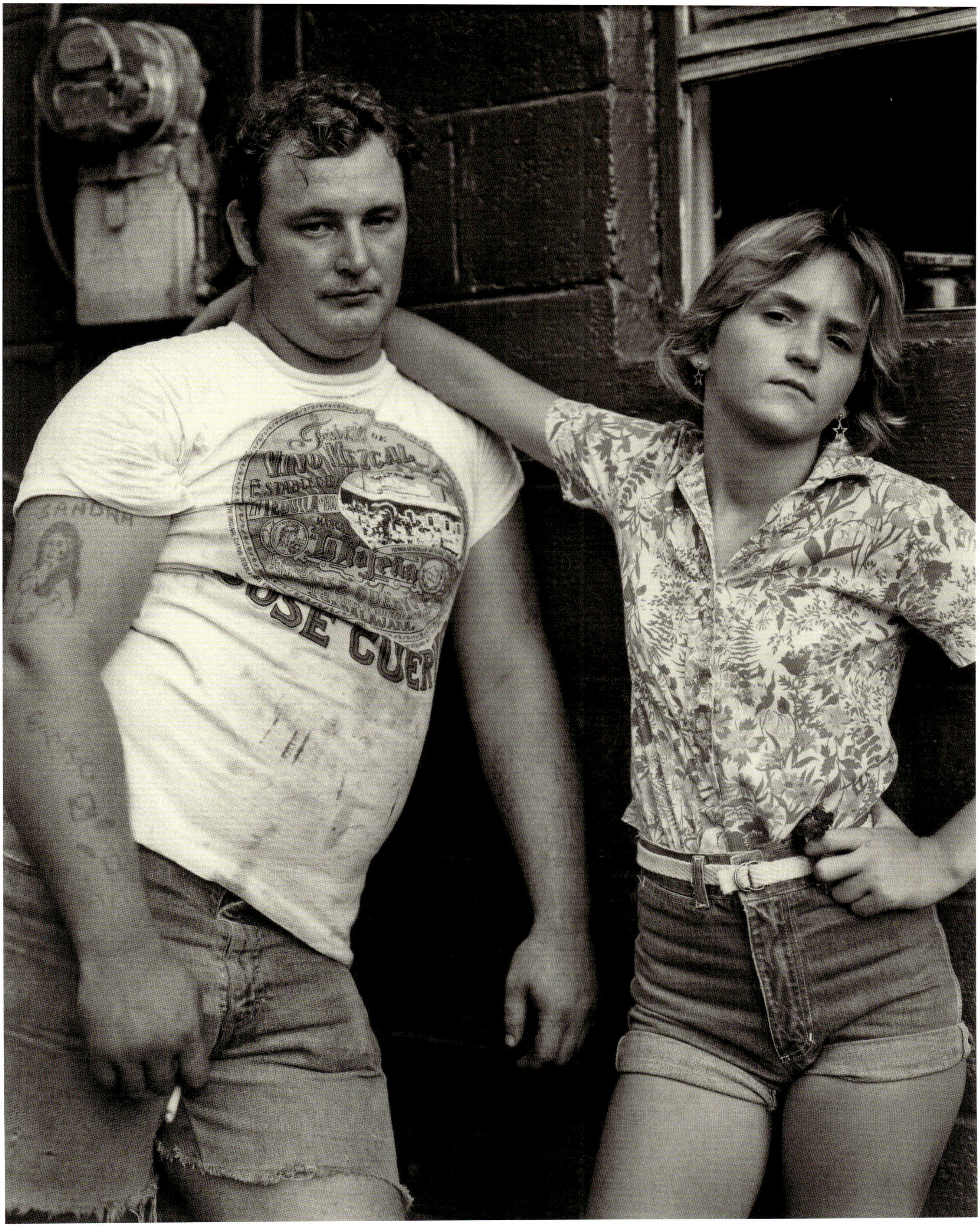
VINO MEZCAL
SANDRA

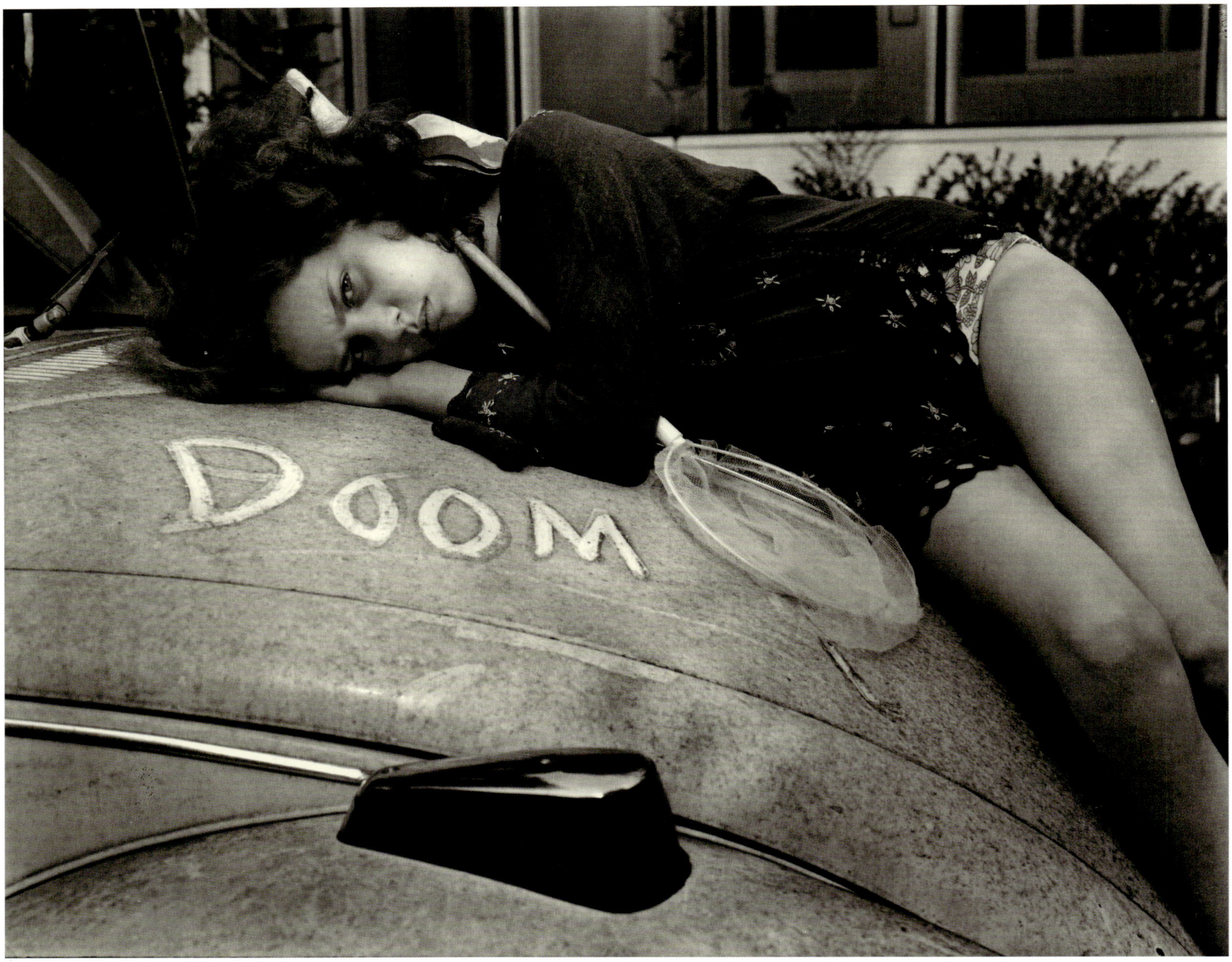
DOOM

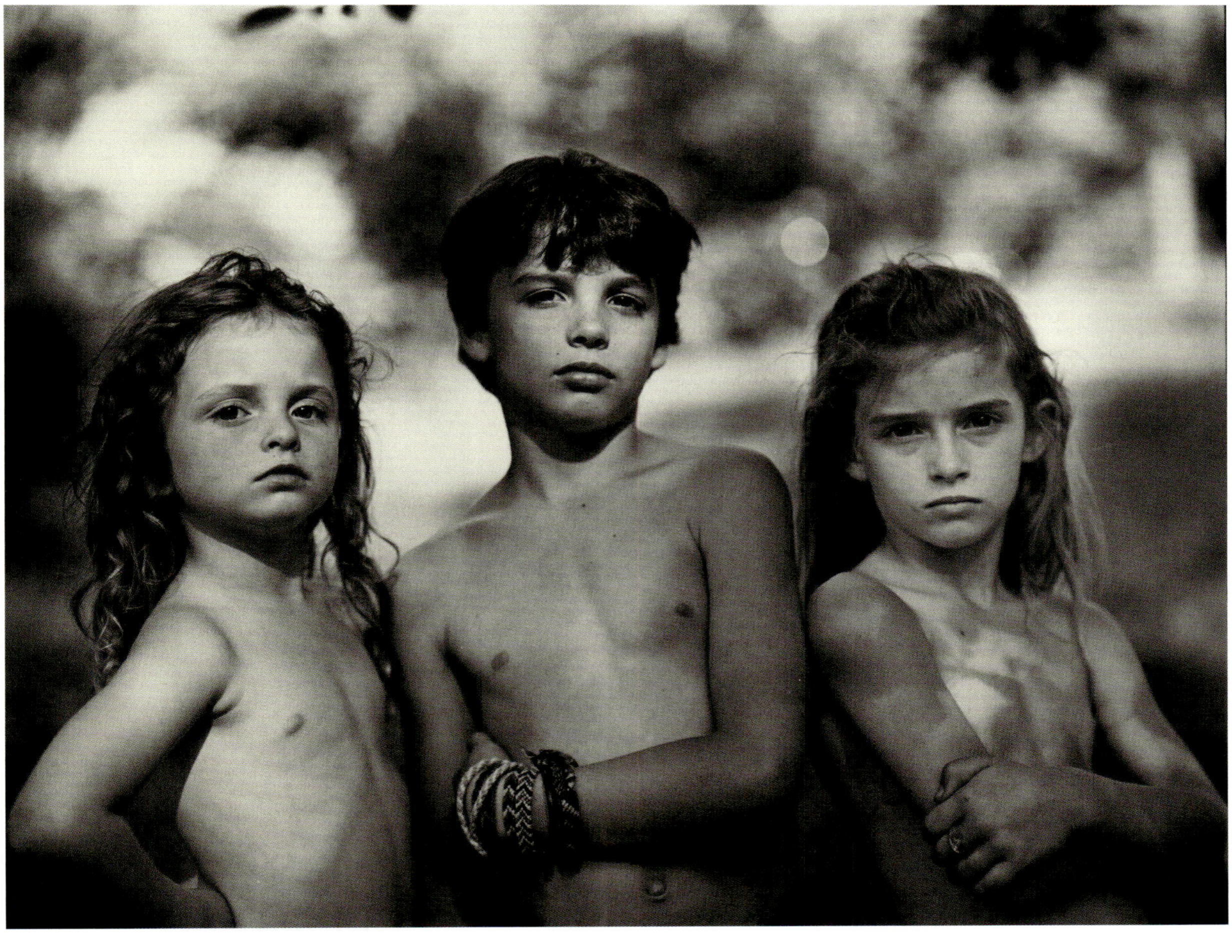

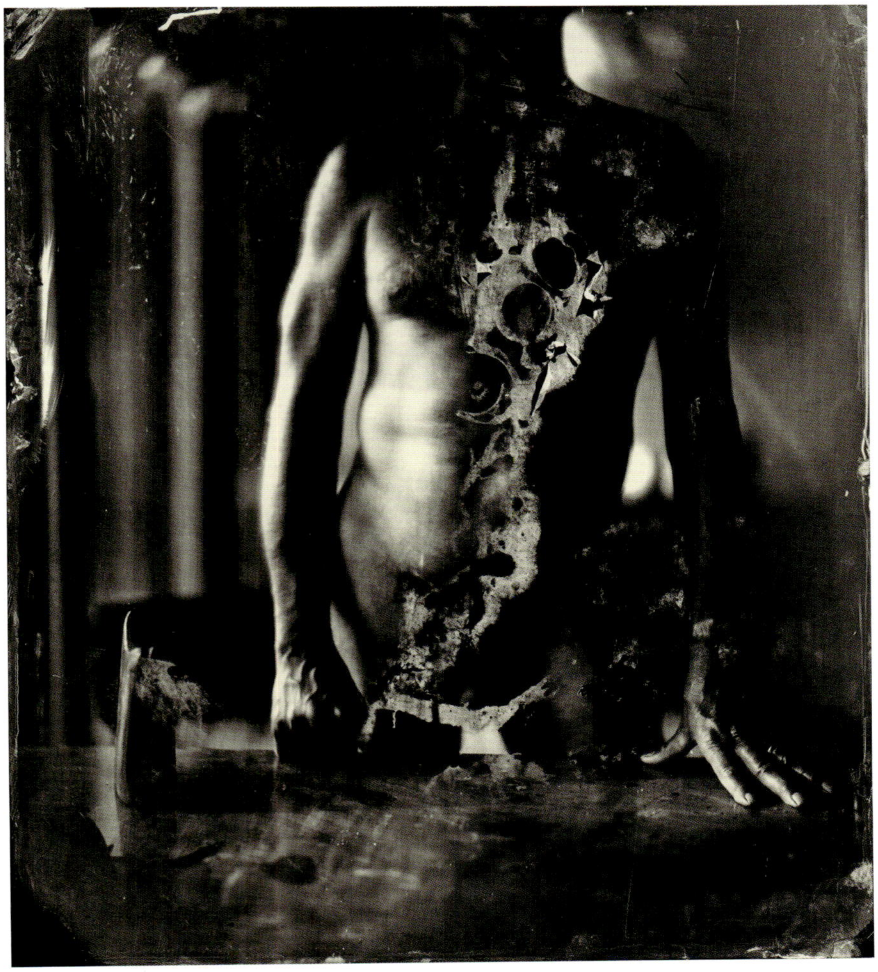

Sally Mann
Ianna and Doom, 1983–5
Gelatin silver print
20.3 × 25.4 cm / 8 × 10 in

Emmett, Jessie and Virginia, 1989
Gelatin silver print
50.8 × 60.9 cm / 20 × 24 in

Hephaestus, 2008
Gelatin silver print
38.1 × 34.3 cm / 15 × 13½ in

John Coplans

John Coplans used the classical form to challenge prejudices towards the aged physical body. Coplans, a writer and curator, and editor of *Artforum*, reinvented himself as an artist in his sixties through photographs that exposed his ageing body. In making his pictures he drew upon his knowledge of the history of photography, painting and sculpture, from Egyptian hieroglyphics and ancient Greek friezes to the classical nude and performance art. Made over the course of twenty-five years, the photographs show the permutations of Coplans' flesh, both life size and larger than life. In place of the ideal proportions of Greek sculpture, we encounter the hairy flesh of this elderly white male. The body loses class, culture and time through the process of its photographic isolation and fragmentation. The specificity of his own fascinating physique at the same time serves as a *memento mori*, a reminder of the way all bodies inevitably succumb to ageing and death. Aesthetics here serves to challenge a social context in which beauty is equated with youth. As Coplans put it: 'These photographs refer to body politics in the sense that "oldness" is a taboo in American society, which tends to worship beauty and youth, consequently the aging of old bodies must be hidden from view, for they are imperfect, very often diseased and soon perish.'[11] In the place of an idealizing vision, he turns the camera on his own aged body to produce pictures of both dignity and freedom.

John Coplans
Self Portrait (Upside Down No. 7), 1992
3 gelatine silver prints
Each 8.9 × 11.4 cm / 3½ × 4½ in

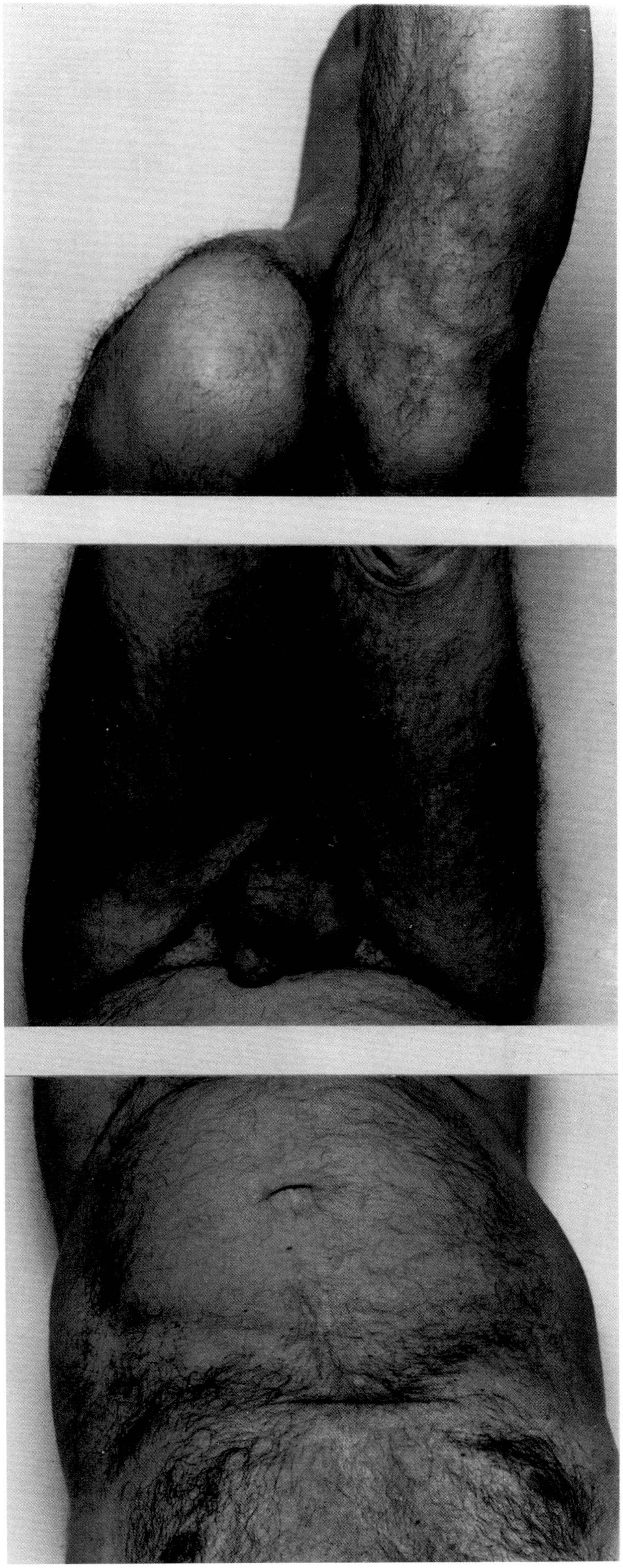

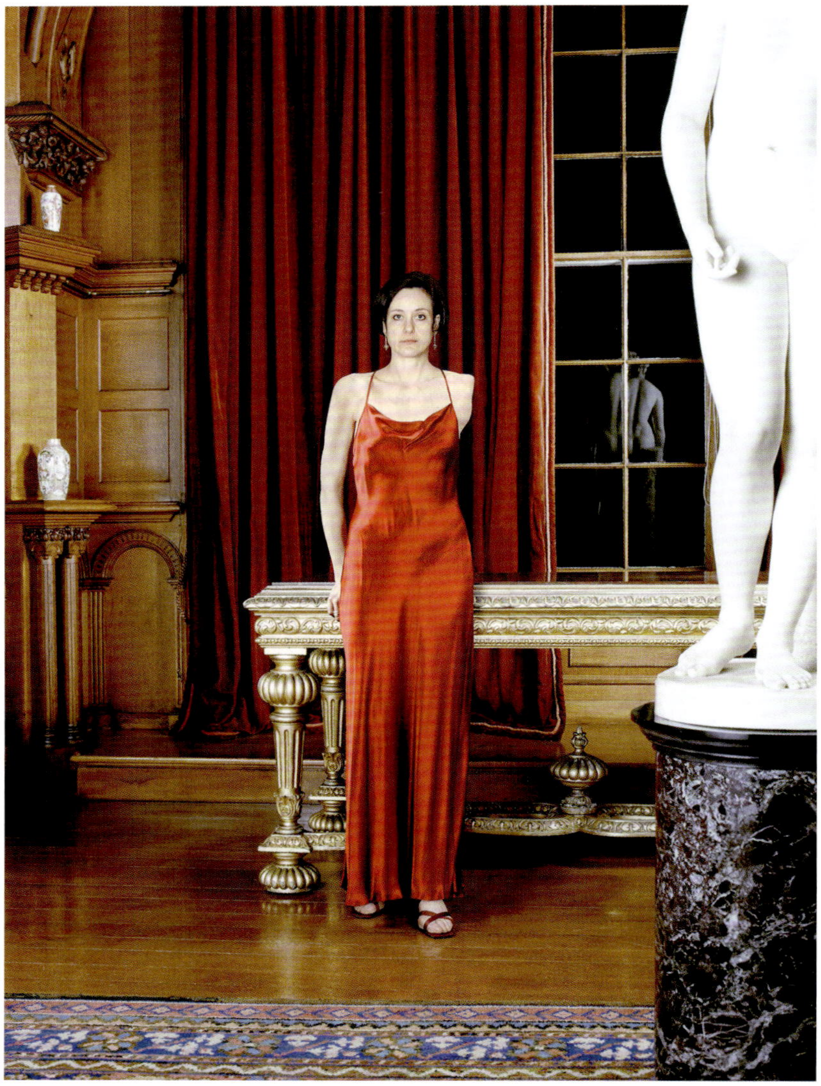

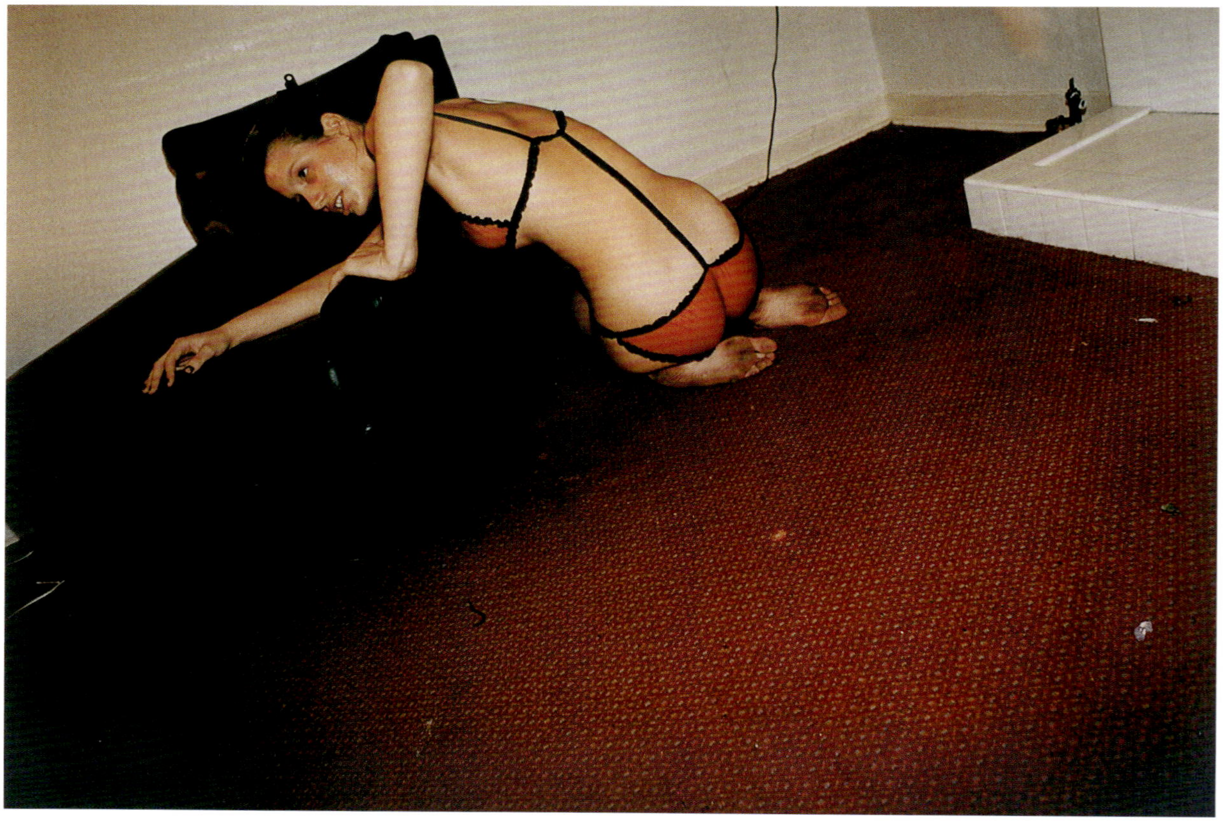

Alexa Wright

Prejudices

In Alexa Wright's digital photographic series *I* (1998/1999), the able-bodied artist makes a remarkable gesture of affiliation and identification, mapping her own facial features onto the bodies of physically disabled women. In this series, the conventions of the stately grandeur of the aristocratic portrait, in which the figure is shown amidst the splendour of his or her wealthy possessions, are radically undermined as the artist deliberately sets up collisions between such settings and the subjects she poses within them. Wright places the bodies of physically disabled women within luxurious spaces in order to raise fundamental questions about assumptions of difference and traditional aesthetic hegemonies, the ideal of beauty. The pictures give grace and dignity to bodies which are culturally marginalized. The work has its basis in collaboration between the artist and her subjects, which manifests itself as an integral and unsettling aspect of the pictures.

Corinne Day

Abjection

In the 1990s fashion photography began to concern itself with unconventional looking models. It was marked by realism, and was not afraid to exploit abject states of the body. British photographer Corrine Day has been instrumental in shifting fashion photography away from stereotyped beauty. The unkempt appearance and skinny bodies of the models tended to be read as signs of drug abuse, and were branded as 'heroin chic', an accusation Day has denied. Her colour photograph *Georgina, Brixton* (1995), mimes the 'bad' look of an amateur snapshot, and shows a thin model in scanty red underwear slumped over a tatty armchair in the grubby interior of a sparse flat. Rebecca Arnold sees such realist-looking fashion pictures as testimony of a shift away from the individual of the 1980s, when the body, 'perceived to be under siege from the threat of death and disease was toned and exercised to form a protective shell.'[12] Instead, we have a display of bodies that appear to have 'given in to illness, thin corpses that flaunt the mortality of the flesh.'

Alexa Wright
'I', 1999
Lightjet digital C-print
100 × 76cm / 30 × 40 in

Corinne Day
Georgina, Brixton, 1995
C-print, 15.3 × 22.8 cm / 6 × 8 in

Cindy Sherman

Cindy Sherman's work shifts from a mimicry of the fetishizing and voyeuristic parade of women as spectacle in the movies to representations of the female form in more brutalized and abject states. If in many senses her use of the mask and costuming accorded with an idea of the female body as constructed, a tissue of signs rather than flesh, the trajectory of Sherman's work is significant in that it challenges this very postmodern idea and, for all the artifice and theatre, returns us to questions integral to the explicit performance work of Carolee Schneemann.

Sherman's work is best seen in terms of 'phases'. In her 'Untitled Film Stills' (1977–80) she portrayed woman as and subject to spectacle, a mirroring and mimesis of heroines in the movies. Film theorist Laura Mulvey has proposed that subsequent works register a significant shift in iconography: 'The female body's metamorphoses, in Sherman's "narrative trajectory", trace a gradual collapse of surface.'[13] This starts in the images commissioned for *Artforum* magazine in the 1980s, horizontal colour centrefolds in which Sherman impersonates women lost in reverie, on sofas, beds or the floor; pictures which, while caught up in a mirroring of stereotypes, begin to suggest interior states. By the time of Sherman's series of pictures from 1985–9, we see beneath the cosmetic façade: the female body has been replaced by decaying food, vomit, menstrual blood, 'the secret stuff of bodily fluids that the cosmetic is designed to conceal'. Mulvey believes such work marks a break with the fetishistic portrayal of women, effecting a corporeal challenge to the mastering male gaze. As the female body disintegrates, the photographs also lose cohesive form.

Sherman's recourse to life-size dummies in subsequent works offered up a symbolic, violent disordering of the body. Such pictures find a certain parallel in the disturbing digital photographs by the Dutch fashion photographer and artist, Inez van Lamsweerde. For *Final Fantasy* (1993), named after a video game, she hired three-year-old models and digitally replaced their mouths with those of adult men. Innocence was disrupted by the leer of males. In the series 'Thankyou Thighmaster' (1993), bodies were digitally mixed with mannequins. Fetishism became edged with abjection, as the shine we associate with glossy magazines could be seen to have condensed into the grease and sweat on the models' hands and feet. Since the bodies are shown without bodily orifices, sealed up, Lamsweerde pushes the fashion model–mannequin analogy to the point of grotesquery. Her art involves a de-eroticizing manipulation of the female form.

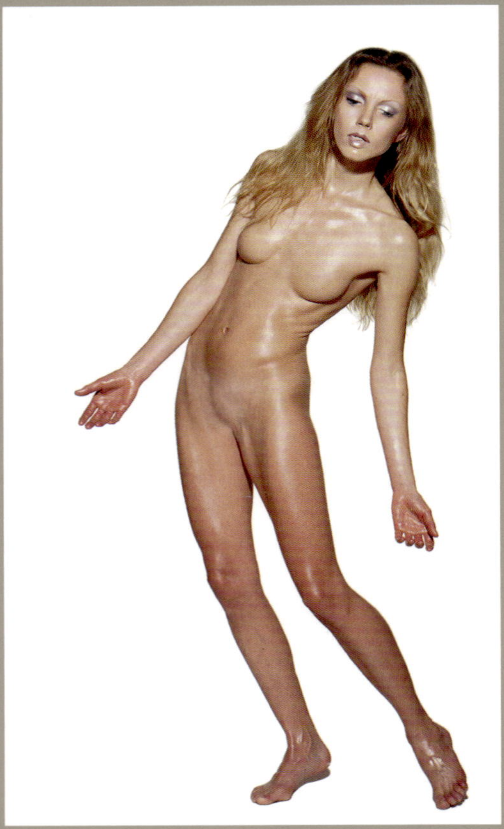

Inez van Lamsweerde
Britt, from the series 'Thankyou Thighmaster', 1993
C-print op perspex
1.9 × 1.2 m / 73¼ × 47¼ in

Cindy Sherman
Untitled #87, 1981
C-print, 59.2 × 122.5 cm / 23 5/16 × 48¼ in

Untitled #96, 1981
C-print, 61 × 121.9 cm / 24 × 48 in

Untitled #173, 1986
C-print, 152.4 × 228.6 cm / 60 × 90 in

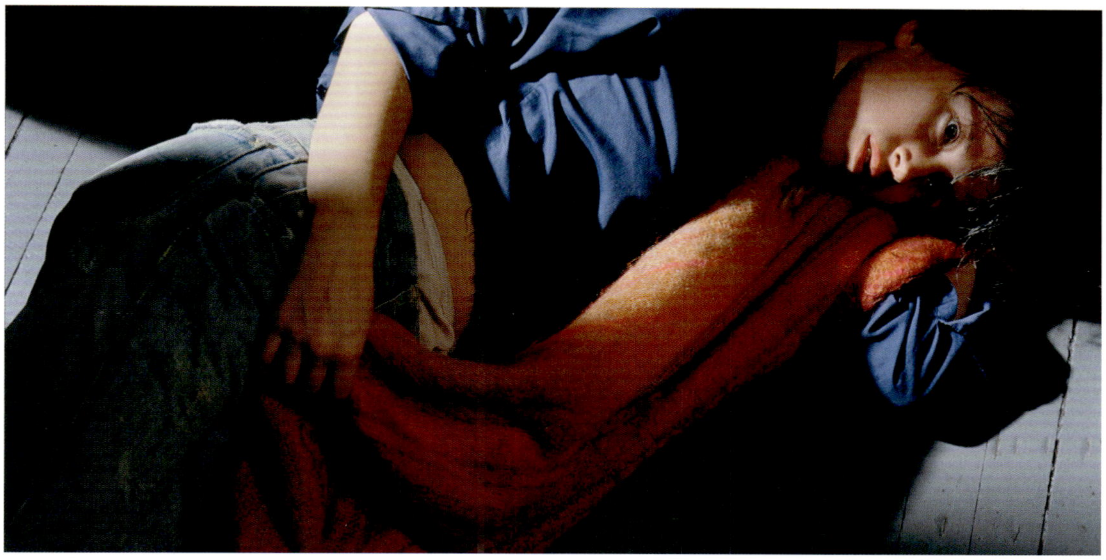

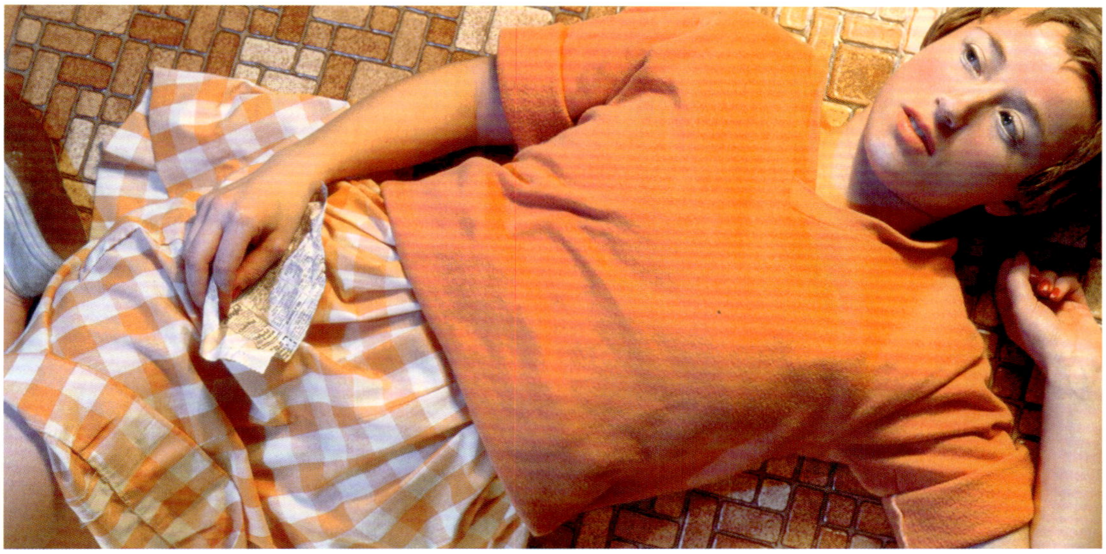

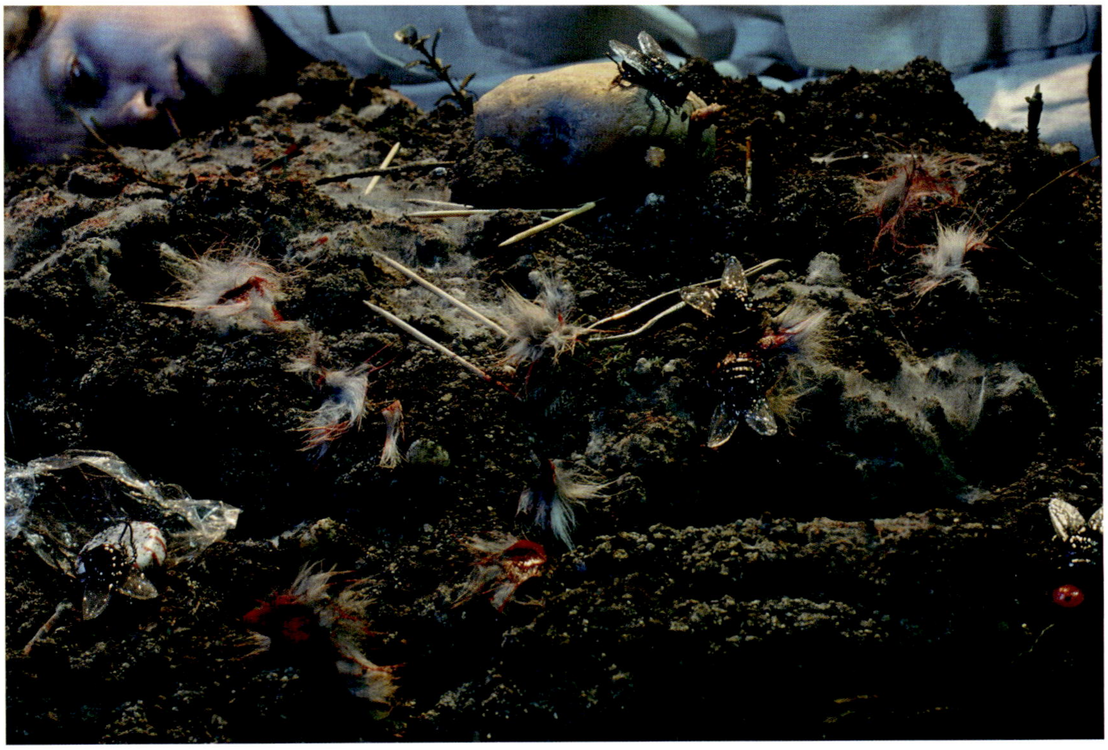

Andres Serrano

Andres Serrano, whose *Piss Christ* (1987) sparked the moral panic that culminated in the obscenity trial of Robert Mapplethorpe's exhibition, has consistently worked against the glossy allure of the advertising image. What created outrage was less the look of his picture, which one critic in *The New York Times* described as reverential, but its blasphemous title. Yet, for Serrano, *Piss Christ* involved 'a duality or contradiction between abstraction and representation, between transforming that little cross into the monumental and mysterious-looking object and then making you reconsider it in another context when you read the label.'[14]

'The Morgue' (1992) extends the oppositions of *Piss Christ*, shifting to the taboo of representing the dead. Serrano's series introduces a particularly disturbing response to the abject body as he exploits the tension between the formal allure of colour and the horror of what is referenced. Many of the large-scale colour Cibachromes in this series deliberately combine a painterly pictorialism with the photographic clarity of his detailed and often fragmentary depiction of dead bodies. Sometimes the dead are given a degree of eroticism, through the close-up detail of mouths, for example, a tactic borrowed from advertising; some images play with iconic allusions, as when cuts on the bodies make analogies with paintings of the dead Christ. Serrano's use of drapery over the corpses in some of the photographs disrupts and counters their shocking viscerality. A formal aesthetic device, it also gives dignity and grace to, for example, the anonymous old woman in *Infectious Pneumonia.* While the cause of deaths are varied – natural, violent and accidental – the overriding impression of the pictures, as Serrano points out, is not one of quiet but 'tragic, violent deaths.'[15] And Serrano knowingly exploits the contradictory aesthetic effect of his depictions of the dead, on one hand giving the corpse a seductive allure and on the other disrupting this through the blunt and explicit nature of the photographic detail.

Andres Serrano
Piss Christ, 1987
Cibachrome, silicone, plexiglass
102 × 152 cm / 40 × 60 in

The Morgue (Infectious Pneumonia), 1992
Cibachrome, plexiglass mounted
127 × 152.4 / 50 × 60 in

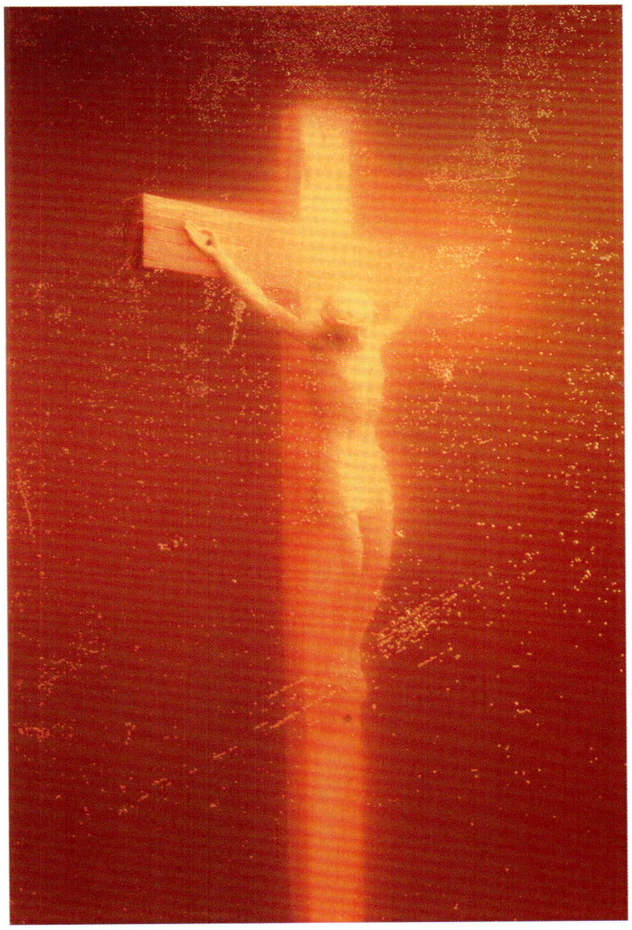

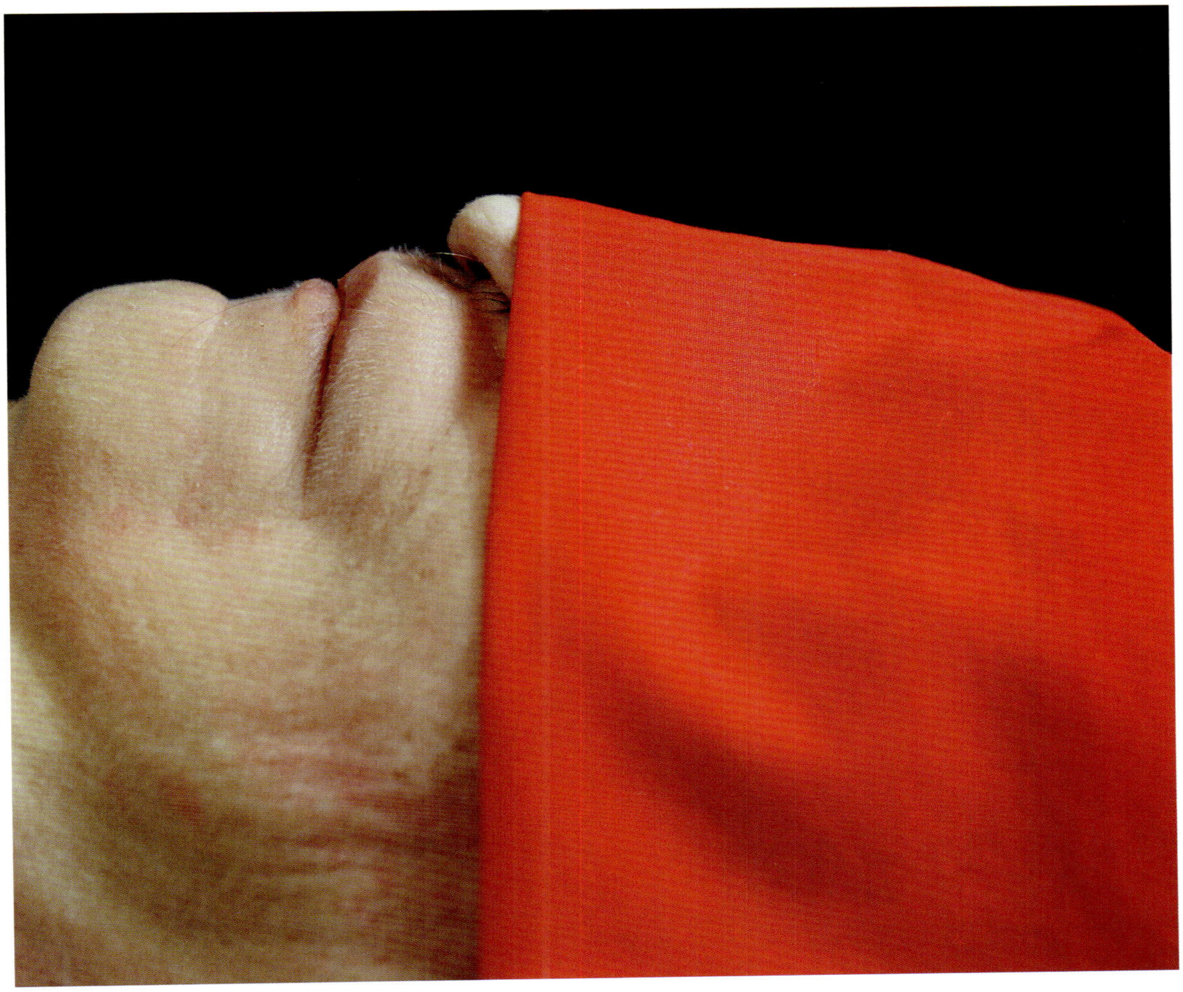

Rineke Dijkstra

Rineke Dijkstra extends Andres Serrano's shocking tactic in her depiction of motherhood. In her portraits of young mothers, all holding their new-born babies to their chests, she taps into the iconographic tradition of the Madonna and Child, but Dijkstra's photography offers a painfully graphic portrayal of the female form: post natal and bereft of any idealization. As Lynda Nead has argued, the history of the female nude involves a succession of bodies sealed, denied their corporeality. Dijkstra's pictures shatter such conventions. Their disruptive exposure is coupled with the fact that all the women look with intensity into the lens, so they appear complicit in their portrayal, and bear expressions that convey a mood of excitement and exhilaration. They have a distinctly proud and triumphant edge. In some senses such pictures echo Diane Arbus's famous 1963 New Jersey photograph of a husband and wife standing in the woods at a nudist camp. Arbus presents the naked couple with a certain rawness and harshness in a graceless picture of Eden that celebrates real human bodies which, much as they might make a poor Adam and Eve, convey a certain pathos and dignity despite the awkwardness of their physical presence.

Richard Learoyd

Richard Learoyd's extraordinarily detailed representations of the human body have a physical impact that is quite unique in contemporary photography. This results from the distinctive way they are produced. Learoyd's camera is also a darkroom, in which images of his flash-lit subjects can be directly imprinted on Ilfochrome positive paper. The camera/darkroom is also attached to one of the few remaining functional Ilfochrome colour printers in the United Kingdom, so the exposed paper can then be immediately fed into the machine and printed out. Such a process gives us a primary and elemental form of analogue picture making, a process of positive printing without negatives and therefore minimum mediation from the real. It is a photography where there is no reproduction or rather a photography that when reproduced will always entail a loss. Each photograph produced is always unique, a one-off.

Ilfochrome is more commonly used for advertising because of its rich saturation and glossiness. Learoyd, however, tempers the saturation; colour intensities are limited to the colour of a dress or the colourful specks of paint on one of the chairs his model sits upon. And the neutrality of the backdrops in the figure studies brings out the subtle range of colours of the skin.

In one extraordinary naked portrait, *Jasmijn Nude* (2008), we see the model's slightly reddened and watery eyes, suggestive of a heightened emotional state that is appropriate to the kind of intensity of response these pictures demand. The photographic translation entails a heightening of the real. The shallow plane of focus highlights a sense of touch and gives a greater physical presence to detailed areas, which in terms of his pictures of the body often concentrates us on the skin of his subjects. Touch is also made integral by the rather awkward and self-conscious gestures many of his subjects adopt in front of camera: the models are often depicted with their hands held together or with one hand holding a wrist or arm. The skin as a sensitive and responsive surface, infinitely rich and variable, is an apt corollary of the photographic surface itself. To picture skin, replete with its traces, marks and imprints, its goose-bumps, hairs, spots, pimples, moles, freckles and so on, can be seen as something intrinsically photographic. Much of the fascination in Learoyd's pictures of women comes from the beauty and eroticism of young skin. With his portraits of men, the skin is coarser and more textured, bearing scars or piercings or heavy with tattoos. The men tend not to face the camera but to turn away or look down and inwards, as in the powerful portrait *Yosef* (2007), with its strong suggestion of restrained and hidden emotions.

Rineke Dijkstra
Tecla, Amsterdam, Netherlands, 1994
C-print, 117.5 × 94.5 cm / 46⅜ × 37¼ in

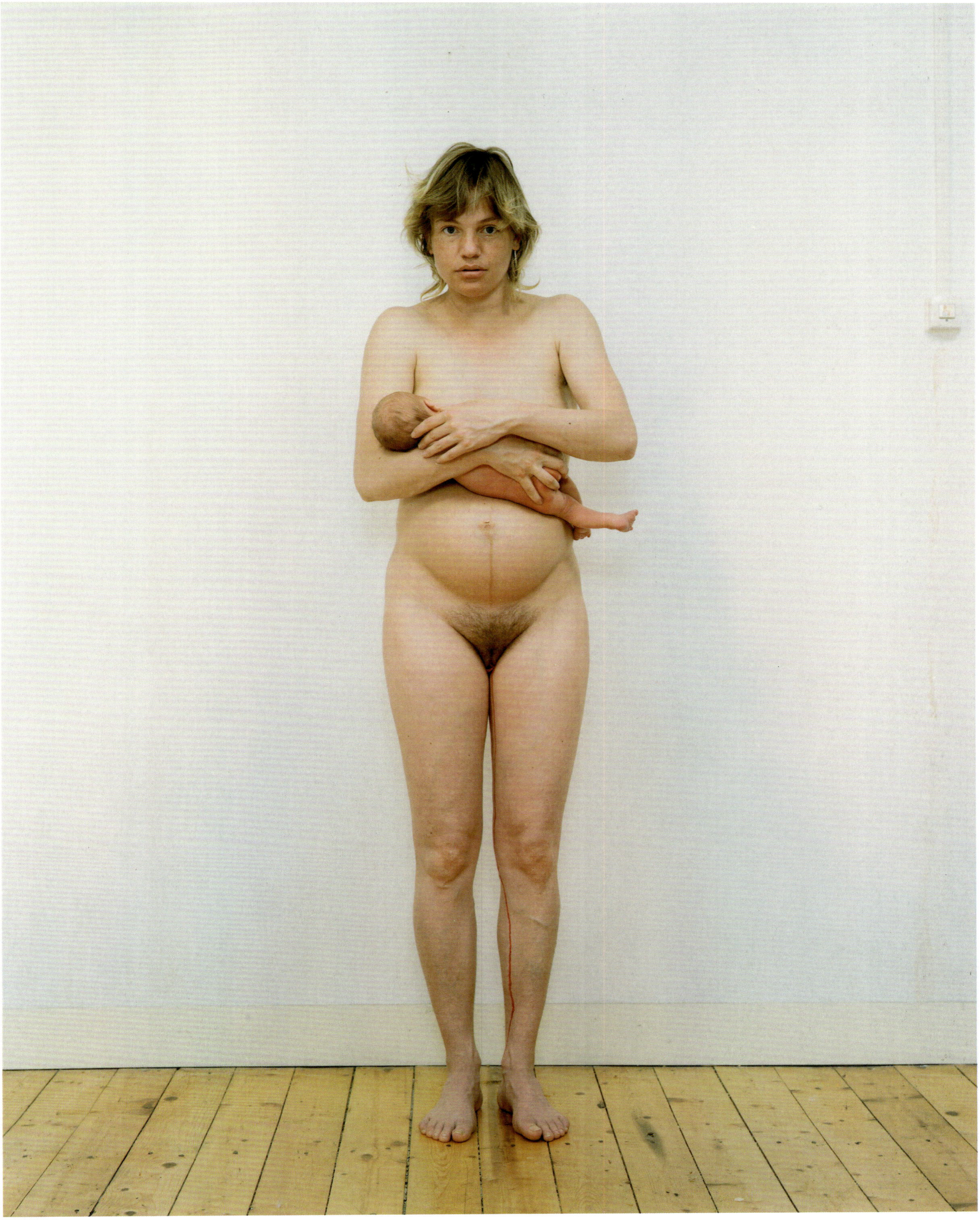

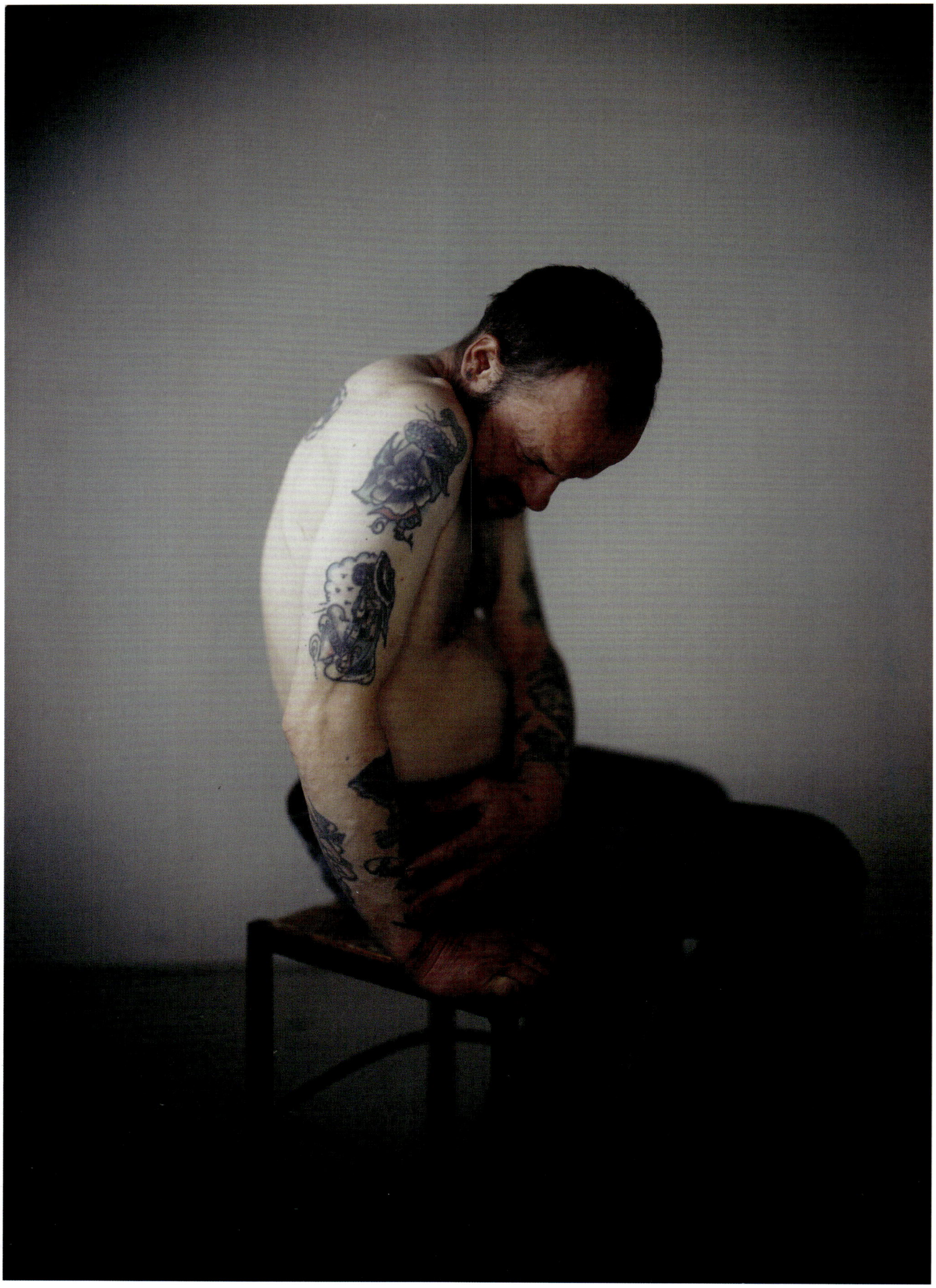

Richard Learoyd
Yosef, 2007
Unique ilfochrome photograph
121.9 × 147.3 cm / 48 × 58 in

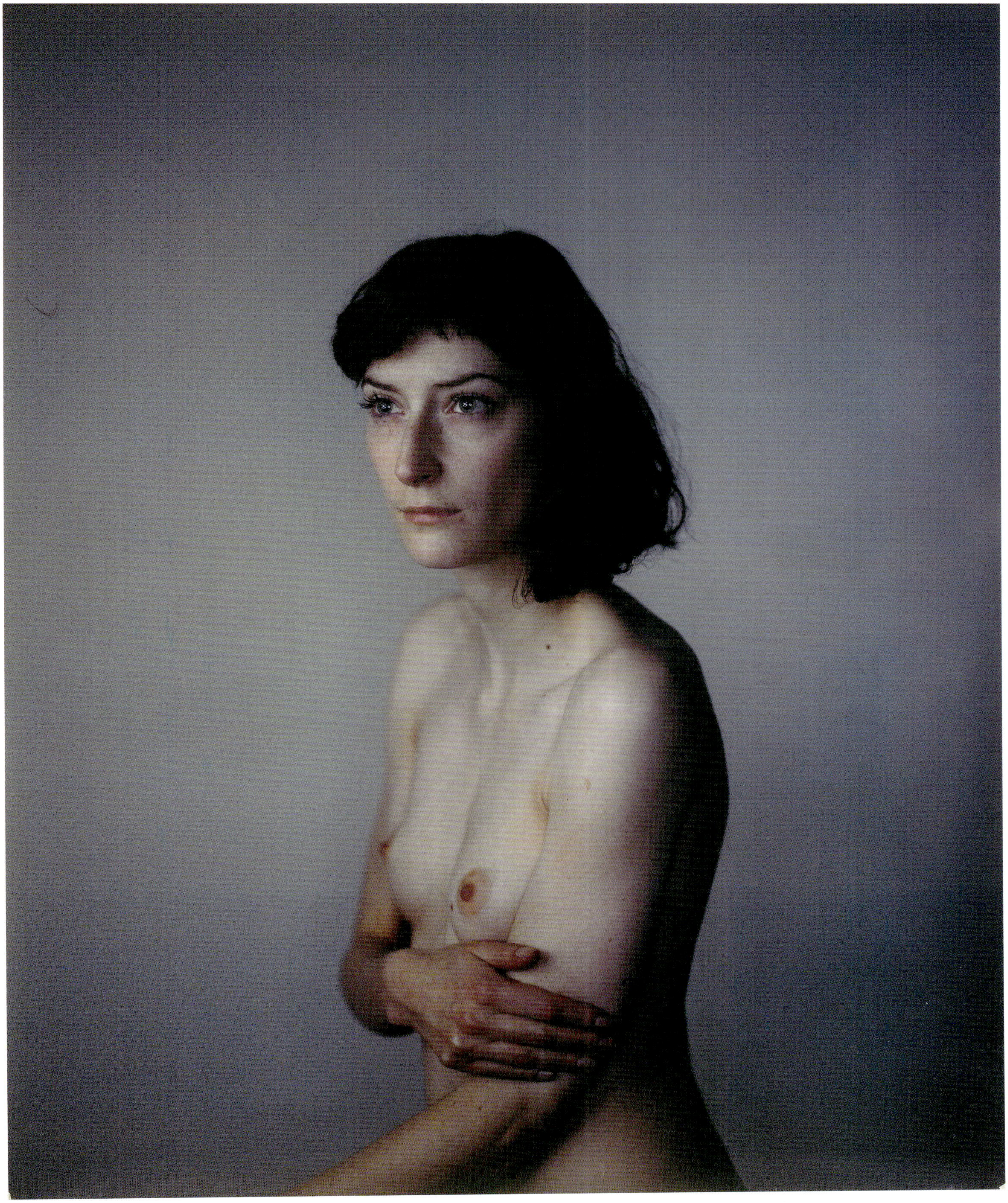

Richard Learoyd
Jasmijn Nude, 2008
Unique ilfochrome photograph
121.9 × 147.3 cm / 48 × 58 in

Jemima Stehli

In using her own body to restage and re-enact famous artworks and photographs, Jemima Stehli's performance and photographic work replays and challenges a misogynistic art historical past. But if she uses her own body to resist its reduction and symbolic appropriation by voyeuristic and fetishizing male artists and viewers, Stehli's work is particularly disturbing in how close it comes to the ultimate reductive act of objectification.

For one of her most-often cited works Stehli performed private stripteases in her studio for an all-male coterie of art dealers, critics and curators, *Strip Series* (1999–2000). The men were also allowed to photograph the event, but in doing so would also picture themselves since Stehli had set up a camera on a tripod pointed at both herself and the men. In some senses this exposé of the mechanics of voyeurism echoed both Helmut Newton's and Guy Bourdin's play with the 'pin-up' conventions.

Stehli's earlier *Table 1*, *Table 2* and *Chair* (1997–8) had gone further. In these works the artist physically re-enacted versions of Allen Jones's sculptures, *Women as Furniture* of 1969. The work takes the form of black-and-white photographs in which Stehli, naked apart from the same spike-heeled boots, adopts the poses of the mannequins in Jones's sculpture. The work is intended to make us aware of the physical awkwardness and impossibility of translating such misogynous artwork into an actual performance.

A similar point of extremity is marked by *Wearing Shoes Chosen by the Curator* (1997). Here Stehli extends her critique to the position of the female artist in relation to the curator and art market: a life-size colour photograph shows her lying face down on the grey concrete floor of a gallery, naked except for a fancy pair of high heel shoes, on display as an art object among the other art objects. One of the two male curators of the show had chosen the shoes from a selection of high heels tried on by the artist during a shopping trip they made together. Carolee Schneemann used her own body to challenge the female body's framing as art; in contrast, Stehli poses as an inert art object, adorned with shoes chosen by the curator. The extremity of her act of subservience and acquiescence, presenting herself like other art objects in the show, spells out the awkward transactions underlying a female artist's status within contemporary art culture. This is the ultimate degradation, but as this is an act of mimicry and re-enactment we are meant to find reassurance in the fact that Stehli remains in control, despite the fact that what we see in the photograph appears to refute this.

Stehli's photographed performances entail an endgame with the problem of representing the body in art. Using her own body to play games with the system and structures of art display, she consciously mimes acts of subservience and compliance.

Santiago Sierra

The Spanish-born but Mexican-based artist Santiago Sierra uses the bodies of others to question the systems and structures of art display. He puts others in demeaning states as the result of payment and in doing so highlights the inequities between the first world spectatorship of his art and the workers, often migrants and illegal workers, whom he pays to perform in the gallery. Sierra often mimes the photo-conceptual look of avant-garde art from the late 1960s and 1970s: texts giving instructions for the performances are accompanied by black-and-white photographs and films that document the events. But the formal correspondence is disrupted by the very different nature of Sierra's events. He deliberately moves art into other contexts, undermining the relatively safe and self-enclosed references of the art world. In a key work from 1998, for example, he persuaded a man in Mexico to have a line tattooed down his back for fifty dollars, a mark he will now carry for the rest of his life. The person subjects his body to such marking not as a result of any aesthetic desire but because of a basic economic need. Minimalist sculpture is a point of critical reference in Sierra's *Eight People Paid to Remain Inside Cardboard Boxes* (1999). The performance first took place in a half-empty office block in Guatemala, with each box containing a person paid to stay inside it for four hours. The social misery of their situation disrupts these abstract geometric forms, abruptly bringing a familiar avant-garde form into relationship to specific economic and social realities.

In his more recent *Campaign Teeth of the Last Gypsies of Ponticelli Naples, Italy* (2009), Sierra subverts the portrait tradition and convention by photographing, in close up, just the teeth of the adults and children from two remaining families of Roma – a people subject to much intolerance, fear and hatred within Italy – before the evacuation of their Ponticelli camp. These pictures were exhibited both within Naples' Madre Museum and on billboards in place of advertisements. This is very much a confrontational intervention: the detailing of teeth, not smiling but clenched and grinding, capped, worn and filled, contrasts with the focus on eyes as a cue to compassion and feeling in the usual documentary portrait. The mouth can be a sign of sensuality and eroticism in advertising, but instead of the cosmetic grins of the models of consumer culture in these pictures the lips are mostly cropped out and emphasis is on the gums and teeth, as if photographed for forensic and clinical inspection. The enlargement and isolation of such dental records presents us with one of the most stark and powerful reductions of the human body in photography. These pictures of clenched teeth imply a gesture of non-compliance, of gritting your teeth as an act of determined resilience, but at the same time the brutal reduction of the body through such pictures speaks about the dehumanization of their subjects.

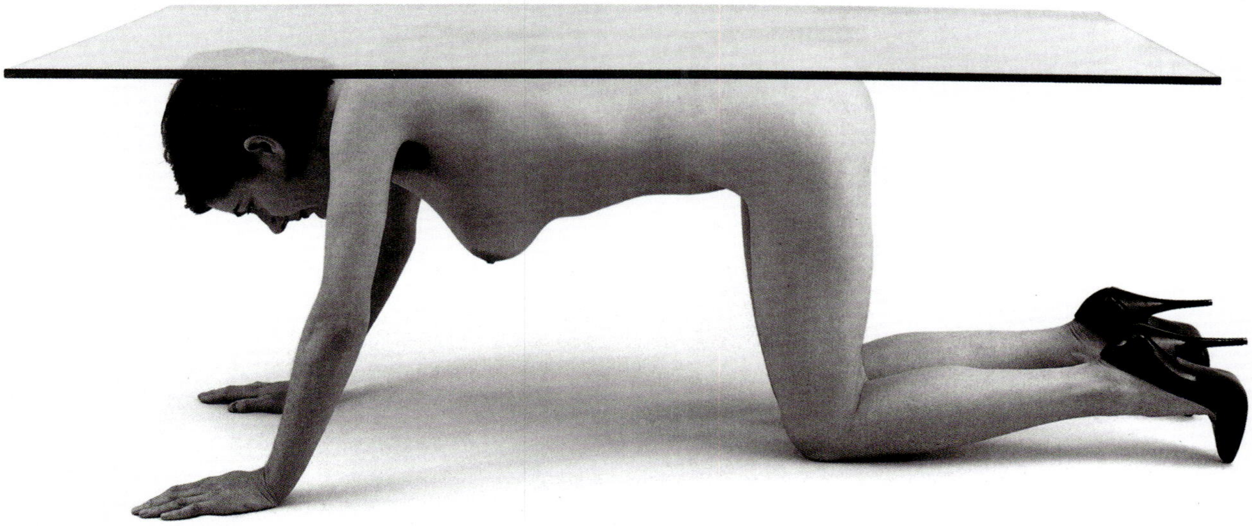

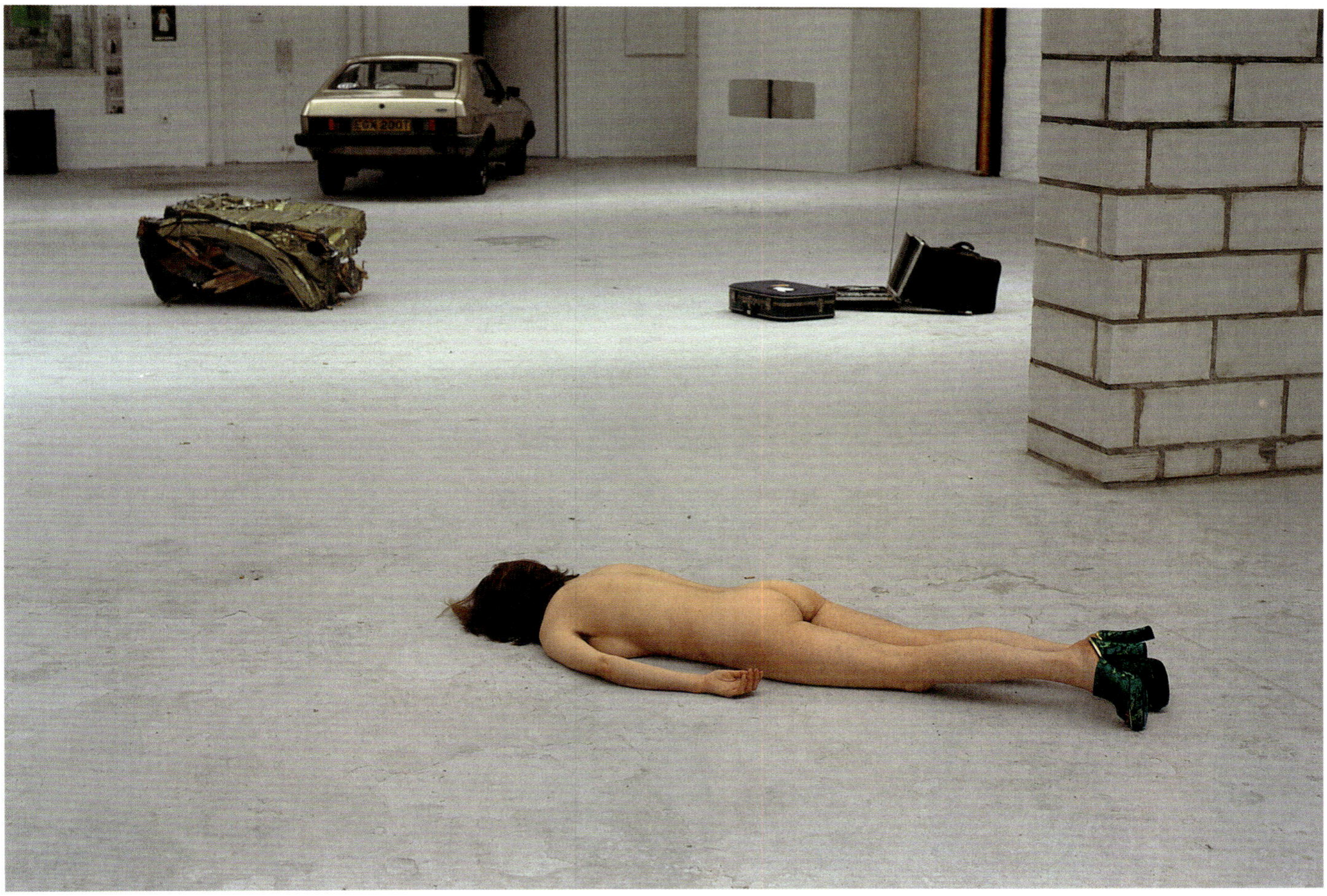

Jemima Stehli
Table 2, 1997–8
Black and white photograph
137 × 241 cm / 54 × 94⅞ in

Wearing Shoes Chosen by the Curator, 1997
Documentation of work at 'Peripheral Visionary' Eindhoven, August 1997

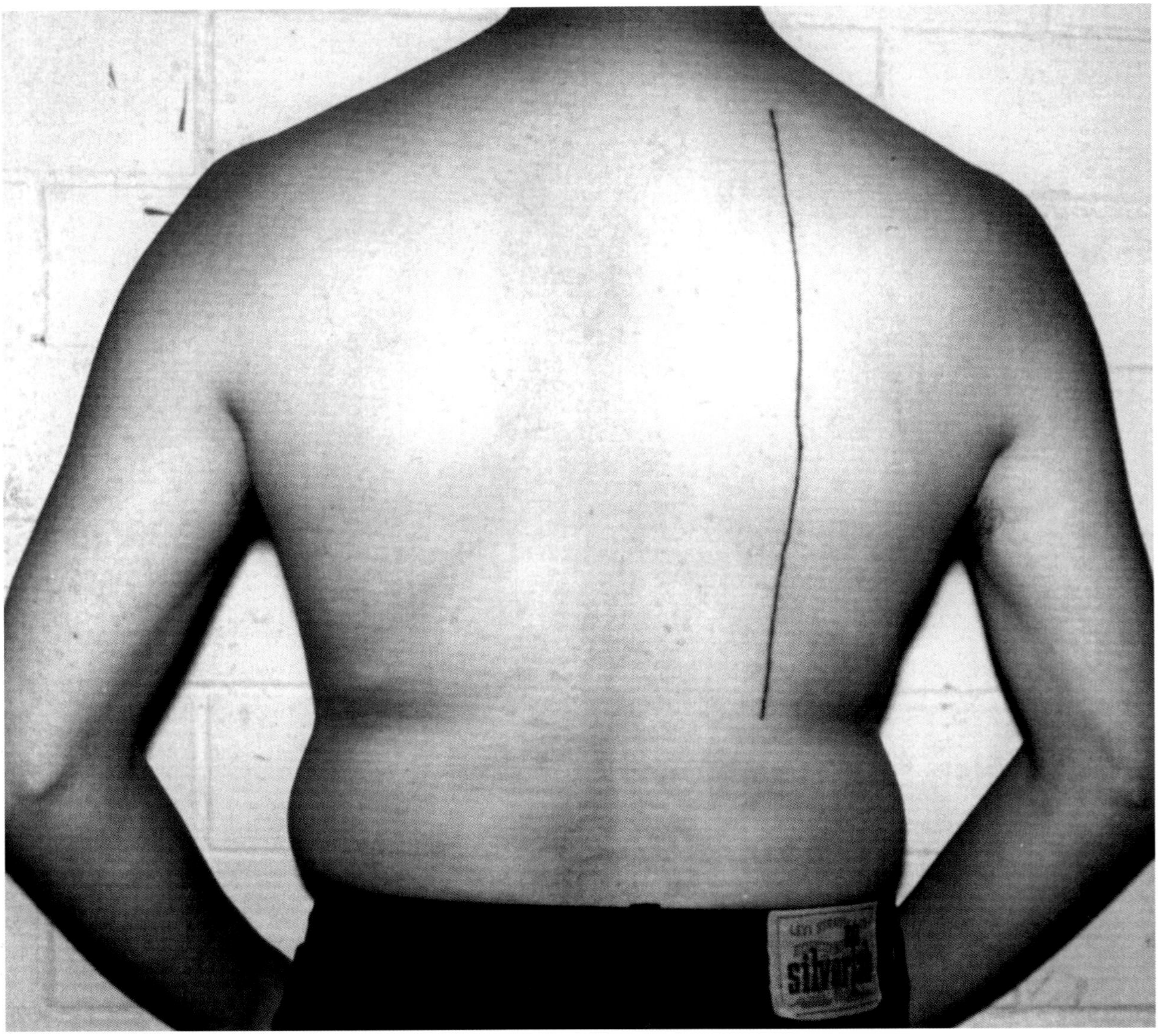

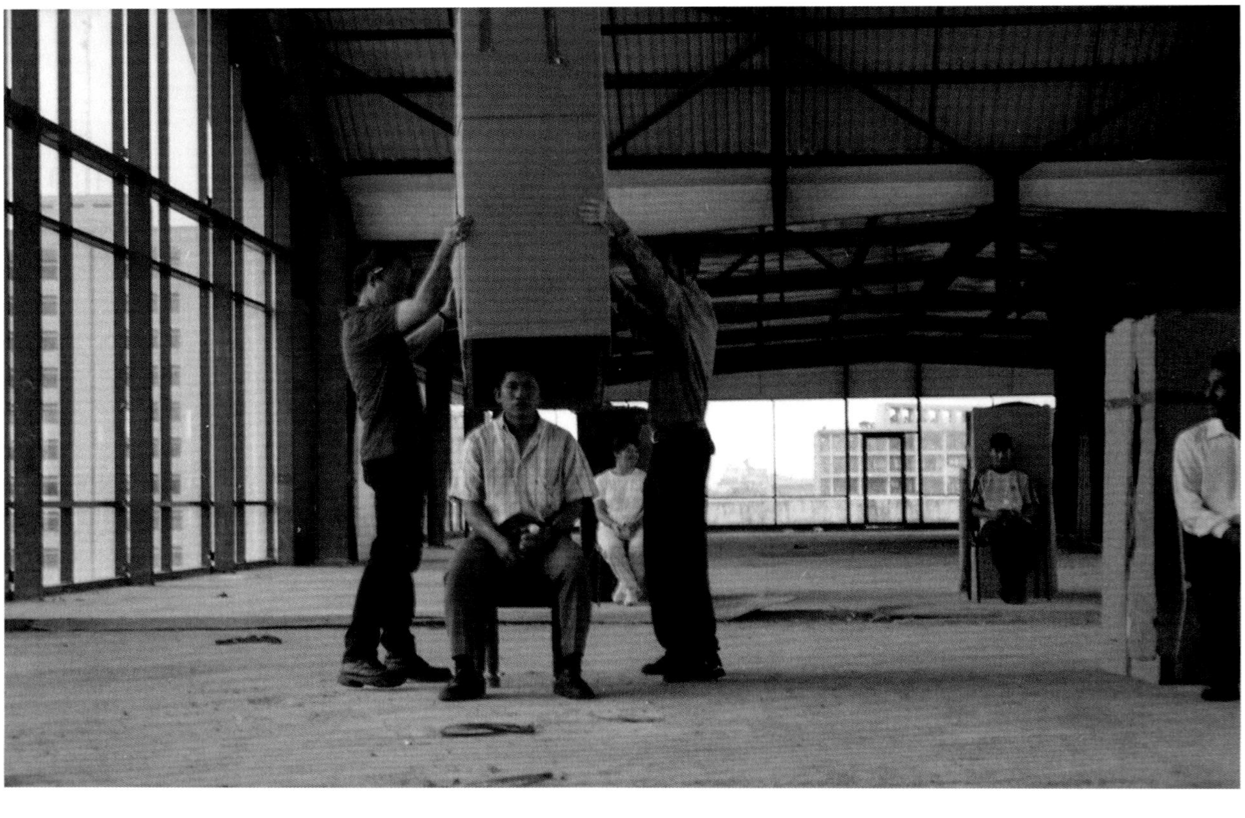

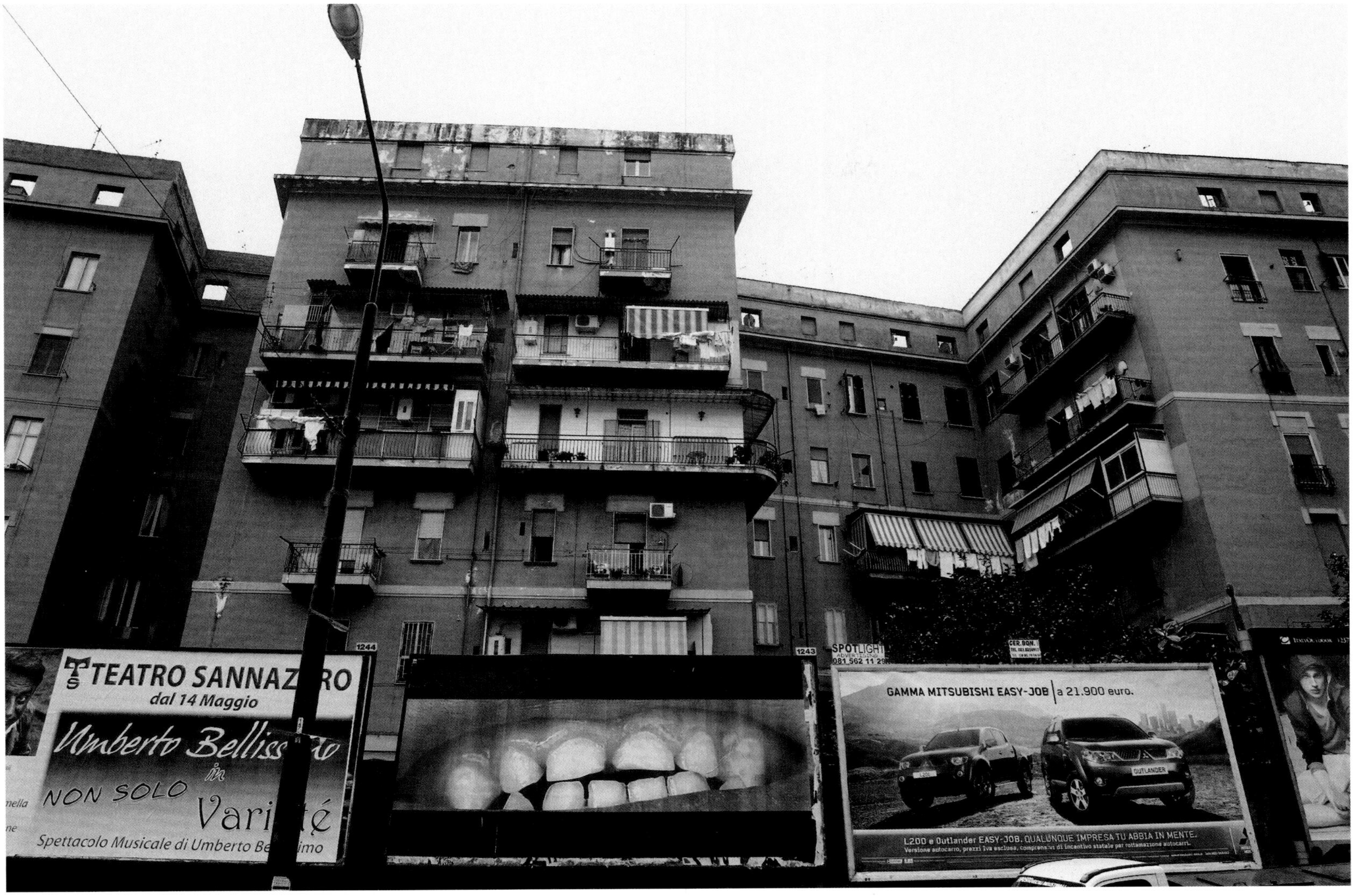

Santiago Sierra
Line of 30 cm Tattooed on a Remunerated Person, 1998
C-print, 150 × 280 cm / 59 × 110 in

8 People Paid to Remain Inside Cardboard Boxes, 1999
C-print, (detail from original diptych) each 29.8 × 21.3 cm / 11 × 8 in

Campaign Teeth of the Last Gipsies of Ponticelli, 2009

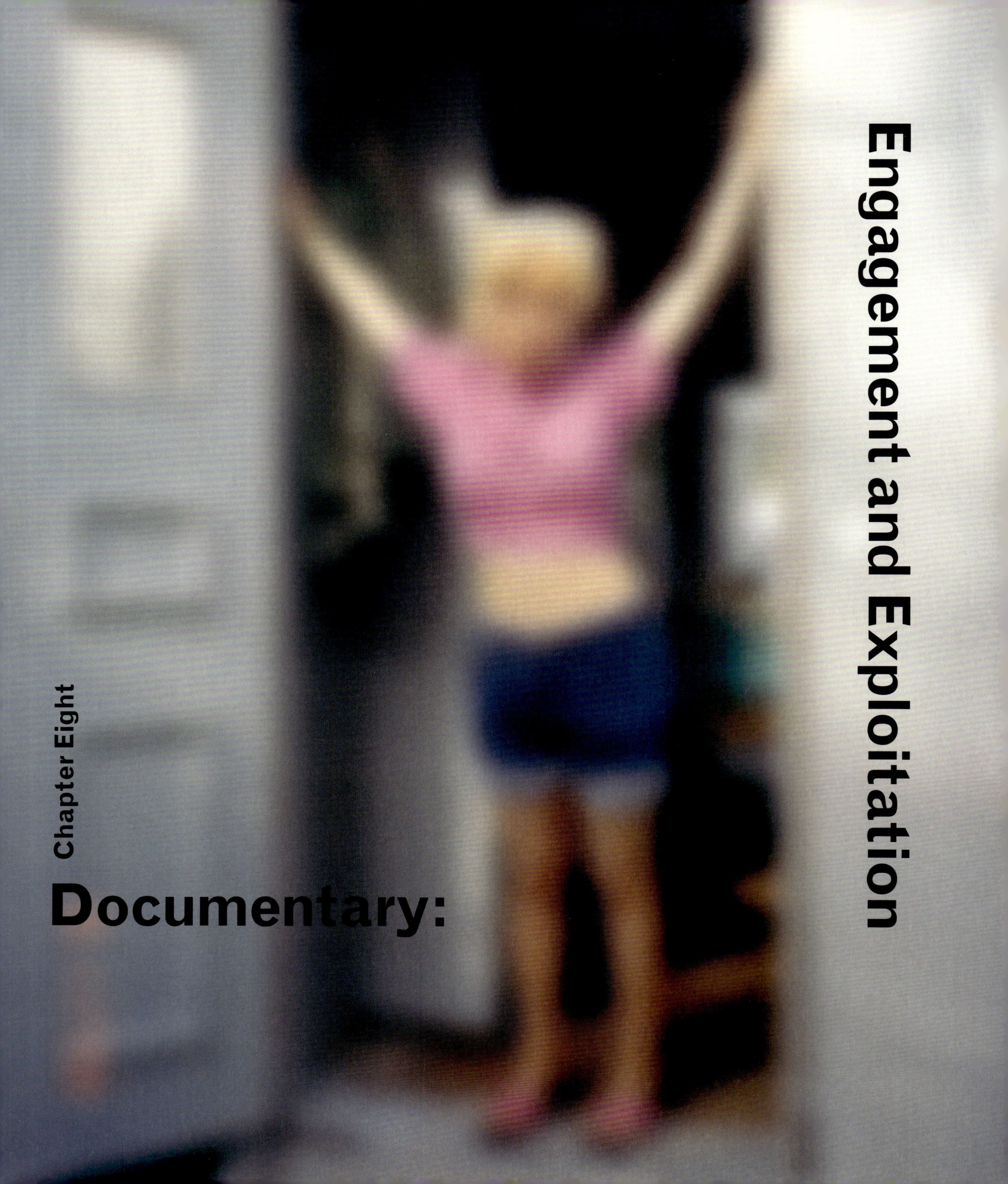

Chapter Eight

Documentary: Engagement and Exploitation

John Szarkowski claimed that by the 1960s the documentary tradition was 'leaden, tired, boring.'[1] Within subsequent postmodern approaches to documentary, the implications of the act of photographing often disadvantaged social groups or individuals was frequently subject to severe scrutiny and critique. Nevertheless, traditional forms of documentary practice remain an important aspect of photography. These forms of documentary often involve some kind of social interaction or exchange between the photographer and those he or she represents. Conscious that this can be an unequal relationship, and of the power relations that characterize the documentary transaction, a number of artists have taken apart the documentary conventions. Such a disassembly produces work that lays bare documentary's voyeuristic and exploitational aspects. Since the 1990s there has been a renewed fascination with documentary, but often in a hyperbolic form in which artists deliberately use shocking and dramatic subject matter.

A touchstone for much documentary photography since the 1960s has been the work of the Farm Security Administration (FSA) photographers, with their dignified representation of the plight of the American rural poor during the Great Depression. Their images became widely known in the United States and beyond in the 1960s, through new editions of such publications as Walker Evans's and James Agee's *Let Us Now Praise Famous Men* (the 1941 original was reprinted in 1960) and such shows as Edward Steichen's exhibition of Depression-era photography, 'The Bitter Years', at New York's Museum of Modern Art in 1962. Such historical documentary work also became meaningful again amidst the tumultuous social and political events of the 1960s and 1970s in the United States.

Dignity and Respect
Danny Lyon
Bruce Davidson
David Goldblatt

Suburbia
Bill Owens

Close Engagement
Mary Ellen Mark
Jacob Holdt
Jim Goldberg

Labour
Sebastião Salgado
Alfredo Jaar
Allan Sekula

Documentary Disassembled
Martha Rosler
Sophie Calle
Kohie Yoshiyuki
Merry Alpern
Shizuka Yokomizo
Nikki S. Lee

Tableaux Documentary
Philip-Lorca diCorcia
Larry Sultan
Philippe Chancel

Excess
Boris Mikhailov
Liu Zheng
Pieter Hugo

Lyrical Observations
Olga Chernysheva

Danny Lyon

From late 1967, for fourteen months, Danny Lyon was given access to photograph six Texas prison units. The project is typical of much documentary, motivated by the need to make public and visible situations and lives that otherwise would remain unrepresented. The blurb on the back of the 1971 book in which the photographs were published, *Conversations with the Dead*, linked the work with Depression-era photography, citing both *Let Us Now Praise Famous Men* (1941) and Margaret Bourke-White and Erskine Caldwell's 1937 *You Have Seen Their Faces*. A number of Lyon's photographs even look uncannily like FSA photographs from the 1930s, such as the images of prisoners cotton picking or those showing a black prisoner collapsed with heat exhaustion in the back of a truck.

But there was one significant difference: Lyon's decision to include personal testimonies from some of the convicts. In particular the voice and paintings (reproduced in colour) of one prisoner, Billy McCune, which in many ways form the affective core of the book. McCune was initially sentenced to death for rape, but the sentence was commuted to life. He had castrated himself in prison and ended up in an area referred to as 'isolation', incarcerated in a nine by five foot cell when Lyon first met and befriended him. On receiving letters and art from McCune, Lyon said 'there was always something incredible, something beautiful, something a man had painted or written from a place where nothing should grow'.[2]

The romantic identification with outlaw and outsider types in many ways continues from Lyon's earlier *The Bikeriders* (1968), a documentary book for which he joined the Chicago Outlaw Motorcycle Club. Transcriptions of taped recordings of Lyon's subjects accompanied the photographs. Lyon takes the relationship with the subject of his photographs much further in *Conversations with the Dead*, establishing a relationship with Billy McCune and giving space and importance to his art alongside Lyon's own photography. Such a gesture of affiliation and identification is important to much documentary, but few photographers have made it so central.

Danny Lyon
Conversations with the Dead: Photographs of Prison Life with the Letters and Drawings of Billy McCune #122055, Holt, Rinehart and Winston, New York, 1971
20.5 × 27.9 cm / 8 × 11 in, 196 pp
Hardback with grey cloth and jacket
75 black and white photographs, 5 colour illustrations and 6 black and white identity photographs,
Foreward by Danny Lyon; introduction, letters and drawings by Billy McCune; design by Danny Lyon and Martin Stephen Moskof

Cotton Pickers, Huntsville, Texas, USA, 1968
Gelatin silver print, dimensions variable
Ferguson is a prison for young men, ages 17–21.

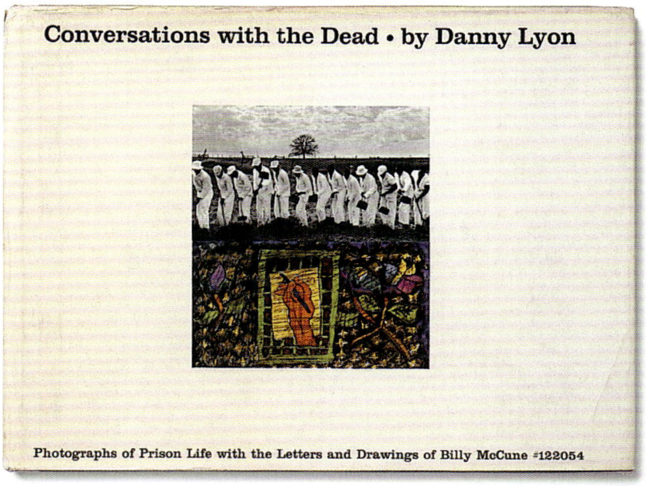
Conversations with the Dead • by Danny Lyon
Photographs of Prison Life with the Letters and Drawings of Billy McCune #122054

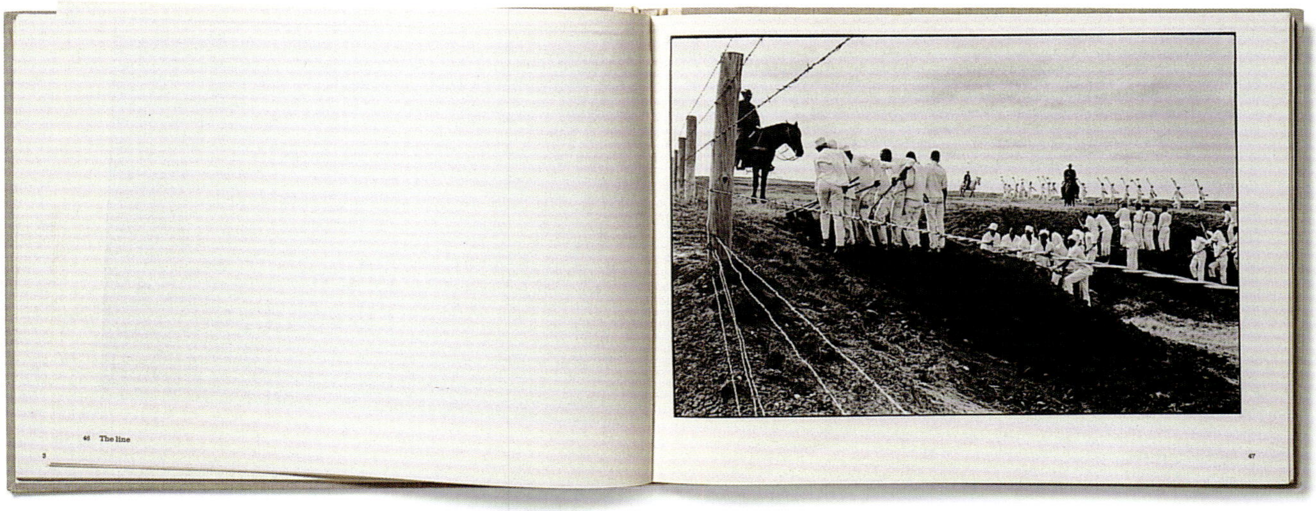
The line

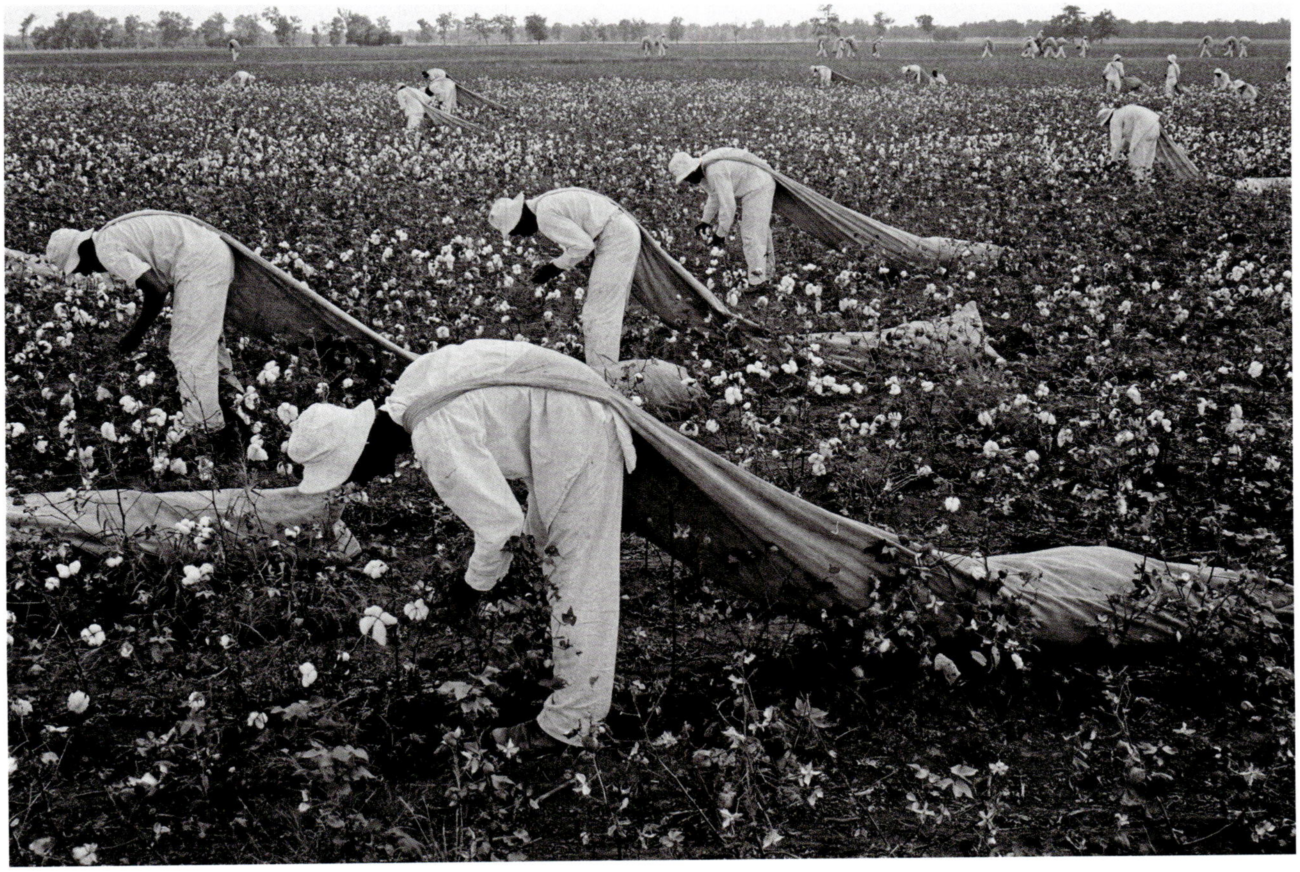

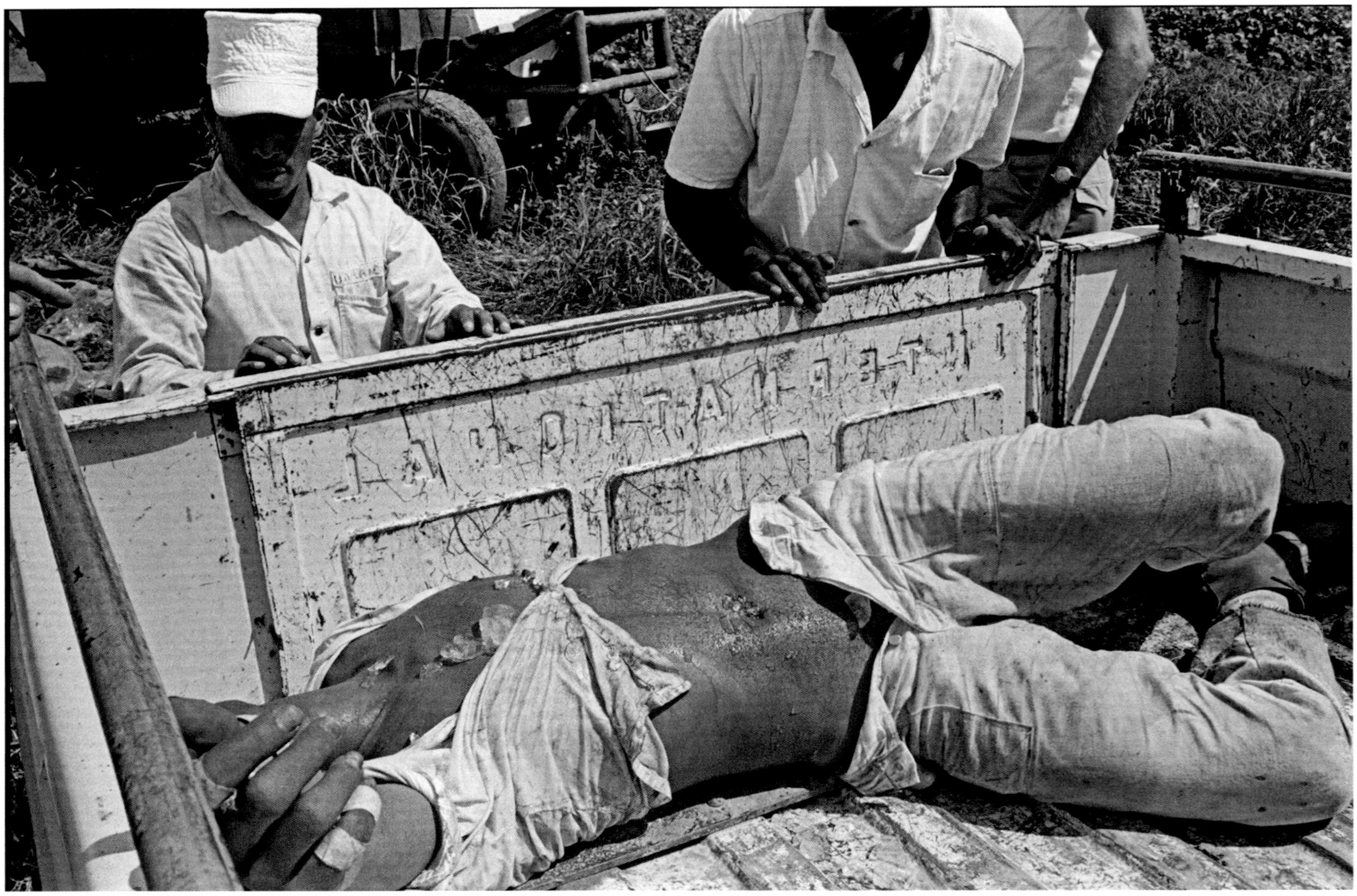

Danny Lyon
From *Conversations with the Dead*, *Heat Exhaustion*, Huntsville, Texas, USA, 1968
Gelatin silver print, dimensions variable
The Ramsey prison farm is set on 16,000 acres of Brazos River bottomland about 30 miles south of Houston and is populated by 1400 men. The prison is divided into a newer and older unit, Ramsey One and Ramsey Two.

From *Conversations with the Dead*
Cell block table, Huntsville, Texas, USA 1968
Gelatin silver print, dimensions variable
The Walls is a walled penitentiary, it is the oldest unit of the system and is located near the center of the town of Huntsville.

From *Conversations with the Dead*, Painting by Billy McCune, 1968
C-print, dimensions variable

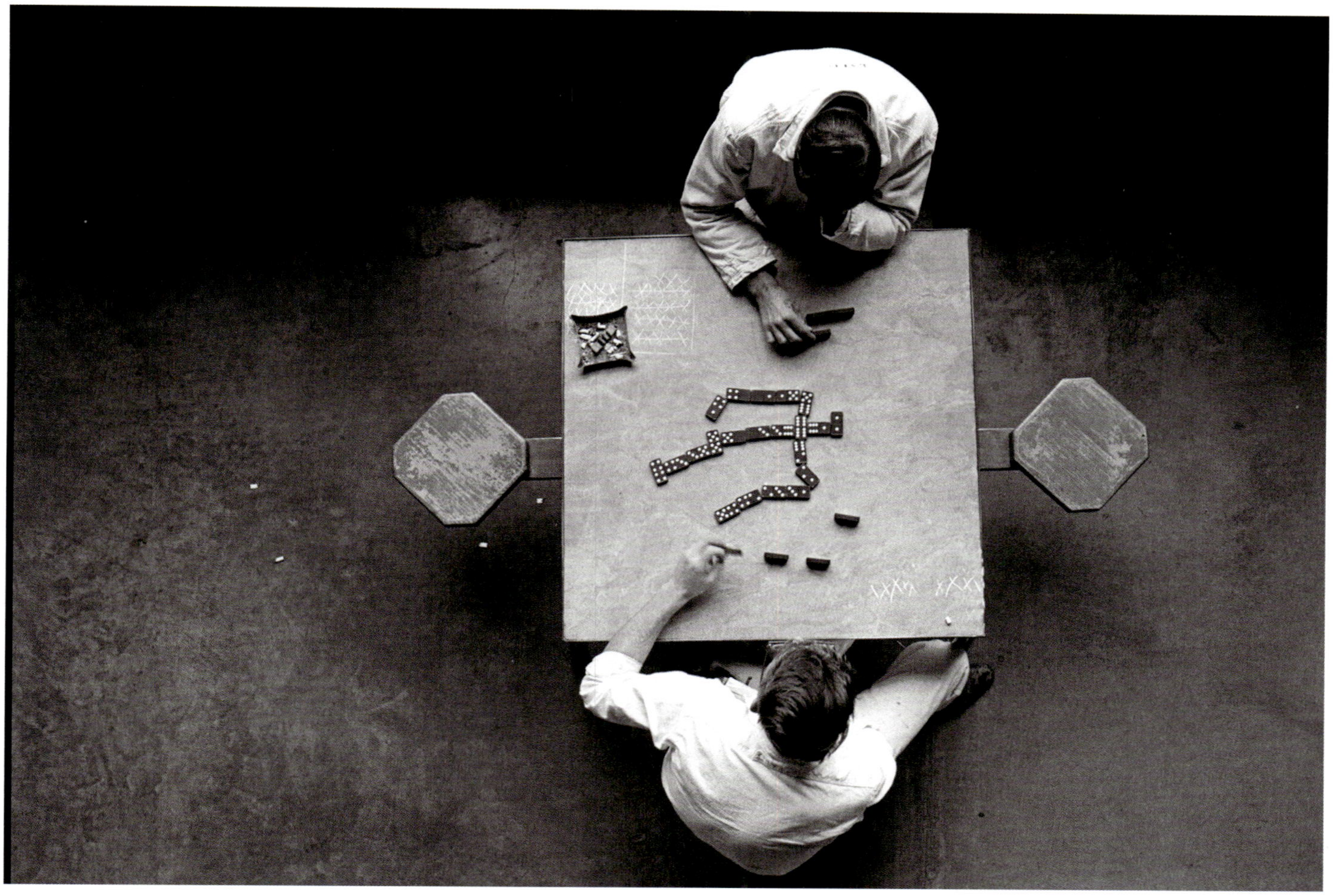

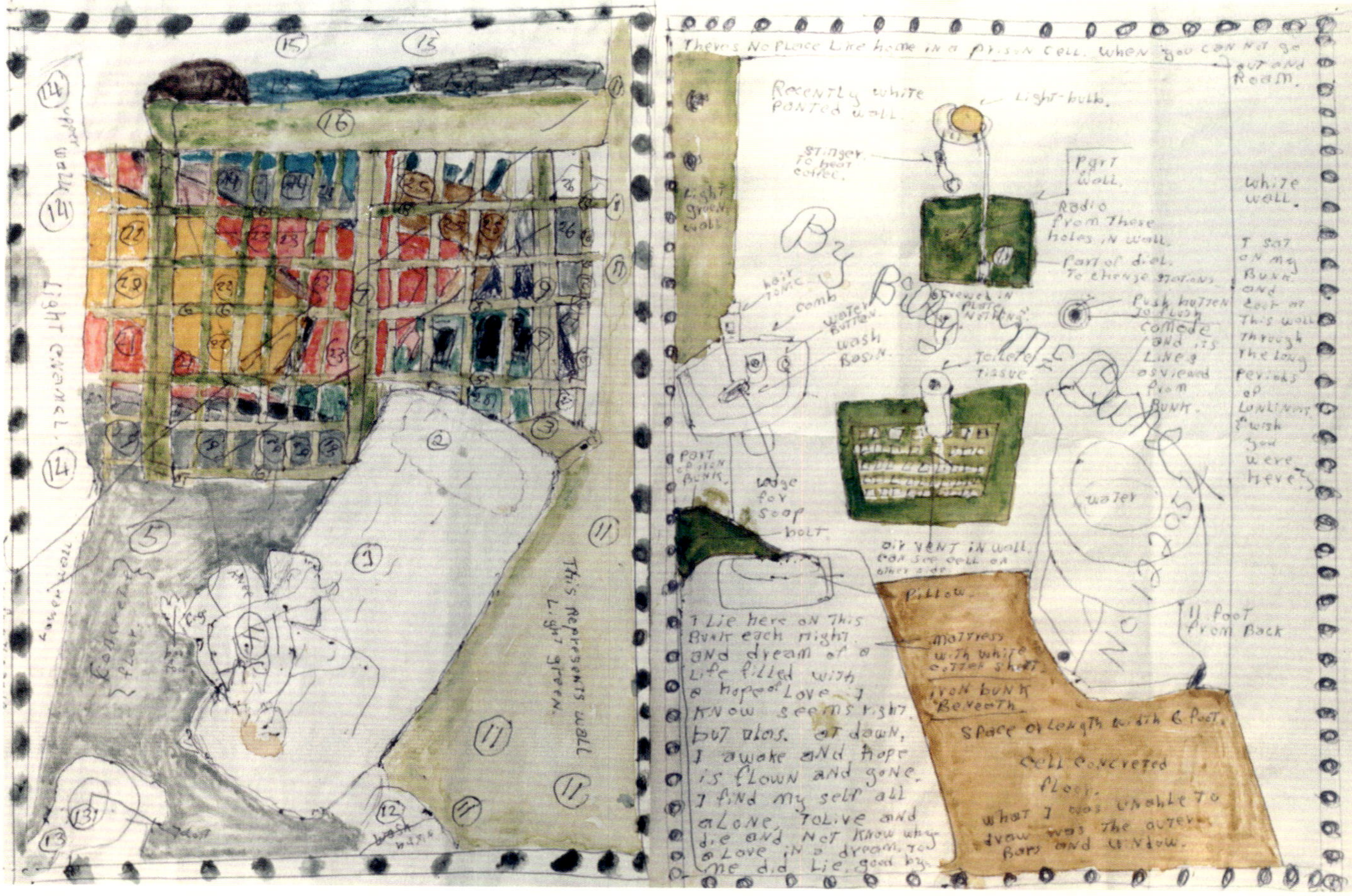
Theres No Place Like home in a prison cell. when you can not go out and Roam.
Recently white Painted wall.
Light-bulb.
Stinger to heat coffee.
Part wall.
Radio from There holes in wall.
Part of dial. To change stations
White wall.
I sat on my Bunk and look at This wall through the long Periods of Lonliness wish you were here.
Light green wall
hair tonic
comb
water button.
wash Basin.
Toilet tissue
Push button to flush
commode and its Lines as viewed from Bunk.
Post of iron Bunk.
Ledge for Soap
bolt.
air vent in wall. can see cell on other side
water
Pillow.
I Lie here on This Bunk each night and dream of a Life filled with a hope of Love I know seems right but alas. at dawn, I awake and hope is flown and gone. I find my self all alone, To Live and die and Not know why a Love in a dream. To me did Lie. good by.
Mattress with white cotton sheet.
Iron bunk Beneath
11 foot from Back
Space of Length with 6 foot.
cell concreted floor.
what I was unable to draw was the outer Bars and window.
This Represents wall Light green.
Light orange.

Bruce Davidson

In Bruce Davidson's book *East 100th Street* (1970) the subjects remain unnamed, although the photography still nevertheless calls upon a dignifying tradition in its mode of representation. While Davidson remained an outsider to the community photographed, he managed to make pictures that exuded warmth, respect and affection; 'I came to 100th Street with a large-format camera on a tripod. I wanted depth and detail and I wanted to meet the people eye to eye.'[3]

The book was the result of two years' work in one of the poorest areas of Spanish Harlem, where Davidson photographed streets, people and interiors. The use of a large-format camera, and the way in which the pose and organization of families in front of his camera often echoed the family portraits decorating their homes, locate these images within a tradition of reverence and respect. Davidson also speaks about giving his subjects prints that were hung up on the walls among other family photographs. The large format creates a particular aesthetic effect and the rich tonality of the original prints, preserved in the 1970 publication – one of the most finely printed, produced and sequenced photography books ever made, according to critic Jonathan Green (writing in 1981) – is integral to his valorizing and idealizing vision. On occasion, Davidson also allows the form of the family pose to be lost in a moment of pure joy and pleasure: one portrait, for example, shows a woman throwing her head back in laughter as a joke is presumably shared with the photographer. Such pictures are rather unusual within documentary, and this photograph was only included in the expanded edition of *East 100th Street*, published over thirty years later.

Bruce Davidson
From *East 100th Street*,
Harvard University Press,
Cambridge, 1970
28.6 × 31.1 cm / 11¼ × 12¼ in,
166pp
Hardcover with printed
acetate jacket
123 photographs, designed
by Elton Robinson

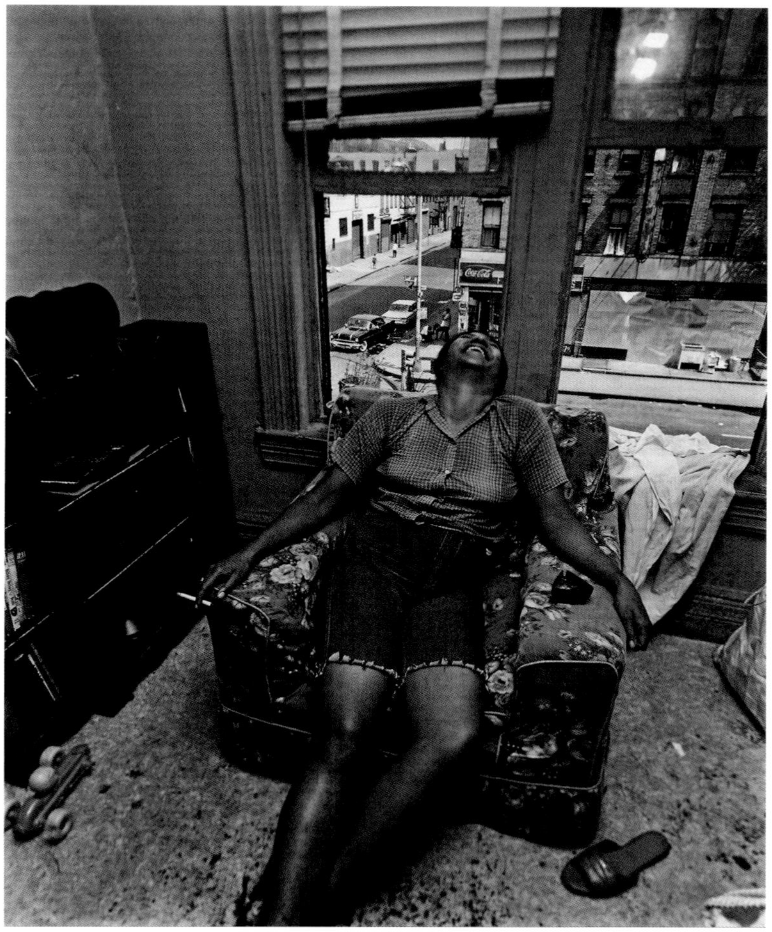
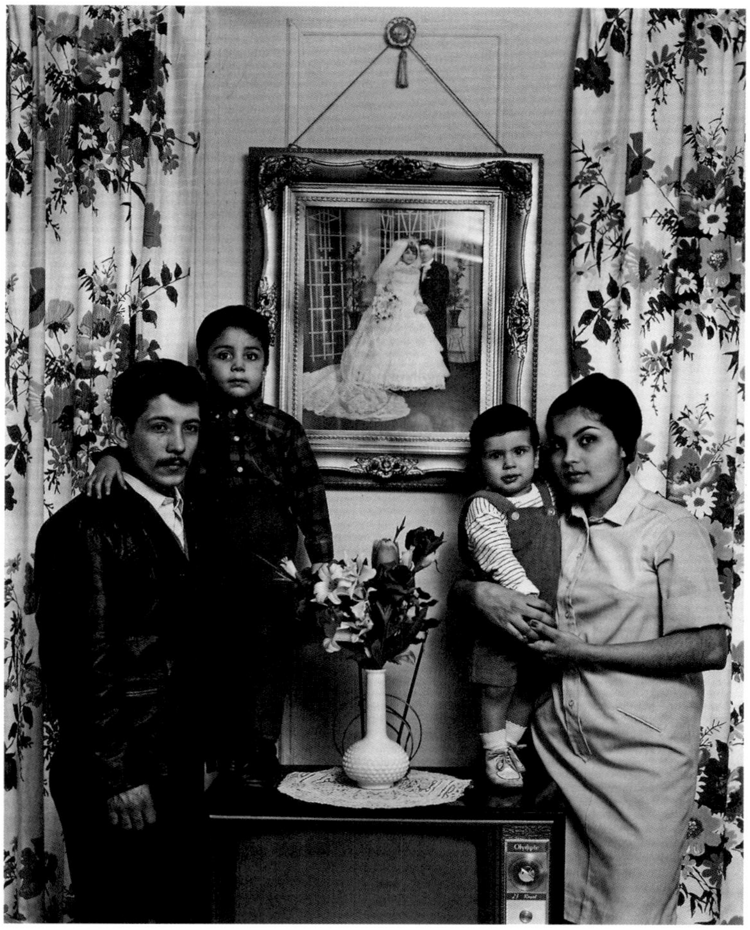
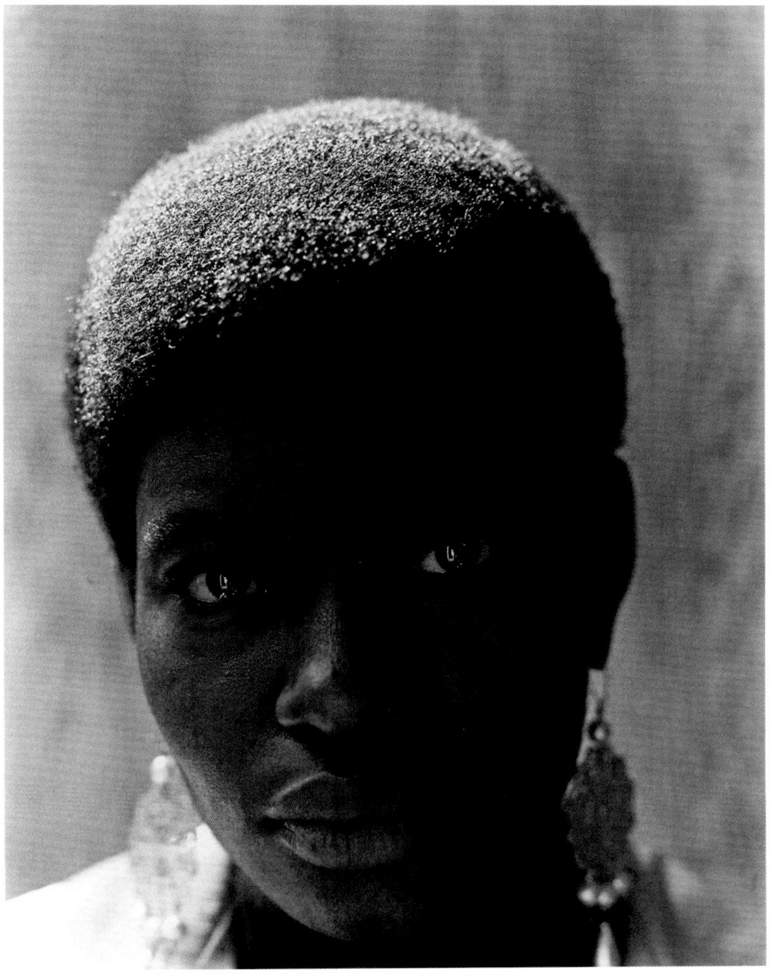
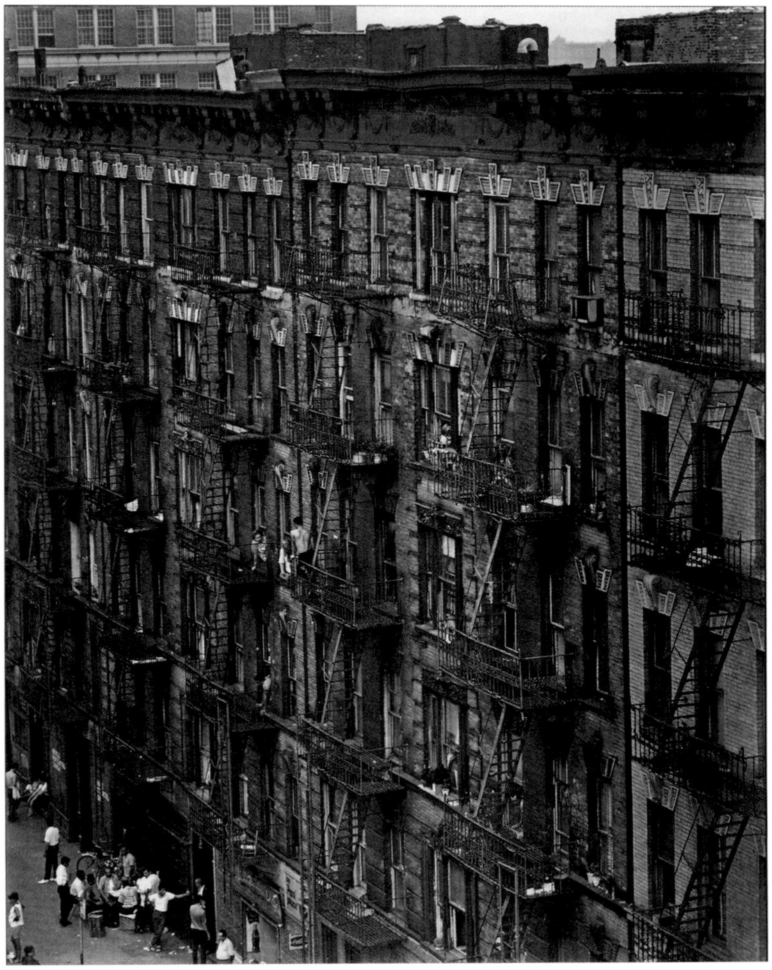

David Goldblatt

David Goldblatt's documentary photography in South Africa has since the 1960s also continued the traditions of FSA photography. His work remains distinct from so much of the photojournalism that has come out of the country's violent history of oppression. Having explained that he 'felt no driving need to record those situations and moments of extremity that were the stuff of the media', Goldblatt was instead drawn to 'the quiet and commonplace where nothing "happened" and yet all was contained and immanent'.[4] As a Jewish white male born to immigrant parents, Goldblatt was brought up in a middle-class family in a town near Johannesburg on the Witwatersrand, the gold-bearing hills of South Africa. In his early series published as *Some Afrikaners Photographed* (1975), his pictures of Afrikaners, responding to the kind of people he grew up with as a child, his fear at their racism and physical confidence, are nevertheless edged with ambivalence. While some evidence confrontational aggression and power – white nationalists staring to camera from horseback – others are more sensitive and tender, such as the symbolically transgressive touch between a white farmer boy and his black nursemaid, whose hand playfully holds the heel of his bare foot. Such signs of human tenderness challenge the ideology and law of apartheid, but at the same time point to the inevitable future when, as an adult, this child will have to deny such intimacy and affection.

Another early project documents the declining mining industries of Goldblatt's hometown: the most visceral and expressive pictures, and certainly the most spectacular, highlight the dangerous work of the shaftsinkers, who drill and blast and dig mines, working up to fourteen hours a day. But in evidencing the physical hardships of labour, his series published in the book *The Transported of KwaNdebele* (1989), is equally powerful. As in the mine photographs, chiaroscuro lighting effects simplify and give graphic force and presence to the pictures. Goldblatt travelled with black South Africans on the crowded buses between their homelands and their places of employment, some journeying up to eight hours per day to get to and from work. The images draw out a general condition of subjugation that is visibly evident in the gestures and expression of the exhausted workers as they try to catch what little sleep they can.

In Boksburg, published in 1982, offers an acerbic observation of the social mores of a middle-class suburbia, similar to the place in which Goldblatt grew up. The pictures testify to a more distanced and anthropological gaze in which one senses the photographer's anger. None of those pictured are engaged with Goldblatt; all are observed going about their daily life. But this catalogue of public and private events is not without a certain ambivalence and contradiction. There is an underlying empathy and fascination with the figure of the child and younger people in this culture: the apprehensive little boy boxer standing rigid in the corner of the ring before a fight; the somewhat awkward display of young girls in the 'Miss Lovely Legs Competition', an exclusive all-white competition which as a result presents us with an unusual exchange of display and gazes between the black people in the audience and those on stage. Or the striking picture of a young teenage girl in her new tutu, proudly pirouetting *en pointe*. Goldblatt pictures her apparently caught in the web of shadows from the trellis on her veranda, just as she is trapped, we are led to infer, by the ideology in which she is being brought up.

David Goldblatt
The commando of National Party stalwarts which escorted prime minister and National Party leader Hendrik Verwoerd and his wife Betsie to the party's 50th anniversary celebrations at de Wildt, Transvaal
Oct. 1964
Gelatin silver photograph on fibre-based paper
Approx. 30 × 40cm / 11⅞ × 15¾ in

A Farmer's Son with his Nursemaid, in the Marico Bushveld, 1964
Gelatin silver photograph on fibre-based paper
22.7 × 33.66 cm / 9 × 13¼ in

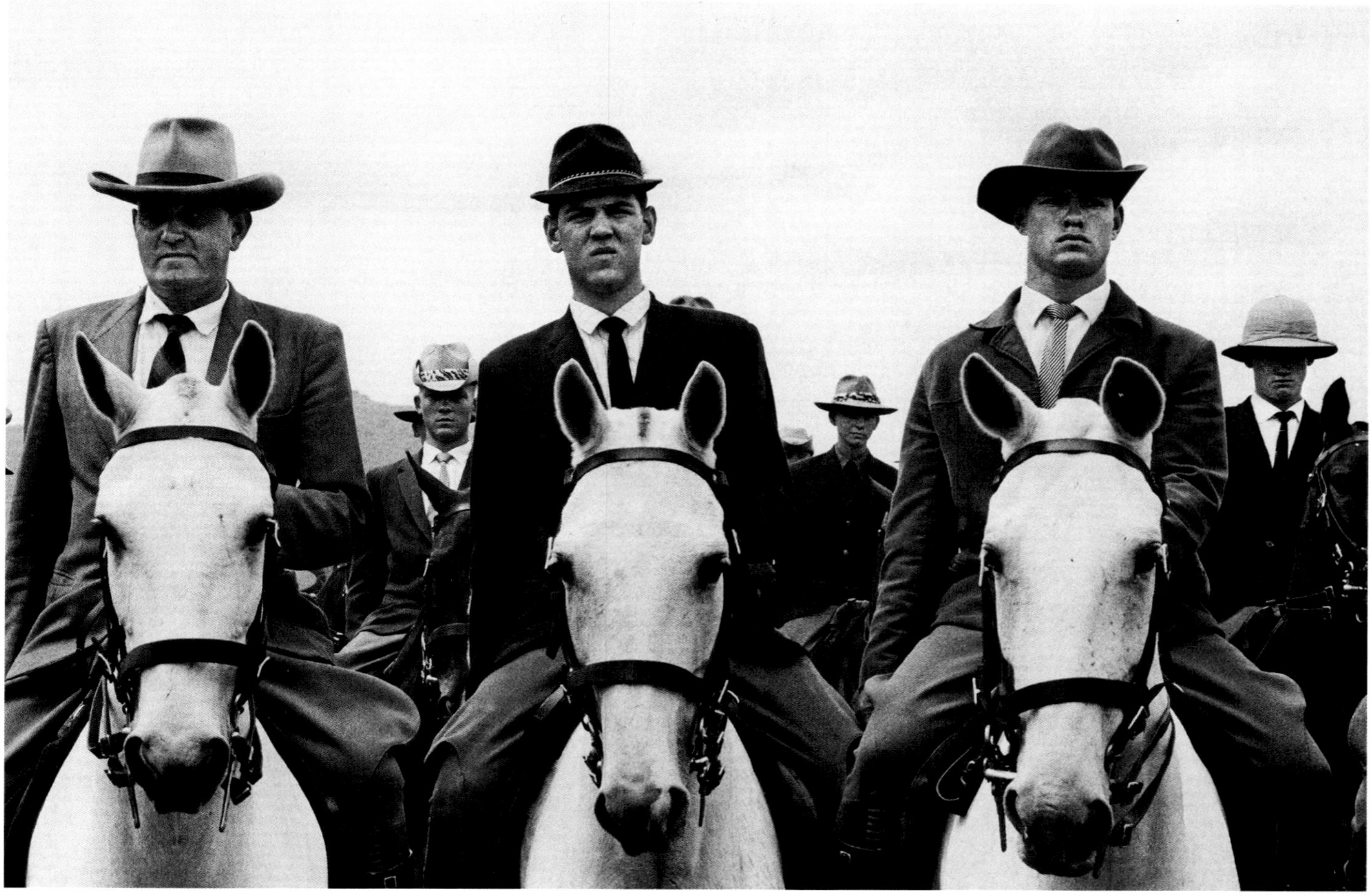

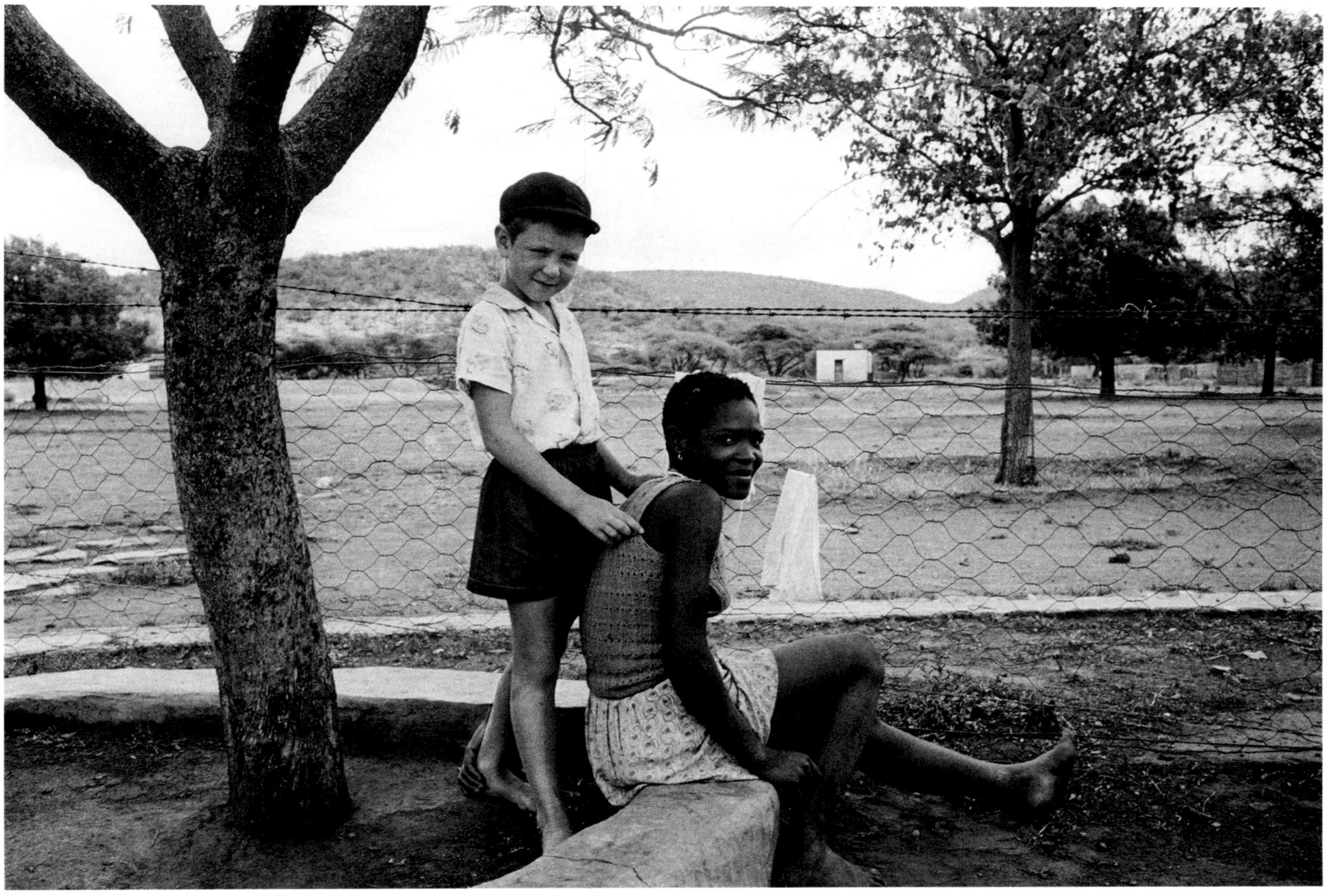

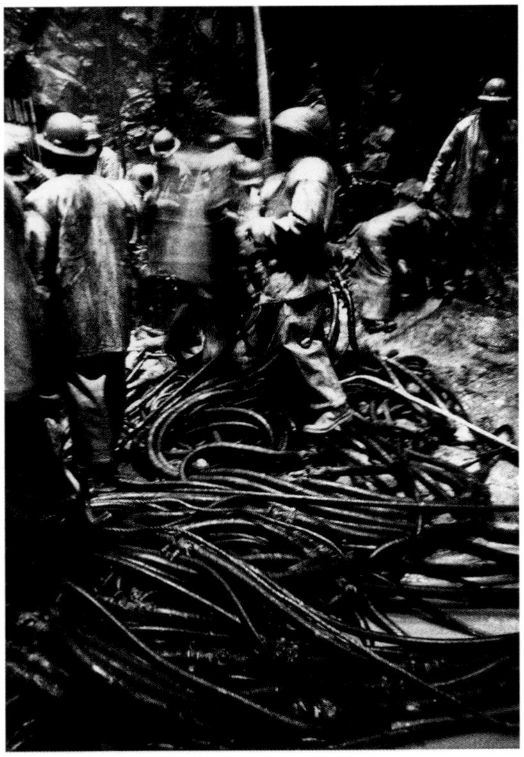

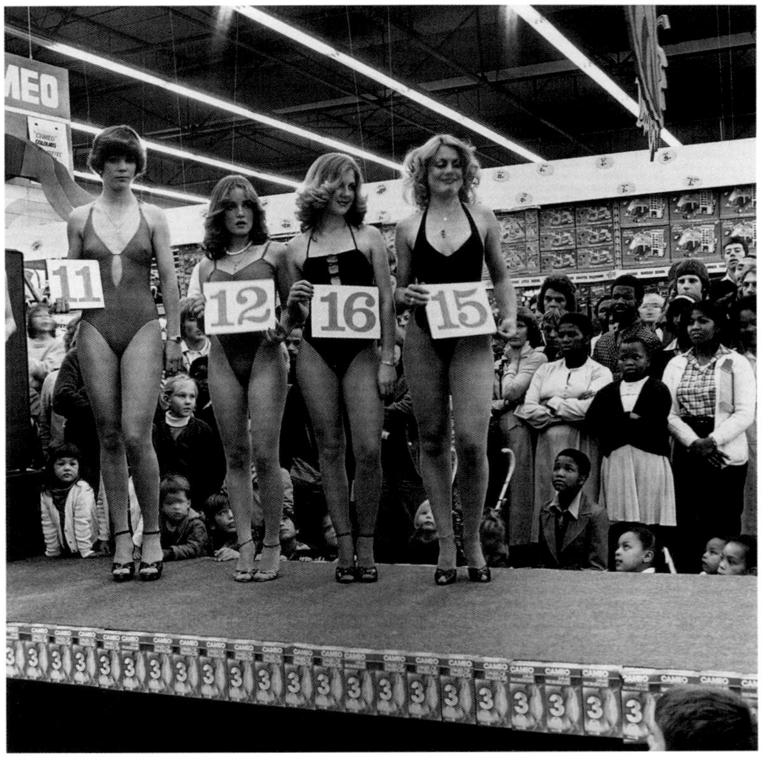

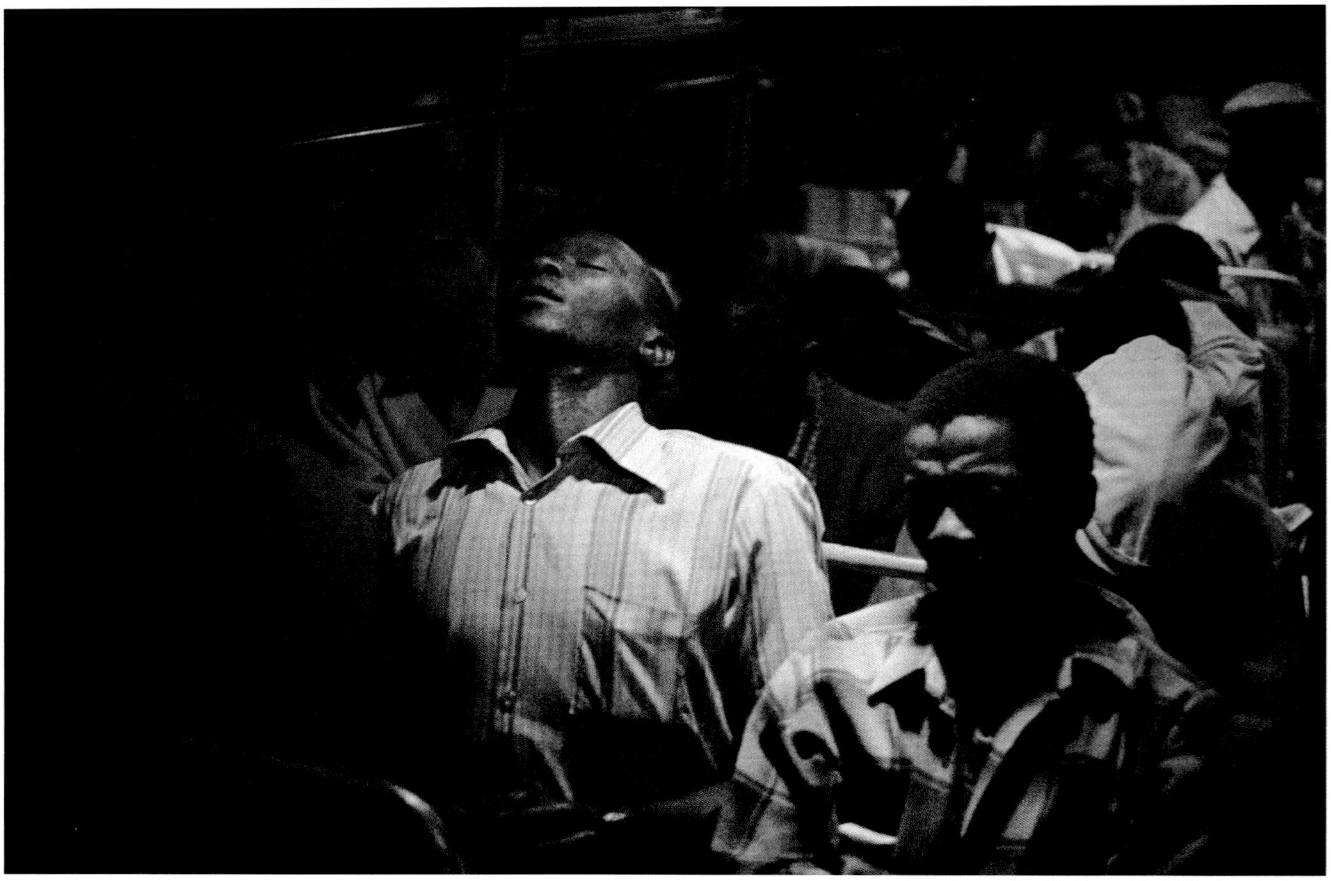

David Goldblatt
Air and Water Hoses Being Connected for Drilling Blast Holes, No. 4 Shaft President Steyn Gold Mine, Welkom, 1970
Gelatin silver photograph on fibre-based paper
Approx. 30 × 40cm / $11\frac{7}{8} \times 15\frac{7}{8}$ in

Saturday at the Hypermarket: Miss Lovely Legs Competition, Boksburg, 1980
Gelatin silver photograph on fibre-based paper
Approx. 30 × 40 cm / $11\frac{7}{8} \times 15\frac{3}{4}$ in

Marabastad-Waterval route: for most of the people in this bus, the cycle will start again tomorrow at between 2 and 3 am, 1984
Gelatin silver hand print
18.5 × 28.5 cm / $7\frac{1}{4} \times 11$ in

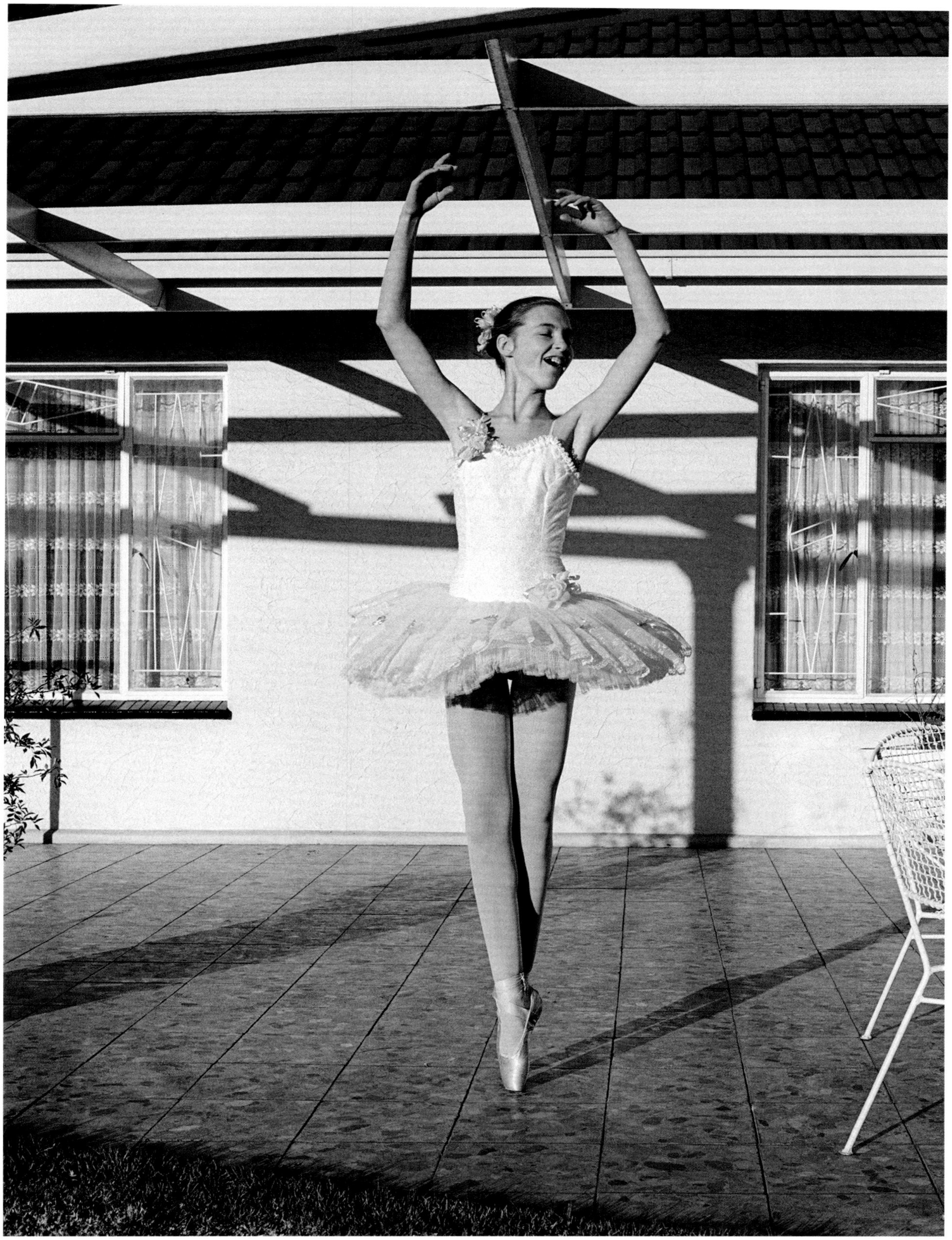

Girl in her new tutu on the stoep,
1980
Silver gelatin photograph on
fibre-based paper
Approx. 30 × 40cm /
$11\frac{7}{8} \times 15\frac{3}{4}$ in

Bill Owens

Bill Owens's *Suburbia* (1972) offers a portrait of a middle-class community, but here the critique is directed against the artifices and fakery of Californian suburban communities where, as Owens says, 'everyone… lives the "good life", which means having attractive homes, high-paying jobs, swimming pools and shiny cars'.[5] One of the themes of the American Dream, salient in the 1950s, was growth. The economy, industries, military were all described as booming, and the nation's new suburbs were the prime examples of rapid, vigorous expansion. Owens wanted to provide 'a visual/anthropological view of America', and adopted a plain documentary style, but this was not without its comic and ironic effects. He introduced the pictures in his book *Suburbia* by explaining that his work as a photographer for a local newspaper enabled him to meet people who 'enjoy the life-style of the suburbs. They have realized the American Dream. They are proud to be homeowners and to have achieved material success'.[6] He advertised his request to photograph suburbia in a local newspaper and accompanied his photographs with captions, intended to say 'what the people feel about themselves'.

One could compare Owens's view of suburbia with Diane Arbus's interior of a middle-class household at Christmas. She sought a hidden America behind a cloistered suburbia, which when pictured served as a symbol and icon of fakery and artifice. Owens extends this approach, but gets under the surface. There is little sense of an indictment of those who live in suburbia. Instead, what comes across are the varied desires and differences of his subjects, often in contrast to the plasticity of their new homes.

Owens presents himself as part of the scene; he revels in the lives of those detailed. His documentary is not harsh but essentially benign, and in this respect one could see *Suburbia* as distinct from the engagement with taste in the work of Martin Parr. Parr's 'Signs of the Times' (1992), which took the form of a television programme, a book and a series of London underground posters, is loaded with irony as texts jar with the pictures, many of which insist upon the vacuity and pointlessness of interior décor that is coded into class distinctions, very often bad middle-class taste. Parr's pictures seem bereft of Owens's humanism: they rely on jokes about aesthetic judgement and values in a suburbia riddled with class distinctions of taste in which an excess of decoration becomes a spectacle for amusement on the part of more discerning and tasteful viewers. The quotes from the subjects that serve as captions tend to flag up their aspirations and are often brought bluntly down to earth in the clear fakery of the interior décor. Marked by misanthropy, Parr's is a darker vision than Owens's. In *Suburbia* Owens's focus is more on the eccentricities of suburban folk, such as climbing a tree to remove the remaining fall leaves, for example.

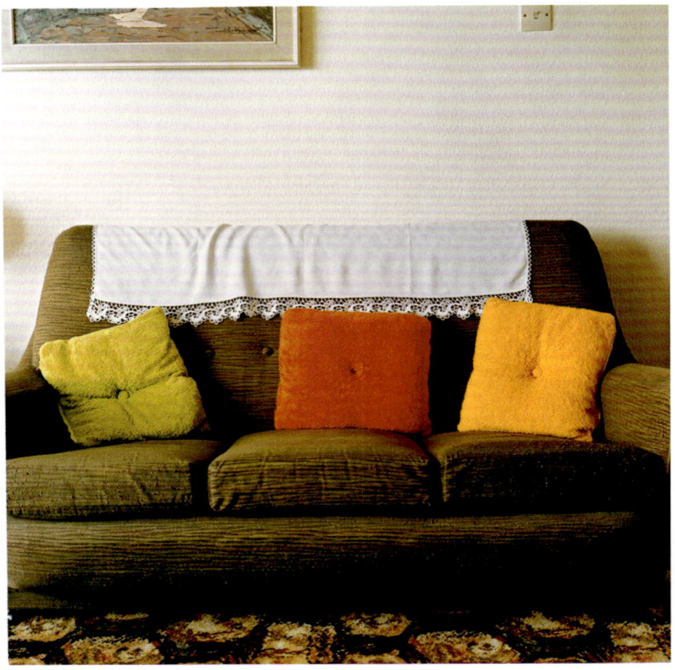

We keep buying things thinking 'that'll look better' and it just doesn't

Martin Parr
From 'Signs of the Times', 1992
C-print, dimensions variable

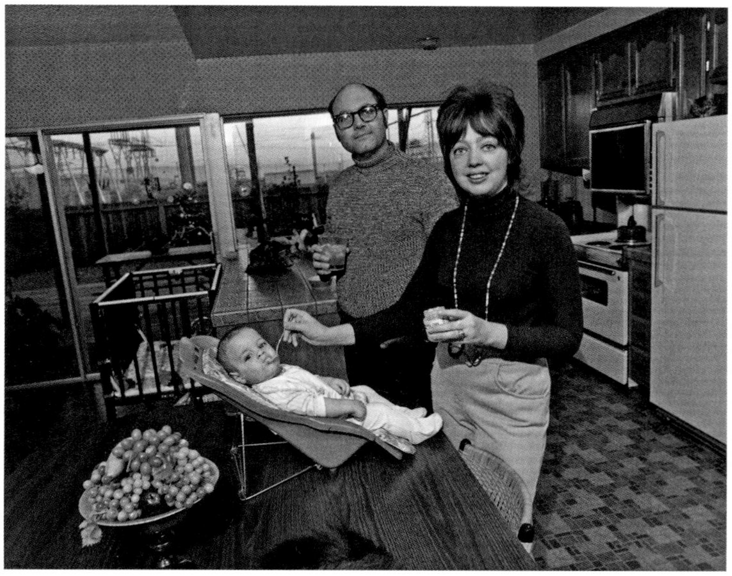

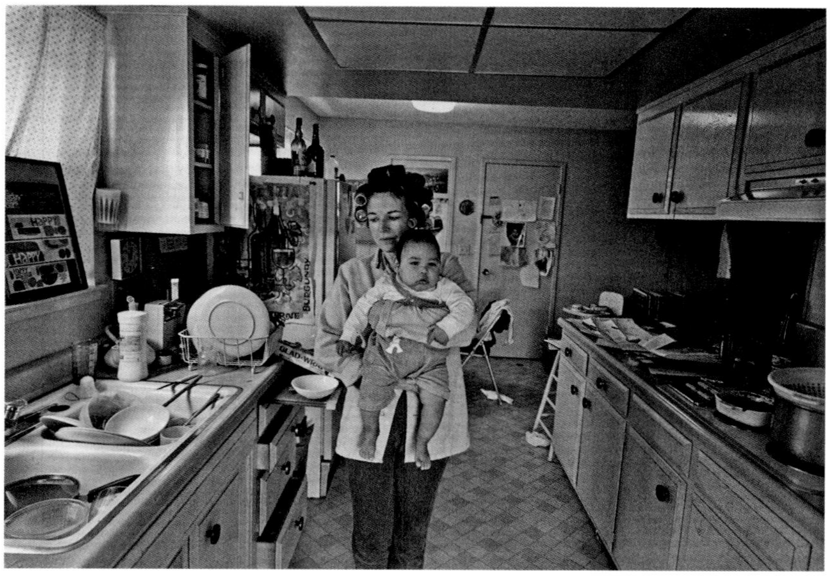

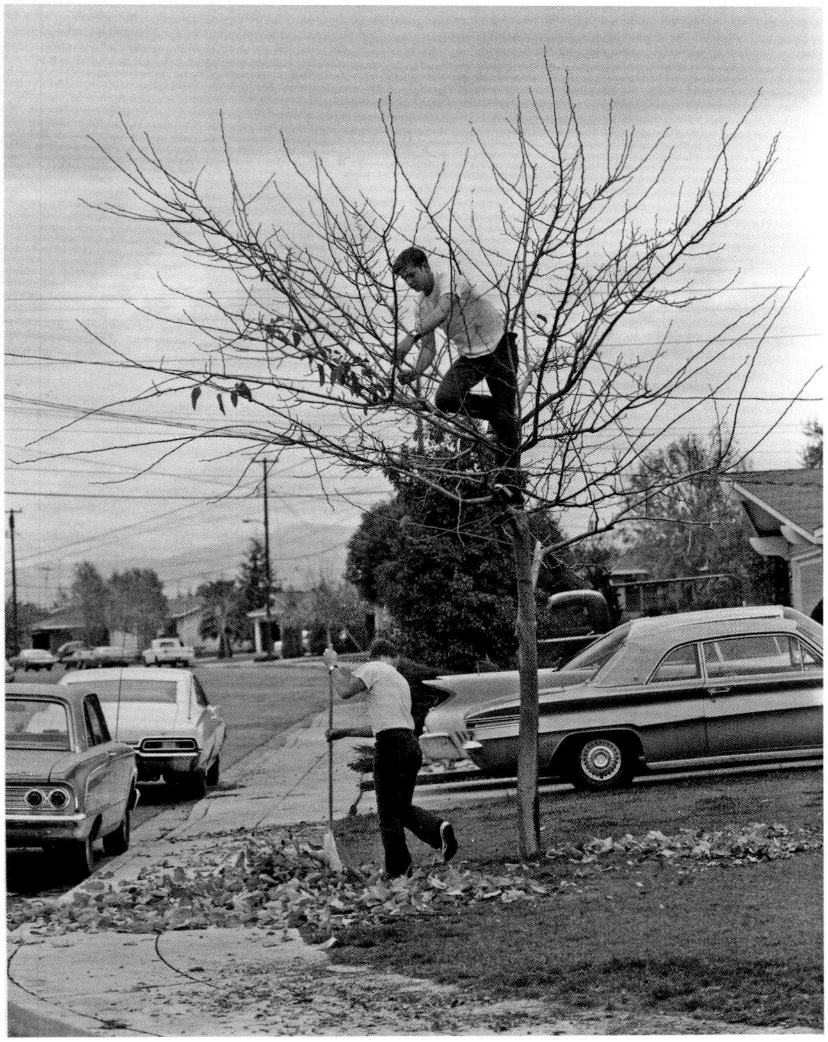

Bill Owens
We're really happy. Our kids are healthy, we eat good food, and we have a really nice home, 1972
Gelatin silver print
20.3 × 25.4 cm / 8 × 10 in

How can I worry about the damn dishes when there are children are dying in Vietnam, 1971
Gelatin silver print
20.3 × 25.4 cm / 8 × 10 in

My dad thinks it's a good idea to take all the leaves off the tree and rake up the yard. I think he's crazy, 1971
Gelatin silver print
20.3 × 25.4 cm / 8 × 10 in

Mary Ellen Mark

Mary Ellen Mark's 'American Odyssey' (1963–99) indicates an important continuity with classic documentary modes. Many of her pictures draw out tensions and potential conflicts between ideological belief systems and individuals. In her exploration of the racism and violent hatred in the United States, she gives a sense of going beyond the public face of extremism to a soft human core. She portrays members of right-wing groups in situations which cast them in a humane light, like the father at an Aryan rally caught at a tender moment, asleep with his young child in his arms. In Mark's picture of a couple of far-right skinheads, *Tim Malone and fellow gang member*, we get the sense of a polarized double portrait: Malone, aggressive and confident, stands on a mattress in his sparse room giving a Nazi salute, while the other youth remains huddled up, face buried in his folded arms, fearful and vulnerable.

Mark's practice is rooted in the humanist documentary tradition. Maya Angelou's poem, 'Human family', with its closing refrain 'We are more alike, my friends, than we are unalike', prefaces the book *American Odyssey*, and serves as an anchoring caption to the photographs. No matter the difference – class, ideology, gender, race, sexuality – Mark's documentary seeks out points of empathy and affiliation. This often entails her having a prolonged relationship with a number of her subjects. Her portraits of Tiny, for example, sensitively document the endurance of a woman whom she first photographed when she was a thirteen-year-old prostitute. The pictures are studies in a developing relationship between the photographer and her subject, from a guarded and confrontational picture of Tiny dressed in black for a funeral – 'her Halloween costume', according to the title – to a photo of her crying at home, comforted by one of her children, taken just over a decade and half later. Mark photographed the Damm family in both 1987 and 1994. Her powerful portrait of this homeless group in their car, in which they were living at the time, attests to their physical bond. Despite all the shit around them, they remain close together: the mother looks wasted, but her husband holds her protectively while the young girl in the back tenderly touches the cheek of her younger brother. The later photographs from 1994 are particularly disturbing because they show the transformation of the children. Mark is clearly interested in their vulnerability. In her intimate photograph of the mother, father and daughter all huddled together in bed, the girl is the only one awake: aloof and thoughtful, her expression conveys a sense of endurance and resilience. As much as she is physically embraced by her father, she is clearly elsewhere, detached. His physical closeness might even be seen to carry more menacing overtones. In a striking profile portrait of her brother, Jesse Damm, now shaven headed, the innocence of earlier pictures has gone; the boy seems troubled by an emotional weight that is disproportionate to his tender age.

Mary Ellen Mark
Crissy, Dean and Linda Damm, Llano, California, 1994
Gelatin silver print, dimensions variable

Jesse Damm, Llano, California, 1994
Gelatin silver print, dimensions variable

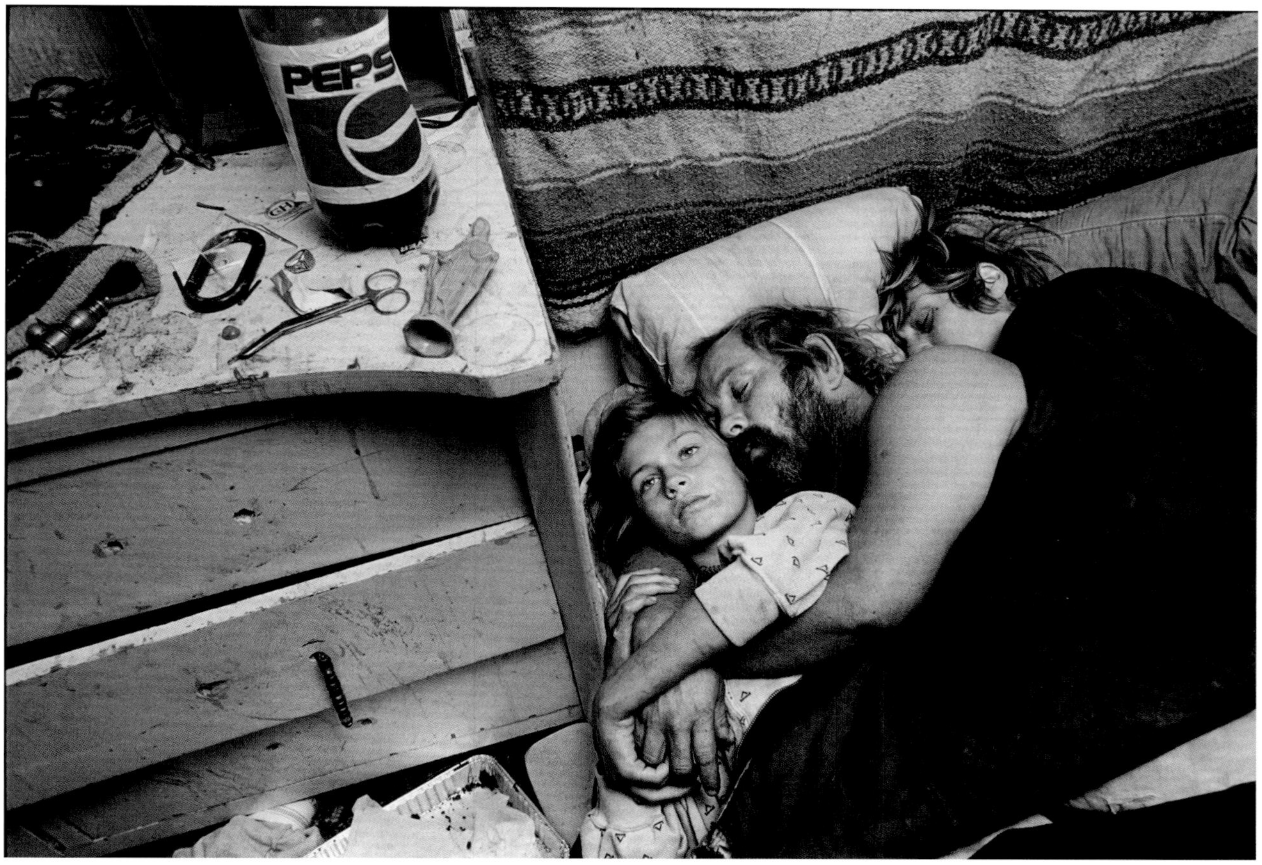
PEPS

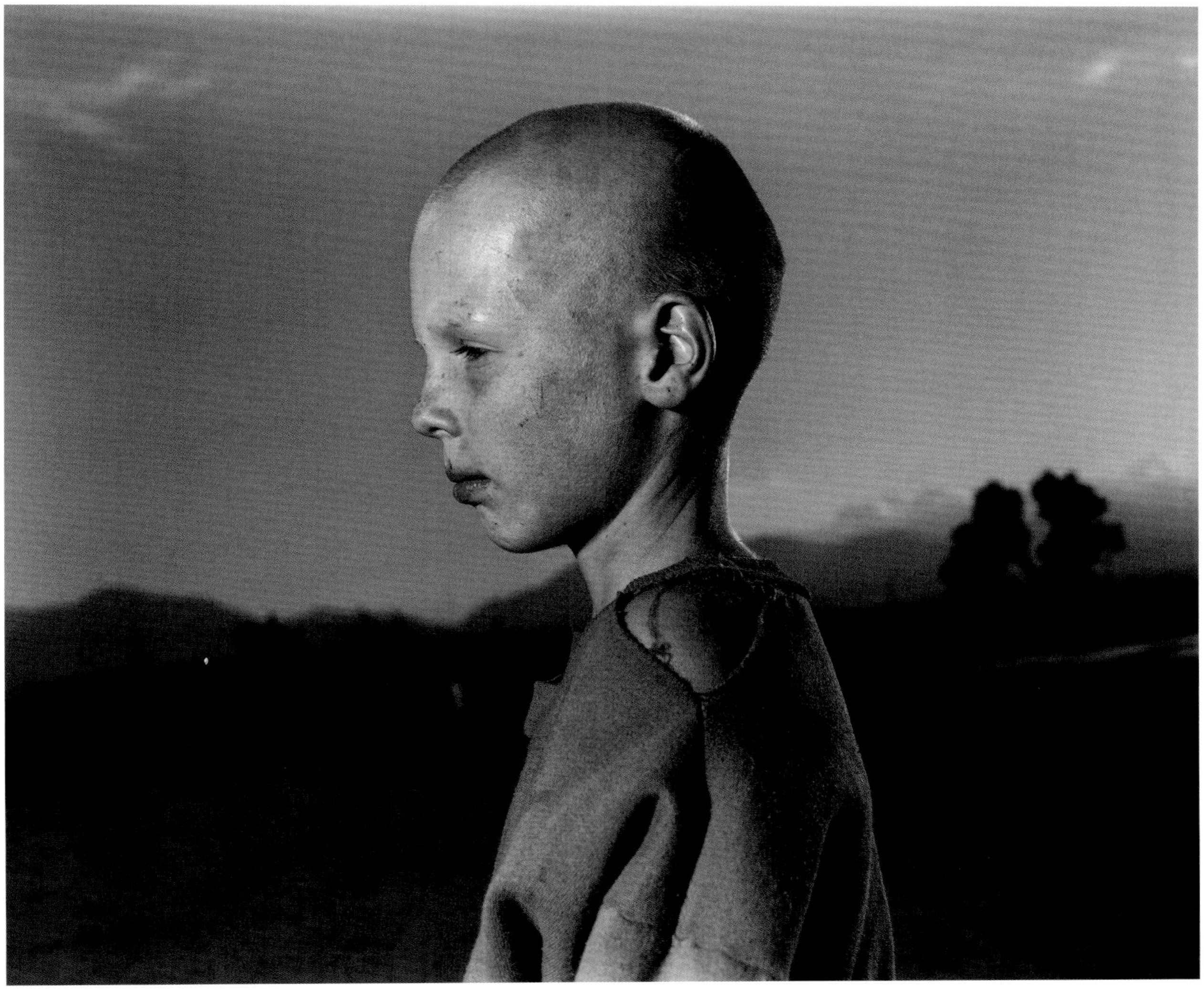

Jacob Holdt

The Danish photographer Jacob Holdt offers a remarkable extension of the reformist ideals of documentary in his 'American Pictures'. Holdt returns us to FSA photography: his subject matter certainly bears affinities, showing the agrarian labour of cotton pickers and cane pickers, and the recurrent evidence of dire poverty and racism. The point seems to be that the United States has not really moved on in terms of the economic suffering and inequalities that are pictured. But there is a difference in the closeness of the relationships from which many of the photographs stem. Holdt's work is best described as an immersive documentary, with many pictures resulting from close affiliation with their subjects. But no matter how close he might get to some of the people he depicts and no matter how little money he had when he made this work, hitchhiking through America with a thirty-dollar camera, shooting with colour-slide film, Holdt, Danish and white, would always still remain an outsider.

Holdt has said: 'I have never been interested in photography as art so very few of my pictures can stand alone. They have all been taken for a cinematic narrative on racism with simple, quickly grasped motives...'.[7] The images rely on the division between the wealthy and poor, and are driven by a love of humanity and the hatred of bigotry. The pictures were also presented as lectures and thousands of images are included on his extensive website, showing startling pictures of poverty, violent death, prostitution, crime and affluence. One remarkable group portrait shows a white family seated on their sofa, the conventionality and innocence of such a portrayal offset by the fact they are all holding guns, armed to the teeth. Others show moments of tenderness: couples in bed, or intimate portraits of his subjects who became his lovers. In some of his pictures of the wealthy, such as the portrait of the lobster-eating and champagne-drinking affluent, the flash-light renders the subjects cold. This awkward freezing of the subject contrasts with the quality of so many of Holdt's pictures of the lives of the poor, in which colour gives warmth and animation to those depicted, finding a certain beauty despite the terrible depravation.

Jim Goldberg

Many of the photographers discussed so far adopt a classical documentary model that endorses and looks back to the work of the FSA photographers. Jim Goldberg is also part of this tradition, only here much of the idealization and romanticism has gone. Goldberg's work signals a more brutal, realist dimension to documentary, as well as extending the collaborative strategy integral to Danny Lyon's photographs. Goldberg's hefty book *Raised by Wolves* (1995) was accompanied by an extensive multimedia exhibition, opening in Zurich and then touring to venues in the United States. Put together with curator Philip Brookman, it was structured around two intertwining stories of runaway teenagers living on the streets of San Francisco and Los Angeles. It is a tale of their lives of abuse, drugs and prostitution. Their desires, fears and loyalties are narrated by means of some one hundred and seventy photographs, video and audio installations, documents and objects in vitrines. Brookman has spoken of both the book and exhibition being 'like a narrative story, we set it up like a film or a novel'.[8] Taking its cue from displays in historical and natural history museums, Goldberg's use of photography extends the forms and modes of documentary representation, but in making more vivid and concrete these damaged and painful lives it nevertheless does not fully avoid still exoticizing them.

Jacob Holdt
Leslie Manselles, from the slideshow 'American Pictures', 1970–5
Leslie was my girlfriend in Hartford, Connecticut... and she still is. We recently celebrated our 35-year anniversary.

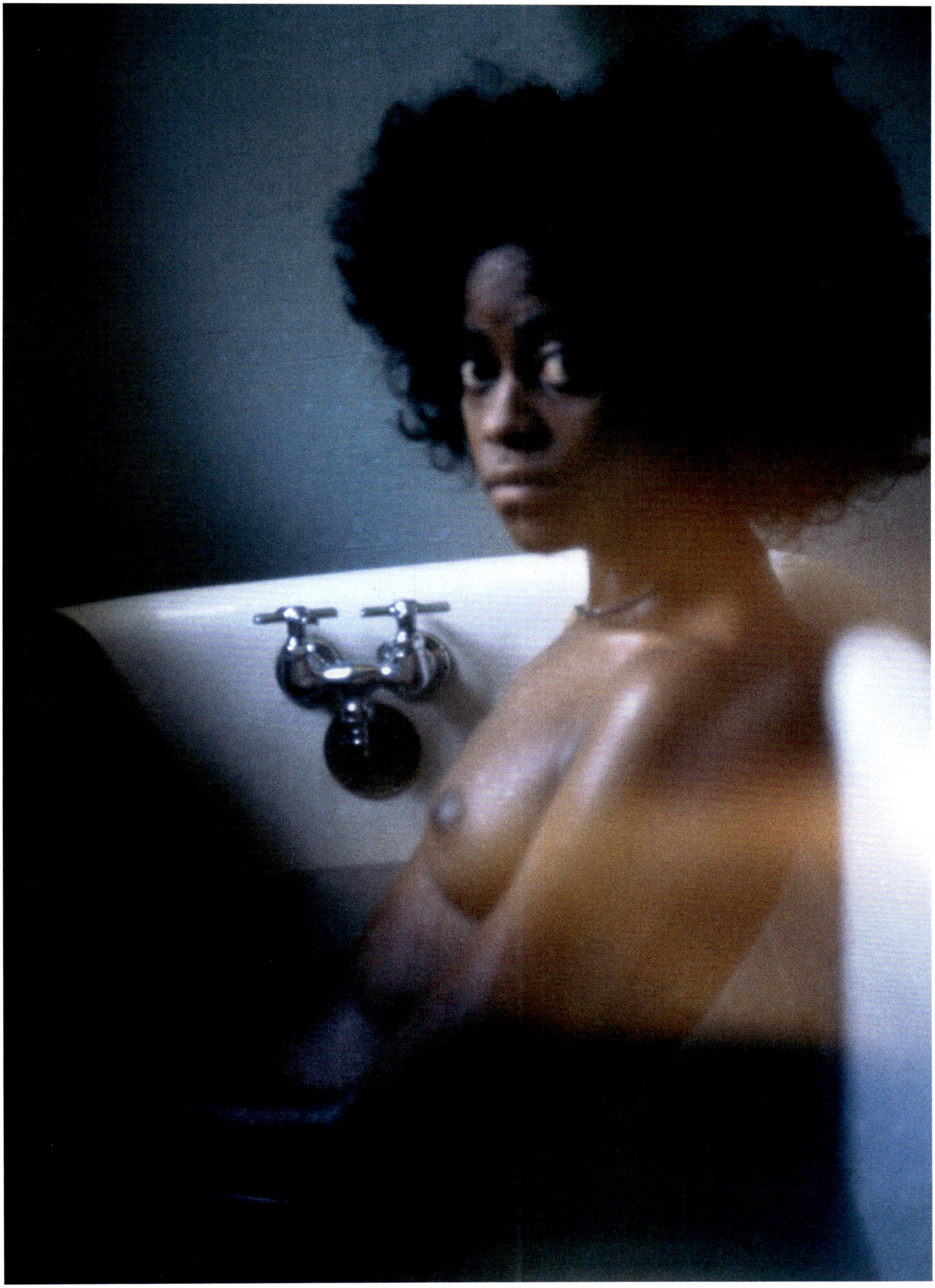

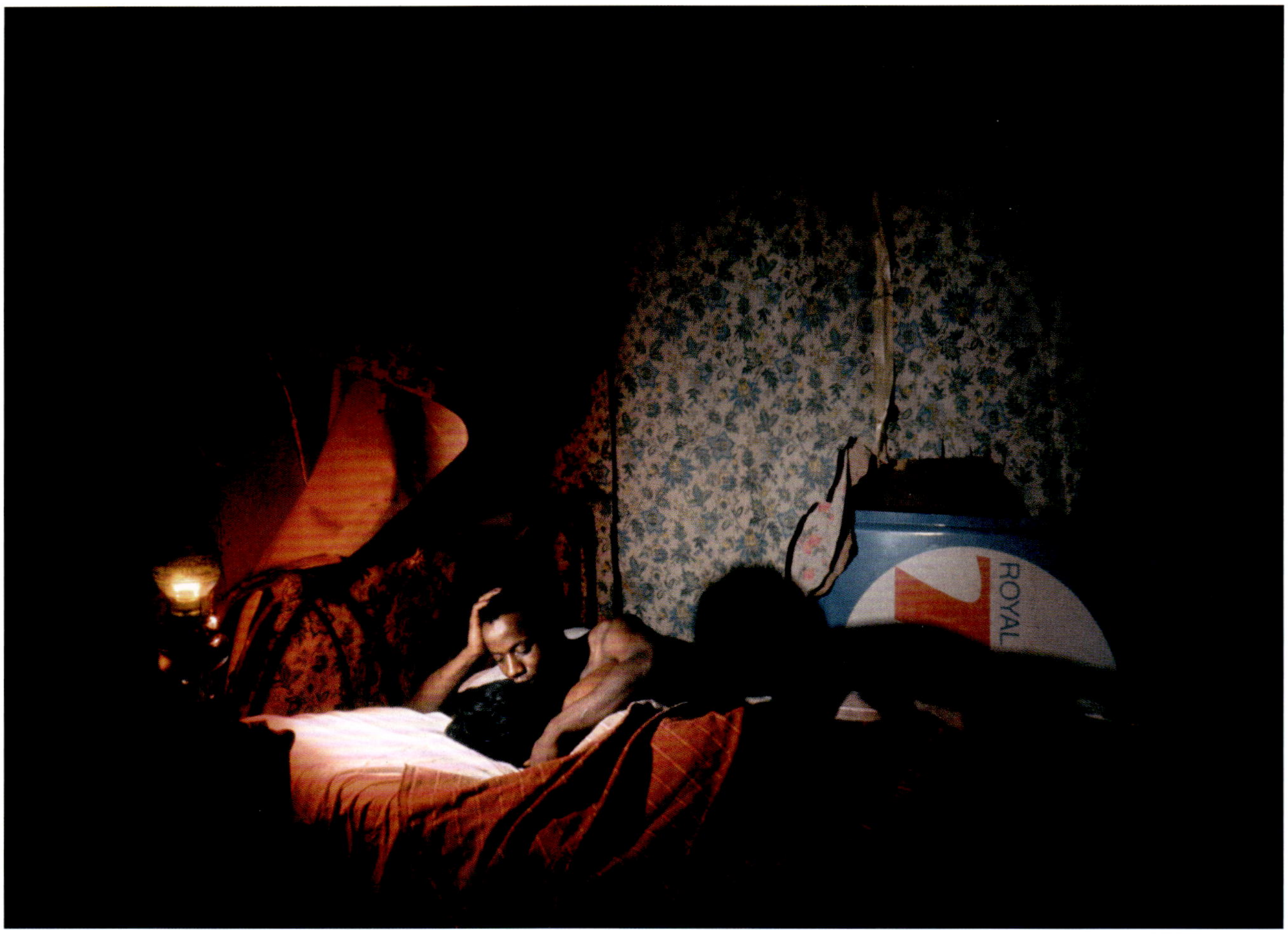

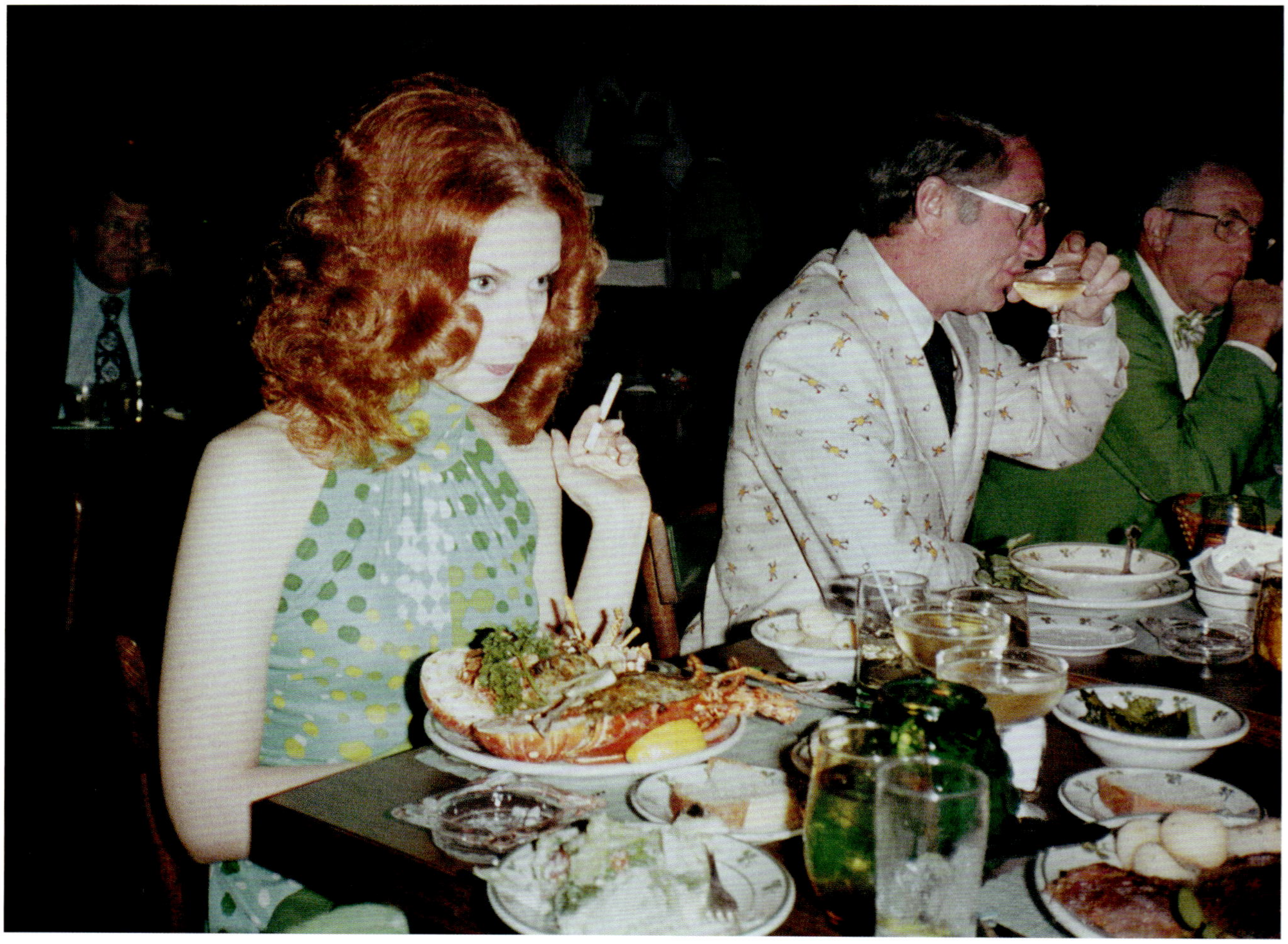

Jacob Holdt
Couple in North Carolina, from the slideshow 'American Pictures', 1970–5
When I lived with this couple in North Carolina I asked if I could take a picture of them in bed. They were a bit shy, but after hitchhiking all over the country and writing them a letter about the beauty of such a picture, they said yes. So I hitchhiked back from California to the tobacco fields of New Carolina and stayed with them again

Palm Beach, from the slideshow 'American Pictures', 1970–5
A leftist millionaire, Bill Gandalls, made me his driver and for a few days I wined and dined with the wealthiest people in the world

Jim Goldberg
101 Pictures, from the series 'Raised by Wolves', 1985–95
Collage with black and white contact sheets, colour snapshots and tape
35.6 × 29.9 cm / 14 × 11 in

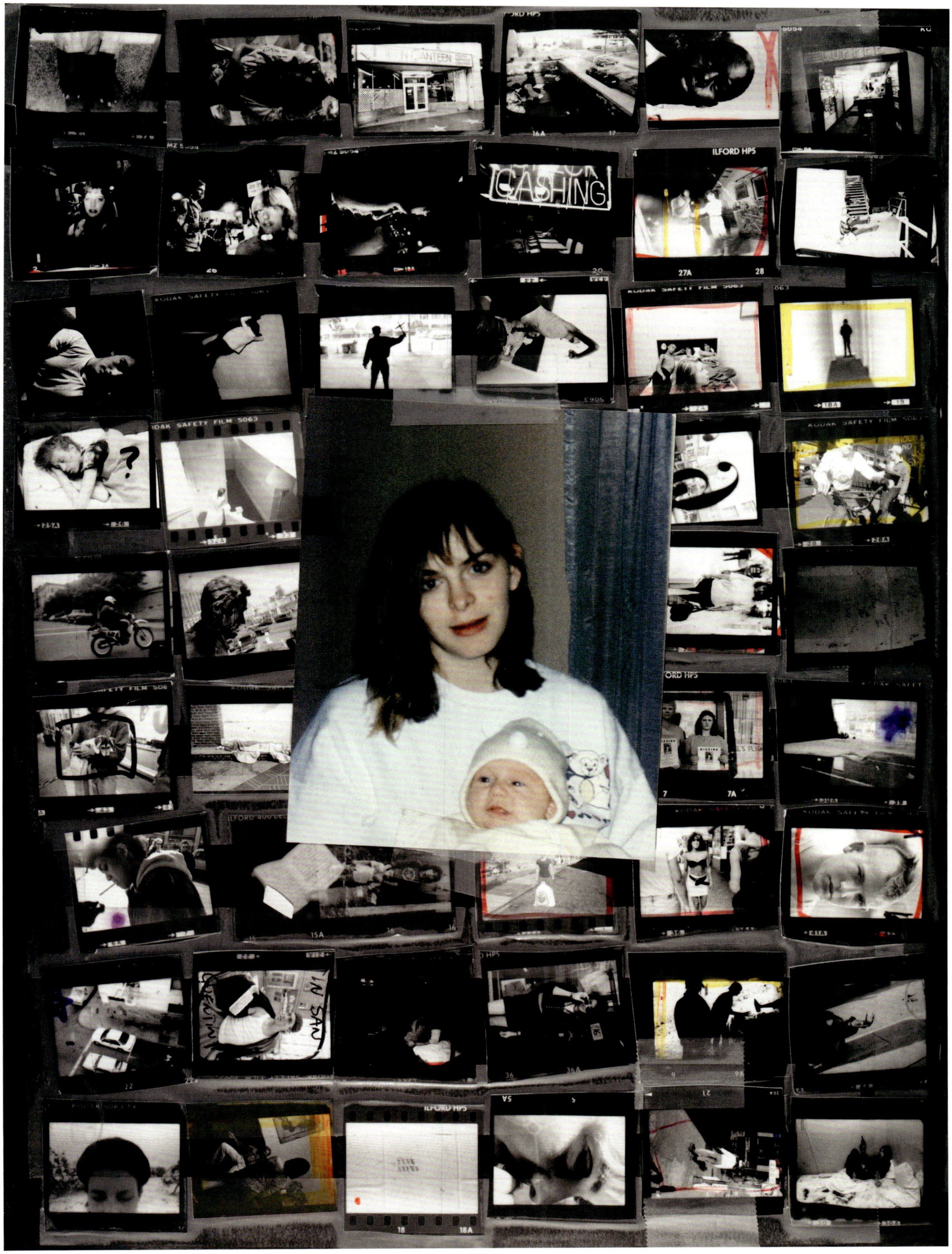

Sebastião Salgado

Sebastião Salgado's 1986 *Serra Pelada* pictures an open-cast mine in Brazil, and shows the workers who dig out the ore with shovels, load it into sacks and haul it up ladders and mud slopes to the top. Some 50,000 workers toiled here, dreaming that they might find gold. The scale of the scene is difficult to comprehend. Viewing such photographs is caught up with an astonishment that something like this could happen in the contemporary world: these are epic scenes of pre-industrial labour in a post-industrial world. The photographs come from Salgado's monumental book, *Workers*, which he describes as 'a homage to workers, a farewell to a world of manual labour that is slowly disappearing and a tribute to those men and women who still work as they have for centuries'.[9] At the core of the book is the intention to show the growing disparity between the Third World and the First World to which it yields its products and services.

Alfredo Jaar

Alfredo Jaar photographed the workers in the mine before Salgado and in colour, but his use of such documentary images is very different. In 1986 Jaar's photographs were presented in place of advertisements in New York's Spring Street Station, close to the heart of the city's financial district; a blunt public intervention in which the photographer sought to counter the abstract relationship to capital with the basic quest for gold. Colourful posters presented among the pictures indicated the market value of gold in various world markets. The collision of commodity culture and the search for gold is awkwardly brought to bear in terms of the fetishizing way in which the gold miners are sometimes depicted. In the way they isolate detailing of the muddied bodies of the labourers, Jaar's colour photographs can be seen as having affinities with the way bodies are represented in adverts. His display of labour is still under the sway of commodification.

Sebastião Salgado
Serra Pelada, State of Pará, Brazil, 1986
Gelatin silver print, dimensions variable

Alfredo Jaar
Rushes, 1986
New York Spring Street, subway station, temporary billboard project
Dimensions variable

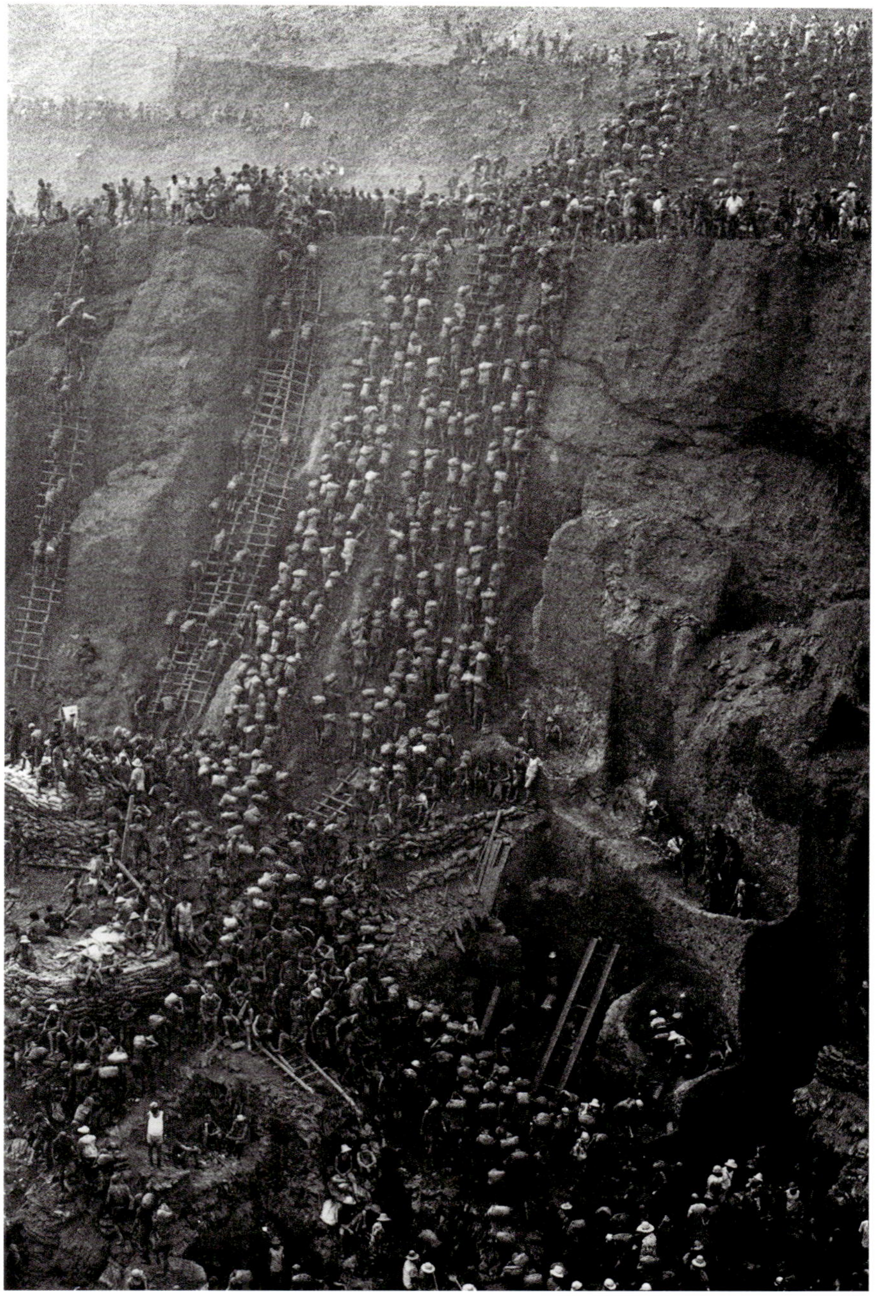

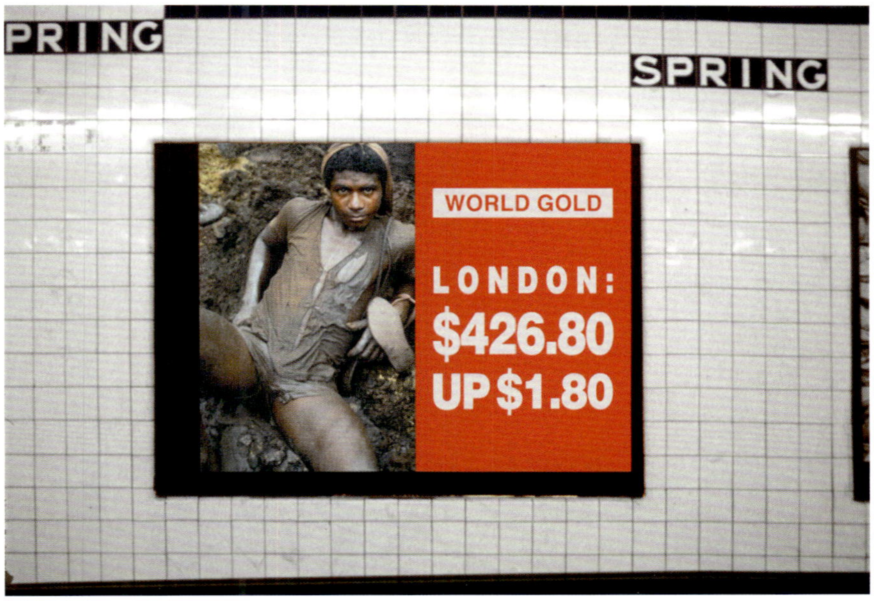
PRING
SPRING
WORLD GOLD
LONDON:
$426.80
UP $1.80

Allan Sekula

Through texts and sequences of colour photographs, Allan Sekula's 'Fish Story' (1990–4) narrates the transformation of seafaring and harbour life around the world. A narrative of epic proportions, it attempts to draw out the economic and social realities beneath the faceless global dominance of late capitalism. It is in many senses a story of the losses brought about by the increasing automation of the maritime world. Sekula opposes the harbour, where material goods appear in bulk, to the stock market where the 'abstract character of money rules',[10] but with the universal containerization of cargo at the end of the 1960s, harbours began to resemble the stock market: 'The boxes, viewed in vertical elevation, have the proportion of slightly elongated banknotes.'

Sekula's photos of rationalized and automated ports – the robot-truck designed to move containers at the automated ECT/Sea-Land cargo terminal at the Port of Rotterdam, for example – contrast with those that show the labour integral to the maritime world. Running through 'Fish Story' are a series of photographs of workers: pipe-fitters finishing the engine room of a tuna-fishing boat, welders in the former Lenin shipyard in Gdansk, women cutting steel in the Hyundai shipyard, a fisherman hauling in the nets on a rain-drenched night after unsuccessfully fishing for sardines off the Portuguese coast. Sekula also makes visible those who live a more precarious existence: the waterfront vendors living in containers in Veracruz, described as 'nomads' who constantly have to move their belongings from one container to the next because the steel boxes rest in one place only for a short time.

Allan Sekula
Unsuccessful fishing for sardines off the Portuguese coast, 1992, from the series 'Fish Story'
Dye transfer print
81.6 × 57.5 cm / 32⅛ × 22⅝ in

Testing robot-truck designed to move containers within automated ECT/Sea-Land cargo terminal. Maasvlakte, Port of Rotterdam, the Netherlands, 1992, from the series 'Fish Story'
Dye transfer print
61.3 × 77.8 cm / 24⅛ × 30⅝ in

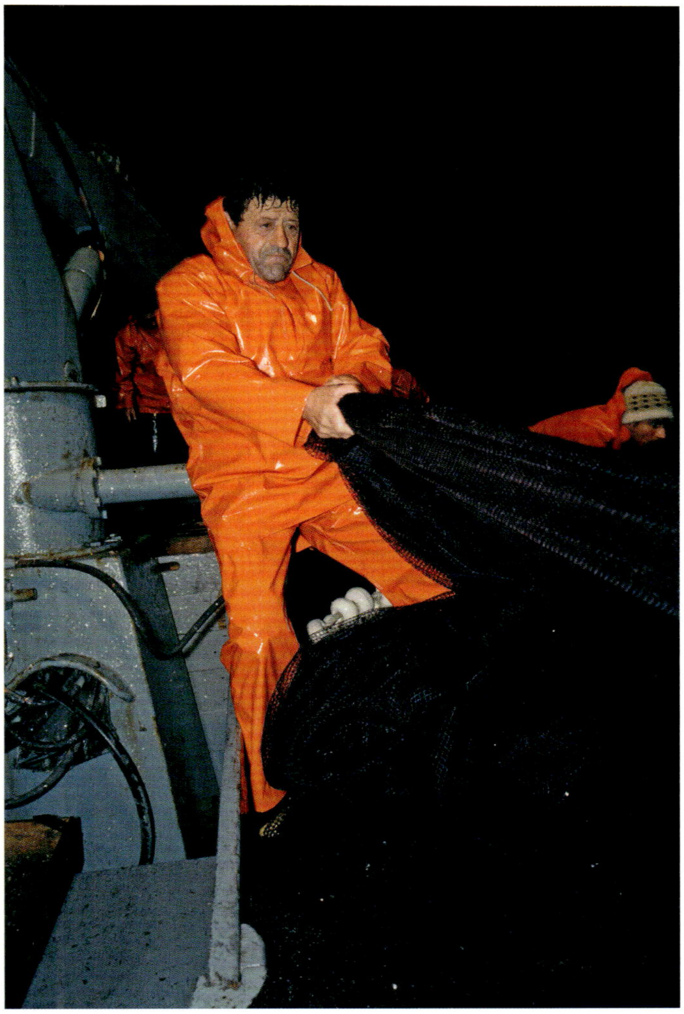

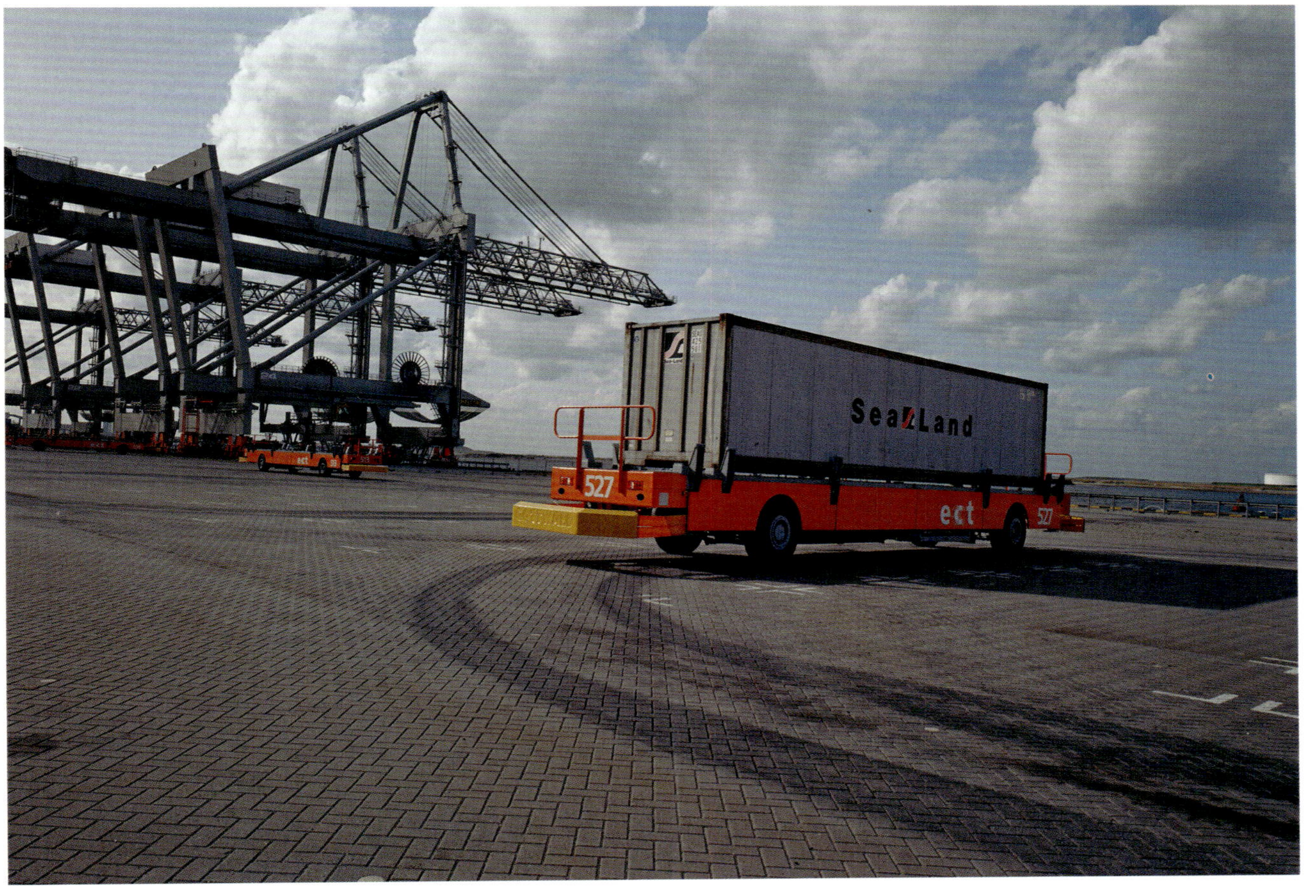
Sea Land
527
ect
527

Martha Rosler

While the humanist documentary tradition has continued it has also been variously challenged, parodied and dismantled. From the 1970s onwards, documentary faced a concerted effort to displace its importance. As photography was taken up and used by Conceptual artists, its documentary form was often subject to parody and critique. Douglas Huebler's photo-text, *Duration Piece 7, Rome* (1973), for example, offers an absurdist variation on a documentary project through a series of pictures that are said to document the movement of water between rocks in the Trevi Fountain. Similarly Robert Barry's *Inert Gas Series* (1969) are impossible documents, as the photographed event of releasing various gases into the atmosphere eludes representation.

Martha Rosler in her documentary critique removes the usual subjects from the frame. Instead, in her phototext work *The Bowery in two inadequate descriptive systems* (1974–5) she shows us the storefronts and walls of the Bowery through black-and-white photographs that look back to the work of photographers like Walker Evans. The pictures are mostly paired with lists of words and phrases for drunkenness (the first three panels have words only) and presented as a grid on the gallery wall. In her landmark 1981 essay 'In, Around, and Afterthoughts (on documentary photography)' she provides a succinct overview of this work: 'If impoverishment is a subject here, it is the impoverishment of representational strategies tottering about alone ... The photographs are powerless to deal with the reality that is yet totally comprehended-in-advance and as diversionary as the word formations (which at least are closer to the culture of drunkenness rather than being framed on it from without). There is a poetics of drunkenness here... The words begin outside the world of skid row and slide into it, as people are thought to slide into alcoholism and skid to the bottom of the row.'[11] As the title suggests, the work draws attention to the way descriptive systems are inadequate, breaking with what she has referred to as 'the underlying humanist notion of the commensurability between representation and experience.'[12] In not giving us portraits of the poor, Rosler raises questions about how the documentarian can adequately begin to represent the experience of other people.

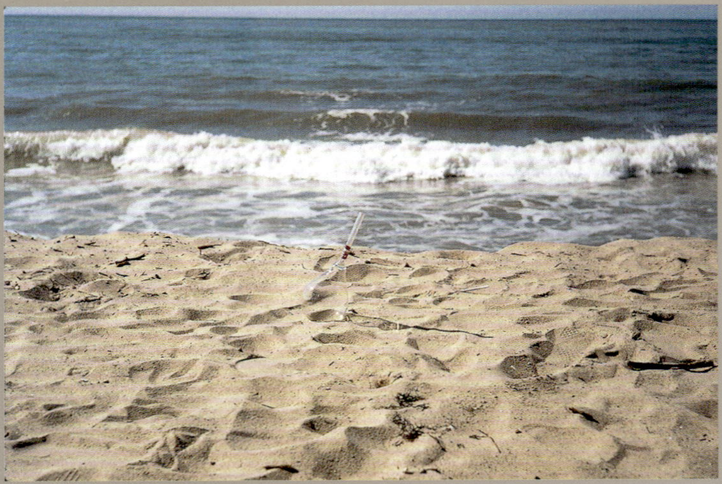

Robert Barry
Inert Gas Series: Argon (from a measured volume to indefinite expansion), 1969, Pacific Ocean, Santa Monica

Martha Rosler
The Bowery in two inadequate descriptive systems, 1974–5
45 gelatin silver prints, each framed board 25.4 × 55.9 cm / 10 × 22 in

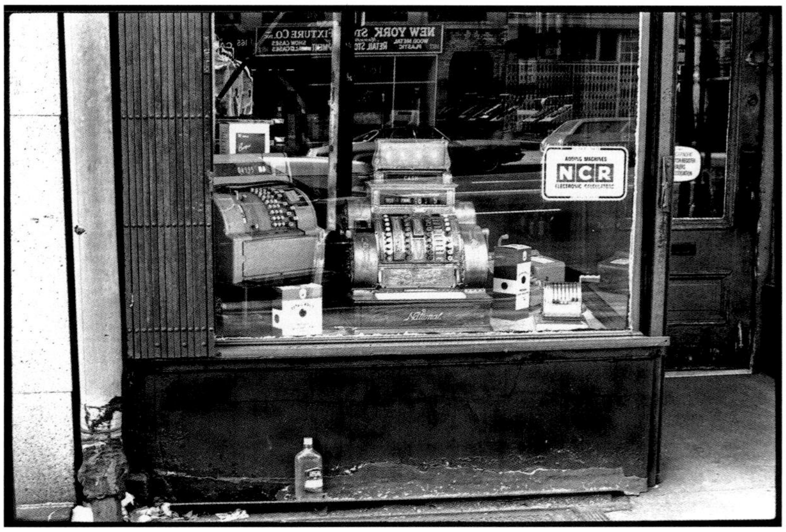

stewed
boiled
potted
corned
pickled
preserved
canned
fried to the hat

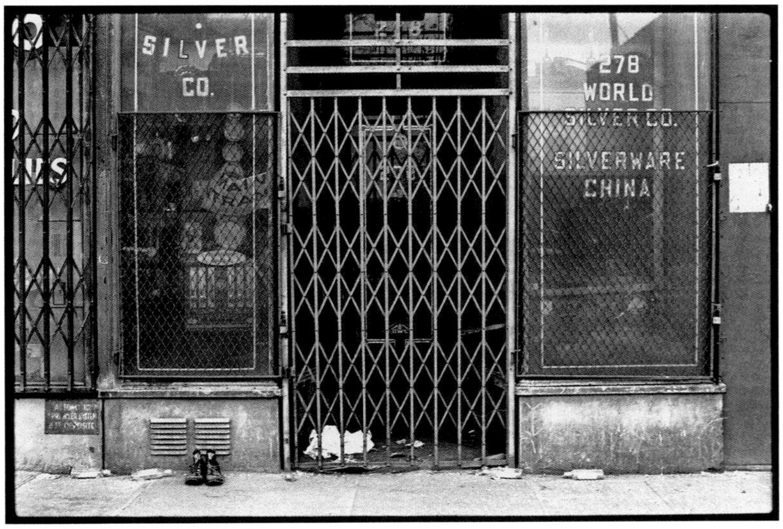

soaked	drenched
sodden	flying the ensign
steeped	over the bay
soused	half-seas-over
sloshed	decks awash
saturated	down with the fish

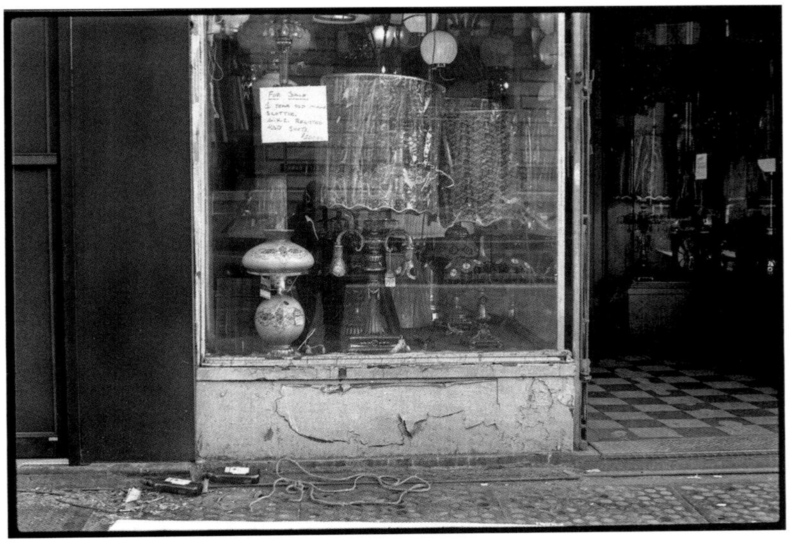

comatose unconscious

passed out knocked out

laid out

out of the picture

out like a light

Sophie Calle

A number of female artists have continued to address the exchange at the heart of documentary practice, combining performance and photography. For Sophie Calle, the modes of voyeurism and curiosity about the other so integral to documentary are isolated and magnified in work that parades itself as autobiographical and confessional. It breaks with the documentary tradition in that the photographer is present and performs in her work.

Calle's photographic and textual documents very often record a performance, a lived experience, in which the artist presents her obsessive fascination with the lives and behaviour of others. For *The Hotel* (1981) she took on the role of a chambermaid so she could snoop among the possessions of the guests in a Venetian hotel. The text and photos which make up this work are about portraits *in absentia*, driven by a quest for clues about the intimacies of other people's lives. The documentation is excessive, with no respect for privacy. Calle empties and photographs the contents of drawers, suitcases and handbags. Private, personal objects are laid out and photographed. She reads people's letters and diaries and reprints their contents in the texts that accompany her photographs.

Other people's lives, actual lives, become the subject of Calle's art – and, importantly, fantasies about those lives. Finding an address book in the street led her to a fantasy about its owner as she pieced together what he might be like through interviews with the people listed in the address book, interviews that were then published in the French newspaper *Liberation*. For this project Calle even left her home 'to move into a more anonymous place so I could immerse myself more fully in his life and habits. I had stopped seeing my friends the better to devote myself to his – whom I envied him, in fact.'[13]

Calle's diary-like book *Suite vénitienne* (1983) narrates through photographs and texts her activity as detective, voyeur and stalker in one of the most beautiful cities in the world. It gives the account of her pursuit of Henri B, a person she had met previously at an opening in Paris and had decided to follow when she learned he would be travelling to Venice. We follow her story, conscious that she is a woman who has adopted a male role and gaze as sleuth and voyeur. She is nevertheless still subject to a male gaze, as the text reveals how she is approached and desired by men, both with her blonde wig disguise and without. As readers of the book, we identify with her looking. The thrill, the perverse pleasure is the way in which the narrative and photos elicit our identification. But while we look with her, no narrative resolution is forthcoming. Instead, there is an odd exchange between Calle and the man she pursues, when he recognizes her eyes and takes her photo. When she tries to takes a photograph of him, he blocks the image. She is only able to take a picture when he leaves and turns his back to her. We never see the face of the person she pursues. Certain power relations are maintained.

Calle's earlier performance as a striptease artist in the Paris district of Pigalle, *The Striptease* (1979–81), highlighted the vulnerability of taking on the guise and life of another. She says she was kicked unconscious by one of her female colleagues after a fight over the only chair in a trailer.[14] Very often, Calle's encounters have no resolution. She might take and wear a discarded pair of shoes she finds in the bin in one of the hotel rooms she cleans, but never gets close to any of those whose possessions she snoops among. The persistent effect is one of disengagement and distancing from people, no matter how much she allows her life to be taken over by another.

In Calle's obsession with unexceptional others, her art involves a displaced kind of homage that we can see as signalling an excessive or parodic version of documentary practice. While containing potential and actual violence and eroticism, her projects essentially lack narrative drama and significance: the detailed cataloguing of possessions in hotel rooms, apart from a few private love letters and disclosures, finally amounts to very little. No secrets are uncovered.

Sophie Calle and Jean Baudrillard
Suite vénitienne. Please Follow Me, Bay Press, Seattle, WA, 1988 (originally published 1983 by Éditions de l'Étoile and Les Cahiers du Cinéma, Paris)
21 × 18 cm / 8¼ × 7 in, 87 pp

At the end of January 1980, on the streets of Paris, I followed a man whom I lost sight of a few minutes later in the crowd. That very evening, quite by chance, he was introduced to me at an opening. During the course of our conversation, he told me he was planning an imminent trip to Venice. I decided to follow him.

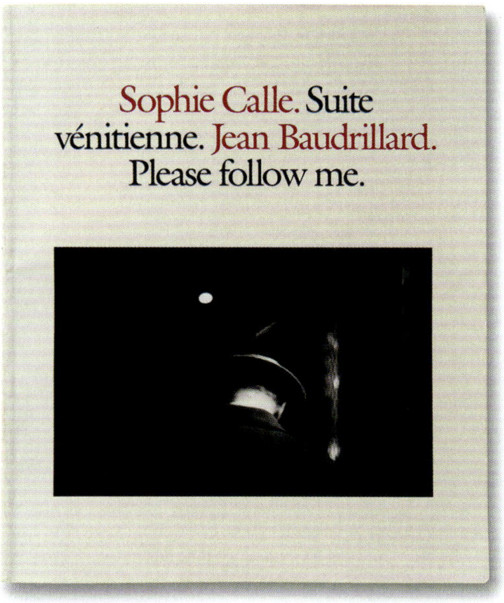

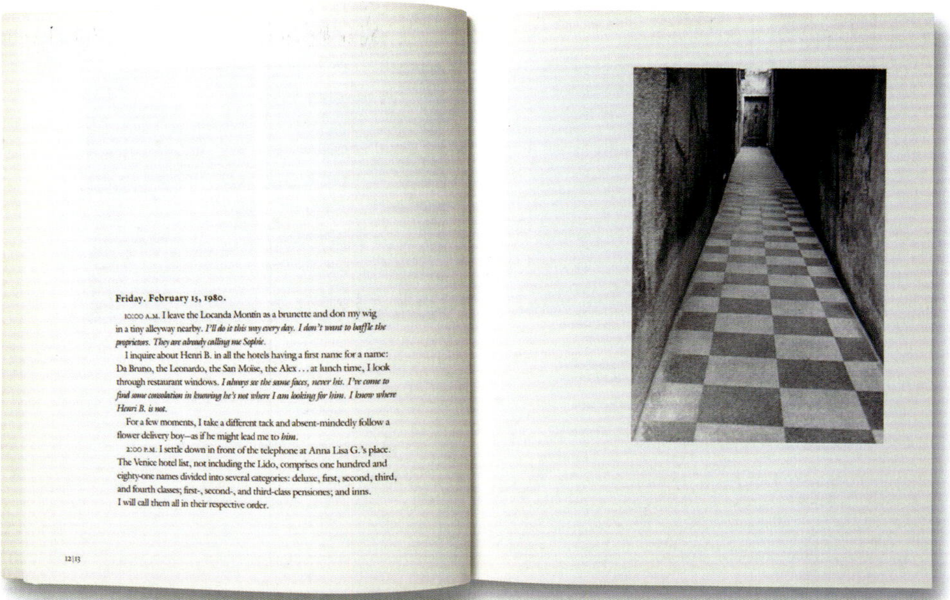

Friday. February 15, 1980.

10:00 A.M. I leave the Locanda Montin as a brunette and don my wig in a tiny alleyway nearby. *I'll do it this way every day. I don't want to baffle the proprietors. They are already calling me Sophie.*

I inquire about Henri B. in all the hotels having a first name for a name: Da Bruno, the Leonardo, the San Moïse, the Alex . . . at lunch time, I look through restaurant windows. *I always see the same faces, never his. I've come to find some consolation in knowing he's not where I am looking for him. I know where Henri B. is not.*

For a few moments, I take a different tack and absent-mindedly follow a flower delivery boy—as if he might lead me to *him*.

2:00 P.M. I settle down in front of the telephone at Anna Lisa G.'s place. The Venice hotel list, not including the Lido, comprises one hundred and eighty-one names divided into several categories: deluxe, first, second, third, and fourth classes; first-, second-, and third-class pensiones; and inns. I will call them all in their respective order.

12|13

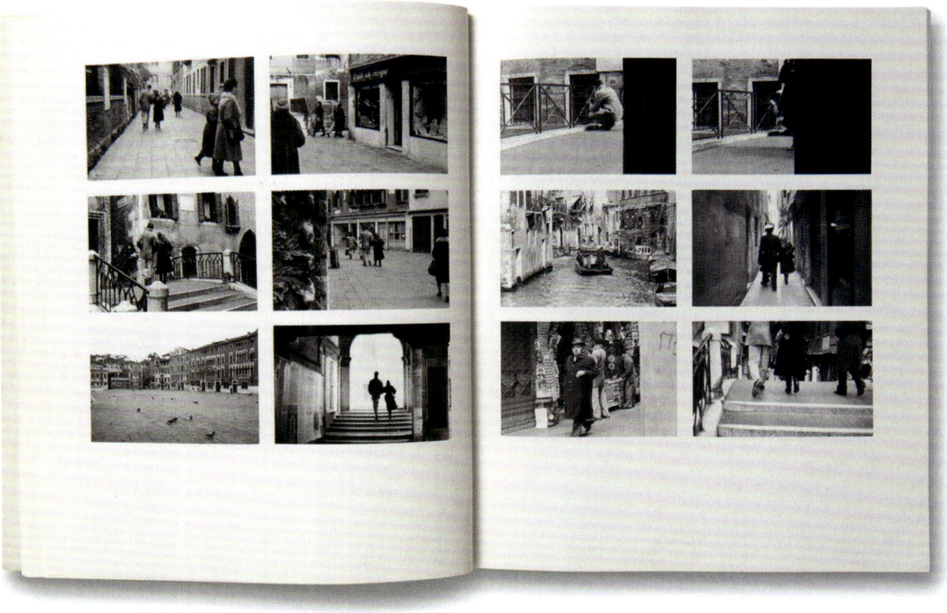

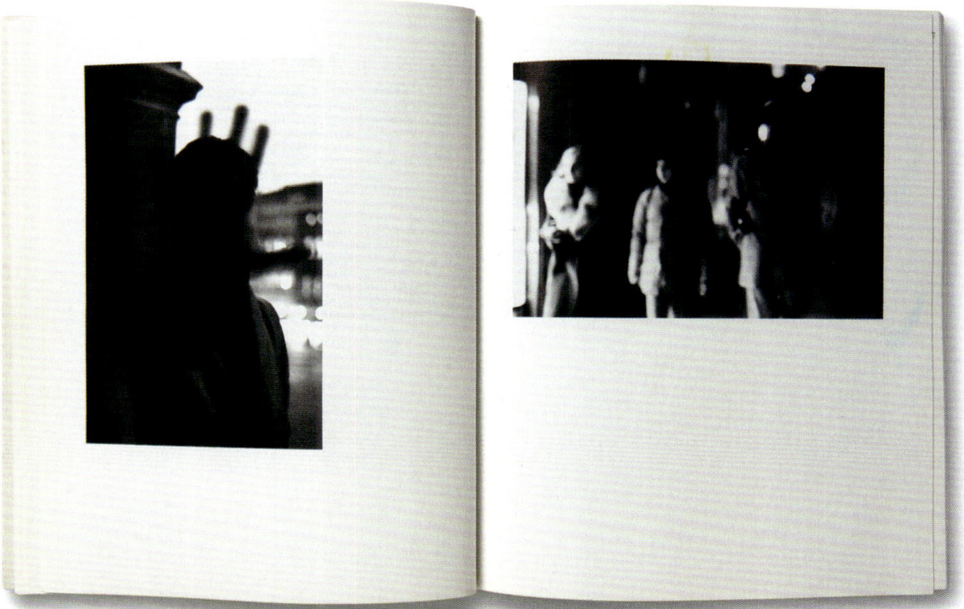

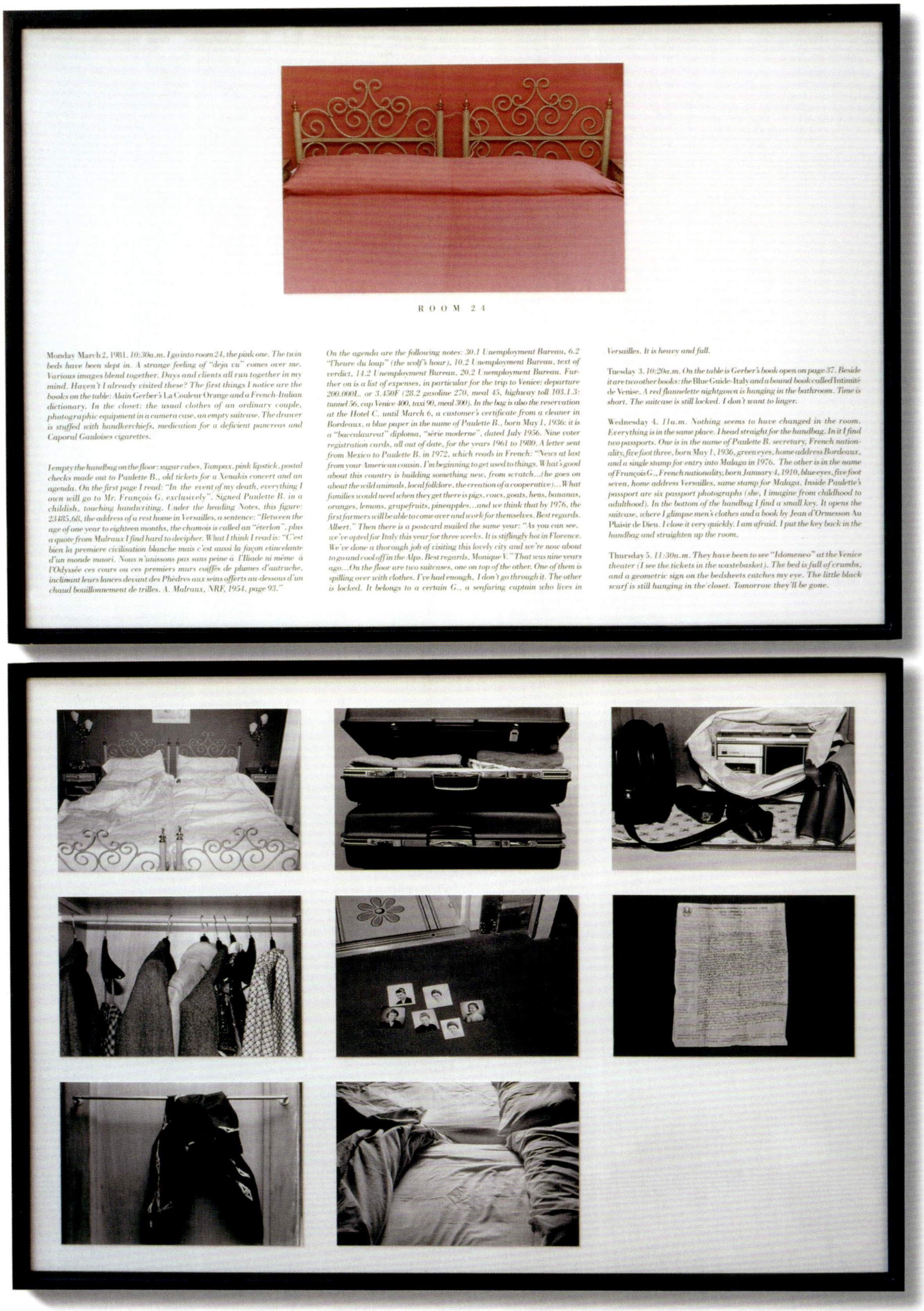

Sophie Calle
Room 24 (2 March), 1981
1 color photograph and 1 text, 8 black and white photographs
Each panel 102 × 142 cm / 40⅛ × 55⅞ in

On Monday, February 16, 1981 I was hired as a temporary chambermaid for three weeks in a Venetian hotel. I was assigned twelve bedrooms on the fourth floor. In the course of my cleaning duties, I examined the personal belongings of the hotel guests and observed through details lives which remained unknown to me. On Friday, March 6 the job came to an end

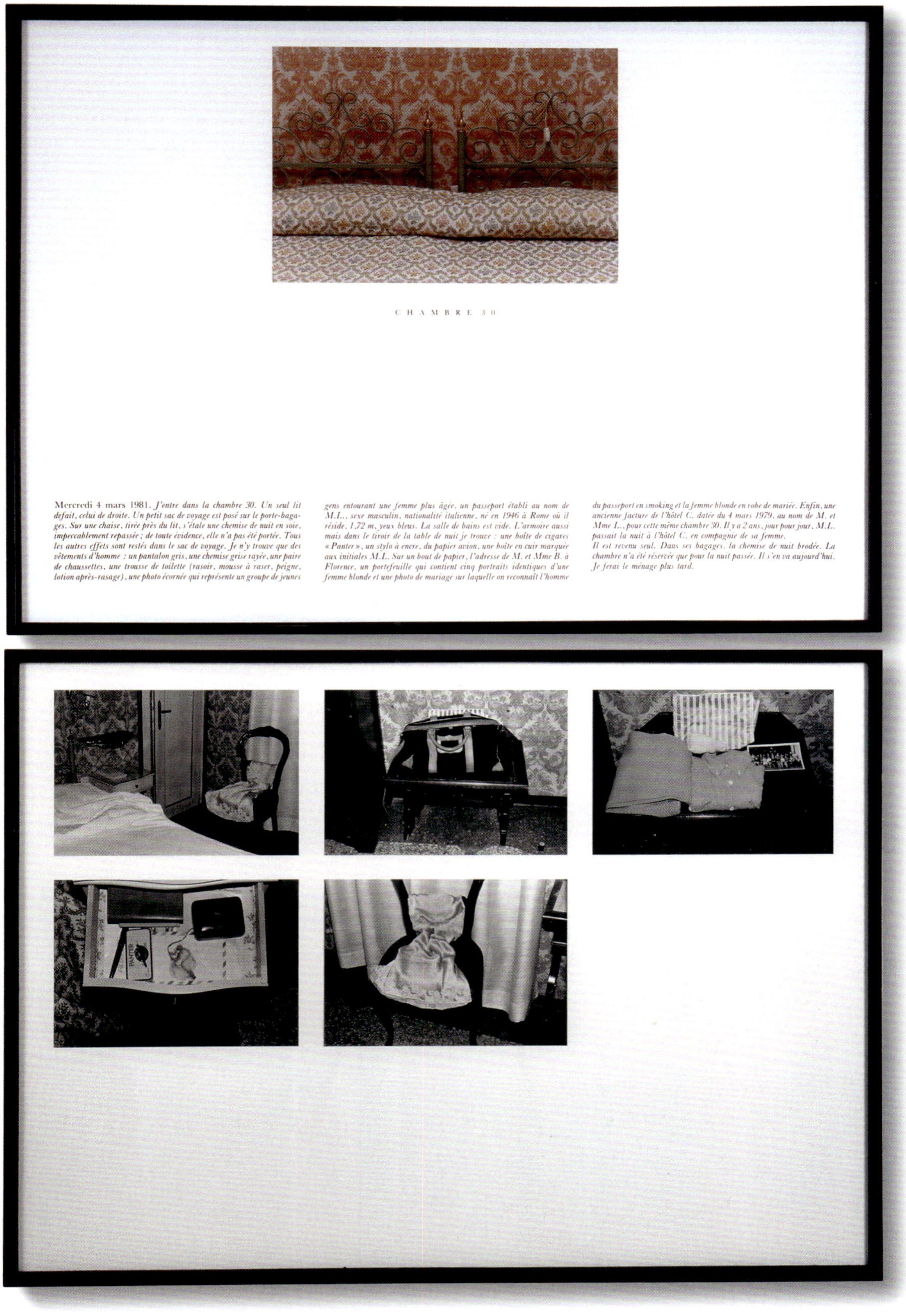

Room 30 (4 March), 1981, 1981
1 color photograph and 1 text, 5 black and white photographs
Each panel 102 × 142 cm / 40⅛ × 55⅞ in

Kohei Yoshiyuki

The work of the Japanese photographer Kohei Yoshiyuki parallels Sophie Calle's voyeuristic fascination with other people's lives. He enjoys the frisson of the peeping tom through his comic and sad documentation of the goings-on in Tokyo's public parks at night using infrared film and flash. The photographer's voyeurism also includes other peepers in the park, and it is his depiction of the interplay between the two groups, voyeurs and lovers, that creates such absorbing spectacles. The photographs are less about the explicit than about the interplay and games playing going on between these two differing groups. When first shown, the photographs were exhibited in a darkened gallery and viewers were invited to look at them with torches.

Merry Alpern

Merry Alpern's book *Dirty Windows* (1995) entails the pure mimicry of voyeuristic transactions. Here the screen of distance protecting the voyeur from his or her subject is not broken; indeed, the screen aids in the fantasy since we get only a partial disclosure of what is going on. The whole is a kind of spectacular tease. As with Sophie Calle, the artist adopts the role of peeping tom. There is a reversal in terms of gender since it is the woman who adopts, or usurps the role of voyeur with these images, secretly taken through the bathroom window of a low-rent sex club near Wall Street. Alpern hid out in a building across an air shaft, capturing blow jobs, stripteases, coke-snorting and a series of other illicit activities with a telephoto lens.

Kohei Yoshiyuki
Untitled, 1971, from the series 'The Park'
Gelatin silver print
60.1 cm × 50.8 / 20 × 24 in

Merry Alpern
Untitled, from the series 'Window Series', 1994
Gelatin silver print
50.8 × 40.6 cm / 16 × 20 in

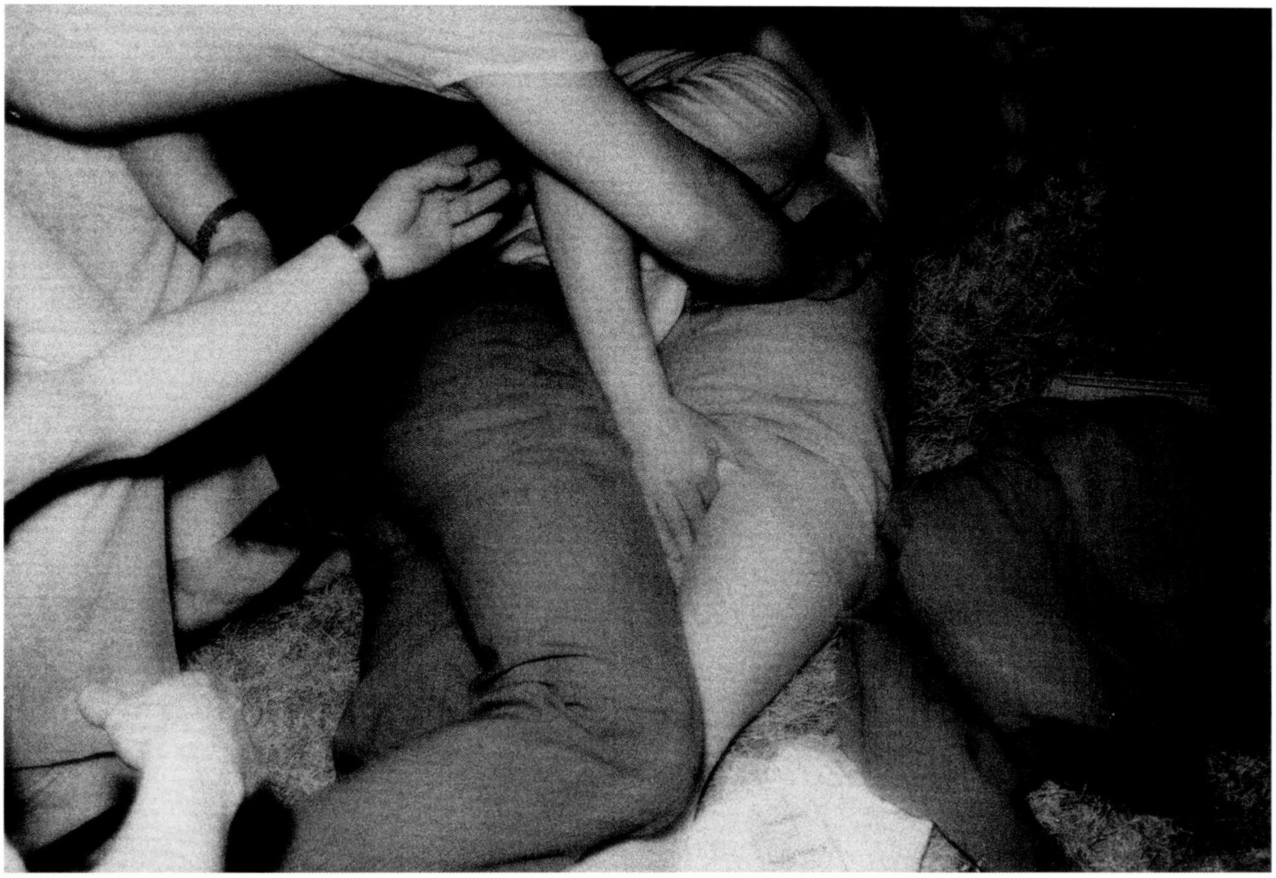

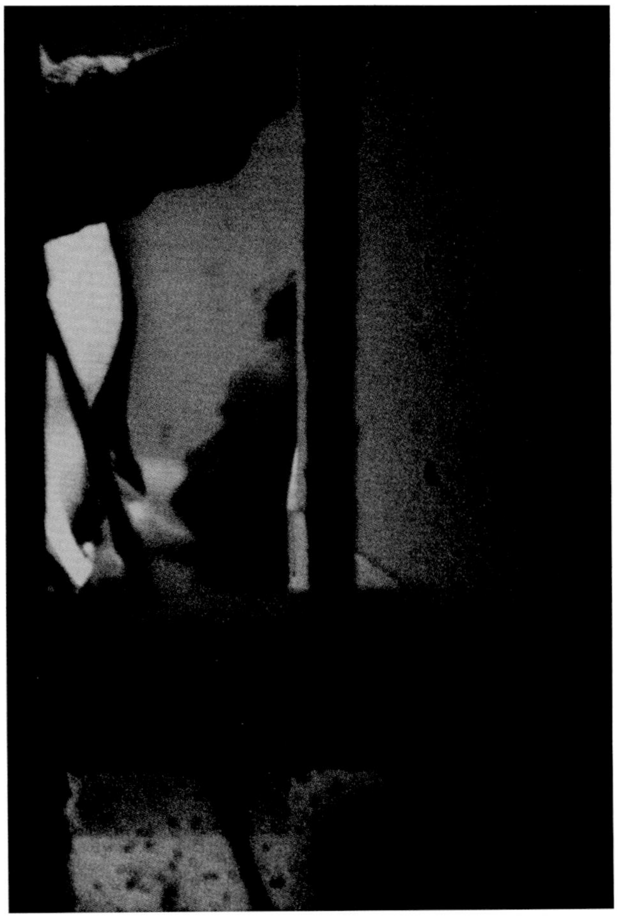

Shizuka Yokomizo

Shizuka Yokomizo's work has affinities with that of Merry Alpern's. Only her photographing through windows is done with complicity. For her series 'Dear Stranger' (1998–2000), she sends her subjects an anonymous letter proposing they stand in their front window at a specified date and time, at which point the artist arrives outside, photographs for a few minutes and then leaves. The subjects are instructed to wear their usual clothing, remain calm, and turn on all their lights. Elements of voyeurism, narcissism and exhibitionism combine in this work. The photographed strangers cannot very easily see the photographer, but they can see themselves reflected in their windows. Yokomizo's photographs disclose the transactional nature of documentary, using windows at night as both an arena of display and as a screen that maintains a distance. She breaks with any sense of closeness and intimacy in this contractual exchange, despite the associations of private and public that the home and the street carry.

Shizuka Yokomizo
Stranger No.1, 1998
C-print
108 × 127 cm / 42½ × 50 in

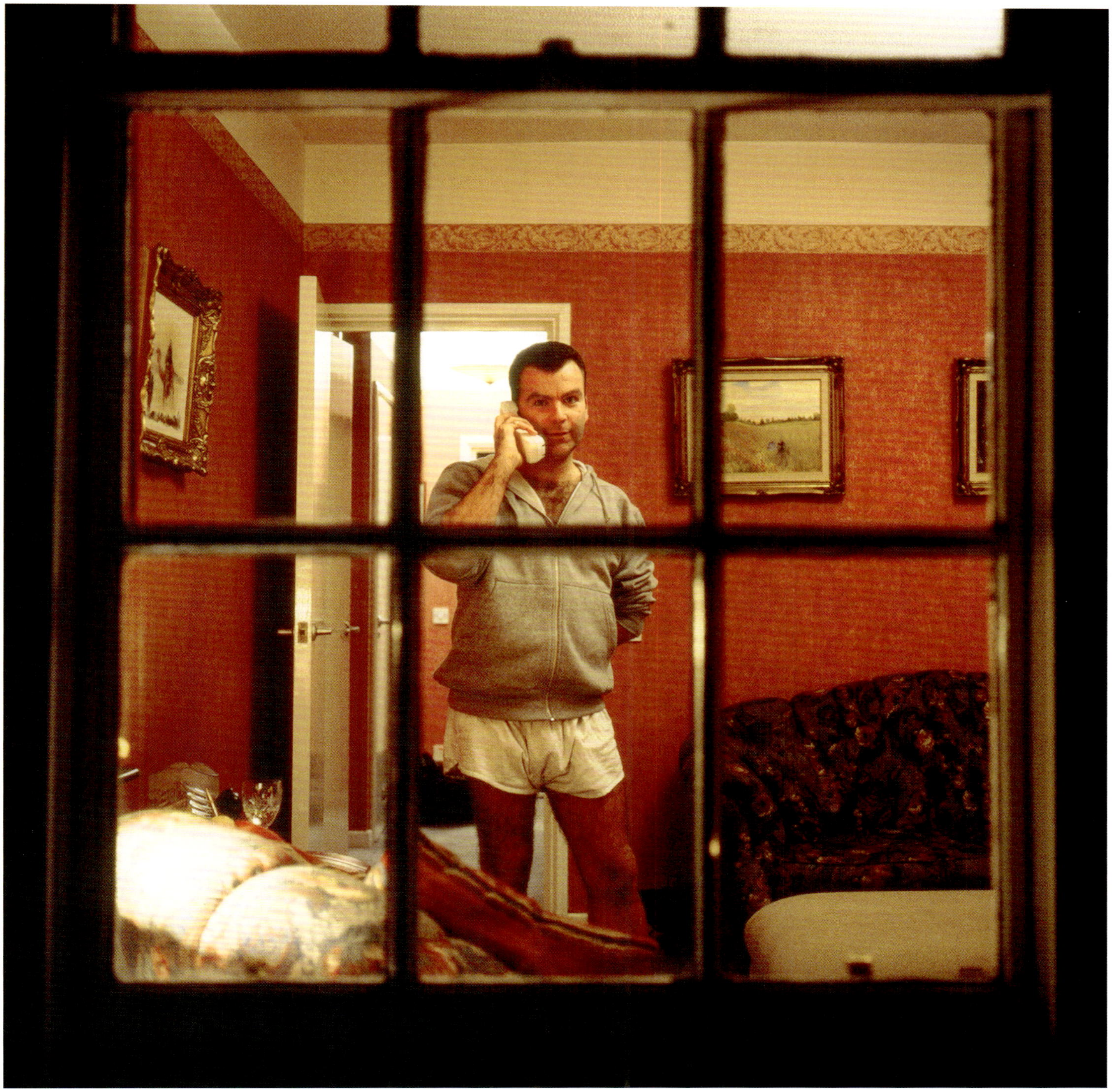

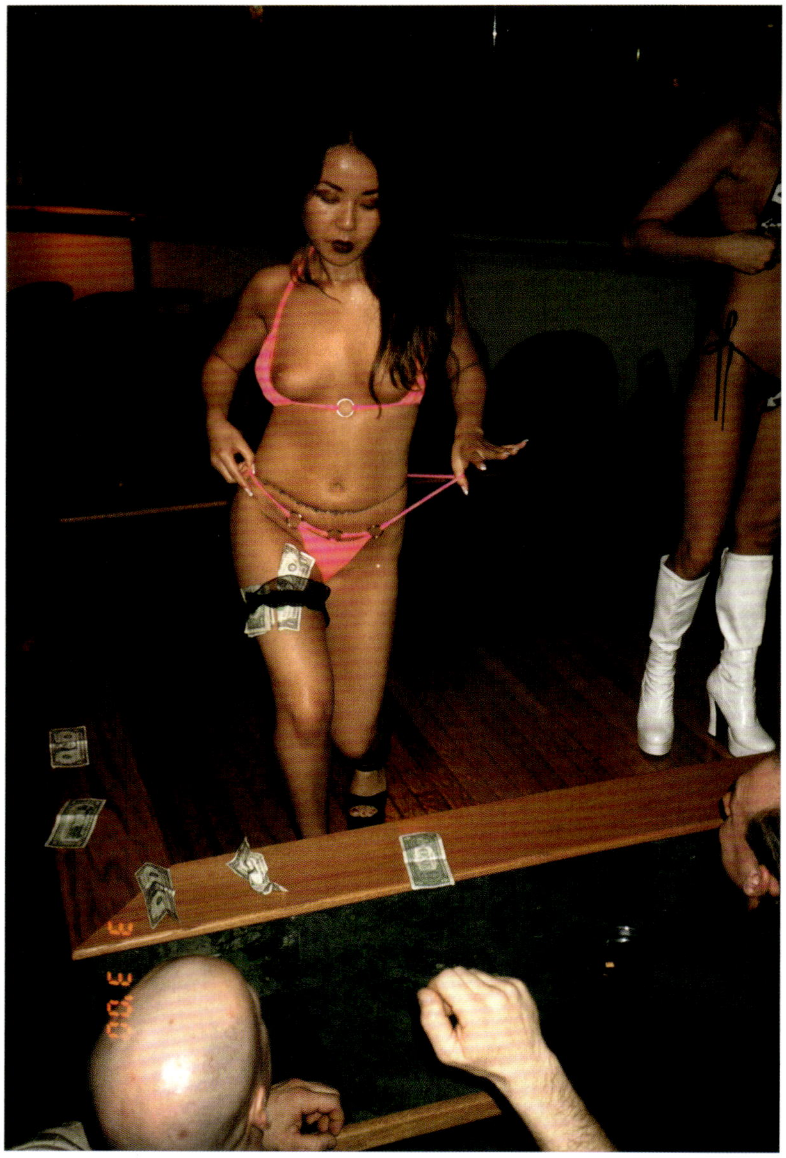

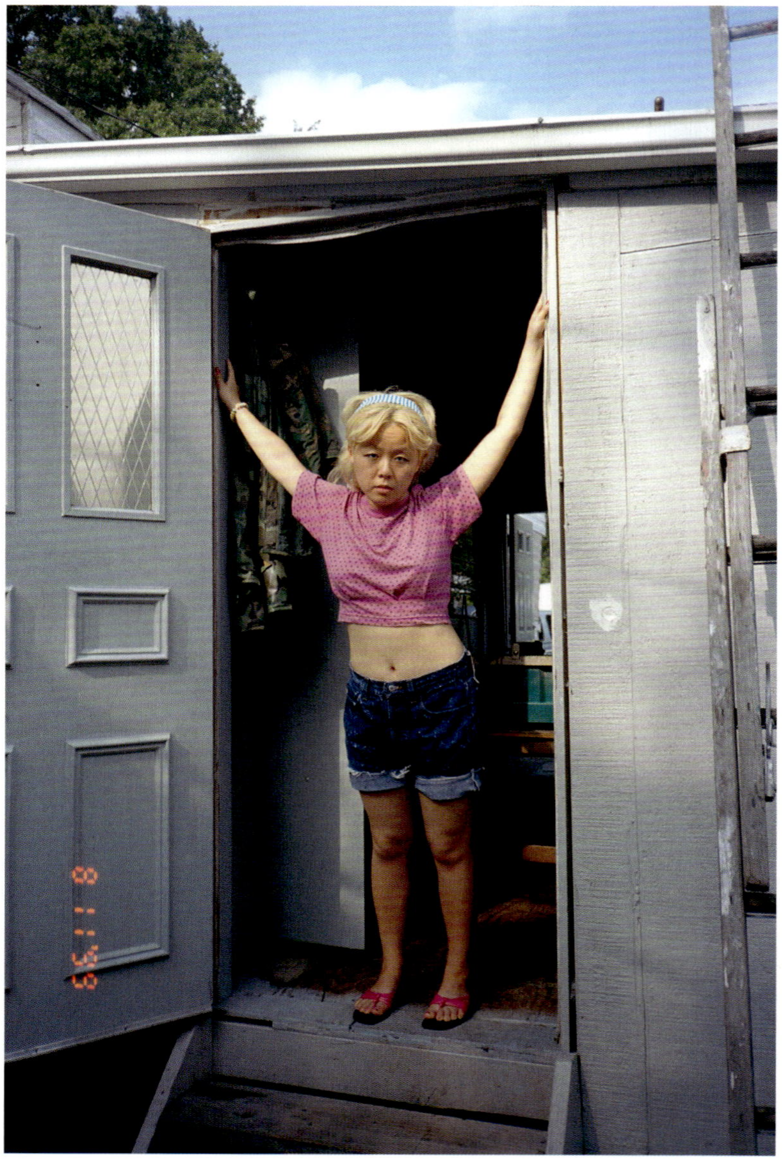

Nikki S. Lee

Documentary Disassembled

Nikki S. Lee gets close to the different people and groups she photographs. In the course of her work 'Projects' (1997–2001) she has transformed herself into a tourist, a Puerto Rican princess, a lesbian, an East Village punk, a table dancer, a Wall Street yuppie and an old-age pensioner. On one hand she could be seen as acting out the collaborative nature of photo-documentary, but on the other she exposes it as phoney. Her work takes the practice of Cindy Sherman out of the studio, extending acts of mimicry to real social contexts. Lee's photographs are the result as much of a performance as of photography; usually she lives with the community she is photographing, and gets to know the dynamics and rituals of the group.

For each of her 'Projects' Lee identifies a particular group which she infiltrates over a period of weeks or months, altering her weight, clothes and hair as necessary in order to assimilate herself. After entering her new identity, she hands a point-and-shoot camera to someone in the group and has her photograph taken with them. Her performances extends the identification and empathy often felt to underlie the documentary transaction. The work is in part about how well Lee can assimilate herself into different social groups, a test of her skills at mimicry, but it also shows us what ordinarily remains invisible in documentary photography: the relationship between photographer and subject. Lee's performances enact the very identifications with others that documentary allows the viewer to do imaginatively. The resulting photographs are inadequate to the complexity of the occasion – they simply evidence signs of her apparent success at affiliation. This is work that formally exposes the limits of documentary. The performances and the potential affinities they set up are much more extended and closer than traditional documentary practice, yet the photographs that record the relation are in many senses much more limited. They do not go beneath the superficialities of the amateur snapshot. Lee's work is bereft of the kind of faith in photography's capacity to speak of the lives of others that informs the extended and crafted documentary sequences found, for example, in projects by Bruce Davidson, David Goldblatt and Mary Ellen Mark.

Nikki S. Lee
The Exotic Dancers Project (1), 2000
C-print, dimensions variable

The Ohio Project (8), 1999
C-print, dimensions variable

Philip-Lorca diCorcia

Philip-Lorca diCorcia's 'Hollywood' (1990–2) gives us the stock subject matter of traditional documentary in its portraits of outsider types from Santa Monica Boulevard, an area of Hollywood often frequented by hustlers, drug users and transients. Yet the pictures are constructed and set up. With the help of an assistant, diCorcia carefully arranged each picture in advance and then began to look for a man off the street he could pay to appear in his photograph. The disclosure of the monetary transaction between photographer and subject as part of each image's title invites us to question the ethics of documentary, and leads us to think of the documentary transaction as a kind of prostitution, with subjects who can be bought like commodities. This is also suggested by the fast food signs against which some of diCorcia's subjects are photographed. Something of the aura and glow of consumer culture persists in the way people are pictured in the tableaux. These scenarios of desire and fantasy, posed and stage-managed by the artist, offer an essentially ethereal and idealized world. Under the glow of capitalism and set against the dream machine of Hollywood, the subjects are portrayed as vulnerable, wistful and melancholic figures.

Eddie Anderson, 21 years old; Houston, Texas; $20 depicts a young male, naked to the waist, through a diner window. His golden flesh is echoed in the bun of the uneaten burger in a tray on the counter, which is set between a tabletop jukebox and a carton of drink. Eddie Anderson becomes fully part of this little still life of cheap fast food and music machine, and is presented as if in a shop-window display. He might be looking in, but it is the viewer who becomes the ultimate window-gazer here. The set-up of this scene, the solitary figure in relationship to the still life and the bored blank look echoes Edouard Manet's A *Bar at the Folies Bergère* (1893) but for diCorcia the blank look suggests compliance rather than defiance, and helps assimilate this subject into the commodified glossed-up worlds his picture–tableaux offer. The shop window reiterates the subject's status as a mere surface upon which fantasies are played out.

Larry Sultan

Documenting the pornography industry in San Fernando Valley, where it rents out affluent middle-class homes for use as film sets, Larry Sultan's 'The Valley' is also caught up with the allure of Hollywood and fantasy. Sultan grew up in the suburbs of the San Fernando Valley, home to approximately eighty per cent of adult film production in the United States. Many of the pictures set up a dynamic between the décor of a lavish middle-class suburbia and the activity being played out within these settings during the shooting of the porn film, an activity that is never explicitly shown but lies always teasingly just out of frame or obstructed by plants or objects. The sense of artifice and fakery conveyed by these extravagantly decorated interiors is unsettled by the specific vulnerability of some of the subjects. The photographs shift between the empathic portrait, which cues a compassionate sense through vulnerability, and others which show us the way people are treated by the sex industry, as yet another commodity awaiting consumption, sitting around between takes, often photographed next to food products that suggest their own refreshment as well as drawing a parallel with their own consumption as a sex worker.

Sharon Wild (2001) offers a portrait of the porn star in high heels, G-String and bra, perched on the edge of a bed in a motel room, or a room made to look like a motel room. A vanity case and the suitcase behind it could be mere props, but they also connote transience and the fluid existence of a porn star, moving from one staged fantasy to another. The grubby and abraded state of the mattress revealed at the edge of the image introduces a realist note that takes us beneath the veneer of the super-lucrative porn industry and makes us think of the labour of porn stars, of bodies gradually getting worn out.

Philip-Lorca diCorcia
Eddie Anderson, 21 years old, Houston, Texas, $20, 1990–2
Fujicolor Crystal Archive print
50.8 × 61 cm / 20 × 24 in

Larry Sultan
Sharon Wild, 2001, from the series 'The Valley'
C-print, dimensions variable

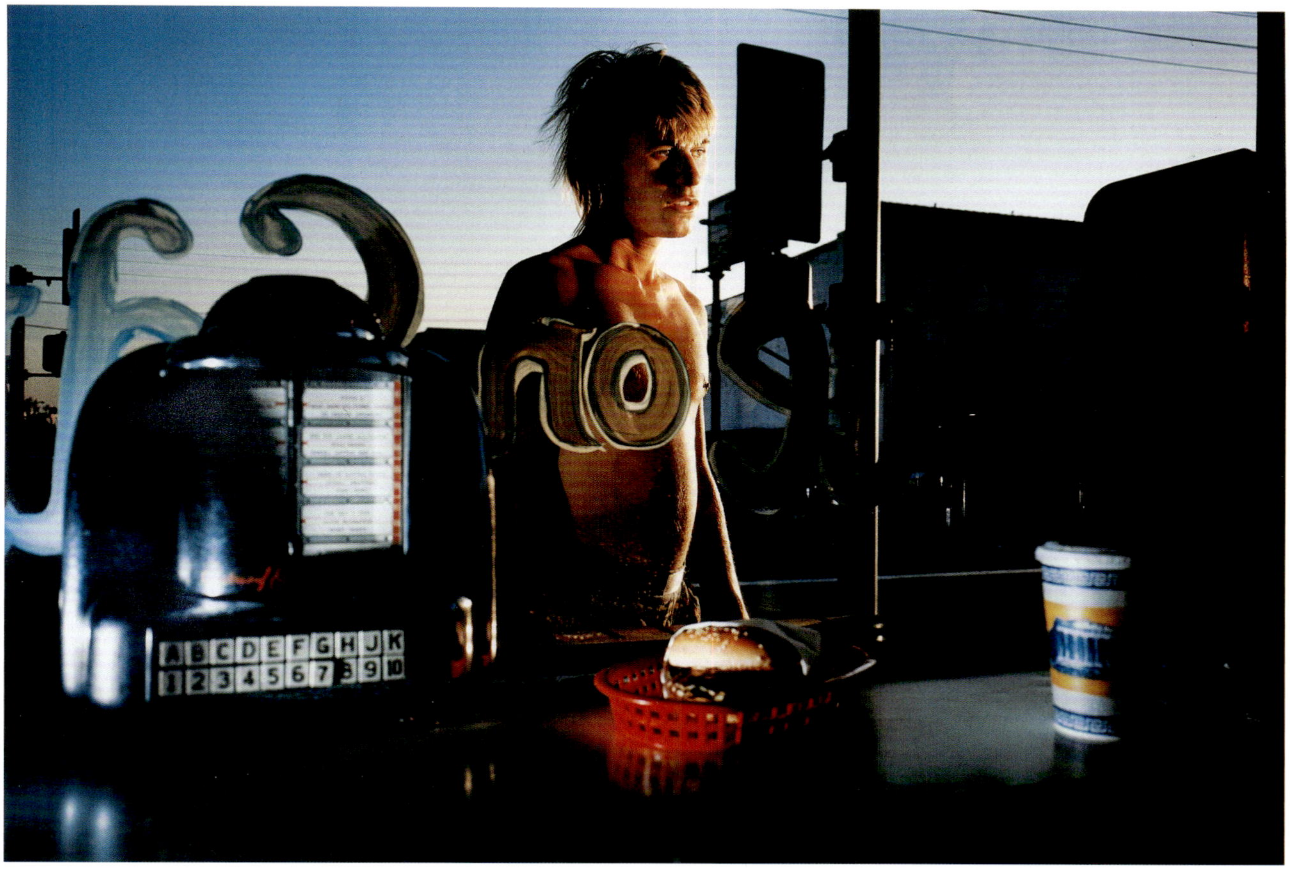

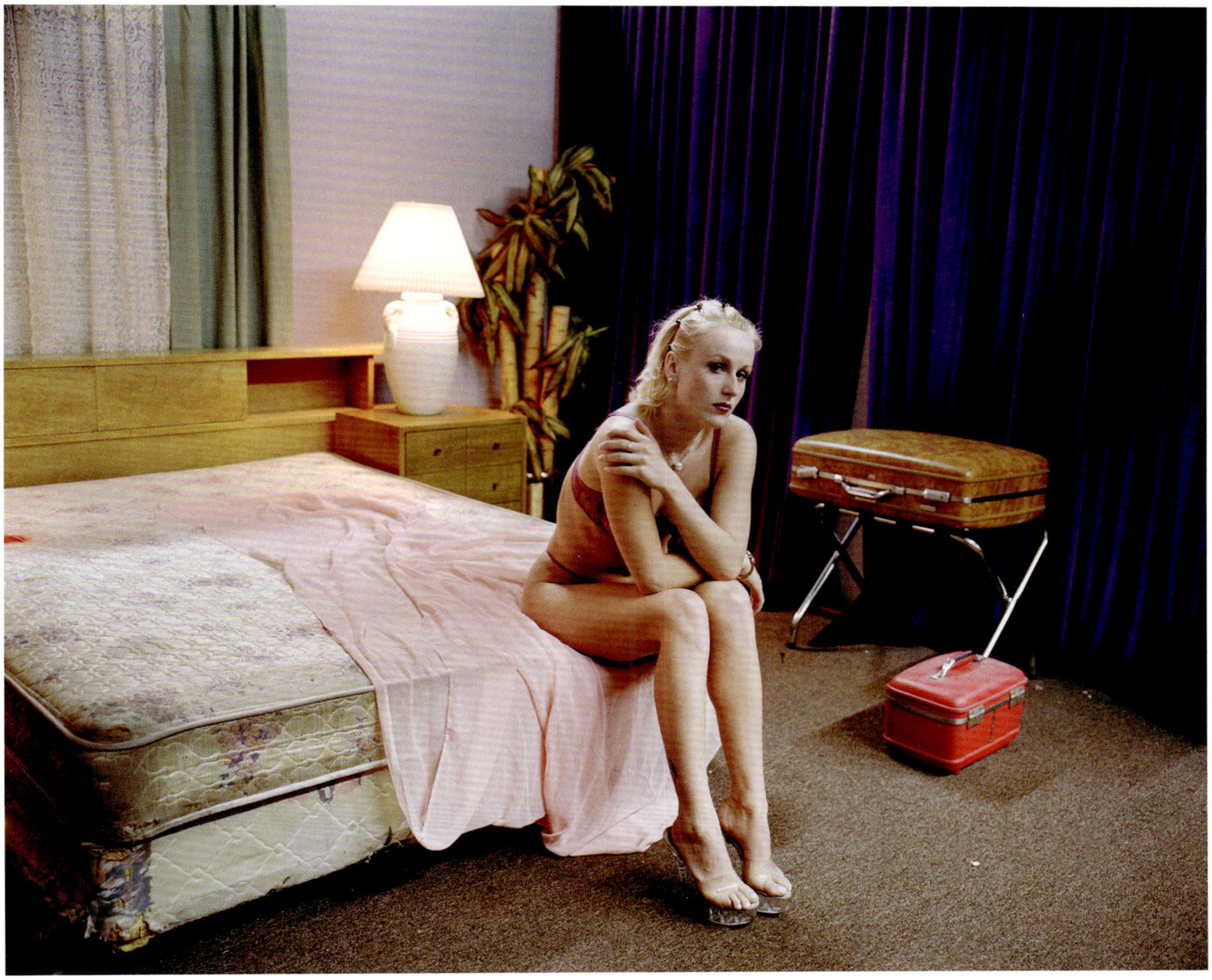

Philippe Chancel

Philippe Chancel's pictures made in response to the tyranny of a regime and the cult of personality in the Communist state in North Korea do not look like documentary photographs. Many of his depictions testify to the restrictions imposed by the totalitarian state. When we see workers, they look as if they are taking part in an heroic tableau. There is in Chancel's photography a constant mirroring of Kim Jong-Il's propaganda. Many photographs look like stage sets, showing the orchestrations of power or portraying a people stripped of emotional expression. This is exemplified by the long-distance views of the celebratory rallies, public spectacles in which the masses hold up images of their Dear Leader. Such pictures show the erasure of the subject through a mass affiliation, and their horror is a result of their calm and order and the way in which their very aesthetic seems to endorse the ideology of the state. For Chancel, however, this is crucially offset by the humanist elements in his photography, the intimacies and sensuousness in his portrayal of mostly female subjects, compliant, beautiful and graceful. Much as such portraits are caught up with an exoticizing erotics, this element serves as a contrast to the anonymous masses who perform in the spectacles of power. Chancel's portraits of people are an important and vital reminder of what's missing from the chilling authoritarian version of the state and also what is so integral to documentary: a humanist vision.

Philippe Chancel
Arirang, 2005
Lambda print, diasec finish
100 × 120 cm / 39⅜ × 47¼ in

DPRK 1, Inside the Koryo Hotel café, Pyongyang, 2005
Lambda print, diasec finish
100 × 120 cm / 39⅜ × 47¼ in

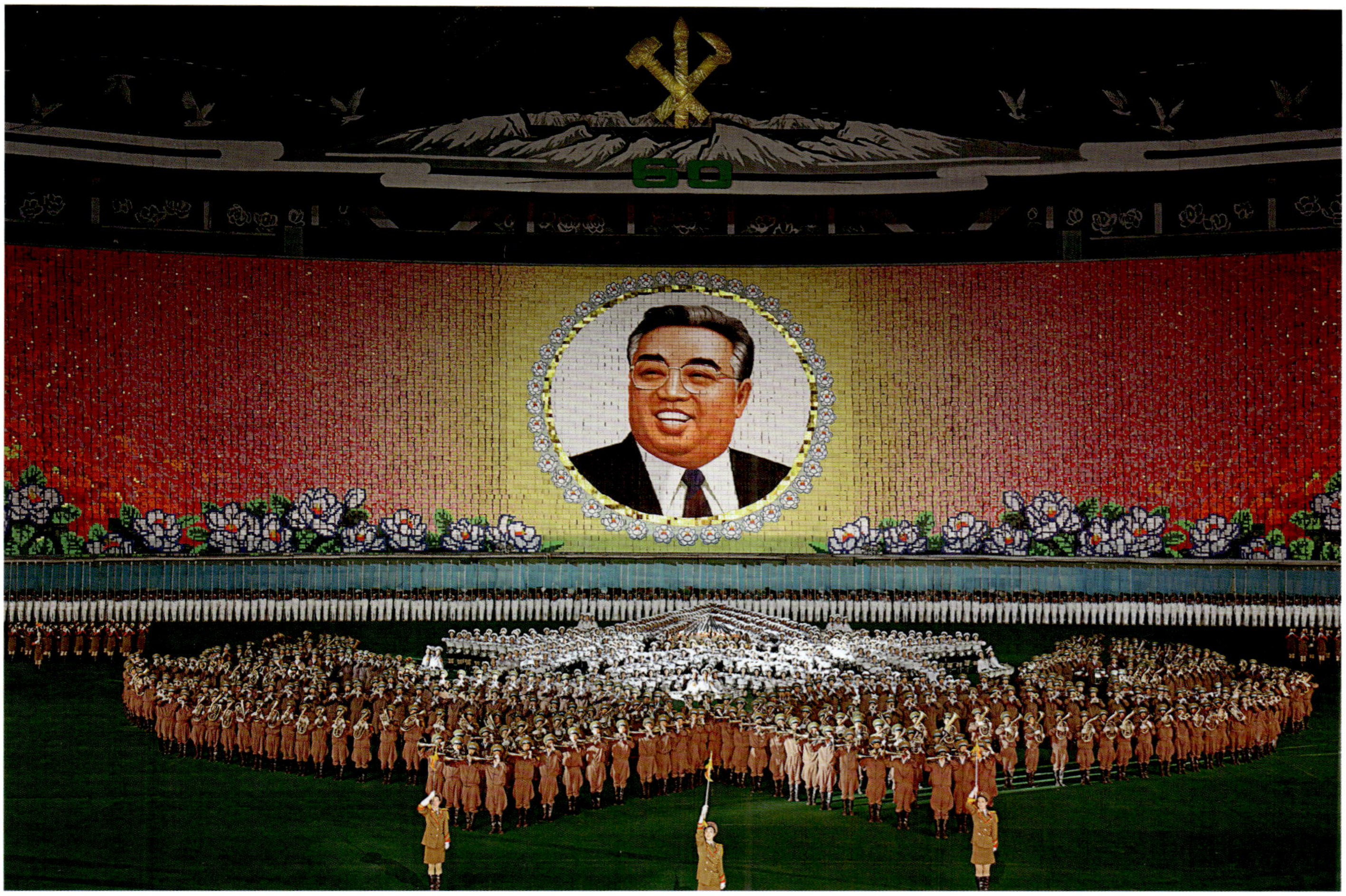
60

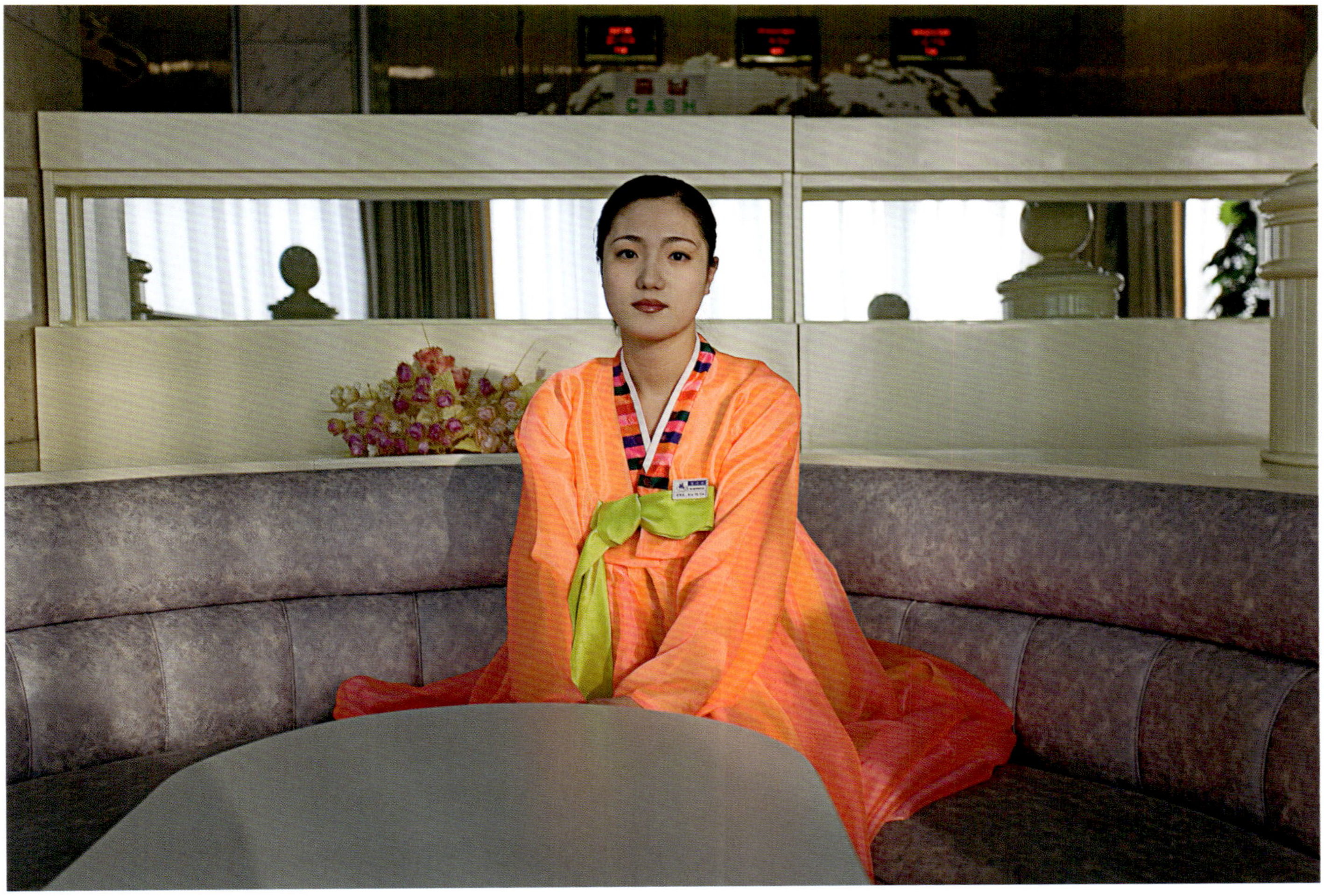
CASH

Boris Mikhailov

The Ukrainian artist, Boris Mikhailov's 'Case History' (1997–8) makes explicit the exploitational dimension of the documentary tradition. As Liz Kotz has pointed out, the 'ethics' of documentary 'demands that the transaction between artist and subject be represented as an exchange': in return for the picture that is taken, the photographer must give something back to those photographed, by endeavoring to 'provide political or reformist help', for example, or simply conferring dignity or humanity upon his or her subjects.[15] Such benevolent liberal myths are taken apart here. Mikhailov evidences the transactions that underscore documentary production, and the effects of capitalism on his country.

Mikhailov pays his subjects, homeless people from his native city Kharkov, to take off their clothes and pose. He says that, if his subjects were simply shown clothed, they would continue to go unnoticed, remaining invisible and inconspicuous. Getting them to undress, he says, removed 'the barrier of dirty, ponging clothes, built between them and others... When naked, they stood like people.'[16] While his pictures vividly evidence the loss of socialist communality in post-Communist Ukraine, Mikhailov seems to be defending his portrayal in terms of the communality of a liberal humanism. Revealing their nakedness invites us to see and recognize them as people, and to acknowledge our common humanity. At the same time, his photographs of these often disfigured, scarred, bleeding and bruised bodies play with Western assumptions about the degraded state of the former Soviet Union. His photographs testify to the death throes of socialism, both through the brutalized realities he depicts and the exploitative way he takes his pictures.

Liu Zheng

Another extreme use of documentary, this time from China in transformation, has been made by Liu Zheng. 'The Chinese', a series of black-and-white square-format-photographs, takes us beneath the surface of consumerist China. From 1994 to 2002, Liu worked on this documentary project as he travelled the country, photographing its people and highlighting the bizarre, dark, marginal, traditional and ritualistic aspect of his country, its non-Westernized and more indigenous aspects. The face of a foreigner, a suited, Western, middle-aged man, crops up only once in the series, and it introduces a degree of unease, as he holds a young Chinese girl close to him. Boris Mikhailov's pictures suggest a relation between the wounded and injured bodies of his subjects and the rotten post-Soviet state, and Liu's subjects also serve as potential symbols of a country in the throes of transformation by capitalism. *Dying Farmer* could be seen as an allegory of the loss of certain rural traditions and ways of life in the new China. What is particularly unsettling is not just the dying and dead, but the way his photographs also include highly illusionistic historical waxwork tableaux, their figures initially indistinguishable from his documents of people. The baroque excesses of the photographs blur into realms of fiction and fantasy. Liu's choice of black and white seems fitting, in that his pictures entail a certain retrospective gazing, fixated upon the persistence of lives, rituals, beliefs and histories, distinct from the radical upheavals and excesses of China's consumerist present. But at the same time the brutality, harshness and grotesquery of his vision reprises a Western cultural documentary fascination with the exotic and returns it to its sender, embellished with clear nods to canonical Western photographers' work, that of Diane Arbus especially. Like Boris Mikhailov, Liu's use of the documentary form is highly conscious of its codes, conventions and limitations.

Boris Mikhailov
Untitled, from the series 'Case History', 1997–8
C-print
148.6 × 99.7 cm / 58½ × 39¼ in

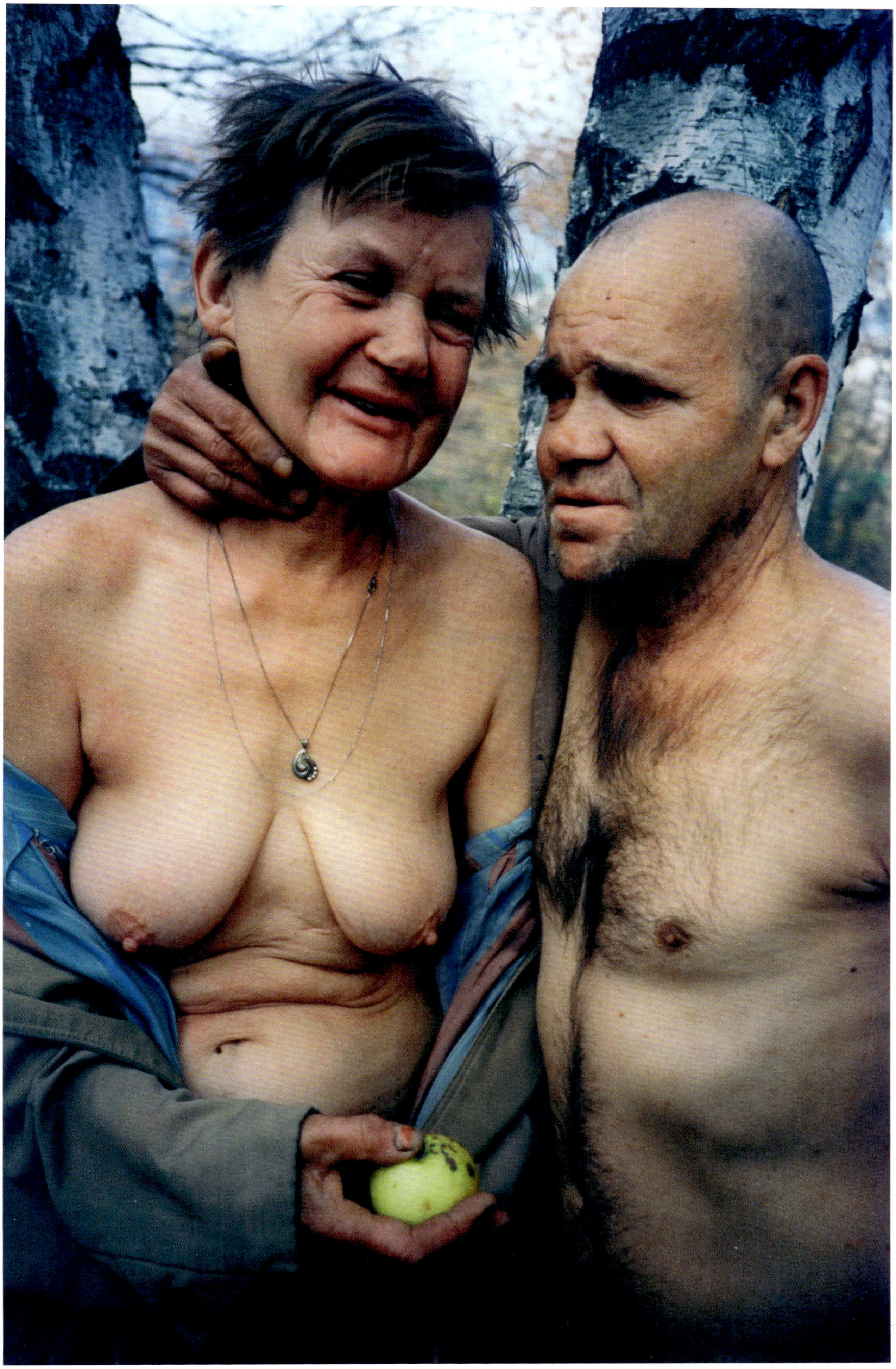

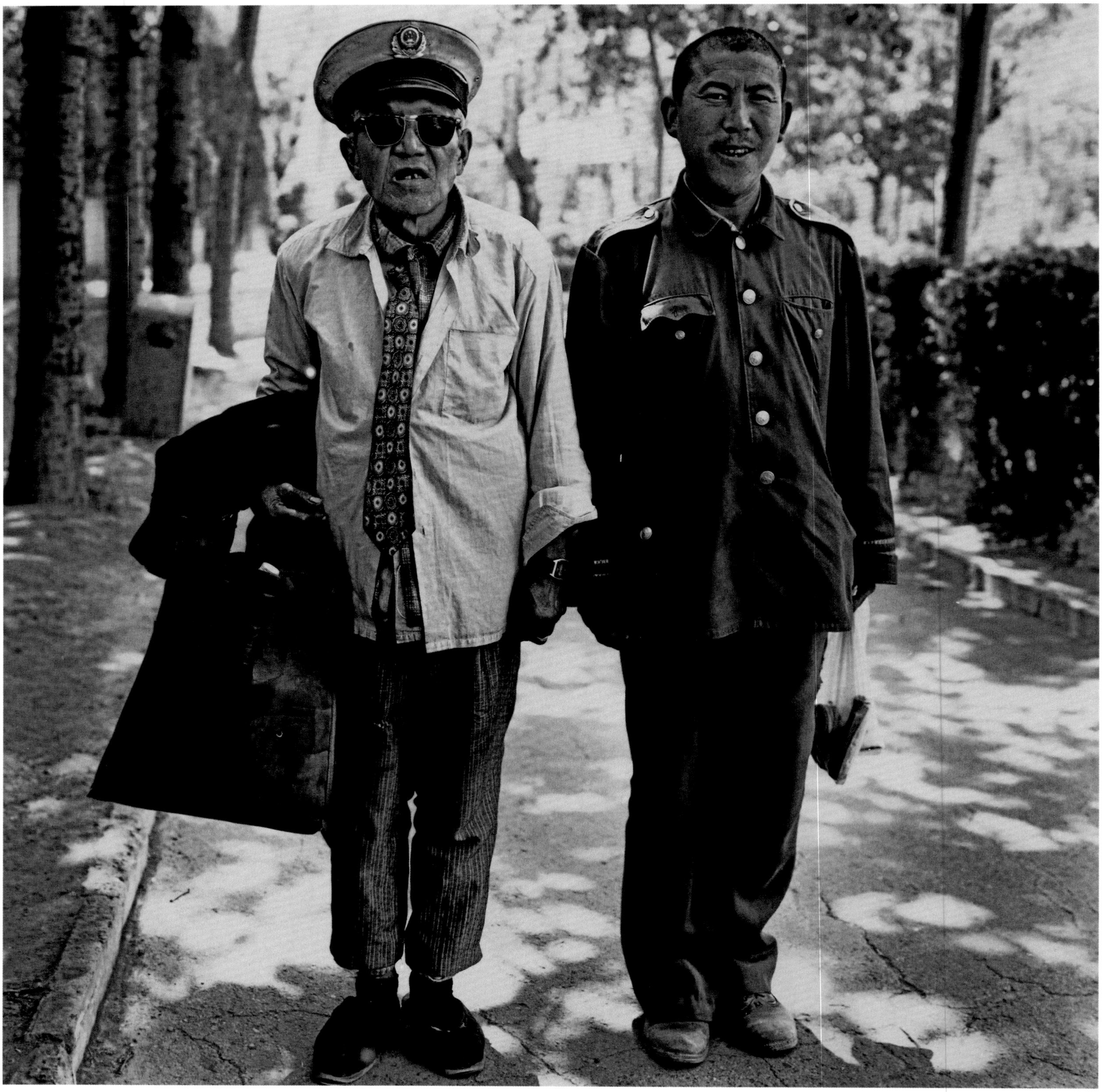

Liu Zheng
Mentally Handicapped Patients, Beijing, 1996, from the series 'The Chinese'
Gelatin silver print
46 × 46 cm / 18⅛ × 18⅛ in

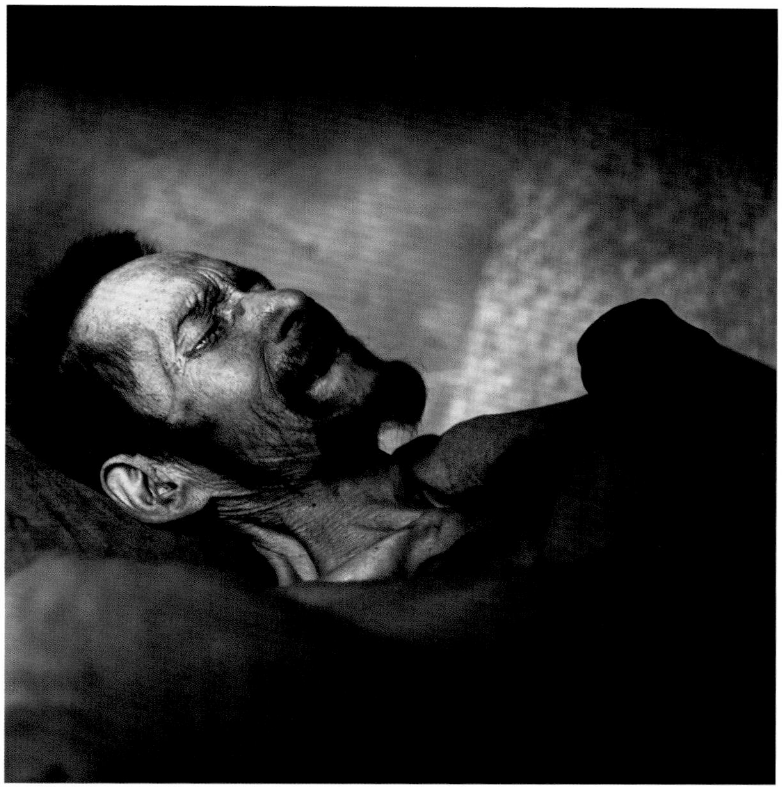

A Dying Farmer, *Xihaigon, Ningxia Province*, 1996, from the series 'The Chinese'
Gelatin silver print
46 × 46 cm / 18⅛ × 18⅛ in

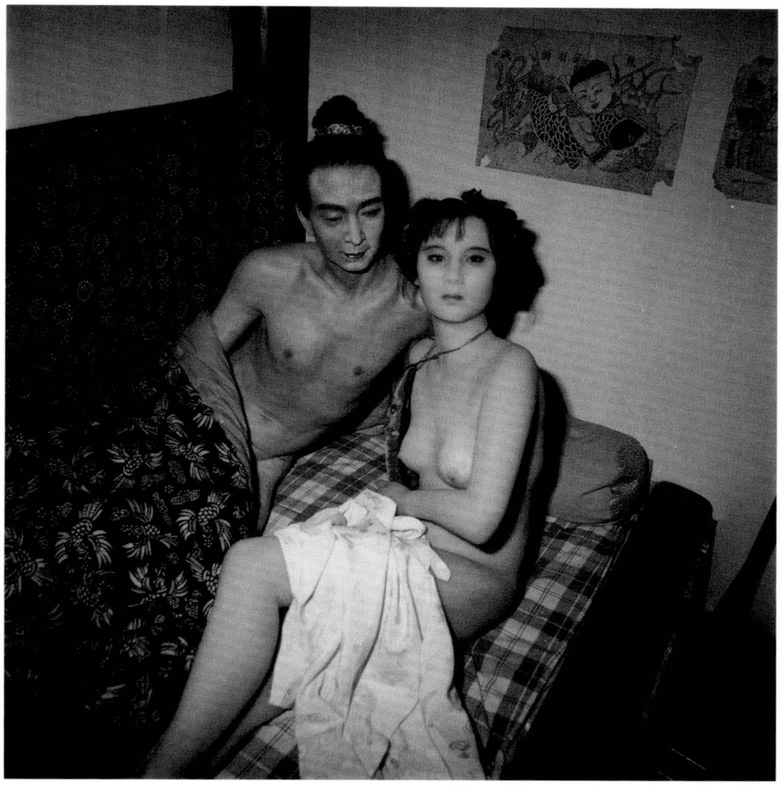

Waxwork, Emperor and Girl in Fornication, *Changping, Beijing*, 2000, from the series 'The Chinese'
Gelatin silver print
46 × 46 cm / 18⅛ × 18⅛ in

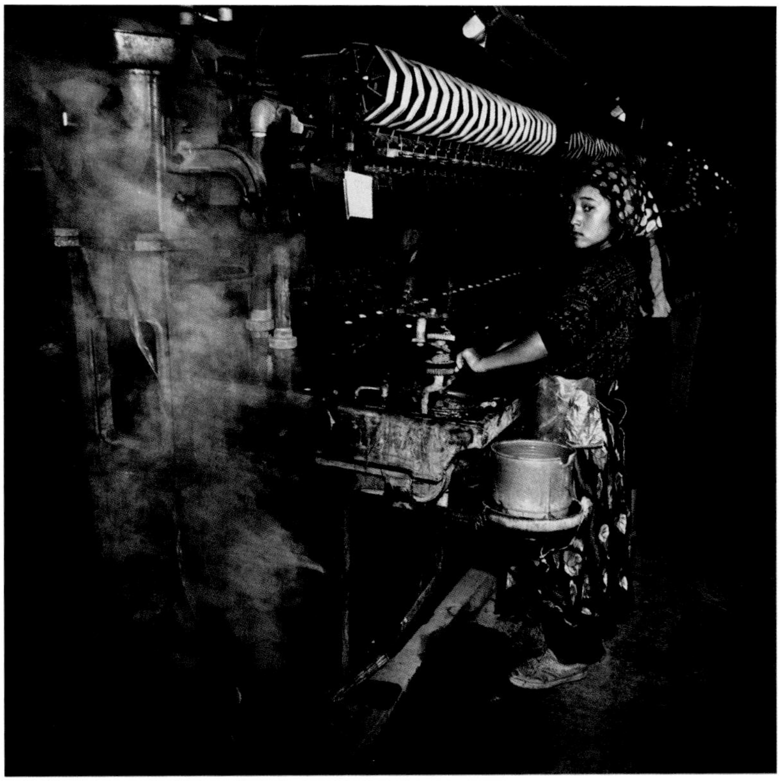

Xinjiang Girl Working in a Textile Factory, *Hetian, Xinjiang Province*, 1996, from the series 'The Chinese'
Gelatin silver print
46 × 46 cm / 18⅛ × 18⅛ in

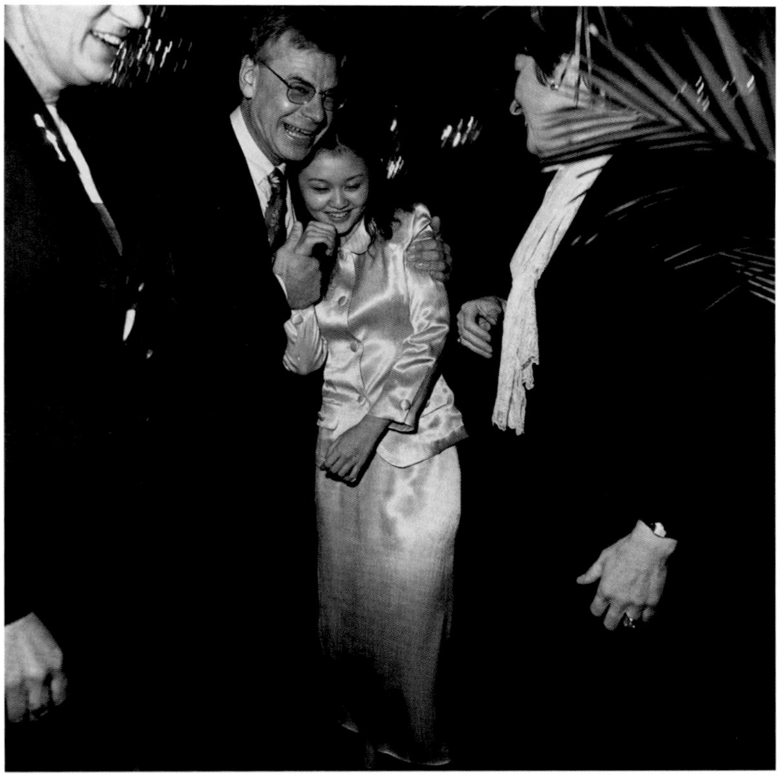

A Chinese Girl with a Foreign Friend, *Beijing*, 1996, from the series 'The Chinese'
Gelatin silver print
46 × 46 cm / 18⅛ × 18⅛ in

Pieter Hugo

The South African photographer Pieter Hugo deliberately exploits liberal fears and racist imaginings about Africa in two extraordinary recent series of photographs taken in Nigeria, *Hyena Men* (2007) and *Nollywood* (2010). The former portrays a troupe of animal charmers and their hyenas, snakes and monkeys. The photographs are taken not during the performance of their street entertainments but at quieter, more reflective moments. The pictures give us the names of both the people and their animals, suggesting a certain affiliation between the subjects and the photographer. In some pictures the men show their bravura – one holds open the jaws of his hyena – but there is also tenderness, as in the portrait showing a chained monkey resting its paw on the knee of its young keeper. The settings are often urban, their economic rawness suggestive of a basic survival. In the face of the affluence of the West, pictures of such people are there to be consumed for their part in an entertaining but slightly troubling exotic art. What we are attracted to here is the novelty of the subject matter, a surprise that this primitive and wild form of entertainment actually takes place.

Nollywood goes further in terms of fantasies to do with Africa, drawing upon the films of Nigeria's low-budget indigenous cinema, the third-largest film industry in the world. Hugo worked with a make-up artist, which gave him access and allowed him to stage scenarios from films, creating a mostly macabre and grotesque horror show of zombies, vampires and devils. What we have here is again something that goes beyond documentary. Hugo's pictures are based upon staged tableaux that are set up to be photographed. What is so unsettling about such work is that it shows us Africans acting out Western stereotypes about their country, but stereotypes and roles that are drawn from their own African cinema. However, in an open letter to Nigeria's Information and Communications Minister, the Nigerian-born filmmaker Oliver O. Mbamara has condemned the photographs, arguing that to portray Nollywood as mostly 'barbaric, devilish and dark' is a serious misrepresentation of the films it produces.[17] Hugo argues that the anger some of his pictures have caused reflects 'collective Western guilt.'[18] This is all very well, but it does not address Mbamara's sense of outrage over the way Hugo's photographs distort Nigeria's film industry. Although Hugo has drawn his iconography from an indigenous mass cultural form, serious questions about accuracy still remain – and such questions are crucially important to documentary.

Pieter Hugo
Mallam Galadima Ahmadu with Jamis, Abuja, Nigeria, 2007
C-print, dimensions variable

Princess Adaobi, Enugu, Nigeria, 2008
C-print, dimensions variable

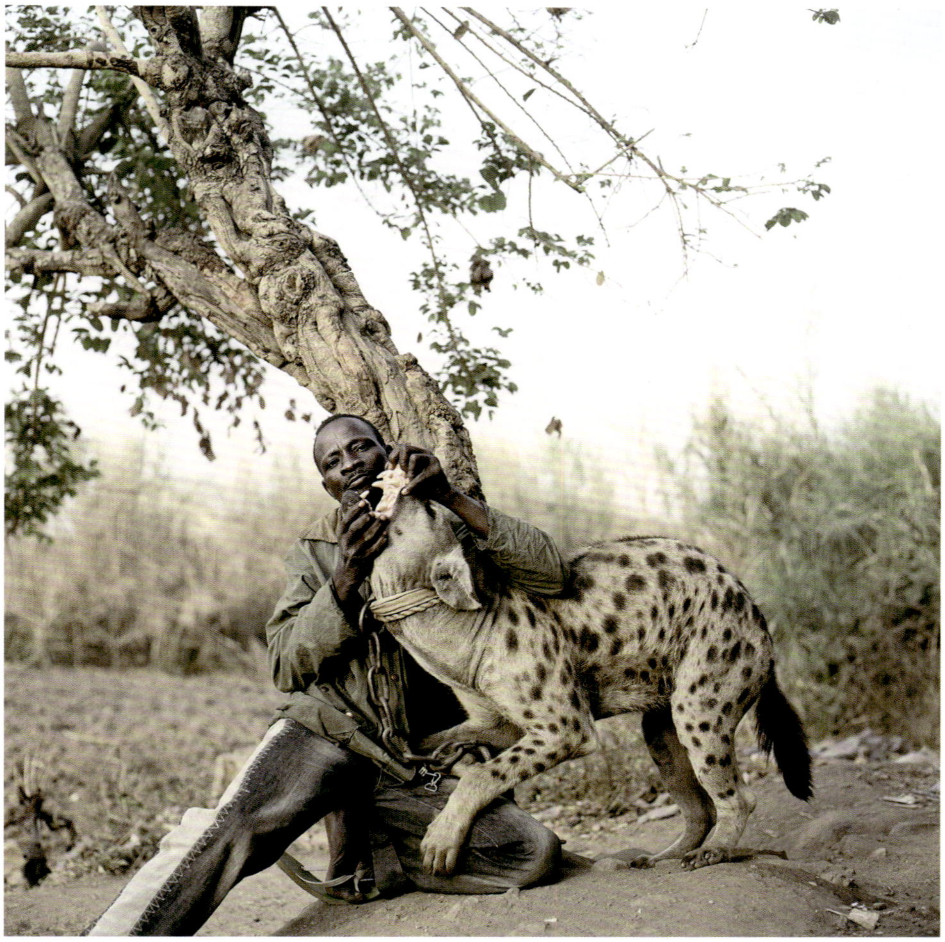

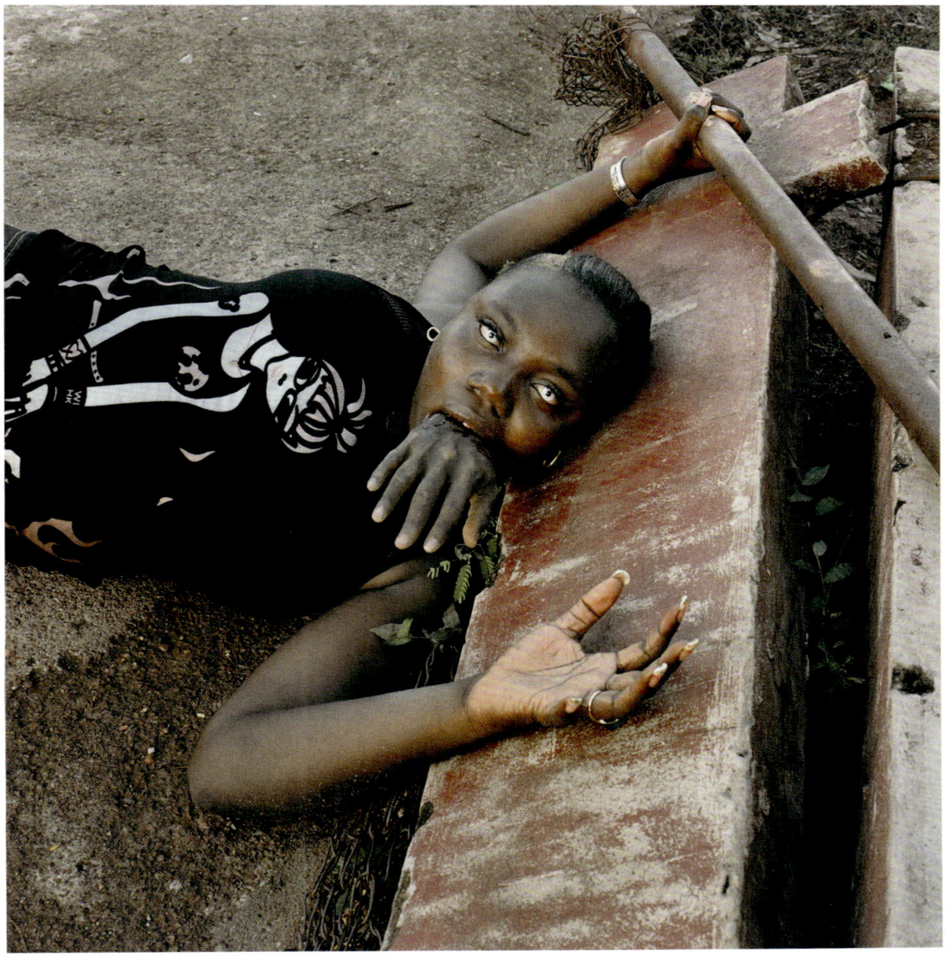

Olga Chernysheva

Olga Chernysheva's photography and video offer lyrical observations of everyday life in Moscow. Her concern, as in 'On Duty' (2007), a series of black-and-white portraits of attendants monitoring escalators from their glass booths on the Moscow Metro, is to give otherwise invisible functionaries a presence and humanity. She refers to these subjects as 'people who attend on the presence of the public' and describes 'empathy' as being integral to what she is doing as an artist.[19] Her use of black and white gives the pictures an historical look: the people pictured appear somewhat out of time, not fully present, used to watching and looking at others but not to be being observed themselves. Such work addresses transition, the sense of a people still caught in a former Soviet role. A similar quality characterizes Chernysheva's 2009 'Cactus Seller', a series of pictures that document both the work of a solitary man tending to the cacti on his stall and its setting among the displays of skeletons, reptiles and fossils within the Moscow Zoo Museum. Chernysheva's portrayal does not distinguish this small trader from the natural history collection of the former Soviet era; in some ways he becomes another specimen. This is accented by the fact the photographs, again all black and white, are displayed in the form of a series of back-lit light boxes mounted on a steel frame that snakes through the gallery space.

In her single channel video, *The Train* (2003), a handheld camera journeys along the carriages of an intercity train from front to back, giving us a collective portrait of Russians, of passengers and staff mostly oblivious to the camera passing them. The film also contains other elements – a beggar reciting a poem by Pushkin, a young boy playing an accordian – that again make us think of the persistence of the Soviet era in the present. The train, like the glass booths within which the guards work, gives the sense of a people separate from the rest of the world, suspended, in limbo; this is underlined in the final shots of the video as we see the train from outside, going off into the distance.

There is an allegorical and non-literal edge to Chernysheva's documentary. Her work conveys a strong sense of the historical past's continuity within and impact upon the present. In this respect it might be described as a haunted documentary. Distinct from the embellished and spectacular tendencies of recent documentary forms, Chernysheva returns us to the ordinary day-to-day in a lyrical engagement with the world around her. Recourse to the back-lit light box is not so much spectacular as a kind of low-grade display, akin to the fluorescence within both the museum cabinets and the cactus-seller's stall in her pictures. We have also shifted towards a more subjective documentary in Chernysheva's art and in this respect her work serves as a fitting point of transition to the concerns of the next chapter – work that is made when the camera is turned upon the artist's own life.

Olga Chernysheva
On Duty, 2007
Gelatin silver print
136 × 90 cm / 53½ × 35⅜ in

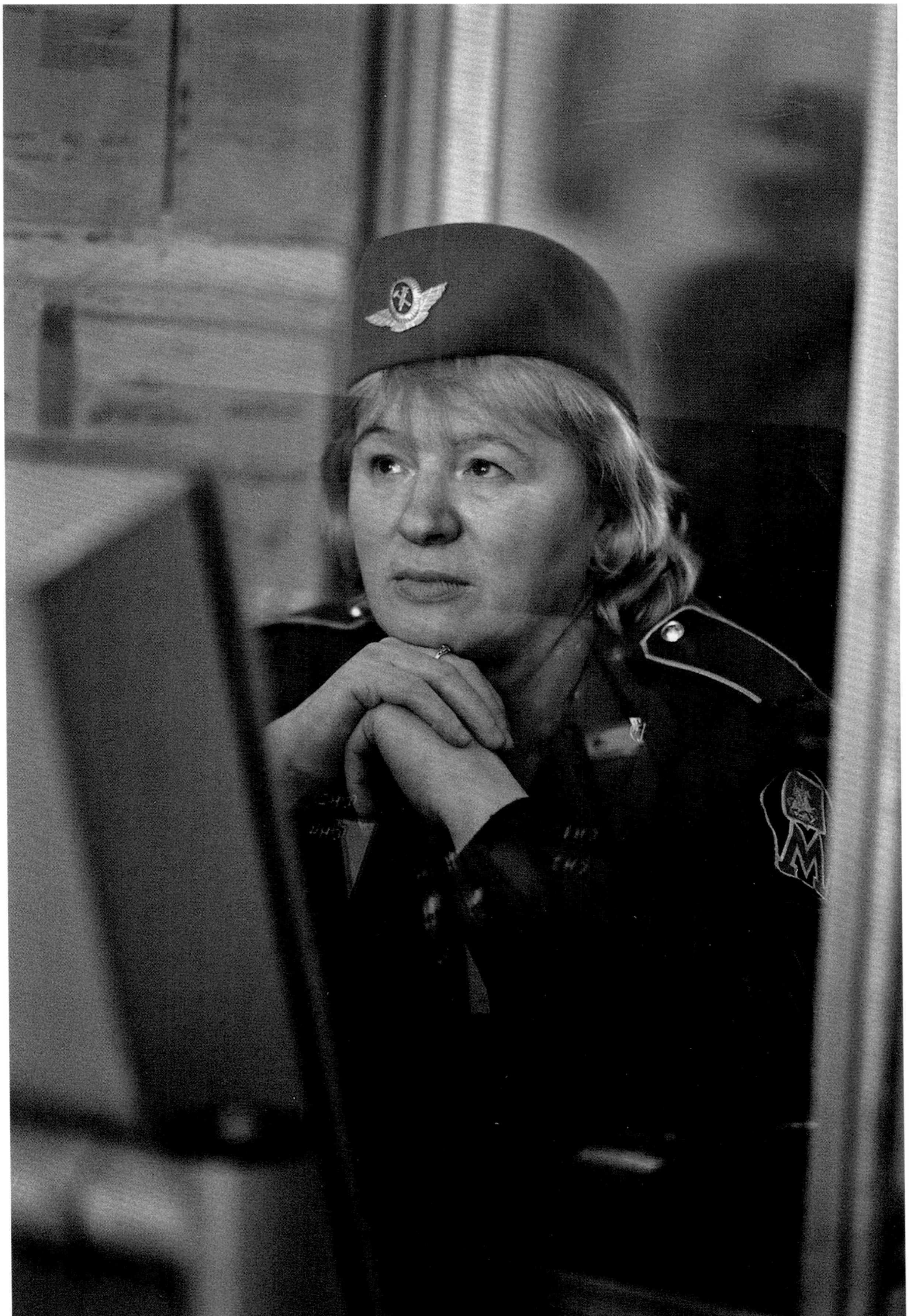

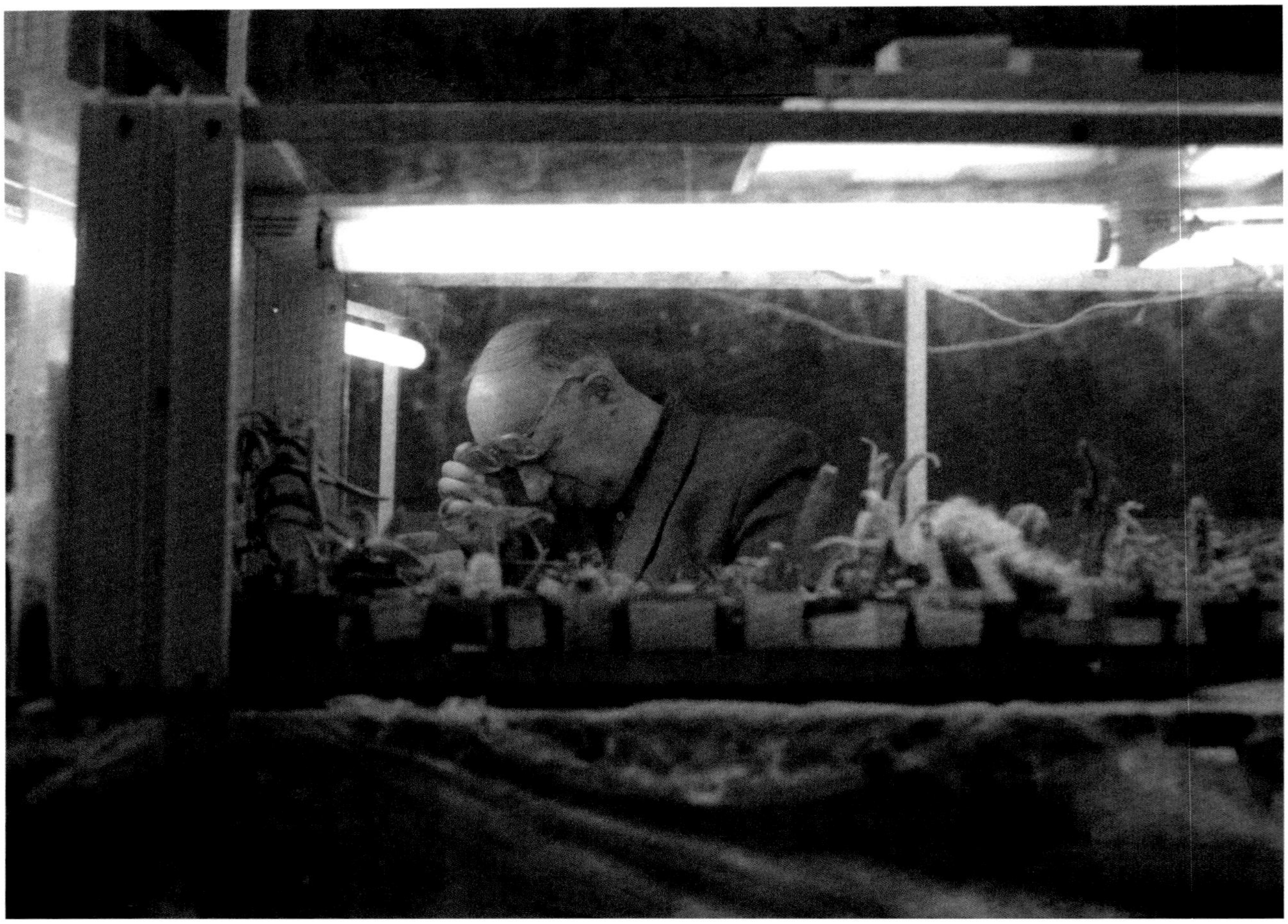

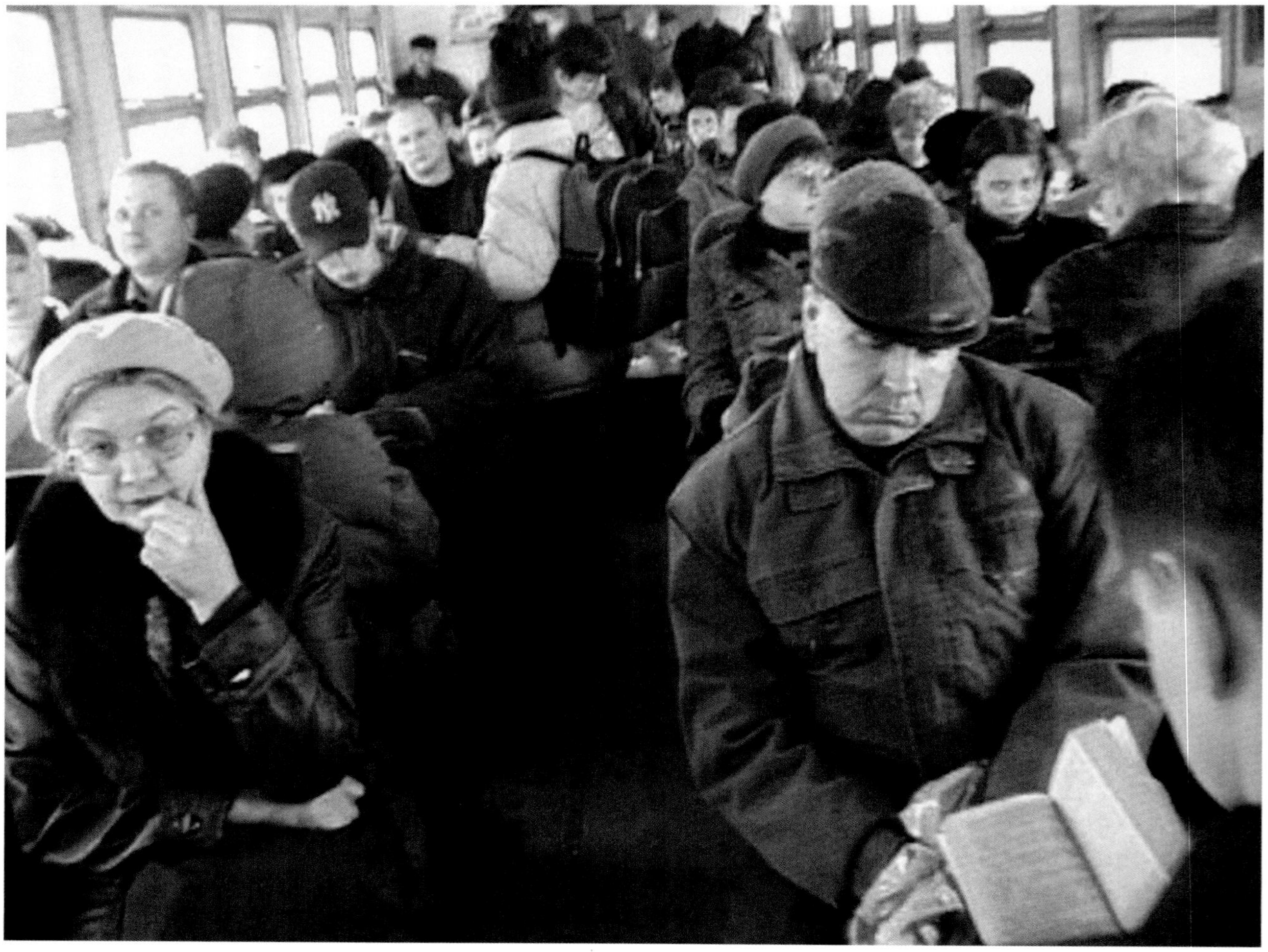

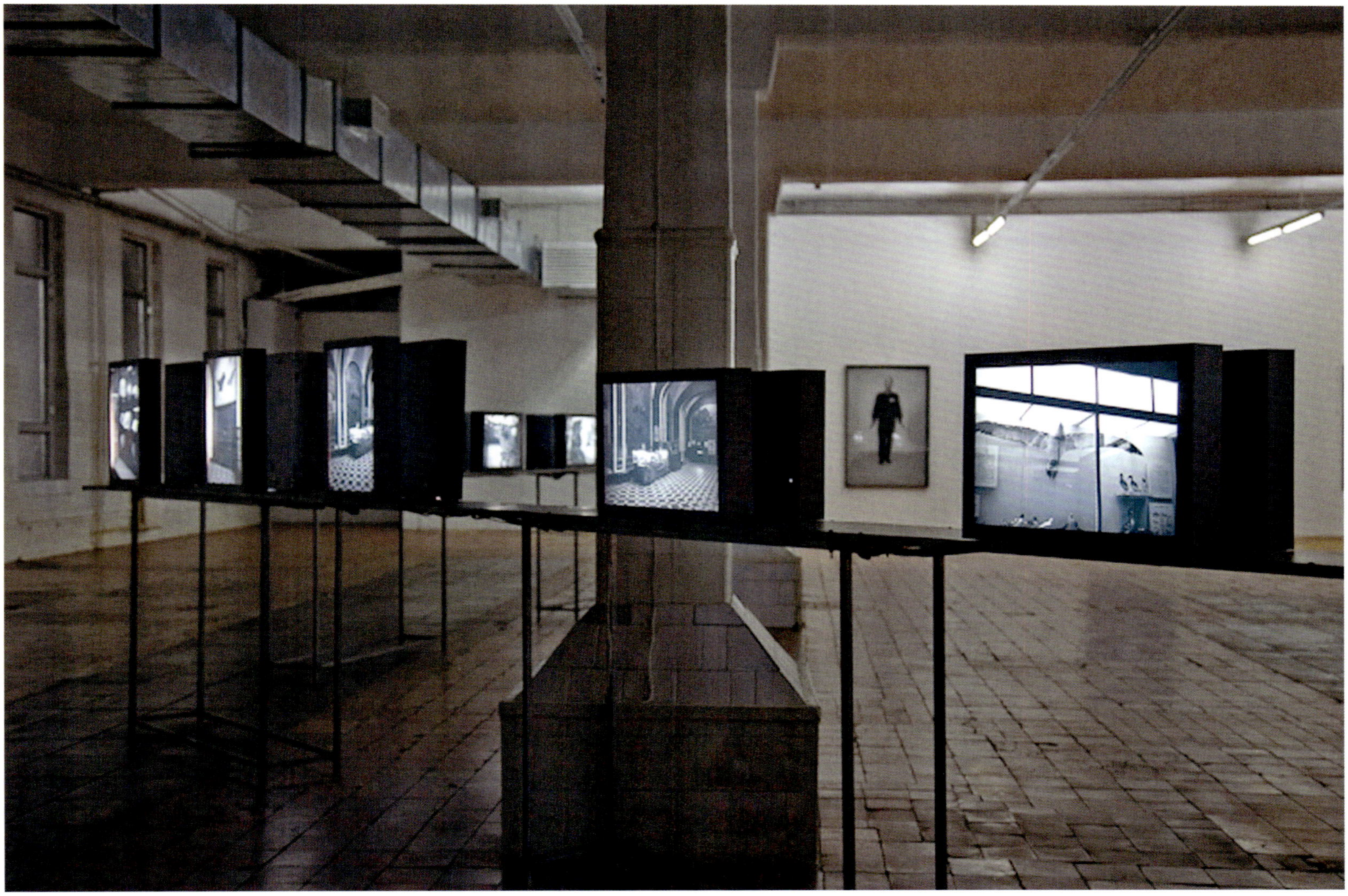

Olga Chernysheva
From the series 'Cactus Seller', 2009
Lightbox, 36 × 51 × 8 cm /
14⅛ × 20 × 3⅛ in

The Train, 2003
Still from video
with sound, 7.30 min

'Cactus Seller', 2009
Installation view, Baibakov Art
Projects, Moscow

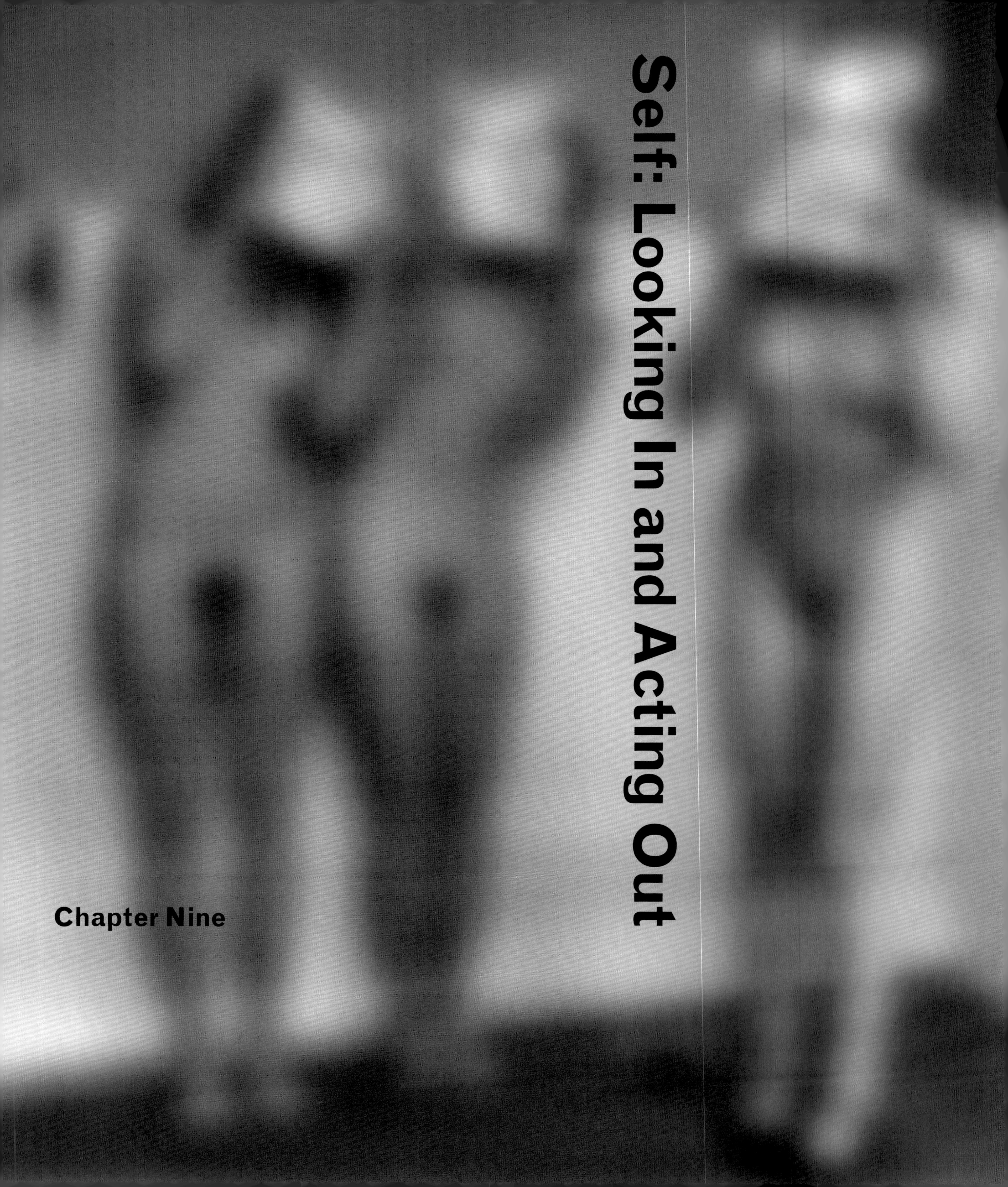

Chapter Nine

Self: Looking In and Acting Out

Documentary is outward facing; it looks at people whose lives and situations are often very different from those of the photographer. This chapter looks at the art produced when the camera is turned the other way to picture aspects of the photographer's immediate lifeworld.

Much of the work discussed in this chapter is about photography as a record of the immediate lives and everyday of the artists. Sometimes such lives can be dramatic and colourful, Larry Clark's and Nan Goldin's especially, but often they are more humdrum and banal. Subjectivity cannot be taken as a universal point of identification, as the specificity of some of the work discussed will highlight. Turning to a more theatrical photographic tradition in the closing section of this chapter the artist often becomes more visible and central in the work. But it is never a straightforward act of disclosure. Identity is often a site of contestation and struggle.

Subjective Documentary

Ed van der Elsken
Larry Clark

Personal Disclosure

Nobuyoshi Araki
Robert Frank
Nan Goldin
Wolfgang Tillmans

Open Form

Felix Gonzalez-Torres

The Everyday

Nigel Shafran
Anna Fox
Keith Arnatt

Theatres of the Self

Jo Spence
Francesca Woodman
Peter Finnemore
Yasumasa Morimura

Ed van der Elsken

Ed van der Elsken's remarkable book *Sweet Life* (1966) is an important testimony to an expressive and romantic reconfiguration of reportage. It is a photobook, still looking out on the world but involving a picturing that is heavily transformed and marked by the feelings of the photographer. With its heavy paper and high-contrast, rich gravure plates it is a lavish book, a baroque travelogue. In the book's inside covers we see contact sheets marked up, indicating how van der Elsken crops and manipulates his photographs. Twenty-two pages of captions and notes precede the photographic plates, as well as a circular typographic composition by a 'letter artist' made out of texts of the names of people, places and things connected with the book. This circular composition is an appropriate cue to the open and receptive relationship to the world that seems to underlie van der Elsken's philosophy. Published six years after a fourteen-month journey around the world together with his wife, his extraordinary photographs show the world as a spectacle of bizarre attractions. His photography is fuelled by passion and a freewheeling, receptive response to the phenomenal world, attentive to both its wonders and violence, but never comprehending:

> I think it's unbelievable, fabulous, this life of ours – everything, the birds and the bees, the deer and the antelope, the spacious skies, the foggy dew, the rockabye babies. Men like John F. and Robert Kennedy, Pablo Picasso, Georges Brassens, Fidel Castro, Pope John XXIII. My wife's embrace, a landing on the moon, space, time, eternity. I don't understand about any of it, except that it's enough to keep me in a constant delirium of delight, surprise, enthusiasm, despair, enough to keep me roaming, stumbling, faltering, cursing, adoring, hating the destruction, the violence in myself and others.[1]

Uniformity and blankness are very much the enemy, typified by what van der Elsken refers to as the 'delirious desert of uniform conformity', pictorially brought out in a high-contrast aerial view of the San Francisco suburbs. When he pictures a crowd, it is not faceless or blank, but caught in the heat of an expressive moment, a point of heightened interest in a horse race. In the caption for this photograph at the races he speaks of the Chinese and the peoples of East Asia having a reputation for self-control and 'faces like masks'. His picture instead shows people at the point at which they forget to keep their emotions under control and when 'delight, hopelessness, excitement – have got the better of them'.

The book begins with pictures about Africans gaining their freedom: a photograph of the sculpture of a defeated slave at the mouth of the Congo is paired against a picture showing the birthday celebrations of a young African in Sierra Leone, a few days before the country gained independence. Van der Elsken's picture of the handover of power (the caption reads 'The British Governor-General taking leave of Sir Milton Margia M.B.E., who in a few days will become Sierra Leone's first African Prime Minister') is unceremonious, a high- contrast picture which shows the dynamic colonial relationship still visible through the gestures of the two men's bodies and their separation underscored by the fold and cut of the book's centrefold, a vertical divide countered by the horizontal black lines of waiting ships that animate the otherwise blank backdrop. The form of the picture and layout linked with political commentary in van der Elsken's portrayal of people on the east coast of Durban, South Africa, in which a solitary male striding across the picture is given a white halo in corroboration of the Apartheid sign on the bench in the picture: "EUROPEANS BLANKES".

The title of the book, *Sweet Life*, comes from the name of a steamer photographed in the Philippines, its associations played off against the foreground depiction of a man weighed down by the crates of empty pop bottles he is carrying, his unsweet life in turn contrasting with the pure joy of the child shown diving from the ship in a picture on the left.

Van der Elsken's photography was subjective: 'I didn't go on this trip for *The New York Times*. I'm not a journalist, an objective reporter; I am a man with likes and dislikes'. He said that he found his truth in 'essential things', and the underworld was his speciality, such as his photographs of Japanese 'toughs' in Kamagasaki, their Westernized look modelled on the gangster style of 1930s' movies. There is an element of fantasy and unreality about such pictures that links with van der Elsken's fascination with lifelike sculptures: the statues in the Tiger Balm Garden in Hong Kong, his pictures of the often gruesome exhibits in the Coney Island wax museum or the uncanny picture showing wax statues of Japanese adulterers, tied up and naked. The book closes with a picture of a painting, Diego Rivera's portrait of his pregnant wife as an allegory of fertility, *Liberated Earth*. The homage signals the desired affinities between van der Elsken's photography and the symbolic and expressive art of the renowned Mexican muralist.

Ed van der Elsken
Sweet Life, Harry N Abrams, New York, 1966
29 × 29 cm / 11½ × 11½ in, 208pp
Hardback, 153 black and white photographs, text and design by Ed van der Elsken

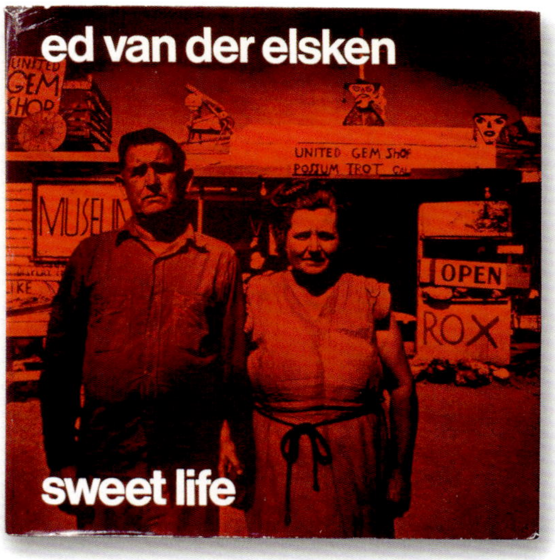
ed van der elsken
UNITED GEM SHOP
OPEN
sweet life

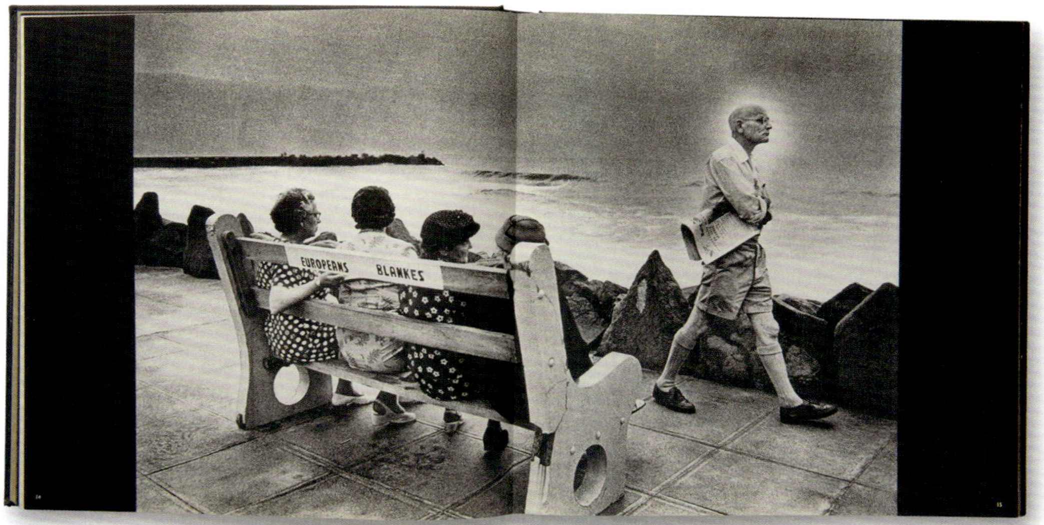
EUROPEANS
BLANKES

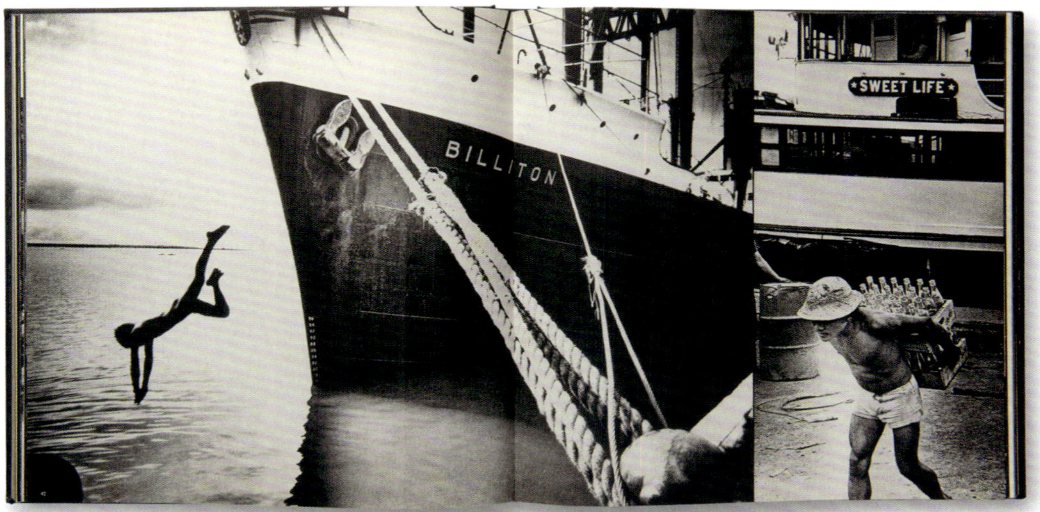
BILLITON
SWEET LIFE

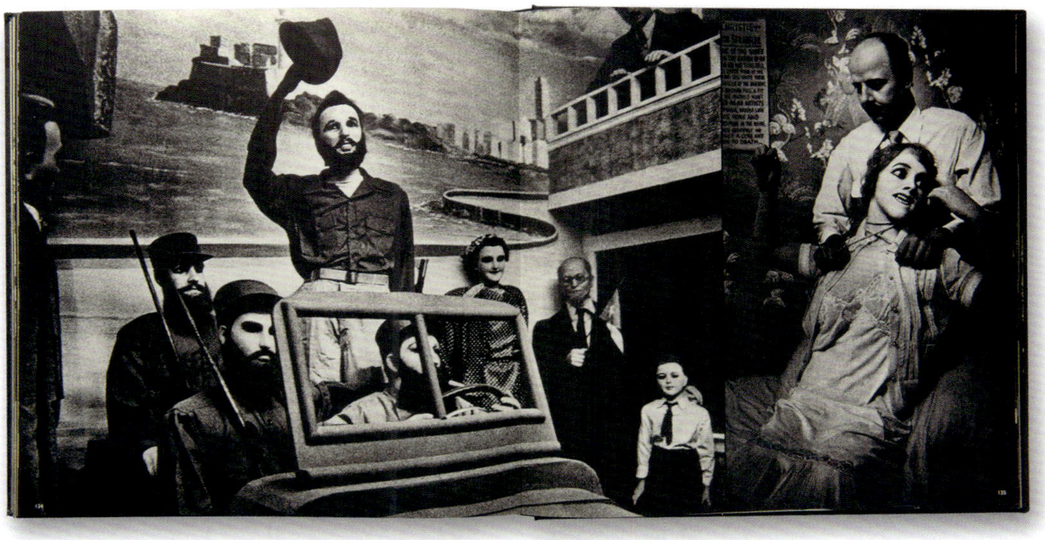

Larry Clark

Larry Clark's ground-breaking book *Tulsa* (1971), with its pictures of drug addiction and violence in his hometown, breaks the usual documentary distance by being taken by someone inside the community photographed. The book is simply introduced by its author: 'i was born in tulsa, Oklahoma in 1943. when i was sixteen i started shooting amphetamine. i shot with my friends everyday for three years and then left town but i've gone back through the years. once the needle goes in it never comes out.' Clark's observation about addition fits the cyclical structure of his pictures, showing drug addiction over time (presented in the form of three sections dated 1963, 1968 and 1971) among successive generations of youths. There is no resolution at the book's close, just a different group of adolescents taking the drugs.

Clark has acknowledged the great photo essays from *Life* magazines of the 1950s as an influence, as well as the movies: 'I grew up in the 50s with all those great B-movies, "film noir" they call it now. Double features, triple features every Saturday… with all the dark shadows in them.'[2] Despite its graphic nature, showing us adolescents with ligatures on their arms and hypodermics in their veins, this is not a seedy or abject portrayal of drug use. It carries a fictive and filmic air. We sense Clark's affiliation with the group he shows, the beauty and idealism in the pictures and a bravura in some of the poses, especially the gun-wielding youth on the cover (its caption indicates that it serves as a memorium image). One of the book's most shocking pictures shocks because of its very beauty, showing a heavily pregnant woman shooting up, her belly and arms irradiated by natural light. At the same time we do see the brutality and consequences of drug use: Clark give us a picture showing a dead baby in an open coffin, the agony of an accidental gun-shot wound, the beating up of an informer (the last presented as a series of film stills). In the last section, one of the teenagers holds up a book bearing a picture of writhing naked figures which could just as easily be an evocation of heaven as hell, an apposite metaphor, perhaps, for the ambiguity underlying this extraordinary book in its portrayal of addiction at the heart of Middle America.

Larry Clark
Dead 1970, 1968
Black and white photograph
35.5 cm × 27.9 / 14 × 11 in

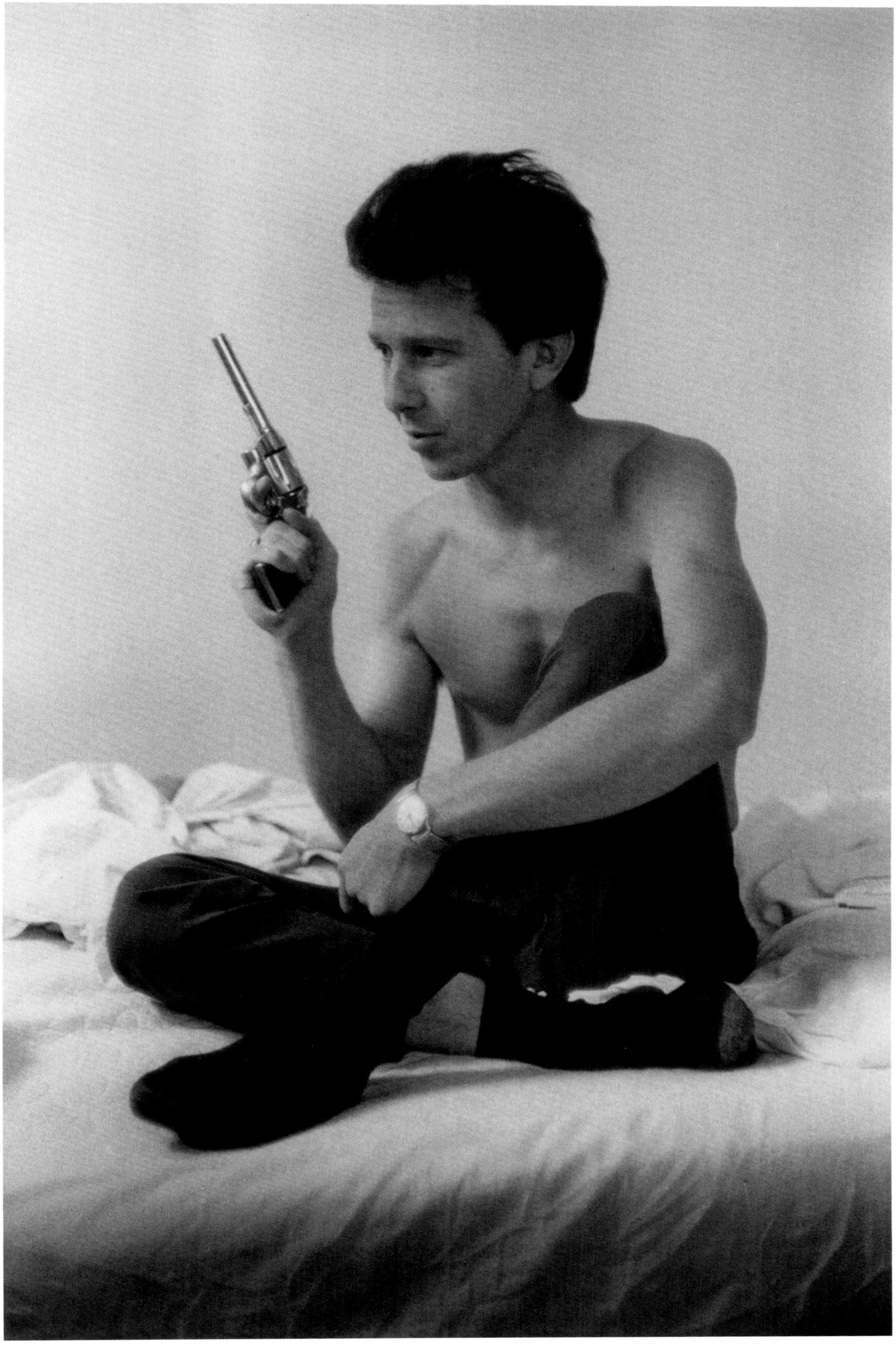

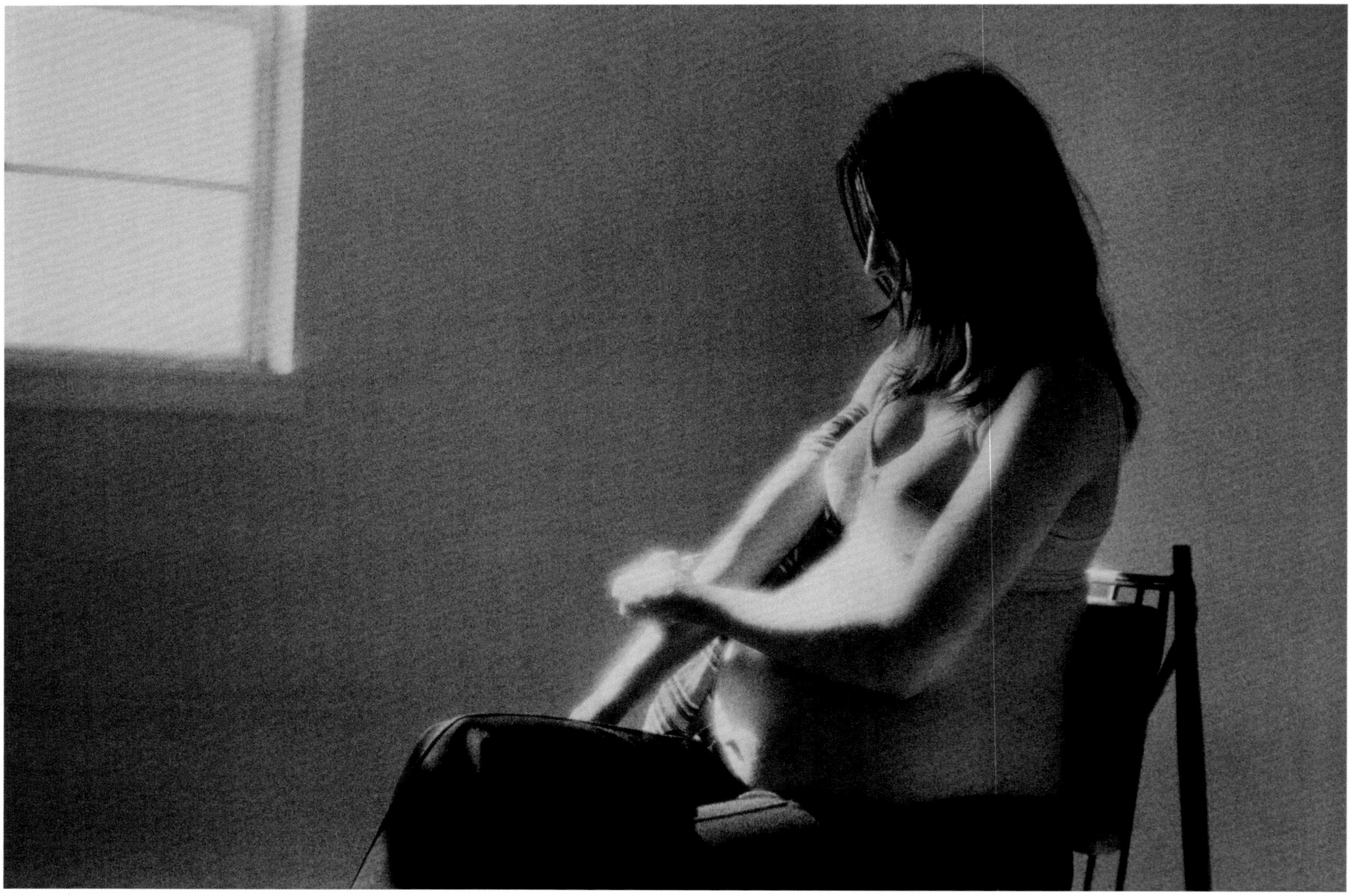

Larry Clark
Untitled, 1971
Black and white photograph
27.9 × 35.6 cm / 11 × 14 in

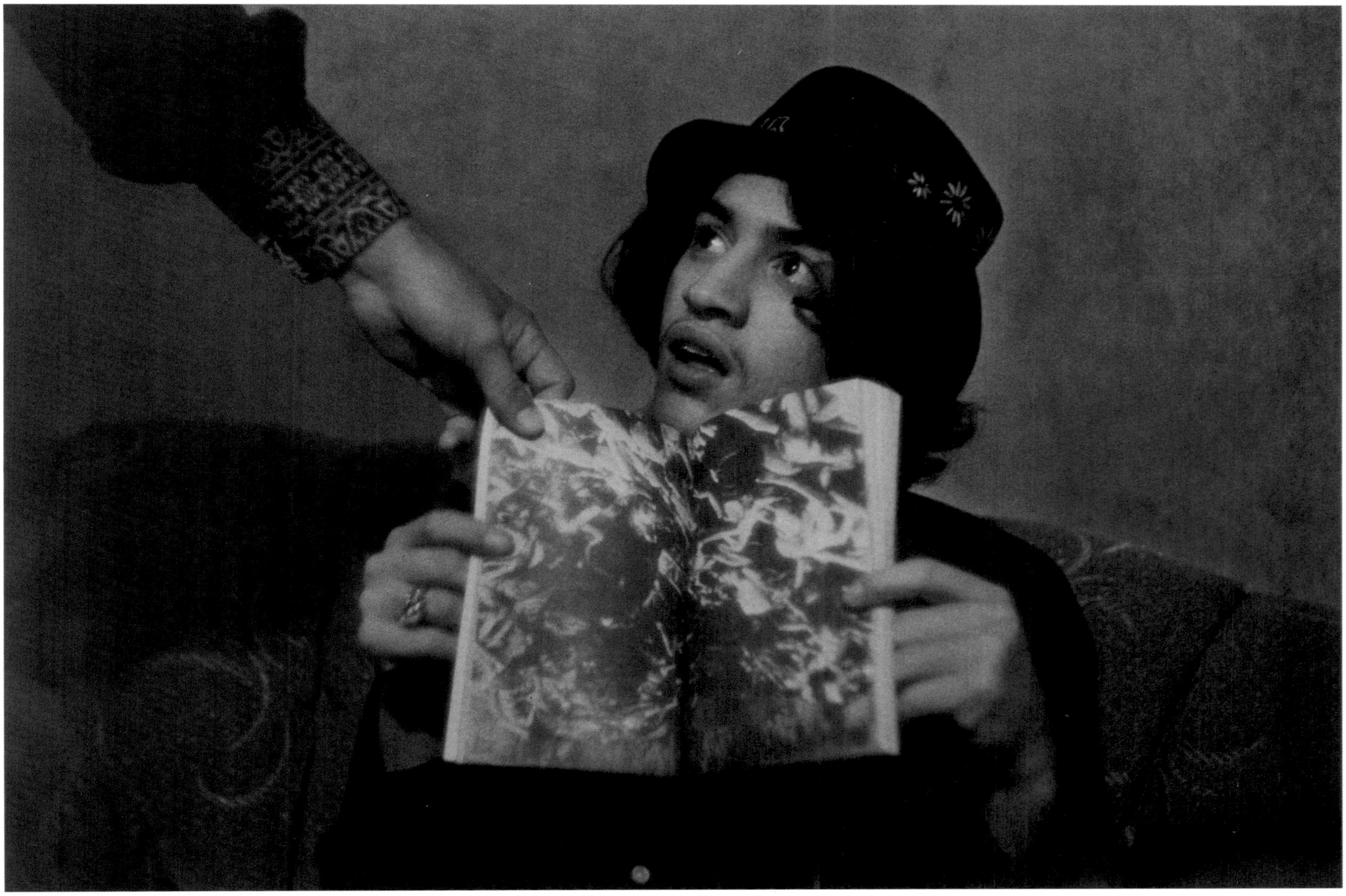

Larry Clark
Untitled, 1971
Black and white photograph
27.9 × 35.6 cm / 11 × 14 in

Nobuyoshi Araki

The sense of personal disclosure through a direct and seemingly uninhibited use of the camera as record is also brought out in Nobuyoshi Araki's intimate photographs of both his honeymoon and his wife's later illness and death, an extraordinary representation of love and death that attempts to bring photography close to the intensity of his feelings. Araki, one of Japan's most notorious and prolific photographers, self-published his book *Sentimental Journey* in 1971, a '*shi-shosetsu*' ('I-novel') made up of a collection of photographs taken during his honeymoon with his bride, Yoko. In an insert to the book, Araki set such an intimate use of photography against the fakery of fashion photography, declaring 'I don't have chronic diarrhea belly middle-ear inflammation, sometimes I am flooded by fashion photographs but it's nothing more than that, this kind of face, this nudity, this private life, this landscape, are total lies; I can't take it.'[3]

Infamous for its eroticism, his photography is characterized by its breadth and excess, its sense of an uninhibited response to the world that will characterize a number of photographers discussed in this chapter. Through a series of ash-grey prints, *Sentimental Journey* provides an intimate portrayal of a relationship. A wedding photograph of the couple adorns the cover of the original book, which opens with a portrait of Yoko on the bullet train about to embark on her honeymoon journey. Araki photographs her both clothed and naked in hotel rooms, gardens and fields. There are moments of tenderness and vulnerability, as in the picture of Yoko curled up asleep in a boat, but Araki also photographs her at a point of ecstasy during lovemaking. At the same time he is aware that such cherished moments are transient, symbolized by his inclusion of a picture of a grave and a butterfly in the series and the closing picture showing just the empty rumpled sheets on the two beds where the couple had slept.

In *Sentimental Journey/Winter Journey* Araki pairs these photographs of his wedding and honeymoon with a later series in response to his wife's illness and death in 1990. From a celebration of love we move to its sombre counterpoint. *Winter Journey* opens with portraits of the couple dancing beside a singer, portraits of Yoko with her cat, then a portrait of her smiling to camera beside a hospital bed. Illness is only implied; Araki's photography is discreet rather than sensational. A picture of an empty sky, edged by the black frame of the window, introduces recurring pictures of nothing or very little, of dark subways, streets, views of anonymous and featureless buildings. In this view of the empty sky, the cord of the window blind hanging in the centre of the picture implies the fragility of such a moment, as if this view of the sky could be suddenly lost to blackness.

Araki photographs a handmade street sign of a little girl holding a black cat over and over again, because it echoes pictures of Yoko and her cat. There are pictures of their cat alone on their apartment terrace or rooftops, then a close-up tender detail of Araki's hand holding his wife's hand and a photograph of her in the hospital bed. In this last image, we do not see her face; she is turned away, and the picture concentrates instead on the flowers and the objects around her. Then Araki photographs a cloth-covered body being wheeled away down a hospital corridor. We assume it's Yoko's. There are pictures of city streets and of melted snow pushed to the side of a road forming the shape of a human form. Araki photographs the funeral, including a final portrait of Yoko in her coffin, her cremation and a view of a smoking chimney. He has himself photographed at the funeral and also includes a picture of himself taken on the subway, wracked with grief. A concluding series of photographs show his empty apartment and the cat, with the book's final image showing the creature prancing in snow. Such photographs seem redolent of Araki's heightened state of receptivity, the emotionally charged context in which he is taking them. The inclusion of digital dates in all the photographs points to the camera as a calendar and clock, a mechanical and anonymous register of time that contrasts with the emotive and subjective context of the photographs. One picture towards the end of the book makes the registering of dates its subject, framing the yearly calendar in a diary with certain dates marked in ink to indicate their importance.

Nobuyoshi Araki
Sentimental Journey, Tokyo, 1971
24 × 24 cm / 9½ in × 9½ in, 108pp
Paperback with green printed sheet tipped in later to first page, 108 black and white photographs

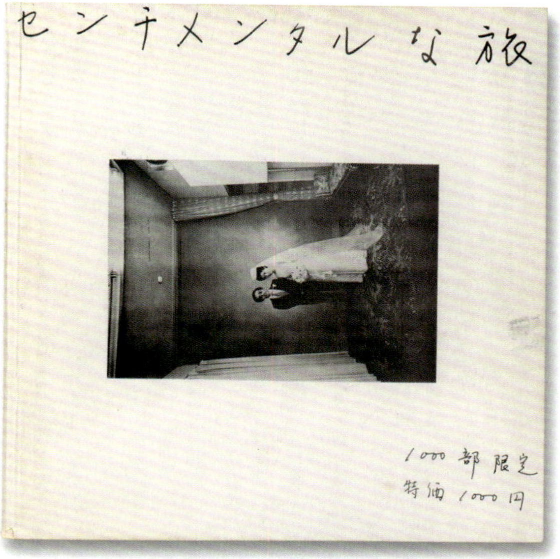
センチメンタルな旅
1000部限定
特価1000円

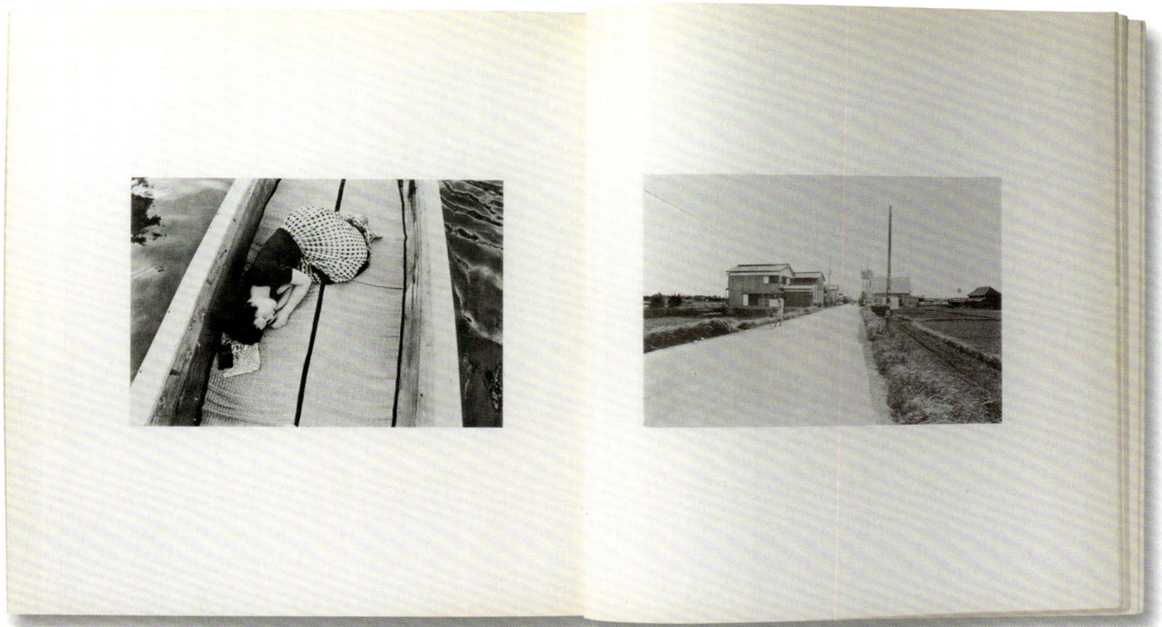

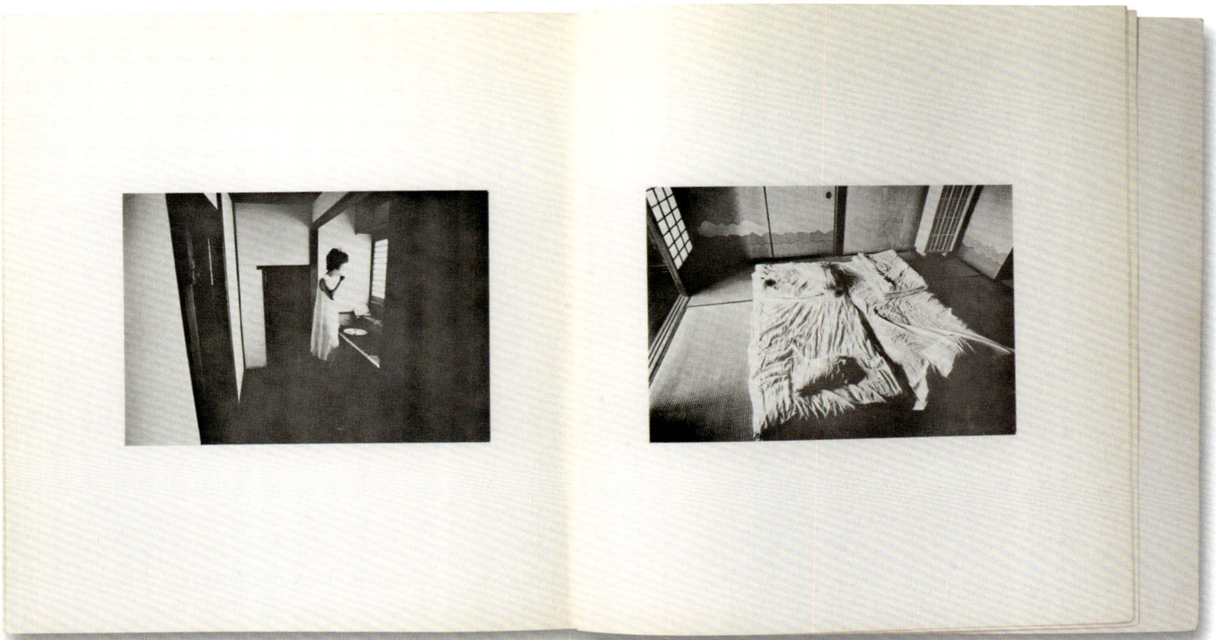

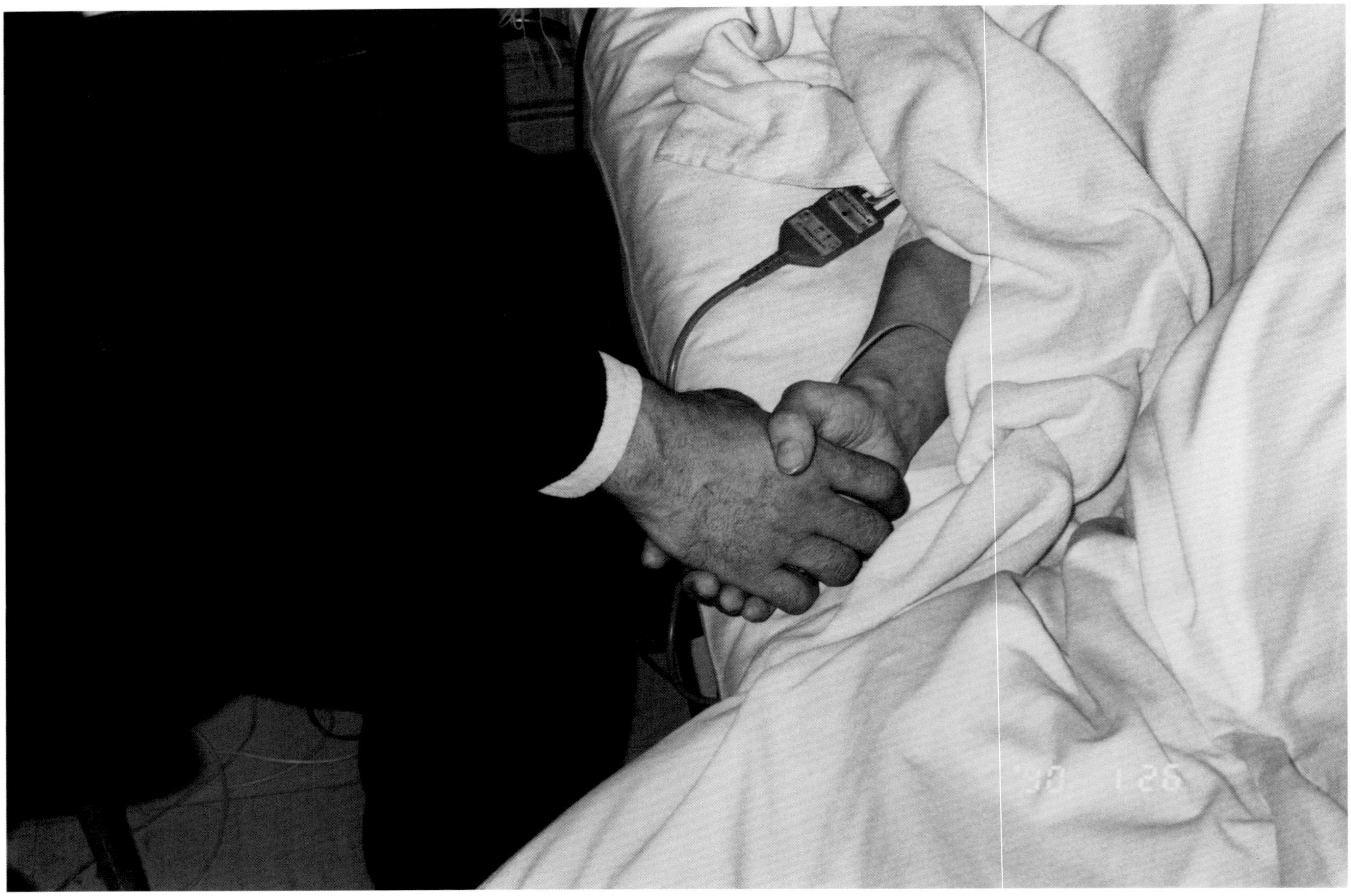

Nobuyoshi Araki
From the series 'Sentimental Journey / Winter Journey', 1991
Gelatin silver print
Dimensions variable

From the series 'Sentimental Journey / Winter Journey', 1991
Gelatin silver print
Dimensions variable

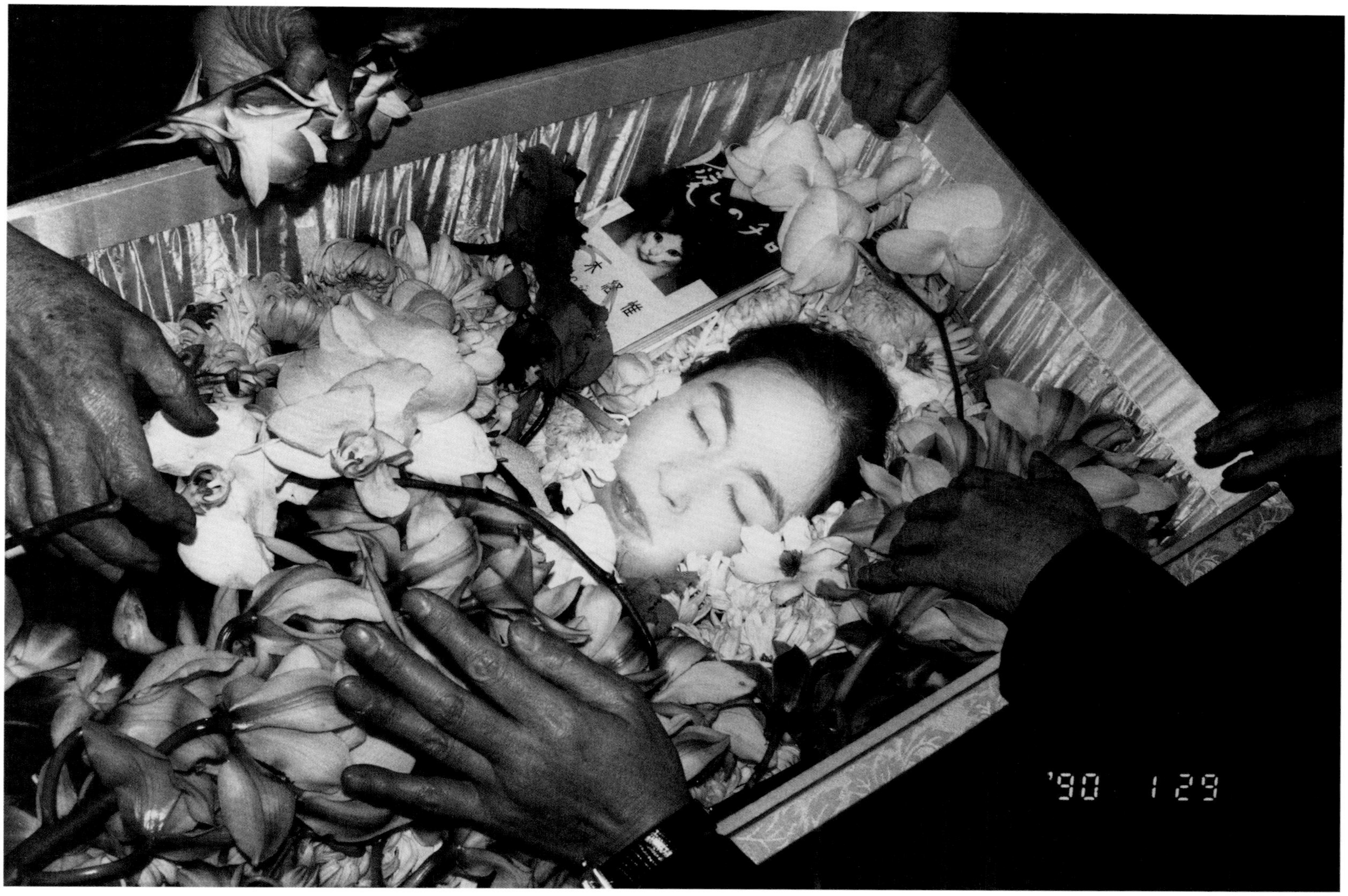
'90 1 29

Robert Frank

Robert Frank essentially reinvented himself in his return to photography in the 1970s after a decade devoted to filmmaking. The documentary aspect of his work of the late 1940s and 1950s unravels in his expressive and self-conscious use of photography in the 1970s. Frank's return to photography, signalled a decisive break from his earlier photography, which came very much from his travels across Europe and America. His work is centred upon his isolated home in Mabou, Nova Scotia, where Frank was working against the very kind of photography for which he had gained his reputation. Photography became the site in which to vent the pain of personal tragedies: the disappearance and presumed death of his friend Danny Seymour, the sudden death of his 20-year-old daughter in a plane crash in 1974 and his son's mental illness. Taken often with a Polaroid camera that used black-and-white positive and negative film, his pictures spiralled inwards, turning back upon themselves and playing with recurring motifs – frames, mirrors, windows, TV screens – while using the often frozen and bleak landscape of Mabou as a setting and backdrop, an elemental void. Frank even re-used pictures from his 1959 book *The Americans*, photographing a couple of well-known prints pegged out on a washing line like laundry – exposed to the harsh elements, blowing in the wind against the empty sea.

The Americans pointed to a sense of vacuity and joylessness in the face of post-war consumerism, but in Frank's work from the 1970s the void is more within than without. The very process of picturing, his recurrent display of the Polaroid image breaking up, underscores a sense of fragility and impermanence. His pictures are edged by a sense of chaos and disorder. Many are given over to measuring and logging time. Dates and the notation of small events recur, often scratched into the negatives: 'FEBRUARY 4 I WAKE UP TURN ON TV'. Outside events still take place but are filtered back through Frank's own world, as in the inclusion of TV stills from the first Gulf War, which are mixed in with photographs of Frank in hospital that play with reflective voids and empty patches of light, all centring upon his own diminutive portrait reflected in a little hospital bedside mirror.

Language itself is inadequate, as the words dripping across walls and mirrors in *Sick of Goodbyes* (1978) suggests. Frank is sick of loss. He's had to say too many farewells. A skeletal toy figure dangles from a hand in the top image, against the sea. The smears and streaks of the improperly processed Polaroid set up their own pictorial drama and match the abrasive sentiment and tone of the picture. Edged with incommunicability, such work unravels the very forms of photography and language. Turning the camera on the everyday context of his life, Frank explores a contingency that is less happenstance and far from the fortuitous finds of shooting from the hip. We move from broad sociological and cultural themes to the confines of home and its environments and the people who are close to him. But the emptiness and darkness at the heart of *The Americans* never goes away.

Robert Frank
Sick of Goodbyes, Mabou, 1978
Gelatin silver print enlarged from
2 Polaroid negatives
34.3 × 22.5 cm / 13½ × 8⅞ in

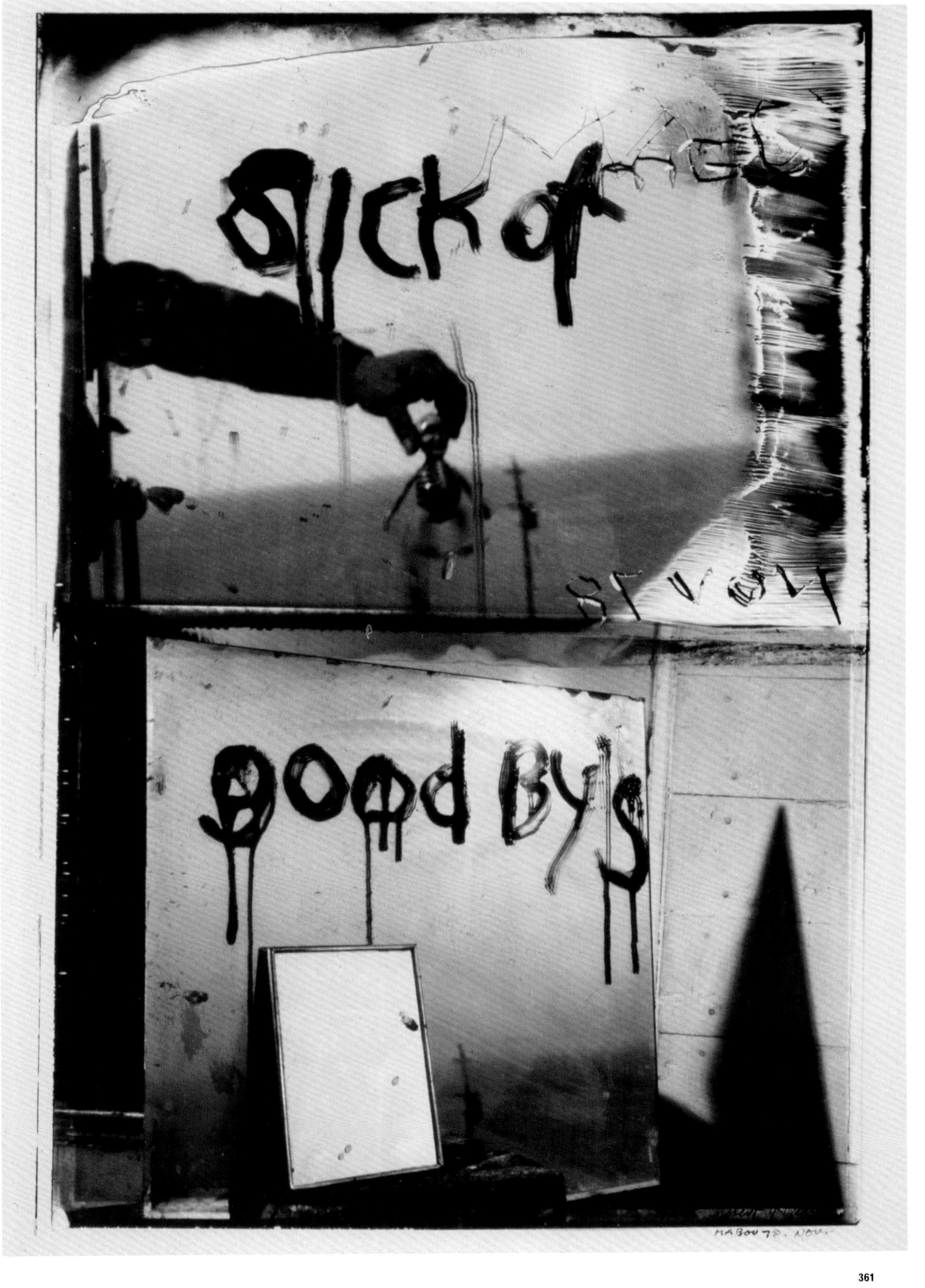
sick of
good bys
MABOU 78. NOV.

Nan Goldin

The 1980s' New York photography scene was characterized by the dominance of the appropriators of *The Pictures Generation* and its accompanying postmodern theories of mediation. Nan Goldin's relentless first-person exposure of her own raw, physical, unadorned dramatic experience breaks with such a model and cues much art of the 1990s and onwards, which is fixated upon questions of the real and the power of the photographic image. Goldin's photography, often painfully self-centred and introspective, can be termed 'insider documentary'. Instead of allowing the usual distance between the photographer and the group depicted, she photographs as a member of the group. Her photographs originated as rock-club entertainment with a total of 800 slides first shown at the Mudd Club in Lower Manhattan in 1979, accompanied by a mixture of taped classical, pop and rock music. A selection of 130 photographs was published as *The Ballad of Sexual Dependency* by Aperture in 1986, after being shown as a slideshow as part of the Whitney Biennial a year earlier.

Goldin's frankness and voracious appetite for the truth could be seen as a reaction against her middle-class upbringing in a Washington, D.C. suburb and her family's silence over her sister's suicide at eighteen. Goldin has described her work as being 'about trying to feel what another person is feeling. There's a glass wall between people, and I want to break it.'[4] The camera becomes a bodily extension of sight: taking a picture is for Goldin a way of 'touching somebody – it's a caress.'

The lyrical use of light, the theatricality and lushness of the colour images offset the blunt depictions of Goldin's rather ordinary and unattractive subjects caught in various situations: crying, pissing, showering, drug taking, masturbating and having sex. 'If it were possible', she says, 'I'd want no mechanism between me and the moment of photographing. The camera is as much part of my everyday life as talking or eating or sex. The instance of photographing, instead of creating distance, is a moment of clarity and emotional connection for me.'[5]

Goldin is as open and frank in showing herself as she is others: 'It's about letting it be what it is. And not trying to make it more or less, or altered. What I'm interested in is capturing life as it's being lived, and the flavour and the smell of it, and maintaining that in the pictures.' A violent climax of the book, *After being battered* (1984), shows the photographer with her eye smashed and bloodshot, staring into the lens after being beaten up by her long-standing boyfriend.

As much as Goldin's photographs are a celebration of her youthful friends and their exuberant lifestyles, they are also about vulnerability, violence and mortality as she pictures the deaths of friends as they gradually succumb to AIDS. Many pictures concern points of self-reflection; mirrors and windows recur as a motif, with lone males and females caught at pensive moments. Women reflected in the mirror suggest an introspection that is evidence of a self-contained pleasure and eroticism. The photographs have a belief in youth and the uninhibited expression of sexual attraction. Even if the relationships are destructive, Goldin's pictures show us how people cling together – they are about the need for the other, an addictive dependency.

Nan Goldin
The Ballad of Sexual Dependency
Aperture, Millerton, New York, 1986
22.8 × 25.4 cm / 9 × 10 in, 144pp
Hardcover with full blue cloth and jacket, 126 colour photographs
Text by Nan Goldin; edited by Marvin Heiferman, Mark Holborn and Suzanne Fletcher; design by Keith Davis

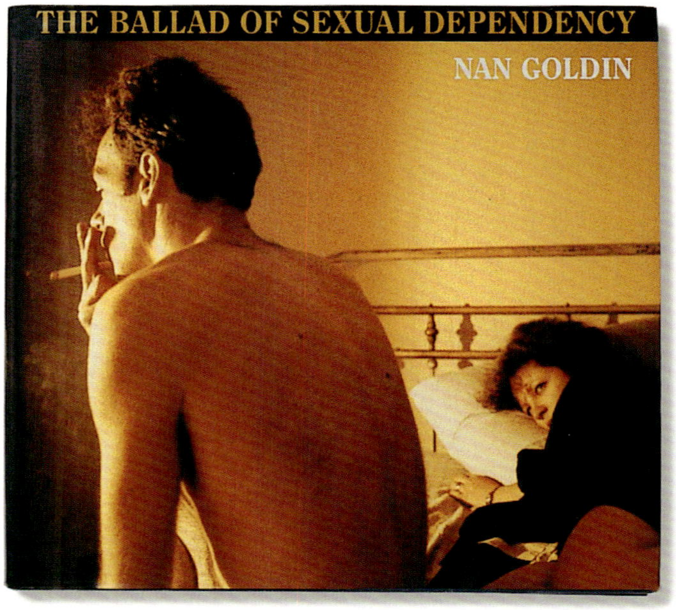
THE BALLAD OF SEXUAL DEPENDENCY
NAN GOLDIN

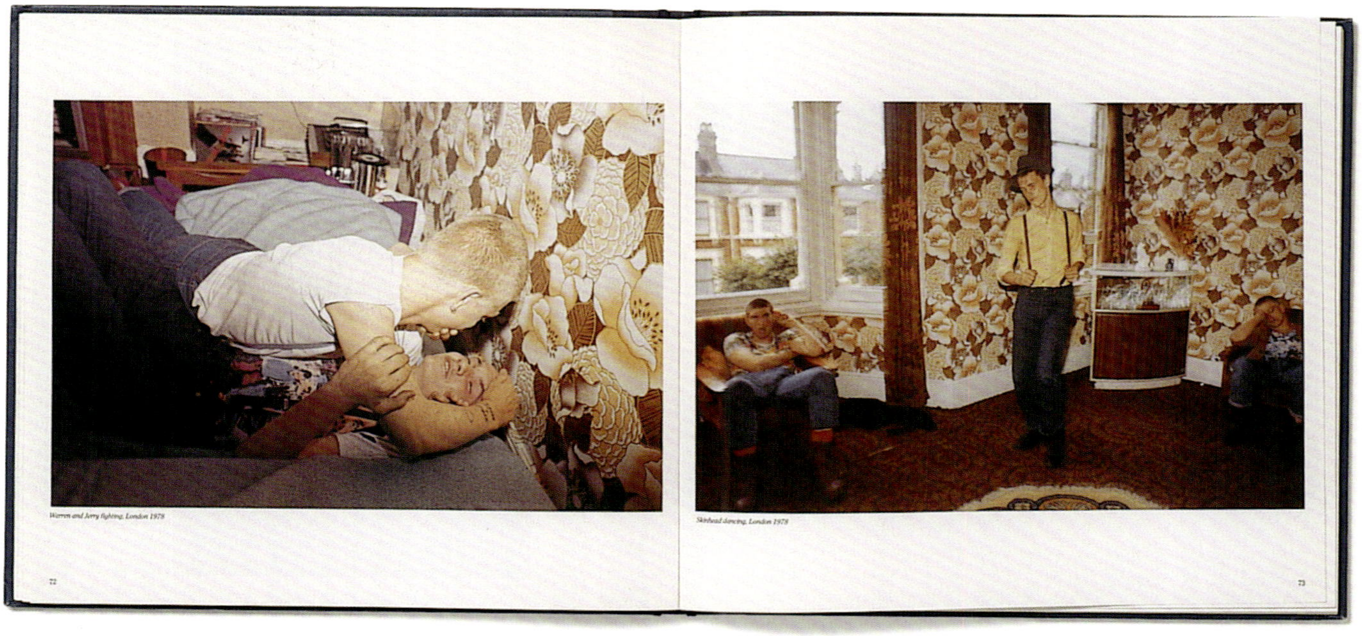
Warren and Jerry fighting, London 1978
Skinhead dancing, London 1978

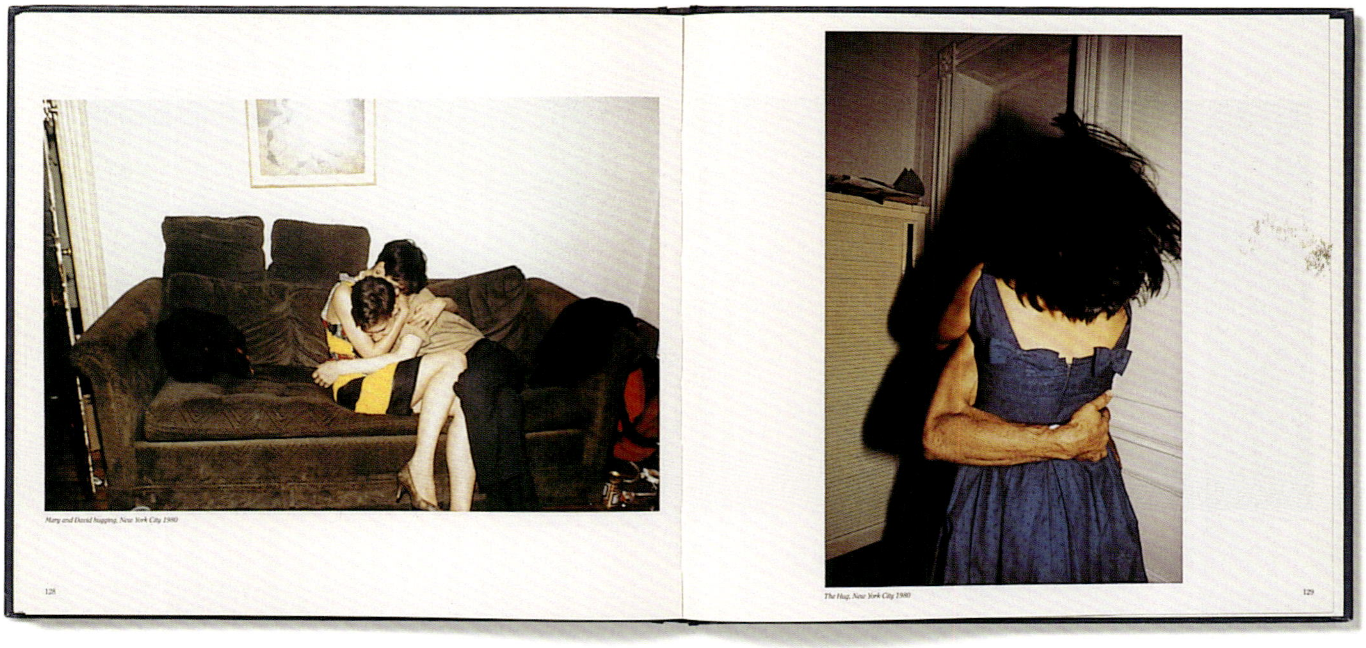
Mary and David hugging, New York City 1980
The Hug, New York City 1980

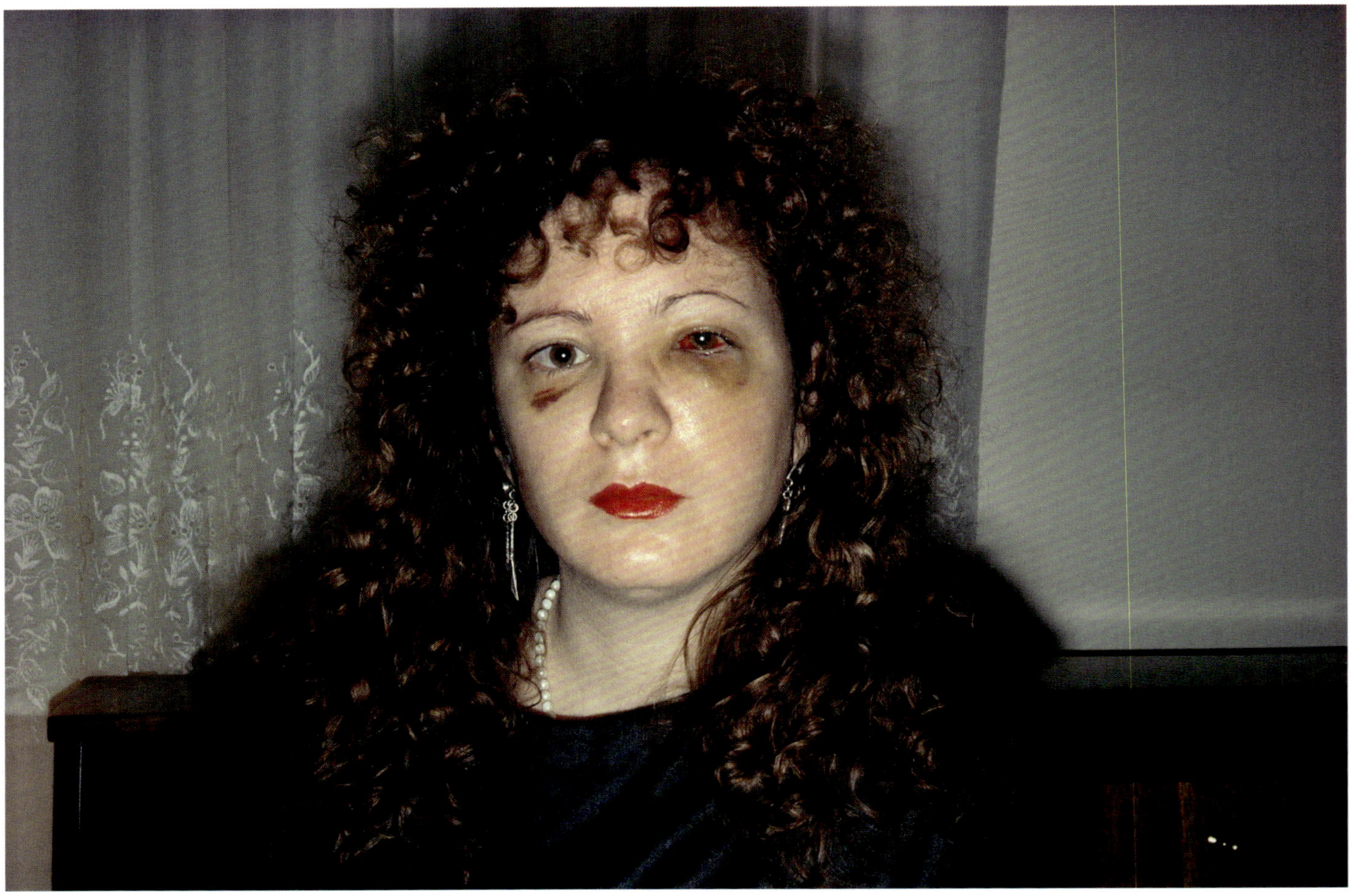

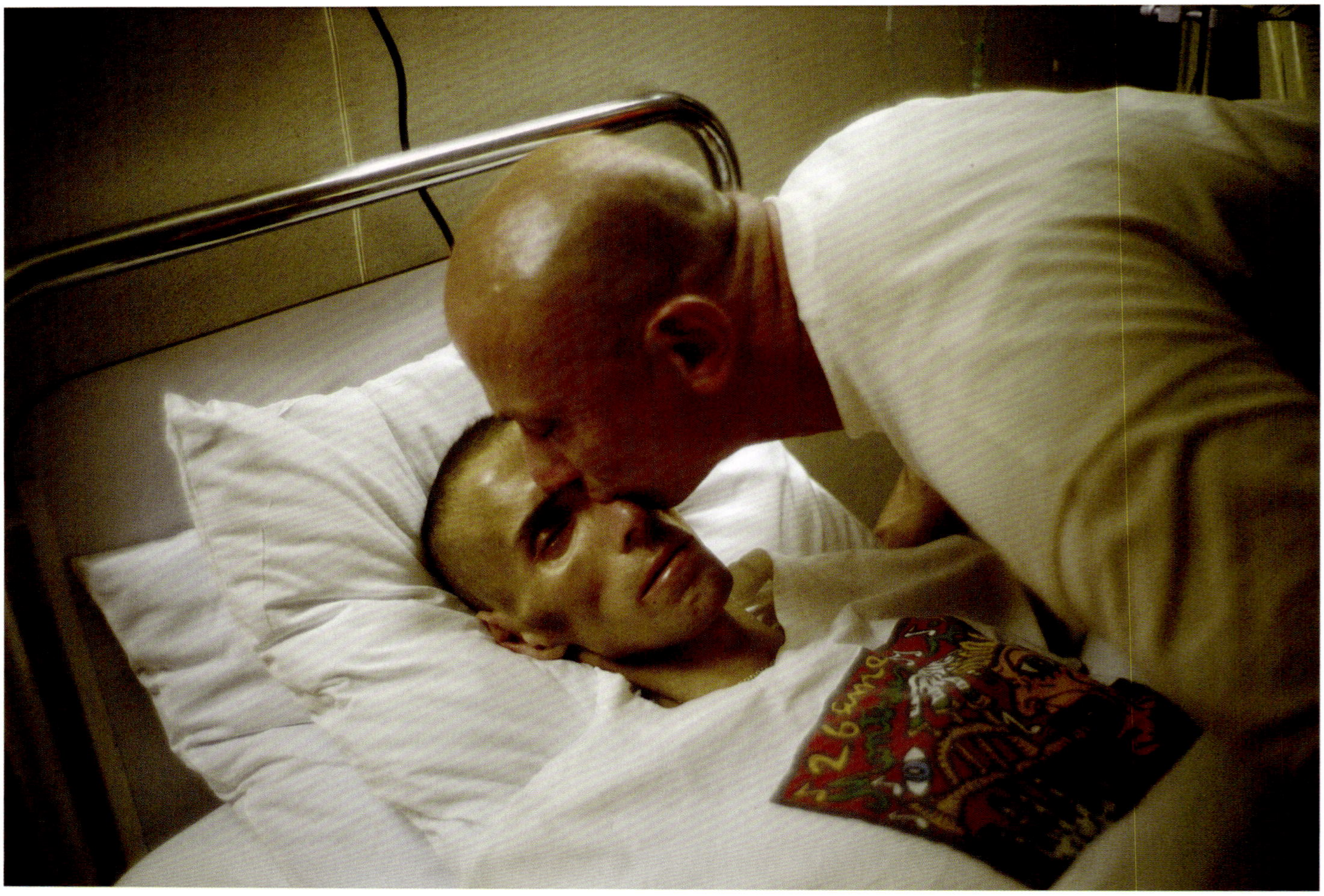

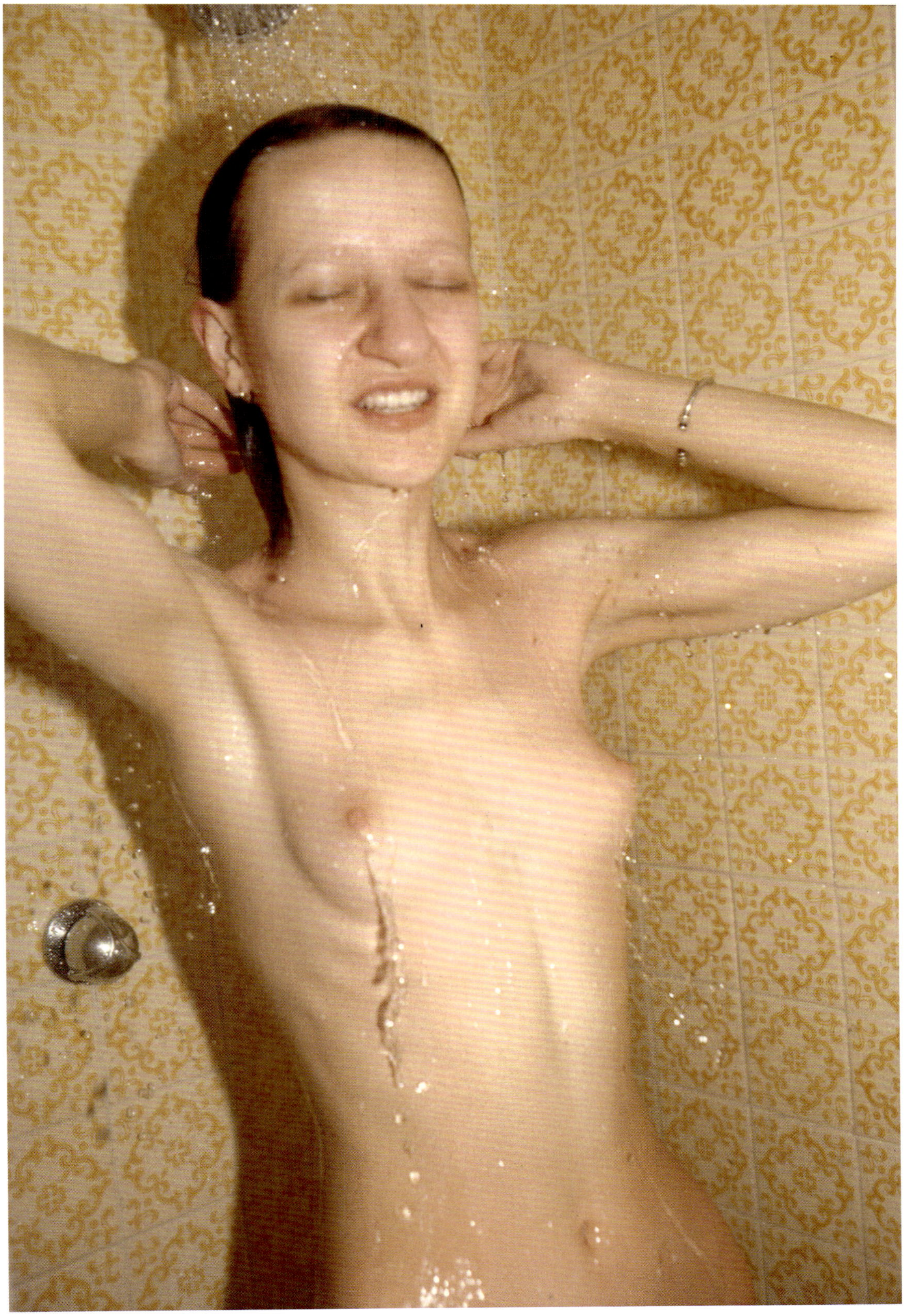

Nan Goldin
After being battered, 1984
Cibachrome print, dimensions variable

Gotscho kissing Gilles, 1993
35mm slide, dimensions variable

Suzanne in the shower, Palenque, Mexico, 1981
35mm slide, dimensions variable

Wolfgang Tillmans

The work of Wolfgang Tillmans is very much characterized by the importance of a nonhierarchical seeing, a sense of a freedom from constraints that not only sets up fresh new formal and iconographic possibilities for photography but also taps into the utopianism and idealism associated with so many of the colourful countercultural young groups Tillmans photographs: clubbers, activists and protesters. His desire for an unprivileged, demotic gaze is further underscored by what has now become his signature style installation of pictures in the gallery – the arrangement of images all over the walls, in different sizes and in different formats.

Driven by a passion for life, a passion for seeing in an open and encompassing, liberating sense, Tillmans' photography is as attentive to the exceptional, the surprising, the beautiful, the sexual, as it is to the more ordinary, everyday and matter-of-fact. Looking at his book, *if one thing matters, everything matters* (2003) – more than 2,400 images, all reduced to the same size, for which he revisited every roll of film he had ever shot – what is immediately striking is the sense of flux and perpetual restlessness, the sense of an addiction to the act of photography. Underlying patterns and threads of imagery emerge, including the reflexive fascination with processes of reproduction: the early digital photocopies, shots from the TV, pictures of one of his own photos showing a youth's face diffused by transparent protective wrapping, the recurrence of stained and colour-manipulated prints, the many abstractions made in the darkroom without a camera. Such a formal strand is mixed in with pictures of youth culture, of parties, clubbers, love parades, demos, peace camps and riot police. There are many still lifes, including the improvised decorative displays of flowers in mineral-water bottles, crumpled clothing, jeans and socks drying on radiators, domestic clutter, the mess left over after partying. The seemingly artless series of plane-spotter-like snaps of Concorde flying overhead. And the predilection for beautiful natural phenomena: photos of the moon through a telescope Tillmans made when a child, sunsets, aerial views from planes, rainbows, a total eclipse of the sun. And the frank and open depictions of sexuality.

Tillmans' photography is very much an affirmation of the sensuality of being in the world. Part of the pleasure we get from his work – and pleasure is key – is the way in which we encounter the joy of both the sensuous form of photography itself and the beauty of the things in the world that photography can so vividly describe. He never shies away from beautiful things. For over a decade he has also explored the abstract formal possibilities of photography. In presentations of his work we now shift between the often unexpected formal beauty and intensity of the photograph as an abstract picture and the sensuality of his rich, evocative and distinctive portrayal of aspects and moments from the contemporary world.

Although increasingly a worldwide vision, Tillmans' photography remains at the same time rooted in the local and specific, as he keeps insisting on details in his own immediate domestic space and the lives of particular social groups and communities. The inertia and fixity associated with the still image seems to be his perpetual point of opposition, a tendency constantly resisted through both his remarkably wide range of subject matter and his distinctively fluid way of installing his pictures. His photography's appeal is very much to do with the overriding attraction of a seemingly uninhibited wonderment and joy before the world, a sense of cherishing moments, people and things, no matter how fragile the present might be. Unlike much insider documentary, and despite the personal tragedy connected with his own life – in 1997 his former partner, the painter Jochen Klein, died from AIDS-related pneumonia – his pictures are bereft of visible signs of pain and suffering. Tillmans avoids what he refers to as the 'mono culture' of 'photographers portraying people as victims or victimized by a social scene.'[6]

Wolfgang Tillmans
Installation, 'Aufsicht'
Deichtorhallen Hamburg, 2001

Still life, Talbot Road, 1991
C-print

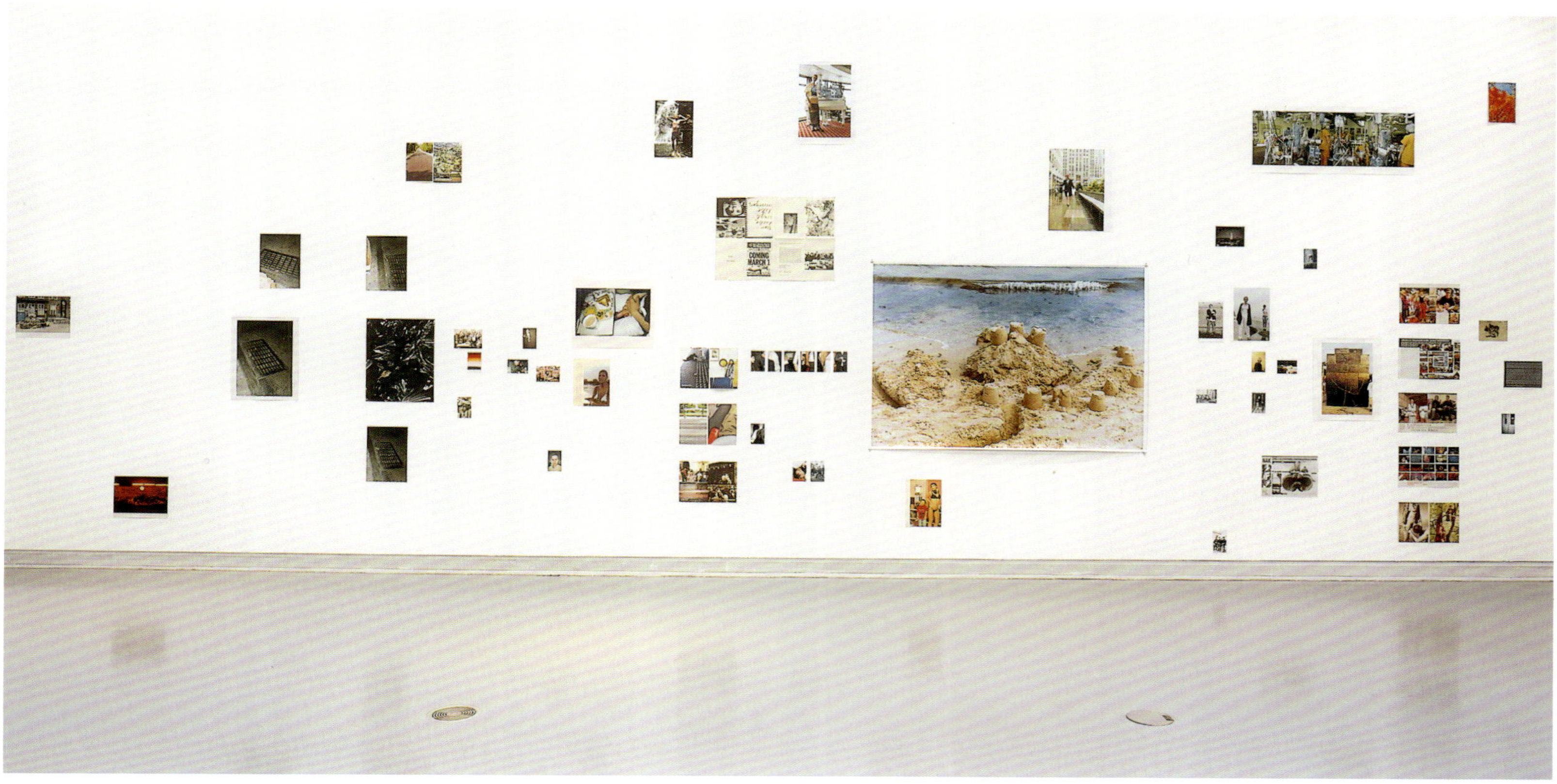

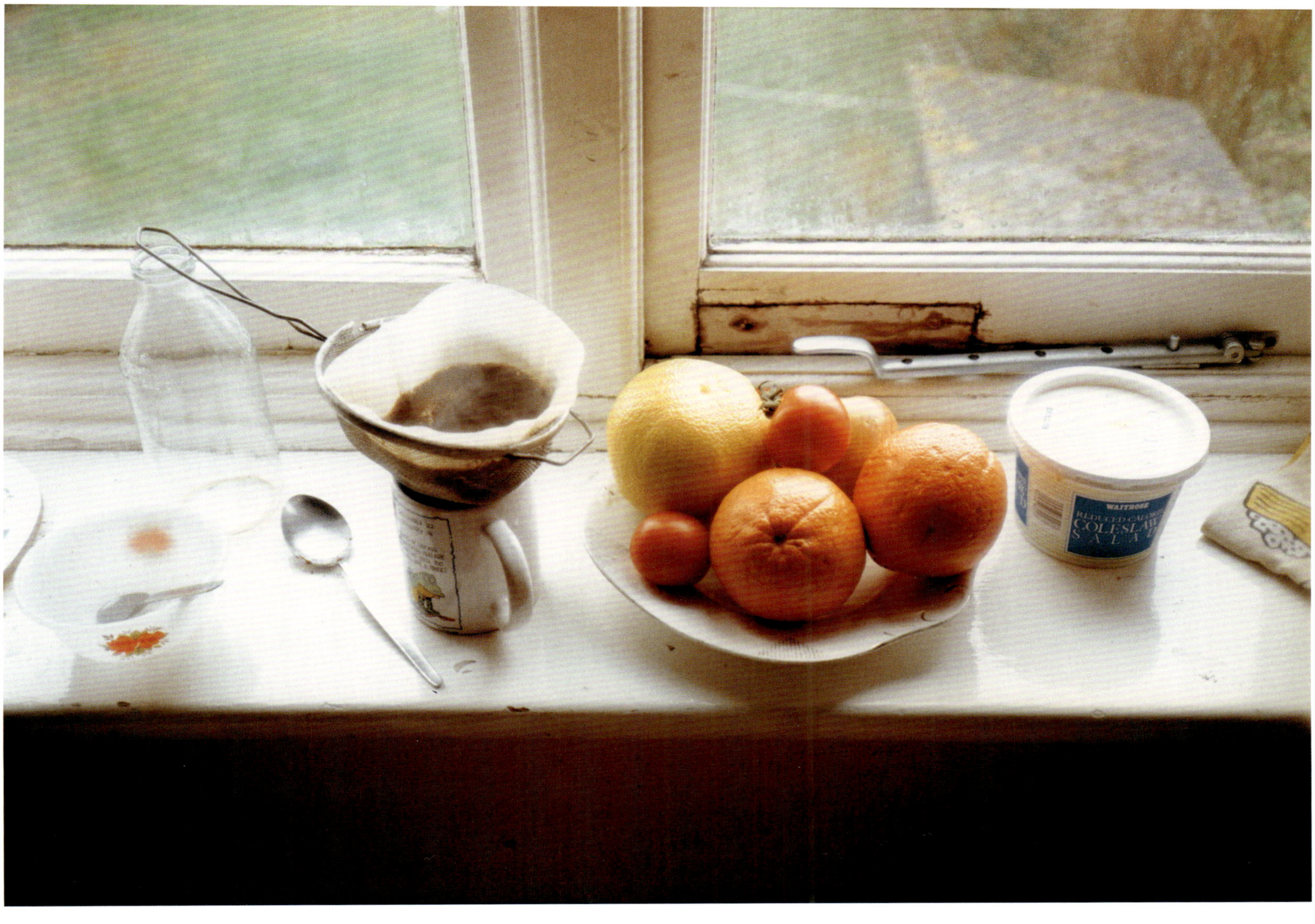
WAITROSE

Felix Gonzalez-Torres

Felix Gonzalez-Torres's poetic and varied work, often understood to be drawn from the exigencies of his lived experience, brought a distinctively subjective approach to minimal and Conceptual art forms. The idea of the art as gift is integral to his practice: the audience is allowed to take away the individual sheets from his stacks of printed paper (which he began making in 1988) or eat one of the sweets piled in corners or spread on the floor (which he began making in 1990). Such works are transitional, both shrinking as the audience consumes them or takes them away and growing as the works are replenished by owners or authorized borrowers of the work. He has said, 'This refusal to make a static form, a monolithic sculpture, in favour of a disappearing, changing, unstable and fragile form was an attempt on my part to rehearse my fears of having Ross disappear day by day right in front of my eyes.'[7] Ross, his lover, died of AIDS in 1991. The weight of the candy is often understood to be based on the specific weight of human bodies: his lover's body in *'Untitled' (Portrait of Ross in L.A.)* (1991). As art critic Adrian Searle has pointed out, the sweet can 'be understood in terms of disease and transmission, as well as devoured in terms of an immediate pleasure, a sugar rush.'[8]

The stacks of prints have included photographic images, such as a lone bird against an expanse of sky in *'Untitled'* (1992/93), its evanescence beautifully in accordance with the work's formal dispersal by viewers as they take prints home. A variant on the idea of the artwork as gift, as something to be taken away, *'Untitled' (Album)* (1992) consisting of nothing more than an empty photo album, and a Certificate of Authenticity had as its condition of purchase a requirement that the owner filled it with his or her own photographs. The work was given as an open form, inviting completion with pictures to do with other people's memories. The subjective and the personal mark all Gonzalez-Torres's work, but without the sense of closure that this can entail.

Personal and emotional imagery appeared in his most public works as billboards, a public, democratic format that extended the openness of his gallery-based work into the street. *'Untitled'* (1991) presented a light-toned black-and-white photographic image of a slightly rumpled empty bed, the indentations left by its recent occupants clearly visible on the two white pillows lying side by side. It is not an unfamiliar photograph – Nobuyoshi Araki photographed the crumpled sheets he had just slept in with Yoko in his book *Sentimental Journey* only the private one-to-one relationship of the book lends itself to the intimacy of such a photograph. Gonzales-Torres's picture was displayed as billboards in twenty-four locations around Manhattan and its surrounding boroughs in 1992, however. It brought the intimate and personal into the public sphere and, in doing so, as Amanda Cruz has pointed out, 'it raises the issue of public scrutiny of private behaviour and also functions as a memorial to those who lay there.'[9] *'Untitled' (For Jeff)* (1992) presented a black-and-white picture of the palm of an open hand on billboards originally in a project for a new museum in Caracas, shown both inside the museum and outside in a neighbourhood of local and immigrant workers. This striking and memorable image can be seen as putting the hand of production in the place of commodities for consumption, but it can also be seen to signify a caring human gesture and accords with the generosity, reciprocity and exchange that is integral to so much of his art.

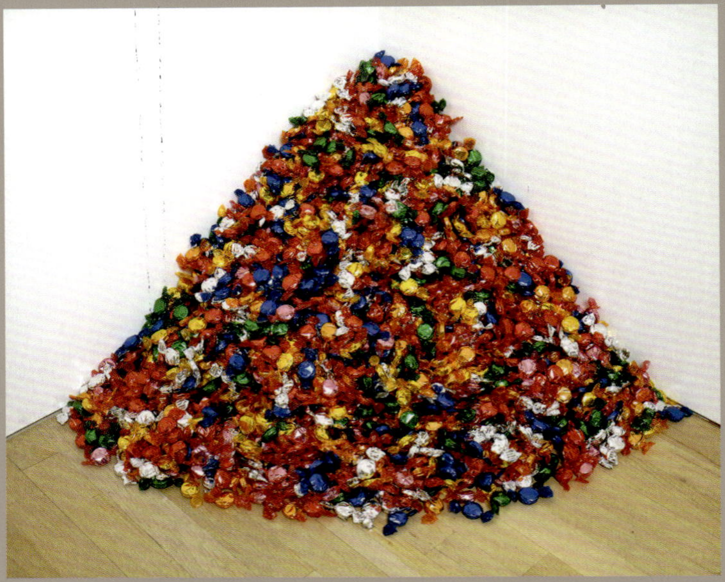

Felix Gonzales Torres
'Untitled' (Portrait of Ross in L.A.), 1991
Candies individually wrapped in multicoloured cellophane, endless supply. Overall dimensions vary with installation. Ideal weight 75 kg / 175 lb

Felix Gonzales Torres
'Untitled', 1992/1993
Print on paper, endless copies
Ideal height 20.3 cm / 8 in
122.5 × 84.4 cm / 48¼ × 33¼ in

'Untitled' (For Jeff), 1992
Billboard, dimensions vary with installation
Installation view of *Felix Gonzalez-Torres*. Magasin 3, Stockholm Konsthall, Stockholm,
15 Oct. 1992 – 15 Jan. 1993

'Untitled', 1991
Billboard, dimensions vary with installation
Installation view of *Projects 34: Felix Gonzalez-Torres.* The Museum of Modern Art, New York.
16 May – 30 June 1992
(Billboards in 24 New York City locations). Location #1: 2511 Third Ave./E. 137th St., Bronx

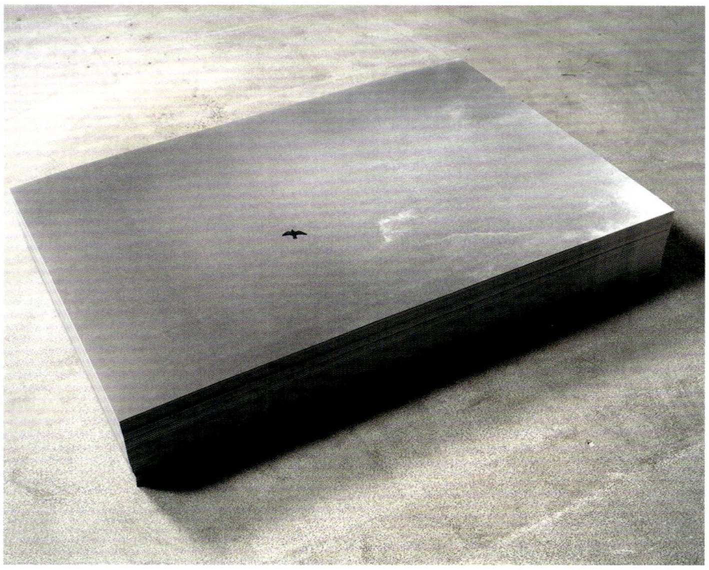

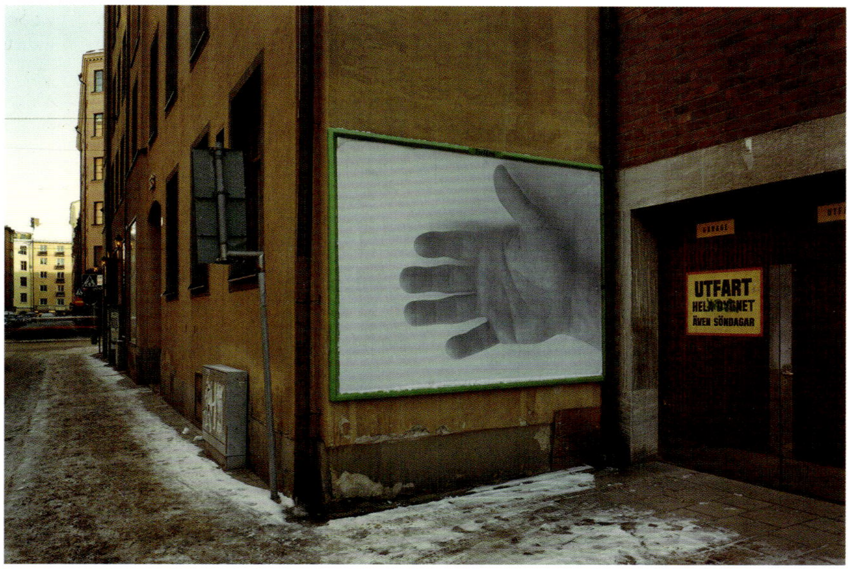

UTFART
ÄVEN SÖNDAGAR

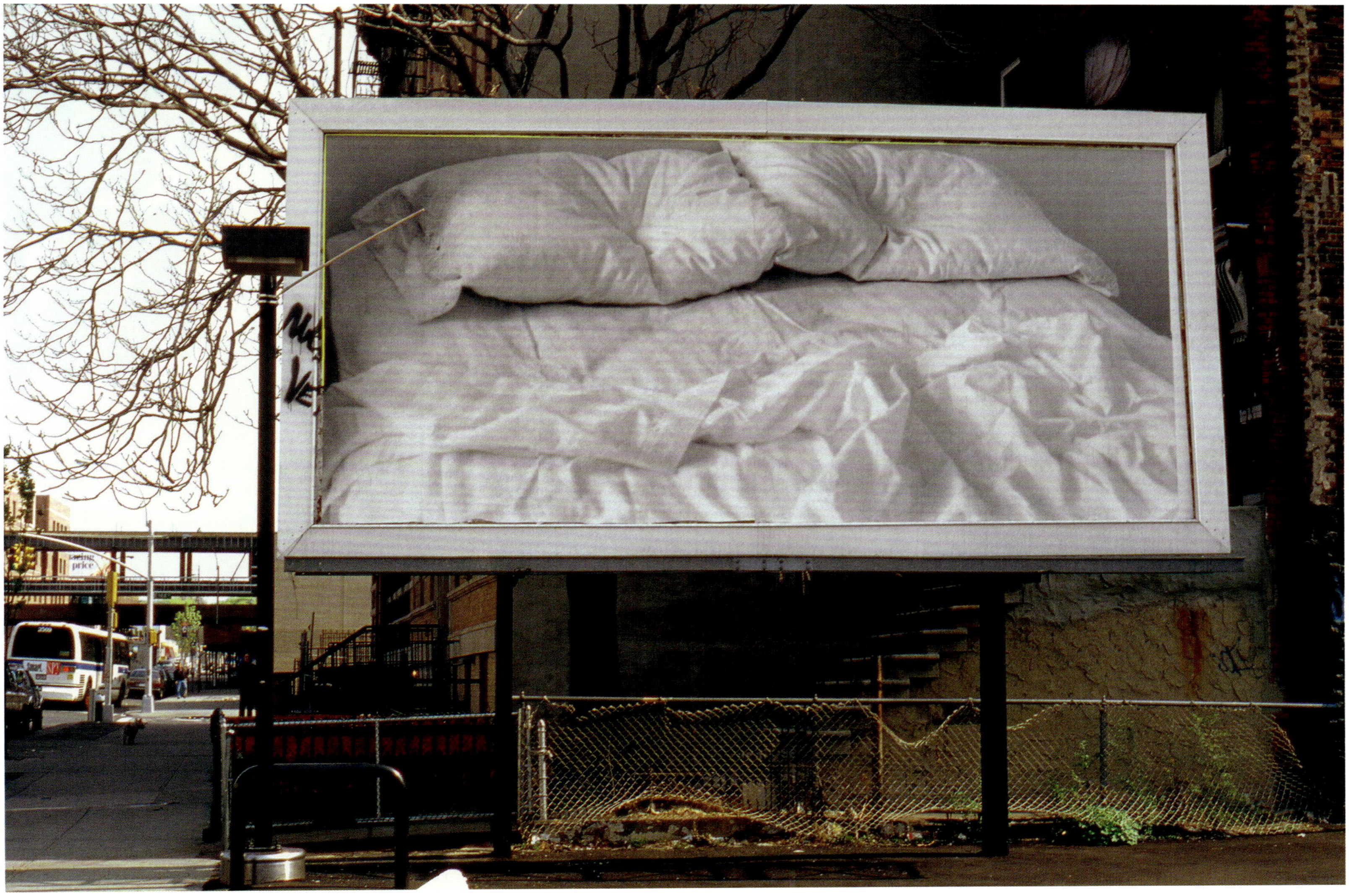

Nigel Shafran

The British photographer Nigel Shafran uses photography to closely observe his own life. His art elevates the everyday and humdrum. *Washing-Up* (2000), for example, makes a *Vanitas* out of a domestic chore, providing a daily record of the differing arrangements of dishes after they have been washed up and are left on the drainer to dry, together with an itemizing of what had been eaten during the meals. Shafran's photography returns us to a basic and simple use of the camera as an index of life, of what is close and personal. The camera becomes a means of slowing down our relation to objects. There is little drama or sensation here. Shafran has said how, 'Sometimes I see old photographs and what's interesting to me are the things on the edges that are not meant to be there – the soap packet, the bit of litter, the things that we can relate to and hold, that everydayness.'[10] Of course, his everyday is not everyone's everyday: it reflects a certain way of life, a certain measure of affluence, domestic comfort and cultural tastes and values.

In his incessant portraiture, 'Ruth on the phone' (1996–2004), he photographs his partner day after day, in the morning, at night, in bed, when she is pregnant and then later, with her new baby. The constancy is her absorption in conversations on the phone and her loss of self-consciousness in such acts of communication. The intimacy of one couple is open to close exchanges with others, and the photographer is not fully possessive; his subject is distracted and elsewhere in this recurrent record. The camera registers her responsiveness to others on the phone, intimacies and expressions to which we sense the photographer is not part. He is certainly not determining the response to his subject, absorbed as she is in whoever she is chatting with on the phone. There is an element in this extensive portrayal of domestic life that recalls the fictional photographer Antonino in Italo Calvino's 1955 story, *The Adventure of a Photographer*, with his ceaseless photography of his girlfriend that eventually drives her away from him. But Shafran is less possessive and controlling than Calvino's fictional character. A close and otherwise closed and private world is valorized quietly and beautifully through a succession of photographs, which in the case of his prolonged portraiture of Ruth registers shifts in time, ageing, changes in the domestic situation and the birth of a child. While their work is distinctive, bell hooks's eloquent account of the effect of Felix Gonzalez-Torres's work is equally apposite for Shafran's photography: 'There is always the insistence that elegance and ecstasy are to be found in daily life, in our habits of being, in the ways we regard one another and the world around us.'[11]

Nigel Shafran
16 March, 2000
1.30pm Second photograph of the day. Breakfast crumpets and tea (mine with cottage cheese and honey, Ruth's with marmite with José and Claudio who I think washed-up), from the series 'Washing-Up', 2000
C-print, 5×4 colour negative

30 January, 2000
Flowers for Lilly Donaldson's 13th Birthday. Crumpets and rosehip tea, left-over squash, pepper soup, homemade pizza, from the series 'Washing-Up', 2000
C-print, 5×4 colour negative

From the series 'Ruth on the phone', 1996–2004
C-print, 5×4 colour negative

From the series 'Ruth on the phone', 1996–2004
C-print, 5×4 colour negative

From the series 'Ruth on the phone', 1996–2004
C-print, 5×4 colour negative

From the series 'Ruth on the phone', 1996–2004
C-print, 5×4 colour negative

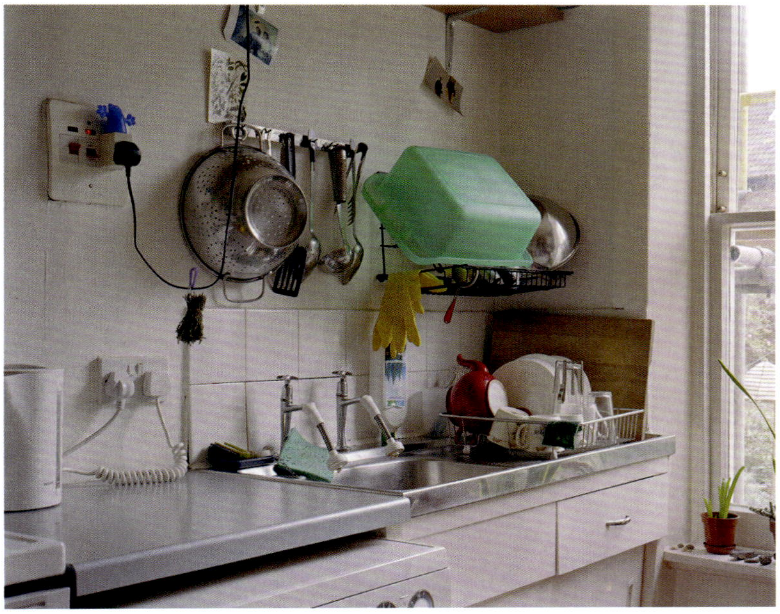

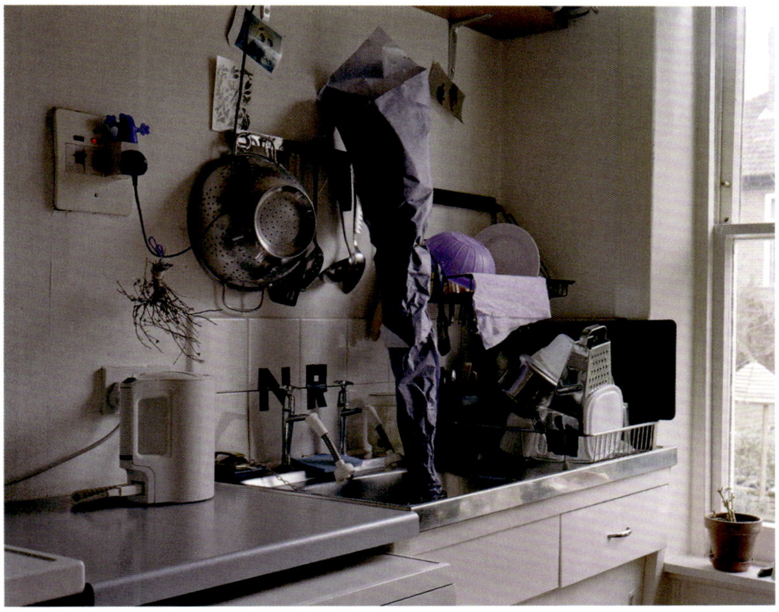

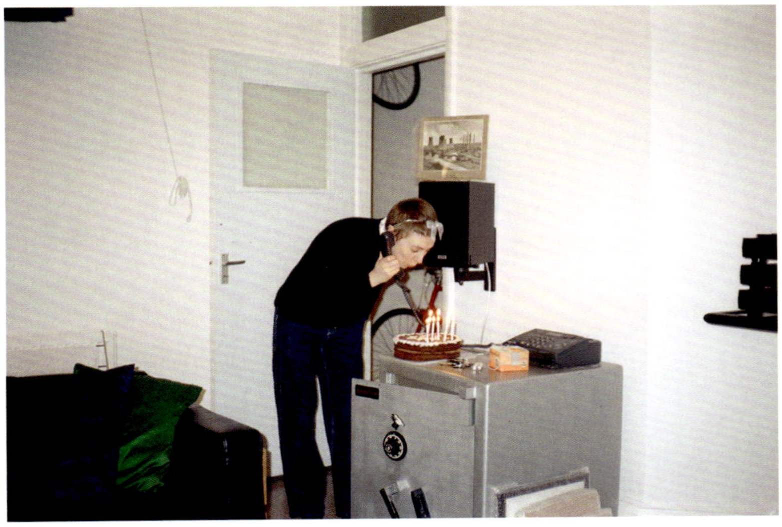

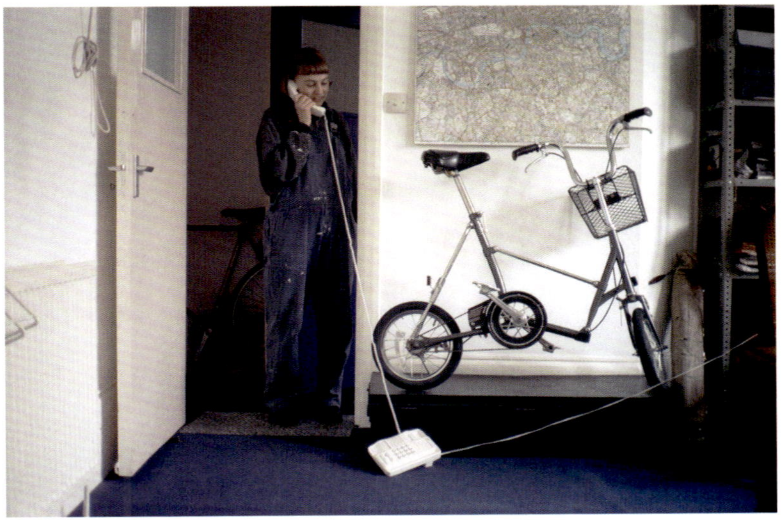

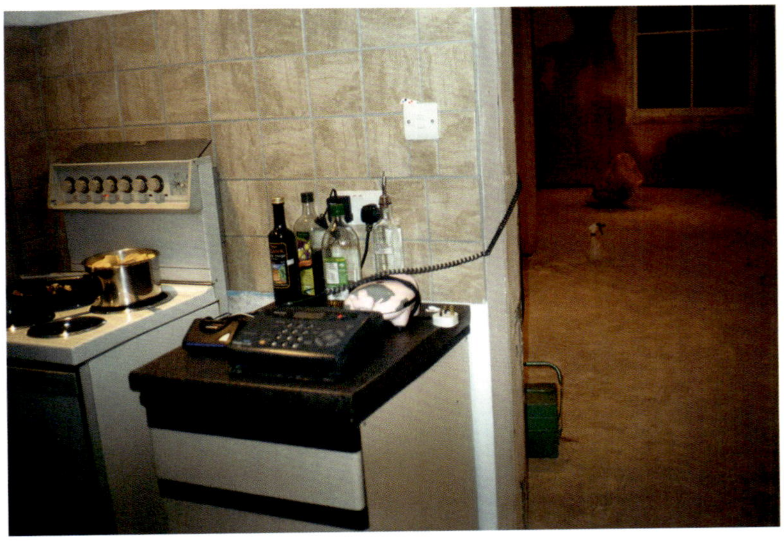

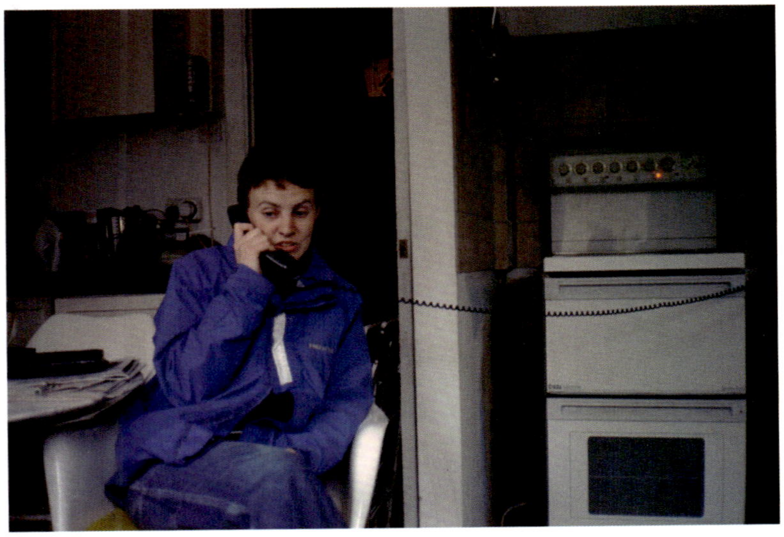

Anna Fox

Anna Fox offers a particularly rich inventive variant on the insider documentary tradition, focusing on particular social situations from her own life. In her books, *Cockroach Diary 1996–1999* (2000) and *My Mother's Cupboards and My Father's Words* (1999), she gives us frank and unsettling responses to dysfunctional family and social relationships. In the latter, meticulous photographs of objects on shelves speak about a bourgeois order and polite front, a facade that is rudely shattered by transcriptions of the abusive language directed at the women in the household by Fox's father as he succumbs to illness. The text recording his words is presented in an elegant calligraphy, an appearance of respectability that corresponds with the neatly arranged objects in the cupboards. *Cockroach Diary*, in contrast, is formally messy. The insects serve as a powerful symbol of all the anxieties, fears and conflicts that erupt among the members of a shared household, a social discord revealed through pages of the diary Fox kept at the time, which are reproduced in facsimile in the book alongside photographs of the cockroaches. The photographs are all taken with a point-and-shoot digital camera, and the low-fi snapshot informality and amateurism fits with the untidy handwritten text. Fox turns her phobia into an obsession and the book charts a strange shift in her relationship with the insects: the attachment provides a therapeutic focus and distraction as everything else seems to be falling apart around her. Fox's obsession with the cockroaches becomes a bit like her mother's fussiness over her cupboards. Such frankness and awkwardness continues to be a characteristic of much of her work. Un-refinement is integral to her pictures in *Notes from Home* (2000–3), domestic photographs made when she moved back into the rural area in which she grew up. Here the rather makeshift aesthetic stems from 'collaborations' (Fox's word) the photographer makes with different members of the household: photographs of the cakes and the Father Christmas papier-maché figure she made with her children, as well as half-eaten animals her cat brought in.

Fox's work tests the form of photography; hers is an impolite and somewhat abject response to the documentary tradition in which she draws upon painful and unseemly aspects of her own life. While her work is intimate, it is not sentimental. Throughout she comes up against the insufficiencies of the photographic medium, testing and pushing its formal potential. Felix Gonzales-Torres meanwhile tests the private in relationship to the public; his images do not seek to document a relationship but evoke it metaphorically through absence. His is a poetic work politicized by the specific context of its making and display and the democratic intentions underlying it.

Keith Arnatt

Keith Arnatt's photographs of the handwritten and scrawled messages his wife left him when he returned home after nights out, 'Notes From Jo' (1991–4), speak about a private life and intimacy of exchange through an emotional language that conveys anger, frustration and affection. These are photographs of words and concern the value of words' directness and immediacy in giving us portraits of a relationship bereft of idealization, revealing how a couple communicate, or rather how one member communicates to the other. Arnatt dares to make such things public, showing how the most seemingly trivial and unimportant aspects of his life are worthy as art. In a similar way, his routine of walking the dog at night led to a series of flash-lit pictures showing the various trails of urine left on the trunks of trees, *Dog Drawings*. The surprisingly sensuous colour pictures also reprise the artist's own earlier photo-conceptual parody of the painterly expressive gesture, in which he would photograph the formless traces left by his own piss. Repetition is important for Arnatt, allowing a certain cumulative force, ensuring and reiterating the value of the seemingly trivial and insignificant things photographed. We see the different notes, the varied scraps of paper that are used, the different coloured pens, and through them the different states of the couple's relationship.

As with Anna Fox's photography, which was inspired by Arnatt's 'Notes from Jo', we get the sense of an inclusive, detailed referencing of a life in a way that is both abrasive and beautiful. Moods and tone vary. There is anger and a strong sense of Arnatt's unreliability, of his wife's need to explain things such as how to use the microwave, reminders to feed their cats and dogs, annoyance – YOU BASTARD! YOU ATE THE LAST OF MY CRACKERS! – but there are other messages that are more inviting and suggestive: IN BED BUT AWAKE! As much as there is comedy here, there is also pathos. Photography gives the throwaway scraps value and importance and makes them permanent and beautiful. The images speak about a relationship through its everyday banalities. The messages pictured have nothing at all to do with the craft or polished use of language; they represent something more immediate, celebrating a basic and direct act of communication between two people, raw, unrefined, but no less moving. Such photography draws on lived experience. It remains intimate and close, and is romantic, expressive and often experimental.

Anna Fox
From the book *My Mother's Cupboards and My Father's Words*,
Shoreditch Biennale, London, 1999
10 × 7 cm / 4 × 2¾ in, 64pp
Paperback, 14 colour illustrations

She
should be
fried
in hot oil

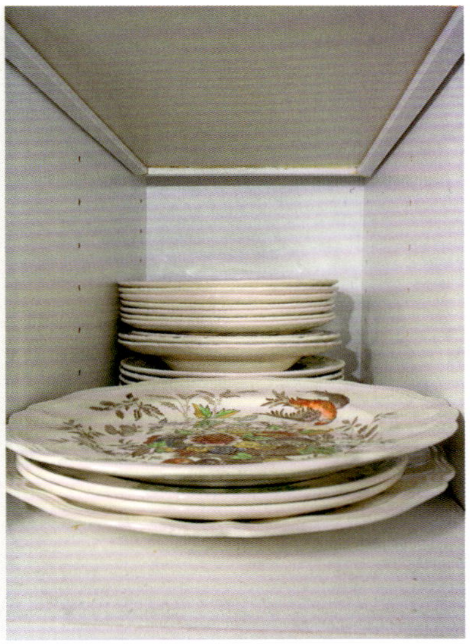

They
shouldn't be
allowed to
breath the same air
as me

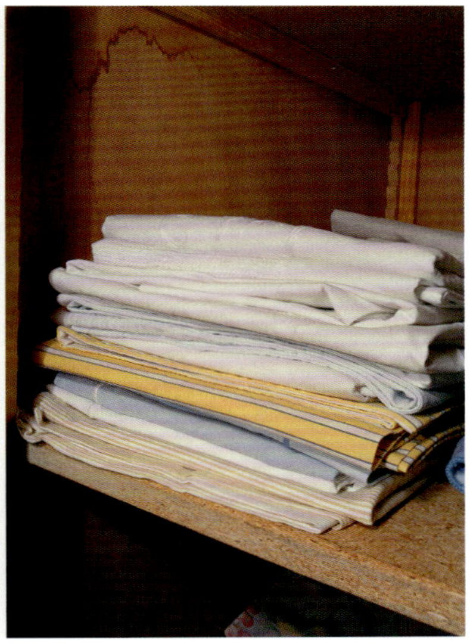

You toad.
Pity I got rid
of the well:
you could have
gone down there
and been
cemented over

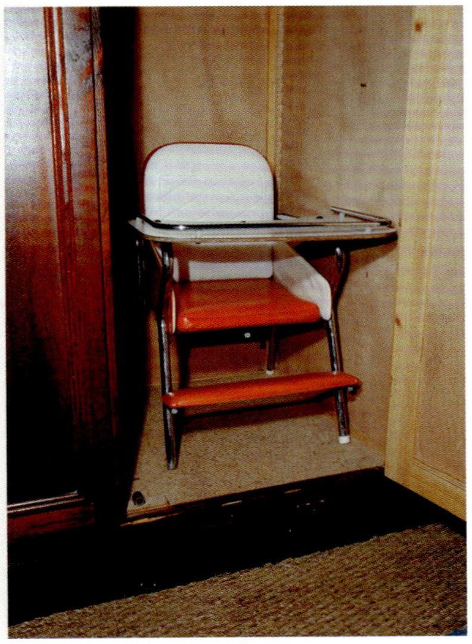

She's rattling again.
Can you stop
your bloody
fucking rattling

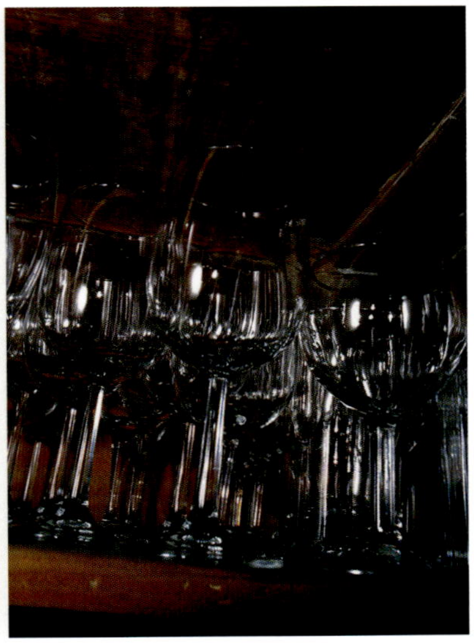

She's
washed so many
dishes her hands
have blown
up like bears
claws

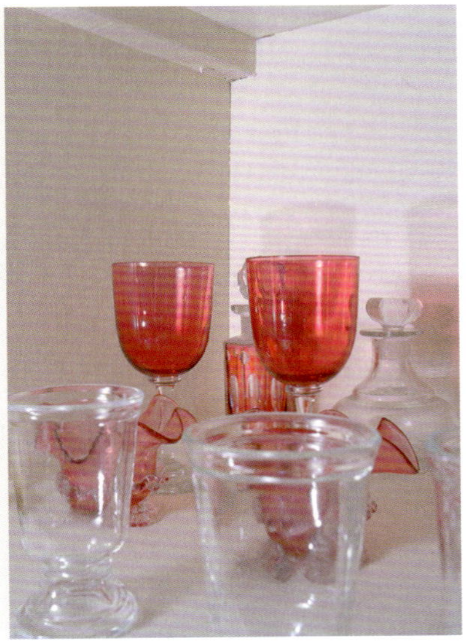

Beastly bitches
Filthy Cows

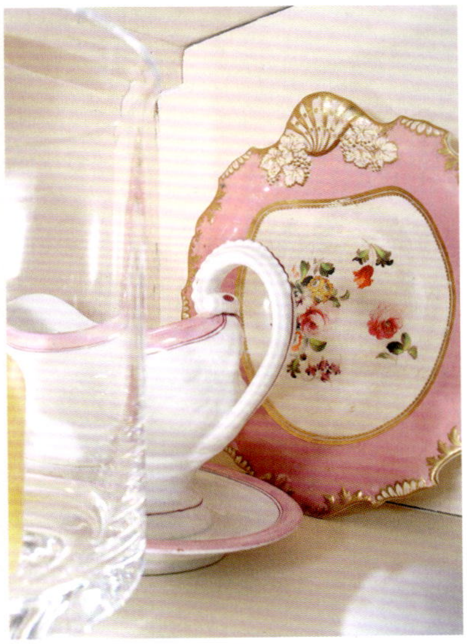

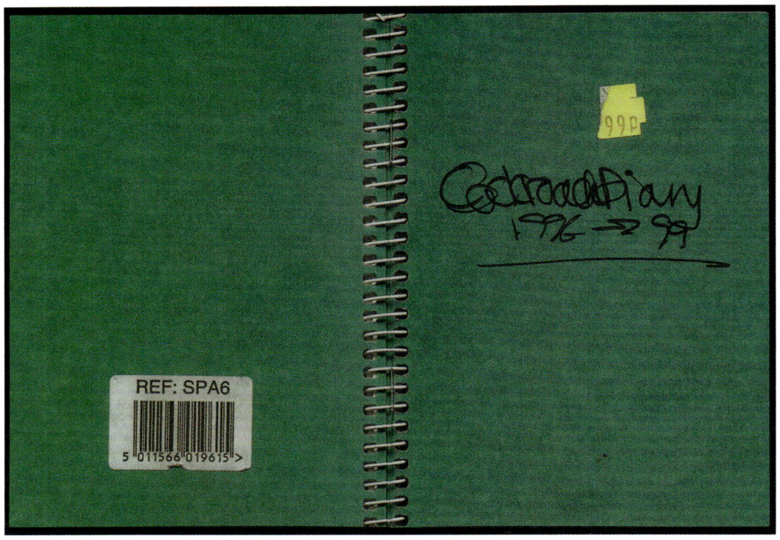

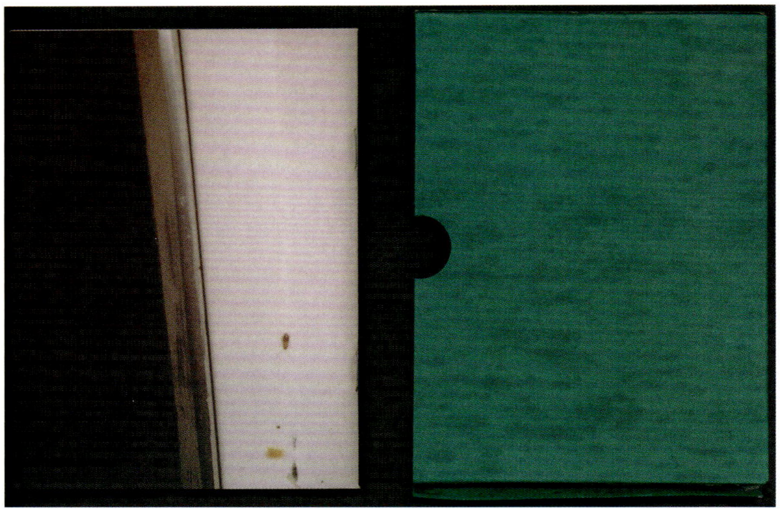

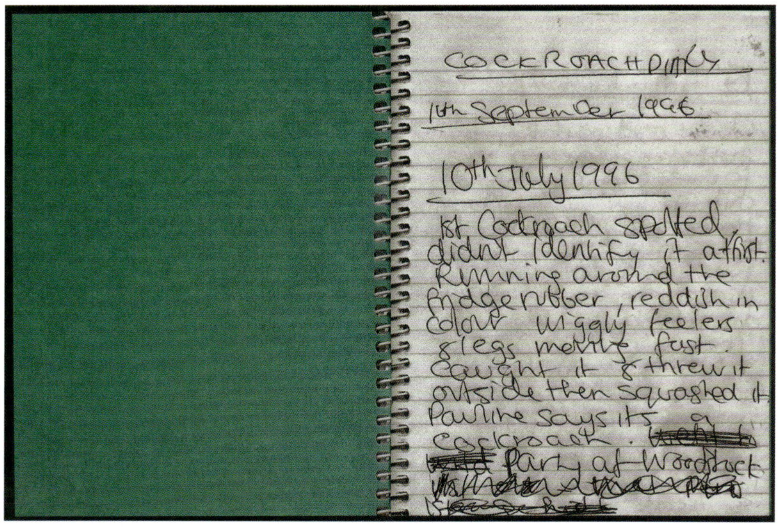

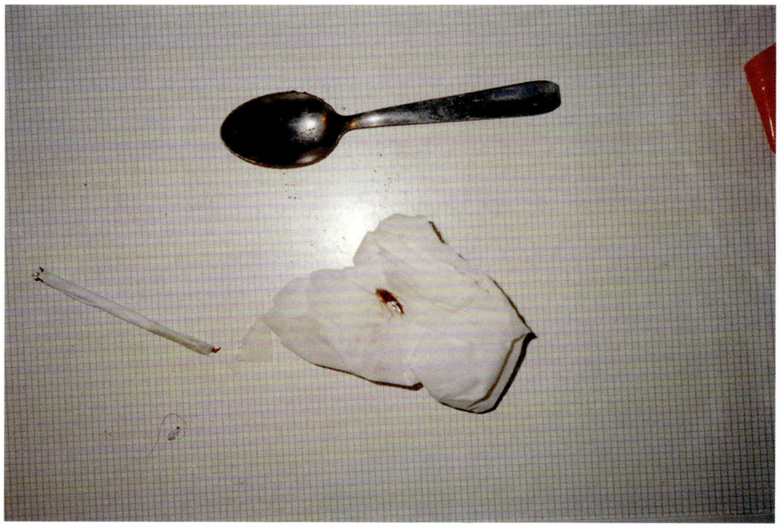

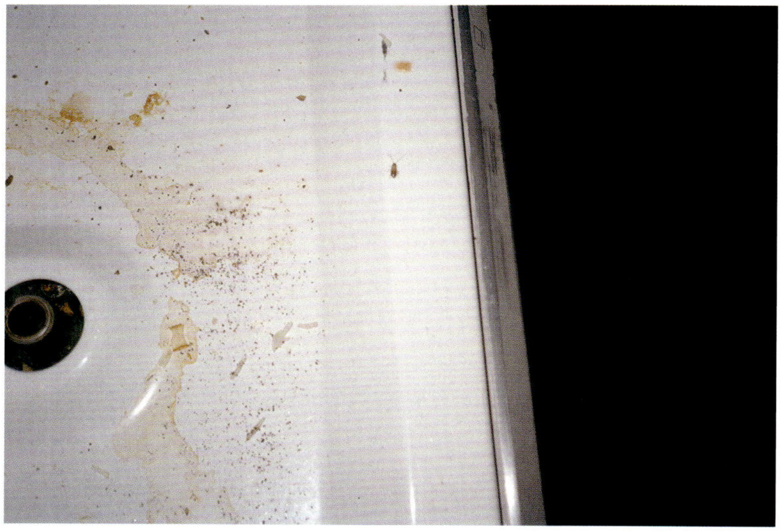

Anna Fox
From the book *Cockroach Diary*
Shoreditch Biennale, London, 2000
15.2 × 10.2 cm / 6 × 4 in
Paperback, 64 pp
14 full-colour plates and 14 texts

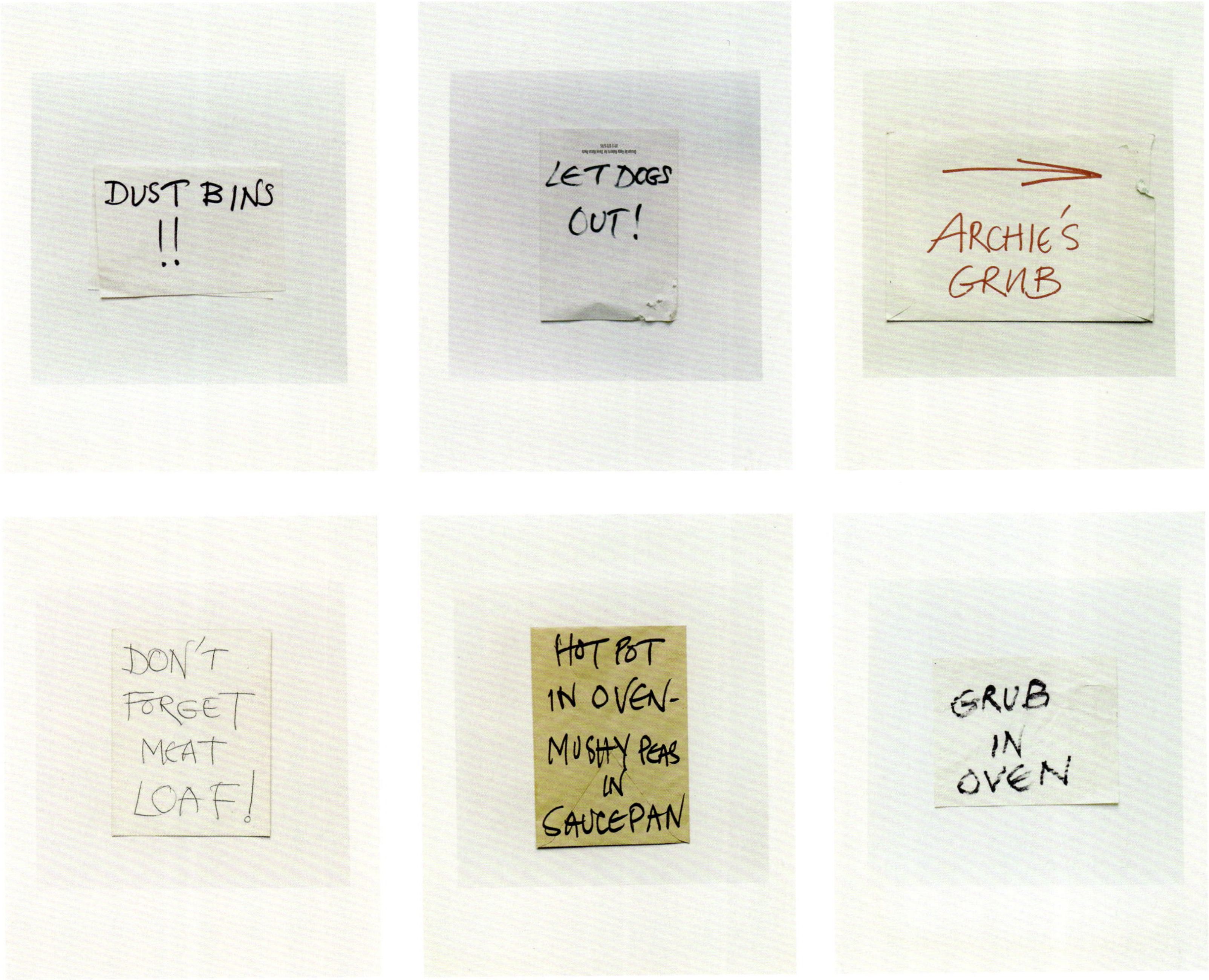

Keith Arnatt
From the series 'Notes from Jo', 1991–4
Colour photographs each
16.5 × 16.5 cm / 6½ × 6½ in

Jo Spence

A combative use of self is powerfully shown through the work of Jo Spence. Describing herself as an educational photographer rather than an artist, photography was important because it was a medium that, as she saw it, 'negates elitism.'[12] Her use of photography and performance offered a comic and angry exposé of the feelings and struggles that marked her experiences as a woman from a working-class background and, following her diagnosis with cancer in 1982, a reflection on the fears and prejudices associated with such illness.

Exhibiting in 1979 at London's Hayward Gallery, in 'Beyond the Family Album,' Spence investigated her personal history, class consciousness and sexuality by displaying pictures from her own family archive accompanied with texts that informed us of what was not told in these images: they held no record of her appalling health, the pointless years of being shunted around schools where she was eventually 'crushed into the mould of typist,' her broken marriage and the havoc the break-up caused her, all the hard work she did for innumerable employers; in short, as she puts it, 'no indication at all of the wider social, economic and political histories of our disgusting class-divided society.'[13] In *Colonization* (1981), part of the series 'Remodelling Photo History,' made collaboratively with Terry Dennett, Spence is photographed standing naked on the doorstep of a working-class home, broom in hand, a rug wrapped round her lower body, breasts exposed and a string of beads around her neck. She presents herself to camera like a species and type, highlighting the primitivizing and anthropological aspect of social documentary. Comic and direct, such photographs are a succinct response to the documentary photographic tradition's fascination with working-class lives.

Spence's later work, notably in 'Phototherapy' and 'On Health,' challenged what is acceptable in photographic depictions of the human body, often involving a blunt and confrontational display of her ageing and scarred body. Taking control of her own representation, Spence refused to portray herself as a victim. In her *Narratives of Dis-ease* (1990), she re-enacted some of her feelings and experiences since being diagnosed and treated for breast cancer. Working back through her mother's illness and death from the same disease, Spence's photography explored ways in which she could take charge of her own illness, claiming agency rather than becoming a passive subject who believes she has no control over what happens or what is done to her. In one of her photographs taken for her exhibition 'A Picture of Health?' (1982–5), she depicts herself naked to the waist and wearing a motorbike helmet, which, as Jessica Evans has pointed out, 'provides a protective shield against those who seek to wound her.' The photograph 'oscillates between a mixture of defiance and damage,' establishing 'a contrast between a shielded "hard" head and a damaged "soft" body.'[14]

Jo Spence
Colonization, 1981
Gelatin silver print
120.3 × 87 cm / 47⅜ × 34¼ in

Picture of Health? / Crisis Project, 1982, (in collaboration with Terry Dennett)
Black and white photograph
69.6 × 49.7 cm / 27⅜ × 19½ in

Untitled (Portrait), c. 1979, from the series 'Beyond the Family Album' (in collaboration with Terry Dennett and Ed Barber)
As illustrated in the book *Putting Myself in the Picture*, Camden Press, London, 1986
Printed text and photograph
23 × 17 cm / 9 × 17⅝ in

Jo Spence as a Sex Object, 1979 from the series 'Beyond the Family Album'
Black and white photographic contact sheets, as illustrated in the book Jo *Spence, Putting Myself in the Picture*, Camden Press, London, 1986
Printed text and photograph
23 × 17 cm / 9 × 17⅝ in

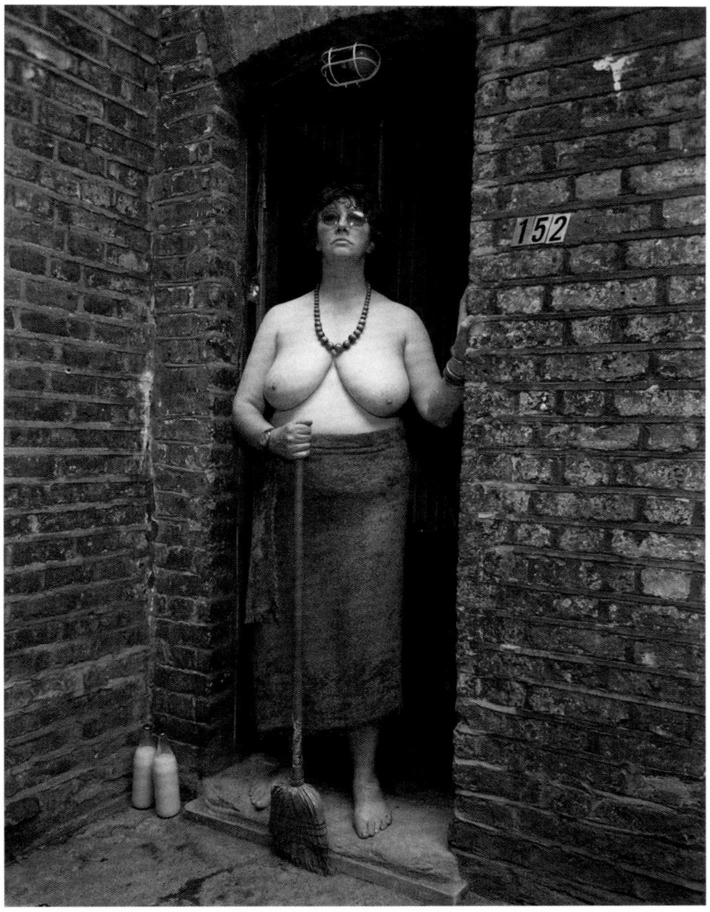

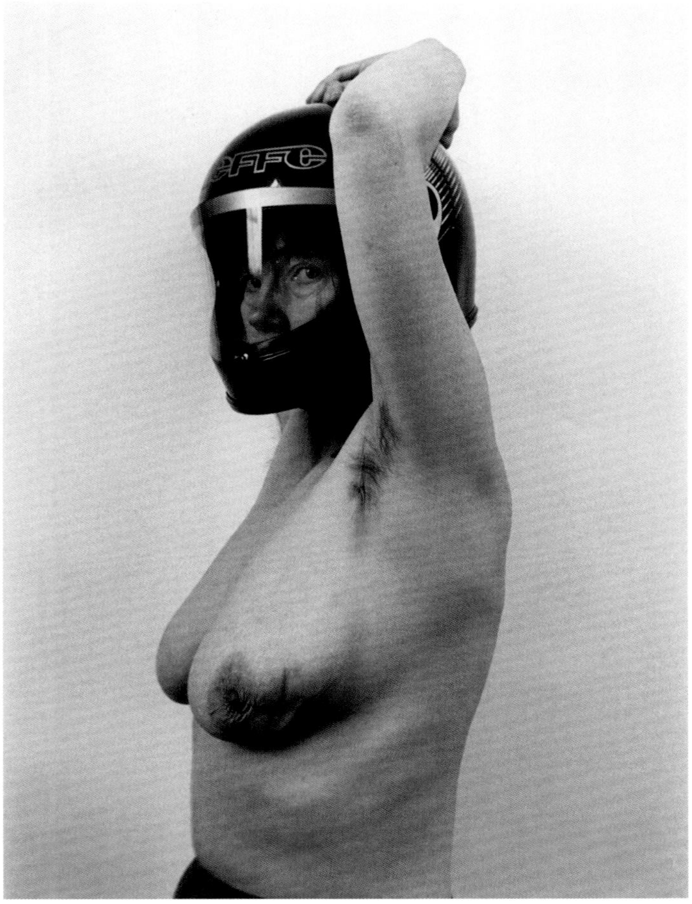

THESE three portraits were all taken for totally different reasons.

1 This was taken by my boyfriend when we were just getting to know each other. I was making an effort to look 'feminine' at the time, curling my hair, wearing earrings, bright colours. I felt good.

I felt poised when it was taken, trying at the same time to look pensive yet affectionate.

It was taken with a large format camera, using the Zone System of exposure control in order to lose skin detail and render the surface white and smooth, yet still retain good tonal detail and deep blacks elsewhere.
(*Terry Dennett/Photography Workshop*)

2 I asked the photographer to take this for me. He used a large, diffused light source – to simulate north light. I wanted to look serious and unfussy. I would be quite happy if this were the only picture to represent me historically, even though it gives very little clue beyond the signs present on the face, emphasized through the use of a particular visual rhetoric.
(*Ed Barber/photographer*)

3 This medical record of me was made five days after I had blown myself up with the gas stove whilst cooking dinner. Wearing my glasses had saved my eyes from damage, but my face was badly singed, my front hair burnt off and my eyebrows mostly missing.

The picture was taken with flat, bounced, lighting in order to record detail. I tried to be devoid of an emotive (pathetic) expression, but wanted to clearly register my shocked condition.
(*Terry Dennett*)

Each of these three pictures has its own field of meanings. For instance they could be read as expressions of my 'womanliness', or my 'intelligence', or my 'stupidity'. I would hardly give photograph 3 to a lover as a keepsake. I could be seen as in control of the situation, or not. What social class am I from in these various pictures? How does this affect the meanings if you don't know anything about me? What value judgements will you start making because I'm not very pretty, or wear these sort of glasses, or don't show my tits? Suppose you had only seen one of them?

In our culture the face is supposedly the repository of our character or our personality. It is used to represent us, and photographed constantly. Quite clearly *how* it is photographed and by whom is a matter for some concern. Quite clearly also *it cannot possibly represent us*, even though we are taught that it can. We must learn to see beyond ourselves and the stereotypes offered, to understand the invisible class and power relationships into which we are structured from birth.

We must begin to question photographs, asking not only what we think they show us (and how much of what we think we perceive is in fact based on the particular type of visual rhetoric worked upon the sitter), but also what they don't (can't?) show us.

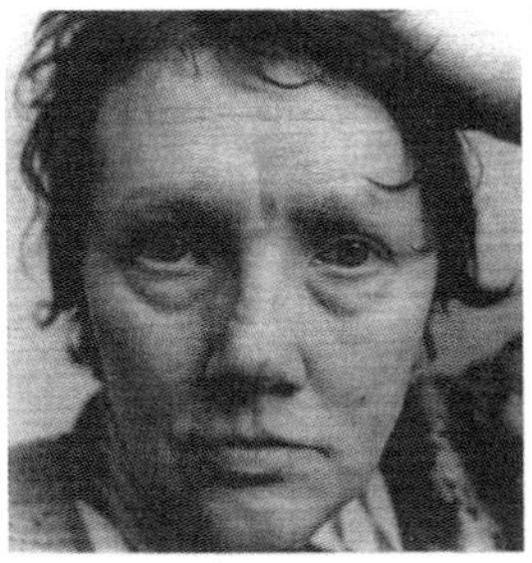
3

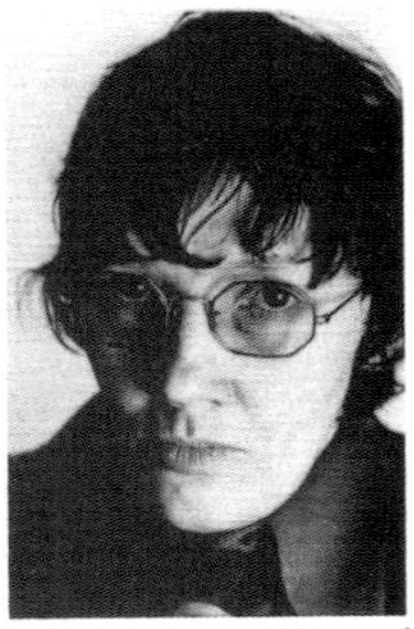
2

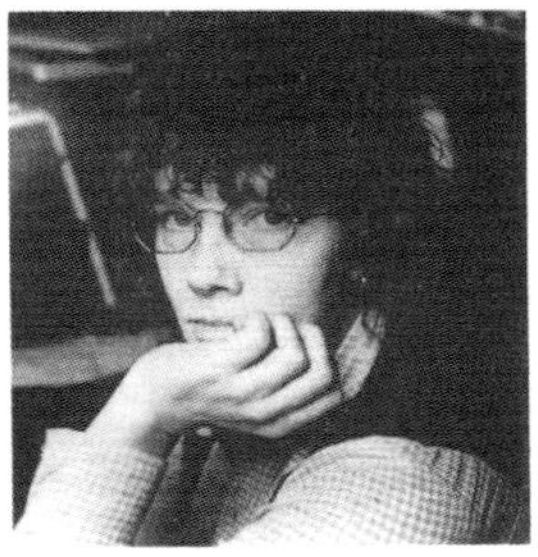
1

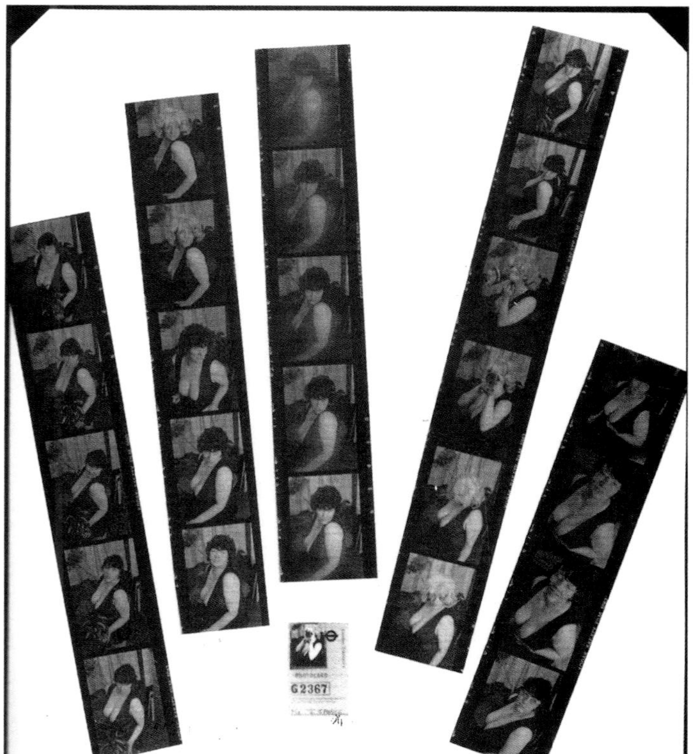

ALLOWING myself to concentrate on the playing out of various imuges for the camera gave me an immense amount of information about myself. Apart from the fun we had from this, I began to conceive of myself as a set of signals or signs, all of which 'meant' something to the viewer (including myself), which I could begin to control more by emphasizing or de-emphasizing as I wished. When these signs (of me) had been transferred into photographs the 'meanings' changed depending on the context in which they were used.
(*Terry Dennett/Photography Workshop*)

Francesca Woodman

A prodigy, Francesca Woodman produced a distinctive body of work before committing suicide in 1981 at the age of twenty-three. Her work has been described as 'obsessively autobiographical', but it reveals no profound truths about the artist.[15] The daughter of artists, she started photographing at the age of thirteen and continued until her twenty-second year. Her archive consists of some eight hundred works, all made between 1972 and 1980. In January 1981 she published her first book, *Some Disordered Interior Geometries*, just a few weeks before she killed herself. During her short life she participated in a number of exhibitions in alternative spaces in New York and Rome, but it was not until 1986, five years after her death, that she had her first solo show, through an exhibition co-organized by the Wellesley College Museum and the Hunter College of Art Gallery. Catalogue essays by Rosalind Krauss and Abigail Solomon-Godeau provided the first sustained assessment of Woodman's work, which since then has invited an extensive and growing body of critical writing.

Between 1975 and 1979, Woodman studied at Rhode Island School of Design and used the framework of student assignments to explore an embodied subject's transformation into a photographic image. Many of her self-portraits explore the tensions between her embodied feminine presence and the disembodiment of producing herself as a two-dimensional picture. In a series of photographs from one student assignment, 'Space²' (1975–6), Woodman challenges the framing structures of the museum by photographing her body in various positions in relationship to a glass and wood display case. In one picture she asserts the femininity of her body by pressing her breasts up against the glass. In another she plays dead, curling her body up on a lower shelf of a glass museum case below a stuffed fox, thus linking taxidermy, the museum display case and the camera as embalming processes. She performs femininity as a stylized submission: the sexuality of her body is made evident but is not acquiescent; there is an 'inner force' (her words) built through the compilation of self-portraits.[16]

In *Untitled* (1976), Woodman presents her face as a mask in the reproduced form of the photographic portrait, as paper prints that are held by three naked women over their own faces, suggesting that Woodman disappears and is interchangeable with other models. The young bodies are present in the photograph in the way the photographic portraits as thin sheets of paper are not. A fourth portrait print is pinned to the wall, in a further iteration of its identity as paper. Woodman does not show herself, and presents the photographic portrait as insufficient: light reflected on the paper portraits shows their surface qualities, in contrast to the sexual and physical presence of the three women's bodies in the photograph. It is this tension between photography and the feminine body that is explored throughout Woodman's work.

Woodman also produced a series of photographs set in a delapidated and derelict house, with paint peeling and plaster falling. In one striking picture, from her 'Space²' series, she is partially hidden by the curl of torn wallpaper: the photograph is beautifully ambiguous, is she emerging from the house or being reduced to the decorative surface of wallpaper? In a group of pictures made in a basement in Rome, her naked body is identified with the scabrous walls and corners against which she is compressed. Covering her body with dirt is suggestive of defilement, but also concerns the woman's body being treated as a photographic surface. At the same time Woodman's hands press against the wall, suggesting she is resisting being merged into it. In one of a series of pictures in which she is depicted moving a mirror, *Self-Deceit #4* (1977–8), she uses it to mask and hide her face. In relationship to women, mirrors are a familiar attribute of vanity and narcissism. Woodman upsets this relationship. The mirror reflects nothing in her picture; it opens a blank void that challenges and refutes the viewer's and the camera's gaze. As Claire Raymond has argued, the camera seeks to fix, measure and contain, while Woodman's performances are a challenge and affront to such a device. Her work also slips out of the self-portrait genre: the blurring of her form, the cropping of her head out of the picture, the play with light or the way she stages containment and fetishism in posing behind and within museum cases, the studio and a dilapidated house all explore her body as a site of resistance to framing, a refusal, as Woodman put it, to be 'flattened to fit paper'.[17]

Francesca Woodman
Self-Deceit #4 (Roma), 1977–8
Gelatin silver print
9.2 × 8.9 cm / 3⅝ × 3½ in

Untitled, Providence Rhode Island, 1976
Gelatin silver print
13.3 × 13.5 cm / 5¼ × 5¼ in

Untitled Rome, 1977–8
Gelatin silver print
14.3 × 12.7 cm / 5⅝ × 5 in

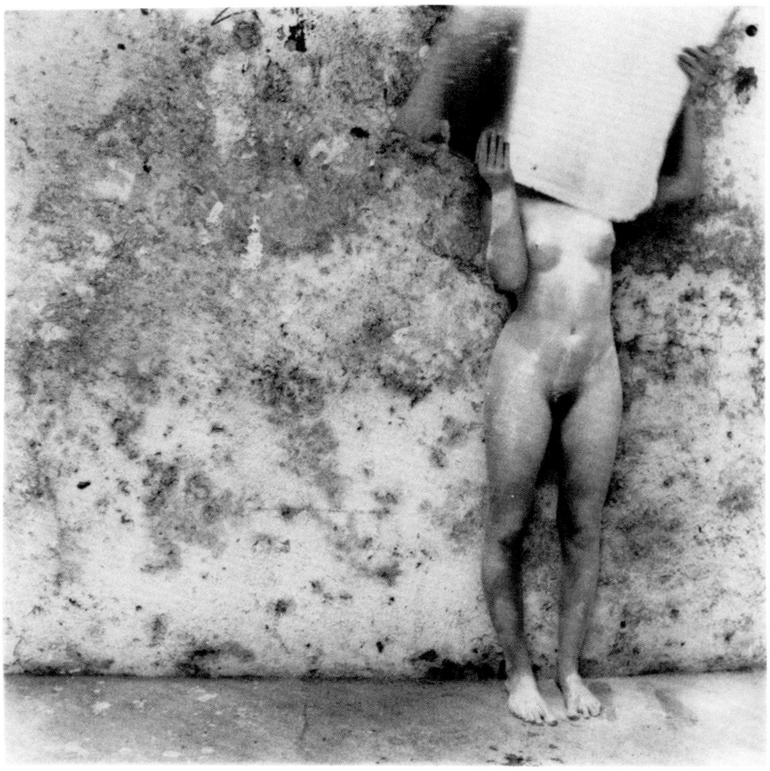
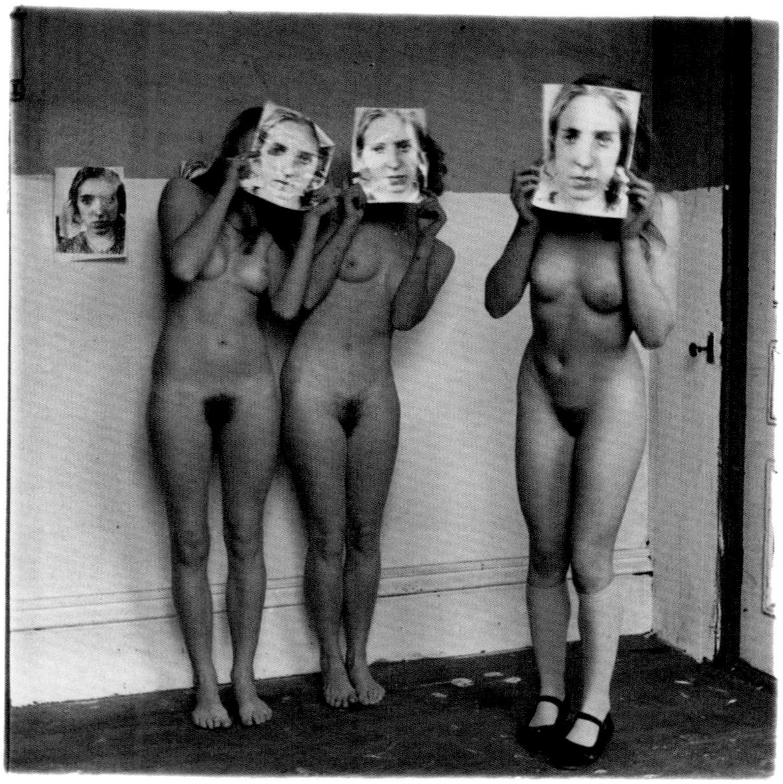
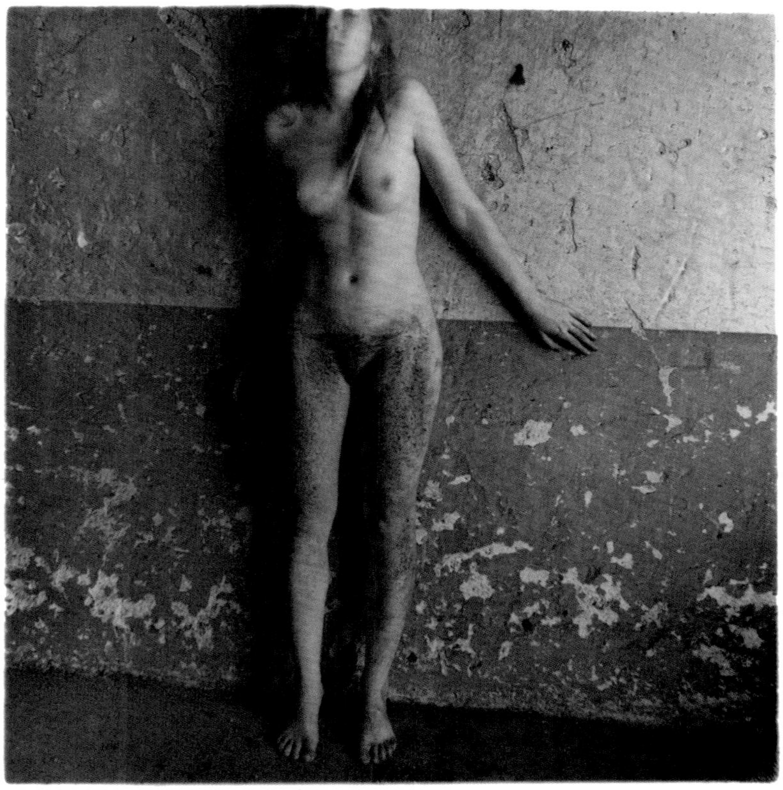

Peter Finnemore

Peter Finnemore's photographs and videos are made in response to his home in the Welsh-speaking heartland of rural west Wales, Gwendraeth House, where his family have lived for five generations. His pictures entail rich and poetic responses to his inheritance and make subtle and shifting commentaries on identity and belonging through a web of symbols that are at once local and more universal. His use of video extends the concerns of his photography, establishing an often comic and bathetic theatre for which the family garden becomes the stage.

Finnemore's 2000 photograph, *My Head is My Only Home*, signals the introspective turn of his practice: it is the world of imagination and play inside his head that will be the source of his photography. Here, the artist stands with his head topped by a little handmade wooden house in a field of sunflowers. This was a key image from his first book, *Gwendraeth House*. The sunflowers are important, signifying a radiant centre linked up with other central and centred forms, in particular the little house. Such images are for Finnemore 'about the search for homes, a central root point of security.'[18]

In recent videos and photographs the shed provides the metaphor of home and belonging. Adorned in camouflage, the figure of the artist alludes to both the threat of a rogue militiaman and to the Green Man, symbolizing rebirth, the cycle of growth of spring each year and an attachment to the land. In *Koan Exercises*, the artist is shown in army fatigues holding onto the roof of his camouflaged shed, implying a desperate measure to hide against some unspecified, outside threat. In a variation of military camouflage, one video shows Finnemore moving around his garden on a bright sunny day, holding a mirror that keeps reflecting sunlight back to a stationary camera and the viewer. Finnemore is both hidden by the light and the source of illumination, someone who challenges our gaze by shining light back to the camera, in a work that has a relationship to Francesca Woodman's play with the mirror, and her resistance to fixity. Finnemore's video has an element of metaphysics. As light bearer and light giver, the artist here can be seen as a divine mystic, but he is also a more mischievous force, with the reflected light cancelling out the image as it hits the camera. What might be seen as transcendence is also a blinding challenge to our vision and gaze. Place and belonging are an integral motivation for Finnemore's art. His work explores both a sense of rootedness and attachment to place and feelings of uncertainty and threat arising from his country's continued marginalization within the United Kingdom.

Gwendraeth House has continued to provide the focus for Finnemore's work. More recently, he has turned inside, from bright light to dark, to produce enigmatic and spare photographs of the spaces of the family home, suggestive of hidden realms with closed doors and dark passageways. Such photographs of the home trace mournful and memorial notes, tempered by occasional animating decorative details such as the floral patterning of carpets or ornamental birds. Here the photograph is charged and imbued with qualities that take us beyond the literal register and document of interior space; a certain Gothicism becomes pervasive, as does a strange sense of attenuated time, of stillness, as we become conscious of the placement and arrangement of objects in time and of the value objects and places have accrued over time.

Peter Finnemore
Koan Exercises, 2004
Lambda print
145 × 94 cm / 57 × 37 in

Threshold, 2010
Fine art HDR archival pigment print
101 × 70 cm / 39¾ × 27½ in

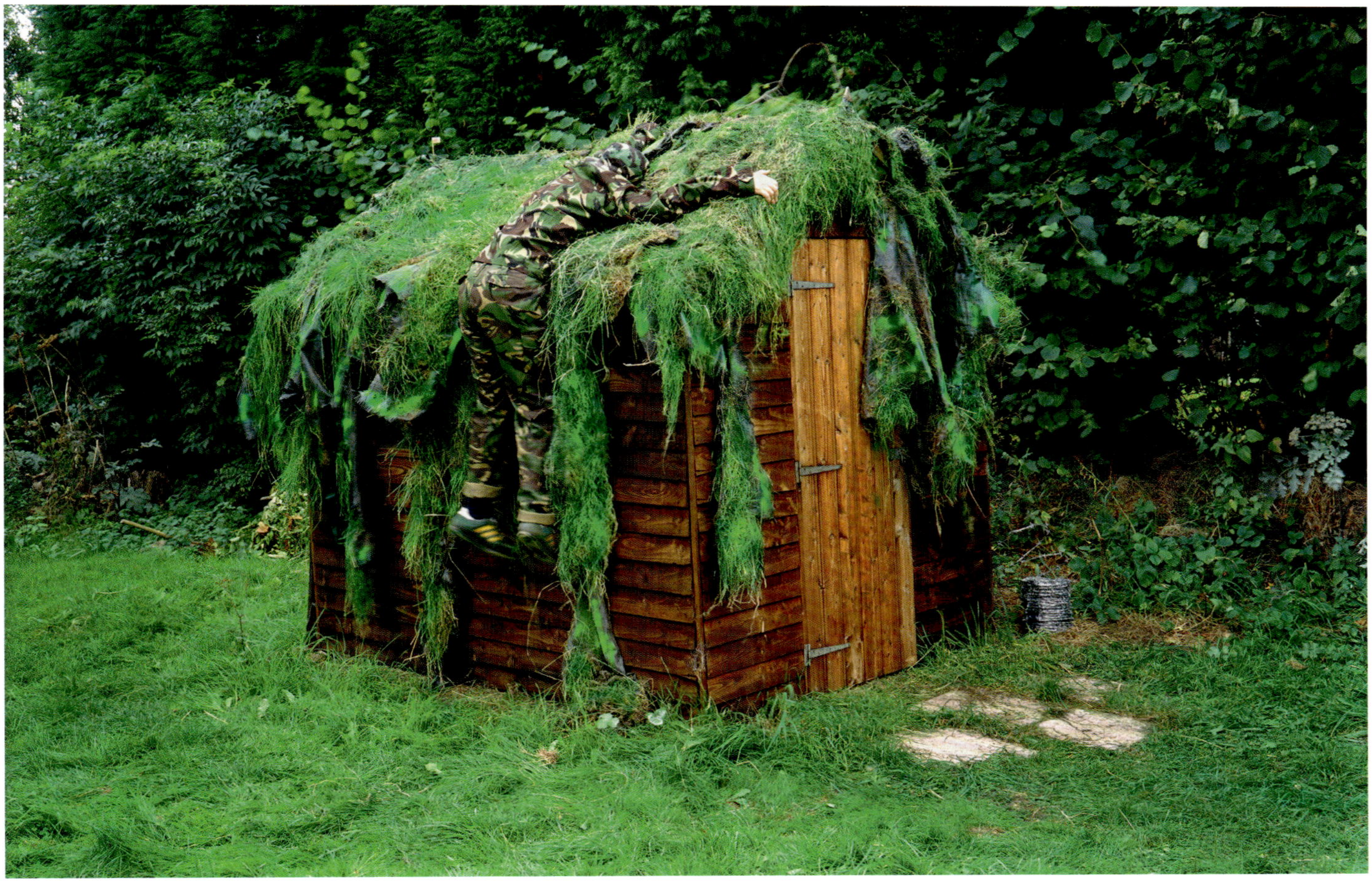

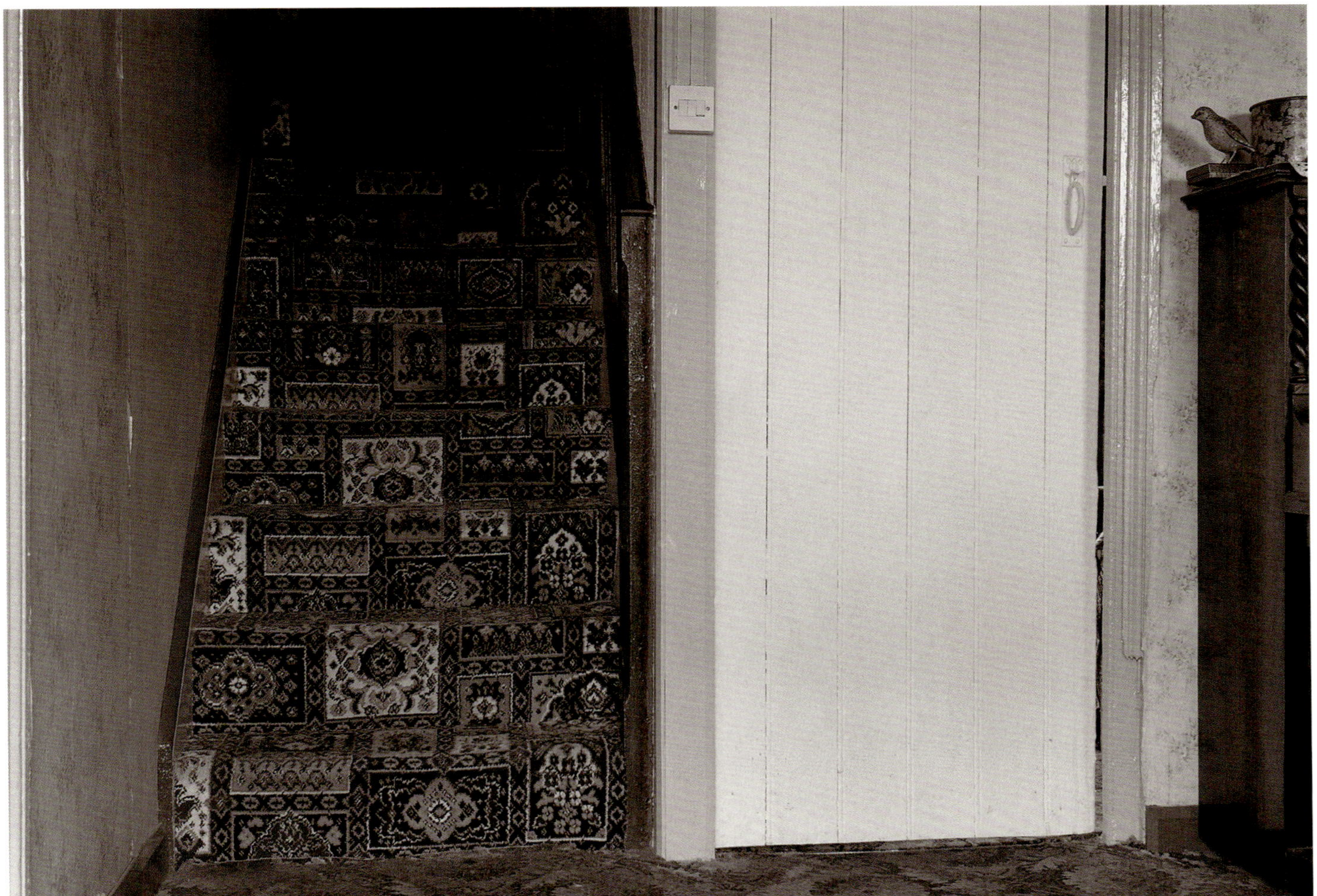

Yasumasa Morimura

The Japanese artist Yasumasa Morimura in many ways dismantles the tradition of self-portraiture. He shows us his face again and again, but it is peculiarly changeable. Make-up and digital cosmetics enable him to pose as figures from the Western history of art, pop celebrities and pin-ups, and more recently as iconic figures and events from twentieth-century history, including photographs from the Vietnam War and portraits of Che Guevara and Adolf Hitler, the latter via Charlie Chaplin's filmic portrayal of the dictator.

Morimura's artistic education in Japanese schools promoted the history of Western art and one can see his work as mirroring the impact of the global hegemony of Western culture on his own country. Morimura's photography is about desire and difference; the mimicry he enacts draws attention to the relationships between the West and Asia. As a Japanese man made-up and photographed to look like one of Van Gogh's famous self-portraits with a bandaged ear, he mimes an expressive icon of Western painting in which the painting is valued as an index of the artist's tortured self. Morimura's crafted impersonation of such paintings requires an abnegation of authorship. Morimura's theatrical mimesis undermines authorship as a measure of meaning and value, especially in the international art market. It also highlights the influence of Japanese prints on Van Gogh's own painting, returning his painting to one of its key sources. In other work, the race and gender of Morimura's Asian body are integral to the photographs' disruption of the codes of Western representations. In *Portrait (Futago)* (1988), he plays both the white prostitute and her African maidservant in Édouard Manet's 1863 painting *Olympia*, performing a relationship the art historical discourse around the painting has often highlighted. By playing a female prostitute, Morimura also draws attention to the long history of affinity between male homosexuals and female prostitutes in the transvestite Japanese theatrical genre of Kabuki.

In 'Requiem for the XX Century', Morimura turns to the male figures associated with the turbulent history of the last century. Extensive and playful, flamboyant and excessive, his global self-portraiture is dispersed throughout Western culture and history, undermining and fracturing that history. This 'maniacal imitation' includes faces and bodies of the turbulent twentieth century, all men, but reset in Japanese scenarios. Osaka provides the setting for Morimura's version of Eddie Adams's photo of an execution in Vietnam – *A Requiem: Vietnam War 1968* (1991) – a reprisal in which he plays all the roles: assassin, victim and grimacing witness. This work (the earliest in the series, produced at the same time he started modelling himself after paintings from Western art history) was made in response to the First Gulf War as a deliberate provocation in the way it called up a traumatic icon of the disastrous US war in Asia. Morimura's recognizability is integral to the criticism that lies within this work: his Asian identity becomes a significant disruption to the dominant forms of Western art history, culture and history that he mimes.

Morimura's art empties out self-portraiture as an expressive genre. Like Francesca Woodman he plays very much with the codes and conventions of representation. Woodman mimed and challenged the processes of photography in her performances, using her feminine body as a site of resistance against the formal exercises that came out of phenomenology, with the idea of the body as universal, unmarked by gender or sexuality. She played with her body's femininity and the challenges this can entail, even while playing games that seem to suggest subjugation or reduce her to a *tabula rasa*, a blank sheet. For Morimura, his body is never neutral; he draws on cultural associations of the Asian body to undermine Western cultural icons. Morimura practices a kind of critical art history. Far from the hollowness and emptiness that might be inferred by some of his actions and performances to camera, this is an assertive, knowing and playful dismantling of dominant forms and models of picturing.

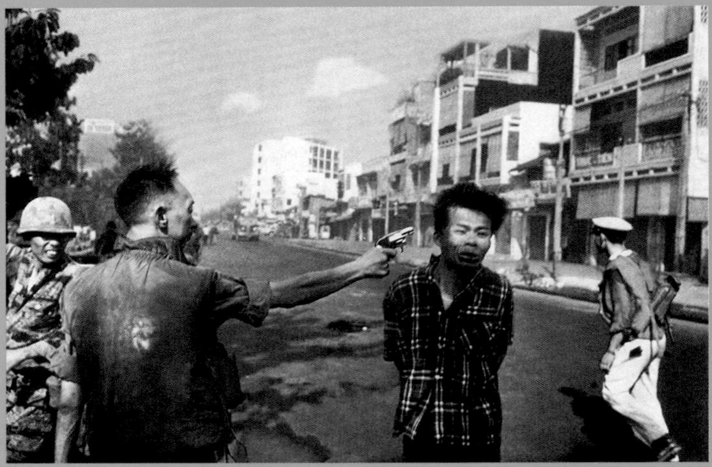

Eddie Adams
Street Execution of a Vietcong Prisoner, 1968
Gelatin silver print, dimensions variable

Yasumasa Morimura
Portrait (Futago), 1988
Colour photograph
Dimensions variable

Portrait (Van Gogh), 1985
Colour photograph
120 × 100.3 cm / 47¼ × 39½ in

A Requiem: Vietnam War, 1968, 1991
Gelatin silver print mounted on alpolic
120 × 150 cm / 47¼ × 59 in

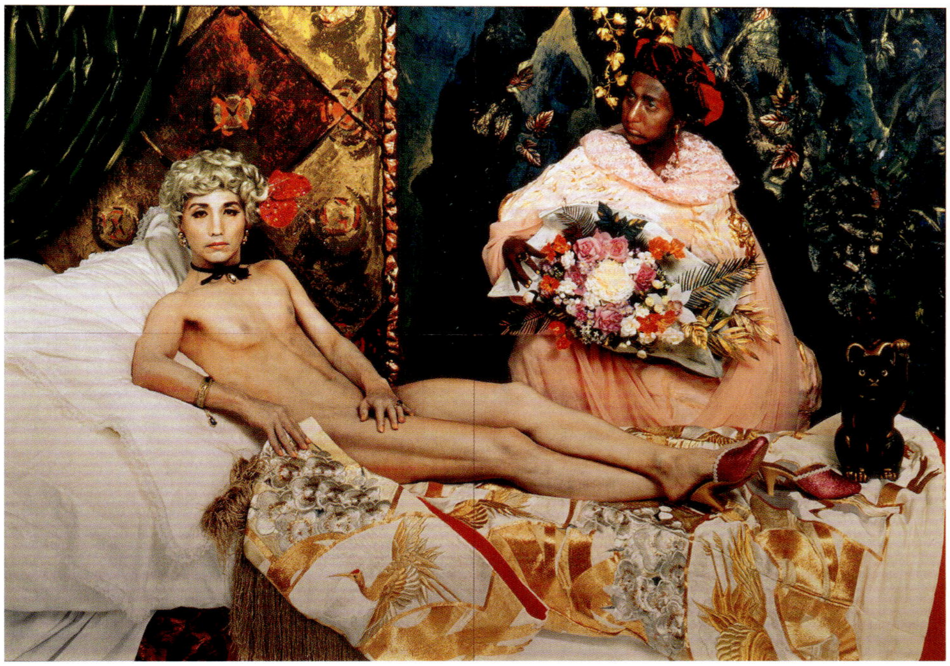

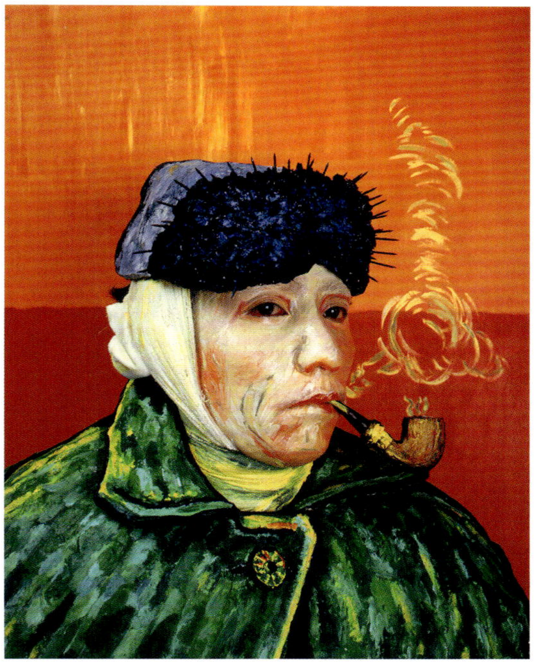

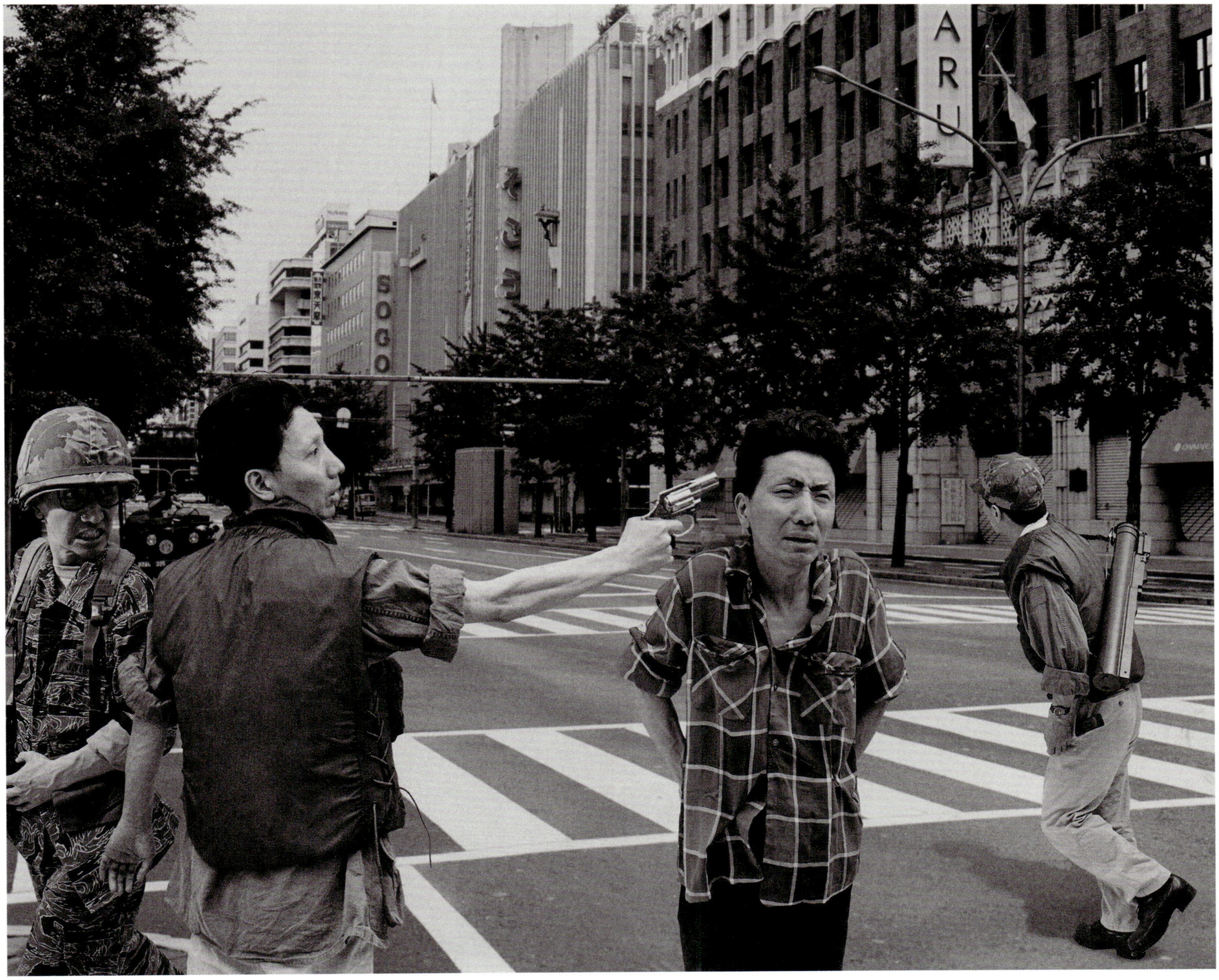
SOGO

Chapter Ten

Constructions: Signs, Fantasy and the Tableau Form

For the American artist Les Krims, 'the greatest potential source of photographic imagery is the mind.'[1] He has spoken critically of certain documentary practices: 'When I started to make photographs, it seemed to me that serious photography was mired in slumming excursions funded by affluent folk eager to see what danger looked like. Art photography used the poor and damaged as its raw materials to manufacture a perverse entertainment.' Such criticism, albeit often less vehement, will recur among the practitioners discussed in this chapter. Instead of treating the world as a given or as raw material, they use photography in various ways to construct, manipulate, alter and stage events and situations. In part, such work recognizes the failure of photography to touch upon the hidden life of the imagination and fantasy. Photography becomes hybrid as it variously encompasses theatrical, performative, cinematic, painterly and textual elements. The advent of digitization has further expanded the potential and possibilities of constructed photography, enabling on the one hand a time-consuming and labour-intensive mimicry of photographic realism, such as in recent tableaux by Jeff Wall, or the production of clearly fantasmatic and over-the-top panoramic spectacles by the Chinese artist Wang Qingsong.

Kathy Grove

Many of the photographers considered in this chapter work against photography's status and identity as document. The position is splendidly illustrated by Kathy Grove's *The Other Series: After Lange* (1989–90), the making of which involved the artist deploying her skills as a commercial retoucher to give Dorothea Lange's iconic Depression photograph, *The Migrant Mother*, what Grove calls 'a face lift'.[2] At the time she was creating her touched-up version of Lange's quintessential documentary image Grove did not have recourse to digital technology, but in many ways her picture has the look of a digitally altered image and cues the radical impact digital technology has had on photography since the late 1980s. Grove's choice of image is also very telling. Subjected to a make-over, a cosmetic job that removes the moles, squints, worry lines and wrinkles of the face in the original, the alteration of the picture also points back to the idealization within *The Migrant Mother*: the stylized and constructed nature of Lange's own photograph, her use of studio portrait techniques out in the field, as well as her removal of the awkward detail of the woman's thumb in one version of the print. But it is the way Grove's image points to a shift in relation to the documentary tradition itself that is of primary interest here. Her 'prettified' portrait signals the defeat of the ideals of the humanist–reformist documentary tradition by the glamour market and consumer culture. It is a response to how suffering can be made chic. Grove has spoken of the work as being in part a reaction against the way the 'fashion industry had cynically begun using poverty to market distressed and torn clothing at obscene prices'.

Kathy Grove
The Other Series: After Lange, 1989–90
Gelatin silver print
71 × 61 cm / 28 × 24 in

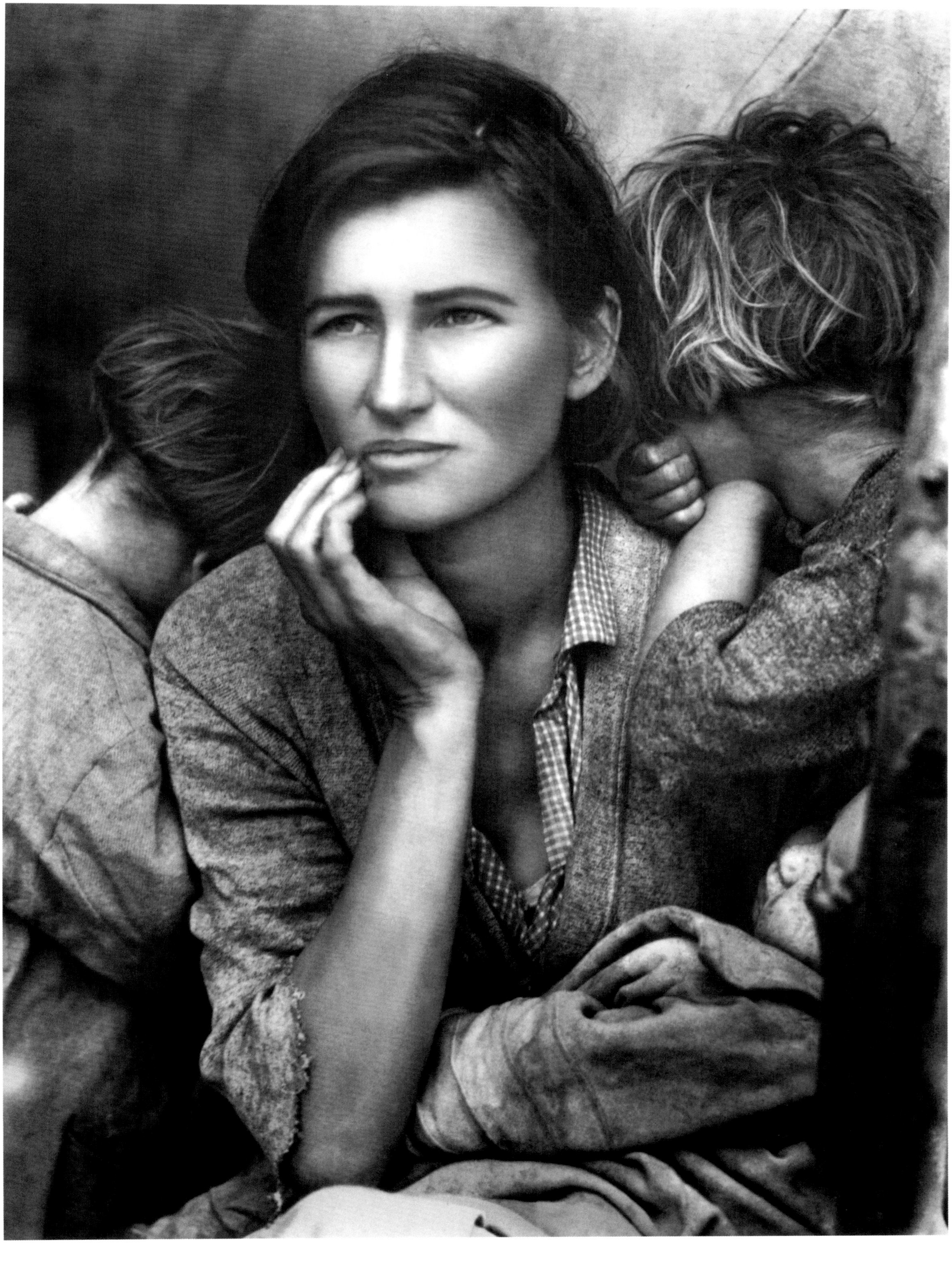

Les Krims

In a 1976 essay for *Artforum*, A.D. Coleman referred to the practice of creating events to be photographed as 'the directorial mode'.[3] Such a term acknowledges the greater authorial control such work can entail. No longer dependent on searching for subjects in the world, the photographer very often creates pictures anew – pictures which can often be much more awkward and disturbing, as they play out the unrestrained desires and fantasies of its authors.

'My pictures relate very much to my own life – sometimes on a symbolic level, often on a quite literal one. There's certainly a sense of satire and irony in many of them, even a vengeful and aggressive tone… I react strongly to events in my life and in the world, and the pictures are meant to be as forceful as I can possibly make them.'[4] This is how Les Krims describes his photography. *Plus One Stop* (1969), for example, shows a young black male seated in an armchair, his arms behind his head, looking back at the camera and viewer with '+ ONE STOP' in white lettering stuck on his bare chest. Krims has said the image is based upon 'the exposure advice given by *Popular Photography* magazine to be followed by amateurs when photographing in the ghetto.' His picture both challenges and draws attention to the indignity of reducing subjects to such a photographic formula: its reductive function becomes fully realized when it is emblazoned across the (correctly exposed) chest of this young male.

Krims produced some of the most upsetting and awkward pictures of the 1970s. One viewer was so outraged and angry by his photographs that he kidnapped the son of a museum official and demanded the removal of Krims's pictures from an exhibition. In another notorious incident connected with Krims, a woman walked into the Special Collections room of the University of California at Santa Cruz library, checked out a set of his photographic prints, tore them up and poured Hershey's chocolate syrup over the remains. The event was photographed, and the action titled *The Incredible Case of the Stack O' Prints Mutilations*.

The pictures that were torn up were from Krims's series 'The Incredible Case of the Stack O' Wheat Murders' (1972), a totally fabricated work suggested by pictures from an archive of crime-scene photographs a student had shown him. Krims was struck by the ambiguity of such forensic photographs – there was no way of telling if the person imaged was dead or pretending to be dead. In his staged photographs, the murderer leaves a stack of pancakes at the scene of the crime and the blood is Hershey's chocolate syrup.

For his 1972 book *Deerslayers* (the title is taken from James Fennimore Cooper's 1841 fictional story of a frontiersman), Krims photographed hunters with their kill, trophy photographs that paid tribute to a group of working-class people much reviled by the left at the time of the Vietnam War. It was made, he has said, in 'response to the politicized, violent liberal response to the war in Vietnam', when every hunter was characterized as a murderer and returning soldiers were spat upon and called 'baby killers'. While the work was not constructed and staged, it had, according to Krims, another premise – to 'suppose the hunters to be conceptual artists making sculptures… I suggested that the deer trussed to cars, pick-ups and campers – commonplace in upstate New York during hunting season – were best understood as sculpture, and a performance Herman Nitzche would enjoy.'

Krims's hand-worked colour Polaroids, *Fictocryptokrimsographs* (1975), opened out photography to an uninhibited imaginary realm fixated upon the body, particularly the naked female form, which becomes as seemingly malleable as the emulsion of the Polaroid itself as flesh is combined with a variety of everyday objects and foodstuffs. Krims lets his fantasies run riot, as the fiction of staged scenarios with models is combined with the ability to move and mix the pigments of the Polaroid image, which remain soft and manipulable for 24 hours after exposure. Such a play against sense and meaning is exacerbated by many of the titles, which instead of pinning the pictures down, as A.D. Coleman has said, 'amplify their imagery': *G.I. Joe Wounded and in Flames Fleeing the Giant Nude Monster*, *The Affect of Kosher Pickles on a Gentile Woman* and so on.[5] Explication founders before such pictures as photography is pulled within the nonsensical world of Krims's darkly comic imaginings and fantasies.

Les Krims
Plus One Stop, 1969
35 mm black and white film
Dimensions variable

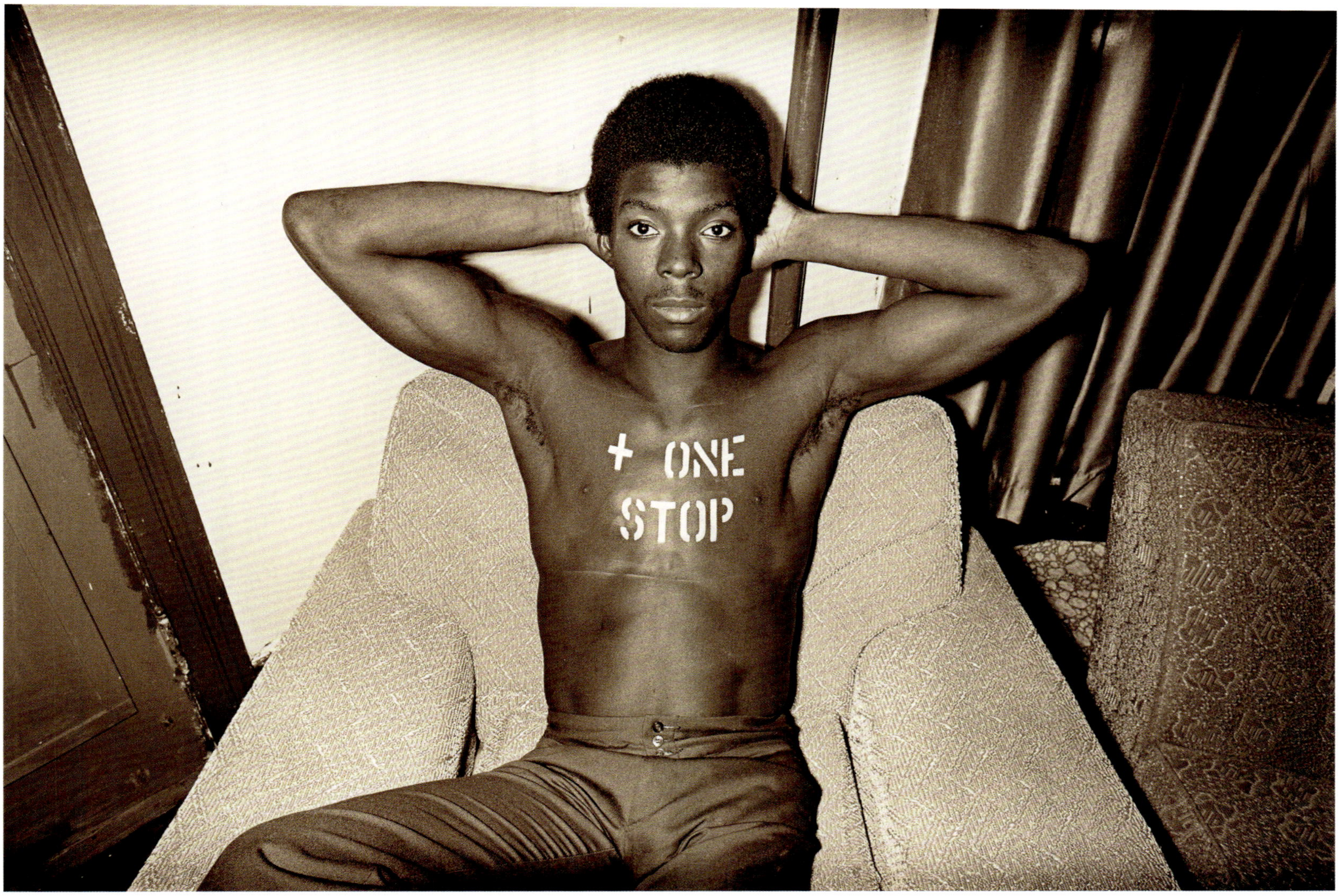
+ ONE
STOP

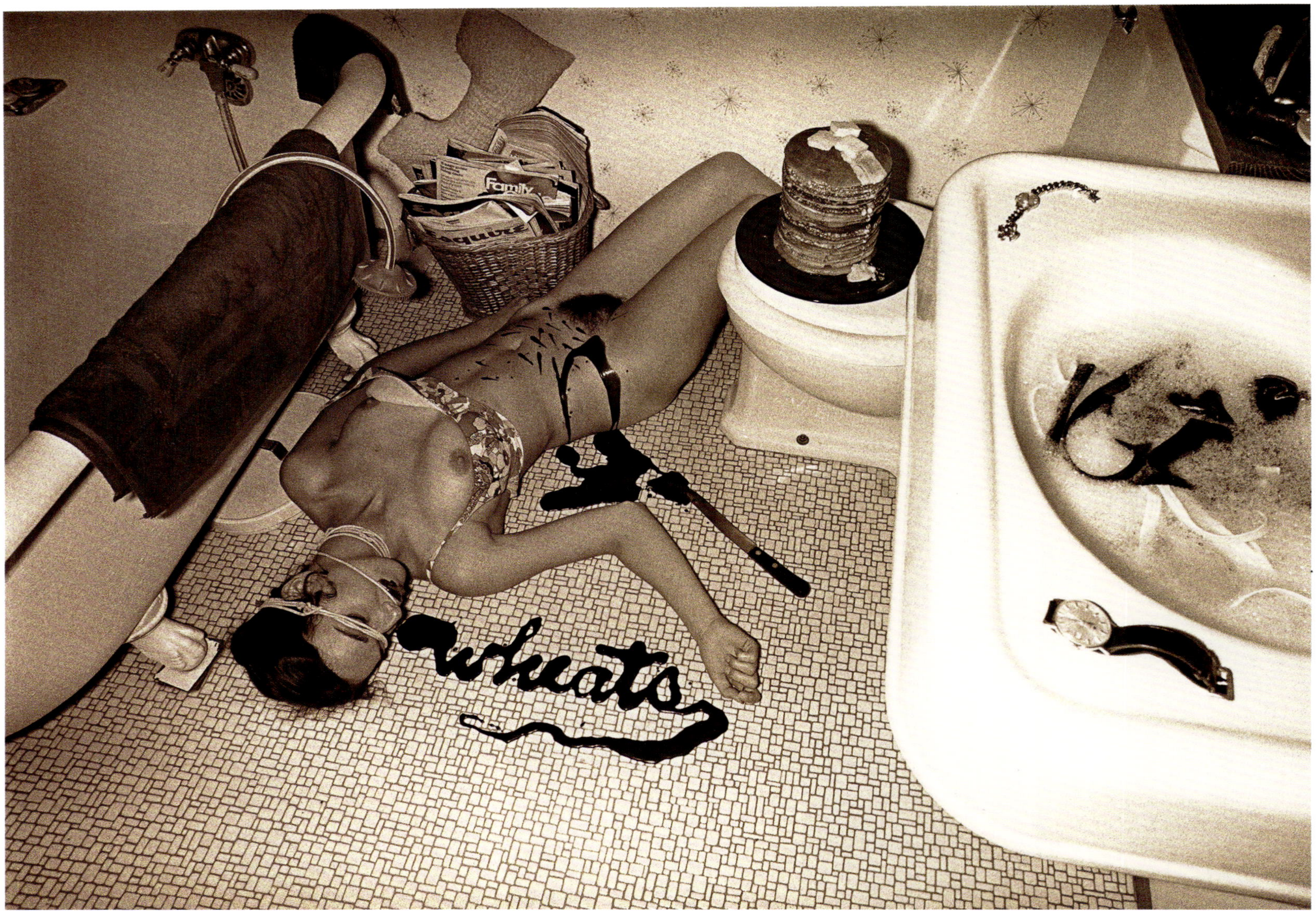

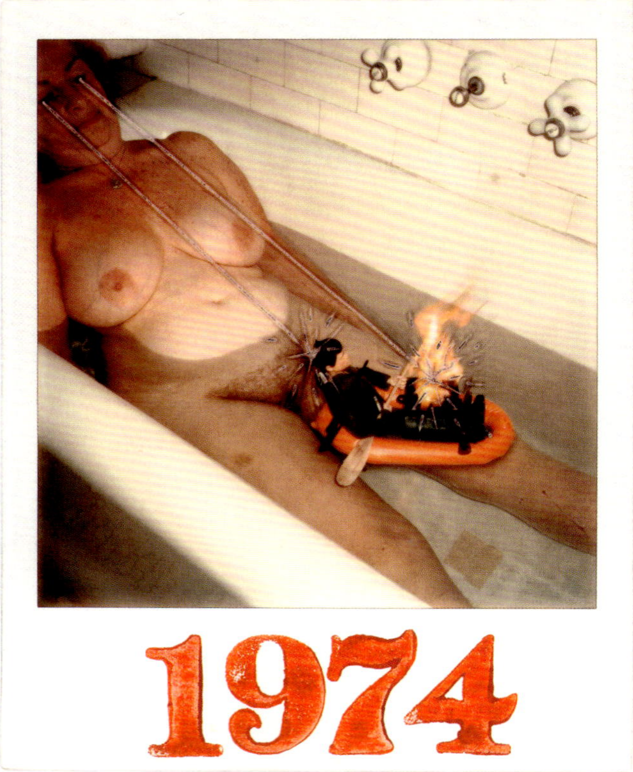

Les Krims
GI Joe Wounded and in Flames Fleeing the Giant Nude Monster, 1974
Polaroid SX-70 print
10.8 × 14 cm / 4¼ × 5½ in

Wheats, 1970 from the series 'The Incredible Case of the Stack o' Wheats Murders' 35 mm
Inkjet print
Dimensions variable

Stacked Double Portrait Deerslayer, 1971
Inkjet print
Dimensions variable

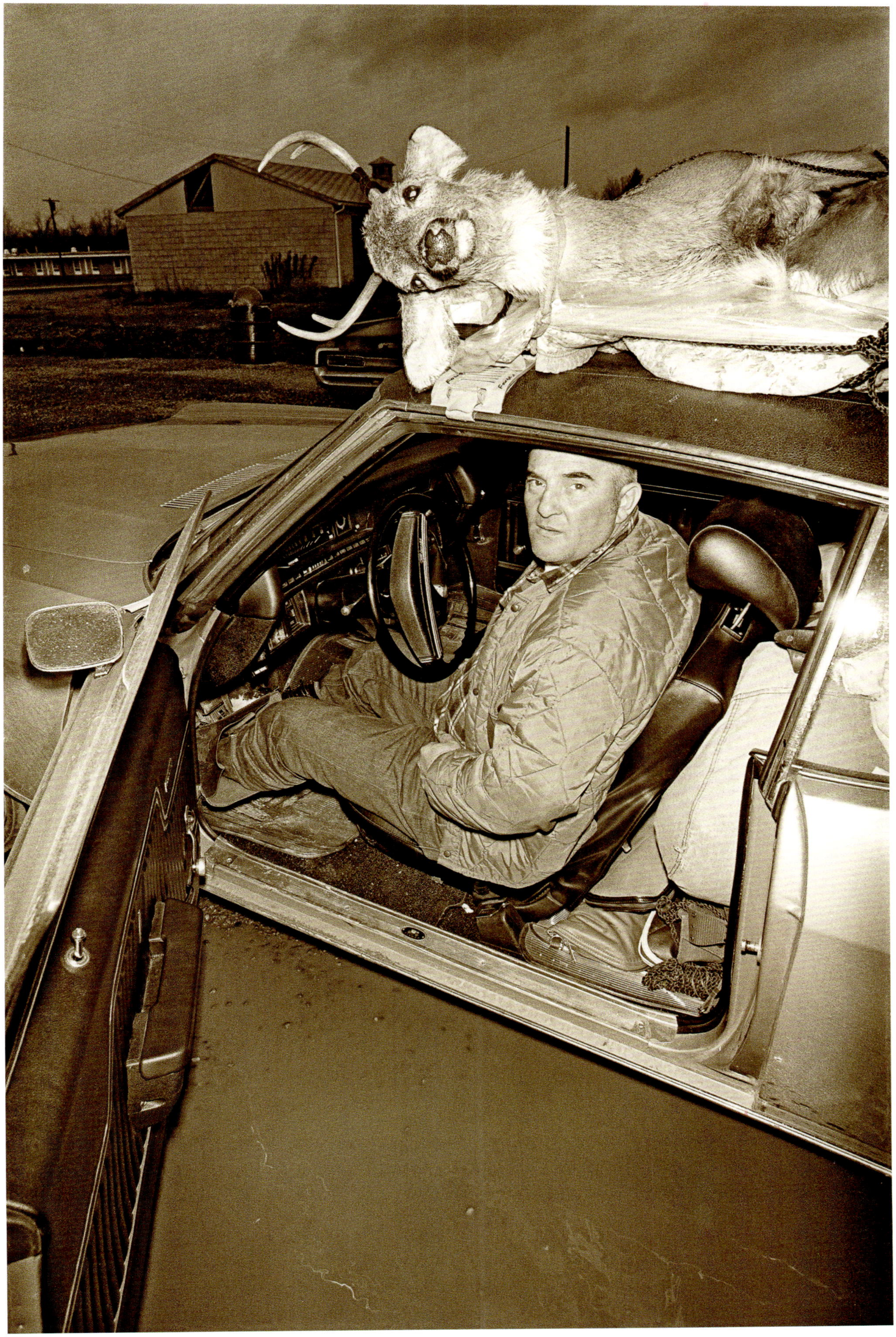

Duane Michals

The American photographer Duane Michals highlights the inadequacies and limitations of the documentary tradition, in which the photographer is, as he says, 'always documenting something, something he knows nothing about.'[6] Michals wants the photographer to 'invent' and be a 'novelist rather than a reporter.' In order to open out the medium to the 'interior landscape' of the imagination, in 1966 Michals started to construct the scenes he wanted to photograph and then convey a narrative through a sequence of images. By 1974 he had also started to write on the borders of photographs in his own hand; replete with cancellations and misspellings, the texts gave a sense of raw immediacy and spontaneity, providing expressive supplements to the photograph that would often inform us of things that could not be conveyed through picture alone. As he said: 'A photograph of my parents or my father doesn't tell me for a second what I thought of my father, which for me is more important than what the man looked like. So I then had to evolve into writing.'[7]

In *A Letter From My Father* (1960–75), Michals supplements an older family photograph he took in 1960 showing his brother in profile under the gaze of his father and mother (a picture suggestive of a family conflict) with a text that speaks about the photographer's own relationship with his father: 'As long as I can remember, my father always said to me that one day he would write me a very special letter.' Michals often wondered what this letter would be about, 'what family secret would be revealed, what intimacy just the two of us would share.' What he really wanted from this letter was his father to tell him where he had hidden his affection. But when his father died, the letter never arrived; Michals 'never found that place where he had hidden his love.'

Black is Ugly (1974) addresses racism through the failure of communication and understanding in terms of the individual, locating the problem not in the endemic racism of American culture but the way in which one unnamed subject has internalized the white lies about his inferiority. Its portrait of a late-middle-aged black male pictured in profile against a bare interior wall suggests a sense of resignation and defeat, and reiterates the message of the text accompanying the picture, which tells us that all his life this man has believed 'that black was ugly and a punishment from God.' Even when the narrator tells him this is not true, 'he would not believe me. It was too late.'

Much of Michals's work is motivated by the desire to overcome the frustrations of non-communication, the tragedy of what goes unspoken. His emotionally direct and affective work often comes up against the limits of the medium, but language enables him to bring to photography thoughts and feelings that might have no visual equivalent. On a number of occasions, Michals has dispensed with the photographic image altogether, presenting instead just a handwritten note on photographic paper. In *A Failed Attempt to Photograph Reality* (1975), for example, he writes about a state of philosophical uncertainty about what is real. In photographing reality the author feels he will always fail, photographing 'only the transient appearances of trees and automobiles and people.'

In the fictional photo sequence *Return of the Prodigal Son* (1982) Michals, in the role of the father, welcomes back a 'son' who has returned in a spirit of repentance from his first encounter with the outside world. Male bonding and companionship is integral to such work. In the last picture, in order to shield and comfort his 'son,' Michals takes off his own clothes and gives them to his 'child.' Here, the enactment of empathy and identification with another's suffering serves as a contrast to the fractured familial bond of *A Letter From My Father*.

Duane Michals
Return of the Prodigal Son, 1982
Sequence of 5 gelatin silver prints with hand-applied text, each
10.1 × 12.7 cm / 4 × 5 in

A Failed Attempt to Photograph Reality, 1975
Ink on paper, 20.3 × 25.4 cm / 8 × 10 in

THE RETURN OF THE PRODIGAL SON

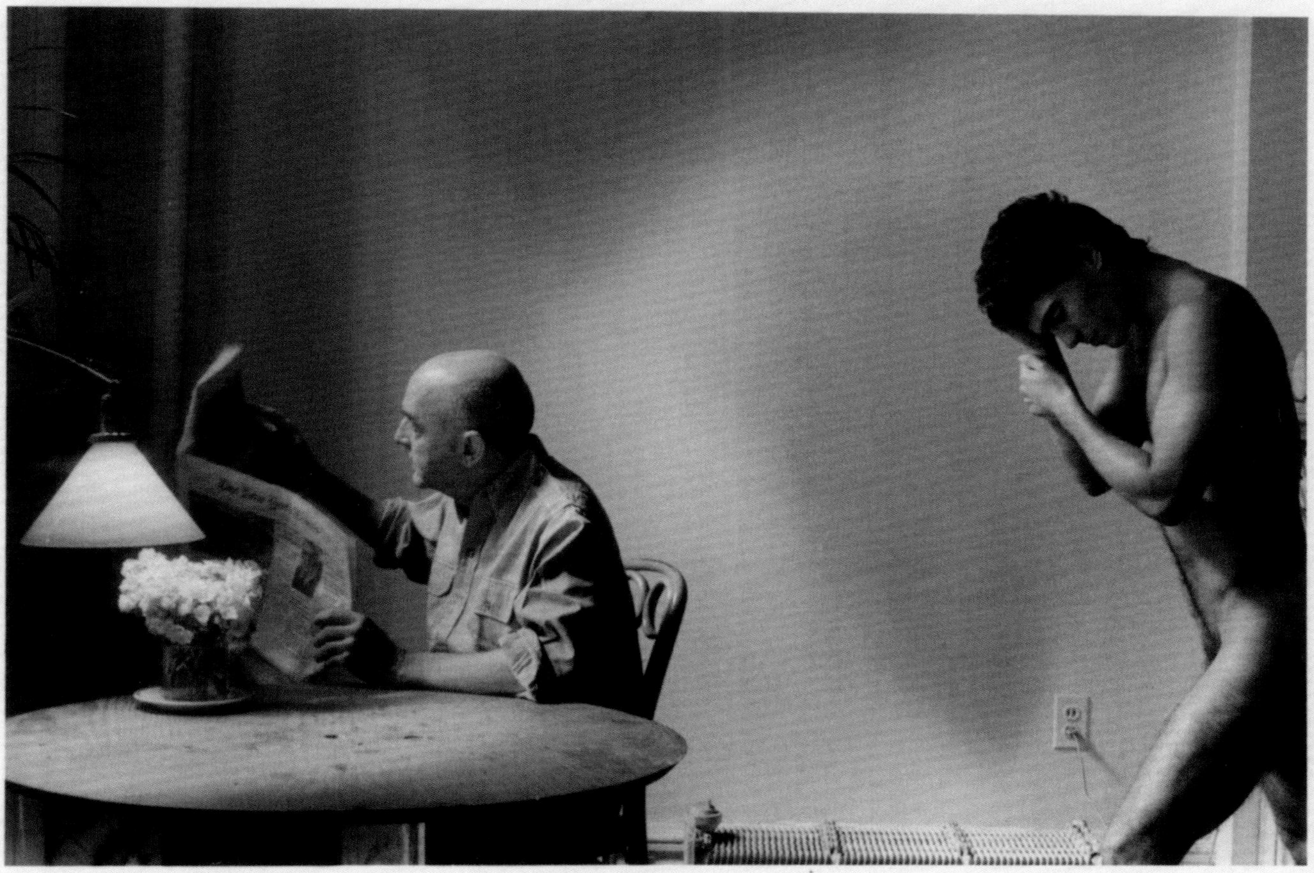

A FAILED ATTEMPT TO PHOTOGRAPH REALITY

How foolish of me to have believed that it would be that easy.
I had confused the appearances of trees and automobiles and people
with reality itself, and believed a photograph of these appearances
to be a photograph of it.
It is a melancholy truth that I will never be able to photograph it.
and can only fail.
I am a reflection photographing other reflections within a reflection.
To photograph reality is to photograph nothing

Duane Michals

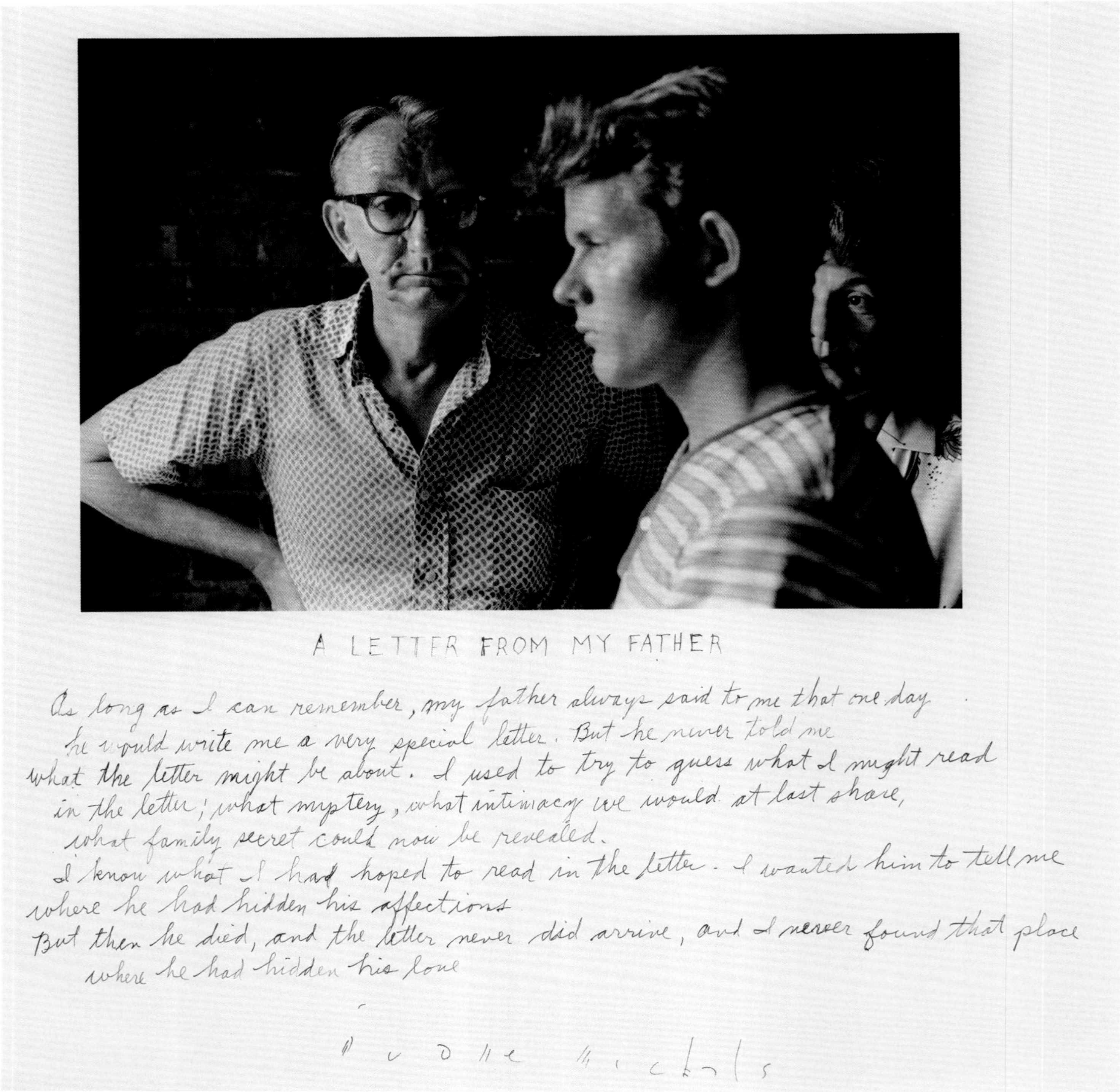

Duane Michals
A Letter from My Father, 1960–75
Gelatin silver print with hand-applied text
14.6 × 22.8 cm / 5¾ × 9 in

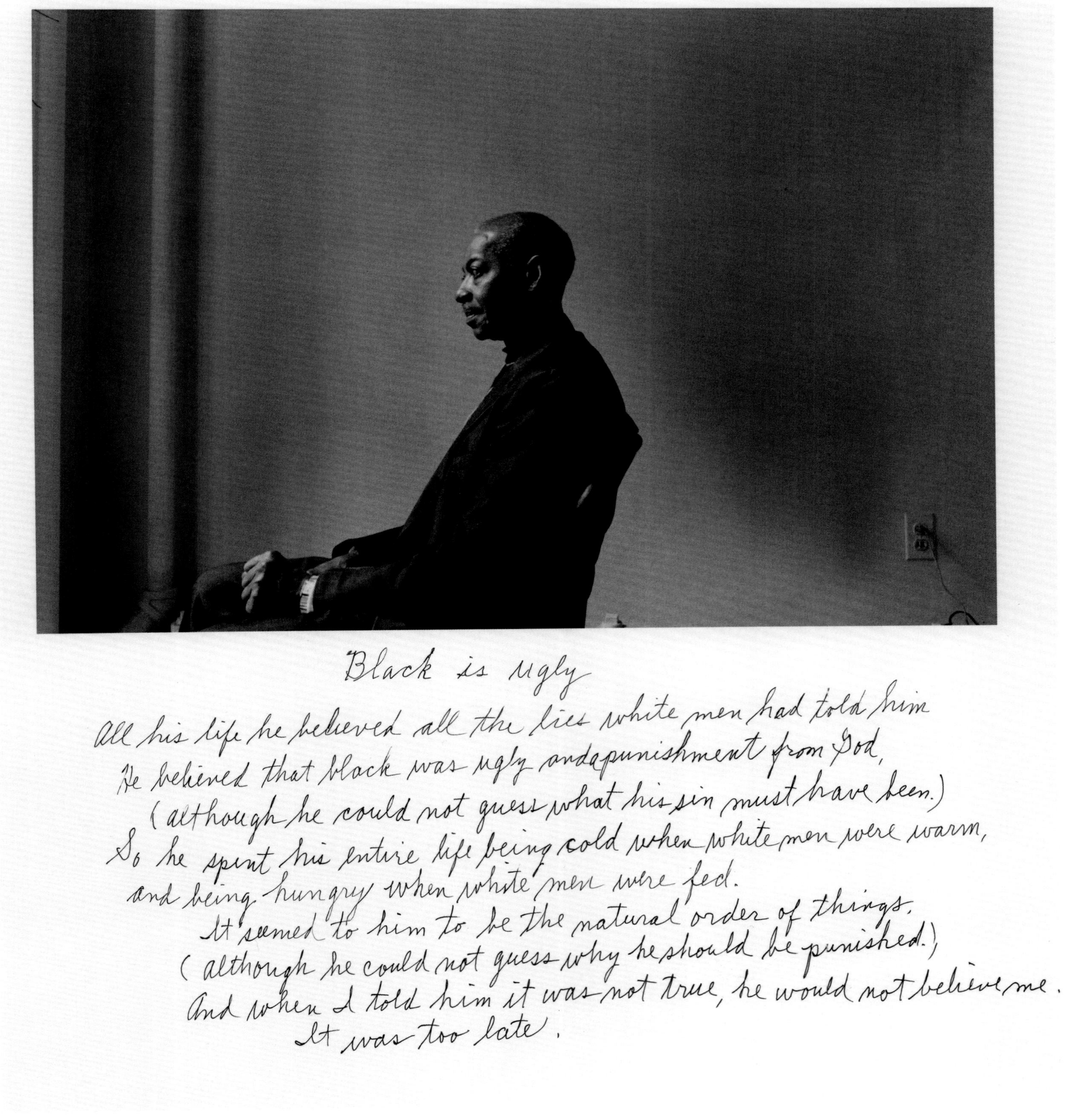

Duane Michals
Black is Ugly, 1974
Gelatin silver print
27.9 × 35 cm / 11 × 14 in

Victor Burgin

A self-consciously intellectual and academic practice began to dominate the critical agendas of photography and art from the late 1970s and throughout the 1980s. In this work, photography was used to variously engage with the forms, rhetoric and address of mass culture.

Victor Burgin's poster *Possession*, five hundred copies of which were flyposted on the streets of Newcastle in 1976, for example, mimed the look of an advertisment with its colour image showing a blond long-haired woman embracing a man. But coupled with a text about the gross economic inequality in the United Kingdom – '7% of our population own 84% of our wealth' (from a 1966 statistic published in the *Economist* on January 15th, also cited as a source on the poster) – the poster was intended to make the viewer think about the relationship between Marxism and feminism, and about how economic power relations are not separate from sexual relations. Women are treated as possessions within the economy of human relationships, the poster implies. Burgin has said he started to get interested in psychoanalysis around the time of *Possession*. The work was meant to be a populist gesture that anybody could understand but, as interviews conducted with people on the street at the time revealed, not everybody understood the poster in the same way.

Such an intervention in advertising – an institution in which Burgin was not 'organically rooted'[18] – was followed by work made solely within the context of art and its institutions, galleries, museums and magazines. His subsequent distinctive photo-textual practice became characterized by the intellectual authority of its cultural references. In the 1980s, Burgin's art, bolstered by his role as a teacher and his academic writings, came to represent a particularly theorized photographic practice. The ideology-critique of such photo-texts as 'US76' and 'US77' (see *Chapter Four: The Street* for discussion of 'US77') was followed by more elliptical sequences of photographs and text which, as he said, were about 'the ways in which our experience of "real life", the "real world", is mediated by our memories and fantasies.' Thus *Zoo 78* (1978) responds not to a real city of Berlin but to what Burgin calls the 'city of the mind', drawing upon both the popular imagery of the Berlin of the Wall as a city of 'enclosure, isolation', and the decadent sexualized Berlin of the 1920s, evoked through citations from Victor Shklovsky's 1923 book about the city, *Zoo, or letters not about love*. Pictures showing Berlin's barren and divided present (as well as its undivided past, evoked through a painting of the Brandenberg Gate) are paired with photographs of its zoo and its peep shows, including one voyeuristic view of a naked woman on all fours on a revolving stage. Berlin allows Burgin to explore and link men's oppressive surveillance of women with the state's surveillance of society in general, a relation reiterated through texts which draw upon an account of voyeurism by Marquis de Sade and Michel Foucault's description of the Panopticon prison, in which all the inmates are watched from a central tower. The two triptychs, *Olympia* (1982), explore obsessions with the enigma of female sexuality through one of Freud's case studies, *Anna O*; E.T.A. Hoffman's story in which a young student falls in love with a woman of wax; Hitchcock's *Rear Window*; and Manet's painting *Olympia*. Burgin also puts himself in the picture, reflected in the mirror through an open door of the women's toilet of a poolside facility. He speaks about the 'dream-logic' of such multi-layered work and says how it is intended neither as an '*object* to be consumed as "spectacle", nor an *opinion* to be consumed as "expression".' Instead 'it is to be *produced* in the active process of looking, reading, comparing, interpreting.'

Victor Burgin
Possession, 1976
Colour lithograph
119 × 84 cm / 46⅞ × 33 in

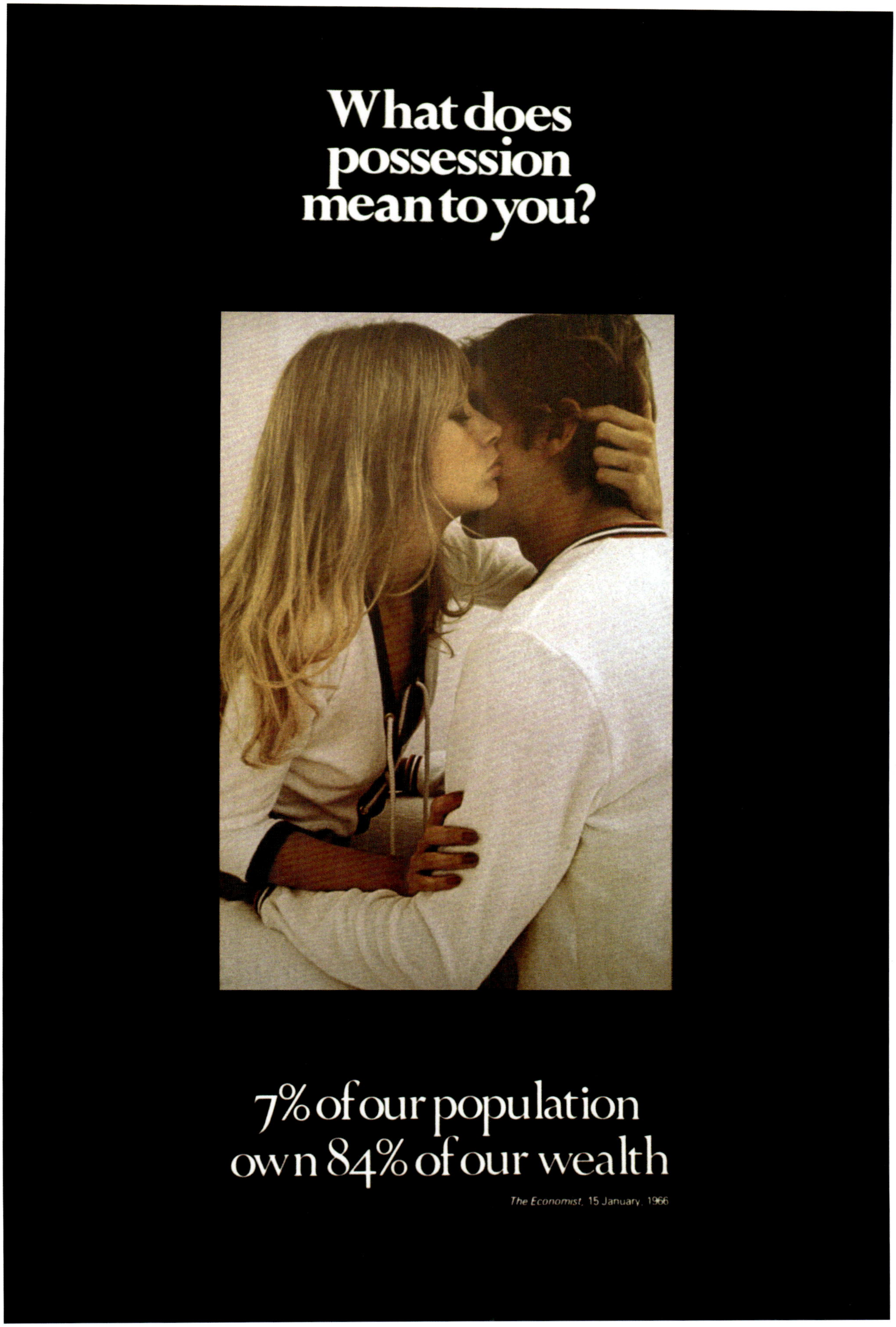
What does
possession
mean to you?
7% of our population
own 84% of our wealth
The Economist, 15 January, 1966

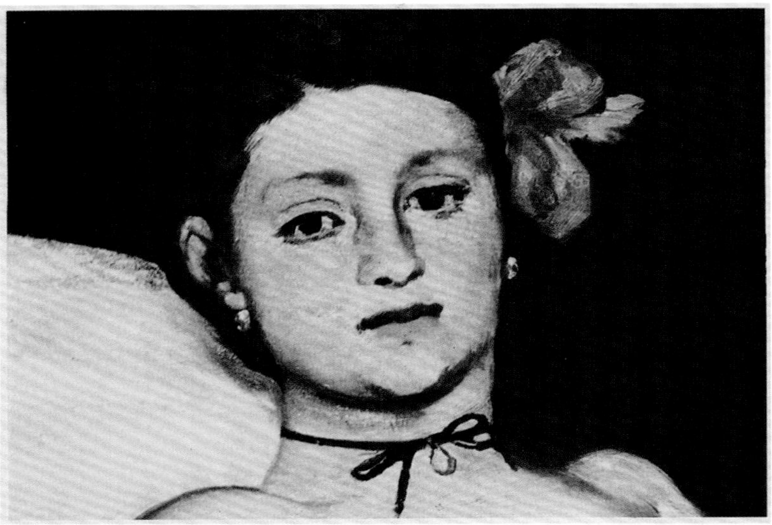

O, is a life-like doll, the creation of a brilliant professor.
Believing her to be real, a young student falls in love with her.
An intruder tries to steal the automaton, but is surprised by the professor.
A fight ensues in which the doll loses her enamelled eyes.
At that moment her admirer, sensing she is in danger,
bursts into the office.

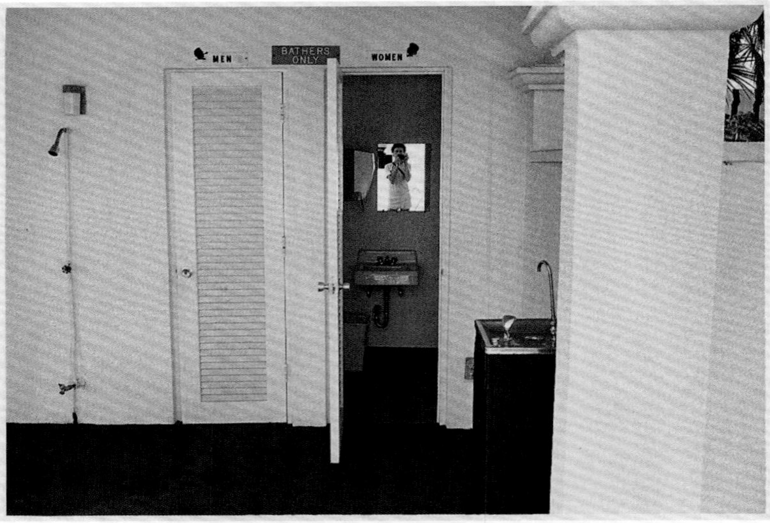

"Oh!"
(A door opens on a memory.)

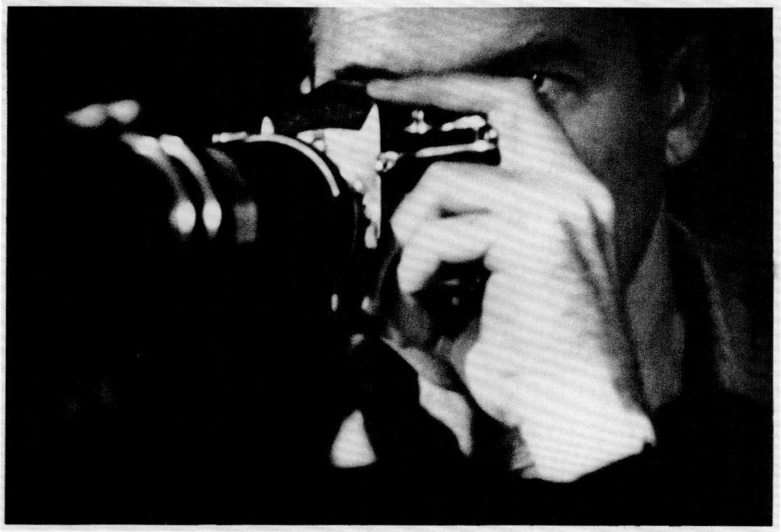

Everything is petrified, frozen for all time, as I watch
the room in which she is to be seen sitting, motionless.
It seems she is staring in my direction,
although I cannot be certain. Sometimes her chair is empty,
but I continue to watch. It is as if the vacant room itself
returns my gaze, holding me spellbound.

Victor Burgin
Olympia (detail), 1982
Photographic prints and text
(2 triptyches)
Each 50 × 61 cm / 19⅝ × 24 in

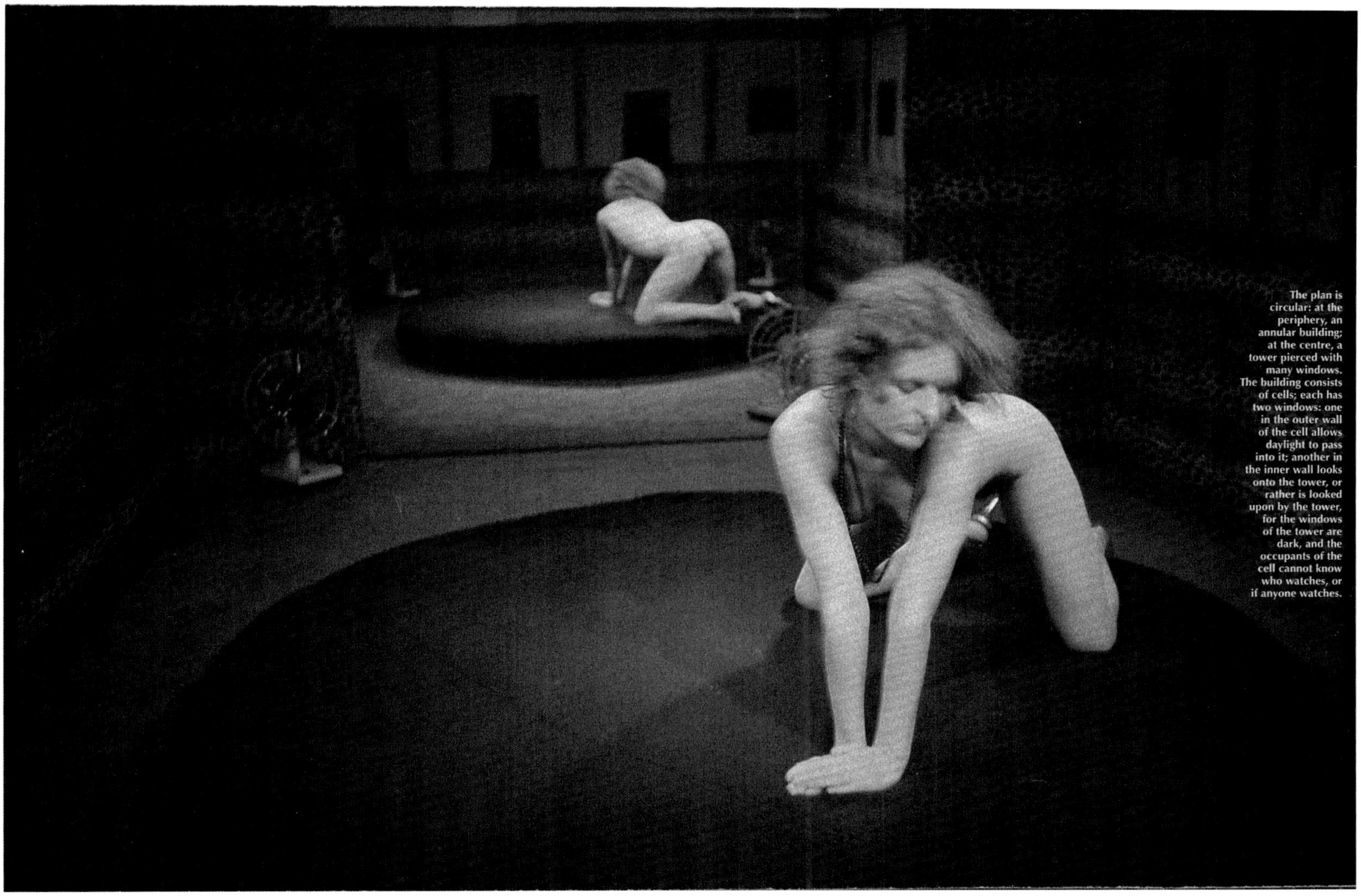

Victor Burgin
Zoo 78 (detail), 1978
Photographic prints and text
(8 diptyches)
Each print 50.5 × 75.5 cm /
19⅞ × 29¾ in

Barbara Kruger

Circulating outside the museum and engaging with the commercial sphere of advertising, publicity and mass media, Barbara Kruger's art was integral to a critical postmodern art practice in the 1980s that was very much concerned with the way in which identities are constructed by representations. In 1982, Hal Foster placed Kruger among a number of practitioners whose work had shifted the position of the artist to one who had become a 'manipulator of signs more than a producer of art objects'; someone who 'sees the status of art as a social sign entangled with other sign systems productive of value, power and prestige.'[9] Kruger studied under Diane Arbus and Marvin Israel at The Parsons School of Design, Syracuse, New York, and it was her relation to Israel, a graphic designer and art director of *Harper's Bazaar,* which led to her becoming chief designer of a national fashion magazine by the age of twenty-two. She cites her experience as a graphic designer as the biggest influence on her artwork: 'I learned to deal with an economy of image and text which beckoned and fixed the spectator.'[10]

Combining image and text, Kruger's graphically dynamic artwork uses the codes and conventions of advertising, playing on and against its direct address to the viewer. In 1981 she first exhibited what has now become her trademark: black-and-white photos that have been cropped and enlarged from different media images (often pictures from the 1940s and 1950s) and combined with strident statements or phrases, all typeset in Futura Bold Italic. Her work confronted the stereotypes and clichés of power, sexuality and representation abundant in the dated images she appropriated from popular mass culture. Many of her source images presented women in states of subjugation or humiliation – Kruger uses language to unsettle and disrupt our relation to such violent visual representations, and says that her work serves to 'intercept the stunned silences of the image with the uncouth impertinences and uncool embarrassments of language.' The aphoristic messages overlaying her appropriated images – 'I am Your Slice of Life,' 'You Thrive on Mistaken Identity,' 'Your Gaze Hits the Side of My Face,' 'We Don't Need Another Hero,' 'We Won't Play Nature To Your Culture,' 'You Construct Intricate Rituals Which Allow You to Touch the Skin of Other Men' – often set up a binary in terms of gender positions in their use of personal pronouns, with 'I' and 'We' implicitly female and the addressee implicitly male. Using language allowed Kruger to, as she puts it, 'welcome the female viewer into the audience of men' and 'to ruin certain representations.' In 1984 Kruger's work expanded to include the subject of money and consumption, a critical concern motivated by her increasing visibility in the art world, but not always separate from questions of gender, as money, very often, reiterates masculine power. Displayed on billboards, posters and electronic signboards, or distributed on such merchandise as mugs, matchbooks, T-shirts and shopping bags, Kruger's art was intended to counter media images as conduits of power and authority; it sent out ambiguous messages, rogue signs that would displace and expose such coercive ideological forces and open up a space for critical awareness. As Kruger's work evolved in the 1990s, her mode of address shifted; language became more dominant, especially in gallery-based installations in which viewers were bombarded by texts, from above and around them.

Barbara Kruger
Your Gaze Hits the Side of My Face, 1981
Black and white photograph
140 × 104 cm / 55 × 41 in

Untitled (We Have Received Orders Not to Move), 1982
Black and white photograph
71 × 49 cm / 28 × 19¼ in

Untitled (You Construct Intricate Rituals Which Allow You To Touch The Skin Of Other Men), 1984
Poster project, Amsterdam

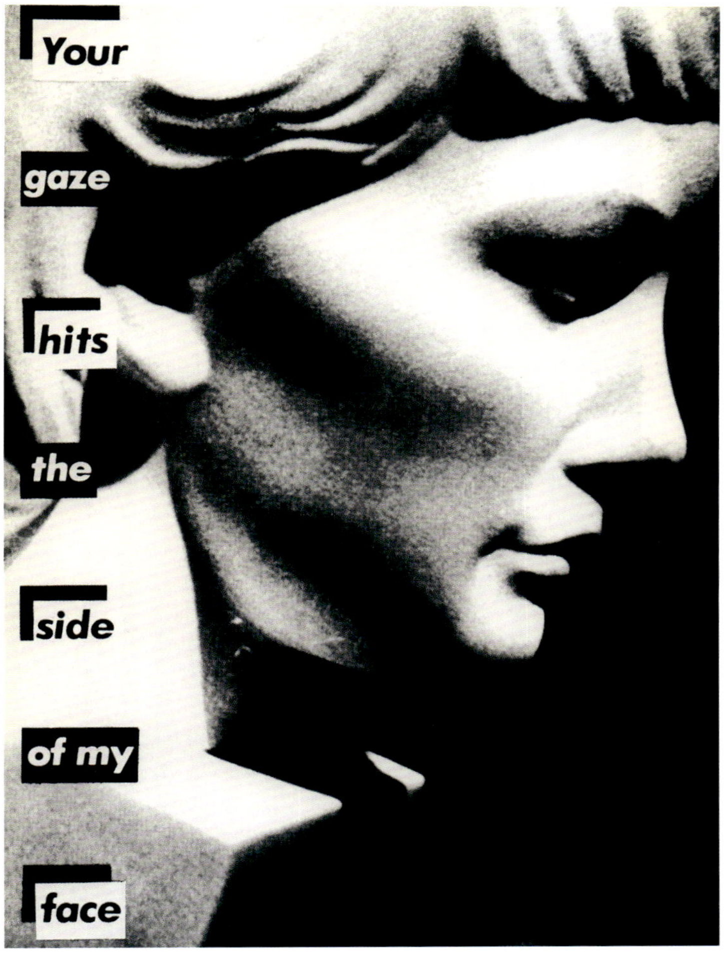
Your
gaze
hits
the
side
of my
face
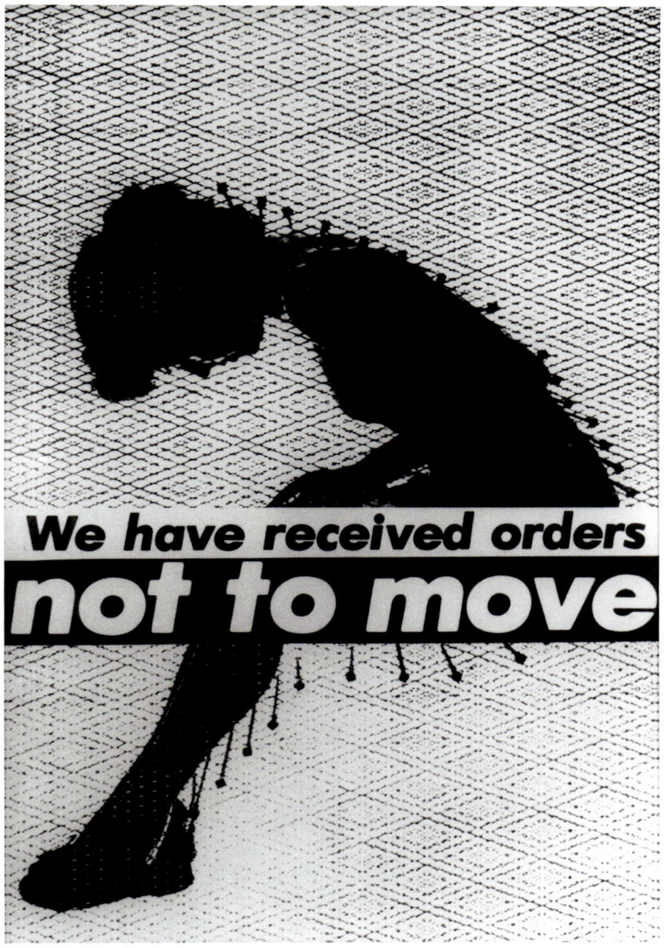
We have received orders
not to move
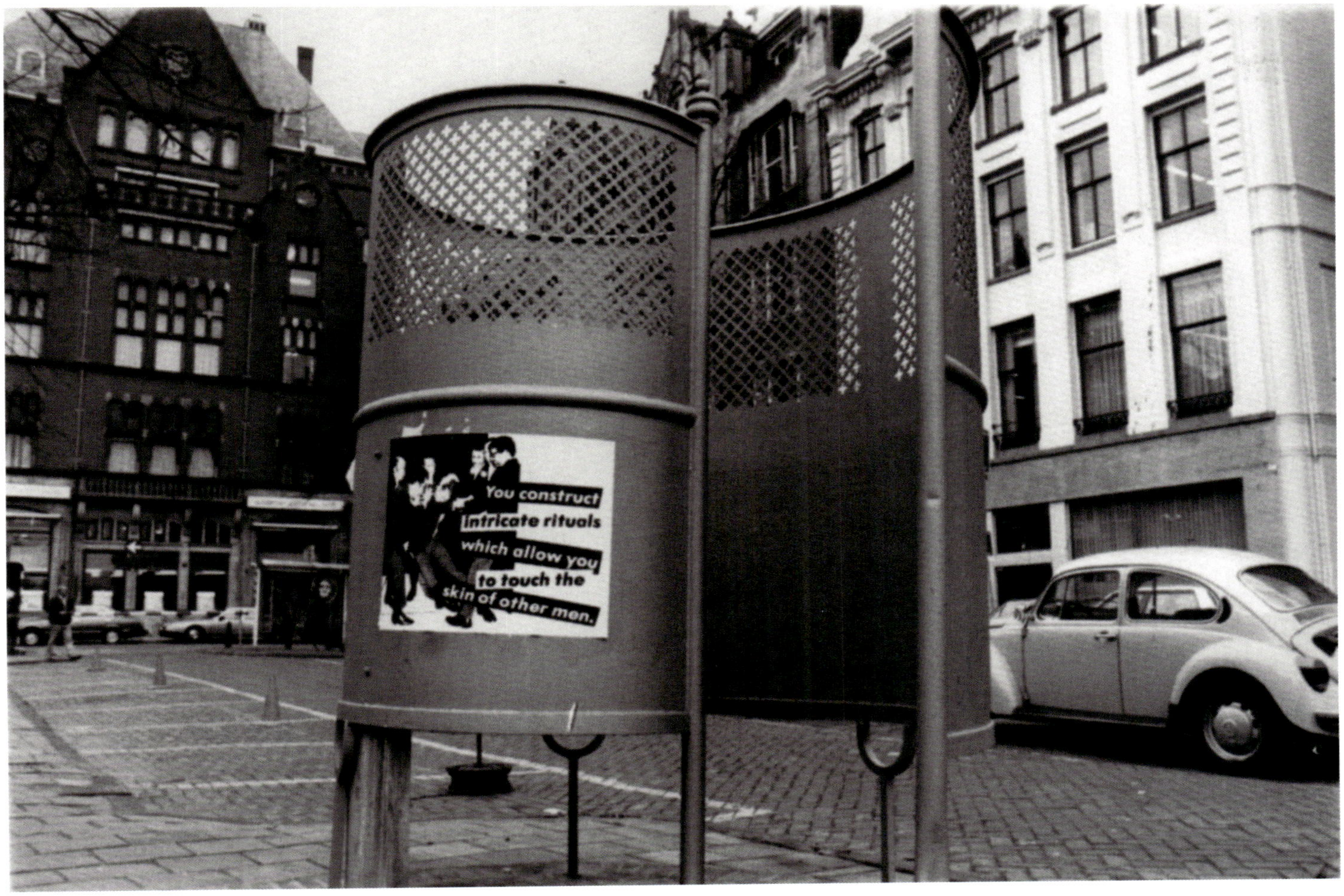
You construct
intricate rituals
which allow you
to touch the
skin of other men.

Shirin Neshat

Shirin Neshat was born and raised in Iran but moved to the United States after high school to study art. When the Islamic Revolution overtook her homeland in 1979, she was exiled and could not return until ten years later. The result of this visit was 'Women of Allah' (1993–7), a series of staged representations showing veiled and unveiled Muslim women embracing guns, a response to the different role women had at the time of the Iran/Iraq War.[11] The display of guns – usually associated with a masculine and colonial power – echoes the fact that, as Neshat puts it, 'women are encouraged to get involved in political affairs, like street protests, voting and fighting in a war.' In this performative work, for some of the images of which she posed herself, Neshat challenges Islamic patriarchal law, not only in the sensuous and erotic portrayal of the female body but also by overlaying the body with the words of celebrated female Iranian poets, including Forough Farrokhzad, Tahereh Saffarzadeh and Simin Behbahani.

In an interview in the book accompanying the photographs, Neshat discusses the contradictions arising from the strict segregation of the sexes within Muslim society. Men dominate the public space and set all codes for social behaviour in order to protect Islamic law, while women take charge of the private, domestic space. For a woman to enter the public space she must be veiled, 'contained, silent and invisible.' But 'a woman wrapped in a veil is extremely sensual and erotic,' and 'eye contact between the sexes is such an arousing sensation in Muslim society.' She speaks of her sister's invisible, imaginary affairs, conducted with men merely through looking.

Neshat's photographs use the veil, the words of female Iranian poets and the gun to challenge both the gaze of the colonizer and the patriarchal structure within Islamic law that confines Muslim women to silence. The veil, while a symbol of repression, can also be seen as a sign of liberation, a resistance against the West. Resistance and confrontation is also the connotation when both the gaze and the gun in the photograph are turned to the viewer. One might also see the Farsi texts inscribed on the female body as an affront to Western viewers, to whom the language is indecipherable, while an Iranian audience would be very familiar with the history and place of the poets in relation to Iranian society. Through the words of the Iranian poets, Neshat makes an important symbolic gesture of identification and affiliation, locating her own practice as an Iranian woman artist in relation to these historical female figures. But made and viewed in the West, the work is ambiguous. The depiction of the female body, while liberating and empowering in relation to the strictures of Islamic law, could nevertheless be seen to be disempowering in relation to the colonial West, feeding Orientalist fantasies.

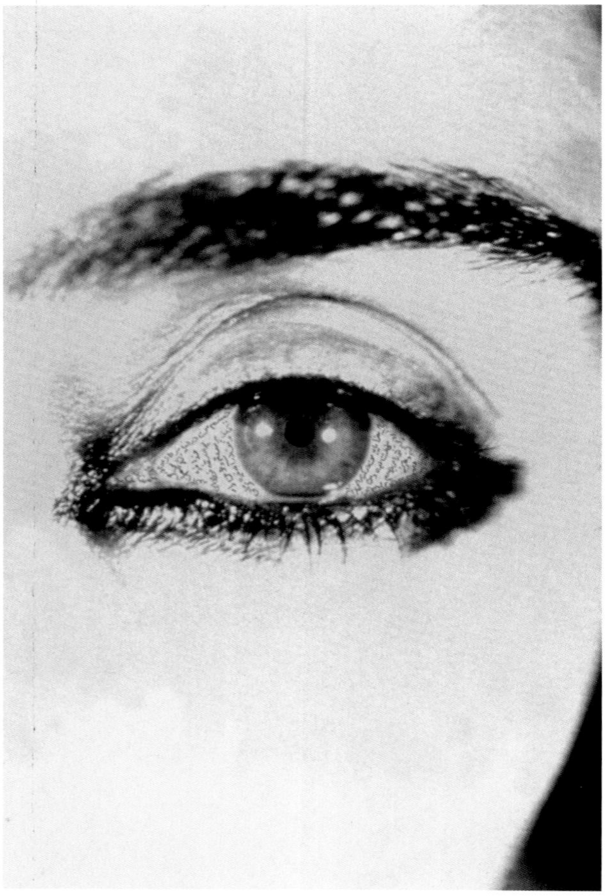

Shirin Neshat
Offered Eyes, 1993
RC print and ink (photograph taken by Plauto), dimensions variable

Rebellious Silence, 1994
Gelatin silver print with ink (photograph taken by Cynthia Preston), dimensions variable

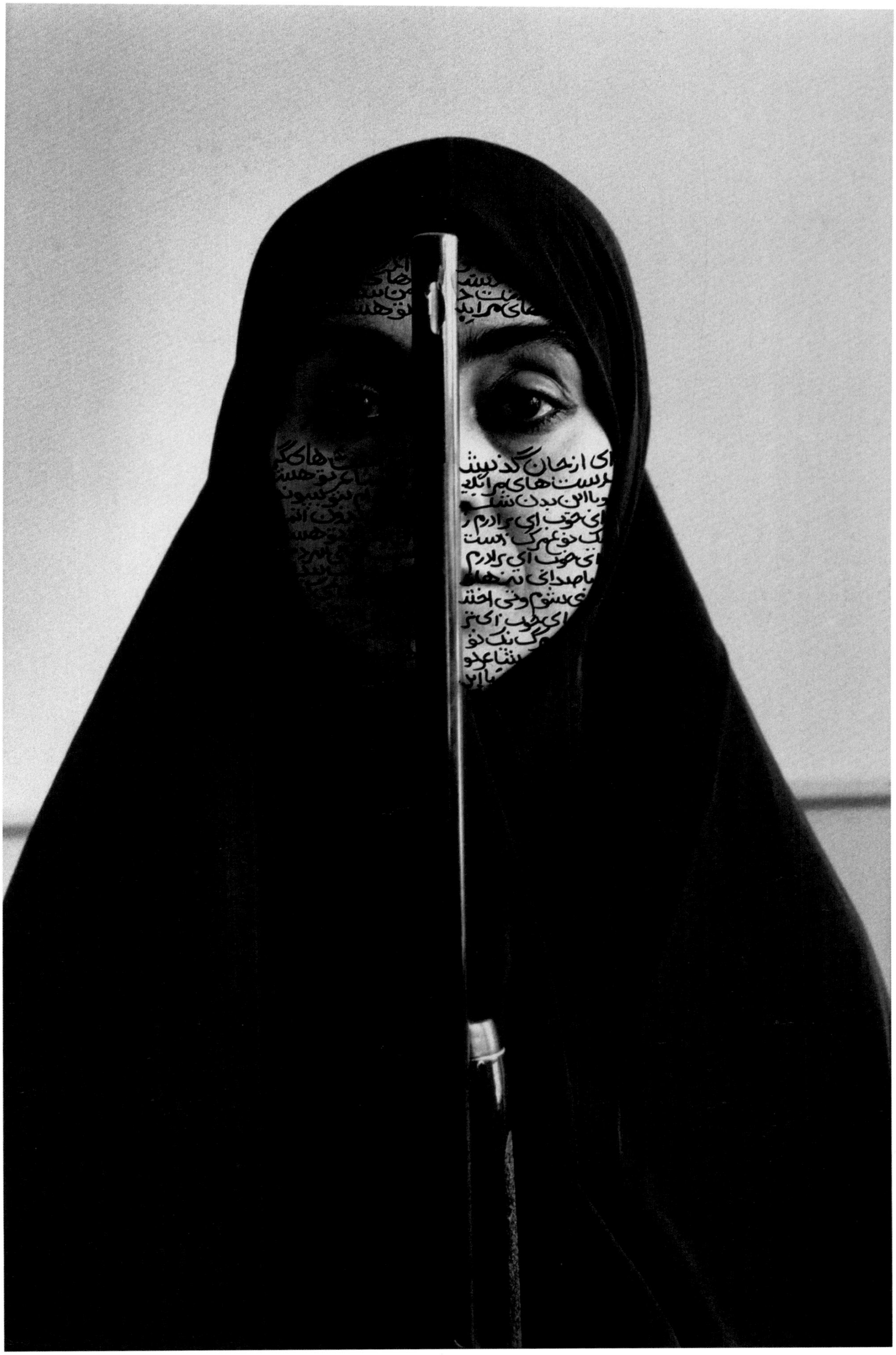

James Casebere

Since the mid-1970s James Casebere has been photographing tabletop-sized models that he constructs from Styrofoam, paper and plaster. The models are based on real and imagined interiors, including prisons, hospitals, schools and asylums, the Berlin sewer system, Thomas Jefferson's Monticello plantation home and more recently interiors inspired by the architecture of the Levant, including the destroyed al-Askari Mosque in the Iraqi city of Samarra.

The selective lighting, minimal furnishings and sepulchral tone of the prison series can be seen in relation to minimalism as well as the solitude of the studio. The fascination with structures of discipline and incarceration shifts to something more visceral in the models of tunnels, which are suggestive of interior bodily organs. In contrast to the quality of the prison cells, with their aura of a spiritual monastic retreat, these pictures imply insurgent subterranean forces and energies. The tunnels' association with a sense of uncontained and excessive forces was further underlined when Casebere 'flooded' them using an artist's resin that dries to a surface that resembles a fluid. The model of an architectural interior of Monticello is also flooded. Its reflections augment the lavishness, but one might also see the water as suggestive of something else, a darker and more troubling stain on history: the continuity of slavery on Jefferson's plantation. In many of the photographs of models based upon the mosques and bath houses of the Levant, the colour and lighting is varied and sensuous; in some the rendition of the colours and surfaces of walls invite allusions to Abstract Expressionist painting. The formal richness of Casebere's envisioning of such architecture becomes meaningful in relation to the fact these models were made at the time when such holy sites were being destroyed in the war in Iraq. Fittingly, his depiction of the al-Askari Mosque is drained of all colour: ashen grey, it serves as a trenchant memorial to the tragic losses, both cultural and human, of such a conflict.

James Casebere
Prison Cell with Skylight, 1993
Cibachrome dye transfer print
76.2 × 101.6 cm / 30 × 40 in

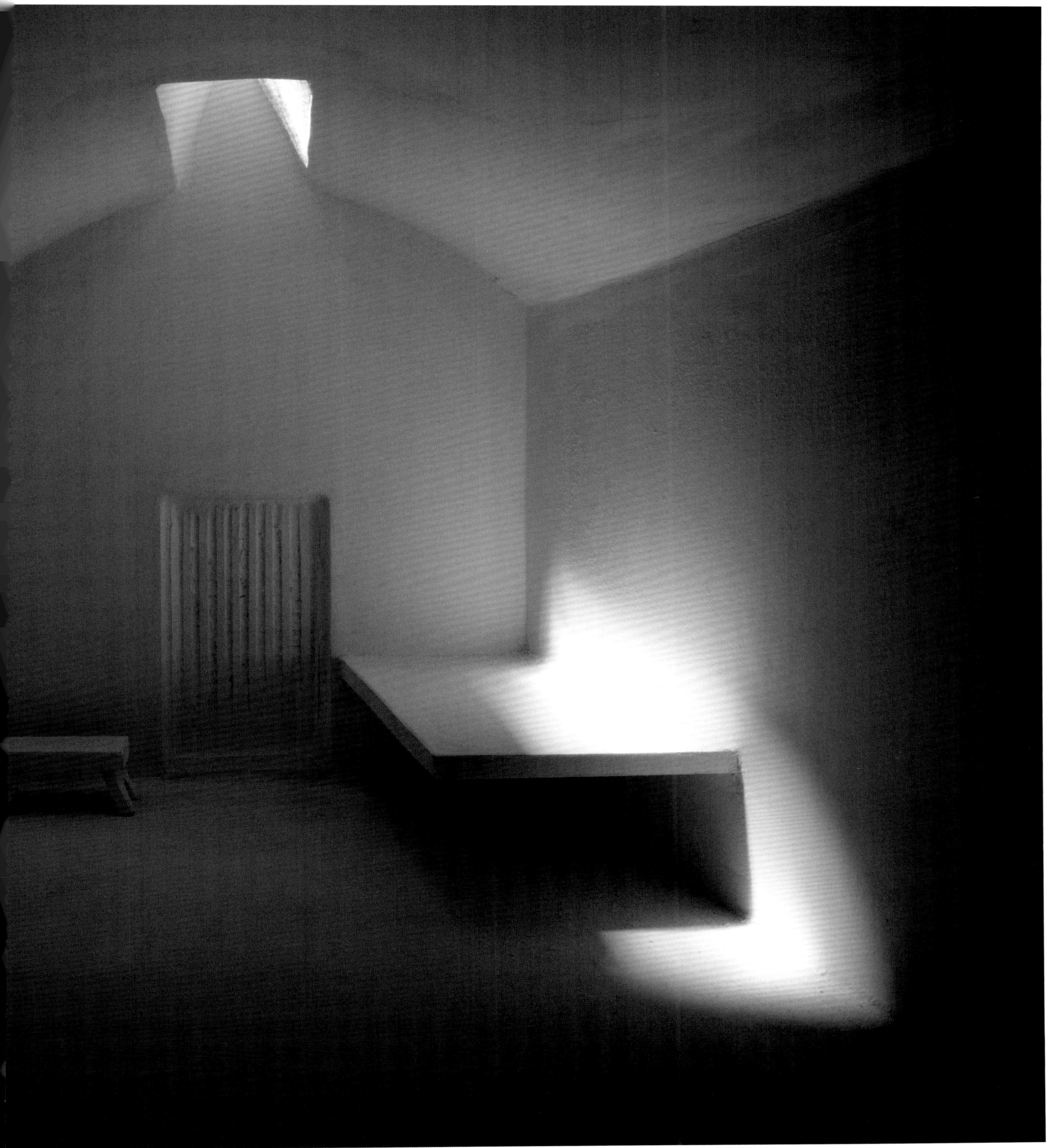

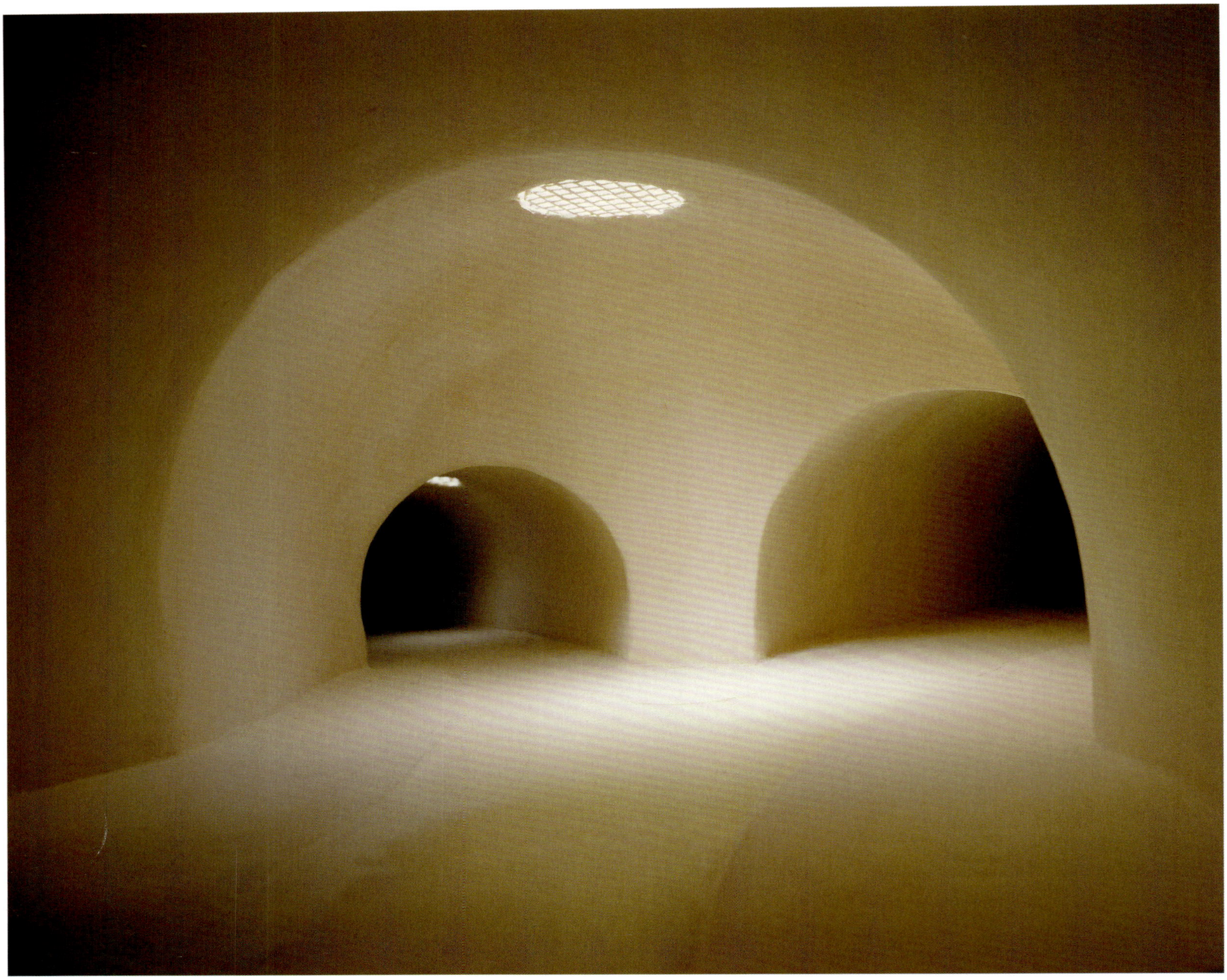

James Casebere
Two Tunnels from Right (Horizontal),
1998
Cibachrome dye transfer print
121.9 × 152.4 cm / 48 × 60 in

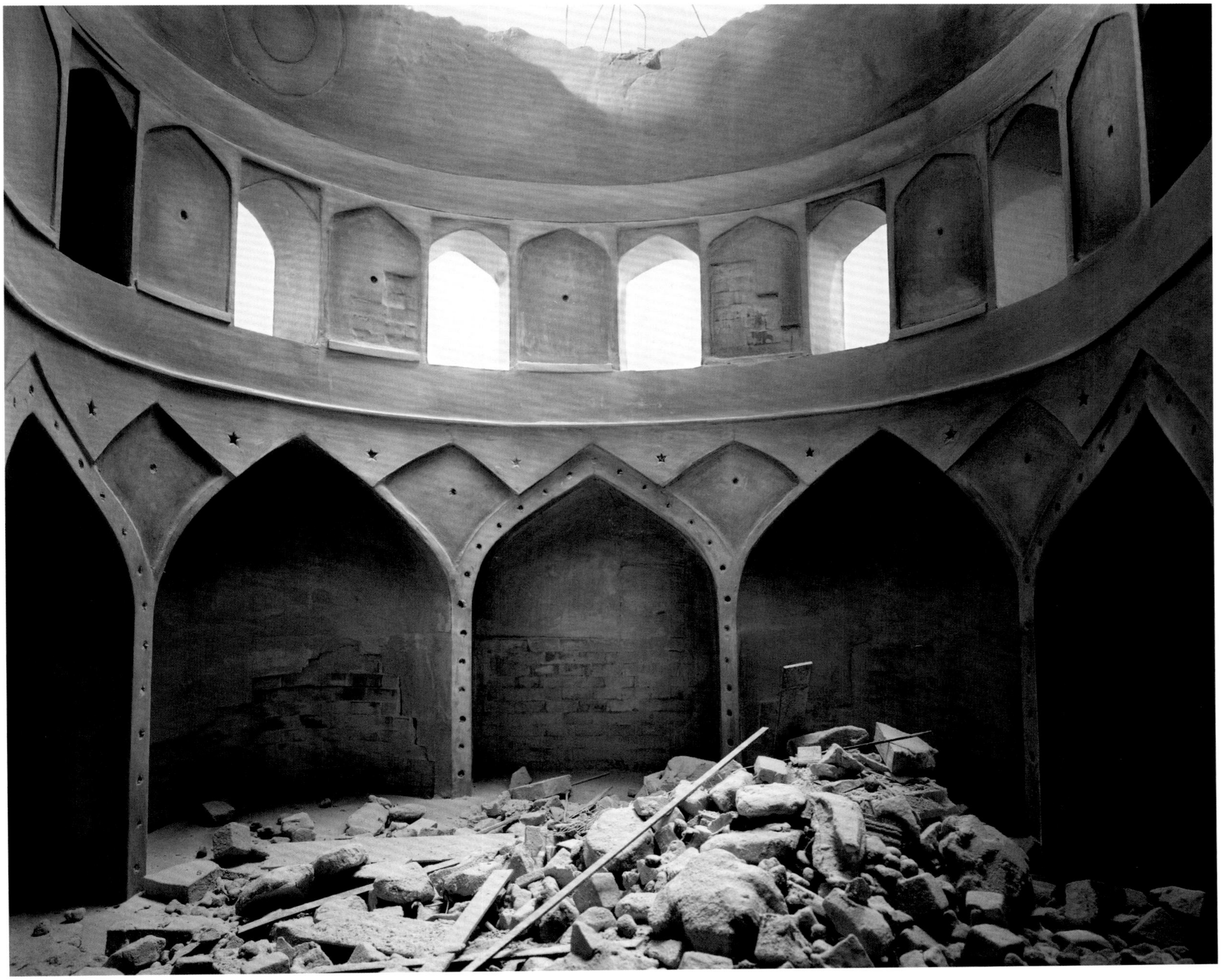

Samarra, 2007
Digital C-print, dimensions variable

David Levinthal

David Levinthal works with model worlds, but rather than fabricating them, he arranges and photographs miniature toy figures. Levinthal taps into American cultural stereotypes with his series 'The Wild West' (1987–9) (informed very much by the omnipresence of the TV Westerns he watched in his childhood in the 1950s) and 'American Beauties' (1989–90), with its lone female bathers, nude or in swimsuits, redolent of the 1950s' pin-up and Hollywood stars. Levinthal keeps the figures in partial focus in order to, as he says, 'submerge the toy-ness of the image, smooth it over.'[12] His set-ups and photographs animate the toys, spinning out the fantasies they prompt but at the same time introducing a sinister and menacing edge, especially with the black skies over the beaches in 'American Beauties.'

Levinthal's darkest and most challenging work is 'Mein Kampf' (1993–4). The work began when Levinthal saw a Hitler figurine in a toyshop in Austria and discovered that someone had moulds from the 1930s and was remaking and hand-painting Nazi figures. 'Mein Kampf' is shocking because of the way its use of toy models seems to ignore the seriousness and solemnity of the Holocaust. The work embodies the artist's own struggle with representing his vicarious experience of the Holocaust, which has been passed down to him through representations in films, books and photographs. Like his earlier series, these are Polaroids made with a 20×24 inch Land Camera, with the aperture wide open to create a shallow focus plane just before or behind the toy objects. This creates an ambiguity intended to draw the viewer in. The 'Mein Kampf' photographs, especially those staging the pageantry of the Nazis, are as he says 'seductively beautiful.' They also involve a deliberate eroticizing of the murder process, with the use of naked Japanese figurines for the portrayal of female victims. Levinthal had used such figures before for his photographs, 'Desire' (1990–1), which explored pornographic fantasies without picturing the explicit body.

In dealing with how the Holocaust circulates through mediated forms of representation, Levinthal's controversial use of sexualized figures as victims made a point about how popular representations have eroticized the Holocaust. As James E. Young has said, 'he was only showing a Holocaust porno-kitsch already at play in the cultural transformations of these terrible scenes.'[13] Levinthal also dramatizes our involvement in the scene of one of these tableaux when he puts the viewer in the position of the implied third gun in a scene showing the figures of SS officers shooting four naked women represented by the Japanese figurines. The shock of the series is his refusal to treat this history any differently than the fantasy realms of the Western and the 1950s' bathers. This might be seen as trivializing the Holocaust, but it could also be seen as acknowledging that we need to think and respond to the Holocaust in ways different from the authority of the documentary material.

David Levinthal
Untitled, from the series 'American Beauties', 1989–90
Polaroid Polacolor ER Land Film
50.8 × 60.9 cm / 20 × 24 in

Untitled, from the series 'Mein Kampf', 1993–4
Polaroid Polacolor ER Land Film
50.8 × 60.9 cm / 20 × 24 in

Untitled, from the series 'Mein Kampf', 1993–4
Polaroid Polacolor ER Land Film
50.8 × 60.9 cm / 20 × 24 in

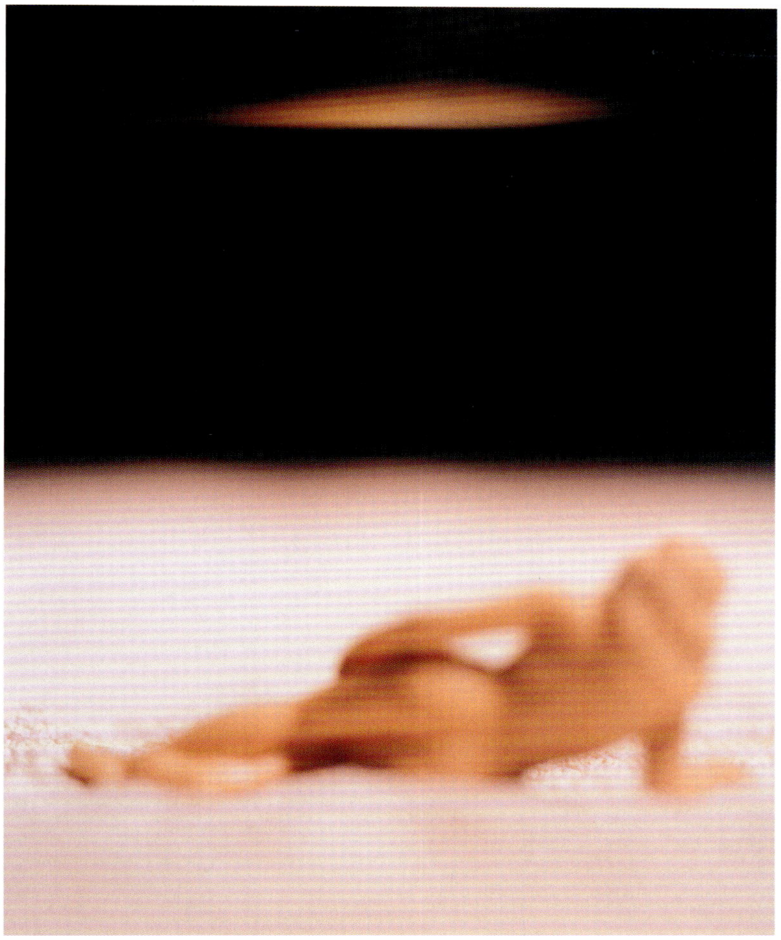

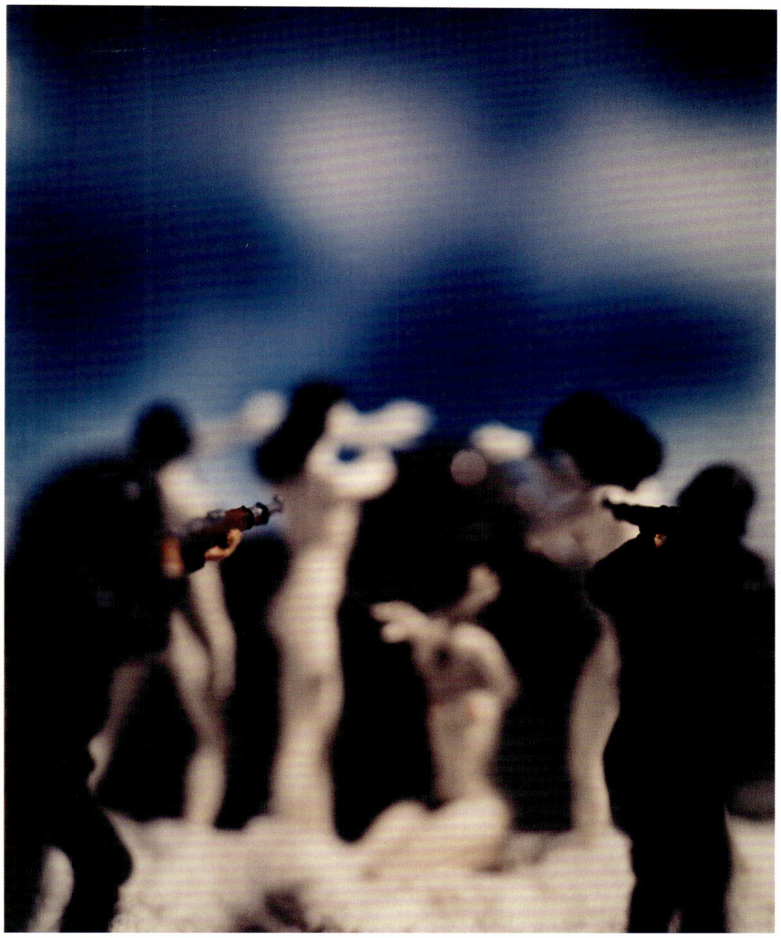

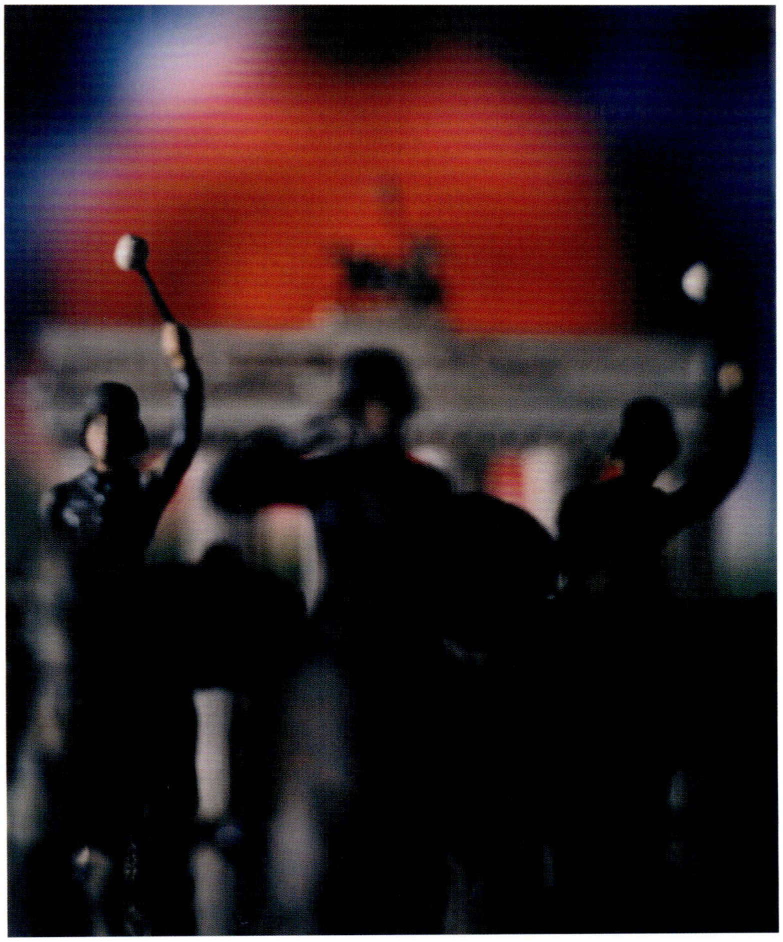

Thomas Demand

The German artist Thomas Demand begins with an image, usually a photograph culled from the media, which he translates into a three-dimensional life-size paper and cardboard model and photographs with a large format camera. His photographs are thus at three levels of remove from the real. The photographed models differ from their source images – they are without contingent details and specific traces of human presence; surfaces are unscuffed, flat and unchanging. Demand's models simplify and abstract, erasing the source photographs to produce both a sense of being out of time and the unnerving sense of an inhuman blankness and detachment. Certain details do, however, give us a sense of a human perspective as his photographs reveal the flaws, wonky perspectives, glued edges, wrinkles and pencil marks in his paper constructions.

Like the work of James Casebere and David Levinthal, Demand's photography could be framed within a postmodern context as a reflection upon a mediated relationship to the world. But the images are distinctive in that they are reliant on source photographs of places that are often notorious because of the events that took place there, and in this respect the elaborate models can be seen as extending and drawing out the aura of the source images and the places they depict. *Corridor* (1995), for example, is based on a hallway in the apartment house where the serial killer Jeffrey Dahmer lived; *Bathroom* (1997) is modelled upon a news photograph of the bathtub in a Geneva hotel where a well-known German politician was found dead under mysterious circumstances. Such crime scene photographs are turned into models and pictures in which forensic detail is lost: Dahmer's florescent-lit hallway appears unreal, like a virtual computer image, while in *Bathroom* the politician is removed from the photograph and only a fold in the bathmat disturbs the order of the scene, an apparent reference to the suspicious detail of the ruffled bathmat in the source photo, with the implication of a struggle and foul play.

Demand's work responds to a faith in things and spaces as carriers of the ghosts of the gruesome or notorious events that took place there. At the same time the images entail the erasure of a distinctive photographic effect. Bereft of contingent traces, they achieve an uncanny and disturbing blankness, the peculiar sense of a photography that has been hollowed out.

Demand has also made models in response to photographs connected with the notoriety of legendary artists. *Archive* (1995) alludes to the film archive of Leni Riefensthal, the maker of *Triumph of the Will* (1935), the infamous propaganda film about the Nazi Party's 1934 Nuremberg Rally. The allusions to the work of such a contentious German filmmaker are deliberate and provocative, but the implications of Demand's source photographs are rarely neutral or banal. The explosive resonance of their associations are set in tension with the quietude of his pictures: the stacks of minimal grey film boxes that make up his Riefensthal picture. *Barn* (1997) is also spare and minimal. Based on Jackson Pollock's Long Island studio as it appeared in photographs taken by Hans Namuth, Demand's version removes the image of the painter and presents us instead with a model of the barn itself, with the only light streaming in through windows and between the barn's wooden slats. What we are left with is in effect a *camera obscura*, a dark room that refers back to the foundations of photography and an aesthetic very distinct from the expressive and subjective art of the painter upon whose studio it is based.

Thomas Demand
Bathroom, 1997
C-print, 160 × 122 cm / 63 × 48 in

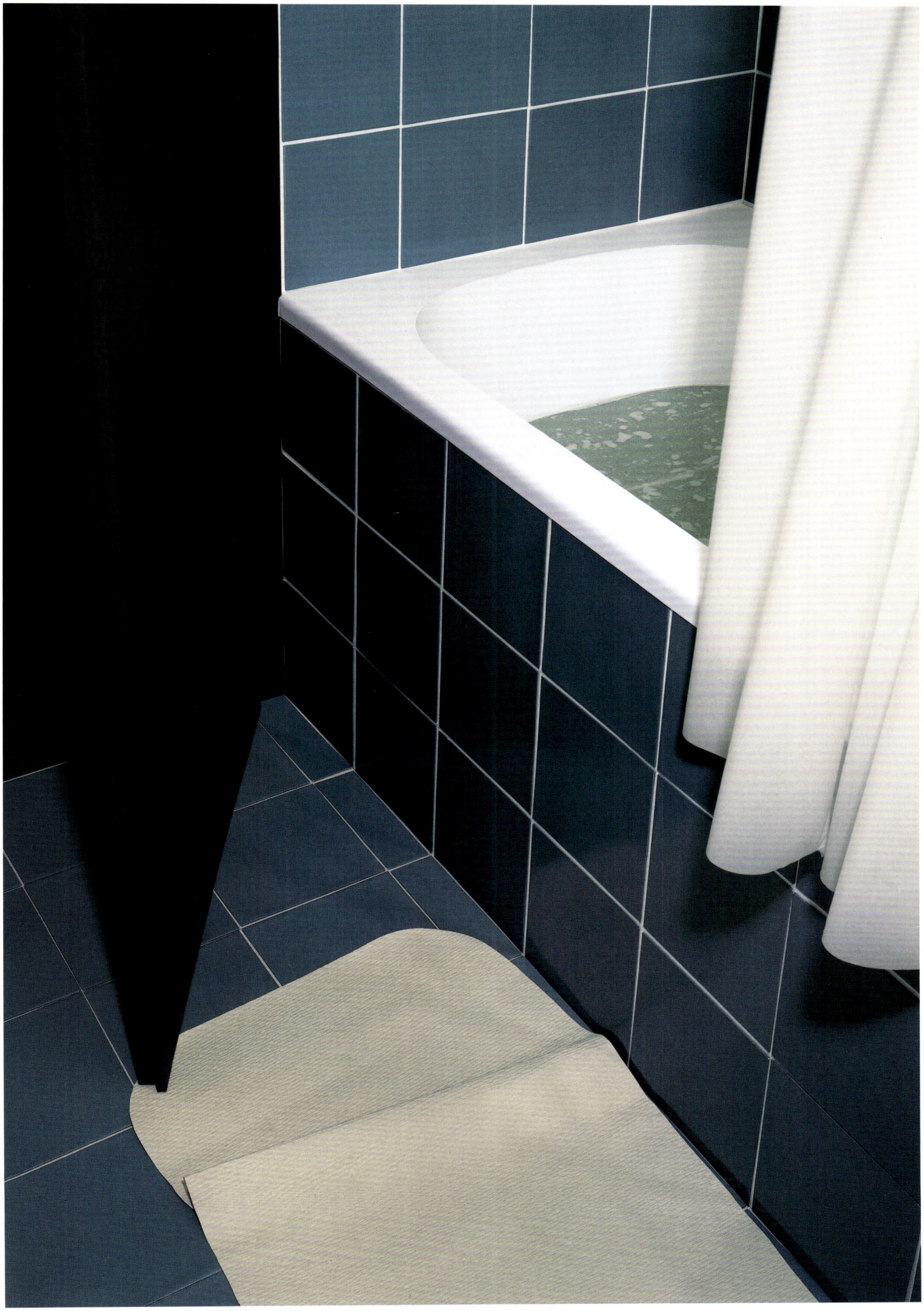

Thomas Demand
Barn, 1997
C-print
183.5 × 254 cm / 72¼ × 100 in

Archive, 1995
C-print
183.5 × 233 cm / 72¼ × 91¾ in

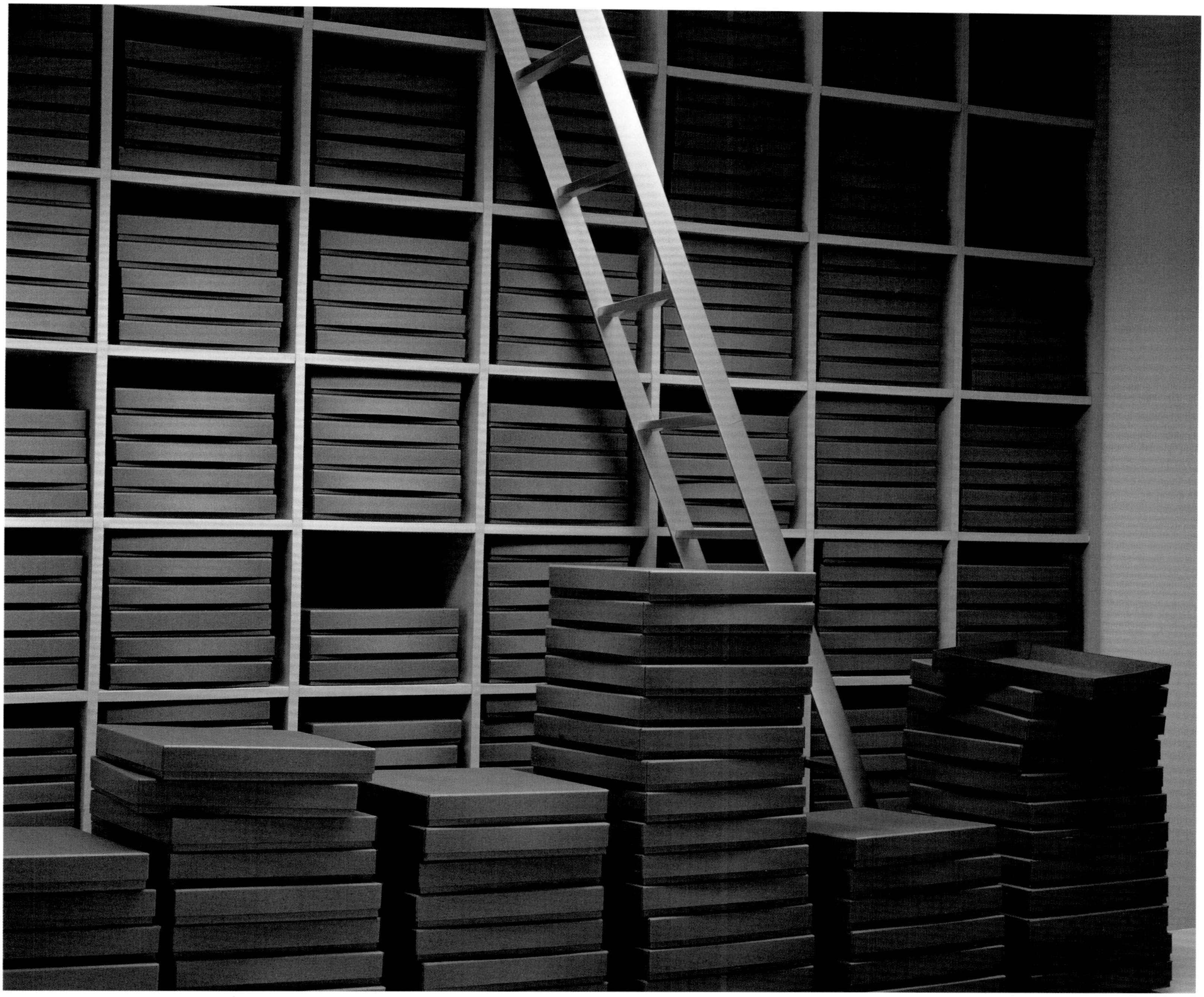

Jeff Wall

Jeff Wall's work has already been introduced in terms of street photography in Chapter Four, but is also highly relevant to the discussion of constructed photography. In many ways Wall inaugurated and shaped much photographic work using human figures and actors in staged tableaux.

For Wall, the tableau became a means of continuing a critique of documentary realism, but without formal strategies of disruption. His work lacked the interruption, the display of fragmentation 'which had become *de rigueur* for serious, critical art since the 1960s'.[14] His work does not have 'any jump cuts which let in the outside, and break up the seamlessness of the illusion'. If much photography of the 1980s was caught up with a critique of the 'straight' image – a deconstructive practice intended to serve as a means to resist the passive consumerist tendencies before late capitalist culture (as borne out by the work of Victor Burgin and Barbara Kruger) – Wall took a different path in his preservation of the picture and his mimicry of the spectacle of public forms of late capitalism through the back-lit lightbox form.

Wall sees his use of the pictorial form in relationship to cinema, and how the films of Rainer Werner Fassbinder, Pier Paolo Pasolini, Luis Buñuel and Jean Eustache accepted technique, generic structure and narrative codes, but introduced new stories and new characters. He mentions Fassbinder's *Ali: Fear Eats the Soul* (1974), a film that borrows its structure from Hollywood melodrama but uses it to tell the story about a transgressive relationship between a middle-aged German widow and a young Arab guest worker. The 'internalized radicalism' in such films is paralleled in Wall's tableaux, where a 'normalized surface' is combined with a subject matter that, certainly with the work from the 1980s, is replete with incidents conveying a sense of social violence and alienation.

One of Wall's first significant and often-cited works, *The Destroyed Room* (1978), presented its staged scene of disaster and violation in a woman's bedroom in the form of a large back-lit transparency that faced the street on its initial exhibition in a Vancouver gallery. It took its cue from and echoed the punk-inspired commercial shop-window displays at that time and it also referred to Eugène Delacroix's 1827 Romantic painting *The Death of Sardanapalus*, in which women are slayed in an orgy of destruction. We are invited to see Wall's picture, then, in terms of an unleashing of destructive male violence, played out within a mock-up of a woman's bedroom; the figurine of a dancer atop a rifled chest of drawers is the only thing left intact. It is clearly an artificial and staged set-up that has been destroyed. While the pictorial surface of Wall's tableaux remains undisrupted, its subject matter shows a series of planar surfaces that have been attacked: the green cover of the slashed mattress, the overturned cream-coloured tabletop and the ripped red back wall, with its orange insulation exposed. The coherence of the pictorial form of the tableau is under pressure from the disorder it displays.

As figures enter the tableaux, they are often used to enact scenarios of alienation, unfreedom and conflict that oppose the normative and conservative pictorial form. In *Diatribe* (1985), a scene showing a heated argument between two young impoverished mothers of differing ethnicity, on a winding lane on a scruffy urban periphery, is combined with allusions to the classical landscape of Poussin. Art historical tradition is here called in to give visibility and importance to a marginalized social group. In *Bad Goods* (1984), the figure of a disenfranchised British Columbian Indian, located within an urban wasteland area, holds an imaginary stand-off with the viewer over a box of discarded lettuces in the foreground. *Outburst* (1989), set within a garment factory, shows us the angry gesticulations of an Asian floor manager as he berates one of the workers.

In a 1999 interview Wall described how his relation to photography was changing. He began by contesting the classical idea of photography as too rooted in fact and putting that factual claim in suspension, emphasizing photography's relation with other arts, mainly cinema and painting; but now he talks about a mimesis of photography as photography.[15] Achieving a seamless photographic look often involved a long, labour-intensive process of production. Even for such fantasmatic scenes as *Flooded Grave* (1998–2000), in which the bottom of a grave opens out onto a slice of the ocean floor, Wall went to great trouble to maintain the illusion that this was a straight photograph, building a tank in his studio from moulds of the dug-out grave which he filled with sea creatures, and digitally combining pictures of this with photographs taken from two cemeteries, all in such a way you could not see the joins.

Morning Cleaning, Mies Van der Rohe Foundation, Barcelona (1999) also involved a seamless combination of different negatives. Nearly 2 by 3.5 metres in size, it celebrates the sumptuous Modernist interior of the reconstruction of Mies's German pavilion (the 1929 original was destroyed), the splendour of its materials brought out by the beautiful early-morning light. The building's windows are covered by soap suds as they are in the process of being cleaned by a black male, a figure that serves as a reminder of the labour that sustains the look of this architecture. But gone is the sense of resistance and conflict characterizing the tableaux of the 1980s. The effect is one of subservience and polite compliance; the art historian Julian Stallabrass has even compared the figure to 'those depictions of farm workers in eighteenth-century England, defined by their fixed place in the natural hierarchical order'.[16]

Jeff Wall
Bad Goods, 1984
Transparency in lightbox
229 × 347 cm / 90⅛ × 136⅝ in

The Destroyed Room, 1978
Transparency in lightbox
159 × 229 cm / 62½ × 90⅛ in

Morning Cleaning, Mies van der Rohe Foundation, Barcelona, 1999
Transparency in lightbox
187 × 351 cm / 73⅝ × 138⅛ in →

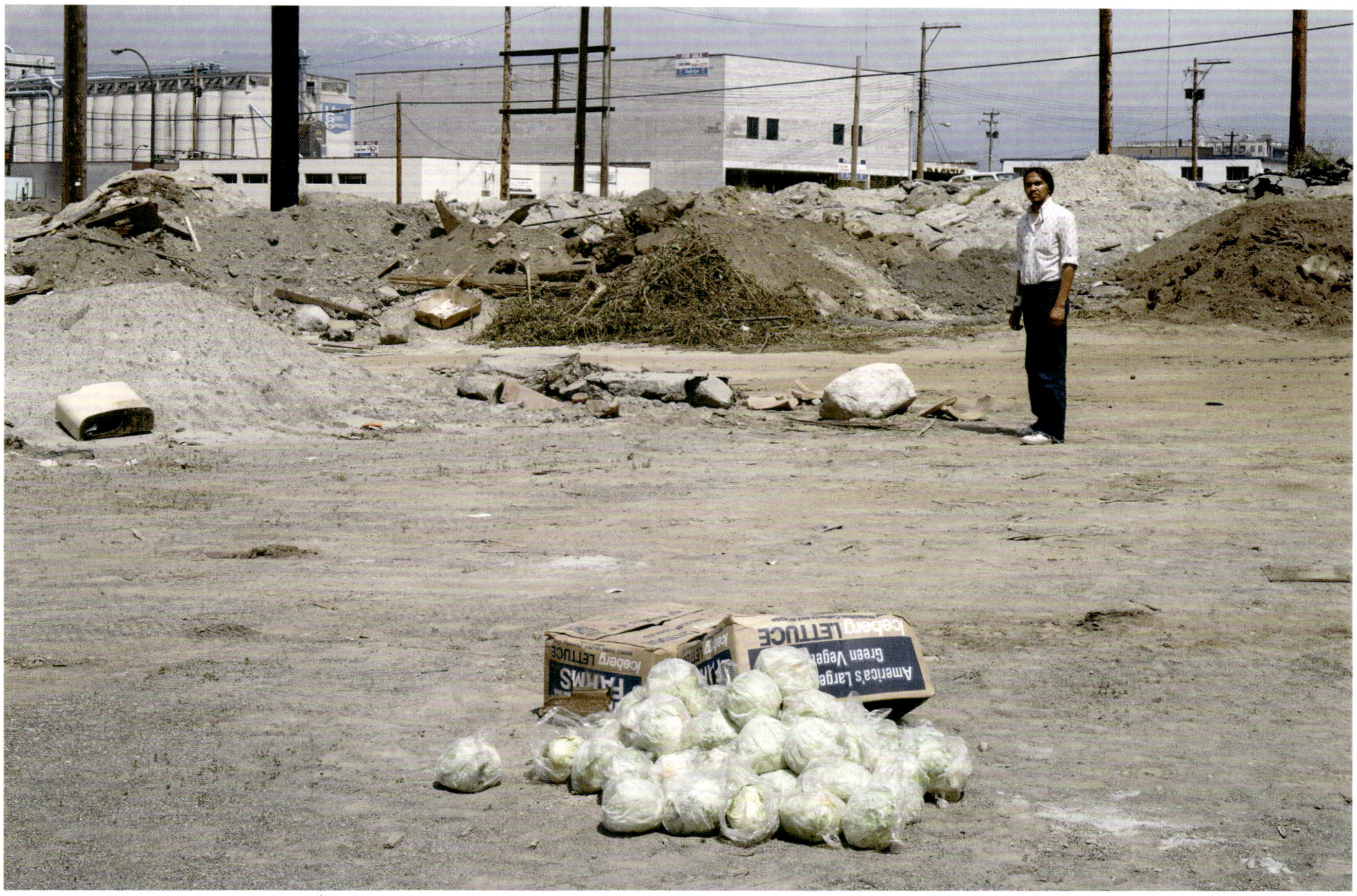

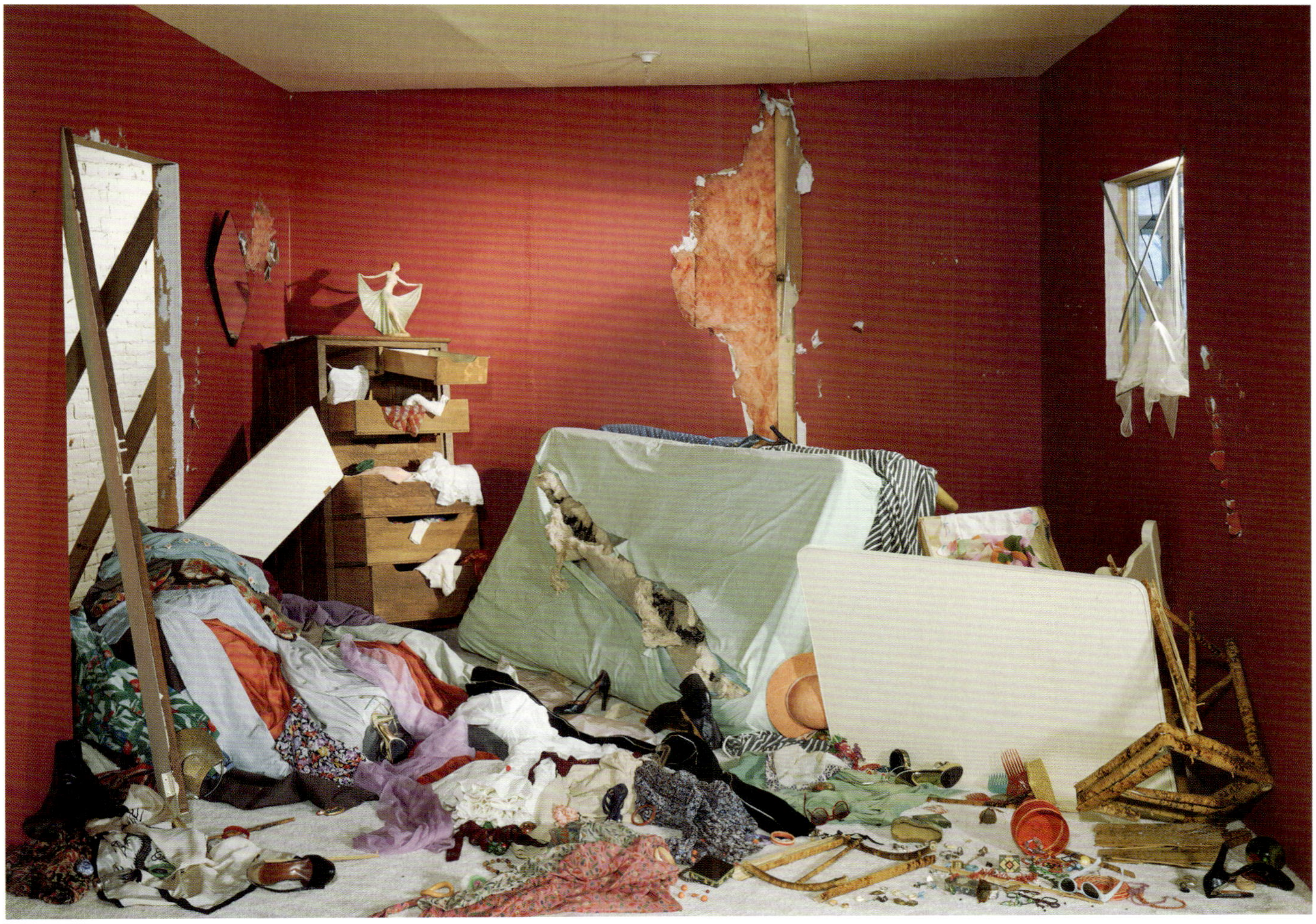

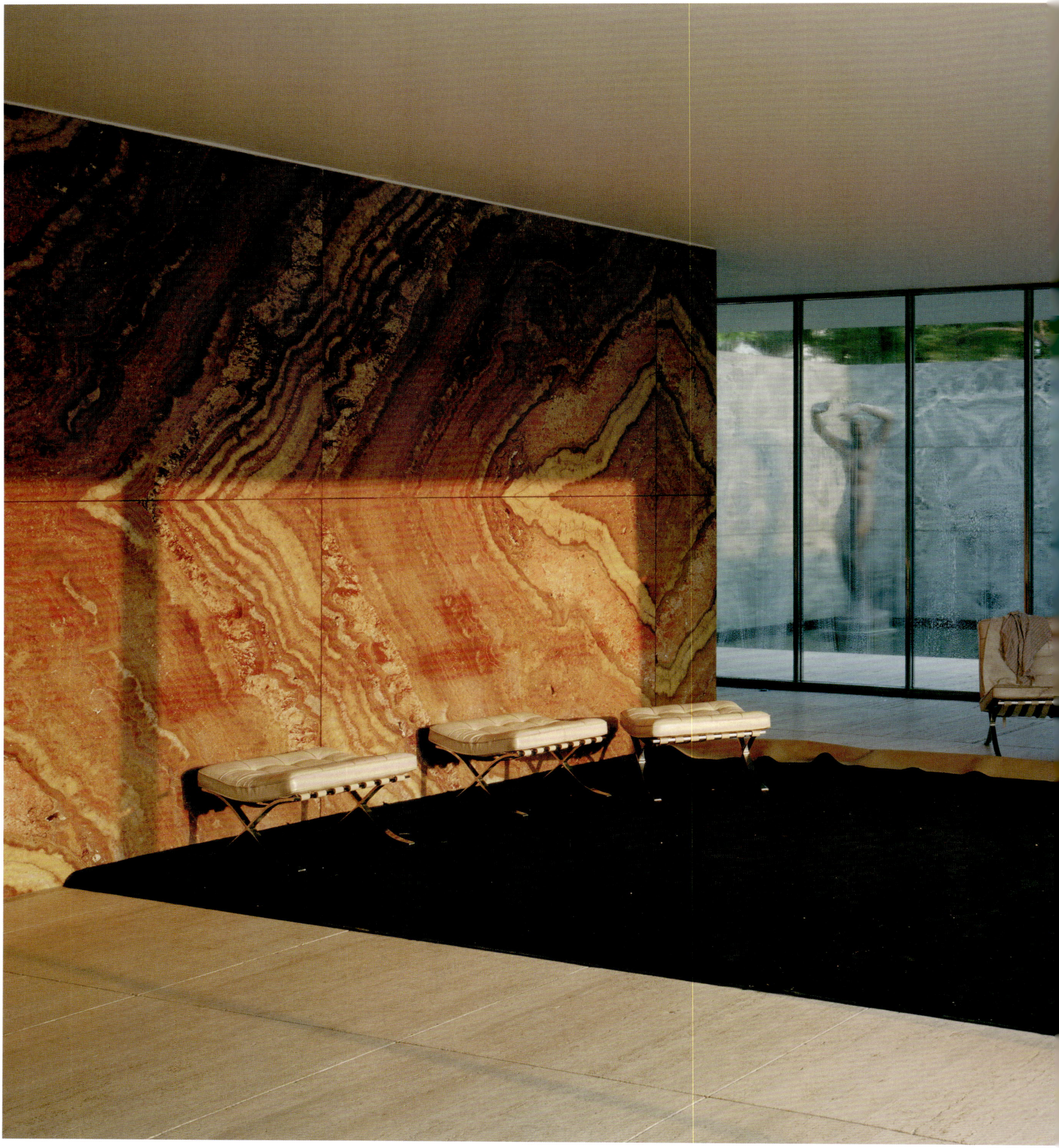

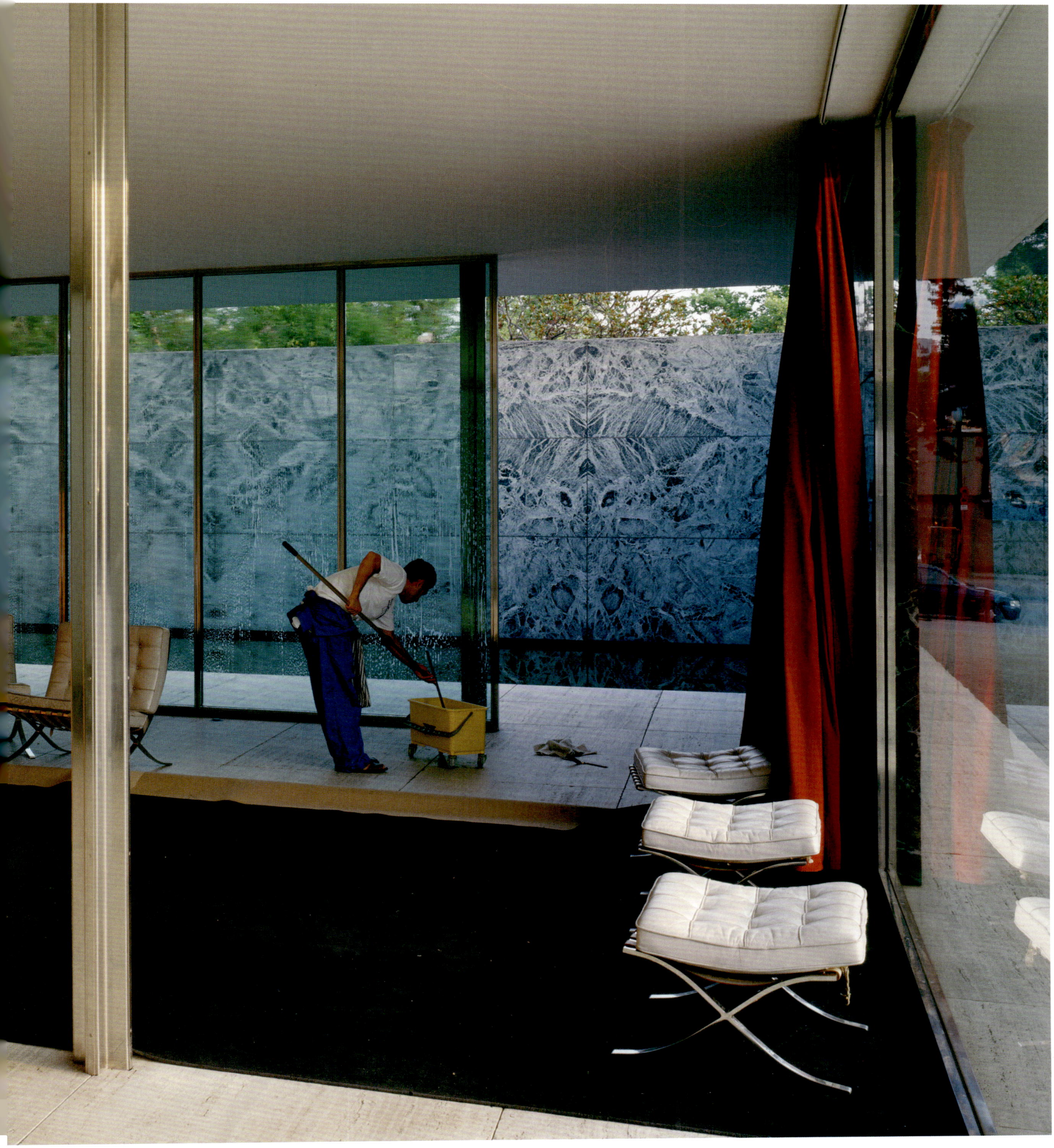

Gregory Crewdson

Gregory Crewdson's pictures are elaborate, involving the labour-intensive production methods of big-budget motion pictures (a crew of forty for his series 'Beneath the Roses' (2003–5), for example). In many respects his photographs can be seen to take their cue from Jeff Wall's staged photographs, but there is an additional cinematic quality as Crewdson has also started to populate his tableaux with recognizable Hollywood film stars. In Wall's pictures, despite their expensive and lavish production, the figures populating them remained anonymous.

Crewdson started using Hollywood actors in his pictures following a commission for a portfolio for *New York Times Magazine*, a feature that formed the series 'Dream House', with its tableaux set in response to a house in Vermont that had been empty for ten years but had much of its furnishings and décor still in place. In the magazine, the use of film stars was a way of linking Crewdson's art to the 'worldy and topical needs of a weekly magazine.'[17] He engaged Hollywood celebrities such as Julianne Moore, Tilda Swinton, Gwyneth Paltrow and Philip Seymour Hoffman as protagonists. Such stars aided in his photographs' blurring with the movies, a relation already in place through the clear allusions earlier work had made to films by David Lynch and Steven Spielberg. At the same time, when Crewdson's photographs are exhibited in galleries or published as artist's monographs, the aura of such stars, like the high-end production values of his photographs, helps underline and maintain their value as luxury art commodities.

Crewdson's lavish tableaux centre on an anxiety-ridden portrayal of small-town American life, populated by somnambulant figures, adrift and alienated from one another. In the pictures that make up 'Twilight' (1998–2002), it is often the suburban home as shelter and refuge that is put under threat by unfathomable forces, symbolized by the cold subterranean world into which the youth's arm reaches down through the drain of the shower of a neatly tiled bathroom, or the dark murky waters that have flooded a living room and in which a cadaverous Ophelia-like figure now floats. Motifs recur and repeat as they do in dreams. In relation to both 'Twilight' and 'Beneath the Roses', Stephan Berg notes, 'the naked women who turn up in trailer doors or bedrooms, mute and disorientated, are like signs of an irretrievably lost paradise.'[18] Cars come to a halt in deserted streets. In one rain-soaked scene, a man stands outside his car, his suitcase by his side, distracted from his routine and the protection of his vehicle by some unexplained moment of revelation or crisis. One picture shows a lone figure in a forest: illuminated by his car headlights, he has been digging up a mass of suitcases and boxes from a deep hole in the ground, in which he is standing up to his waist. What secrets might be revealed remain undisclosed and hidden. The picture stands as an allegory, perhaps for its maker's own obsessive fascination in his art with what can be dredged up from the unconscious.

We get the impression that Crewdson controls the construction of each picture right down to every detail. As in Wall's tableaux, there are dangers inherent in such authored and controlled works: the banishment of the fortuitous and contingent can mean that the pictures are overdetermined and overcoded. Compared with William Eggleston's and Joel Sternfeld's documents of America, Crewdson's spectacles seem rather mannered, glossy cinematic embellishments on the existential cast of an earlier generation's art.

Gregory Crewdson
Untitled, from the series 'Twilight', 2001
Digital C-print
121.9 × 152.4 cm / 48 × 60 in

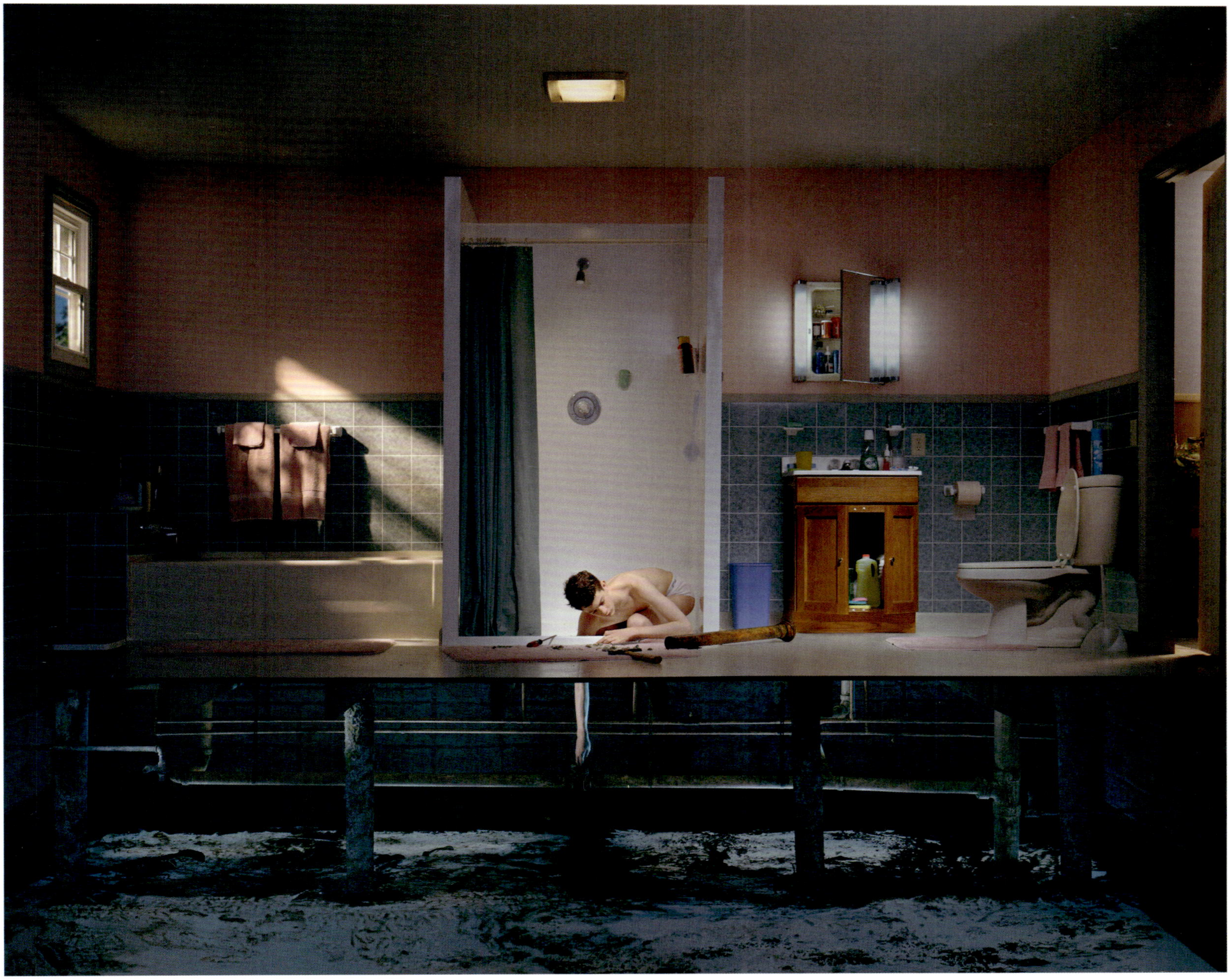

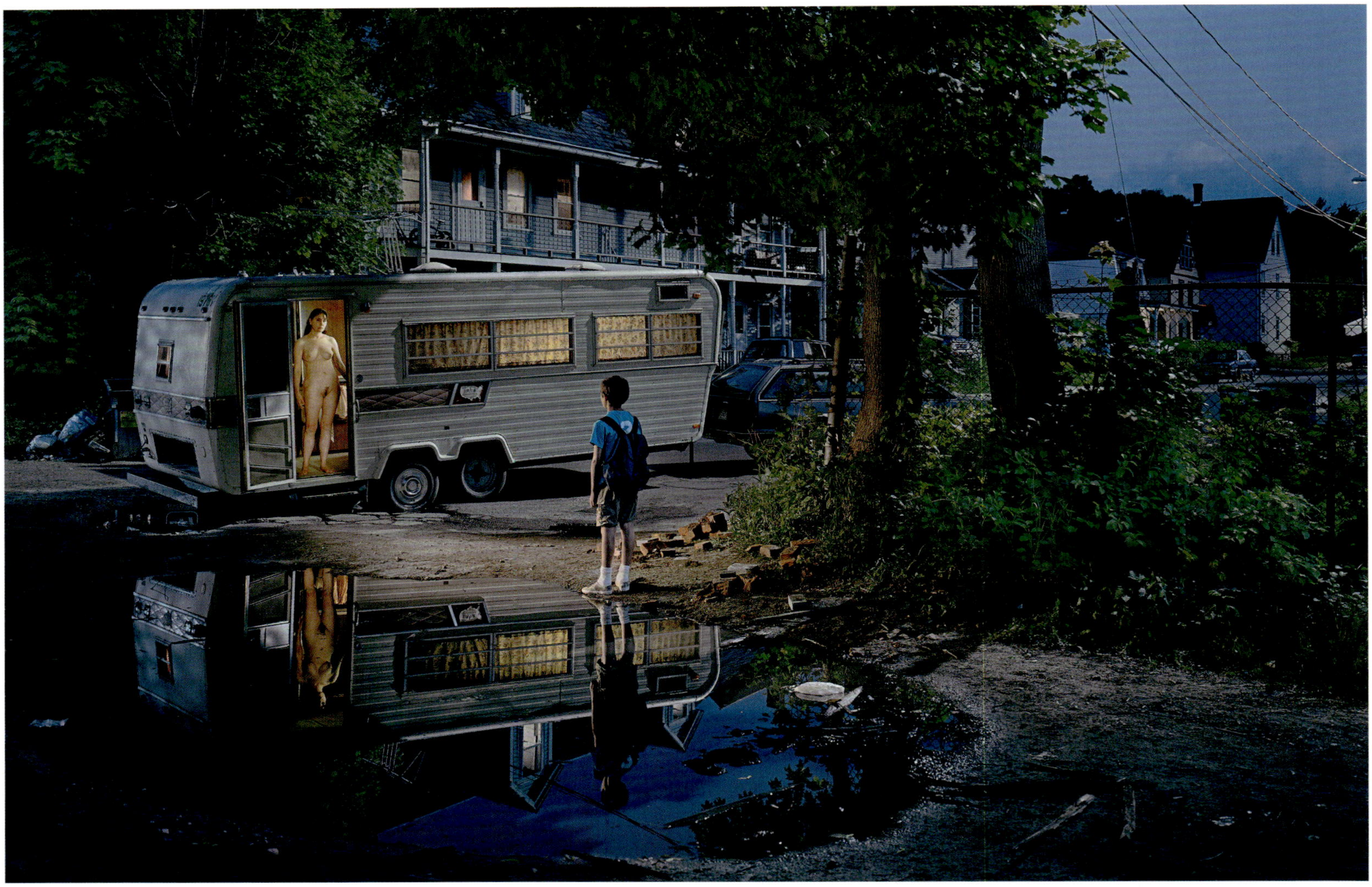

Gregory Crewdson
Untitled, from the series 'Twilight',
2002
Digital C-print
121.9 × 152.4 cm / 48 × 60 in

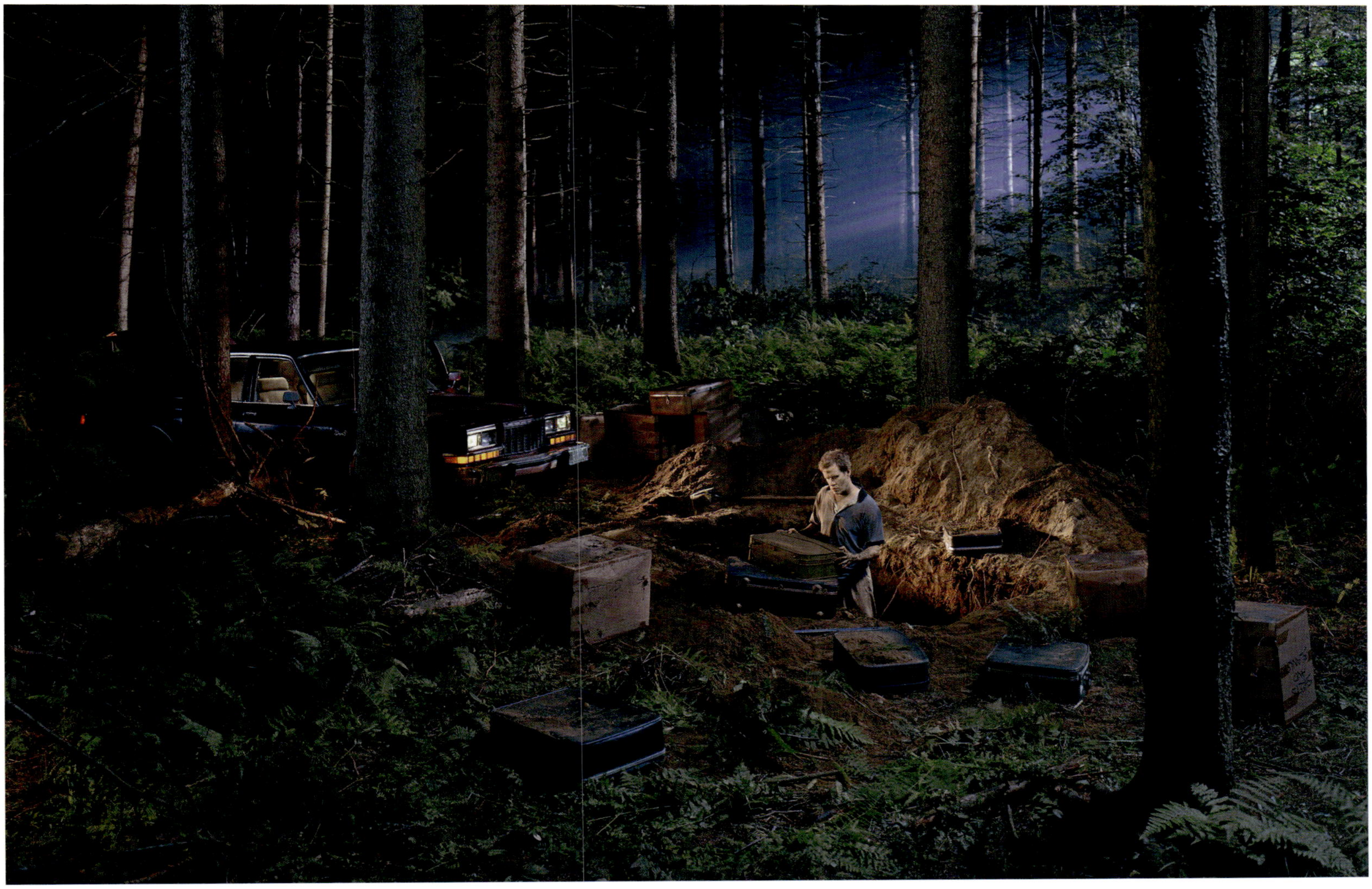

Untitled from the series 'Beneath the Roses', 2003
Digital C-print
144.8 × 223.5 cm / 57 × 88 in

Carrie Mae Weems

The economic and direct mode of production of Carrie Mae Weems's work is very different from the lavish, spectacular and expensive tableaux of Gregory Crewdson and Jeff Wall. 'The Kitchen Table Series' (1990) combines photographs and texts (containing lines from songs, children's rhymes and games, colloquial speech, familiar phrases) to weave a story about a woman's romance with a man, its break-up, her relationship with her daughter, her women friends and herself. Weems acts the part of the woman. The story is told from within an ordinary domestic setting, involving a spare studio set-up, with an overhead lamp and kitchen table. Of this series Weems has said: 'One of the things I was thinking about was whether it might be possible to use black subjects to represent universal concerns...'.[19]

As a viewer we are positioned at the end of the kitchen table looking in. The series opens with the woman sitting with a man leaning against her, his head buried in her neck. There is a mirror placed in front of her, but she looks back at the viewer in a direct, face-to-face confrontation across the table that takes place again a little later in *Untitled (Woman Standing)*, a testimony to the woman's independence and strength. Weems has acknowledged that her work responded to her problems with Laura Mulvey's 1975 influential article 'Visual Pleasure and Narrative Cinema', which identified women with the image and spectacle in cinema and men as the bearer of the look. Mulvey's article came out while Weems was constructing the series and, Weems says, 'Everyone and their mama was using it, talking about the politics of the gaze and I kept thinking of the gaps in her text.' Weems's response in the 'Kitchen Table' series was 'to flip all that shit around, and to start creating a space in which black women are looking back... and challenging all of those assumptions about the gaze, and also questioning who is in fact looking.'

Carrie Mae Weems
Untitled (Woman Standing), from the series 'The Kitchen Table Series', 1990
Gelatin silver print
71 × 71 cm / 28¼ × 28¼ in

Untitled (Woman and Phone), from the series 'The Kitchen Table Series', 1990
Gelatin silver print
71 × 71 cm / 28¼ × 28¼ in

Untitled (Man Smoking), from the series 'The Kitchen Table Series', 1990
Gelatin silver print
71 × 71 cm / 28¼ × 28¼ in

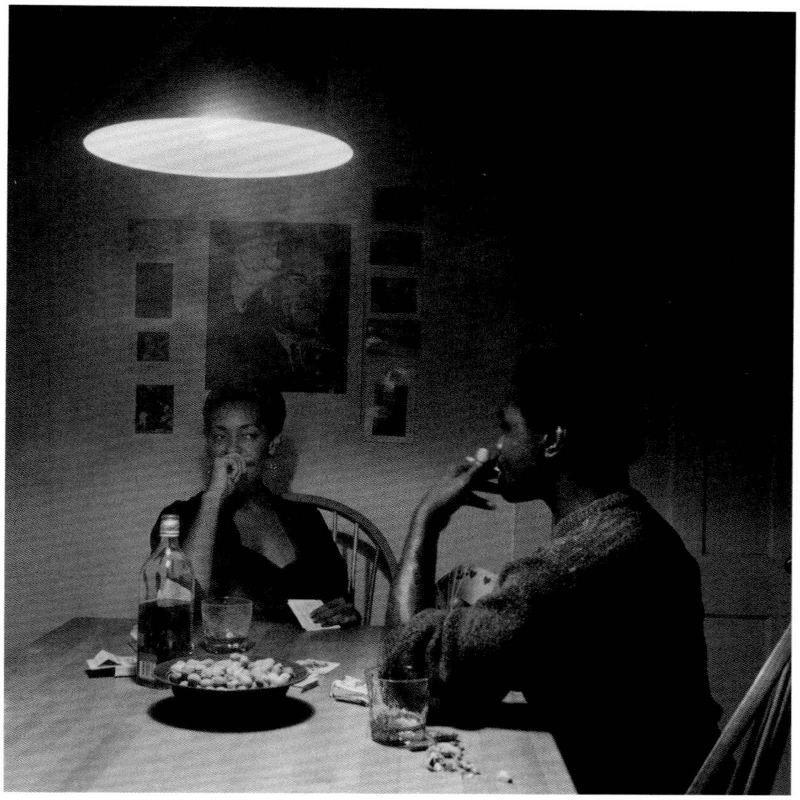
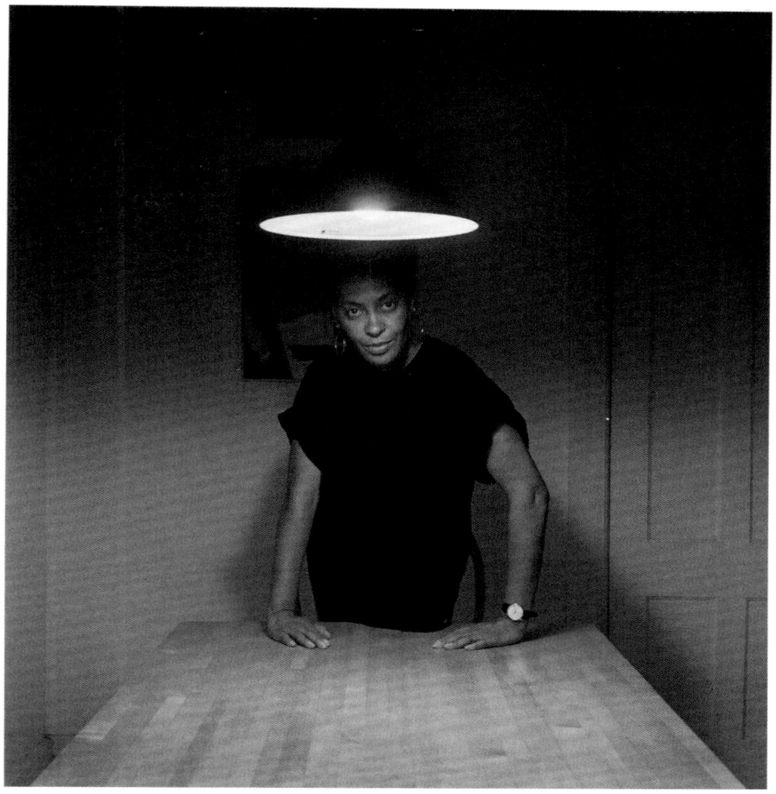
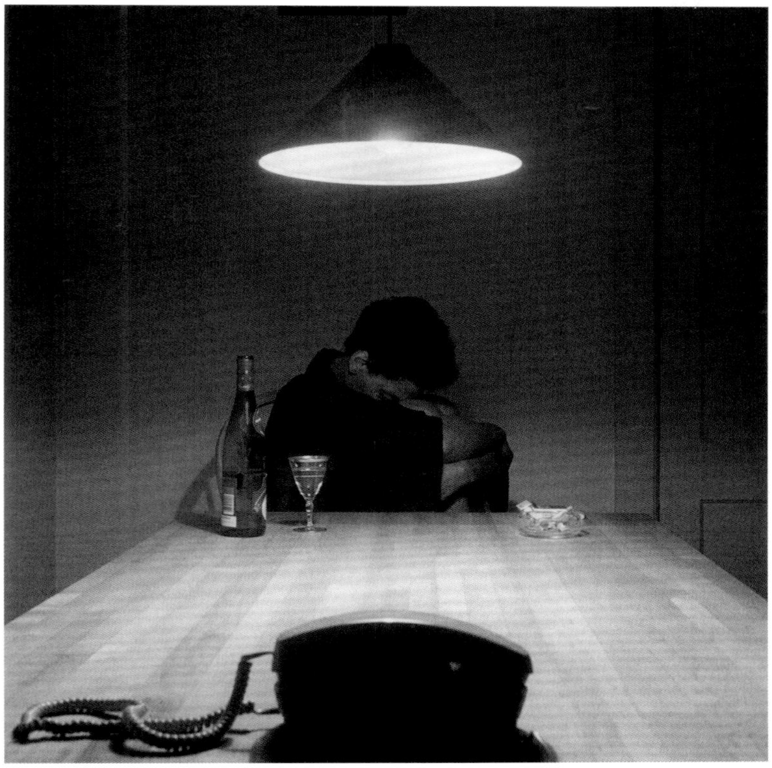

Tracey Moffatt

Until the early 1970s it was the Australian government's official policy to remove Aboriginal children from the care of their parents and place them with white foster parents. Tracey Moffatt's natural mother was Aboriginal, but she was brought up by white foster parents, along with her brother and two sisters, in a working-class suburb of Brisbane. She describes a childhood and adolescence spent 'glued to the television,' watching everything from 'schlock to the sophisticated.'[20] She trained as a filmmaker and her use of tableaux photographs in series is particularly filmic. The photograph in Moffatt's work, as Régis Durand has said, seems like a '"freeze frame" plucked from the unfolding of a film – an impression reinforced by the fact that it never exists in an isolated state, but always within a group, a series, which seems to point toward a possible narrative content, or at least an intention, an energy turned in that direction.'[21]

Regarding her series 'Up in the Sky' (1997), Moffatt says, 'there is a story line, but the hanging order of the pictures can change it around. There isn't a traditional beginning, middle and end. You can be in the present and shift to the past and come back to the present.'[22] The twenty-five off-set photographs, printed in ochre or steel blue, have an uncanny, dream-like quality. They were all taken in an abandoned mining area of Broken Hill in southeastern Australia, where George Miller shot his dystopian futurist *Mad Max* films (1979 and 1982). While some images show what Moffatt saw and photographed, most are staged and set up. The photographs showing female wreckers, sledge-hammering engine parts on the edge of the desert, come closest to the imagery of the *Mad Max* films. Not tied to the narrative, they function more symbolically, suggesting the battles and hardships going on between the poor whites and deracinated Aborigines in the tableaux.

There is a sensitivity to mood and feeling in Moffatt's pictures. Certain looks or gestures, isolated and frozen, take on particular significance. The young white woman in the child's bathing pool, her face caught in light, appears to be longing for a world far from her bleak surroundings. Another image shows her pregnant outside her home, looking sad, with one hand on her swollen belly; a tall scrawny smiling white male stands by her side, one hand on her shoulder and the other holding a gun. An older male figure in the foreground has a distracted look and holds a white bird in his hands. The narrative seems to centre on the woman, who in the opening photograph holds a dark-skinned infant to the window of a dilapidated house while three nuns wait outside. Images showing the nuns holding the child up in the sky, having taken it from the mother, seem to speak about the complicity of the church in the destruction of many Aboriginal communities. Another image shows the woman running to the camera holding the baby, while both white and Aboriginal people appear to be pursuing her. Many pictures show some kind of conflict. One shows a young Aboriginal man standing in the middle of the road, aggressively confronting the camera. Four images show two youths, one white, the other dark-skinned, tangled together as they fight in the dust. Two other pictures from inside a shack show the baby serenely lying on a bed. In one sequence, the sleeping baby is paired with a contrasting picture showing a dark-skinned Aboriginal man staring up into the sky, eyes wide open, his face frozen in fear. The detail of the broken wall in the shack above the baby's head disturbs the calm and seems to presage what we see in the following image, suggesting that the conflict and violent death within this Outback community centres on this child.

'Up In The Sky' has something of the quality of the filmmaker Pier Paolo Pasolini's poetic realism, particularly his *Accattone* (1961), with its moving portrayal of a poor and criminal underworld on the fringes of Rome. Moffatt's photo series 'GUAPA (Good Looking)' (1995), takes us in a very different direction. The ten images are drawn from her childhood TV days. Modelled on the American roller derbies, popular since the late 1930s and shown on television in the artist's youth, the pictures show big, tough women of various races having violent encounters with one another and with the white referee. Moffatt staged and photographed the roller girls against a white studio wall and printed the images so they were half-toned and slightly underexposed or bleached. Tinted in soft-rose shades, evoking the quality 'of a long-lost television show,' these beautiful pictures tend to de-realize the violence of the sport. The series reflects on the base violent impulses sublimated through the spectacle of sporting activities. 'GUAPA's' conscious aestheticizing of violence is, however, offset by the ambivalent closing image, showing one of the women with her skates off, seated on the circular railing, bruised and beaten.

Tracey Moffatt
Up In The Sky #23, 1997
Off-set print
61 × 76 cm / 24 × 30 in

Up In The Sky #11, 1997
Off-set print
61 × 76 cm / 24 × 30 in

Up In The Sky #1, 1997
Off-set print
61 × 76 cm / 24 × 30 in

Up In The Sky #7, 1997
Off-set print
61 × 76 cm / 24 × 30 in

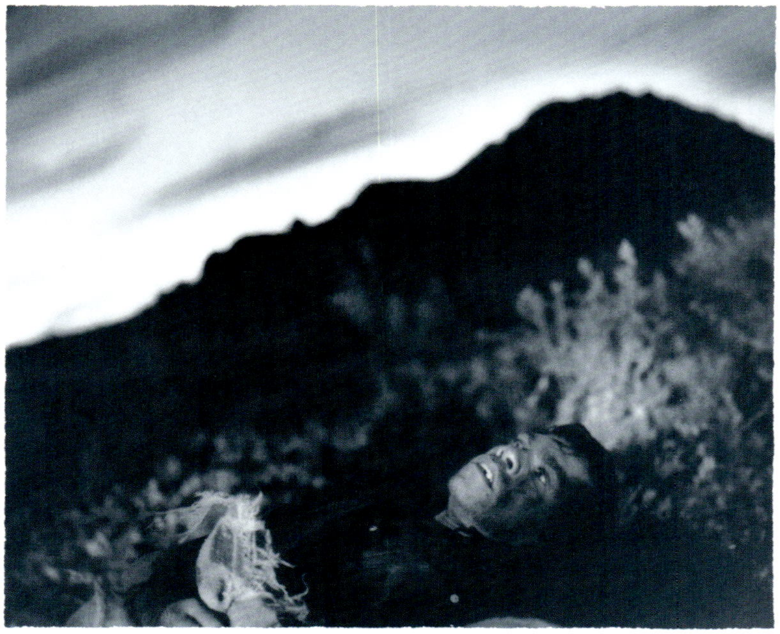

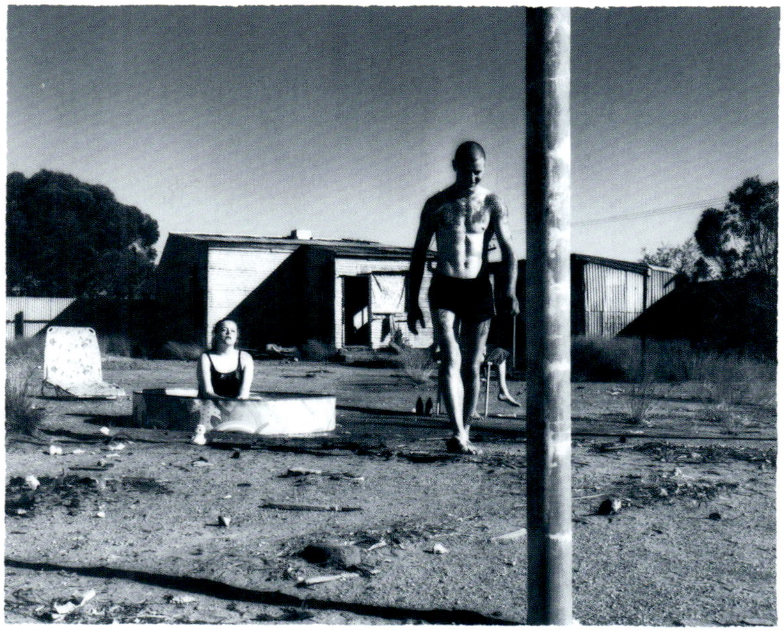

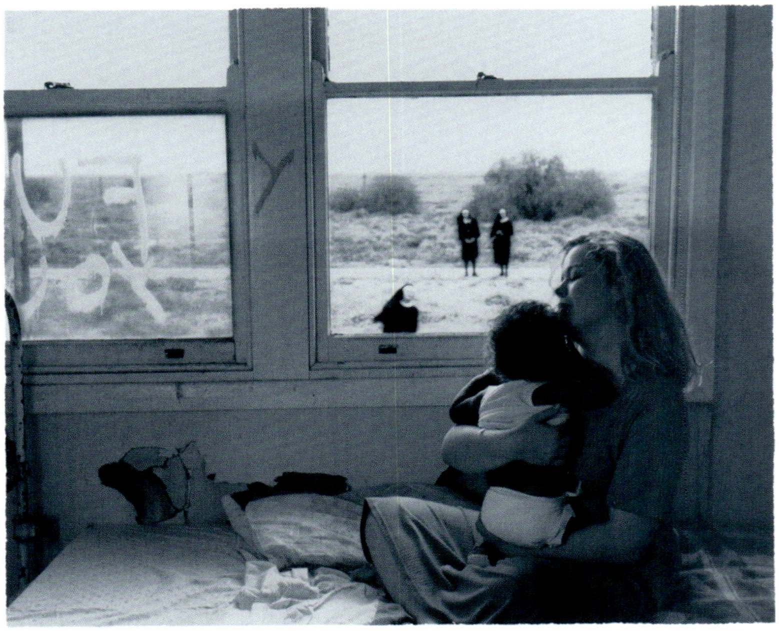

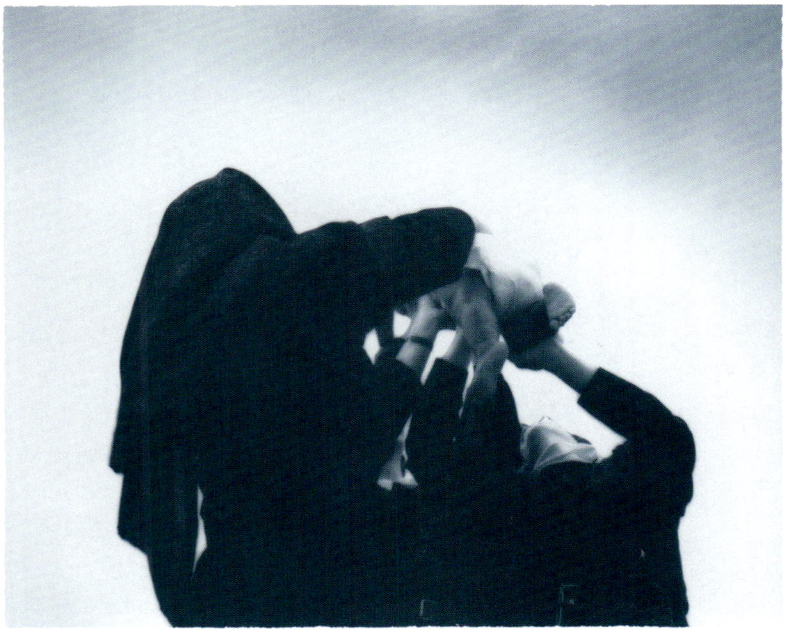

John Goto

The British artist John Goto looks back to political montage through his digitally composited photographs. *Capital Arcade* (1997–9) forms the first of three series of works that Goto has collectively entitled and branded *Ukadia*. Together they provide a distinctive satirical reflection on the cultural and political landscape of Britain under New Labour. While the digitally constructed pictures of *Capital Arcade* are formally modelled on the artifice and colourful excesses associated with advertising, what Goto himself refers to as 'the neon glitz'[23] of mall culture, their citations from well-known paintings effects a significant collision as the quick consumerist take associated with the shopping arcade is mixed in with the evidently more discerning gaze of the connoisseur art historian. The high art of Mantegna, Raphael, El Greco and Poussin lifts the pictures away from the mindlessness connected with consumerism and provides an important utopian counterpoint and ballast to the work. *Capital Arcade*'s glitzy and kitsch spectacle of shopping-mall consumerism contrasts with Goto's following series, *High Summer* (2000–1), which draws upon the genre and conventions of landscape painting to provide beautiful settings for contemporary land use. The idylls associated with the pictures' allusions – the eighteenth-century landscape gardens of Stourhead, Stowe and Rousham and the seventeenth-century French paintings of Poussin and Claude – are rudely interrupted by the groups of figures that populate Goto's landscapes: Ascot toffs, hunters, sporty types, joyriders, drunks, the military, eco warriors, muggers.

Gilt City (2002–3), the final part of *Ukadia*, takes its cue from documentary and street photography. Documentary's tradition of looking at the other is replayed here through the full-figure portraits of outsider and colourful street types. The low trade of shady dealings and goings-on among Goto's street figures provides a parodic echo of the no-less-dodgy trading associated with the pompous city buildings behind them, buildings which come to stand for the architecture of the banking worlds of the overdeveloped West. Many of the pictures play on an unexpected disparity of codes, a joining of sign systems that seem inappropriate. The stylishness of his subjects rubs up against our assumptions of difference. Much as they may appear to stand apart in Goto's tableaux, such figures are partly assimilated by the globalism of commodity culture. Goto seems to direct his satire at the liberal humanist viewer. The punning title of the series draws attention to the guilty unease with which the middle-class tend to view such outsider types, misfits and marginals. In contrast to much documentary, then, Goto is not trying to speak for the socially disempowered; instead he uses signs of difference – albeit skewed and reconfigured – to say something about the value systems that keep such types in their place, on the streets, begging, dealing, hawking or performing. Capitalism, in Goto's pictures, becomes a pervasive monolithic force, readily assimilating and commodifying any signs of subversion or deviance.

Wang Qingsong

Wang Qingsong's work is extraordinary in terms of its excess, critically engaging with the rapid transformation of China in the grip of a fever of modernization.[24] Having trained as a painter, Qingsong first made use of digital composites in such pictures as *Thinker* (1988), which shows him seated on a giant cabbage leaf, meditating before a dazzling night-time cityscape. Just above his hands, which are clasped on his chest, one can see the logo of McDonald's stamped into his flesh, an emblem of China's upheaval. Qingsong has moved away from digital manipulation since 2000, arranging more complex groups of figures in the space of his studio and landscape. His series 'Another Battle' (2001) drew upon the memories of patriotic films he saw as a child. These films portrayed the struggle of soldiers to defeat the Japanese invaders and defend China. Now modernization in China has given rise to a situation that can be compared to a new war between ancient Chinese civilization and modern Western commercial culture. Photographed in the hills of Hebei province outside Beijing, Qingsong's images show traditional military banners replaced by the logos of multinationals such as McDonald's and Coca-Cola. Qingsong plays the defeated commander in this confrontation between East and West; he acknowledges that, 'Mindless pride in our nation is now replaced by a mindless desire for Western consumption.'

Qingsong's work responds to the decadence and glut of capitalism, and the excesses of his work mirror the excesses of consumerism. This might well explain the blatant narcissism and self-promotion of such a work as *Billboard* (2004), which depicts a huge advertisement with ARTWORKS OF WANG QINGSONG in English and Chinese, the address of the artist's English language website and a phone number. Figures are set before this promotional display; some seem involved in completing its installation while others mime everyday street activities. The detail of the fruit and vegetable sellers who have set up store in front of this banner serves as a reminder of China's agrarian past, displaced by the crude and garish promotional and commercial strategies of capitalism. *Competition* (2004) presents the glut of advertising as a contemporary Babel. A surfeit of competing signage leads to breakdowns in communication. Giant walls are covered with hundreds of handwritten and hand-drawn signs, bearing the slogans and phrases of advertisements from multinationals to small businesses. Much as this work comments upon present China, it also recalls the past. The advertising is not unlike the *Da zi Bao* posters littering streets during the Chinese Revolution, handwritten accusations that targeted and condemned landlords, rich farmers, counter-revolutionaries, rightists and criminals.

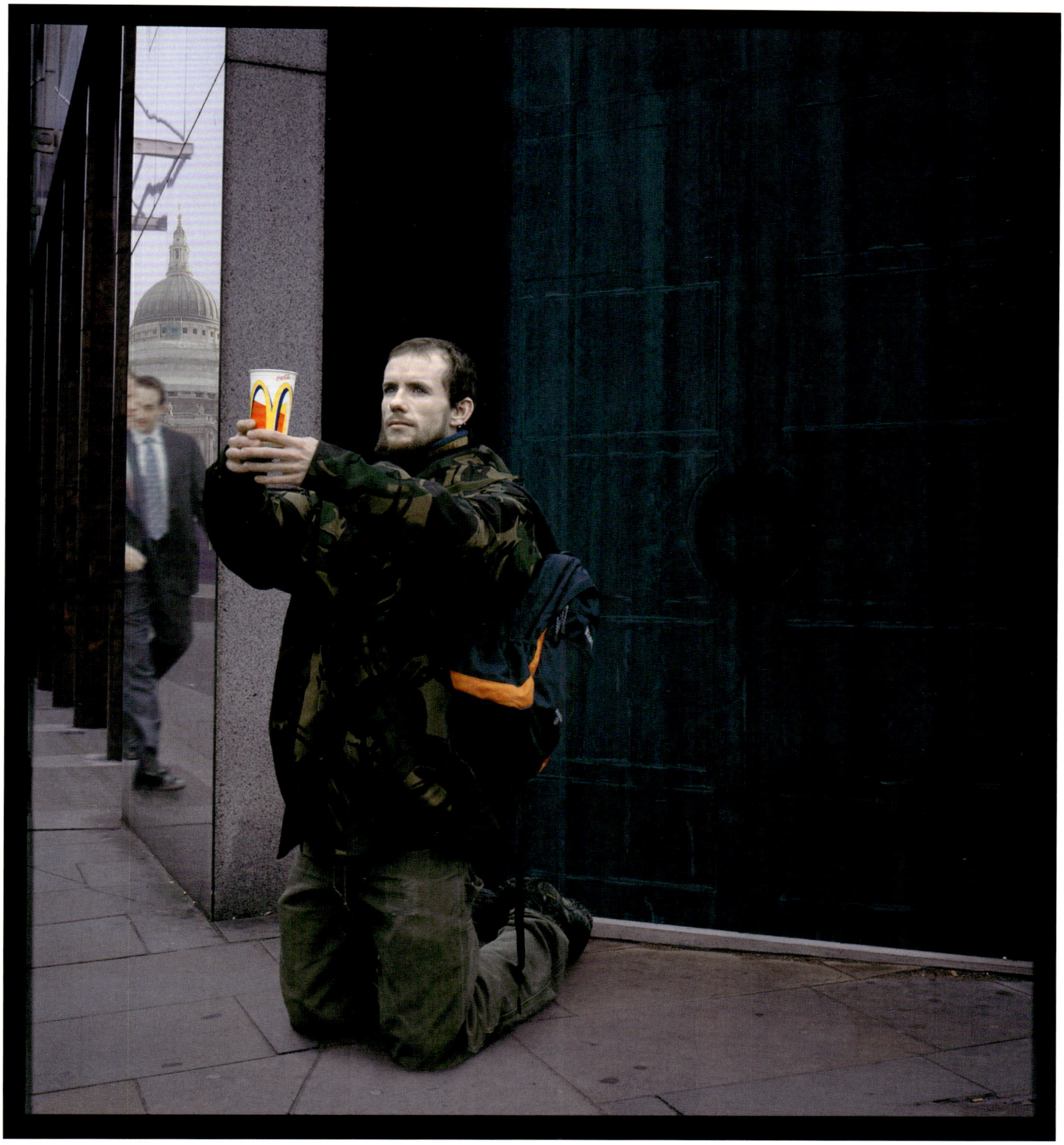

John Goto
Beggar, from *Gilt City*, 2002–3
Micro Piezo print on cotton paper
79 × 74 cm / 31⅛ × 29⅛ in

Unit 3, from *Capital Arcade*, 1997–9
Micro Piezo print on cotton paper
110 × 157 cm / 43¼ × 61⅞ in →

Society, from *High Summer*, 2000–1
Micro Piezo print on cotton paper
72.5 × 110 cm / 28½ × 43¼ in →

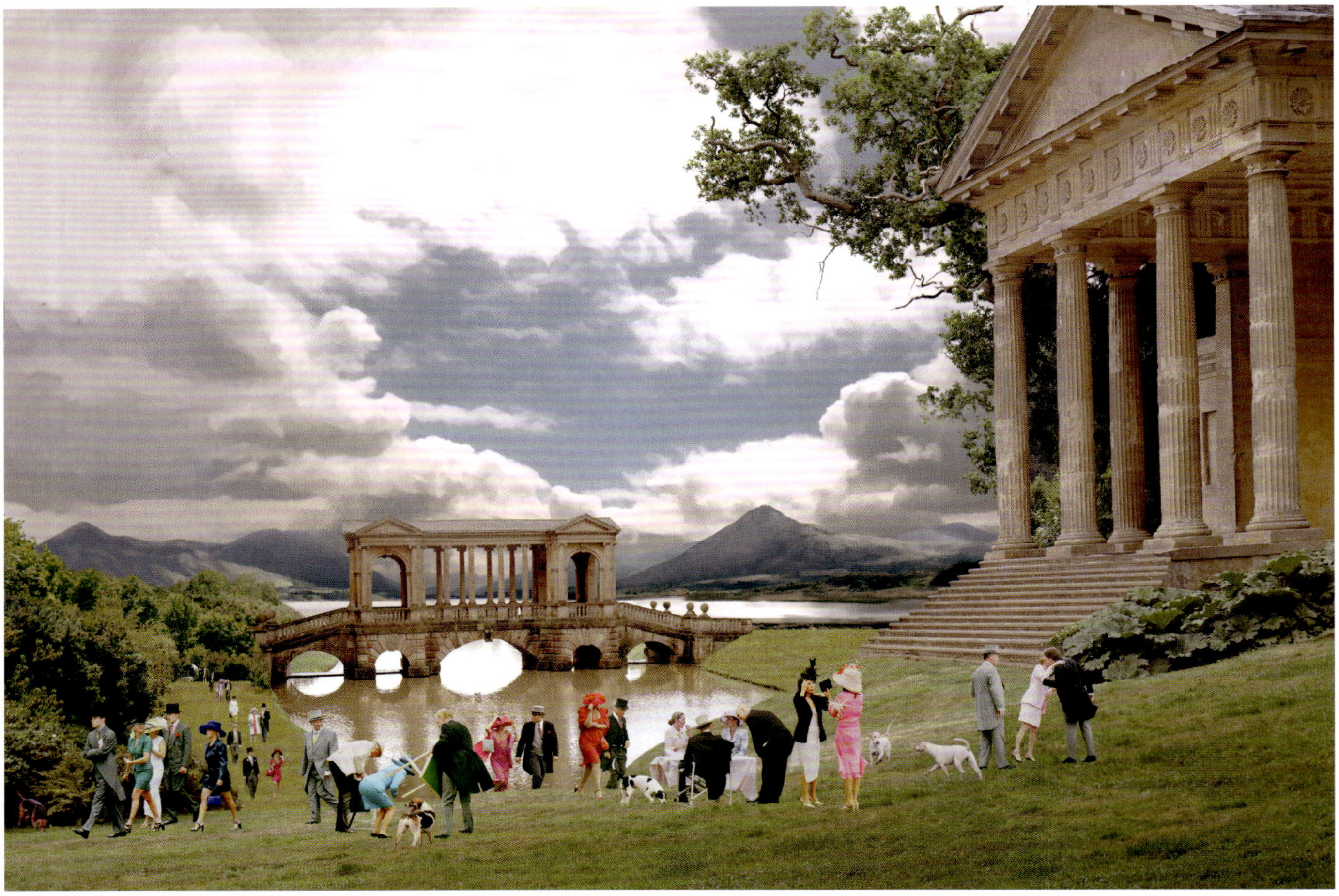

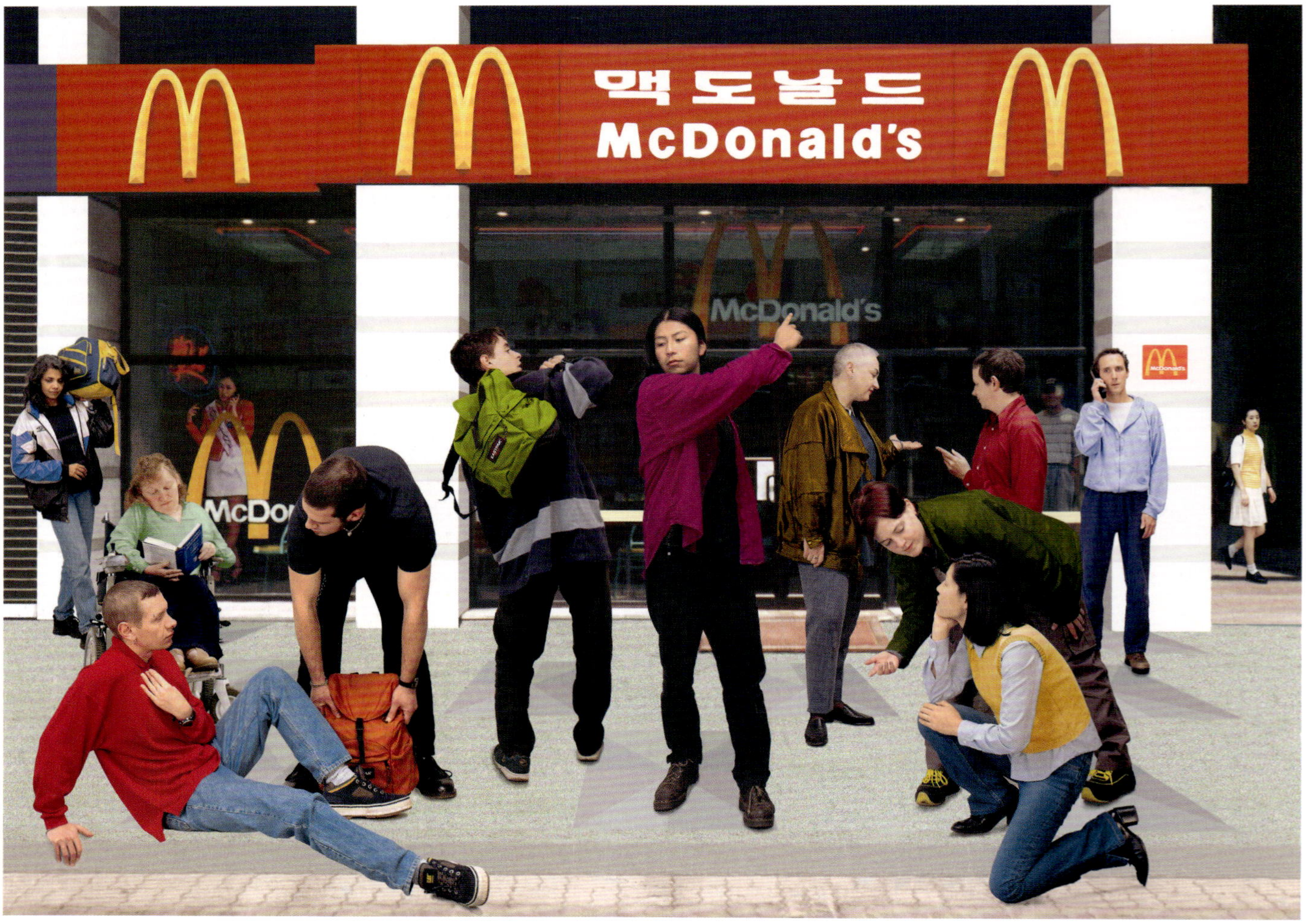

Wang Qingsong
Competition, 2004
C-print, 170 × 300 cm /
66⅞ × 118⅛ in →

Billboard, 2004
C-print
170 × 300 cm /
66⅞ × 118⅛ in →

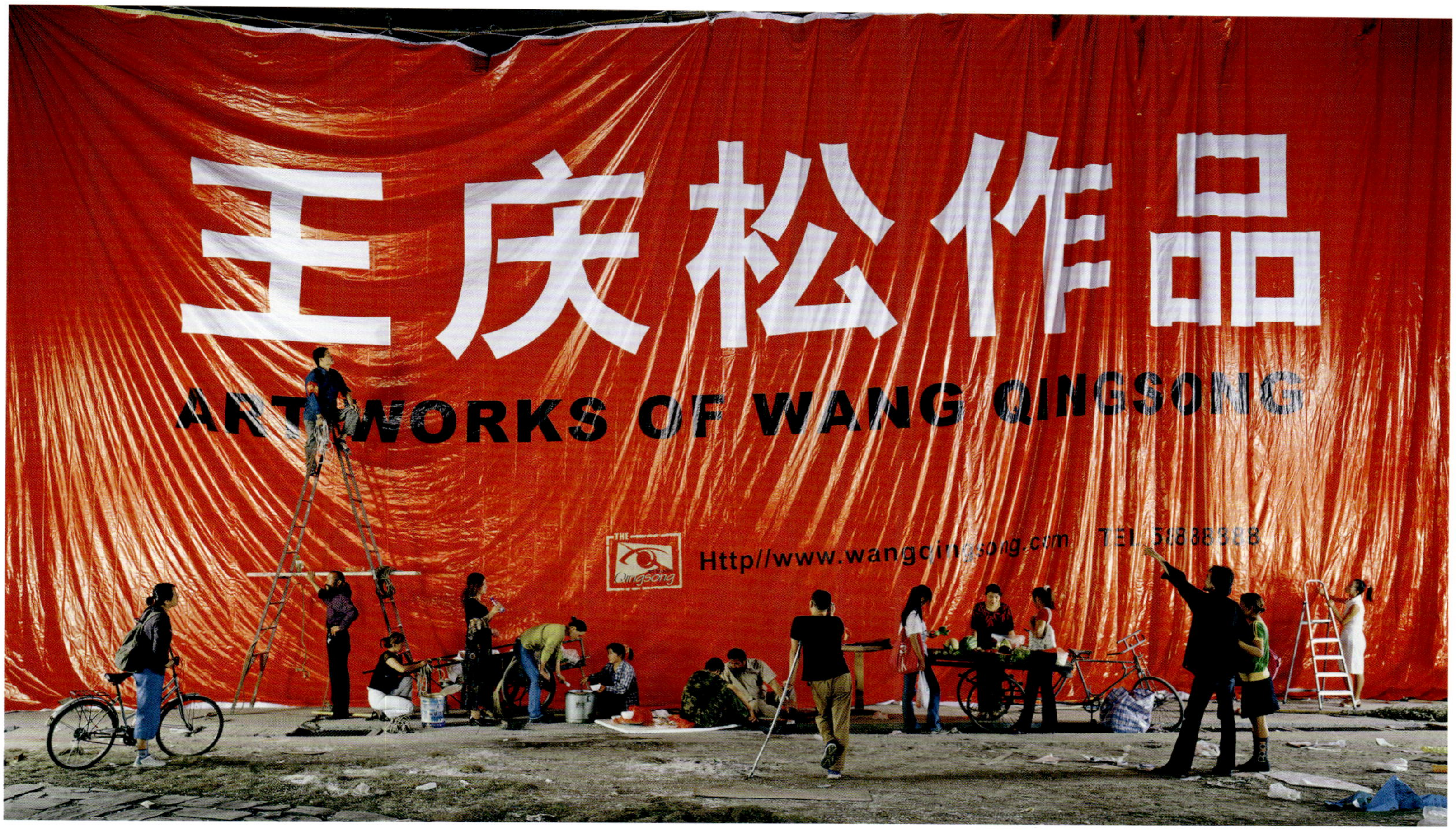
王庆松作品
ARTWORKS OF WANG QINGSONG

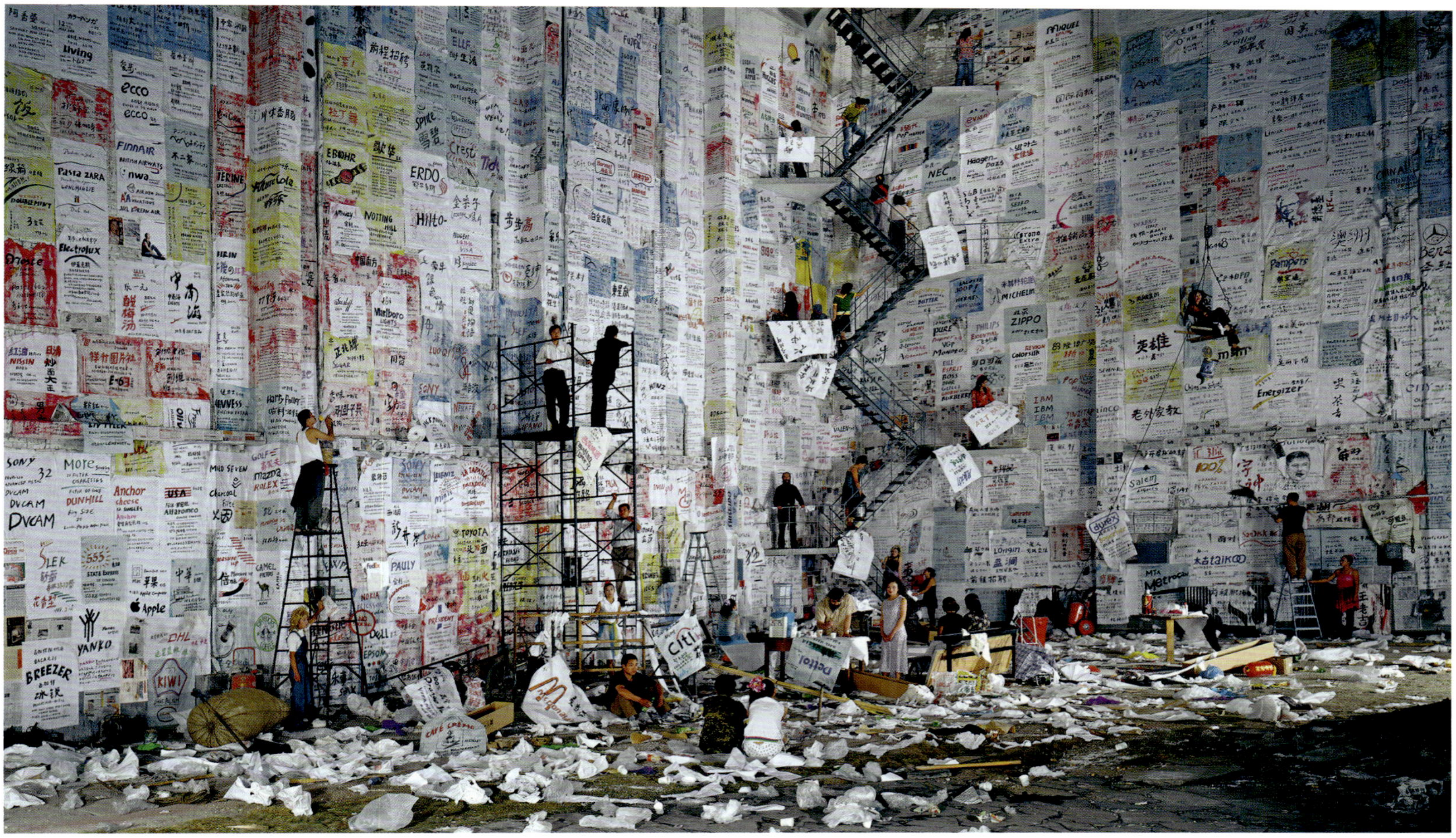

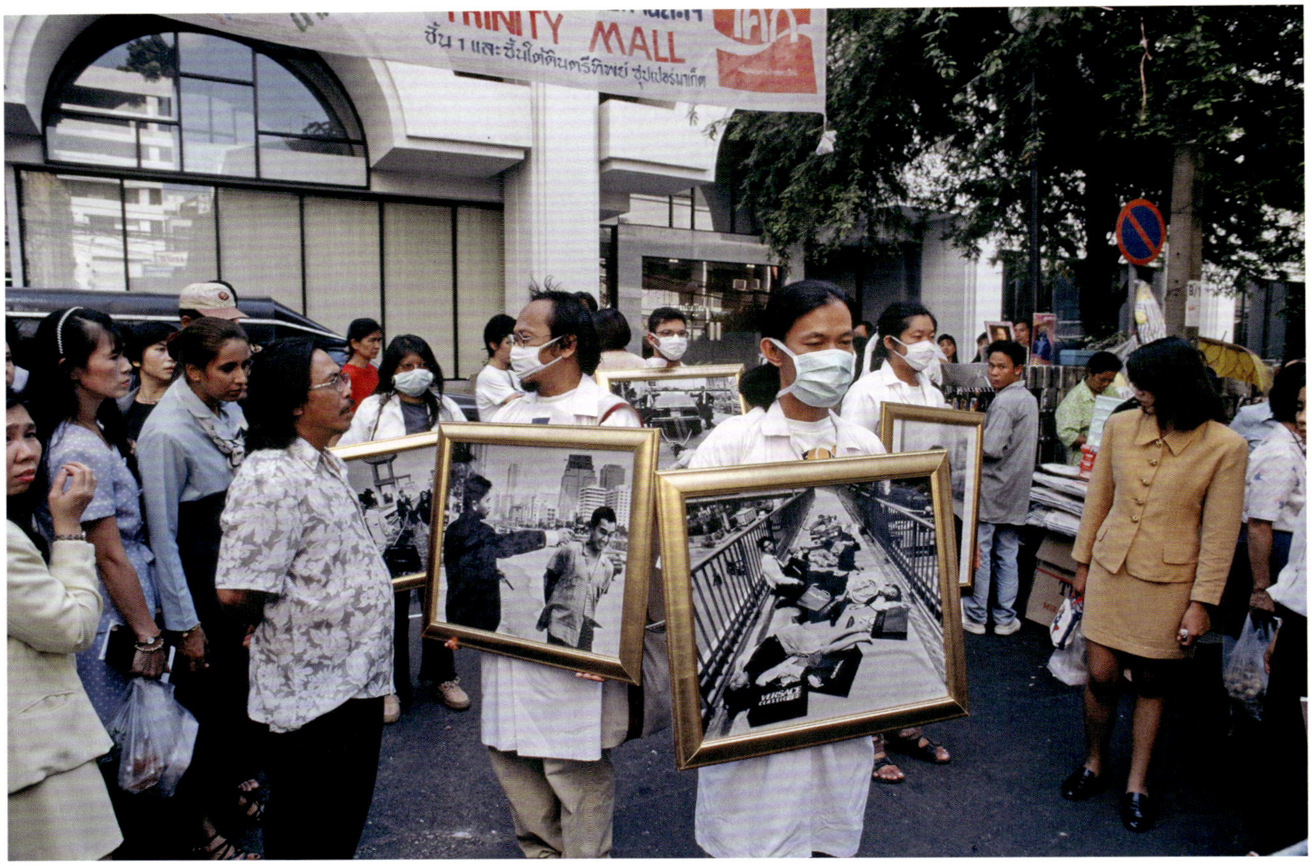
TRINITY MALL

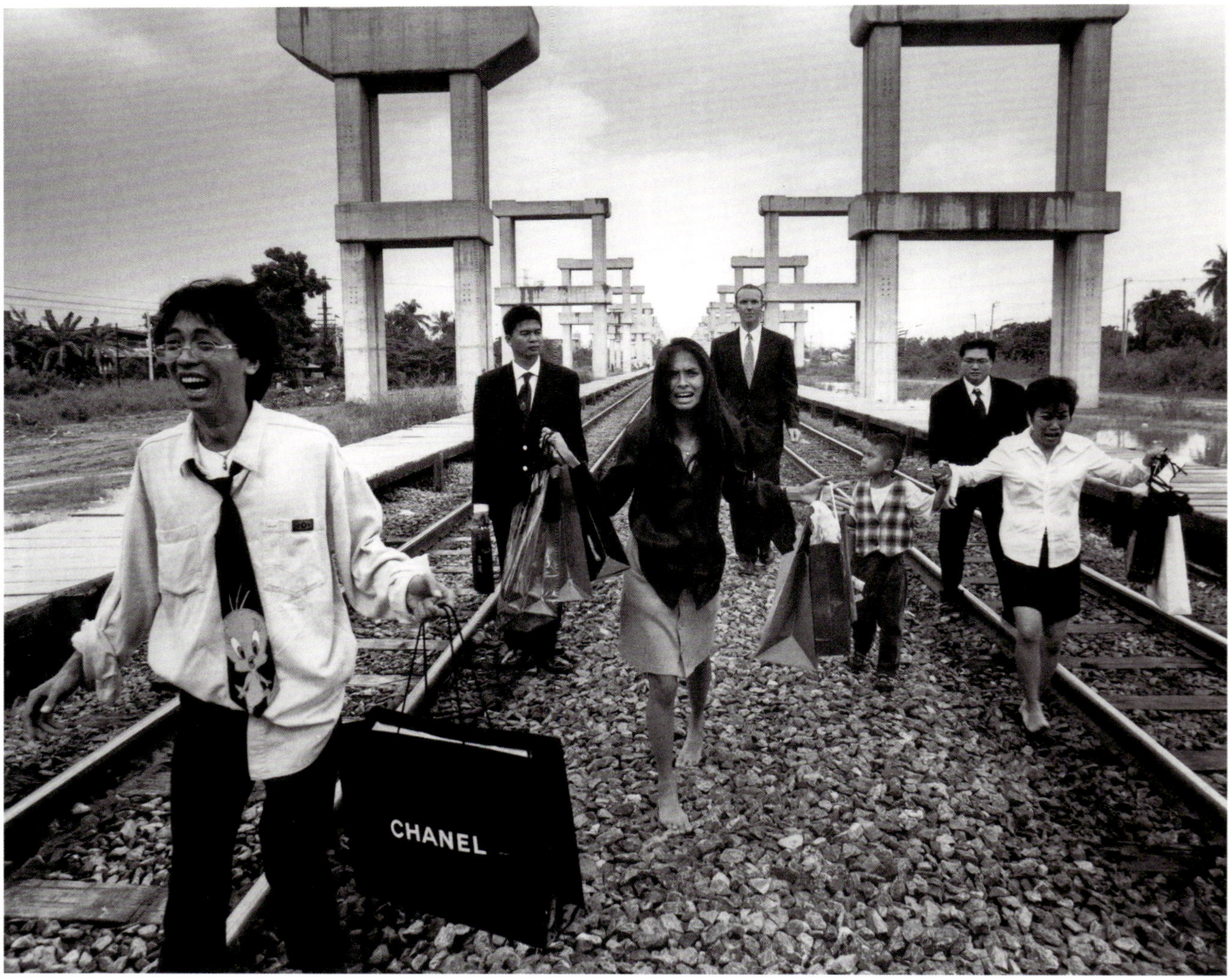
CHANEL

Manit Sriwanichpoom

The extraordinary work of Thai artist Manit Sriwanichpoom moves between two very different kinds of photography.[25] As a documentarian, he produced a year-long photographic record of the many different people allowed to publicly protest against the Thai government every Tuesday: 'Protest' (April 2002–3). He also constructs photographs. For his series 'This Bloodless War – Greed, Globalization and the end of Independence' (1997), Sriwanichpoom restaged well-known photographs from the Vietnam War and the bombing of Nagasaki in scenarios involving consumption. The black-and-white photographs were mounted on large boards and exhibited along the roadside in a central Bangkok street and also hung on the shoulders of a group of fellow artists and transported by foot around Bangkok's business district. Such an activist display brings the photographs closer to the protests Sriwanichpoom later documented. Much as we might see the two series as being distinct, they can be seen to inform one another. The staged images use savage humour to contest the notion of Asian people as powerless victims, provoking us not only to recognize the corporate powers which impact on developing economies but also to question the way the histories of these Asian countries have been framed by Western news media. As with Wang Qingsong's pictures, consumerism is seen in terms of warfare. Here, the excessive consumerism of the present – in which, as the artist has said, 'Outrageously expensive, imported luxury items became the new barometers of status as people appeared to consume indiscriminately' – is seen as another form of colonialism, with happy shoppers now posing in tableaux that recall the horrors of Western imperialism. Here the artifice of the staged photograph lends itself to the shallow and superficial act of consumerism. Sriwanichpoom moves between parody and the classic petitioning documentary tradition evident in 'Protest' with its year-long document of citizens' theatrical and desperate attempts to call attention to their cause in his year-long document of contemporary protests.

Manit Sriwanichpoom
From 'This Bloodless War', 1997
6 gelatin silver prints
Each 50.8 × 61 cm / 20 × 24 in

This Bloodless War #2, 1997
Gelatin silver print
50.8 × 61 cm / 20 × 24 in

Wawi Navarroza

Wawi Navarroza's *Not Today* (2010) is a photograph of a re-enactment of a massacre in Maguindanao province, on Mindanao island in the Philippines, the most gruesome act of election-related violence in the country's history, in which fifty eight people (mostly women and media reporters) were massacred in cold blood in a sudden ambush. This tableau involved, as the artist has said, 'real persons with real jobs and real reasons for agreeing to join this re-enactment of a disquieting event, a fresh wound. Some of them played cameos of themselves (a real artist, real designer, real nurse, real journalist, real celebrity, real popular figure, real movie actor) mixed with totally anonymous and unknown 'real people' masquerading as actors and fake ones (fake soldiers, fake guns, fake blood).'[26]

In many respects the use of the tableau acknowledges the insufficiency of the documents, the widespread internet news photos of the aftermath of the massacre. The tableau was also erected as a public advocacy billboard against election-related violence along Manila's main thoroughfare, its billboard capital. The re-enactment involved in this extraordinary scene is involved in, as Navarroza puts it, 're-creating a shared pathos'. The work opens out photography to political action. Those involved are affected by the recent terrible event, the 'fresh wound' they collectively restage.

Navarroza's use of the tableau is interesting in its deliberate artifice and theatre. But to see this as somehow shallow or inadequate in relation to the event is to miss the point. One should recall David Levinthal's 'Mein Kampf' series, and the anxiety about his use of toys to restage the Holocaust. Do they cheapen or belittle such a sacrosanct subject, or speak about a greater truth concerning our relationship to the Holocaust? Much of the work discussed in this chapter rethinks our relation to documentary. Navarroza's 'Theatre of the Absurd' (her words) is an attempt to begin to respond to the 'senseless killings' her own country had recently witnessed. As her commentary posted on her Facebook page (February 2010) indicates, the work was very much born out of a concern with how we respond to such atrocious images and events, observed from a country riven by violence, the second-most dangerous place for journalists: 'We are safe behind our TV screens and computer screens, on Facebook where we have seen and passed around the monstrous pictures, scared, shocked, and saddened, for a pause, then we take a deep breath and go on with the continuum of our lives separate from the tragedy. It weighs on the shoulders. We are festered and frustrated... but in the privacy of our own little thoughts we ask, what can we do about it?' Navarroza does not give us an answer. But her use of the staged photograph so soon after the massacre involves an important political gesture of affiliation and identification between the artists and the people she uses, as well as making visible on a grand pictorial scale a massacre, 'a harrowing crime', that many in the West may well hardly be aware of. Such an approach to photography opens up the tableau form and takes us beyond the limits of raw documents of atrocity.

Wawi Navarroza
Not Today, 2010
In situ on a public billboard, Epifanio De
Dimensions variable

Not Today, 2010
Lambda Durst colour print
Dimensions variable

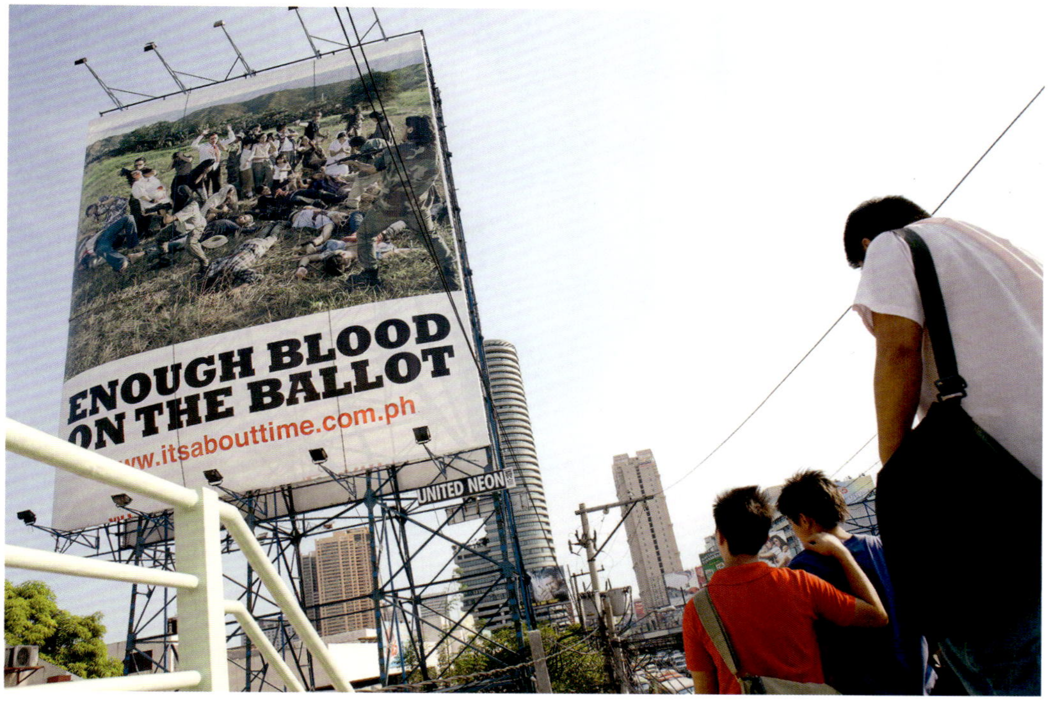
ENOUGH BLOOD
ON THE BALLOT
www.itsabouttime.com.ph
UNITED NEON

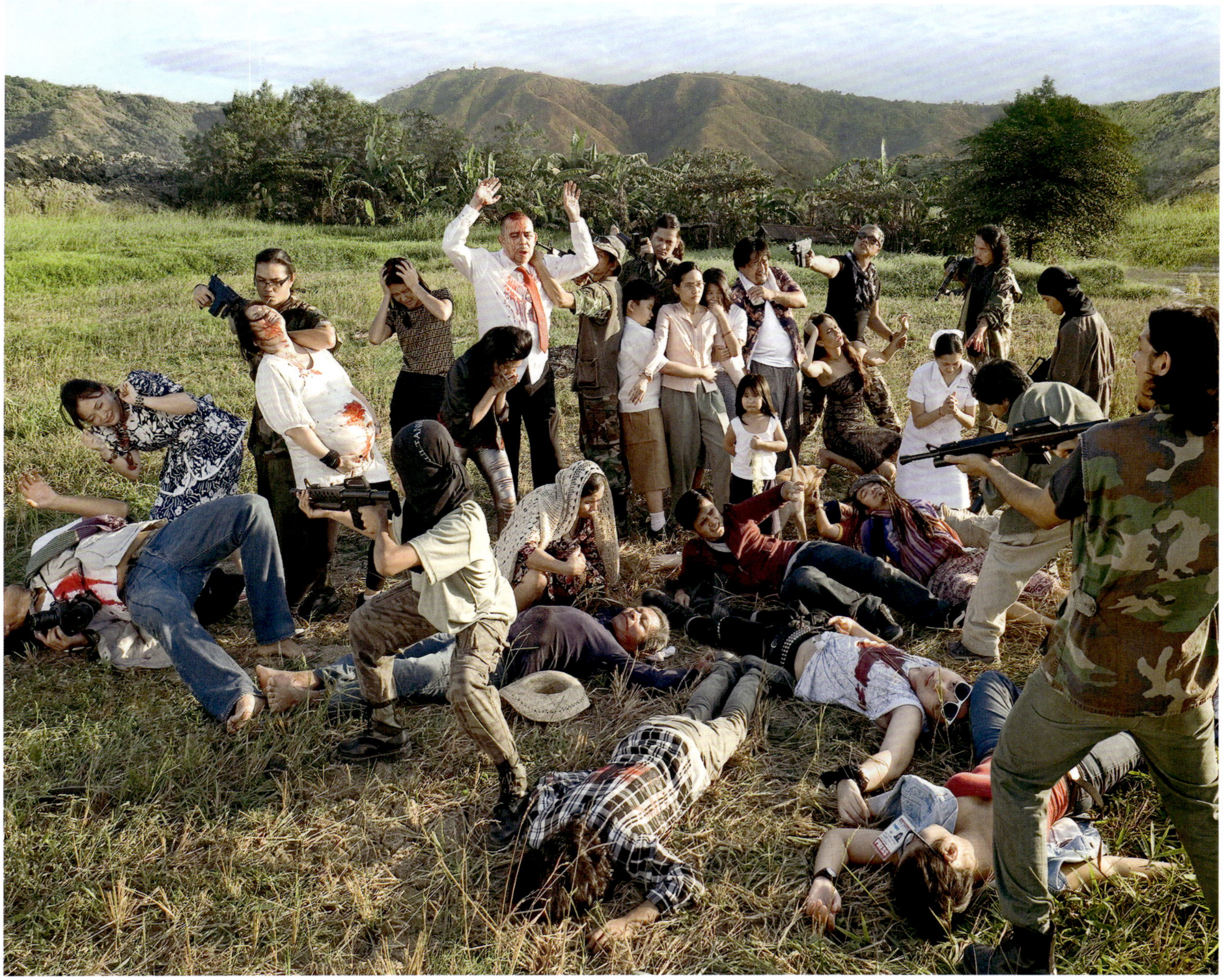

Chapter Eleven

Photography Tomorrow

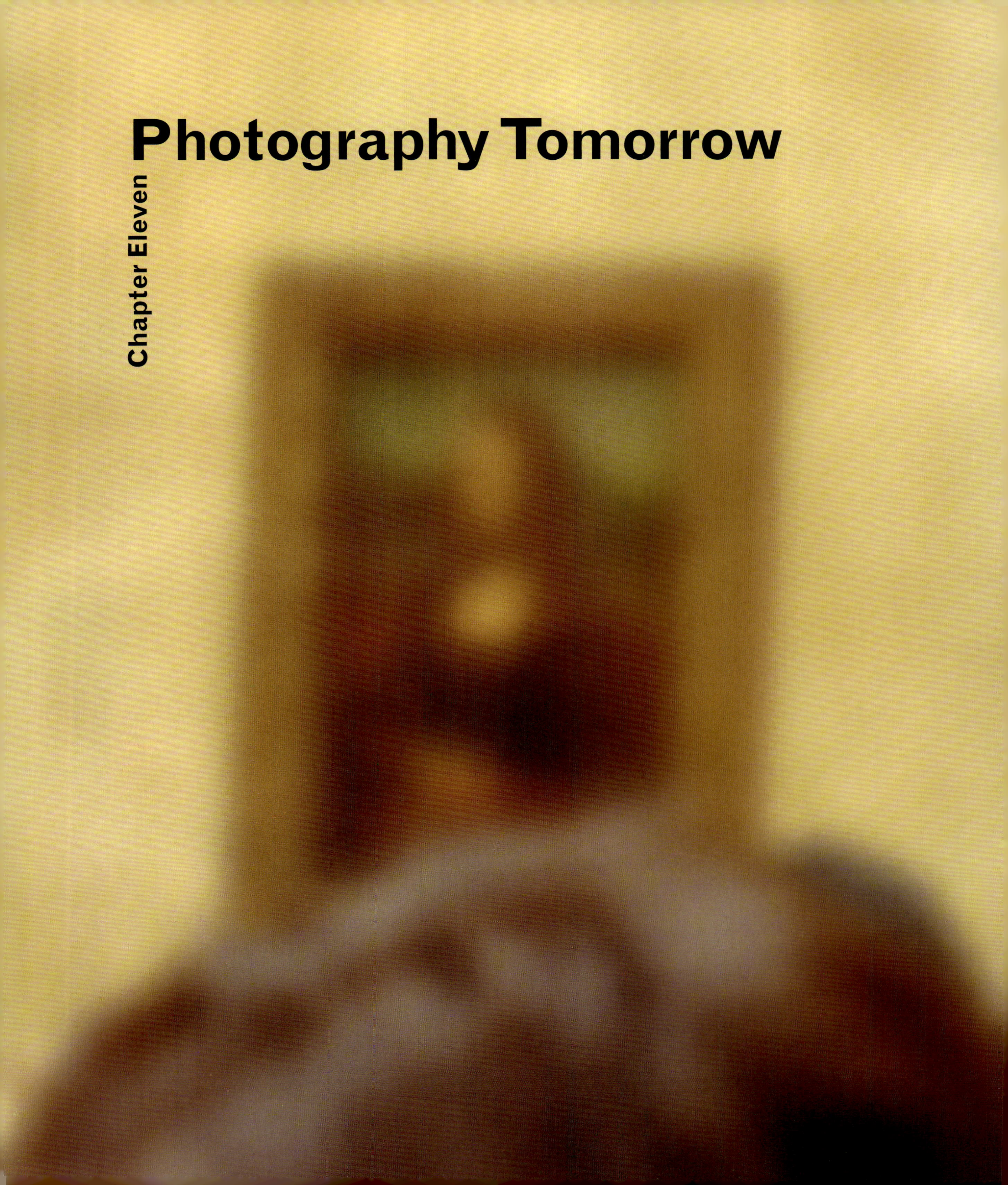

‘I think we live in a great paradox today. On the one hand we are bombarded by thousands of images, but on the other hand it has never before been so controlled, be it by the government or by a certain part of the private sector. Therefore, I believe that we have lost the ability to see and be moved by images. Nothing moves us anymore, nothing has any meaning.’[1]

These powerful remarks, made by the artist Alfredo Jaar at the start of the twenty-first century, provide an appropriate way of beginning to think about photography in the future. Lots of extreme statements are made in terms of photography, none greater perhaps than the claims of photography’s death in the late 1980s – claims made in the face of digital technology’s perceived fundamental alteration of photography’s identity as a reliable evidential medium. Jaar’s is an extreme statement, but it reflects an emphasis here on an extreme photography, practices that take photography to a limit or raise questions about its value and use.

Photography did not die as predicted; neither has its value as a medium of witnessing. But we are now faced with the inevitability of film photography’s obsolescence, as film manufacturing and processing, the production of film cameras, the availability of darkrooms all come to an end. At the same time, images are proliferating because of new digital technologies. More people are taking pictures than ever before. The photographic landscape and environment is changing dramatically, and this will inevitably impact on artists’ relationship to photography.

Alfredo Jaar
Taryn Simon
Joachim Schmid
Paul Graham
Erik Kessels

Alfredo Jaar's statement was made in relationship to one of the most powerful and distinctive responses to photography in its history. Marked by a strong sense of crisis, his 2002 installation *Lament of the Images* – made for Documenta 11, Kassel, Germany, one of the world's biggest and most important exhibitions of contemporary art – did not show us any pictures but instead blinded us with a blaze of projected light, a forceful reiteration of the sense of an ending, of a limit point having been reached. Like other examples that will be discussed in this closing chapter, it is a work very much concerned with fundamental issues about how we think and relate to photographic images in a culture characterized by the contradictions and problems arising from greater image proliferation, greater image control and a seeming greater diminishment of the value – both emotional and intellectual – of images.

Rather than a despairing nihilist gesture, *Lament of the Images* was integral to a strongly held argument that images mattered. Our encounter with Jaar's blinding field of light was preceded by three glowing panels of back-lit texts presented in a darkened room. In an allusion to the specificity of the captioning of documentary photographs, each panel was titled with a location and a precise date: Cape Town, South Africa, February 15th, 1990; Pennsylvania, USA, April 15th, 2001 and Kabul, Afghanistan, October 7th, 2001. The date of the first text references the global media event of Nelson Mandela squinting into the light on his release from prison, which is linked to the fact that prisoners were blinded by the limestone as they broke rocks in a quarry on the centre of Robben Island. The closing line of the text informs us that no pictures of Mandela's release show him crying, as the blinding light from the quarry had taken away his ability to cry. The highlighting of such a detail is important in that it implicitly accords with the problem of an emotional numbing that Jaar feels characterizes our wider disconnected relationship to photographs today. Texts two and three consider the loss and control of images in relationship to two significant events. The first refers to the burial of 17 million photographic images from Bettmann and United Press International, purchased by Microsoft chairman, Bill Gates, in a limestone mine, a collection including 'images of the Wright Brothers in flight, JFK Jr. saluting his father's coffin, important images from the Vietnam War, and Nelson Mandela in prison.' The final panel informs us that, just before launching airstrikes against Afghanistan, the United States Defense Department had bought all rights to satellite imagery of Afghanistan and neighbouring countries, creating an 'effective white-out of the operation, preventing western media from seeing the effects of the bombing…'.

The metaphor of blindness and not seeing is made palpable through the light of the installation in *Lament of the Images*. In a response to a culture of visual overload, and amidst the inevitable image glut and spectacle of Documenta, Jaar's absence of images forcibly makes us reflect upon the political implications of image use and control. It is a lament for lost images, explicit in its fears that as Gates's private company Corbis puts millions of pictures into storage in its underground vault, the slow process of their digitization (as the text panel informs us, between 1995–2001, only 2 per cent of them had been scanned) will make them 'totally inaccessible.'

Jaar's work speaks about the loss of pictures, using searing light as a lament for the mass of images we do not and may never see. The blindness his art forcibly reflects upon is a statement about our relationship to images today, a call for the need to respond to images, to recognize their value.

Alfredo Jaar
Lament of the Images (detail), 2002
Plexiglass text panels, light wall and mixed media
Dimensions variable

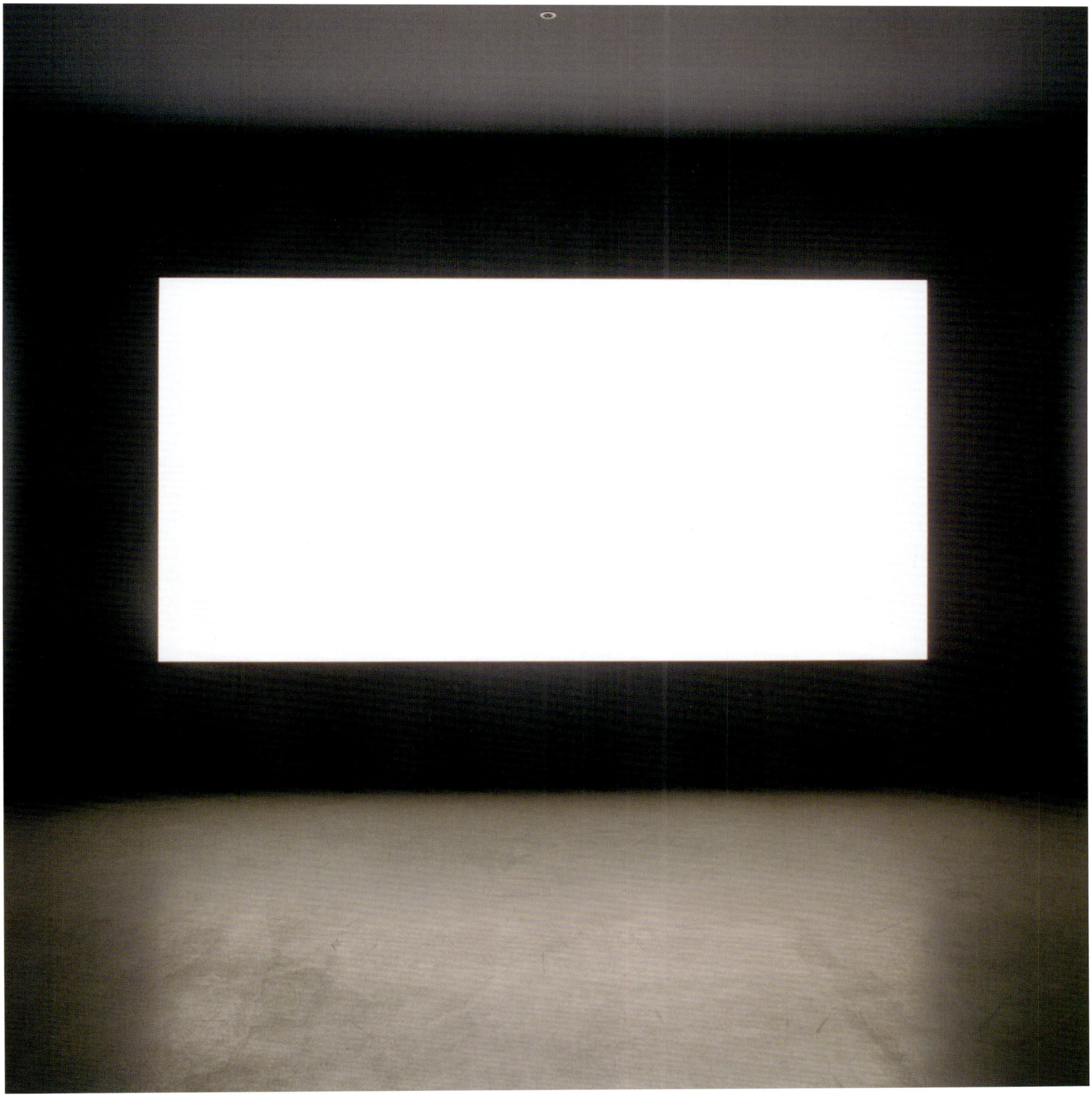

Taryn Simon

Taryn Simon's ambitious 'A Living Man Declared Dead and Other Chapters I – XVIII', (2008–11), highlights the space between image and text, absence and presence and order and disorder. In this four-year project, encyclopedic in scope, she travelled around the world to research and photograph the bloodlines of people whose lives have been affected by extraordinary, and quite often tragic, events. As she has said of this project: 'I was interested in ideas surrounding fate and whether our fate is determined by blood, chance or circumstance.'[2]

For all the differences in nationalities, the same poses and portrait conventions recur – her subjects are photographed seated with their hands on their laps, looking straight to camera and fairly inexpressive, all against the same neutral back-drop. Simon treats portraiture as a machine-like process in such photographs, with all her pictures lacking, as she puts it, 'embellishment'. Tracing descendants in terms of bloodline meant the photography is systematic and controlled: 'I wanted to find an absolute catalogue – one that couldn't be edited, interrupted or curated by choice.'

Simon's medium consists of three equal elements: photography, text and graphic design. The portraits are followed by a text panel in which Simon constructs the narratives and collects details of the bloodlines. Each story constitutes a chapter made up of varying numbers of panels, the number of which is determined by the length of the bloodline. Examples include a blood feud between families in Brazil; the descendants of Hitler's personal legal adviser Hans Frank; the descendants of Calbrera Antero, who, as part of the Igorot community of Filipinos, was put on display in the 1904 St Louis World Fair (and in accordance with colonial assumptions compelled to eat up to 20 dogs a week); an Iraqi man employed as the body double of Saddam Hussein's son; an Indian man who, (together with his two brothers and cousin), was declared dead in official records so that his relatives could claim his land.

Simon makes use of absences in her inventories, presenting blank pictures to indicate where people declined or refused to participate. A number of the descendants of the Nazi Hans Frank, for example, did not agree to being photographed. Some allowed Simon to represent them through their clothing. The chapter concerning the bloodlines of victims of the 1995 Srebenica massacre is the only one that includes the dead. Instead of portraits we are presented with pictures of teeth or bone fragments, identified by DNA tests. These forensic pictures were printed the same size and placed in relation to the portraits of their living blood relatives. In her chapter on Ukrainian children from orphanages there are of course no bloodlines to follow. Indeed it is the consequences of being without the protection of a family that the many portraits, ordered by age, invite us to reflect upon – when they leave these orphanages, we are told, they are vulnerable to being used in child pornography or human trafficking.

In some senses this project is about making people visible, using the photograph as evidence for identity. This is clear in the first chapter that gives us the title for the whole series, the living man (and other relations) declared dead by a corrupt legal system so relatives can claim his inherited land. A number of chapters are focused on problems of identity and identification: Latif Yahia, Saddam Hussein's son's double; the first female hijacker, Leila Khaled, who had several facial surgeries to hide her appearances; and the map of the bloodline of Ribal Btaddini, part of the Druze religious sect in the Middle East, which is the most complex in the series since it involves repeat portraits in recognition of Btaddini and the community's belief that he is the reincarnation of his paternal grandfather.

Each chapter contains another panel which Simon calls a 'footnote', collecting traces that provide further evidentiary material relating to the stories, including the shirts of children killed in the blood feud in Brazil, interior photographs of the Ukranian orphanages, stills from a video used in the war crime trial evidencing Serbian paramilitary units' involvement in the Srebenica massacre and pictures of gold-plated guns found in Saddam Hussein's palace. Disrupting the order of the systematic portraits, they introduce a more open and suggestive means of evidencing each chapter's narrative stories.

Simon has said that her project examines how: 'the forces of economics, geography, religion, governance, are butting up against the internal forces of psychological and physical inheritance.' Such internal forces cannot be pictured but are implicit through the recurrence of the portraits of people and their placement and organization according to bloodlines. The photographs might be seen to affirm and confirm presence and life to camera – important especially when the accompanying story is about a person missing or legally declared dead, or those who have lost their identity or need to hide their identity. But the images are at the same time very unsettling in terms of the overall systematic mode of depiction. These grids of faces reduce their subjects to specimens, sorted and classed within a system. One large chapter, concerning the government's control of the rabbit population in Australia and portraying three bloodlines of rabbits injected with lethal diseases to test their virulence, is a reminder of the terrible underside to this obsession with bloodlines. The dark shadows of eugenics and the Holocaust mark this work. Simon's 'A Living Man Declared Dead…' is in this respect very distinct from The Museum of Modern Art's famous 1955 worldwide photography exhibition, 'The Family of Man', with its essentially restorative vision of humankind after the atrocities of World War II.

Taryn Simon
Excerpt from 'Chapter XI, A Living Man Declared Dead and Other Chapters I–XVIII'

'Chapter XI, from A Living Man Declared Dead and Other Chapters I-XVIII', 2008–11
Photographs, digital prints on paper and transfer lettering on paper on board
213.5 × 302.8 cm / 84 × 119¼ in

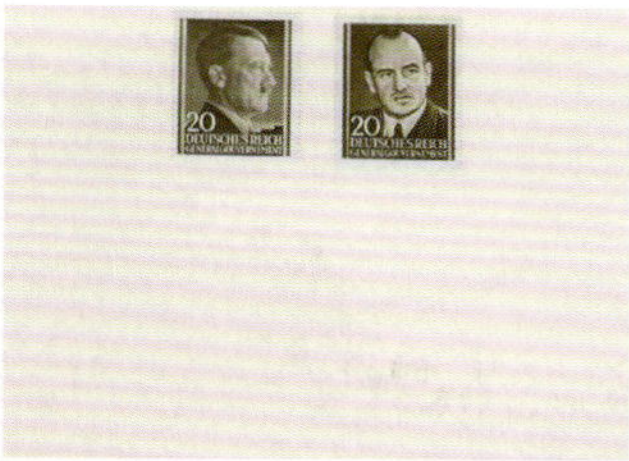

c.

XI

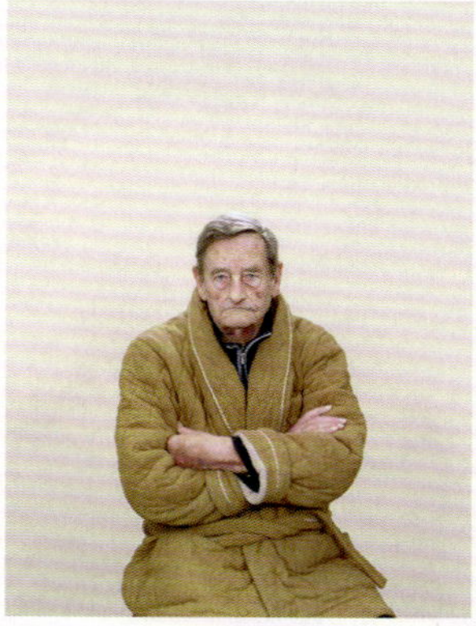

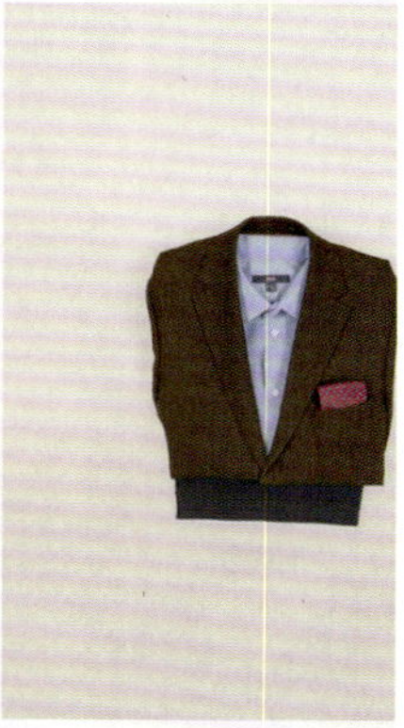

7.

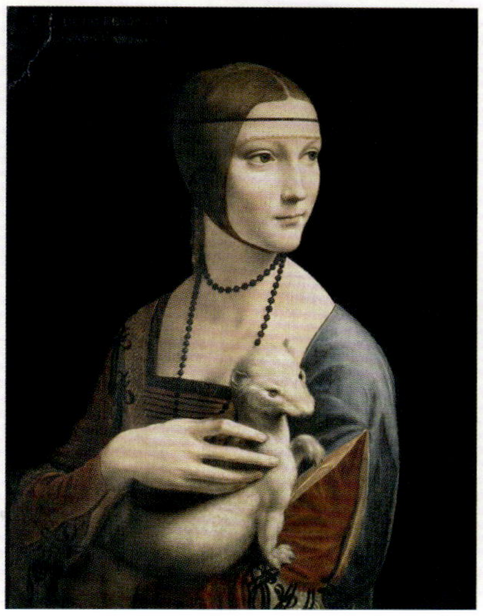

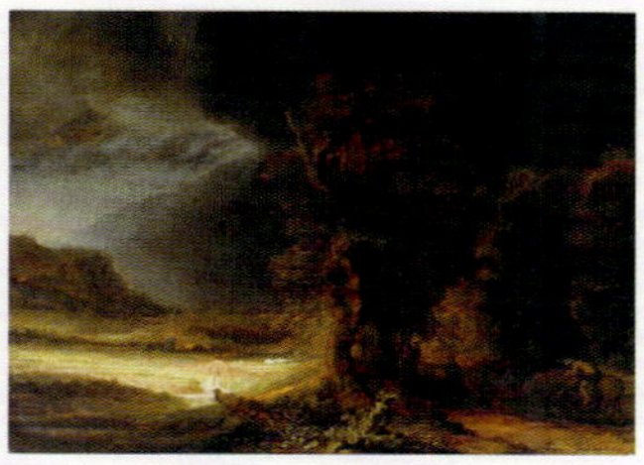

f.

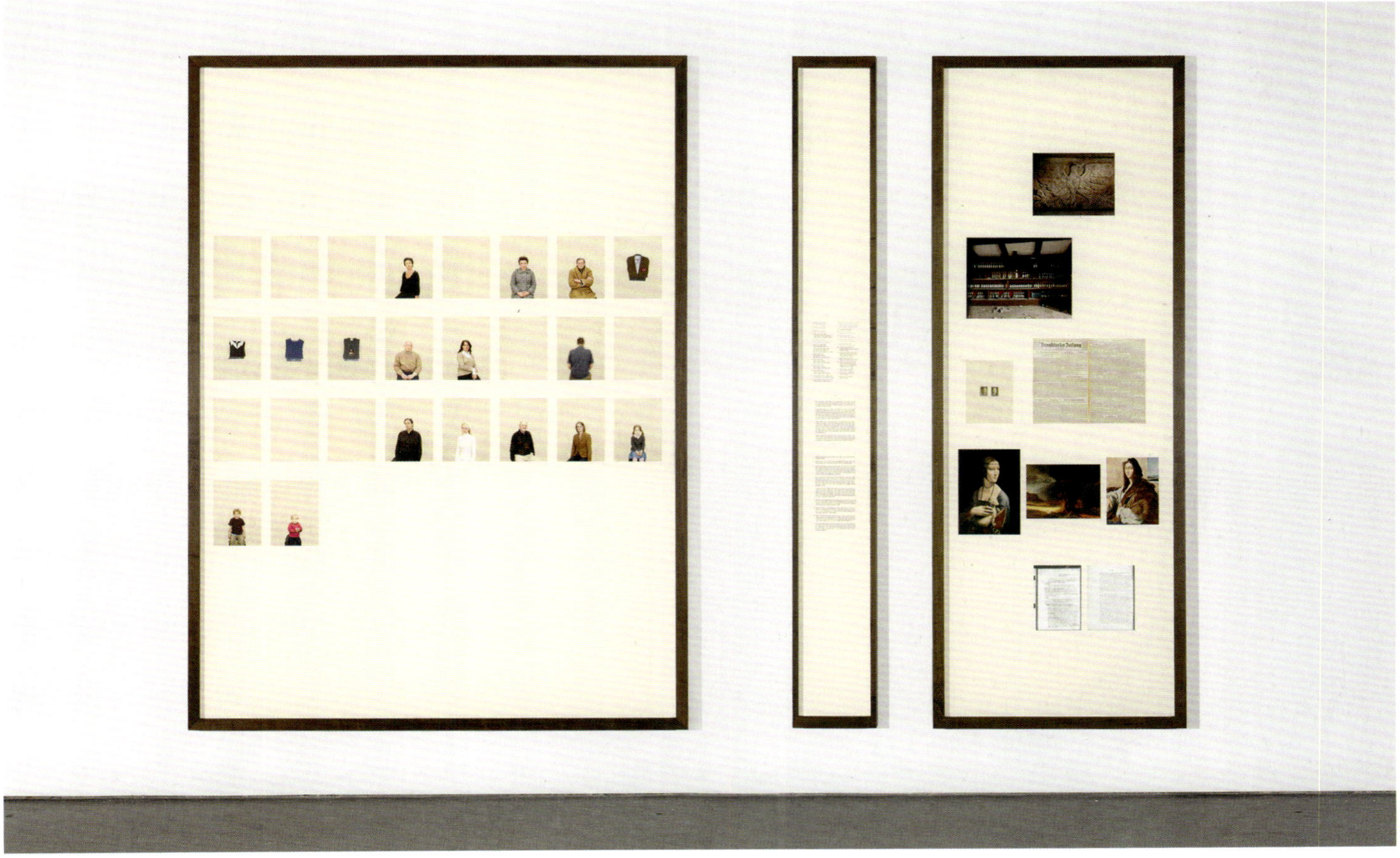

Joachim Schmid

The premise of Joachim Schmid's use of photography is very different to Taryn Simon's. He does not go out in the world to make his pictures. Behind Simon's approach is a certain conceptual mandate. A sense that she is gathering and organizing stories from around the world in an attempt to make sense of the chaos; 'This mass pile of images and stories forms an archive. Within this accumulation of images and text, there is a struggle to find patterns and to consider that perhaps the narratives surrounding the lives we lead are as coded as blood itself.' Simon's photographs are presented as tables, mapping generations according to a particular order and system. And it is in terms of the catalogue we find a point of relationship to Schmid's use of photography – in the way he also subjects photography to systems and structures of classification.

In Chapter One, Schmid's work was introduced through 'Bilder von der Straße', a project that involved him collecting photographs found from the street. His recent extensive and encyclopedic project, *Other People's Photographs*, collected in ninety-six books and published between 2008 and 2011, involves more than three thousand images selected and edited from the photo-sharing site Flickr.com. Founded in 2004, Flickr has since become what Schmid calls, 'the biggest image pool ever accumulated in the history of humankind', storing billions of photographs and with millions uploaded to the site every single day.[3]

As more and more people take and share photographs, we are faced with a substantial shift in what photography is today. Schmid confronts this problem or crisis in photography head-on. He challenges tradition by embracing mass photography, celebrating its ceaseless and expanding iconography, and taking us towards another, messier side to photography, distinct from those more authored and artistic photographic works that make up its history.

Other People's Photographs is very much about the instant and the moment, a sociality of image use and display, of pleasure and fun in taking pictures, of snapshots in the fullest sense. Schmid's editing is organized not through authorship but by content, and is stripped of any of the tags or messages that accompany the pictures online. The images are assembled as volumes according to a quirky mode of ordering and classification, with each devoted to a specific subject set out in alphabetical order, from photographs of airline meals to details of maps bearing the location sign 'You Are Here'. In many senses it is an absurd archive, reflecting the chaos and disorder of the web.

Schmid's books address photography as a form of consumerism by showing us again and again repetitive acts of documentation, often of the most commonplace and banal aspects of day-to-day to lives: pictures of food recur, including airline meals, bread, pizzas, birthday cakes, fish and so on. Photography is caught up in a record of what we do, what we buy and consume. One volume, entitled *First Shots*, even includes a series of photographs showing the different camera boxes in which, we assume, the cameras that took the pictures came. Photography in the digital age is easy: we can now spend more of our time photographing our lives, the food we are served, the commodities we have bought.

In *The Picture*, another volume from *Other People's Photographs*, Schmid has collected photographs posted online that people have taken of Leonardo da Vinci's *Mona Lisa*. Blurred, crooked and in a variety of colour casts, these pictures are taken among the daily crowds that come to see the most famous painting in the world, yet all but two manage to avoid the heads of other museum-goers. What we get with Schmid's book of pictures of the painting is to all intents and purposes bad photography. We sense how far away the tourist snap is from the elevated and culturally valued artwork in the museum, but we also realize how we cannot really see such a painting any more.

Schmid claims there are many undiscovered artists on Flickr, yet his selection and editing erases authorship, as does his organization of books by subject matter. His aesthetic – if we can call it that – is broad-ranging, mischievous and messy. His obsessive engagement with contemporary vernacular photography on the web comes close to and even courts chaos and incoherence, but at the same time *Other People's Photographs* is affirmative in its relishing of the obsessions, absurdities and pleasures found within a photography of the ordinary and day-to-day.

With Alfredo Jaar's *Lament of the Images* there was, of course, no photography. Photography was discussed and reflected upon through the text panels and the dramatic visceral light installation. But there were no images. Simon's 'A Living Man Declared Dead and Other Chapters I – XVIII' while deploying photography, was still dependent upon texts to present the stories associated with each bloodline. Both epic projects are conceptually-led. Schmid's books prioritize pictures over words. Titles identify each volume – and that is it.

Joachim Schmid
Other People's Photographs, 2008–11
Series of 96 books each
18 × 18 cm / 7 × 7 in, 36 pp
32 photographs, hardcover with dust jacket

Details from the books *First Shots*, *Airline Meals*, *Big Fish*, *Coffee*

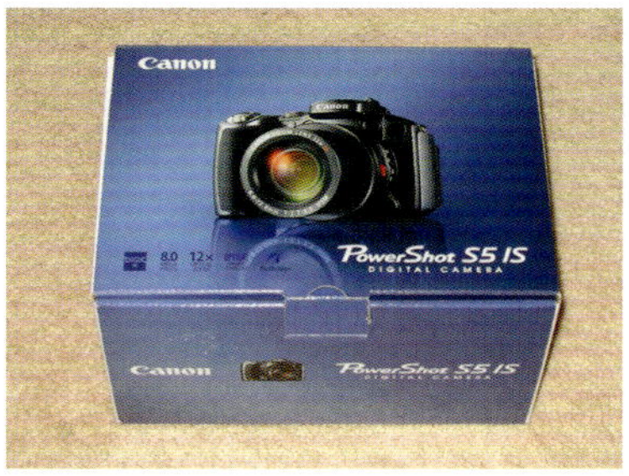
Canon
PowerShot S5 IS
DIGITAL CAMERA
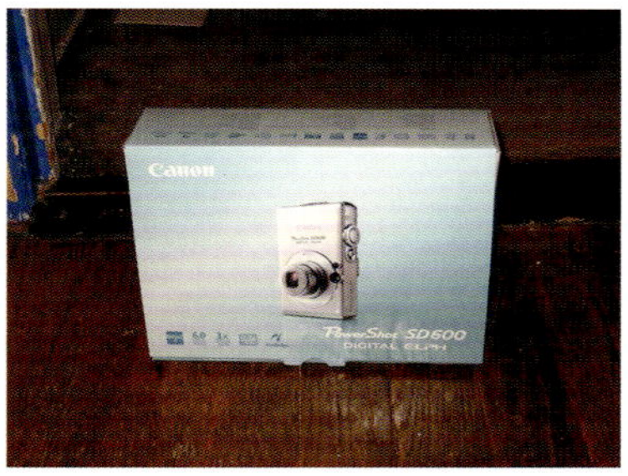
Canon
PowerShot SD600
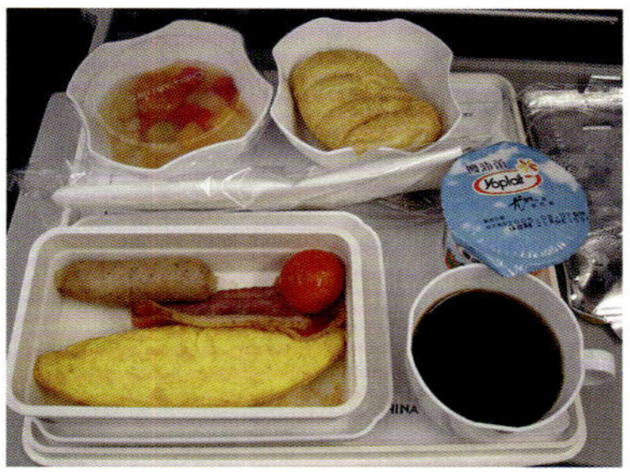
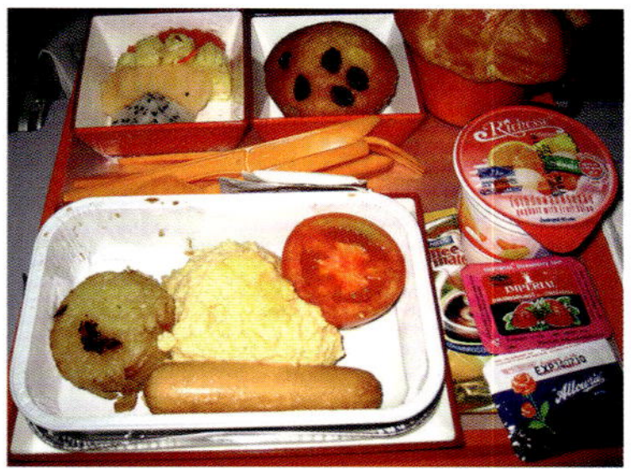
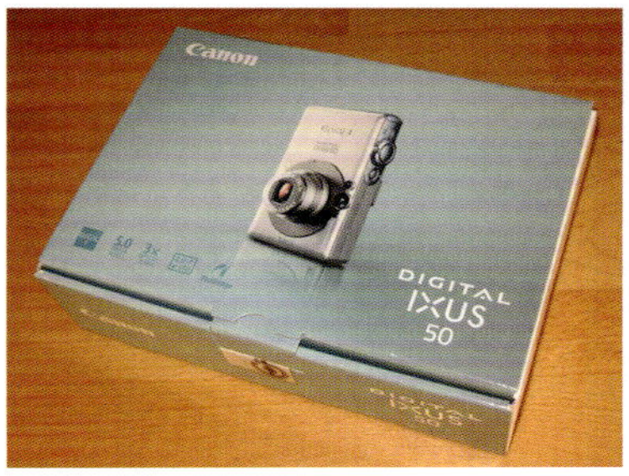
Canon
DIGITAL
IXUS
50
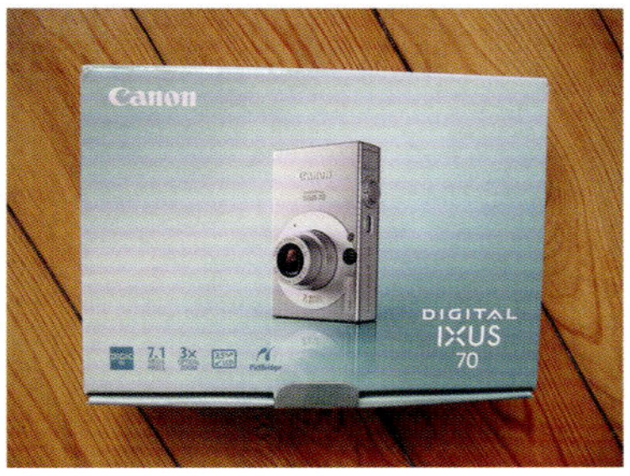
Canon
DIGITAL
IXUS
70
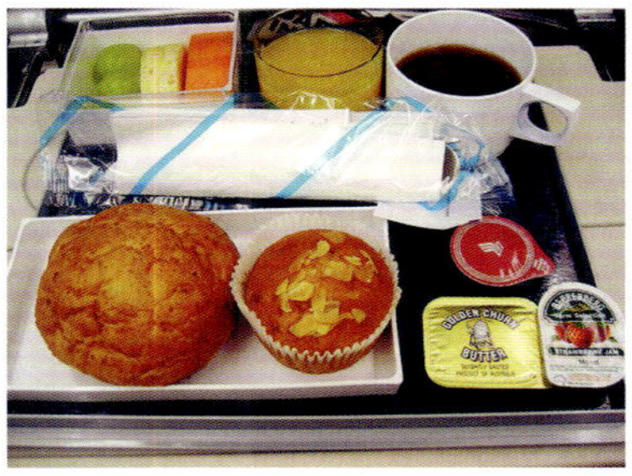
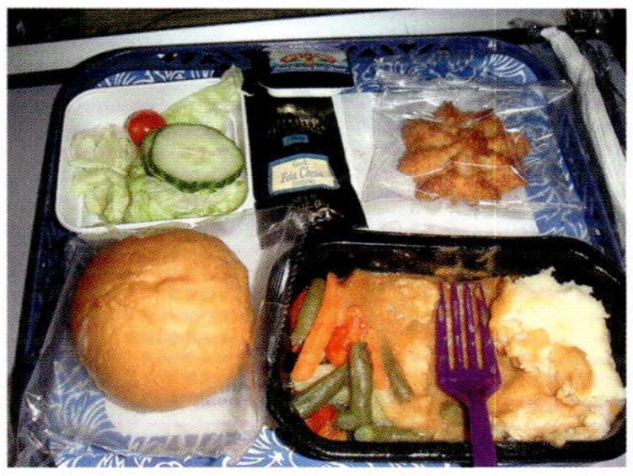
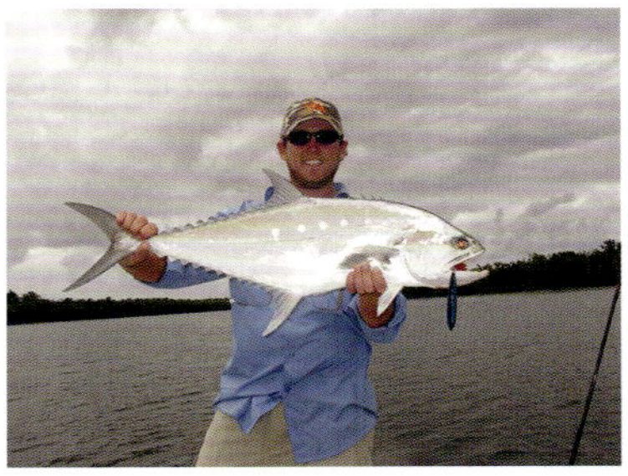
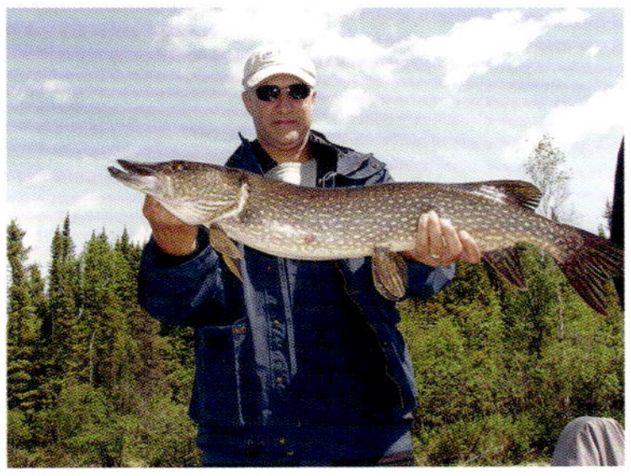
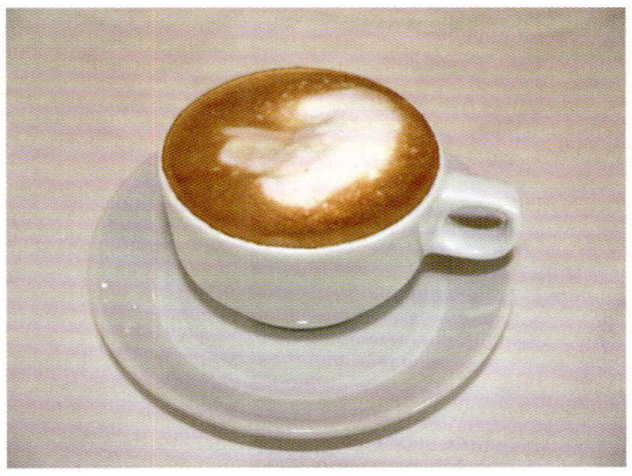
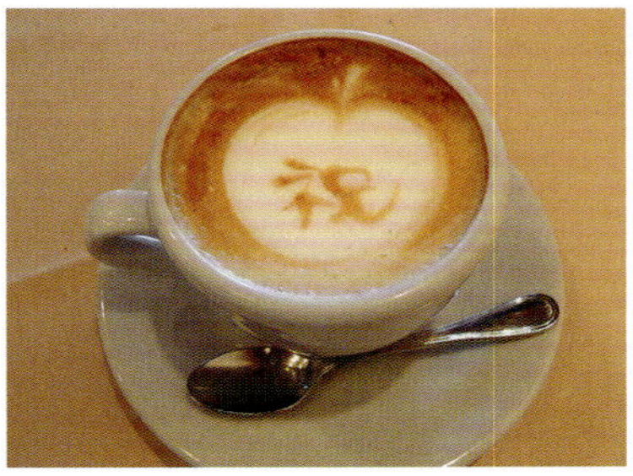
祝
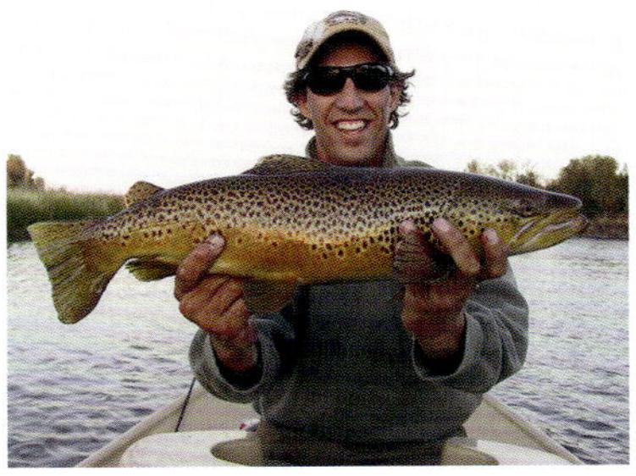
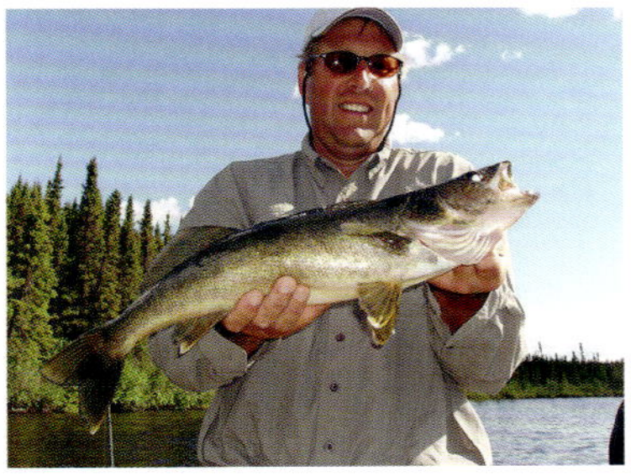
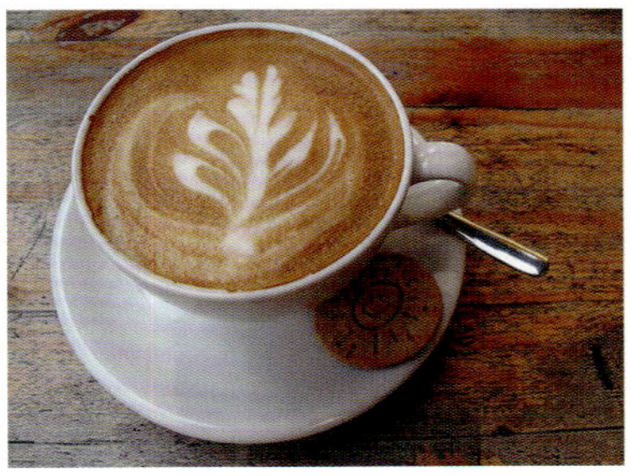
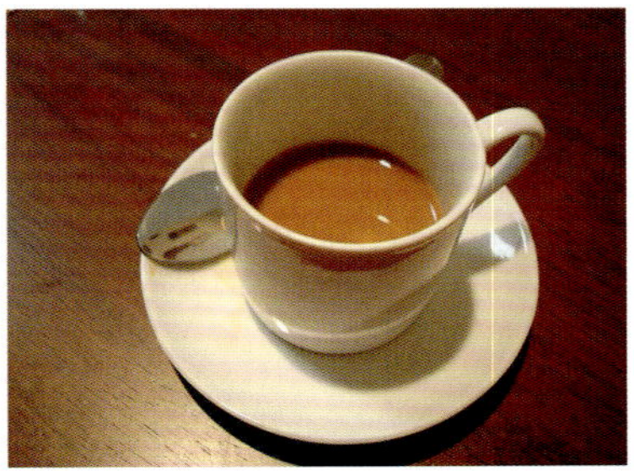

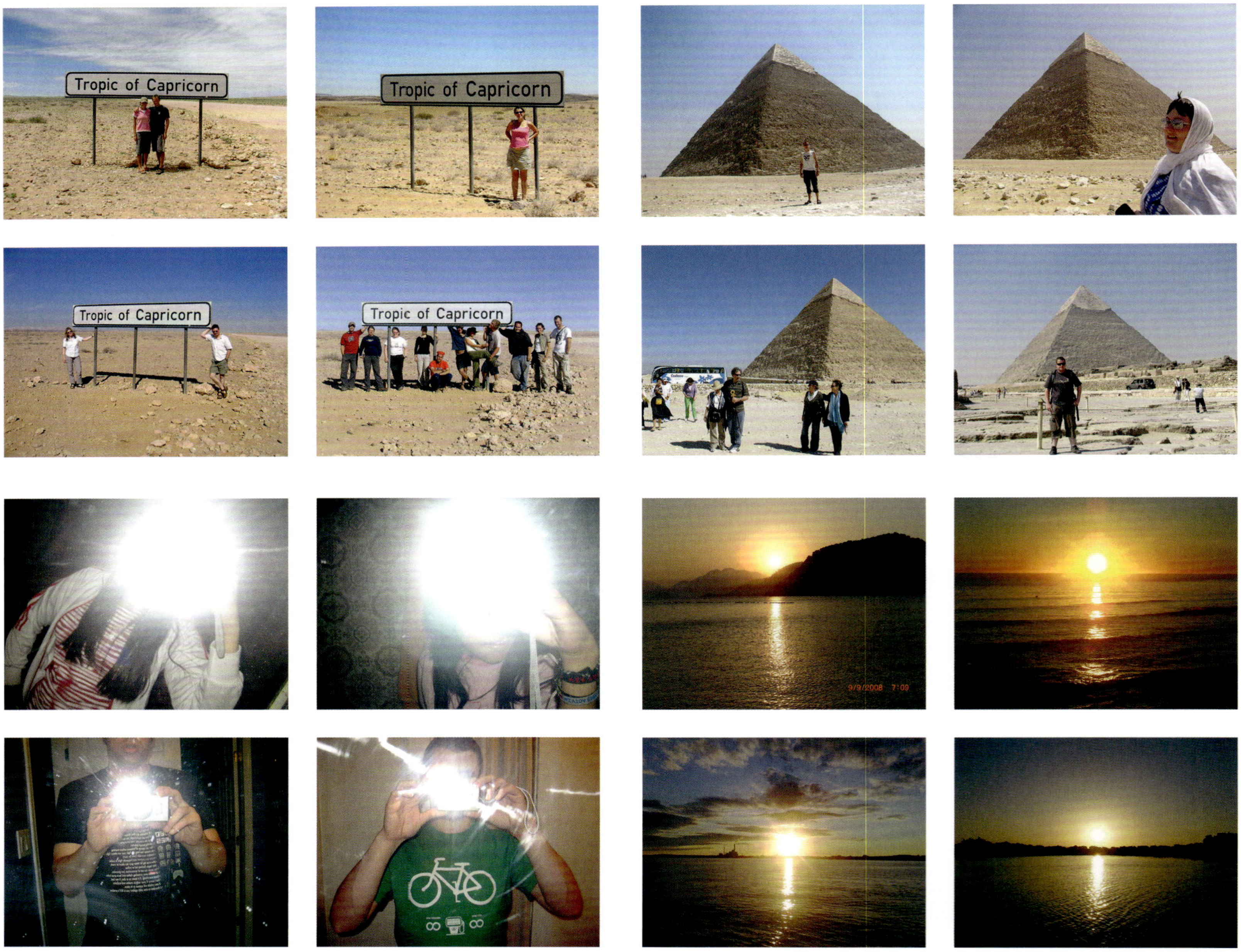

Joachim Schmid
Details from the books *Tropic of Capricorn*, *Pyramids*, *Flashing* and *Sunset*

Opposite:
Details from the books *The Picture* and *Bread*

Spines of selected books from the series 'Other People's Photographs'

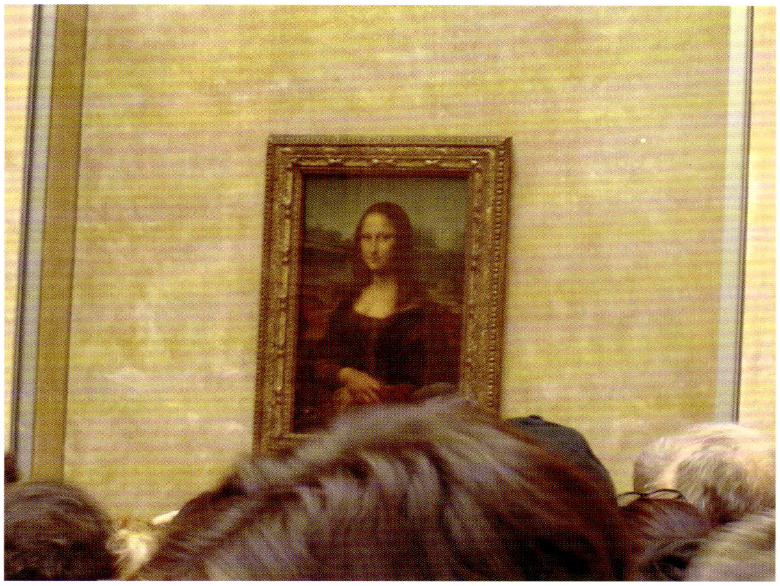

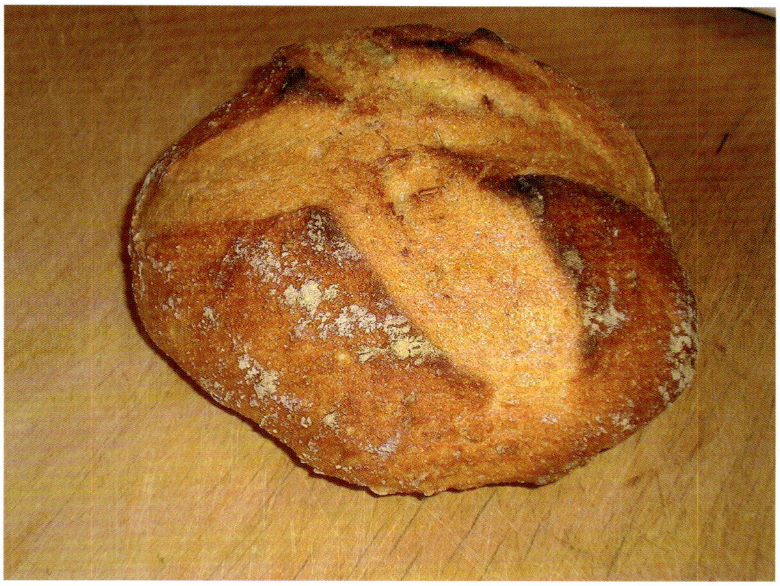

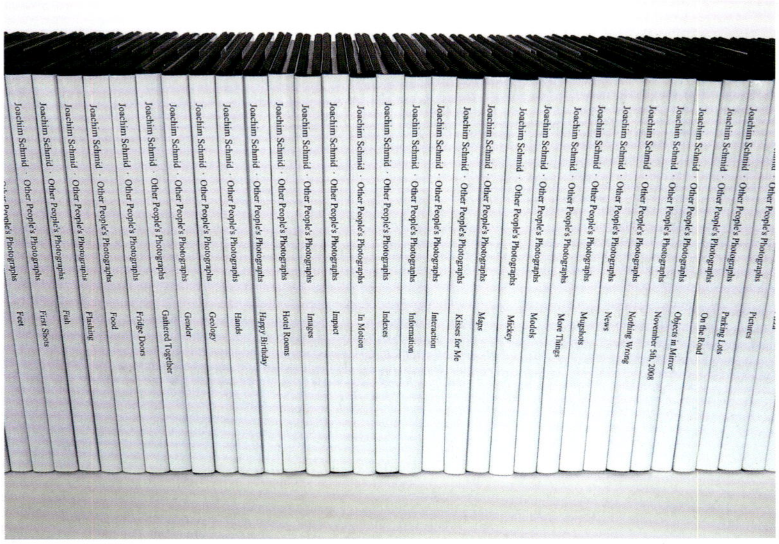
Joachim Schmid · Other People's Photographs Feet
Joachim Schmid · Other People's Photographs First Shots
Joachim Schmid · Other People's Photographs Fish
Joachim Schmid · Other People's Photographs Flashing
Joachim Schmid · Other People's Photographs Food
Joachim Schmid · Other People's Photographs Fridge Doors
Joachim Schmid · Other People's Photographs Gathered Together
Joachim Schmid · Other People's Photographs Gender
Joachim Schmid · Other People's Photographs Geology
Joachim Schmid · Other People's Photographs Hands
Joachim Schmid · Other People's Photographs Happy Birthday
Joachim Schmid · Other People's Photographs Hotel Rooms
Joachim Schmid · Other People's Photographs Images
Joachim Schmid · Other People's Photographs Impact
Joachim Schmid · Other People's Photographs In Motion
Joachim Schmid · Other People's Photographs Indexes
Joachim Schmid · Other People's Photographs Information
Joachim Schmid · Other People's Photographs Interaction
Joachim Schmid · Other People's Photographs Kisses for Me
Joachim Schmid · Other People's Photographs Maps
Joachim Schmid · Other People's Photographs Mickey
Joachim Schmid · Other People's Photographs Models
Joachim Schmid · Other People's Photographs More Things
Joachim Schmid · Other People's Photographs Mugshots
Joachim Schmid · Other People's Photographs News
Joachim Schmid · Other People's Photographs Nothing Wrong
Joachim Schmid · Other People's Photographs November 5th, 2008
Joachim Schmid · Other People's Photographs Objects in Mirror
Joachim Schmid · Other People's Photographs On the Road
Joachim Schmid · Other People's Photographs Parking Lots
Joachim Schmid · Other People's Photographs Pictures

Paul Graham

Paul Graham's response to everyday street life – presented in the form of another beautiful publishing phenomenon, *a shimmer of possibility* (2007), made up of twelve books – acknowledges the literary influence of Anton Chekov's short stories. But, like Joachim Schmid, Graham values and emphasizes photography as a pictorial form. He organizes one hundred and sixty-seven colour photographs within the differently coloured individual volumes, the fullest containing sixty-four photographs and the slimmest just one. There are no captions. All we are given is an indication as to where and when each series or suite of pictures was taken.

The photographs reflect a clear excitement with the pictorial possibilities of things seen in the world, a return to something basic and primary in the act of photography, a wandering, drifting succession of observations resulting from road trips made across America. Graham has said: 'I don't get tired of trying to understand and look at the wonderful and amazing nature of what's around us.'[4] The books present clusters and sequences of pictures, often tracking small and seemingly inconsequential everyday events drawn from American life. The pictures benefited from the new flexibility of digital photography, which allowed Graham to 'shoot and shoot' and maintain a remarkable quality, close to that achieved from a 4x5 inch plate camera.

With many pictures showing the dispossessed and poor, there is still a certain documentary tone to the book, but the work is much more open, not being driven by social messages. The pictures are full of surprises, a sense of wonderment with things in the world: the detail of rich floral patterning of a tattooed arm as someone reaches out from a car to collect an order from a drive-in, the textured surface of the bonnet of a battered car (felt sufficient enough to be given a book to itself) or the sudden epiphany of the sun breaking through during a shower of rain, a moment that breaks the rhythm of Graham's sequence of pictures showing a black worker mowing the grass outside a motel in Pittsburgh.

Graham says he is a 'street person' and does not want to 'feign being intimate with somebody I met five minutes ago. I accept and embrace that so much in life is "ships passing in the dark."' The aesthetic of drifting that characterizes many of his pictures echoes the transience and nomadism that is a condition of the lives of many of the people he photographs. In one volume, he depicts a young African American from behind as she wanders past New York's shop fronts. She is wearing a brown hooded coat, with a grid pattern of white and blue lines. Such details of dress are integral to the pictorial qualities of Graham's pictures. The photographs pick out the woman's repeated gesture of putting her hand to the back of her neck or on top of her bowed head as she walks, implying some inner anguish or trouble. The gesture of hand to head is repeated in the last picture of a claustrophobic and painful suite in another volume, showing a black man in a wheelchair who appears trapped and confined in the city, his movement seemingly blocked by the blue concrete base of a street sign. In this sequence the photographs are interleaved with a series of pictures showing stormy evening clouds that seem to echo the inner state of the figure. In the New York series, the sequence is intercut with a group of photographs showing shifting views of a dramatic sunset over the hills of North Dakota. The resplendent but transient beauty of the sunset, a photographer's cliché, takes on a new meaning and value in terms of the street photography to which it is linked. The relationship between pictures amplifies the momentary sense of the lives that pass before us on the street. Sunsets and falling and fading light recur in the books, giving an overall elegiac cast to *shimmer* as a whole.

One suite of pictures focuses on a white male figure in his 60s, standing in the grey shade of a featureless wall. Initially he is seen looking at something to his side, then we see him looking down to the ground, holding his cigarette. The sunlight catches the top of his head and also illumines a wisp of exhaled smoke. In two closing profile portraits the man looks up and out at the world again, his right hand raised to his chest in an almost spiritual gesture. The spiritual hint in the last image is echoed in the book's other pictures which, taken at night, portray a Christ-like long-haired figure on the roadside. In the first image he is shown staring to camera and holding the flowers he is presumably selling. Two more pictures take us closer to his face, but he does not engage the camera. Pictures of the flowers, showing them fallen rather than upright, are followed by a detail showing cuts on his wrist.

While the volumes of *shimmer* make us conscious of different economies and social relations, Graham is not driven by a documentary mandate. He is much more distracted by the surprising and unexpected beauty he observes on the street. The detail of hands holding a large white supersize polystyrene food or drink container that opens and closes one volume's sequences of images, for example, could be seen as an allusion to begging, but Graham's interest is also in the shift in light between the two pictures, how the cup and hands change between light and shade. Many pictures are about food and eating, acts of consumption: people coming and going from a supermarket, pictures of shelves bearing paltry foodstuffs, a display of drinks from a liquor store. One sequence of pictures shows a woman about to eat a meal that rests on her lap on its tray, wrapped in a plastic bag, the orange colour of its oily and fatty meat content rhyming with the colouring of her hair. We do not see her eating the meal; instead we are given two views of the ground, with shifts in focus, showing discarded bones, white scraps of fast food packaging and an empty soda can in the gutter. The final picture in the sequence is a vivid close-up profile portrait of the woman as she inhales from her cigarette. Although we are still aware that so many of those Graham portrays are dispossessed and poor, the new pictorial accent in these pictures loosens the documentary expectations of this mode of photography. Such lyrical and affirmative responses to life on the street do not make statements or give us messages to consume.

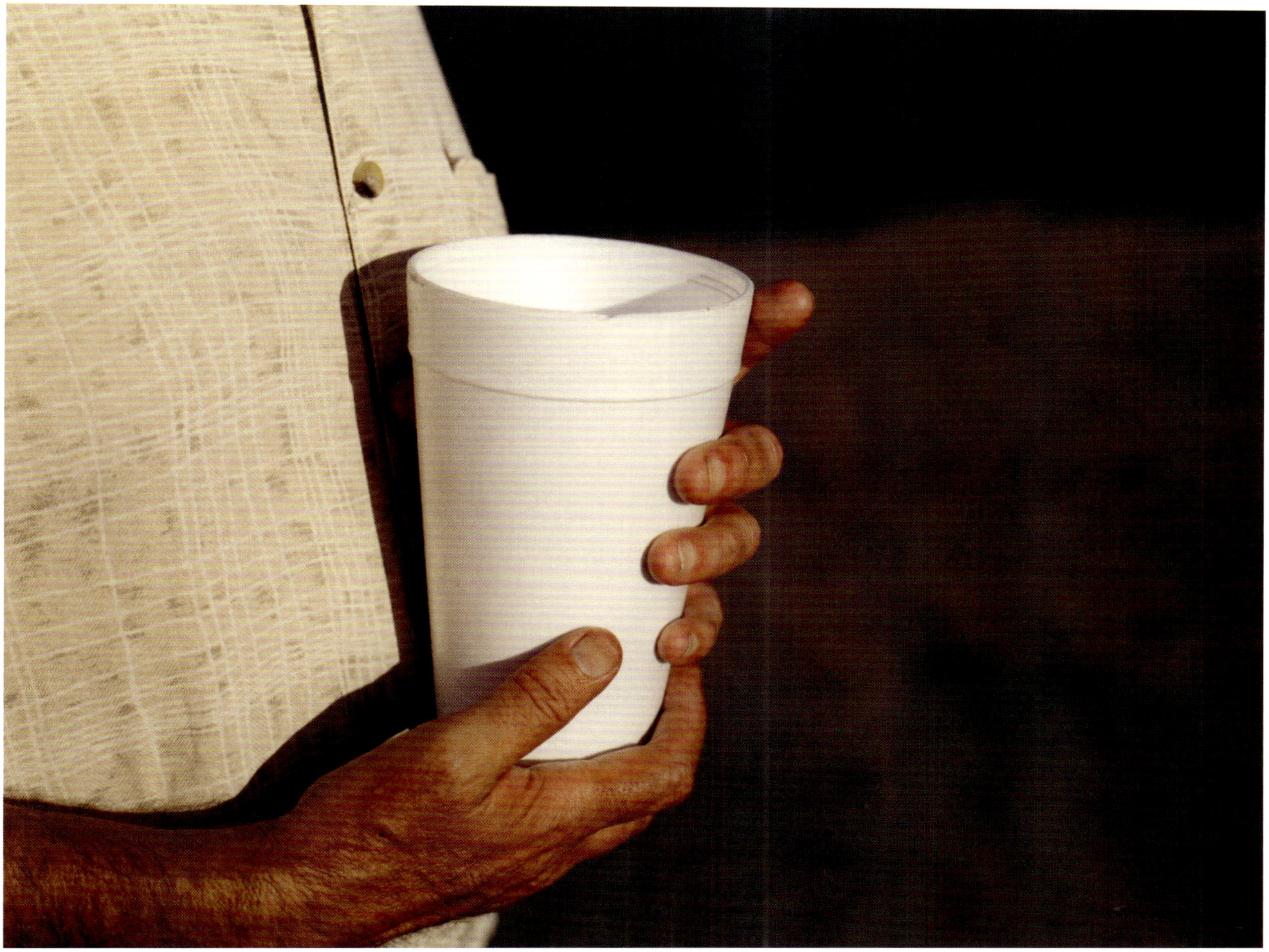

Paul Graham
California, 2006, from the series
'a shimmer of possibility'
Pigment print, 105.4 × 132 cm /
41½ × 52 in

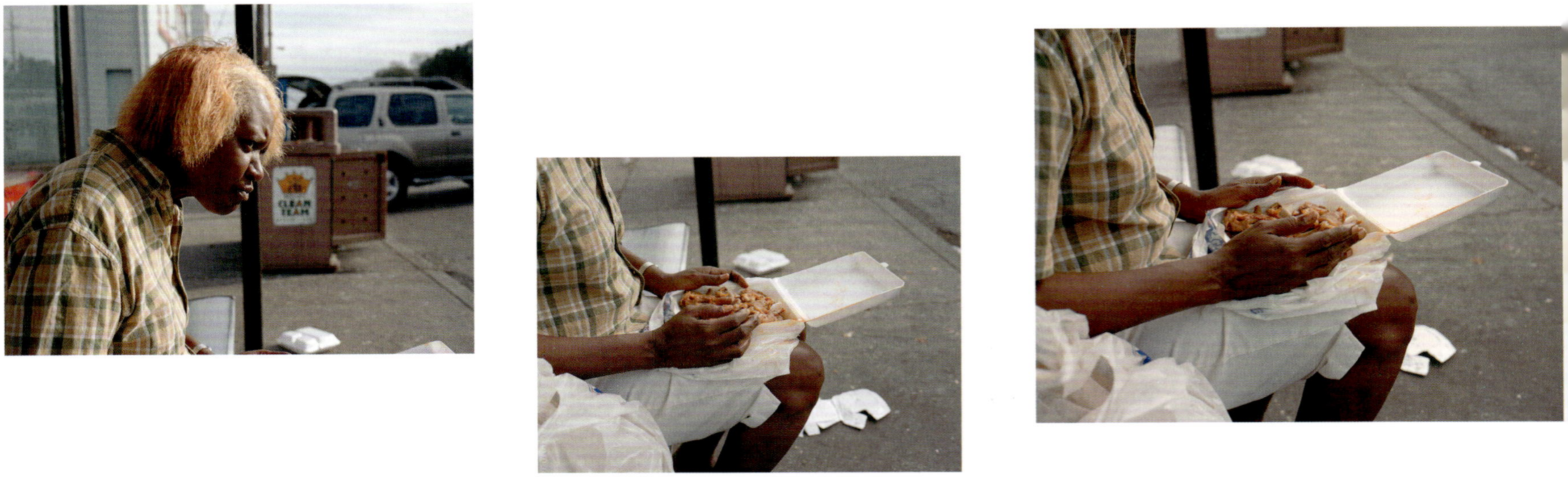

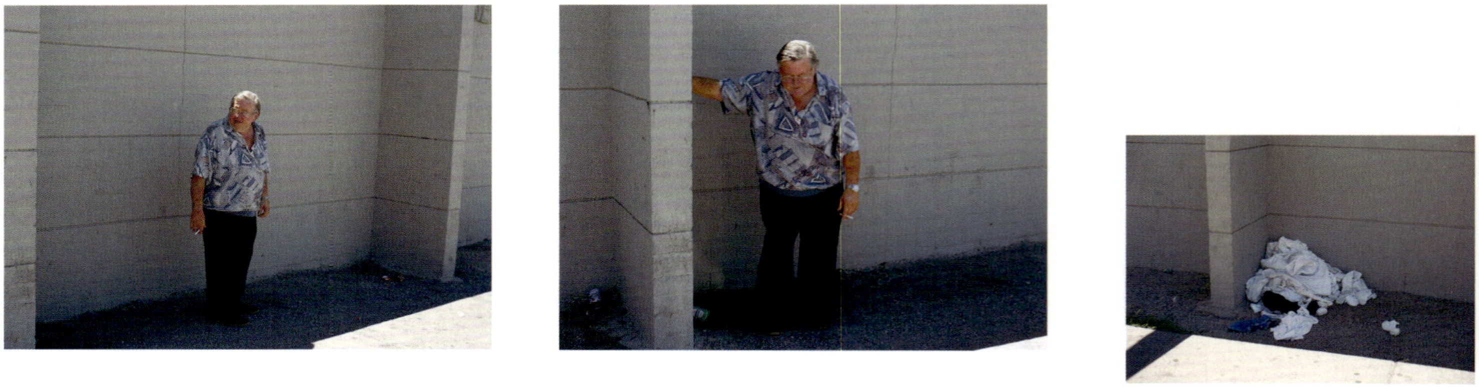

Paul Graham

New Orleans, 2004, from the series
'a shimmer of possibility'
Six pigment ink prints each mounted to Dibond
61 × 81.3 cm / 24 × 32 in
55.9 × 71.1 cm / 22 × 28 in
68.6 × 91.4 cm / 27 × 36 in
38.1 × 50.8 cm / 15 × 20 in
38.1 × 50.8 cm / 15 × 20 in
61 × 81.3 cm / 24 × 32 in

Las Vegas, 2005, from the series
'a shimmer of possibility',
Six pigment ink prints each mounted to Dibond
61 × 81.3 cm / 24 × 32 in
55.9 × 71.1 cm / 22 × 28 in
68.6 × 91.4 cm / 27 × 36 in
38.1 × 50.8 cm / 15 × 20 in
38.1 × 50.8 cm / 15 × 20 in
61 × 81.3 cm / 24 × 32 in

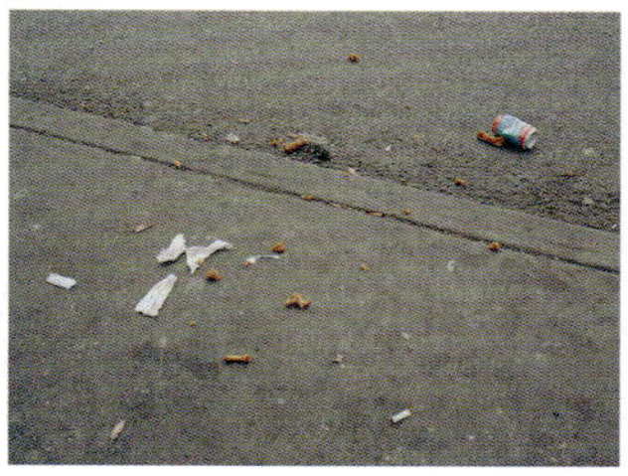
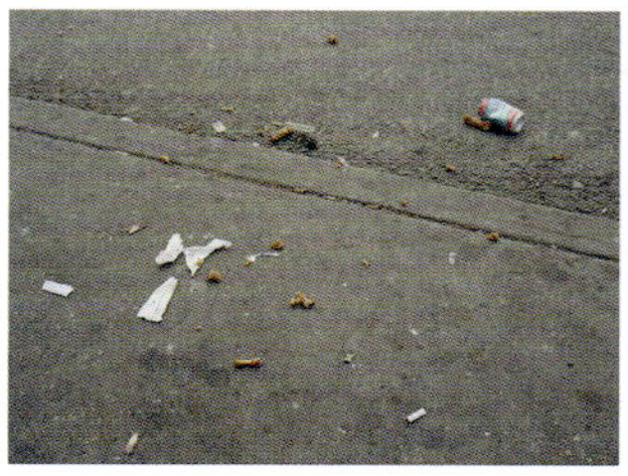
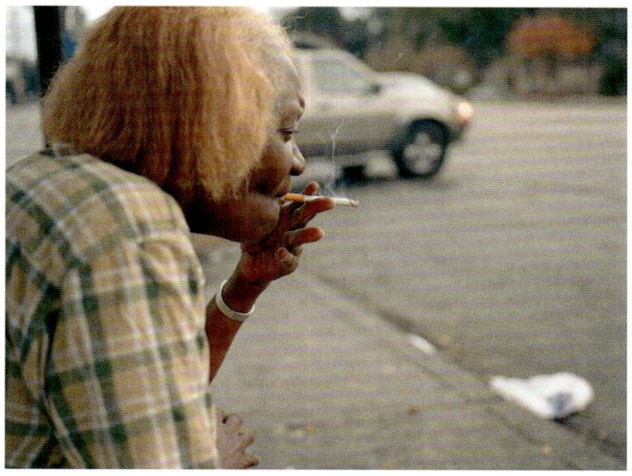
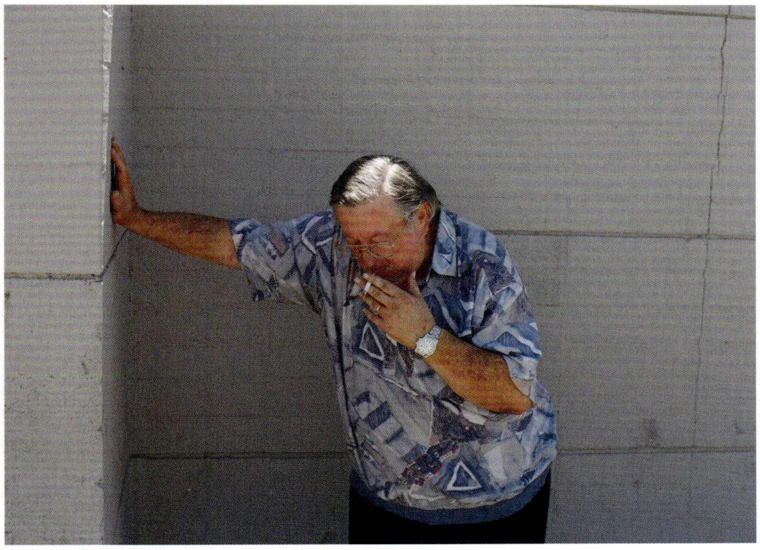
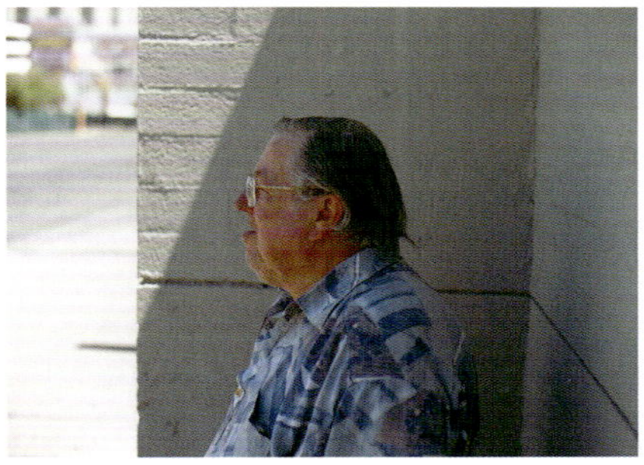
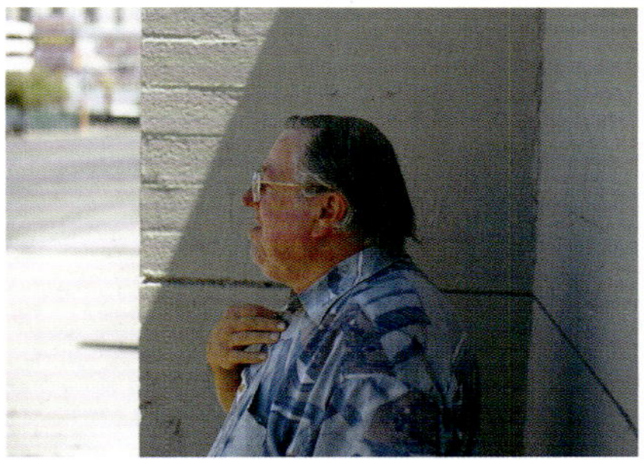

Erik Kessels

This chapter began with the absence of photographs in Alfredo Jaar's installation *Lament of the Images*. It would have been a good way to end this long book. But it is only part of an ending. Jaar himself did not intend us to see it as an end of photography. Since then photography has, as I have shown, proliferated beyond all bounds of comprehension, and it is with a beautiful and memorable installation made in response to this crisis in the face of the ubiquity of photography that one can end this book. Nearly a decade after *Lament of the Images*, in November 2011, Erik Kessels filled an Amsterdam gallery with prints of images uploaded to Flickr over twenty-four hours. It was an exhibition of 350,000 pictures that opened only days before a picture by Andreas Gurksy became the most expensive photograph ever sold at auction. My book began with Gursky and the millions that secured and underscored photography's status as art in the museum. It seems fitting, then, that it should close with Kessels's brilliant critical intervention, physically bringing into the gallery the problem and issues of mass photography, a photography that normally circulates virtually, from screen to screen. Printing these pictures stabilizes and fixes them. There is something about stalling the flicker and speed of our relationship to internet images in this installation. Piling the prints up in the gallery, Kessels presents us with a sea of images intended, as the artist says, to 'visualize the feeling of drowning in representations of other peoples' experiences'.[5] It is an extreme gesture made as part of a show about the future of photography. The work does not give us any answers, but succinctly and effectively presents us with a particular contemporary photographic reality, a reality that the photographic artists of today and tomorrow will all have to begin to make their way through, one way or another.

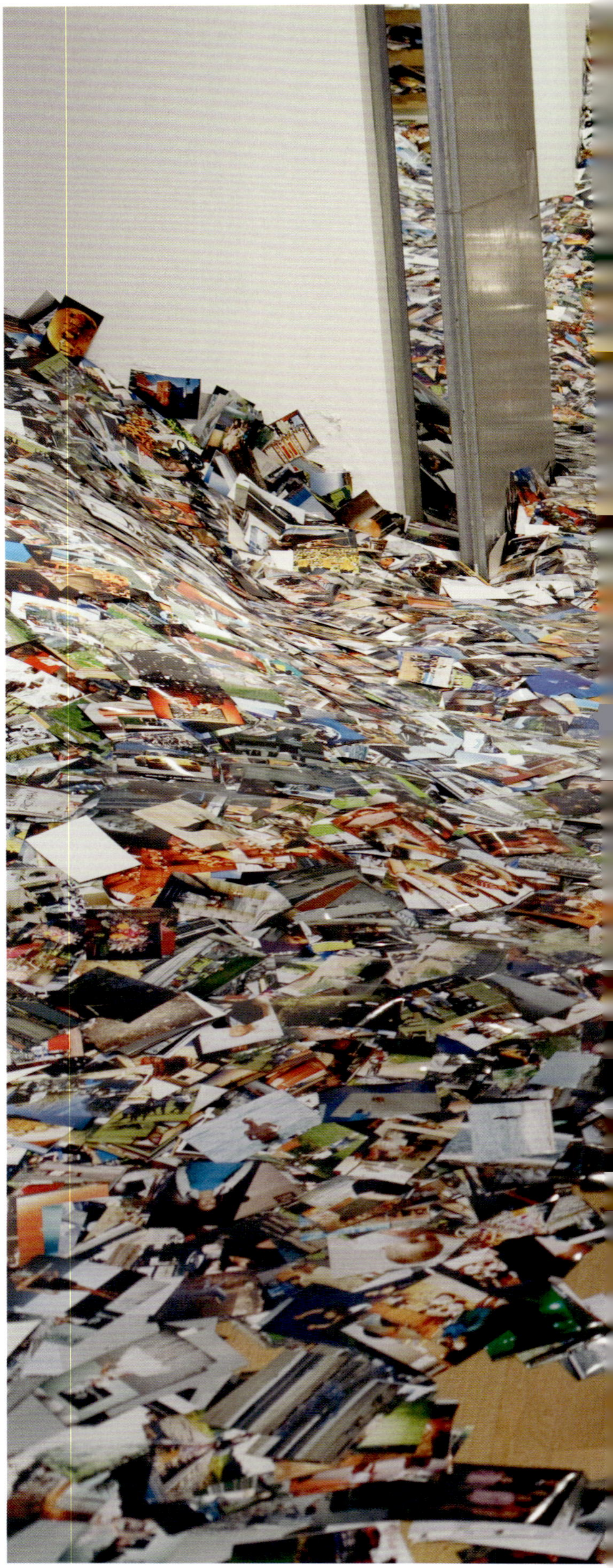

Erik Kessels
24 Hrs In Photos, Dec 2011–Jan 2012
350,000 photos, dimensions variable

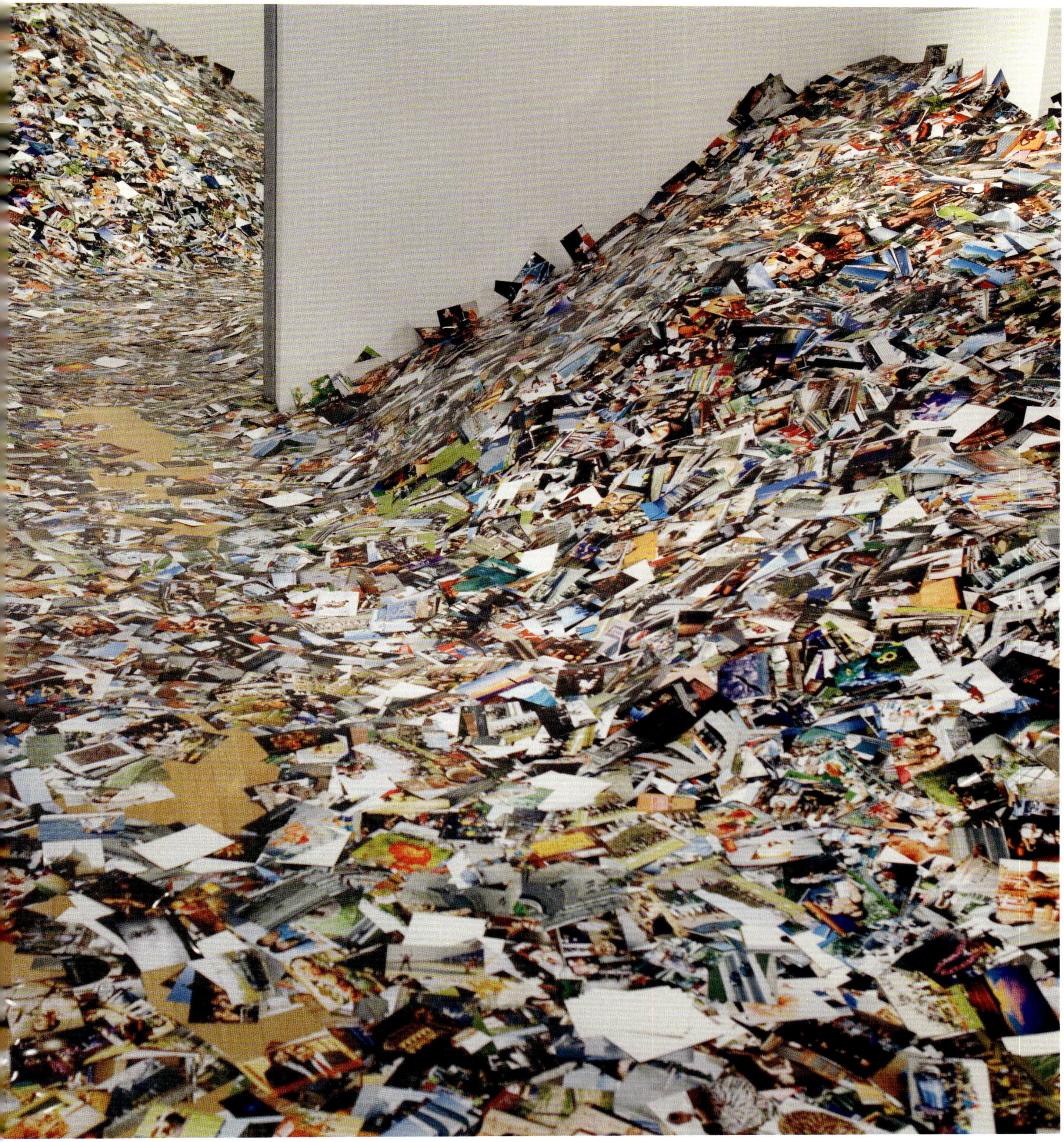

Introduction

1. M. Fried, *Why Photography Matters as Art as Never Before*, New Haven and London, 2008, p. 14.

Chapter One: The Copy

1. Quoted in R. Hughes, *The Shock of the New*, London, 1980, p. 345.
2. B. O'Doherty, 'Rauschenberg and the Vernacular Glance' in *Art in America*, Vol. 63, No.5, 1973, pp. 82–8.
3 This and following quotes, W. Klein, *New York 1954–1955*, Stockport, 1995, p. 13, p. 16 and p. 15
4. K. McShine, *Andy Warhol: A Retrospective*, New York,1989, p. 16.
5. T. Crow, *Art in the Common Culture*, New Haven and London,1996, p. 53.
6. D. Moriyama interviewed in L. A. Martin, and K. Wada, *Japanese Photobooks of the 1960s and 1970s*, New York, 2009, p. 29.
7. N. Araki in *D. Moriyama*, Paris, 2003, p. 135.
8. D. Moriyama interviewed in L. A. Martin, and K. Wada, *Japanese Photobooks of the 1960s and 1970s*, New York, 2009, p. 29.
9. L. Steinberg, *Other Criteria: Confrontations with Twentieth-Century Art*, London, Oxford, New York, 1972, p. 88.
10. J. Wall, '"Marks of Indifference": Aspects of Photography in, or as, Conceptual Art' in *Selected Essays and Interviews*, New York, 2007.
11. All quotes from E. Ruscha taken from A. Schwarz, ed., *Leave Any Information at the Signal: Writings, Interviews, Bits, Pages*, Cambridge, MA and London, 2004, p. 24, p. 53, p. 223 and p. 252.
12. This and following quotes by the artist are from C. Van Bruggen, *John Baldessasri*, New York, 1990, p. 29, p. 30, p. 30.
13. This and the following quote from G. Brett, *Mapa: The Airmail Paintings of Eugenio Dittborn, 1984–1992*, London, 1993, p. 75, p. 81.
14. R. Storr's *Gerhard Richter, October 18, 1977*, New York, 2000, p. 132.
15. This and following quote from the Bechers in D. Birnbaum, 'Bernd and Hilla Becher', *Artforum*, Vol. 42, No.9., May 2004, p. 203 and p. 204.
16. V. Liebermann, *Thomas Ruff* London, 2001, n.p.
17. H. Sugimoto, *Time Exposed*, London, 1995, p. 91.
18. M. Durden, 'Photography, Anonymity and the Archive: Joachim Schmid', *Parachute*, 109, 2003, p. 120.

Chapter Two: The Portrait

1. R. Barthes, *Camera Lucida*, London, 1982, p. 3.
2. C. Owens, *Beyond Recogntion*, Berkeley, Los Angeles and Oxford, 1992, p. 183.
3. P. Adams, *The Emptiness of the Image*, London, 1996, p. 145.
4. All quotes by Arbus taken from *Diane Arbus*, Aperture, New York, 1972, n.p.
5. This and following quote from R. Dijkstra, 'Interview with Jessica Morgan' in *Portraits*, Boston, 2001, p. 76.
6. C. Bishop, 'The Naked Immediacy of Photography', *Flash Art*, November/December 1998, p. 88.
7. M. Hirsch, *Family Frames*, Cambridge, MA and London, 1997, p. 100.
8. A. D. Coleman, 'Mysteries on the Verge of the Vernacular' *Portfolio*, Issue 17, 1993, p. 24.
9. S. Furuya, *Christine Furuya-Gössler: Mémoires, 1978–85*, Kyoto,1997, n.p.
10. M. Faber in S. Furuya, *alive*, Zurich, 2004, p. 167.
11. P. Galassi, *Nicholas Nixon: Pictures of People*, New York, 1988, p. 26.
12. R. Avedon, *In The American West*, New York, 1985, n.p.
13. V. Liebermann, *Thomas Ruff* London, 2001, n.p.
14. R. Durand, 'An Interview with Thomas Ruff' in *Thomas Ruff*, Paris, 1997, p. 31
15. S. Watney, 'Interview with Andres Serrano' in A. Searle, ed., *Talking Art*, London, 1993, p. 127.
16. M. Diawara, 'The Sixties in Bamako: Malick Sididé and James Brown', *Malick Sidibé*, Göttingen, 2003, p. 10.
17. http://www.thephilanthropicmuseum.org/?portfolio=t-h-o-h-y-the-hall-of-hyperdelic-youths (accessed 10/7/13).

Chapter Three: Colour

1. Quoted in J. Keller, 'At Fortune' in *Walker Evans: The Getty Museum Collection*, London, 1995, p. 304.
2. This and subsequent quotes by Eggleston taken from W. Eggleston, *Ancient and Modern*, New York, 1992, p. 18, p. 28, p. 13, p. 22, p. 82, p. 82, p. 82.
3. J. Szarkowski, *Eggleston's Guide*, New York, 1976, p. 10.
4. M. Holborn in W. Eggleston, *Ancient and Modern*, New York, 1992, p. 12.
5. Quoted in C. Lange, M. Fried and J. Sternfeld, *Stephen Shore*, London, 2007, p. 14.
6. This and following quote by Shore taken from S. Shore, *Uncommon Places*, London, 2004, p. 179 and p. 6.
7: This and following quote in b. hooks, 'The Radiance of Red' in *Art on my Mind*, New York, 1995, p. 213 and p. 219.
8. Quoted in M. Kozloff, 'The Coming of Age of Color' in *Photography and Fascination*, Danbury, CT, 1979, p. 189.
9. Quoted in A. D. Weinberg, *On the Line: The New Color Photojournalism*, Minneapolis, 1986, p. 41.
10. Quoted in S. D. Moeller, *Shooting War: Photography and the American Experience of Combat*, New York, 1989, p. 391.
11. This and following quote in S. D. Moeller, *Shooting War: Photography and the American Experience of Combat*, New York, 1989, p. 410 and p. 412.
12. K. Light, *Witness in our Time*, Washington and London, 2000, p. 105.
13. A. D. Weinberg, *On the Line: The New Color Photojournalism*, Minneapolis, 1986, p. 43.
14. A. Webb, *Under a Grudging Sun*, London, 1989, p. 10.
15. This and following quote from M. E. Mark, *Falkland Road*, London,1981, p. 7.
16. This and following quote from R. Singh, *River of Colour*, London, 1998, p. 10.
17. D. Chandler, *Paul Graham*, Göttingen, p. 30.
18. D. Rossell, *Ricas y Famosas*, London, 2008, n.p.
19. B. H. D. Buchloh, 'Cosmic Reification: Gabriel Orozco's Photographs' in Y-A Bois, ed., *Gabriel Orozco*, Cambridge, MA and London, 2009, p. 147.
20. G. Orozco, 'Lecture 2001' in Y-A Bois, ed., *Gabriel Orozco*, Cambridge, MA and London, 2009, p. 101.

Chapter Four: The Street

1. C. Westerbeck and J. Meyerowitz, *Bystander: A History of Street Photography*, London, 1994, p. 34.
2. H. Cartier-Bresson, 'The Decisive Moment' in *The Mind's Eye: Writings on Photography and Photographers*, New York, 1999 [1952], p. 42.
3. This and subsequent quotes from Meyerowitz all taken from C. Westerbeck, *Joel Meyerowitz*, London, 2005, n.p.
4. J. Szarkowski, MoMA wall label for *New Documents*, available at: http://www.moma.org/docs/press_archives/3860/releases/MOMA_1967_Jan-June_0034_21.pdf?2010 (accessed 21/6/13).
5. This and following quote in B. Diamonstein, ed., *Visions and Images: Photographers on Photography*, London, 1982, p. 181 and p. 185.
6. G. Winogrand quoted in D. Longwell, ed., 'Monkeys Make the Problem More Difficult: A Collective Interview with Garry Winogrand', *Image* 15, no.2, July 1972, p. 4.
7. This and the following quote by J. Szarkowski in G. Winogrand, *Animals*, New York, 2004 [1969], p. 45, p. 46.
8. G. Winogrand, *Public Relations*, New York, 2004 [1977], p. 14.
9. T. Papageorge in G. Winogrand, *Public Relations*, New York, 2004 [1977], p. 15.
10. J. Green, *American Photography: A Critical History*, New York, 1984, p. 110
11. P. Galassi, *Friedlander*, New York, 2005, p. 39.
12. This and following quotes by R. DeCarava, unless indicated, quoted in P. Galassi, *Roy DeCarava: A Retrospective*, New York, 1996, p. 19, p. 19. p. 31
13. This and following quote by P. Galassi from his *Roy DeCarava: A Retrospective*, New York, 1996, p. 29 and p. 11.
14. Quoted in S. T. DeCarava, 'Introduction; Celebration', in J. Alinder, ed., *Roy DeCarava/ Photographs*, Carmel, 1981, pp. 18–19.
15. This and following quote taken from D. Moriyama, *Memories of a Dog* Tucson, 2004, p. 9.
16. D. Moriyama quoted in accompanying pamphlet essay to *Daido Moriyama: The Complete Works*, Vol.3, Tokyo, 2004, p. 5.
17. From Wall's interview with A. Pelenc in *Jeff Wall*, London, 2002, p. 17.
18. T. deDuve, A. Pelene, B. Groys and J-F Chevrier, *Jeff Wall*, London, 2002, p. 90.
19. This and following quotes from the artist in M. Fleming, *Ken Lum: Recent Work*, Oakville, 1994, all p. 5.
20. J. Agee in *Helen Levitt, A Way of Seeing*, Durham and London, 1989, p. viii.
21. R. Barthes, 'The Great Family of Man' in *Mythologies*, New York, 2012, p. 197.
22. Quoted in T. Smith 'Everyday Arcadias' at http://www.beatstreuli.com/beatstreuli/information/trevorsmith.html (accessed 1/7/13).
23. A. Pace, 'An interview with Beat Streuli' in *Beat Streuli*, Turin, 2000, p. 117.
24. H. Cartier-Bresson, 'The Decisive Moment' in *The Mind's Eye: Writings on Photography and Photographers*, New York, 1999 [1952], p. 22.

Chapter Five: Landscapes

1. J. Szarkowski, *Ansel Adams at 100*, New York, 2001, p. 26
2. M. Fried, *Why Photography Matters as Art as Never Before*, New Haven and London, 2008, p. 180.
3. Quoted in L. Cooke, 'Andreas Gursky: Vision (Per)versions' in M. L. Syring, *Andreas Gursky: Photographs from 1984 to the Present*, Munich, Paris, London, 1998, p. 14.
4. R. Adams, *Along Some Rivers*, New York, 2006, p. 26
5. M. Kozloff, 'Bad News from Epic Landscapes' in *Lone Visions*, Albuquerque, 1994, p. 199.
6. T. Papageorge, 'Robert Adams—What We Bought: The New World' [2001] in his *Core Curriculum*, New York, 2011, p. 145.
7. R. Adams, *The New West*, [1974] New York, 2008, xii.
8. W. Scheppe, 'Lewis Baltz and the Garden of False Reality' in L. Baltz, *Candlestick Point*, Göttingen, 2011, p. 102.
9. D. Green, 'Between Object and Image' [1996] in D. Brittain ed., *Creative Camera: 30 Years of Writing* Manchester, 1999, p. 266.
10. From an email exchange between the artist and author in March 2011.
11. R. Misrach, *Violent Legacies*, Manchester, 1992, p. 88.
12. M. Kozloff, 'Bad News from Epic Landscapes' in *Lone Visions*, Albuquerque, 1994, p. 205.
13. http://www.prixpictet.com/portfolios/earth-shortlist/edward-burtynsky/statement/ttp (accessed 12/6/13).
14. http://www.edwardburtynsky.com/ (accessed 12/1/13).
15. W. Doherty, email correspondence with author, March 2005.
16. Quoted in E. Edwards, *Raw Histories*, Oxford 2001, p. 222.
17. J. Carville, 'Re-Negotiated Territory', *Afterimage*, July/August 2001, p. 7.
18. This and following quote, Y. Barrada, *A Life Full of Holes: The Strait Project*, London, 2005, p. 58 and p. 57.
19. http://www.georgegeorgiou.net/gallery.php?ProjectID=148 (accessed 12/12/2012).
20. C. Pantall 'Parallel Lines' BJP, 7/1/ 2009 at: http://www.bjp-online.com/british-journal-of-photography/feature/1638654/parallel-lines (accessed 12/1/2011).

Chapter Six: History

1. This and following quote by A. Grundberg, *The Crisis of the Real*, New York, 1990, p. 185 and p. 190.
2. J. Nachtwey interviewed by E. Farnsworth, (16/5/2000) at http://www.pbs.org/newshour/gergen/jan-june/nachtwey_5-15.html (accessed 12/11/13)
3. L. Sante, Introduction, J. Nachtwey, *Inferno*, London, 1999, p. 10.
4. J. Stallabrass, 'Sebastião Salgado and Fine Art Photojournalism', *New Left Review*, 1/223, 1997, p. 148.
5. Quoted in J. Stallabrass 1997, p. 149.
6. F. Ritchin, Introduction, S. Salgado, *Sahel: The End of the Road*, Berkeley and Los Angeles, 2004, p. 4.
7. Quoted in K. Light, *Witness in Our Time*, Washington and London, 2000, p. 111.
8. S. D. Moeller, *Shooting War: Photography and the American Experience of Combat*, New York, 1989, p. 405.
9. A-M. Lê, *Small Wars*, New York, 2005, p. 124.
10. I. Jeffrey, *Shomei Tomatsu*, London, 2001, p. 9.
11. M. Durden and L. Papadimitriou, '*Sans-Souci*: Christian Boltanski Interviewed' in, D. Brittain, ed., *Creative Camera: Thirty years of Writing*, Manchester, 1999, p. 217.
12. G. Marsh, 'The White and the Black: An Interview with Christian Boltanski', *Parkett* No.22, 1989, p. 39.
13. M. Durden and L. Papadimitriou, p. 215.

14. Quoted in G. Peress, *U.S.News*, October 6, 1997 available at http://www.artsmia.org/get-the-picture/print/peress.shtml (accessed May 4, 2012).
15. C. Horsfield, *Relation*, Paris, Lisboa, Sydney, 2006, p. 218.
16. 'Faith and Doubt at Ground Zero: Interview' at http://www.pbs.org/wgbh/pages/frontline/shows/faith/interviews/meyerowitz.html (accessed 5/6/12).
17. J. Meyerowitz, *Aftermath*, London, 2006, p. 185
18. M. Durden, 'Interview with Geert van Kesteren', *8 The Photography Biannual*, Issue 25, Spring 2009, p. 39.

Chapter Seven: The Body

1. J. Tumler, 'Bas Jan Ader: Artist and Time Traveller' in B. Spence, ed., *Bas Jan Ader*, Irvine, 1999, p. 24.
2. Quoted in B. Spence, 'Painfully Ironic' in *Bas Jan Ader*, Irvine, 1999, p. 36.
3. M. Newman, 'Photography and Video as Sculpture in the Work of Erwin Wurm' in *Erwin Wurm*, London, 2000, p. 4.
4. D. English, 'Stripped Bare: Nude Girls and Naked Truths' in S. Meiselas, *Carnival Strippers*, Göttingen, 2003, p. 153.
5. R. Brookes, 'Fashion Photography: The Double-Page Spread: Helmut Newton, Guy Bourdin & Deborah Turbeville' in M. Barnard ed., *Fashion Theory*, London and New York, 2007, p. 521.
6. R. Brookes, 'Sighs and Whispers' in *Guy Bourdin*, London, 2003, p. 129.
7. This and following quotes by Mercer in 'Reading Racial Fetishism' in his *Welcome to the Jungle*, London, 1994, p. 179, p. 191 and p. 200.
8. S. Sontag, 'Fascinating Fascism' in *Under The Sign of Saturn*, New York, 1981, p. 86.
9. P. Phelan, *Unmarked: The Politics of Performance*, London and New York, 1993, p. 51.
10. M. Hirsch, *Family Frames*, Cambridge, MA and London, 1997, p. 165.
11. J. Coplans quoted in S. Morgan and F. Morris, *Rites of Passage*, London, 1995, p. 76.
12. This and following quote in R. Arnold, 'Heroin Chic' in *Fashion Theory*, Volume 3, Issue.3, August 1999, p. 285.
13. L. Mulvey, 'Cosmetics and Abjection: Cindy Sherman, 1977–87' in *Fetishism and Curiosity*, London and Indiana, 1996, p. 72 and p. 71.
14. A. Serrano quoted in W. Steiner, *The Scandal of Pleasure*, Chicago and London, 1995, p. 11.
15. A. Serrano quoted in R. Hobbs, 'Andres Serrano: The Body Politic' in *Andres Serrano: Works 1983–1993*, Philadelphia, 1994, p. 42.

Chapter Eight: Documentary

1. A. Grundberg, 'An Interview with J. Szarkowski' in *Afterimage*, October 1984, p. 13.
2. D. Lyon, *Conversations with the Dead*, New York, Chicago, San Francisco, 1971, p. 12.
3. B. Davidson, *East 100th Street*, Los Angeles, 2003, p. 157.
4. D. Goldblatt, *South Africa: The Structure of Things Then*, Oxford, 1998, p. 7.
5. This and the following quote by B. Owens from J. Guimond, *American Photography and the American Dream*, Chapel Hill and London, 1991, p. 261 and p. 262.
6. B. Owens, *Suburbia*, San Francisco, 1974, n.p.
7. http://www.american-pictures.com/gallery/index.html (accessed 1/6/13)
8. Quoted in J. Ballerini, 'A Tale of Two Teens: The Saved and the Doomed in *Raised by Wolves*', *Afterimage*, Summer 1996, p. 12.
9. S. Salgado, *Workers: An Archaeology of the Industrial Age*, New York, 1993, p. 6.
10. Both quotes from A. Sekula, *Fish Story*, Düsseldorf, 1995, p. 12.
11. M. Rosler, 'In, around, and afterthoughts (on documentary photography)' in ed., R. Bolton, *The Contest of Meaning*, Cambridge, MA and London, 1989, pp. 322–24.
12. B. Buchloh: 'A Conversation with Martha Rosler' in C. de Zegher, ed., *Martha Rosler: Positions in the Life World*, Cambridge, MA and London, 1999, p. 44.
13. S. Calle, *Double Games*, London, 1999, p. 192.
14. S. Calle, *Double Games*, London, 1999, p. 67.
15. L. Kotz, 'aesthetics of intimacy' in D. Bright, ed., *Passionate Camera*, New York and London, 1999, p. 208.
16. B. Mikhailov, *Case History*, Zurich, Berlin, New York, p. 9.
17. This 2009 letter was originally published on http://www.africanevents.com but is no longer available. (Originally accessed 15/5/2012).
18. Interview with Pieter Hugo, 2010 available at http://www.electronicbeats.net/en/features/pieter-hugo-nollywood/ (accessed 15/5/2012).
19. O. Chernysheva, *Acquaintances*, London, 2010, p. 56.

Chapter Nine: Self

1. All quotes taken from unpaginated notes in E. V. Elsken's *Sweet Life*, New York, 1966.
2. M. Kelley interview 'Larry Clark: In Youth is Pleasure', *Flash Art*, July/Sept, 2008, p. 175
3. N. Araki quoted in R. Keneko and I. Vartanian, *Japanese Photobooks of the 1960s and '70s*, New York, 2009, p. 108.
4. All quotes, unless otherwise indicated, from N. Goldin, *I'll Be Your Mirror*, New York, 1996, p. 448, p. 452, p. 452.
5. N. Goldin, *The Ballad of Sexual Dependency*, New York, 1996 [1986], p. 6.
6. Quote taken from email exchange with the author, September, 2003.
7. L. G. Corrin, 'Self Questioning Monuments' in *Felix Gonzales-Torres*, London, 2000, p. 14.
8. A. Searle, *The Guardian*, 6/6/2000 http://www.guardian.co.uk/culture/2000/jun/06/artsfeatures1 (accessed 12/12/13)
9. A. Cruz, 'The Means of Pleasure' in R. Fergusson, ed., *Felix Gonzales-Torres*, Los Angeles, 1994, p. 18.
10. N. Shafran, *edited photographs 1992–2004*, Göttingen and Brighton, 2004, p. 120.
11. b. hooks, 'subversive beauty: new modes of contestation' in R. Fergusson, ed., *Felix Gonzales-Torres*, Los Angeles, 1994, p. 46.
12. J. Spence, *Putting Myself in the Picture*, Seattle, 1988, p. 35.
13. Both quotes from J. Spence, *Putting Myself in the Picture*, Seattle, 1988, p. 82 and p. 83.
14. J. Evans, 'An affront to taste? The Disturbances of Jo Spence' in *The Camerwork Essays*, London 1997, p. 244.
15. C. Townsend, *Francesca Woodman*, London, 2006, p. 55.
16. Quoted in C. Raymond, *Francesca Woodman and the Inner Sublime*, Farnham, 2010, p. 89.
17. Quoted in R. E. Krauss, *Bachelors*, Cambridge, MA and London, 1999, p. 166.
18. Quoted in P. Finnemore, *Gwendraeth House*, Cardiff, 2000, n. p.

Chapter Ten: Constructions

1. This quote from Krims taken from his website *www.leskrims.com/* (accessed 11/11/09).
2. This and the following quote by Grove are taken from an artist's statement communicated by email to the author in March 2011.
3. A. D. Coleman, 'The Directorial Mode: Notes Toward a Definition', *Light Readings*, New York, 1979 [1976] pp. 246–257.
4. This and following quotes from Krims taken from his website *www.leskrims.com/* (accessed 11/11/09).
5. A. D. Coleman, 'Lucas Samaras and Les Krims' in *Light Readings*, New York, 1979, p. 241
6. All quotes, unless otherwise indicated, are from B. Diamonstein, *Visions and Images: Photographers on Photography*, London, 1982, p. 128, p. 128, p. 118.
7. M. Livingstone, *Duane Michals: Photographs/Sequences/Texts*, Oxford, 1984, n.p.
8. This and subsequent quotes taken from V. Burgin, *Between*, Oxford and London, 1986, p. 21, p. 135, p. 78 and p. 137.
9. H. Foster, 'Subversive Signs' in *Recodings: Art, Spectacle, Cultural Politics*, Port Townsend, 1985, p. 100.
10. All quotes from Kruger taken from K. Linker, *Love for Sale*, New York, 1990, p. 14, p. 29, p. 62.
11. All quotes from Neshat from her catalogue *Women of Allah*, Turin, 1997, n.p.
12. This and following quotes from Levinthal in C. Stainback and R. B. Woodward, *D. Levinthal, Work from 1975–1995*, New York, 1997, p. 128 and p. 153.
13. J. E. Young, *At Memory's Edge: After-Images of the Holocaust in Contemporary Art and Culture*, New Haven and London, 2000, p. 55.
14. All quotes from his interview with A. Pelenc in *Jeff Wall*, London, 2002, p. 11.
15. 'Boris Groys in Conversation with Jeff Wall' in *Jeff Wall*, London, 2002, p. 152.
16. J. Stallabrass, 'Art-Photography Lite' in *New Left Review*, 65, Sept/Oct 2010, p. 122.
17. K. Ryan, *Dream House: Gregory Crewdson*, Milan, 2008, n.p.
18. S. Berg, 'The Dark Side of the American Dream' in ed., Stephan Berg, *Gregory Crewdson 1985–2005*, Ostfildern, 2007, p. 19.
19. This and the following quotes taken from 'Talking Art with Carrie Mae Weems' in b. hooks, *Art on My Mind: Visual Politics*, New York, 1995, p. 76, p. 84 and p. 85.
20. T. Moffatt, *Fever Pitch*, Annandale, 1995, p. 5
21. R. Durand, 'Specific climates' in *Tracey Moffatt*, Barcelona, 1999, p. 103.
22. Interview with G. Matt in M. Hentechel, ed., *Tracey Moffatt*, Stuttgart, 1998, p. 19.
23. From a discussion with the artist by the author, October 1996.
24. All quotes from the artist taken from his website: www.wangqingsong.com (accessed 12/12/10).
25. All quotes from the artist are taken from his website http://www.rama9art.org/manit_s/ (accessed 12/12/10).
26. This and subsequent quotes are taken from the following website resource, 'Artist's Note on new work Not Today' at http://www.facebook.com/note.php?note_id=108632549178131 (accessed 12/12/10).

Chapter Eleven: Photography Tomorrow

1. This quote by Alfredo Jaar is taken from a 2002 interview for Documenta: http://universes-in-universe.de/car/documenta/11/frid/e-jaar-2.htm (accessed 12/1/13).
2. This and all following quotes by the artist were originally taken from Taryn Simon's talk, 'The Stories Behind the Bloodlines', November 2011, video posted on line at http://www.ted.com/talks/taryn_simon_the_stories_behind_the_bloodlines.html (accessed 12/3/ 2013). Simon subsequently modified some of the quotes during the completion of this text.
3. This and following quotes by Schmid taken from his article 'Reload Currywurst, Photo Sharing: You Can Eat Your Sausage and Have It, Too' (2008) available on line at http://fotokritik.wordpress.com/2008/11/11/reload-currywurst/ (accessed 1/9/12).
4. All quotes taken from R. Woodward's interview with Paul Graham in *Photo-Eye* Fall 2007 available at http://issuu.com/photo-eye/docs/photo-eye_magazine_fall_2007 (accessed 1/7/13).
5. Quote taken from Creative Review blog posted on 11 November 2011, http://www.creativereview.co.uk/cr-blog/2011/november/24-hours-in-photos (accessed 12/6/13).

The brief biographies of the photographers featured in this book given here are not intended to be complete. Their purpose is to offer the reader a guide to further research. Wherever possible each biography includes the following information: the photographer's date and place of birth, place of residence, title of retrospective book, if applicable, and one or two solo exhibitions.

Bas Jan Ader
1942–1975. Born Winschoten, The Netherlands. Lived Los Angeles, CA, USA.
Lit.: Spence, B., *The Case of Bas Jan Ader*, Irvine, 2000
Exh.: 'Bas Jan Ader: Please Don't Leave Me', Boijmans Van Beuninge, Rotterdam, 2006; 'Bas Jan Ader Retrospective', Sweeney Art Gallery, Riverside, CA, 1999

Merry Alpern
Born 1955, New York, USA.
Lives Brooklyn, NY, USA.
Exh.: 'Private', Schirn Kunsthalle Frankfurt, 2013; 'Exposed: Voyeurism, Surveillance, and the Camera since 1870', Tate Modern, London, 2010

Laurie Anderson
Born 1947, Glen Ellyn, IL, USA.
Lives New York, NY, USA.
Lit.: Goldberg, R., and Anderson, L., *Laurie Anderson*, New York, 2000
Exh.: 'The Record of the Time: Sound in the Work of Laurie Anderson', The Musée Art Contemporain of Lyon, 2003; 'The Waters Reglitterized', Sean Kelly Gallery, New York, 2005

Nobuyoshi Araki
Born 1940, Taito-ku, Tokyo, Japan.
Lives Tokyo, Japan.
Lit.: Miki, A., Isshiki, Y. and Sato, T., *Nobuyoshi Araki: Self, Life, Death*, London, 2005
Exh.: 'Nobuyoshi Araki Photobook Exhibition: Ararchy', Izu Photo Museum, Shizuoka, 2012; 'Nobuyoshi Araki: Self, Life, Death', Barbican Art Gallery, London, 2005

Diane Arbus
1923–1971. Born New York, USA.
Lived New York, USA.
Lit.: Arbus, D., *Diane Arbus Revelations*, London, 2003
Exh.: 'Diane Arbus Revelations', SFMOMA, CA, 2004; 'Diane Arbus', MoMA, New York, 1972

Keith Arnatt
1930–2008. Born Oxford, UK.
Lived Tintern, Wales, UK.
Lit.: Hurn, D., Grafik, C., *I'm a Real Photographer: Photographs by Keith Arnatt*, London, 2007
Exh.: 'Keith Arnatt: Sausages and Food', Collection In-Focus Display, Tate Britain, London, 2013; 'Keith Arnatt: I'm A Real Photographer', The Photographers' Gallery, London, 2007

Richard Avedon
1923–2004. Born New York, USA.
Lived New York, USA.
Lit.: Avedon, R., Squiers, C., Aletti V., Garne P., *Avedon Fashion 1944–2000*, New York, 2009
Exh.: 'Avedon Fashion 1944–2000', International Center of Photography, New York, 2009; 'Richard Avedon Photographs 1946–2004', Louisiana Museum of Modern Art, Humlebæk, 2007

John Baldessari
Born 1931, National City, CA, USA.
Lives Santa Monica, CA, USA.
Lit.: Pardo, P., Dean R., *John Baldessari Catalogue Raisonné, Volume One: 1956–1974*, New Haven, CT, 2012
Exh.: 'John Baldessari: Pure Beauty', The Metropolitan Museum of Art, New York, 2010; 'John Baldessari: A print retrospective', Museum of Contemporary Photography, Chicago, IL, 2010

Lewis Baltz
Born 1945, Newport Beach, CA, USA. Lives Paris, France and Venice, Italy.
Lit.: Baltz, L., *Lewis Baltz: Works*, Göttingen, 2010.
Exh.: 'Lewis Baltz', Kunstmuseum Bonn, 2012; 'Lewis Baltz: Prototypes/Ronde de Nuit', National Gallery of Art, Washington D.C., 2011

Yto Barrada
Born, 1971, Paris, France. Lives Tangier, Morocco.
Lit.: Chévrier, J., Bovier, L., Dirié, C., Barrada, Y., *Yto Barrada*, Zurich, 2013
Exh.: 'Yto Barrada: Riffs', Deutsche Guggenheim, Berlin, 2011; 'Yto Barrada, Jeu de Paume', Paris, 2006

Bernd & Hilla Becher
Bernd Becher 1931–2007. Born Siegen, Germany. Lived in Düsseldorf, Germany.
Hilla Becher Born 1934, Potsdam, Germany. Lives in Düsseldorf, Germany.
Lit.: Lange S., Gaines, J., *Bernd and Hilla Becher: Life and Work*, Cambridge, MA, 2006
Exh.: 'Bernd and Hilla Becher: A Survey 1972–2006', Fraenkel Gallery, San Francisco, CA, USA, 2009; 'Bernd and Hilla Becher: Landscape/Typology', MoMA, New York, 2008

Richard Billingham
Born 1970, Birmingham, UK.
Lives Stourbridge, UK.
Exh.: 'Richard Billingham', Anthony Reynolds Gallery, London, 2010; 'Richard Billingham: People, Places, Animals', Melbourne, 2007

Christian Boltanski
Born 1944, Paris, France. Lives Malakoff, France.
Lit.: Boltanski, C., Grenier, C., Sante L., *The Possible Life of Christian Boltanski*, Boston, 2009
Exh.: 'Christian Boltanski: La vie possible', Kunstmuseum Liechtenstein, 2009 'Christian Boltanski', Centre Georges Pompidou Paris, 1984

Guy Bourdin
1928–1991. Born Paris, France.
Lived Paris, France.
Lit.: Gingeras, A., Bourdin, A., *Guy Bourdin*, London, 2005
Exh.: 'Guy Bourdin: Retrospective', Deichtorhallen, Hamburg, 2013; 'The first retrospective of Guy Bourdin (1928–1991)', V&A, London, 2003

Daniel Blaufuks
Born 1963, Lisbon, Portugal.
Lives in Lisbon, Portugal.
Lit.: Blaufuks, D., *Daniel Blaufuks – Works on Memory: Selected Writings and Images*, Cardiff, 2012
Exh.: 'Works on Memory', Ffotogallery, Cardiff, Wales, 2012 'Daniel Blaufuks: Utz', Vera Cortes, Lisbon, 2012

Victor Burgin
Born 1941, Sheffield, UK
Lives Somerset, UK and Paris, France.
Lit.: Burgin, V., *Parallel Texts. Interviews and Interventions about Art*, London, 2011
Exh.: 'The Burgin Position: Victor Burgin Retrospective 1967–2014', Museum für Gegenwartskunst, Siegen, Germany, 2014; 'Victor Burgin – A Sense of Place', Ambika P3, University of Westminster, London, 2013

Larry Burrows
1926–1971. Born London, UK.
Lived London, UK.
Lit.: Burrows, L., *Larry Burrows: Vietnam*, New York, 2002
Exh.: 'Larry Burrows: War & Peace', Laurence Miller Gallery, New York, 2005

Edward Burtynsky
Born 1955, St Catharines, Canada
Lives Toronto, Canada.
Lit.: Burtynsky, E., Pauli L., Haworth-Booth, M., Baker, K., *Manufactured Landscapes: The Photographs of Edward Burtynsky*, New Haven, CT, 2009
Exh.: 'Edward Burtynsky: The Landscape That We Change', McMichael Canadian Art Collection, Kleinberg, 2013; 'Edward Burtynsky: Mid-Career Retrospective', The National Gallery of Canada, Ottawa, 2003

Sophie Calle
Born 1953, Paris, France. Lives Paris, France.
Lit.: Calle, S., Macel, C., Bois, Y., Rolin, O., Racine, B., *Sophie Calle: M'as tu vue? – Did you see me?*, New York, 2003
Exh.: 'Sophie Calle: Talking to Strangers', Whitechapel Gallery, London, 2009; 'Sophie Calle: Take Care of Yourself', Paula Cooper Gallery, New York, 2009

James Casebere
Born 1953, Lansing, Michigan, USA. Lives New York, NY, USA.
Lit.: Okwui E., *James Casebere: Works*, Bologna, 2011
Exh.: 'Picture Show: James Casebere', SECCA, Winston Salem, NC, 2002; 'James Casebere: Model Culture, Photographs, 1975–1996', The Ansel Adams Center for Photography, San Francisco, CA, 1996

Philippe Chancel
Born 1959, Paris, France. Lives Paris France.
Exh.: *Workers Emirates*, Ikono Gallery, Brussels, 2012; 'The Narcissism of power', Columbia University, New York, 2011

Olga Chernysheva
Born 1962, Moscow, Russia. Lives Moscow, Russia.
Exh.: 'Compossibilities', Kunsthalle Erfurt, 2013; 'Olga Chernysheva', Calvert 22, London, 2010

Larry Clark
Born 1943, Tulsa, OK, USA. Lives New York and Los Angeles, USA.
Exh.: 'Larry Clark', c/o Berlin, Germany, 2012; 'Kiss the past hello', Musée d'Art Moderne de la Ville de Paris, 2010

Anne Collier
Born 1970, Los Angeles, CA, USA.
Lives New York, NY, USA.
Exh.: 'Anne Collier, (2002–present)', The Museum of Contemporary Art, Chicago, 2014; 'Anne Collier', Nottingham Contemporary, 2011

Thomas Joshua Cooper
Born 1946, San Francisco, CA, USA.
Lives Glasgow, Scotland.
Exh.: 'Selections from True: Photographs by Thomas Joshua Cooper', Lannan Foundation, Santa Fe, NM, 2009; 'Simply Counting Waves', European City of Culture Exhibition, Centre for Modern Art, Gulbenkian Foundation, Lisbon, 1994

John Coplans
1920–2003. Born London, UK.
Lived New York, NY, USA.
Lit.: Coplans. C., *A Body: John Coplans*, powerHouse Books, New York, US, 2002.
Exh.: 'Body Parts', Tang Teaching Museum and Art Gallery, Skidmore College, Saratoga Springs, NY, 2004; 'John Coplans: A Retrospective', Gulbenkian Foundation, Lisbon, 1992

Gregory Crewdson
Born 1962, Brooklyn, New York, USA. Lives New York, NY, USA.
Lit.: Burnett. C., af Malmborg, E., Hoffman, *Gregory Crewdson: In a Lonely Place*, New York, 2011
Exh.: 'Gregory Crewdson: In A Lonely Place', City Gallery, Wellington New Zealand, 2013; 'Gregory Crewdson: 1985–2005', Kunstverein Hannover, 2005

Bruce Davidson
Born 1933, Oak Park, IL, USA
Lives New York, NY, USA.
Lit.: Davidson, E., *Bruce Davidson: Black and White: Circus, Brooklyn Gang, Time of Change, East 100th Street, Central Park*, Göttingen, 2010
Exh.: 'Bruce Davidson: Witness', Robert Klein Gallery, and Ars Libri, Boston, MA, 2013; 'Bruce Davidson', Beetles+Huxley, London, 2011

Corinne Day
1962–2010. Born London, UK.
Lived London, UK.
Lit.: Day, C., Cotton, C., O'Brien, G., Correia, A., *May the Circle Remain Unbroken*, London, 2011
Exh.: 'May the Circle Remain Unbroken', Gimpel Fils Gallery, London, 2013

Roy DeCarava
1919–2009. Born New York, USA.
Lived New York, USA.
Lit.: Galassi, P., DeCarava, R., Turner, DeCarava, S., *Roy DeCarava: A Retrospective*, New York, 1996 Exh.: 'Roy Decarava: A Retrospective', MoMA, New York, 1996

Luc Delahaye
Born 1962, Tours, France. Lives Paris, France.
Lit.: Delahaye, L., 'Luc Delahaye: 2006–2010', Göttingen, 2012
Exh.: 'Luc Delahaye: 2006–2010', Galerie Nathalie Obadia, Paris, 2011; 'Recent History: Photographs by Luc Delahaye', Getty Museum, Los Angeles, 2007

Thomas Demand
Born 1964, Munich, Germany.
Lives Berlin, Germany.
Exh.: 'Thomas Demand', Museum of Contemporary Art, Tokyo, 2012; 'Thomas Demand', MoMA, New York, 2005

Ad Van Denderen
Born 1943, Zeist, The Netherlands.
Lives Amsterdam, The Netherlands.
Exh.: 'Baladia', Gallery West, The Hague, 2012; 'GoNoGo', Museo Nacional de Bellas Artes, Santiago de Chile, 2010

Saïdou Dicko
Born 1979, Déou, Burkina Faso, Lives Paris, France.
Exh.: 'Saïdou Dicko', Schattendieb Der Artco Gallery, Herzogenrath, 2012; 'Photography, painting and video installation', Centre Culture Franco-Mozambique, Maputo, 2009

Philip-Lorca diCorcia
Born 1953, Hartford, CT, USA.
Lives New York, NY, USA.
Lit.: diCorcia, P., *A Storybook Life*, Sante Fe, NM, 2003
Exh.: 'Philip-Lorca Dicorcia: Photographs 1975–2012', Schirn Kunsthalle Frankfurt, 2013; 'Philip-Lorca diCorcia', Los Angeles County Museum of Art, CA, 2008

Rineke Dijkstra
Born 1959, Sittard, The Netherlands. Lives Amsterdam, The Netherlands.
Lit.: Blessing, J., Philips, S., Dijkstra, R., Adrichem, van J., *Rineke Dijkstra: A Retrospective*, New York, 2012
Exh.: 'Rineke Dijkstra: The Krazy House', Museum fur Moderne Kunst, Frankfurt, 2013; 'Rineke Dijkstra: A Retrospective', SFMOMA, San Francisco, CA, 2012

Eugenio Dittborn
Born 1943, Santiago de Chile, Chile. Lives Santiago de Chile, Chile.
Exh.: 'Eugenio Dittborn: Your Letters. Pinturas Aeropostales 1986–2012', Museum Het Domein, Sittard, 2013; 'Airmail Paintings' Bienal do Mercosul, Porto Alegre, 2011

Willie Doherty
Born 1959, Derry, Northern Ireland. Lives Derry, Northern Ireland.
Exh.: 'Willie Doherty: DISTURBANCE', Dublin City Gallery, 2011; 'Willie Doherty: Traces', Speed Art Museum, Louisville, KY, 2011

William Eggleston
Born 1939, Memphis, TN, USA. Lives Memphis, TN, USA.
Lit.: Sussman, E., and Weski, T., eds., *William Eggleston: Democratic Camera*, New Haven, CT and London, 2009
Exh.: 'At War with the Obvious Photographs by William Eggleston', The Metropolitan Museum of Art, New York, 2013; 'William Eggleston: Democratic Camera Photographs and Video, 1961–2008', Whitney Museum of American Art, New York, 2008

Ed van der Elsken
1925–1990. Born Amsterdam, The Netherlands. Lived Amsterdam and Edam, The Netherlands and Paris, France.
Lit.: Elsken E. V., Parr, M., ed., *My Amsterdam: Ed van der Elsken*, Amsterdam, 2005
Exh.: 'Ed Van Der Elsken – Look. Ed!', Annet Gelink Gallery, Amsterdam, 2012; 'Ed van der Elsken: My Amsterdam', Mireille Mosler Ltd, New York, 2009

Peter Finnemore
Born 1963, Lanelli, Wales. Lives Llanelli, Wales, UK.
Exh.: 'The Silent Village', DOX – Centre for Contemporary Art, Prague, 2012; 'Project Object', Oriel Myrddin, Carmarthen, 2011

Anna Fox
Born, 1961, Alton, Hampshire, UK. Lives Hampshire, UK.
Lit.: Williams, V., ed., *Anna Fox Photographs 1983–2007*, London, 2007
Exh.: 'RESORT. An exhibition chartering life in British holiday camp, Butlins', Pallant House Gallery, Chichester, 2011; 'Cockroach Diaries & Other Stories', Impressions Gallery, Bradford, 2008

Robert Frank
Born 1924, Zurich, Switzerland. Lives New York, NY, USA and Nova Scotia, Canada.
Exh.: 'Looking in: Robert Frank "The Americans"', SFMOMA, San Francisco, CA, 2009; Robert Frank: Storylines', Tate Modern, London, 2004

Peter Fraser
Born 1953, Cardiff, Wales. Lives London, UK.
Lit.: Chandler, D., *Peter Fraser*, London, 2013
Exh.: 'Peter Fraser', Tate St Ives, Cornwall, 2013; 'Peter Fraser', The Photographers' Gallery, London, 2002

Lee Friedlander
Born 1934, Aberdeen, WA, USA. Lives New York, NY, USA.
Lit.: Galassi, P., Benson, R., Friedlander, L., *Friedlander*, New York, 2008
Exh.: 'Lee Friedlander: America by Car', Whitney Museum of American Art, New York, 2010; 'Friedlander', MoMA, New York, 2005

Seiichi Furyua
Born 1950, Izu, Japan. Lives Graz, Austria.
Exh.: 'I prefer to be on this side', Galerie Thomas Fischer, Berlin, 2013; 'Seiichi Furuya', Albertina, Vienna, 2004

George Georgiou
Born 1961, London, UK. Lives London, UK.
Exh.: 'New Photography 2011', MoMA, New York, 2012; 'Fault Lines/Turkey/East/West', Side Gallery, Newcastle, 2010

Luigi Ghirri
1943–1992. Born Scandiano, Italy. Lived Roncocoesi, Italy.
Lit.: Celant, G., *It's Beautiful Here Isn't It*, New York, 2008
Exh.: 'Luigi Ghirri: Pensare per immagini', MAXXI Museum, Rome, 2013; 'It's beautiful here, isn't it', Aperture Foundation, New York, 2008

Jim Goldberg
Born 1953, New Haven, CT, USA Lives San Francisco, USA.
Exh.: 'Face of Our Time', SFMOMA, San Francisco, 2011; 'Deutsche Börse Photography Prize', The Photographers' Gallery, London, 2011

David Goldblatt
Born 1930, Randfontein, South Africa. Lives Johannesburg, South Africa.
Lit.: Goldblatt, D., *David Goldblatt Fifty-One Years*, Museu d'Art Contemporani de Barcelona, 2002
Exh.: 'David Goldblatt Fifty-One Years', Museu d'Art Contemporani de Barcelona, 2002

Nan Goldin
Born 1953, Washington, D.C., USA Lives Paris, France and New York, USA.
Lit.: Goldin, N., Costa, G., *Nan Goldin The Devil's Playground*, London, 2003
Exh.: 'Nan Goldin', Whitney Museum of American Art, New York, 1996; 'Nan Goldin', Centre Pompidou, Paris, 2001

John Goto
Born 1949, Stockport, UK. Lives Oxford, UK.
Exh.: 'Sweet Augmentations', Dominique Fiat Gallery, Paris, 2012; 'Goto, Photographs 1971–81', The Photographers' Gallery, London, 1981

Paul Graham
Born 1956, Harlow, UK. Lives New York, NY, USA.
Lit.: Graham, P., Chandler, D., Almereyda, M., Ferguson, R., *Paul Graham*, London, 2009
Exh.: 'The Present', Pace Gallery, New York, 2012; 'Paul Graham: Photographs 1981–2006', Whitechapel Art Gallery, London, 2011

Kathy Grove
Born 1948, Pittsburgh, PA. Lives New York, NY, USA.
Exh.: 'Kathy Grove: The Other Series', Fotografie Forum International, Frankfurt, 2002; 'Kathy Grove: This is Not a Woman', Musee de l'Elysee, Lausanne, 2001

Andreas Gursky
Born 1955, Leipzig, Germany. Lives Düsseldorf, Germany.
Lit.: Hentschel, M., ed., Gusky, A., *Andreas Gursky: Works 80–08*, Ostfildern, 2011
Exh.: 'Andreas Gurksy', The National Art Center, Tokyo, 2013; 'Andreas Gursky: Works 80–08' Vancouver Art Gallery, Vancouver, 2009

John Hilliard
Born 1945, Lancaster, UK. Lives London, UK.
Lit.: Nusser, U., Hilliard, J., *John Hilliard*, Heidelberg, 1999
Exh.: 'John Hilliard' Galleria Artra, Milan, 2010; 'John Hilliard: Profiles' L.A.Galerie-Frankfurt, 2009

Thomas Hirschhorn
Born 1957. Bern, Switzerland. Lives Paris, France.
Lit.: Buchloh, B., Gingeras, A. M., Basualdo, C., Hirschhorn, T., *Thomas Hirschhorn*, London, 2004
Exh.: 'Flamme Eternelle', Palais de Tokyo, Paris, 2014; 'Drift Topography', Tate Modern, London, 2003

Jacob Holdt
Born 1947, Copenhagen, Denmark. Lives Copenhagen, Denmark.
Lit.: Holdt, J., *United States 1970–1975*, Göttingen, 2007
Exh.: 'United States 1970–1975', Kunsthal Rotterdam, 2009; 'Faith, Hope and Love', Louisiana Museum of Modern Art, Humlebæk, 2009

Roni Horn
Born 1955, New York, USA. Lives New York, NY, USA and Reykjavik, Iceland.
Lit.: Neri, L., Cooke, L., Duve, T., Horn, R., *Roni Horn*, London, 2000
Exh.: 'Roni Horn, Double Mobius', FLAG Art Foundation, New York, 2011; 'Roni Horn aka Roni Horn', Tate Modern, London, 2009

Craigie Horsfield
Born 1949, Cambridge, UK. Lives London, UK and New York, USA.
Lit.: De Zegher, C., *Craigie Horsfield: Relation*, Paris, Lisbon and Sydney, 2006.
Exh.: 'Schering en inslag/ Confluence and consequence', Museum of Contemporary Art, Antwerp, 2010

Tehching Hsieh
Born 1950, Nan-chou, Taiwan. Lives Brooklyn, New York, USA.
Lit.: Heathfield, A., Hsieh T., *Out of Now: The Lifeworks of Tehching Hsieh*, Cambridge, MA, 2009
Exh.: 'Tehching Hsieh' Franklin Street Works, New York, 2012; 'Tehching Hsieh: The Imminence of Poetics', São Paulo Biennale, 2012

Pieter Hugo
Born 1976, Capetown, South Africa. Lives Cape Town, South Africa.
Lit.: Hugo P., Demons, T. J., Schuman, A., *Pieter Hugo: This Must Be The Place: Selected Works*, 2012
Exh.: 'Pieter Hugo, This Must Be the Place, Selected Works 2002–2011', Musée de l'Elysée, Lausanne, 2012; 'Pieter Hugo: Nollywood', Institute of Modern Art, Brisbane, 2010

Alfredo Jaar
Born 1956, Santiago, Chile. Lives New York, NY, USA.
Lit.: Jacob, M. J., Jaar, A., ed., Princethal, N., ed., *Alfredo Jaar: The Fire This Time: Public Interventions 1979–2005*, Milan, 2005
Exh.: 'Alfredo Jaar: Abbiamo amato tanto la rivoluzione', Fondazione Merz, Turin, 2014; 'Alfredo Jaar: The Ashes of Pasolini', Musée d'art de Joliette, Joliette, 2011

Sarah Jones
Born 1959, London, UK. Lives London, UK.
Lit.: Jones, S., Dillon, B., Campany, D., *Sarah Jones*, London, 2013
Exh.: 'New Pictures 8: Sarah Jones', Minneapolis Institute of Arts, Minneapolis, 2013; 'Sarah Jones: Photographs', National Media Museum, Bradford, 2007

Seydou Keïta
1923–2001. Born Bamako, Mali. Lived in Bamako, Mali.
Lit.: Keïta S., *Seydou Keïta: Photographs, Bamako, Mali 1948–1963*, Göttingen, 2011
Exh.: 'Seydou Keïta, from the Jean Pigozzi collection', The Moscow Multimedia Art Museum, Moscow, 2013; 'Seydou Keïta', Tate Modern, London, 2008

Erik Kessels
Born 1966, Roermond, The Netherlands. Lives Amsterdam, The Netherlands.
Lit.: KesselsKramer, 2 kilo of KesselsKramer, Tokyo, 2005
'24HRS of Photos', FOAM Amsterdam, 2011; 'Album Beauty', FOAM, Amsterdam, 2012

Geert Van Kesteren
Born 1966, Amsterdam, The Netherlands. Lives Amsterdam, The Netherlands.
Exh.: 'Why Mister, Why?', Nederlands Fotomuseum, Rotterdam, 2005; 'Mwendanjangula! Aids in Zambia – Intern'. Human Rights Documentary Film Festival, Langhans Gallery, Prague, 2005

Idris Khan
Born 1978, Birmingham, UK. Lives London, UK.
Exh.: 'Beyond the Black', Victoria Miro Gallery, London, 2013; 'Idris Khan', Fraenkel Gallery, San Francisco, CA, 2012

Sanggil Kim
Born 1974, South Korea. Lives Seoul, South Korea.
Exh.: 'Layer', PKM Trinity Gallery, Seoul, 2008

William Klein
Born 1928, New York, USA. Lives Paris, France.
Lit.: Klein, W., *William Klein: Retrospective*, 2006
Exh.: 'William Klein Retrospective', Foam, Amsterdam, 2013; 'William Klein + Daido Moriyama', Tate Modern, London, 2012

Yves Klein
1928–1962. Born Nice, France. Lived in Paris, France.
Lit.: Klein, Y., Brougher, K., Cabañas, K., Hickey, A., Ottmann, K., Vergn, P., *Yves Klein: With the Void, Full Powers*, Ostfildern, 2010
Exh.: 'The Show is Over', Gagosian Gallery, London, 2013; 'Yves Klein: With the Void, Full Powers', Hirshhorn Museum and Sculpture Garden, Smithsonian Institution, Washington, D.C., 2010

Bohnchang Koo
Born 1953, Seoul, South Korea. Lives Seoul, South Korea.
Exh.: 'Slow Talk', ivorypress, Madrid, Spain, 2013; 'Bohnchang Koo', Kukje gallery, Seoul, 2011

Les Krims
Born 1943, New York, USA. Lives Buffalo, NY, USA.
Exh.: 'Les Krims: Retrospective', Galerie Baudoin Lebon, Paris, 2007; 'Fictions 1969–1974', Laurence Miller Gallery, New York, 2004

Barbara Kruger
Born 1945, Newark, NJ, USA. Lives New York and Los Angeles, USA.
Lit.: Kruger, B., Foster, H., Kwon, M., Gever, M., Squiers, C., *Barbara Kruger*, New York, 2010
Exh.: 'Barbara Kruger: Belief+Doubt', Hirshhorn Museum and Sculpture Garden, Smithsonian Institution, Washington, D.C., 2012; 'Barbara Kruger: Retrospective', Whitney Museum of Art, New York, 2000

Louise Lawler
Born 1947, Bronxville, New York, USA. Lives New York, NY, USA.
Lit.: Baker, G., Bankowsky, J., Kravagna, C., Pelzer, B., Fraser, A., Lawler, L., Graw, I., *Louise Lawler And Others*, Ostfildern, 2004
Exh.: 'Louise Lawler: Adjusted', Museum Ludwig, Cologne, 2013; 'Louise Lawler: Twice Untitled and Other Pictures (looking back)', Wexner Center for the Arts, OH, 2006

An-My Lê
Born 1960, Ho Chi Minh City, Vietnam. Lives New York, NY, USA.
Exh.: 'Front Room: An-My Lê', Baltimore Museum of Art, MD, 2013; 'The Photographs of An-My Lê', University of Kentucky Art Museum, Lexington, KY, 2008

Richard Learoyd
Born 1966, Lancashire, UK. Lives London, UK.
Exh.: 'Richard Learoyd: The Outside World', Fraenkel Gallery, San Francisco, CA, 2013

Nikki S. Lee
Born 1970, Lee Seung-Hee, Korea. Lives New York, NY, USA.
Exh.: 'Nikki S Lee: Projects and Parts', GAK, Bremen, 2007; 'Nikki S. Lee: Parts', Kemper Museum of Contemporary Art, Kansas City, MO, 2005

Catherine LeRoy
1945–2006. Born Paris, France. Lived in Los Angeles, CA, USA.
Exh.: 'Under Fire: Vietnam War', Center for Photography, Berkeley Graduate School of Journalism, Berkeley, CA, 2005

Sherrie Levine
Born 1947, Hazleton, PA, USA. Lives New York, NY, USA.
Lit.: Burton, J., Sussman, E., *Sherrie Levine: Mayhem*, New Haven, CT, 2012
Exh.: 'Sherrie Levine', Simon Lee Gallery, London, 2012; 'Sherrie Levine: Mayhem', Whitney Museum of American Art, New York, 2011

David Levinthal
Born 1949, San Francisco, CA, USA Lives New York, NY, USA.
Exh.: 'David Levinthal: War Games', Corcoran Gallery of Art, Washington, D.C., 2013; 'David Levinthal: Photographs 1974–2008', 169 Gallery, Santa Monica, CA, 2011

Liu Zheng
Born 1969
Wuqiang Hsien, Hebei Province, China. Lives Beijing, China.
Exh.: 'Liu Zheng', Zen Foto Gallery, Tokyo, 2009; 'Liu Zheng: Survians', SOHO New Town, Beijing, 2006

Richard Long
Born 1945, Bristol, UK. Lives Bristol, UK.
Lit.: Long, R., Hooker, D., *Richard Long: Walking the Line*, London, 2005
Exh.: 'Richard Long – Prints 1970–2013', Museum Kurhaus, Kleve, 2013; 'Richard Long: Heaven and Earth', Tate Britain, London, 2009

Ken Lum
Born 1956, Vancouver, Canada. Lives Philadelphia, USA.
Lit.: Arnold, G., Enwezor, O., Schoeny, R., *Ken Lum*, Madeira Park, 2011
Exh.: 'The Mini-Mall Series', Marc Jancou Contemporary, New York, 2013; 'Ken Lum', Vancouver Art Gallery, Vancouver, 2011

Danny Lyon
Born 1942, New York, USA. Lives New Mexico and Maine, USA.
Lit.: Lyon, D., Edwards, H., *Memories of Myself*, London, 2009
Exh.: 'This World Is Not My Home: Danny Lyon Photographs', The Menil Collection, Houston, Texas, 2012; 'Danny Lyon: Montage, Film and Still Photography', Whitney Museum of American Art, New York, 2007

Mike Mandel
Born 1950, Los Angeles, CA, USA. Lives Watertown, MA, USA.
Lit.: Sultan, L., Mandel, M., Cotton C., Lethem, J., Lewallen, C., Ratcliff, C., Wagner, T., *'Larry Sultan & Mike Mandel'*, Cologne, 2012
Exh.: '7 Turkish Artists: Mike Mandel & Chantal Zakari', Photographic Resource Centre, Boston University, Boston, MA, 2011; 'Evidence: Mike Mandel and Larry Sultan', Winterthur Museum, Zurich, 2010

Sally Mann
Born 1951, Lexington, VA, USA. Lives Virginia, USA.
Exh.: 'Sally Mann: Upon Reflection', Edwynn Houk Gallery, New York, 2012; 'Sally Mann: The Family and the Land', The Photographers' Gallery, London, UK, 2010

Robert Mapplethorpe
1946–1989. Born New York, USA. Lived in New York, USA.
Lit.: Mapplethorpe, R., *Mapplethorpe*, Krefeld, 2007
Exh.: 'Robert Mapplethorpe: Works from 1980–1989', Galería Elvira González, Madrid, 2013; 'Robert Mapplethorpe', Scottish National Gallery of Modern Art, Edinburgh, 2006

Mary Ellen Mark
Born 1940, Philadelphia, PA, USA. Lives New York, NY, USA.
Lit.: Naef, W., *Exposure: Mary Ellen Mark*, London, 2006
Exh.: 'Mary Ellen Mark', Galerie Anne de Villepoix, Paris, 2013; 'Mary Ellen Mark: American Odyssey', International Center of Photography, New York, 2001

Ralph Eugene Meatyard
1925–1972. Born Normal, IL, USA. Lived in Lexington, Kentucky, USA.
Lit.: Meatyard, R. E., Parry, E., Siegel, E., *Ralph Eugene Meatyard: Dolls and Masks*, Sante Fe, NM, 2011
Exh.: 'Ralph Eugene Meatyard: Dolls and Masks', Art Institute of Chicago, IL, 2011; 'Ralph Eugene Meatyard', International Center of Photography, New York, 2005

Susan Meiselas
Born 1948, Baltimore, MD, USA. Lived in New York, USA.
Lit.: Meiselas, S., Brothers, C., Desnoes, E., Lubben, K., *Susan Meiselas: In History*, Göttingen, 2008
Exh.: 'Susan Meiselas: In History', International Center of Photography, New York, 2009; 'Susan Meiselas: Pandora's Box', Amador Gallery, New York, 2007

Ana Mendieta
1948–1985. Born Havana, Cuba. Lived in New York, USA.
Lit.: Bryan-Wilson, J., Heathfield, A., Rugoff, R., Rosenthal, S., *Ana Mendieta: Traces*, London, 2013
Exh.: 'Ana Mendieta: Traces', Hayward Gallery, Southbank Centre, London, 2013; 'Ana Mendieta: She Got Love', Castello di Rivoli, Turin, 2013

Joel Meyerowitz
Born 1938, New York, USA. Lives New York, NY, USA.
Lit.: Meyerowitz, J., *Joel Meyerowitz: Taking My Time*, London, 2012
Exh.: 'Joel Meyerowitz: 'Part I' and 'Part II', Howard Greenberg Gallery, New York, USA, 2012; 'Joel Meyerowitz: Out of the Ordinary, 1970–1980', Jeu de Paume, Paris, 2006

Duane Michals
Born 1932, McKeepsort, PA, USA. Lives New York, NY, USA.
Lit.: Livingstone, M., *The Essential Duane Michals*, London, 1997
Exh.: 'Storyteller: The Photographs of Duane Michals', Carnegie Museum of Art, Pittsburgh, PA, 2014; 'Duane Michals: A Retrospective', Thessaloniki Museum of Photography, Thessaloniki, 2008

Boris Mikhailov
Born 1938, Kharkov, Ukraine, Lives Kharkov, Ukraine and Berlin, Germany.
Lit.: Mikhailov, B., *Boris Mikhailov: A Retrospective*, Zurich, 2003
Exh.: 'Boris Mikhailov, The Books 1968–2012', Sprengel Museum, Hannover, 2013; 'Boris Mikhailov, A Retrospective', Institute of Contemporary Art, Boston, 2004

Mintio
Born 1986, Singapore. Lives Singapore and Bali, Indonesia.
Exh.: 'Kebon Indah' in collaboration with Budi Agung Kuswara, Baba House, National University Singapore Museum, 2013; 'The Wax on Our Fingers' (collaboration with Budi Agung Kuswara), ICAN (Indonesia Contemporary Arts Network), Yogyakarta, 2012

Richard Misrach
Born 1949, Los Angeles, CA, USA Lives Berkley, CA, USA.
Exh.: 'Richard Misrach: On The Beach 2.0', Pace Gallery, New York, 2013; 'Revisiting the South: Richard Misrach's Cancer Alley', High Museum of Art, Atlanta, 2012

Yasumasa Morimuri
Born 1951, Osaka, Japan. Lives Osaka, Japan.
Exh.: 'Yasumasa Morimura: Theater of the Self', The Andy Warhol Museum, Pennsylvania, PA, 2013; 'Las Meninas Renacen de Noche', The Shiseido Gallery, Tokyo, 2013

Daido Moriyama
Born 1938, Osaka, Japan. Lives Tokyo, Japan.
Lit.: Nishi, K., *Daido Moriyama*, London, 2012
Exh.: 'William Klein + Daido Moriyama', Tate Modern, London, 2012; 'On the Road', Osaka National Museum Osaka, 2011

Tracey Moffatt
Born 1960, Brisbane, Australia. Lives Sydney, Australia and New York, NY, USA.
Lit.: Summerhayes C., 'The Moving Images of Tracey Moffatt', Milan, 2007
Exh.: 'Tracey Moffatt: Narratives' Art Gallery of South Australia, Adelaide, 2011; 'Tracey Moffatt: Between Dreams and Reality', Spazio Oberdan, Milan, 2006

James Nachtwey
Born 1948, New York, USA. Lives New York, NY, USA.
Lit.: Nachtwey, J., *Inferno: James Nachtwey*, London, 1999
Exh.: 'W. Eugene Smith and James Nachtwey', The Museum of Fine Arts, Houston, TX, 2012; 'James Nachtwey: Testimony', International Center of Photography, New York, 2000

Wawi Navarroza
Born 1979, Manila, Phillipines. Lives Manila, Phillipines.
Exh.: 'ULTRAMAR PT.I: Gathered Throng, Falling Into Place', Silverlens Gallery, Makati, 2012 / 'ULTRAMAR, PT.II: Hunt & Gather, Terraria by Wawi Navarroza', Makati, 2013; 'On Landscape & Some Dislocations', Galería Patrick Domken, Cadaqués, Costa Brava, 2012

Shirin Neshat
Born 1957, Qazin, Iran. Lives New York, NY, USA.
Lit.: Abramovic, M., Danto, A. C., *Shirin Neshat*, Milan, 2010
Exh.: 'Shirin Neshat', Detroit Institute of Arts, Detroit, MI, 2013; 'The Book of Kings', Gladstone Gallery, New York, 2012

Helmut Newton
1920–2004. Born Berlin, Germany. Lived in Berlin, Germany, Paris, France and California, USA.
Lit.: Newton, H., Newton, J., *Helmut Newton: Sumo*, Cologne, 2009
Exh.: 'Helmut Newton retrospective', Grand Palais, Paris, 2012; 'Helmut Newton: Selected Works', Hamiltons Gallery, London, 2011

Nicholas Nixon
Born 1947, Detriot, MI, USA. Lives Boston, USA.
Lit.: Nixon, N., *Nicholas Nixon*, Madrid, 2003
Exh.: 'Nicholas Nixon: Family Album', Museum of Fine Arts, Boston, 2011; 'Nicholas Nixon: The Brown Sisters 1975–2009', Netherlands Photo Museum, Rotterdam, 2010

Simon Norfolk
Born 1963, Lagos, Nigeria. Lives Brighton, UK.
Exh.: 'Burke + Norfolk: Photographs From the War in Afghanistan', Tate Modern, London, 2011; 'Simon Norfolk: A Retrospective', Andulsian Centre of Photography, Almeria, 2010

Gabriel Orozco
Born 1962, Xalapa, Mexico. Lives New York, NY, USA, Paris, France and Mexico City, Mexico.
Lit.: Rosenweig, P., Fineman, M., Orozco, G., *Gabriel Orozco: Photographs*, Göttingen, 2004
Exh.: 'Gabriel Orozco', Tate Modern, London, 2011; 'Gabriel Orozco', MoMA, New York, USA, 2009

Bill Owens
Born 1938, San Jose, CA, USA. Lives Hayward, CA, USA.
Lit.: Owens, B., Homes, A. M., *Bill Owens*, Bologna, 2008

Exh.: 'Bill Owens: Suburbia', Brigham Young University Museum of Art, Provost, UT, 2010; 'Bill Owens: Suburbia Revisited', Arnolfini Gallery, Bristol, 2008

Roger Palmer
Born 1946, Portsmouth, UK. Lives Glasgow, Scotland.
Lit.: Palmer, R., *Roger Palmer: Circulation*, Salzburg, 2012
Exh.: 'Latitude/Tropic: Photography Projects from the Tropic of Capricorn, (with Jeremy Wafer)' PSL Project Space Leeds, 2010; 'Dislocated: Roger Palmer/ Paulina Eglé' Pukyté, Gallery Vartai, Vilnius, 2009

Tod Papageorge
Born 1940, Portsmouth, NH, USA. Lives New York, NY, USA.
Exh.: 'John McLaughlin, Tod Papageorge', Studio 54, Galerie Thomas Zander, Cologne, 2014; 'Tod Papageorge – Passing through Eden', Michael Hoppen Contemporary, London, 2008

Martin Parr
Born 1952, Epsom, UK. Lives in Bristol, UK.
Lit.: Williams, V., *Martin Parr*, London, 2014
Exh.: 'Martin Parr / Retrospective', Galerie Paris-Beijing, Brussels, 2013; 'Martin Parr: Photographic Works 1971–2000', Barbican Art Gallery, London, 2002

Gilles Peress
Born 1946, Neuilly-sur-Seine, France. Lives New York, NY, USA.
Exh.: 'Photography from The New Yorker', Howard Greenberg Gallery, New York, 2011; 'Anti-photojournalism', La Virreina, Barcelona, 2010

Richard Prince
Born 1949, Panama Canal Zone, USA. Lives New York, NY, USA.
Lit.: Prince, R., Bankowsky, J., Dogg, J., O'Brien, G., Spector, N., *Richard Prince*, New York, 2007
Exh.: 'Richard Prince', Sadie Coles HQ, London, UK, 2013; 'Richard Prince: Spiritual America', New York, 2008

Jorma Puranen
Born 1951, Helskinki, Finland. Lives Helsinki, Finland.
Exh.: 'Museum Meditations, Rehearsals for a Good Life, Landscapes in Full Colour', Galerie Anhava, Helsinki, 2013; 'Jorma Puranen (1992–2010)', Emma Museum of Modern Art, Espoo, 2010

Wang Qingsong
Born 1966, Heilongjiang Province, China. Lives Beijing, China.
Lit.: Butt, Z., ed., *Wang Qingsong*, Ostfildern, 2006
Exh.: 'Wang Qingsong', Gallery 100, Taipei, 2012; 'When the World Collides', International Center of Photography, New York, 2011

Vandy Rattana
Born 1980, Phnom Penh, Cambodia. Lives Phnom Penh, Cambodia, Paris, France and Taipei, Taiwan.
Exh.: 'Bomb Ponds', Asia Society Museum, New York, 2013; 'Surface', SA SA BASSAC, Phnom Penh, 2012

Robert Rauschenberg
1925–2008. Born Port Arthur, TX, USA. Lived in New York and Florida, USA.
Lit.: Kotz, M. L., '*Rauschenberg: Art and Life*', New York, 2004
Exh.: 'Robert Rauschenberg: Combines', The Museum of Contemporary Art, Los Angeles, CA, 2006; 'Robert Rauschenberg: Retrospective', The Guggenheim Museum, New York, 1997

Gerhard Richter
Born 1932, Dresden, Germany. Lives Cologne, Germany.
Lit.: Friedel, H., *Gerhard Richter: Atlas*, London, 2007
Exh.: 'Gerhard Richter: Strips and Glass', Kunstmuseum Winterthur, 2014; 'Gerhard Richter: Panorama', Tate Modern, London, 2012

Sophy Rickett
Born 1970, London, UK. Lives London, UK.
Exh.: 'Sophy Rickett: Objects in the Field', Kettle's Yard, Cambridge, 2013; 'To the River', Arnolfini, Bristol, 2012

Martha Rosler
Born 1943, New York, USA. Lives Brooklyn, New York, USA.
Exh.: 'Martha Rosler: As if', Galleria Civica d'Arte Moderna e Contemporanea, Turin, 2010; 'Martha Rosler: Positions in the Life World (1998–2000)', International Center of Photography, New York, 2000

Judith Joy Ross
Born 1946, Hazleton, PA, USA. Lives Bethlehem, Pennsylvania.
Lit.: Ross, J. J., *Judith Joy Ross: Photographs*, Munich, 2011
Exh.: 'Judith Joy Ross. Photographs since 1982', SK Stiftung Kultur Köln, Cologne, 2011; 'Judith Joy Ross: The Devil Today and Reading to Dogs', Pace/MacGill, New York, 2012

Daniela Rossell
Born 1973, Mexico. Lives New York, NY, USA.
Exh.: 'Daniela Rossell', Blaffer Gallery, University of Houston, Texas, TX, 2004; 'Daniela Rossell: Terror Chic', Sprüth Magers Projekte, Munich, 2003

Thomas Ruff
Born 1958, Zell am Hammerbach, Germany. Lives Düsseldorf, Germany.
Lit.: Ruff, T., Weski, T., Enwezor, O., *Thomas Ruff: Photographs 1979–2011*, Munich, 2012
Exh.: 'photograms and ma.r.s', David Zwirner, New York, 2013; 'Thomas Ruff', Galerie Rüdiger Schöttle, Munich, 2012

Ed Ruscha
Born 1937, Omaha, NE, USA. Lives Los Angeles, CA, USA.
Lit.: Marshall, R. D., *Ed Ruscha*, London, 2005
Exh.: 'In Focus: Ed Ruscha', The Getty Museum, Los Angeles, CA, 2013; 'Ed Ruscha: 50 Years of Painting', Hayward Gallery, London, 2009

Sebastião Salgado
Born 1944, Aimores, Brazil. Lives Paris, France.
Exh.: 'Sebastião Salgado' Galerie Polka, Paris Photo, 2013; 'Then and Now: Photographs by Sebastião Salgado', David Brower Center, Berkeley, CA, 2009

Joachim Schmid
Born 1955, Balingen, Germany. Lives Berlin, Germany.
Lit.: Weber, J. S., MacDonald, G., '*Joachim Schmid: Photoworks 1982–2007*', Göttingen, 2007
Exh.: 'Joachim Schmid e le fotografie degli altri', Museo di Fotografia Contemporanea, Cinisello-Balsamo/Milan, 2012; 'Joachim Schmid Selected Photoworks 1982–2007', The Photographers' Gallery, London, 2007

Carolee Schneeman
Born 1939, Philadelphia, PA, USA. Lives New Paltz, NY, USA.
Lit.: Schneeman, C., *Imaging Her Erotics*, Cambridge, MA, 2002
Exh.: 'Then and Now Carolee Schneemann', Oeuvres d'Histoire, Musee departemental d'art contemporain Rochechouart, 2013; 'Carolee Schneemann: Remains to be Seen', Edinburgh Art Festival, 2012

Andres Serrano
Born 1950, New York, USA. Lives New York, NY, USA.
Lit.: Heartney, E., Hanson, D., *Andres Serrano, America and Other Work*, Cologne, 2004
Exh.: 'Works 1985–2002', Andre Simoens Gallery, Knokke, 2003; 'Body and Soul', Barbican Art Center, London, 2001

Allan Sekula
1951–2013. Born Erie, PA, USA. Lived in Los Angeles, CA, USA.
Lit.: Risberg, D., '*Allan Sekula: Dismal Science Photoworks 1972–1996*', Normal, IL, 1999
Exh.: 'Allan Sekula: Disassembled Movies 1972–2012', Akbank Art Center, Ali Akay, Istanbul, 2012; 'Allan Sekula: Retrospective', Zacheta Gallery, Warsaw, 2009

Nigel Shafran
Born 1964, London, UK. Lives London, UK.
Exh.: 'Compost pictures', Charleston, 2010; 'Photographs by Nigel Shafran, 1992–2000', Taka Ishi Gallery, Tokyo, 2000

Fazal Sheikh
Born 1965, New York, USA. Lives Zurich, Switzerland, New York, USA and Kenya.
Lit.: Sheikh, F., *The Portrait*, Göttingen, 2011
Exh.: 'Beloved Daughters – Photographs by Fazal Sheikh', List Art Center, Brown University, Providence, Rhode Island, 2010; 'Fazal Sheikh', Huis Marseille – Museum voor fotografie, Amsterdam, 2009

Cindy Sherman
Born 1954, Glen Ridge, NJ, USA Lives New York, NY, USA.
Lit.: Respini, E., Burton, J., *Cindy Sherman*, New York, 2012
Exh.: 'Cindy Sherman', MoMA, New York, 2012; 'Cindy Sherman', Serpentine Gallery, London, 2003

Stephen Shore
Born 1947, New York, USA. Lives New York and Tivoli, USA.
Lit.: Lang, C., Fried, M., Sternfeld, J., Shore, S., *Stephen Shore*, London, 2008
Exh.: 'Something + Nothing' Sprüth Magers, London, 2013; 'Uncommon Places', Photobiennale 2012, Manege Hall, Moscow, 2012

Malik Sidibé
Born 1936, Solonba, Mali. Lives Bamako, Mali.
Lit.: Sidibé, M., *Malick Sidibé*, Cotonou, 2009
Exh.: 'Studio Malick', DePaul University Art Museum, Chicago, IL, 2012; 'Malick Sidibé', Jack Shainman Gallery, New York, 2011

Santiago Sierra
Born 1966, Madrid, Spain. Lives Madrid, Spain.
Exh.: 'Santiago Sierra, Sculpture, photography, Film', Sammlung Falckenberg, Hamburg, 2013; 'Santiago Sierra: Dedicated to the Workers and Unemployed', Lisson Gallery, London, 2012

Taryn Simon
Born 1975, New York, USA. Lives New York, NY, USA.
Exh.: 'Taryn Simon: Photographs and Texts', Multimedia Art Museum, Moscow, 2012; 'A Living Man Declared Dead and Other Chapters I-XVIII', Tate Modern, London, 2011

Raghubir Singh
1942–1999. Born Jaipur, India. Lived in Paris, France and New York, USA.
Lit.: Singh, R., Travis, D., *River of Colour: The India of Raghubir Singh*, London, 2006
Exh.: 'Raghubir Singh: Retrospective', Sepia International, New York, 2004; 'River of Color: The India of Raghubir Singh', The Art Institute of Chicago, 1999

Robert Smithson
1938–1973. Born New Jersey. Lived in New Jersey and New York, USA.
Lit.: Smithson, R., *Robert Smithson retrospective: Works 1955–1973*, Oslo, 1999
Exh.: 'Robert Smithson in Texas', The Dallas Museum of Art, Texas, 2013; 'Robert Smithson Retrospective', The Museum of Contemporary Art, Los Angeles, 2004

Jem Southam
Born 1950, Bristol, UK. Lives South West England.
Lit.: Southam, J., *Landscape Stories*, New York, 2005
Exh.: 'Jem Southam: British Landscapes', PhotoEspana, Real Jardín Botánico, Madrid, 2010; 'Jem Southam: Path to a Picture', V&A, London, 2006

Jo Spence
1934–1992, London, UK. Lived in London, UK.
Lit.: Spence, J., *Jo Spence Beyond the Perfect Image. Photography, Subjectivity, Antagonism*, Museu d'Art Contemporani de Barcelona, 2005
Exh.: 'Jo Spence: Work Part 1', Space, London, UK, 2012/ 'Jo Spence: Work Part 2', Studio Voltaire, London, UK, 2012; 'Jo Spence and Alexis Hunter', Richard Saltoun, London, 2013

Manit Sriwanichipoom
Born 1961, Bangkok, Thailand. Lives Bangkok, Thailand.
Exh.: 'Obscene', H Gallery, Bangkok, 2012; 'The Lambs of God', Centre for Contemporary Photography, Melbourne, 2008

Jemima Stehli
Born 1961, London, UK. Lives London, UK.
Lit.: Burrows, D., Slyce, J., *Jemima Stehli*, Birmingham, 2002
Exh.: 'Jemima Stehli: set up, sound check, end', Vegas Gallery, London, 2011; 'Jemima Stehli', ARTRA, Milan, 2010

Joel Sternfeld
Born 1944, New York, USA. Lives New York, NY, USA.
Exh.: 'Joel Sternfeld: Color Photographs since 1970', The Albertina Museum, Vienna, 2012; 'Joel Sternfeld: First Pictures', Luhring Augustine, New York, 2012

Beat Streuli
Born 1957, Altdorf, Switzerland. Lives Zurich, Brussels and Düsseldorf, Germany.
Lit.: Streuli, B., Bellour, R., Valtorta, R., Watkins, J., Schnetz, S., *Beat Streuli: Public Works 1996–2011*, Zurich, 2012
Exh.: 'Beat Streuli: New Street', Eacc Espai D'Art Contemporani de Castelló, Castellón de la Plana, 2013; 'Beat Streuli' Museo di Fotografia Contemporanea, Cinisello-Balsamo, Milan, 2012

Thomas Struth
Born 1954, Geldern, Germany. Lives Düsseldorf, Germany.
Lit.: T., Lingwood, J., Kruzynski, A., *Thomas Struth: Photographs 1978–2010*, New York, 2010
Exh.: 'Thomas Struth: Photographs 1978–2010', Whitechapel Gallery, London, 2011; 'Thomas Struth', Kunst in Weidingen, 2013

Hiroshi Sugimoto
Born 1948, Tokyo, Japan. Lives New York, NY, USA.
Exh.: 'Hèrmes Editeur', Couleurs de l'Ombre, Tyler Print Institute, Singapore, 2013; 'Revolution', Museum Brandhorst, Munich, 2012

Larry Sultan
1946–2009. Born New York, USA Lived in Greenbrae, CA, USA.
Lit.: Sultan, L., Germann, M., *Katherine Avenue, Larry Sultan*, Göttingen, 2010
Exh.: 'Larry Sultan: Here / Home', Los Angeles County Museum of Art, CA, 2014; 'Larry Sultan's Homeland: American Story', Amon Carter Museum of American Art, Texas, 2012

Wolfgang Tillmans
Born 1968, Remscheid, Germany. Lives Berlin, Germany and London, UK.
Lit.: Tillmans, W., 'Wolfgang Tillmans: Manual', Cologne, 2007
Exh.: 'Wolfgang Tillmans', Maureen Paley Gallery, London, 2013; 'Wolfgang Tillmans', Serpentine Gallery, London, 2010

Shomei Tomatsu
Born 1930, Nagoya-shi, Japan. Lives Nagasaki, Japan.
Lit.: Phillips, S., Rubinfien, L., Dower, J. W., *Shomei Tomatsu: Skin of the Nation*, New Haven, CT, 2004
Exh.: 'Shomei Tomatsu: Skin of the Nation', SFMOMA, 2006; 'Aichi Mandala: Early Works of Tomatsu Shomei', Aichi Prefectural Museum of Art, Nagoya, 2006

Felix Gonzales-Torres
1957–1996. Guâimiro, Cuba. Lived New York, USA.
Lit.: Gonzalez-Torres, F., Corrin, L. G., *Felix Gonzalez-Torres*, Ostfildern, 2007
Exh.: 'Felix Gonzalez-Torres', PLATEAU, Seoul and Leeum, Samsung Museum of Art, Seoul, 2012; 'Felix Gonzalez-Torres: Specific Objects without Specific Form', MMK Museum für Moderne Kunst, Frankfurt am Main, 2011

Jeff Wall
Born 1946, Vancouver, Canada. Lives Vancouver, Canada.
Lit.: Duve, de T., Pelenc, A., Groys, B., Chevrier, J., Lewis, M., *Jeff Wall: The Complete Edition*, London, 2009
Exh.: 'Jeff Wall Photographs', National Gallery of Victoria, Melbourne, Australia, 2013; 'Jeff Wall', MoMA, New York, 2007

Andy Warhol
1928–1987. Born Pittsburgh, PA, USA. Lived in New York, USA.
Lit.: *Andy Warhol "Giant" Size*, New York and London, 2006
Exh.: 'Reading Andy Warhol', Museum Brandhorst Munich, Germany, 2013; 'Andy Warhol Retrospective', Museum of Contemporary Art, Los Angeles, 2002

Gillian Wearing
Born 1963, Birmingham, UK. Lives London, UK.
Lit.: Herrmann, D. F., Krystof, D., Schwenk, B., Deamer, D., *Gillian Wearing*, London, 2012
Exh.: 'Gillian Wearing', Whitechapel Art Gallery, London, 2012; 'Gillian Wearing', Museum Brandhorst, Munich, 2013

Alex Webb
Born 1952, San Francisco, CA, USA. Lives Brooklyn, New York, USA.
Lit.: Webb, A., Dyer, G., '*The Suffering of Light: Thirty Years of Photographs by Alex Webb*', London, 2011
Exh.: 'The Suffering of Light: Thirty Years of Photographs by Alex Webb', Brigham Young University Museum of Art, Provo, UT, 2012; 'The Webbs' 11 trips to Cuba, Discovering the Poetry of the 'Violet Isle'', Museum of Fine Arts, Boston, 2012

Carrie Mae Weems
Born 1953, Portland, Oregon, USA. Lives New York, NY, USA.
Lit.: Delmez, K. E., Gates Jr, H. E., Sirmans, F., Storr, R., Willis, D., *Carrie Mae Weems: Three Decades of Photography and Video*, New Haven, CT, 2012
Exh.: 'Carrie Mae Weems: 3 Decades of Photography and Video', Frist Center for the Visual Arts, Nashville, 2012; 'Maddening Crowd', McNay Art Museum, San Antonio, TX, 2012

Garry Winogrand
Born 1928, New York, USA. Lived New York, NY, USA.
Lit.: Rubinfien, L., *Garry Winogrand*, San Francisco, New Haven, CT and London, 2013
Exh.: 'Garry Winogrand', SFMOMA, San Francisco, 2013; 'Garry Winogrand: Some Animals', MOMA PS1, New York, 2010

Michael Wolf
Born 1954, Munich, Germany. Lives Hong Kong, China.
Exh.: 'Architecture of Density', Flowers Gallery, London, 2014; 'Pieces of China: A Retrospective of Michael Wolf's China Projects', Museum Center Vapriikki, Tampere, 2007

Tom Wood
Born 1951, County Mayo, Ireland. Lives North Wales, UK.
Exh.: 'Tom Wood: Photographs 1973–2013', National Media Museum, Bradford, 2013; 'Men and Women', The Photographers Gallery, London, 2012

Francesca Woodman
1958–1981. Born Denver, CO, USA. Lived in New York, USA.
Lit.: Townsend, C., *Francesca Woodman*' London, 2007
Exh.: Francesca Woodman: Retrospective, SFMOMA, San Francisco, 2011; 'Photographs: 1977/1981', Libreria-Galleria il Museo del Louvre, Rome, 2011

Alexa Wright
Born 1962, London, UK. Lives London, UK.
Exh.: 'Out of Order', London Gallery West, University of Westminster, Harrow; 'Alter Ego', Scottish National Portrait Gallery, Edinburgh

Erwin Wurm
Born 1954, Bruck an der Mur, Austria. Lives Vienna and Limberg, Austria.
Lit.: Wurm, E., 'Erwin Wurm', Cologne, 2009
Exh.: 'Synthesa', Xavier Hufkens Gallery, Brussels, 2013; 'Erwin Wurm – New Sculptures', Baltic Centre for Contemporary Art, Newcastle, 2006

Shizuka Yokomizo
Tokyo, Japan. Lives London, UK.
Exh.: 'Shizuka Yokomizo', Galería Leyendecker, Tenerife, 2009; 'I Can Feel It (But I Can't See It)', Wako Works of Art, Tokyo, 2008

Kohei Yoshiyuki
Born 1946, Hiroshima Prefecture, Japan. Lives Tokyo, Japan.
Exh.: 'Kohei Yoshiyuki: The Park', Presentation House Gallery, Vancouver, 2011; 'The Park', Galerie Gebr. Lehmann, Dresden, 2010

General

Barthes, R., *Mythologies*, New York, 2012 [1957]

Bate, D., *Photography: the Key Concepts*, London, 2009

Benjamin, W., *Illuminations*, London, 1973

Berger, J., and Mohr, J., *Another Way of Telling*, London, 1982

Berger, J., *Ways of Seeing*, Harmondsworth, 1972

Bolton, R., ed., *The Contest of Meaning*, Cambridge, MA and London, 1989

Burgin, V., ed., *Thinking Photography*, London, 1982

Burgin, V., *The End of Art Theory*, London, 1982

Campany, D., *Art and Photography*, London, 2007

Clarke, G., *The Photograph*, Oxford, 1997

Coleman, A. D., *Light Readings*, Oxford,1979

Cotton, C., *The Photograph as Contemporary Art*, London, 2009

Durden, M., ed., *Fifty Key Writers on Photography*, London, 2012

Durden, M. and Richardson, C., eds., *Face On: Photography as Social Exchange*, London, 2000

Fogle, D., *The Last Picture Show: Artists Using Photography 1960–1982*, Minneapolis, 2003

Fried, M., *Why Photography Matters As Art As Never Before*, New Haven CT and London, 2008

Guimond, J., *American Photography and the American Dream*, Chapel Hill and London,1991

Green, D. ed., *Where is the Photograph?* Brighton, 2003

Green, J., *A Critical History of American Photography*, New York, 1984

Grundberg, A., *Crisis of the Real, Writings on Photography, 1974–1989*, New York, 1990

Hand, M., *Ubiquitous Photography*, Cambridge, 2012

Hirsch, M., *Family Frames: Photography, Narrative and Postmemory* Cambridge, MA and London, 1997

hooks, b., *Art on My Mind: Visual Politics*, New York, 1995

Jeffrey, I., *A Concise History of Photography*, London, 1981

Kozloff, M., *The Privileged Eye*, Albuquerque, 1987

Kozloff, M., *Photography and Fascination*, Danbury, 1979

Papageorge, T., *Core Curriculum*, New York, 2011

Parr, M., Badger, G., *The Photobook, A History volume I*, London, 2004

Parr, M., Badger, G., *The Photobook, A History volume II*, London, 2006

Roberts, J., *The Art of Interruption: Realism, Photography and the Everyday*, Manchester, 1998

Rosler, M., *Decoys and Disruptions: Selected Writings, 1975–2001*, Cambridge, MA and London, 2004

Solomon-Godeau, A., *Photography at the Dock*, Minneapolis, 1991

Sontag, S., *On Photography*, Harmondsworth, 1977

Steichen, E., and Sandburg, C., *The Family of Man*, New York, 1996 [1955]

Strauss, D. L., *Between the Eyes: Essays on Art and Politics*, New York, 2000

Szarkowski, J., *The Photographer's Eye*, New York, 1966

Szarkowski, J., *Looking at Photographs*, New York, 1976

Szarkowski, J., *Photography Until Now*, New York, 1989

Wells, L., ed., *The Photography Reader*, London, 2002

Wells, L., ed., *Photography: A Critical Introduction*, London, 2009

Chapter One: The Copy

Aarsmann, H., de Cleen, C., G., Germain, J., Kessels, E., van der Meer, H., *Useful Photography # 003*, Amsterdam, 2003

Andre, C., 'A Note on Bernhard and Hilla Becher', *Artforum*, Vol 11., No. 5., December 1972, p. 59

Belting, H., *Thomas Struth: Museum Photographs*, Munich, 1998

Birnbaum, D., 'Bernd and Hilla Becher', *Artforum*, Vol. 42, No.9., May 2004

Branden W. J., *Random Order: Robert Rauschenberg and the Neo-Avant-Garde*, London and Cambridge, MA, 2003

Brett, G., *Mapa: The Airmail Paintings of Eugenio Dittborn, 1984–1992*, London, 1993

Chevrier, J-F., and Lingwood, J., *Another Objectivity*, Milan, 1989

Crimp, D., *On The Museum's Ruins*, Cambridge, MA and London, 1993

Crow, T., *Art in the Common Culture*, New Haven CT and London, 1996

Eklund, D., *The Pictures Generation, 1974–84*, New York, 2009

Evans, W., *American Photographs*, New York, 1938

Greenberg, C., 'Avant-Garde and Kitsch', *The Collected Essays and Criticism, Volume 1*, Chicago and London, 1986

Hambourg, M. M., *Walker Evans*, New York, 2000

Hopps, W., and Davidson, S., *Robert Rauschenberg: A Retrospective*, New York, 1998

Kaiser, P., ed., *Louise Lawler and Others*, Ostfildern-Ruit, 2004

Klein, W., *Life is Good and Good for You in New York*, New York, 2010 [1956]

Lange, S., *Bernd and Hilla Becher: Life and Work*, Cambridge, MA and London, 2006

Lawler, L., *Twice Untitled and Other Pictures looking back*, Columbus, 2006

Lubben, K., ed., *Susan Meiselas: In History*, New York and Göttingen, 2008

McShine, K., *Andy Warhol: A Retrospective*, New York, 1989

Mandel, M., and Sultan, L., *Evidence*, New York, 2003 [1977]

Martin, L. A., and Wada, K., *Japanese Photobooks of the 1960s and 1970s*, New York, 2009

Moriyama, Daido, *Farewell Photography*, Tokyo, 2006 [1972]

O'Doherty, B., 'Rauschenberg and the Vernacular Glance' in *Art in America*, Vol. 63, 1973, pp. 82–8

Phillips, L., *Richard Prince* New York, 1992

Ruscha, E., *Leave Any Information at the Signal*, Cambridge, MA and London, 2002

Schmid, J., *Bilder von der Strasse*, North Carolina, 2012

Schwartz, A., *Ed Ruscha's Los Angeles*, Cambridge, MA and London, 2010

Singerman, H., *Art History After Sherrie Levine*, Berkeley, Los Angeles and London, 2012

Spector, N., *Richard Prince*, New York, 2007

Storr, R., *Gerhard Richter, October 18, 1977*, New York, 2000

Szarkowski, J., 'Photography and the Mass Media' in David Brittain, ed., *Creative Camera: 30 Years of Writing*, Manchester, 1999 [1967]

Szarkowski, J., *From the Picture Press*, New York, 1973

Szarkowski, J., *Walker Evans*, New York, 1971

Van Bruggen, C., *John Baldessari*, New York, 1990

Wall. J., *Selected Essays and Interviews*, New York, 2007

Witkovsky, M. S., *Light Years: Conceptual Art and the Photograph, 1964–1977*, Chicago, 2012

Chapter Two: The Face

Aarsmann, H., de Cleen, C., Germain, J., Kessels, E., and Van der Meer, H., *Useful Photography # 004*, Amsterdam, 2004

Adams, P., *The Emptiness of the Image* London, 1996

Arbus, D., *Diane Arbus*, New York, Aperture, 2012 [1972]

Armstrong, C., 'Biology, Destiny and Photography: Difference According to Diane Arbus', *October* 66, Fall 1993, pp. 29–54

Avedon, R., *In The American West*, New York, 1985

Barthes, R., *Camera Lucida*, New York, 1981

Cadava, E., *Fazal Sheikh: Portraits*, Göttingen, 2011

Crimp, D., *Melancholia and Moralism*, Cambridge, MA and London, 2002

Diawara, M., *Malick Sidibé*, Göttingen, 2004

Ferguson, R., *Gillian Wearing*, London, 1999

Fox, A., *Zwarte Piet*, London, 1999

Furuya, S., *alive*, Zurich, 2004

Furuya, S., *Mémoires*, Zurich, 1995

Furuya, S., *Portrait*, Salzburg, 2000

Furuya, S., *Christine Furuya-Gössler Mémoires, 1978–1985*, Kyoto, 1997

Kozloff, M., *The Theatre of the Face*, London, 2007

Lee, A. W., *Diane Arbus: Family Albums*, New Haven, CT and London, 2003

Magnin, A., ed., *Malick Sidibé*, Zurich, Berlin and New York, 1998

Magnin, A., ed., *Seydou Keïta*, Zurich, Berlin and New York, 1997

Meatyard, R. E., *The Family Album of Lucybelle Crater*, New York, 1974

Morgan, J., ed., *Portraits: Rineke Dijkstra*, Boston and Ostfildern-Ruit, 2001

Searle, A., ed., *Talking Art*, London, 1993

Sheikh, F., *A Sense of Common Ground*, Zurich, Berlin and New York, 1996

Sheikh, F., *The Victor Weeps*, Zurich, Berlin and New York, 1998

Silverman, K., *The Threshold of the Visible World*, London and New York, 1996

Slyce, J., *Sarah Jones*, Essen, 2000

Wallis, B., ed., *Andres Serrano: Body and Soul*, New York, 1995

Winzen, M., ed., *Thomas Ruff*, Cologne 2001

Chapter Three: Colour

Billingham, R., *Ray's a Laugh*, New York, 1997

Buchloh, B. H. D., 'Cosmic Reification: Gabriel Orozco's Photographs' in Bois, Y-A., ed., *Gabriel Orozco*, Cambridge, MA and London, 2009

Burrows, L., *Compassionate Photographer*, New York, 1972

Celant, G., *Luigi Ghirri: It's beautiful here isn't it…*, New York, 2008

Chandler, D., *Peter Fraser* London, 2013

Chandler, D., Ferguson, R., *Paul Graham*, Göttingen, 2009

Dicko, S., *Le voleur d'ombres*, Brussels, 2007

Euclaire, S. *American Independents*, New York, 1984

Euclaire, S. *The New Color Photography*, New York, 1981

Fineman, M., *Gabriel Orozco: Photographs*, Göttingen, 2004

Fraser, P., *Two Blue Buckets*, Manchester, 1988

Graham, P., *Paul Graham: Beyond Caring*, New York, 2007 [1986]

Grundberg, A., 'Magnum's Postwar Paradox' in *Crisis of the Real*, New York, 1990

Holborn, M., *William Eggleston: Ancient and Modern*, New York, 1992

Keller, J., *Walker Evans: The Getty Museum Collection*, Los Angeles, 1995

Lange, C., Fried, M., and Sternfeld, J., *Stephen Shore*, London, 2007

Leroy, C., *Under Fire* New York, 2005

Light, K., *Witness in our Time*, Washington and London, 2000

Mark, M. E., *Falkland Road* New York, 1981

Meiselas, S., *Nicaragua*, London, 1981

Norfolk, S., *Bleed*, Stockport, 2005

Parr, M., *Common Sense*, Stockport, 1999

Parr, M., *The Last Resort*, Stockport, 1998

Rosler, M., 'Wars and Metaphors' in *Decoys and Disruptions, Selected Writings, 1975–2001*, Cambridge, MA and London, 2004

Rossell, D., *Ricas y Famosas*, London, 2008

Shore, S., *American Surfaces*, London, 2005

Shore, S., *Uncommon Places: The Complete Works*, London, 2004

Singh, R., *The River of Colour*, London, 1998

Singh, R., *A Way Into India*, London, 2002

Stein, S., 'FSA Color: The Forgotten Document', *Modern Photography*, January 1979, pp. 90–98, pp. 162–166

Sussman, E., and Weski, T., *William Eggleston: Democratic Camera*, New York, 2008

Szarkowski, J., *William Eggleston's Guide*, New York, 2002 [1974]

Szarkowski, J., *Slide Show: The Color Photographs of Helen Levitt*, New York, 2005

Temkin, A., *Gabriel Orozco*, London, 2010

Webb, A., *Under a Grudging Sun*, London, 1989

Weinberg, A. D., *On the Line: The New Color Photojournalism*, Minneapolis, 1986

Chapter Four: The Street

Agee, J., *Helen Levitt: A Way of Seeing*, Durham and London, 1989

Alinder, J., *Roy DeCarava*, New York, 1981

Burgin, V., *Between*, Oxford, 1986

Cartier-Bresson, H., *The Mind's Eye: Writings on Photography and Photographers*, New York, 1999

diCorcia, P-L., *Heads*, Göttingen, 2001

Elskildsen, U., ed., *Street and Studio*, London, 2008

Frank, R., *The Americans*, New York, 1958

Galassi, P., *Lee Friedlander*, New York, 2005

Galassi, P., *Roy DeCarava: A Retrospective*, New York, 1996

Friedlander, L., *Self Portrait*, New York, 2005 [1970]

Papageorge, T., *American Sports, 1970, or, How We Spent the War in Vietnam*, New York, 2007

Stallabrass, J., *High Art Lite*, London, 1999

Sternfeld, J., *Passing Strangers*, New York, Boston, London, 2001

Szarkowski, J., *Winogrand: Figments from the Real World*, New York, 1988

Wearing, G., *Signs that Say What You Want Them to Say and Not Signs that Say What Someone Else Wants You to Say*, London, 1997

Westerbeck, C., *Joel Meyerowitz*, London, 2005

Westerbeck, C., Meyerowitz, J., *Bystander: A History of Street Photography*, New York, 1994

Winogrand, G., *Public Relations*, New York, 1977

Winogrand, G., *The Animals*, New York, 2004 [1969]

Winogrand, G., *Women Are Beautiful* New York, 1975

Wolf, M., *Tokyo Compression Revisited*, Hong Kong and Berlin, 2011

Wolf, M., *A Series of Unfortuante Events*, Bad Münder, 2010

Wood, T., *All Zones Off Peak*, Stockport, 1998

Wood, T., *Photieman*, Göttingen, 2005

Chapter Five: Landscapes

Adams, R., *Along Some Rivers*, New York, 2006

Adams, R., *The New West*, New York, 2008 [1974]

Adams, R., *Los Angeles Spring*, New York 1986

Adams, R., *California*, San Francisco 2000

Adams, R., *Pine Valley*, Portland, OR, 2005

Baltz, L., *The Prototype Works, The Tract Houses, The New Industrial Parks Near Irvine, California*, Göttingen, 2005

Baltz, L., *Rule Without Exception*, Alburquerque, 1990

Baltz, L., *Candlestick Point*, Göttingen, 2011 [1989]

Baltz, L., *Park City*, New York, 1981

Barrada, Y., *A Life Full of Holes: The Strait Project*, London, 2005

Bezzola, T., Lingwood, J., *Thomas Struth: Photographs 1978–2010*, Munich 2010

Chandler, D., *Sophy Rickett*, Brighton and Göttingen, 2005

Cooper, T. J., *point of no return*, London, 2004

Cooper, T. J., *Ojo de Agua*, New York, 2006

Cooper, T. J., *True*, London, 2009

Durden, M. and Stathatos, J., *Paul Seawright: Hidden*, London, 2003

Edwards, E., 'Jorma Puranen – Imaginary Homecoming – A Study in Re-engagement', *Raw Histories: Photographs, Anthropology and Museums*, Oxford and New York, 2001, pp. 211–233

Fisher, J., *Willie Doherty: Unknown Depths*, Cardiff, 1990

Georgiou, G., *Fault Lines: Turkey from West to East*, Amsterdam, 2010

Hobbs, R., *Robert Smithson*, Ithaca and London, 1981

Horn, R., *Another Water*, Zurich, Berlin, New York, 2000

Kozloff, M., *Lone Visions*, Albuquerque, 1994

Misrach, R., *Violent Legacies*, Manchester, 1992

Misrach, R., *Destroy This Memory*, New York, 2010

Nusser, U., ed., *John Hilliard*, Heidelberg, 1999

Parr, M., *Small World*, Stockport, 1995

Palmer, R., *Overseas*, Salzburg, 2004

Palmer, R., *Circulation*, Salzburg, 2012

Pauli, L., *Manufactured Landscapes: The Photographs of Edward Burtynsky*, New York, 2009

Salveson, B., *New Topographics*, Göttingen, 2009

Schubert, M., *Edward Burtynsky: Oil*, Göttingen, 2009

Sternfeld, J., *American Prospects* Göttingen, 2004 [1987]

Southam, Jem, *Landscape Stories*, New York, 2005

Syring, M. L., ed., *Andreas Gursky*, Munich, Paris, London, 1998

Szarkowski, J., *Ansel Adams at 100*, New York, 2001

Tucker, A. W., *Crimes and Splendors: The Desert Cantos of Richard Misrach*, Boston, 1996

Chapter Six: History

Blaufuks, D., *Álbum*, Lisbon, 2008

Blaufuks, D., *Works on Memory*, Cardiff, 2011

Blaufuks, D., *Terezin*, Göttingen, 2010

Burrows, L., *Vietnam*, London, 2002

Burrows, L., *Compassionate Photographer*, New York, 1972

Delahaye, L., *History*, London, 2003

Durden, M., Papadimitriou, L., 'Sans Souci: Christian Boltanski Interviewed', *Creative Camera: 30 Years of Writing*, Manchester, 1999 pp. 213–19

Durden, M., 'Interview: Geert Van Kesteren', *8: The Photography Biannual*, Issue 25, Spring 2009, pp. 34–39

Gumpert, L., *Christian Boltanski*, Paris, 1994

Gumpert, L., *Christian Boltanski: Lessons of Darkness*, Chicago, 1988

Geert van Kesteren, *Why Mister, Why?*, Utrecht, 2004

Geert van Kesteren, *Baghdad Calling*, Utrecht, 2008

Horsfield, C., *Relation*, Paris, Lisbon, Sydney, 2007

Jaar, A., *It is Difficult*, Barcelona, 1998

Jaar, A., *Let There Be Light: The Rwanda Project 1994–1998*, Barcelona, 1998

Jeffrey, I., *Shomei Tomatsu*, London, 2001

Meyerowitz, J., *Aftermath*, London, 2006

Moeller, S. D., *Shooting War: Photography and the American Experience of Combat*, New York, 1989

Nachtwey, J., *Inferno*, London, 1999

Kismaric, S., *Judith Jay Ross*, New York, 1995

Peress, G., *The Silence*, Zurich, 1995

Rienhardt, M., Edwards, H. and Duganne, E., *Beautiful Suffering: Photography and the Traffic in Pain*, Chicago 2007

Rubinfien, L., and Phillips, S. S., *Shomei Tomatsu: Skin of the Nation*, New Haven, CT and London, 2004

Salgado, S., *Sahel: The End of the Road*, Berkeley and Los Angeles, 2004

Sebald, W. G., *Austerlitz*, Harmondsworth, 2002

Sontag, S., *Regarding the Pain of Others*, New York, 2003

Stover, E., Peress, G., *The Graves: Srebrenica and Vukovar*, Zurich, Berlin, New York, 1998

Woodward, R. B., *Small Wars: An-My Lê* New York, 2005

Chapter Seven: The Body

Arnold, R., 'Heroin Chic', *Fashion Theory*, Volume 3, Issue 3, September 1999, pp. 279–295

Blocker, J., *Where is Ana Mendieta? Identity, Performativity, and Exile*, Durham and London, 1999

Brookes, R., 'Fashion Photography: The Double-Page Spread: Helmut Newton, Guy Bourdin and Deborah Turbeville', in M. Barnard ed., *Fashion Theory*, London and New York, 2007 pp. 520–526

Brookes, R., 'Sighs and Whispers' in C. Cotton ed., *Guy Bourdin*, London, 2003, p. 129

Burgin, V., *In/Different Spaces*, Berkeley, Los Angeles, London, 1996

Burrows, D., ed., *Jemima Stehli*, Birmingham, 2002

Cousins, M., 'Alexandra Wright: Disabling Beauty', *Portfolio*, No. 30, December 1999, pp. 52–3

Heathfield, A. and Hsieh, T., *Out of Now: The Life Works of Tehching Hsieh*, Cambridge, MA, 2009

Jones, A., 'Jemima Stehli: On All Fours Naked in High Heels – A Critical Position?', *Women: A Cultural Review*, Vol.10. No.3, 1999, pp. 297–307

Mann, S., *Immediate Family*, New York, 1992

Mann, S., *At Twelve: Portraits of Young Women*, New York, 1988

Mann, S., *Proud Flesh*, New York, 2009

Mavor, C., *Becoming*, Durham and London, 1999

Mercer, K., *Welcome to the Jungle: New Positions in Black Cultural Studies*, New York and London, 1994

Meiselas, S., *Carnival Strippers*, Göttingen, 2003

Morgan, S., Morris, F., *Rites of Passage: Art for the end of the Century*, London, 1995

Mulvey, L., 'Cosmetics and Abjection: Cindy Sherman 1977–87' in *Fetishism and Curiosity*, London and Indiana, 1996, pp. 65–76

Nead, L., *The Female Nude*, London and New York, 1992

Newman, M., *Erwin Wurm*, London, 2000

Phelan, P., *Unmarked: The Politics of Performance*, London and New York, 1993

Riefensthal, L., *The Last of the Nuba*, London, 1995 [1973]

Schneider, E., *Santiago Sierra: 300 Tons*, Köln, 2004

Schneider, R., *The Explicit Body in Performance*, London and New York, 1997

Sontag, S., 'Fascinating Fascism' in *Under The Sign of Saturn*, New York, 1980, pp. 73–105

Spence, B., ed., *Bas Jan Ader*, Irvine, 1999

Steiner, W., *The Scandal of Pleasure*, Chicago, 1995

Stiles, K., *Carolee Schneemann: Imaging Her Erotics:* Cambridge, MA and London, 2003

Chapter Eight: Documentary

Blazwick, I., *Sophie Calle: The Reader*, London, 2009

Chancel, P., *North Korea*, London, 2006

Davidson, B., *East 100th Street*, Cambridge, MA, 1970

Davidson, B., *East 100th Street*, Los Angeles, 2003

Diserens, C., *David Goldblatt: Fifty-One Years*, Barcelona, 2002

Ferguson, R., *Nikki S. Lee: Projects*, Osfildern-Ruit, 2001

Galassi, P., *Philip-Lorca diCorcia: Hollywood*, New York, 1995

Goldberg, J., *Raised by Wolves*, Zurich, 1995

Goldblatt, D., *In Boksburg*, Cape Town, 1982

Goldblatt, D., *The Transported of KwaNdebele*, New York, 1989

Holdt, J., *American Pictures: A Personal Journey Through the American Underclass*, Copenhagen, 1985

Holdt, J., *American Photographs: 1970–75*, Göttingen, 2007

Hugo, P., *The Hyena and Other Men*, New York, 2007

Hugo, P., *Nollywood*, New York, 2009

Liu, Z., *The Chinese*, New York and Göttingen, 2004

Lyon, D., *Conversations with the Dead*, New York, 1971

Lyon, D., *The Bikeriders*, San Francisco, 2003 [1968]

Mark, M. E., *American Odyssey*, New York, 1999

Mikhailov, B., *Case History*, Zurich, Berlin and New York, 1999

Owens, B., *Suburbia*, San Francisco, 1972

Owens, B., *Suburbia*, New York, 1999

Parr, M., Barker, N., *Signs of the Times*, Manchester, 1992

Salgado, S., *Workers: An Archaeology of the Industrial Age*, New York, 1993

Salgado, S., *An Uncertain Grace*, New York, 1990

Sekula, A., *Fish Story*, Düsseldorf, 1995

Sekula, A., *Photography Against the Grain: Essays and Photoworks 1973–83*, Halifax, 1984

Sultan, L., *The Valley*, Göttingen, 2004

Storr, R., *Olga Chernysheva: Acquaintances*, London, 2010

Woodward, R. B., *Merry Alpern: Dirty Windows*, Zurich, Berlin and New York, 1995

Chapter Nine: Self

Araki, N., *Sentimental Journey/ Winter Journey*, Tokyo, 1991

Ault, J., *Wolfgang Tillmans*, New Haven, CT and London, 2007

Bright, D., *The Passionate Camera: Photography and Bodies of Desire*, London and New York, 1998

Calvino, I., 'The Adventure of a Photographer' in *Difficult Loves*, London, 1985 [1955], pp. 40–52.

Clark, L., *Tulsa*, New York, 2000 [1971]

Ferguson, R., *Felix Gonzales-Torres*, Los Angeles, 1994

Finnemore, P., *Gwendraeth House*, Cardiff, 2000

Finnemore, P., *Zen Gardener*, Llandudno, 2004

Fox, A., *Cockroach Diary: 1996–1999*, London, 2000

Fox, A., *My Mother's Cupboards, My Father's Words*, London, 2000

Goldin, N., *The Ballad of Sexual Dependency*, New York, 1986

Goldin, N., Armstrong, D., Holzwarth, H. W., eds. *Nan Goldin: I'll Be Your Mirror*, Zurich, 1997

Greenough, S., and Brookman, P., *Robert Frank: Moving Out*, Zurich, Berlin, New York, 1994

Hurn, D., *I'm a Real Photographer: Photographs by Keith Arnatt*, London, 2007

Kuspit, D., *Yasumasa Morimura: Daughter of Art History*, New York, 2003

Miki, A., Isshiki, Y., Sato, T., *Nobuyoshi Araki: Self, Life, Death*, London, 2005

Morimura, Y., *Requiem for the XX Century: Twilight of the Turbulent Gods*, Milan, 2008

Raymond, C., *Francesca Woodman and the Kantian Sublime*, Farnham, 2010

Ribalta, J., ed., *Jo Spence: Beyond the Perfect Image: Photography, Subjectivity, Antagonism*, Barcelona, 2005

Roberts, R., *Silent Village*, Cardiff, 2010

Shafran, N. *edited photographs 1992–2004*, Göttingen and Brighton, 2004

Spence, J., *Cultural Sniping: The Art of Transgression*, London, 1995

Tillmans, W., *if one thing matters, everything matters*, London, 2003

Townsend, C., *Francesca Woodman*, London, 2006

Verwoert,. J. Halley, P., Matsui, M., *Wolfgang Tillmans*, London, 2002

Williams, V., *Anna Fox: Photographs 1983–2007*, Brighton, 2007

Chapter Ten: Constructions

Banks, R., *Gregory Crewdson: Beneath the Roses*, New York, 2008

Berg, S., *Gregory Crewdson 1985–2005*, Ostfildern, 2007

Burgin, V., *Between*, Oxford, 1986

Coleman, A. D., *Light Readings*, New York, 1979

Cooke, L., *Tracey Moffatt: Free-Falling*, New York, 1998

Dabashi, H., *Shirin Neshat: Women of Allah*, Turin, 1997

De Duve, T., Pelenc, A., Groys., B. and Chevrier, J-F., *Jeff Wall*, London, 2009

Goldstein, A., *Barbara Kruger: Thinking of You*, Cambridge, MA and London, 1999

Goto, J., *Ukadia*, Nottingham, 2003

Isaak, J. A., *Feminism in Contemporary Art*, London and New York, 1996

Kirsh, A., and Sterling, S. F., *Carrie Mae Weems*, Washington D.C., 1993

Krims, L., *The Little People of America*, Buffalo, 1971

Krims, L., *The Deerlsayers*, Buffalo, 1972

Krims, L., *The Incredible Case of the Stack O'Wheats Murders*, Buffalo, 1972

Krims, L., *Making Chicken Soup*, Buffalo, 1972

Krims, L., *Fictocryptokrimsographs*, Buffalo, 1975

Levinthal, D., *Mein Kampf*, Sante Fe, 1996

Linker, K., *Love for Sale*, New York, 1990

Livingstone, M., *Duane Michals: Photographs/Sequences/Texts* Oxford, 1984

Marcoci, R., *Thomas Demand*, New York, 2005

Ryan, K., *Dream House: Gregory Crewdson*, Milan, 2008

Stainback, C., and Woodward, R. B., *David Levinthal: Work from 1975–1996*, New York, 1997

Vidler, A., *James Casebere: The Spatial Uncanny*, Milan, 2001

Young, J. E., *At Memory's Edge: After-Images of the Holocaust in Contemporary Art and Architecture*, New Haven, CT and London, 2000

Photography Tomorrow

Graham, P., *a shimmer of possibility*, Göttingen, 2007

Schmid., J., *Other People's Photographs*, London and San Francisco, 2008–2011

Simon, T., *A Living Man Declared Dead And Other Chapters: I-XVIII*, London, 2011

Valdes, A., *Alfredo Jaar: Santiago de Chile*, Barcelona, 2006

Page numbers in **bold** indicate main references and page numbers in *italics* indicate illustrations.

Author's Acknowledgments

Putting together a book of this size has accrued debts of gratitude to many people. Firstly I'd like to thank all those at Phaidon who worked so hard in getting this complex publication to press, especially my editor Rosie Pickles for her care and precision in seeing through the final stages of this book's completion; my previous editor, Jennifer Lawson, who did so much to get the book underway; Amanda Renshaw for her continued support for this book throughout the overly long time of its writing; and Pablo Martín for his wonderful design. I feel very privileged that we have been able to get permission to reproduce so many of the photographs I wanted in this book and I would like to give thanks to the picture researchers for making this possible: Emmanuelle Peri, Sarah Bell and Louise Thomas. I'd also like to thank Tim Cooke for his clarity in copy-editing my text and Paul McGuiness for managing the book's production.

This book has evolved in relationship to the many lectures and seminars I have given on photography at both the University of Derby and the University of Wales, Newport (now the University of South Wales), as well as seminars held at the Instituto Politécnico do Porto, Portugal, and guest lectures delivered at numerous academic venues, museums and galleries, in both the UK and Europe. This book has also drawn from some of the reviews and articles on photography and contemporary art I have regularly published throughout the last two decades. Among the students, colleagues, artists, photographers, writers, curators and editors that have impacted on this book, as well as friends outside the academic, photographic and art worlds, I would especially like to thank the following: Stephen Bann, Malcolm Barnard, David Bate, Halla Beloff, Caroline Blinder, Henry Bond, David Brittain, Wolfgang Brückle, Stephen Bull, Kate Bush, David Campany, Gloria Chalmers, David Chandler, Robert Clark, Chris Clarke, Louise Clements, Jim Cook, Chris Coppock, Stephen Curtis, Olivia Maria Marques Da Silva, KayLynn Deveney, Liam Devlin, David Evans, Sonja Fessel, Peter Finnemore, Jane Fletcher, Anna Fox, Peter Fraser, Mick Gidley, Tony Godfrey, John Goto, Ken Grant, Juliet Hacking, Sissy Helff, Inge Henneman, Steven Hoelscher, Ian Jeffrey, Sarah Jones, Dragana Jurisic, Idris Khan, Peter Kramer, Vered Lahav, Jo Longhurst, Joanna Lowry, Amak Mahmoodian, David Manley, Carol Mavor, Penny McCarthy, Paul Morris, Gary Needham, Roger Palmer, Colin Pantall, Penelope Petsini, Grant Pooke, Angus Pryor, Melissa Renn, Sophy Rickett, Russell Roberts, Steve Schofield, Mark Sealy, Helen Sear, Paul Seawright, Oded Shimshon, Ulli Sieglohr, Theodoros, Sam Thorne, Ian Walker, Richard West, Val Williams, Tom Wood, Richard Wright and Gillian Youngs.

The libraries of both the University of Derby and the University of South Wales house some of the most extensive collections of books on photography in the UK. I would like to thank the librarians from both institutions in helping me research this book and especially Heather Watkins and Angharad Evans. Martin Parr also kindly made his remarkable photography book collection readily available.

Throughout the writing of this book, I have also gained tremendously from the abundant wit, intelligence, humour and criticism of artists David Campbell and Ian Brown, with whom I make art in collaboration under the name of Common Culture.

Finally, I'd like to dedicate this book with love to my family, Lydia, Anna, Alexis and Nikolas.

99, 100, 101: Courtesy the artist and 303 Gallery, New York; 181: © Robert Adams, courtesy Fraenkel Gallery, San Francisco; 265b: Courtesy of Mary Sue Ader-Andersen, Bas Jan Ader Estate, Patrick Painter Inc., Santa Monica CA; 37t: © the artist/courtesy Alexander & Bonin Gallery; 213: Courtesy the artist; Alexander and Bonin, New York; Kerlin Gallery, Dublin; Galerie Peter Kilchmann, Zurich; Matt's Gallery, London; and Galeria Moises Perez de Albeniz, Madrid; 329b: Courtesy Merry Alpern; 27b: © Carl Andre. DACS, London/VAGA, New York 2014; 54, 55: Courtesy the artist, Anton Kern Gallery, New York; Corvi-Mora, London; Marc Foxx, Los Angeles; 63: © The Estate of Diane Arbus; 375: © Keith Arnatt Estate. Courtesy Maureen Paley, London; 27t: © ARS, NY and DACS, London 2014; 186: © ARS, NY and DACS, London 2014; 232, 382: The Associated Press Ltd; 78: Photograph by Richard Avedon and © The Richard Avedon Foundation; 174, 182, 183: © Lewis Baltz, courtesy Galerie Thomas Zander, Cologne; 219: © Yto Barrada, Galerie Polaris, Paris; 322: Courtesy Robert Barry; 121: © Richard Billingham, courtesy Anthony Reynolds Gallery, London; 245, 246, 247: Courtesy Daniel Blaufuks; 274, 275: © Estate of Guy Bourdin. Reproduced by permission of Art + Commerce; 193: Courtesy the artist and Brancolini Grimaldi, London; 30: © Chris Burden. Courtesy Gagosian Gallery; 11, 26, 158, 159, 397, 398, 399: © Victor Burgin, courtesy Galerie Thomas Zander, Cologne; 106t: Larry Burrows/Katz Pictures Limited; 209, 210, 211: © Edward Burtynsky, courtesy Nicholas Metivier Gallery Toronto/Flowers, London; 405, 406, 407: © James Casebere. Image courtesy James Casebere and Lisson Gallery, London/NY; 345, 346, 347: Courtesy DIEHL Berlin; Foxy Production, New York; 283: Courtesy John Coplans and London projects; 409: Courtesy David Levinthal; 439: Courtesy Taryn Simon; 419, 420, 421: © Gregory Crewdson. Courtesy Gagosian Gallery; 168t: Courtesy the artist and David Zwirner, New York/London; 335t: Courtesy the artist and David Zwirner, New York/London; 305: © Bruce Davidson/Magnum Photos; 393, 394, 395: Courtesy the artist and DC Moore Gallery, New York; 149, 150, 151: © Sherry Turner DeCarava 2013. All rights reserved; 253b, 254: Courtesy Luc Delahaye & Nathalie Obadia Gallery; 411, 412, 413: © DACS 2014. Thomas Demand/Artists' Rights Society (ARS), New York/ Courtesy Matthew Marks Gallery; 85: Courtesy Ad Van Denderen; 135: © Saïdou Dicko; 36: Courtesy Eugenio Dittborn Studio; 7l, 95, 96, 97: © Eggleston Artistic Trust. Courtesy Cheim & Read, New York; 154: © Ed van der Elsken/ Nederlands Fotomuseum; 337: Courtesy the artist, Eric Franck Fine Art, London; 381: © Peter Finnemore; 83t, 373, 374: © Anna Fox, courtesy James Hyman Photography, London and Tasveer Arts, Bangalore; 355: Robert Frank; courtesy Pace/MacGill Gallery, New York; 127, 128, 129: Peter Fraser; 8l, 146, 147: © Lee Friedlander, courtesy Fraenkel Gallery, San Francisco; 58, 69, 70, 71: © the Artist, Courtesy Galerie Thomas Fischer; 168t: Courtesy the artist and Galerie Eva Presenhuber, Zurich; 321: Courtesy the artist and Galerie Michel Rein, Paris; 327: © Adagp, Paris 2013. Courtesy Galerie Perrotin; 221: George Georgiou; 92, 103, 104: © Estate of Luigi Ghirri, courtesy Matthew Marks Gallery; 402, 403: Courtesy Gladstone Gallery, New York and Brussels; 317: Courtesy Jim Goldberg; 307, 308, 309: David Goldblatt and Marian Goodman Gallery, Paris; 364, 365: © Nan Goldin; 368: Photo: Raluca Blider © The Felix Gonzalez-Torres Foundation, Courtesy of Andrea Rosen Gallery, New York; 369: © The Felix Gonzalez-Torres Foundation. Courtesy of Andrea Rosen Gallery, New York; 369: Photo: Neil Goldstein © The Felix Gonzalez-Torres Foundation. Courtesy of Andrea Rosen Gallery, New York; 427, 438: John Goto; 119, 237, 445, 446, 447: © Paul Graham/courtesy Pace/MacGill Gallery, New York; 123: Courtesy Greene Naftali; 387: Kathy Grove; 6r, 47, 179: Andreas Gursky/ © Courtesy: Sprüth Magers Berlin London/DACS 2014; 197: Courtesy the artist and Hauser & Wirth Gallery; 253t: © Thomas Hirschhorn. Courtesy the artist and Stephen Friedman Gallery, London. Photography Philip Carr; 315, 316: Courtesy Jacob Holdt; 257t: Courtesy Craigie Horsfield; 267b: © 1981 Tehching Hsieh. Courtesy the artist and Sean Kelly Gallery, New York; 343: © Pieter Hugo. Courtesy of Stevenson, Cape Town and Yossi Milo, New York; 195: © the artist/courtesy Ingleby Gallery; 9l, 224, 249, 319: Courtesy Alfredo Jaar; 437: Courtesy of Galerie Lelong, New York, Louisiana Museum of Modern Art, Humlebæk, Museum of Modern Art, New York, and the artist, New York; 89b: Courtesy the artist and Jack Shainman Gallery, New York; 89t: Courtesy CAAC–The Pigozzi Collection © Seydou Keïta/SKPEAC; 9r, 448: © Erik Kessels/Photo: Gijs van den Berg; 261: © Geert van Kesteren; 50: Courtesy of Idris Khan and Victoria Miro Gallery; 51, 91t: Courtesy the artist and PKM Gallery © Sanggil Kim; 265t: © ADAGP, Paris and DACS, London 2014; 53: Bohnchang Koo; 389: © Les Krims 1969; 390: © Les Krims 1974; 390: © Les Krims 1970; 391: © Les Krims 1971; 286: Inez Van Lamswerde; 292, 293: Courtesy Richard Learoyd; 298, 332: © Nikki S. Lee/Courtesy Sikkema Jenkins & Co; 29t: © Sherrie Levine, courtesy of Paula Cooper Gallery, New York; 29b © Sherrie Levine, courtesy Whitney Museum of American Art, N.Y. Photograph by Sheldan C. Collins; 340, 341: © Liu Zheng, Courtesy Yossi Milo Gallery, New York; 189: © Richard Long. All Rights Reserved, DACS 2014; 167, 201, 202, 203, 353, 354, 355, 383: Courtesy the artist and Luhring Augustine, New York; 301, 302, 303: © Danny Lyon/Magnum Photos; 279, 280, 281: © Sally Mann. Courtesy Gagosian Gallery; 277: © Copyright The Robert Mapplethorpe Foundation. Courtesy Art + Commerce; 163: Courtesy the artist and Marc Jancou Contemporary, New York/ Geneva; 25, 64, 131, 132, 133, 291: Courtesy the artist and Marian Goodman Gallery, New York/ Paris; 243: © ADAGP, Paris and DACS, London 2014. Courtesy the artist and Marian Goodman Gallery, New York/Paris/Photo credit: Elke Walford; 243: © ADAGP, Paris and DACS, London 2014. Courtesy the artist and Marian Goodman Gallery, New York/Paris/Photo credit: Marc Domage; 15: © Mary Ellen Mark/ courtesy Falkland Road, Inc; 313: © Mary Ellen Mark; 401: Courtesy Mary Boone Galery, New York; 66, 77, 164, 367: © the artist. Courtesy Maureen Paley, London; 67: © The Estate of Ralph Eugene Meatyard, courtesy Fraenkel Gallery, San Francisco; 109, 270: © Susan Meiselas/Magnum Photos; 269r: © The Estate of Ana Mendieta Collection Courtesy Galerie Lelong, New York; 33: Courtesy the artist, Metro Pictures, New York, and Sprüth Magers Berlin London/Metro Pictures; 61, 262, 287, 296: Courtesy the artist and Metro Pictures, New York; 139, 257b, 258: © Joel Meyerowitz, courtesy Howard Greenberg Gallery; 339: © Boris Mikhailov/ courtesy Pace/MacGill Gallery, New York; 91b: Mintio (Samantha Tio); 205, 206, 207: © Richard Misrach, courtesy Fraenkel Gallery, San Francisco; 153, 154, 155: Daido Moriyama Courtesy of Daido Moriyama Photo Foundation; 239: Courtesy Murray Guy, New York; 226: Courtesy James Nachtwey; 433: © Wawi Navarroza/Silverlens Galleries; 273: © The Helmut Newton Estate; 73, 74, 75: © Nicholas Nixon, courtesy Fraenkel Gallery, San Francisco; 111: © Simon Norfolk/NB Pictures; 60: Courtesy ORLAN; 311: Courtesy Bill Owens; 190, 191: Courtesy Roger Palmer; 221: © the artist/ Panos Pictures; 145: © Tod Papageorge/courtesy Pace/MacGill Gallery, New York; 124, 125, 176, 310: © Martin Parr/Magnum Photos; 6l, 35: © Richard Prince; 215: The Artist, courtesy Purdy Hicks Gallery; 384, 429: © Wang Qingsong/courtesy the artist studio; 13: © Estate of Robert Rauschenberg. DACS, London/VAGA, New York 2014; 37b: © Gerhard Richter 2014; 323: Courtesy Martha Rosler; 425: Courtesy the artist and Roslyn Oxley9 Gallery, Sydney; 235: © Judith Joy Ross/ courtesy Pace/MacGill Gallery, New York; 45, 46, 81t: © DACS 2014/Thomas Ruff; 19, 21: © Ed Ruscha. Courtesy the artist and Gagosian Gallery; 231, 319: © Sebastião Salgado/NB Pictures; 8r, 57, 434, 441, 442, 443: Joachim Schmid; 269l: © ARS, NY and DACS, London 2014; 216, 217: Courtesy Paul Seawright; 83b, 105, 289: Courtesy Andreas Serrano; 371: Nigel Shafran; 86, 87: © Fazal Sheikh/courtesy Pace/MacGill Gallery, New York; 296, 297: Courtesy of Santiago Sierra studio/ © DACS 2014; 116, 117: Photograph © 2013 Succession Raghubir Singh; 184, 196: © Estate of Robert Smithson/DACS, London/VAGA, New York 2014. Image courtesy James Cohan Gallery, New York/Shanghai; 43: Courtesy Sonnabend Gallery; 198, 199: © Jem Southam/courtesy James Hyman Gallery; 377: © Estate of Jo Spence, Courtesy Richard Saltoun; 377: Jo Spence Memorial Archive/The Estate of Jo Spence, courtesy Richard Saltoun Gallery, London; 430: Photograph by Manit Sriwanichpoom; 295: © Jemima Stehli; 39, 40, 41, 81b, 177: © Thomas Struth; 49: © Hiroshi Sugimoto, courtesy Pace Gallery; 335b: © The Estate of Larry Sultan, courtesy Galerie Thomas Zander, Cologne; 358: Courtesy of Taka Ishii Gallery, Tokyo; 359, 240: Tepper Takayama Fine Arts, Boston and Y. Tomatsu; 187: © the artist; 284b: © the artist; 157: Courtesy Vito Schnabel Gallery; 136, 160, 415, 416: Courtesy Jeff Wall; 16: © 2014 The Andy Warhol Foundation for the Visual Arts, Inc. / Artists Rights Society (ARS), New York and DACS, London; 112, 113: © Alex Webb/Magnum Photos; 423: © Carrie Mae Weems. Courtesy the artist and Jack Shainman Gallery, New York; 421: © the artist, Courtesy White Cube; 173: Courtesy Michael Wolf; 7c, 141, 142, 143: © The Estate of Garry Winogrand, courtesy Fraenkel Gallery, San Francisco; 171, 172: Courtesy Tom Wood; 348, 379: Courtesy George and Betty Woodman; 284t: Courtesy Alexa Wright; 267t: Photo Studio Wurm/© the artist; 331: Courtesy Shizuka Yokomizo; 329: © Kohei Yoshiyuki, Courtesy Yossi Milo Gallery, New York

Additional photography Ian Bavington-Jones

Phaidon Press Limited
Regent's Wharf
All Saints Street
London N1 9PA

Phaidon Press Inc.
65 Bleecker Street
New York NY 10012

www.phaidon.com

First published 2014

ISBN 978 0 7148 4563 0

A CIP catalogue record for this book is available from the British Library.

Designed by Pablo Martín

Printed in Hong Kong

Front cover: Sarah Jones, *Dining Room (Francis Place) (II)*, 1997 © the artist, courtesy Maureen Paley, London

Back cover: Liu Zheng, *Mentally Handicapped Patients, Beijing*, 1996 © Liu Zheng, courtesy Yossi Milo Gallery, New York